Best Damn Garage in Town
My Life & Adventures

ALSO BY SMOKEY YUNICK

Best Damn Garage in Town...The World According to Smokey
(3 volume boxed set version of this book)

Track Tech

Power Secrets

Portions of *Best Damn Garage in Town* are available as audio books:

Sex, Lies & Superspeedways

MORE Sex, Lies & Superspeedways

STILL MORE Sex, Lies & Superspeedways
(Summer 2005)

OTHER TITLES FROM CARBON PRESS

FIREBALL: Legends Don't Fall From the Sky
by Godwin Kelly

Best Damn Garage in Town
My Life & Advetnures

by Henry "Smokey" Yunick

Racer   Patriot   Mechanic   Inventor   Casanova

It's not politically correct
or grammatically correct,
but then again,
neither was Smokey.

Daytona Beach
Florida

For electronic browsing and ordering of this, and other Carbon Press books, visit www.carbonpressonline.com

The publisher offers discounts on this book when ordered in quantity. For more information, please contact:
    Carbon Press, LC
    520 Ridgewood Ave
    Holly Hill, Florida 32117
    866-SMOKEY2 (766-5392)
    www.carbonpressonline.com

Best Damn Garage in Town: My Life & Adventures
by Henry "Smokey" Yunick
Copyright © 2001-2005 by Carbon Press, LC

All rights reserved. No part of the contents of this book may be reproduced in any form or by any means without the written permission of the publisher.

Published in the United States by Carbon Press, LC, Daytona Beach, Florida.

Design: Wade Caldwell
Additional Photography: Wayne Allen, Russell Williams, Wade Caldwell
Manufactured in the United States of America.

First Edition (5th Printing)

ISBN: 0-9724378-3-5

Best Damn Garage in Town
My Life & Advetnures

Table of Contents

Where Do Racers Come From? 1

Tail End Charlie Goes to Europe 23

The Watch, The Ring and the Jacket 51

The Mule Ain't Blind 76

Albert the Alleygator 91

One Step Ahead of Castro 93

Carnie 98

Lord Calvert Takes Her Through the Turns 112

The Fabulous Hudson Hornet 123

The Cover of the Saturday Evening Post 135

About Tars	150
Society of Heads-up-asses Surface Transportation Manufacturers	170
The Hole Gets Bigger Everyday	177
If the World Had More Deweys…	183
The System: Don't Get Mad, Get Even	216
Racing with one Arm	221
Dear Bill	223
Mexican Road Race	225
It Didn't Say You Couldn't	232
Pontiac…How the Sweater Got Knit	239
Wore Out and Dead at 50	262
The Little Car That Could…But Didn't	265
50 Good Drivers and an Asshole	273
Family	348
Real Racer's Proving Ground	351
The Fan	433
Indy Qualifying	439
Indy Pace Car	442
The Beaver Patrol	444
What Did You Invent Smokey?	446
Flow Bench	508

A Greased Chute to Shitsville 512

The Smokey BTU Juggling Contest 519

Slippin' Outta Sync 526

Ocelot 573

Smokey Yunick, PhD 578

Funny Lookin Grasshoppers 582

Champion Hound Dog Tamer 588

Eleven Rose Bushes 594

Since I Quit Racing 602

Dale Earnhardt 619

The Smoketron 621

Power Secrets 626

Across the Pond 633

Back in the Game 636

The Final Final Chapter 638

The Dictionary According to Smokey 641

vii

Foreskin

I know much that's in this collection of memories, experiences and adventures, will be controversial...some will offend...some of it will be doubted.

I'm 75, and half way to 76 today...so in spite of taking three years to do this...maybe, just maybe, some of it is not 100% accurate. I've checked, double checked, and talked to the players still able talk...that in itself is a problem. If I ask Bud Moore, Ralph Moody, Tim Flock or Jack Smith, they all remember it a little different. I had, and have collected more data, and I've had a lot of help from people like Gene Granger and Don O'Reilly, (who had the foresight to hang on to a lot of data and pictures...that helps in reference to compiling a history book on stock car racing).

Anything without a past cannot have a future...rite? Auto racing history in the United States from day one till ten years ago is very, very fragmented, in reference to an accurate history of it's conception and growth. Mainly because not a single sanctioning body has survived the journey, except NASCAR, and they threw the record of their first 20 years in the Daytona dump.

Margie, Kilroy and I, by 2001, have spent five years working on this project.

I decided three years ago this had to be two books, now it looks like it will be three. One about my life and two on the technical adventures and evolution. Since I'm an amateur book author I think first the year-and-a-half was wasted...I've since done it over ('bout three times). I now think I know what I'm doing. I'm sure I'll be notified how you judge our project.

I'll now save words and time, in reference to this collection as books.

What are these books about?

My interest is to recreate, as accurately as I can, the history of stock car racing in the United States, as I knew it, from 1938 to 2000.

I've injected myself into these pages as your guide. I believe I'm qualified for the guide job...I "talked the talk and walked the walk" from 1938...it's now 2001, and I'm still talking and walking.

I realize no one is perfect, I realize that my observations and opinions are just that: one man's view of a complex 60 or so years of racing history.

I think one of the most interesting questions a race fan has is "what is a racer?" So as an example, I include my journey through life and racing.

I think up to 1980, I was a typical example. I know the current racer is a different breed of cat.

Why did I spend so much time and effort to do this? To glorify Smokey Yunick? To make money? Because I hate NASCAR? Because I got a hard-on for the France's? I've now learned fame is 99 percent limited to a very, very short span of time. My belief is, if this book was simply about myself, it would surprise me if 10,000 copies were sold. But I'm expecting, because it is a history book, it will be read by many people interested in auto racing for many reasons and that some good will be accomplished with it.

I'm not a rich man, but I can make it to the end without any hand outs. So it's not for money.

About hating nascar. There ain't no such thing. NASCAR is the France's.

OK...we are down to not liking the France's. I knew Big Bill as good as anybody did from 1946 till 1975.

I doubt Bill's kids know that in the last two years of his life he would come to my shop and invite me to go fishing with him, fly with him to St. Louis to get an option on a super piece of property to build a race track – and I would own part of it. Bill then was a very sick man...I think he had Alzheimer's disease (I don't know that). It was obvious his memory was gone. He was, even on his last visit, happy. He had a special look on his face when he was happy. I can only describe it as the look on a little kid's face when he's just shit in his pants and he don't want you to know it.

I was shocked at the visits. But when I realized Bill was no longer in a position to defend hisself, my negative feelings for him personally were gone.

One day, he said, "Smokey, I'm lonesome. We all worked so hard to get this thing going, I lost sight of some things, like friendship. Let's go to the islands and go fishing and chase some pussy."

Well, I had to turn away from him. I damn near cried. 'Bout that time his male escort herded him up and put him in the car. No, we never went fishing or to St. Louis to buy a track property. And we never went to any of the fifty lunch dates he made with me.

What are my feelings today about Big Bill?

Simply sadness. It could have and should have had a much nicer ending.

Now the rest of the France's:

Annie...how the hell could anyone be mad at her? If she wasn't a straight arrow there never was one.

Little Billy...you go by how people treat you in your process of categorizing each person who is involved in your personal life. My experiences with Little Bill were with a snotty, shit-head, rich and powerful man's son. Remember, I left NASCAR in 1970. There's no question in my mind Bill Jr. is no Smokey fan. And I can tell you I don't light up with happiness every time I see him. Matter of fact last I saw him I got thinking, "if that dumb ass don't lose some weight and quit puffing on all those cigarettes he ain't gonna be here much longer." But obviously my opinion of him in 1970 was way off the mark. He's running a billion dollar circus and apparently doing it well.

Jim France…I know him very sparingly. He is a neighbor of mine, but if he walked in here rite now I'm not sure I'd recognize him. What little I knew about him, I rated him the "keeper" of the two.

So I got nothing to not like abut him. Matter of fact, my boy Smokey told me 'bout ten years ago that Jim France, in reply to a question about whether he would run NASCAR with Bill Jr., answered, "I'm 42 years old now. I never worked a day in my life and don't intend to start now." I liked that – I like honest people.

The son and daughter of Bill Jr., I don't know them. I've heard the daughter is sharp, and the son is an asshole. Sure nothing 'bout them for me not to like (I don't know them). My boy Sam went to high school with Brian and he seconded his asshole rating. (This has been confirmed by some press members that I know pretty good.)

Last thing: Is this book aimed at making me some sort of a hero? How you feel about yourself is the real reward if you operate in an arena where what you do or did gathers a lot of media attention. Daily, I still get an "atta boy" from one or more people, and when I shave in the morning, looking in the mirror, I'm at peace with myself. Sure, I did a lot of things I wouldn't care to see on front page of the newspaper. But if you find some of them, and correctly print them, I'll have no animosity to you.

I can handle the bad stuff when it's the truth.

I wish I hadn't done some of it, but I have another defense as well…half of the bad stuff I done I had no control over: "the devil made me do it." As I've gotten older, I'm seeing the mistakes of judging people. I realize now it's OK to have an opinion, just don't play God and judge people. So now, instead of saying, "He is an asshole," I say, "In my opinion he is an asshole." Do you follow me?

Also, as I look in the mirror I think, "Goddam…you are lookin' more and more every day like ten miles of bad road."

Well, I'm well into the "golden years"…you know…where you're half blind and deaf and all the stuff on your body you broke and abused is hurting and falling off. You got ten teeth left that have cost you fifty grand in the last fifteen years.

If hair on your head is to keep your brain warm, my brain would be froze solid.

One of the good things that happened to me in last twenty years is my wife Margie. She said this book needed to be. She has typed and retyped this thing for one million hours. She takes such good care of me, once in awhile I forget I'm out of warranty.

She says you are gonna enjoy reading this. If you're not, chew her out, not me. It was her idea.

Really, I can't tell you how good it makes me feel when people ask for my autograph or tell me what a great kid I was back in 19-0-something. That's why I know the real reward is only how you feel about yourself. Everything else is temporary.

What you will read happened. Some will be offended by the language, how we lived, what we did…as I said earlier, I'm your guide. I lived it. If you don't like the way it unfolds close the lid and call Margie and ask for your money back. (I doubt she'll refund it though.)

I have no intentions of changing any of it to keep from pissing off major or minor players.

The things we did, said or tried to do can't be changed. That's the way it was.

For my part, it was an adventure that only a few got to take. I'm actually grateful I had a hand in the game. Would I change anything if I had the power to do it again with my changes? Yes…three changes.

#1 – Nobody would have been crippled or killed.
#2 – We would have won every race we run in.
#3 – I would have got to lay Marilyn Monroe one time.

I've discovered as you age, you run out of room for all that happened. I guess then, as the brain runs out of storage space, all medium and normal things are thrown out of memory, and you end up with just the very good and the very bad stuff that happened. So for those I don't thank or mention who helped me, or for that matter were against me, I apologize in advance. Actually, now I don't feel hard about people who gave me a hard time. How in the hell could you separate the good from the bad without some bad days? An example: Ray Fox did some things I considered very wrong. I wasted twenty years hating him, then got to revisit and spend some time with him, and discovered hell, he really is a very nice person, that used to be an asshole. Now I'm starting to have second thoughts about him again. Auto racing and its participants deserve a lot more attention from the hi-powered big business wizards. It's the only profession in the world where you pay a fee for the right to work for nothing. How's that for a way to cut the overhead?

The magnetism that auto racing projects I believe, is stronger than "day one," and gets a little stronger every week. Why would a grown man cry when he failed to qualify for a race that could cost him his life? Pretty powerful stuff for those who deal in the behavior of modern humans.

The following I wrote for the readers of a book called Smokey Yunick's Track Tech. To introduce and explain myself to the readers. I re-read the thing and decided why try to do it again – nothing has changed:

First thing I saw on the office wall at GM, when they hired me to run Chevrolet Racing (1955) was, "The price of progress is trouble" (Kettering). That man knew what the hell he was talking about.

1946-1976 – those 30 years were a blur of stock cars, trucks, boats, motorcycles, Indy cars, airplanes and helicopters. I worked 18 hours a day, seven days a week and found time besides to investigate most all of the immoral pleasures of socially unacceptable behavior. I lived like a running Southern dog, belly to the ground – tail straight out – ears straight back.

My formal education ended in the 10th grade, because by then I had developed a habit of eating two or three times a day. I've always had an attraction for speed and mechanical things. In the after World War II time frame, everything in life is timing. I didn't know that, but for a curious-minded person addicted to speed, I was there at exactly the right time. Stock car racing was a format whereby everyone started even, next to no education and no money. A racer was a social outcast, no chance for credit, no insurance, not wanted in hotels, social status just a little better than an ex-con or a "mon-backer."

In spite of all the drawbacks, to me, it was still a thrill on race day morning to walk into the pits, pull up my pants, look around and say, "All right you sons-of-bitches…let's have a race."

Being short on education, money, and friends – really all we had was each other. While we fought like tigers at the race track, we lived like gypsies and took care of each other in our own way. My adventures educated me to whatever status you give me. I'm grateful for the help, opportunities, knowledge, friendships and honors that have been afforded me in the now, 60-plus years. Although financial rewards are unbelievable now compared to then, I wouldn't trade then for now for the world.

The only thing that I would change, had I the power, would be to delete the accidents where men were injured and suffered for the rest of their lives. For those who died quickly, I have no tears. We all knew what the risk was and accepted it. Respect and sadness were my emotions…the sadness passed, but the respect stays.

My mental justification was the world benefited with better surface transportation from our learning curve. I still observe what's going on with great interest – puzzled by some of it…admire some of it. Some of it gives me a sense of nostalgic sadness but, I realize nothing is forever.

I'm 72 now, and I suppose as time passes, it's hard to accept change from the way you thought was best. Racing as I lived it was an unknown sport. It's now a mature modern complex engineering marvel. Maybe more of an entertainment event than a sport. I hope you find my adventures in racing interesting and for some who are headed up in racing, hopefully you'll find something that will help you. I'm sure it is nowhere near as easy now as it was 55 years ago, but I think if you have the talent and desire, any average IQ can make it in racing. Some things are better: barriers for race, color or gender are gone. But racing is a Missouri sport show – "Show me."

In the technical part of this book, even though it is dated, consider this, that which deals with physics and chemistry will never change. Nature and this planet dictates what we can and can't do. However, there are many ways to skin a cat…and "how you skin the cat" is what will never stop changing. There are no limits to man's ingenuity, just as man's ingenuity will never conquer the forces and behavior of this planet.

What did I get out of 55 years? When I shave in the mornings and look at myself, I'm comfortable with myself and my life. I had my chance and feel in some special way, a sense of well being, as I continue to probe into another "what if" idea at my shop. Got no bosses, do what I want, don't give a damn what any one thinks about it. Still work seven days a week because I want to. I'm a lucky man.

One winter day 'bout Christmas, 1970…a writer was here interviewing me for a story 'bout alternate energy. Said he was shocked with my small dirty office…dog bones on the floor…my greasy clothes. He asked me what kind of friends I had.

There was a pile of Christmas cards on the desk.

The phone rang…it was a call from Sweden on a Chevy problem.

As I talked he picked through the cards.

A couple of days ago, as I'm searching for something I wrote for Popular Science back then, I found the draft of his story. The cards he was impressed to see were from:

(Current, past or soon to be)
Pete Peterson, President, Ford Motor Company
Henry Ford, President, Ford Motor Company
Semon Knudsen, President, Ford Motor Company
Pete Estes, President, General Motors
McDonald, President, General Motors
Ed Cole, President, General Motors
Bob Anderson, Chairman, Rockwell International
Bob Mercer, Chairman, Goodyear
Lloyd Ruess, President, General Motors
John DeLorean, Vice President, General Motors
Bob Stemple, President, General Motors

So…would you agree I had some goddam good teachers?

Nope…no card from "Big Bill."

My life from 1939 to 1975 was like a wide open train ride on the Orange Blossom Special…where it ran on parallel tracks to the Wabash Cannonball…seemed like it was never quite fast enough, and always so close to leaving the rails.

You know I don't know how to exactly say this, but somehow in the background I could always hear this powerful, mournful whistle as we rocketed past dangerous breath-taking situations.

If there was ever a dull moment, I missed it.

A goofy idea I got in 1958 – I'd have liked to have Marty Robbins leading his band playing The Wabash Cannonball as we rolled out on pit road at Indy, race morning.

I asked him, 'bout it, he said "Yup, we'll do it someday." "Someday" will never happen.

Smokey

Best Damn Garage in Town
My Life & Adventures

Where Do Racers Come From?

As far back as I can remember (I was 'bout 12-13 years old), I lived in a place called Neshaminy, Pennsylvania. My family lived on a 15 to 20 acre farm. My mother's name was Lena. She was an immigrant from Poland. Father, named John, was an immigrant from the Ukraine. The house we lived in, didn't have electricity and never had a phone. All of the heat for the house came from one big stove in the basement. This stove used coal for fuel and had about a four foot diametrical grating in the middle of the house where the heat came up for the whole house. When it got cold, small farm animals as well as dogs and cats crowded around the heat source. At times the baby goats and rabbits used this warm area as a bathroom. I cannot describe the odor of baked goat and rabbit shit, but it is bad.

My mother and father apparently didn't like each other. Even in my earliest recollection, their idea of a normal weekend was where they fought and smashed up the furniture. My father, who I never got to know very well, worked out of town as a carpenter. He was a great believer in beating hell out of kids to keep 'em straight. I have a sister named Irene (Renee). She is two years younger than I, and I really didn't get to know her very well until I was 70.

I think the European culture was "work seven days a week, and raise your own food." In short, become self-sufficient. As I remember it, if you were born poor, you stayed poor. We lived under the European attitude of "control the kids closely, work the shit out of them, and train them to take care of the elderly – 100 percent if it became necessary." In short the philosophy was, "take care of your own and ask or expect no help from anyone, civil charity or the government." Great idea, 'cept I think if we hadn't got a little government help we'd have starved.

The cost of living was very different then. As I remember it $25 a week was good pay. A loaf of bread (not sliced, six to seven cents. A quart of milk cost a dime,

My mom Lena in the back yard of my boyhood home in Neshaminy, Pennsylvania.

Old lady "Gertrude" Haldeman – State Road School in Neshaminy – they thought I was cute and I got away with murder.

Coke a nickel, hamburgers 15 cents, movies 25 cents, and newspaper two cents (Sunday was a nickel.) Gasoline cost 20 to 25 cents a gallon. I think that farm we lived on cost five or six thousand dollars. There was no income or sales tax and beer was 10 cents a glass.

My school (first to eighth grade) was in one room, first to eighth grades all together. The school was in an old creamery building in a beautiful setting, on a small river. One lady teacher taught all those kids. The teacher even had to keep the heater going.

Well, with my father gone most of the time I got stuck with farm duty – the whole nine yards. There was always a lot of work to do. Milk the cows and goats, do the plowing, planting and cultivating, take care of couple hundred chickens, four or five pigs, two cows and clean the barn and chicken coops. Also take care of one big-big plow horse. Man, I'll tell, you there ain't nuthin' in my childhood and teens worth remembering.

To get a bicycle I had to run a paper and magazine route (six miles twice a day). I won the bicycle in a magazine selling contest. When my father found out I paid for 'bout five dollars worth of the books I couldn't sell in order to win, he beat the shit out of me and wouldn't let me use the bike for three or four months. When we got electricity a year or so later, I won a radio selling newspapers. Again, I paid for a couple bucks worth to win and my dad smashed the radio on the porch. By now you can figure we really weren't "asshole buddies." He did have a problem. (He was an alcoholic in my opinion.) He didn't especially care for beer, he was a whiskey drinker. Well, finally it's high school time. Only one small problem. High school is six miles one way. There are no school buses…you can't imagine the world without school buses can you? In those days it was the student and family's job to get the kids to and from school and to feed them. You brought your own lunch with you, or bought it, or just didn't eat. No one ever complained and most kids had something to eat. Well I got that bike, but after experimenting, I did better by parking my bike at the end of my paper route ('bout five miles from school) and doing a walking hitch-hike. Worked pretty good, and very seldom did I get to school late, but I did do a lot of fast walking for two years and two months. This routine and farming kept me in really good shape.

Back those days nothing went right for me. For a few years everything I tried turned to shit. While still in high school I wanted to play football so bad, but I only weighed 135 pounds. The coach was a nice 250 pound dago who had been a star at the University of Pennsylvania. In those days you had to buy your own football cleats (shoes). Of course I didn't have the

The goats weren't bad as long as they were outside.

Me and my dad in one of our better moments. This was in Washington, DC, just before he died.

money. I practiced in work shoes, you know, the kind that laced above ankles. They had cow shit all around where the soles were sewed to the shoe. Well, I guess the coach could see how bad I wanted to play. At that time I could really haul-ass running and I was strong as hell. I could pick up one wheel of the rear end of a Fordson tractor off the ground with my back and knees. (That was the "rite of passage" at the time. If you could pass that test you had a license to drink and chase pussy.) Back to football. It's the first game and we are losing our ass. My father forbid me to play football, so nobody knew I was trying to make the team (Willow Grove High School). The coach puts me in with a borrowed pair of shoes 'bout two sizes too big. I'm really giving it hell, and doing pretty good, but I cracked my left arm between the elbow and shoulder.

Shit, I've gotta go to the hospital…with no insurance. Man, I was so low I could have walked under a snake's belly standing full up with a big hat on. Okay, gotta go get a cast on it. How the hell am I gonna be able to milk cows, and husk the corn, and all that other shit with just one arm? Things don't look good, but hell, it gets a lot better. I leave from x-ray to get a cast put on. The terrazzo floors and football cleats don't go together. My feet flip…zingo…and I'm on my ass. Now bones sticking out of the skin (same arm) and I need an operation and a cast. By now my mother has found me and my father wants to kill my ass. Well, as you can guess, my career as a football player is over.

Had one big horse named "Big Bill." Actually Bill was a huge horse (I'm pretty sure he was a Budweiser kind of horse) but he hurt one of his hind legs by working too hard and he had a condition called "milk leg." If it got all swelled up from too much work, old Bill's leg, from knee to hoof, would get huge and I couldn't work him. (Well hell…I only gave six bucks for him at a sale.) Plowing with a pair of horses is an experience. I'd borrow a neighbor's horse, and off we'd go. Hand guiding a plow with two horses pulling it ain't all that hard till you hit a rock or a root. You get one foot in the bottom of the furrow six inches deep. The other foot is pushing the dirt spinning off the moldboard. You kinda had to squash it down as you went. When the tip of the plow hits a rock, the two handles you're guiding the plow with pick you clean up off the ground. There is a wooden cross-bar between

Me and Irene (Renee) around 1928.

the handles and that son-of-a-bitch comes up and catches you in the chest or on the chin. This is where you learn how to say "motherfucker" and every other dirty word known to man (in English...and in my case Polish and Ukrainian). Man that hurt! What made it worse was Bill would look back with what I swear was a shit-eatin' grin which I took to mean "How did that feel, big farmer?"

Next came the cultivator. This was a one horse deal that you used to kill the weeds and loosen the soil and kinda hill up the plants. Well, corn needs lots of this, and as corn is growing, it is delicious to horses. So here's what makes a young boy a foul-mouthed nervous wreck. At the end of each row, Big Bill reached down and ate the last corn plant. Then, as I turned him and the cultivator around, (this too is a hand held deal.) Bill also ate the first corn plant on the next row. By the time I'm done cultivating five or six times the field is 10 to 12 corn plants short on each row and Bill's fatter than hell.

One day I'm going back to the barn. I've been fighting with Bill for 'bout eight hours, so going back in I

If I wasn't hot shit in high school, I sure thought I was.

ride him, kinda sideways, no saddle, just sittin' on his pulling harness. I'd just gotten a six foot steel ruler. This type of ruler was a new-new deal. You pulled it out of a pocket-sized circular container. When you wanted to put it away, you pushed a button on side and it made a lot of noise as it recovered the six foot of steel tape. There is a problem here that I'm not aware of it yet. The problem is that the noise this rule makes when it retracts sounds like a rattlesnake. Apparently Bill knew about rattlesnakes and I guess, simply stated, he was afraid of 'em. Well I'm sitting up there, tired as hell and half dozing. Bill walks slow...in fact the goddam horse had two speeds: low-low, and wide-ass open. Now, for as big as he was (and even with that bad leg), when he shifted to wide open, he covered a lot of ground quick. I pulled out 'bout half that rule, hit the button to wind it in and Bill thought, "Holy shit...a 10 foot rattler!" With that he accelerated to 30 mph in about two seconds and headed for the barn about a half a mile away at top speed. Another problem is coming up. I built Bill's stall, but by not keeping it too clean, and letting it build up probably a foot of straw, corn fodder and horse shit, there remains only a couple inches clearance above Bill's back. I don't know or think about this till I notice Bill is going in the barn at full throttle. Bill went in fine, but I caught the top of the barn sideways and came forcibly to a dead stop way over what the body can stand. I swear, when Bill got stopped in the barn, and seen what happened to me, he really enjoyed it. He had the weirdest grin I ever saw on a horse.

Well in a week or so I recovered enough to make a major decision. Bill and I were through. I decided to build a tractor. I was trying to sell Bill, but nobody wanted him at any price 'cause of that leg. The only taker was dog food guy. He offered no money, offered just to take him. Well, I wasn't so pissed that I wanted him in dog food cans, so I just kept him. Well Bill watched me work on the tractor project for

Big Bills's replacement – my first stab at inventing. It was great as long as it was running, but there were lots of times when we had to push it back to the barn.

three months doing nothing but getting fat as hell. Really Bill had helped me, but it took 50 years for me to realize it. (Margie just brought this to my attention: I was to have many more days-hours-months-years of pissin' and moaning 'bout another "Big Bill.") I can't remember the ending of "Big Bill" the horse. Anyway, for the tractor I bought a Dodge car with a big-ass engine and transmission for 10 bucks and a Ford truck worm gear rear end with dual wheels, but no tires, for five bucks. I was gonna make steel wheels, like a Fordson, but in the end put tires and chains on…that was a mistake. I built the tractor with hacksaw, files, hand-powered drill, and chisels. When I burned, cut, or hit my hands, fingers or whatever other ways you damage yourself up with just plain old man-powered tools, you needed to know all those cuss words to keep going. I guess it's a therapeutic form of first aid. Luckily I had a wide vocabulary from all those days plowing with Big Bill. Finally, the tractor is a success…but not a sensation. It lacked traction, got hot and broke a lot. But when it was going, I pulled two plows, and did more in one day than I could in two weeks with Bill. The year of the tractor I was 14 years old.

My next adventure was selling produce I grew…going house-to-house in Doylestown, Pennsylvania. First I pulled my produce wagon six miles by hand. Later, I loaded the produce in an old small stage coach, with Bill doing the work. Through this I got enough money to buy a Indian motorcycle. It was a beauty, a real nice, damn-near new, Indian "Bonneville Chief" – actually, Indian's race model. It cost 20 bucks at two dollars a week with no finance charge. After two and a half months, it's all mine. I replanted the next spring, but when school got out my sophomore year, I was taken to Washington, D.C., to learn the carpenter business working for my father. Man, I hated that job. Carpentry is very hard work. The only amusement I got all week was trying to screw the land lady's daughter. Came close, but no-cigar. Even with my newly learned story from the experts, "Just let me put it in a little bit, and if you don't like it I'll stop." The daughter was married to a nice hard-working executive, but she was a "10" regarding sex, and he was probably a "three" or "four." Best I could do was get my first blow job (it lasted 'bout 45 seconds.)

I rode the cycle from Washington home every week or two. One day in the rain I got to

One of my more attractive outfits…but it worked with the girls. (OK, one's my sister.)

5

showing off to some girls driving in front of me and really busted my ass. Back then helmets were a starched white cloth deal. With a head wound, the blood really looks serious on the white. It was actually nothing serious, but lots of blood. However, the motorcycle was wounded bad. It's destiny was to become a part of my first racing experience.

And now things are going to really pick up speed. I got to end of October in my junior year when my father had a heart attack and passed away. I had to quit school and go to work to help my mother and sister make it. Well really just my mother, my sister found a family she could live with, earning her keep by doing chores. I tried to finish high school, but after two months, there ain't no way we can afford it, so I quit and go to work. I remember the day I quit, it was Friday, I turned my books back in and just said "I have to quit." They just said, "Fine, sign these papers." They couldn't have cared less.

I'm now an "official high school dropout," another poor dumb shit who was doomed to work his ass off and be poor till he croaked. Here's an episode that made me wonder. For two years and two months, before I got out of school, I walked one-half mile to the top of a very steep hill. In those days all transmissions were manual. A car was in first or second gear climbing to the top of a long hill. Just at the top the car's speed is very slow and it is easy to stop. Almost every day when I was in school, a black Essex coupe with a male driver would go by me at 'bout 15 mph. He never-ever stopped, except that last day. I was dumbfounded. I had quit even putting my thumb up after the first year. As a matter of fact, I grown to hate him when I stood there in the rain or snow or cold and he just rolled past inside that car. But he gave me a ride on the last day. As I recall, he didn't want any conversation, but was pleasant.

My first job was for a Ford dealership, Konroy Ford, in Doylestown. I was to dig a 150 foot tunnel under a cement garage floor for a steam line. Underneath the floor was like a dump: oil cans, mattress springs, old 55 gallon drums, broken glass, shit…you name it. Working under there was a son-of-a-bitch. You had to crawl in, dig a bushel basket full, and drag the basket back out. It was a one man deal. I got 'bout sixty or seventy feet in there and then they said, "We want to teach you how to be a mechanic" it paid 10 bucks a week. I worked six days, 7:30 am till 5:30 pm weekdays, Saturday we got off at 3:00.

I still can't make it with those wages, so I work at night at a small wrecker, general repair, and Studebaker dealer called Hall's Garage. Hall loved the wrecker business, but his hobby was guns. (He was a good gunsmith I was told). So my job there was the "big stuff…transmission rebuild, replace crank, etc. Hall supervised me enough to get by…but half the time I was lost. Right in here I decided I wanted to be connected with engines or anything that went fast. In the late '30s, cars and airplanes were still simple really, so I started trying to learn the physics of the engines, axles, and transmissions. I also started trying to understand gasoline, diesel fuel and oil. I found the right books or it would have never worked. I got a physics book that was fun to read. It explained what energy was and how it could occur in all the different mediums society was using and/or knew about. For example: nuclear energy – it had zero on that – it was not discovered yet, and jet and turbine engines were just the dreams of a "crack pot" Englishman. But it turned out to understand the physics, you had to understand simple chemistry. Well the chemistry books I found were like the physics books. They were relatively simple, and very interesting. I learned what air, dirt, water, rocks, oil, steel, aluminum, glass, etc., were. I learned how they were made, and how some of them allowed various changes and what form of resulting energy you could derive benefit from. For example: water power to electricity ain't that simple. Sure, it is neat, clean, damn-near perfect at first glance. But, if you considered it as a man made form, such as a hydroelectric dam, and looked closer, you saw massive environmental damage. So I decided the number one rule for my thinking would be "Don't fuck with the natural world."

Example: if you don't like cold weather don't try and heat all of Minnesota, move to Florida.

But what I noticed most, was the people in charge of maintaining all the prime movers did not really have a clue on what made the deal tick. They depended on manuals, and cut-and-try experience. So all the guidance they received came out of a "Chiltons" repair manual, or a manufacturer's manual. My favorite comment after getting an answer from one of my peers was "why?" I came to realize that if an expert is explaining a subject, and they really don't understand it completely, when you simply ask "why?" the conversation continues in circles (which always go to same place… nowhere). Asking "why?" is the only way to learn anything.

In 1935 to 1950 if a new car burned a valve at 20,000 miles or burned a rod bearing at 40,000 miles, nobody bitched…that was normal. I can remember after an engine overhaul (in the frame) engines were so tight that no starter in the world would turn the engine. We'd have to tow 'em and hit the starter at the same time. This was the accepted practice. I decide to assemble the motors without all the parasitic drag that required the tow job to get a fresh motor rebuild started. Hell, the rope seals at both ends of crankshaft alone had the crankshaft 'bout locked, and oil leaked forever anyway.

At Hall's Garage I got to work on all odd-ball Oaklands, Willys Knights, Packards, Studebakers, REOs, Pierce Arrows all very different 4-cycle engines. The Willys Knight had a sleeve valve – damnedest deal you ever saw. Like a lot of other setups, it was not worth a shit, but "cut-and-try" was running wild. Hell, most of the stuff then had splash lubrication to mains, and dippers on the rods (no oil pump). Compression was a big number, 'bout 6:1. Gasoline 'bout 80 octane with three cc of lead per gallon.

Believe it or not, Chrysler at the time, had the best stuff, but blew it. They just got too far ahead of theirselves when they came out with that air-flow car. If they hadn't put that fucked up vacuum clutch and vacuum shift on all of them, and had fixed the engine compartment so you could get at the engine to work on it, I believe that car would have torn the world up. But nobody, including Chrysler, knew how to keep the goofy clutch-trans deal working. (The first one I ever saw, I was working in a Chrysler dealership in Fayetteville, North Carolina – and was 16 years old). Basically, the dealer can't fix it so he hands me manual and suddenly "I'm the new expert." How in the hell do you get to a North Carolina town when your working in Pennsylvania? OK I've shifted gears, this story has to back up a li'l bit first.

Believe it or not, my mother tried to have me put in jail for non-support when I was sixteen. I have two boxes I bought at a farm sale 'bout six months before the "non-support" deal. I don't know what's in 'em. This turned out to be a brand new U.S. Army motorcycle in a crate for five bucks, and a new side car to go with it for $2.50 in the other. (Auction rules can't open boxes.) Well now, sitting around in a crate for 20 years hurt the piston rings and valve springs, but not too bad…the cycle just burned quite a bit of oil. It had a big engine in it, and it would haul-ass. The first time I rode it hard, at 90 mph, it threw both treads off the original tires. The lights on it were "prest-o-lite gas." (Yes, it had a tank you could get re-filled, and you lit head light and tail light with a match.) Well, I put the side-car on and it was some kind of a flexible deal that really made that rig un-spinable. In rain, snow, or ice, I'd pass anything going, and be in complete control.

At the time I had a dog who looked like Disney's Pluto. Yes, "Mickey Mouse" had just begun about then, (the mid-30's) so I named my dog "Pluto." Well Pluto was a dumb dog, always screwing up, but Pluto loved motorcycles. He jumped up on the tank in front of me (I guess he weighed 100 pounds.) and was just a pain in ass 'cause if I took him along on the motorcycle, he would take off when we stopped. With the sidecar Pluto has it made and he won't get out of it when I stop for at least half an hour.

He was a boy dog, a puppy I picked up 'bout 1938 after he'd been nicked by a car. Nothing broke, just soaking wet, sore, cold, scared and hungry. I put him in my jacket and he got his first motorcycle ride. He showed his appreciation by pissing all over me as we rode. Well, what the hell, it could have been worse. It could have come from little closer to his tail. He shivered all the way home. I thought this was because he was wet and cold, but I guess the motorcycle noise scared him also. Since my parent's were immigrants, and barely making it, my mattress was a hand-made, big cloth bag filled with hay or straw. This bag was then laid on the floor to make a bed. From this I learned that newspaper was very useful as a cold insulator, so under the bag of straw was 'bout a quarter inch of paper.

You know, Pluto was really my only real friend then, and as I journey through life, every once in awhile I get reminded of that dog. In the late 70s, I was in Ecuador working on a jungle oil field engine problem. En route I stayed in a mountain town overnight in a private home. The llama was their horse, their heater, their clothing raw material, and their pet. And you'll find this hard to believe, but when the llama got old and died, they ate him-or-her. What's a llama got to do with this? Well, the family I stayed with slept all around and on the llama for heat. I thought of Pluto, (as he had slept with me), and when it got cold, he got under covers with me and we got heat from each other. No, I never remember getting fleas from him, 'cept once.

My Indian Chief

Well, I need to haul stuff like lumber and cement to keep the house from falling down so I remove the sidecar body and replace it with a flat deck like a pickup box with six inch sides. On this Pluto rides standing up. Well, I learn how to pick sidecar up to jump fire hydrants and how to get sidecar wheel up and keep it up. All through this, I notice Pluto has unbelievable balance. You cannot throw him off that sidecar.

I like the dog, but he at times is a real pain in the ass. There was a bridge in Neshaminy that crossed a small river. I guess the bridge was about 150 years old (I believe I saw "G.W." carved on it). It's sides started even with the road. They were rock and mortar with a cement cap 'bout 24 inches wide. They went from nothing to four feet above the road in the middle of the bridge. It is 20 feet down to the river. Under the bridge the river is three to seven feet deep. A favorite trick I learned was to pass a car on the right on the bridge cap, with sidecar up at a 30 degree angle with Pluto standing up balanced in the sidecar. Well one winter night, with one too many beers, I tried this one time too many. I'm gonna cross the river at 50 mph, on the 24 inch wide top of the bridge sides with sidecar and Pluto out in space. About midway, I made a mistake that caused me to drop off of bridge cap.

There was an inch or two of ice on the river and the old Harley, Pluto, and I hit it 'bout flat. We went through the ice into 'bout three feet of water. I can still damn-near hear Pluto when we hit that icy water. It was a bright moon, and as we crawled out of the river and got up the bank I looked at Pluto. He had a way of drawing his gums up and showing all his teeth. Sometimes it looked like he was grinning (a sarcastic grin), or sometimes it looked like he was laughing. That night his look was like he was shitting razor blades, and he was shaking like a jitterbug sander.

You could drive down to either side of the river. Cars stopped that had seen the accident and believe it or not in 45 minutes, we pulled cycle out (I had a rope). It was always fouling plugs, so I had spare plugs in my jacket. I bet I got it started in 10 minutes. In less than an hour, Pluto and I were at home in bed. It didn't hurt the cycle in any way, the lights even still worked when I re-lit them. The next night this led to a big problem with the local police regarding a non-support warrant.

I felt like jail was likely to be my next new adventure, so I got away from the cops, parked the Harley about a mile from the house. I slipped in and got my clothes and possessions, all five bucks worth, and walked back to the cycle and goddam, there's Pluto sleeping in the side car. I thought it would be better to go back to barn and get my tent, a gas stove, and some blankets. Now all I needed was my tools. They were six miles north at Hall's Garage, so I slipped up there 'bout seven in the morning. I didn't say anything, just got my tool box and slipped out. I decided to head south. I'd guess I had five or six bucks.

Where am I headed? I have no plan 'cept to get a long way from home. By getting odd jobs, Pluto and I get to Hercules, Virginia – the place they make dynamite. On edge of town I see a diner that looked like an old railroad car 'cept it's fancied up with chrome and neon lights. It's late, 'bout 9:30 pm, and raining like a son-of-a-bitch. When you ride a cycle in the rain it stings like needles. Poor old Pluto (he was a short haired dog) is getting it all over. Pluto had real long floppy ears. And he walked like all his leg joints were unhooked. He had absolutely the most "I don't give a shit" attitude I've ever seen. Well, Pluto would let me put goggles on him as long as it wasn't raining or snowing…maybe they fogged up, I don't know. So Pluto's in misery, I'm hungry, soaked, and tired. I notice they got rooms so I stop. Yup, rooms 50 cents a night, dog OK. I rent a room and go to the back of the kitchen and get some scraps for Pluto. Actually a good meal for him, and I got a hot (used) roast beef sandwich (only been eaten a little) for a quarter (new price 60 cents). We eat in back of kitchen. Finally I'm warming up and drying out. I hear somebody singing and playing a guitar. Sounds good so we go up front. The place ain't crowded so we sit and listen with a cup of coffee. (five cents – man that heat felt good) The singer was a colored man named "Blind Boy Smith." I thought he was super, just right for a cool, rainy, miserable night.

Pluto wasn't the best looking passenger I ever had.

Well, "let's get to bed." The mattress is a hay-in-a-bag deal, not too bad. The light is one bulb. There is no pillow, no sheets, but a good enough blanket. The place has one toilet for all the men and one for all the women. I noticed six or seven fairly attractive women sitting around and coming and going while I drank the coffee and listening to the singer. Well here's the scoop. The "room deal" used to be a stockyard. The gals are "working ladies," selling pussy to the factory workers that made explosives. Pluto and I are spending the night in a whore house. Well, hell, what's wrong with that? I don't have no money, and I'm a lot more tired than I am horny. I try to get some sleep, but in five minutes I start to itch and Pluto is scratching and whining. Finally I can't stand it anymore plus all hell breaks loose outside. I turn light on and quickly figure the problem out. I'm covered with lice, and so is poor Pluto. The noise outside is explained to me by a cop who comes busting in with gun drawn…a raid on the whore house.

I can't stay the night. It's still raining and Pluto's going nuts so we get back on the road. In half mile here's 'bout eight to 10 of the ladies walking down the road soaked to the bone and hitch-hiking in their high heels. What a sorry, sad bunch of ladies. We ride till morning. Had 'bout a full tank of fuel and two-gallon spare can on the side car. I pull into gas station and ask the attendant for a cheap "home remedy" for the bugs. Man, by now I'm in misery and Pluto is worse. He laughs. He apparently has had experience with this type of problem. "You simply get in barrel of kerosene for a couple of minutes, or rub yourself with kerosene generously." The medical advice was free, as was use of the kerosene, but let me offer this suggestion. If you ever have the same experience and use this remedy, do not rub kerosene on your peter and balls and do not get it in the crack of your ass (and the same for your dog). 'Cause if you do you will experience a sensation similar to having your peter, balls and asshole set on fire. And judging by Pluto's vocal and footwork demonstration, I'm not sure it wasn't worse for him. I mentioned the terrible discomfort I was having to the attendant, his reply was, "You don't itch do you?" There was a mountain stream 'bout 50 yards from gas station with water was about 33 degrees fahrenheit. Pluto and I finished the deal off by drowning some of the remaining lice, and freezing the rest of 'em to death.

Next stop Fayetteville – here's how I ended up getting a job in North Carolina. While eating at diner, the man on the next stool is telling me he can't find a mechanic to hire and bitching 'bout new Chrysler air flow car. Turns out he is a Chrysler-Plymouth dealer. He also owns the hotel-restaurant. He asks me if I know anything about Chrysler air flow. I said, "a little"…and he was desperate, so that's how I got a job. I'm broke, and get offered $10 a week with room and board. (Remember… boss owns rooming house and restaurant). His rooming house was an interesting place, especially the first night. Pluto and I are shedding the skin of our wounded parts. (Sleep don't come easy if all the skin on your peter is coming off.) I don't know this, but room is 'bout five feet from a railroad track. About five o'clock in the morning a goddam train come roaring down through there running 'bout 60 mph with horn wide open. "Holy shit!" I jumped up in bed and Pluto lands on top of me scared silly. No, we couldn't get a quieter room, so early every morning we just semi-consciously sat in bed and waited for that son-of-a-bitch to pass. We got used to it, but it still was a very undesirable experience. Well, it took two-and-a-half days, but I finally got the air flow to move and do kind of what it was supposed to. But I was afraid if I promised it was fixed and it wasn't, I might not get paid. So I had them order a 50 cent part under the ruse that soon as I got it, "problem solved." If anybody reads this that worked in that dealership, would you drop me a note and tell me if that deal was fixed, or did it go to hell again?

Well, 'bout now I've decide that Pluto and I have had enough fun. We got our ten bucks and decided to return to the frozen north. Pluto could have been a model for Walt Disney's Pluto. He was just 'bout same color with the same spots. Pluto moved like a bowl of Jell-o. Everything just wobbled when he was in "normal" travel mode, and he had two gears; "normal and overdrive." Full grown he weighed 'bout 85-90 pounds, had long ears, two-tone eyes, one light gray and one kinda dark brown. He had two expressions. One was a very sad look, and the other was kinda a sneery look. Pluto's legs were very long, and he had a long, big tail. He was a short-haired dog with whopper power. Pluto, I guess, was a hunting dog with defective lineage. I doubt all his ancestors were from same tribe. Matter of fact, a certain part of his anatomy, I think came from elephants…that dog was blessed with humongous sexual equipment.

Although he never saw a race car, or was ever around them, he had pre-1960 racers traits. He was either looking for, trying to, or doing "it" 24 hours a day, seven days a week. One day a reporter asked me some questions 'bout how we planned to run Darlington, and I told him "Southern style." That was about Pluto. He chased anything that would run, from a mouse to a horse or bull. But when he ran he shifted into overdrive, his belly would almost rub the ground. He'd put his big tail straight out, his nose to the ground and ears straight back. I was told by hunting dog experts, that's how good southern hunting hounds ran: "belly to the ground, tail straight out, and ears straight back." Pluto's tail was his secret in catching everything. He had front steer, and rear steer. His big long heavy tail steered his ass end like a rudder on a boat or airplane.

Oh man, he could flat haul ass and catch anything he was after. Even tractors and trailers, but sometimes he had the problem of "now that you've caught it, what the hell you gonna do with it?"

Remember "Big Bill" my horse? One day ol' Bill quit running and taught Pluto how to fly (about 40 yards) with one good kick.

Watching Pluto chasing stuff reinforced a lesson taught me. "Be careful what you wish for, you may get it" (like chasing a skunk). Remember I told you Pluto could catch anything? Well, I made some money trapping muskrats and weasels. The area I lived in had lots of skunks. A good, 'bout all black skunk was worth 'bout four bucks skinned and stretched. In the worst case, a small one with lots of white brought 'bout 75 cents. We found if we drove an old car slow at night down country roads, (mostly unpaved) the skunks would be blinded and immobilized by the head lights. One boy driving and one boy on each running board. As you get close, you grab skunk by tail and jerk him off the ground. (If he can't plant his rear legs he can't spray) As you can guess, before night was over, both catchers got "skunked" good. Well now, how 'bout Pluto? Damn right, with ol' "never miss Pluto," our income 'bout doubled. But I can't describe what he smelled like as result regarding skunk piss. He'd jump all over us when we took skunk away from him to dump it in a burlap.

He taught me a lot about women. Yup, that dog helped me understand women. You ever have a male dog that would put his front paws around a female's legs and simulate intercourse? Well Pluto was bad 'bout doin' that. As a rule the lady would be very annoyed, and I'd have to holler and bang him to stop. But being a half-assed farmer, I noticed when big dogs, cows or horses were mating, the women watching would behave strangely. (It makes them horny.) But problem was, if I did what Pluto did (get hard and big and parade around, jump and hump on the closest lady) I might end up in jail. What I did learn was, whether it be for pleasure or for profit, it pays to advertise. And if you do your best, and are unsuccessful, just grin, shrug your shoulders, and, as you walk away, convince yourself that "Hell…I didn't want it anyhow." (I can remember trying and striking out, Fireball scored, and guess who got the clap?)

So anyway, I'm trying to get to Richmond, Virginia on the way back to Pennsylvania from my brief career as an air flow expert in Fayetteville. I'm 'bout 100 miles short, and it's raining like hell. I doubt I got two bucks in total. I'm riding a motorcycle with a side car for Pluto. Neither has a wind screen and the rain stings so bad I stop in front of nice farmhouse under some trees, get out a piece of canvas to wrap around me and the dog. In a few minutes he takes off, and a few minutes later a teenage girl comes down 'bout 50 yards to see what's wrong. She talks to me 'bout 30 seconds before a woman on porch calls her. The rain slows quite a bit, but I want to ask the lady to let us stay in barn, or some place, till morning. I don't know how to ask, so Pluto handles it. The farm lady has a fancy female dog (I guess with sex on her mind). As we walk toward the porch, Pluto has already "docked" with the "100 miles from Richmond" lady dog. I hear the commotion, and dog yelping, so I run up there. Pluto not only got the lady dog, but he's stuck and can't get loose. 'Bout half hour later we get dogs apart. The farmer lady's "sure cure" (cold water) didn't help. Her daughter brought piece of meat out, and 'cause by now Pluto is more hungry than sexy – the problem was solved.

We get invited to supper, and a place to sleep. We left 10 days later. Me with a sore peter, and both mother and daughter grinning and waving "bye-bye." If Rose happens to read this, the reason I didn't come back when I said, was because World War II started, and I was focusing on a war-related job, and I knew the farm deal would end shortly with me getting verbally abused. The father? I don't know, never asked, and nobody told me anything.

Took about two weeks to get back to Pennsylvania. Everybody seemed glad to see us. No jail if I'm a good boy. I get a pretty good job, best I ever had. The second World War is coming so a couple of real nice guys start a machine shop in Doylestown. They are doing munitions work. I'm a millwright's helper. The man I work for is sharp, quiet, and a super teacher. I'd been there three or four months, getting paid 25 bucks a week, straight time (with overtime, my pay came to 'round 40 bucks). Man, I'm practically a millionaire. I've got a girlfriend and I'm trying to screw myself to death. And I have backed way off on the drinking. The US motorcycle champion lives close by so I decide I will be a motorcycle racer and get a whole lot of money. Why the hell not? He runs an Indian Bonneville Scout. I've got one, but I need to, the phrase then was, "soup it up."

Well this racer's name was Bob Halloway (I think). He has a big ad in the magazines. In it he smokes Camels. Hell, I smoked a pipe, but I switch to Camels. As it turned out, he never really smoked in his life. I go watch him race at Langhorne. He's got 2 legs, 2 arms and 1 head just like me. I find out he don't smoke or drink. He is what they called an "up-country Dutchman." But I lose some respect for him, 'cause up till now I figured if they printed it…that was it. When I digested what I learned that day at Langhorne. I thought, "He likes to go fast and so do I…I'm just a little short on weight, but I'm strong." I figure, "Hell, in a couple years, I'll do the Camel ad, and be on the level…I'll smoke 'em."

First race is at Hatboro…a one-half mile (I think) dirt track. Things ain't going that well, my motorcycle smokes like hell. My "soup-up" job seems to be lacking something 'cause some of those other guys are running all over me. Here's where I get my nickname. I'm trying hard, I'm all over the track, getting in everybody's way. But with a lot of luck…and remember the word "desire?" What I'm doing excites the fans. The announcer forgets my name and I'm the new kid, "Smokey," named for the "Smoking Indian" I was riding. Well Hatboro's not gonna get me the Camel ad, so I work on the engine some more. I talked to the guy who built Halloway's engines and he really helped me. There's gonna be a big race soon in Langhorne.

I don't qualify or even try to, but I get in the feature through a non-qualifiers heat race. There are rules requiring credentials to run here, (experience rules) but I learn how to beat the system. Simply put, by lying and giving bum information, I get a license. Later in the day I realized they had a pretty good plan…experience was indeed important. In a few laps, (I guess there were 40 cycles in the race) I realize I'm really in over my head. Langhorne is a fast mile dirt track. The cycle runs half-decent, but going fast on a track by yourself is not quite the same as running in a pack of 40. In about three laps, as I'm going into turn one, I'm suddenly face-to-face with a rider who was in front of me. I believe his last name was "Fox." Well, we are both gonna need the same spot on the racetrack. He is going backwards trying to stop, and I'm going sideways, balls out, trying to miss him. Well, it didn't work out. The poor "Indian" of mine is all bent to shit, I've got a couple broken toes in my left foot, a broken left foot, a broken left hand, a four inch circle of skin missing on my left shoulder, and three or four broken ribs. I'm 30 miles from home, don't have a soul with me, and I'm using an assumed name. To top it off, it's getting dark, and there are no lights on the cycle (I rode it to the track.) Well, really, all the physical problems I had weren't that serious, but I'd never broken any ribs before and well, hell, you know what that feels like. I got home – finally. I lucked out and the machine shop doctors patched me up. And they gave me a machining job that took 'bout all day to make one cut. I never missed a day's work. I never rode the Indian again, don't know what happened to it. There was no hospital free treatment for racers then, and no insurance, so I just sweated out the healing. I still have one little toe on top of the next toe, that's the way it healed. My broken hand bones healed and lined up perfect. I retired as a motorcycle racer. Fuck the Camel cigarette ad. I decided to quit cigarettes too and go back to the pipe.

By now I had a fairly good car (a Plymouth four-cylinder coupe) a fifteen buck deal. I bought it, thinking, "if the cycle deal didn't work out it had a really neat big bore four-cylinder, and would make a hell of a sprint car motor." I knew a guy who has a home-made sprint car chassis made out of a 1934 Ford. We'll put my Plymouth engine in it. It had a Model B Ford four-cylinder with the Howe kit on it. Hell, I work in machine shop got everything in the world to make stuff. The sprint car never happens, and here's why.

My slightly worn scrapbook from the war – it also has lots of photos of my family and early life.

The machine shop buys an old lathe. (I believe George Washington used it in revolutionary war.) Big son-of-a-bitch, 'bout 30 feet between centers or more. The millwright modifies it and rebuilds it completely and I helped, so I am the number two expert on that lathe. They had just got a contract to rough machine 90 mm anti-aircraft gun barrels. They were very heavy as forged, looked like a big steel tree trunk. After we got the lathe running, the millwright runs a couple of these gun barrels through himself with his trusted helper "Smokey" (by now everybody called me "Smokey"). Well, the plant don't have a lathe operator qualified to do the job, so it's decided "let Smokey try it." I'm no Einstein, but I'm not plumb stupid. I figure if I goof up, a ruined gun barrel would cost the company a fortune, so I let them know "I don't want to." One of the partners (guy named "Doc," a pretty savvy gent), he says, "Yeah, I guess that would be too much for you to know how to do." Well, that done it, now I gotta have the job to prove I can. I was probably the best 90 mm gun barrel roughing out man they ever had. With this, the sprint car plan had a problem. I could work any amount of overtime I wanted, so if I worked on race car parts it was expensive to me because of lost overtime. Plus, the guy who had the car was a lazy drunk and a pain in the ass.

In case you never seen one, here's an old ad that shows a Pitcairn Autogio – and no, none of the guys who flew 'em looked like that.

The sprint car ambition would end soon enough. One Sunday I got real curious 'bout air-planes. Five miles down the road there is a town called Pitcairn. The town has a big airport and a factory that built airplanes and autogyros. You know what an autogyro is, or was? Well actually it was the father of the helicopter. Who invented the autogyro? I don't know. I thought Pitcairn did, but later I was told "Bullshit, a Spanish cat dreamt it up." What did it look like? Like a regular two seat low wing airplane, with a radial engine in the nose, but with short wings and conventional tail. But over the cockpit a rotor mounted horizontally. The forward speed of the machine was pulled by standard propeller. This causes the rotor to spin, so you could land at a very slow speed…say five to 10 mph. Another plus was, if engine quit, it didn't crash hard. But it never come close to winning the Nobel prize for aircraft wizardry.

"Mr. Pitcairn," the owner of all this, was quite a man. I think his ancestors came over on the Mayflower, and the king of England gave his ancestors 50 square miles of southeastern Pennsylvania. He owned the town of "Pitcairn," as a matter of fact Mr. Pitcairn started the US Air Mail service. He actually built a special airplane to carry the mail called "the Pitcairn Mail Wing." Well, at that airport I saw and sat in an old "mail wing," and had a ten minute ride in one. I guess it was a good airplane for 1920-something. Even after the airlines took over the mail hauling, Mr. Pitcairn continued to pay and employ his old mail wing pilots who chose to stay with him. I guess they did some giro flying and worked on them. Well after a few visits to his airport, I got a flaming desire to be a pilot.

Anyway, at the airport is a beautiful girl 'bout my age. I find out her dad is the head welder for Pitcairn. He's a Swede, still talks kinda funny…yes, he needs a welder (gas). All Air Force frames had to be gas welded, and to work on aircraft you had to become Army-Navy certified. Pitcairn pays for my certification, and gives me enough money to eat on. I'm finished with cars, motorcycles, and race cars…I'm gonna become a pilot and seduce my boss's daughter. Well, the "seduce" part had a snowball's chance in hell. He got me aside and said "he was young once and knew everything I was thinking…and that if I did get her to take her panties off, he will 'cut my nuts out.'" Could be that's an old Swedish saying, I never heard it before. Actually, he knew me a lot better than he knew his own daughter. I had mentally given up, but I learned another lesson, "all things come to those who wait." (Yup, she did.)

Why did Pitcairn spend money to train me? World War number two had just started. I soon find out he's signed contract to lease his factory to Firestone. They are in a joint venture to build huge wooden gliders. (Yep, I said wooden, but they had many metal parts). Well, I'm still working on autogiro airplane stuff, but the future is gliders. By now I see my future clearly…"Air Force fighter pilot." So I talk to Mr. Pitcairn about it, and surprisingly, he says "Do it," and "here's the road map." Man they were really hurtin' terrible for pilots…timing is everything in life. I go to Philadelphia and take the Aviation Cadets test. The rules say you "must be a college graduate, or pass a college level test for knowledge and skill." Boy, the test was a bitch. Kinda like a picture of a jackass, a bulldozer, an airplane and a mule, with instructions to "circle the airplane." In a week a letter from Air Force says, "Congratulations, you passed. Bring birth certificate and get a medical exam. The FBI will interview you for security check."

Well, step one is a bitch, I've got no birth certificate. "Born where" has two or three answers, "real first name" take your pick: Henry, Gregory, or Harold…"born when," that too is a little shaky. Matter of fact, there were two or four spellings of my last name. So I'm screwed…World War II ace shot in the ass…never made it off the ground. Pitcairn says, "How did you do in the test?" I tell him my problems. He's a quiet, unexciteable person, and he says

What the well-dressed future pilot wears.

"Let me think about it." In an hour he walks up and gives me a slip of paper with a Catholic priest's name and address in Philadelphia ,which is an hour away. As he leaves, he turns around and says, "Do you have 10 dollars?" I don't, so he gives me a 10 and says, "It will be subtracted from your pay." By 10 o'clock the next morning, I have a birth certificate that hasn't been questioned, to this day 60 years later. The priest chose "Henry" from my three names, and "sometime in May around 1923" became "May 25, 1923." My "place of birth" became Philadelphia. I swear, I was in and out the door in 10 minutes after the priest comes in the room. OK, next get physical. Half of that is "Do you like boys or girls best?" And "Have you ever tried to screw a dog or a sheep or cow?" (A joke going around was "I didn't 'cause every time I tried to kiss the cow it slipped out.")

Only problem is I have is some teeth problems that I had put off for two reasons. One, I was scared silly of dentists, and two, I didn't have the money. But here comes the "hooker." First thing is, I get sworn into the regular Army Air Force. Second thing is I get sworn into the Aviation Cadets. They know only about one third are gonna become air crew, so if you don't make it, you stay and do other enlisted people stuff...you know, grunt work. I never even knew what the hell was going on. All I can think is "in a year or so, I'm gonna shoot more goddam German's and Jap's than Eddie Rickenbacker did!" Yahoooo, I'm an Air Force pilot. Remember when I told you I hit a point in my life where for 'bout three years everything that could go wrong did? Well it happens again within a week.

The future "Eddie Rickenbacker."

It's just before Christmas, right after lunch – I'm welding some tubes in a new autogiro and one of the other welders has filled tube I'm welding with acetylene during lunch. I don't see him (this is a standard belly slapper trick) and my goggles are real loose with a big gap at the top. "Pow!" The big bang. Boy, this one ain't funny. My left eye gets hot metal in it. A day later I'm blind in my left eye. No chance for 20/20 eyesight again the company doctor says. The next day the Air Force says "report for transport to Air Force cadet training." Well, they ain't ready for one-eyed pilots yet," so inside of three hours I'm an ex-Aviation Cadet and loading up on a train for Miami Beach, Florida for basic training in the Air Force. I took my motorcycle goggles with me (they come in handy flying, right?) When I get to Miami, story is: you're gonna be anything from a dish washer to maybe a radio operator (on a plane)... "What you want to do?" Actually by now I'm crushed...I really don't give a shit. "Radio operator"..."Oh, OK, we need some. Finish basic training," which is basically switch you from a human to a robot doing calisthenics in a sand spur filled field in 90 to 95 degree weather. Swim in ocean? (Miami) Not in that movie.

Three day train ride from Miami (90 degrees) to Sioux Falls, South Dakota (40 degrees below zero, with snow and ice with 40 mph winds), in wood and tar paper barracks using soft coal for heat. Soft coal when burned really stinks, and also turns the snow black. Spinal meningitis hits like a freight train. Lots of young "would be heroes" died there. Man, I got low. I can't stand cold weather. Standing in the chow line 45 minutes in the cold and ice, covered with snot and phlegm from the sick did wonders for those who

Women mechancis and refuelers... hot damn services with a smile (all kinds).

were overweight.

Two months later I could build radio, take and send 18 words a minute in Morse code. The army dentist repaired my teeth and taught me to take care of 'em and consider what I ate carefully. Ha… what in the hell did I have to say about what I ate? People who flew (then) in unpressurized planes, experience terrible pain if they have fillings that leak (pressure changes), so the Air Force dentist used what felt like air hammers, crowbars and chain saws to fix our teeth.

Part of training requires flying in a twin engine bamboo bomber. I believe not much of a plane, and with a pilot that was a fuck-up pilot if there ever was one. Every landing was a miraculous recovery from the jaws of death. He was a pimple-faced, snot-nosed, li'l mamma's boy, scared plumb shitless. He was an example of how desperate they were for pilots. (If you read this Mr. Radio School pilot, I'd appreciate a card from you. I'll be happy to rescind my observations about your piloting and offer you a public apology if you lived through it flying.)

Anyhow, I asked to be reassigned to a different pilot, and damn if I wasn't. But the second Mr. Looney, snot-nose pilot cornered me and ends up saying, "If you think it's so easy, why don't you fly instead of turning radios off and on?" For the hell of it, next day I ask for an eye check. Doc says "Hey, that things looking much-much better." Then, you know the deal, "Which line can you read? etc." When he's finished the doc says "Come back in a month, I want to recheck. You're getting close to 20/20." Three weeks later I'm about to graduate radio school and I am gonna be assigned someplace else; probably a bomber group. I slide over

Some of my primary gang and a BT-13.

for recheck in desperation to beat the reassignment. I had a little trouble, and the Doc let me cheat a little. Goddam…he passed me again! (They really needed plane drivers). The next day I'm on a train headed to Santa Ana, California and pre-flight school. Lieutenant snot-nose 'ground looped' in a night landing night before I left. (Nope…nobody got hurt bad.)

Man, life sure switches fast. In a ten minute eye exam, a World War II flying ace is reinvented. But all the great feelings are kinda gone now. I find Santa Ana is gonna be double tough. There the college bit is real and the tests are gonna be real. Now here's the bad part. If you don't cut it here as a potential pilot, you got three roads: navigator, bombardier, or back to non-commissioned Air Force. Pilot, navigator and bombardier graduated as second lieutenants. There was a fourth slim chance, warrant officer infantry pilot. To me anything less than pilot was almost like a super-dishonorable failure. You see, I thought at this stage, "how well you learned to fly" was the boogie. Nope, not so, you had to absorb the math, physics, weather, engineering, aerodynamics and take or send 18 words of Morse code a minute. The college requirements were real. Well that 90 days were 20 hour days seven days a week. The college kids had hell with radio, engines and aerodynamics. I had no real trouble there. The math, physics, military code, and chemistry, were all way out of reach for me. I decided to try and memorize the stuff I was totally lost in. Believe it or not I found I could hold it a day or two. They always tested within 48 hours. In 'bout three months I cleared the toughest hurdle.

I get sent to Visalia, California for primary. PT-19 Ryans, a monocoupe low wing. Air Force then believes 40 years old is too old to fly and best way to see if a kid can make a pilot is to give him two hours of aerobatics as a passenger. Your first flying day they try to make you sick in spins, snap rolls, chandelles, upside down loops and slow rolls. I had a little trouble, never puked but came awful close. If you puked, off to bombardier or navigator school you went. After that it was all down hill. You got eight hours instruction and then your solo. Shit man, no way to describe it 'cause you never know whether you

Me and Mr. Waters – the guy who taught me how to fly.

get a chance to solo or wash out. Wash out is a term for "couldn't cut it, fucked duck, ain't got it." The Aviation Cadets was a string of cliffhangers…five to be exact. (Pre-flight, primary, basic, advanced, operational training). Any of these 'bout 90 courses could be your washing out. If you washed out they could make a navigator, bombardier or hell any kind of an Air Force officer out of you or even a dish washer. My instructor is a nice man, civilian pilot Mr. Waters. In 'bout a week of flying Mr. Waters says "Henry, I don't think you're gonna make it." Brother that done it, I'm now one flying son-of-a-bitch. I couldn't even come close to accepting a wash-out mentally.

The day you or anyone solos an airplane is very special (by the way, where I was you got eight days to do it or else... Hours?…'bout eight to 12). That feeling you get when you fire the engine and line 'er up on the runway, see the green lite and shove the throttle all the way up and when you feel the wheels come off the ground and now it's you …man…what a thrill. You fly 30-40 minutes. Time to land…that last 15 feet to the ground, your ass holes so puckered up you couldn't drive a ten penny nail up it with a four pound hammer. You land and start breathing again. I think they cut or jerk the sleeve off of your shirt or flying suit (a solo ritual). The day I soloed I knew "Eddie Rickenbacker the second" was on his way. I loved the

WHERE DO RACERS COME FROM?

Yep, that's me after my first solo.

aerobatics, and in primary and basic flight training, aerobatics were a big-big part of the deal.

Mr. Waters and I never really got on same page. I don't know how to explain it, but it's like in racing if the driver, mechanic and money can't communicate, ain't nuthin' gonna happen. He was, I'm sure, a very good pilot and instructor, but I couldn't dig him.

Well I graduate. "What you want to be?"…"A fighter pilot"…"OK, go to Taft, California (at the time a deserted half-assed oil field). I think we got BT-13s. Some kind of canvas-wood-metal single engine trainer, 'bout twice the everything of the Ryan also a low wing, I believe with retractable wheels. I can't remember too much 'bout Taft. It was a hot, undesirable area with next to no vegetation and no nonsense. Hard nose training: day, night, cross country and aerobatics out the ass. I'm becoming a robot. No pussy in three months in Miami, no pussy in three more in South Dakota, two quickies in Santa Ana, a couple "almosts" in Visalia, flat zero in Taft. Good thing story 'bout masturbation and eyesight is not a fact or by now most pilots in training would have been half-blind.

As you read along you may think "this screwball's a sex fanatic." Check this out: my adventures in a space of 300 yards.

– 12 years old: playing football at friend's house, just two of us. I get kicked in the balls. Mommy says, "I need to put ice on it"(Yeah, sure), and then says "I need to kiss it to make it better," then decides to have sex – with her boy watching and her on her period?

– 13 years old: I'm a paper and magazine boy. Lady told me, "don't leave paper or magazine outside, bring it inside." "Sure." Uh, oh, with a big police dog?

– 14 years old: got a girlfriend. Her momma says, "I know what's going on. It's OK, but here's how to do it and not get pregnant." My first blow job, and suddenly I can't see. Yup, right on my face. She says "Did you like that?" Yuck, hell no. But what can you say to your girlfriend's mother?

While in advanced training – the "Dear John" letter…yup my girlfriend couldn't wait. A sailor was taking over for me…I wonder if he got the mother too?

Jr. Wylie, me and Billy Wilson.

19

My buddy Zack that I trained with in Marfa – you'll hear more about him later.

Anyway, the two li'l deals in Santa Ana: first one – double my age, wants to get married (insurance and allotment.); second one – telling her young husband how much she misses him on the phone while doing "it" with me (he's in an Army camp). The Air Force spent 10% of your time telling you and showing films of the horrors of venereal disease. In the film a soldier with his face mouth and tongue eat up with syphyllis would scare you half to death. But if you got a leave, it was the same ol' deal; the sun went down and our peckers went up. They taught us about and furnished us with prophylactic kits. You know, right after sex put a, b, and c on and wrap it up and put it in a bag (like a Bull Durham bag). I lost my best girlfriend on account of these things. I think party's over, so I put this mess on. But the li'l lady says if you don't do it to me again, I will die. Well in trying to get the black goop off of me, the sink, my hands, my underclothes get covered with this seemingly unremoveable mess. The lady accidentally sees the mess and my useless attempt to clean. Man, when she finds out I put this stuff on 'cause she may be diseased, I found myself in the street in six seconds. I took a week to really get it all off. Nope never again. Instead I always asked the lady if she had any problems I ought to know about. But really blind faith in penicillin did away with any second experience with a pro kit.

OK, I graduate primary so the next step is basic in Taft. BT-13 (I think)…single engine, bigger, heavier, more power. They concentrated on cross country, instruments and aerobatics. Man I'm sure I'm on my way to PT-6s. Taft was 18 hours a day wide-ass open calisthenics. I think they wanted us all to do a mile in one minute. But we had to do two miles in 10 minutes along with ground school and flying. Any of you who knew Taft in 1941 know why I'm not writing about all the fun I had there. Time I left Taft I could fly an airplane. Up till then the airplane flew me. I've got three of the five hurdles conquered. I'm still a pilot.

Advanced was in Marfa, Texas. I knew when I got assigned to Marfa I was on wrong road to being a fighter pilot ace, so I asked for reconsideration to fighter pilot, and find out 95% of all pilots ask for fighters. "OK, I'll switch to fighters after the bombers." Well, turns out it could

Me and Renee after graduation.

be worse, I could be in line for air transport command flying freighters – passenger flying airplane delivery boys.

Marfa, Texas in the early forties ain't nobody's favorite place, 'cept if you're a rattlesnake or a coyote. We flew the UC-78 bamboo bombers, wood and cloth twin engine quickie trainers, (el cheapo's) but plenty good enough. Only fun I had there was to get down to locomotive level with one landing lite on at night and pull up 'bout 50 feet before the locomotive. But it had to be on a dark night 'cause if they got our tail number it was "adios." Other fun was to drop Coke bottle close to farm tractors or horses. The noise was real – they whistled like bombs in a movie. Horses would set world records for a standing quarter mile.

I have a friend in advanced, Willie Walker from Memphis, ain't got too much family either. In the military everything went by last name, first initial. So no matter what it was, good or bad, I either got it last or next to last. Believe it or not, this system really had a bearing on your military adventures. I meet this nice guy from Memphis, Willie Walker 'cause we sleep close together ("w"-"y"...get it?). Yippe-ki-ay, we both make it.

Me and Bill showin' off our new metal.

My sister Renee wants to come pin my wings on (a big Air Force deal for some)...the girlfriend I had at home by now has given me the "Dear John" letter and the Navy has taken over. Well nothing's forever is it? Here's the deal: When you get your wings and commission some "very important somebody" in your life is supposed to pin your wings and 2nd Lieutenant bars on for the first time. Well my sister Renee did it for both Willie and me. Willie Walker was a super nice guy. I think they have had a very happy marriage. Willie went on to fly B-29s and photographed the atomic destruction of Japan. I didn't think he could ever make a real good pilot, he didn't drink, gamble or chase pussy enough. I suppose after this book's published they'll probably prefer not to be identified with me. (To shorten up this part, they have been married 'bout 55 years and still seem to like each other.)

Renee, Willie and I enjoyed the graduation. I understand in my exuberance, and with maybe a li'l too much tequila, Renee had to pay for some damage. Except for occasional pranks and graduation, my three months at Marfa were not fun. Only safe thing I enjoyed was visit to Pecos

Me and Renee after graduation and tequila.

to see Judge Roy Bean's old bar and the town. You know living in that country in late 1800s must have been rough sledding.

OK, I'm a genuine Air Force pilot – 2nd Lieutenant, fancy uniform, "hot shot charlie" hat, white silk scarf, big ol' shiny wings. It felt 'bout like winning at Indy. Got a couple weeks off so I'm going back to see my unfaithful girl who deep sixed me and make her sorry she did. Also to see Pluto and fire up my Indian Chief and go for a ride. Gonna strut through town and show 'em that goddam, wild-assed kid was a big success. Well the town didn't give a shit. I did get my ex-girlfriend's bloomers off again, but I knew 'fore

Just a big operator.

I was one day gone, the Navy would take back over. But I needed that to walk away and forget I ever had anything there. You hear the deal "you can't go back home once you left"…it's a fact.

Within a week it was all a memory and a dim neutral one. I wasn't pissed at my ex-girl. The motorcycle was no longer important. Pluto didn't even recognize me – barked at me and I thought he was gonna bite me. I remember thinking "You son-of-a-bitch, how could you forget so quick?" But it was 18 months. I forgave him. Hell, I doubt my girlfriend lasted six months, but that's life…ain't no use getting pissed. If I'd had a gal chasing my ass 'round once or twice a week I wouldn't have lasted one week. My mother's real happy. Big jump in 2nd Lieutenant's send-home money: $21 a month for a private, I think around $400 a month for a 2nd Lt., with flight pay.

Off to Roswell New Mexico, hello B-17.

Tail End Charlie Goes to Europe

Three months of Roswell, New Mexico B-17 transition. Simple translation: learn how to fly a B-17.

I need to set the movie up for some later happenings. In Marfa a big-big cat named "Zackerson," a 19-year-old kid named "Yunick," a big blond German "Von"-something and a guy named "Willie Walker" hung around together. With our initials, our beds are next to each other. Once a month the Army performed a ritual called "short arm inspection." You get up at 5:30 am (no clothes) stand in front of your foot locker. A doctor (could be, and in Marfa was, a female) examined your peter for venereal disease. As she stepped in front of you she'd bark "skin it back. Some guys that weren't circumcised couldn't get the skin back. How would you like to inspect 300 penises a day for three or four days in a row? Could that get boring considering the up side of this medical procedure? Now to make it a less embarrassing deal, the doc gave a red ribbon for the biggest and littlest. "Von-Something" won the "whopper award," (which I was jealous of) and poor Zack got the "midget peter" red ribbon. Zack wasn't circumcised and that led to some trouble soon after. "Where's Zack?"…"In base hospital"…"Why?"…"He got married and his new wife got his foreskin back…it swelled up so he was circumcised three days ago." "Where's Von-something?"…"Emergency three day extra leave"…"He got married and new wife's got badly wounded pussy." ("Von-Something" married a little-bitty, cute blond nurse, who seemed to just love to get put in the hospital for a wounded pussy.)

Roswell is a hot-hot place…120 degrees plus on the runway. But right over the runway, at 30,000 feet, it's 65 degrees F… below zero. I'm not pulling your leg. I can still remember my first experience doing a walk around pre-flight inspection with a little major that was my assigned instructor. A 19-year-old kid, who would have been a gas station mechanic if no war had started, is supposed to know how to fly this

Do I look old enough to be flying a B-17?

180,000 pound mother of 'bout 200 foot wing span night or day, clear weather or instrument weather anywhere in the world. Why do I mention night flying? 'Cause during the war we were not allowed illuminated runways or use of landing light. Airport lights under combat conditions would make airports sitting ducks. Hell you weren't even supposed to light a cigarette outside at night (here or in combat). Sound goofy? I think it was but that was our leader's rule. Where's the runway? When you flare out during a night landing and your ass is 30 feet in the air and you can't see in front, you're looking at your own plane's nose. As I crawled up into the pilot's seat for the first time (and it was at night) the li'l major said sure is big ain't it? I said wow, I can't believe this thing can fly it's so big. He said, "After four hours of instruction, you'll solo this thing. I'll be your co-pilot." He also said every time you crawl in this thing it will get smaller and smaller. When you walk out and it looks like a Piper Cub watch out, that's ass busting time. He said this is the toughest airplane in the world but if you fuck up this thing will wind your clock quicker than a cat can clean it's ass.

The classroom training was not my favorite part.

Other than learn to fly, there is flat nothing to do. Roswell is a neat li'l western horse town. It's got a big cave nearby and if you like bats you got it made. But I found a cabin deal in Ruidoso, New Mexico run by a lady bout 85 to 90 that had posters of all the old time bad guys and Indians. She also had a big collection of saddles, guns, knives, bows, arrows, spears and Indian and early Western clothes. I never tired of her stories of the West in the late 1800s. Geronimo lived within five miles of her place at one time…I guess that it's still part of an Apache reservation. Man, she sure put the "bad mouth" on how we treated the Indians, and said 90 percent of the outlaw stories and lawmen stories were bullshit dreamt up by a couple of Eastern paperback magazine writers. If there is such a place as "God's country" that might have been it. The air smelled like pine needles…big, beautiful trees…big green meadows with a cold-clean creek running through, and quiet. So quiet you could hear a skunk fart.

Here I am at the threshold of step five (the last step) to qualify as a combat pilot. The alternative here is you become a copilot on a bomber or in the air transportation commands. Co-pilot can be a bad deal where all you do is say "flaps open, flaps closed," "gear down, gear up" and your life is in the hands of God knows who. When you get right down to it, quite a few who would be between 76 and 85 years old in 2000 ain't here because they were sitting in airplanes that stopped too quick from 1941 to 1946. After

Eager cadets.

I made it through the two engines on one side landing and take off I thought, "Yeah…I can fly this thing." "Hey…where's the runway lights?…Hell…It's pitch black." The li'l major says "calm down – think 'bout flying this thing and forget 'bout it's dark – don't worry 'bout it. Hell, you got 10 grand free insurance."

I meet a rich 17-year-old nymphomaniac who lives with her grandma. She had a new car. Here's the deal: she sees two dogs and one sniffs the other's ass, she's sexy. If she sees a boy horse with his cock out, she's sexy. No big deal. Here's the big deal. She gets her kicks with the danger of getting caught at a stop lite. She'd climb on you while you're driving, or behind a gas station, or in a restaurant parking lot (in the daytime). She'd follow me into men's room and do it on the toilet or in the next room from where grandma's sleeping…with door open. She would do it in the car, on the car hood, anywhere all the time. And to top it all off, you could hear her for 50 yards.

I don't know which is the hardest on the nerves; two weeks learning to land at night without lights, or possibly getting caught with her (17?). I get used to night landing with no lights, but not her. Suddenly she dumps me for a "30-something" colonel…zingo!…I'm history. Won't take phone calls and if I see her she ignores me. That really wounded my ego. It was the first time I got deep-sixed by a girl. I'd sure love to know what her adventures were from there on. Man, that was 100 pounds of "something else."

We finish up our training. 'Bout half become co-pilots for multi-engine heavy aircraft. The rest become multi-engine heavy aircraft commanders. Some go to transport, some to B-24s, some to B-17s. Willie Walker and I get multi-engine heavy air craft command of B-17s at Dyersburg, Tennessee for crew, bombing, gunnery, and combat operational training. At the time Dyersburg was hottest place I'd seen on earth. It was 100 degrees with 100% humidity, 24 hours a day, seven days a week. No air conditioning, so you'd sleep bare-assed naked and wake up at 5:00 am, soaking wet with sweat. Man, you'd climb up in the cockpit at noon and with the windows closed, it's 135 to 140 degrees in there. Hell, if you didn't wear gloves, stuff in there would burn you. You're more than likely to be going to 30,000 feet to fly formation. Up there it's 65 to 70 degrees below. Heater?…not that I could find. It was unpressurized as well, so we breathed oxygen out of bottles.

Yep, that's me after my first solo.

So here's how it goes:
Layer 1: silk everything head to toe.
Layer 2: wool underwear head to toe with electric connections head to toe.
Layer 3: GI khaki wool pants and shirt.
Layer 4: sheepskin pants with suspenders, sheepskin boots, sheepskin jacket and leather gloves.

I wore a wool head sock for flash burn protection, silk, and a heated wool and sheepskin buckled head cover. Three head coverings so far. Now a pair of wide goggles (orange lens) to prevent flash blindness. On top of all this, an iron flak helmet. Next we wear a flak suit, kinda looks like a catcher's chest protector canvas with steel inserts. I'll guess it's about 35 pounds. I ain't done yet. We also have to put on a back pack parachute and a chest reserve chute.

What's a back pack chute? First, it's a parachute – and a good one. Second, it has in it an escape kit. It goes like this: if your mission is across Yugoslavia and into Germany, you have a silk map of every country you fly over, and a series of language books. Silk maps because it's "light, strong and waterproof." The language books work this way: I point to a sentence in English "I'm hungry," or "I need a doctor." The Pollock then looks in my book and points to his answer in Polish, and right along side is the English interpretation. The kit also has 300 or 400 American dollars in it. Language is a nice touch, but that's what makes shit happen.

A Boeing B-17-E Flying Fortress.

In the kit there is also a medical section. It has medicine for infections, bleeding, pain, diarrhea, and "stay awake" pills. In this section there are several heart-shaped orange colored pills marked in four sections. Two of these sections are enough to make you climb laughing on the top of a missile and tell 'em to light it. A kinda "brave" pill which gives you ungodly stamina for 'bout 36 hours. When that son-of-a-bitch wears off, you are gonna sleep for 24 to 30 hours, I don't care where you are when it poops out. You guessed it, the little orange pill was always disappearing. One hundred bucks apiece was the going rate in combat area bars. (Nope, they were not in the state-side backpacks.) There is some powerful food in there too. It'll keep you going for a week, and if desert fly over is involved, a water ration is included. Oh yeah, I almost forgot, also had a .45 pistol and about 75 rounds, a GI Knife and an oxygen bottle in your left pant leg. There is also an altimeter by the oxygen bottle.

You wear this shit for 10 or 12 hours at a time, and you climb into a 17 from below, under the cockpit. You have to be assisted because you can't make it with your own power. It's 135 degrees in there and you got nearly 100 pounds of stuff on plus your GI shoes are tied to your belt (you need shoes to walk in if you bail out). When you pull the rip cord and the chute opens, the second thing you notice is that your shoes break the laces and hit you in the face as they leave (you're right – leather laces)…you could tell who had been down that road by the knots in his shoe laces.

The Dyersburg deal was to teach real combat conditions. We used the guns, dropped the bombs, flew formation, did it all 'cept no fighters shooting at us and no flak coming up. Good thing too or all the pilots would have resigned. Well some rotten bastard shot up a colored man's house and killed the occupants, so my whole time there I was listening to "Who shot Sam Bass?" 'Cause he was a poor colored cat, it was treated like a joke.

I'm nearly ready to go overseas. All this training is with the nine others who will crew your plane in combat. Any of you ever read "Smiling Jack," a war time cartoon 'bout the Flying Tigers in this time frame?…A guy named Zack Mosley from I believe Vero Beach, Florida was the author.

My co-pilot was Lieutenant Charles Charles, a small, mustachioed "would be" fighter pilot. Later "Smiling Jack" had a "Hot Shot Charlie" as an ace Flying Tiger pilot. It will turn out that "Hot Shot Charlie" was Lt. Charles Charles.

We are close to graduation. One tough part was formation. A "group" was 400 bombers – 16 in a squadron – a diamond of four diamonds. Each wing half on a 17 was 60 feet long. We had to overlap wings bout 20 feet and keep about a 20 feet vertical for 10 hours. Worse part of the deal was vapor trails. When the weather was wrong, as we disturbed the super saturated air with our wings the pressure and temperature change would result in turning that air into a whitish vapor. Well, after about 30 minutes of white trails whipping past your cockpit, you'd lose your orientation and get vertigo – (delusions in reference to other planes), So you had to give it to co-pilot for 5 to 10 minutes to reorient yourself. There is no alternative except a collision.

When you're flying right wing, the co-pilot in the other plane is close enough to recognize his face. In all the airplanes the pilot sits on the left, the co-pilot on right. The job kept you busy with prop wash, rough air, spent bullet shells coming through your props and into your windshield plus watching enemy fighters positioning themselves, waiting for you to come through the flak.

It's kinda like driving a race car at 200 mph, 'cept race cars are inches apart and weigh 1,500 to 3,500 pounds. But concentration is 'bout the same and the rookie-expert movie is real.

That is "what can I do if that fucker on either side or above or below me goofs, panics, or gets scared shitless?" Airplanes are like open wheel race cars, touch wings or wheels and the shit's in the fan.

Dyersburg was close to Memphis, so a leave day was Memphis honky tonks, booze and virgins, and also the annual state fair. This is a big-big deal. Waaaay too much to drink. I get back to base by the skin of my teeth in reference to being late, no sleep, get to flight line. We go up into hi-altitude formation, 28,000 feet and my appendix breaks. Co-pilot has never considered learning how to fly this big mother. Now his ass is damn near six miles up in formation with an unconscious pilot. I'm in and out of consciousness. I wake up with the co-pilot trying to land plane while the tower gives him verbal help. I come to and try to help with "do's, dont's and oh shits." Remember, I told you when you hurt bad enough fear of death doesn't exist? He misses three approaches. I'm tired of the suspense and either wanna die landing or get to the doctor. Next one I land it with trim tabs. Ain't got enough strength to simply hand fly it.

I wake up in the hospital minus the appendix. (this was before air conditioning). I think, "Hell ain't much different than earth…'bout as hot…people look the same…nobody's got horns…wooden building? A voice says, "How you feel?" I answer "I've got world's biggest headache, I'm so sore it hurts to breathe and

I'm thirsty." "Nope – can't drink" (something 'bout anesthesia). I gotta go to bathroom and I want to puke. "How do you feel?" another asks. I start to completely destroy any chance for good relations with medical staff. "Like a tiger that just got run over by a tank." The nurse outranks me and chews my ass out. The doctor says "Shut your damn mouth and don't move for at least one hour." I'm now sure this is hell. Well, how many people told me that's where I was headed? I see bout three of the crew members coming towards me. Holy shit! I guess I killed whole damn crew. Turns out they just come to hospital to see if I survived the broke appendix operation. Well hell, I feel a little better, I ain't dead. "Bye-bye crew." It turns out the operation stops combat for me for 90 to 120 days. They give my crew to another pilot. I'm pissed…it looks like I'm never gonna get to blow those German mothers all to shit. I'm an engineering test pilot now.

The test pilot job is a boring eight-hour ride around in circles. I'm supposed to see if the mechanics did a good job rebuilding the engines and plane. After a week I start to make the circle bigger and bigger. (Remember, no radar, no transponder, nobody knows where the hell I am.) I get braver and braver. Finally, I'm over Daytona Beach, site of the world's land speed record. Damn, Daytona was a beautiful place in 1941. Big, wide, smooth, beach. Main streets covered by big oak trees with Spanish moss hanging all over 'em. US Highway 1 is so covered with trees you have to put your lights on for six miles in the daytime

…Ormond to Allendale big green tunnel.

I decide when I leave the service I'm gonna live in Daytona. (Nope, never got caught)

When time was up I got a crew someone else started and I suppose a medical problem broke up.

"Go to Lincoln, Nebraska with your crew." Nine guys in a crew: co-pilot, navigator, bombardier, flight engineer, radio operator, ball turret gunner, left and right waist gunner, and tail gunner. I was so happy to get out of Dyersburg. I was bored, reckless and bound for trouble. The unauthorized roaming during those engineering check rides plus a little unauthorized maneuver like doing a loop with a B-17 once in awhile. (I did it 'cause an older pilot I admired told me how to do it.) I also got a little reckless in the lady department (like "doing it" on a bus station bench at 5:00 pm with a PX employee). I needed to get a lot more serious with my job before I got caught.

The new crew and I didn't really hit it off too good. Kinda same deal. The co-pilot is a gum-chewing, zoot-suiter, with a little "womb broom" mustache and sideburns; a "would-be" fighter pilot. (Remember I'd already seen that movie). I got orders: "Report to blabbady blah unit, Marrakesh, Africa ASAP!" "Marrakesh…where the hell is that?" "French Morocco, the gold coast of West Africa." "OK." Go to Lincoln, Nebraska and pick up your new shiny B-17. We fly from Lincoln, Nebraska back to Dyersberg, then to an Air Force base in Maine. When we get to Maine old "zoot suit," a kid named Borch, is one sick puppy (like a bad cold). Fuel up and go to Gander Lake, Newfoundland. The weather is bad-bad. By the time we got to Gander field the co-pilot's a basket case. Take him from plane to hospital (pneumonia). I said weather was bad…do you believe I flew through a hurricane from Maine to just out of Newfoundland? The hurricane caught up with us 'bout midnight.

We are at Gander Lake. Operations says, "Go to your plane and keep outboard engines running and keep nose of plane into the wind." After two hours of this and the eye of the storm gets there. Now no wind. Go back to operations to get a weather briefing. They say they are loading my crew and filling fuel tanks. They give me an estimated departure and "To the Azores Islands in one hour." "Hey, ain't got a co-pilot…go without?" "Nope, when you get back to plane, a co-pilot will meet you; an air transport command pilot." "Can he fly a 17?"…"Sure, he can fly anything."

You wanna guess who I find sitting in the co-pilot's seat? Gene Autry, civilian aircraft Transport Command pilot.

Well shit, if he brought his guitar we can…nope. Gene Autry hands me his papers. They order him to fly co-pilot to the Azores Islands. The island we land on is 'bout one mile long and half mile wide. Find that son-of-a-bitch with a rookie, scared shitless New York hebe navigator, we did! And, ain't got enough fuel left for an alternate airport. Know why? The alternate is 10 hours away. I've got ten hours time on the ground there. Lindbergh in my mind was ten foot tall. Boy, that cat must of had the balls of a dinosaur to pull that deal off in the li'l shit box at low level.

The singing cowboy did not say one fucking word to me the whole 10 and a half hour trip except repeat my control commands: "15 degree flaps… full cowl flaps…gear up." I could still hear pretty good then and hell, he never even hummed a cowboy song, never showed me a picture of his horse…nuthin.' But he was a brave man. He could not fly a 17, yet he crawls into one with rookie nineteen year old cat who at best is half-qualified in case all don't go right. Plus we left in the eye of a hurricane, which meant at least one hour of very, very turbulent weather, and we can't go back to Gander if we have a problem 'cause of the

This is what Daytona looked like back them. (Courtesy of Daytona Beach News Journal)

weather. Was I scared? You're damn right I was till I seen the island. Even then, it was a very hairy landing. The runway starts at ocean edge and ends at ocean edge. I get it "whoaed" with 'bout 20 feet to spare. The brakes are red hot. Go to briefing…now I'm puffed up like I got ten years ocean flying. I'm starting to use ol' pilot's slang. "How was the hurricane?" "Oh shit, nuthin' to it." "Have trouble finding the island?" "Nope, hit it rite on the head" (more like shithouse luck). "Really a short runway ain't it?" "I never noticed" (what a crock… last 100 yards, my asshole was so puckered up you couldn't have driven a 20 penny nail up it with a ten pound sledge hammer).

In the morning we head out to Marrakesh. The weather's good and I've got a new co-pilot. This cat's a talker. "Heard you had Gene Autry yesterday as a co-pilot, what kind of guy is he?"

"Oh wonderful…played his guitar all the way over and sang. Told me if I ever get to Hollywood when war was over, to stop in to see him…said he'd let me ride his horse around the block." "Guns?"… "Yup, had one on each side – chrome plated and genuine ivory grips." New co-pilot says "Damn! You're lucky." Autry died a year ago. For 55 years I kept thinking I'd run into him and remind him of the li'l trip in the hurricane. I got even…I never went to see any of his movies.

I'm on final approach at Marrakesh, down to 100 foot. A big sign on side of runway to "watch out for lions on the runway." (in English) Lions?…I did see a couple of burros. Hot damn! It's hot.

"When we gonna bomb the Germans?"… "Don't know, ain't ready yet."

I meet an American engineer representing the company that made the AT-20s across on the other side of the air base. Who are they?…"The French Foreign Legion!" There is a problem. The "frogs" are metric trained. All the stuff in the "20s" is in pounds, you know, in English. He says, "Wonder if you'd consider helping me check some of 'em out while you wait here for your assignment?" "Hell no…too damn hot." Anyway, only thing I know in French is "we-we" or something like that, supposed to mean "yes." That night at the local night club I notice the Foreign Legion pilots got a corner on all the fancy pussy in the joint. "Hmmmmmmm, maybe I should go help them tomorrow." Next day I fly with two of 'em. This don't help much, but with an interpreter sitting on my lap the next day, we hit the jackpot. The interpreter is 'bout five foot four, 95 pounds, long-haired, and beautiful. I'm sure long ago her ancestors were related to the mink family. I played that game for 'bout a month.

I've seen Foreign Legion movies where the legionnaires go through hell. Take my word for it, any tears shed for the Legion pilot's are wasted. Those cats lived one day at a time and did one thing at a time. I decided part of their training must have required demonstrating they could fuck eight hours a night seven days a week. They were good pilots, crazy as hell, but they flew the plane like a good horseman rides a horse. The plane did not fly or intimidate them. They taught me the "virgin routine." "Love me tonight, I've never did it before and tomorrow I may die." They helped me with a touch of racism I believe I had before then. I overcame my concern for skin color. In truth, I should have been considered a good will ambassador for the US. They also taught me to "understand what you intend to do, and then fucking do it." They taught me to "be sure and live through today, or maybe I"ll miss something really good tomorrow." They taught me "make the best you can of what you're handed and never complain." I'm positive they taught me things in several weeks that extended my life considerably. (I should mention wherever we went, I'd come into contact with a unique pussy marketing ploy. A young boy approached us with six to eight pictures of his 18 year old sister. Yes, nude and suggestive. For this transaction, language was not a barrier the world over, "fig-fig" or "zig-zig" did it.)

As I think bout them, they reminded me of a joke I heard later. A pilot, co-pilot and engineer are flying a DC-3 in India. They've got five USO "movie stars" on board and plane trouble that means bail out, but the plane's got only enough chutes for the crew. Pilot says, "Bail out!" Co-pilot says, "What 'bout the girls without chutes?" Pilot says "Fuck 'em." Co-pilot says, "Do you think we have enough time?" This last line was how those cats lived. Soon it is time for me to go. Tunis, Bizerte, lots of destruction, killing and misery.

I go to Bizerte. Same army deal, "Hurry up and wait." Well hell, at least there is lots of bars and plenty of gals. Somebody says, "Best deal going is in the Casbah." I say "Well, I've already been there." He says, "Bullshit…you couldn't find it in a week." I say, "Hell, the Legion pilots had me all over it." Turns out all old African cities have a Casbah. It's a name of the core of the city (and it's walled), that means "here's where the poor, real nationals live." It has it's own laws, customs, and life style. An example: hell, they use every form of dope known to man openly, and it's for sale dirt cheap. You could also still buy slaves in there. (Interestingly, the sellers were black or arabs). So for you world travelers on the west side of Africa, when you ask to be taken to the Casbah, you may regret it.

I don't have the Legion pilots to help me in Bizerte, so I get a bartender to teach me French (seemed like French was main language on the Gold Coast.) Probably ain't real correct, but as I remember it "Vulevo coushae de wette ava qua?" means "Will you sleep with me tonight?"

This approach is not bullet proof. You either get a "Oui" or a slap in the snoot. I was working on a response to the slap in the snoot where I would say in French "In that case, I guess a blow job is out of the question?" (I did not master this.)

Here it is, an assignment. "Take your plane and crew to Bari, Italy for next assignment." 'Bout a week of "hurry up and wait," so we decide to investigate the sex habits of the Italian female and to learn what the different wine words meant. Money was easy – a lira was a penny – 100 lire one buck. I meet a neat li'l lady 'bout 17-18 years old. Grandmother's sick and she needs ten bucks to save her life. How's this work? I give ten bucks, save grandma, then tonite I go to her house and she will teach me Italian and explain the country. I'm leery of the deal, but my pecker over rules my brain. I do have enough sense to take the "equalizer" inside a boot (a la the Legion pilots). It was kinda chilly there, but I guess she didn't notice it. Anyhow, I find myself 50% shit-faced drunk, disrobed, and engaged in a spirited fucking contest. Well suddenly the little Italian "good will ambassador" disappears and so do my clothes. But because in true "western style," I did not remove my boots and throw 'em down…I had put 'em back on. When I go into the next room looking for the girl, there's two or three mean lookin' uncles and grandma – and grandma don't look sick to me. We have a language barrier. It becomes clear that if I don't leave (less clothes) and quick, I may get seriously injured. I grabbed my Italian-American language interpreter out of my boot, put one in the floor by their feet, and the clothes miraculously reappeared (minus 'bout 15 bucks).

I'd already learned that if things go to shit and you can negotiate without physical damage, haul ass and return with reinforcements. I grabbed my clothes and left. An MP was right there in the street. He asked me why I was undressed. I explained my failed "romance." I'm pretty sure several MPs went up to the room and ruined the uncles' evening.

Air Force people had two major problems in this war area. The Germans and, in some places, the dagos. Someone would pay handsomely for Air Force uniforms and Air Force credentials. Why? I can only guess (probably for some sort of espionage). It seems many adventurous American air crew members would disrobe at the drop of an attractive (and some not so attractive) lady's panties. As a rule the air crewman had enough alcohol in him to ignore potential trouble and, getting rite to the point, often ended up one drunk, naked, lost, scared American male who just entered into an arrangement with the devil and the venereal disease experts at the base hospital. At this time he did not know of the near term problem his li'l pecker created. I guess the moral of this story is "Fuck with your clothes on and a .45 in one hand when in unfamiliar territory." I had a bombardier, Frank Bartlet, who stared in a movie just as I described. Penicillin saved his ass from being a star in an Air Force training film.

I get to experience combat in Italy. After ten minutes of flak, fighters shooting real live bullets, and seeing what was happening to some of the others, combat don't seem so great. There is no way to describe the helplessness of a big plane like a 17 spinning down tail first and burning. That was the one and only time I looked and tried to count chutes coming out. Why? In that minute I damn near joined them by not paying attention to all the evil intentions the German fighter pilots and the German aircraft gunners had regarding my survival. In short, ten minutes of real danger scared the "give a shit" out of me. Hell, it's like my plane is a sitting duck. When you hit the IP and you lock on the auto pilot, some scared shitless bombardier is up in front fiddling with the Norden bomb sight and driving the plane. He can move the plane up or down left or right with his control of the auto pilot. (That, by the way, lasted three minutes for my whole career. From then on I'd tell the bombardier, "You talk to me – I'm flying this mother.") Remember, we are in a very-very tight formation. The tighter you flew, the tougher our gun power was in total. If you for any reason got unhooked from formation, Hogan's goat had a better chance than that loner.

You know, after I landed and looked at the holes the flak and the fighter bullets made in our plane, I no longer felt very superior and 90% (maybe 98%) of my anticipation of jumping in a plane to go "bomb the shit out of 'em" seemed to have disappeared. Matter of fact I got to wondering if they could use a 17 pilot back at Roswell as an instructor. I find out our next step is Foggia, Italy as part of the 97th Bomb Group.

In Foggia a couple of days later I hear, "Gentlemen, you are in the 97th Group of 15th Air Force"…some of the bullshit… "We are the greatest taught, best fuckin' air fighters in the world." You know what I noticed loud and clear? In all the training they had two especially noticeable themes. (A) "You are the cream of American malehood. You are the best trained and toughest aircraft fighter in the world." (B) They taught us – pounded into us every day "Germans and Japs were dirty rotten bastards. The Germans would strafe you in your chute and the Japs jabbed pregnant women in the belly with bayonets. Both starved and beat prisoners."

Let me tell you, brain washing works. No matter how bad things got, no matter how stupid some the orders I received, it seemed I never-ever, for a second, ever thought of arguing, questioning, or disobeying any order I received from a superior. Now I did a lot of shit I knew they would disapprove regarding how I accomplished what they told me to do, but I always did it.

The airplane I got in Lincoln, Nebraska, and flew over to Italy is assigned to me and my crew. No one else uses it so we can name our planes. I'm impressed with a newspaper cartoon of the time called "Smokey Stover," (a fireman). We name our plane "Smokey and his Firemen." I paint it on left side just under pilot's window. The "S" is like a fireman's nozzle and hose just like in the cartoon. Next to your name, you leave a place for missions. Missions were indicated one at a time in groups of five with 25 missions as a "tour." After a tour, you go home on leave to find out who is screwing your wife or girlfriend, then come back or go to another theater for a second tour. A B-17 pilot's nightmare was to survive 25 in Europe then go home on leave and get transferred to a B-24 in the Pacific. That ain't gonna happen to me.

I get to Foggia when weather is cooled off. We fly off of steel mats on the dirt or mud, 5,000 feet of it. In whatever weather you take off and land every 15 seconds. On a dry day you can't see if your gonna run over the guy who's in front of you. His four fans give a solid dust storm.

If it's raining you get same deal, can't see shit. You pilots think about the spacing today for take off and landing. We'd get green light from tower and green flag from controller on the ground by my left wing. He's holding a stop watch and waving the flag every 15 seconds. Why both a flag and a light? Sometimes you couldn't see the tower for dust, water spray, or fog. Fog? Damn right. In the Army Air Corps, when they said "take off at 0400," that meant 0400. I can't remember ever where a mission was changed because of weather 'cept in the air. When the shit got serious, the weather sometimes canceled missions for two to three days. But once it was "on," it was on.

Oil refineries at Polesti – boy, that was a motherfucker. First raid, went in at 1,500 feet. (Yup, hundred – not thousand) They had about 800 88 mm anti-aircraft guns. These anti-aircraft guns shot a bullet bout 3 inches in diameter and it didn't operate as to go through your plane. It was designed to explode very close to your plane, and then pass many pieces of shrapnel into your plane's parts, including the human parts in it. We called this "flak." When these things exploded they omitted black smoke. The gun shot in a rectangular pattern of four shots in either left hand or right hand rotation. Soon as you saw the second one, you knew where "three and four" would be. You guessed it, I tried very hard not to be there. OK, with 800 guns and four shots every five seconds that's 48 shells a minute times 800 equals 9,600 shells a minute. That's why it looked like we flew through black clouds. The big deal was "altitude." They blew at a given altitude to the foot. You wanna get back to your base? One way only – be either at least 10 feet above or below the fuse altitude.

"Fear" – I notice now days people wear clothing saying "No Fear." Let me tell you 'bout how that word that's followed me most of my life, "F-e-a-r." I'm in Foggia, Italy. We go to eat at 6:00 pm. We stand in line outside an old farmhouse that is the chow hall. Just as you got to the door to go in, there was a bulletin board. You look up on this board (in my case I look to the bottom of the list) and if it says "Yunick," here's where "fear" lives. Shit, I ain't hungry now. I went today and about a third of

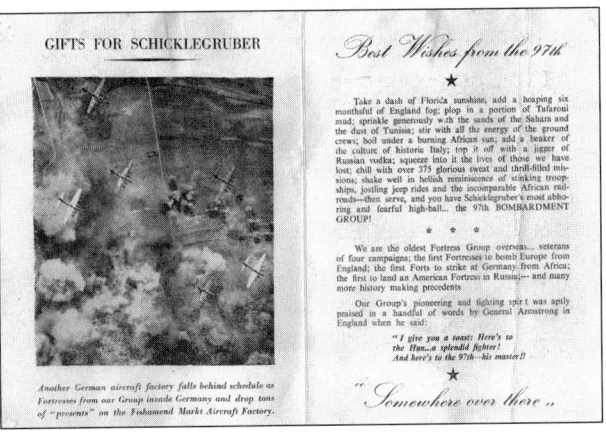

The type of stuff they used to get us to hate the Germans.

the planes ain't back yet. Nope, no chance they'll be back, they'd be out of fuel three hours ago. I nibble on the food quietly while all the pilots not on the list are happily laughing. Uneaten food gets banged out of my mess kit into 55 gallon garbage can.

Rite here I start to loosen up. How come old, sick, crippled people and little kids – three, four and five years-old are eating out of our garbage cans? Hell they are all Catholics, 200 miles from Rome. (I'm a Catholic then). Why ain't they got shoes? Old and young feet are wrapped in burlap tied with twine. We got an Officer's Club. "Gimme a double Three Feathers with a beer chaser." Officer's Club used to be a chicken coop so it's got no heat. "One more double"…9:30 pm. I go back to my no heat, no shower, no bath room, wash in wash basin, toilet 100 yards away tent. (Really impressive latrine though, 'bout a 20 holer). Fear is gone now. I start to wonder "Where we gonna go?" Goddam, I hope not back to Polesti, and that

A look at my artistic abilities.

deal at 1,500 feet. On that run we flew through smoke, fire, pieces of the refinery, pieces of planes…kinda like three or four minutes through hell. I told you I'd tell it like it was. This was no 35 mm movie, it was 88 mm and 50 caliber real. Maybe it was just me, though I don't think so. If you were in the briefing room, you heard the murmur of "oh shits."

I'm starting to depend on the alcohol, but I have no idea it's happening. I have no trouble going to sleep but the other end is rough. Waking up at 2:00 am, with no heat and cold water is a bitch.

Climb up in a big GI truck at 2:30 am, going to briefing in an old barn with benches. MPs check us in. As I enter the barn I can see the target for today. It's an aircraft bearing factory in Regansburg Germany. I've never been there. Next, we get the most important part of the deal, "How many 88s? How many 105s? (That's the size of the anti-aircraft guns in millimeters, roughly three or three and three-quarter inches) "What altitude we going in?" Answer: "Four hundred 88s…eighty-five 105s…30,000 feet"…not bad. If we go in at 32,000 feet 88s can only go to 28,000 feet and 105s to 32,000. "Fighters?"…Oh, shit! "Goerings," "yellow noses," 109 Messerschmidts, the best they got. Hard-nosed, sharp, and damn good gunners. "Who's gonna help us?" "The colored fighter pilots in the Air Cobras and P-40s." "Oh shit!"

Now I've heard about how effective they were recently on TV, and I know this is gonna piss a mess of people off, but those cats (the checker tails), couldn't hit a bull in the ass if they had him by the tail. In fairness to their pilots, their planes and support were a hell of a ways from Goerings flying circus. It was kinda like a high school football team against the Dallas cowboys. I heard one of 'em down real low hollering for "help," and one of 'em answered back, "That's what you're getting extra combat pay for black boy."

Next I see the 51s from up around Remini will take us the last 100 miles to the IP and bring us back out from the other side of the bomb run. Phew! That's better. Why the difference? I have no idea. Training maybe? Certainly the Air Cobras and P-40s were shit boxes by P-51 or P-47 standards. (Note: all P-51s were not equal). Early models were half of the later ships. I'm gonna clear up some bullshit that the movies and war propaganda played up. A P-40 or a P-38 wasn't in same league of a P-51, P-47, Focke Wolfe or Messerschmidt. Too heavy, too slow, wouldn't turn. Flying a 38 or 40 or Air Cobra against the Germans was a real good way to get dead quick. I loved the planes, but war deals in facts – bullshit don't cut it.

You old cats reading this, you ever hear of Berlin Sally? Well she was a broad who broadcast on our standby frequency. 'Bout an hour out of Foggia, here it comes; "Lieutenant Jim Brown, is it cold up there?"

(Hell yes, 65 degrees below zero) She continued, "Don't worry 'bout your wife Mary, (we are six hours ahead of eastern time). She's sleeping with her boss Jack Walker and he's keeping her nice and warm. You know she may be a tiny bit pregnant from what I've heard." This shit's real accurate. The names are correct. Can you imagine Jim Brown flying formation not being bothered by this? Then Sally says "I hear you're going to Regansburg and you got the black birds for fighter protection. Herman's yellow noses will probably get every one of 'em. They can catch you before you get 100 miles from the IP." Now we usually had three IPs. If she names the IP one, two or three that you were briefed to use, you'd get kinda a chill in your spine. That meant they moved all the guns over to the route we are gonna use. Flight commander can break radio silence or shoot a specific flare color combination and change the IP. The whole time I'm sitting there shitting my pants waiting for us to bang into another 17 or get a 88 shell up my ass.

What the hell's the IP?… "Initial Point"…that's where you turn your true heading and start your bomb run. This is ten minutes of auto pilot flying and the bombardier has auto pilot course correction. He's looking into the Norden bomb site and making flight path corrections.

Every time we'd turn the IP, I'd have to piss. (Reckon that scared the piss out of me?) I've got a steel flak helmet on. I take it off, get my pecker aimed – I've got so much clothes on and the belts and check chute

Me and "The Firemen."

in the way – and piss. Maybe 75% makes the helmet. In a minute it's froze. I bang it out on the flight deck and put my helmet back on.

The bomb run is fighter free. You can see why can't you? If they followed us in they'd be just as vulnerable to the flak as we were, so during those ten minutes their fighters and our fighter escorts would play "Eddie Rickenbacker and the Red Baron." I'm busy watching the flak.

I forgot to tell you, when the shit got serious down the IP, I flick auto pilot off and tell the bombardier to talk to me 'bout correction. I now had the freedom to change altitude 30 to 50 feet. How come? Ever hear of "Tail End Charlie?" That was me. Hardest to fly because of prop wash and shell casings from other 17s raining into my windshield and props. Nobody wanted that spot, so I had no trouble to get it. Another reason was the way they attacked. As a rule, we flew north to within 15 to 20 miles of target and turned left into the bombing run. This puts you on a southeasterly heading. 'Bout time we get to the target, say 11:00 am, the wiener guzzlers can do what Hollywood taught 'em flying out of the sun in the 12 o'clock high routine. So, the bombers would be blinded by the sun and the heinies would come at us head on. Again, tail end charlie is the place to be for this, sort of last in line. Also, once the bombs are gone I can slide around 100 yards and up or down 50 feet. Plus, being last in formation, every gun we have can shoot, 'cept the bombardier, and hell, if he did shoot I doubt he ever hit anything.

You wanna know something interesting? Many air crew would not pull the trigger. Believe it or not, when we got, say ten minutes from expected fighter contact, I'd tell all gunners to clear their guns…that meant shoot 15 to 20 rounds to make sure guns worked. I had one waist gunner that I doubt ever fired a round. Bravest cat in the crew but scared absolutely shitless about killing somebody. Flights were eight to 11 hours and he never complained, did everything perfect, 'cept the 50s scared the hell out of him. Every mission I'd decide to shit-can him cause his only real job was waist gunner. I didn't catch on till I'd check left over ammunition after we got back and all his would still be in the can. Him and his gun was 500 pounds of waste. I guess I was pretty sure a court martial and dishonorable discharge would ruin him. Believe it or not, he was not by himself by a longshot. I'd guess 15 to 20 percent never pulled the trigger. Talk about 50s scaring the hell out of you. Every plane I flew that had a top turret with a pair of 50s the engineer used… if it wasn't for lap belt and shoulder harness, I'd of went through roof of cockpit every time he squeezed them triggers. They were at my ear level, say 18 inches away… goddam!…what a noise.

On the bomb run the fighter's circus I never saw, but before and after the IP (if there was no flak), I watched and helped. We as a rule had ten 50s and some of the kids were pretty good with 'em. But the fighter pilots were like race drivers. Some few (theirs and ours) were light years better than the average cat. They played a lot of chicken. You could see a few would never give an inch. Some missed each other by inches and the closure speed was 500-600 mph. I've always believed some of our fighter pilots were like serial killers, they loved it. (I guess they had to to stay alive.) My experience was that the mouthy bullshit artist with the floppy hat, silk scarf, and starched and pressed clothing wasn't the one. The quiet, moody loner, the one who hung around his plane all the time making sure everything worked, the cat who came back with all his ammo gone and 25 gallons of fuel left; he was a paid legal killer who liked his job. You know something – those kind kept living. That kind didn't remember how many kills he had credited and didn't care. When he did get credit, his crew chief painted it on his plane. To get credit for a "shoot down" or a "kill" required gun camera film and/or a witness. If you know some old cat who you heard shot down ten Germans, someplace it's officially recorded.

In Italy, I was stationed at Foggia. The bombers had several satellite air bases to the main (paved) airport at Foggia. My first tour I flew with the 97th off the steel mats. Second tour I moved to the main, Foggia base. The commanding general of the 15th Air Force was an iron ass real Air Force general – General Curtis LeMay. I didn't like him worth a shit. But is it possible to like a man that yesterday sent a bunch of people you knew on a one-way trip they'd never come back from? Who everyday chewed your ass out for missing the target and doing a lousy job? (The truth was he was right). A man that did this for six months, everyday?

Our Italian castle in Foggia…that's my left-handed guitar… never got the hang of Wabash Cannonball.

Life is funny. As a rule I'd of never got to meet LeMay 'cept one morning LeMay was gonna take us up to Berlin on a long-long haul. I think I need to say this 'bout in here. That son-of-a-bitch would crawl in a 17, (and he could fly it as good as any man going) and sit there and take it for 10 or 11 hours like we did. He did this maybe 2-3 times a month. Well, this morning I got on Berlin Sally's program. LeMay's plane fucked up so I was told to move from "charlie" to "the point." I'm a 2nd lieutenant, so the only thing I can think of is I had a lot of experience. The deal is this: drive around and form the wing (400 planes) and take off to the IP. They are getting another plane ready for LeMay if and when he catches up he will take over, I go back to being Charlie. I doubt they knew LeMay was going until then.

Sally's making fun of a second lieutenant forming up a wing, and asks me how I like the point and tells me how I'll soon get to meet Goering's Focke Wolfe 190s head on. 'Bout two hours out a kernel (I don't know how to spell colonel yet – sixty years later), slides up from bottom and takes the point. I slide down and pull in Tail End Charlie's hole. This was a dandy…as we started crossing the Alps, the weather's half-assed good I notice a straggler 17 with a big diamond on his tail. I know he's not part of the 97th, but he could be legitimate cause I've seen that insignia before. He slides in closer and closer. I know the krauts got some various planes of ours in flying condition and use 'em for spying and espionage. This cat is a wrong ass.

I notice our escort slide up and sniff him (we are radio silent) Here's how the escort deal works. No fighter can go from Foggia to Berlin and back…can't carry enough fuel. But they can come with tip tanks, catch up to us, take us across the Alps. Then they've got to turn back.

At same time P-51s with tip tanks from England meet us 'bout the time the first group leave. They take us up to the bombing run, and help for 20 minutes on the way home before they have to peel off and go home. All this can happen because a loaded 17 cruises at 160 mph and the fighters fast cruise at damn near double that.

37

Anyway, we are rite over highest part of the Alps. This is a day when one bombardier in whole wing (LeMay's plane) drops all the bombs. All the planes have a radio activated trigger, so when he drops, all 400 planes drop also (secret shit). Now when you turn onto your bombing run, you open your bomb doors to let the bombs out. We're still over the Alps and ol' diamond tail has the frequency and triggers the deal. In a few seconds the Air Force needs 400 pairs of bomb bay doors, and has dumped 3,200 tons of bombs on 56 billy goats and two yodelers. This has a built in problem. Also, when you lighten a plane up 10 tons, it rises sharply, so three or four crews earned the eternal respect of the people for whom they sacrificed their lives. No, you never read about it. Nope, it didn't count as a mission – it was an "aborted" mission.

Ain't too much longer after this terrible experience on losing bomb bay doors and I'm on a mission in Poland (Krakov maybe). We're high – 32,000 feet – but just barely over the clouds, so I can't see the flak. Half way down the IP, things go terribly wrong. My side window (4 inch thick plexi-glass) gets blowed out. Bango! 65 degrees below zero, with wind chill at 160 mph. The instruments instantly ice over, forward visibility zero. I can see out the hole where my window was. Number two engine next to my seat is burning (a gas fire). Some of the flak hits my flak helmet, I don't have it hooked, and it knocks it off. Now I get a terrible pain in my back. I shut down number two, side slip it to put fire out and ask the flight engineer to see how big the hole is in my back and how much blood's leaking out. Goddam it's cold!

I quit the Catholic religion 'bout four months ago and the squadron priest told me I was headed to hell. I figure hell to be 'bout 200 degrees. (doesn't sound too bad). Engineer says "no blood at all, no hole." Goddam, I'm cold. I push back in the seat and "Oh shit! It really hurts, look again, I'm dying!" The co-pilot takes over, "See if you can dial into God's frequency, you're gonna need him for the next five-and-a-half hours." (Didn't know how to fly, the son-of-a-bitch). In about five minutes the engineer finds the trouble. Three red hot pieces of shrapnel hit the helmet, knocked it off, then fell between my inner wool electrified suit and me. We can't smell the burning flesh. I learn we can't distinguish between extreme heat and extreme cold without visual help. That was a bad, long day. We were a cripple, and we play hide and seek in and out of the clouds for 'bout an hour with three JU-88s. We get 'er back with 'bout five minutes fuel left. I also decide next time, if there was a next time, that plane was gonna get very light trying to get back to base. If you ever see me in a "penguin suit" look at my shirt cuffs – you'll probably see two of the three pieces of flak. I had cuff links made out of 'em.

Kinda hard to tell, but that's them.

Soon after this my trouble with General LeMay started. I've noticed as I run around the world on my mission to save the world from the Nazis, that after I park my plane, about half an hour later a big GI truck comes to pick us up. But a general has a red flag with his rank on it that they put out the pilot's window as they taxi and a couple Jeeps come to get him immediately. Well hell, what about same kinda flag with a second lieutenant's gold bar on it? I make the flag and flag holder.

Works great every time. I'm sure they get pissed when they see the lone yellow bar, but I suppose they figure "what the hell, we're here so we might as well run him in."

I get a li'l braver. I was born and raised in boots. I got a pair of black boots the Legion pilots gave me and I wear em 'cept on missions. I start wearing them on missions. Next I grow a mustache and beard (we called this the "Jesus look").... Let me tell you, the appearance change was wonderful with the ladies, but one day as I climbed out of the pickup jeep. Here is the grand wizard LeMay. I get 30 minutes to get rid of the flag, shave the womb broom and beard and get into brown, as he said, "fuckin' goddam brown shoes!" Well any chance to get more money and a silver bar just went down the tube.

I can't help but notice the captains, majors and colonels. Around there were second lieutenants when I got there. That li'l Army major who taught me how to fly 17s in Roswell said "Smokey, don't ever volunteer for anything." So as time passed and they from time to time said, "Would you like to be/or do something maybe more important than a bomber driver?" I'd say "No...I'd like to do what I do now." I noticed that after 'bout eight months very, very few of the people I came with were still around. Luckily, I learned from the mistakes of others.

The pickup flag worked great until my "buddy" General LeMay found out about it.

A friend of mine was hit by flak from below. It came through the seat and blew his balls into such bad shape they had to remove 'em. Before the next mission I had a 50 pound piece of armor for my seat. I drug that plate along with me and put it in the bottom of my seat from then on. In those days, the possibility of a life without sex was a fate more horrible to contemplate than death.

Shortly after the disastrous day with LeMay, I was called to operations to see if I'd be interested in learning night bombing. A li'l voice said "Tell 'em no," so I did. They said, "You're very friendly with the limeys and the pollocks here, so you're gonna fly couple night bombing missions with the limey's in a flying corrugated barn with wings (I think they called it a Lancaster).

This plane is a work of art – primitive art. I believe Fred Flintstone designed it. Even at the top speed of 140 mph, it was clumsy, heavy, and slow. But it turned out to be very reliable. I fly co-pilot to learn the night bomber defense, "the corkscrew." I can't seem to get away from it – now I'm gonna learn how to screw with an airplane. The game is hide and seek in the clouds. You fly in constantly rolling, twisting motion making the bomber harder to hit with a 20 mm cannon. The enemy defense is a very fast twin engine attack fighter a JU-88 with big nasty bullets that blow up like 88s.

In my spare time I cultivated friendships with the Pollock fighter pilots that flew the clipped wing Spitfires and the limeys that flew those Mosquito's. Here's the deal, "You show me how to fly your Spitfire or Mosquito, and I'll take you on a bombing mission and let you solo a 17 (with me in it). The pollocks were a weird bunch. Apparently the German's did some horrible things to their kinfolk and country. These quiet, crazy bastards seemed to all have a death wish. I saw 'em in action. They flew those Spitfires like they and the plane were one. They were also utterly fearless, but they did it better and kept living, well considering their bitter fierceness. "When you guys take a break, a leave?" I would ask. "How many missions?" (For us it was 25). Answer "never" or "till we win the war and kill every living German that caused this war." In racer's lingo of yesterday, they would be considered "extremely pissed."

The Mosquito was a complete wooden air plane. I believe it was laminated spruce. Now let me tell you, this son-of-a-bitch could haul ass. It was light, with short wings, could turn on a dime and climb like a jet. Their Spitfires performed well too. Landing the Spitfire with it's narrow wheels and ass backwards brake-rudder control and tiny wings was a handful for me (this was a tail dragger), but once in the air it would compare to fastest race cars in the world. All you had to do was aim it and shove it all the way up. You then had enough guns and engine to do anything you were man enough to try. All the other Royal Air Force stuff (to me) seemed to be junk, but these two planes were in a class of their own. Nope, I never flew either in combat.

I get 12 or 15 missions in and squadron says "take three or four days off – your plane's busted and we've got no parts." 'Bout every time you went on a mission you'd get bullet holes or some flak damage or oil or fuel system damage. The 17 was the toughest, most reliable and forgiving air plane in the Air Force. Hell, I came home once on two engines on one side (but you couldn't hold altitude). But as tough as they were, they didn't heal themselves, so I got a few days off.

Couple of the Polish fighter pilots I'd taken on missions knew Rome pretty good and had time off for the same reason. They said, "We show you how to forget this shit"…and took me to a place in Rome called "Broadway Bill's." Broadway Bill's was a night club and whore house across the street from the Victoria Hotel. In that place every vice known to man was in process or being arranged.

German and American spies, OSS people, Italian secret service, partisans, Yugoslavian underground cats…and pussy out the ass. Place had only one rest room for both male and female. You're standing there taking a piss while watching a girl put her lip stick on or combing her hair. The ladies are trying to survive, and have recently had to switch from German pilots to American. Why pilots? We were only ones with a couple bucks (combat flight pay). My Polish guides introduce me to Marilyn Monroe's Italian sister. (Yup…Northern Italy's got blondes and red heads.) First night we go to my room at the Victoria. For you who have stayed there during WW II, you know. And for you who have stayed there as a tourist since, I want you to know that one block probably broke more of the ten commandments per night than did any other five cities in Europe combined. Sin was everywhere. In the elevators, the phone booths, the bathrooms, in the hallways and alleys.

The three of us pilots had one room (all we could get), but I got two new life experiences. The combination male and female bathroom and sex in a kinda three way deal. I was a li'l spooky, so next day we went to her apartment. Big mistake. Some cat comes bailing out of her bedroom. Picture on bureau is German pilot (same cat). I guess he was a deserter (wouldn't have blamed him). She says "He don't care – don't worry." I can't handle getting killed over a piece of ass, (even if it was the real Marilyn) so our beautiful friendship came to an end in less than 24 hours.

Wouldn't have worked anyhow…"How did you two meet?"…"Well I was taking a leak, and so was she, and we started a conversation and…"

I'm pretty de-sexed for a li'l bit here, so I go to the Vatican (I'm a Catholic rite?) I want to see the Pope and the famous church. The Polish pilots?

You wonder why I never use their names? Answer is I didn't know their names because they didn't want anybody to know their names. Yes, they knew my name and they spoke half-assed English but when I asked they said they had no names. So to me they were "Pollock One" and "Pollock Two." They had a Polish word for me which I think meant 'bout the same as "jack-off" in English. To me it sounded like "smukee." They advise me against going, but I'm going to the Vatican. They walk me to it. It's a long walk, across a river (Tiber, I think). It's walled in like a separate country inside several blocks. It's got it's own law and post office.

They have tours (for a small donation). The tour shows, among other things, the gold and the expensive ornaments of the Vatican, and there is a lot of them. The Pope's chair is even half gold. This place drips money. I spend seven or eight hours there…hell, I even go to the catacombs. (Why?…I don't know, everybody there is dead, and has been for a long-long time.) As I walk around, I develop a giant problem. Foggia's 200 miles east of Rome (about). How come little kids and old people (Catholics) eat our garbage and ain't got shoes or a home? I go to a church service. They worship stained glass windows and statues and crosses. The altar's gold – gold is everywhere. In the ceiling, walls, doors, altars, chairs, chains. They carry the pope in on a gold chair (yet looks like he can walk fine). On top of this, ten percent of your assets were supposed to go to the church. (They hounded you like Jim Baker the preacher…"send money, and often.") During the mass, I can't understand one damn word. The service is either Latin or dago. They swing pots of stinky, smokin' stuff. To make a long story short, I'm lost as to the spirit of these ceremonies. Near as I can figure, they only have one good useful feature. If I fuck your wife and I go and confess to a priest, "it never happened." There was one other very interesting plan. If you say, had been married fifteen years and your wife got fat and ugly and wouldn't give you any, but your good lookin' 20 year old secretary was fucking your brains out…if you had enough money to grease the cash register, you could get the marriage annulled…as in "It never happened." A third feature that looked good: if you got divorced you could never remarry…so at worst you can only be a "one-time loser." Right, wrong or indifferent, when I walked out the gate that afternoon they needed to subtract one off of the total number of Catholics. I was long gone.

The Polish pilots get us a good ride back to Foggia. Yup, I do feel better. But back at the base, it's getting cold and the tent's not good enough any more. I buy limestone blocks from a quarry and build a square five feet tall house with a doorway and put tent on top of the limestone walls for a roof. I then built a heater out of a 50-gallon drum that used aviation gas for fuel. I pay ten bucks a month for electric that works most of the time. The heater has 30 gallons of water on top, so I get some hot water. I'm in pretty good shape for the winter coming. Soon I hear maybe in a few more missions I'm gonna be sent home for a leave. Oh shit, here it is, the dreaded deal where you end up in 24s. I put in for permission to do a second tour without leave.

'Bout two weeks back from Rome, Pollock Number Two is gone. Pollock Number One ain't talking, just silent, staring. Rumor is Number Two was strafing a train going to Germany, just above northern Italy and Yugoslavia. General Rommel "The Desert Fox" out of Africa, was on the train. When Number Two ran out of ammo they said he drove the Spitfire right into the side of a car he thought Rommel was in.

I need to tell you 'bout the Red Cross and the USO efforts to help us. There was a lady, "Flip Frame" by name, a Red Cross gal who, with her helpers, met us when we returned from a mission and gave us a big shot of whiskey for sure, and maybe two if we asked, just before debriefing.

Same in the morning, only it was hot coffee and donuts (course darn few of us were hungry at 3:00 am). She called the deal "Flip's Frying Fortress" and you got a 50 mission card from her when you did two tours. She was also with some of us in Africa. Those Red Cross gals lived the same shitty existence we had. I'd look forward to jumping down out of the truck and when she handed me the shot of whiskey that was kinda the last sentence on the story of "today." She and I knew when I came out the door of the briefing room at 3:00 am and I said "See you in about 12 hours – don't run out of booze" that was one big-assed "maybe." The USO girls I know helped out, but I never went to their stuff. I always felt uncomfortable in crowds and I preferred to read and drink three or four shots and go to sleep early.

I don't know how we would have survived without Flip.

Yup, we had good gasoline lanterns you could read by if there was no electricity most of the time.

The reading I done was my college. The Cadet pre-flight school stirred up all kinds of desire to know more bout physics, chemistry, aerodynamics and internal combustion engines. Simply stated, I wanted to be able to understand enough 'bout all parts of the airplanes I flew, so that I could maybe know enough someday to build them better. But most important, I wanted to know enough to figure out a band-aid to get back to the ground when disaster was nibbling on my ass. My number one reading choice was "dirty" books. If you ordered a sex book there were two problems: "not listed" or "never came." But the text books were easy to get. The real problem was to find 'em written in language I could understand. (Then and now, I think no word in the English language should have over six letters in it.)

When my friend the Polish pilot disappeared (Pollock Number Two) I started re-thinking the "don't plan over one day" philosophy. I decided I'd done enough stuff to earn my US citizenship good boy badge. I got experience out the ass and no rank. I'm in the best possible position to become a professional fuck off.

"Oh hell, tomorrow I go again. Headed to Vienna, the marshaling yards (rail yard), long haul.

Weather is shitty and a very late take off is scheduled, it's daylight, ceiling 'bout 150 to 200 feet – visibility bout half mile. Remember Zackerson? the big guy with the little uncircumcised peter from B-17 transition in Roswell? He is in another squadron and is last in his group to take off. We take off every fifteen seconds. I'm right behind him, first in my squadron 'cause the colonel has got oxygen supply trouble. Zack goes and must have lost an engine. There is a telephone line bout 40 feet up. Zack takes it out, left wing low. He twists full down with left wing just as I pass over him. Hitting and blowing up – smoke and pieces rise up in a cloud layer. You can't see shit. Hold heading! Climb at 750 feet per minute (145 mph)…hope the hell you don't run over the guy in front of you, or get run over by guy behind you. 'Bout ten minutes (seems like two hours) I break out 'tween cloud layers. "Did we get any damage?" I look out my side to check for holes. The left wing, number one and number two engines seem good. Then I see it, a goddam arm – blowed off at the shoulder. It is hooked, elbow on the leading edge, between number two engine and me, held there by air pressure. Zack's arm? I had to look at that for ten hours. Who's arm was it? Who knows…to me it was Zackerson's.

I don't know what it was, but from that day on, if I smelled a real bad smell I'd puke instantly. The arm stayed on till plane slowed down to bout 60, then it dropped off. I could feel bump as left landing gear run over it. Zack was having a portrait painted of himself off of a photo. This was a common deal because Italy was full of artists (pretty good ones). I got job to write letter to his wife and go through his things. For example, some guys had a girlfriend and a wife, and in their foot locker were letters that sure didn't need to go to the grieving widow. Plus other potential trouble making deals. Hell, I saw one case where the pilot was fucking his wife's mother and her sister. I also found out there were at least two "dickey lickers" in the Air Force.

Zack was clean, I found nothing that was bad. I made final payment on

This one made it back 500 miles.

portrait and sent it and his belongings to Seattle. I became a pen pal with Zackey's wife. This ends when I come home. "I'll meet you someplace and tell you all about it," never happened. I realize how lucky I am my girlfriend gave me the "Dear John" treatment when I was in advanced so I don't have to write anybody. In mail call I don't stand there chewing my fingernails hoping for a letter. I seen many of them Dear John letters destroy men.

It's close to Christmas – it's cold as hell in Italy with a lot of snow-sleet. A 16-year-old mess hall and clean up girl is pregnant…'bout eight months gone. Everybody is joking 'bout who did it. It's decided "Kilroy" did it. When I came back from Rome I had a long talk with the Catholic priest 'bout idol worship, sick and hungry kids and the elderly. The answers I got are double-talk bullshit. Around 8:00 pm a pilot comes in Officer's Chicken Coop Club, "Say, that girl outside is in labor." We run out, get her and a bunch of blankets. She's laying on the floor screaming for a priest (she's strict Catholic and thinks she's dying). I send Frank, my bombardier, to get the priest.

Frank comes back, says he won't come. Apparently she's fucked up her Catholic license "serves her right, let her rot in hell." In 'bout two hours, baby was born. Lucky both didn't die. It wasn't till the baby was out we found a doctor who finished it off. Do I need to tell you what I

Me, as the WACS pinup, and Jim Stancifer

thought about Catholicism then? I wouldn't even come close to their blessing meeting after each briefing. (A priest blessed and prayed for all Catholics lucky enough to be fighting for their country on this mission, but his stuff didn't work on other religion, so they had Jewish and some other religions also…but I can tell you their batting average was piss poor.)

I gotta tell you how we got a little satisfaction from the priest. My bombardier Frank was also club bartender. Shortly after the baby deal, Frank made a bucket of eggnog…

Christmas, I think. Well Frank was drunk as hell and had to piss. The eggnog bucket was on the floor under the bar. I saw Frank whip it out and piss in the eggnog. I didn't say anything till it was nearly gone, then told them all what gave it it's special flavor. You're rite if you guess Frank got the shit kicked out of him, plus forced to drink a cup of it. Here comes the priest. Yup, He had two cups of it and bragged on it's taste. I later found out there is a religion in India where piss is drank daily…and I was told fresh piss is sterile. If you cut yourself with a rusty knife, piss on it (the cut, not the knife). You don't believe me do you?…well ask your doctor.

"Smokey, come to squadron headquarters." "Tonight at 11:00 pm. You take eight tons of acid fuse bombs up to Buda, Hungary." Budapest is, I come to find, two cities separated by the Danube River. Buda is west, and Pest is east bank. "Your target is the railroad yards in Buda. The Russians have captured Pest, and your IP will be ten minutes east of Pest and across the river to the target. "The Germans still have Buda, you will have special flare pistol sequence the Russians will look for, and pass you across without firing the AA stuff at you." "Oh boy thank you, I was wondering what I'd do tonight to keep from being bored."

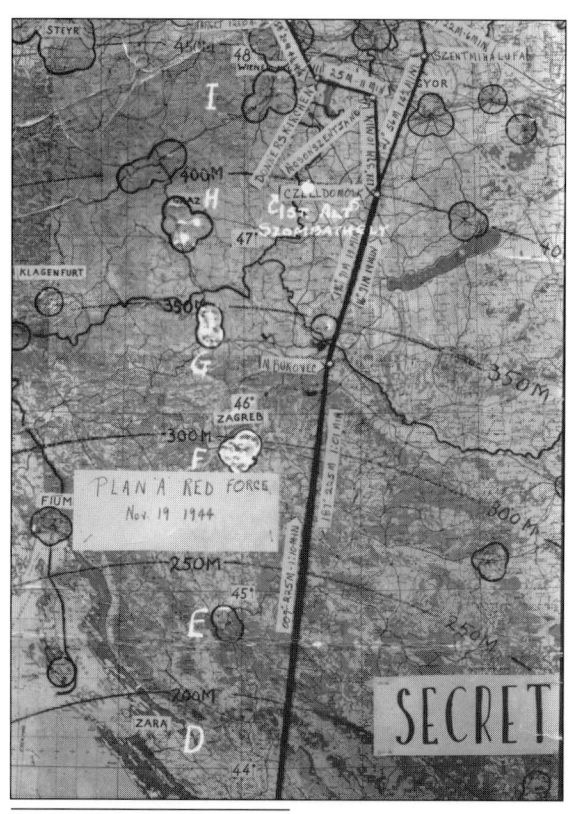

One of the maps from a mission.

Part of the limey training is "never let the blue light at night get on you." The AA gunners have spot lights to help pinpoint you for aiming. If they can put the blue light on you, the guns get the super best aiming dope and odds are you will shortly be history. Over and over they say, "Don't let them get the blue lite on you." This info would serve me well over Hungary.

I took off at 11 pm in a blinding snow storm and began climbing out pretty directly on a five to 10 degree heading. As soon as we got 100 miles into Yugoslavia and the weather started to clear…"Oh shit…here they come!" Two or three JU-88s. I can't see my gunners having a chance with 50s against 20 mm cannons, so into the clouds we go. I don't think I should fly a stable heading, so I move left and to the right 40 to 50 degrees. We pop out of the clouds and in a minute they find us. This shit went on for over an hour. I cork-

44

screwed the 17 till it was dizzy. We got the 11th crew member on board – a radar man. This is a brand new plane a Boeing B-17H. This has been four hours and he is gonna have about five and a half more hours of ass puckering tough sledding. We are gonna be the mouse and the JU-88s are gonna be the cats. Finally, I guess they had to break it off because of fuel, but maybe weather, cause 'bout then I'm at 32,000 feet, and it's weather all the way to 50 miles east of Budapest. I notice I'm 'bout five mph short on indicated air speed for power settings. What I don't know is the 88's hit the leading edge of wing by number four engine and we got a hole in there 'bout eight inches round. Well the radar operator got us there right on the money. We give the veri pistol color codes.

I'm on the bombing run over Buda, hand flying to bombardier calls. Remember weather is clear here and it's a moon lit night, but below not even a li'l match, no lights. I get five miles from target and suddenly there's lights everywheres and flak everywhere. I look and the blue light gets close then dances away then comes back right on us…blinds me damn near.

The orange salvo ball is right there on the panel in front of me. (An emergency deal, so you don't have to land with a load of bombs if something fucks up in bomb bay from flak or fighter damage. You salvo the bombs…that is, pull on orange ball – bomb bay doors drop off and so does everything else in bomb bay.) I grabbed that son-of-a-bitch and pulled it plumb out of the panel. The bomb bay doors were open so the bomb racks empty. As soon as I salvo, I'm corkscrewing and twisting, trying to get away from that motherfucker blue light. In a couple minutes no lights of any kind. The bombs will start to blow, but they are acid fuses, it will take from five minutes to 24 hours for acid to eat through for detonation. When lights go out I turn 90 degrees left and put all the shit to the firewall. First time I ever turned the turbos to #10 (8 was max)…I want to get back to weather before the JU-88s find us in the open.

Little do I know, but I've made history. The bombs dropped on the Russians and missed the target by five miles. I gave the Russians the flare signal twice and they were supposed to acknowledge with a certain color flare. Never happened. I assumed Germans had crossed the river and run the Russians off. How much time have I got for diplomatic posturing…three maybe four seconds?

Anyway, so now I've got to get home. There are several issues we need to work through.

Item A: we got a wounded number four engine. I shut it down but can't feather its prop. In getting out of there at extra high engine boost with pretty good pitch in props, the dead engine wind milling with lots of prop pitch costs us bout 10 mph.

Item B: number four engine has no oil pressure so the prop will either lock up or burn shaft up and drop off.

I then realize we may have a fuel shortage problem. Well, maybe I can go to the Isle of Vis, or Remini, a couple hundred miles shorter. "Oh shit…here they come again!" I'm saving every inch of altitude I can, but I have to drop down quick to get in a cloud layer. I can't go up, not enough engines…down only. It's just a bad day period. It is rougher than a bitch. I figure we are going to find icing soon.

Those JU-88s chased our asses for an hour and a half or two hours. Finally they wound number three engine. We got an oil leak. To me an oil fire on an airplane is worse than getting AIDS, cancer, a heart attack, brain tumor and colon cancer all at once. Nope, it never burned. I guess they have to abort because of fuel. When I get to the coast, the weather's lousy, I can't get either Vis or Remini on the radio so I decide to try to get back to Foggia. We got close to ten hours in now. (Oh yeah, we lost bunch of oxygen from German's inhospitable reception.) Some crew stations are at 18,000 feet with no oxygen.

Here's the plan: everything, guns, ammo, radios, ball turret, flak suits, flak helmets and anything else not welded down, goes in the drink. We are over the Adriatic now. Consider this, all of us except the tail gunner can go anyplace in the plane, but the tail gunner has got one option…the silk elevator…and with a very dangerous exit percentage. So if I ditch it, the tail gunner might not be able to get out without help (no tunnel). Soon number three runs out of oil and has to be shut down. The prop off of number four engine had fell off about half way over Yugoslavia. When we get down to 2,000 feet, we break out of the clouds and we've picked up some ice. Fortunately the wing boots are working so we are able to shed the ice. I find the runway for a straight in, but it's got 45 mph cross wind.

I've pumped all remaining fuel to two good engines. I have to run them at the forbidden #10 position on boost for enough power to land. All that cross wind and two engines out one side – shit, I was plumb sideways at 50 feet. It took all the foot power the engineer and I had to work the rudder. The co-pilot's leg gave out. If you ever have to push real hard with one leg, you find after the leg muscles are exhausted the leg will start jumping up and down. That happened to co-pilot, so flight engineer helped. We had a very shitty, rough landing. The airplane is actually bent down in the middle a little. I forgot to tell you, they sent another crew up there with a different IP. No, didn't tell me till debriefing when I left six months later to go to India (he hadn't got back yet).

Here come trucks and off we "go to be debriefed." "Flip give us a drink," I tell her, "and I'll need the second shot big time…or a pint." Just then here comes his majesty, Ol' Iron Ass (General LeMay). First question, "Where's my flak suit?" Then, "Congratulations on being the first son-of-a-bitchin' American to bomb the Russian tank corp." Third statement, "The American tax payers will really appreciate you ruining a brand new 25 million dollar air plane." I thought – horse shit. I hear they only cost five million. And last, "We really appreciate you throwing the first radar equipment in the ocean." While he gets his breath Flip slips me double number three. "Colonel" (Whoops! This is only general I've ever talked to.) "Ah, general the flak suit deal was, well the supply sergeant said the regular bombing run crews needed every flak suit there was but ten, and I had an 11th man (the radar operator). "I saw a tan leather flak suit hanging up all by itself," (our flak suits were dark green canvas) "and I asked the sergeant for it and he refused. So, I jumped the counter and took it." "Yes sir he tole me it was yours, but I never dreamt I'd fling it into the ocean. I'm sorry I took it sir." (But really, I wasn't, and nope, I didn't wear it)

Every time I got half-way through the bomb salvo deal he'd interrupt and start raising hell.

I said "yes sir" and "no sir" 112 times and "I'm sorry sir" 50 times. While doing this, I notice his number two man ain't too unhappy. I do believe I detected a grin on his snoot when I tell 'em 'bout jerking the salvo cord clean out of the instrument panel. That third double shot is getting to me now and I get to thinking. "I ought to ask him 'bout getting promoted to first lieutenant." Nope, never got a chance, he abruptly hauled ass. In my mind I did a good job with the circumstances being what they were. The sway back airplane? Considering two left engines only in a 45 mph cross wind, even today I wonder how much better any one could do. Why land in a cross wind? We only had one runway aimed at prevailing winds. I'm also thinking 'bout the one I landed and it broke in two pieces, half eaten up with flak. No one chewed my ass 'bout that. As they left the colonel who grinned said, "Lieutenant, you dropped that whole fuckin' load rite in the middle of the pride of the Russians. They fucked up on the veri pistol code and were shooting at you." (Hell I knew that).

Couple days later, we got to take another load of acid fuses to an oil refinery, a place called Polesti. I think weather or something bad happens so they abort the mission. "Go out over the ocean to blababyblah…dump 'em and go back to base." Well the fucking bombs won't release. Even the salvo deal won't let 'em go. We wear out a couple of fire axes trying to chop 'em loose. (You know, with bomb bay doors open it's hard not to fall out, all you got is a catwalk between left and right bomb racks). Over the radio I hear, "Bail out!"…"put it on automatic pilot," try this and that and somebody says "land it at base." Suits me. Yes, they get 'em defused before first one went off, but guess who happens to be listening to all this shit on the radio…LeMay.

One week later I get the orders, "Report to first emergency rescue at Foggia main airport with your plane and crew" ('bout 15 miles away). Yup, I'm no longer a bomber pilot. I've been reassigned to the 1st Emergency Rescue unit. This is really a CIA/ OSS outfit that deals in rescues, spies, and the like; a sort of taxi service for every sneaky deal going on all over Europe. We work anything unusual or clandestine as far east as Poland and everything else but England, and as far down and including Greece on other side of the Adriatic sea. Why the 17? A company named "Higgins" invented a boat big enough for 16 men to live on for 30 days. It's a combo sail boat with an inflatable cover over it's center. It's a hell of a deal. Built to fit under a B-17.

Ain't heavy but damn near no ground clearance in taxi and landing mode with that thing on board. We drop it with three big cargo chutes. There is no warranty on the drop part of the deal. You either get two million toothpicks or a nice boat. When it hits the water 'bout eight lines shot out to help people grab on for help getting on board.

I survived General LeMay, but not without getting reassigned.

I moved so fast from my limestone house at the 97th to a bombed out hotel in Foggia, I never got a nickel for the house I'd built. In the hotel room, I had no electricity, no running water and toilet you couldn't flush. The room also had an unusual accessory I'd never seen before for the ladies, a kinda toilet they sat on with plumbed in water to wash their li'l pussies and asses (I guessed). Sure didn't look like it was planned for hands and faces. (Yup, I got it figured later.) Being the move was so close I knew all the nurses and Red Cross ladies. I soon found that with the local ladies, silk parachutes, K rations, silk stockings (PX stuff)…you could have a harem for pennies. The parachutes were the prize. Panties, bras, all kinds of women's clothing was made out of them. They could dye the stuff any color, and they used every silk thread in a chute. Yup, there were times when parachutes were on the endangered species list. Remember, you can't fly without one.

You could have a sleep in maid for 'bout nothing. I didn't and them Italian gals were very jealous. They could really be a pain in the ass if you ran your mouth too much. I kinda stuck to nurses and Red Cross gals, who I could understand, to help me through at least one more day before I died. I have to believe regardless of what they looked like, our gals were the most thoroughly fucked women on the face of the earth. I doubt a day went by they got less than ten offers. My observation is based on my trip around the world. These women deserved a ton of credit for the big job they did in, most cases, very substandard and dangerous conditions.

I heard some hell raising outside the hotel one night, and went down to the street to find a young pilot dumped off by the hotel with his balls in his pocket. Nope, he didn't make it, had lost too much blood. Some of the local men really weren't big US boosters.

I get a new 17 because that last mission in the 97th ruined the second "Smokey and his Firemen." We named the plane "Smokey and his Firemen" (same as others). I have long ago given up on my patriotic zeal to blow Germany into submission. In this period of my career as an Air Force pilot, I really make a business out of staying alive and living a little better and more comfortable life. I've had quite a bit of combat experience, even without gaining rank. And I am using these experiences to avoid as many stressful, dangerous and unpleasant assignments as I can.

I notice film, cameras and picture developing equipment are in very high demand, so I become a photo officer on the side. This funded my education as a poker player, which later helped me establish an educational fund, in case I choose to educate myself when war was over. My master plan was programmed in such a way that there was no possibility I wouldn't survive in good shape…well maybe.

OK, we go to Naples, big deal. The Air Force announces jet planes, helicopter and Higgins boats as our newest weapons. Nope, there were no jets before this, no helicopters before this, and no Higgins boats. I go first, the chutes fuck up and boat is nothing but splinters. The jet is a fighter, I think a "Bell," burns its tail off in takeoff attempt. Only the helicopter "does it" like it's supposed to. I was fascinated by the chopper. I tried to swap rides with pilot. "Nope, no deal." I get to wondering how bad you have to fuck up to get put in them things…looked like a grasshopper with a big propeller coming out of it's head and a li'l propeller coming out of it's ass sideways.

That's the early helicopter.

The night before this "big show and tell," a colonel stationed in Naples says, "You want to have some fun tonight? Go to the Arizona club." "OK. How you get there?"…"Easy, get on the subway… and blahbeddy-blah…and you're there." Subway? this was a really a spooky ride. Good thing they could see the .45. I get to the club, man is it ever hard for my pussy happy mind to comprehend. This place is packed with a couple hundred military men, 150 to 175 girls, and 50 or 60 waitresses. You tipped the waitress with folded up paper bills, or a 50 cent piece standing on edge of table and they could, and did, grab either with their pussies. Any you old codgers who went there ever have nerve enough to tell anybody 'bout it? How bout the screwing exhibition the li'l gal had with the world's biggest cock. Hercules! Any of you ever tell 'bout the girl who took on a burro?

Here's the deal. The colonel I'd met and a couple other officers owned and operated this club. The food and drinks looked like they mighta come from a PX warehouse. Well, later as I thought 'bout it, I decided they had a good plan. Run a business on the side. Now stealing Army stuff, I didn't think much of that. I started buying all the German and Italian uniforms, swords, helmets, watches (military issue), medals, all kinds of stuff like that. All kinda American, German, Italian stuff, old parachutes, GI knives, parachute escape kits (the ones with the orange heart-shaped pill in the escape kit that was powerful enough that half a pill would keep you wide awake for 48 hours). My eager "sucker" customers were either new crew coming in, or old crew going home on leave. Damn right, cash only. One day I was surprised to see the colonel who owned the Arizona club in Naples. He says "He needs a Higgins boat in Naples, and general so-and-so said for me to give him one." I say "OK…come on, I'll let you talk to CO."…"Oh no, it will be a hush-hush deal," and I get one grand to drop it off of the coast of Corsica on a phony rescue deal. Hell, there are only four or five of 'em in the whole theater. I can see it in the Stars and Stripes magazine, front page…"second lieutenant gets firing squad for selling Air Force boat." I tell the Colonel I'm not interested. I say "Colonel, sir, my plan calls for me to have a happy, easy going life. I'm in no hurry to be rich, and most importantly, I want the freedom to come and go subject to military rules only." If there were a surplus of boats, and they were being wasted it would have been a whole new ball game, but they were scarce and effective. But from here on out, I gave the Air Force 40 hours a week and freelanced the rest of the time.

One of the Higgins boats.

We had Catalinas to land in the ocean to pick you up (no sharks, don't know why). We also had L-5s and a B-25. We seemed to be air taxis for people who dealt with Italian Guerrillas, Yugoslavian partisans, Polish patriots and French freedom fighters. A lot of rough, quick trips to (as a rule) hostile, unfriendly places, which quite a few times, simply put, would scare the shit out of us. (Like landing a P-boat at night on Lake Constance without lights). We didn't as a rule know any more than destination and weather conditions. The weather drops were usually very inaccurate. Being photo officer with access to a little Stinson L-5 aircraft got me to meet Mussolini and his girlfriend. Not personally, but in a cold mountainous town in northern Italy. Unfortunately for Mussolini (and his girlfriend), the Italian partisans, had just killed them both and hung them up like slaughtered hogs…head down and with some sex organ mutilation and exchange of location. So I can't say I knew them very well. (It may be of some interest to you, Mussolini's pecker wasn't too big.) The 10 pictures I took were my best sellers of all time. I doubt you'll ever see the actual pictures. Yes, I had some. The brass took 'em and my negatives.

A typical day in the 1st Emergency Rescue. We'd land the 17 on the Isle of Vis, 'bout 15 miles off the

49

coast of Yugoslavia, where Tito had his army. The reg's had their women living with them. In his plan, women were allowed among the troops and fought with the men. Matter of fact Tito had a very attractive blonde young wife with him. We'd land on Isle of Vis to wait, fuel, or load passengers. Vis had one steel mat runway bout 5,000 feet long. So all crash landed planes had to be immediately bull-dozed into a ravine at end of runway. Tito's air force was 'bout one 1930 200-horsepower bi-plane with machine guns that fired through the propeller. I believe he could fly it. I had a kind of personal plane – a B-25 I got out of Tunisia, when I used to go down there from Foggia for a day or two at a time. I took it to the Isle of Vis, and offered to sell it to Tito for five grand. He didn't want it. Good thing, this might have been my undoing. He couldn't speak English but his young wife could.

There were hundreds of 25s in a field in Bizarte, so I picked the best one and rebuilt it from other planes. I removed all armament and armor plate. A souped-up B-25 was my personal transportation. Course I had to let others use it, but hell, only two or three other pilots were checked out in a 25. Now that thing would flat haul ass. I kept it until I left China. Yup, over there we did our own maintenance on the 25s and 17s.

The PBY Catalina's were a good size sea plane (amphibious). They were twin engine, slow, heavy, tough, goofy looking things. The wing and two engines were mounted above the fuselage, 20 feet in the air for rough sea considerations. They were effective in the ocean, but could be "bad news." You'd suspect in a rough sea, bad to land in and take off of – and it was. But on a dead smooth sea or water body, you could not get them out of the water. Water suction on the hull kept you from rotating up. You'd have to get a boat to cut back and forth to roughen water up, and maybe get out.

You know where Venice, Italy is? I'm sure you heard 'bout it. The city in a bay with water for streets. I could not then, nor even today, figure out what the reason was for 'em to do it the hard way. Plus, how clean was that water with the human waste, garbage, trash runnin' into it all the time? Open window or door and into the water she goes. Well, hell, without the water streets where the hell could they row those gondolas around? Anyway, the harbor is bout six miles of shallow water. We land, pick up a crew that ditched pretty close to land. The German's are there and their shore batteries can damn near reach us. The sea is dead calm so there's no way rite now to get out. We taxi out further from shore. Gunfire?!? Whoops, a German submarine starts shooting. After five fucking hours of this, the wind finally gets the water up and we get out. If that water out there'd been 10 inches deeper you'd never be reading this. That submarine would of ate our ass up.

After 'bout six months of this I get order to go to Agratela, India and join the 7th American Rescue squadron. This assignment is in Flying Tiger country and in the heart of the bengal tiger homeland.

They had a custom there at Foggia, if you transferred out you played out your aerial antenna with 'bout a 10 pound lead weight on the tail end (kinda like a big electric fishing reel). Then got down on the deck and buzzed your tower while listening to the tower. If you did it right, the lead weight pulled the tower's antenna down. If the radio went silent you'd done it. Yup, we busted it and made two guys jump off the wings of a P-boat.

The Watch, The Ring and the Jacket

As I left Italy headed for Cairo, I thought about the 1st Emergency Rescue adventure: the "007" cats who parachuted into various parts of Europe, the Italian partisans in northern Italy, Tito's underground, L-5 landings at night in pastures for pick ups, P-boat landing on lakes at night, B-25 quickies (land on a road, unload, load and fly), hauling weapons and medical supplies in some little, unknown place with no real navigation help 'cept blinking lights, smoke signals, (yup, smoke, real Indian stuff), colored flares, or letters stamped out in the snow. The "Isle of Vis" experience, watching Tito operate a two-bit operation and driving the Germans goofy. Of watching 'bout 10 B-24s ditch, and not one successful (as a rule pilot and co-pilot came through windshield seat and all). The excitement of playing with the Spitfire and the Mosquito. Watching colored pilots trying to land P-40s on a carrier off of Corsica. (Matter of fact, carrier pilots had to be the most skillful and bravest pilots in the world. Every landing looked like from a 90 percent to 25 percent crash. Can you imagine landing on a runway that rises or lowers 25 to 30 feet at your stall speed in landing? Then at night? How 'bout finding that postage stamp in bad weather, and you're low on fuel, nothing but the radio range to guide you? In the fighters you can't see shit when you flare out to land. Having to shoot ditched B-17s full of holes to sink 'em and arguing with Italian boat captain 'bout transferring air crew they'd rescued (a money deal), opening up escape kits for more money…yup, they'd ask 'bout $500 a piece rescue money. (I'd usually get it done for one hundred. Watching the British HSLs (high speed launches). Yup, those suckers ran 55-60 mph. They picked up parachuted survivors that we'd spot on a B-17 sea search, or even with a Catalina, if there was over 8 to 12 foot sea. I had seen a lot of shit, some good, some ugly.

Next, here we go to India and the Flying Tigers.

We get to Cairo and luck out, delayed orders for Cairo to Baghdad and from Baghdad to Abadam, Iran. I need to go back to Italy and get the B-25 started to India. I hitch a ride back to Foggia. I've got the 25 in Cairo in 'bout 18 hours. Still no orders, (I need 'em to be able to get fuel) so I'm off to the "Great Sheppard Hotel." Man, this is pilot's heaven. Every color of woman on earth, many wealthy. I meet a young gal from Alexandria who's family owns a horse race track there. She's got a new car. We get to the race track at 2:00 am. I can't wait no more. Into her daddy's office and on his couch we make love on the "I've never had sex before and may be dead tomorrow" routine. Come to think of it, I believe the same thing would have happened if I was an army truck driver. Couple days later we're cleared to Karachi, Pakistan by way of Cairo,

Baghdad and Abadam. We follow the Iraq pipeline (oil). The next day to Baghdad then due south to Abadam, Iran. Abadam is right on the Dead Sea (Sarragosa), also known as the Persian Gulf. This is oil country…hot…130 degrees at 11:00 am. I stand on sand just off a wooden walk way and shift my weight from foot to foot and here comes oil. The air smells like stinking hot crude. I luck out and get cleared out at 5:00 am the next day. I had to put on gloves to handle the controls – they did not cool off at night. In couple minutes after take off from Abadam, we're over the ocean going east to Karachi, (I believe it was in India then) that's a long haul – from Abadam to Karachi. It's a long way over desolate desert, ocean and mountains – no place to land.

The sea we go over at take off has no waves and no current. Floating on the surface is a 500 mile long garbage dump: old crates, wood, dead camels, abandoned parts of boats…and you could smell the stink at the airport and flying low leaving with all air ducts open. It smelled like rotten meat and rotting fowl. Birds? One zillion birds picking this stuff over. This is in early 40s, wonder what it looks like now? Where did it come from? I don't know, never found out. Looked like you could walk on it.

Once you hit the PONR (Point Of No Return), your ass is mud if the plane don't make it to Karachi. We get the job done. But nobody knows anything about us so we can't get fuel…again. Looks like the British are running the movie and for whatever reason, at the airport they have housing for about 200 Polish nurses. In the bomb bay we got an upright piano, (yup, a piano). Clifford Reckling, the navigator, could run it pretty good. So we unload it under the plane.

Yeah…we really did have the jacket and the scarf.

This place is 'bout 95 degrees and 100 percent humidity. We sleep in bed rolls. I decide to invite the Polish nurses to a party at the plane while waiting for an "OK to fuel" (I need 8,000 gallons). I've now come from the US, half-way around the world to India. (I eventually went clean around the world and back to Indianapolis, Indiana). We were there three days awaiting OK to fuel.

The world's sexiest women are Polish. We had about 20 men. Us and some English air crew, and 'bout 100 nurses (not all my crew participated). Those Polish nurses could fuck 24 hours a day.

Before I could get half-way through my "never had any before" routine I find out Polish girls know all about oral sex. Remember, I'm half pollock. I decide rite then when I get out of Air Force – I'm gonna move to Poland. I doubt there was any sexual position or act those ladies did not know and perform to perfection.

Could it be because they lived without electricity, radios or movies and sex was only form of entertainment? (I think my Margie could be part Polish.)

I don't know whether I was glad or sad when we got fueled up, but sex sure wasn't heavy on my mind anymore. Karachi to Calcutta is another long haul, but over civilization, some of it looked real good.

Dum Dum Airport, Calcutta – here's the deal. This is kinda the headquarters and the Flying Tigers home. I refuel (no problem here) new orders "go to Agratala on the Assam-India border, 5,500 foot concrete runway (no buildings of any kind). I'm in the 7th Emergency Rescue now and a Flying Tiger.

Agratala is the capitol of the province of Tripura, now this is Bengal, this is "tiger out the ass country." Real live mothers with huge heads and huge paws. I'd see live ones almost every day and especially at night. We lived in bamboo, palm and thatch quarters called "bashas"…dirt floor, mosquito netting a "must." We hired an Indian servant (individually) called a "basha boy" a la British army custom of every officer having his own "bat man." Our camp area was 'bout five or six miles from the airport. There were no paved roads.

It was a jungle, but not in the say "Amazon" sense, where you needed a machete to chop your way. We lived under a tree canopy where black panthers could fall into a newly dug latrine 'bout 20 inch deep, where hyenas would get in our garbage cans, where tigers jumped over your head while you were in a moving Jeep, where python snakes were real and big. Where if you didn't watch it, you could step in a pile of fresh elephant shit or if you landed a P-boat in the Brakmaputra river in upper Assam (big-big tea plantation country) and didn't look close,

B-29 and a C-54 in Luliyang.

you might land on a hippopotamus. It was a place where tamed elephants did what bulldozers do here and where it could rain for over a month non-stop (they called it the monsoon).

Judging from the number of kids the natives had, I figured out what they did in the monsoon, but we would go half-goofy, play cards. We couldn't fly because the monsoon is half the year in India. This is not a thunder storm deal. It starts raining couple hours a day, then in a week or so just pours like a cow pissing on a flat rock 24 hours a day. All leather and brass turns green. I believe a couple of monsoons would be very hard on male eyesight if that story about going blind is true. Consider this: my basha boy has two wives now and wants a raise to buy number three. His name is "Zypher." I say "Zep…if you let me screw her too, you got a deal." He says "Well she's only nine years old and…" "Never mind Zep." (Nope, no raise.) "What's her mother look like?"

I got a small monkey I call "Gargantua." He sleeps on top of my mosquito netting, either playing with his peter or pissing in my face. During a monsoon card game in poor light with $1,500 bucks in the pot and two of us left in game and I'm deciding to "call" or "fold." In middle of table is a can of Planter's peanuts. As the monkey scoots over and grabs a handful of nuts he flips the call or fold hole cards. A very-very loud noise, a lot of smoke, fur, flesh and blood. Mr. "Call or Fold" shoots my monkey with his .45. My first instinct was anger. I objected but he outranked me and really, I was getting tired of the monkey piss showers. Take away the monsoon and I believe the monkey would have lived much longer.

We got a rich neighbor – the Maharajah of Tripora. He is really a nice guy 'bout five foot four tall and five foot four around…educated at Cambridge and Yale. His pay annually is his weight in gold. Believe he got paid in June. (He stays on porky side). His house of 'bout 200 rooms is in Agratala.

He also has a special house, for his 150 wives (I ain't shittin' you, this cat had 150 or so wives. Nope, he was one way in that deal.) He'd feed us every Wednesday night, then let us ride around on his elephants. Had a pickup truck body strapped on elephant's back (with a powerful battery operated light). He'd loan you a gun (you could damn near stick your thumb in the barrel) and tie a goat or sheep or calf to a tree. When tiger got close enough the scared animal hollered, on comes the light, the tiger is temporarily blinded, and the "brave" hunter shoots (half the time misses, and an Indian hunter does the job). If you got a buddy who has given you a line 'bout killing a tiger when he was a Flying Tiger in India, he might have, but it would be the equivalent of catching a hungry fish from a rain barrel. Did I? Hell no! If I had my way, all wild animals would die of old age.

I liked taking a Catalina north to visit a tea plantation in upper Assam land on the Bramhapur river which had lots of hippopotamus in it. Then go to the plantation watch elephants work and fuck. Boy they had a lot of fun – wild and tame. Damn those things are strong. Be glad you ain't an elephant. You'd have to dig a six foot hole for the lady elephant first to have sex. Nope can't use another elephant's hole. The English plantation owner liked our visits but not nearly as much as his teenage daughter…remember what I said 'bout women watching big animals having sex.

Gargantua was fun when he wasn't pissing on me.

A bit more on tigers. Every time I drove from airport to base camp when it was dark, and it usually was, I'd always see several tigers jumping across our dirt road. Man, they are beautiful creatures and some were huge. I saw some (skinned) in the Maharajah's palace their nose touching 15 foot ceiling and tail partly curled up on the floor with huge, huge paws.

Once I went with the Maharajah on a wife buying deal in case I decided to live in India. X-number of

A Flying Tiger B-25 with a 75mm…the one that turned that elephant into dust.

cows, goats, and some money. Day I was with him he bought a 13-year-old girl. He seemed to like 'em young. Man he could of used Viagra by the barrel. If you think that's terrible, you're wrong. That was a great honor for bride's family and herself.

This place had snakes – I hate those damn things. I'd have killed a couple of big snakes there, but they scared me so bad when I first saw 'em, by the time I got ready to shoot the snake was gone.

I've seen an Indian stick his goddam leg in a python snake hole (his leg was wrapped in burlap) This was a constrictor snake, not venomous. (15 foot long average big one) The snake swallows his leg up to his knee, then they pull Indian out of the hole with snake on his leg, pull snake off his leg and kill it (for the skin). This was a standard hunting procedure then.

In here someplace, I get promoted to a first lieutenant and a squadron leader. Our job was "search and rescue, plus OSS stuff." Course I never really knew what the secret shit was. I doubt our operations manager knew the whole story. We had a really good commanding officer…a West Pointer…well maybe just to me. He'd never been involved in any knock down, drag 'em out dead or alive deals. I got some extra points for stuff I did in Africa and Europe. That's over. In India, now I'm gonna play "survive." Though I'm now a flight commander, if a particularly dangerous mission comes up, I've got an ear infection…"can't go." Ironically I did get a serious ear infection from flying very high with a head cold, which eventually led to a broken ear drum because of an inexperienced flight surgeon. (We lost our oxygen supply and had to drop from 30,000 to 14,000 in a hurry.)

I hear 'bout the CNAC (Chinese National Air Carriers) in Calcutta needing cargo space from Dum Dum to Luliyang, China. ("The Hump"…ever hear of it?) Let's start this off with "flying the Hump was a piss poor way to get old." No bullet or flack problems, the enemy was weather, very unreliable and crude navigation equipment, plus poor plane maintenance. I think I had the only B-17 in India. I'd rather fly the Hump than do a European bombing mission but I'm not sure the Hump wasn't a slimmer bet. Man, there are a shit-pot full of B-24s, C-47s and DC-6s in that rock pile in eastern Burma to Kunming. The Hump was our supply line to the goon non-communist freedom fighters. The Hump was in real-life a Chinese shake down racket run by Chiang Kai-Shek, his wife, an American – General Chennault and a couple of

US Air Force officers. Whatever it was, it was a bitch to fly. Number one…the weather was always bad. Number two…once you passed the PONR, there was absolutely no place to land, actually no place to even bail out, walk out and live. (I doubt anyone lives in that pile of rocks even today.) Number three…Luliyang had one long 10,000 foot runway, but the runway was at 10,000 foot elevation, and rimmed like a coffee cup with about 15,000 rim. To land, you screwed your way down, and also to get out you had to make a climbing 360 degree turns. (Note: all fuel had to be flown in.)

I decide it's time to start a business…photography and a freight service, India to China and back.

CNAC Headquarters is in a new apartment building they own called the "Kanarni Estates"… next to the horse track on "Chowringee Road" in Calcutta, 'bout four miles from my apartment…25 cents by rickshaw…35 cents by cab. I go down there and ask for the "top cat" regarding the Hump. I see General Chennault. Oh yes, he lives there. Who runs the apartments? They say Tony Martin and Alice Faye, a couple of movie stars. I see 'em. One's a master sergeant the other's a WAC tech sergeant. (I might have names off, but movie famous for sure.)

"Who's that girl over there?"

"Oh that's General Chennault's wife."

"Huh?…I know I saw her in a cat house in Chittgong Burma not long ago."

They say, "That couldn't be."(Bullshit)

"Can you use a B-17 to haul on the Hump, Colonel?"

"Yes, we can."

"Is it legal?"

"Yes, it's legal, the Air Force knows all 'bout it, you can haul a load any time you want. We'll pay you $5,000 bucks in rupees, you figure it out from there. We will furnish you with a safety deposit box here at the Kanarni Estates if you wish."

"Sounds dangerous. 'Bout the five grand, I'll let you know Colonel. Thank you sir."

I go to bar and talk to a bunch of ATC pilots. Everybody seems wired in and it's an everyday deal, the Air Force is all for it. I go to Dum Dum to look around and see what I can learn.

I see a fancy DC-3, "Who's plane is that?"

"Chiang Kai-Shek's."

"What's he doing?"

"Hell, he's head of the CNAC, lives in Formosa and has a freight contract with US Government."

I finally decide the deal's a shade of gray. Not white…but I decide it's "OK."

I go back to Colonel so-and-so, and say, "When you want me to fly a load?"

He says, "Right now if you want."

I say, "You got a co-pilot and flight engineer type I can use?"

He says "No problem."

I say, "How 'bout a navigator?"

He laughs and says "Lieutenant, you got one radio range in and out, you won't be able to do celestial navigation 'cause you're gonna be in cloud cover all the way. What the hell will a navigator do for you? But if you want one I'll find one."

"OK. You're right…where do I park?"

A radio range has in it the "a" and the "n" side; "Da-dit" or "dit-da." The center of the signal is a a steady "da." That's all you got for eight hours and the mountains twists the beam because of ore deposits.

After about an hour and I got it over there. They load it up with 8,000 pounds of heavy canvas mail sacks. I can't help but notice they have been cut open and sewn shut on one side just under the cable that locked 'em.

From the beginning of the rocks on the west side of Burma it was riding a bucking horse for five hours. I luck out, Luliyang is clear with a few scattered cirrus. Whew! I taxi up to unload.

A Navy guy, a Lieutenant Commander (what the hell's the Navy doing here?") signs my delivery forms. He says, "I'll have you loaded and fueled in two-and-a-half to three hours."

I say, "I want a bunk and a shower, I'll leave at daybreak."

After checking weather (all they have is pilot's reports…no weather stations past Burma, so as a pilot goes up and back past each other we'd exchange information), I leave 'bout 6:00 am, guessing the weather. As I get on board, I think I notice that Navy guy's last name was Dempsey, (on his flight suit) first name is "Jack." (Nope, no bells ring yet.)

We get load signed in at Dum Dum and I ask, "Where do I get paid?" "Kanarni Estates, CNAC office." When I get there, a Chinese lady pays me five grand in rupees and tells me I can exchange them for American (at a 2 percent loss) down the street at "blabbdy-blah" and Chowringee.

I betcha they owned that deal also. Later, I ask "Who's the Chinese broad?"

"The General's wife you dumb shit"

"Chiang Kai-Shek?"

"Yes, don't you ever read a paper?"

Have you ever thought about the fact Chennault nor any of the top brass of the Flying Tigers ever came back to the States? If you knew the real truth 'bout the Flying Tigers and the CNAC most of you'd puke. Chiang Kai-Shek fucked the US government out of at least 100 million bucks, which today would be more like a billion. Hell, he built a country out of the money now called Taiwan.

Next trip load's not ready, so I wait while an incoming plane from the States unloads all mail sacks. Then a crew comes along, slices the mail bags open just below locking cable, dumps all the stuff out and burns it.

"What, they are burning the mail headed for China?" They refill the bags with nylon stockings, Life Buoy and Ivory soap, aspirin, toothbrushes, toothpaste, non-prescription drugs, all sorts of drug store stuff. I found out that stockings were a big-big deal (women's stockings). American-made hose were way better 'bout not running. Don't make sense to me, but that's what I hauled over "the Hump." Coming back, I checked what's in the bags. They're filled with snake and animal skins, carved ivory objects, jade and other precious gems raw and finished, antiques (vases for example), money, gold, and silver.

Does this bother me regarding the obvious fact that it's illegal? Nope, I figured I was doing this on my own time and our government knew about it. I saw it as a huge waste of money. But, of course, what is war? A huge waste of life, money, ruined lives, horrible pain and suffering. All because of the world leader's ego trips of 30 or 40 years duration. Remember the wooden gliders Firestone built in Pitcairn's plant I told you about? I saw 'em again. 'Bout a 100 of 'em towed by C-47s, (the gooney bird) to a big field all filled with troops gonna go into Burma and chase the japs out (that ain't there no more). Well, the japs cut three to 4 inch diameter bamboo, planted it into the ground 'bout three feet on a 45 degree angle with two feet of it sharpened above ground. The gliders can only land one way based on the terrain. I can't tell you how bad that was. Those bamboo poles went into the wooden bottom of those gliders and into the troops sitting damn near to on the floor. This was a surprise night time deal. It was a surprise all right…you didn't hear about it…want to know why? How much money, how many lives, how much suffering, because of fucked up intelligence?

By now, to me everything went into the same pile. Take it a day at a time, keep alive and comfortable, figure out ways to make a buck and try to do the above the easiest way possible. 'Bout every trip I'd have one or two national passengers. 500 bucks each was the accepted fare (one way). Nope, no taxes. Course I told 'em they had $10,000 life insurance also. (Hell no there was no real insurance.) They were never on the manifest. In another deal, you got any idea how much a genuine Flying Tiger leather jacket would bring from a visiting politician or movie personality at the Kanarni Estates? I could buy 100 of 'em for 10 bucks apiece, and in right place, 100 to 200 each was like falling off a log. I had one little deal to do, promote all jackets to Colonel, Lieutenant Colonel or Major. Yup, I'd leave an officer's name on the jacket. Japanese flags, swords, pistols and uniforms sold very well, too. The ATC pilots bought 'em from me, flew 'em to the states and got mucho bucks for the junk. A jap soldier's wallet with personal papers and pictures were also a hot item. Same deal for Japanese GI watches, medals, knives and insignias.

I need to tell you this. Our outfit did very little regarding missions in India. Cover some B-29 stuff from India to Rangoon, an air taxi for "so-called" secret stuff, and long distance stuff where a Catalina would have to be refueled by a submarine to get back. (Not a good way to live long) Here's where an "ear infection" comes in handy…I can't very well drop the boat in the jungle…the bay of Bengal is our only ocean. It's a big bay all the way down to Rangoon. Yup, plenty rice burner military there. Why? Hell, I don't know.

I had a navigator friend from Alabama, Sharon Elabesh. His family was big in jewelry stores. We had some L-5s, a small air plane, single engine. Somehow Sharon's bought a bunch of semi precious stones from a broker in Calcutta in the market but it was his job to pick 'em up. They are damn near to Rangoon. So I take an L-5 and we leave to get 'em. We fuel at Chittagong (south end of Burma) and sneak down to just north of Rangoon, Henzada. Sharon bought about 100 pounds of semi precious stones (unfinished rubys, emeralds, opals, sapphires, etc.) We had a limey spy help us with fuel half way between Chittagong and Henzada. He looked in the bag and paid the money – I never shut engine off.

Sharon got a royal screwing from the "so-called" dumb gooks. The bottom half of the bag was bottoms of 7-Up bottles for uncut emeralds, pieces of yellow runway light lenses for amethyst, etc. He found out when we got back to the base at Agratala. Sharon, do you ever tell that story to your audience? (Sharon became a singing motivational speaker-comedian, world class.) I got to go back to Cairo to get the B-25 I'd left there.

I hitch a ride from Calcutta to Karachi. Yup, "Hello Polish nurses, I'm back and hornier than a three-peckered billy goat." But I got a ride leaving in morning to Cairo – a two day deal on an ATC DC-8, so I take a nurse that has a week leave coming. She stays in the "up to a mile high, and over a mile high" club for 23 hours ('bout 30 minutes less than total flight time). Hell, everybody, the pilot, co-pilot, engineer, and navigator. I guess you'd have to say she was a very friendly person. Well, maybe kinda over friendly.

The 25 is fueled and I pay somebody 25 bucks for a note to take to Baghdad to make sure I get fuel. (I ain't got orders for this. Yup…the Colonel knew, but didn't want to write up orders for the trip). We sleep in plane at Baghdad, but when we get to Abadam…its way, way too hot. We have to split up for night. I was afraid of a major fuel problem here. Not a word of trouble. "Fill 'er up?" he asked and didn't even ask me to sign for it. Flying a B-25, climbing out with a lady sitting on your lap pretending she ain't been laid in a year is a good movie, but I imagine if a plane was following us our wiggley flight path would probably look weird…kinda like the evasive action the boats did to keep from getting a big hole from a torpedo. On the

5th day we are back in Karachi. Fuel…no problem. (Imagine how much money was wasted on fuel alone? For example, all the fuel in Kunming had to be flown in there – no pipe lines, no roads.) Americans filled the tanks in Karachi – the limeys owned a pipeline from Karachi to Agratala. They charged us one dollar a gallon to ship it via their pipeline – plus they used all they needed free. You gotta remember in the early 40s the British run India like they owned it (maybe they did).

I stayed the night in Karachi and promised the nurse I'd never screw anybody else 'till the war was over and I went to Poland to marry her. Well, all this was her idea and of course she would live by same code. I forgot to get her Polish address in the saying goodbye part. If you read this li'l Polish nurse, you now know why I didn't come back to get you. If you read this, would you mind dropping me a note and let me know if you made 48 hours on your vow?... (I made it 'bout a week).

I gotta tell you 'bout last Hump trip. I've just returned and it was hairy weather. I see a guy in operations in Calcutta…I think "Damn, he looks familiar." 'Bout that time he comes over and says "Remember me Henry?" I got it now, its Mr. Waters, the primary instructor who told me first flying day I wasn't gonna make it as a pilot. I answer "Yeah…you soloed me and said I'd never make it." Mr. Waters is a civilian ATC pilot now, riding right seat on a DC-8. Gonna make his first Hump trip. I think, "Holy shit, what horrible weather to do a virgin Hump ride." What makes it worse, in right seat you don't control your destiny, and if the left seater screws up your ass is mud. He asks me, "How's it going where I've been," but I need to get fueled and get back to Agratala, so I tell him the short version. He asks, "Any tips?" I could give him and I think "Yeah, start hollering you got a sore ear." But I decide he ain't gonna really listen. I do tell him "Monitor the guys in front of you and all those coming back for pilot weather reports and mainly 'bout ice." I think half of those that went down either got lost or iced up. Every trip I had ice. We

Me on some steps somewhere.

had boots on wings for ice removal but still not enough. The trick was, climb above it, or drop down if you could. Fish altitude (for no ice). I threw in, "Keep good track of the PONR." I also said, "Follow the range tight from leaving Burma to the cone." I warned him where the beam bent, even showed him on the map. I don't believe he ever came back from that trip.

They were flying a load of fuel in 50 gallon drums. Can you imagine a couple of them babies getting loose in the bucking bronco mode? They weighed 'bout 575 pounds apiece. But, Mr. Waters, if you're still going, thanks for the "You'll never make it" speech, I then shifted gears and tried even harder to get it done.

As big as the world is, ain't it funny how sometimes it's small? Well, guess who they shove in the rear door of the 17 a week later at the Chinese end? A very-very sick cat named Jack Dempsey (that was the name on his flight suit, had yellow jaundice). He was even more yellow than the Chinese. I told him he got sick "cause he didn't eat enough pussy." He said "Nope, more like too much." He's damn near dead when they load him, and that first five hours out of Kunming wasn't of any help to him. Nope, he recovered and returned to the States and lived quite awhile longer.

As we sometimes spent a night or a day in China (breaks en route because of weather), I decided I wanted to know something 'bout the firecracker kings. I ate their food close by the airport (by the way the runway was 10,000 feet long at 10,000 feet altitude and was built by women, by hand…no dozers, no drag lines…by hand (don't know why men didn't participate) and they did a good job. I know a Chinese/Russian girl who works in operations and she understands the Chinese spoken in that area, and is fluent in English.

Listen to this…how would you like to fight a soldier that really and truly believes getting killed in battle is the most wonderful thing that can happen to him?

The average Chinese who lived there had a big hat, the blouse, the skirt or pants made of roots and various plants (including footwear). All hand-made with no undergarments and no change of clothes. At best they lived in a self-made shelter of plants and bushes and trees, or rock and dirt. These shelters had no windows or doors, no heat, no water, no lights, no medicine, and no dental or doctors. These people could carry all their worldly possessions on their backs. You could buy a baby girl for five bucks ten times a day. The saddest part was they seemed to all have six to ten kids. Death by starvation was as real as night and day – actually a kinda natural expected event. It was almost like they were talking animals who could be educated to do most all things "so-called" modern society considered "normal" way of life.

I met an American/German doctor there (in Luliyang), a civilian. He'd lived there for five or six years studying the people. His whole life, 'bout 40 years of medical adventures, was dedicated to a single topic. "What race of people are the most intelligent?"

At the time, I thought the Germans were and figured the negro to be least intelligent. His answer, "All, given same opportunities and motivation are damn near equal, but the Chinese could have a slight edge as smartest, and yes, if there was a race that came up a little short it would be the negro." Nope, he never said "Afro-American" once. Really, he separated us into groups defined by color: white, black, yellow and dark skinned. Religion to him was an important characteristic because he believed certain religions were designed to keep the "believer" ignorant and dependent on the leaders. He claimed these "animal-like" people, in a two to three generation span, could fly or design the most complex airplane going if given the same lifestyle and education as the "so-called" super powers offered.

I tried every drug known to man while there. Opium, heroin, stuff you drank, sniffed, smoked, injected or ate, you name it, were all available dirt cheap. I just didn't get it. My impression was "you never felt good without some bad parts." My ability to pleasure the ladies was next to zero. Plus I was very aware that if I got put in a dangerous situation, my ability to defend myself was near 'bout zero. I've never knowingly fooled with that stuff since 1945. Did I inhale? Ha, I did everything I was told to do by the "experts" and the Chinese/Russian lady was a connoisseur of hallucinatory drug stimulation. I did play with peyote for a couple years here in Daytona, supervised by my drunken, metallurgist professor from Northwestern University (for educational purposes only).

In conclusion, Americans ain't got a clue how well off we are as compared to about 80 percent of the rest of the world. I've always believed the only thing the war did for me, considering it took me completely around the world and exposed me to so many countries, customs and life styles was that deep down I realized how lucky I was to live in the States and have so many choices and options to aim at a life-style I liked (or thought I liked). And equally important, I could have more than one chance at the brass ring.

Ever hear of the Burma Road? Well the US decided to build a road from Burma to China. I think a general named "Merrill" took a bunch of tough engineers in there to do it. At first they had to put up with the japs sniping at them, then I think when the japs realized how impossible the task was, they went south to Rangoon. We called 'em "Merrill's Marauders." Them poor bastards lived in the mud, rain, jungle, and impossible engineering conditions. After the Japanese harassment as the road went north and east the Chinese communists were an ever increasing and effective enemy. I believe if that road was done as it should have been it would have taken 40 years and 40 billion dollars.

They ate K-rations, slept in leaky tents – a great breakfast was "shit on a shingle" (chipped beef in a thick brown gravy on a hard thin biscuit). You don't like the menu?...ask your dad or granddad, or maybe great granddad. A K-ration was a cardboard box 'bout 10 inches long and five inches wide by two inches thick, sealed in heavy wax paper. Hell if you dropped it in water it would float. As I remember there were 'bout three or 4 different menus. You could live off of it completely. I never liked it, but I can't say I starved because of it. They were big on cheese (we called it "choke ass") and the crackers were, I think, of a wheat derivative. SPAM must have cleaned up during the war, that was a favorite meat substitute. You know, I believe if you found an unopened box of k-rations today, 55 years later, I betcha it's still edible.

If General Merrill gets to Kunming, China, we've got a problem. The Chinese communists are not allies of ours, as a matter of fact they want to kill all our asses and take over the airport. Remember, Chiang Kai-Shek is a communist enemy and the hump is a Chiang Kai-Shek operation, part of the so-called "Free Chinese Movement." It operates on the support we give them by air.

Merrill has his gang surrounding the airport. That's our only protection from communist capture as we wait for whatever wonderful ending this movie will have.

I ride around India in the 17 or the 25. I have to take a bunch of visiting politicians to New Delhi. Why? To see the Taj Mahal. New Delhi has 2,650,000 buzzards flying around it at 500 to 2,000 feet so naturally I hit one. They weigh 'bout 150 pounds, got an eight foot wing-span and stink like rotten meat. That damn buzzard went through the wing's leading edge right next to number four engine. I must have puked 10 times patching the hole back in Agratala. Later I had a couple trips to Kashmir (where the Kashmir sweaters come from). Everybody lives on house boats. I flew a bunch of limey military brass there in my 25 on a trip to Islamabad and the Khyber pass. On the way we have to go over Mount Everest (29,000 feet) just so I could say "Oh, shit yes...I flew over and pissed on it with my "piss tube." Nope, not even a goat walking around. You know, I think there's a rock pile north of Islamabad I flew over that I think is 400 or 500 feet higher. (Actually, I guess it's in Russia.) Man, that ain't no damn place to live (maybe my altimeter was off). While in Calcutta I meet a British "fanny." Nope, I didn't make it up...kinda like our WACs. She was 'bout 17 years old, cute as a bug in a rug, and dying to get laid. Her boss is a lesbian and conquered my li'l fanny. We're going to a big party at the Kanarni estates, our first date in an Oakland touring car cab. She's got on a maroon evening gown...can't wait...and it ain't even really good and dark yet. My first experience with a messy, bloody wildcat real virgin. We went back to my apartment and then found out what looks like an obvious cleaning tool if soaped up good, is a big mistake (the soap got into some very sensitive areas). I had to take some British brass to Delhi in my 25 so I took the li'l fanny with me. Two bad things happened. I hit a buzzard at 'bout 900 feet on the final. It hit right on the plexi-glass dome of the engineer's twin 50's turret right behind me. Man, that buzzard flesh, stink, feathers, blood…I instantly puked. We had a pretty bad landing as a result. My "so-called" co-pilot could fly, but never was inside a B-25 before this trip. Second bad thing, the British general went ape-shit over my li'l fanny, transferred her to an island we called "Candy," some maps called it "Ceylon." They now call it "Sri Lanka."

New adventure coming up. We have to go to Okinawa for re-assignment of the 7th Emergency Air-Sea Rescue.

I had 'bout a month to be in Okinawa and met a pilot who flew B-25s with a cannon in it's nose. I think it was called a "French 75." (I believe this was a projectile about two-and-a-half inches in diameter.) He was based in Burma (Chittagong I believe). This was not a real nice place. The women chewed "beetle" (like chewing tobacco), 'cept the juice they spit was maroon. Their teeth were mostly rotten. They also smoked grey cheroots, which were like a cigar, but looked like two-week-old grey dog turds. This guy knew I kept our 25 flying. His outfit didn't have a mechanic or parts for engines of a B-25. He could not get the number two engine started for a month because he was waiting on a new carburetor from the States (which I bet ain't come yet). The engines used a Holley pressure carburetor that weighed 'bout 45 pounds and were 'bout a foot square and 'bout seven inches tall. So my very first Holley carburetor experience was not on a race car or passenger car, it was on an airplane. (Actually the problem wasn't carburetor at all… the fuel system was filthy through dirty gasoline for couple years and nobody to clean it.) When I got it running we went for a ride. His cannoneer went with us. I wanted to experience what I'd heard it felt like when plane dead stopped for an instant. This happened when you fired that big gun. We're at 'bout 25 feet, running 'bout 150 and an elephant steps out to cross the road. The cannoneer pulled the trigger and the elephant disappeared…the road had 15 foot hole in it. We flew through what was an elephant and dirt. I had a .45 on. It pissed me off so bad I fuckin' near shot the son-of-a-bitch in his seat. He was a basket case. A perfect example of "the ugly American." He loved to kill and to him Burmese people were "trash."

I thought it'd be good for a laugh.

When that cannoneer pulled the trigger the noise and sudden sensation of stopping. (If I was honest with you I believe I'd have to say I might have soiled my bloomers a little bit.) Without a lap belt, I'd have broke my neck on the ceiling of the cockpit. I betcha every time the thing fired, 100 rivets in the plane sheared. I got to visit a couple weeks later asking to fly that particular plane "to use it kinda like dynamite." We wanted to remove a real construction problem where they couldn't get dozers or crew in. I asked 'bout the pilot I'd worked with. Not much of an answer. More like "he just disappeared." (I betcha the Burmese got tired of his shit and he disappeared in a hole with sharpened bamboo.) The Burmese had very cruel customs of punishment (more like "two eyes for an eye"). All in all, I think I flew the thing two or three times.

This move to Okinawa is kinda like loading Noah's ark…whatcha gonna take?

Ain't got room for it all. I've been collecting stuff since Marrakesh, Africa, and so has the crew. Ever since I was a kid I wanted to play a guitar. In Italy I bought a good guitar for peanuts then sent away for guitar lessons. I'm left handed, so I have to re-string the guitar (it was built for a right hander). I sent away for and received 'bout three different sets of lessons. The Wabash Cannonball and The Orange Blossom Special were my favorites. I banged away on the damn thing must have been 1,000 hours. Everything I played sounded like a half-assed Wabash Cannonball. You know I still remember most of the words?

Well my guitar playing is now a topic of conversation wherever I go. Folks say my "music and singing is good to chase rats," or that I should "make a record and play it at bar closing time to clear bar out." Later in Okinawa they say, "play it to get japs to come out of the caves and surrender." (It was pretty bad.) I start to leave it, but decide just having had Gene Autry around for eight hours had to eventually have some "good" rub off (yes, one of those lesson books was from his company). No pets, no furniture, no booze can go. I decide the piano will go with us to Okinawa, but the B-25 I'll just leave at the Dum Dum airport. I only made a li'l over 700 a month, but I had a B-25 to use as my own, with fuel and maintenance furnished and zero payments. Even at that I figured it would be of no use on Okinawa because the closest "goof-off" places were Shanghai or Hong Kong.

My master plan is "figure out a way to get assigned in the Philippines or Australia till the war is over." I've mentally retired from my patriotic duty to save the world from the "Nazis" and the "sneaky japs." I think subconsciously, I must have decided I'd done enough. Did I? Hell…you decide. They named the major air battles by name and you got a point for each. At this time I've got stuff saying, "Without you, we'd of never won the air battles of the Northern Apennines, Air Combat Balkans, Southern France, Rhineland, Central Europe, Po Valley, Central Burma, the China Offensive, and ended up with one more "air offensive Japan,"…no points for the African adventure (that kinda pissed me off). I got something from the French for the Foreign Legion stuff, but can't find it and I can't remember what it was for (looked powerful as all hell).

The day orders come to Okinawa via the Phillipines, I decide I'll go to Luliyang, to Manila and then to Okinawa. There is big trouble at Luliyang. The Chinese government with the head cat there directing the movie…commies. I called him "General Mayonnaise" (three words Mao Tse Tung). Our General Merrill ain't got enough of anything, looks like airport is gonna fall any minute. I get to Luliyang 'bout 5:00 pm and I bribe the gas man 50 bucks to get fueled (fuel is short). I check weather and never a dull moment. They think there is a typhoon dead en route to Manila…Manila? Where the hell else can you go. Can't go back to India tonight, weather there bad, too. What's typhoon?…an oriental hurricane, no more, no less. Well, I'll have to wait. Around 6:00 pm a C-54 (big 4 engine) transport crashes on take-off. (He was gonna try and out wrassle the weather back to Calcutta.) All pilots that came in that afternoon (including myself) figured that to be 'bout suicide. I noticed all the "Gooney birds" C-47s and the "Tokyo Trolleys" C-46s and the B-24s have adiosed the place. The whole airport is weirdly deserted.

"Crash on take-off?" Man, that don't make any sense. We roar down there with a Jeep. In the six or seven minutes it takes us to get there the Communist Chinese have stripped the bodies (it didn't burn, just busted open like it was dropped 200 feet). The Chinese stripped the corpses of rings, watches, wallets, papers, shoes, hats, pistols; all GI issue. They even knocked out any teeth with gold fillings, and had already disappeared in the hills and vegetation like magic. I'm scared now. I sure don't have any plans to become a Chinese communist prisoner of war.

I decide a lucky rifle shot or two knocked the C-54 down. We haul ass back to operations. I tell crew "get on" and tell navigator, "File a visual fight plan for Manila." By 8:45 pm, I'm climbing out of the coffee cup airport at 15,550 feet I swing to 160 degrees, aimed at Manila. I know I want to cross out of China over a town, I believe called "Charles." (Yeah…not very Chinese is it?) It's gotta be a pure celestial navigation and shit-house luck deal. No radio range till 100 miles out of Manila.

Well, the navigator goes ape-shit. He's giving headings that sound impossible to me. I refuse to change course and don't know the winds aloft. As we get close to the Chinese coast I get a big surprise. Towns and lights are not blacked out. The lights help me guess the drift. It's not a real dark night and I'm up there at 30,000. A Colonel at Luliyang said he'd flew that trip a couple times for the OSS and the winds were not bad, but out of the west. Over time, we run up on a city or town. About the time we got almost up on 'em the lights would go out. As I remember, Charles might have been an island rite at the Chinese coast. I feel pretty good because I think we are on course leaving China.

"Hello typhoon." We are in rough air and clouds, rain, lightning, every fucking, nasty thing you could experience. And with another negative, the nagging doubt concerning, "are we close to course?" 'Cause there ain't no turning back and we are borderline on fuel even if we are close to course. Are we in a tail, cross, or head wind? Navigator goes plumb ape-shit 'bout the course. His station is in front and under the cockpit. He's coming through the tunnel to raise hell with me. As he gets his head out of the tunnel I had my .45 by the barrel and "cold-cocked" him. (He had switched to the emergency air bottle we had in our flight suits. I forgot 'bout him.) I don't think anyone else knew what happened. I guess he had enough air till he woke up and went back to his station. OK, we hit the eye of the typhoon. Luckily it was actually a "big moon" night, and there were no clouds above the eye. The navigator takes a celestial fix and says he "thinks we are in good shape." I've decided when we crossed over the coast and hit the typhoon, the winds would rotate the full 360 degrees constantly, so actually there would be zero wind effect by the time we found Manila.

Was I right? Hell, I'm not sure, but I'm still alive 55 years later. 'Bout 6:00 am the typhoon seems to be behind us. I see islands. "Hot damn! We made it!" then I make big mistake fuel-wise. I slowly start down, all I got is frequency of radio range and tower. The mistake was the Phillipines were a long, long chain of islands. What I saw was the most northern part of the Phillipines.

Clark Field in Manila is way, way south, and the Colonel's tip…"look for a volcano…Corregador and a big city and airport is right there"…took a while to come true. No volcano, no big cities and fuel is low. A new deal pops up kinda like a stranger who wants to be a pen pal. I'm monitoring an international distress channel and getting transmissions, asking questions. These are both American and Japanese spies so I ignore them. It now dawns on me "Hell, nobody at Clark Field knows we are coming." Now I'm starting to sweat. I dropped down to 5,000 feet too soon I can't see as far as I need to and lower flying consumes more fuel. I decide, at best we got 15 to 20 minutes fuel.

Then, Halleluia! "There's the volcano and Corregador…there's a big town. Hell, it's Manila, and Yup, there's the airport like the Colonel said." I call tower for landing instructions and the tower says "Don't come any closer, as a matter of fact, back up ten miles and circle" or they will shoot us down. So I call tower and say "Sir, I don't know your rank, but I'm "so and so from so and so" and explain the trip. I tell him "I'm gonna land on a "straight in." I've decided in five to 10 minutes at best, "Smokey and his Firemen" is gonna be on the ground…on it's wheels or in pieces. Tower says "Who's Babe Ruth?"

I say, "Baseball player."

"What do you know about him?"

Not being a big baseball fan I say, "Not much, he hit most home runs ever hit, has a candy bar company and was first famous white man to endorse colored pussy."

I hear a laugh…we land. They taxi me to a way-out location. They surround the plane with GIs.

As I stop two engines quit, no fuel. I drop down out of the pilot's hatch and I'm a happy son-of-a-bitch. The other crew men, they think I've done a hell of a job. (They didn't know what a squeaker I'd just put them through.) What happened in Luliyang?…I never heard.

The people at Clark really never were very nice to us, and next day made me move to another airport and town (I think called Angeles)…make sense to you old Manila hands?

I have to wait for orders to proceed to Okinawa. At Angeles we have to live in and under the plane, no quarters. I think we were there two, maybe three weeks.

Now the hospitality here was more like it. Pretty li'l ladies came and cooked for us, washed our clothes and I think they were second only to Polish girls as to sexual positions, frequency and duration. It was warm and dry most of the time, so it, to me at least, got very boring.

I learned Clark Field was a huge aircraft repair center. I found out "no Jeeps available" (officially), but went over to supply side of things (Sergeants). They had a kinda "Hertz" deal of their own. "One buck a day – includes fuel"…and I get a brand new one. I go to fighter overhaul center. I've always wanted to fly a P-38, P-51 and P-47. Hell, they got 'em all there. I sniff around, asking, "Any chance I could get a cockpit check and fly one each?" (Especially if I made a contribution to their Officer's Club). Nope…"No way" says the unit's "CO" (That usually bought you anything.) So I talk to Master Sergeant in charge of the flight line. He says "Hey, we are short of check pilots, we could damn sure use you if you promise not to do any dumb shit and make us more work." Turns out the pilots assigned to flight check are way short of people, so they bust their ass to check me out on all three. The P-38 was a big disappointment. It was slow and couldn't turn. It was 'bout like when you think you got a shot at getting in your girlfriend's pants tonight and then you discover she's having her period. The P-51s were everything I expected, but I was surprised…not as nimble as the clipped wing Spitfire. Straight down full throttle was some serious speed. But the big ol' P-47…what a surprise. It weighed eight tons (big mother fucker), but it was like a race car, when you punched the throttle on that sucker…it didn't stay in one place very long. Straight down full throttle? You'd need more balls than I had.

The P-47 had a red button right next to gun trigger (said water injection) Flight manual said, "If you use this system in extreme emergency, you must red line the airplane." What's that mean? If a Second Lieutenant "red lined" an airplane (meaning it had a problem of some kind), nobody, including the commanding general of the Air Force, could fly it until the red lining was cleared up…including a test flight. Here's the deal, if you pushed the injection button, water and alcohol shot in the engine. This increased the cylinder pressure tremendously and that sucker would leave a big trail of black smoke, jar you back in your seat and really-really haul ass.

Idea was, in a combat situation could save your ass, but engine-wise this possibly cause serious structural failure, so all engines that had been water injected had to be pulled and overhauled.

I bet you're starting to catch on aren't you? My next goal is to figure out how can I fly one of these with the red button down? I bring a nude picture of my elderly house keeper (18 and she is a pretty thing). I show it to Captain in charge of flight check and ask him if there is "some way he could help me fly a 47 with the button down?"

This was a big mistake, damn near got into some serious trouble in that maneuver. This way I found out, "If you want to get something done in the Air Force, find a tech or Master Sergeant and be discrete." (That means "keep your mouth shut.") The Sergeant says if I "get my housekeeper to move to Clark with him when I leave, it's not a problem. I jump in a 47 that was already red lined for water injection and get above clouds where they can't see black smoke and stay close to the field, so if a piston lets go I can make it back "dead stick." Holy shit! When that juice hit those cylinders I think fuel flow increased 10 to 15 percent at the same time. For the next two or three minutes I had the thrill of a lifetime. I'd have to compare it to 'bout like your first sex climax. The engine run good after the "squirt" so "no harm done." Nope, never flew any fighter in the Philippines in combat. (My housekeeper moved in with the Sergeant two days before I left).

I believe if you wanted to shoot at a jap then you'd have had to send away for one to be imported. That don't include those in hiding that got left behind when their outfits pulled out. I really enjoyed those three weeks.

I did decide the Philippines really needed a quality birth control program. Seemed like all those girls had some hormones similar to the mink. While I was there I seriously thought 'bout coming back after the war (if I made it) and buying a small island and living there. I think 30 bucks a week gave ten of us food, laundry, minor clean up and major sexual favors. I was very impressed at how happy they were with really hardly any worldly possessions, and their ability to accept life as it was with no worries. I liked their diet too…fish, fruit, vegetables, rice and breadfruit all bought on the barter system. They ate nothing store-bought.

I get the orders. "Proceed to Buckner Bay Airport, Okinawa." I go to operations to file a flight plan and check weather. Would you believe a typhoon bigger and nastier than the one we run through three weeks ago is coming across the South Asia Sea. It's a long haul, another dead reckoning, and some celestial navigation, but with the typhoon you gotta get it done before and after the storm. Well hell, I'm an old typhoon runner now. I'm pretty sure the wings won't break off though. Believe it or not, two or three of the crew got pukey riding this bucking bronco for two or three hours. 300 miles out of Okinawa the sun's out and visibility is very good (no smog)…other than mistaking Iwo Jima for Okinawa, we found it. For you "now" instrument-rated pilots, you can't imagine getting lost. I think 20 percent of the total of lost planes and crews were just plain-assed lost and run out of fuel. This is in reference to other than combat missions. As time passed my opinion of Lindbergh and the size of his balls appreciated by about a factor of ten. No weather info ('cept pilot's reports), no winds aloft info, no alternate airport, one radio range 2,000 miles away.

Buckner Bay was another steel mat runway 'bout 5,000 feet long. Damn sure ain't no problem to find a jap to shoot at here. Big deal here is, half the US Navy is within sight of the bay.

We fly the 17 with boat on underneath. B-29s are going back and forth to Japan from Okinawa and other islands. If you drop a boat to a crew, say 200 miles out, a flying boat (a Catalina) comes within six or eight hours and picks guys up off of the boat we dropped 'em. A new wrinkle, "We want to sail the boat to Okinawa and keep the boat." (Normally after the people were rescued we'd sink the boat with a .50 caliber out of the waist.) They won't get out of the boat and into the Cat.

I live in a big tent with 'bout 20 others. I later find out we are on a Japanese ammunition dump (covered with three foot of dirt). Here's the movie. Now we've gotten in position to invade Japan (after 'bout six months of heavy European-style bombing). We, the emergency rescue, will cover the water routes for ditching and parachutists. Business is slow and boring. I count my loot.

I got 'bout 125 grand. You can see rite there I was a half-decent poker player and a major part of the money had Madame Chiang Kai-Shek's fingerprints on the bills. My Flying Tiger days are over, but business is booming. Remember I'm the photo officer. I'm getting tons of pictures for nearly nothing from Guadalcanal all the way up to Iwo Jima and Okinawa. (The gruesome stuff was what the new-comers wanted.)

Okinawa has got a million caves. In three-quarters of the caves are japs who've been barbequed by flame throwers. An absolutely horrible way to die I think…course I'm only guessing. The caves are booby trapped with land mines everywheres (jap placed). They have maps to know where not to walk. The Navy supply ships and air transports had a market in the States for Japanese soldier GI issue and personal possessions. This includes weapons, flags, military records, clothes, medals, and insignias. Those Navy guys offered damn near double the money you can get on the island. After a couple days I retired as a "cave looker-in-ner." There were three good reasons for this career decision. First, there were still plenty of undiscovered land mines and booby traps. Every day somebody triggered a land mine. Second, remember my weakness about puking? A friend of mine found a highest ranking Jap in the end of a long cave. All his stuff in good shape, but I'd say been dead a week and didn't smell too good. My friend moved the body in collecting personal effects and clothing and the body was booby trapped. He was splattered all around inside the cave. What do you tell his family? "The dumb shit got blowed to pieces by a dead rice burner?" Or do you say "He flung his body over a hand grenade to protect his fellow soldiers?" And finally, all the japs in the caves were not dead and some were very, very pissed off and still had weapons and ammunition.

I transferred my commercial ambitions to natural treasure. The island had a sea shell called a cat's eye. These are yellow, shiny and rather small. They were used as jewelry world wide, and as money in some islands. Apparently, Okinawa was the only place they lived in the world. I cornered the market on cat's eyes and sold what cost me 200 bucks for five grand. Much easier than enemy cave exploration.

Okinawa is a beautiful island, but mostly mountain, with lots of vegetation. When I was there it was not really a good idea to go sight seeing. There must have been 500 rice burners militarily abandoned there in the jap's hasty retreat. I told you place was loaded with caves. They used 'em for both living quarters and also as burial tombs. All I remember about the burial deal is that grandpop was in a big vase as ashes or bone, I don't know which.

Okinawan women seemed to vary in two classes…either petite little things that would rather die than fraternize with "Americans," or shapeless-plump kinda b-class persons (by their standards). The japs used these ladies to keep their troops from going totally blind from playing with their peters too much. As you look at history books, notice all World War II vintage japs had glasses half inch thick. In particular, notice the emperor Hiro Hito. His glasses 'bout three-quarter inch thick.

Wanna guess why?

Seemed like our brass decided those unemployed ladies should be medically checked daily and bathe often. They did so in mess hall garbage containers. (No, not old dirty ones…new ones.) As I watched them bathe, even in my prime I would have needed Viagra. The Navy guys covered it with a catchy phrase "any port in a storm." OK, maybe some day, but I ain't been on the deserted island near long enough. For other reasons though I'm suddenly getting twitchy. I decide that I've been drinking way too much using an unhealthy "Smokey-made" formula consisting of alcohol from the hospital, pineapple juice, Aqua Velva shaving lotion, and various other tune-ups, like fermented potato juice.

I'm not flying too much for a month, it's just routine patrol. By accident I'm asked by a Red Cross lady to photograph a friend's wedding on a Navy ship in the harbor. (Remember I'm the squadron's photo officer.) Turns out photo paper, film, etc., is in very short supply on Okinawa and I had brought a ton from India.

A naval officer and a very wealthy Red Cross lady from St. Louis are due to be hitched. (She's got enough miles on 'er that she looks out of warranty) This is a deal that you're gonna see in a few pages will show how small the world can be, and how fate can cause stuff to happen almost beyond comprehension. The groom is 101 percent Navy pilot stud. Kinda looks to me like a barter deal. Where money and sex have more to do with it than love.

Believe this or not, I've never been on a ship before. This wedding has to be 12 miles out so ship captain can marry them. I find out the Navy has real whiskey, steaks, chocolate cake…the works, and out the ass too. Ever notice how fat the sailors get? I found out why. I drank too much, and to shorten the story, two days later as I developed the 200 wedding pictures, I goofed bad.

None were worth a shit, none! Well as you can guess that ruined my career as an excellent photographer. But it did create a dialogue between Smokey and the Red Cross ladies. And hell, in a blacked out tent with poor lighting, I can't say it wasn't good.

Stop and think about it…who could have in their wildest dreams imagined photo supplies as a strong barter tool for pussy on Okinawa? 'Bout this time I'm trying to figure out how to pull a scam and go back to the Philippines. Things on Okinawa are not ideal, and with a little bad luck a man could get killed without trying too hard.

Just in time a miracle! The goddam war is over! Two atomic bombs in 'bout a week ended the son-of-a-bitch. Atom bomb? What the hell is that? In a couple days I go to Tokyo, pick up fuel to complete a patrol and I see why the japs gave up so quick. From what I saw from the air, and now with 55 years of improved technology…God help this world if that shit ever gets turned loose again.

Hooray war's over! We let our hair down and had a big party in our tent with my home-made whiskey. I play Wabash Cannonball one more time, and let the guys destroy the guitar. A strong rain and windstorm tears tent up. Next morning I'm sleeping under an army truck, soaking wet, and with the goddamdest headache and bellyache I ever had.

Guess what? The sneaky mother fuckin' japs sent a bunch of kamikaze pilots in and I can see from where I'm laying, the whole son-of-a-bitch war starts over again. Man they are plowing into those ships, everything is blowing up, burning, exploding. Can you imagine a 20 to 25 year-old cat aiming his plane for the middle of a carrier or battleship and hitting it wide-assed open? What kind of pills do you reckon they fed them? Suddenly, as quick as it restarted, it's over again.

Surrender on a battleship. Pictures are going to be a "big deal" and I'm in perfect position to furnish film. Did I get to watch? Nope. If I had my way they'd of signed a surrender with a General and hung the li'l piss ant that caused all this misery by his balls from the ship's flag pole.

I didn't, of course, know MacArthur, but the word from Burma to China to the Philippines and in Okinawa, was that he ran instead of fighting. Yep, he got on a submarine and hauled ass to Australia while all his men were captured, starved, tortured. In a few days story gets worse.

With war ended we've got too many people and nothing to do. Only place to go is biggest city on Okinawa "Naha"…but it's blowed all to shit. The people openly hate us. I'm down at operations, kinda bored. A Marine pilot we picked up out of the drink some time ago said, "Wanna have some fun?" I said, "Not with the local hookers." (I'd seen him come out of there a week before.) He laughed and said, "Go get your stuff for two or three days if you can get away." I say "Yeah, I can leave, but I don't have wheels to go get my stuff." He sends his driver and Jeep to get my stuff. (Hell it's all in a bag.) I climb up in the Marine's C-54 and get off in Shanghai where 'bout 20 Marine officers and myself check in hotel. It was the first bath tub and hot water I'd seen in four months. They also had store bought whiskey.

Now, around 7:00 pm, I'm in a restaurant eating a wonderful seafood dinner. Shanghai had no war effects, no blackouts, had paved streets, rickshaws and cabs, and a species of women called "White Russians." These creatures were beautiful, kinda tall, with less than white skin, who walked in such a way that you got a hard-on just watching. In India, Burma and China I got exposed to every drug there was. Here in Shanghai in two-and-a-half days, I got exposed to every sexual configuration ever invented. To me, up till then, sex was a "two people game." (Well, I did have a few others.) In Shanghai I played various games that had as many as 20 people. I knew life as "drink, food, sex." They showed me how to combine all three without the need for the normal table setting equipment. Those ladies made a career out of the art of pleasing a man.

There was (to me) a sad side of this. I found out that when these ladies passed 35 years of age, they were like beautiful flowers that had shriveled up and needed to be replaced. The two-and-a-half days cost 'bout 100 bucks, and that included by their standards, generous tips. The Marines said "load 'er up – this adventure is over, we'll be back in a month." Hell…when I got back to Okinawa, nobody knew I had been gone.

I was "Officer of the Day" twice in my Air Force adventure. Couple days after I got back from Shanghai, I'm "it." Do you know what Officer of the Day is? It's a military custom when all officers take turns being the camp's military law enforcer. Maybe you can compare it to jury duty. Some hate it, some love it. I did not want it, but you do what you're told without comment.

Around 2:00 am there is a noise in the mess hall. MP says, "Some one's in the mess hall." Remember we still got lots of live, hungry, pissed off japs around. I unlock the rear mess hall screen door. I've got a flashlight in one hand, a .45 in the other. Here "it" comes. (The MPs were coming in from front.) "It's" coming right at me. The .45 goes off. The "brave" lieutenant "Officer of the Day" has just shot and killed an unarmed man with nothing but a pair of shorts on, holding a one-gallon can of stewed tomatoes. By the time the bullet flattened out from going through the can, it damn near cut the skinny jap in half. On come the lights. You can imagine the sight. Tomatoes, blood and guts are all over.

I puked. I had no intention of killing anybody. I guess being startled, reflex action caused me to pull the trigger before I got my brain in gear. Maybe it was a signal I'd reached a saturation point of a very unnormal lifestyle. No, I didn't get criticized as a matter of fact the story was "Don't fool with that fuckin' Smokey – he'll shoot your ass in a heartbeat." The victim was a Japanese soldier left behind, living in a cave 'bout half mile beyond the mess hall and 'bout half-starved.

I hang out around flight operations at the Buckner Bay air strip. There's a couple B-29s sitting there, but crew for only one. A major asks me if I'm "checked out in a 29?" I say, "Nope, never even seen inside one."

He asks if "I'd be interested in getting checked out?"

I ask, "What's the plan?"

He says "They need the 29s because of their range to go way up in China, maybe Mongolia, to bring back 100 prisoners of war."

I say, "What 'bout rest of the crew?"

He says, "All we need is a pilot."

I ask 'bout co-pilot… "Can he fly it?"

"Nope…he's a pissed off wanna be fighter pilot…never made a landing or take-off."

I'm most concerned 'bout navigation and as it turns out he is a dandy. "OK, who's gonna check me out?"

"Flight engineer." Yup…the usual instrument orientation.

For the checkout, the pilot is blindfolded, someone calls instrument or control by name and you touch it with your finger. In a 29 the flight engineer 'bout handles the engines (pilot can override) and the co-pilot handles gear, flaps, and radio.

Hour-and-a-half later I'm off the ground, North bound to way the hell up in China.

"Say, what kind of airport is this? How long is runway?"

"'Bout 6,000 feet, dirt"… "Huh?…Dirt??"

"Holy shit! This plane weighs tons."

"No problem…it's been done with a 29."

Land in daylight with plenty of pure shit-house luck. Landing a 29 ain't bad, but when you flare out, (it's a tricycle gear) the pilot's ass is 50 feet in the air and the pilot is blind as far as seeing the ground (so you wait to see how hard you hit).

The passengers we pick up are pathetic. Some men are six feet and over, weighing 115 pounds; nothing but skin and bones (some of 'em Generals). They had fuel there, how the hell it got there I have no idea. I guess we load 'bout 100 men and no possessions 'cept maybe two pounds of stuff in a paper bag. It's quite cool, but all they have is shirts and pants. Some are bare footed.

We've got Navy doctors, blankets, snacks.

Take-off is no problem and the trip back is no problem. On the way back all the ex-prisoners are asked what they want for a coming home meal at the Navy hospital mess hall. Steaks, lobsters, big salads, shrimp, oysters, roast beef, baked potatoes, french fries, chocolate cake, strawberry short cake, beer, wine, champagne, whiskey. Each request was filled by name. Yup, the Navy had all this good stuff. This kinda pissed me off. We were on K-rations and pretty simple, common food. Hell, it may be better diet, but it sure wasn't anything you'd order in a restaurant.

Of all these passengers, there was not one MacArthur fan. Matter of fact they were quite bitter 'bout him. The mess hall act was pitiful. Hardly any of the poor bastards got past a drink or appetizer. Why? The doctor told me their stomachs had shrunk. I couldn't help but think "maybe if we hadn't got out of China that night, our asses could be getting a taste of what these poor devils went through."

Who were they? In general, captured officers from Corregador and Bataan.

I heard what sounded like "quite a few of them perished during the time of their capture." I forgot to tell you…the landing at Buckner Bay closed the airport for two days. I bounced 'er in too hard, blew a couple tires and rolled up half mile of steel mat runway. Also messed up one prop. Nope, nobody got a scratch…just a jolt and a lot of noise. No, they never asked me again. Matter of fact, I heard some derogatory remarks 'bout my ability as a pilot. And not one of the passengers thanked me for the trip. To me the fact I could walk away from it, I consider it a success. (At the time, if they'd grounded me, I wouldn't have give a shit.)

I get word when I first get to Okinawa, "Smokey and his Firemen" are scheduled to fly back to the States and play the "Memphis Belle" deal, to sell war bonds. I didn't like the idea. I was afraid it would be a six month deal, and then get throwed on a B-24 outfit and end up back close to Japan. I'd already seen the damn deal restart once. I had quit writing letters a year ago and had just concentrated on surviving with a half-decent lifestyle. Twisting through the sky in a 24 ain't my idea of anything good. So I tell our Colonel "I'd rather not do it if he'd like me to stay." (I was "brown-nosing" him to get him to kill the deal.) I even offered "to take him to Shanghai."

He said, "The publicity would be good for the 7th American Rescue...I should go." So deal's off right? Bullshit. "Fly her back to Frisco next week."

Man, I had a weird early life.

A freighter, an old banana boat (the "something" Mauro) has a captain, who is hauling supplies from Hawaii to Okinawa that wants pictures and jap stuff. He invites me to dinner on his ship.

I bring what he wants, we both drink too much, and I wake up and the ship's sailed from Okinawa headed for Hawaii. Nope, can't get off, jap submarines might sink some boats like the kamikaze deal in Buckner Bay. Salt water showers and this slo' poke ol' boat (I doubt she goes over 12 mph). The radio says, "No problem – your plane will meet you in Hawaii – you can take 'er from there." All I've got is clothes I'm wearing.

This boat is operated by the US Army, not the Navy, so I get some clothes. I arrive in Hawaii, and goddam, I can't wait to get off of this slo' poke relic. "Lieutenant Henry Yunick, Officer of the Day." Son-of-a-bitch! I'm headed off for the airport when I hear this. This, I suppose let some ship's officer off the boat who had family on Hawaii. "Well," I think, "No problem, I get off duty 6:00 am and my plane will be waiting for me." I'm up most of the night and drinking. I wake up 9:00 am and the boat's sailed again but this time for Frisco. By the way, this boat's full of GIs going home. "OK, my plane will be in Frisco." New orders say that when I get there, I'm to go to Camp Ernie Pyle. (They named the camp after a very famous war reporter who played the odds too far and got his ass killed on Iwo Jima.)

In military, everything is done alphabetically, so a "Yunick" gets off last, gets on last, and so on. Takes four to five hours to unload passengers. By the time they get to the Ys it's 'bout 7:30 am the dock is getting covered up with women waving to home coming service heroes (by the way, some are injured and immobile). I guess patriotic women who want to make you feel good waving flags and blowing kisses. From my position on the boat I could talk to someone on the dock 'bout 25 feet away. There's a lady there that turns out to be lonely and horny. I'm supposed to get off the boat and get on a ferry boat to Camp Ernie Pyle. My pecker overruled my brains (after all, it's been two or three weeks) and I end up in a room at a hotel called "Top of the Mark" (hotel with expensive doors). En route from the boat to the hotel we stopped and I bought a hammer and some nails, some food, booze, and fruit. I asked for and got highest available room. We never made it to the bed, did it right on the floor. Woke up three or four hours later then nailed the door shut. On the third day I got concerned 'bout not showing up at the camp to go meet the plane. Plus my li'l peter is ruined and lady just had to go work. It's agreed when I get reassigned I will come back to Frisco and marry her and take her to my new assignment. (Oh yes, we had also run out of whiskey, ice and mixer) The door? It was 90 dollars.

I get to the camp fully expecting serious trouble. "Have you had your homecoming meal yet?" "Nope."

"Well here's a menu. You write out what you want and it will be ready to eat at 12:30."

I call the airport, my plane's there and our bond tour has been canceled.

"Go to Camp Attaberry near Indianapolis, Indiana for debriefing and reassignment, or for discharge." No arrest, no MPs to drag me off. Nobody even said, "Where you been?"

They got a point deal going. If you got "so many points" you're eligible for discharge. I've got enough to get five guys out, but hell, I ain't going no place. I'd have 20 years in by age 37, so I'm just gonna drive airplanes and start trying to get promoted (with the war over I want rank). I got 125 grand in a tomato can and I ain't got a mark on me, 'cept a bad eardrum. Never got any venereal disease. My worst deal was malaria. (I got it in India, it comes and goes. Man that's tough sledding – fever and chills.)

By the way it kept coming back off and on for damn near 20 years, then never bothered me again. You people who had it know what I'm talking about (that's how the phrase "shivering like a dog shitting razor blades" got going). We first took quinine, then attabrine was perfected and 'bout three or four days it would go away. Here's a tip, if you're overweight get someone to give you the malaria bug. In 'bout four days you'll lose 10 to 15 pounds and your food bill will be zero. (Course there is a possibility it may kill you.) Over there, without medicine it was a top three killer, a mosquito bite was how you got it. We slept under a mosquito net in Africa, India, Burma, China, Philippines. We had a medicine we smeared on, mosquito was supposed to eat it and fall over dead, but I doubt it worked. (I think it softened the skin and the mosquito snoot went in deeper.)

I can't believe it. Bad as I fucked up in last three weeks, no trouble of any kind. "Get on the train tomorrow, 6:00 am." A thru train to Indianapolis, Camp Attaberry." And check this out. With a seat that turned into a bed. The train ride was a three day deal, but this train has several USO hostesses. A small world. One of 'em was a classmate of Red Cross gal I bum photographed her wedding on a ship. She was stacked like a brick shit house, but she needed a new head. Well, high heels, silk stockings and kinda a short skirt. After watching that thing prance around the train, I decided to violate one more rule "Don't fuck the USO girls." I got the bartender (yup, there was a free bar) to make be 'bout 4 martinis in one bottle, I fed her half the bottle in the dining car and listened to her explanation of how she was a virgin. (Gonna be married in a month – gonna get off tomorrow in St. Louis, so "Don't get any ideas, cause it was absolutely not in her character.) At same time I felt a foot in a silk stocking sliding up and down my leg. We walk by her seat/bed deal (she shares it with another hostess). "Can I come in and…well have one last drink before she disappears forever?"

"Oh, no." she says, "I'm not falling for that."

But she does have a light that don't work, "Maybe I could quick fix it…?"

"Oh hell yes – I'm an electrical whiz."

Hmmmmmm…seems strange. The light seems to work fine. But I'm confused, why is this girl unbuttoning my pants and acting like a cannibal? And how would a virgin be so good at it the first time? The rest of the martini's, the ritual of being liberated from her virgin status, plus the swinging of the rail car, took six hours including a little sleep. We are past St. Louis. She's lost all sense of embarrassment 'cause her roommate can't not know what's going on (matter of fact I thought "how 'bout a 3-way," but neither voted with me). I believe if I had one more day I could have pulled it off with some help from some margaritas.

But it's "Indy time." I'm picked up by a pair of WACs: a Sergeant and a 2nd Lieutenant.

It's night, "Do you want to go to the camp barracks or stop and have dinner some place?" Oh yes, they know the town. "Can I take you two to dinner?"…"We'd love that but we got to put civilian clothes on." After the food and some drinks they say, "You wanna go to camp now, or maybe stay at our place tonight, and we'll go in together in the morning?" How in the hell can an officer and enlisted person live together off base? I'm pretty tired, but not that tired. As I got in the shower I got the message, they decided to wash me real good. My first legitimate three-way (with added entertainment). It seemed like they enjoyed each other 'bout as much as me. This was a movie I hadn't seen before (different than Shanghai). You think I should have reported those perverted women? I woke up 6:00 am, I guess honeymoon's over. "I'll shower and dress."

The 2nd Lieutenant says "We've got the weekend off and if you don't report till Monday there won't be any problem."

"How do you know?" I ask.

She says, "We cut the orders for the Commandant."

I was able to corrupt them some more by explaining the sexual, eating and drinking habits of the Shanghai ladies. I opt to stay in the Air Force and they accept me. I get a three week leave. Then go to Germany to fly coal…yes, coal…in a C-54 (or Tokyo Trolley) to a city that's fucked up by the Russians. As long as it's not a B-24, it's fine with me. Three days later I completely started fucking up my life good.

Had some leave…"Where you gonna go?"

"Shanghai."

I ask 'em at Indy "Need any airplanes delivered to Shanghai?"

"Nope, and if we did no first lieutenant is gonna get the job…you ain't the only one who knows about Shanghai."

"OK, how 'bout Hong Kong?" Same answer.

I got a sister living around Philadelphia, "I'll go see her for a couple days." This was the decision I should have never made. My sister had a recent minor operation and was impressed with a student nurse that cared for her. My sister thinks I should meet this girl. This starts a romance.

So many deals like this must have happened then. The returning, confused service person and ladies who lived in a man-short world.

The lady's name was Elizabeth Parker. In reality, we were like a magnet that has opposing poles.

I should say rite now, I'm sure if she'd paired up with the correct man for her she'd probably have been great. In three weeks this baby is talking serious shit and I'm staying at her house.

For you young, unmarried cats reading this, pay close attention. I'm positive this movie plays every day a thousand times, the only difference are the male and female stars. I didn't know it at the time, but really my whole world was airplanes, my ass, food and pussy. I didn't have a clue 'bout this "love shit." My whole world for four years was maybe like a lion tamer…I kept teasing the lions for some kind of a thrill I got out of getting away with it.

For three years I had blind faith in a .45 pistol and a parachute. Hell, sometimes I slept with 'em on. I never-ever flew in the Air Force without at least one parachute on, and overseas I never was over two feet from my .45 automatic when I wasn't wearing it. I liked a back pack chute and helped the technician pack it. I never left it anywhere. I took it with me and kept it in my barracks bag. In my life I figured plans for two weeks out were worthless.

The leave is up.

I go back to Indy.

The two WACs say, "We can get you two more weeks"…I say "I don't want to go to Germany and fly coal…what can I do around Philadelphia?"

"How 'bout assistant Officer's Club manager in Greensboro, North Carolina?"

"I'll try that."

Two more week leave.

I fall deeper in the web.

I'm starting to get scared. "Why don't you resign from Air Force and take a job around here?"

Well hell, I want to fly and retire at 37.

I get to Greensboro. The manager is a Major, a pilot and a typical "Hot Shot Charlie." He is also a crook.

Every vendor who sells supplies to officer's club pays him under the table. In the Air Force, you have to fly at least four hours a month to receive flight pay (then – I don't know 'bout now). Well, hell, that was 'bout half my pay. I was getting 'bout 700 a month in combat, here it would be down to around 400 and less if I couldn't claim flight pay. They have an advanced trainer there…AT-6s and we can use 'em and get the hours. I try to borrow one to go to Philadelphia to see Bette. "Nope, can't get it."

The Major can get it though, he's got enough rank and he needs the hours. At departure time, 8:00 am, the runway is covered with ice. Yes, goddam ice in Greensboro, NC. He is going to Philadelphia with me and we'll switch coming back, and both will get the hours we need.

He's been up all night and simply put, is drunk.

He climbs in rear seat, the pilot seat. The front seat is for the student. I say "Charlie, get up front, you're so shit-faced you'll ground loop this motherfucker in the first 100 yards."

(You see rudder don't get control till 'bout 60 mph, so you use left brake to keep 'er straight till rudder works…get it?)

Left brake, on an ice runway, and drunk is a piss poor plan. In 150 yards, ground loop dug a wing tip in and got the prop tip also. He jumps out, goes back to operations, tells them I'm flying it. He jumps in his car and disappears. I filed the flight plan and signed it before he tried to take off.

Well, other than that shitty landing in Okinawa with that 29, I've never put a mark on a plane. I'd rather eat dog shit as have this on my record. I fought this like a tiger. Finally a tech Sergeant on the flight line testified he heard me tell the major he was too drunk. He testified the Major was in the back seat. In the Major's deposition he got caught in two lies. They stuck it up his ass but good. He got grounded and transferred out to I suppose, a shitty job in the Aleutians. I didn't wanna be there when they find the payoff deal, and I bet every club officer did it, so I pulled the biggest mistake of my life…I resign.

End of the Air Force and start of civilian transition. Now I'm in the web deeper.

I get a job in a Ford garage, I'm living with her parents, I'm a fucked duck.

I don't want to get married, but I figure I have to do it 'cause somewhere here I must have mentioned marriage.

Men…if you get in one of these deals, tell the truth and haul ass. They'll be hurting for a month or so, as opposed to stuff much, much worse later. I'm over 76 now, and I still wonder what my life would have been like if I'd made my decisions based on my head instead of my heart. That's it. Suddenly my whole life changed…I'm free to dress as I please, but I'm really lost. Suddenly I've switched from an expert to a rank amateur in a sea of pros. I had a chance to get back in twice – Korea and Vietnam and if I hadn't had children, I would have. But you gotta play the hand you're dealt.

So four years of my life gave me the above.

As I stood outside the door of the Air Force, my possessions in life were a leather Flying Tigers flying jacket, a 97th Bomb Group official ring (a little corny…silver skull and cross bones and I had rubies put in for eyes and diamonds for teeth in India). Plus an Air Force wrist watch with a band made out of a piece of stainless off a crashed zero (hot dog jap fighter), and lastly, a can with 125 Gs in it. Actually a rectangular tea can I got in the market place on Chowringee Road in Calcutta.

The tin can got buried in Daytona with 135 grand in it for fifteen years.

The ring, the jacket and the wrist watch I left in a gas station rest room coming home from Darlington in '51. We'd won the race and I was so physically and emotionally tired, I never missed any of it till next day. (I cleaned up in the rest room – I was covered with grease and mud.) I can't hardly tell you how much that stuff meant to me.

I'd found a way within a year to totally blank those four years out.

I never questioned the orders I was given, not even for a millionth of a second. But when I seen recon pictures of where we missed targets and hit homes, hospitals and prisoner of war camps, I can't say it didn't bother me (but I was able to shift the blame to Hitler and his staff, and to the li'l piss-ant jap and his staff).

Take my word for this. I truly hated the radicals who plunged us into the misery, terror, pain, death, destruction and starvation almost world wide.

Whoever got my ring, watch and jacket. You stole my only life's possessions that I thought I needed.

They were my secret badge of manhood. On other hand, maybe you did me a favor. I needed to get rid of all yesterdays and try to look at life a lot longer than a day at a time.

Sure 'nuff…I really didn't need 'em.

I've lived 55 years since and still peddling. The Wabash Cannonball carried me back to the civilian world. As the years passed the whistle, the rumble and the roar became even fainter. The "what if" got stronger by 1948. I knew the destination but no idea of the route.

The Mule Ain't Blind

After World War II, a lot of couples got married that didn't really know each other and a lot of time was wasted which caused many bad endings for doomed marriages, and worse yet, the children.

I bought a house trailer and I had a '38 Ford. I got a job in New Jersey at a Ford dealership. (Jersey was where my sister and the nurse lived.) As happens every year in New Jersey, the weather turned to shit. I hated cold weather, ice, snow. (Don't even like reindeer cause they run on snow) The service manager was a draft dodging asshole named Al "something"…("Pierce" maybe). My stall was next to a big main door. This door had a small, person-size door you could manually open and close. The big door also opened and closed electrically by pushing a big red button. Every time Al opened the big door, I froze. So, I asked him to use the little door when he could. Well, he just ignored me. I guess he was "gonna show a war hero he was nothing." So after he continued using the big door and freezing my ass off, I got up from under a car and told him, "If you open that big door one more time you don't have too, I'm leaving!" He just looked at me and pushed the big red button.

I was putting a clutch in a Ford truck. I dropped the transmission. Picked up my tools, threw 'em in my car. Took a hammer and busted the red button. And left the dealership. I went to trailer park, hooked up the trailer we were living in and waited for my wife (she got home at 5:00 pm). When she got there I said, "I'm going to Florida, either get in the car or I'll help you get your stuff out"…too bad…she decided to go to Florida. (It was close…I had most of her stuff out and on the ground and she reversed). I shut engine off when I got to South Daytona, US 1, Reid Canal trailer park. (I had a '38 Ford two-door, and a 28 foot Shultz house trailer).

First, I got a job with Eastern Air Lines as a co-pilot, $250 a month, flying a DC-3 at night. Seemed like thunder storms every time. Flying the da-dit or dit-da. Hunting the steady…and then the cone of silence. Two weeks was more than enough. By then I knew I couldn't work for anybody and would have to start a business…so I started doing the only thing I knew how to do: fixing cars and trucks in trailer parks and gas stations.

What I didn't know was, "How can a 20-year-old man, who has lived a very fast and interesting life, racing motorcycles, working on airplanes, autogyros, fly with French Foreign Legion, the Flying Tigers, B-17s in Africa and Europe, China, Burma, India and the Pacific, and seen so much trouble and dying, or been in so many experiences where it all hung on a thread…and lucked out. How can such a man be happy in Florida?" Right in here, a racer is born. It was the only thing I could really get a thrill out of. My wife said, "No driving or else." Should have let the "or else" happen, but I took the easy way and built race cars for others.

Daytona had Bill France, a race driver, promoter, garage owner. There was also Marshall Teague, mechanic and driver and Fireball Roberts, race driver. Daytona also had Frank Swain, Indian stooge for France. Called "the Indian," Frank never-ever got credit for his part in the birth and teething of NASCAR. 24 hours a day, seven days a week, he'd have died for his "Big Bill." Too bad Frank would get shit-faced drunk just smelling the cork out of a whiskey bottle. This tendency eventually hurt NASCAR and himself. He had a sad ending.

France was a promoter and a good one. As a mechanic or driver, he wouldn't have made a pimple for real one's ass. Teague, on the other hand, was a great racer. He was unusual in that he was both expert driver and mechanic. Fireball was getting good as driver, fair as a mechanic. I started into stock car racing helping Teague and the others. Fireball's modified ran out of our shop a short time. Hudson came along and paid me the outrageous sum of $200 an engine to build race motors for them. But that included going to races to baby-sit them. All told that came to about $2 an hour.

In here someplace I found what I needed to replace the Air Force excitement.

I met a man – Harry Neal…185 pounds of solid muscle…65 years of age…an old fashioned straight arrow who worked like an elephant. He had a big tin building rented for his blacksmith shop right in the middle of Daytona on Beach Street. He only needed 'bout half of it and once in awhile he needed help. I had a little knowledge of blacksmithing from the farm, so we made a deal. I help him when he needs it "no charge" and I get place to work "no charge." Really worked good for both of us.

I didn't have to worry 'bout getting fat working at a forge in 95 degree outside temperature…in a tin building…swinging an eight pound hammer making truck springs. (I had no trouble keeping a 30 inch waist.) After 'bout six months I had saved $400 working on cars out of Harry's shop so I started looking for a place of my own. I found what would become "Smokey's." The man wanted $2,400 for the river front lot, agreed to take $400 down and a two year mortgage and free repair work for his butcher shop delivery truck…a hell of a deal.

A young builder I met (Buddy Nims) said he'd build me a 24 x 30 shop for $1,000 labor, if I helped. I got concrete block company and lumber yard to sell me material for a second mortgage at a high rate of interest (four percent). Well, it turned out I ain't too good in real

Yup…you can see the river at the back door.

estate, 'cause the first load of lumber needed to construct the foundation was delivered at 4:00 pm at edge of the road (Beach Street). At 6:00 am the next morning it's half mile down the river. At high tide the bargain piece of real estate was 100% under water. Well, everybody's got to have a few bad days mixed in with the good days to know the difference. My new friend and I got some fill dirt on credit, and in a month "Smokey's Automotive" had a roof on, electricity, a phone, and had two locking doors. I got loans paid off in time and it was the beginning.

That was 1947...now its 2000. It's always been same piece of swamp. Over the years I expanded it, so by 1970, "Smokey's" was 25 mechanics and parts people. The original 24 x 30 building was built into a three-acre building. All during that, I raced 40 times a year, and was at various times a GMC, International Harvester, Caterpillar, Cummins, and Detroit Diesel dealer. I often had an inventory of about two million in new trucks in stock. I was the only salesperson. On top of that, we did 'bout two million a year in parts and service. (Remember, back then, two million was 'bout like 12 or 14 now.) Back then you worked 14 hours a day, seven days a week to compete. There were many independent garages...just 'bout like mom and pop grocery stores...so if you worked your ass off and figured out how to collect for the work you would make out. (Back then everything was on credit and no interest paid.) But you could make it. It used to be that parts stores and dealers would not sell parts at any discount unless you had a garage license. The discounts were for 33 to 50 percent. Without that margin from selling the parts you installed, I'm gonna compare the chances of doing today what I did then..."No way in hell." Now everybody gets discount same as garage owner.

The first shop and Army surplus wrecker.

I'm gonna back up and fill in a little. In 1948 the Stewart Neon Sign Company built and installed the original and only neon sign..."Smokey's Automotive Service – Best Damn Garage in Town." It cost $285...$25 down and $15 a month, or credit on bill for repairs to Stewart's truck.

That original neon sign still exists...in new condition. It's in Floyd Garrett's museum at Sieverville, Tennessee. A good investment though. It cost me $300 to get the neon redone (on a $285 total sign) and $500 labor to redo the metal work before it sold for $5,000 to Floyd. Do you think he got screwed? Nope, it happened in an auction. So if he got screwed, we'd have to call it a form of masturbation 'cause he was the bidder.

First night that sign lit up (it had a timer, on at 7:00 pm, off at 6:00 am) I sat there, looked at that sign and got shit-faced drunk by midnight. To me that was the final touch...I was a success. I still got original office chair I bought used. It and my first desk were $4. The poor desk is gone. I sat a Hudson Hornet engine on it, and in twisting the engine around, the goddam desk collapsed. (In trying to save engine from damage, I broke my left hand. Once it starts to fall, there is no stopping a Hudson engine.) The chair was, and still is fire engine red (used some paint I had left over when I painted a Holly Hill fire truck).

I also still have the "lion-tamer chair." Back in early '50s, a day before Christmas, I get a call to tow a bus in and fix it. I had a wrecker then (surplus Army auction acquisition, a nearly new Dodge 4x4 for $400 from air base in Melbourne, Florida on which we built our own wrecker equipment). So I tow this bus in and guess what? It was a Flexible bus that had a GMC 4-71 Diesel engine installed in a half-assed conversion. (Originally, they had straight eight Buicks.) Well, this 4-71 engine had its rods knocked out.

It was a cold, nasty, rainy day and we've got more work than we can do already. But we are also the only diesel shop for 60 miles. I tell the guy, "Can't fix it till after Christmas." I also notice bad smell coming from the bus. What I don't know is, I smell lion shit and decaying meat. Turns out the bus owner is a lion tamer (six lions) with a traveling show out of West Palm Beach.

Well, this is a smooth talking son-of-a-bitch, and he's got a damn nice looking wife.

I get thinkin,' "Maybe…when he's not lookin'"…and I agree to fix the bus. The mechanic I gave the job to, Harry Van Driel (yup, he is still going today)…he's pissed. It's cold and overtime on a shit-box vehicle,

We got a little bigger.

where all we can do is patch it is a shitty way to spend an evening. I grind two rod throws in the bus with a Winnona wheel drive crankshaft grinder (still got the grinder). We finish next day round noon and the bill's 'bout $600. Out comes madam lion tamer's check book. Well, back then checks are bad news, don't take any out-of-town stuff, and they had been told bill would be "cash." So he calls bank and lets me talk to them – "Oh, hell yeah…got millions." Like a damn fool I let him go, but I haul ass to the bank to deposit their check.

What I don't know, is when he got five miles down the road at Port Orange, he called his bank and stopped payment.

OK, "The lion tamer's chair." Remember the kitchen-looking kind of chairs lion tamer's used along with their whips (and they sat on 'em backwards)? Well, while we were working on the bus, (and most of it was laying down on a creeper) madam lion tamer is sitting on the lion tamer's chair with no panties on, (goddam wonder I didn't kill myself) watching us work. When they left they forgot the chair. Also where they dumped some lion shit it killed the grass. Did we ever get paid? Nope, 'cept the chair. (Need a good genuine lion tamer chair for 600 bucks? Course I've used it to sit down weld with for 50 years).

The above gives you an idea why I was attracted to racing. The Air Force life was always just one cliff hanger to the next, so I never got bored. Now there's a medium sized problem…maybe even more than that. In the Air Force, I didn't realize till the late '50s, I must have depended on alcohol for some part of my being able to climb into that airplane and say "yes-sa-boss" and do it day after day. Well, I decided, I might as well face the fact…I was an alcoholic. I liked the feeling, not the taste. As a rule I drank as I worked at night. I had my last drink January 4, 1961. It was a dandy. Four quarts of beer and two and a half quarts of Seagrams V.O. (this was about a 24 hour deal). Curtis Turner, Paul Goldsmith and I had been racing in Nassau with an experimental Corvette (the first Sting Ray) out of the GM styling department. When we came home, I bought a gallon of V.O. for 12 bucks. This trip back, Paul Goldsmith got his first flying lesson from Nassau to Palm Beach to Daytona. Yup, landed both places without no help. You guessed it, Curtis and I didn't quit drinking early enough.

On with the story of the 12 dollar gallon of Seagrams V.O. from Nassau. It was a Saturday afternoon and hot (90 degrees - January 4th). One of my guys had overhauled a Road Ranger transmission in William's Welding Supplies Autocar (where I get my nitrous gas). This is a heavy duty tranny that weighs 900 pounds. It's not right. The mechanic's got a young family so I say, "Go home, I'll fix it." I finished 'bout 11:00 pm. It checks out, but I'm at 15 thousand feet because I decide to drink the Nassau Seagrams V.O. while I work.

I'm sure the lion tamer was laughin' when he saw this in the rear view

I've got no home, I live in machine shop on an army cot. Don't bust out crying here, I caused the divorce by chasing pussy worse than Clinton. Oh hell yes, I knew the terms for what I was doing…just let the little head think too often. To shorten the story, 24 hours later I come to. It's around 3:30 pm and I'm lying in my cot. I reach around, find the whiskey bottle and stand it up. Hell, it's got maybe a little over a quart in it. My goal was to drink it all.

So I decide what I'm doing is stupid. I feel awful. As I lay there I decide, "That's it…I'm gonna quit drinking and replace it with sex" (which don't make you feel bad when it's over…'cept maybe a little sore). Besides, if I put the energy into the car I was building for the Beach Race, I might just win.

So next Monday morning I'm a reformed alcoholic (or drunk, which ever suits you). I've been drink free for 18 hours. Jim Stephens, the Pontiac dealer comes by about 11 am…"Let's have a drink." (Jim's a drunk, but don't know it.) A social climber and big buddy of Bill France Sr. He's into politics, social clubs…you know the drill…a good-natured asshole. Even gives 25 bucks a year to the Boy Scouts. Fucks everything that he can get his paws on. Basically, a typical car dealer circa 1960. He is astonished, but says, "Well hell, he will quit also." Next door is Freddy's Paleface Harbor Bar and Restaurant, so I go over with Jim and drink black coffee while Jim drinks a coke. There, Stephens proposes a bet. One thousand bucks if either one of us has a drink before Beach Race in February. This is 'bout a six week deal. I give Freddy a bum check for a grand and Jim gives Freddy ten "C" bills.

Well I die a million deaths yearning for a drink, but I make it, and we win the race. Jim, the prick, got drunk twice but lied about it. You know when I found out 'bout his lying I never had any use for him again. After winning I decide to celebrate and get shit-faced drunk. Now all my friends are trying to force me to have a drink. This pisses me off. "I'm gonna have a drink when I want to, not because you're pushing me." I go off to get cleaned up and then…well, I woke up 5:00 am Monday morning on the Army cot. I was so tired I just conked out. I avoided a bath 'cause my bathtub was a cast concrete dual clothes washing tub. One side hot, one side cold (the hot side was broke and it was cold that evening). The machine shop where my bathing facilities were located used to be a "do-it-yourself" laundry.

As primitive as this sounds, the bathing facilities were luxurious compared to the climate control system. My dog was sleeping with me…no heater. My dog slept on the air mattress I had. He had long ago bit holes in it. It still held air in half the places, so I gave it to him. I need to tell you an army cot with nothing is a good way to sleep 'cept in cold weather. The best deal then is lots of newspapers (and overdue bills) and sleep with your clothes on ('cept your boots). If it got real cold you'd have to put 'em back on.

Anyway, after missing the post-race festivities, I decided to try to stay sober till after Indy. I figured maybe I'd have better chance by thinking better outside an alcohol haze. But I also decided not to avoid bars or temptation. If I changed too much then alcohol was still controlling my life. So I hung what was left of the Seagrams V.O.…just above my tool box. I had access to whiskey 24 hours a day.

But we didn't win Indy. We were leading the race and had magneto trouble. Now I'm gonna get really drunk, probably a four-five day deal in Vegas. To my surprise I could not swallow the first drink. I spit it out and decided never to drink again. By the middle of June I'd decided to quit for good. This is January, 2001 and the deal's still on…the Pontiac dealer? Long-long gone.

Even after that I kept the Seagram's bottle above my tool box. Well in a year or so I noticed the whiskey bottle would seem to lose some liquid, so I marked it, and sure enough, it slowly went down. So remembering the old up country Dutchman's story of how to break someone of sucking eggs, I pissed in the bottle a little. Then after a month I told my helpers 'bout pissing in the bottle (by now I know who it is). I notice in next three years it never leaves my mark. Since then the sneaky drinker (and he is still alive, and still a friend of mine) is very concerned I don't name him in this book. (I can make him do 'bout anything if I threaten to put his name in here). After 'bout ten years of bottle hanging over my tool box, somebody unties and drops it. "Adios" the Seagrams "special blend."

I need to back up a little again.

By 1947, Marshall Teague, Fireball Roberts and myself are pretty good friends. Bill France I know well, but we never got real buddy-buddy. He had an Indian Friend named Frank Swain, who was France's 365 day a year stooge. Frank worshiped France and I never knew why. France couldn't drive worth a shit, he was a terrible mechanic, he was always broke, and he owed everybody in town, and he paid Frank very little. I gotta mention Frank Swain because in my opinion he, as well as Bill France, Joe Epton, Ed Otto, Bill Tuthill, (Marshall called him "the white-haired bastard") Pat Purcell, Enoch Staley, Paul Sawyer, Judy Jones, Annie France, (no, Bill France Jr. didn't have a damn thing to do with it) Harold Brazington, Clay Earles, Red Byron, Red Vogt, Marshall Teague, Fireball Roberts, Jack Smith, Raymond Parks, Joe

Littlejohn, Bud Moore, Glen Wood, "The Flying Flocks," (Fonty, Bob, Tim, and Ethel) Gober Soseby, Jim Paschal, Johnny and Mary Brunner, Bernie Kahn, Alvin Hawkins, Don and Edith O'Reilly, Herb Thomas, Lee Petty, Buck Baker, Joe Weatherly, Curtis Turner, Junior Johnson, Ray Fox, Houston Lawing, Morris Metcalfe, and about 20 more…they built NASCAR. It was never a one man band. Yup, France led the band, but the music came from the above.

I know some of the original gang that's still in fair shape that I've left out will be pissed. That's about all I can remember. Hell…nobody's perfect. I bet you didn't know Bruton Smith (his real first name is Olin) was involved in stock car racing from the beginning. He actually was 'rassling France for all us racers. His outfit was called NSCRA. Well really, in those days he was no candidate for a "model citizen award." Today I marvel at his meteoric rise to fame and fortune. Take a bow Bruton, you came a long way buddy (I read today worth $1.2 billion).

Back to Frank Swain, he was a big part of NASCAR's start-up, plus he was our first starter. Remember, I told you Frank was a genuine Indian. Two beers and he was totally obnoxious, shit-faced drunk. And, when he slipped off the wagon, it was for several or more days. Plus, some drunks, like me, just drank and kept our mouths shut. Frank never quit running his mouth when he was drinking. Sober, he worked 24 hours a day and give you the shirt off his back. Frank loved Marshall also, and worked for him part-time. Frank had enough on France to hang him, and 'bout all Frank knew, I knew. I don't know exactly what happened or how (or if I knew I've forgotten), but Frank gets booted out of NASCAR just 'bout the time NASCAR starts rolling. Frank never complained or explained it but it damn near killed him. He lived a lonely life in an old house trailer on the side west of the St. Johns River. He loved to fish, and was a world class fishing guide. He died in the late '80s, I think I found out about it a year or so later by accident.

Anyway, the beginning of NASCAR. In the '50s Daytona was a beautiful hick town run by a bunch of local crooks (judges, lawyers, councilmen). Hell, we even had a justice of the peace, a guy named judge Roy Beard who operated exactly like judge Roy Bean, even tried murder cases. In the midst of this small time civic politics, I notice some interesting goings on. My then father-in-law was the district attorney, a man named Billy Judge. He was a tough, small, scrappy, fair, pretty honest cat. 'Bout five foot four, 130-pound ball of energy, and, I'm told, a damn good lawyer. (Is there such a thing as a good lawyer today?) Well, I noticed Billy didn't like France worth a damn. (Oh, I forgot to tell you, Billy was in deep trouble regarding the "elixir of the devil.") Hooo-he. So one day both of us are 'bout three sheets in the wind. I asked him why he always called France a "no good son-of-a-bitch." Cause outside of the drivers, car owners, and mechanics, all the local politicians and business types loved him. Hell, everybody in Detroit loved France, which is how NASCAR started bringing a few bucks into Daytona beginning in '47. (Now the amount is in the seven-eight hundred millions – probably even more. I have no real info 'cept what I get as a stock holder…yup, I got a couple shares.) Well, maybe today Daytona half-ass appreciates the income racing brings it, but first 30 years Daytona ignored NASCAR.

Getting back to Billy Judge and his low opinion of France. Turns out during World War number two tires and gas were hard to get (both were rationed). France, for whatever reason didn't spend any time killing Germans or japs. He stayed home. (I used to call him a holy roller draft dodger.) While at home he apparently pissed the government off by selling stolen government merchandise; hot rationing stamps for tires and fuel. They wanted to penalize him with a lengthy stay in prison. I guess by the time Billy got to it, the government had a "done deal," and France's ass was mud. Well, Billy goes to work and convinces the government that nothing really bad happened, and the government, said "Sorry we bothered you." Billy then says, "You owe me $1,500 France." To which France says, "Send you money tomorrow" (check is in the mail). Fifteen years later, just before Billy died, this came up and Billy said, "that son-of-a-bitch has never paid one dime of it." Who knows? This one thing might have canceled the whole NASCAR adventure. (The thing that really pissed Billy off was that by then France was in jets.)

I left NASCAR in 1971 over a dispute regarding rules. When I left, I told France Sr, I'm gone, I've had all of your shit I can handle." He said, "You'll be back." I said, "If you don't believe I'm gone, count the days till I get back." This is 28 years later, I ain't been back yet. It's no secret NASCAR don't give a damn 'bout Smokey. In reality, they may have total justification. I do not in any way feel I've been singled out for mistreatment. I got same deal every other racer got back then…France Sr. just shit all over all of us.

Now, let's really look at NASCAR, Bill France Sr., and his treatment of the original gang. It's very possible we were such an odd lot of humanity that any method other than the one he chose would not have worked. We will never know. France ran NASCAR like a dictatorship. Some he crushed (like Curtis Turner, Marshall Teague, Frank Mundy, Herb Thomas, Tim Flock, and Fonty Flock). He had to be something special, cause I don't know of any racer that liked him, but we kept going back for more. France was a world class bull-shitter, and had the balls of an elephant with regards to gambling with finances, and he'd work 20 hours a day, seven days a week if necessary. The Detroit and Akron money and manufacturers loved him. He had some Barnam in him.

I remember Champion Spark Plug (one of very first to put money in NASCAR). France met Champion's executives at the Eastern Air Line plane with an elephant. The elephant had a thing like a pickup box strapped on it's back for them to ride in, and came equipped with two hookers and booze. The two Champion "big shots" (Dick McGeorge and I forgot other cat's name) rode elephant to the Streamline Hotel, a trip of 'bout three or four miles. I'll let you guess how that ended. Well Champion put lots of money in NASCAR for 'bout 40 years and in the end they got screwed out of a building they built and paid for at the Daytona track. But don't cry many tears for Champion. During the last 40 years it's been run by a bunch of incompetent assholes, and maybe that's best way to purge a defective outfit.

Sometime late in 1947 Red Vogt and Raymond Parks came to Daytona to see France 'bout using a Georgia charter Raymond and Red had formed and called the National Stock Car Racing Association…they couldn't use that name so they copied it. Yup, that's where it come from. Next thing I knew France's lawyer, Lewis Ossinskey, has changed the deal to a Florida

The party was just gettin' started.

corporation with France as president. Marshall Teague is secretary, but Vogt or Parks ain't there.

Up to that point, we were having a big problem with the promoters. Quite often, promoter couldn't put purse up till he collected the gate, and for various reasons (including just being goddam crooks) they'd take off with money while we raced. You know rest, phone calls, "The check's in the mail." You wouldn't believe me if I told you the name of a now very rich and famous track owner who did this to us sometime…maybe Bruton Smith? This was included in the learning process.

Course, if you towed 1,100 miles and won the race, then didn't get paid…well, it sucked. We're tired, had a half a snootful, and still had to tow all night to get back home and go to work. It could put you in a pretty bad mood. (Maybe that's why I'd quit racing once or twice a year).

NASCAR was a sanctioning organization structured to prevent this practice. They got the prize money first then sanctioned the race.

In the beginning we raced 40 or more times a year. We had one car with one engine (in the car). We towed with a passenger car and carried all our wheels, tires, spare parts, and tools in the tow car and the race car. Usually I had a free helper as a passenger. I think those free race fan helpers were goofier than us. Course they could quit going anytime and not be out a dime. Sometimes the driver went with us and towed all night then raced next day. Ever hear of a "yellow bar?" Well, that was the best we had…a tow bar from tow car bumper to race car bumper. They cost 'bout 75 bucks. (15 dollars extra for steering and brake cables) Only way you could tow and relax, was at 80 mph. Any speed under that, and you'd steer your ass off trying to hold it on your half of those skinny two lane roads that we used 30 percent of the trip. Your back would get wringing wet going from "almost" to "almost."

Well, this also made another problem. Before police radios, we just kept going. By the time cops got going, we'd out-run 'em. But soon came science, and them upstanding upholders of the law (as a rule some dumb shit with a power complex, especially in the little hick towns in Georgia, North Carolina, South Carolina, Florida, and Tennessee) got radios! Hot damn y'all! Then here come those hi-speed police cruisers with V8s and hi-speed "tars." Man it was over. They invented road blocks and we became their worst enemy (smart-assed racers). Sirens, flashing red lights, spot lite in the roof to check 'em out. A speeding violation took a minimum of two hours. Had to go to see the judge. (As a rule some ignorant son-of-a-bitch who hated racers.)

One night 'bout 4:00 am, Herb Thomas and I are going to Darlington. I think we were in South Georgia, in pulpwood and swamp country. Bingo! I look in the mirror and see a red light blinkin'. Herb flat footed it. (We were already running 85 in a Hornet towing a Hornet.) Well, three or four miles down the road they've got a road block. Well, there we get to meet all the "would-be racer" deputies. None of which like us worth a shit. They are all Ford lovers and we are Hudson Hornet racers. We get told "can't outrun them ray-dee-o's" The judge gets up. (He lives right close to court house.) Man, he is one nasty son-of-a-bitch. He decides, "40 bucks and costs." I think, "not too bad," but Herb's a little snarley (tired, running one or two hours late by now), so he gives judge some lip. "80 bucks plus cost, and one more word, and your ass is in the filthy-assed jail."

That last day before we left to go race, was almost always like this. Work Thursday to 6:00 pm at your regular job…eat…then work on the race car. That night you'd start drinking whiskey with beer chasers to keep going and stay awake and work all Thursday night. You'd continue all day Friday till midnight, then hook up and tow all night to start inspection at 8:00 am someplace. Then you'd qualify Saturday afternoon around 6:00 pm…leave the track taking the engine with us. Back at the motel, you'd work on engine Saturday night and install back in race car starting 5:00 to 5:30 am the next morning. The race was on Sunday afternoon. If you crashed, you had to get race car "yellow bar" towable, then tow back home. We wanted to be home by 8:00 am Monday morning so we could do our day work Monday. Finally, Monday night we get to bed. We were nuts, because at best all you could hope for was to break even and live. I've been where a speeding ticket took the eating and gas money and had to find a gas station where owner was goofy. We'd have to get gas with a promise we'd give him a race day ticket, or trade tools for fuel. He needed to be as goofy as we were but I always found one anyway.

One night I was flat towing a '61 Pontiac to Charlotte by myself. Fireball was driver at the time, and as great as a race driver he was, he also was a lazy son-of-a-bitch who didn't care to tow. I get damn near to Charlotte, coming into a town called "Rock Hill" 'bout 5:00 am. (I think) (I remember reading 'bout it a year or two ago. Years ago the locals stole the land from the Indian occupants. Now the Indians want the land back. Seems like nobody ever legally bought the land from 'em. Now there's a slight problem. That is, there now is a big city on the Indian's land. Wanna guess who will get the shaft on that deal?) It was a usual race weekend, so now I haven't slept in 48 hours. I want to show you somehow how twisted justice is. The deadly realization your "ass is had" – the feared blue flashing light. (used to be red). "Well, hello Mr. State trooper" with his tight fittin' pants, (wonder how they could get them and their shirt buttoned without castrating themselves). Well, first the lecture of unsafe driving. "Well, when you are all alone on the road, running 75 in a 30 mile per hour zone, watch out for school kids." (At 5:00 am, you don't sit there wondering if "that" means you.) Then the ticket – 75 mph in school zone, $50 payable right now – "in cash." Well, that took all I had but 'bout four bucks. Next, here's the part that blowed my mind, Mr. State trooper…Mr. "Dudley-do-right" of the North Carolina mounted police…in a special law enforcement Ford…with his hi-speed "tars" and a roof mounted spotlight (that was to lite up area he wrote ticket in)…needed two tickets for the race and could I help him? "Course," I said "Hell yes, Curtis Turner owned the track and he was a good friend of mine…was two enough?"…Talk about balls!

Needless to say, I ignored his phone calls. Don't get me wrong, most police are great. Hell, my boy Steve is a police officer for Daytona Beach. And is a motorcycle policeman who also does jobs, like for the NASCAR tracks. So if you get a ticket from some tall, good-looking, skinny motorcycle cop with big shiny black boots on up to his balls…wearing a 4 inch big shiny belt with guns, pepper spray, and three or four radios strapped on, with a gen-u-ine black leather "Marlon Brando" cop jacket on…and I almost forgot, a wooden cop's club and a shiny helmet…and most important, those big dark sun glasses that you see yourself in, (he tells me these sun glasses fix it so you ain't got a clue what he is really thinkin'…this is "shut up and sit down time") and the guy is named officer Yunick…tell him you read this book. He likes me, so maybe he'll take it easy on you. Hell, he was sent to arrest me at the Beach Race in 1997.

Listen to this. I get along so well with NASCAR, I haven't been in the pits there for a race since I last ran in 1970. So I always wait till 'bout 10 minutes before race, then drive to track in the Fiesta. (Yup, never bought a new car in my life.) The Fiesta is small, so I can usually find a tight parking spot fairly close to tunnel. You know why? All cops are trying to get inside to watch start of the race, and I leave at around half-way, so no problem… back to February 1997. I get ticket from man at tunnel and hand him $35 bucks. He says "20 more." I say "I just want to walk in…no car or nuthin'." He says he understands, "That's 55 bucks." I think "Holy-shit…the France's need another jet or boat." OK, I pay it. (It's their fuckin' track so I guess they can charge any damn thing they want.) When I quit, I told France Sr., "If he asked me time of day it would cost him 100 bucks"… so whatever's fair I always say.

Reminds me of "Big Bill"…as he was known by his many friends and admirers…this remember, didn't include any racers. (We had our own pet name for him…none of it you'd ever hear Billy Graham say it!) Big Bill's favorite expression was, "Load the wagon boys, the mule is blind," and he always used his "shit-eating grin" when he said it. (The look reminded me kinda' of like Steve looked like when he was two years old and had just pooped in his pants and didn't want to admit it.)

Well I pay the $55. A hand grabs both the $55 and the ticket. A voice hooked to the hand says, "He don't pay here," and explains to the poor ticket seller that, "the man in the dirty work clothes and greasy Crane Cam race jacket is a "big deal…and without him NASCAR would have never happened." (Obviously, given the disposition of his employer, we can't mention hands owner's name…I never saw him before in my life). Well, ticket seller apologizes for even thinkin' 'bout sellin' me the well-priced ticket.

In 1947, we bought an engine from junkyard to build into a race winning engine for 20 bucks. Fifty years makes big difference doesn't it? In 1997 A "no-seat" ticket equals two and three-quarter 1947 race engines. 'Course a Coke was a nickel in '47. (Actually we didn't call it "Coke"…called it "dope." You'd hand the man a nickel and say, "Gimme a dope." They kept 'em cold with ice, 100 pound block ice, chopped up with an ice pick.)

Back to '97 ticket deal. Now I'm comin' out of the tunnel walking. The guard says, "You Smokey?" I puff up and say "Yes." (Maybe I did something wrong? But I can tell this isn't the case 'cause guards don't stay long. I doubt they get paid very much. They love racing, but as a rule they are where they can't see shit.) He reappears with his family. (The guard's family is always close by at the track.) So we take picture and sign autographs. Then he says "Would you like to go on top of the tunnel?" That's really what I'm hoping for. Damn good place to watch the whole turn three and four action (notice all the cameramen in that area). OK, I'm on tunnel, no ticket, no credentials. After 50 miles I see it's gonna be a boring, "follow the leader" deal for 450 miles till the last 50 mile shoot-out where everybody loses their brains and goes ape-shit. I start walking towards race traffic along the fence (on the track side of the fence). I decide to go a li'l further, li'l further…into turns four and three, then down back stretch into turn two. I head for turn one, slowly walking by the inner guard rail all way around and seeing stuff I never knew before. Example: the back stretch, half way down, is too narrow. I see Kenny Schrader "go to sleep," and is 'bout to get passed by Steve Grissom. (Kenny in the outer lane, Steve comin' in the middle. Don't know who was on the fence, probably Andretti…he always seems to be in wrong place at wrong time.) Kenny gets left wheel off pavement an inch and farm is gone, it's eight inches down to the dirt.

I go to the race to see who's got the power, who's got the chassis, who is racin' and who is out there lost. You can see things like who's got too much wedge in left rear. (That means driver is now rich don't like to do this any more 'cause it scares the shit out of 'em.) And see things like "Damn!.. Bill Elliot is racing again," etc. I also notice that "Mr. Goody-two-shoes Gordon" is behavin' like Earnhardt. He didn't actually hit Earnhardt, but he damn sure put him in the wall. And I had a feelin' as he left Earnhardt in the wall he didn't even feel bad. No opinions – "just the facts ma'am."

Well, I get to turn two and here comes motorcycle cop. Big-assed dark glasses, siren goes "woo-woo." Here is Officer Yunick of the imperial palace guard, with the weirdest look on his face I ever seen. I put my hands behind my back to get handcuffed. I offer to walk out, but he is busy on the radio. I'm told "caught without credentials is immediate expulsion." "No shit…it's a serious offense." I get to wonderin,' "How do I get out?" They send a police car, but "control" tells Steve "Let him go wherever he wants…just don't walk on the track." (Might scare the drivers I guess). I thought that was nice of 'em really, so I have another experience walking back out.

The fan fence is the way back. There is a big ditch just below fan fence. Going back I notice people wavin' wanting autographs, so I walked the fence 'bout a mile and a half, signing autographs. But it really made me feel bad. These are my fellow 55 buckers. Some with cars or pickups (cost more)…most with kids, (this cost more money). They can't see shit packed in like worms. They must be in there all night long…broke, hungry, tired. Some half shit-faced on beer have no idea what's going on in the race.

But this is the very heart of NASCAR. They love one driver or they love one make of car. They get treated like a herd of cattle – $3.50 hot dogs, drinks same. 15 to 25 buck programs, stand in the heat, mud, rain, no seat…stand in line to piss. (Women have terrible wait on their side.)…toilets plug up. Man, lot's going on in there that's not pretty. I guess no way to do it real good but you wouldn't have to try real hard to do it a lot better. (Remember, "Load the wagon, the mule's blind) Apparently that is still part of company constitution. Well here's what got me good as I walked past the fans. You don't sign hi-buck programs, you don't sign new t-shirts, you don't sign new baseball caps.

You sign ol'-old hats, old t-shirts with holes.

You sign one dollar bills and li'l ol' scraps of paper out of wallets.

You sign for li'l kids that wonder "Who is that old bastard?" with their daddies and mommies and grandfathers and grandmothers ravin' on 'bout when I was a racer.

Well it 'bout put tears in my eyes to realize that so many people even knew me and were proud of my part in the evolution of auto racing. They'd push their hands through the fence just to touch you.

My son Steve on his motorcycle.

If I had my way, I'd put tents up in four or five places where those poor fans (poor in reference to money only) could meet retired and wounded racers without any goddamned extra cost. That's where the sponsors should give away some shirts and hats and racers pictures with autographs in this…the very heart of "NASCAR fan land." No other so-called sporting event in the world has the loyalty of a Winston Cup race fan. I think racers got to cultivate the fans. I believe you can overload the wagon for the blind mule. Baseball did it. Basketball and football keep playing Russian roulette with their fans. I sure hope the racing promoters control their greed before they fuck up the fan base that took 45 years to build. I notice some of the "now" racing stars are getting very wealthy by the standards I knew. And I notice they have become quite unhappy with some of the fan attention, and are pretty nasty. I say, "Watch your step racer," if you keep it up, you can soon leave your race souvenir trailers back in the barn. I know what it's like to sign autographs for two hours straight…or even eight…and you ain't got the time, etc. But, goddammit, learn how to do what you can, thank 'em, give a brief reason, then haul ass. Truman said it best, "If you can't stand the heat, get the fuck out of the kitchen"

I've noticed as time passes, racing is picking up more and more vultures and leaches. You know, the fucking "would-be racers" that are writers, press agents, sponsor hunters, souvenir venders, promoters for trading cards, miniature cars, personal appearances, book writers, food and drink sales schemes, race car memorabilia, parking, new track promoters, new sanctioning bodies, official soft drink, water, food products, radio, TV, magazine…every fuckin' thing with a fat price tag. Motels and hotels do it best. They've got a five day minimum at two to three times normal rate. The Daytona Beach Motel Association should be renamed the "Fuck More Vultures Club" with our city's blessing. (This will piss my neighbor off, his honor Bud Asher, the current mayor, and the head man in the motel association, "Triple Fuck 'em" Tom Staed.) In general, all this has put a few bucks in racer's pockets, but as a rule a very small percentage goes to the racers (between five and 15 percent). The rest goes to the vultures and leaches. (Do you think my attitude will hinder my chances the city fathers will do something nice for me someday?)

But the real damage is slapped on the fan's ass. They pay exorbitant prices. Now I see the "king daddy of all vultures," the lawyers, are getting in the act big time. Fan suits against high prices is just the beginning. Wait till car gets into grand stand, watch the lawyers act then.

Back to cops and speeding tickets. During the 1950s running hard and late cross-country to races caused a serious money problem. I found through some Chicago racer that ten bucks got you a license in 'bout any state…issued in any name. So, I'd carry 'bout five states. And for a couple years we could get them to take a check if the name was printed on the check. So, we had four or five licenses, and checks with four or five names. We only used this plan for, what was in our opinion "unfair taxation." Kinda' like Jr. Johnson's clan looked at whiskey taxation. Back in them days a check, if drawn correctly on a blank piece of paper, was legal and acceptable. (I once paid John Holman $10,000 – under protest – on a piece of a brown paper bag, and it went through. The next one on toilet paper for $500 didn't make the cut.) Obviously, once we played the "check game," you could never use that road again (that had some bad implications).

In 1947, 1948, 1949 'bout all we raced were modifieds. I helped Marshall Teague and Fireball Roberts. They were Daytona neighbors. Matter of fact, in 1949 Fireball kept his modified at my shop. A friend I met when I worked that short time in New Jersey, a guy named Roy Jones, had migrated to Daytona and came to work for me. Roy was a world-class welder and pretty damn fair mechanic, but he got so race happy, (and he was single at the time) that he, Fireball, and the car, got to be a pain in the ass. So they soon told me to "shove it," and loaded up and went to the Charlotte area to seek their fame and fortune. And they did pretty good. I think they both lived off their take. 'Course that kind of living was hand to mouth.

Back then a '37 to '40 Ford coupe or two-door was "it." It was very rare to see any other make . Fords were called "'Henry's" then…Chevys were "stove bolts"…Buicks were "Joe Lewises."

Lincolns were "Big Henry's." Chryslers and all others were scooped into one category…"trash cars." That is, till the hemi's came, then they were re-christened "Mopars." Race cars came from local junk yards and cost from 20 to 50 bucks apiece. Junkyard engines cost 'bout 10 to 25 bucks apiece or nuthin,' if you'd let him put a small sign on-it your car like "Joe's Junkyard." We had to use all stock stuff with three possible exceptions: cylinder heads, cams and intake manifold. These all varied from track to track. Sometimes they allowed custom heads from California, (like Edelbrock or Offenhauser). When we could run a race cam, there were four or five vendors: Harmon Collins, Offy, Ed "Isky" Iskenderian, Winfield, and Erickson. (Man, his cams were wild.) Winfield made the best, but he was a little guy with big demand from Indy and sports cars, even car manufacturers, so in stock car racing, he'd only sell to a chosen few. Marshall teague was on Winfield's qualified "short list." I was allowed to buy, but no conversation. "Isky" too had the good stuff for the time. Sometimes a California hot rod manifold was OK'd, and them things came with one to five carbs. All we had then was tiny two barrel Stromberg 97s. For exhausts we had three choices; stock, nuthin', or "zoomie." Sometimes I think lots of racers died early because of this. No headers were faster than stock headers, zoomies were best, but outlawed mostly. I think the "no header deal" caused Banjo Mathews' rather early departure from our world.

Poor Banjo, he spent his whole life racing 365 days a year. He gave so much for so little and suffered too much in his last 10 years. Finally, as he struggled with death in such a painful-awful way, the racing world threw him a few crumbs. He received the Charlotte Motor Speedway "Smokey Yunick Award for Life Mechanical Achievement," then the "National Motor Sports Writer's Award" (Darlington Hall of Fame). Then the "Champion Spark Plug Award" at victory banquet in NY. Hopefully soon, the International Racing Hall of Fame at Talladega, Alabama (but it's in Eastabooga, Alabama), will induct him.

Note: late news flash…he made into the Hall of Fame in 1998. Too late, though, he is gone.

OK, the flathead Ford engine came really in three flavors.

The Ford 60, which meant 60 HP, the Ford 85, (85 HP), and the Lincoln Zepher V12, (actually one and a half 60's end-to-end on a common crank). This engine was really a pile of shit. Never did anything for anybody 'cept wore out any human being who ever had to pull the heads off of one.

But the Ford 60 and it's big brother, were really what stock car racing was born around.

The Ford 85 spawned the original after-market racing industry. The grandfathers of stock car racing. These guys still have never been recognized for what they done. Harmon Collins, Edelbrock Sr., Offenhauser, Ed Iskenderian, Mickey Thompson, plus the guys who did Spalding, Winfield, Grant, Crower, Carrillo, Sparks, Vertex, Ericson, Schrader. Hell, it's 55 years later. I'm sorry. I'm sure I missed quite a few. How 'bout "Honest Charlie's in Chattanooga," first speed shop this side of the Mississippi? Then there was, and still is, "Smitty," from Lincoln, Nebraska – Clay Smith. I almost forgot him and he was maybe the smartest of us all. How 'bout racer Brown?

Actually, in cams and ignition there was overkill…especially in ignition. Crazy magnetos and dual distributors were really not a hell of a lot of help. But with cams the difference between too much and just right was day and night. With cams, Winfield was the master, Clay Smith the genius and Ed Iskenderian the "Henry Ford" of the deal. Ed got the price down, and marketed to the masses. He really was the gas dumped on stock car racing and set it on fire. In stock car racing there were a generation of mechanics who built the cars that made the deal work. Men like the grandfather of all stock car engine men, Red Vogt, and Wolfie from the east, and Bud Moore and Ray Fox (south). There were others I'm sure. Man this is tough trying to remember 50 years or more…knowing you leave out some who did so much.

There was a real sad-sorry part to the story. The manufacturers have been the "Society of Head-up-asses Surface Transportation Manufacturers." True, they invented affordable surface transportation for the masses. Hell, for the whole world. I think there were as many as 700 different American car companies from 1910 to 1940. When the smoke cleared out, there were three left: Ford, GM and Chrysler. Sure, we still had some walking wounded. Nash- Kelvinator…what a story that cat was that owned Nash…Hudson, Prest-O-Lite, Autolite, and much-much more…"Ol' man Mason," Pancho Villa's finance manager (I'll tell you 'bout him later.)…Packard, Kaiser, Sears and Roebuck, Crosley. Maybe missed one or two, but hell, what difference does it make? (Oh yeah…"Tucker.") They were all out of the game soon enough.

The sorry part of the story was in about the real "thinking about making it better," was shot in the ass and traded for, gotta make a 10 percent net profit." The philosophy was: "Don't change a fuckin' thing, cause we're gonna make at least one million of everything." Then a system of rating, or quality, was changed from a scale of one to ten on quality…to a scale of one to ten on "how do we stack up against each other (the big three)." I worked in a Ford garage in 1937. List price on a new Ford 60 coupe was $675. In 1955 GMs cost on a 255 cubic inch small block V-8 was $84.65. (For you GM experts, if you choose to contest that price, I got that from Ed Cole, who I worked for personally) Hell, I bought a new Crosley convertible for five hundred bucks (well, almost new just had it's snoot punched in by a deer). You say, "You didn't get much"…well, did you forget what kind of car won the first Sebring race? Yup, a Crosley.

That Chevy engine is now almost 45 years old, conceived May 10, 1952…and with 75 semi-fathers, was born September 1954…and is concrete exception to all the rest of my comments regarding the dead mental period from 1935 to the present. They still produce that small block Chevy. Over 65 million have been built, still going like the energizer rabbit. I've got a 1955 small V-8 block. I could bore out the main journal and bolt every single thing off of Dale Earnhardt's engine he won the 1998 February Beach Race with…and it wouldn't surprise me if his engine didn't use the small journal crank…and his crank would have bolted rite in. And all the rest of it as well.

In the year of 1995, I, with the help of Steve Lewis and his gang at PRI, (well probably, it is the other way around, but I suggested it) found the remaining survivors, about 20 of the original 75 engineers that built the small block Chevy. We gave a grand party to honor them during the December, 1995 PRI trade show extravaganza. Here's an interesting fact. In soliciting funds to help pay for this dinner and it's awards, Chevrolet Motor Company, all the current drivers, and all the current Chevrolet car owners in NASCAR Winston Cup refused to give us a fucking dime toward the party. (That party cost $110,000…thanks PRI!) Now of the $110,000, many after market vendors chipped in $85,000 and Steve added 25 Gs. Don't that tell you a lot about where their heads are? Shit, most of them assholes would be pumping gas in some service station without that engine. If those in the above are unhappy 'bout what I've said, "Fuck you all!" I think your answers were chicken-shit then and I still do now.

I also know you as a group do some very nice things. But, from where I sit, I see it as a PR service…not from your hearts. Hey, you who are today's heroes. Every single one of you will fade away. In 50 years from today, only two or three percent of you will be acknowledged as having ever existed. Well, nothing wrong with that, that's what makes the world work. But you gotta give back while you can. Nothing is for nothing in this life.

What the hell is happening to words like "thank you," "please" and "you're welcome"? Today's racer lives a stressful, very dangerous life, that part is no different than it was 50 years ago. I don't begrudge a dime of your hi-buck salaries. Compared to what the various players get for playing with their balls and whackers…you guys are grossly underpaid. What's a life worth?

How much is it worth to sit in a damn wheelchair for 40 years? Or life like a vegetable for 20 years? But goddamit, if you're born with a size seven and a quarter head, keep wearing a size seven hat. Some of you assholes are up to a size 12 in your own minds. Nobody makes you climb into those son-of-a-bitchin' cars and strap your ass in…your ego does that.

I admire and respect your talents and courage…some of you really are heroes. But most are .200 hitters. I admire and respect you also. You try your asses off. You never make it, but you never give up. The real truth is, you're needed. They got to have cars to run over and blow off. They can't race without you, no more than they can race without special tires. But there isn't one single person in the world we can't get along without, and that will never change.

Albert the Alleygator

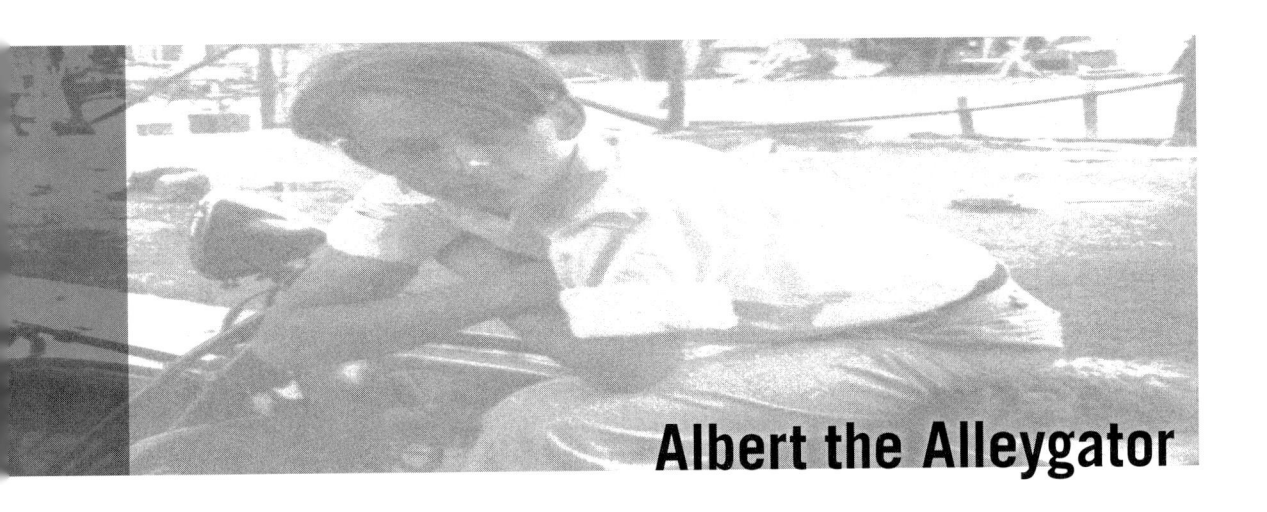

When I first built the garage in 1947, alligators frequented the area all around us. Matter of fact, where the Park Inn Cleaners is, across the street from my shop, we killed 'bout seven gators five to seven foot long before they starting filling the swamp in. A gator 'bout three feet long hung out beside back door at garage. At high tide the water at back door used to be two foot from the building. (At low tide it was fifty feet out). Well, we started feeding our "friend" and named him "Albert." Albert got his name from a daily cartoon character. When I added the first addition and built a parts department, Albert started sleeping under the parts counter.

Albert is growing, and he is 'bout four foot now. About here Albert is getting to be a pain in the ass. Nope, it's not his fault, every son-of-a-bitch has seen a gator farm where they see performers tap gators on the snoot to get it open then put their arm through his jaws only to move it quickly when he snaps them shut. They then grab his snoot with two fingers and hold it shut. The other trick, is get him on his back, rub his belly and put him to sleep. All good shit in a gator farm, but if you're drunk, or goof up, alligators' teeth are like sharp nails, and it's mouth don't open unless you help him with a crow bar.

I had a friend, John Morgan, a hard working brick and block mason. Every weekend he got shit-faced drunk. He'd come to the garage Saturday afternoon, grab Albert by the tail, drag him or her out from under the counter and around the shop. (Note: I never did figure out how to know the sex of an alligator – I spent my time around them watching what the mouth was doing, and where it was in reference to my body parts). Albert (or Alberta, I guess) was not particularly fond of this.

Well, one Saturday was John Morgan and Albert's training session, but only cause John said so. What John don't understand is alleygators figure they have a God given right to eat any block mason or brick layer slap up. One day John Morgan, "the alligator trainer" found his self in a position where two of his fingers were causing Albert's jaws to lack an inch in closing. I'm trying to calm down the famous drunk reptile tamer, and with a tire iron, trying to get Albert to remove his teeth from John's fingers. This gets to be a real problem 'cause Albert has learned somewheres, after you clamp down, then you start spinning. John panicked and used Albert's two teeth to slice both fingers their last inch. You'd think "that's end of story." Nope.

John kicked Albert. Now Albert's got him by the foot. For those of you reading this who really know alligators must be amused reading this, but I'm really getting pissed now 'cause in trying to help solve the problem, Albert lets go of John and gets me. Well, no problem, I've got steel tipped boots on. Soon I have steel tipped boot on, 'cause one boot comes off so I'm two inches short on one leg. Albert apparently figured he had a foot to eat and hauls ass out the door into the river; yup, boot and all. How fast can a gator run? One inch a minute slower than any average human when going wide open, but plenty faster than a human with one leg suddenly two inches shorter than the other.

OK, before all this started, I'm putting a trailer hitch on. The customer is there waiting. First I throw John's bloody ass out. The customer is concerned how we mistreat Albert. How 'bout me? How do I get my boot back? I get back to the hitch to get him gone. Without my boot, sparks from stick welder burns my foot. The day is not improving with age. I got a friend who stops in with two quarts of beer. I clean up the blood. (I mean, old John must have bled pint of blood.) 'Bout an hour later, or a quart and a half of beer later, here comes Mrs. Drunken Block Mason in John's pick up with a friend of the family, a new lawyer…with a camera. He wants crime scene pictures, especially the bloody parts, and of photos of Albert.

By the way, my friend with the beer is a Daytona policeman who's had trouble with John in regard to "nasty drunk." We are both feeling extra frisky, so I say, "You can start with your picture of Albert, he is somewheres close by in the river trying to eat my boot." We then heave "Mr. Legal Eagle" into the river to find Albert. His camera falls off, so I throw it to him. If it wasn't waterproof there would have been a problem. I hadn't started to hate lawyers yet, but the idea of a law suit about the deal was the last straw.

We still got the wife of the drunken defective alligator trainer to deal with. I say "Mrs. Morgan, you're a fine lady, too bad you're married to that asshole John." (And she really was a nice lady) "But I've had all the Morgan shit I can handle today, so get into the pickup and go home and heal the defective gator wizard, 'cause I bet he won't be able to lay any stuff for quite awhile." The lawyer reappears in the street and seems very annoyed, he's very wet and yelling about law suits.

At that particular time I was wired in with the crooks who ran the county so good. I could have murdered the son-of-a-bitch and got away with it. (Nope, never did.)

Well it's plain Albert has to be deported. I had another, real problem with him. His spot under the parts counter was such he could bite you if he wanted to. Your toes were inches from his mouth either side of the parts counter. If you happen to bump his snout with toes of your shoes, Albert would emit a very loud "hisssssssssssss." Needless to say, when a customer discovered the source of the hissing, he was very reluctant to stand at that counter. No, Albert never bit anyone but John, but he sorta was bad for business.

Next day here come ol' Albert, looking for some food. I drug him to the river by the tail and flung him into it 'bout four or five days until finally Albert gave me kinda a sneerey look and swam off.

If I ever saw Albert again I never knew it. To me you seen one gator you seen 'em all. If Albert's still alleygatoring he would be 'bout 52 to 54 years old, and 'bout 15 feet long.

The moral to this story is "don't fuck with wild anythings…don't try and feed them or domesticate them." Course no alligators come around anymore. The goddamned river is so polluted by the politicians and ignorant greedy business types that fish, snakes and gators can't stand it.

One Step Ahead of Castro

I believe around Christmas, either 1954 or 1955, I had a visit from a well known sports car racer. I really can't remember for sure, but I believe it was Lance Reventlow, to work on engines for his team at a race in Cuba. (Not Castro yet...Batista was the asshole dictator at the time.) Don't ask me why, but Batista lived in a house in Daytona part-time. His house was 'bout a mile from my shop. His stooges tell me "Come to Cuba! When you are there we'll show you the best time of your life...wine, women and song." I jumped at the offer to help race in Cuba.

The Cuban dictator stooges met me at the airport. I showed up at pits a day late with a terrible hangover and a wounded pecker, but I did have a sorta big grin.

All I remember was meeting Doris Duke's husband who, by the way, drove a race car there. This cat was named Rubioso...a world-famous fucker. At a party I asked him for some tips. (Well, how often you gonna get a chance to be tutored by a world class cocksman?) Only advice I remember is, "Wear a silk scarf tucked in your shirt, but first masturbate till you ejaculate into the scarf...the odor now renders women helpless and very sexually stimulated." Well, only scarf I had was made out of a parachute (French Foreign Legion stuff). It was at home in Daytona. (Who the hell packs a scarf for Cuba?) Later though, when I returned, I decided to test his advice, but never could find the damn scarf.

The other thing I remember about Cuba is there was a world class sports car driver I met. He always wore black everything, was very handsome, and a world class stud (or so I was told). Maybe his name was "Count Portofino," or something like that. And he had a beautiful American movie star there who was absolutely ape-shit over him. He had a mouth full of rotten teeth, and his breath would run a skunk off. No, I never got to see "it"...but it must have been a dandy.

OK...'bout fifteen years later I'm a GMC dealer, and the Atlanta zone manager for GMC envies my adventures. So after one night of partying here, he is still half-shit faced. He wants to experience an orgy. I wouldn't tell you his name, but after I helped him out in business, he ended up doing something bad to me which really pissed me off. In a nutshell, I got him the horsepower to move from Atlanta zone general manager to national sales manager because of my friendship with Mr. Knudsen. Among other things, this 'bout tripled his salary. He later canceled my franchise and gave it to my asshole buddy, the local Pontiac dealer, Jim Stephens to make points with Pete Estes who was pissed at me for going to work with Knudsen at Ford when I quit him. (Pete was president of GM at the time). I was working for John Delorean then. John was general manager of Chevy. I asked John to talk to Pete Estes about holding the dealership cancellation for a year to give me a chance to get rid of the new and used trucks. Also I had 'bout half million bucks worth of GMC parts. It didn't work. I asked John what happened when he was trying to get Pete to back off of the franchise jerking. John said, "I gave up when he lost his composure." When Pete got angry he'd go ape-shit… holler, throw shit, want to fight.

My Benedict Arnold "friend" Bob Stelter, he was a big cat, 'bout six foot three, really intelligent, funny and very qualified for his position. Man…he really disappointed me. I know I wasn't a good dealer, but I really wasn't a bad dealer either. The proof is in the dealership transfer. GMC has never recovered 'cept in pickups. I guess too that the double-double cross made it harder to accept. The Pontiac dealer Jim Stephens was supposed to be my friend. Really, he rode my back free for four years as car sponsor and then at the end even had car registered as himself as the owner. I never noticed it till couple years ago. Even after he and Stelter had the meetings to transfer the franchise and we met from time to time…he never ever mentioned it. Jim Stephens, in my world you were a sorry bullshitting parasite who wormed your way into politics…the upper social world and into NASCAR's inner circle. How'd he do it?…whiskey, pussy, a few greenies and an exceptional line of name dropping and half-truths. He would have made a perfect stand-in for Bill Clinton.

OK…Let's get back to Cuba. In the late 60s, an ex-world champion boxer named Rocky Marciano shows up at some races. I meet him and he says "Man, I got a night club in Havana where all the women are beautiful sex maniacs who really love racers." Yeah, Holy shit! Sounds like racer's heaven, so I go see. Yup! All Rocky said and more. OK…Bob wants some action, big time. I have a junk airplane. It's 'bout 7:00 pm and getting dark. I got 'bout 300 bucks in my pocket. Bob wants to go to Cuba to Rocky's bar. I don't even change clothes, I'm pretty dirty, and I ain't got no anything 'cept I grabbed my passport. Don't know why, really didn't need it then. A hundred dollar bill got anything done. We jump in my old plane (a Stinson) and haul ass to Miami to catch last flight to Cuba at 9:30 pm. We catch it by the skin of our teeth…a four engine turbo prop.

When we get there I noticed everything is weird and fucked up. I am hearing guns firing, but get a taxi to take us to Rocky's 'bout 11:00 pm. There I find out Castro's taking over Havana tonight! Well Stelter has seen the girls. He gets the jukebox going and is doing his best to dance his ass off. And he and I are only two customers with about ten or twelve scared girls. Turned out Castro was rough on hookers and I think the gals knew it. I find out what the skinny is from the manager, and notice he is frightened also. Meanwhile, Bob picked a pretty little redhead who was scared of the shooting, got very drunk and kept passing out. Bob would pick her up, she'd hold onto the jukebox, then slide down to the floor. He carried her to his room. I'm not sure he violated his matrimonial vows. I believe the li'l redhead was unconscious till I put her in the shower to wake her up.

Remember I'm not a drunk anymore, I'm dead sober. 'Bout 5:00 am I decide to get the hell out of Cuba. A plane, same one we came in on is supposed to leave at 7:00 am. I've got tickets, but Stelter won't wake up. I get his girlfriend up and get her going. Bob finally wakes up and finds out the cute li'l redhead is gone. He opens window and there she is getting in a cab. The dumb shit then throws half his clothes out the window at her. I finally get him dressed and get to the airport late. 'Bout 7:00 am all hell broke loose. Castro has taken Havana and with 'bout ninety seats on the plane…1,000 people want to ride. I quickly start to use my experience that demonstrates the power of the "greenie." One hundred won't do it…two hundred…OK, it's a deal, "Get on." But Stelter is outside trying to get a cab back to Rocky's. Man, luck is everything. Bango! I see one of Batista's guys. He's going to Miami, but he's still got horsepower at the airport. We get two guys

Attention Truck Buyers

18th ANNIVERSARY
GIGANTIC SALE!
NEW & USED TRUCKS

1953 to 1970

Our sale is a little premature since this was planned for our 20th anniversary as a GMC truck dealer. But my strong connections and personal friendships with the top brass of GMC have sped this sale up. I have been notified, as of October 31, 1970, our GMC franchise has been cancelled.

So, as of November 1, 1970 with a heavy hearf we say goodbye to the world's only truck engineered by two sets of engineers, Chevrolet does the truck and GMC does the emblems and hub caps.

As you can guess, these ads are expensive so, we must include some advertising on the remaining line of trucks we have. We now believe, which I think you can understand,

"INTERNATIONAL"
is a much better truck.

HERE ARE THE TREMENDOUS BARGAINS!

NEW 1970 GMC ASTRO SLEEPER
V-8,-8V-71 Detroit Diesel 13 speed Road Ranger all chromed up. Air conditioning, twin screw with many other comforts, appearance and performance options. A real good truck for the West Coast & Eastern States. The reason we're stuck with this one is, it's on the heavy side but will work out O.K. if you haul a bulky light material like feathers or potato chips. We are really worried about dumping this baby.
LIST $28,900 .... SPECIAL SALE PRICE $21,500

NEW 1970 RED GMC 5500 SERIES
Right length for a 14 ft. body, 4 speed-2 speed, 8.25x20 tires, V-6 engine, heavy duty suspension. Good for about a 5 ton pay load.
LIST $4925 .... SPECIAL SALE PRICE $4450

NEW 1970 GMC PICK-UP
Yellow & white. Wideside, long wheelbase, straight 6, soft seat & gauges.
LIST $2829 ... If no trade-in $150 over invoice & service.

1970 GMC
Long wheelbase, wideside, Real fancy deal. This is a demo, broke in and operated by Louis Hobbs. Has very low mileage, speedometer has not been set back. 350 V-8, power steering & brakes and a lot more in comfort and appearance options.
LIST $3425 .... SPECIAL PRICE AROUND $3000

REMEMBER these prices above are 1970 and 5% or more cheaper than the '71 models and there isn't enough difference in a '71 to put in your eye.

1969 GMC 5500 SERIES
C&C 396 V-8. Blue, will take 12 ft.-14 ft. body or up to 20 ft. with a stretch job. This truck is in real good shape, no patching, no abuse, but a lot of miles on it. Basic purpose of specs. are bulky med. weight load that you can fly with for 1,000 mile range without hurting it. '71 price on this is well over 5 grand.
SALE PRICE $2850

1968 GMC HANDI BUSSES
We have 4 of these damn things we are stuck with & it has me puzzled. These are all real nice trucks well equipped. Low mileage & in very good condition. We got them from GMC where they were used as transportation and on the proving grounds (remember, I said I had big wheel friends up there) but we can't seem to sell them. Let's face it, the strike has got everything messed up & looks like it's going to last a long time. If you can't get or afford a new one, these will do the job for less than ½ price & you can haul 8 to 10 people in comfort. Well, reasonably comfortable. V-8 engines, automatic trans., power steering & brakes, H/D suspension, heat & vents & lots of glass & new paint.
SALE PRICE .... EACH $1700

1966 GMC 12 FT. 1 TON STAKE
V-6, new paint, looks good & runs good. Former Dunn Bros. Lumber Truck, already builder trained. If you need a truck & things aren't going good enough for a new one, smoke this one over & ride it. This will tide you over 'til next boom & still keep you looking good.
SALE PRICE $1500

1964 GMC TILT CAB TRAILER PULLER
Will take 9 to 10 ft. body. Big V-6 engine, 4 speed single speed, 2½ ton (not a cut down). This ol' gal looks pretty good & it runs good, but it's got a blue million miles on it. It was pretty raggedy when we got it, but we did a lot of work on it & there's still a lot of good in her yet.

1971 GMC PICK-UP

Metallic green, long wheelbase, wideside, 350 V-8. Loaded executive type truck too nice to even put a load in it and get it dirty. Everything but air conditioning and we can do that here. I think we made a mistake when we ordered it without air, but what's done is done. Glen Durham bought the 1st new GMC I ever sold for $1200 and I made a $100, this was in 1963. This truck lists for $3848 and to make a $100 I'd have to get $3263, but times have changed and we have to get $200 over to come out at all. Who ever buys this one will probably buy the last GMC we sell. Don't worry about the warranty, a new dealer is on the way and will handle the problems, if any.

I JUST HAPPENED TO THINK OF SOME MORE JUNK WE HAVE AROUND HERE.

Two new Bock Tandem Axle Trailers, 5,000 lb. rating. Special built for transporting a full size car or a race car. Real dandies! Brakes and lights all set. **$1350** each. ALSO one new 9 ft. Stake Body. Will fit any truck with a 60 inch C.A. complete with full removable 42 inch stakes **$295**

NOW...
LET'S GET ON TO THE BETTER TRUCKS!

NEW 1971 INTERNATIONAL TRANSTAR SLEEPER

Treadway Orange sleeper. 6-71 Detroit Diesel 10 speed Road Ranger and many other goodies like air conditioning. This truck is perfect for Fla., Ga., Ala. and not bad for the entire East Coast. Perfect furniture hauler for all over. If you're not happy at home and want to get away from it all and still make a living, come smoke this motel on wheels over and enjoy your work.

LIST $20,800 .... SALE PRICE **$18,750**

1970 INTERNATIONAL 1600 SERIES

C&C, white, 8.25x20 tires, pretty much H/D equipment, 304 V-8 4 speed-single speed, 'bout right for 12 ft. body, real good chassis for fuel oil.

LIST $4506 .... SALE PRICE **$4050**

> REMEMBER these International list prices are without the new 5% increase that comes in October — '70.

1970 INTERNATIONAL SCOUT

4 wheel drive, Blue & White. A damn good on and off the road vehicle not too loaded up, but enough to get the job done off the road. A small V-8.

LIST $3805 (Old Price) .... SALE PRICE **$3495**

1971 INTERNATIONAL 1200 PICK-UP

This is set up for H/D work or camper. If you don't already know it, International Pick-Ups & Travelalls are considered the best campers & towing rigs in the business.

LIST $3463 .... SALE PRICE **$3050**

USED TRUCKS

1960 GMC

2 axle, 6V-71 W Detroit Diesel Road Ranger, aluminum tilt cab sleeper. Tagged, inspected and use tax paid, some states. Runs like a stripped ape, no skeletons in the closet, I know of.

SPECIAL SALE PRICE **$4800**

1966 GMC ½ TON PICK-UP

Long wheelbase, W/S. Another one of our famous proving ground jobs. V-6 automatic, new red & white paint. It's got about everything GMC ever made in the way of extras, on it. Runs like a new one, very low mileage and remember, they don't make the good ol' V-6 pick-up anymore. This was the last of the real GMC's. Had a little rust on it when we got it, so we patched it up so, don't wait too long or it will start back again. That salt on the roads up there gives 'em hell.

SPECIAL PRICE OF ONLY **$1250**

1964 CHEVY ¾ TON PICK-UP

6 cyl., color — Rusty Beige, runs good, not a junker, but too old and too rusty for us to recondition. As is ...

GUARANTEED 1 MILE **$350**

1969 FORD

C&C, 10,000 miles (no baloney) I got it new when I worked for Ford. Used it for a race truck. It is flat loaded! The biggest, toughest, gas job they make and it's got an idiot-proof gear box, The Allison. It's a tilt cab, air conditioned sleeper with too many options to really list out. It's good for short or long haul, or as a box from 14 to 22 ft. (course, for over 15 ft. it would have to have a stretch job) or as a road tractor with a shrink job. Never been titled, cost around $13,000 on '69 prices now over 14. So, if you have need for something like this, don't buy a new one, come over here & get ...

A REAL BARGAIN AT **$8,000**

I never lied to you before, did I?

1966 FORD 2 TON DIESEL

Boy! This has got to be Ford's biggest flop. Cost about 6 grand then, we pulled it all the way down & rebuilt it. It's got very low mileage, not a dent in it, runs & looks brand new & we can't even come close to selling it. Look! This truck will do a hell of a job if you don't over load it and do it cheap. It's very, very good on mileage. It will carry about 4 tons 55 to 60 MPH with no problem. Makes a good fuel oil chassis or Inter-city like Orlando or Jax. Somebody put this thing to work, I'm tired of looking at it and now it's starting to rust.

SALE PRICE **$2500**

1966 FORD 13 FT. VAN

6 cyl. A real good truck. Just selling it for a fellow, can't waste much money on it, just take my word ...

A VERY GOOD BUY AT **$1300**

40 FT. FRUEHAUF DRY FREIGHT TRAILER

With Todco rear roll up door, not buggered up inside or out. Real clean & straight, tires are not much & I don't know too much about the brakes. Bought it in Detroit to do a job & now would like to get rid of it. In comparing trailer prices, if you're interested, it's probably as good or better than anything you can find ....

FOR **$2400**

NOTE:

Our sales force is not too well run, as you probably know, if you've been here before (I run it) but that's because you're used to the other dealers ways. But all you do here is walk in, ask for a salesman, then they will page one of us. You see, it's easy to get lost around here and still be here with another customer. The two best salesmen are Louie Hobbs & John Sabatka and I ain't too bad myself.

I hope this ad stirs your soul and we get some action, because this is going to cost a ton.

YOUR EX-GMC DEALER
Smokey Yunick
(Owner & Chief Ad Writer)

"THE BEST DAMN GARAGE IN TOWN"
Smokey's Automotive Service
957 N. Beach St., Daytona Bch, Fla. Ph. 255-2558 - 253-3300

to damn near carry Bob, kicking and screaming to the plane. All seats are full. Two asses get booted out and we get to Miami. I don't believe there has been another scheduled airliner with no special restrictions yet and this is damn near thirty years later. Six months later Stelter stuck it up my ass.

Bob, I should have left you over there you asshole. I bet your wife and family would have laughed when you got back to the states a year or so later, and GM would have taken you back into a high position, maybe even paid you for time you were stuck in Cuba. If you're still living and read this I hope you're pissed. 'Cause I didn't give a shit about the GMC franchise, but I lost a lot of what I didn't have (money) getting rid of the GMC parts and trucks. "Take 'em back" your ass. The contract read that way, but in real life it was "Adios and fuck you." (The goddam parts are still here.)

I believe your road got a little rocky later didn't it Bob? Mr. Knudsen didn't care much for your act with me and in Detroit they have a system called "Don't show your anger...get even." But Bob, I'm not mad at you any more. (Good thing I forgot about you...I find out (June 1999) that quite a while ago you were peddling a bike on vacation and your living permit got canceled.)

Nope, I've never been back to Cuba since. Too bad...I thought Cuba was a nice place till Castro took it over. Castro, if you'd retire that place could be a hell of a vacation spot, and a good place to build a race track. So why don't you fold and take it easy before your breathing permit runs out? He runs that place like NASCAR, but without "greenies."

Now you got a rough idea of why I heard the dreaded word "sue" from GMC. When I heard the words "lawsuit" about the ad, I said, "Give my response to Mr. Stelter...one word...Cuba."

I've noticed that there was a large difference in social etiquette over the years in how disputes were settled. Working people just started kicking the shit out of each other till reason or pain helped us form a mutual agreement of some sort. The corporate bullshitters years ago formed a system using certain humans with genes from vultures (I'm not sure how they were conceived). Society gave these things a title called lawyers. I've been watching the adventures of a male and female pair of them recently. They may cause a new adjective to be coined to specifically describe the part some lawyers play in today's social structure. The word "Clinton" could replace about 10 words describing various bad and illegal acts. Would you believe fifty years ago being a lawyer or doctor was 'bout most honored profession there was? As a rule...were relatively poor and worked 14 hours a day...and were loved and respected by damn near all? Back then the only crooks you had to watch out for were bankers and politicians. Even preachers were straight then...you know the old deal..."Do unto others as they do on to you?" If it was practiced now 100 percent, the world population would drop six billion in a month.

Carnie

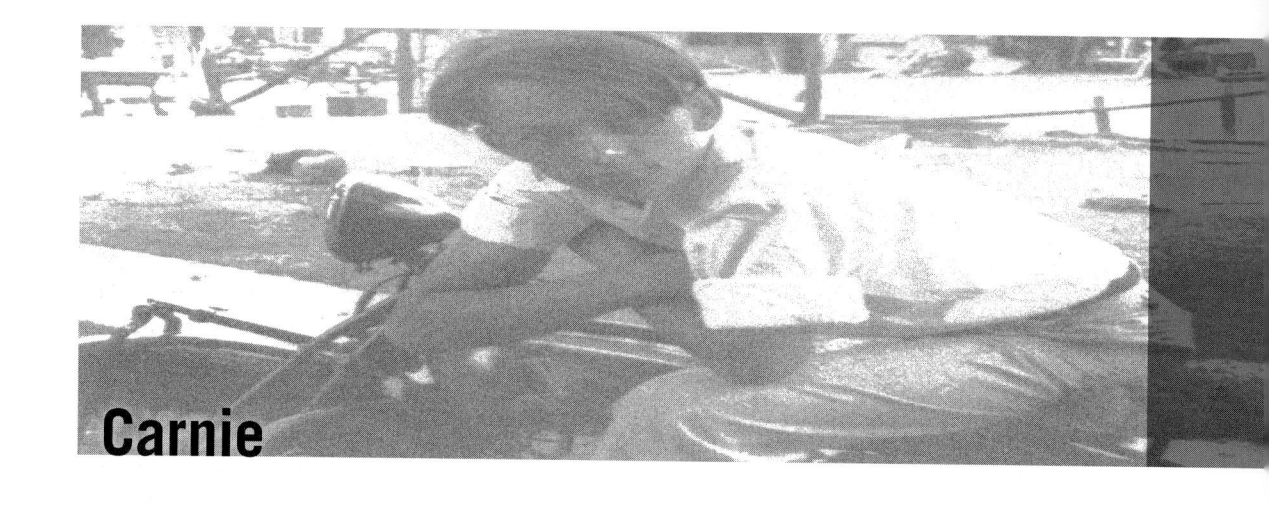

One great big difference in racing in 1950 and 2000 is what the news media did for it. Yup, the underpaid, pain in the ass reporters from newspapers, magazine, and especially TV, for 50 years. I'll bet you the media is 30 percent of NASCAR's success. The drivers are 60 percent of the story. The other 10 percent of us are behind 12 inches of concrete. The drivers are badly underpaid as compared to the stick and ballers and the entertainers (music, TV, movies). What risk do they really take, other than football or boxing? A race driver has a very real risk of death or a crippling injury. All the rest of those hi-bucker stick and ballers biggest risk is that somebody is gonna kill them for screwing their wives, sisters or girlfriends (or catching AIDS). The media gave auto racing every week and every day stories and pictures of the drivers. Since 1960, but especially now, a major part of the population, not just race fans, know who the drivers are and quite a bit about their personal lives.

You know what Clinton looks like. You read every day about him, hardly any of it good. I don't know him (and don't want to). All I know about him I got from the media They have told me he is a draft-dodging-hippie, lying asshole, who has never worked a day in his life. They say he screwed two-thirds of Arkansas financially, and the other third sexually. I got a letter yesterday says, "Send money, we are going to impeach Clinton." (I sent 10 bucks.) I hear he stole millions in the election process, has sold favors and secrets to bad countries. Really, my opinion of him a la the media is, if we hung him by the balls that would be too good. Yet today he is the most famous, most popular human on the face of the earth. Take a bow media, you invented him.

You know, he could gain a few points from me if he quit driving that fucking 400 passenger airplane around like it was a pickup truck, jumping out of it flinging millions of our money around like it was plain paper. When you know how much those trips costs you want to puke. (Actually, if any one of those women said he was a super fucker, that would help too).

Well, the problem is, what really is the truth? Could it be that I got him all wrong because of the media and he is a sweet, lovable, genius doing a wonderful job and saving us from poverty and pestilence?

I'll bet you there has been more stuff written about Richard Petty over the last 35 years, than Clinton in the last six years, and Richard's was all good shit. ('Cept his bumper banging, election losing deal with his Ram Charger nasty pickup.) The big deal in NASCAR is not how many felt tip pens you've worn out, the big deal is that the people know what you look like. I'll give you an example. In an airport, Richard or Earnhardt or Gordon walk in, wearing dark glasses or not, and the whole airport goes ape-shit. OK, at the same time, Michael Shumacher (the Formula One ace that gets paid 80 million a year), is walking to a plane. There wouldn't be three people in a US airport who knew him from an IBM salesman.

Richard Petty is a big cowboy type hat with 10 pounds of fancy shit around the brim, sun glasses, a big mustache, a work-lookin' shirt, blue jeans, cowboy boots and a big-big belt buckle, wearing a shit-eating grin. He carries dual felt tips all the time, and really, he can write "Richard Petty" beautifully on anything. You can really read his name. The new deal driver's love is to scratch a weird-ass thing that looks like it's written in Arabic. (A hand writing expert couldn't figure out what it meant in 10 years). Truth is, if you signed your ass off for an hour, the best you can do if you write legibly is a hundred an hour (not counting clothing and personal treasures), so they had to speed it up.

Now the new racket is, charge more and more every race for a ticket that lets you in the cage with the monkeys. The problem is, it would take the drivers every minute of the day up to the race and three hours after it to sign half of the autograph requests. So, the driver has to sneak in the track, hide in the motor home, then hide in the transport trailer, the "star's dressing room." At times, they have a police escort in order to get to various PR duties connected with being "the head monkey" (or damn near it).

Well, now another little problem. The stars get 10 to 15 grand for a one hour personal appearance, or a million dollars a year in a hundred hour personal service contract to a sponsor, sometimes more. This means that two hours of free autograph signing is 30 grand "shot in the ass," right?

As I think back to the early fifties, we too got police escorts. Usually from the bars, nightclubs and racetracks, but to jail or hospitals, not to our race cars or personal appearances. These cats nowadays can read and write and count too. If we could find some of the early year "sign in sheets" for entry or pit passes, you'd be surprised at how many of us used an "x." I'm not trying to be critical, I'm just telling you the different worlds 1950 and 2001.

The reason the media made racers and racing is 'cause the reporters…damn near all of you are "wanna-be-racers" And you are as excited and appreciative of the duel as are the best fans. In fact, you reporters are racing's greatest fans. And you dumb shits never realized how rich you made so many and the shamefully small financial rewards you get for what you do.

What the hell does the word "race" mean? I think a more appropriate description would be a "duel." 25 or more drivers, each with a deadly weapon, try to cover a given distance first. They must follow a strict set of rules that prohibits deliberate killing of any of your opponents. But if one or more of the contestants, crew or spectators is accidentally killed, that's OK…am I wrong? There are, interestingly enough, legal procedures attempting to prove criminal charges against the track owners and technical people. For example: Ayrton Senna's fatal accident in Italy, (I believe) five years ago.

So the driver rapport with fans is headed for the "shitter." Actually, this can't be helped. A human can only do so much. (Maybe we need race driver doubles like in the movies, or Elvis). I believe if Jeff Gordon had 10 doubles at a track that would cover the autographing.

In the forties and fifties, only two kinds of racers made sports page one. For the Indy 500 winner the media did a job the world wide. There was only one other way, "you have to be killed to be written about,"…"Yhtbktbwa" was the abbreviation.

In 1950 sports writers ignored auto racing. Not enough fan following to be worth their time. In 1955 Ed Cole, boss of Chevrolet knew this, and felt we had to fix that or start to fix it. He told me to give away (that's right, give away, not loan) 200 new Chevrolets to sports writers nationwide. He said average cost was $1,500.00 bucks per car and the liability if they were loaned was too high — it was cheaper to give them away. I got my ass chewed out every week for not giving them away fast enough. Newspapers and fan rag correspondents were first in line, radio reporters were next, then TV people. (Note: TV was low man on the media totem pole in 1955.)

With no grease to reporters, it was "car 92, Herb Thomas, driver." With a 100 dollar bill grease job, it was "a 1955 'Motoramic' Chevrolet car #92 with Herb Thomas driving." The early newspaper and radio reporters didn't know a damn thing about auto racing, and didn't want to know. I had an idea that being sent to a race track to report was then a form of punishment for a reporter who fucked up. I can remember George Moore was a reporter for an Atlanta paper. He interviewed me and printed that we, "removed and threw away shocks as part of preparation for racing." At the time George was totally ignorant technically. (He eventually became very good at race reporting.)

In 1964, he interviews me at Atlanta. I'm really way too busy, and he's too goddamned dumb to notice it. He asks about a car I built to run Indy, that originally was to have a turbine engine in it. He kept calling it a rocket engine. No matter how much I tried to get him to understand there was a huge difference, he would not listen. So he says, "Why did you change your mind and put a regular engine in instead of the rocket?" (The real reason was that I thought I was getting engine free to use, but they wanted $36,000 in advance for a rebuild cost when I finished and at the time I couldn't have handled $3,600, but I did have a good Offenhauser.)

Anyway, I'm really up to my ears with him by then, so I said, "You know how they make the rocket fuel here close by Atlanta?" (And they did, I don't remember the town) He said, "Yes, he knew." I said, "We found out all rocket fuel was made in square shapes and there were no small enough fuel lines manufactured in square shapes, so for lack of fuel lines, we switched to alcohol and an Otto cycle engine." He printed it. George finally earned his master's in race reporting ten years later.

Three of the very best reporters that really helped NASCAR and the racers were Max Muhleman, Bennie Kahn and Don O'Reilly. Max Muhleman was with the Charlotte paper and Max loved Fireball. Then the Daytona Journal had a little guy named Bennie Kahn, and there was Don O'Reilly. Don and his wife started a magazine called Speed Age, the first good real race fan magazine. All three of these reporters loved racing, and got fairly technically oriented so they knew to ask good questions. Those three invented Fireball and Smokey. We could blow up 100 miles short, but if you read their stories, we were the whole damn race.

Chris Economacki is the "dean of racing," his reporting rag the National Speed Sports News, is the bible of racing. In the beginning Chris was open wheel happy and not much help, but since 'bout 1960, I believe Chris became a NASCAR fan. Chris never innovated anything, he just reported the race results and gave the news of the killing or crippling wrecks, in four inch headlines. The real inventor of the racing rag was Walter Bull.

Atlanta had a very famous sports writer who I guess was as good as it gets in stick and ball. But he wouldn't make a pimple on a race reporter's ass He wrote, but he was no fan: Furman Bisher, say hello. Sports Illustrated sent a guy named Ken Rudine in and he became a fan, and half-assed knew what he was writing about, but I doubt anyone else did. There were others. I can't recall them all (But a couple are Al Thomy and Herman Hickman) Gene Granger from Spartanburg really was up to speed. The first 15 years of NASCAR would be totally lost without Gene's foresight.

Two photographers really did a hell of a job to help us get flying, T. Taylor Warren and Don Hunter. I can't remember the other five or six including NASCAR's Houston Lawling. These men worked 80 hours

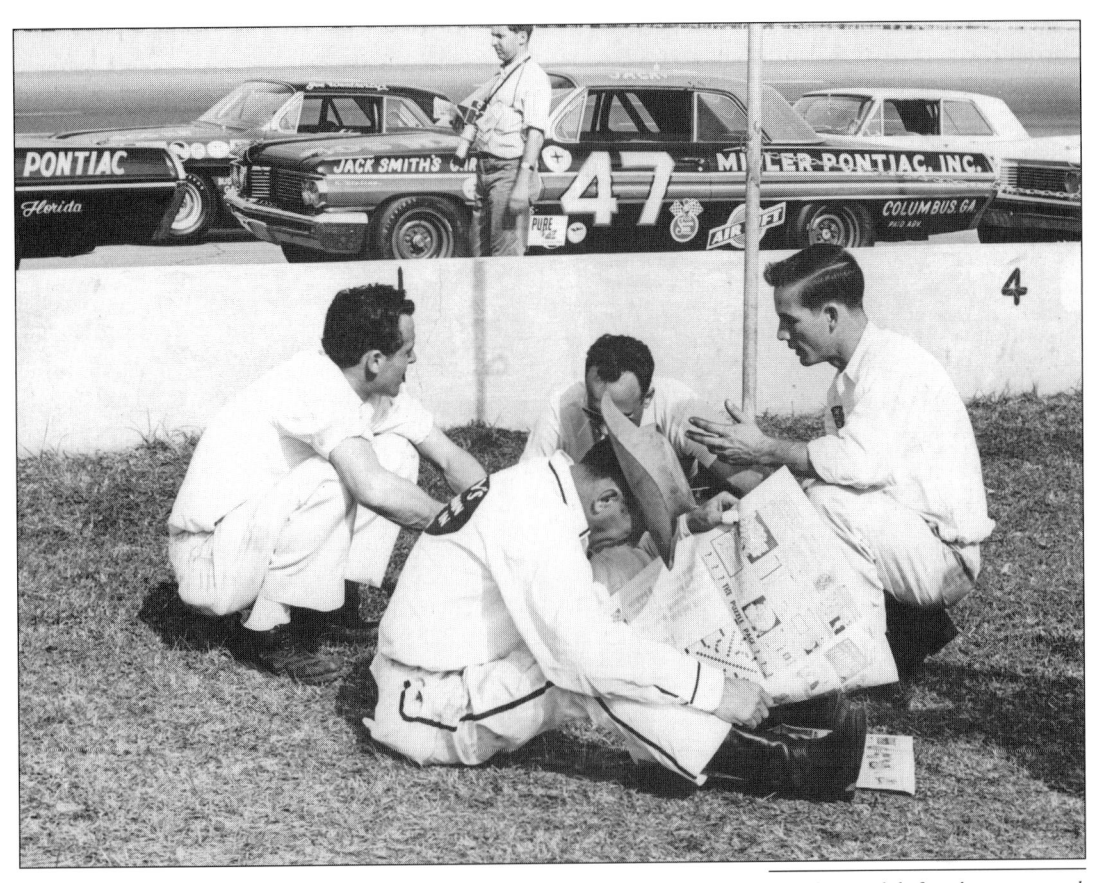

Hard at work before the race started.

a week for less money than a "mon backer" and sold stock car racing to America. Bob Meyers took over the Charlotte paper's race coverage when Max went Hollywood and went off to be Dan Gurney's PR man. (Believe it or not, Max was one hell of a racer before he hit the "big time." Hopefully, he will get back to earth before he slips into outer space.) (Another thing Max, you're too damn fat now. Your high-buck lifestyle is gonna kill you.) Bob Myers knows his stuff, but it took him a long time to catch up (I think he was overworked with too many sports). I read a story he wrote about the first Atlanta race for the November '97 Atlanta race program. If I didn't know better I'd of thought he went back to drinking, "Bobbie, you're getting lazy in your old age."

Reporters should be neutral, but they weren't and aren't. They had their favorites. I'm missing some of the very good reporters who helped the sport, but you're not, by human nature, too apt to remember some asshole who kept putting you down every couple months in his paper. You know, very seldom does a reporter know the whole story. Many times reporters get "snowed" by some person with a vested interest. I really got better than a fair deal while some got the shitty end of the stick.

One time a reporter tore my ass up. I half-assed deserved it, the guy's still around, and writing. He lives in Charlotte and worked on a paper there. (He's now retired and a free lancer). I was working for Knudsen then at Chevrolet. I told Knudsen about what a bad deal I got, and, "I was gonna get even." Bunkie said, "Smokey, my dad told me," and his dad was president of General Motors at one time, "Never get in a pissing contest with a skunk." Also, a thought worth considering: don't get in a popularity contest with someone who buys ink by the barrel. I thought about it, and have lived by it ever since comfortably.

I also got another opinion from a racer the reporter run down He just shrugged it off with a simple comment, "Whatever's fair." I figure if you fought the battle, what ever it was, in this country, you have a license to praise or criticize. But at the same time, so does everybody else, assuming that they too were involved in the battle.

But you know race magazines and some newspapers are still doing the same damn dumb shit they did 20 years ago. I wrote for a magazine called Circle Track for eleven years beginning in 1984. They did then, and still do now, give you race reports that are three months old, do a lot of ass-kissing to get advertisements, and many times print candied up bullshit to keep from unfavorable treatment tomorrow from the race sanctioning bodies and their customers. News is news. As I see it, if you have to step on Bill France Jr's balls, and it's the truth, do it. Hell, he'll live through it, and it will help him build a better character.

When Billy came back from the Army he did something that ticked me off. I was complaining about it to his dad. I said, "It will take him five years in the 5th grade to get an idiot's license." Big Bill said, "I think he can do it in four." Now 40 years later, I'd guess the France family holdings at probably several billion bucks. When Billy goes over the rule books, all Detroit is holding their breath and he's got Japan's hi-rollers kissing his ass for a part of the action. (Not bad for a jack-off who I didn't think could pour piss out of a boot.) 'Course, I'm the smart-ass know-it-all still working in a junky dump of a garage. The "dumb shit" has got three or four jets, five or six ocean going boats, and enough money to buy Cuba. I've learned that my opinions and assessments of people and events are subject to quite a bit of error as the years pass by. I've also learned not to take myself too seriously. You know, the only thing that matters is, when you shave in the morning and you see yourself, what you think of yourself. If you feel good about yourself, and can take a deep breath, stand them aching bones up a little straighter, and walk off, you're a lucky man. That is, if at the same time you ain't hungry, and your shoes ain't got holes in 'em and the roof don't leak where you sleep. Newsflash: Billy gets pulled over by the big "C" the year of 2000. It is pretty serious but I've read he is gonna pull through. This is a good example of sun don't shine on the same dog's ass all the time.

One giant difference in racing is the amount of money available. I knew a crew chief of a winning Indy car in the '50s who got $150 a week. I know a crew chief in Winston Cup that gets a million a year (1998). Drivers back then got at best 50 percent of purse and no other moneys. Most race track help was free, or permanent "go-fers" that got 50 to 70 bucks a week, or 20 bucks a week, food and permission to sleep in the garage.

I can remember Jim McGee, chief on Patrick's Cart team. (Scott Pruett driver.) His first year as a race mechanic for Dean Van Lines. He was at Indy, working for one of the best, Clint Brawner. Jim had to sleep in his car in the racer's parking lot. But hell, I can remember being "chief" and owner, and sleeping in the car many-many times. From what I can see now, the "grunts" do the work. Looks like now there's so many young people wanting to be career racers, they are now willing to work 70 hours a week for minimum wages.

Here's a big difference: education. Yesterday with desire, hard work, and "cut-and-try," you could make it because the technology was so crude and inaccurate. Also, the learning process was slow So you could grow with the science. Today in competition for big time racing jobs, your knowledge of physics, petro-chemistry, aerodynamics, mathematics and computers, dictates your chances of success.

One of the considerations in high-performance vehicle manufacturing and maintenance is, if you make a mistake in a critical area, you can kill someone just as surely as if you stuck a loaded pistol in the driver's ear and pulled the trigger. Of course many jobs carry that sort of responsibility. Even in the wildest of the wild days, the code of the hills was "zero tolerance" on poor workmanship. There's a hell of a difference between not knowing what you're doing and shitty workmanship. Actually the difference is ignorance, or murder.

But there is a third equation that is called "a mistake." Sometimes you have to call a shot in a split second when your options are limited. (Usually two – kinda like "go right or left") Naturally, sometimes you zig when you should have zagged. Some of these calls were so critical that someone paid the ultimate price. Someone, years ago coined a phrase that covers all the negatives that are associated with racing, the simple statement, "That's racing." In the earlier days you'd think about that lot while you were carrying part of the casket of your buddy who zigged when he should have zagged. I should add, when you complete your explanation of what happened, as you say, "That's racing" it's required you hold up your hands and shrug your shoulders just right, then it is official. You do it just about like Bobby Labonte when he holds his hands up in the Pontiac commercial and says, "Wider is better."

Some parts of racing are the same today as from day one, the first race. It concerns the human part of it. What it takes to be a racer and how much the human body can stand have not changed. Racing may become more or less dangerous and life styles will vary, as will the cost and rewards of racing. But the amount of desire, and the natural physical qualities a human needs to be a winning racer, they are still, and always will be, the same.

Probably the greatest difference in racing was the effort per driver that it took to race. The sacrifices regarding health, fitness, finances, families, the low social status, and the near poverty so many racers lived in were all hard burdens to bear. Most of us had to keep a full time job, or run a small business to pay for the time we raced. Sure, there were exceptions, but very few. Raymond Parks, one of the building blocks of NASCARs foundation, paid Red Vogt, the father of all stock car mechanics, to build and maintain cars for Red Byron, Tim Flock and Fonty Flock, and some others. I don't know what Raymond really did for a living, but I do remember some law enforcement people were quite curious about it. Finally, a couple years ago, Raymond got put in the Darlington International Hall of Fame ('bout 20 years too late).

This was an unusual deal back then (1950s). Actually, the car dealers were our sugar daddies. We'd get from 75 to 200 bucks to let a sign painter put the dealer's name on the car. Many times he gave us a new car to build into a race car and many times he gave us sheet metal and parts. Remember, in the beginning, everything was actually "stock." There were no "after market" parts manufacturers for strictly stock Grand National racers. Even if there were, it would have been illegal to run them. Back in the 40s, 50s and 60s, the car dealer was the best known businessman in all small cities and towns. He was a flashy, well dressed, hard drinkin,' pussy chasing, wild party lovin' cat – and as a rule a straight faced lying son-of-a-bitch. No, of course, not all of them were just this way, but by a large percentage they fit this mold. This cat was a fair golfer, he went to church quite a bit, belonged to the Lions, Raccoon, Kiwanis, Rotary and any other social place where he had contact with potential customers. He was a charter member of the country club, knew all the politicians (Hell, he owned part of 'em) and as a rule, was a pretty nice guy. But he liked racers and racing. We had what he wanted: the wildest parties, the best lookin,' wildest "old" women (19 to 25 years old), and we stood on the gas every night, all night long. Every night 'cept Saturday.

Back then, we actually stayed longer in town than they do now, and we run more races (40 to 50 a year). We usually came twice a year to each track. Most dealers liked to go fast. Some drove race cars, and some were pretty damn good at it, but 'bout best you could expect from him was 'bout $500 a race.

OK, tow from Daytona to Lincoln, Nebraska for $500 if you win. But you wreck and get 25 bucks at pay-off. We are about 2,800 miles from home: myself and a helper, the driver and his wife. Man that was rough sledding on 25 bucks. Why did we go? Points! The fucking points! The point system was not designed to enrich a racer's life. Actually, it was an additive designed to first punish and lastly, to reward racers (make every race "or else"). Our natural instincts said, "Only go to close – good paying races." "The Mustache" (one of the France's stooges, Bob Latford), dreamt up the current point system in a bar, on a napkin 40 years ago. Amazingly, he must have done a superb job. It's been criticized and maligned the whole 40 years and yet it still stands. (He is still some kind official working for NASCAR, I think he runs the media facilities some places.) You want to be champion, then you better run every race. Thus, the point system is an invincible ring in the nose of every serious challenger for the championship.

For those of you who are not old enough to remember the "Uncle Tom" customs of the old south, watch and listen to top ten award winners at victory dinner. Watch and listen to the "yas sir boss – yas sir mista France – thank you, thank you suh." Is a point system bad? I don't think, so but it should be applied in a more democratic form where all competitors can vote and agree on format. Yesterday we towed the race cars with another car. Sometimes a heavily financed older car, or a late model "loaner" from a dealer. (No trucks, trucks were too slow and had no place to sleep) Believe this or not, I did it, and so did 90 percent of the rest.

We worked on race cars at night, from 'bout 6:00 pm till 2:00 am every night, and worked eight to 10 hours in our garages, or for someone else during the day. Most of us made our living at some part of the car business, garage work, parts houses, junk yards, used car lots, body shops, wrecker services, and dealerships were the favorite occupations of yesterday's racers. Oh, I left out one of the biggest category, gas station owners.

One sentence says it best: birds of a feather flock together. We needed to invent a new ethnic group and did with the category "racer." In this kind of grouping there is always a clear leader. He sets the pace and has the courage and brains to innovate. The sheep follow. From there on money takes over. Penske is a good example of this. It becomes simple; hire the best, pay the highest wages and the rest is automatic.

All our sponsor money was from automobile oriented businesses. If we could get 15 to 20 thousand a year total sponsorship money, a car and parts, a tow car, and some tires, we had the best deal in racing. For say 45 races, coast to coast, we had one car. The chief mechanic was engine builder, car builder, chassis man and drive train man, body man, and car painter. Some could also sign paint. The chief mechanic was also the main tow man, rounded up sponsors, and once in awhile drove the goddam thing in the race. The chief mechanic usually had one unpaid idiot helper. "Idiot" because he worked so goddam hard for nothing, but he loved racing.

We usually got to the track (nine times out of 10 it was an all night tow job) at 7:00 or 8:00 in the morning, (Saturday morning for little tracks, Wednesdays at big tracks), only to go through an aggravating four to five hour inspection process. We'd then eat a cold hot dog and drink two day old cold coffee for lunch as we worked. We'd get to practice a couple hours late in the afternoon and have to leave the garage area by 5:00 or 6:00 pm. Many times I pulled the engine and took it to the motel or a gas station or some nearby dealership, to put in bearings and do a valve job till two or three in the morning. It wasn't anything special to go two days and two nights without going to bed. We learned how to sleep in car 30 minutes and go at it again.

If we drank too much whiskey it backfired – you couldn't stay awake. If you drank too much coffee you'd get the "heebie-jeebies" and shake like a dog shittin' razor blades and do goofy stuff. There also were pills. "California turnarounds," "No-Doz," and all the truck driver's specials. These didn't help me keep awake. The only thing worked for me was coffee, and I had to recognize that point where I felt funny, where the next cup would start the shakes.

'Bout 30 minutes of sleep always worked for four or five hours. I can remember some of the long tows. It was Daytona to Langhorne, or maybe to Indy, or Daytona to Riverside – 56 hours non-stop. I'd been without sleep 40 hours or so once I got the trailer loaded and then have a 24 hour tow. I'd have a female to keep me awake by trying every sexy game known to women, while my helper slept in the back seat. I still fell asleep, but a stop for a 30 minute nap and I would be OK for a while. It's a miracle half of us didn't get killed towing half asleep.

Well, I'm ahead of myself here. Up until Kiekhaefer in 1953, who had a tractor and trailers (4 of 'em if I remember), we all towed our race cars with a car. We also carried spare parts, tires, wheels and tools in the race car and tow car. We didn't take (or usually even have) a spare engine. We maybe had a set of cylinder heads ready to go on, with us and a spare crank, a couple of rods, a few pistons, and lots of little stuff. We might also bring a spare transmission, clutch and one or two gear changes for rear axle for ratio. By gear changes, I mean a ring and pinion, not a spare third member to swap out. We had no spare sheet metal, so if we wrecked in practice, or qualifying we had to fix it. I never-ever missed a race. Somehow, we'd fix it if there was time.

I didn't get a truck to haul parts till 1955, and that was a wore-out, shit-box 12 foot van – Chevrolet one ton – and I was running the Chevrolet factory effort. They had 200 cars to give away to reporters and zero trucks for racers (no budget). Our biggest problem was how to haul wheels and tires, spare parts, tools, fuel equipment (55 gallon drum and funnel), a couple floor jacks, hand lug wrenches (no air or electric wrenches yet, and when they were available, we wasn't allowed to use them for awhile.) The tow car was filled inside so your free helper/relief driver ended up sleeping on a creeper, with his head in the headliner.

How 'bout this? Many times we travelled with a "go-pher" sitting in driver's seat of race car asleep, being towed on a windy-rainy night at 80 miles an hour. For the go-pher, there was no pay, just food, and maybe a place to sleep (and they say drivers are the only heroes). The first tow-bars we made were crude, but got it done. The car dealers flat towed so many passenger cars, people started making tow-bars to sell. The "Red-Devil" came first. It wasn't much, but I never had a problem with it 'cept for "seat-gap." Man, those early tow-bar jobs were probably the cause of many ulcers and colon problems.

You could not tow slow at 55 miles an hour. When you did, your arms were so busy you looked like a monkey trying to fuck a football. At 70 you quit sweating. At 80 you could slide down, lean back in the seat, and drive with one hand and pick your nose with the other. Colon problems? Yes, cause when you sit there for 10 or 12 hours with your ass so puckered up that there's a name for it ("scared shitless"), there are repercussions. I want to tell you rite here and now, we wore seat belts. I would not run without them. Actually, we could install a seat belt in 15 to 20 minutes.

Next came the "yellow-bar," with steering cables and brakes. They were flimsy, and half-assed, but if you knew how to adjust them, worked pretty good. There was however, a major problem. If in the race you bent up front bumper on race car there was no way to hook the bar on to go home. So, sometimes we had hell to pay before we could get tow bar on.

Stop and think about it, the race car had built in "turn left" in it, so when you needed it to go straight or right, it didn't want to do it. The combined weight of race car and tow car and 'bout 3,000 pounds tools, part and equipment meant the whole deal probably weighed 11,000 pounds. It was a handful to control, accelerate and decelerate. Also, on a hot day, which we didn't do much of, the tow-car would run pressure cap off it's seat and blow all the water out of the engine and radiator.

You know, 40 or 50 of these a year or so and, man we must have really been having fun to do this, and keep on doing it for eight or 10 years. We had other problems. Stock cars got some people's attention, but an Indy car in fifties and early sixties, they caught everybody's eye. A friend of mine named Bill Cheesboro was towing an Indy car on a two-axle trailer with a Ford pickup, when a car load of colored males in a big-assed Buick straight eight, wanted to see the car. This is late on a dark night. Well, to see the race car, bright lights on the Buick were better, but these lights hit Bill's mirrors and really blinded him. So after being followed for 10 minutes, at a stop sign Bill opened driver's door and hollered back to the Buick's six occupants, admirers of Bill's racer to, "Get off the brights and back off." Well that don't do a thing 'cept get the phrase "motherfucker" used quite a bit. Bill gets back in, and goes 'bout five more minutes with the same problem. A red light stops Bill's progress. At the last light on way out of town Bill stops, jumps out with a hammer in his hand and taps both headlights. Now it's all dark in front of the Buick as Bill leaves – problem solved.

But it worked both ways. The first Indy race for me as mechanic and owner of car was 1958. I left Daytona kinda short on money. The trailer I was using, had new looking tires, but they were dry rotted. I had to buy a tire in Chattanooga. 'Bout 200 miles out of Indy I'm out of gas, and out of money. I explained my financial embarrassment to a gas station owner while offering a drill or some kind of collateral for the gas. He is really enjoying looking race car over, particularly the engine. It had an Offenhauser. Those engines were beautiful examples of rugged, powerful simplicity. He don't even look up and says, "Forget it, I always wanted to see one of these" And he says, "If you need gas on the way back home, come back." I said, "Same price?" He laughed and said, "Yup." Got him so charged up he came to the race.

I did stop there on way home. We wrecked on 1st lap while leading it, but so did 20 or 21 others. It was bum start. Dick Rathman and Ed Elisian got together and all hell broke loose. This was a pretty bad deal as Pat O'Connor got killed in the wreck.

Next, France started making alliances with Wynn's Friction Proof, Bardal. These, and other various "snake oil" companies, apparently contributed to the cause via Bill France. They paid some prize money, and "mechanic of the year" type stuff. I won the Wynn's deal once. They gave me a diamond pin. Well, it was nice, but you needed a magnifying glass to find diamond. Best pawn offer I got was a ten spot. I got more for the Champion red jacket.

These companies offered oil and fuel additives. They weren't worth a shit, but "don't confuse people with the facts." Anyhow, I decided to make my own additives for fuel, but not to apply for certification and approval under the rules. The rules said, "If you advertised it, you had to be NASCAR approved." (To get said approval you had to pay-off.) Well, I didn't want to advertise, the last thing I wanted was for NASCAR to know about it. Finally, anything I did that made car go faster ended up getting disqualified with a catch phrase France invented, "not within the spirit of the rules." He could do every dirty rotten deal you could think of (kinda like Clinton) then laugh at you and suspend your ass for "what ever was fair" as he saw it.

So, in the first 20 years, Big Bill had control and was loved by Detroit brass and the parasites (the people who contributed nothing, but found a way to make a living out of racing). But the racer wouldn't have pissed up his ass if his guts were on fire (Big Bad Bill). In that 20 years he suspended enough of us for violating his holy doctrines. Those who felt they had to race, shut up and took it, but a smoldering resentment was just under what you saw. Again, maybe that was really the secret of NASCAR's success.

The buzz words are, "NASCAR was run as a dictatorship"…and that's why it worked, maybe. How you gonna prove otherwise? I've been around quite a bit of this world and many of life's problems. My experiences lead me to conclude that we were an ignorant bunch of lower class society all right. 'Cause the only place a dictatorship works is when the subjects are uneducated, and if they have a wise and fair dictator, he manages their lives for them. France never had our respect and cooperation. If you questioned a stupid call by the chief inspector, and asked why, the standard answer of one of the ignorant assholes France had for chief inspector (Norris Friel being one of 'em) was, "Because I said so."

In the early sixties a major problem we had was "heads-up-their-asses engineers" in Detroit put a flimsy 20 to 25 gallon steel gas tank within an inch of rear bumper, and dropped down below the car 'bout six inches, totally unprotected. Soon as you got tapped in the ass there would be a tank fire. Well, they were great in the films, but very hard on drivers. So in '63 I built a chrome alloy guard to prevent that happening. Friel made me take it off. I asked, "Why?" You want to guess the answer? In '64 guess what wiped poor ol' Fireball's ass out? If this offends any of you old inspectors from my day, I don't give a damn. Racing continued in spite of your obstructions.

How does NASCAR inspection today compare with yesterday? I really can't answer that. I think if you are gonna judge something, anything, you really have to have all the facts. I'm not qualified to judge today. But I have noticed all competitors seem to be much more subdued today regarding making any political comments. NASCAR was like phone or electric company in Daytona then (only got one of each). Point is, if you don't like it, what are you gonna do about it? (This was then.)

But I always go by track record, and with the way NASCAR's growing, how in the hell can anyone stand back and say they don't know, or they are doing a lousy job? They can't build seats fast enough for the fans. Looks like the tracks are getting (I think) too greedy. I can't believe what I'm seeing. I see people giving up alcohol and drugs to have enough money to go to a race.

Yesterday we had a nasty li'l problem. A lot of drug money slipped into NASCAR. I think that's been handled.

With all the hell raising and social violations, I only seen two of what I consider "no question" drug users, and both were soon gone. I consider that real important in reference to the quality of the contestants as compared to the other hi-buck sports figures. For the multi-billion dollar industry racing has become, it's amazing how it continues to prosper, with really no guidance.

I'm talking about it nationwide, and to a degree internationally. It's a group of separate kingdoms. However, that is about to change. Little kingdoms want to be bigger kingdoms and the big fish are gonna eat all the little fish. The main ingredient is the "greenies." Winston Cup type racing is so lucrative, and the promoter's profits so obscene, that in nature's normal pattern of behavior, a war will start very soon.

There is a big need for a "NASCAR Two" type deal, so that racing can be available to all who want to enjoy watching the stock car races. NASCAR, I think, would have a more than full plate with 35 races. In November 1994, I wrote a story for Circle Track about splittin NASCAR into two leagues. I noticed in the February 2000 Sports Illustrated some of NASCAR's money men share my opinion. But mainly "bigger" will create some monstrous control problems. Yeah, the word monopoly would appear in six-inch letters.

But that ain't enough, there is demand and enough interest for about 35 to 40 locations nationally racing, say, twice a year. Getting 55 new race teams for a "NASCAR Two" is no problem, nor is getting new tracks built at strategic locations. Hell, in five years there will be 35 tracks. That's 70 races a year, right?

The real problem is where the hell you gonna get 100 more sponsors for eight million a year or more? Did you say drivers? There are 100 or more drivers today that, in two years, could have you as a spectator pissing in your pants. For example, Tony Stewart. Three years ago had you ever heard of him? Racing is not all skill and balls. It's entertainment furnished by men with a very special sense of balance and varying degrees of desire. Interestingly, I believe the top ten drivers will go just as hard the last lap if it's for $1,000 or a million. Racing didn't do enough for sponsors, or race fans at day one. And now, 50 years later, racing is still screwing the fans and sponsors. You can only do that so long and then the ball game's over.

Ain't no sponsor gonna plunk down 25 million to sponsor a race car that don't get least 30 million back. You say "nobody in Winston gets 25 million." I agree, but let's look at it like it is. For every dollar a sponsor spends on car and driver, he spends two more dollars promoting the deal cause if they don't, their whole investment is junk. Guess how much it costs (in year 2000) to be a prime sponsor of a competitive car? Eight and a half to nine million to the car and fifteen to twenty million to exploit the investment. 25 million ain't exactly petty cash for any company. They really have a way of knowing what they are getting back.

For the Charlotte October 1999 race there were 11,000 people in hospitality tents at ($25 bucks apiece). It's 'bout like what the monkey said when he pissed in the cash register, "This is gonna run into money." How 'bout if a heavy sponsored team misses qualifying and 500 customers are brought in for the race? Is there a major flaw in here? I think racing needs to wean themselves away from car manufacturers and the plan they have now, and sell sponsorship of car name for "so much a season." Then switch to a common body for all cars with grill and engines being the only distinctive feature. The body'd be three or four piece fiberglass, with paint in the gel coat, then quit the wind tunnel shit and control speed by engine displacement.

For example, McDonalds says, "We are quitting racing." Do you think, as sharp as their management is, if they got good value for their racing dollars, they would quit the program? Because in reality, McDonalds has got more hamburgers than hamburger-eaters today. They changed their minds and stayed 1998, 99 and 2000, but why would they quit something that sold hamburgers at a profit? So instead of car "#94, Bill

When I got ged up with Bill and NASCAR, I'd start aiming for Indy.

Elliott,"…get rid of the number. It's the "McDonalds," or "McDonalds Ford," or "Bill Elliott McDonalds Ford." I think sponsorship should also be planned whereby sponsor can plan a marketing theme for specific races. Simply stated, "Mr. Sponsor, what would you like for your 15 million? How can we help you to feel good about the money your spending?"

There is another puzzle, if racing is so good why is Goodyear saying adios? Why is Goodyear's stock in the shit-house? You know something? I bet if Goodyear charged a fair price for every tire used in Winston Cup, including amortization of development cost, the price of the tires alone would exceed the total prize money paid by all the Winston Cup tracks for the 30 something races The same would apply to all other racing as well. (This does not include vendor's prize money – an example.) That's assuming competitor runs every race.

The manufacturers too, invest a fortune, yet many times gets treated like a dog. If just Ford and General Motors go home tomorrow, the wonderful world of NASCAR would be in deep shit ('bout six feet of it). I've been there – I saw 'em go home in June, 1957. Man the next 10 years were like pissing into a 50 mile an hour wind.

When I worked for Champion Spark Plug in 1990-95, including all racing cost, every racing spark plug we built cost over 40 bucks apiece and we gave them away. Each engine used 'bout 40 plugs average…five plugs changes per engine and…five engines a race. The point is, sponsors and manufacturers need justification for request for funding. Stock car racing never operated this way. How 'bout the NASCAR fees, and the rest of the cost? It's always been the old southern saying, "Load the wagon, the mule's blind."

The greatest race promoter there has ever been in the United States is Humpy Wheeler. He should collectively be paid 'bout five million a year by all race sanctioning groups, to be the "high commissioner of racing." As high commissioner, he should organize racing to identify and offer value to the sponsor-manufacturer and give the fan, who pays racing's mortgages, more comfortable and convenient accommodations. Why in the hell do you sit his ass down on an uncovered metal or concrete seat, 95 degrees in the sun or in the cold rain ? The goddam seat cost 160 to 175 bucks. You get your money back the first year at $95 a race and now you're talking, "Gotta buy the seat for two days for $180 bucks." Get it all back in one race. That's bullshit! Spend another ten bucks a seat, and put a roof on it.

They should also give away earplugs and require everybody to use them. And for Christ's sake quit fooling around and put sound suppression on all race cars. I loved the noise as much as anybody, but the noise is a very serious offense to all human ears, particularly to infants. I look down in the front row (cheapest seats) and see momma, pappa and two kids, both under three years old, and I know, that at the start of race, when cars are all bunched up, it's gonna be 135 decibels when they go by. Promoters, track owners, you don't realize how medically bad that is, or you would have stopped it years ago. Bruton Smith talks about putting a roof over Bristol (a one-half mile track) with, at the time you read this 150,000 seats. If you do Bruton, the hearing aid companies collectively should pay you a couple million a year. But with noise suppression on race cars, you could maybe have some hi-tech roofs.

We began with all clay (mud), called "dirt tracks." Now, that's exciting, dirty, nasty racing (maybe the best), but it makes a tough job tougher. Then asphalt started, that's better really, but concrete is best. Oh yes, all the race experts and bull-shitters pile on me and say I'm nuts. But the best racing surface in NASCAR is Dover, Delaware. If Mel Josephs refinished the track a little smoother (regarding roughness of finish and surface), and took out the highs and lows with a laser machine, tire wear would be best in NASCAR. A concrete track runs cooler, and track temperature will not change enough due to cloud movement or minor temperature changes to effect car handling in a major way. Concrete tracks can be cleaned, as airport runways are today, so spillage of oil, grease, anti-freeze, etc., can be totally controlled. Oil-dry wouldn't be needed, a blast of water at high pressure will remove spillage instantly.

No asphalt can stand a 3,500 pound racer at 150 miles an hour, pulling one-and-a-quarter to three Gs, for four hours on a 90 degree day with the sun out. Asphalt gets to about 140 degrees, but what's worse is damage to asphalt that comes from ultraviolet rays of the sun. This is a negative on track and tires as well. In short, it reduces lateral traction where tires and asphalt react to the ultra violet. Black is a heat conductor and storage medium. White, like silver, reflects radiant energy. Concrete makes a better thermal deflector than an absorber. All early asphalt tracks, big tracks especially, broke up first time we got on 'em. Darlington, Charlotte, Daytona, Atlanta. Also, most half miles would break up in 500 laps or less. Martinsville and Bristol never did. Martinsville is concrete turns, and Bristol concrete all the way.

Well, at Darlington they invented a fix. By second year no asphalt could stand the load. The better the tires and chassis got, the higher the lateral tearing and kneading forces were. So Bob Colvin and the rest of brains at Darlington came up with a good "farmer type thinking" answer. "Pour some slick shit on track surface and reduce lateral traction." The first time I saw it was race morning 1953 (They put in on at night). It looked shiny. The track looked like patent leather (like a Marine's shoe). We called it "bear grease" in public, but the slickest substance known to a farm boy was owl shit. (Never-never step in owl shit. Why is it so slippery? Hell, I don't know. Turn on your computer and poke in "www.SmithsonianInstitute.com" and enter "owl shit." If they don't know, who would?) So in the inner-racing communication, the track was pronounced "slicker than owl shit." I could write a book about how many race cars were destroyed and how many drivers did how much sheet-time, because of the invention of "bear grease." It is still being used today, but some track experts have been able to use it effectively without totally destroying the car's handling traits.

My vote for the world's expert track builder and paver is Clarence Cagle. He was maintenance supervisor at Indy Speedway for 30 years or more. This cat knows asphalt. I'd say he has had input in 85 percent of all big time asphalt tracks in United States. I think his footprints could have been found on circle race tracks in Europe, Australia, Japan, and maybe South America. But Clarance is a stubborn old fart, and refuses to consider concrete. He is a neighbor of mine now, 'bout five miles up the road. He is what we called a "snowbird," but I think he has been here long enough now to have a "Southerner's license."

One time I was planning on building sixteen one and one-half mile tracks all off of the same blueprints. I hired Clarence and A.J. Foyt as consultants. Well, not really, I wanted Clarence bad, but knew A.J. was so goddam opinionated and with zero foresight, I didn't want him closer than one mile. But the "money man" figured A.J. would be a flashy "big name" (and he was) and this would get some public support. Well, my plan was "all tracks concrete paved." Clarence and A.J. in unison said, "Bullshit!" They said, "Concrete would buckle from cold, crack, get rough, and eat tires up…no way." Well, the track deal blew up, but I would have quit rather than back off of concrete track surface. You need covered grand stands, lights, concrete track, and tires that can run in the rain. That way you will cut rain-outs to about zero. Concrete tracks give much better traction in wet conditions.

Clarence and A.J. weren't alone in their very negative position on concrete tracks. I called Leo Mehl (boss man at Goodyear Racing) and told him I needed a tire for a concrete track. He said I was out of my fucking mind. I told him we were gonna use spec tires from one tire company for a year, at a bid price for the racing tire. "One tire for all sixteen tracks for one year, and we take a bid for one year spec tire exclusive."

He liked that part. 'Bout a year later Dover Delaware announces a concrete track. They collectively have tried all known to man to pave it with asphalt, and have a tire that can handle the loads. Goodyear has exhausted their technology and given up.

My curiosity went to work. I knew Melvin Josephs (one of Dover's owners) was as good an asphalt paver as there was maybe in the world. I figured him to have enough balls to be a "lone ranger." So, if asphalt couldn't do it, what's left? Dirt? Well, not today, not at a super track. One reason — too dirty. Boards? Not hardly. So it had to be concrete. I knew Goodyear gave up on an asphalt Dover unless the track's configuration was changed, so when I heard "Dover concrete," I figured it to be a joint venture between Goodyear and Dover. Leo, how close did I get? Melvin?

Day one, the garage and pit area were unbelievable. They were unpaved, with no guard wall, one shit house, and no pit assignments. You just found a spot in the mud, unloaded and got to work. Well can you imagine jacking up a two-ton car in the mud? Most places didn't even have electricity in pits for each car. At the first race in Darlington, the starter's stand is on left side of track 'bout 25 feet up a tower. The lower eight of this tower is "one-holer" and sink. The urinal was outside. Next to the shit-house door is the one pay phone at the track. On race day you got 100 people in line, including racers, standing there cross-legged, or holding their ass. The odor in that area was so bad that all phone conversations were, as a rule, 30 seconds or less. But it did one good thing. Back in them days, they had small black gnat by the millions 'round Darlington. (I guess maybe it was agriculturally oriented.) If you opened your mouth to talk, you just swallowed 30 of 'em. Well, believe it or not, the toilet area was gnat free.

Mauri Rose, a friend of mine, gave me a picture of a very famous Italian racer (I believe "Nuvolari") at a race in Italy. In this picture he is holding his peter, taking a piss in the open, with one hand around his peter, and holding a cigarette in other while talking to the Queen of Italy. So, I guess we were about average. Yup, apparently in the early 30s. they still had kings and queens. So, when the lines at toilet were a problem, I just walked over to the "monkey fence," took a piss, and signed autographs with the other hand. (No, I never got the deal to work when I asked lady to hold it while I used two hands to sign.) You do what you gotta do.

Lord Calvert
Takes Her Through the Turns

I'm not able to give a report on automobile racing from day one, but let's look at what I should be knowledgeable about.

Racing started 'bout 1920, soon after World War I. Yes, I know there were many races before that, but it was on an experimental basis. Races were usually organized as advertisements, or commemorative events. In the twenty years from 1920 to 1940, racing's message was "danger," and rightfully so. The human body is still the same as it was, say, 500 years ago. 40 Gs for .05 of a second in deceleration, or acceleration, was the maximum a human could, and can still stand. We humans, in the last 100 years, have come to live damn near twice as long as we used to, but all our parts are no more or no less capable of standing unusual punishment or abuse.

I started my adventures in auto racing 'bout 1938. I was 'bout 14 or 15 years old, and for some reason, I was attracted to speed, and go-fast machines of any kind. For some goofy reason, I liked those, "Oh shit!" moments that you experience when you realized you had overstepped your ability to be in command, moments just before the vehicle was out of control and then stopped, as a rule, much quicker than you wanted. The public always has, and I guess, always will, have some fascination with watching a human gamble with his (or her) life, and strangely, there have always been those who are more than willing to oblige.

The Roman gladiator had no choice. They threw his ass in a cage with a lion and it was a dead lion, or your ass was inside the lion. If you examine what little there is recorded about auto racing's early years, you'll be shocked to know what a large percentage of drivers that got killed, or incapacitated by the few races that we had annually.

Consider 1940. We had four kinds of racing. Cars (open wheel), boats, airplanes and motorcycles.

Probably in 1940, 2,000 people total were involved in all forms of racing in the United States. (And Chris Economaki was one of 'em…that's how old he is.) Today we probably have 300 forms of racing, and 150 sanctioning bodies…from motorized roller skates, to 6,000 horsepower draggers including racing cockroaches.

In 1940 an automobile or motorcycle racer had a social status even with a leper, or a "mon backer" on a garbage truck. (That's the guy hanging on end of truck saying "mon back.") Except, except an Indy 500 winner! Don't ask me why, but everybody in the word knew who won Indy that year. The Indy winner was instantly promoted from "social trash" to "royalty," with all it's privileges (except financially).

Racing was then the only business I know of where you paid (entry fee and license) for the right to work you ass off 90 hours a week for nothing. The promoters of the races were, as a rule, bullshitting con-men barely making it. The racing associations were run by pompous old farts, most with a racing history, but none ever won the Nobel prize for business.

But they were the foundation of what? Condoning a sport? Because if killing, crippling – bankrupting, teaching drinking and chasing pussy is a sport…then racing was a sport. No, I think Lucky Teeter had it right. He called his outfit, "Hell Drivers Thrill Show."

When I am asked to compare racing in 1940 to racing in 1990, people ask, "What's the difference, if any?" My answer is, "If I was a racer, today's people are not, and if today's people are racers, I never was." In 1940, racing was a series of thrill shows. We were never a sport. Back then racer equipment had the potential to kill if driver error or a mechanical goof-up occurred. And they still can, but by comparison, today's race vehicles are five times safer. The doubling of speed hasn't made it more dangerous. If you hit a concrete wall, steel reinforced, head-on at 160 miles an hour, there ain't no difference than the same deal at 80 miles an hour. The driver's a dead player either way. Only difference is there's about five hundredths of a second difference in when they were terminally injured.

There is a huge difference in the social status, and in the educational and business qualities today's racer has as compared to 1940. You won't believe this, but I can remember when 10 or 15 percent of racers could not read or write. Hell, I had a driver win several national championships, that couldn't read or write. I never realized what a handicap that was, but today I'm deaf, so I have a handicap that makes it difficult to compete with "normal" humans. I have an employee who's been here 40 years. He can't read or write. Can you imagine how difficult that is for he and I? Racing today has engineers educated to the peer level in their respective categories. (Hell, up to 1955, I spelled engineers "engine ears.")

When you compare drivers then, 1940, and drivers now, 2001 one thing is clear. No driver will make the "big time" who can't read and write. No driver with any sort of social stigma, morally or legally, can make it anymore. (It's OK to lie 'bout pussy.) Driver's today are much better educated. They adapt to the pattern of social behavior required of a celebrity. They are actors in movies, TV, and real life. As a result, as compared to yesterday, most racers in the current crop are actually a bunch of egotistical, uninteresting assholes.

Yesterday's driver was much more of a natural born expert on extracting the maximum performances out of a race car. Yesterday's driver had to prove himself in no more than 10 races.

One of the greatest all time racing heroes, Richard Petty, would have died by this rule. But his dad financed him, he kept learning, and finally Richard figured it out.

It turns out there's more than one way to skin a coon, and they did. Bill Vukovich, Curtis Turner, Fireball Roberts, Paul Goldsmith, A.J. Foyt, Bobby and Al Unser, Herb Thomas, Ayrton Senna, Fangio, Shumacher, Mark Donahue, Bobby Allison, Dale Earnhardt, Jeff Gordon…these are off the top of my mind, I've left out 25 others. My point is, these people went fast "rite now," in about any damn thing with wheels, including motorcycles.

There is one hell of a difference in drivers. For example: in Winston Cup 1997 there's only about 10 real "honest to God race drivers," in the 60 or 70 names registered. Cart has about four or five, IRL 'bout the same and Formula One 'bout four. Money 50 to 60 years ago couldn't buy the race as it can today. Back then all equipment was pretty equal with the real contenders, but the talent was the key. Of course luck is almost as important as skill and equipment.

Today you see equipment, personnel and money 'bout equal. One driver wins 10 out of 30 times and another driver crashes 10 out of 30. Guts and balls don't get it done. Most of yesterday's drivers had more than enough of both. But to run consistent and fast for every lap, that's the hard part. The winner simply wants to win so bad he'll do anything to get it done. Jeff Gordon's crew used a catch phrase, "refuse to lose." Every really good, successful driver, crew member, owner, office personnel, technicians are a team who communicate almost perfectly and consider second place a failure.

Example: I was with Herb Thomas, racing at Langhorne. He blew a tire with three laps to go while leading. He came roarin' in and said, "Change 'er quick, we'll win it yet." Remember this: Be a good loser? Show me a good loser, and I'll show you a loser!

It was not uncommon yesterday for a driver to run Indy only, and sometimes win. Today with the kind

Fireball, me and Jack Sullivan at the Firetone truck. (photo by Jerry B. Howard)

of prize money, and the kind of experience necessary, run Indy only and win the odds would be 'bout like winning a 40 million buck lottery.

It is possible for a driver to educate himself through driving schools, buying rides, being a sponsor (rich daddy) having an attractive personality, and learn; how to win some races. But I think that approach is running out of gas. I see us heading for a change. Where driver candidate goes to driving school for two to three years (at a college education cost, say $250,000) then fights for development driving job on a wealthy team. That's the Formula One scenario now. That approach makes the most sense. The candidate's grades are reflective of his talent. Today's machines are much too expensive to be entrusted to unqualified candidate drivers – even those with wealthy parents or backers.

I see a space and aviation-oriented test procedure that exists today capable of testing with a 95 percent success ratio, to qualify a potential driver, or to disqualify him or her, without running a single lap. But a change in next two or three years is coming. Driver is given a test that requires a middle ear that can recognize his attitude degree by degree, ref., to a 360 degree rotation in both the vertical and horizontal plane. In short: a sense of balance test. This equipment and technology is in Huntsville, Alabama and is controlled by the military (Naval doctor Angus Rupert in Pensacola).

I consider the routine of training a Winston Cup driver in the Busch stuff first bullshit. The qualified new driver would have (from his testing job), learned all the tracks by the time his opportunity came. And would be capable of going fast. All he would have left, would be learning how to race, right? Sure, that's no minor, easy feat, but two thirds of current Formula One drivers started this way and I'd say, are more successful than with any other plan.

Yesterday's driver was a social disaster. He drank too much and much of his time was consumed in personal problems, usually female oriented. He was financially 'embarrassed 'bout all the time, a poor parent 'cause he simply wasn't home hardly ever. Socially, the guy was an outcast. No insurance possible. No financing available to him. Hell, if you went to a hotel for a room and filled in the "occupation" blank with "racer," suddenly the hotel was out of rooms. (We hid our race cars so bellman couldn't see it).

Today's racer is a whole new ball game. Probably has the highest social rating going in all of the entertainment venues. Who would you like as a party guest or business representative, Jeff Gordon or "Shack-up-O'neil?" Yesterday's "ace" driver got 50 percent of prize money and nothing else. And as a rule, he had to do a little work on the car. Today's "ace" makes a million and up to five million plus a lot from collectibles and "fan frenzy junk." (Racer's take?...In the millions!)

Hell…a "Winston Cupper" without a jet is hurting, the driver with a turbo-prop, is looked down on. I can remember when the sign of success was when the car company of the make you raced, loaned you a new car to drive.

Today, if driver ain't got a one million buck motorhome he's a third-stringer. Even the chief mechanic has a five to seven hundred thousand buck dressing room, and 'night before the race' bed room inside the track. In the early days most driver's drove to about all the races. They couldn't afford to fly. Well, how 'bout towing from Daytona Beach to Lincoln, Nebraska for $500 to win?

After flying to the track, today's driver hides up in the air conditioned office part of his trailer or a one million buck motorhome. The day one driver was working on a car, with his uniform pulled half way down, or with a greasy white t-shirt on.

Yesterday's driver ran Indy and Darlington in street shoes, slacks and a tee shirt, with a pack of cigarettes rolled up in the shirtsleeve and an open face helmet (about as protective as strapping a turtle shell on your head). They very seldom wore gloves. Nine out of ten finishing drivers had bleeding hands, and some with bleeding asses (Yes asses!) and two out of 10 with burns on throttle foot from the heat. I've seen Jimmy Bryan climb out of an Indy car with his ass and clothes soaked in blood. Some would not wear helmets, or use safety belts, until it was mandated by the sanctioning body.

Today's drivers train as athletes in exercise and diet. Yesterday's drivers ate steak and eggs and roast beef sandwiches with a half pound of gravy when they won and cold "tube steaks" (hot dogs) the rest of the time. They were drunk every night at track's local bars. Driver training amounted to "no drinking or screwing on Saturday night." (Which caused a lot of mechanics to show up Sunday morning very sleepy and half-drunk with a sore peter.) You may not believe this, but it wasn't unusual for driver to take a pint of whiskey with him, and take a "snort" on the "yellow."

I kept a fifth laying in tool box on race day. Around 1950, France said, "No liquor in pits." He wasn't any "holy-roller," back then he was shit-faced about half the time also. He also got as much pussy as any pornographic film star. I remember, as a joke, I took pint from under Frank "Rebel" Mundy's seat at a modified race I was helping him at. First caution, he came in raising hell 'bout the missing pint. (He liked the expensive stuff, how could you blame us for drinking it?) One time an old racer friend, Buddy Shuman, was being interviewed by a female reporter at Darlington. She was a Southern Baptist and was very concerned over the bravery required to go so fast with the number of serious accidents. Buddy's "gone" now, he was a friend of mine, but he got to where you couldn't tell if he was drinking or not (just kind of acted goofy all the time). Anyway, the gal asked him about the "brave part of it." I could see it coming, and didn't know how to stop it. He said, "Ma'am, I just take 'er down the straightaway. 'Lord Calvert' takes her through the turns" and she printed it. ("Lord Calvert" was his favorite whiskey.)

I don't want to leave impression that all racers were wild, drunk, womanizers – just 80 percent of us. Herb Thomas, Ralph Moody, the Petty's, Fred Lorenzen, they wouldn't come play with us. And there were others. But if drinking, playing with the ladies, and getting to meet quite a few law officers in their place of business, dooms those who lived that lifestyle for some part of their lives to some sort of punishment in the hereafter, most of us early racers are in bad shape. If a quorum is needed, I'm afraid it will be in the most unrewarding atmosphere. I don't worry about it, I figure when I quit, I got back all my points in five years. If not consider this, all you have done up to five seconds ago is irreversible history. If there is a "hereafter" I want to be with my friends regardless of conditions. Tim, Curtis, Fireball, Joe, Paul, Buddy, Fonty. You know, it's now January, 2001 and there is damn near nobody left of that wild-assed bunch of gypsies. Glen Wood, (I may not get to see him if we are judged) Jack Smith, Bud Moore, Buck Baker, Ray Fox, and Frank Mundy are 'bout all that's left.

Fireball was the original "thinking driver." He rated all drivers, and rated them as "race drivers" or "squirrels." He had a plan on how to handle every one. Had he been able to continue racing as a car owner, he might have been, and still be, very successful. He handled racing as a business…it's a sad story (but hell, they were all sad stories). His plan was to retire as a driver after race he got burned in. He had just got a good job with beer company in Chicago. He stopped in to see me at Indy to tell me I was right about it being over for him as a driver. The coming Sunday was my last qualifying chance at Indy and his last race. Sunday we wrecked my car at Indy. An hour later I got word he crashed and burned in Charlotte and was messed up bad. I towed my wreck back to Charlotte (got there at 5:00 am) but they wouldn't let me see him, too hurting. Next time I saw him, I helped carry him to a place 'bout quarter mile from the Daytona track, within 100 yards of his friend Marshall Teague.

Teague was a rare breed. He was as good a mechanic and car builder as there was and could drive 'bout good as any. Actually, he got the first car company and the first oil company into NASCAR racing (Hudson and Pure Oil – now Unocal), when racing got going in the tail end of the 40s. Most drivers were car owners and mechanics as well, and usually operated with one or two go-fers or helpers, as a rule not paid. Or at best got food, lodging, and some clothing. Marshall Teague and Jack McGrath were probably best known for this special talent. Anyway, other successful combination drivers, owners and mechanics were Lee Petty, Cotton Owens, Ralph Moody, Herb Thomas, A.J. Foyt, Jim Reed, Fireball Roberts (Yup, believe it or not, if he had to, he could.) Buddy Shuman, the Terrible Thompsons, Junior Johnson, and others I can't recall. Back then we had the blind leading the blind. Guys who'd never been in a "fast lap" in a race car talking and reasoning with drivers over how, or what to do to correct a problem that's totally different than what we assumed. We were all just guessing, just using the farmer "cut-and-try" approach to build race cars.

Most of the original drivers in NASCAR were at best, high school grads, with menial low paid jobs. And as a rule, worked in a car oriented business like a gas station. Most got started driving a few modified races in flat head Fords, 200 dollar races. Some broke into "Grand National" cold turkey, first race, Whammo! "Hello thrills!" Most ran a year or two and disappeared, but each has his own, unbelievable story of how it developed.

I need to get off subject for a little bit. Going back 50 or more years in memory is not easy. You'll find out. As you get older your memory gets worse. Not only does it get worse, sometimes you remember it totally incorrectly. But you're so sure you're right, and you refuse to reason. One time I said a car was green (1950). Turned out, while I was arguing the car was green, I suddenly remembered where and why Marshall got the car, and that yes, it was maroon. So, as I mention drivers and mechanics, I forget some (many) names of those who had so much to do with it, or more than the one I remember. I want to apologize in advance. I'd like to be 100 percent accurate, but then again, why? The most successful people from a monetary point of view, and the most successful political figures are the biggest bunch of lying, scheming, crooked bunch of son-a-bitches I've ever seen.

As you've read before, some of NASCAR's early drivers were well known by a group of people connected with the manufacture of whiskey, and other intoxicating liquids without a license and without submitting part of the money to the government. You've read about Junior Johnson's absence from society for some period of time. (Junior's story needs a finish. Some time after Junior was released, the government decided they had made a mistake, and said, "We're sorry we locked your ass up old boy" and removed his social stigma with a pardon. (Junior, say "Thank you, Ronnie.") But I'll say 50 percent of NASCAR drivers then had personal experience in the geographical movement of a liquid that gave you a hell of a headache and made you very bad from an expected normal citizen point of view.

Guys like Jack Smith, Raymond Parks, Billy Watson…these are some of the few still breathing. I'm not saying they actually did any of this illegal stuff, but they sure knew a lot about it. Shit, it reminds me of Clinton and the Monica Lewinsky story. I heard those type explanations 'bout bootlegging and bedroom adventures, "Are you gonna believe me, or you goddam lying eyes?" NASCAR, I think, got quite a bit of support early on from bootlegger money in the form of race cars, race tracks, and car sponsors. (I've always been suspicious that Wilkesboro was built with a few bucks of moonshine money.)

I knew quite a bit about it, cause part of my customers were moon shiners, and part was the local sheriff's fleet. Both used Hudson Hornets. My job was to make 'em go like hell. Everybody knew everyone's pedigree, and around midnight the contest would start. (Actually, it would start at about 11:00 pm.) The bootleggers would come and give me some dirty movies. The sheriff's office was across the street. The deputies came over and would be watching the movies. The projector would break down. As a rule, all the sheriffs would fix projector till they saw the whole movie.

By then most of the job was done, the "shine" had been delivered.

The subject of female drivers; once in a while now, a woman driver shows up and the press gives the impression that's historic and unheard of. Hell, the second NASCAR race run had 28 starters, three of which were women – Ethel Mobley, Sara Christian and Louise Smith .

In the first 10 years of NASCAR, the driver's didn't make enough to hardly live on. I noticed, as time passed, when it came time to pay a food or whiskey bill as we left the local saloon, a driver never made a move to pay. Well, in the beginning he couldn't, but have you noticed it's still that way today?

Here's an example: Bill Holland had just won Indy, and has about three second places as well. He came to NASCAR after AAA threw him out for running three laps in a "Lions Club benefit for the blind race." (not AAA sanctioned). He was the hottest name in racing at the time. France brought him into NASCAR. He ran in seven races, and made less than 550 bucks total. That's from late January 1951 to early may 1951 and the races were from Daytona to Phoenix, and back to Charlotte. Today, you'd have to pay that much just to sniff Gordon's jock strap.

NASCAR today has developed the cars, the technical specifications, driver experience and qualifications, track qualifications, and criteria in regard to medical, fire and emergency services through 50 years of "cut-and-try." That's a lot of hurt guys. This includes race track construction and configuration, to where it's much-much safer for all involved, but in particular, the drivers.

In NASCAR from 1949 to 1958, 'bout ten years and about 400 total races, some 27 racers were injured fatally on the race track with plenty more doing tough sheet time. Most all good race tracks today have pretty damn good hospital on the racetrack infield. Back then, a local doctor with a bag and an ambulance or a hearse, or maybe just a fire truck was all we had. With all changes in the science of vehicles, track shapes and surfaces, and driver wearables, the concrete retaining wall still remains as a giant badge of stupidity for the sanctioning bodies and track owners. They have not been improved one damn bit. The cost in driver and vehicle related damage is beyond any reasonable explanation. I think the sanctioning bodies and all concrete retaining wall track owners should receive a six-foot tall trophy called the "Heads-up-your-ass Championship" sponsored by the national league of morticians, and the society of "Stick-it-up-your-ass" hospitals and doctors.

In the 60 years I've been involved in racing, the second most important issue I tried to understand was, "How do you find a good driver?" What qualities, physically, morally or socially, do you look for? When I started, to win races the driver was the number one factor. Number two was power, and number three was chassis. In 1940 to 1975, the basic standards of a good race driver were, a hard-drinking, pussy-chasing, wild, party-loving, male between 20 and 40 years old, not over 160 pounds and not over six feet tall with balls so big he had to walk with his legs spread to keep from banging his ankles. It was assumed you had to be born with special traits and attributes, which mated a human to a machine in such a way as may be described in "how to ride a horse properly."

Instant and lightning quick reflexes, and of course courage that was unquestioned. You know, courage was the commodity almost every driver candidate had. It was also believed then, that you cannot learn to be a race driver. If you weren't born with it, you'd be doomed to a noisy bright-colored field filler. "Strokers" we called them. It was believed by most, and I still believe this, that "racing is for young people."

A.J. Foyt used to be a good friend of mine, or at least I thought so. For a long time I raced with him and against him. He perhaps, is best example of the truth that "racing is for young people."

I think Richard Petty came close to same story. A.J. Foyt, I believe, was greatest race driver we've ever had and surely one of the top three of all time (US). Most of you reading this are thinking, "Bull-shit, no way." That's cause you never saw him race. From 1956 to 1975 it didn't make a shit what he drove, he would manhandle, abuse, cheat, lie (I think he was clean on stealing) to win a race. With his skill and courage, he was damn near impossible to beat in any goddam thing with wheels he sat his ass in that made noise and moved when he mashed the gasser. And I mean "rite now," not any "after a year or two of experience" stuff. He developed a Texas-size ego, and a bad habit. After 20 years of being the boss, he felt that if there wasn't a story about him in every morning sports section, he would die. So he went past his real "get-off-here" place. So did Richard. But it's really not their fault. A good racer don't ever want to quit. Actually, those who did, like Bobby Unser, Dan Gurney, Rick Mears, Junior Johnson, Johnny Parsons, David Pearson, Benny Parsons, Ned Jarrett, Fred Lorenzen, Paul Goldsmith, (just a few who quit early) maybe they had more courage than usual. To walk away while still very competitive, and not trying to get it done with experience rather than quickness, took guts. I've observed over 55 years the "come-back" driver is a likely candidate for much "sheet time" or the "deep-six."

Well, what's the most important single thing a winner has to have? Believe it or not, it's "desire." The winner is so consumed by the need to win that everything, I mean everything and anything else in his life is in second place. No human can keep this up forever. I'd say 20 years of it is the most I've ever seen, and 10 years the average.

Very few people have any idea of all the sacrifices a truly great driver, or any competitive driver, has to accept. It's many times, just two degrees cooler than hell. Blood boils at 140 degrees F, and when blood boils, death follows in a couple of minutes. And how 'bout sitting in same position for four hours, tightly strapped in at temperatures round 130 degrees traveling at 200 to 300 feet per second, two to 12 inches from a competitor with restricted vision, (Windshield covered with oil and rubber and the last hour running into the sun on a quarter of each lap) breathing carbon monoxide five to ten times above normal till you're fuckin' dingy. Where the real story is your asshole is so puckered-up you couldn't drive a 10 penny nail into it with a four pound hammer. Then do that 30 or more times a year. If nothing else, by now you must realize that anybody who does this is out of his fucking mind.

Listen to this...until a driver hits the end of the road, just before a race starts they are nervous and apprehensive. This is what made it so hard for me to digest this bullshit from Darlington '97. "Dale Earnhardt goes to sleep waiting for race to start," bullshit...Dale was sick. No cat's that cool.

But, and this is true. When the green flag falls, and race starts, the driver is enjoying the hell out of it.

Finally, the day comes when you brush your teeth race morning and you puke. Yup, competition, racing is an unnatural event physically. Desire and physical make-up combined with mental conditioning very definitely limit how many times you can do this. Dick Trickle is a very special person. I don't know how in the hell he has been able to go so long. Actually, he' still pretty competitive. (But watch the tail end of a long race, you can see Father Time talkin' to Dick.) The driver's pay for this life style abuse with poor health in their so-called "golden years." You don't see many of the old hands around the track after they quit. Know why? When they aren't in it, they don't want to admit they abused their selves that badly, or they're in a wheel chair, walking wounded, bed-ridden, or dying. Maybe they realize they foolishly wasted their lives.

One thing that really retires 'em as race fans is when they find out tickets are available to them the same way as a person going to their first race as a spectator. Next they find the pit and garage entrance is closed to them, same as any other fan. Is this right?... Is it wrong?...I don't know. But I sure consider it chicken shit on the part of the sanctioning bodies and race tracks. Why shouldn't the retired racers have a gold pass to any race, any place? They would in my world.

Being a race driver for 20 years will never be a formula for a long healthy life. I notice somebody asked Tom Kendall if he ever thought about the accident where he tore his legs up so bad. (This is when he had just won 11 out of 11 Trans Am races). His answer was, "Yeah, every time I stand up." Ask the families of long time racers if loud TV is a problem. Hell, 80 percent of 'em are half deaf and on hearing aids. Watch Rick Mears and A.J. walk. Used to be you could tell an Indy driver by burn scars on his face and hands, (right, Jerry Grant?) but that's been whipped with technology (well, pretty much). The burn situation was much the same in NASCAR. Rubber fuel cells made a big-big difference. Believe this, in 1966 I had a car rejected in NASCAR tech inspection 'cause it had a rubber fuel cell instead of a legal steel tank hanging out and down, (so soon as somebody tapped you in the ass you weren't burning). That's why Fireball ain't here.

In the 30 years I ran race cars I had 53 or more drivers. I think this list either shows I was hard to get along with, or my cars were no good, or the way life was back in the "old days." But one thing is for sure. I had an awfully good education on "what a real racer is." Underneath that racing uniform I used to think main attribute besides balls, was lightning reflexes, so I built a box with a spring-loaded raccoon tail. I'd get driver candidate to open box and see what happened. (Did he catch it or not?).

Curtis Turner did poorly, 'cause he drank so much and had so many great ladies chasing him. during our off-hours at a race. The drinkin' caused racers to get a black eye as poor lovers. So it was only rite that I as his team mate would substitute for him to try and maintain a racer's expected performance. We had a simple phrase for this activity …"poon-tang." I must say, racing with Curtis was one of the nicer parts of my adventures. (Other than it got me educated in the divorce part of our society, which was anything but nice.) But, remember what they say, "If you wanna play, you must be prepared to pay." Curtis, if I had it to do over again, I'd do the same thing 'cept I wish I'd caught on to your shortcomings as a lover quicker.

Well, the raccoon tail deal got old. So I got a new game, a tin container with about a 15-inch snake-looking spring. Take the lid off to get some candy and out comes snake. Well, nobody comes close, it can't be caught. Fireball couldn't grab it even knowing it was coming. I see a motorcycle rider, Paul Goldsmith. I'm looking for a new driver, a "virgin" to try and team up with, that don't have any bad habits to cause trouble. Well, first shot, Goldy grabs the snake. You know, I believe Goldy was the most natural-born racer I ever raced with. And Herb Thomas was right behind him.

Here are the drivers I raced with.

Let me tell you this, I consider my being able to race with these cats a very special privilege and honor (except one). They are a very special class of humans.

Bobby Allison	Tim Flock	Banjo Mathews	Sammy Sessions
Donny Allison	Paul Goldsmith	Ralph Moody	Swede Savage
Mario Andretti	Charles Glotzhatch	Frank Mundy	Les Snow
Buck Baker	Jerry Grant	Cotton Owens	Betty Skelton
Bunky Blackburn	Jim Hall	Marvin Panch	Marshall Teague
Tony Bettenhausen	Dennis Hulme	Johnny Patterson	Herb Thomas
Duane Carter	David Hobbs	Fireball Roberts	Mickey Thompson
Darel Derringer	Bobby Isaac	Dick Rathman	Curtis Turner
Zora Duntov	Junior Johnson	Lloyd Ruby	Bobby Unser
Joe Eubanks	Bobby Johns	Johnny Rutherford	Al Unser
AJ Foyt	Gordon Johncock	Jim Reed	Billy Vulkevitch, Jr.
John Fitch	Jerry Karl	Mauri Rose	Joe Weatherly
Fonty Flock	Joe Leonard	Paul Russo	Dempsey Wilson

Jim Rathman was special to me. He was the sorriest SOB I ever knew that was a race driver.

I believe if Goldsmith had stayed with me a while longer, he would have done even better. But greed reared it's ugly head and he went for the "Firestone test driver" money and I guess a much better deal. But he and Ray Nichols never clicked like Paul and I clicked. I rode with Paul on a road course and at Darlington. He was one cool cat. He did it so effortlessly it looked like your grandmother could do it. Riding with him at Darlington, when he got the car hot lapping for the first time, it looked to me like going into turn one was 'bout like trying to put a bulldozer through the eye of a needle at 200 miles an hour. Goldy acted like he was just going down the street to get a pack of Camels.

Herb Thomas was a natural. He had a short career, but I bet his winning percentage is highest of any driver. A severe race injury shut him down. But his real problem in the beginning was lack of education and poor social communication. Herb would lean into driver's door, slouch down so you could just see his eyes. I remember him leading Darlington, driving with one hand and picking his nose with the other.

Freddie Lorenzen. I admired him cause he won so many races and, in my opinion, was scared shitless most of the time. Remember the word "desire?" Man, he had it. I remember first time I saw him. It was 1955 in West Memphis Arkansas – BC ("Before Clinton"). He and tiny Lund raced with us for the first time. Each had a '55 Chevy. It looked like each were owners, drivers, and chief mechanics.

Tiny was the most unlikely driver I've ever seen. 'bout six foot three and weighed 100 pounds too much. But that son-of-a-bitch could, and did, mash the pedal. Driver's weight is very-very important.

Now, with power steering, Jeff Gordon is the perfect size. 100 pounds of weight on a half mile is 'bout .15 of a second one way or other, even on tracks where acceleration is not a factor, weight dictates corner speed. Mario Andretti, believe it or not, came onto the scene 'bout 130 pounds (That cat got it done even before power steering at 130 lbs.)

It's hard to remember "all-and-who" after 55 years, but we've always had one or two that just stood out as Jeff Gordon does today. (Kinda looks like he now has some company in Jeff Burton and Tony Stewart.) I'm surprised that Ward Burton's not done any better. In the beginning, I thought he could out-drive Jeff a little. Now, a good driver, and a fast car is not enough to do it. It takes a team of money, driver, and mechanic or nothing happens. I don't know yet what the great driver has that's so special but I think it's a sense of balance. As I try to figure out what the magic of a super driver is, I've decided "ears" may be the ingredient that has the magic in it.

Yup, your ears, by the pressure on them, tell you if you're accelerating, or the reverse, and I believe now, they help you identify the limits of lateral traction, front and rear.

You and I really drive by the feel in our asses, even on the highway (that and your middle ear). Some are comfortable at over one G, some have a comfort level way down round seven-tenths of a G.

So, if you have superior powers, to identify the absolute end of lateral traction, you do have an advantage, and I think a big one. The more you steer, the slower you go, so if you can identify the limits of lateral acceleration, and therefore are comfortable driving a car just under where it will loose traction, you will steer less and this in itself will increase speed.

But as important, or even more so, this gives driver a considerable edge on absolute corner entry and exit speed. For example: at Darlington, how fast you get into number one turn ain't near as important as being able, at the apex of one and two, to flat-foot it coming off and hold it there till you lift for turn three. Increased corner speed coming off a corner multiplies straight away speed and you gain in lap speed. David Pearson's secret was all based on this style. He didn't go in particularly fast, but he came off the corners like a rocket. Now that's my observation, you'll have to ask David if I'm right. One thing was for sure, when he and the Wood boys got dialed in, it was "Katie bar the door." David was a long gone mother. I think I see some Pearson in Jeff Burton. Do you agree David?

All of us have been in a jam of some kind, where simply stated, "you were scared or apprehensive." Stuff like racing, flying, hunting dangerous animals or snakes, or getting shot at.

A sure sign you ain't happy, is when your central back starts sweating, and your clothes show it. It's dark, it's wet. It's kinda like when your buddy asks you if you laid "so and so" last night, you lie about it and say, "Hell no!" and your buddy says, "That's good…she has AIDS." Well, in a race car, when driver is enjoying being 'bout roasted to death driving a fair-handling car, he sits back in the seat relaxed, especially if things are going good. You'll never see his back. But when, for whatever reason, it's not fun any more, you will see his back. I call that "seat gap." At same time, you'll notice back of his clothing is wet. That is a giant sign that "the ball game is over."

I lived through that with two great drivers, Herb Thomas and Fireball Roberts. I didn't want to be any part of a driver's death or serious permanent injury. I quit both soon as I was sure. One, a year later, Fireball came and admitted I was rite. The other, Herb Thomas, was crippled for life shortly after (but through no fault of his). All good race drivers know it's a dangerous deal that will kill some of them, but they are totally sure, "It will be the other guy, not them." There is never a seat gap with this attitude.

Here's what I'll call a "golden rule." It takes four things to win a race: driver, mechanic, money and luck. If the driver, mechanic and money are as good as it gets, but the money, driver and mechanic don't like and respect each other, nothing good's gonna happen. It must be a team. Now luck is the one uncontrollable ingredient. It visits all competitors from time to time. But if your driver wrecks 11 times in 30 races, that ain't just bad luck, that's a junk driver. I watched every new driver, new to me or just new to that type of racing. Some with little or even no experience, and some with 10 to 15 years in. I watched when they practiced, and particularly when qualifying, especially on four laps, like Indy. A good driver will run a groove, identical to within inches, every lap. The driver who changes groove, or corner pattern every lap is lost and will never be a winner.

He may go fast, but he is following the car and then saving it. He is not in control.

Also, I've seen drivers who truly understood the physics of racing who, given the whole track when qualifying, did very well. But when they did not have the luxury of being able to run in the best groove, they were hopelessly outrun by the real racers. I know this is gonna piss a lot of people off, but I've never seen a good "big time circle racing female." I've seen females with super skill, but I never saw one that could race. No big deal as I see it, I never saw a male have a baby.

My guess is we will someday have a very good female driver, but I wonder if she will pee standing up or sitting down.

I've seen it a lot with rich kids, and the rich and famous say, movie and TV stars, maybe a sports writer or two, and lots of rich foreign drivers. I think most anyone could be taught how to drive a race car. No-one can be taught how to race. An example: flying a helicopter compared to flying an airplane. A helicopter is very hard to learn how to fly, but I believe 90 percent of the people who want to can be taught. But I also believe, if all helicopter pilots flew 1,000 hours a year, 75 percent would be dead in five years. So, there are some very special traits, genes, what ever the hell we are made of, that you're either born with, or were standing behind the door when they were handed out. Without these magical genes you are gonna be what we called "strokers," "field fillers" or "cannon fodder."

The Fabulous Hudson Hornet

In 1951, when Marshall Teague was finishing up the 1950 season with the big, heavy Lincoln, he started dickering with the Hudson Motor Company for a race car and a couple bucks to go racing. Quite a bit was going on Bill France didn't know about. Hudson's PR guy was a sharpie named Tom Rhoades. Hudson was owned by Queen of Holland, a babe named Wilhamena, and was about to go down the drain. 27,000 cars a year was 'bout it. The shame of it was, at the time, the Hudson Hornet was best buy in the United States. It had the best power, handling, safety, was cheap, and was a good looking car to boot.

Now Rhoades couldn't swing the deal by himself, but Marshall had a Pure Oil gas station in Daytona. Pure was the "daddy" of what is now "Union Oil Company." Pure Oil had a real sharp cat named Mal Middlesworth as PR Manager, who was young, and wanted to take Pure Oil "big time." Pure Oil was then a loser oil company too – it has been for 55 years. (How do I know, I've had stock in it. Must be run by a truck load of idiots. How in the hell can an oil company lose money for 50 straight fucking years?) Pay close attention here now. It gets complex. Pure Oil had their own tire manufacturing company (and were loosing their ass), and the oil company ain't exactly "setting the woods on fire." Talk about timing in your life's experiences, Marshall's got a possible "full-house." He's as good a driver as there is, he is very unusual in that he is also "that good" as a mechanic and race car builder, he sells Pure Oil stuff, and Hudson is "nibbling" on the worm.

Rhoades and Middlesworth bankroll Teague for "peanuts." France is over at his gas station fixing flat tires and Teague delivers him Hudson Motor and Pure Oil, a fuel and tire company. Teague didn't get enough money to pay Jeff Gordon's jet fuel bill for two months, but it was the start of motor companies' direct involvement, and of a major sponsorship for oil marketing companies. Well everybody involved got a lot more out of the deal than Marshall, who was a real personable man. Good looking, well-mannered. Only negative was he was a fat-ass. Newspaper described him as "portly." (I called him "lard-ass"). In summation: a damn nice human. Later France demonstrated his appreciation to Marshall by flinging his ass out of NASCAR for running in an AAA stock car race.

A side note: Do you know congress was, in the early fifties, in process of banning automobile racing in the United States? I've got to give France a gold star here. He played a big part in defeating that idea. By then Bill had now learned how to live with, deal with and sometimes out-hustle the crooked politicians. My observation was, with "greenies," "pussy," and "booze." All things are possible. (This was "then" 1947, in 2001 I don't know, but I doubt there's much difference in the mix.) Also, if you decide to pursue this approach in your life's adventures, keep a good camera loaded and handy. Remember 'bout what I said, "When you got 'em by the balls, their hearts and minds will follow."

Mal Middlesworth was headed for bigger things, and he had a young assistant named Dick Dolan. Poor Dick, an innocent, dumb kid from Chicago, ended up goddam near controlling stock car racing. One of those unknown heroes here which stock car racing has never thanked in any form. For Christ's sake, the least they could have done was put Dick in the "International Motorsports Hall of Fame." (Henry Ford's in it and hell, he was dead before we got going). But goddam it, that's the way life goes I guess – "Don't tell me what you did for me yesterday. What are you gonna do for me today?" As you people sit down in the "Marshall Teague grandstand" in Daytona (at a ticket price you'd expect an air-conditioned, gold-plated seat), look over to "turn one." Maybe you can see the spot on the track where he died while trying to get back into NASCAR.

France wanted to set a world closed-course speed record. Teague tried to drive the most viable car: Chapman Root's Indy Streamliner. The car belonged to a very rich man. And very unusual for a rich man, he was also one hell of a nice man. His name was Chapman Root. At this time Chapman lived in Daytona and had big soft drink factory here. His family owned the Coke bottle design patents. He was an adopted son and lived a fairy tale child's book. Nope, Chapman never did anything for Smokey. He used a lot of trucks as a Coca-Cola mogul. I was a GMC and International Harvester dealer, but no matter how hard I tried, Chapman never spent one damn buck at Smokey's. What happened? The goddam car took off into a wall, the seat came out and Marshall never knew what hit him.

He called me Saturday morning at 8:00 am begging for help. I said, "I can't help you, the body design is upside-down, it wants to fly. If Chapman OK's a new body I'll help, but I ain't going out there to help you commit suicide." He said if he hit 180 miles an hour France would rescind his life time NASCAR ban. I said, "put a passenger seat in the car and ride that fucker around 'bout four hard laps and I believe he'll be cured." By 10 am he was gone. No, I'm not talking "murder." Marshall knew the game and nobody chained his ass in there. But France should have known there was gonna be some "ass-busting" if Marshall continued to pursue that impossible goal (a 180 mph lap in a car that was seven or eight mph short). Aerodynamically the car was ass-backwards. For it's day it was a beautiful looking "Streamliner" (that's what they called 'em). But in reality the car was a poor design for speed, it simply wanted to fly.

OK, Here's the deal. How did Smokey get involved with Hudson? The real quick version is: Marshall would build 90 percent of best race car in NASCAR then run out of time and shove last 10 percent together half-assed. He got me to help on the last 10 percent at night. Money? Hell no. I got paid the same as the rest of the racers, nothing. Well, Marshall likes the driving of Herb Thomas, and talks Hudson into another car for Herb to drive. As usual, he runs slap out of time to get the car ready, so I help finish them, and they run one-two in the 1951 "beach race." This deal wasn't just me, Marshall and Herb. Marshall had a good friend, a limey named Bill Cannon. Bill was a super mechanic, and he probably did more for Teague than I did. I don't know what I was officially, but I ran the pits for both cars. I noticed here four or five years ago, Marshall was "crew-chief" according to some reports written by other people. How do you run the race in the pits if your driving the car?

Now you need to meet another important player in Hudson-Nascar-and Chevrolet, a guy named Vince Piggins. He was a nice young Hudson engineer, who had an Air Force-World War II background as an Allison aircraft factory representative to the Airfare. Now he is Hudson's liaison engineer between Teague and Hudson. We had a crying need for stronger suspension parts. Remember, those cars were goddam near "showroom stock," and quite a few drivers died as those parts failed. For example, Hudson's rear quarter panels were deep and strong and the rear axle shafts were weak by racing standards. So, when the axle broke, rear wheel was loose, but trapped in this strong wheel housing. This caused the Hudson to bounce ass-over-head violently. The axle would always break in the middle of a corner. As the loose wheel tried to get out of the wheel well, it would get between the wheel well and the car floor. This height increase would cause the car to tumble in the direction of the wheel rotation. The tail of the car got nearly vertical and then dropped over forward as kinetic energy completed the violent roll.

Also, we were always pushing for more power. But power had to either have a factory part number, or had to come from sometimes puzzling "interpretation" of the rules. By now, France, whenever a technical dispute was involved that was over his head, had a "cure-all" phrase to settle it. He simply said that, "It was not in the spirit of the competition and/or the rules." A real dumb, chickenshit cop-out, but it did the trick.

Well, the Hornet was really hurting for intake air to run the engine. For horsepower it had a little chickenshit carburetor, a one barrel that was not even half big enough. Teague and Piggins got Hudson to develop and release for production a twin carburetor package and the start of a twin exhaust system. This "Twin H Package" as it was called, was the first "automotive manufacturer 'cheater' racing ploy." Hudson sold quite a few of these performance parts. They also modified the block slightly, and called the whole deal "the 7-X engine" 308 cubic inch in-line six cylinder.

This was actually the best stock car engine for the four years before the small block Chevrolet (1951-2-3-4). It had several weaknesses though. The connecting rods, just below wrist pin were 'bout size of your little finger, and it had a weak, cork lined clutch plate that run in liquid. It also had weak, goofy pistons with pinned piston rings.

So Teague, Piggins, Tom Rhoades (Tom was Hudson PR manager) and Mal Middlesworth constructed the foundation of the current sponsorship methods, while Dick Dolan watched and learned. As a side note: Dick Dolan became extremely powerful, and lasted till the early 90s. No, he didn't get fired as a reward, he retired. He's still going as a consultant. Piggins decides the Thomas deal needs to be separated from the Teague deal, so I'm offered the fabulous sum of $200 an engine (period) to build engines for Herb Thomas. That includes everything…spark plugs, oil, rings (which were free from vendors). And I got any part Hudson made for their engine at no cost. I also have to "baby-sit" engine at races, and be crew chief for expenses only. Like the dumb race happy cat I was, I say, "Sure, it's a deal." Ain't too much longer and I'm building cars as well as rebuilding them. Herb's collecting prize money, both as driver and owner. I'm still getting 200 bucks and expenses.

Herb passed on in 2000. He'd probably deny this, but his wife Helen, she was the money man

Twin H Package. (photo: T. Taylor Warren)

at the track. She had a whopper brown alligator hand bag. All the money went in there at the track. That thing had a time lock on it, and I never seen it open but just once at a race for the "going in" deal. Now Herb and Helen, don't get too upset about this, but Herb was a "bush hillbilly" – dirt poor. Course none of us did any better than hand-to-mouth then and none of us looked like movie stars, but Herb's wardrobe, hairdo, and teeth were particularly bad. When I first met him I thought, "How in the hell did Marshall pick him?" Well, after 50 practice laps at Darlington, I knew why. That son-of-a-bitch could flat haul-ass, and you could see he was in total control. He'd sit there slouched down in the seat, driving one handed, pickin' his nose with the other, and out-running anybody's ass, lap after lap, race after race. His record of victories per number of races run, I believe, would still be best of any driver. He was only in it 'bout seven years and won Darlington three times. Would have been four times, but a rod broke with only three or four laps to go in one race. Herb Thomas was the most natural born race driver I ever saw. Paul Goldsmith was next.

We used to get paid mostly in cash. Herb and Helen were born poor, worked like dogs and they were honest. However, Herb did have a big negative. He was a PR disaster in personal appearances and in dealing with the media. Poor ol' Vince Piggins, his budget was so small he couldn't help. I wouldn't go so far as to say I was screwed in those four years of Hudson, but I will say this: many times I woke up after the first sleep I'd get after a race with a very tender asshole.

What I hope you get out of these various adventures is a description and/or a picture of how stock car racing was brewed. Start with a man who had a piece of land and a relative with a small bulldozer. Next thing you know you've got a race track. Next, you throw in a con-man who envisions a series of annual races that he can live off of comfortably. Then, to these few tracks and some organization, you add small garage owners, or young people associated with surface transportation, who like to drive and build noisy, fast cars. Lastly, you add some parts and capital from the local car dealer, bribe the local sports editor, wait for a week, stir well, open the gates to the fans Sunday, milk a few bucks from 'em to get in plus sell 'em hot dogs, Cokes and beer for double the price and presto – stock car racing. Really a weird cross-section of Americans, that today would get into social trouble (as they were then).

It was a good thing he could drive like hell.

Automobile racing was 100 percent "white" in the beginning. It's 50 years later now, and still no one's noticed what fueled the explosion of interest in stock car racing, and the fact it's still 99 percent white.

Why? I'll probably get tarred and feathered for this, but I've never seen a person of African descent who could drive worth a shit. Just as we've seen African-Americans excel in music (if you can call it that), baseball, basketball, football and throw in soccer and dancing. Will black America ever have a racing champion? Yeah, I think so. Why? I believe their sense of balance is above average enough, but I believe there is a reluctance to poke their fingers in the crocodile's asshole too deep (maybe they just know better).

The fan has paid for the whole goddamned deal! Chrysler, GM and Ford didn't, and still aren't, spending their money in racing to sell cars to people who have no interest in auto racing. They spend the money for one reason only. That is to sell cars to people who like to see their favorite driver in their favorite brand car win. The money the auto manufacturers spend on car racing is added to the price of the car. Race fans don't get pissed, all buyers pay that tax, but only 25 percent of 'em are race fans. Get my point? The race fan was as goofy and as different as we were.

In 1954, for Darlington, I build new car and engine for the race. The inspection is in an old dirt floor barn 'bout couple miles west of the track. Well, Buddy Shuman (Lord Calvert's co-driver), is chief technical inspector. Buddy looks over the engine. Back then we had to pull the cylinder head and the oil pan as well as pull the cam out. After he looks he says, "The cylinder block, and cylinder head are illegal." That means another engine.

How 'bout that grandstand.

Well, I don't have a spare engine. So I think, "Smokey, you're in a hell of a jam here. You're about to lose your $1.00 an hour major league racing job. You got two days to build another engine, and won't get paid, 'cause they can't use the "illegal" one. You've got no parts, and no tools 'cept hand tools." About that time I see a board on the side of the inspection barn move. Buck Baker's running an Olds '88. His mechanic, Boise, has got Buck's Olds' nose right against the side of the barn. I see cam come out of block, go through the wall (where the board magically moved) and another cam coming in. Buddy's 20 feet away, having another shot of Lord Calvert.

So, I decide "Yeah. When confused always take a good drink, maybe a couple." I got a fifth of "Three Feathers" (tasty beverage, four or five bucks a fifth). There is a couple of big-big trees outside the barn, it's hotter than hell and the goddam black gnats are eatin' my ass up. So I get under a tree, sit down and have a li'l drink. Well 'bout 3:30 pm here comes my world famous 'baccy farmer Herb, and the world's first stock car factory liaison engineer Vince Piggins. "What's wrong?" they ask.

Well, that pissed me off. By now everybody in North and South Carolina knows I've been caught cheating and our car has no engine. So I say, "Take me to a bus station or truck stop. I'm going home." They say, "You can't do that, we have to win the race first." I say, "Fuck the race, NASCAR, Hudson Motor Company, Buddy Shuman, Darlington, the black gnats, boll weevils," and then threw in Herb and Piggins as well. Here comes the "Got 'em by the balls" deal again. Piggins says, "We'll pay you to build another engine. Take the engine out of the tow car and make a racer out of it." I'm the "lone ranger," no help at all so I say, "If I have to, I'm gonna buy a mule across the street and ride out of here."

Meanwhile, a couple of my competitors made some smart-ass remarks about cheating. (Buck Baker and Bud Moore for starters) Remember the barn/cam deal? Well, Bud was also as slippery as an eel. That pissed me off. I'm about 92 percent drunk by now, so I agree to build another engine. Also I'm now remembering that starting tonight I have a motel room courtesy of the bank president's lonely, neglected nymphomaniac wife (but that also meant a maximum of two hours sleep a night).

Well, I pull the engine out of our tow car under the tree, using the tree to hang a chain hoist on (honest to God shade tree mechanic job). I got the engine inside. (Did I tell you this place had a dirt floor and that it was dark inside?) We worked with mechanic's drop lights till we get throwed out at 8:00 pm.

The banker's wife has been sitting outside, blowing the horn for an hour. I hate to "porno" this up by telling you the truth…like telling you she oral sexed me from "parked at the barn to parked at the motel." But, you know there ain't nothing like a fifth of whiskey and three or four hours of screwing to get your brain working. So early in the morning I bought a big galvanized washtub, and got 10 gallons of gas in GI cans. (I still wonder how she explained why the trunk of the Cadillac smelled of gas so strong to her husband when he put his golf clubs in?) I've got a plan now how I'm gonna do this deal and show 'em I'm really worth the goddam dollar an hour they pay me.

They didn't call it the bath tub for no reason.

On the way in I stop at "Sad Sam's Gas Station and Fireworks…factory sales…best prices in South Carolina." I buy two dozen cherry bombs (2 bucks, with a special "race discount'). My sexy friend wants to know, "Can we go back to motel for a quickie?" I say, "Hell no! I've got to get to work." I pull in behind the barn and carry the big tub into the inspection barn. I can't believe what I'm seeing. Buddy and NASCAR, and I imagine Darlington's Bob Colvin had a hand in it. A bleacher has been erected, with over 100 seats, and I'm to build engine on a bench in front of the bleachers while 100 or so people watch me. Also, a deputy sheriff is to watch and keep things orderly.

Well, it pissed me off, but I thought, "Hell, this is even better." I fill big tub up with gasoline to wash some parts from the original engine. The washtub's even big enough for engine block. So I put everything back in that is in both new block and the old block 'cept the blocks themselves (got the gas black now).

Now with all the parts from the old and the new engine in the tub full of dirty gas, I just have to pull out the pieces I need (legal or not) and slap them in the block, right? I realize it ain't quite that simple, so I have to remind you again about "when you got 'em by the balls."

I know if you light a cherry bomb fuse and throw it hard into a container of gasoline, all that will happen is nothing. The fuse will go out, no oxygen, but 9,999 people out of 10,000 don't know that. Do you want to guess what the bleachers looked like when the first cherry bomb went into the tub? And how much time I had to do what I wanted in between cherry bombs into the tub? I forgot to mention that every other cherry bomb I threw went under the bleachers. You wonder why after a couple of cherry bombs into the tub and no explosion why they didn't catch on? I don't know. But I'll bet you even after I told you this, if I did same thing around you rite now, you'd haul ass. I think it comes under the heading of self-preservation.

NASCAR…Buddy Schuman? After I threw a few cherry bombs at them, they stayed at other end of the barn. The deputy sheriff? He was a Herb Thomas-Smokey fan. There was, however, a problem. Kiekhafer brought in a cam shaft checking machine and loaned it to NASCAR. The cam I was using had legal lobe dimensions, but I had moved the lobe centers quite a bit. You know, it's a small world. The man who checked cams worked for Carl Kiekhafer, a Mr. Charlie Strang. (He later became president and chairman of the board at Outboard Marine and was commissioner of racing for NASCAR 1998). "Hi Charlie." Well, they check lift and total lobe contour, but not lobe centers. I'm not sure they knew how. Then after checking, he puts a secret marking on cam to preclude cam switching.

I only have one good cam, so I have to pull a switch in the dirty gasoline. He hands me the "stocker" with secret mark. I have to rinse it off and make the "switcheroo." (He don't know there's another cam in bottom of the tub). But it ain't that simple. I drop the "stocker cam" and lose track of which is which in the tub. After 10 or 15 seconds, I realize I'd pulled the wrong one out of the tub. Luckily, the inspector says, "Wait a minute, I want to re-check our secret mark." In the process, I drop the cam on purpose on the dirt floor. (Got to re-clean rite?) This time no mistake and in goes the Hudson cam duplicate (with some errors on lobe centers).

There was nothing in rule book 'bout lobe centers. Sure, there was a confusing, unclear sentence 'bout "cam had to have stock dimensions, (stock cam dimensions varied from .002 to .005 and the lobe centers I used only varied 'bout 12 degrees). Well, my engine ends up all the same but the block. You're thinking, dirty cheater, right? Well, of the seventy-five cams Charley checked, I bet that, at most, ten were run in the race. Go figure. (Remember Boise and Buck's Olds?)

OK, here comes another curve, that on surface, meant nothing to me then. They ran two steel bands over cylinder head, through intake and exhaust manifolds, and around the oil pan. They then put another band around the engine long-ways to preclude removing timing cover. These bands were then locked with a banding lock and seal. I was the only one to receive this pioneering attempt to enforce the rules.

The cars go to the track from inspection barn and we practice and qualify. We qualify in the shit-house, 23rd. "OK," say our competitors. "See that, that son-of-a-bitch ain't nothin' when he's legal." (Truth is the qualify was a con job.) Now the impound area is a fence around a choice section of Darlington red mud hole just off of turn four. It is locked at night, impounded like Fort Knox. Only way to get in there is with 20 dollar bill. (I wasn't sure guards didn't race 'em after we left)

Bud Moore's still going good, and maybe he'll say it never happened, but I was told he reported seeing me in the impound area at night cutting the fore and aft banding strap, and changing cams in the darkness. Don't it get you wondering what the hell Bud was doing around impound area at night? Plus, it was considered impossible to change cams in a Hornet without pulling cylinder head and manifolds.

Well, after 354 laps around the "Lady in Black" Herb captures the $6,850 winner's reward. Ya-hoooo – we are the only two-time winners. Well, I'm starting to get drunk and get ready to tow car back to Daytona, and Buddy says, "Take 'er to the barn, we are gonna inspect again." They say they are gonna re-check the first three finishers. Curtis Turner ran second in an Olds 88, (some young kid named Bradley Dennis from Atlanta built the engine and it was a running son-of-a-bitch). Course Curtis driving it was worth an extra 50 horsepower.

Curtis and Bradley have a car owner who was a super bull-shitter, who loved racing and knew enough about it to be dangerous. I guess he had some money. He was from Kentucky and I believe had some sort of right to call hisself "Colonel Ernie Woods." Well, he protests us. I suppose even the people like Colonel so-and-so, who were a pain in the ass, were needed to help stir up sponsors.

Well, inspection gets underway 'bout 6:00 pm. I refuse to do anything without a written request. So finally they say, "We want the cam." By now I'm half gone. The banker's wife got pissed and left with somebody else. (Never saw or heard from her again – guess I did lousy work.) They ask me, "What I want to see on Turner's engine?" I say, "I don't give a shit what he or anybody else has got, I just want to go home." Well 'bout 7:00 pm we got a crowd around the old barn. 'Bout 500 Herb and Smokey fans, and 'bout 500 Turner fans. And there's a lot of drinking and mouthing-off going on. I don't pull the cylinder head. I can't, it's illegal as hell. (This comes under heading of "defensive cheating.") I found if I used gasoline to measure capacity of cylinder head cavity, and cooled the gas with dry ice, I got a lot better higher compression ratio. (Rule book didn't say type of fluid, or temperature.) I had a hunch that shit wasn't gonna work here, so I quickly invent a way to get cam out with head on.

I got cam out, and deal is "just want to check for secret mark." I ask, and insist inspector tell me where secret mark is in reference: front, middle, or back. He finally said he wouldn't tell me. The bench had four inch wooden top on it. I grabbed cam by front and smacked bench hard as I could with back end. We now had a four piece cam. (Cams then were chilled cast iron.) I then asked inspector again which part he wanted to check. He finally said "Rear." He left barn, went into inspection room. Came out five minutes later and said cam was OK. I kept the other three pieces. Also got back rear "secret mark" piece. Well, that done it. (I'm not gonna tell you how I happened to have that piece.) The 500 Turner fans, and "Colonel Kentucky" by now are so drunk they couldn't hit a bull in the ass if they were holding it by the tail. They decide to whip our asses 'cause, "They have been screwed."

Now they want the head bad, but I refuse. We're going by written request. Well, by now Piggins and Herb Thomas (sober) are dying a million deaths. I get cam out 'bout 10:00 pm. By now we have been joined by the National Guard and the sheriff has a "no vacancy" sign out at the jail. Curtis said some smart-ass thing to me that offended me "by the code of the hills," so I smacked him in the mouth. He then knocked me on my ass and so on and so on. One inspector who was giving me a rash of shit really got to me. I took him out back of the barn and locked him in a trunk. Nope, it was easy with about ten pissed off Hornet fans to help me.

I don't remember much more, 'cept there was a Hudson waiting outside the sheriff's office, and jail 'bout 4:00 am and I went to Daytona in it without the race car. Herb had taken it to his home in Sanford, North Carolina. Bill France? He did his usual, when the race is over if there is trouble, "haul ass." Probably only man left living who was sober and witnessed it would be Bradley Dennis, the sharp kid that built Turner's motor. Well, after Darlington '54, we finished out the season with Hudson. In 1954 Hudson sales double from 27,000 to 55,000 cars. By the end of the season though, I'm seeing some cracks in the Hudson dynasty and the engine is starting to have trouble keeping up and winning. The cars are built in an antique, terribly located plant and the company is losing money.

Star Quality. (photo: Jack Cansler)

Along comes a roly-poly cat named Mason. He owns Prest-o-lite, Autolite, Nash Motor Company and Kelvinator refrigerators. He buys Hudson. Ol' man Mason. Now people, that cat's life story should be told. He sure changed my way of thinking.

We always had spark plug trouble. Only one company made a so-called "race plug." That was Champion. But they made these plugs only for Indy cars, racing airplanes and big race boats. In say, 1950, a movie comedian named Jerry Colona buys a spark plug company called "Blue Crown." He decides stock car racing will sell Blue Crown spark plugs, because his company made some plugs for Lou Moore's Blue Crown Offy's, and when they won Indy, plug sales picked up. Well, Jerry's people offer me 500 bucks a race to run Blue Crowns, (Herb, you never knew that did you?) Well, those plugs ain't worth a shit. Even worse than the Champions. Blue Crowns had a nasty habit of failing the shell roll lock on the ceramic and would, once in a while, blow chunks of insulator right into the hood. Hard enough sometimes, to stick in hole they made. Regardless, when you race for 500 bucks to win, and you get 500 just to use a certain plug, you can see how easy it would be to become a spark plug prostitute. But I had to quit after a year, money or no money, because of poor plug quality.

Soon as I quit, Mr. Mason, owner of Prest-O-Lite and Autolite, calls me and says, "I'll pay you anything you want to run our plugs in your Hudson, up to 1,000 bucks a year." I'm up to my ass in "Mickey Mouse" spark plugs by now, so I tell Mr. Mason I have no interest in his plugs. He says, "Smokey, any two reasonable men can solve any problem if they talk." I say, "Talk ain't the problem, shitty spark plugs are the problem."

Well, that ol' boy, he could bullshit the balls off a brass monkey. So we met and talked.

It turns out, before he shows up in Toledo and buys Prest-O-Lite, Kelvinator and Nash, he was Pancho Villa's male secretary. Now if this ain't the way it was, don't blame me. This is what Mason told me. By the way, when I met Mr. Mason (I don't remember his first name. I always just called him Mr. Mason) he was 'bout five foot five tall and five foot three around the middle. He was bald, smoked a cigar that looked like it was one inch in diameter and a foot long, wore a straw hat winter or summer. He had two kinds of suits: brown and white and black and white (herringbone maybe?). Same with shoes, two/tone, brown and white or black and white. He loved race horses, pussy, and money. I don't remember him drinking but do remember that he was a Mormon, and had a male secretary named George Romney. Yup, the same guy who became Governor of Michigan.

The more we talked the more I liked him. As I told you, he was working for the Mexican reformist (reformist my ass, more like bandit), Pancho Villa. I can't get too explanatory about Villa, I never really got into revolutions. Mason's explanation and his right-hand man's story differed about the money part. Apparently Pancho gets into deep shit and his hand is about to run out. He's got a wife, some kids, and quite a lot of money (gold). So Mason is to take the wife and kids and the loot to Toledo, Ohio. (Why Toledo? I have no idea.) Then the wife and kids go to Cuba from Toledo. While this is underway, Pancho bites the dust. (I'm sure that was not in original plan.) The widow and kids get to Cuba, but the money stays in Toledo, and Mason ends up owning a bunch of big companies. Did he use Pancho's money? I don't know. They only had one lottery then, "the Irish Sweepstakes." Nah, I doubt it. When I asked him if he did, he said, "Do I look like somebody who would do that?" I said, "Yes." He just left it at that, he didn't argue.

Well, to get 500 bucks a race to run the plugs, I had to resort to some "race negotiating." The deal worked like this. I walk out of meeting and go home. A contract follows in 'bout a week which you throw in the trash can, or tell 'em you wiped your ass with it. Next week another contract comes like it should be and I always sign it "Smokey," the lawyers always send it back to get me to sign it "Henry."

Mason and I got along good. No problem 'bout blowing ceramic out. (Got a threaded deal instead of being rolled). But the plug still fouled out almost always for same reason. They had very poor dielectric character from moisture in center wire sealing system, and poor ceramic quality. In general plugs were too cold. There is a good reason spark plug didn't get a lot of hi-tech fixes in that time frame. I'll give you an example: I worked for Champion Spark Plug in 1957. Ford Motor Company paid four cents a piece for plugs, and Champion had to keep six million Ford plugs in stock. (Champion was original equipment.) I kept after Mr. Mason about a better race plug. He says "do it," and gives me a young engineer to work with (Paul Atwell). Remember me, Paul?

Well, in here Mason buys Hudson and makes Romney president of Nash and Hudson, and renames it American Motors. Remember I work for Hudson with Herb Thomas racing Hornets.

OK, it's time for 1955 race plans. I go to Toledo to a big meeting chaired by George Romney, president of American Motors. The meeting is at big long table, elliptical in shape, with I'd guess 30 people. Well, we got Romney, who's president of the deal. An engineer named Roy Chapin, who was president of Hudson. (The Chapin family were "Hudson" from day one.) Marshall Teague is at meeting also. "Are we gonna have a frame or unit construction common to both Hudson and Nash?" Hudson is at this time a half-frame, half-unit construction and Nash is full unit construction (no frame). I see prototype 1955 Hudson and damn near puke. It's a smaller car with a smaller straight six engine than the Hornet called a "Jet." It's also an up-side-down bathtub Nash design with no frame. Marshall sides with the "bathtub engineers," because he wants to continue with Hudson. Hell, by now half the United States called the Hornet the "Teague-mobile." I see the car as a loser and I'm dead against it. I can see too that the deck is stacked as Roy Chapin battled the "bathtubbers" tooth and nail. For every question he puts up, Romney says, "What's the answer?" and one of twenty engineers sitting at table jumps up like he has a right front spring under his ass, and answers. Piggins can't say anything. He's trying to hang on. When it comes my turn to comment, I call it an up-side-down, under-powered bathtub, with a much too weak suspension system and too short a wheel base. Mentally, I'd quit an hour ago. So when it's time to vote, and by then it's about 25 to 5, I stand up. Say, "I quit." I go to airport and home to Daytona. Hudson's like a 10 foot snake with head cut off: It will, and does die at sundown in a year or two.

When I switch to Chevy (This is the next adventure I have, and this one was a dandy.) We really are having plug trouble. (I'm now running Champions.) Mason has also bought Autolite spark plug company. He calls me about a plug deal and I say "nope." (His plug is actually a little worse than Champion's.) We run mostly on the dirt, and the calcium they used to glue the clay together would get in plug gap and ground the plug. (We only run .020 to .025 gap.) So he said, "Build your own plug, we'll manufacture it, and sell it." So I said, "OK." My idea then was to extend the tip of the plug into the oncoming fuel charge, and let fuel keep the plugs clean by washing them with high velocity gas-air-vapor charge. I make up a set of modified Autolite spark plugs with extended tips. In here Prest-O-Lite and Autolite are kinda the same deal. Atwell is an engineer at Autolite assigned to help me make the extended tip spark plug and experiment with it. Paul was a junior advanced engineering brain. Results were very good in the dyno, more than I had hoped for. When plug location was nailed down in the Chevy head in the beginning, I objected because during a cold start, or when fuel level got too high in the carburetor fuel bowl from high cornering forces, the over-rich condition would foul the plug, as it was at the lowest point in combustion chamber. And like a baby bird's mouth, the fuel would run in and drowned it out. Well, finally Paul Atwell makes a sample set of plugs. I get 'em just as I'm leaving with the 55 Chevy Herb Thomas is gonna drive at Lakewood, a mile dirt track in Atlanta.

Now I gotta tell you about a man who was about as nice a human as it gets. His name was Earl Twining and he was an engineer who represented Champion at the race tracks. Earl didn't have any of our bad habits. Actually he was more like a preacher than a racer. But at the time, Champion was asleep with their head up their asses. Their plugs just weren't any good. As a matter of fact, that is my observation of Champion in general for the last 55 years. I think its actual story would make good post graduate college material for a course on "how not to run an international company."

Well, I've tried to get Earl to make the extended nose plugs for a year or so, but he is not sold. He don't think plug can be made to stay cold enough in the extended tip region of hi-temperature. Well, we qualify on pole with the new Autolite deal. 'Bout one-half hour before race, Earl comes over with a box of plugs, and the usual "good luck" deal. He tells me he thinks I'll really like these plugs. He "had 'em made special for me to try, be sure to use 'em."

Oh shit. I ain't got the heart to tell him I don't want them, so I say "thanks a lot, etc." But how am I gonna use them? I figure, well hell. I'll just tell him they were a little better, but to keep from lying about it, I have to find a way to use them.

Lakewood is a muddy, radiator plugging track, so we have to run what we called "shaker-screens." These were made of two to four screens, one in front of the other, and on the front screen, we'd wire big bolts or lug nuts to jump around and beat mud through the screens. You guessed it. I wired the new champions to the shaker screen, so if I said I used 'em, I wouldn't be lying.

OK, the race is over (we won) and here comes Earl. "Congratulations, can I have plugs out of winning engine to take back to Toledo to look at, and show engineering?" Well, I wish the earth would have opened up and swallowed me when I seen the look on Earl's face when he got the picture. You know, I don't think he ever talked to me again, even when later I built and operated a Champion plug testing laboratory at my shop in Daytona.

Back to Autolite. After the race is over I call Mason at home to report the success of extended tip plug. Mason asks, "Will it work in passenger car?" I say "Hell yes. Much better than in racing." (What's an extended tip spark plug? Pull one out of your car and look at it. Everybody uses 'em since the late/mid fifties.) Mason says, "OK, come up Wednesday, I'll have contract ready" After our conversation, we have verbal agreement where I'm to get one mil per plug. (there's 10 mil's per one cent) Well, at a million plugs a day from 55 to 2000, go figure. (Probably two times that with world-wide patents.) Wanna guess who had a stroke and dies within 24 hours? Well, without Mason, everybody at Autolite gets amnesia. Hell, can't really blame 'em I guess. You know, my recollection of Mason yet today is a little fat man with balls so big, that he had to walk spread legged to keep from banging them with his ankles. What did I get out of the deal? Same as for the carburetor that 80 percent of all stock car racers in the world use.

Another Hudson win.

Smokey's Hudson track record:

First Hudson factory race team:
- Started Detroit August 12th 1951, 250 miles. Qualified 6th, finished 57th, overheated 27 laps.
- Darlington, 82 starters, September '51, Herb wins had 2nd fastest time, Teague crashes.
- We won championship '51, finished second in '52, won the championship again in '53, and got second place again in '54.

- 1st points, '51, seven wins
- 2nd points -'52 , eight wins
- 1st points - '53, 12 wins
- 2nd points -'54, 12 wins

We won 39 races total. Won at damn near every track at least once, and Darlington twice.

The Cover of the Saturday Evening Post

Every US motor company and division was operating in a "dream world" up to 1974, 'cause when business was good they made money ass over head and when business was fair they still did OK. But when business turned bad, they lost their ass by the hundreds of millions. Each year in this period, year after year cars were just new cosmetics on the same old junk. They made 'em look pretty good from 15 feet, but up close you can't make a 40 year old broad look like a 18 year old beauty queen.

One man, Ed Cole, had the foresight and balls to stick his neck out and "go for broke" with a whole new ball game — car, engine and concept. He "shit-canned" the Chevy straight six cheapo "poor mans" car for a light, simple, hi-mileage, inexpensive hi-performance car that young and old would quickly learn to really like. This car, this engine, the 55 Chevy V8, totally dated the whole world's other car manufacturers obsolete. I was lucky enough to work for him personally for three years. Course at the time I didn't realize what was really going on.

In the fall of 1954 I was in a "quit racing" mode, drinking and partying around like there would be no tomorrow. Just doing what I goddamned felt like, with no thought about the consequences.

Back to "the hell with tomorrow, tomorrow may never happen" thinkin'. Ed called me and offered me a job. I wasn't very nice to him, and turned it down. A month later he come to visit me to talk about a job. I refused to talk and ran his ass off. I had all the two dollar an hour racing experience I needed. Plus, I knew how it destroyed my social life.

In spring of 55, Bill France asked me to take a job with Chevy so he could get 'em hooked into NASCAR. I said, "Bullshit, every time you do me a favor, I end up with the shitty end of the stick." He had a little piss-ant airplane, a Tripacer, and he could fly it half way decent. He bribed me with "wine, women and song" to go to North Wilkesboro. Why there I don't know.

I met with Ed Cole, Mauri Rose, Russ Saunders, Mac Mckenzie, and I don't remember the fifth man. Might have been Rosey, or Harry Barr. This is the Chevrolet brains. On the hill where the fans sat, on what was the front downhill straightaway, no fence. And if you didn't make it through #1 you went through a barbed wire fence into cow shit and cows (dirt track five-eighths mile long).

Deal was, I run one race, Darlington 1955, and I get car and $10,000. Really, a hell of a deal. I was feeling no pain so I signed the contract. I'd already smoked the engine over, actually raced one once and won with it. But I didn't tell them. Before I signed I told them I didn't like the "Mickey Mouse" valve gear, and got them and France to agree I could make a shaft rocker prototype, and if it was better, Chevy would offer

Me and Herb after a win...they said posing for a photo was in the contract, so I made myself look pretty.

a hi-performance conversion kit to shaft rockers, and France would accept it.

This was the first time I had "Big Bill" by the balls. A very smart old man, at whose gas station I sometimes worked told me this when I was 'bout 14. He said, "When you get a man by the balls, do what you want to, that man's heart and mind will follow." I don't think he was the originator of that phrase. I think it was Will Rogers or Confucius (philosophy comes from wherever you find it). At first France said "no" to the valve train deal. I said, "OK, this party is over take me back to Daytona." When he realized I meant it, he agreed and signed a short agreement.

Well, as it turned out at the speeds we were running, 5800 rpm, the shaft didn't help enough to go to all the trouble. So we went with "Mickey Mouse" valve mechanism. But this stuff had poor durability. I didn't take that into consideration, all I looked at was power.

While I was screwing around, not racing before the Chevy job, I built a '55 Buick for Herb Thomas to drive for Buick Motor Company. The car ran good at its first race at Langhorne and we run off with the race. Then with five or six laps to go, we picked up a nail in the left rear tire. It was a horse track then, and it was an old fence nail 'bout six inches long. (I think we did win one, maybe two races with it later.) Buick decided not to pay me, or to continue, so I quit. Herb kept car in Sanford, North Carolina and decided to race it at the Charlotte fairground. I said "no." Hell, it was my car. The stubborn bastard did what I figured, he run it without changing rear axles. As a result, the right rear broke and he goes through fence. He busts his leg and the car's junk he tells me. I never see car again, it just disappears.

Herb had been champion several times, and would have been again in 1956 till France dealt him a bad-bad hand. He is in his 70s now, and still going, but kinda puny. His racing wounds ain't making his days any better. Too bad racing hasn't found a way to say "thanks" before it's too late. (Newsflash 2000: it's too late. He's crossed over.) Same with Lee, Tim Flock, Cotten Owens, Ralph Moody, Jack Smith, Frank Mundy, and about 15 more. Red Vogt "left" and we never gave him a proper thanks.

Well, with Darlington coming on, and my concern 'bout Chevy engine durability, I decide to test it at a relatively new track, a hi-bank, dirt, one and a half mile killer track in West Memphis, Arkansas.

Mauri Rose, by then was assigned to me as a liaison between myself and Chevy engineering. (Actually, he lived with me for a year.) Man, he was a hard working, sharp "run to win or bust" cat. One hell of a helper. No, really one hell of a partner. Mauri had a problem with everybody but me. Nobody liked him 'cept Ed Cole and me, and they fought him tooth and nail. Ed Cole liked him, well actually Mauri reported to Cole personally and only, but even Cole would get weary of Mauri's battles.

Herb healed up enough to run West Memphis, but in the race the "real" Herb Thomas didn't live there any more. That busted leg in the Buick changed him. No more did he lay back in the seat, driving with one hand and pickin his nose with the other. Well, 100 miles into race, Mauri says "Smokey, what the hell's going on? (He never saw Herb run before.) Well, Herb ain't doing it. No way. I guess the sheet time hurt him because before that Herb Thomas had highest winning percentage of any driver NASCAR ever had. That cat hauled ass, and usually kept her between the fences and he finished. He had also always qualified strong. Hell, 'bout half the time he was on the pole. But at West Memphis, he was a "stroker."

(Tiny Lund and Fred Lorenzen ran their first NASCAR races there. Both in '55 Chevys in 1957.)

Now this track was a dangerous son-of-a-bitch 'cause it gets great big holes in it. You see it was 'bout a 30 degree bank, and banks were Mississippi river bottom (a fine silt). No way to get it stabilized. I think somebody got killed every time it was run. Hell, Lee Petty went through the fence in turn 3. Over a power line 40 feet from the ground and landed in parking lot on his wheels. Well, track got so goddam rough, that gas tanks fell out, real axles broke out, front suspensions jerked off, and engines overheated real bad. The guys runnin' the race were trying to keep track wet to hold dust down. The first part of the race the mud was slicker than owl shit. Man, when it plugged radiator, it took four or five hours in a radiator tank to get it out from between the fins on a 12 to 14 fins to inch core (ain't much room between fins).

Well, I realize I'm 30 horsepower short, my "Fearless Fosdick" driver is pullin' up a little lame, and the engine has a very weak valve gear, so I decide only way we can get job done at Darlington is by brains, trickery, or shit-house luck. We got smallest engine in the race (265 cubic inches) so we are a 200 to one shot in regard to winning. I tell Mauri to "go travel the world and find me a good tire." I found a hole in the rules which paid a lot of attention to wheel width and tread patterns and bolt holes, but not a damn thing about diameter. (I wanted a 20 inch tire if I could get it.)

Well, Mauri's gone for a couple weeks. You see, he knew everybody in the tire business from all over the world (he had won Indy three times). And he had one friend, Otto Wolfer, who maybe at the time was the world's best tire expert. Otto worked for Pure Oil at the time as the head tire man. Yes, Pure Oil actually made their own tires then. Wolfer had worked most of his life at Firestone, and he had designed a sports car tire for Firestone to be used by Briggs Cunningham at LeMans, on a very heavy Chrysler Hemi powered car, probably an Allard. This tire was for a 16 diameter rim, with white wall on one side, and non-directional tread. Wolfer knew Briggs, who took 25 of 200 to LeMans to test, and decided he liked Dunlop better, so the 175 remaining tires got sent to a junkyard in Akron. Here's where Mauri finds the tires. The junk man decides we have to buy all 175 of 'em. Mauri calls me and says, "The best is here, I can buy 'em for $1.50 each." I get the junk man to take a buck apiece.

You race fans who know the Darlington race track today, I'd like to give you a racer's description of Darlington, 1955, for the September 500 mile race. We flat tow our cars there. No trailers, no trucks, and all our tools, parts, and pit equipment are in tow car and race car. You can't get a motel room for love nor money. They ain't got any. Darlington is a sleepy farm town. Biggest deal is the Lucky Strike tobacco warehouse. All of the tobacco was auctioned in the dried leaf form to the "cancer vendors." (Note: I smoked cigarettes, pipes and cigars for fifty years – so I can call that shit anything I want.) The auctioneer was regarded as extra special, and they were a colorful bunch of bandits.

Darlington had a bug that was kinda like cotton-tobacco country symbol – black gnat. (I think they were race fans). Anytime you opened your mouth you swallowed ten of 'em.

The first ten years of Darlington were special. To us stock car racers, it was our answer to Indy. The Darlington 500 was hands down the most prestigious stock car race in the world. I'd count the last thirty days, and the morning I got there every year I'd slip into a small world three miles in diameter. I loved to

Lined up for the start of an early Beach Race.

race there. It took several days to qualify all the cars so we'd have to be there 'bout ten days total. They started about seventy cars in '55. Don't know how they arrived at the number of qualifiers, but back then they made up the rules as they come to the problems. It was all based on the almighty greenie.

The track was a fucking mess actually. There was no way to get car good at both ends 'cause turns are all different turns. The number one and two turns are fucked up because of a track neighbor's minnow pond. It was in the way when they started grading so one end is narrower than the other. The track surface was asphalt, and no known asphalt could stand the weight, speed, and lateral forces of that many race cars on a hot day. So, like the farmers they were, the track management, the night before the race would coat the turns with "owl shit" or "bear grease." This band aid reduced the lateral traction to a point it didn't knead the asphalt, and it pretty well stayed in place.

Simply put, the track could now last the race but the race cars were running on black ice. There was one way in and out except across track at turn four. To get an ambulance in or out, stop the race.

It always rained. The pits didn't even have a guard rail and when you'd jack a car up on a hot day the jack would sink into the mud. The control tower was in the infield two stories up. Underneath tower was message center. That was one wall phone on the outside of a one-holer outhouse. There was just one toilet for all of us, so phone calls would be brief as you swallowed the black gnats and smelled the over-ripe shit house. If you complained, you were reminded, "Nobody made you come. If you don't like it, it's a 100 yards to the road out of here".

So I ended up pissing at the pit fence behind the car. Sure, the fans were there. But what the hell you gonna do with the two quarts of beer you drank last night? I can remember pissing and signing autographs at same time, and a favorite of mine was to ask the lady to "hold it while I signed" (no one ever did, but I did have a little drunk offer to kiss it, but her boyfriend stopped her. Sure I'd of let her – didn't want to offend a race fan.)

Well in practice it looks like tires will go 'bout 5,000 miles. They are hard as hell, but we can run 'em at a lower air pressure. Our corner speed is better, but we are short on the straight. Kiekhaefer catches on in three or four days and he asks Firestone for some like it. They actually don't even know what the hell he is talking about. In 1955 Goodyear built special tires for Kiekhaefer only. Suddenly Firestone big shots want to be my friend. John Laux is my good friend and John works for Firestone. John says, "His bosses want me to sell some tires to Kiekhaefer." I tell John, "Hell will freeze over first." John says "I didn't expect you to be so nice about it."

At this time Firestone racing is run by what I called the "three Mac's." McCreary, and I don't remember the other two Mac'somthings. If the United States would have had an Olympic drinking team, those three would have received the gold-silver and the bronze. Well here comes the three Mac's. I've never met any of them before. They introduce themselves then tell me to "give Kiekhaefer fifty tires and they will replace them later." I say, "No." They say, "If I expect any cooperation from Firestone in the future, I'd better cooperate, 'cause they have the key to success in racing." I guess they thought if they were nice to him, he'd switch over to Firestone. Kiekhaefer was winning everything 'cause he had four cars and 50 or 60 men. They seem to be a pretty congenial bunch of what I've discovered is pretty much standard issue corporation "do-nothing bullshitters" with very little knowledge of their products. So I tell them to "go fuck themselves" in the nicest way I could. The dumb bastards didn't even know about me buying the tires in the junkyard. They didn't realize they threw away the best tire they had. The "Super Sport" at that time was considered a failure, a flop, money wasted and they had been around six months. Well, of course I'd ruined my chance for a wonderful friendship with the brass at Firestone.

'Bout thirty minutes later here comes the "Imperial Wizard" himself known by his many good friends as "Big Bill" France. Big Bill says, "Smokey, I promised Kiehaefer you'd loan or sell him tires." I say, "I've got to race that motherfucker in a couple days, and I really don't like him to boot. So you tell him Smokey said, 'Fuck you and your horse, too.'" At the time I really disliked Kiekhaefer. He drove into NASCAR with money out the ass so NASCAR was playing, "We love Chrysler" at the time. Again the power of the "greenies" reared it's ugly head. Big Bill says, "You don't understand Smokey, if you don't give him the tires I'll have to outlaw your tires." Here comes the second and last ball crunching I ever had for "Mr. NAS-

CAR." I laughed and said, "Bill, you're sitting there with you fishing pole and the hook is in Chevy's mouth. Your waiting for them to swallow the hook. That will probably come race day. You know me well enough to know if you go through with your threat, I and the race car will be in Daytona in eight hours." He knew I wasn't bullshitting. I wish I could have heard his explanation to Kiekhaefer.

I'm short on horsepower and am betting all my marbles on tires. The tires are called "Super Sport." (They are white wall). We decided to mount them white wall "in," (we could do this because they were non directional) and cut half the tread off. I got what in my thinking is the best tire by far. And our game is the "rabbit and the turtle." It worked and we qualified, practiced and raced on one set of four tires that cost me one buck apiece. (Mauri brought back 173 tires for 175 bucks) We never changed a tire. Other cars were heavier and had two to three miles an hour lap times better, but they blew their tires all to shit. Herb could have won race by five laps, but he was smart and just kept a comfortable margin. Actually, it was like taking candy from a baby. The engine made it fine, we didn't really have to push it hard all day.

It was a rough day for the Tempest. (photo: Larry Tomaras.)

We won the race. Kiekhaefer blew one hundred tires with his four or five cars. Chevy swallowed the hook. After the race here comes the Olympic drinking team. They wanna take pictures. I say, "No pictures," but it turned out I had to. In entering the race the entry blank said I agree to ads. I personally don't have to, but car and driver can be used. I say, "OK, you got me." I put on farmer two strapper overalls, a red bandanna, a straw hat, paint two of my front of my teeth black with shoe polish, take my shoes off and say, "Let 'er rip." You guessed it. I won that round too. That's why you never saw the Darlington Firestone victory pictures in a Firestone ad.

Yup, they got Herb Thomas to do one they did use. Firestone stayed fifteen more years, but never ever did get the tire caught up with the race car. The 1955 Chevy victory was very unpopular.

The south was "Henry" country. Chevy in 1955 was considered "grandma's car."

That victory did some good in Darlington. A struggling auto alignment shop with Bear Alignment equipment loaned me the use of his equipment to set the Chevy front end. The fact the car went the full race with no tire changes, and fast enough to win, and maybe advertising that he put in a miraculous front end setting that made this possible kept him very busy for a long time.

I think stock car racing started a transition in that time frame. Around 11:00 pm, I'm towing back to Daytona and I hear a very famous radio commentator (Keltenborn was maybe the guy's name?) included in his daily news delivery that "a '55 Chevy driven by Herb Thomas…," plus a few names and a few highlights. They actually reported the race result. (That's when car radios could hold a station for three or four hours or more of traveling). I don't know who got the best of the deal – NASCAR or Chevy. I think that li'l adventure did boost the Smokey fan club some, and caused me to receive some Detroit work offers.

Well, within five weeks we got 15 inch "Super Sport" Firestones out the ass, Chevy is big into NASCAR, and my 16 inch tires get outlawed. France don't need me anymore. There are 15 Chevys running in three months. The ball game's on and still going strong 45 years and many-many millions of dollars later.

What happened to the car? Don't know, Herb made that one disappear too. But I did keep the winning engine. It's in Don Gartlits' museum in Ocala. I rebuilt it a couple years ago and it runs good. You ought to visit Gartlits' museum. He has a big, beautiful display of drag cars and old passenger cars, and old garage equipment.

I bought that Chevy new in '55 from local dealer for $100 bucks over cost. It was a model without a back seat built to sell to tobacco company's cigarette salesmen and cost $1,812. Just to give you an idea of how much race cars have changed in price, my tire bill for the race was $4.00 or a buck each. Compare that to a top team in 1997 that, at Darlington, to practice, qualify and race, today's team uses 'bout 25 sets at $1,200 per set or $30,000 clams.

Remember the deal, "Load the wagon, the mule's blind." Well the "one race" deal with Chevy ended up on "plan-B." How about a 24-hour record at Darlington at 100 mph. Plus, a new closed course world record? It pays another 10 grand, 'cept we want two cars in case one breaks. (These cars must be strictly stock showroom stuff). Well, we are really all whores at heart, and for the right price, we'll do most anything. I agree, and we get the job done.

Now, what about 1956? How about $1,000 a month and expenses? And also run the Chevy racing program from your shop in Daytona. (I must have really been drunk when I signed that)

They worked my ass 80 hours a week, 365 days a year, for the princely sum of $12,000. In beginning race on the beach in February 1956, rightfully or wrongfully, I decide Herb's had it, and he's gonna bust his ass if he keeps racing.

Of course he don't see it that way, so I give him the cars and engines we had ready, and Ray Fox, who worked for me at the time, and expense money to run out of a shop where Herb lived in Sanford, North Carolina. Remember, I run the Chevy race program then. In a weird and fucked up plan I give Herb new Grand National and convertible circuit cars and 'bout five engines. Admittedly, the Chevy money wasn't much, but he had the same deal I had. Well, soon as they get started they suddenly quit and go to work for Kiekhaefer. Then 'bout two-thirds way into season, quit Kiekhaefer and go back to the '56 Chevy deal. Herb and Fox did real good and won the championship, but Chrysler and Kiekhaefer, and the mighty green back reared its ugly head again. France adds two more races at Hickory, North Carolina on November 11th and Wilson, North Carolina on November 18th. Herb's still ahead in points after one extra race. In the second additional race, Herb gets his brains knocked out in a weird little accident with a Kiekhaefer car and Buck Baker wins race and championship for Kiekhaefer.

After Herb and I separated I noticed Paul Goldsmith on his motorcycle. He won the '54 beach race on a Harley. I asked him when he came by to visit after the race if he'd like to race stock cars. He said, "Yup, that's why he came by." So I gave him "the driver's test," the old mongoose deal. I had a snakeskin with a foot long metal tube spring inside, loaded out the ass with a spring in a can that says peanut brittle. You get him to take top off of the can to get some candy and BOING!

He caught the son-of-a-bitch snake coming out of the can. I've never seen anybody else that could catch it, even knowing what was going on.

Nope…we weren't using radios yet.

Well, he was a sensation in the car, but he lacked experience and sometimes the car would look all wrinkled up, and we'd have a real job on our hands to get it to tow back. But he worked his ass off helping us. I didn't mention it, but Herb Thomas was the same way. Those two spoiled me, 'cause none of the others worked on cars. Herb worked on chassis, and was a big help. But he wasn't worth a shit on engines, transmissions or drive axle. Well, neither was Paul, but in 1956, Paul starting to really get going really good and starting to win.

By now the Chevy program is over my head. Mauri and I need help, so I try to get Cole to hire Vince Piggins, who I worked with in the Hudson Hornet days. He was Hudson's liaison engineer that worked with Marshall, Herb and myself, as well as all other Hudson racers. I can remember in late 1953, when the whole goddamned field was Hudson Hornets.

Well Mackenzie, Cole's number two man in racing, had picked a guy named Jim Wangers for the job. Mauri and I couldn't stand him. He was a PR Guy from Campbell-Ewald, Chevy's PR firm. Jim didn't know his ass from a hole in the ground, but tried to bullshit his way in. Piggins wanted the job bad. But for some reason, even though Piggins was by far more qualified, Mackenzie didn't want him, so he hires Wangers. Jim don't know it, but I saved his life. If he'd got in then, Mauri would have killed him. So I call Cole and tell him, "I quit" ('bout 10:00 am). He said, "Too bad." 'Bout 9:00 pm that night he called and said, "Get your ass back to work, I just hired Piggins and Wangers is out of the deal."

As soon as Vince gets in, he shoots a weird deal at me. And Cole loves Vince's plan. Chevy starts a race team in Atlanta at a big Chevy dealer, Nalley Chevrolet. The deal is called "Operation Sedco" which stands for Southern Engineering and Development Company. A la Kiekhaefer they build the cars for all Chevy racers, at no charge, and I build all the engines in Daytona.

Well, I'm against race teams cause by now we got another one. Pete DePaolo is running a race team out of Charlotte for Ford. Pete DePaolo, nobody in the world can not like him – nifty super person. (Pete's a racer, has won Indy as a driver.) But this team shit is busting up the poor racers and new comers. They ain't got a prayer. It was really wrong.

France is thinking it was great. Well, if we look at what France accomplished, maybe I was wrong. But I was defending the system that racing was born on, so I did what I thought was right. The talented drivers and mechanics could rise to the top if everybody had same chance. Back then, nobody got going because of lots of money and no talent. Today there are 100 "Jeff Gordon's" and "Dale Earnhardt's" out there that will never get a shot at it cause they don't have the "know how" or political connections to get the financial support or the PR skills to present themselves favorably. Look at the Indy cars, and some of Winston Cuppers, and other racing divisions. Rides are outright bought, or procured by bringing in hi-buck sponsor. What does a sponsor pay for first class action in Winston Cup in 2000, 10 to 15 million? CART got up to 'bout eight million or more per good car, now I imagine it's less. They are headed down the tube. I think Indy cars are damn lucky to get two million. To sponsor a Formula One car, 200 million isn't out of the question, but that's a whole different deal. A Busch car, $200,000 to three million is 'bout it.

Well anyway, Piggins gets his wish (over my objections) didn't take him long to bite the hand that fed him. But I'm not sure he ever knew exactly how he got the job. Well, I have a last ditch meeting with Cole on Monday morning at 7:00 am. This is in March of '57.

Ralph Johnson and I had spent all winter getting the junk Rochester fuel injector to work in a race car. This was a weird deal, with 2-4 barrels. We make a little over one horsepower per cubic inch with stock motor. Course, this was using the GM "Test code 20" which included motoring friction added to real out the crank number. But in a race version, loosened and cheated up a little, we got a real one horsepower per cubic inch. But Cole wanted the romance of fuel injection. Big-big secret . He paid to put 12 foot fence around my race shop and had it guarded 24 hours a day, seven days a week with Wackenhut guards.

He sent one of his favorite young engineers to help me develop it. Ralph Johnson was his name, he was perfect. He worked his ass off, drank like a fish, chased women like a wild man and we both hated the "goddamned injector." But for the amazing salary of $1,000 a month, we did it – well in the dyno it worked. In the car it wouldn't pull a sick whore off a piss-pot. Finally, one day, Paul and I are testing on the "jungle road." A stretch of empty road through Tomoka State Park about eight miles north of my shop. I'm sitting on the floor reading a manometer, checking the under hood pressure. I see it's to the moon.

The '57 Chevy didn't come standard with a heater but had a door in the fire wall that you could twist the handle and it would come out, and then the heater kit replaced this door.

I decided, "We'll just try and open door, maybe drain some underhood

Fireball and me.

pressure, and see what happens."

This is at night, with no lights, we're running 'bout 120. I snap the handle. The air pressure slams me into rear firewall where back seat was. Damn near knocked me dingy. Paul's laughing his ass off and the car's now running 'bout 140 miles an hour, problem solved. The under hood pressure drove the injector dead rich. Turns out I had my head up my ass for a month. The injector totally operated on pressure differential and I knew that.

Well, we put two 90 degree tunnels in front fire wall through floor board, one on each side. This got rid of under hood pressure and the car ran strong, but in the qualifying commotion (we still raced on beach sand), I couldn't find Goldy. We were about to run out of time so I qualified car. Ray Fox hadn't gotten all the plug wires on tight. One had some moisture in it, and it blew off but I actually won the pole position running on just seven cylinders.

Now in the race Paul led it all the way until, with 'bout 25 miles to go, an injection nozzle partially plugged up. Adios one piston. Smokey's car looked like a mosquito spraying rig, ball game over, no cigar, Pontiac wins.

Back to Detroit. Meeting with Ed Cole Monday morning. (My contract has expired.)

I guess Ed's got a big fire to put out. I wait and still no meeting. The receptionist says, "Postponed, maybe 11 am." Damn, I got other things to do.

They want to build a "street-able" version of our race car, and call it "the Black Widow." This was the beginning of street "muscle cars." Dumbest goddamn deal I ever heard of. This type of car should have been sponsored by the "Funeral Directors of the United States." You guessed it, the rich kid's daddies bought 'em for junior. Two in the morning, junior's had three beers, got a car full of kids, he mashes that gas and starts a demonstration of hi-speed driving skills and thrills. We still had a wrecker service at the shop. Man, that was bad shit.

Piggins has been at Chevy 'bout a year now. And has a Chevy factory race team going.

Ed Cole likes that idea cause we're racing Pete Depaolo's Ford team and "Kiekhaefer's Chrysler locomotives." I'm saying "no team, just help any person who races Chevy with parts and tech help, and give the producers enough money to operate." 'Course I've already lost the argument, but don't know it. Piggins has already made a deal with a Chevy dealer in Atlanta called Nalley, and has started the company called "SEDCO" – Southern Engineering and Development Company.

The 11:00 am meeting is canceled. More fires. How 'bout 2:00 pm? To make a long story short, no meeting Monday. The meeting was about "Smokey builds engines only for SEDCO and parks his race car." This was Cole's agenda.

My message was to be, "If you start a race team, I quit." By now I've learned only way to get those bastards attention was to quit. OK, the meeting now is set for 7:30 am, Tuesday morning. Canceled, moved to 11:00 am. I'm starting to get really pissed. But Ed runs through the office and is such a good bull-shitter, I'm convinced he can't help it.

Back then one horsepower per cubic inch was best we could do. Chevy had the smallest engine by far, and I'm wanting more cubic inches, so I built a pair of 427 out of the new four-inch small blocks I got. I'm bustin' at the seams to tell Ed about my new invention. At 5500 I got 550 horsepower with one four barrel. That's 250 more horsepower than we ever saw before, and rite in here superchargers, fuel injection and double four-barrels, 3-2 barrels get shit-canned by NASCAR.

(A blessing really for Chevy 'cause the fuel injector was never gonna get the Nobel prize for engineering.)

OK, 11:00 am and the meeting is moved to 2:00 pm, "Thanks for being so patient." I'm sitting there at 1:30 pm and in zooms Bill France, "Hi, how-ya-doin?" "Great, really enjoying sitting on my ass waiting a day and a half. What you doin' here?" "Well, I had a meeting in town with Ford, just dropped in to see Cole." 'Bout 1:35 Cole comes roaring in and two minutes later calls Bill in his office. I sit there 'bout 20 minutes with smoke comin' out my ears.

When stock cars were really stock.

I finally get so fuckin' mad I tell Cole's secretary "I'm leavin', and if Cole wants to talk to me," he can call me. (I give her Pete DePaolo's phone number at Ford in Dearborn.) I had a standing offer from Pete for 40 grand a year to do anything I wanted: race, develop engines, run Indy cars (with the Ford pushrod). I was getting $1,000 a month from Chevy. The line was always, "You'll get a raise some time, but right now engineering budget used up." I called DePaolo and asked if he still wanted me. He said, "Hell yes." I said, "Get a three-year contract ready. I'll sign it in one hour." So at 3:30 I signed a three year deal with Ford.

It was a good deal, I got 40 grand a year, a free million dollar life insurance policy, free medical and dental (staff engineer stuff) and get this, they buy me an airplane, and give Thunderbirds to Paul Goldsmith and I (Goldy goes with me to Ford). I also get free trucks, free station wagons, free everything, free clothes (even agree to pay expenses for "traveling secretary"). We got new dynos, and they would pay for any new equipment. What's more, the contract was noncancelable. (The GM deal could be cancelled in 90 days and was a one year contract). On top of that I had an expense account. Never before or since had I ever had an expense account. It didn't make a damn what I charged, they paid it.

Ford flies me back to Daytona that evening. (I had never even seen inside of a GM plane, let alone get to use one for personal transportation). At 8:00 am the next day, Cole calls and says, "Hey, what happened?

I was ready to meet 10 minutes after you left." I said, "Ed, you never renewed my contract. The old one expired 90 days ago. I don't work for you any more. I signed at 3:30 yesterday with Ford for three years, for five or six times more than you paid me." I told him, "After you hang up, go look in a mirror. You'll notice you got one head, two arms, and two legs just like me and I got feelings just like you. I know you get paid many-many more dollars than me, but I don't feel you're any damn bit better than I as a human. As a matter of fact, I got better manners than you. If you came to Daytona for a 7:30 am Monday meeting, and I kept your ass waiting till past 2:00 pm the next day, and then met with someone who just walked in, would you continue to sit there till I got good and ready to see you?" He hung up.

SEDCO and Piggins were in business, Rathman and Pistone got in the deal. SEDCO was the racing version of un-employment, food stamps, small business loans. This lasted actually less than a year.

I signed with Ford early March of '57, ran a few races. First race I run with Ford the supercharger was still in. Ford had never won with it. The Supercharger was a junk McCullough with a governer in it. I pulled it into high gear and welded it. Then the carburetor could not furnish enough fuel. The needle valve was too small so I opened it up. Then it flooded so I threw the float, needle and seat away. Instead of that junk, I put in an electric pump to maintain fuel level in carburetor. We took it to Langhorne. Man that thing hauled ass.

A bad day at Atlanta.

Langhorne then was one mile dirt, fast, and would dig out bad. Well, fans knew when championship cars were there, "stay out of front rows," but stock cars "get right up front."

When Paul qualified, he covered them people 10 rows deep with mud. Run it like a champ car, sideways all around the joint. Course that was the pole at 100 miles per hour plus. Ford says, "Go on TV tonight." I said, "You didn't tell me, all I got is work clothes." DePaolo has a tailor measure me up in pits. At 5:30 pm in my motel room is a new suit, shoes, everything but a hat. I work for Ford twice, and both times they treated me like a king. GM paid very little, and they treated me like a dog. Maybe I deserved it, but how do you say nice things about a bunch of fuck-up pelicans? (You know what a pelican is? It's something that all it does is eat, squawk and shit. I'm talking yesterday.) I'm sure it's better now. I'm also sure Detroit can build a race car or race engine by itself. 'Bout time don't you think? (I'm writing this in June of '97.)

In the Langhorne race Paul laps the field. Fireball is running a Holman and Moody Ford in second. Holman comes down says "Hey, Ford really needs to win with a supercharger. Why don't you slow Paul down?" I say, "OK." I notice Fireball un-laps himself, and then toward end of race passes Paul for the lead, so I go to Holman and say, "What the fuck's going on?" He says, "We're here to race ain't we?" I tell Paul, "Get going." Next lap, coming off of four, Paul throws both rear tire treads into the grand stand. By the time we changed tires, we're out of the game. Can't catch up.

John Holman wasn't too bad a guy, but he sure had some chicken-shit ways. But his partner Ralph Moody, he was a different breed of cat. He was a racer, as good as it could ever get. His word was his bond, and let me tell you, he knew his shit about racing, chassis in particular.

Pete DePaolo, what a guy. He was a real racer. Working for him was a pleasure. He was the funniest guy I ever met, yet he was capable of corporate, political, and public relations at any level, comfortably and efficiently. But he was too trusting, and finally John Holman and Jack Passino got a wheel under him, and out of the ball park he went. I got along with John H, but after I got him figured, I handled him like a 16 foot crocodile. I never let him get behind me again after Langhorne '57. Pete, you're long gone, but not forgotten in my world.

In early May, I get a call at the track in Indianapolis from Ford telling me all manufacturers were gonna quit racing June first. They would honor my contract in full and would release me immediately if I wanted to go work for someone else. This is very secret time, kinda interesting. Nobody in Ford racing knows this yet – secrets and politics.

Well, it's now after Langhorne and I'm having some fun. Holman don't know, and Piggins and SEDCO don't know their world ends June 1st. I decide I'm gonna keep racing Fords till I use up my stuff because they were so good to me. The next race, I think, is on the hi-bank dirt "killer track" in West Memphis. Ray Fox is back helping me. He's on the way to the track towing a new Ford race car with a new Ford tow car. He runs into a mule and wagon en route and lowers both roofs (flipped 'em both). Hell yes, I was pissed, but that was part of our lives – "In every life a little mule must fall." I don't remember how we did. I remember all the "real good" and all the "real bad" shit, so that means we didn't do very good.

Well, it's Darlington time 1957. I got two race cars in good shape, the "mule killer," and another one. Curtis, Weatherly and I were on a drunk in the Carolinas, and Curtis asked me 'bout driving one of my cars at Darlington. I think he was in Holman or Ford's dog-house for something, so I said, "Sure, great idea." So we go to Darlington as a two car team with myself, two part-time mechanics (Emory Lunsford and "Snake") and a full-timer who has had enough of racing and is there under protest, Harry Van Driel. Harry is a damn good race mechanic, did a couple years with Marshall Teague first.

Well, all kinds of stuff's going on. Remember "Saturday Evening Post"? (A big seller magazine). They get a hold of me and say, "You've won Darlington three times. If you win this year, we'd like to do a feature story 'bout you." I do the right thing. I'm half-drunk and don't want to be bothered, so I say, "Don't bother me, I'm partying," and hang up. Next couple days they call again so I ask, "You get four or five pages of pictures and words, and people pay money for it, what do I get?" He says, "I'll call you back." A couple of days later he finds me in Atlanta, but I'm in a very serious drinking situation with very interesting companions (biggest tits I ever saw in my life attached to some kind of a sex maniac). He says, "We'll pay you $10,000. Well, if I wasn't so drunk, I'd have fainted. But after years of watching France operate, I said, "Not interested. $25,000 or forget it."

The next day in Daytona a telegram comes, "OK, we'll pay 25 (if this and if that)…man, that telegram sobered my ass up quick.

At the time I've got a single engine airplane and in a good head wind some birds can pass me. There is a new twin engine Piper Apache and I know a dealer who's got a demo that he'll sell for 25 grand. I say, "Bring that bird to Darlington, I'll buy it race day night." Well, everything goes pretty good in the racing department. It looks like Goldsmith in one car, and Curtis Turner in the other are, by quite a bit, the fastest in practice. They qualify one-two.

Now things are starting to change and some problems start to rear their ugly heads. On Saturday before the race, there is no practice and big parade in Darlington. I'm working on the cars while Goldy and Curtis are in the parade on a float. A messenger arrives, out of breath, and says, "Goldsmith's and Turner's wives will be arriving at the Florence airport in 20 minutes." Now that don't sound too bad does it? But it really is bad news. I've got a "secretary" with me, and to keep cost down, she stays in my room. My wife has a Daytona detective staying in same motel I'm in. (Very wasteful, you can imagine the expense: airfare, motel, food. Whew!) Paul, for some reason or other, was kind enough to be sharing his room with an Eastern Airlines stewardess who loved racing and racers. Curtis had a "cousin" staying with him. She was in our lingo "an import" – when that baby moved, all eyes were on it. Anyway, Turner's and Goldy's wives will be at motel in 45 minutes. Holy shit, I gotta move.

I haul ass to our motel, collect up the two gals, all their luggage and put this and them in my room. (I don't have to tell you what my secretary and the other two ladies thought about this, do I?) I dive back in their rooms, clean out the panties, hair pins, and personal effects 'bout one minute ahead of the wives. (Found an interesting looking, I guess you'd call it a sexual toy, under one bed. I guess this was before cigars were popular for such things.) I'd sent a messenger to notify Goldsmith and Turner of their good fortune and unexpected company, but without information on my cleanup and the temporary housing changes. (They are in the parade in Darlington.)

Well, my secretary stays, Turner's "cousin" leaves town, Goldy's stewardess says "She ain't goin' no place." (Apparently Goldy has been particularly nice to her.) I manage to get her a room, same motel. You'd think that would be enough trouble for a poor hard workin' racer. Hell no. Not even close.

The "big deal" for gamblers then was to bet on who'd lead the first lap. Big-big money movin' in this deal. Well, Goldy falls in with one bunch, and agrees that "Turner leads first lap." At the same time, Turner has been approached by another group of gamblers, and agrees that "Goldy will lead the first lap." Nobody knows anything about what the other side is doing 'cept me. On the pace lap, I find out about the double-deal.

So in first lap of the race Goldsmith leads going across start finish line with both rear wheels locked-up and Turner pushing. After that the two Fords are long gone, for a while. Around 25 laps into the race, a hell of a wreck happens going into turn three. Fonty Flock, Goldy, and Billy Myers, are some of those collected. Myers dies and Goldy is pretty wounded. We got a hospital tent behind garage area. At first it looked like Goldy was hurt real bad (he really wasn't). Matter of fact he won a race someplace three or four days later.

The hospital tent has a wife in it, and a very concerned stewardess outside who is positive she should be in there with Paul. I notice she ain't listening to me and I still got Turner racing (and leading the race) and don't forget the 25 grand deal, so I decide "fuck-it." I leave a friend in charge of the mess and go back to the race. Well, we were getting pretty well into the race, and are having no trouble controlling the race car, when Lee Petty goes roaring into three underneath, and slides up into Turner. (If this pisses you off Lee, I don't give a shit)

Four or five years ago, I got job of puttin Lee in a hall of fame. (Nobody else wanted to do it.) But in truth, he deserved it. He and about eight or nine other guys got NASCAR going and never got credit, or pay for it either. Lee didn't travel with the gang, or stay in same motels we did. He took his family. Momma was Lee's scorekeeper (for NASCAR). Maurice and Richard were 'bout 12 and 14 years old when I first remember them. I particularly remember Richard, sitting in dirt at Darlington, sanding the ports in a flathead six

Plymouth block. (Lee run a Plymouth coupe then.) I used to call him "Richard One Finger" cause he'd sit and smooth car parts with one finger pushin' emory cloth.

Lee seemed like he was always in a pissing contest with somebody. I remember a race in West Palm Beach. As I remember it, Herb Thomas and I won it and Lee and Curtis were second and third. I don't remember who was which. Anyway, we are at local Hudson dealer's shop for a post race tear down. Lee and Curtis get in big argument. Lee swings at Curtis, who ducks it. Turner's back is against a plywood partition where, about a foot over his head, a piece of Bear aligning equipment weighing 'bout 40 or 50 pounds was hung on a couple of hooks. Lee's fist hit the plywood and down comes the piece of iron on Turner's head. Turner needs a few minutes to wake up. While I'm giving him a drink he says, "Damn, the ol' sonna-bitch can hit Smoke!"

Another time, I think it was Richard's first race in Canada and we're on a half mile dirt track in a cow pasture. The race is damn near over and Richard's leading, on his way to winning his first race. Damn if Lee don't go out of his way to spin his son Richard out. In that Hall of Fame induction, Richard was in the audience, and I asked him to confirm it. He did. Lee got up and said, (looking at me) "I never did like you either." Actually, if Lee had been just a little better as a baseball pitcher, we would have never had heard of "the Petty's" in auto racing. Lee damn near made it in the St. Louis baseball organization as a pitcher.

Well shit, with Turner in the wall, there goes the Apache. I patch up Turner's car but he is hurt, so he can't drive. Joe Weatherly jumps in. The car looks like a bow-legged, cross-eyed, flying junkyard but he finishes 10th with it. That's enough for one day right? Wrong, Weatherly teaches Lee not to fuck with his buddy Curtis – put him into the turn three wall.

Goldy and Turner are both in hospital. I have removed engine out of Goldy's car and sold what's left of it for $8 to the junkman. (That was a brand new race car a week before). I'm towing Turner's wreck on a trailer, and am trying to get out of track to see Goldy and Turner at the hospital in Florence. I'm damn near out of the traffic, and someone cuts me off in a brand new Desoto. Yes, Desoto. So I get out and say "Mister, please stay put. I'm actually ahead of you and you got bad manners." He gives me some shit (course by now I've had four good pulls on a fifth). I can see, he don't see my point, so I try another approach. I say, "If you squeeze up again, your "new shiny" is gonna look awful funny without a front-end." You know the rest. He did and I did. Just about tore left front fender, grill and hood off that poor little Desoto. I did a good job too, didn't hurt the radiator or right front suspension, or the new Ford tow car. (Remember the other new '57 Ford tow car had just had the roof lowered by mule). A couple troopers standing there arrested Mr. Desoto for some terrible offense like "using auto to hurt people" then gave me a police escort to the hospital.

In September, 2001, it will be 44 years later, and I still haven't seen the guy from the "Saturday Evening Post." Guess the deal's off huh? (Never even got a ride in the damn Apache.) They say everything happens for the best, but I still don't see, 40 years later, why it's better. I don't see why we didn't win and why I didn't get the Apache. How'd the deal turn out at the hospital? Ask Paul, he's still around. When I got there Paul still had one too many worried ladies around.

My secretary? She got pissed and flew back to Daytona with the detective.

About Tars

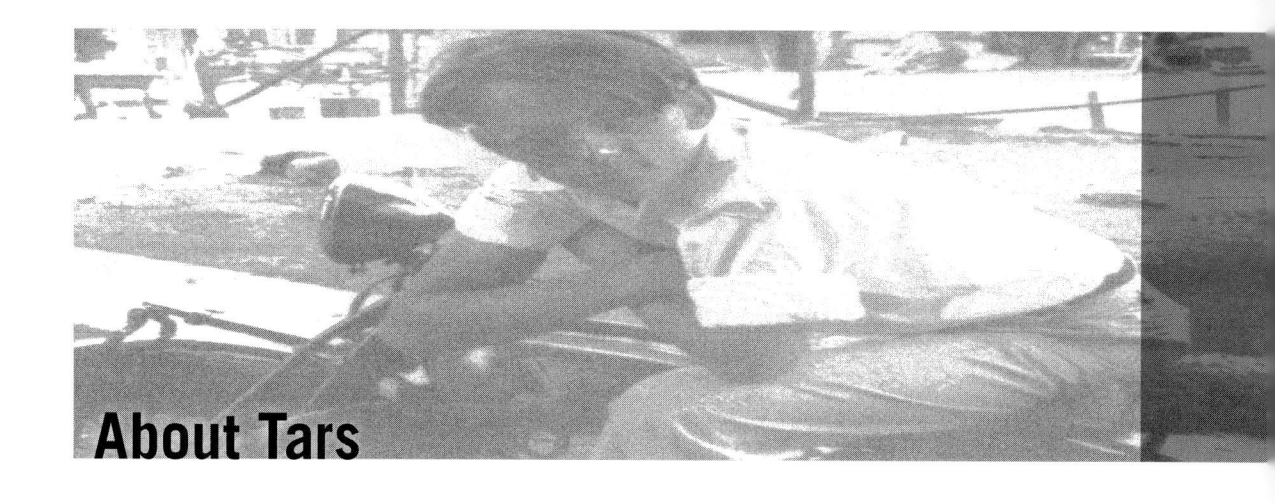

The biggest single problem a stock car racer had in 1947 was tires. Up till about 1975 was 28 years of pure hell regarding blowed "tars." (Southern for "tires"). The cars as primitive as they were, were years ahead of the tires. In racing blowed tires killed and injured more people than any other single thing. Blowed tires were the biggest expense in all of racing. Blowed tires also probably made more race fans than any other single item. The crashes, the excitement of race cars smacking into walls and each other with the busted shit flying all over the damn place, and the excitement of any second, any lap, the double boom of tire and the wall kept the fans just one notch below heart attack.

This part of the story features a young tire engineer (self taught). He was my and about every other stock car racer's first interface into the mysteries and how to transfer the power from the engine into the race track, and how to do it in such a way that a wrecker was not necessary between the start and finish of the race. This was part "A." Part "B" has not and never will be solved. That is to run every race track flat out all the way around. In 2001 the Goodyear stock car racing tire is light years better than in 1947, but the search for "better" will continue as long as racing exists.

Read this as if you and I were talking and I answered your questions for two days. From time to time I didn't know the answer, but knew someone who had the information and called and talked with them. I started off wanting to just tell you 'bout a guy named John Laux, who played a tremendous part in developing a better stock car and Indy tire, but his memory I guess went through too many power outages, and some of the dope got lost. I wanted you all to know about and credit this man for dedicating his adult life to racing tires. I damn sure don't want to see a tombstone "John Laux, Firestone tire changer."

I can't make the story come out chronologically. There is just too damn much to remember and so many players. So as I jump around in years it is because this is how it unfolded from my and the other's memories, and/or records. Give me a little break. Some of this was over 50 years ago.

Where were you on June 17, 1947 at 2:00 pm? What were you doing? See what I mean?

Some of this is funny. Some was serious — up to and including permanent injury and death.

Some of this was poorly thought out and executed. Really, the history concerning the development of racing tires from 1947 to 1975 is about like my story, not well planned, but considering what happened in real life, probably couldn't have been much different. Consider this: as of December 1, 1998, Goodyear tires is the only US product that carries world class racing ranking. So somehow, some way, tires got done. This was a terribly expensive evolution. If you don't get anything else out of this part, and you are a racer, think very carefully before you send our tire companies to hell about something that angers you regarding race tires. If Goodyear, Hoosier and Firestone quit this week, what would we do? (Open wheel racers, this could be your world very soon).

I betcha tire company profits from race tires is not a lucrative business as it's relationship to big time auto racing is structured. I doubt it would be enough to keep the blimps running. So consider starting a "race tire manufacturer" national holiday, like say, Goodyear or Firestone's birthday.

Might be a good idea if some of you do learn how to manufacture good race tires. If we have one strong lawsuit loss to a major tire manufacturer, our lawyers have got the laws so screwed up, automobile racing could be history in a year or less. Nope, I don't work for any tire company. This is just racer to racer. Hell, half of the time I can't get them to answer the phone, 'bout like "genuine" Perkins was at the end at Chevy.

Jim was the Buick sales manager that quit and went to work for Honda (or maybe it was Toyota) and really set their asses on fire. Chevy was headed to the shithouse at 100 miles-an-hour when Jim was the first hi-bucker GM ever took back at a hell of a raise and position to manage Chevy. He was general manager the year they put that hi-buck, piece of shit, junk English engine in the Corvette. I told him that engine and car was gonna cause him more trouble than all of Chevy. Two-and-a-half years later when he was half shit-faced he told me I was right. His reign at Chevy wasn't genuine. He did busy work for three years then they fired his ass. In the last six months Jim wouldn't take my calls so I saved some money.

We have heard many stories about how Edison invented the light bulb, Goodyear and Firestone invented tires, Henry Ford invented the first practical car and Bill France invented stock car racing. But in real life none of them did, or could have pulled it off without a hell of a lot of good help. Who was the first guy who stuck his finger in Edison's light bulb socket and hollered "Goddam! Shut it off!" We'll never know, but I can tell you about one of those guys. This part is about an unsung hero of racing, John Frank Laux, the first human representative of a major tire company (Firestone) sent to the deep South, Darlington, South Carolina, to stick his finger into a socket built by Harold Brasington, called the Darlington Raceway.

This tire eating son-of-a-bitch was 1 3/8 mile, but kinda like John's real first name, changed depending who introduced him and the track size according to who measured it. It had lots of bank to it. Both ends of the track were different. It had four different turns. Well, what do you expect? Harold did it with mules and about as much money as one new hi-buck eyetalian sports car costs now. Harold is still going strong. (Nope. Now gone, guess I'm writing too slow.)

The inventor of paved hi-bank stock car racing. He says now he didn't use mules, but there are pictures around.

Well, lets get to it. All we had to race were regular store bought tars from the gas station, Montgomery Wards or Sears Roebuck catalog, parts stores, recappers and tire rationing coupon crooks. We were just barely starting to get tar stores. Hell, in 1946, to buy a tire you had to have a tire rationing coupon. To get the coupon you had to show the tar rationing board a good reason (like to get to work). Or we had crooks who sold us coupons. Some of our early racing heroes and pioneers believe it or not hung on the edge of going to the penitentiary 'bout this. Maybe I shouldn't call them crooks. Maybe it was just that they had trouble interpreting the laws. My father-in-law saved one cats ass from a long vacation in government furnished housing. If I told you who it was, you would fall out of your chair. (I may decide to tell the story before I finish. I'll give you a clue. His initials were B.F. My father-in-law was district attorney for the Daytona Beach area.)

Can you imagine going to a tire rationing board and asking for ten coupons to buy tires to use on a race car? Tires weren't cheap, good price was six to ten bucks apiece. Consider this, with average price we paid for a '37 coupe to make a race car out of was $35. So some tires got borrowed from unwilling donors and never returned. Tires were our major problem. No way could we build or modify a tire to make a satisfactory race tire. You know there was a factory tire man before John Laux. Otto Wolfer, an honest to God tire engineer with Indy race car experience.

Marshall Teague (a stock car Christopher Columbus) was a Pure Oil gas station owner, and Marshall got Otto, who worked for Pure Oil then, and believe it or not, Pure Oil built their own tires. Marshall got Otto to build a so called "stock car racing tar." Otto missed it and it ended up "just a tire." I'm sure Otto was limited by financial and other considerations, but the cold facts were that the tire wasn't worth a shit either.

When we first began racing stock cars, tires have total control over our progress. For a while there the speeds were stuck because of no tire technology. Tire companies didn't seem to be interested enough to make a tire for stock car racing, and who could blame them really. Problem was, street tires just didn't hold up under racing conditions. Another problem, even if we could afford a bunch of tires, we just couldn't take that many with us. Remember, we had to carry our tires from race to race, with no trucks and no trailers. All your spare parts and tires had to go in the race car or tow car.

In 1950, at the first Darlington race, over 80 cars started. Before the race was over, Speedy Thompson had the record: 21 blown tires. And I can't remember if he even finished. I was there helping Marshall Teague. We showed up there with a Lincoln and about 20 tires. Turned out that was just 'bout enough rubber for the warm up.

Darlington, from day one, was a mud hole both inside and outside the track. Hell, part of the pits were mud and the best parts were mud and gravel. Seems like I changed a hundred tires slippin' around in those nasty pits.

It was the first 500 mile race we ever had. The most elaborate team had twelve spares mounted at the start of the race. In the race, 635 tires were blown. What saved our asses was the fact that the race fans in general were Southern Baptists. Very religious folk, no drinking, but they were partial to medicinal beverages called tonics.

During that first race some snake oil peddler from "Luzzeanna" brought up a forty foot trailer full of a tonic called "Hadacol." I tried some and believe we could have run it for fuel in a midget car. (they ran on alcohol) Well, this stuff tuned up the spectators so that when they saw us running out of "tars," the infield fans started offering us their tires, wheels and all. They pleaded, "take my tars," now these were real race fans. Would you loan Earnhardt the wheels and tires off your car today?, I don't think so.

We took wheels and tires all afternoon. When we jacked up their cars and pickups, we put wooden coke boxes under each wheel. (Back then cokes came in little eight ounce bottles delivered in useful wooden crates.) When the race was over, the infield is a mud hole, the fan's tires were blown and in the process their wheels ruined. As we load up they are all hangin' on the fence wanting their tars back. Since we can't solve the problem in a satisfactory way, we move on. I can still see all of those cars sitting on coke boxes in the rear view mirror as we were dragging what was left of our racer out with a tow bar. That began a night trip back home and back to work round 8:00 am or whenever we got there.

From 1947 to 1955 we somehow made it on cotton fabric, natural rubber or some percentage of synthetic and natural rubber. Seems like about everybody's tire had about the same general construction. None could stand any temperature over 250 degrees. All had too much tread depth.

We swapped stories of success and failure reference various tire manufacturers. Firestone had one tire I believed called 'The Champion,' but as I remember it, I believe the only thing it did better than any other tire was it made more noise when it blew. I played around with recaps quite a bit, and it seemed like if I widened the rims and cut down on tread thickness and headed towards a slick, things got better. But France figured out where I was headed and ruled five inch maximum rim width and no slicks allowed. In those days standard tires were four ply (real) and six ply (real) was the heavy duty deal. We thought six ply would be better, but not so. They ran hotter plus they were heavy and hurt acceleration. We looked at Indy tires. They were 16 inch and 18 inch rim sizes, very heavy, no good for rough dirt or rough asphalt, and next to no footprint (too skinny). Sprint car tires were not strong enough. We weighed about 4,000 pounds or better from 1946 to 1953. We get by the best we can 'cept for help Pure Oil gave Marshall Teague.

In 1953 an ex-driver, a knowledgeable tire person shows up. Dave Evans, as Goodyear tire company is helping Chrysler who jumps into NASCAR with Kiekhaefer. This is a Chrysler factory deal with strong NASCAR support. These were heavy, big-engined, powerful cars like Chrysler 300's. This started with a tire Goodyear made for the Mexican Road Race. 120 to 135 miles an hour, all day long on skinny asphalt rough roads from Central America clean through Mexico to El Paso, Texas. Mountains 80 percent of the way. Now it turns out that Firestone also made a Mexican Road Race tire, but neither of these two or the Otto Wolfer Pure Oil tire helped us. Still blistered and blew. But yes, they were some better. All this is serious enough that quite a few drivers got crippled or killed.

We are learning that natural rubber takes heat better than synthetics and the tire companies recognize cord angles, and carcass materials also contribute both positively and negatively to the tires ability to stand the abuse and at the same time we found tread material composition and thickness played a big part in tire development. 99 percent of what I'm gonna discuss is circle track, US in regards to lateral traction and temperature behavior and control and in regards to wear characteristics.

We are now finding out that tire pressure is critical and starting to notice best tire for the right front ain't best for the left front and same for rear. Up to September, 1955, tire manufacturers support is mostly hot air and bullshit. Stock car racing is with very serious problems in reference to safety. Got so bad for Fireball that his official song was "Hello Walls." (I like the song they usually played when I walked in, "On Top of Ole Smokey.")

The first Darlington race was won with a slow car, on secret Firestone Mexican Road Race tires. Johnny Mantz driving a Plymouth owned by Bill France and Enoch Staley, mechanicized by a little sharp hillbilly named Hubert Westmoreland. He had no tire trouble and beat us so bad he stopped long enough to drink a coke on his last pit stop. We were using lug wrenches, (no air) and jacking in the mud, dirt and gravel. You think that is crude? How about two open 50 gallon barrels, one full of water and one full of gas. (Them days you supplied your own fuel). Darlington, first race. Yup, some had a lot of trouble running hot then. Needed lots of water.

From 1950 to 1955 very little happened to get a better tire. September 1955, we gained.

Chevrolet wanted to race. I took the job. A one shot deal to run the new '55 Chevrolet V8 car in the Darlington 500. I found out the car was three or four miles an hour short on speed. In five or six hours that was 12 to 15 laps down. So I had help from Mauri Rose, a Chevy engineer who won Indy three times. He not only knew tires, knew everybody in the world who knew tires, including Otto Wolfer. Mauri and I worked for Ed Cole, the daddy of the small block '55 Chevy. I told Mauri our only chance to win was a better tire. So, I sent him to go anywhere in the world looking for a better tire. I wanted an 18 inch tire. (I found a loop-hole in the rules. No rim diameter specified) I told Mauri, "See if you can find some 18 inch tires" "Why?" he asked. "They would run cooler than 15 inch tire." Again, "Why?" "Takes 'em longer to make a round."

After three weeks Mauri said that he had talked to Otto Wolfer about this, and Otto told him that Firestone had made a special tire for Briggs Cunningham to use at Le Mans in 1955. Briggs took 25 of them to France to test against Dunlop and chose Dunlop. Firestone had 175 left and decided they were no good. This was a new tire named "Super Sport." White wall on one side and 16 inches in diameter. Mauri found the tires in an Akron junk yard. (Nate Rothkins' place) Nate, if you had burned those tires racing history would be different. The day they were going to burn them Mauri bought them for one buck apiece (Nate wanted $1.50). We practiced, qualified and won the race on one set of tires that I cut 100 thou off the top of the tread. Still could have run 500 more miles on same tires. Four bucks worth of tires won the 1955 Darlington 500 mile race. I made the local Bear frame alignment man famous. I credited his superior front end alignment to the sensational tire wear.

Firestone then made a 15 inch copy of the Super Sport, and stock car racing finally got a race tire in 1956, but without white walls. Now Goodyear has been picking up race cars from 1953 to 1956 because Firestone didn't think stock cars were worth the expense and trouble. In the Darlington, September '56 for the 500 mile race, John Laux shows up with two tire changing machines and a helper, Bobby Summers. They get a place in the mud to put their air compressor and tire machine and a light bulb. Only thing missing was pedal powered DC electrical generator and John and Bobby in coonskin caps. This was the wild frontier.

Pete DePaolo engineered the Ford team. He gives Laux 200 wheels to mount for starters. There were 90 cars entered. This is day one for the big time auto racers, big trucks are now standard for Keikhaefer, (Chrysler) and Depaolo racing (Ford). Up until now I mount all of my own tires, 45 pounds of air on the right side, 20 pounds in the left front, and 30 pounds in the left rear. Hell, it hardly touched the ground. My equipment for testing tread for hardness is an ice pick. We used talcum powder in mounting tires. Same stuff used on babies tails. John scares me to death. He slops liquid lube on tire bead in mounting. I know this is gonna make the tire slip on rim and pull the valve stem but it don't seem to cause that problem. John borrowed another tire machine from Depaolo Engineering. For the record, knowing and racing with Pete DePaolo was a privilege in my memories. (He was Holman and Moody's "grandfather.")

John also hired another local man who, as near as I can remember screwed up about all he touched. The first Afro-southern American race tire technician, but when the smoke cleared away, changing tires from 8:00 am to midnight every practice day. Firestone was on 73 of the 75 qualified cars. Goodyear had 2 cars, Kiekhaefer's stuff. The two Chryslers on Goodyear were Speedy Thompson (Chrysler) switched to Firestone in 18 laps and Frank Mundy (Dodge) switched in 28 laps. Well, time the race was over I'm impressed with John and also gave good marks to Bobby. Hopefully Ginger, John's wife, won't get upset by my evaluation score I gave John but he worked hard and I mean hard. 18 hours a day in the 90 degree heat and 90 percent humidity, in the mud and rain, in the open with no shade, with one more character builder. If you opened your mouth to talk, 50 black gnats flew in. Part one of the test, both got A+.

Part two of the test was the ability to perform during the day after three to five hours of heavy drinking at night and at the same time doing our best to convince the local young (some were middle age) women to become race fans. Well, John passed this test handily and got extra points because he was considered a yankee. Bobby, it turned out, was a world Olympic class drinker. Actually he could out drink Firestone's managers, and they were definitely Olympic quality. But Bobby did little to entice women to become race fans. Well what can anyone do when you are unconscious? Both were voted genuine racers membership and part of our family. (One part of the test genuine racers had to pass that I'm omitting). When all survivors pass on, the rest of the test should be described by a historian (kinda like last guy out, lock the door). Yes it did have something to do with women and nationality origin.

John Laux's arrival really made us feel that we would shortly get help. Up to '56 we were helpless. Nothing we could do to fix the tires and all help up to then was ineffective, inconsistent, irregular and subject to cancellation at any second. Dave Evans (Goodyear), was a good guy and a racer but he didn't have enough power or money to really run a hi-buck tire program. All tire companies acted like we didn't have enough to offer to be worth the cost. (Boy, that's sure changed hasn't it?) When John got enough hi-test in him he would talk like help was coming. He knew everybody in racing and Firestone and he made sense. Well, too bad he spent so much time getting his southern real racer's membership. The company didn't appreciate his experience and solid relationship with the racers and John missed out on an opportunity to manage the program.

All big companies were alike back then. Probably still are. The brown-nosing, good bull slingers got the top jobs and therefore control.

The rest of the story played out the same whether it was tires or engines, etc. The technology for example on how to make a stock car race tire was a total unknown. Sports cars, Indy cars, sprinters or midgets and motorcycles were known, but they too had limited know-how and experience. Let me take you from ground zero to 1956. Tires we could buy in 1947 (war was over I believe 'bout September 1946), were synthetic rubber and totally hopeless. Got hot and blew. Guaranteed to 35 miles an hour, so the tip was to find pre-war tires or police or military natural rubber tires. They are one to six years old, and sometimes used. We tried recaps, and that as a rule was no good. In late '47 and '48 we could with some luck, get new six ply natural rubber 6.70 x 15, 7.10 x 15 and 7 60 x 15. The 6.70, 7.10, 7.60 Numbers were maximum width of tire inflated on a 5 or 5.5 inch rim (wide) The 15 was dimension of the diameter of the bead where it slid on the rim. The 5.5 inch maximum rim width was NASCAR law, but there was no diameter rule up to October 1955.

The fabric was a good Egyptian cotton. Ball park cord angles were 48 degrees on passenger cars and more around 54 degrees on high performance tires. Tires had, and still have about three different kinds of rubber in them. The tread was special for wear and ability to stand heat, just under the tread is a layer called "under base." This is aimed at bonding and heat control excellence. Thirdly, every cord and every wire in the tire has a rubber coating, again for best heat and bonding results. Next, is side wall rubber and it's stiff, hard and inflexible rubber. Tip here: use a very thin layer particularly the outside we see. Why? Thinner is cooler. Why is stiffer better? The tire is fastened to the road at one end and to the rim at the other. Consider walls flex. You, for example, turn steering wheel five degrees and footprint only turns one degree with deep flexible side walls. Now go to stiff-short sidewalls and five degrees of steering wheel gives you four degrees at the road.

Going back to cord angle for a minute, why is more cord angle better? Because more cord angle resist tire getting bigger in outer diameter from centrifugal force at speed. (Ever notice how tires "grow" on Kenny Bernstein's car when he does a burn out?) Beads then and now were steel, but bead sole angle where tire slid onto rim to hold the tire from turning was only about five degrees then and tires did rotate on us on the rims. A real problem. We ran tubes 100 percent. No such thing as tubeless yet. We ran very good natural rubber tubes but if tires rotated, valve stems were pulled loose from the tube. Some of us tried drilling into bead flange and putting in sheet metal screws. This created a cause for concern, like where do these screws go if they fall out? Eventually this gets fixed in a much better way.

Back then, blowing and blistering tires was a way of life. Happened to everybody. Winners and losers alike. Those who ran up front were used as a barometer for some of the sharpies who ran a "just don't get lapped pace." We used regular compressor air. Yup, with lots of moisture, which caused the tire pressure to build up, say ten pounds. Well, this was supposed to be bad regarding handling. The harder the tires, as a general rule, the less your lateral traction will be. So I tried nitrogen. My observation was, hell, that didn't help. Maybe made it even worse. How come?

That nitrogen was not totally moisture free so we got a little better lateral traction, but blew and blistered worse. Why? The wet air out of a compressor on a hot humid day would condense the moisture to steam in the tire. Water boils at 212 degrees at sea level, right? Tire air temperature 250 to 300 degrees F, so even at 50 pounds pressure the moisture turns to steam, the steam evened out the hot spots in the tire. This gave us a few more miles before the shotgun went off. Yup, that is how it sounded. You could hear it over the engines.

We found another band-aid. Tread as a rule never wore out. Seemed like the hot tip was a hard tread. We called Firestones "Flintstones." The tire blistered first and a good driver could feel it. But what the hell could you do about it? You sweated it out, hoping someone else blew a tire and brought out the yellow flag before you blew one and totaled your car. The band-aid was to cut the tread off except for 180, 125 or 80 thousandths in depth. The tires run cooler and it prolonged the tire's misery. Can you imagine running 40 to 45 times a year (yup, the early racing schedule for NASCAR was that many races a year). Running from 100 to 150 miles per hour, waiting for a goddam tire to blow? Then with the paved high banks, waiting for it to happen at 180 mph? I think back then the better drivers banged their balls with their ankles when they walked.

Now. Let's get back to John Laux. So you can see the big part he played in getting good raceable tires on stock cars. John has rolled his speedometer over a couple of times. Born a Hoosier in Bedford Indiana on November 24, 1921 (if you want to send him a birthday card). Still married to Ginger, had one daughter, Sharon, and now has a great grandson named George. He spent three-and-a-half years with the Army in Europe, with a tank outfit to help tear the German's asses up. I want you to know John as he is. A 60 year racing veteran who loves racing and spent his whole life racing, and is still around racing. This year, 1995 at Indy, he helped all of Dick Simon's sponsors and their friends get loaded up on cholesterol and alcohol. He has been there and done that with race tires for 50 years.

He wanted to drive a midget like every other boy in Indiana, but ended up a test driver for Firestone tires at Indy with a motorcycle. He worked for the tire Einstein, Otto Wolfer who, on the side, rode the motorcycle in the tire tests also. When the motorcycle wore out John lost his job. By now he knows everybody in Firestone racing and a fair number of the Indy racers.

In 1950 John got a job with Firestone to go to Darlington race track to help with tires for a championship car race (Indy cars). This track really wasn't good for those cars. Too fast. They call the track "the lady in black." What a stupid name. The track is 100 percent male, and is a son-of-a-bitch on tires, chassis and driver. By 1951 John is following the championship cars for Firestone with Bill McCreary, the open wheel racing boss (but not in engineering). John must have been hired and fired or laid off by Firestone six times in six years because of budget reasons. No tire company took stock car racing seriously. An awful lot happens in here reference to racing tires, but it's all Indy stuff.

Firestone is trying a heavier, more powerful car for a Indy test car. Ed cole tries to solve the power problem with a Caddy engine (he is chief engineer at Caddy), but doesn't work out.

Next a Chrysler engine goes in and it has the power and does the job. General LeMay has become a half-assed expert in sport car racing. He and France, plus George Wallace, became ass-hole buddies. LeMay and Wallace run for president and vice president. (I guess France would be secretary of treasury.) The world, including NASCAR and Firestone gets involved in sports car racing at Air Force bases. LeMay does stir it up enough that Firestone does get with it and some progress is made. John Laux comes through again like a champ, rightfully criticizing LeMay and race officials as a bunch of stupid assholes who are screwing up the races. This works great. Lemay gets John fired in five seconds, all of this is happening from 1950 to 1955.

1953 Dave Evans is working for Goodyear and shows up in NASCAR. He gets Lee Petty to run a tire test in West Palm Beach in '53. Now we got Goodyear tread patterns on NASCAR tracks. Dave is an ex-racer and he knows enough 'bout tires to be dangerous ('bout like us). Dave is a lucky cat. In 1960 he, Paul McDuffie and I are on edge of Darlington apron walking up the pits in front of the pit wall after Paul's and my cars pitted. We both are on Goodyears. Dave is on the outside, Paul is in the middle and I'm on inside. A car out of control kills McDuffie and two other mechanics. Evans and I don't get a scratch even though our three heads were touching each other when we got hit.

Well, now I notice Firestone is starting to be nicer, but in lip service only. I think Goodyear is making Firestone nervous. Goodyear could have taken over real easy in '53, '54 and '55, but they didn't give Evans the support he needed when the iron was hot. In those days, one man built the car, the engine and painted it, did it all. Usually with free help at night. So learning about tires was crammed in tightly in each chief mechanic's brain along with all the rest. By now the driver is starting to get very interested in tire technology. I guess they were getting tired of crashing and doing sheet time. So when John Laux shows up in '56 at all races, and is starting to address our needs and pushing hard for Firestone's solutions, I for one could put up with getting drunk to find out what was happening in total for tires. Cause John ate, drank and lived with us at the tracks, and during our tests and off time as well. He saw all of our problems.

I spent most of my time hunting horsepower. I was short on chassis and long on aerodynamics, so my car was a great test car up to the time I quit running NASCAR in 1970. I never found a tire that we couldn't destroy in 30 laps. John fed info to me to try and help the chassis and kept on suggesting changes to Firestone engineers, and really by late '56 John knew more about tires than any of us, including most of the engineers. Man, he was dead serious about Firestone racing tires. If Goodyear won, John would get so upset that if he had been a rice burner he would have committed hari kari.

Some facts: 1956, 57, early '58 race tires cost $49.00 apiece mounted. Tubes extra. Goodyear and Firestone didn't think balancing was needed until 1958. Then they went to bubble balancing (no spin). Even Indy bubble balanced only. There was no charge for mounting or balancing. I never bought a race tire in my life. I guess I lucked out. And in the late '60s I got paid $120,000 tire (Goodyear) money to run Indy only (driver got half of it). Some got $250,000 to run a season (Indy cars). By the end of 1956 the world according to John said every race track required a different tire. The right front and right rear tire would be the same. The left front a tire all by itself. And the left rear another tire all by itself, plus it needed to be at least 1/4 to 1/2 or maybe as much as 1 inch smaller in diameter. (Hell, now how 'bout three or four inches smaller) We called that "stagger." Any stagger we got was by stretch from over pressurization, inter change

157

of tire models, and/or manufacturer. In 1965 the Wood Brothers went to Indy and did the tire changing for Colin Chapman's Lotus, driven by Jim Clark. The team won the race. Chapman had the juice to have stagger built into his tires, big time stagger. The Woods got special stock car tires with mucho stagger. They kept their traps shut about it. They had Pearson for a driver and they simply tore our asses up for a couple years before they lost their secret advantage.

Tire pressure would be different for each tire. John found out that rim width and rim offset were critical and affective. John brought to my attention the difference in new pavement and old pavement, clean track and greasy track, cold track, hot track, what happens to a track after a hard rain, clouds, or bright sun. Sometimes tires need to be broke in, some needed to be run as stickers (new). Some tires get greasy and slow down (Goodyears) some tires get better when hot (Firestone). What happens if you run in worn rubber out of the groove? The importance of keeping tires clean on a yellow.

Now by 1957 we have 15 to 20 different Firestone tires and same for Goodyear. Who the hell can keep up with this? John.

Plus Norris Friel, NASCAR's chief inspector, he wants all tires to be the same. So tire companies start secret coding of special phony tires. We got to the edge of having specific Fireball, Richard Petty or curtis Turner tires. All drivers liked different chassis and tire combinations. Hell, by 1958 I am so lost I give up. All of the hot dogs test every couple of weeks. I don't have time to test and go by what John tells me. If he bum steers me, I park the car in front of the grandstands with a sign by the bad tire sending that particular tire to hell for all to see. I'm sorry now because some of this probably will reduce his life span by something. ('Bout in here John's got enough inside dope he can about win a race for you.)

By 1970 some race shops like the Petty's, looked like a tire factory warehouse from left over race test tires, all different. I have a problem keeping up with John because some times I'd run Goodyear for awhile and in January, 1961 I quit drinking, so I lost out on the 12 beer tire engineering sessions three or four nights a week that John chaired. Holman and Moody and Ford were running wide open in here and them cats did some kind of testing and chassis setup testing. That information didn't get into non-Ford ears or eyes. Well hell, can we fault them for that? Nope!

By 1967, Goodyear and Firestone had 'bout an even tire and the tire companies decided to buy drivers for the Indy thing. Each had about 15 drivers from $250,000 a year on down per driver. Ten years before this, the two tire companies are concerned about just development and tire manufacturing cost, and in 1959 Goodyear and Firestone have a secret motel meeting to cut cost. Today a deal like this probably would put ten people in the penitentiary for 20 years. Firestone says, "All we want is Darlington and Daytona." Goodyear says "OK," and gets the rest of the tracks by default. The expense of a factory tire race program was so huge the tire companies cleverly devised an accounting system so even the top management people who managed the total corporation couldn't really know what the real cost was. I don't think anyone knows what it cost to build each race tire. Race tires are all certified up to x-raying the complete tire. Race tires are all hand built. My guess is a set of Winston Cup tires today cost Goodyear two grand, and they sell them for fifteen hundred. Indy tires cost more.

Remember you have to include engineering, testing, servicing and unused stock left over. 1998 Indy tires are junk after checker flag falls. Every track has it's own tire just about. At Indy one hot dog driver can use 100 sets in practice, and the Indy race. The 1999 Indy had a whole new tire, but the word "Eagle" was not on any of the 500 mile race cars. Goodyear is starting to disappear on race tires. It's gone from Formula One. Indy?

Suppose they cost $4,000 a set to make. Run that through your calculator x 33, plus how many unqualified cars and back up cars that don't race, say another 40. It's like the monkey said when he pissed in the cash register, "This is gonna run into money." By the way most of these Indy tires are free. Many times when I see and hear tire company's getting verbal and news media abuse, I wonder what the hell racing would do if say, Goodyear said, "Adios." Firestone? Yeah. Now the only goddam American part we had on an Indy car goes foreign. The 2000 Indy race will be run on Japanese tires, Goodyear has folded and is out of the game.

I was told '95 Firestone Indy tires were made in Japan because of poor workmanship in the US. Can that be? Now only way to see a Goodyear Eagle at Indy time is tie one to the fence. Goodyear is very proud of their name. 'Bout 20 years ago I invented and patented a silent tire and obtained a copyright name. "The Bald Eagle." It was a slick tire, cut in such a way to evacuate the water, not displace it. Hell yes, it worked very well, but less than totally developed. We tested it at the Goodyear proving ground at San Angelo, Texas. When Goodyear's lawyers woke up all hell broke loose and my partner Ken and I lost that legal argument in a day (and some loot). Moral of the story: don't fuck with Eagles. I guess the Indians sold 'em to Goodyear long-long time ago.

In 1974 Firestone said "good-bye" to Indy also. Goodyear won the tire war. 20 years of confusion, screw ups, wasted millions. In that 20 years I had to rearrange my priorities regarding speed. Tires are the biggest control in speed, chassis second, aerodynamics third, and power fourth. In regard to driver ranking, we are at a point that a driver can no longer carry a poor handling race car and be competitive. So now I rate driver in a human way, the car in a mechanical way. I started out thinking power number one, driver number two, aerodynamics number three, chassis number four and then tires number five. Now, (2000) the order of importance is tires, engine, vehicle dynamics, aerodynamics, driver.

In the late '40s and all of the '50s, stock cars were considered junk (hillbilly taxi cab racing). All other established forms of racing looked down on us kinda like trash. But for some reason John, the tar man, comes to NASCAR in 1956 and inside of two years he is considered one of us and the head man regarding tire performance, politics, personality, engineering and the Dear Abby of racing tires regarding stock car racing. We depended and trusted him far more than any other tire expert. John was not a store bought tire engineer, but he was a damn good home-made tire expert and in about any kind of racing 'cept draggers.

In the beginning of stock car racing there was a zero percent of stock car tire expertise, for that matter not much better for all kinds of racing. I believe a fair statement would be "and neither did any tire company in the world really understand race tires." John Laux, being a "home-mader" without any brown-nosing hormones, constantly got the short end of the stick, and never to this day, never came close to getting credit for his contribution to racing. He is remembered as a Firestone tire changer. He was manager of Firestone's stock car racing from 1956 to 1963. Then he quit and switched to Goodyear. In 1964 he got the inverted valve done while in his new job at Goodyear. Why was this important? We used to cut off valve stems with wheel nut hammers on open wheel cars and stock car when fender rubbing. I feel he was responsible for getting Goodyear off on the right foot at Indy in 1964, '65 and '66. He forced a speed up to get away from a skinny stock car tire to a wide-wide asphalt grabber and gets everybody to try them.

When he leaves Goodyear in July, 1966, pissed off by inter-company politics, he has a chance to manage an Indy race team and other race team possibilities and to run Gene White's Firestone race tire distributorship in Atlanta for the whole eastern US. This apparently included building team's own cars. I think a fair assessment would be, the operation was a success. In looking through pictures John saved, I noticed quite a few of O.J. Simpson. I wonder what that was all about?

(I noticed one of John, Lloyd Ruby and Gene White and Simpson in a race car titled "The 4 Losers"). This operation wore out in 1974 and John was scheduled to go to England and run the European race deal for Firestone, but they pulled the plug and Firestone racing ends.

John is still going, 78 years old. Still working around race cars and race tars. He is still healthy and sharp (well, maybe a li'l bit wobbly). I believe there are a few more good miles left in that cat.

I'd like to give you a detailed explanation of the evolution from 1956 to 1975 but here is what I run into: memories 20 years old are a little dim. 30 years old dimmer with missing parts and at 40 years it depends on what day it is. 50 years back nothing in writing, just depends on who's telling the story.

'Bout all you can remember is the super bad or the super good days. Also, if you ask four old-timers who were there how it was, you would get four different versions. I'd like to show how and what was done regarding technology, not just saying in 19 so-and-so tires got better. I've questioned about 20 of the people who lived through it. These people developed the tires from day one until now. I've tried to check and double check to be half way correct. I've been collecting bits and pieces for about a year. I have noticed the real history of race tires has been badly misstated in most available written books etc.

Race tire history is like 90 percent of the rest of racing history, or any other history for that matter:

– Usually bullshit as told by the most powerful liar with a vested interest.

– The correct information up to 1970 is so dim and clouded and unrecorded that in another 20 years what really happened will be forever lost.

Well hell, maybe the fact is who gives a damn, but I think it is important.

Steve Petrasek, a Firestone race tire engineer, was sent to NASCAR in 1956 to represent his company and design and test stock car tires in addition to his other duties, such as Indy tires. He was in charge till 1965. I've picked Steve's brain and memory for weeks. I also found an engineer at Goodyear who was very involved in the birth and evolution of stock car race tires. Walt Devinney. Steve is retired with 50 years of tire engineering. Steve is now a flower grower and tractor driver for his wife. Walt is still engineering and trying to keep Firestone and other tire cats from taking away Goodyear's "#1 in tires" sign. How about some sample tire stuff to start with?

You can't wear rubber down without heat and friction. Get a piece of tire tread, a grinder and a garden hose and check it out. If you just heat a tire without friction it will only melt, turn the water on tire tread at the grinding wheel nothing will happen. So if heat is an enemy of tires they should be white, and race track should be white to repel solar rays (the ultra violet). White tracks are easy. How about concrete? White tires? Why not white silicone? Did you know original tires were white? Natural rubber is pure white. I've worked around it for years in the oil fields in Ecuador. Comes out of tree like maple syrup. Misters Goodyear, Firestone and Goodrich figured out how to transform this gooey liquid stuff into an automobile tire, but without carbon and sulfur the rubber tree would only make pencil erasers, waterproofing apparel and rubber balls. For those of you who were in favor of killing all the vegetation in Vietnam not too long ago, guess where the biggest pile of natural rubber comes from today?

Although we consider Firestone first into NASCAR and we tried to use their heavy duty natural rubber tires first (police, military and hi-buck big car tires) really nothing got better. Goodyear got started tire testing in the spring of '53. Dave Evans from Goodyear brought a special tire they had for the 1952 Mexican Road Race to test. Right here the "Blue Streak" is born (name of Goodyear race tires). Next step was the Firestone 16 inch "Super Sport" I used in the September '55 Darlington 500 race. Then in 1956

Firestone comes with the 15 inch Super Sport but this tire was never as good as the original 16 inch Super Sport. John Laux, along with Firestone's race engineer Steve Petrasek are Firestone main players. For the next pretty good ways I'm gonna give you Steve's answers to my questions. The 1956 super sport came as a 6:70, 7:10 or 7:60 x 15 built for a 5.5 inch wide rim. The tread, a non directional tread resembling a twisted rope, was natural rubber from .125 to .180 thick. The tire bead was changed to nine degree bead sole from a production 5 degrees. The tire needed a humped rim flange to help eliminate tire carcass from rotating (to stop pulled valve stems). Side walls had very thin coating of sidewall stiff rubber to reduce heat and lighten. The fabric was nylon type 6 and the cord angle was 62 degrees (Firestone measured cord angle in reverse of other tire companies). Tread underbase was reduced in thickness to .125 from normal .200 to .250, again a maneuver to reduce tire temperature. This created a problem about tread cutting and/or tearing. Clark Stair, a Firestone engineer, brainstormed not only a tread fix, but a better under base rubber called WJ heat resistant compound (this was the thin underbase).

In this period, decision is made, all tracks will have a special tire to itself. Every week tire specifications are reconfigured. We now have about 20 different tires for various racing or hi-performance activity for each company. From 1960 on, tire company tire testing has been a never ending man hour and financial sewer. The tire companies hired various race car owners and drivers and they tested year round. In some cases, owned the test car. What was bad 'bout this is we were now at a point where better race tires are useless for standard (1975) surface transportation, race tires were too hard to be useable on passenger cars. So in reality tire companies' race support is getting very expensive. Firestone says the stock holders are being screwed by the racing expense and gets out of stock car tires in '68.

1956 saw the beginning of tubeless racing tires. This required a special rubber applied in two or three layers to inner tire carcass to preclude air loss. Decision now made race tires be nylon 6 ply. The original nylon, called "type 6," got limber when hot. This allowed tire to grow in both outer diameter and in width. We had a problem when width increases. Sidewall got in upper ball joint and this caused sheet metal on cars to change dramatically (big crashes). Also made some chiefs look dumb. This was solved though by a new nylon called "type 66." This solved problem, period. Matter of fact type 66 is still used today.

Every tire made has a point where it can carry a maximum load but only if the tire pressure is correct for the load. Regarding lateral traction, any change in weight, or pressure away from ideal, will incur some loss in cornering ability. Nitrogen was tried at Indy the first time in 1950 and didn't really help. It still had some water in it that expanded just like the water in air. There is available now a product called "dry nitrogen." Yup, it's much better.

In 1957 Firestone came out with a secret liquid to put in a racing tire to make it run cooler. I've heard it called "tiger piss" or "camouflaged water." The idea being it switched to steam and increased tire pressure 10 to 12 pounds, and end result was cooler running tire, but with a harder tire (more pressure), lateral traction was penalized. This idea was continued until 1961 by Firestone, but kinda looked like biggest benefit was it seemed to amuse and entertain the Goodyear engineers. If you see any pictures in that time frame of Goodyear engineers, they are always laughing. I can tell you tiger piss didn't like natural rubber at all (reference inner tubes).

In the late fifties we get a new trick in tire test. Pull off track and quick stab outer, center and inner edge of tire and record temperature. If you looked up in corner tires smoked, but temperature gauge in pits said 200 degrees to 285 degrees, I cut a piece of tire tread and put it on a hot plate and it smoked at 320 degrees. At a Goodyear tire test I was doing at Rockingham I decided temperature reading was wrong. A Chevy engineer named Don Gates was helping me instrument my car. We decided to read temperature on the fly. Don bought some parts in an army-navy store in Rockingham, North Carolina, and glued them in a cigar box. It didn't work till we blocked out the ultra violet with paint brush bristles screwed to the fender edge. We could transmit this to pits. Now when you saw tire smoke you saw 320 degrees F. I decided "what difference does it make?" Even if temperature was inaccurate it was relative and if it got to 250 degrees or higher we knew tire was gonna blister and blow. For drivers it must have been hell knowing and waiting for a tire to let go. By 1970 I got so spooky about this that if my boots were fastened the ground I'd of come plum out of 'em any time I'd hear the double boom.

In 1957 tread stock is getting much better in handling the heat, but wear suddenly gets out of hand. Wears out much too fast. Tire tread is quite a mixture of ingredients, some very unlikely things in tread compound. Natural rubber and carbon black being be far the main stuff. Carbon black is what gives you the wear. What is carbon black? Only a little more complicated than cutting a slash in a tree trunk and catching what bleeds out (natural rubber). You stand a heavy steel plate up and aim an over rich flame mixture of water, gas or oil up against the plate. Then scrape off the black soot, and you got carbon black. Water is used in this over rich burning process, and by adjusting the amount of fuel, air and water, the carbon black is controlled in reference to quality and type. I believe real fine molecular carbon is best for traction. Heavy coarse carbon helps a tire run cool, but is bad in lateral traction. Well, bad in any traction mode. If you are gonna build your own tire, don't forget to throw in some sulfur, rosin, clay, paraffin, oil, silicone, zinc, stearate , and more with the rubber and carbon to get the stuff to plasticize and vulcanize. How much of each? I don't have a clue.

I studied it for one reason. I still believe a white tire is better than a black tire. If I was Stu Grant at Goodyear, I'd make white tires and decorate 'em with blue and yellow dirigibles showing Stan Gault as pilot. Consider what solar rays (ultra violet) can do to much of a tire's chemistry. I'm puzzled why this hasn't been addressed yet. This also includes the asphalt.

1956, 1957 spinning the tire to balance it is starting. I'm still using a bubble balancer, carrying it with us. 1957 we got three different tires. Right front and right rear are the same. Left front is a pretty plain tire, don't do much. Left rear is special. First, it is a quarter inch to one inch smaller in outer diameter than he right rear. Remember, we called this "stagger." This makes the unsteerable rear wheels want to turn to the left. You want to see how this works? Lay a paper cup on it's side and push it with your toe. Notice it's the big end describes the outer diameter of a circle. Catch on? Also, each wheel carries a different air pressure. We find out a quarter inch of stagger can make a hell of a difference when we got dialed in. We find tire pressure is critical to half a pound.

Let me quickly finish up tire temperatures: with the 3 temperatures across the tire and the 4 wheel positions, the name of the game is "have temperature across the tire even, and have all four wheels have same temperature." Not really do-able. But game is to get as close as you can.

Caster and camber, springs, shocks, toe steer, air pressure, wheel base stagger, static and actual weight, also aerodynamics down force devices and shocks, are our major weapons to try and get all tires to do the same amount of work.

Now, we find the size of the footprint or tire contact area is a very, maybe most important factor.

Also, the wider the tire the better. But to a point. Another control point is sidewall flex. You need a little, but damn little. Here we keep jumping to wider rims and wide tires. Matter of fact, 1957 and 1958 and forward, tire sizes were phony as hell. I get lost trying to keep up. In 1958, we are running a 8.20 X 15 but that don't mean a thing. It could measure 9 inches instead of 8.20. (Remember this number is the tire width). Finally, NASCAR says "It's gotta roll through this template without touching or else." Price of tire is kicked up to $75 each late in '58. In this 1958 to 1965 time frame there are so many tire subtle changes, codes start getting used so the tire companies could separate the various designs. No, you couldn't see it with the naked eye. They all looked the same. The chief NASCAR inspector, Norris Friel, raises hell to try and keep it simple. One tire specification, only one tire manufacturer if keeping it down to 20 different kinds of tires per manufacturer per year was really Friel's goal. He won. The sad thing here is that the chosen few, simply had better tires than the majority. Man we had red dots, white dots, yellow dots, blue dots. NASCAR would have had to hire a World War II spy code breaker to really police this adventure.

In 1958, bead slippage got some more help with a rim manufacturer bead change and a bead change on the tire sole contact surface. This got a new double angle 8 degree and 12 degree. Now this really helped the air seal and slippage. In these times an awful lot learned on the race track within two years showed up in production tires, but I'd say by 1975 racing turned left and passenger tires turned right. I don't see the technology transfer I used to see in tires. 1959, 60, 61, 62 not much happened in passenger car tires to make them better. Firestone only cares 'bout Daytona and Darlington. (Remember the motel deal.)

So, by 1962, Goodyear got damn near everyone on their race tires. 1959 Firestone comes up with a wide tire named "Darlington," Firestone's answer to the "Blue Streak." This tire has a gold band.

Right behind this is a "Charlotte" tire (this was a pretty good tire). By 1962, drivers are making a lot of noise about some help with right front tire blowout.

In 1959, I put power steering on my cars so Fireball could steer. No man living could over power a blowed right front tire with manual steering. With power steering Fireball said he could at least say, "Oh shit" before it hit. 1962 Firestone is trying to stuff a tire inside of a race tire, so when the main tire blew, you would have the inner tire for some help. This was introduced at Indy first in a test. But never used in an Indy car race. Drivers like Fireball weren't sold on the Firestone deal and ask Goodyear for action, and were impressed with Goodyear's test program that ran from 1962 to 1965.

Firestone's tire inside of a tire, and Goodyear's also, were take-offs on a premium tire and also used on vehicles that transported governmental big shooters. Rich and famous types and law enforcement people, gangsters and rich old ladies. Firestone's deal was like a wet firecracker. Fizzled but nothing happened. Goodyear put a guy named Joe Hawkes in charge of inner tire program. Bill Shaffer, race tire engineer, was assigned as a consultant to Joe. They really got with the program after two of their tire testers got killed. In September '64, Jimmy Pardue's fatal accident in a tire test gave Goodyear extra incentive to perfect the safety tire aspect.

Then in January 1965, Billy Wade has a fatal accident racing, not testing and this fatal injury again showed a serious failure of the driver safety belt system. Billy Shaffer designs the crotch strap from under the front of the seat to the buckle up area to prevent driver from sliding down in the belts, which then caused severe stomach and chest injuries. This was adapted by racing in general and has saved many a driver. Nobody ever gave Bill the gold star he deserves. 1965, crotch strap and inner tire debut, Daytona 500 mile race. Bud Moore cars and Darrell Deringer driving, did almost all the testing. Richard petty did some testing also. The test wasn't for the faint hearted. We all credit Darrell Deringer for the test pilot medal. Hit a sharpened, angled short piece of pipe welded to a plate with a front tire at 180 miles an hour. Idea being, blow outer tire and still maintain control with inner tire. Well, it worked pretty damn good. But not without problems.

It had a tube inside the inner tire so it was heavy as hell (unsprung weight), the whole mess was hard to mount, and it required a tricky dual action filler valve. With this valve, the inflation of the outer tire wasn't super reliable, but without question worked. But it wasn't perfect.

Inner tires are still used on the extra hi-speed tracks in the NASCAR track system.

They are now better, with a different rim and air valve design (now use two air valves).

When tubes were removed from the inner tire, the tires could equalize in pressure. When tire pressure equalized, tire vibrated so badly you would have to stop and change. Why? I don't know. Heard 3 or 4 reasons, all different. Man, it would shake the balls off a brass monkey.

Really what difference does it make? You had to stop and get lapped.

When you sit back and consider the tires as they progress (Goodyear and Firestone), some things I think stood out. Goodyear liked some synthetics material in the tread and Firestone didn't. Goodyear tires started great and got greasy. Firestone didn't work until it got hot. Both were hot for wider rims and wider tread. I think, if NASCAR hadn't stopped them, we would have ended up with one rim 36 inch wide and one tire with a 36 inch footprint on the rear. Both started reducing tread thickness everywhere. Goodyear won a few races from 1953 off and on, but in 1960 Junior Johnson won the Daytona 500 on Goodyears and they had finally hit the big time.

Actually, from a racer's point of view it seemed like the tread compound was all of it. How hard or soft it was seemed to be the major contributor to a good or bad tire for a particular race. So, in here comes el gumball, "the qualifier." Here's another can of worms. Kinda unfair. Not all knew about them, or could get them. Finally, we end up with right side and left side. Two kinds of tires only allowed, but left side compound could have various smaller outer diameters for stagger in the rear. Qualifying tires are out. You start race on your qualifying tires. All through this now I'm talking about 1963, 1964.

I got to back up here: for 3 or 4 years, say from 1959 to 1965, at times these tires would start to go nuts on the long high banks. They would start jumping or shudder, then get real hot, then blister and blow. Turns out heavy cars and high speed put a standing wave into effect that starts going around the tire until the leading wave eventually catches up with the last wave, they then overlap and go berserk. John Laux found this in a tire test at Indy with Granatelli's World War II gun camera on a test car.

In 1963, the latest Firestone is a low squatty tire, a gold striper, 6 ply type 66 nylon cord with very high cord angle, 64 degrees to 66 degrees, a .060 underbase, tread from .125 to .180 thick, real wide footprint, 'bout 9 inch size 8.20 / 8.90 x 15 (a wide cheater), rim width 'bout 9." The tire is tubeless with a dual angle bead sole. Very thin and very stiff side wall rubber. This 'bout got rid of the standing wave problem but not rid of the standing wave. A bias ply, non-radial tire runs flat where the tire meets the track (not round). This flat touches the ground in the front and in the back and the middle is raised up into the tire in the form of a wave. Radial tires don't do this. They stay round. They have steel cords instead of nylon and it doesn't stretch. We now know the tire footprint flat on track, period (without the wave), gives biggest footprint (assuming you have front to rear lateral traction balance). Caster, camber and tire pressure are main contributors to percentage of correct. Aiming at this is one thing, doing it is something else. Today, late 2000, some hi-buck cars come damn close to doing it and with their down force aids, the corner speeds are astounding.

Big-big item: put 1964 shocks on a 1998 Indy racer and you'll lose 25 miles per hour in the turns.

What's also important is not just how you look at the contact area. How long do you stay in full contact. Shocks and changing wheel geometry due to uneven surface and changing tire loads regarding lateral traction and down force, velocity and air pressure all play a part in what percentage of time and where you will have the maximum foot print. Remember, once lateral traction is lost and car starts to slide, either or both ends. You may as well be 10 feet in the air.

Traction in every plain is zero. It used to be most all attention was given to a better friction coefficient and a big footprint. That is switched around now. Tire footprint and percentage of time you can maintain this is the game. And of course, size of footprint is very much a part of it and is where biggest gains are. So you are talking suspension, shocks and aerodynamics here. Land speed record Bonneville tires have big trouble in resisting serious deformation which causes too much heat, also this condition is a rough, unbalanced, dangerous speed losing mode. This goes on in draggers and sprint cars. Land speed records are another world and not really related to stock car racing problems. 8 Ply tires helped the standing wave as did very high cord angles, but 8 ply is heavy and very steep cord angles are not best across the board. I believe at speeds over 400 miles per hour tires will have to be out of material not subject to deformation (even metal), regarding very high OD speeds. (Centrifugal force).

By 1964, most tires are in the 62 to 64 durometer (getting pretty soft). We've learned 51 percent weight on front tires and 49 percent on rear tires is best, or in this neighborhood. But 25 pounds (of weight) plus or minus on a tire is critical, when we are fighting for balance. Don't lose the ass end and don't push. Just an even drift when you hit the limit of lateral accelerations. Then the word "grip" comes to live with us. Which means driving is solid and predictable or poor and unpredictable.

This is a neat word. Lets everybody know you listen to Formula One driver interviews.

1 pound of air pressure, one quarter degrees of caster or camber, 60 thousandths of toe steer in the wrong direction or the wheel base half an inch longer or shorter side to side is a night and day difference. Also, any wheel travel on any of the four wheels that changes toe, caster or camber or wheel base either side is a possible night and day difference. Rim width, rim offset affect tire performance, but we learn shocks can make a tremendous difference in handling. Why? They determine how long you can enjoy maximum footprint in reference to a full lap. In whatever groove you choose to run or race in.

In the real world, in the fifties, sixties, seventies and eighties, forty years we are totally ignorant of the technology and physics of wheel dampening, plus all our shocks suffered from tremendous changes in operation linearly to length of the race as race conditions caused shocks to heat up and totally change function and sometimes up to a total failed mode. All this was dumped onto tires for solution. So tires were actually aimed at a rapidly moving target. Chassis and track kept changing every lap.

I believe shock technology got overrated. A shock with the most correct average of resistance in both compression and rebound, and a close average in frequency with a fluid that is able to operate under 350 degrees F is in general all you can do. In the 1962 time frame the ground work is getting started for a modern new player. Leo Mehl is put to work as compound policeman on production tires at Goodyear. He was there one year and got transferred to race tire development. He worked in this area for two years, sports cars and stock cars. Goodyear is still working with passenger car molds and Leo is head tread compounder for sports cars. The tread is mostly natural rubber and the big game is carbon black. But sports cars ran rain or shine, so Leo had to have a special rain tire. Somehow he found a synthetic and natural rubber mix made a better rain tire. Some of the new synthetic oil technology helped as Leo played with the chemistry and vulcanization and sulfur, synthetic rubber know how is getting better. By the mid '60s, Goodyear is starting to use more and more synthetics in racing tread stock. This was biggest gains for racing as well as passenger tires and truck or commercial tires as well. By 1970, Goodyear really got good crew of long hairs who are getting a good grip on polymers and this know how is used to make just about 100 percent synthetic tread tires stock.

Let's back up to 1965. Leo is now Indy, stock car and sports car head guru. After some exciting Indy races 1965 and '66, where Foyt last minute switches from Goodyear to Firestone, and wins with a Goodyear driver's uniform. Finally, Leo gets his giant hero badge. Foyt wins Indy '67 on Goodyear tars. Hot damn. Blue Streak did it. Yup, what a goofy name. Well, Leo gets rewarded for winning Indy. (But was it really?) The reward was that they dump the Formula One job on him. Also, he is absolute ruler of Goodyear Racing. I think including go-carts. Man when he talks the earth shakes. Simply stated, he got the job done every damn place. Goodyear had a lock on the world's racing tire deal. (Hey, how could you miss in the US? Ain't nobody else.) Win on Sunday, sell on Monday, maybe. I had some Goodyear stock. The more they won the more the stock dropped. As a matter of fact, as they took over world racing the company damn near went bankrupt. Lucky for racing the guy who saved Goodyear's ass liked racing and Leo. He got stock going again and I sold out like a damn fool way too early. Stanley Gault is that cat's name. Lucky for us he liked racing and dirigibles.

Well, right in here Michelin starts kicking Goodyear's ass big time in premium tire sales. So Leo, the genius is brought back to the US, is pulled out of racing and starts Goodyear playing catch up with Michelin radial tires. Well, he got two years of that game which really wasn't any trip to Paris. (If I got some of this mixed up, Leo will probably call me and chew my ass out.) But end of '74 he got moved back as grand dragon of race tars. His official desk sign said "director of marketing of race tires." I ask Leo what he considered his best shot. Answer was, "The transition from a heavy skinny tire to a light very wide tire. Also the molding know-how that let you mold the tire without losing the center line." He also said that the reverse moulding process in the late '60s was the biggest contributor to a wide bias ply race tire. 1975 was Goodyear's racing radial tire debut. If I remember right, in those next two years Leo's black hair kinda got a lot of silver or gray in it. This is mid June 1995, Leo is still emperor of all racing with 30 years of "been there and done that." I bet they name a blimp after him when he quits. (Shortly Leo is retired, and then takes over Indy car). Nope. Still haven't seen a Leo Mehl blimp as of March '99. I hope so. (This story ought to help if I want free tars some day). Ha! Found out at Indy in '97, "Your free shit ended with your last homer."

Can you tell by now how many hours of my life were used to try and understand race tars? You know, if racers got pensions or retirement, I wouldn't have to spend six months trying to outwit the slow toll Alzheimer's has on the survivors to write this. Who the hell was Alzheimer? The first victim, or the sawbones who first figured out what the hell went wrong? Does anybody know?

Remember, we the old farts who renamed ourselves "senior citizens" call it C.R.S. ("Can't remember shit").

I'm starting to notice that there are more questions than answers. In the evolution of a satisfactory or capable racing tire for stock cars there is a major problem. The racing rules of nearly every separate sanctioning body are legislating and using tire spec. And rules to control or reduce race car speeds. In general, Winston Cup tires are simply too small diameter for durability. I keep saying tires control race car speeds. Talking 1995 talk, there is no incentive for a better tire except for competition between tire companies. Maybe a safer tire but safe equates to slower.

In this story 1948 to 1975, it is always how to go faster. We find wider rims and wider tire footprint are a sure way to go faster, and we get in trouble in the early '50s because we assume wider rim is better. We put tires designed for a five-and-a-half inch wide rim on a eight inch wide rim. Nope, didn't work.

I got to go through a set of NASCAR rule books, 1957 to 1975 thanks to Jerry Cook, NASCAR's 'modified' five-star general.

Here is how the rim and tread width evolution played out.

1947 To 1955 not much attention paid, so four-and-a-half inch, five inch and five-and-a-half inch wide rims was about it. Hell. They were all stock and we cared more about strength of the wheel than any other thing. We didn't have trouble with the big Ford bolt circle, but the four-and-a-half on five, or the five on five wheels, they weren't even close to being strong enough. But rules said "stock" and here is where things got hard to control.

Example: 1957 Rule book, Chevy could run a seven inch wide rim. A Cadillac nine-and-a-half inch wide rim. All car makes had a personal rim width spec., lite cheap cars, seven inches. Hi-buck locomotives up to nine-and-a-half inches.

Yup, you put Caddy wheels on a Ford, etc., inspector says, "How wide are your rims?" You prove it by saying, "May a lightening bolt strike me dead (and raise your right hand) if I'm lying. Same as my peter, five inches." How you going to measure 'em if they are tire mounted?

Darlington, 1950. Inspector is gonna demount 400 wheels to measure rim width. 'Bout 100 car entries? OK, Sure. Special equipment could have done it, but would it work outside in the mud? The standard method was measure unmounted rim.

1958, Special bulletin give rim width and special tire rules. "Can't find bulletin."

1959, Same deal. Special specification sheet (missing). 15 inch or 14 inch only. (No more Darlington trickery - 16 inchers remember?)

1960, Same deal.

1961, Rule book missing.

1962, '63 , '64-All of these years same as 1959.

Through all of this most of the cars are running seven inch to eight-and-a-half inch rims, and the tire footprint runs from six inch to seven inch wide on the tars.

1965, Rims width, loud and clear. Maximum eight-and-a-half inches wide.

1966, NASCAR is tired of all the tricks and games about actual tire specs and reported or claimed specs, so they construct out of angle iron a rectangle that is 29 5/16 inches long and 11 11/16 inches wide.

You air up the tire to 60 psi and it has to go through the fixture with moderate human effort "or else." What did "or else" mean? "Sorry, confidential or classified."

Remember. Now the biggest or widest tire is a 8:60 x 15, which is 8.6 inch wide. Long way to 11 11/16 ain't it?

Also, rule book says "maximum tread width 8 inches"

1966 is where inner safety tire is required to run any super speedway.

1967, Maximum tread width eight inch maximum rim width 8.5 inches."

1968, Maximum rim width 8.5 inches, maximum tread width 10 inches."

Inner tire now is a "must" as was started in 1966. Matter of fact still required as of now on hi-speed tracks.

1969, Tire template idea expands to three sizes. Goodyear only now gets whole mess of new rules:

Tire template is 11.85 inches for 8.5 inch rim, 12.35 inches for 9 inch rim, 12.85 inches for 10 inch rim. But rules also say "9 inch rim maximum." Here's where qualifying tires (gum balls) get wounded. This is an expensive game that needs ending. "This year start the race on the tires you qualified with"

1970, Rims can be 8.5 inches to 10 inches wide and tires up to 12.85 inches wide, but finally. 1971, A 9.5 inch maximum rim width, but tread jumps to 11 inches maximum.

"Start race on qualifiers," is still the rule.

1972, Rules are 'bout the same for wheels and tires.

1973, Rules stay the same but "slicks" arrive. (No tread).

Finally. 18 years after I got in trouble for running slicks. They are all there is.

1974 and 1975, wheels and tires stay the same.

So in twenty years we come from 4 1/2 and 5 inch wide rims with 4 to 5 inches of tread width to 9.5 inch wide rims with tires 12.70 inches wide in section with 11 inch wide tread width. Tires from 1975 on I'll leave for someone with hands on experience. From 1975 on, in all of racing records started being kept by all involved, and I doubt the history will be lost on all racing subjects forward of 1975.

In my search for facts and details for this story I ran upon an interesting accomplishment of A.J. Foyt. I never knew 'bout all of the tire engineers who ever worked with A. J. in tire testing. They say he was the best they ever worked with for development. One said that he seemed to have radar in his ass.

In 1959, a seed was planted at Goodyear. A famous Italian inventor named Guillo Nata (spelling of first name may be incorrect) invented a synthetic rubber called polybutadiene, known as B R. (Natural rubber is symboled NR, makes sense doesn't it?) Frank Jenkins, a compound specialist at Goodyear, is assigned to find ways to use BR in race tires. Frank's long suit is long hair math, and of course, chemistry. So in 1960 (secretly), this tricky Frank is sliding some percentage of BR into the racing tire. Only his big boss knows about it. By 1962 Frank has got a different tread compound formula for every NASCAR Grand National track. (Now called "Winston Cup")

(Why change? Grand National is just two words out of the dictionary. Winston has a large generous check book that writes in "NASCAR" where it says "pay to" quite often. And a phrase used by the educated business types "for special consideration" in as much as seven figures.)

So, in 1960, Goodyear race tires are part BR and part NR rubber. Frank got moved out of racing in 1963 and was involved as a consultant until 1965. A very high percentage of BR was used. But in those days not yet 100 percent. I'm told now there can be 100 percent synthetic rubber race tires that can do the job better. I'm of the belief that's not a world wide accepted tire expert's opinion. By 1965 some serious work gets going to correct the carcass manufacturing technique which more or less built the tires with a crown to a carcass that presented a flat wide contact patch as manufactured. But by adding a lot of rubber in right and left shoulders of tread and side wall intersections. This extra rubber acted like a heat sink and cooled the working surface and the tread carcass bond. Stu Grant, current leader of the Goodyear "super team" helped me find some of the answers, but he is too young really. I doubt he could even spell butadiene in 1972, and that is about where this story ends.

I thought I ought to mention all the Firestone people who contributed in one way or another up to 1975 and hell, Steve Petrasek's list had over 60 names on it. No room here. But it should be recorded. If you decide to write a book call me, and I'll give you the list and I got one for Goodyear also. You know, when you look at a worn out tire which nobody wants, you got to give 'em two bucks to take it. (Well let's face it, up until today only good for mosquito condos).

Without tars, courtesy of messieurs Goodyear, Firestone and Goodrich, what a different world we'd live in. Think about it. Tires are really like magic.

One last thing. If I used your tires and wheels in the 1950 Darlington race, specially if I left you in a bad situation, like no wheels or tars, I'd at least finally want you to know that I felt bad about it and apologize. So much of racing back then operated on an old southern saying, "Load the wagon, the mules are blind."

At the time, I think racers in general, without noticing it, had developed some bad manners. We started biting the hand that was feeding us. John Frank Laux: as a racer I say "thank you" for your work and concern for a better, which at the same time was a safer tire. Many racers were able to retire in a reasonably good physical condition. I know your working career didn't make you a wealthy man from a financial point of view. But, if friends are worth 10 bucks apiece you were a wealthy man.

Your path was strewn with quite a few "pelicans" and the residual pelicans produce. Having been exposed to that environment quite often myself, I appreciate your efforts and dedication that much more. As near as I can find out, in 1947 racing tires represented a 5,000 tire demand. A tire executive who pays a lot of income tax estimated today it is about two million. Isn't that about 400 times more tars in the 48 years? Damn John, it seems like at the very least somebody would give you a golden tire iron or something.

Seems to me it just ain't right not to mention the names of the players. So below are those I can remember with some help from Goodyear race engineering: Gene Mamannio, Jim Louian, Elmer Wasko, Tony Webner, Jim Early, Ed Long, Ted Lobringer, Harold Mills, Ed Alexander, Paul Lawritzen, Don Knight, Mike Babick, Larry Truesdale.

And here are their counterparts, the pioneers who wore Firestone uniforms up to their surrender:

E. Waldo Stein, Clark Stair, Otto J. Wolfer, Steve Petrasek, Mel Hershey, Barry Davis, Bob Age, Cal Clark, Don Kohseik, Al Speyer, Bill Rians, John Moore, Bill Hanion, Bill McCreary, Bert Thomas, Bob Casseday, Gene White Company, Ann Rolushwall, John Laux.

Society of Heads-up-asses Surface Transportation Manufacturers

The engine problems we had as "just born strictly stock car racers" were as follows, numbered as to frequency of failure.

#1 Engine bearings burned up or hammered out because of poor oil, no decent oil filters, poor oil pressure or cheap materials

#2 Burnt and broken pistons resulting from poor materials, poor fuel delivery and heavy design

#3 Over-heating from plugged radiators

#4 Poor head gasket design causing blown gaskets

#5 Poor block and head clamping border line to terrible caused leaks between cylinders and blown gaskets

#6 Spark plugs fouling due to component failure, ceramic would just blow out of the shell, or center wire would come loose and move, and fractured ceramics that then leaked to ground.

#7 Valve spring failure 'cause of too much cam at too many rpm and too little spring

#8 Cylinder scoring from poor oil and poor oiling at high rpm

#9 Connecting rod and rod bolt failure

#10 Crankshaft breakage from too much rpm and vibration

#11 Cam shaft lobe failure mostly from poor oiling or heavy springs

Actually, every goddamned piece of all the engine makes were at least 50 percent short in design criteria for what we were trying to do in the horsepower department. The combustion chamber design, along with induction, fueling and exhaust conduits, were best described as woefully inadequate. In the working fluids flow design, Detroit was a lost ball in the high weeds.

OK, let's compare, or examine the 2001 "stock" Ford or Chevy racing engine as approved by NASCAR. Not one goddamned piece, gasket, seal, or fastener, is used on a production engine. As a matter of fact, the Ford engine, as raced, hasn't been used by Ford for years. I'm not necessarily criticizing, except to say "why in the hell don't they tell the truth?" (When's the last time you could buy a V8 Pontiac?) A model name the manufacturer's claim as it's corporate name costs $25,000. Try and buy a spare car the day after the Daytona 500 for $100,000. You'd have same luck as trying to buy $100 bills for $85.00. This "win on Sunday" bullshit is a phony sales pitch based on outright lies. You're welcome, Detroit. "We win-you win," Ford says. Chevy and Pontiac say, "Because of what we developed for, and learned from racing, you get a better, safer car." Bullshit, Detroit hasn't used a carburetor for years. All NASCAR racers use carburetors.

Today's production car, as built by American and foreign car manufacturers are all to varying degree shit-box death traps regarding safety. If Ford and General Motors used what they learned on the race tracks regarding the ability to survive accidents, 75 percent of the wrecks that cripple and kill today would not require medical attention, and within a week, people would be back to normal. I believe the above with all my heart. If auto and truck manufacturers used technology NASCAR has perfected, car insurance would be one-third of what it is now. Sure, these cars would be kinda shitty lookin' inside, but what's the game? You wanna keep truckin' or do you mind dying a little?

In NASCAR, Busch or Winston Cup, the cars survive 150 to 200 mile an hour collisions with other cars or barriers, and in 30 minutes are back running around the race track. If a 2001 passenger car hits a tree at 65 miles an hour, it breaks in half. When I look at the new stuff, all glass all the way around and roof held on by next-to-nothing, there ain't no car above your elbows in sitting position. Sure the crash survival data shows cars are safer, but notice that standard crash tests are performed at 35 miles an hour. How real is that number? For example on October 5, 1997 there was a 21 car crash at Eastabooga (Talladega) at 195 plus miles an hour. 21 race cars crash and all the drivers walk away.

I bet it cost one million bucks to fix the 21 racers. Well, maybe more, a complete car, "race ready," today is 'bout 150 grand. What did a good Winston Cup (Grand National) car cost in 1948?…'bout a grand. I bought a new 1955 Chevy for $1,812 (the car Herb won Darlington with). I worked for a Ford dealer in 1937 and a new Ford 60 coupe was $675 List price. Those $675 Ford coupes and a $15 junkyard 85 horsepower Ford engine were the foundation NASCAR was built on. (Those $675 Coupes in 1947-1948, were 15 to 25 bucks at the junkyard.) It was possible to buy a race ready, not too shabby, race car in 1949 for 500 bucks (modified).

The 1948 cars were probably twice or more times stronger than today's cars. I'm talking an accident, at a given speed. Hold it, "Mr. Expert," I know statistics say "today's cars are safer." I say bullshit! Put 2001 tires, brakes, suspension system, (in reference to correct suspension geometry) safety belts, and air bags on a 48 car and crash test it. The car would be twice as easy on passengers and driver. Those cars had steel frames and body metal twice as heavy and strong. NASCAR cars do not use unit construction. Unit construction and glass roofs are bullshit, suicide. And in my opinion, a badge of stupidity for the current car designer. I'm soft peddling those comments, I don't want to piss off the car manufacturers too much. Hell, what's more important? Living with a car that has padded bars, a single left rear door and an interior that don't look too fancy, with a frame which makes car cost 100 bucks more (Yes, $100 will more than cover it) or dying in a greenhouse shitbox? Weight is important, but hey, a Winston Cup car with 750 horsepower weighs 3,500 pounds. How 'bout a 200 horsepower car at 2,600 pounds? That would be as easy as falling off a bicycle.

It boils down to this. The average human being operates with his head up his ass. I think it's because we all think "Sure, it can happen, but not to me." That's what every good performer in a dangerous profession lives by. You, the reader, you believe this too, so do I, but if i'm gonna walk through an area full of poisonous snakes in a tuxedo, I'm still gonna put on a pair of ugly snake-proof boots. Fuck what it looks like, I wanna keep on living.

Automotive News, the bible for production surface vehicles (cars and trucks – Keith Crane publisher, sharp cat, raised in the car business) in October '97, some dumb shit-head who works for him tells him, "1997 cars are twice as safe as yesterday." Now goddamn it, when you own and publish such a prestigious magazine, whether you want it or not, you have the responsibility to be correct. I assume you have to kiss all the advertisers asses to keep their business, but I doubt you spend enough time researching personally, so you "parrot" information to us furnished by manufacturers, or some computer wizard. That's a perfect example of "bull-shit in, bullshit out."

In 1948 the road system in the United States was probably 75 percent more dangerous than now. I had a wrecker service here (Daytona) from 1947 to 1964. To compare the remains of today's accidents, I see a difference of maybe comparing a brick shit-house to a plastic and glass shit-house.

Cosmetically the cars are great. Detroit finally figured out a jelly bean was dynamically more stable than a Kraft cheese box, and the shape of a flounder better still. But hell, a 12-year-old kid could have seen that if he watched fast moving water over a jelly bean, or a dead fish. Years ago, I noticed in Ecuador where I worked in oil and gold fields, that most all rocks were smooth, and for the most part, shaped like a rock jelly bean or a rock flounder. This is in fast moving shallow water (mountain-jungle). If I turned rock 90 degrees, all hell broke loose, in reference to turbulent water flow. I learned more in an hour in a water tunnel than I could in a week in a wind tunnel. Remember, I'm talking surface speeds up to 300 miles an hour.

What's this all got to do with day-one stock car racing? Just this, the first 20 years of stock car racing wiped out and seriously crippled about thirty men. All cars should have about a front 49 percent- rear 51 percent weight bias, with driver only. All cars should have enough down force to sustain that ratio to the vehicles terminal speed. Also, all vehicles should have at least one "G" of down force at 60 miles an our and two "G" at 120. The above came from "learning by doing" in NASCAR. In the beginning, roll bars were not mandatory. When rules said "roll bars," some cars, so help me god, ran with 2x4 wooden roll bars and a leather belt wrapped around rear post of driver's door and roof center post. We took the windshield wiper blades off, taped up the headlights, and removed the muffler. We ran with full glass, we were not allowed to remove glass, or replace it with plastic. Hell, I've driven cars and trucks that, at 100 to 120 miles an hour, the front wheels lifted off the ground. We had to find answers, and quick.

I drove a Chevy pickup on the beach in February 1955 time trial, that when it got up to 120 miles an hour…front wheels were two to three inches off the ground. I had to count the turns, lock to lock, and then put steering wheel in middle to land the front wheels straight. The first prototype Chevy Corvette (of the manta-ray style), at 120 miles an hour, the front wheels were totally off the ground. (This was 1960, not 1918) In my report, I suggested "we turn the body around on the chassis, or turn seat around to face other way, and reverse drive train." Bill Mitchell was chief of GM design at the time, and the Corvette was his pet. In addition to telling him "body was ass-backwards aerodynamically," I told him, "Car had a transmission and brakes that were 50 percent or more short of being rated fair." The car was supposed to be capable of racing a Ferrari. I suggested they, "Junk the proto-type, and start over." (In about five years Bill started talking to me again.)

So, aerodynamics, brakes, drive train, shocks, wheels, tires, suspension systems, in regard to strength and correctness of geometry, were all woefully short, and the sad part about it was NASCAR refused to let us strengthen the suspension, and the manufacturer's ignored us like we had "AIDS," or if they nibbled at racing they played with a half-assed strategy of heavy duty parts, which did very little better. Actually, in most cases, "heavy duty," was a trade name for making certain suspension parts with opened up dies, and/or, filed core patterns.

We raced in 1955 with front spindles and bearings, and wheels and rear axles same as off the show room floor. If you broke a rear axle, you lost that wheel. This was generally an interesting experience, considering you have no way to steer the ass end and no brakes. We broke front spindles every race. That's also interesting, when you lose a front wheel, or even more so when you broke an idler arm, and had no steering. All this was made more interesting 'cause you had one master cylinder working all four wheels, so when real axle or front spindle broke, you were tested physically and psychologically, to see how you reacted at over 100 miles an hour, with no steering or brakes, and surrounded by 20 other race cars trying to turn. A complaint to NASCAR would usually get you the standard answer, "Nobody's forcing you to do it. If you can't stand the heat, get out of the kitchen." (Didn't Harry Truman invent that saying?)

Fire, goddam, we had hell with fire. 28 Gallon steel tanks, (yeah I know 22 gallon maximum) Bullshit! Up till 1968 most were from 25 to 28 gallons. How come? Well they half-assed checked the tank before the race, but last thing any race sanctioning body wants to do is disqualify the winner of a race, especially a big race. So after race inspection, worse could happen is get your ass slapped and a "finger waving" ("If you ever do that again we'll make you stand in the corner or have to write 'don't cheat' 1,000 times.") We had steel tanks two inches in front of rear bumper, and drooping eight inches below the bumper. Most cars, filler cap is rite in middle of tank, one inch from bumper. Well, soon as someone tapped you in the ass, (no matter how easy), cap and gooseneck were gone. The rules and the inspectors said, "Ain't allowed to move 'em 'Strictly Stock.'"

OK, the fans loved it. Goddam fire every place, 28 gallons, about six pounds per gallon, 120,000 BTU's per gallon, 'bout three and a half million BTU's right under your ass. So I decided in 1963 to build and install a 'moly' steel guard to stop a "tap in the ass" from starting a fire. Well, the chief inspector was "Iron-ass, Bird-brain, Norris Friel," he says, "Take it off, it's illegal." I say, "Why?" and get standard answer. "'Cause I said so." I noticed in 2000 at the July 4th race in Daytona some drivers complaining 'bout restrictor plates make racing much more dangerous. In some paper Earnhardt's (Mustachio) reply calls those drivers a common phrase from the 50s, "candy-asses" and suggested an old Southern remedy. Soak old sox in kerosene and tie one around each ankle to keep ants from eating their candy asses. So, the code of the hills was and is, never, never complain 'bout danger. Even if you shit your pants in the race.

I'm at Indy, 1964, trying to get capsule car, with Bobby Johns driving it, qualified. It didn't pan out. The car has brake problem, and it's backed into the first turn wall with no time to fix it. So I get the hell out of there. Boy, that's a "shitty" feeling – missed the race. Kinda like you get all the buttons cut off your work shirt, and you're "drummed out" of the track. "Ain't good enough, couldn't make the cut."

Well, this car had very complex fuel tank shapes. So with help of Firestone and Goodyear, I build rubber fuel cells, with standard military helicopter specification materials. (So, now I know how to build a rubber fuel cell). Well, same hour we wreck the capsule car, (this is in May, 1964), Muhleman says, "Smokey, I hate to make your lousy day worse, but Fireball was in a bad wreck in Charlotte and badly burned. He's not expected to make it."

I load up my junk. This was still in my "poor boy" days, and I towed a two axle trailer and had a one ton truck to haul parts, tools, and one helper. The helper was a dandy, "T.A. Toomes," from "Richard Pettyville." This cat had never seen an Indy car, or ever been to an open wheel race yet he helped me build that car from scratch. I drew plans New Year's day, we started the next day, and had car in Indy, May 1. (four months, two men) It's in Hall of Fame at Indy. Look at it, and besides wondering what the goofy bastard was like that dreamt it up, consider two men built it all in four months.

Well, I get to Charlotte 'bout 5:00 am Monday morning. I want to see Fireball but I can't see him.

The conversation I get is, "It don't look good, maybe a 10 percent chance." But, I find out fire destroyed the favorite part of his body. Well, at that particular point of our lives, (I knew Fireball very well.) I knew, that if it was me, life was over. I'd rather be dead. But fate wasn't too nice to him, and he lingered in much pain for a month before he "checked out." As we buried him, I vowed to myself "If I never raced again, there would never be a metal tank, or metal fuel line."

I'm also starting to have trouble justifying what I'm doing. I've helped carry out both Fireball and Marshall. They are about one or two hundred yards apart. My mental justification up till then was, "Well maybe racing does extract a high premium, but what we learned will make ordinary surface transportation safer." That justification was starting to get wobbly. We are racing "killer cars" we know how to make better, and racing's requirements are now turning left. Normal surface transportation is turning right. My excuse is now flawed. We've wore out the "rear view mirror story," (a race car invention in early Indy days) the tires we need are not good for passenger cars, etc.

Well, I built a 1965 Chevy and put a rubber fuel cell, 22 gallons, with a non metal fuel line (Firestone made it for me.). It was a prototype Chevelle, but I entered it in 1966 Beach Race with Mario Andretti as driver. Well, France wanted Mario so bad, when the inspectors told me, "Take the rubber tank out, and put in steel death trap," I simply said "Go fuck yourself." (Remember the "When you got 'em by the balls.") Well, we never heard no more 'bout the tank, but Mario crashed the car early in the race.

Same inspection again. In 1967 I built a Chevelle. It had same 22 gallon Firestone rubber and fabric tank (a la helicopter technology), and a turn over check valve. Getting through inspection was a story in itself. Turner put it on the pole by a ton, but the engine was a 650 horsepower time bomb. Turner was supposed to run at 75 percent, but he forgot about it when he got behind on a bad pit stop we gave him. When he went 100 percent, in about three laps car looked like a mosquito sprayer, adios engine. We burnt a piston and smoked 'er down.

We start 1947 5,000 rpm "flat head" Fords, we squeezed them Hornets to 52 and 54 hundred. Then the small block Chevy in 1956, 6,000 rpm with a three inch stroke. By 1966 we have learned how to turn a three 9/16 stroke to 6,800. Then the three-and-a-half inch stroke small block Chevy's to 7,600 in 1980, and three-and-a-half inch stroke Chryslers and Fords the same. With the the 302 Chevys and Fords, we learned how to make a three inch stroke live for four hours at 8,000 to 8,200 rpm, but boy, if I have one little rod bolt with bad specs "there went the farm." Well, up to 1970 we had to use stock stuff turning even the three-and-a-half inch inch strokes 7,800 with factory heavy duty parts.

In 1947, '48 and '49 'bout all we raced were Modifieds. I helped Marshall Teague and Fireball Roberts, they were Daytona neighbors. As a matter of fact, in 1949 Fireball kept his modified at my shop. A friend I met when I worked that short time in New Jersey, Roy Jones, had migrated to Daytona and came to work for me. Roy was a world class welder and pretty damn fair mechanic, but he got so race-happy (and he was single at the time), that he, Fireball and the car got to be a pain in the ass. I gave them some new rules. They told me to "shove it," loaded up, and went to Charlotte area to seek their fame and fortune and they did pretty good. I think they both lived off their take. 'Course that kind of living was hand to mouth.

Back then a 37 to 40 Ford coupe or two-door was "it." Very rare to see any other make.

Fords were called "Henrys" then, Chevys were "Stove Bolts", Buicks were "Joe Lewises".

Lincolns were "Big Henrys," Chryslers and all others were scooped into one category "Trash cars" (that is, till the hemi's came). Then they were re-christened "Mopars."

Race cars came from local junk yards and cost from 20 to 50 bucks apiece. Engines the same but 10 to 25 bucks apiece, or nothin' if you'd let him put a small sign on it, like "Joe's Junkyard."

Had to use all stock stuff 'cept three exceptions:

1, Cylinder heads: Sometimes they allowed custom heads from California (like Edelbrock or Offenhauser).

2, Cams: We could run a race cam, and there were four or five vendors. Harmon Collins, Offy, Ed "Isky" Iskenderian, Erickson (man his cams were wild). Actually, in cams and ignition there was over-kill. And really nothing in ignition was a lot of help, but in cams the difference was day and night. Winfield made the best, but he was a little guy with big demand by Indy and sports cars, etc., even car manufacturers. So in stock car racing he'd only sell to a chosen few. Marshall Teague was on Winfield's qualified "short list." I was allowed to buy, but no conversation. "Isky" too had the good stuff for the time.

3, Manifold: The other change was, sometimes a California hot rod manifold was OK'd and them things came with one to five carbs. All we had then was tiny two-barrel Stromberg.

For exhausts we had three choices…stock, nothin' or zoomie. Sometimes I think lots of racers died early because of this. No headers were faster than stock headers and zoomies were best, but outlawed mostly. I think "no header deal" caused Banjo Matthews rather early departure from our world. Poor Banjo, he spent his whole life racing – 365 days a year – gave so much for so little and suffered too much in his last ten years. Finally, as he struggles with death in such a painful, awful way, the racing world threw him a few crumbs. He received the "Charlotte Motor Speedway Smokey Yunick Award for Life Mechanical Achievement" – then "National Motor Sports Writer's Award" (Darlington Hall of Fame) - then the "Champion Spark Plug award" at victory banquet in New York. In 1998 he made it into the International Motorsports Hall of Fame at Talladega, Alabama (actually Eastabooga, Alabama) but it was too late, he was gone.

OK, the flat head Ford engine came really in three flavors. The Ford 60, which meant 60 horsepower. The Ford 85 (85 hp) and the Lincoln zephyr V12, (actually one and a half 60s end-to-end on a common crank) This engine was really a pile of shit. It never did anything for anybody, cept wore out any human being who ever had to pull the heads off of one. But the Ford 60 and it's big brother the 85 were really what stock car racing was born around.

The Ford 85 spawned the original after-market racing industry. The grandfathers of stock car racing…they still have never been recognized for what they done: Harman Collins, Vic Edelbrock Senior, Offenhauser, Ed Iskenderian, Mickey Thompson, Spalding, Windfield, Grant, Bruce Crower, Fred Carrillo, Sparks, Vertex, Erickson, Schrader. Hell, it's 55 years later. I'm sorry, I'm sure I missed quite a few. How 'bout "Honest Charlie", first speed parts shop this side of the Mississippi? Ed Iskenderian was the "Henry Ford" of the deal. He got the price down and marketed to the masses.

Mechanics did a lot to build the sport too. Mechanics then, like the grandfather of all stock car engine men, Red Vogt, Wolfie from the east, Bud Moore and Ray Fox from the south. Then there was, and still is, "Smitty" from Lincoln, Nebraska; Clay Smith. I almost forgot, and he was maybe the smartest of us all – Clay Smith the genius. He really was the gas that was dumped on stock car racing and set it on fire. Man this is tough trying to remember 50 years or more…knowing you leave out some who did so much.

There was a real sad-sorry part to the story: the manufacturers. OEM (Original Equipment Manufacturer) should have been "Society of Head-up-asses Surface Transportation Manufacturers."

True, they invented affordable surface transportation for the masses, hell, for the whole world. I think there were as many as 700 different American car companies from 1910 to 1940. But when the smoke cleared out there were three left: Ford, GM, and Chrysler. Sure, we still had some walking wounded – Nash, Kelvinator, Packard, Kaiser, Crosley. Maybe missed one or two, but hell, what difference does it make? (Oh yeah, "Tucker") They were out of the game soon enough.

The sorry part of the story was in about the real "thinking about making it better," was shot in the ass and traded for "got to make a 10 percent net profit"…"Don't change a fuckin' thing, cause we're gonna make at lest one million of everything." Then a system of rating, or quality, was changed from a scale of one to ten on quality to a scale of one to ten on how do we stack up against each other (in the Big Three)?

I worked in a Ford garage in 1937. List price on a new Ford '60 coupe was $675. In 1955 GM's cost on a 255 cubic inch small block V8 was $84.65. (For you GM experts, if you choose to contest that price, I got that from Ed Cole – I worked for him personally.) Hell, I bought a new Crosley convertible for five hundred bucks. You say, "You didn't get much." Well, did you forget what kind of car won the first Sebring race? Yup, a Crosley! In the 50s everybody in the US mass surface transportation manufacturing drifted off in a dream world, where they had the world by the ass. I got a smell of it working for Hudson '51 through '54. They doubled their sales and went bankrupt. Next, I worked one year with Packard in it's last years death throes. Run by a guy who made electrical appliances up till his take-over of Packard, "Jack Nance," by name. He didn't know a goddam crankshaft from an electric toaster. Yet he called the shots. Well, he put that company in it's grave quicker than a "cat-can-lick-it's-ass." 'Course he had a lot of help from his staff…but who picked the staff? It just illustrates what happens when you worry about selling cars more than you worry about making cars.

The Hole Gets Bigger Everyday

"What did you change or invent Smokey, that eventually became a standard practice, or a truly better deal, and is now used by all?" This question is always a can of worms. No matter what I say, someplace, somebody will say, "Bullshit, I started that two years before he did." In the case of a part that looked different enough that there's no question someone invented something, the accompanying problem is to prove "who did it?" I'll give you a quick example: the four-cylinder Pontiac Tempest.

I was working for Pontiac. Mr. Bunkie Knudsen, the boss man at Pontiac, was told to sell the Corvair under different name. He hates the Corvair for reasons that probably have merit. (He later has to love it when he next becomes Chevrolet General Manager.) Bunk says, "We will build our own little car." John Delorean (number three at Pontiac then), had been developing a new line of belt driven overhead cam engines for Pontiac in four, six, and eight cylinder versions. Well, the development of these engines get into trouble, and there is no time to fix the four cylinder. So I'm asked for suggestions. I'd seen the trouble coming and knew the time table and knew they couldn't fix the engine's problem's in time. As a quick fix I made a four cylinder out of a current Pontiac 389 cubic inch V8 engine. I'd done it before as a band-aid for a truck company. I had a running prototype the day of meeting and three days later we are running it at Pontiac headquarters. Thirty years later I find out I had nothing to do with it. Pete Estes chewed my ass out 'bout it, but John Delorean remembers it kinda like I do.

You know, this system works also in reverse. If an engine, or parts of it, or any part of the total car, are really fucked up, you'll never find out who to hang. The American auto manufacturer had created a bullet proof system over the years that kinda reminds me of Saddam Hussein. His country is in terrible shape, but he still gets a good enough grade to keep the job.

So, knowing there will be some bullshit ("He didn't do it – I did.") I'm gonna tell you about various changes I made to the cars, and engines. I believe in my advanced age, that some of my contributions, or attempted solutions to serious problems regarding engines and automobiles in general were incorporated in "band-aid" fixes and future design. I think what needs to be said here, is that there has always been a very strong resistance to changes to a specific engine, or any part of a product manufactured by the American car companies, suggested by anyone except the official engineering team. It's usually referred to by brave writers as "the not invented here" syndrome. There are two sides to this.

Verbal recitations on changes as compared to doing it in hardware a million times a year, and 50 billion actual miles, there is a hell of a difference. In the 40s through the early 70s, any change was tested to death.

A change to any part of an engine or car costing .25 cents more was a major concession. A million vehicles a year, times six replacement market pieces. Well man…you're looking at a million and a half bucks. An example: I was told by Chevrolet in 1956, that to change a part number cost at least 35,000 bucks (regarding parts catalogue change). Today that would probably be 10 times that.

Sure, it was done sometimes. But I considered it to be the equivalent of walking on water barefooted. Stop and think about it. It's part of life, and it's always gonna be that way in all industry the psychology has to be changed to where change is good and expected. Look at the communications stuff. Hell, it changes every 10 minutes and people are making tons of money.

This was the biggest problem Detroit had, and probably still does.

There is also a major problem. At what point do you stop changing and inventing and go into production? It's not possible to invent a new complex product that is perfect at conception. Let's go back to 50s. A general manager of a motor company at General Motors, Ford, or Chrysler was a vice president and had the power of an emperor. Nobody ever questioned him in public.

Sure, when employees talked to each other, (out of hearing as a rule) they sent him to hell – but not always. Marion Rosenberger, Ed Cole, Bunkie Knudsen, and some others I didn't know, were worshipped by their employees in general.

But in General Motors, and it was the same at all manufacturers, when the top cats retired, it was as if they died the day after they were retired. You can't find one goddam statue at any motor company to any of the past leaders…none, zero, period. I worked for Pete Estes when he was at Pontiac as chief engineer, and as General Manager. And when he was General manager at Chevrolet, and when he became president of GM. Six months after they retired him, we met and talked. He said that on his last day as president, he had to attend meetings away from his office till 4:00 pm. When he got back, his personal effects from his office were boxed up and sitting in the hall, his name was off the door, and the lock had been changed. When he got back outside to leave, he then noticed his name in parking place was already changed to new president's name. He was to get an office and a secretary and be used as a consultant. The office he got was "junk," he never got the secretary, and they never used him as a consultant. I said, "Hell Pete, if you'd have looked, you'd have noticed that they took your picture down in the lobby the same day." But what surprised me was to hear him complain. I said, "Pete, it was the same way the day you took over president, and it was the same 40 years ago when you started." (I think Cole preceded him). With all Ed Cole had done, soon after he retired all I ever heard was all the mistakes he made (the Corvair, the Wankel engine, the '58 Chevy, the 348, the 409 and air suspension, and the sorry Chevy automatic transmission).

The rest of the "power story" is that the staff of a motor company ('bout 20 to 25 people then) and general manager run the deal. The staff voted on replacement, or addition to staff.

Before they would reach down and pull you up to their level, you had to understand the staff "invented" you. And could also "kill" you. So in any major change, the inventor of the change would send a memo to all the staff and say, "I'm gonna make a change, what do you think about my idea?" Well, all staff always said, "Man, that's a hell of an idea." and endorsed the memo. Now if idea bombs, and costs corporation a fortune, who do you blame? Who do you fire? The deal is, if you hang one you got to hang 'em all. So the "fuck-ups" never got wounded, but instead, got promoted, as the chain of command continued it's slow evolution. With this system of mutual dependence within the staff, there was no way an "outsider" could be brought in.

Sometimes two cats would get to be in line for major promotion, like Ed Cole and Bunkie Knudsen for the president of GM. Well, odds were about even. Henry Ford had a bellyful of Iaccoca, and wanted to get out of the car business to be the "Secretary of Housing and Urban Renewal" for President Johnson. No other "Ford" even close to being able to run Ford Motor Company, so he had to consider candidates from outside Ford. Knudsen and Cole were the "super stars" of automobile manufacturers. So Henry said to Ed, "If you don't get the presidency of General Motors, I'd like you to run Ford Motor." Then made Bunkie the same deal. This is no bullshit. Remember, I worked for Ed and Bunkie, and got to know Ford when I went to work at Ford Motor Company in 1969.

Well, Ed told General Motors, "If I don't get the deal, I'm gone to Ford." Bunkie never advertised his Ford offer, and actually it kinda looked like Bunkie was the chosen one by the insiders. Here's an item: both are same age, so the loser has no chance of the job tomorrow. Well, the big day comes, and Cole wins. Knudsen gets the shaft. Well, I haven't told you this yet, but Knudsen and Cole really disliked each other "big time." Cole told me, "Knudsen was an asshole." Knudsen said, "Cole was a little prick." Pete Estes keeps his mouth shut and switches from a "Knudsen man" to Cole. John Delorean stays John Delorean, and he never agrees with Cole, and the bad part about it is that John turns out to be correct nine out of ten times.

Now big corporations are no different than little ones. They never work as a team. It's always team "A" against team "B." I believe if GM was run as a team in the '50s, they would have ended up with 98 percent of the car business, because by then both Ford and Chrysler were in the process of committing suicide. (Both damn near succeeded.) Well, Ed Cole's now president and Knudsen is GM everywhere but North America. Well, Cole's apparently training Knudsen to eat crap, but Knudsen can't swallow the shit, so Ford wins. Knudsen tells Cole to shove it up his ass. And boy, this must have been a bitter decision for Knudsen to make, because his dad was once president of GM, but his dad also worked for Henry Ford Sr. for awhile. Knudsen calls and tells me he is "going to Ford and that I should come with him." Well, as much as I loved Knudsen, I'd already had one "go-round" with Ford in 1957. The pay was great but as fucked up as GM was, Ford made GM look brilliant. Meanwhile, Chrysler was being run into extinction by a buddy of Knudsen's named Townsend. (In spite of King Petty's help). I barely knew him, but I didn't like him as a "top cat." (Actually, I didn't think he had enough sense to pour piss out of a boot.)

OK, Cole's running GM, Pete Estes is running Chevrolet, I'm working for Pete. (12 Grand a year) 1969, Knudsen's been at Ford 10 months, and Cole has switched from a race car loving cat to a holy roller…"Get out of racing, and stay out." I can't believe it, but I can't talk to him. He is still pissed about me quitting him in 1957. You know something that surprised me, and I still don't understand it – the GM system said, "We can fire you in an instant, that's OK, but if you quit us, your ass is mud." Going back a-ways: I think Knudsen really believed in Smokey. After Knudsen left Pontiac and GM had been out of racing, Knudsen brought me back to Chevrolet in 1963. Pete Estes inherited me at Chevy when Knudsen went to GM overseas and Pete got the Chevy General Manager job. (remember I quit Pete Estes at Pontiac in 1963, or he fired me. Actually, I quit and he fired me at same time.)

Well, what the hell, to get paid $10,000 a year and a free car I only had to work 70 hours a week, 365 days a year, and furnish a shop with $300,000 worth of tools and pay insurance for the deal. Well hell, that insurance was only 'bout 10 grand a year. I think I can analyze the whole deal now. I was on a 25 year ego trip but didn't know it. I reported to the general manager or president. I was in on lots of big time deals.

Soon as I learned the difference between General Manager and President (and remembered to write "General Manager" with capital letters, and put "vice president" on the address). They started picking me up at the airport and furnishing me with a chauffeur. If I had a new driver I hadn't met, I'd sit back watching him recover from his shock of picking up a "big shooter" at midnight with a race jacket, cowboy boots, hat and dungarees, and then wait 20 minutes for the stewardess to come with us, (while I was signing autographs for 15 percent of the passengers). I doubt he picked up many "big shooters" who were 'bout 51percent drunk carrying more whiskey than they had luggage.

Really, I didn't want or like the chauffeur deal. I lost a lot of flexibility. If I said I'd be at a 8:00 am meeting at Chevy, Pontiac, styling, etc., and I met someone on the airplane going to Chicago, I had to go to Detroit, and the Chicago adventure never happened. Well, in my way of thinking, "never put anything off till tomorrow – tomorrow may never come." I'd have no way to tell driver about change, and he's be waiting outside airport for hours. Bill Mitchell was vice president in charge of GM Styling. He was the one who insisted on the chauffeur deal. So, even if you could notify GM, "Don't send the ego car," how could you tell a secretary, "Don't send circus wagon. I'm gonna get laid and will get there by a last minute different deal?" You never knew a smile, a look and suddenly a whole new adventure presented itself. I suppose my attitude was flawed but I believed it was a racer's duty to never knowingly refuse to help a sexy woman, even if he was a stranger and the adventure created some cliff hanger timing problems.

To just not show for the meeting, that violated one of my 10 commandments. "Never do something for your own personal gain." That is, something that would be a problem for someone else. (This only includes things on the level). I could have solved this many times by lying, but I consider lying unacceptable except when it concerns women. In regards to women it was OK to lie your ass off without penalty in your adventures. You want to know why? 'Cause women lie to men something awful and remember Confucius said, "When in China, talk Chinese. (Boy I'm glad I never had to deal with Clinton. I wouldn't have had a clue on how to handle a word magician of his class – "World class hell," I'm sure he could be "universe class!") There are three things I never have been able to understand or live with, a drunk (and I was one), a damn good liar, and a pissed-off woman.

Well, back to Bill Mitchell and limos. One day a strange driver picked me up. He came with a Buick "dream car." I was supposed to "oooh and aaah" about how wonderful it was. It was nice, but when we got back to styling, Bill came to garage to meet me. He immediately looked in front ash tray (I smoked a pipe then). There were several cigarette butts and ashes in it. Bill apparently suspected driver was breaking "no smoking" rule and he fired that cat's ass on the spot. The guy had 27 years of service and seemed real nice to me. I waited 'bout an hour to give Bill time to cool down. (I've already found out he was a "dead player" from the driver's actual boss.) I asked Bill to reconsider. Well, that ended badly. I said some things I shouldn't have (I guess nobody likes to be called "a fat-assed, bald, cross-dressing, son-of-a-bitch.) I knew, and so did he, and a couple of cops and one hooker, that Bill wasn't perfect either. (Matter of fact, I still have a couple of pictures I had to have taken to get him to be a good boy and give the lady her clothes back.)

Bill Mitchell was a damn good stylist, and a pretty good guy. But that fancy office, his title and power made a prick out of him sometimes. But hell, none of us are perfect. You know what I noticed? We all start off with one head, two arms, and two legs, so no one of us is really special enough to abuse other humans.

Mitchell's boss, before he retired was a real "war horse," Harley Earl. That fucker was what we in Florida call a "he-coon." He was big, rough, tough, and talented. A good match for Bill France Sr. I know Harley really liked France, but I don't know how France felt 'bout Harley. I went to Harley's funeral with Mr. Knudsen. I don't remember seeing Bill there, but he could have been off to the side praying.

Well, Bill Mitchell shut off the limo service and didn't talk to me for five years. You won't believe this, but we got to be buddies again a couple of times. I'd piss him off if I criticized him while he was blowing his top. I'd say, "Why did you ask me you dumb shit, you knew I didn't like it?" Bill was real proud of his friendship with Porsche. Every year he went to Germany and drove the new kraut "hot" cars, and dined with the genius himself. No, I never talked to him (Doctor Porsche). I don't even remember meeting him. Well, I'd always get Bill pissed off by criticizing his friendship with a German and a competitor to boot. (Remember, my relationship with the Germans in the early 40s wasn't on the best of terms)

Bill couldn't drive a nail. It's a wonder he didn't kill hisself 50 times in his hairy test rides. I was racing a very special Corvette in Nassau. The concept car of the wide Corvette (a nose flying dog) the Manta Ray, Sting Ray series. I had introduced Bill to a young lady we called the "Island Princess" the night before at a big-big social dinner and dance. You know the sort of dance, Rocky-fellers, Roosevelts, senators, movie stars, hi-buck greasers. The Nassau races were a big deal socially world wide. Anyway, at this dance Bill's had one drink too many. He is cherry red, talking to Roosevelt's son, and some other famous bullshitters. The Princess should have commanded some respect. After all, her great grandfather was the King of Nassau at one time.

Yup, she was very dark complected. A nice girl, and had sexual talents that left me speechless (and with a couple hundred mosquito bites, I mean all over) Can you imagine making love to a 150 pound wildcat on the front seat of a Morris Minor? Well, as I introduce "Her Highness" to Bill, right in front of Roosevelt, God and the whole damn ballroom, he grabs her by the ass and tells her he'd "like a blow job."

Next morning, he's got her in a Corvette, coming down a 12 foot wide road, with rock walls on both sides, running 'bout 90 miles an hour. He loses it, spins, (and don't touch a wall) right in front of the Volkswagen garage I had rented to work on the Corvette. I ran outside, saw that everything was OK then grabbed the keys out of switch and threw them far as I could into a field full of 'bout two to three feet high grass. While he blew his cork I said, "Bill wouldn't this be dandy if you hurt or killed the princess? Wouldn't your wife and GM be proud of you?" I said, "Go hunt the keys, by the time you find them you'll be sober enough to drive again." Yes, the keys were found in a couple hours by some native boy I hired. Did he look? Hell no, he walked off and it was five years before he'd talk to me again. I hope you don't misunderstand my experiences with Bill Mitchell. I liked him and admired his talent, but sure didn't have much use for some of his "hen-house ways."

When they built the tech center in Warren, Michigan in 1955, Harley Earl's people at styling designed the whole deal. The masterpiece was the stairway up to, and Harley's office, dining room and apartment. I can't even describe it. I haven't been in it since 1987. Yup, in 1987 I finally wore out my front door key. They changed the lock and I'm even more forgotten than Bob Stemple and Lloyd Ruess. I'll tell you the whole story later. Yup, if you're the writer you can do stuff like this.

Back to the beautiful dining room at styling.

This was a private "big shooter" dining room. In the middle of the table was a rotating upper table offering of every before and after meal pleasure ever thought of. Each diner had a button by his seat. You pushed the button, and it came to you. You could order from menu, or chef came out and you told him what you wanted. I don't know why, but I'd eat there a lot for a year or so, then it seemed I'd be in the dog house and miss four or five years. We played that game from 1955 to 1987.

Styling is operated as secret as the military weapons classified materials. Every day in certain areas, the lock combinations changed. Guards every goddam place. I got my "hero badge" there in late '50s. They had a "cold room" built in a very awkward location to get a big car in. Like a "fish tail Caddy" was a pure son-of-a-bitch to get in or out. Well, I'm screwing with ground effects on land, even bought and learned to fly a helicopter I used in my tests. If I'd had my way, Indy cars would have had tail rotors and controllable air foils front and rear. I don't know why, but I really dug aerodynamics (even though it took me 10 or 15 years to be able to spell it, usually came out aero-dynomouse). Anyway, I got my "hero rating" by saying, "Get a big piece of aluminum one inch thick, drill the plate full of holes, connect the holes with grooves, fasten a half inch plate over the one inch plate, drive a Cadillac on it, hook an air hose to it, and move it with one hand. Hell yes…like a dream! Next adventure is three-foot circle of plywood, the holes, and a vacuum cleaner motor, and a 100 foot cord, then races around the room, body English steered the deal one inch up from the floor.

Larry Shinoda was Bill Mitchell's right hand man for awhile. He was a character. He loved Corvettes, and did an awful lot of work on their concepts. Larry just "checked out" in November 1997. I guess I liked Larry also cause he loved racing. Especially open wheel cars. Indy was his second home. He "fucked up" when he followed Knudsen to Ford. Knudsen liked Larry especially, and put him on the Mustang at Ford. Larry was a Knudsen man, and when Bunk got it up the gazoo, Larry knew he would be next. He was, and there is no going back to GM. Only man in the world ever pulled that off was Jim Perkins, but eventually it caught up with him, and they "deep-sixed" him, too.

You know Bill Mitchell was famous for one other thing. He was first man to survive a divorce and not get drummed out of GM. Now that took some balls. When I first worked for GM, an unwritten code of the hills was "no jews, no colored, no divorce." Many big shooters lived with their wives for 20 or 30 years in misery cause of the no divorce code. Ed Cole was probably number two to beat the no divorce rap and live to talk 'bout it. By and large, the corporate giants in all the "big three" were nice people, but they sure had more than an acceptable percentage of untalented assholes. Once the assholes got plugged into the system, the code kept them in. But what was worse, every so often they get promoted higher. Somebody invented the "peter principle," an observation where if any of us continuing to be elevated in business or socially, or in the world of athletics or politics, we finally reach a point where we are in over our heads. No one man ever come close to being a peer in all the vocations the complexity of our lifestyle encompasses, from both a business or social point of view, so you finally reach a point like GM did in 1970. Their chairman and president just could not call all the shots in a timely forward thinking five year business plan. The foundation, being old, old, started to crumble it was like the hole in a dyke when it started in 1970. This is 2000…the hole gets bigger every day.

The strangest thing I notice GM and Ford are climbing in bed with the rice burners now. It's awesome. They had over 54 percent of vehicle business. Went to sleep with their heads up their asses and when they woke up the "rice burners" and Europeans had dynamited the foundation the US vehicle business was built on. I can remember a speech Henry Ford made in 1969. He said he had no fear of the "jap's making a competitive product." After he finished, I said, "I got a feeling in a couple years you're gonna wish you hadn't made that speech." A couple of years later he told me he couldn't have imagined the inroads the Japanese were making in marketing and product.

By then, Ford's was out of dough and headed for the shit house doing about 100 miles an hour (1972-3).

You know, I think there is a point at which something, anything, can get too big to control. I believe that's what knocked GM, Ford and Chrysler on their collective asses. In government, same deal. Now I watch every day, more and more mergers, and we talk 'bout biggest, second biggest etc, in the world, save money, hell of a deal. I suspect 10 years from now this consolidation will backfire and the process will reverse itself. I noticed when 10 experts are asked for an opinion on same question, you actually get 10 different answers. In my opinion that means no one really knows. It's just their best guess.

If the World Had More Deweys...

This chapter is about the people who were influential in my thinking, people who I learned from, and people who were peers in their specific niche of life history and/or racing. Some were leaders and made significant contributions to racing, to science, to the mechanics of auto racing in regard to entertainment value, finance, safety, medical solutions for an extremely hostile human environment. And some of these people apparently had extreme forward vision that moved the so-called sport of auto racing to increasingly higher plateaus. Some I liked and admired. Some I'd have hung by their balls if I had the authority. I can remember at best, about sixty-five years. So, I will start from about age twelve, and try to introduce them to you. Hopefully, accurately, but with no warranty except that I'll try to be accurate.

John Yunick

Not all, in my opinion, were what I call "good people." I can't start off by what as a rule is "number one," my father, John Yunick. I hardly knew him. He was a Ukrainian. Came here 'bout 1920. Worked and drank hard. I believe he was a pussy-hound. I was afraid of him. Seemed like his favorite activity was to either beat the shit out of me or my mother. I hate to admit it, but I in no way liked or respected him. He died of a heart attack I think, when he was 42 and I was 'bout fifteen years old. As I write and try to recollect, I've noticed my memory works best in recalling the very good or very bad parts. The "in between" is very clouded.

In September of '98, I read and envied Mark Martin's description of his recent experience coping with his dad's accidental death in an aviation accident. Mark said his dad was his idol and life model. It also made me feel bad. In the beginning, I let racing consume so much of my time I believe I deserved a rating of "defective father." I'm gonna have to tell you, I was a loser as a father.

You know something, I never was aware of it till I quit racing. Maybe my adventures in the war twisted my sense of values as well. What happened to me I think, the challenges, the excitement and the danger, plus the thrills of winning, consumed me to the point that I saw the responsibility to support my family in a medium lifestyle, as secondary issue to my main goal in life: to win every race I would ever participate in. You may or may not believe this, but from 1948 till 1975 my work schedule was from 7:00 am to 1:00 am, eighteen hour days, seven days a week, three-hundred-sixty-five days a year.

Sure I was nuts. Maybe that's why I quit racing so many times. Kinda like a drunk or a smoker or a doper trying to quit. It's hard to tell you this. I guess none of us like to admit to our warts, pimples and our closet collection of bad things. You know, if it's locked, you never open it.

LENA YUNICK

I can't say much for my mother, Lena. She was Polish. Came here 'bout same time my father did. She had a tough life. I think the European conception of raising children did not promote a close family. My parents' code of the hills was, "We made you, so you must work from the day you can walk and talk to help. And children must care for parents in their old age." In this way of thinking, more kids are better (more hands to work).

My mom, Lena Yunick, and me.

RENEE AND BILL WALKER

I had a sister a couple of years younger than I, Renee. (pronounced Ree-Nee, short for Irene) She had her hands full to survive and find a road to a good American life-style with two kids, nice house and a dog. She got lucky and married a classmate of mine from Aviation Cadets in advanced training. She met him when he and I got our wings as Air Force pilots in Marfa, Texas. Willie Walker is his name. He was a B-29 pilot involved in convincing the rice burners they made a mistake at Pearl Harbor what seems like a million years ago.

Though she was my only kin, I didn't try to keep track of her much after that. I was totally engrossed in auto racing and the mysteries of the internal combustion engine and it's fuels and its lubrication problems. From that I was forced into vehicle dynamics and slowly to apply what I'd learned regards aerodynamics in the Air Force to a race car. Actually, all aspects of the challenge to make a race car go fast and last. Kinda was like trying to eat an elephant. (Actually easier, since the information necessary to accomplish this was not perishable). It dawned on me, if I ate a little bit every day, eventually I would consume the whole damn elephant.

This approach is not a task where the effort needed is a fixed value. The elephant I ate weighed 4,000 pounds. With the giant strides in technology, today the elephant weighs 7,500 pounds or more. No longer will a high school drop out be able to eat the new elephant. Nor will a PhD be able to do it. The mass is just beyond one man's capacity.

I was considered the ultimate loner. A species I believe now extinct. Competition forces departmentalization. This forces a collection of three or more individuals in various categories to team up to arrive competitively at a given contest at a given day. Ray

My sister Renee.

Evernham, I consider to be the dean of the current faculty of crew chiefs. They each operate with 25 to 35 technicians. The school I went to gave you one or two racing assistants, who as a rule, they donated their time. I guess for same reasons as us, just to race.

MR. DETWEILLER

Mr. Detweiller, the older up-country Dutchman, gave me all the moral and social guidance I ever got. Well, put it another way, the only person I listened to and tried to absorb. He ran the Sunoco in Neshaminy. Maybe the only adult I trusted besides my school teacher. I had a female teacher, in our one room deal. She taught first to eighth grade. I admired and trusted her. She was my role model of what was good in the female category. Both she and Mr. Detweiller had deceased mates. I tried to get the two together. (The school was only 100 yards from his gas station.) Nope, never did happen.

I didn't get any help from religion. I was a Catholic and forced to go to church fairly often, but when I was driving B-17s out of Foggia, Italy, my views on religion took a different set. I spent a winter there. This was 'bout 200 miles east of Rome and the Vatican. When we ate with our mess kits, we'd dump the left over food into big garbage cans outside the mess tents. Here, there were many very old and very young people, with their feet wrapped in burlap or nothing, standing on ice or snow eating what we threw away. The closest civilian housing was one and a half miles away. There were five and six year old kids there, and it's dark, and snowing – bad shit. Well, everybody in Italy is Catholic but the church is doing nothin' for these people.

Just 'fore Christmas, a sixteen-year-old girl is 'bout to give birth; she's unmarried. I imagine the father was probably a German pilot or German air crew. We haven't been there long enough for the baby to be American. She's in the officer's club laying on a couple tables. The weather is beyond horrible – cold, snow, wind. I run to our squadron priest, "Come give us a hand." The girl and us are all scared. She wants a priest, she thinks she's dying. That son-of-a-bitch would not come. Fucking "out of wedlock," and she's a dead player. Well, the baby was born OK and the mother didn't die, but the Catholic religion has a shaky disciple now.

Month later I finish my twenty five missions, and I go to Rome for a week to drink, party and fuck. I got to go to see the Vatican right? I do. I see gold everywheres. They carry the Pope on gold stuff. I'm told Vatican is really rich. Must be 'cause there is gold on the roof, ceiling, every damn place. So when I get back I go see the priest, "How come church don't help people eating our slop? Hell, it's right in the Vatican's backyard." One Catholic customer shot in the ass. Haven't been to church except for marriage and funerals since.

I'm for helping the living, screw the dead. We can't help them. Simply put, I do not understand a system where we have a right to inflict punishment on people who do things that are not criminal.

How 'bout ol' Jim Baker? Explain that deal to me. How many did he fuck in the name of religion?

Before Vatican visit, when I'd get scared, man I give it the "Hail Mary" and all the stuff I learned at confession. I found out if I screwed a married woman all I had to do was tell it to a priest, say a few prayers and when I got finished it never happened. Nope, never had a priest ask for her phone number.

Well, close to where I lived in Neshaminy, Pennsylvania there lived a motorcycle racer named Bob Hollowell. He was a religious up-country Dutchman 'bout 28 years old. I wanted to be just like him. Bob was national motorcycle champion, rode an Indian motorcycle. I finally got together twenty bucks, buy an Indian Bonneville Scout just like Bob rides ('cept Bob's is new) and start racing it. I know Bob pretty good, not as a friend, but by being around him. He does not smoke, period.

In order to finance my racing career, I sell the Saturday Evening Post (magazine) and have to deliver them. One issue there is a big advertisement on the rear page, of "National motorcycle champion" Bob Hollowell smoking a Camel cigarette and telling how great it tastes. Adios Bob as a role model hero. Now to me he is just another lying motherfucker. At that age you want to drive a race car, fly airplanes, run a submarine, drive a fire truck, be a professional ball player, go out west and be a cowboy. So it's very easy to be influenced in that period of a man's life.

Mr. Garth Pitcairn

OK, war's started, World War II, man I gotta get in the Air Force, drive a P-40, paint a shark head on it, and be a war ace. I started my war contribution by roughing out 90 millimeter gun barrels, at a machine shop. Next I learned to weld and passed the Army/Navy aviation welding test at Pitcairn Aviation. Gonna make autogiro's (half-airplane, half- helicopter). My main boss is Mr. Garth Pitcairn, a very-very rich man. Up till I met him all rich people were bad people. He taught me we all have one head, two arms and two legs and that, educated equally, all people of all colors were equal. From there on my opinions or judgments had no reference to color or financial implications.

He taught me to avoid religion, unions and politics in conversation. His opinion of this was, "All three were forms of control of the masses manipulated by authority – happy egotists with nearly blind faithful and extremely opinionated followers. A necessary evil in democracy, but the best option man had." One day I couldn't stand it anymore. I asked, "Mr. P. how do I get to be an Air Force pilot?" He did that in a couple hours. (That is to create a legal birth certificate out of nothing.) I was grateful to Mr. P. for this till ten minutes after first German bullets started zinging around my plane. At that time Mr. P, all your good guy points were used up.

My first flight instructor in primary flight training, Mr. Waters, was also a big help to me. After our second instructional flight he told me my chances of becoming a good pilot or to avoid washing out were damn near zero. That done it. I then tried twice as hard and got it done.

Life's strange and full of surprises. I bumped into Mr. Waters much later during the war in Calcutta, India. I had just returned from a Hump round trip, and there he was, an ATC co-pilot on a C-54 getting ready to go on his first Hump run. He ain't got back yet, and I doubt he ever will be.

I write a lot about my war years elsewhere in this book. My ass-chewing by General LeMay, meeting Chiang Kai-Shek and his wife, General Chennault, the colonels who run the Flying Tigers, the Army people who run the Kanarni Estates (Alice Faye was a WAC and Tony Martin a master sergeant), Jack Dempsey, the fighter who I delivered in China, the neat West Pointer who run the Sixth Emergency rescue (my boss in India), the Maharajah of Tri Pora with whom we ate once a week.

I was very disappointed in the open violation of mail laws…smuggling, no other word for it. The deception and waste of money. And the stealing actually of military fuel and equipment use. Chiang Kai-Shek, under the guise of eventual Chinese return to democratic form of government, really raped the US taxpayers out of hundreds of millions of dollars. The real story of the Flying Tigers as opposed to how it was presented to the US citizens. A very deceptive story. I'm afraid my social and moral targets were lowered considerably by the adventures in the China-Burma-India theater of war.

I tried every single kind of drug invented up till then in China and India, but was very puzzled by the results. My expectations were disastrous – way above what I remember about the effects. (Sex and drugs as I experienced them did not mix.) You know, I think that part helped me. I never again ever tried any of that stuff (let alone inhale). But I'm only 77, I may start up later.

General Merrill was real. I didn't know or meet him, but I knew about, and was around the stuff he and his men did regarding the Burma road and China. His act helped me recover from the CNAC (Chinese National Air Corps) act. Merrill did what I thought Army generals were supposed to do. The actual Flying Tiger story makes me kinda ashamed. It was really a very expensive crooked PR exercise, where the firecracker expert and his wife made enough money to buy Formosa.

I'm now twenty years old. One fourth of my life has been either making killing equipment or killing with bombs. I've been brainwashed to hate Germans and japs. I've met quite a few famous people, but I'm really disappointed and disillusioned. Hell, the story I got in the Philippines was MacArthur was a bumbling coward who ran when the shit hit the fan. By now I'm sure I will not live through this, and the fear of dying only appears in those few minutes (or more like seconds) when something ain't going worth a shit.

In late '45 when the japs came back in the kamikaze deal, I'm laying on an army cot in a tent on top of a buried Japanese ammunition dump in sight of Buckner Bay on Okinawa, laughing and drinking home made alcohol from medical supplies, shaving lotion and pineapple juice. A week before the war's over and they lied to us again. If the war was already over why did the shooting and bombing start again? My character is in bad shape. For first time I disobey standard operating procedure drunk and off-post when the planes hit. Up till then I hadn't ever even considered it. Nothing happened. No punishment.

Next I'm to start a bond tour in the US with the B-17 (Smokey and his Firemen). I get drunk on a ship, fall asleep, it sailed to Hawaii. I'm stuck on board so I've got to go to Hawaii. Still no punishment. Plane is in Hawaii waiting for me. Another mix up over drinking and I end up on same ship going to San Francisco. In Frisco, I'm AWOL for four days. Still no punishment. Now I get two month leave, then a discharge into the Reserves. Man, if ever there was a lost soul it was me.

Next step is working in a Ford garage in cold country. It lasted a month. I also found myself committed to marriage, and didn't have the balls to say, "Time out, I've changed my mind." I've got a house trailer, I quit my job and tell my wife that I'm going to Florida with or without her. Just goddam gone inside of six hours. I got to Daytona, I started to calm down and started to try and join a world where maybe it was OK to think forward as much as a year. I try a job as co-pilot for Eastern Airlines one month (at $250 a month). I was flying C-47s at night, in thunderstorms most of the way, flying the beam "a" and "n" signal. No radar, just right into the weather.

I hate to be a quitter but I'd rather starve than continue. Well, I started working on cars in the trailer park and made enough to live on. Inside of six months the demons were gone. I found peace I guess.

Daytona was a beautiful place to live then. Beautiful trees, best beach in the world, very cheap place to live, really nice people. I was outsider, but accepted. Back then, Daytona had an on-off switch. Thanksgiving to June first switch was "on" to wealthy vacationers. June first, that switch went "off." The lower income tourist switch came "on" July first, and switched "off" August fifteenth. From school out to school in. Remember, I told you 'bout flying over Daytona four years previous. Now I knew why I parked car and trailer here and didn't go further.

By the end of '47, I've built a small garage on, or I guess in the Halifax River. The last piece of property on the north side of Daytona Beach (957 North Beach Street, Daytona Beach FL 32117. But if you think you got gypped when you bought this book, don't write me. I won't give you your money back.) This property was land at low tide and water at high tide. The 1947 labor rate for auto-truck repair charged two dollars per hour against the flat rate.

Coca-Cola, or by it's Southern name "dope" was a nickel, newspaper (daily) two cents, gasoline twenty cents a gallon, hamburger a quarter, beer a quarter. Motive Parts is my main parts supplier, they have a machine shop, and Marshall Teague works there as an automotive machinist, and Fireball Roberts drives their delivery truck. Both keep their race cars just in back of machine shop, and at night they push 'em in to work on them. Bob, the owner of the machine shop loves auto racing. He don't know it, but his generosity helped start NASCAR.

Daytona's full of little chickenshit garages like mine, and to make a living you got to hustle. I worked seven days a week from 7:00 am to 7:00 pm and many days till midnight. This was a pretty big drop in social status for a "war hero." But by now I know I'm too damn opinionated to ever work for anybody. I'd already found out it was very easy to improve the performance of about any engine, but no one would pay for the extra time to do it. But stock car racing was the road where people who got excited by noisy, fast cars could satisfy this strange urge to experiment with auto engines.

FRED GARD

My first good customer, was Fred Gard, of the "Home Ice Company." Yup, then ice man still brought ice to your ice box. Delivered right to your kitchen for ten cents, maybe more. Fred was a drunk, freckle-faced, red-headed Irishman, maybe Scotch. Fred gave me back humor and a different kind of inner peace. He was always in trouble, always broke, lied worse than Clinton, but no matter how bad it was, he'd find something funny 'bout it. Worry? Hell no, somehow, someway it would be OK, if the roof don't leak, your shoes ain't got holes in 'em, you ain't hungry and you feel good physically. Hell, what else is there? Fred, you were my first and worst customer. When you went out of business you owed me quite a bit of money by the standards then. We seen each other off and on till about 1975.

'Bout 1990 he shows up here at the shop driving by himself. He is ninety years old. (If you've heard that drinking will kill you, Fred Gard had to be the 8th wonder of the world). He says, "Smokey. They're gonna ground me, take my driver's license. I forget where I live and I get lost." I haven't seen him in fifteen years. I'm astounded he is alive, and goddam he looks great. But like most bad actors when they get up in years, they find a crutch to lean on. For him it was religion.

Fred says, "I know I'm gonna die soon. I've made peace with every person living 'cept you. I don't want to die knowing you hate me." I hugged the old son-of-a-bitch and I said, "Freddie, I never ever hated you. And about the money, I doubt I even thought about it for thirty five years. When you first became a customer, watching and listening to you and drinking with you really put me back in the real world again." Really, if I just did everything opposite of what he did, that would be the right thing to do. So I said, "Fred, you could have died years ago and been clear of any damnation by me."

Let me tell you something, maybe being the ice man was very hard, poorly paid common labor, but them cats had more options for pussy than even the preachers do. You can imagine taking forty five minutes to deliver a twenty-five cent piece of ice. Yup, Fred and I had quite a few adventures where he couldn't get the truck started and the customer was lonely and had a quart of whiskey or lots of beer. Even ice men could only fill so many boxes a day. Fred had a super nice lady for a wife. I imagine she and Fred were probably married 65 or 70 years. She, I'm sure should be a candidate for sainthood.

What made you think you were a mechanic, Smokey? Well, while I was flying in the war, I worked on my own planes, B-17 and B-25 and I'm still alive. I signed off of all my repairs as tech sergeant Goofaldo Shadetree. I believe that was my mental image of my mechanic qualifications.

BILL FRANCE, SR.

There was a big bullshitter in Daytona named Bill France who had a garage across the river. He was a "would be" race driver and race promoter. We all (garage owners) built reputations. I decided when I was a kid to try and be the best at what ever I did. So I buy a sign for out front, "Smokey's Best Damn Garage in Town." This sign prompted a visit to my shop by Bill, because that day I was re-doing a job France had screwed up in his gas station garage. During our first meting, I decided France wouldn't make a pimple on a real mechanic's ass. And I doubt he left singing the praises of Smokey.

Back then the parts houses bankrolled the little garages. We had 40 days to pay, and we got a big discount no one else but a licensed garage could get. Not quite the same today is it? (I think Motive Parts was a NAPA store, but I'm not sure). I always appreciated what the parts people did for us, knowing that without their help "Smokey's Automotive" would have never been.

Well, Bill was bad about paying, which hurt those of us who did. And I, having been involved in World War II, did not expect anything special from society, and was offended by males who managed to avoid losing four or five years of their lives, especially considering the various negatives that went with the deal. France got a draft dodging, no paying, shitty workmanship rating in my book. Then when I seen him drive in a race at Langhorne, I gave him a one star rating on a scale of one to five. OK, you can see, our relationship was no love affair to start off with. I watched him operate from 1947 till 1959. A lot closer than any person except Joe Epton or Pat Purcell. After 1959 I got to know less and less about what was really happening. It would take 100 pages to describe France as I knew him. But Bill Clinton does it for us in a simple

Before the Daytona Speedway was finished – Big Bill is the tall guy and I am standing with Jim Stephens.

phrase. (Picture a six foot three Bill Clinton without wavy hair.)

France divided himself into two people. The one the racers knew, and the one the "money people" knew. France could manipulate people like the pied piper. You couldn't believe a goddam thing he said. He's used Lindbergh's plane name, "we." It was always "we" doing the work, and "I" gets the money. France was as ruthless as Hitler. People who crossed him, like Teague, Turner, Flock, were immediately banished from stock car racing. Kinda like getting thrown out of the French Foreign Legion. (They cut all the buttons off your coat, and take your citizenship and camel away.) As you read this, I guess you wonder how come you had a NASCAR license for 23 years? How come France didn't kick you out? Confucius said it best with, "When you got 'em by the balls, their hearts and minds will follow." Put another way, he liked what I brought to the track: my cars and the fans to see my cars.

Bill, in his furious struggle to establish NASCAR, did some things society would frown on, and some of his maneuvers, if examined by the law, would have interrupted his rise to fame and fortune quite drastically. And to be honest with you, my personal life socially, was not exactly a role model for the American male behavior from 1946 till 1970. But from a legal point of view, I can't ever remember being a candidate for incarceration; well perhaps nothing other than abusing the recommended driving code. You may be thinking now that I hate Bill France, and this book is aimed at smearing France. A vendetta for the abuse I got from him – you're wrong. We all have warts and bad stuff. I decided this book was gonna be the way things were.

When Bill got so ill, last couple years he lived, I quit writing or saying anything critical of him. I considered him helpless to defend himself. Two years before he died he called me at least 500 times, sometimes five times in 15 minutes, and visited me at the shop at least ten times. The last time I saw him alive, he asked me to go to St. Louis with him in his jet to look at, and get option on some land that "we'd" build a race track on. This is the first time I ever heard the "we" word regarding profit. Yup, I'd "Own part of the track in St. Louis". No, don't go looking for the track, it never happened. I'm convinced he meant it, but by now, I'm seeing Bill France number three – an old, sick man. But he looked great, and lived in his own private "Disney World," a make believe happy world.

He actually seemed quite happy. He smiled and laughed. Course he couldn't drive. Had a chauffeur with a portable phone, and what looked like a nurse in the back seat. Oh yeah, a great big free "Pony-ack." He was pretty mobile still, just mind and memory adrift like an eagle feather in a 20 mile per hour wind on a gusty day. "What time are we gonna leave for St. Louis?" he'd say. I would answer, "Well hell, right now I guess." He says, "Go home, get some clothes, 'cause when we finish in St.Louis we'll go to the islands." He has a couple boats there, and "We will go fishing and chase some pussy, like the old days." Then he puts his arm around me and says "he misses us." (The original bunch) Now he has money, and wants to "spend lots of time with us and help us enjoy our remaining years." Well, I turned away and damn near cried. I got all choked up. I thought, "What a fucking shame, most of us were either dead or crippled or sick, and as a rule very poorly equipped financially in our medically much more expensive years. Here Bill's got the world by the ass financially, but he's out of time." But something inside his brain made him aware of yesterday in a way I guess that bothered him, and he aimed to remedy it.

No, my true feelings for Bill France, Sr. are sadness. He did live a long life, but I doubt he was comfortable with his conscience as the days wound down. All males, at least all with beards, have to look at their faces every morning in a mirror. I'm of the belief: if you don't feel pretty good about yourself, and the trails you leave behind in your life's adventures, each time you really look in the mirror, it's an uncomfortable sensation that you would like to remedy somehow.

All successful people I spent time with, I tried to learn something from my close observation of how they operated. Now I'm to the point where I've decided what's yours is yours, and same for me. I will not run up your back and over your head to get where I want to go, but to left, right, or under is OK. I figure any deal you and I get into has got to be good for both of us. I had four or five rules I lived with. There was only one rule that France and I shared. That was, "Whatever I think is OK is OK." Even here, we differed though. His deal was also, "Anything I do is OK." So if I learned anything from him, it was about how not to treat people you potentially have direct or indirect control over.

But to try and reduce the credit or fault what he did for stock car racing would be idiotic. I'm not sure anyone could have done what he did. Maybe his chicken-shit method was the only was it could have been done. When Harry Truman ordered the atomic bomb into Japan it probably was the most humane way to end the war. But I doubt anybody from Hiroshima sent Harry a thank-you card. In retrospect, the most effective method to do something has got much to do with whose ass is getting eat up. Of the 23, 24 years I played "NASCAR," I think 20 of 'em I had a big need for Vaseline. Yes, Vaseline not Valvoline (mixed with 10% novacaine).

In those years there were at least 10 times I decided, "That's it, I've been fucked enough." Three times France himself talked me into coming back. The other times it was "greenies" and ego.

In '58 I entered Indy and France said, "If you run Indy your ass is mud in NASCAR." I said, "Maybe in a couple of years I'll figure out how to keep living without your crap." The day before I left for Indy in '58 with race car, I got good news from France, "You can run Indy. We will remove your pictures from the Porta John toilet seats. Come out to race track with your race car for a picture." I was in a good mood, remember that was done the day I tore up the five grand check from "Halifax Recreation Area" with the mayor (on TV). Well, I get there and no France. I notice that, even though track's not finished (Daytona), it looks like a man could get around it. So I thought, "I'll never get another chance like this to piss France off." By now I've heard he's gonna drive a race car around the thing for the first time for TV. So I jump back in tow car and took the Indy car, with a good name "the City of Daytona Beach Special," around the track on a trailer. I got back to starting point as France got out of his car.

You're right – he was pissed. Not a bad day's work. I royally pissed off Owen Eubanks, the mayor and local bank president, and France in one hour! Really, he should have thanked me. The black and gold Indy car with the name it had would have made a better first race car around Daytona picture story, but as I guessed, no picture, no story. Well, even as pissed as he was, he couldn't very well throw me out of NASCAR again – he just put me back in the day before.

Now here's a part of France's world I admired. He charged us for a NASCAR membership and entry fee for each race. For which we were guaranteed the right to work our asses off for nothing, no insurance, no pension, no vacation, no paycheck. Back then 500 bucks to win as a rule. In the beginning, you could tow clean out to Riverside, California for not a hell of a lot more. And ol' Bill, with all of the above negatives, would still hold suspension over your head if you weren't a good boy and do as you were told. If you know of anybody else in the world ever did this (and did it for 50 years), write me and tell me about what they did and how it worked. I think if the Nobel people ever offer a prize for con games, NASCAR would win it in a clean sweep every year.

A final salute to "Big Bill." 'Bout two years ago, during one of the patch jobs doctors have to do from time to time, to keep me mobile enough to work, two nurses that worked part-time taking care of Bill at his house told me kinda how it was taking care of him. They both said they hated it. Why? Well, seems like he never got over his racing days habits. And too much "grab ass" and "feeling" was always going on with graphic language about "fucking and blow-jobs." But as you now know (a la Clinton), this is of an non-sexual nature. Bill was in his eighties and still peddling!

Marshall Teague

Anyway, the garage is planted in middle of '47, Smokey Albert Yunick was born September, '48. I sold the trailer and bought a house ($6,500). In the middle of '48 I started getting bored. I don't know why, but I kept my war stuff to myself. Marshall Teague was curious 'bout it. He was a flight engineer on a B-29 and was very proud of it, so a friendship was started even though I refused to participate in an Air Force dialogue with Marshall. Nope, don't know why. Guess I was ashamed of all the innocent people I knew I had helped kill with my B-17.

Fireball worked part time with Marshall, so I start getting included in race talk and am now a part-time free helper for Teague. Fireball starts using my shop for his race car. All this starts with modifieds. In 1951 Teague wins beach race with a Hornet. I meet Vince Piggins and Mal Middlesworth. Piggins is the Hudson Motor Company liaison engineer for the Teague deal. Vince did the engineering and managed the Hudson stock car effort. Middlesworth is the Pure Oil PR honcho. This is start of factory and large corporate sponsorship.

In 1951 Marshall decided to run a second Hornet with Herb Thomas as driver. Well, Marshall couldn't hardly get to the race track on time with his own car, so two cars was just too much. I had already been working with Marshall before Piggins offered me $200 an engine to build Herb's race engines for '51. Goddam, I'm about to get important, I'm in my first factory deal! I already know it took close to 100 hours to build a new race engine from scratch, by the end I found out how to spend nearly 200 hours per engine. The straight up stuff took 50 hours but off-setting the crank, dropping the deck, playing with the ports so they couldn't tell – the little things took a lot of time. But hell, the flat rate per engine is only 50 hours, so I'm getting a hell of a deal – double the flat rate!

Vince Piggins and I go back to Hudson Hornet days. This whole Hudson factory racing support system is very fragile, amount of money is very minor, but it was important for NASCAR's development. They pay your expenses and you go baby sit engines at track. No pay, just expenses. For anything over 400 miles, you can fly. But you can't rent car, "Herb will pick you up, OK? And you'll share a room with another helper." I said, "Bullshit! Deal's off." They said, "OK, have your own room, single rate only." Vince ain't a bad engineer but Hudson allows such a small budget for stock car racing, no one could have made it any better. Actually, by late 1954 Vince was the only engineer in Detroit who knew his ass from a hole in the ground regarding stock car racing. Well, before it's over, I'm building the whole car and I have cars coming back to Daytona for overhaul. No more money, but the exposure to me surely is supposedly "worth millions." OK, '51 to '54, two NASCAR championships and two second places. "Vince, I need you to pay me for all this extra work." "Well Smoke, Herb said he'd pay you," etc.

It's the end '54 season, "Fuck it! I quit!" "Wait a minute, Hudson is gonna give you a new car built to your specifications, and give you a diamond ring." "OK, Black two door sports coupe and every extra you got." Ever see a red diamond? Well that's what my ring had. Still got the ring? Nope, I lost it in a card game soon after. How much was it worth? Got no idea. What the hell would I know about diamonds?

Well, shortly after that, the Queen Wilhamena (who owns Hudson) said piss on this money losing deal, and sells the farm to American Motors. I'm invited to Detroit to a big meeting about 1955 race program plan. The car looks like junk to me. Marshall's taking their shit, trying to hang on. I'm like a guy in jail for life. I got nothing to lose, so I said, "Stick your '55 deal up your ass," and left the meeting. Started home to Daytona. 'Bout a week later noticed I was in Las Vegas – got lost on the way home I guess. Vince took all the shit and shortly got his ass fired anyhow. Poor Marshall worked his ass of with a Hudson jet. It wouldn't get out of a shower of shit, and he was done. Good bye ol' Hornet, you were a dandy in your time.

Through all this France and the promoters give us a lesson in character building. Every racer should have kept a quart of Vaseline handy to help accommodate France, the promoters and sponsors…to ease our pain. Man, we got used. But no one really knew where we were going. I played the game 35 years. I tried to rock along in life giving priority to how I handle daily and short term problems or goals. I can say I don't think I ever really thought about next year till I was 55 years old. In the back of my mind 65 years old was the end of any sort of life worth living. At the time, my number one priority was still to enjoy life. "The hell with tomorrow." By late 1954 I decided I was just a damn fool, working my ass off for the "Bill France Benefit Fund." (I had that part right.) I'd found out you didn't have to be a racer to enjoy life. Sure I missed the racing, but how much can you miss anything when you're playing with one of the local nymphomaniac beauty queens with no clothes on?

Pat Purcell

Pat Purcell was France's number two man in the fifties. Pat was a carnie, a con man, and an Irish alcoholic (he knew his shit). He was fair and square, but crazy. He'd never turn his back to any shooter. Probably the perfect man for the time and condition of stock car racing. France could have been caught screwing some gal with four witnesses and Pat could prove France was in Africa at the time. I had an old plane then. Once in a while I'd take Pat with me to a race. He said that a couple times I tried to kill him, but it was his whiskey we were drinking. Pat had a real neat wife, "Agnes" who I felt, managed to keep him going the last ten years he was with us. He taught me a lot, but not much of real use to me. Stuff kinda based on the carnie way of life like, "Never, ever give a sucker a break." And, "The hell with tomorrow, tomorrow may never happen." (I already knew that part.) He was only guy I ever saw that could get France to listen and consider his comments.

Red Vogt

I got to tell you about Red Vogt. He influenced me quite a bit. He's gone now. Left 'bout six or seven years ago. If he was still here he'd be in his 90s. Red Vogt was the grandfather of every stock car engine builder there will ever be. Red-headed, freckle-faced, burr haircut, coffin nail puffin,' 18-hour-a-day, seven-day-a-week workin' robot. He was the Christopher Columbus of discovery regarding turning a sow's ear (stock car engine) into a silk purse. If he hadn't already had a nickname, I'd called him either "Merlin" or "Magic." In the beginning, all of us run for second unless his car either failed or crashed.

He was 15 years older than me. Hell, he was in a pit crew at Indy in the late twenties. His favorite engine was the flat head V-8 Ford, which was stock car racing's foundation. In 1947, he and his car owner Raymond Parks (another very important contributor to stock car racing's foundation), come to Daytona and approached Bill France with a Georgia corporate charter called "NASCAR."

Bruton Smith

About in here I need to bring up Bruton Smith. He and France were promoters who competed for track, drivers and cars. And remember within a year Bruton is trying to compete with NASCAR for the contestants with his remarkably same sounding outfit "NSCRA" (National Stock Car Racing Association). The reason racers were interested was for honest control of prize money and future growth. Bruton ain't gonna like this part, but he too got forgetful from time to time and disappeared with the prize money.

People ask me if, "I ever envisioned the growth of stock car racing as it is today?" Hell no! Not in any mental fantasy I could have conceived, even when well-tuned by the devil and his thirst remedies. But even more is the transformation of a zoot-suiter to a billionaire, with the second largest vested interest in motorsports in the world. (Hello again Bruton). A "zoot-suiter" to me was a dandy dresser in 1948, and their costumes were, even down pedaled, very unusual, it was a national fad. Well, in 1949 thru 1959, Bruton run second to France, 'bout five laps down, 100 to go and 'bout 1959 blows on the front straight away running last, and disappears (at least to me).

"Where'd Bruton go Curtis?" "Don't know Smoke. Let's start a bran' new party!"

Back to Red Vogt. I don't know why Red nor Raymond Park were not officers in the new NASCAR (now a Florida charter). This shit's way over my head. But Marshall Teague has been nominated secretary and treasurer of NASCAR, and every few days he fills me in. According to Teague, France had Cannonball Baker, Eddie Bland, and Bill Tuthill in his back pocket. France ran NASCAR like it was "his store." Well, Teague wasn't a "yes" man, so shortly he had as much to say about running NASCAR as NASCAR's official dog. Marshall gets rewarded for his efforts by getting flung out of NASCAR. A remarkable item came to my attention in the listing of NASCAR race driver's points, Marshall Teague never existed in 1949, '50, '51, '52. I guess France run 'er like the French Foreign Legion. If you fucked up they cut the buttons off your

Richard Petty in the pits.

coat and removed your name as having ever been there. Or they just shot your ass. Well, France didn't have the juice then to get away with deep-sixing just anybody. Hell, what difference it make anyhow?

Teague only won seven races in stocks, and the modifieds didn't count any more. Curtis Turner, Tim Flock and Richard Petty got the same reward. Richard did quite a bit of ass-kissin' and got back "in" in 1965. Yup, King Richard was "out" for awhile over a rule dispute 'bout engines. In 1965 Turner got reinstated 'cause NASCAR was hurting from loss of manufacturers backing racing.

The world kinda caught up to Red Vogt 'bout 1951 or '52. He was operating on a very low budget and there was some dealer and accessory manufacturing money out there in this time frame. His star started to fade by 1958. Red was socially classed a "has-been" all because he couldn't handle the bullshitting and political ass-kissing. He was a very simple man who's hand shake was as good as a forty page contract. Simple fact was, Red refused to, or couldn't accept the "new world" we got flung into. So he lived out his working life doing what he enjoyed. Some racing, some passenger car repairs. By 1970 racing had forgotten him. It's 1998 now, and people are brushing off the cobwebs and dirt of the years, and are starting to discover and honor this deserving racer. In 1998 he had a garage named after him at the new Atlanta garage area, and was first recipient of the "Smokey Yunick Racing Pioneer Award." Red, you were a dandy. I miss your knowledgeable comments, wisdom and humor. Too bad the racing world didn't know you and your achievements. One of my un-favorite days was when I delivered the eulogy at his journey's end.

He was kinda like Babe Ruth, he'd just point his wrenches and when the smoke cleared, he'd done it again.

ED COLE

In spring of '54 Ed Cole from Chevy called me to work for him and race a Chevy. I said, "Don't want to." In fall he came to Daytona. I again said, "Not interested." By now I've had a Hudson "character builder," the Packard "disaster" and a royal screwing from Buick. Never got paid to build the Buick Herb Thomas broke his leg in, and later used. Meanwhile, I've noticed France is doing great. Herb Thomas is on top of the racing world, but in all fairness to him, champion twice, runner up twice in four years. His prize money totaled $98,000. In spring of '55 France talks me into meeting Ed Cole and his staff on a hill, front straightaway, North Wilkesboro. This meeting changed my life – again.

I was so taken by Cole and my ego was stimulated to where my brain quit thinking. 'Bout a close to even deal like when you engage in a very dangerous sexual adventure. (We had a saying, "Your peter run away with your brains.") Ed had four of his top helpers, Mauri Rose, Mac Mckenzie, Russ Saunders, and Harry Barr with him on the hill. Why did we meet in such a remote place? I don't have a clue. Inside of an hour Cole snowed me so bad I agreed. Hell, I couldn't wait to start building a Chevy race car.

My first Detroit meeting was rigged to convince me I was special. They piled on the praise bullshit. I assumed the chief engineer of Chevrolet to be the smartest engineer on earth with the most important engineering job in the world. Kinda like he won the "Indy of car brains." Cole was not only a good engineer, but a world class leader. I learned a lot about engineering from him, but as hard as I tried, I never even came close to his ability to motivate people into the blind faith his people and myself gave him. Hell, hours meant nothing. He could get you to work you ass off for him and enjoy it.

He'd visit me in Daytona, eat at the house, sit there, talk and drink for hours. Ed Cole was a real example of the American way. First two years around Ed I was so impressed with his manner and knowledge I pumped him every second for information. I had no idea then he was a self-taught engineer, nope. Kinda like after you win Indy without a driver's license, then you get one next year. You know he still didn't have an engineering degree when he was general manager of Chevy? And he'd already been chief engineer at Cadillac! He worked his ass off. This, coupled with his fantastic ability to lead, and his compassion for his fellow workers and people in general made him a success.

Here's an example: I'm with him in the tech center. It's brand new, not officially open yet. A janitor stops him in the hallway and explains a way to make Chevys better. Ed listens for three or four minutes (and we were in a hurry). The idea was not good. As we moved on I asked him, "How come he listened to that deal?" He said "Smokey, you never can tell…might've been a good idea." For sure that janitor was a Cole ass-breaker as long as Cole was running Chevy. If you didn't get it done he wouldn't chew your ass out. He had a way to make you feel ashamed of striking out without one word of criticism.

Well, Ed Cole not only was a super smart son-of-a-bitch he was also a leader. He knew how to get you to work your ass off but he also knew how to say "thanks." (This part Bill France never ever come close to learning.) If you knew the Ed Cole I did, you'd have liked him. If you didn't know he was a big deal, only way you'd have a clue would be by his clothing. Ed was a kinda medium size man, a dandy dresser. I can't even imagine him in dungarees. He was also not afraid of alcohol, and he did appreciate attractive ladies. In short, he had some pretty good qualifications you needed then to be a racer.

Once, about three months after I went to work for Cole I said, "I know my job is to win Darlington. But really, where the hell are you trying to go? Knowing your final goal will help me do a better job for you." He said, "I want you to make the '55 Chevy a desirable car for 15 and 16 year olds." I said, "I don't get it, they don't have any money." He said, "Yes, but I think in five to ten years they will and I want to make their dream car a 'Stove Bolt.'" We called 'em Stove Bolts down south because Chevy was the only company left using a carriage head bolt. (Dome head bolts with a square shank under the head that was supposed to keep it from turning) You couldn't put two wrenches on 'em. This was bad news if bolt turned 90 degrees. Yup, we even had Cole calling his car by it's Southern nickname.

If you wanted change he would listen, then decide his response in thirty seconds. Then all hell wouldn't budge him. In my opinion, the spark plug was in absolute wrong place (lowest point in cylinder), so any collected fluids – fuel, oil, and water – would run into the spark plug cavity and foul it. I had to move it on my own. Two years later they put it in production. But very seldom did Ed turn me down unless it had pretty expensive costs (a new cylinder head line be 'bout 50 million). I've been in the middle or around the edges of US car manufacturing for fifty years. If they ever build a facility to honor the "heros" of surface transportation, Ed's statue should be on highest place on the building.

Ed, John Delorean and Harold Sperlich were only three I met in my thirty years adventures with the elite brains of Detroit that had the balls to call it like they saw it, and the horsepower to get away with it, Knudsen a close fourth. Make no mistake about it, Ed Cole is the father of the 1955 Chevy, and the small block engine. Sure, he had some really great help. But he found 'em, he picked 'em (75 men in total).

That small block Chevy engine which he guided from it's inception and through it's first 15 years has as of now surpassed 65 million copies. 46 years later it's still in production (2000). It was born May 12, 1952. That man, with a staff of 75 engineers, designed and built the '55 Chevy with a V8 engine using only two components from 1954 – the transmission and brake systems.

It started May 1952, was in Chevy dealer show rooms September 1954. Don't that make Ed kinda special? Hell. They can't do it in less than three years now with 2,000 engineers. Plus, in '52 they were still pulling the handle down on the adding machine. In '52, every engineer had a slide rule in his coat pocket. Ed Cole's pick of the 75 engineers that changed Chevy's world varied in their lovability (a few were really assholes), but all were above average in talent, and team players.

How many did they sell in 1955? One million cars, that's how many. That engine will probably win the NASCAR Winston Cup championship in '01, it did in '00. Twenty-eight months from first drawing to show room floor. No car company in the world can come close to that even now. How good was his engine? It is still in production 48 years later. The Chevy small block engine is still the heart and soul of automobile racing.

NASCAR would have never been if it weren't for the Chevy small block engine! In 1995 Steve Lewis, owner of Performance Racing Industries magazine, liked my idea of a dinner and celebration of those 75 men (yup, all men). Steve put a program together (cost over a hundred grand). Twenty-one of 'em came (only 'bout twenty four living then). The after-market racing vendors underwrote about 80 percent of it through donations. Steve paid the rest. Guess who wouldn't give one goddam nickel to help pay for it? Chevrolet Motor Company. And not a single current Winston Cup Chevy driver or car owner. Not one racing association gave a dime either. Hell, if it wasn't for that engine Gordon, Earnhardt, Childress, and most of the other drivers would be pumping gas at some filling station. Just because things turned out the way they did, with everybody ape-shit over stock car racing, doesn't mean that it had to be that way. Part of the success is having a good motor to run.

Ed treated me like an equal, he listened and he taught me. A couple weeks before the Warren Michigan "Tech Center" was finished, Ed, Mauri Rose and I, were in the engineering shop with a '55 Chevy that had a chronic ignition problem. I was showing Ed what I considered a solution. This required a couple holes to be drilled, but where we were there was no electricity. One hundred feet away they had juice, so Mauri was going to try and get permission from the building people to run a an extension chord. They said, "No." I got pissed, hooked the cord up, and drilled the holes. Soon after, fifteen hundred men walked out of the building Saturday afternoon 'bout 2:00 pm, and stood by the lake in front of the Tech Center. Ed and the union guys went 'round and 'round, but stupidity prevailed. Fifteen hundred men got paid time and a half for two-and-a-half hours, and went home.

I consider him the best mass production engine man the world has ever seen, but he should have stayed and run Chevy or gone over to run GM Research till he retired. After the '55 and '56 Chevy, he got in a hurry and OK'd some bad shit (the 348, 409 engines). He let the bean counters wreck the big block 427 engine then let the '58 Chevy styling and the Corvair slip through. These bad calls, plus the wasted trip in air suspension and steer by ball instead of conventional steering wheel, the Wankel engine, a terrible automatic transmission made me question his direction. As I saw it, if he didn't personally guide the deals they didn't work. He even turned against racing in late '57. He was not worried about making cars, he was on his way to be GM's president, in a close race with Knudsen.

You ever hear of the "Peter Principle?" Well it's about we all have limits in our ability to perform, and 99 percent of us, especially the most ambitious, as a rule get into situations or jobs we can't handle. When Ed got the job as president I think he was in over his ass. He was an engineer, and a really special one, but as a paper shuffler and corporate planner he was out in left field. That's for bullshitting bean counters with a special talent to know what the public wants. In early '57 Ed's plate was way over full and I noticed his effectiveness to lead was slipping. Seemed like he went from a hero to a politician. Less decisive and influenced by opinions from unqualified people. Soon after a day came when I was demoted socially and rated as a "less than important." Sure, who the hell am I to criticize the president of GM? If I was so goddam smart, how come I'm still working at 77?

One day Ed overloaded my ability to adjust to his changing from engineer into executive and I quit. Well that pissed him off and he never spoke to me till nearly eight years later. I'm sitting on the pit wall at Indy by myself, looking at my Indy car. The capsule car had just failed because of my only, very special cross-flow aluminum radiator ('cause my method of mounting it was flawed). I knew how to fix it, but only people in the world that could make me a duplicate radiator at the time were Harrison Radiator, and the last I heard from them was, "Don't bother us again. This job was an expensive pain in the ass." You didn't need to be a social behavior specialist to not notice. I'm so low I can walk under a snake's belly standing up with a hat on. I hear a voice that says, "What's wrong Smokey?" I look up and it's Ed Cole. I'm 75 yards from anyone else. He sat down beside me. I explained the problem and he talked just like as if we were back in Daytona at the house. Nothing was said about the past eight years. He asked 'bout my family, you know, stuff you ask about if an old friend came by you hadn't been in contact with for a long time. He had some personal problems he told me about which amused me. I'm thinking, "I'll be damned, Ed's discovered pussy. Even GM presidents have experience with such a common problem." I'd guess he left me 'bout 3:00 pm.

At 8:00 am the next morning, an engineer from Harrison Radiator handed me a new radiator and said a spare would follow next morning. Yup, he brought it on a special GM flight from their New York factory.

Ed always wanted to have a good airplane and fly it himself. We talked about it many times. Well, I'll be goddamned if the Peter Principle didn't wipe him out. He tried flying a junky airplane in instrument weather, which he couldn't handle yet. And this great car hero loses his ration of the golden years. Someplace, somebody needs to really honor Ed Cole. Racing sure owes him. Ed, you're gone, long-long gone. I'm very grateful and proud to have worked for you and to have known you pretty well. If a stranger asks me if I knew you I say, "Hell yes, he was a friend of mine," and puff up a little. My personal gain from Ed Cole was a lot of engineering knowledge, but most important help or lesson I received was "all humans are about equal, and we all have 'bout same opportunity to attain what ever goal we set for ourselves if we work at it, and have the wisdom to target a goal we have the special talent for." I don't think Mark Maguire is ever gonna win Indy, and I doubt Jeff Gordon will ever hit 70 homers in the big leagues. Get it?

MARION ROSENBERGER

Ed Cole had an assistant chief engineer (worked under Harry Barr) I called Rosey. Marion Rosenberger was his legal handle. This man was a smart, hard-working, dedicated team player. He treated me like an equal in all ways. He was the best sounding board I had for my ideas. I learned plenty from his simple down to earth know-how. I admired him and tried to adopt to his easy going, unhurried and deliberate method of analysis and solution but I couldn't. I was never able to drop the cut-and-try or farmer approach. When they decided to use independent suspension on the Corvette, (I believe in '63) Rosey asked me to write a set of specs for an optional aluminum rear axle assembly. These specs will include how to adjust carrier bearing and how much back lash. I said, "OK, I'm gonna put one in an Indy car I'm building" (the capsule car). I had already gotten a prototype and done the job, so I wrote the deal up that night at the motel and gave it to him next morning. He was shocked and asked me, "How the hell I arrived at the figures?" I said, "Easy, I just put the third member on hot plate and set pre-load and ring gear clearance when it got to 300 degrees Fahrenheit." He was thinking, "Ten grand and a month for two engineers, plus a week at proving ground."

No one could work around Rosey and not learn. He was a natural born teacher. Rosey was a Chevy man clean through. I bet his shorts had the bow tie all over 'em. When I quit Cole, and later in '61 was running a Pontiac, Rosey was a real race fan, so he came to Daytona for the races.

We remained good friends and talked to each other fairly frequently, picking each other's thinking.

Well, Fireball's leading the race and no one can beat him "unless." Well "unless" happens. The engine breaks a rod near the end, knocks starter off, and car comes in pits dragging starter by battery cable. The oil pan has got big hole in it and there is oil all over hell. Rosey needles me 'cause a Chevy wins. He asks what happened. I don't want to give him the satisfaction of knowing connecting rod failed, so I say, "Piece of a tire knocked starter off, which then knocked hole in oil pan." Rosey buys it, then finds out the truth six months later (Tried to get even till he retired.)

I talked to him six weeks before we were gonna have a big party for the survivors of the 75 engineers (he being one of the key players) who did the small block. He sounded the same as he did in '62. Two weeks before the party (he is in his 90s, but in good shape) he was walking down the street and his breathing permit expired. We missed you at the party Rosey. I hope some day the world gives you a gold star for your contribution to automotive advancement.

Mauri Rose

Mauri Rose – boy, there was a dandy. A little bitty guy, 'bout like a little 800 pound gorilla. If you worked with him and goofed off, or didn't know what you were doing, you got your ass bit hard constantly. For a self-taught engineer he was plenty good. Mauri won the Indy race three times back in the '40s when it was tough to steer. Really a job best suited to a gorilla. Mauri drove damn near standing up, so he could steer stiff-armed with his upper body and shoulders. Now, Mauri's journey through life didn't in anyway endear him to his associates, but from 1955 till 1957 Mauri was in Daytona as Chevy's liaison engineer. We worked 'bout 14 hours a day, seven days a week. It turned out it was best he lived with us, rather than a motel. I worked with him for damn near three years, and kept in touch with him till he checked out.

Early in my association with Mauri Rose we had a bean counter as a boss (MacKenzie). He was the lead speaker and listening to him you were led to believe he did it all. Actually, he did nothing but hold us up. I got very angry. We had about 2,000 students in the audience. I look at Mauri, he waved down and had a look on his face, "I'll take care of it." He said MacKenzie's speech reminded him of a story in India. There was a new bridge and lots of cars and animals (like elephants) going across. An elephant in line was asked by a flea if he could ride on him over the bridge. Mr. Elephant said, "Sure." Well, the bridge groaned and squeaked and when they got to the other side the flea said, "We sure shook that bridge, didn't we big boy?" I used this fable many times when forced to speak with a high ranking bull shitter. The friendship – what friendship?

I'm proud to say I was his friend. I learned a lot from him. (Some of it "what not to do.") He and I were the Chevrolet racing team in 1955, 1956 and the start of 1957. That is, we ran the deal. I enjoyed his weird humor, his goofy kids, li'l Mauri and Doris. Eating in a public restaurant with the kids was an experience. If a restaurant ever has a waiter or waitress they wanted to quit, just train a male adult and two kids to put on the Rose's standard restaurant act, and that would shortly get the job done. That was the loudest, runnin'-aroundest deal most places ever saw. Mauri Rose, you were a real racer. It's too bad more about what you really were is not known. All you Chevy race fans say, "Thanks Mauri," he helped lay the foundation Chevy racing is built on.

Zora Duntov

Zora Duntov was the other big name Chevrolet racer I worked with. Now he was a dandy. Zora was a European engineer with a rich talent in engine design, who migrated to this country I guess in the late forty's. He built the "Ardun" cylinder head system for the flat head Ford. This was really a very far-sighted, financially risky challenge which did not pay off either financially or in appreciable power. Zora drove sports cars in Europe. I don't remember how Ed Cole picked him to head the Corvette program, but I believe they met in Sebring. Ed was a half-assed boat and sports car racer when he was chief engineer at Cadillac, and even though I admired Zora, I have to say he really was not in my list of the 500 best drivers. I don't know where Zora could have taken Corvette if he had the same opportunities the European engineers had. At Chevy the program was "try and make a silk purse out of a camel's asshole." Kinda like the buildings in the old west, a fancy front view and junk behind.

Yeah, I know Corvette lovers, but be a li'l bit honest with yourself. Your Corvette is a "tuxedo tiger." Actually is kinda like a "swoose" – half duck and half goose.

You know, I'm writing this, at 40,000 feet between Atlanta and Detroit, 3-27-98. First time I've been back to Detroit since 1987. My last visit was to drive all '87 new GM Models, and meet with all the GM brass, including Lloyd Ruess (then president of GM) on a Saturday morning, and describe my opinions on the various models. In a nutshell, I said, "All were still shit-boxes." Lloyd said, "What's your proposed solution?" I said, "Stop production on all models Monday. Take a couple years off, and fix them." You're right, that meeting was over in five minutes. I've never been hired or talked to by GM since. Word must have got to Ford and Chrysler, no calls from them either.

What do you think? Have you even owned a '87 GM Anything? I'll tell you this, if you know what the hell you're talking about, and are honest in your responses to questions from your peers and the media, you will tend to be as thoroughly avoided as people are with contagious diseases.

Back to Zora. As he approached the mid-sixties in age his health began to fail. I continued my friendship and contact with him till about a month before his living privileges were revoked. He attended the small block Chevy engineer's 40th anniversary celebration at the PRI Columbus show. He, I think, gave his last public appearance and speech that afternoon. Zora's wife Alfie is still going. Shortly a book on Zora's life will be offered. She commissioned a very good writer, Howard Walker, to do the book. Zora, it's too bad the five or six special engines you built weren't preserved for all to look at in some museum for all to observe. Museum? I tried for 15 years to get GM to build a museum to keep the "dream cars" and engines, and milestone development prototypes. I tried with Cole, Knudsen, Estes, Bill Mitchell, John Delorian, Lloyd Ruess, and Bob Stemple. Not even a spark. I guess politically that idea had "kiss of death" on it. You gotta believe some GM people knew it needed doing.

RALPH JOHNSON

In mid-'56, Cole said, "Smokey, I want to have fuel injection for '57. When you're resting, between racing '56 Chevy and '56 Chevy convertible, we have a fuel injector that Rochester built for us that needs to be developed, but it's a big secret." So GM sent the injector stuff down and paid to have a 12 foot fence installed around my race shop. They even hired a 24 hour a day guard security system. Wackenhut supplied the "Fearless Fosdicks."

That's Ralph in the Champion jacket., Rex (my son) and Curtis

He said, "I'll send an engineer down to help you." So along with the fuel injection setup he sent Ralph Johnson – six foot three inches of young, wild-assed something. He hated fuel injection, loved alcohol, and if anybody would have said, "What's a pussy-hound look like?" I'd recommend they look at Ralph second, and myself first (of course). Ralph was my kind of man. He worked his ass off, didn't bitch, and drank and partied every night. We worked till 1:00 am, seven days a week. He'd go to the Five O'Clock Club, sit there and drink till it closed at 5:00 am, then go home with the number one stripper and fuck till 7:30 am, before coming back to work at 8:30 am. Don't ask me how he stood it. I'd get three or four hours sleep and was hurting. Sure, sometimes I'd find him face down on the injector table asleep, but as a rule he could handle it.

This went on for 10 months straight. Ralph was funny, and as a rule, likeable. But drunk, that son-of-a-bitch made a mule look like a push-over. Stubborn, nasty, aggressive, bad news if you tried to influence him in any way. Ralph was also a hell of a good engineer. I'm sure if he'd have kept his nose clean, he would have been Chevy's chief engineer by 1970 or 74. When I quit Chevy in spring of '57, Ralph went to Atlanta with the Chevrolet race team, and the injector came and went. Well Ralph's mouth, aggressiveness and partying wounded his career at Chevy, and he goes to Holley carburetor. When I go to Ford I get him job there, but he shortly blows it too. Now he is running damn near out of control.

I lose track of him until one day in early 70s he shows up at shop broke and out of work, on his ass and wants a job. Well, I'm very hard to work for, a know-it-all, son-of-a-bitch and I don't like any discussion over five minutes about what I want to do. Ralph likes to argue so I said, "It won't work, you can't keep your goddam mouth shut – all we do is fight." Well, he swears that shit is over. We worked together for maybe fifteen years after that. Did we have trouble, hell yes. But he worked so hard, and was so faithful that somehow we made it.

Ralph worked so hard when we were trying to train a turbocharged 207 Chevy to run Indy it amazed me. This was the biggest challenge of my life. (Well maybe second to getting out of that whore house in Rangoon in early '45) I've seen him at Indy, hang onto a chain link fence, puking 'cause he was exhausted, then come back in ten minutes and work till seven the next night.

Ralph Johnson was a racer, but his lifestyle and all those hours screwed up his health. When I sold the hot vapor engine, I had a chance to give him a couple of bucks. After battling the world to sell the hot vapor engine, I think I mentally gave up. The whole deal collapsed, and in '87 I decided to force Ralph to get a better job before we killed each other.

He got a job at Crane Cams, and I think his health improved, but his disposition seemed to get shittier (if that was possible). In 1995 he pulled a deal on me that took the rag off the bush. Being one of the 75 engineers that created and developed the small block Chevy, he was invited to the PRI 40th Anniversary celebration for the Chevy motor. This was an all expense paid deal and he was supposed to get a fancy ring to boot.

Well, Ralph comes up, don't like the hotel we used. So he turns around and goes back to Daytona the next morning. I haven't seen him since and have no plans to do so in the limited future we both have. I'm through babying that no-handling asshole.

PETE DEPAOLO

In the spring of '57, I quit Chevy and went to work the same day for Ford. My boss there was Pete DePaolo. Pete was good people. I never met anyone who had a bad thing to say about him. He was a racer. He had won Indy once as the first guy to average over 100 miles an hour for 500 miles. That don't sound too impressive today, but considering the rough, slippery bricks with oil all over them and the skinny, rock hard tires they used on those spindly, no handling shit-boxes, it was a very-very rough ride.

Working for Pete was a pleasure. A 400 percent pay increase, a paid-for airplane I used to commute to Charlotte, a paid, full-time traveling secretary, and an expense account for food, booze, anything. My only instructions were to race wherever and whenever I wanted and develop Ford engines for high performance. I though I had died and gone to heaven. Pete was, I think, the funniest, best public speaker I ever heard. Still today I consider myself lucky to have known and worked for Pete.

PETE PETERSON

Ford, at the time, had a pretty good engineer I worked with and for, a guy named Pete Peterson. We worked together on the '57 Ford and later the Trans Am car. Pete ended up running Ford Motor Company and did a pretty good job. But I guess they didn't see it that way and put him out to pasture early.

I first met Jack Passino in this time frame. He was director of Ford Motorsports. I couldn't get comfortable with him. In 1969 we crossed paths again. This time I was in the driver's seat. To my face he was great, but behind my back he did every rotten, dirty trick in the book to wipe me out. He ended up hanging himself before I could get to him. I doubt there will ever be any statues to him at Ford.

Mr. Semon "Bunkie" Knudsen

Mr. Semon Knudsen, also known as "Bunkie" (why I never knew) was probably the biggest influence on me of any male human (except Mr. Detweiller). Mr. Knudsen did more for NASCAR from 1957 to 1970 than all the rest of Detroit put together. Mr. K was one of the superstars in Detroit. He and Ed Cole were kinda like, at the time, Jeff Gordon and Dale Earnhardt today. Rite here, I'm gonna quit calling Mr. Knudsen by his real name and substitute my name for him. I called him "Boss," 'cause I couldn't handle the "Bunkie" deal. (and me with a name like "Smokey," which suits me just fine – go figure). His credibility, his economic horse power, his really genuine love for racing built the economic foundation for advertisement, entertainment value and credibility for NASCAR. I worked for, or with, the Boss from 1958 till 1985. I met him in 1957. He came by and visited me in the early winter of '57. Wanted me to run a '58 Pontiac in the February Beach Race (last one on the ocean sands). "Nope. Thank you. I don't want no more stock car stuff. I'm going to Indy somehow." Month later he calls and says, "Come on up, I'll pay your expenses." "Thanks a lot, but I don't have time." "I'll pay you $1,500 plus your expenses." "OK, I'm ready." The deal is, run one race ('58 Beach Race) for ten grand and I own race car and purse. I'm broke and I see trouble coming, my hunch is the trouble is unavoidable and expensive. (I see a canceled husband license coming.)

Ten grand for two months night work and maybe a few bucks prize money. "Got a contract?"

"Nope! Five grand today and five grand race morning." The checks were drawn on Knudsen's personal bank account, not Pontiac Motor Company. One race, ten grand, and I own car. I thought, "Shit, I'm hooked up with an insane man." So I asked him, "Why was he willing to use his own money?" He said, "I'll get it back several times over in bonuses." You see, in June '57, GM quit racing and boycotted NASCAR. The "Big Three" – Ford, GM and Chrysler – said, "Adios France, your act is too expensive and a pain in the ass." Actually, the Boss took a risk fucking with a corporate edict to abandon stock car racing which was in force at the time. This man is different. Kinda like Ed Cole. I know he is very

Bunkie Knudsen

rich, born rich. His dad was president of GM once and had a trainload of stock. Yet he talked to me like I was important and talented. I wasn't used to that. Cole was only other big shot that got, I guess, my ego going. I agree for one race only. "That's fine," he says.

Paul Goldsmith drives it. We sit on the pole and win the race. $4,500 bucks is the reward, plus we are judges in the beauty contest, with the education furnished to me by the world's greatest authority regarding selecting beauty contest winners – Fonty Flock. Those adventures in selecting the queen may have been of value almost equal to the money. For you mothers and fathers reading this, CAUTION: some beauty contests really couldn't stand to be televised in their entirety if they still operate the same as they did in the '50s and '60s.

The beauty contest jusges.

I sold the race car for ten bucks to Cotton Owens ten minutes after I drove it back to the shop. Because of a deal I suspected was on it's way. (The Boss wanting me to continue racing the car).

Time he got to my shop the racer was gone. But I was so impressed with this man, that after I tried Indy in '58 (wrecked) I'm slap out of money, so he has very little trouble talking me into a deal to run a '59 Pontiac. The pay ain't much, ten grand a year and all expenses. I keep winnings. I can take off for Indy, I can sell used and obsolete stuff. (You know that's part of a stock car racer's deal. Then it was what he lived on.) I had a problem, in that I felt I should pass used junk on behind me to struggling newcomers trying to race a Pontiac. This habit shot that possible subsidy in the ass.

Remember by 1959, I'm an Olympic class alcoholic, and I'm supporting divorce lawyers and detectives. Also, taxed alcoholic beverages were not free. So I'm back to living one day at a time in the corner of the

203

garage machine shop. I now wonder why the Boss was interested in me. He lived a pure, socially correct life with out the usual habits of the inherited rich; that of being lazy, money-wasting, pussy-chasing, alcoholics, and with less than nice personalities. I didn't realize it at the time, but in about 18 months, without my even suspecting it, he planted the seed to get me to retire as the active drinking champion of NASCAR. I think that by giving me his confidence, I developed enough desire and confidence to get serious about racing. A few years later I realized you can't be drinking champion and racing champion at the same time.

The Boss made Pontiac the official NASCAR car. For the last forty years Pontiac is still the major choice of surface transportation of the royalty of NASCAR. In them days, I called it "grease." I don't believe it was bribery, but money and or free, big ticket items do, as a rule, in normal humans, affect their hearts and minds. Yup, the inspection process and approval of changes in durability and in the power category went much smoother under Knudsen's watch. NASCAR had a full-time ambassador in the Boss. He not only supported racing, he enjoyed it. He went to quite a few races and mingled with drivers and mechanics in the garage area. The Pontiac management team in '58 was Knudsen, Peter Estes and John Delorean. My job was to race a Pontiac, help all Pontiac racers, technically and with some parts, and my job was to decide on power and durability improvements and to do the development. First day the Boss introduced me to the staff he said, "Smokey's in charge of the racing. Don't any of you second guess him. If he fails us I'll send his ass to Siberia."

History don't show or tell about Knudsen's amazing resurrection of Pontiac. When he got there Pontiacs were a heavy, no-power, no-handling, overloaded with chrome, Kraft cheese box on wheels. A world class "dog" in 1957. By 1962 Pontiac was a hot-selling, styling leader, hot performer on the racing scene. Ed Cole's leading the charge for GM, but suddenly Knudsen's hot on Cole's ass for the "Car Boss of the Year World-wide Championship." Knudsen wanted to win every race, sell every car. He taught me to win. Get the best managers in all departments and give them a free hand. (But I didn't follow his example. How the hell could you on a grand a month?)

He give 'em all enough time, and if it didn't happen he called you in and talked it over. If you still didn't get it done he'd send a hatchet man in to wind your clock, and watch you pack your bags.

He never personally did anything bad to anyone and the "Don't get mad, get even" philosophy is a GM invention. I attended some board meetings in the early sixties that if duplicated today, and made available on video, would cause 100 billion bucks worth of law suits. 1963 Knudsen slides over to run Chevy. Pete Estes takes over Pontiac. Knudsen says, "Come with me." I want too, but feel like I should stay at Pontiac. I now notice Pete's not the gung-ho racer Knudsen is. Inside of eight months I'm not too happy either.

I'll make this part shorter. Pete and I had a hell of a fight over a meeting I had with Knudsen and Cole. He apologized later in the day, but the divorce was born and four months later, without any tears on Pontiac's part, I'm back with Knudsen at Chevy. Still at $12,000 a year. But hell, I only have to work 70 to 80 hours a week to get staff engineer perks with janitor's pay. Well hell, money ain't everything is it?

I really liked my new job at Chevy…to work on the development of the Chevy "Mystery Engine." A brain child of, as I saw it, Dick Keineth. A young engineer who reported to Duntov. By now the Boss and I are close, and I'm exposed to all the in-fighting and good stuff. Chevy's building 10,000 vehicles a day. GM's got 55 percent of car market and Congress is gonna put GM in jail for having a monopoly and every kind of crime short of lying to grand jury. I asked the Boss, "Ain't you worried?" He says, "Hell no! If Congress wants to put somebody in jail for selling 60 percent of all the vehicles in the US, I'm their man."

Around '67 Knudsen moves up in GM. He's in charge over everything 'cept North America. In this time frame the Boss or Cole is gonna be GM's next president. Cole wins. This really hurt the Boss 'cause that meant he'd never "drive" GM. Ed and Knudsen are the same age. After a few months of Ed's direction at GM, the boss can't handle it. He's got standing offer to "drive" Ford Motor Company from the southwest corner of the glass house (Ford's headquarters), and he takes it. He says, "Come with me" (again). I'd been at Ford once and they treated me like a king and paid me 'bout four times what GM did. But they were twice as fucked up as GM and I didn't want anymore, so I said, "Thanks, but I'd rather finish my Chevy stuff, then leave and go into the oil business and gold exploration in Ecuador." I'm working for Pete Estes now, he is Chevy general manager. I'm trying to get out of racing. I've finally wised up. I've been on a big ego trip at about two bucks an hour. And only money I got was from inventions, a couple bucks out of the dealerships and a little from the oil business. (Between 1961 and 1966 I run 100 grand into five million and back to zero, so I knew I could do it).

In late '69 there's a knock on race shop door round 8:00 am. A well-dressed man asks if I'm Smokey. "I have a package for you from Mr. Knudsen. Will you sign this receipt and note the time please?" "Sure." It was a big brown envelope from Ford Motor Company, Office of the President. Letter from Knudsen, must be important but rite now, I was working for one of his proteges, John Delorean, when the GM presidency battles between Knudsen and Ed Cole came up. I'm running the dyno trying to run two to one valve rocker deal. Round 4:00 pm the phone rings, "Smokey, it's the boss." I get on the line, "What do you think of contract?" "Oh shit Boss, I ain't had time to read it. If it's important I'll do it now." He hangs up. He is pissed. I open deal up. First a letter. "I need help Smoke, only real backer I got is Henry Ford, all the rest are hostile Iacocca people. Look over contract, call me 3:00 pm today, please." I better go wash my hands, sit down, and read this deal.

He gave me the greatest contract any mechanic ever had then. It's a five year, uncancellable contract, giving me the right to race any kind of race car, any place in the world at Ford's expense. My shop and myself will work full time on Ford engine and vehicle development. The pay is $500,000 a year for me and the shop. Any further needs, man-power, tools, building or equipment and all operating costs, Ford pays. One million a year free insurance, staff engineer privileges including medical and dental. Ford furnishes all passenger and truck vehicles needed. Hell, I had to read it twice to believe it. Well, I call the Boss 'bout 5:00 pm and say, "OK." He says, "Be at airport 8:00 am tomorrow, there will be a Ford plane to bring you up and we are gonna have lunch with Henry Ford. I want him to meet you." You hear that? Sending a jet to pick you up, Henry Ford wants to meet you, half a million a year. Must be true, I haven't had a drink in nine years.

At the meeting and meal I asked Ford why he was leaving job and turning it over to Mr. K. He said, "I want to do something for my fellow man, President Johnson is gonna appoint me Secretary of Housing and Urban renewal very soon, and I believe Bunkie can take Ford to the next level."

I'm back in Daytona 8:00 pm, contract signed. Hot damn, I'm really a big shot. I've arrived.

My deal with GM is a one year-cancelable by either party in 90 days, 12 grand a year and they pay for all supplies they don't furnish. The contract had expired 60 days ago. Well I've got to tell Pete, I call him at home 9:00 pm the same day. Before I can say anything he says, "Glad you called, our engineering budget at Chevy's been cut, I'm gonna have to cut you two grand a year, we'll make it up to you later." I tell him the Ford deal. "Congratulations, at that money see if they got room for me too. Hate to see you go, but…" 8:00 am the next morning it's Pete says, "Smoke, got Ed (Cole) on a conference call here. We ain't gonna let them sons-a-bitches steal you away. We can't give you a five year deal, but you got a job with us for life you know that will pay you $585,000 a year. Course we can't give you a paid million buck insurance." All of a sudden I get hot. I feel absolutely stupid. I say, "Ed, what in the hell have I done to raise my value to GM $573,000 in twenty-four hours, or have you guys been screwing me for ten or fifteen years?"

Why I agreed to this I don't know, but I agree to ask Knudsen to release me from contract. But I insist on doing it face-to-face. I arrange a seven-thirty am meeting with the Boss. (Day after I'd already signed the Ford contract). We meet. "Let's talk on way to Mercury styling studio." I ask him about a release. He gets so pissed he turns around, he's gonna go wrong way on freeway. He chews my ass up one side and down the other. And I keep saying, "All I did was promise to ask you. Let's go to Mercury, the deal's on." This turns out to be not too good a day.

I've pissed off the Boss, and when I tell Pete "Adios" that cost me a fair weather friend and the GMC dealership, but hell, the dealership was a low buck pain in the ass deal anyway.

Well, Lee and I didn't cross paths but a couple times. The second time I called him a "loud mouth lying dago bastard" and walked out of meeting. The deal was, Iacocca wanted to put 429 dry sump NASCAR engine into a Mustang and he wants to build 50,000 of 'em. Knudsen was pretty fair engineer, and could half-assed mash the pedal and keep her aimed pretty decent, so he says the obvious, "That car will be nose heavy and push it's ass off and there will be no way to fix it." Lee persists, so Knudsen's answer is, "If it don't weigh over 2,550 pounds we'll do it."

50,000 cars is a lot of money and they would have weighed 3,600 pounds and been a dangerous, no-handling shitbox. That's when I blew up.

The Boss really gets me involved into Ford's planning and future engine programs, but all ain't well. Henry's mother wanted ol' vicuna coat (Lee Iacocca) to be president instead of the Boss. Henry hated Lee. I don't know why, only thing I heard was "lying son-of-a-bitch." Things ain't going too cool. Knudsen sends me to Cleveland to look at engine plant and see if it's good place to produce the later- called Cleveland 351. When I got there equipment was already being installed. (Knudsen didn't know it). Iacocca wanted to build 50,000 Mustangs with 429s "the shotgun motor" in 'em. Cars with a lot of power and 750 pounds of engine on the front wheels. I tell Knudsen, "Don't do it, it will be a handling pig, push it's ass off and kill bunch of rich kids."

Knudsen says, "What's the most the car can weigh and steer?" I say, "2,500 pounds." Lee says he's already had one built that weighs 2,500 pounds. "OK, Lee, we'll build 'em if they don't go over 2,500 pounds." Lee don't know it, but I got the finished "2,550 pound car" at my shop in Daytona. It's been acid dipped, had one lightweight Recaro seat, no upholstery, no back seat, 'bout two pound fiber glass bumpers front and rear, no floor mats, and no sound proofing. I put my elbow on the roof when talking to Bruce McClaren, and the roof sunk in two inches and didn't come back. It was thinned and lightened and it still weighed 3,200 pounds.

Big meeting to decide the issue in Dearborn. I say, "Lee, the car will go over 3,700 pounds." "Nope, we have already built and weighed a car," Lee says. Turns out in a meeting that Lee's in, if there are eight people in it, he never quits bullshitting, butting in or flat out lying. I say, "Hold it Lee, that car's in Daytona sitting on four scales." Three times I told Lee I had the car sitting on scales, and it weighed a whisker over 3,200 (goddamned engine was 700 pounds). He wouldn't shut up long enough to hear me. At the time a real Mustang weighs 3,250 pounds. Well, the shotgun motor weighs 240 pounds more, so a Mustang with the 429 engine is gonna weigh 'bout 3,750 pounds at least. He keeps on lying so I start to leave meeting. Knudsen says, "Where you going?" I say, "Home. I ain't going to sit here and listen to this lying dago anymore." I had to stay. Now you know why Lee won't come to my funeral.

Note: you know, shortly after they fired Knudsen's ass and put Lee in as president, they built a bunch of 'em anyhow.

You can see by now things ain't going too good for the Boss at Ford. Momma Ford's is gaining on getting the skids greased under Mr. K's ass. The quiet underground is hard at work. The Boss gives an interview in 1970 to a fancy car buff magazine. He said, "Way to get a good car designed is give the prototype car to Smokey, give him a green light to change anything he wants, then copy his modified prototype." Yea boy, that did it. Ford's chief engineer is Bill Ennis, a pretty good engineer, but would never get to claim Nobel prize in automotive engineering. Smoked big cigars like Clinton likes. (Who knows? Never thought about it then). At the Atlanta race Mr. K. grabs me at track. " Ennis is on the way to chew your ass out, you take it. If you smack him in the snoot you're gonna make my deal rough." "OK, Boss." Ennis chews my ass up one side and down the other. I don't know what the problem is, I've not seen the story. Ya-sa, ya-sa Mr. Ennis. He's screaming, "Hell, I can lay off all of Ford research and development people, send all the shit to Daytona, save millions."

Course Holman, Passino, Charley and the rest are watching and laughing their asses off. Ennis is the guy who got his hero badge by putting the oil pan on a Ford engine backwards in 1957 to get the engine in the frame and off of the drag link and tie rods. Why? The dumb bastards in engine and chassis were pissed at each other. Then found engine wouldn't fit in the frame. I didn't blame him in a way. But hell, I had nothing to do with it. Mr. Knudsen was his man but he wasn't that brave (yet). Well Bill, I wasn't too fond of you either at the time, and if it hadn't been for Mr. K., I'd of shoved that cigar lit end first up your ass (right there in the pit area).

Rite in here the Boss is a dead player and don't know it. Most all the big shots in the glass house seem to be leaning against the doorways of their offices doing what they please and daring the Boss to say something. He tells me to build a cheap building and gather up all the four cam Indy engines, and store 'em. Then build an aluminum small block, 350 to 400 cubic inch push rod for Indy. Ford purchasing refuses to accept PO for the building. Engineering fights me on block and cylinder heads, tooth and nail. Bill Ennis, the engineering chief, is giving me a rough time, and I knew he heard Knudsen tell me what to do.

'Bout that time, I had a chance to talk to Ford himself. It was our second meeting, the first one was Knudsen introducing me to Henry. Then Ford had said Knudsen or Cole were only two guys he would have felt comfortable turning Ford over to – I mean he is high on Knudsen. Well, in second meeting, I can't help but notice a different attitude 'bout Knudsen. During that conversation, he's really cooled off. But one thing's still loud and clear. He hates Lee Iacocca. Now I'm starting to catch on. The underground says "Momma Ford" has got the votes for Iacocca, so "Knudsen's got to go," and Henry can't stop it. I've already told the Boss I've heard they are gonna "have his ass" right after fourth of July. You know, there is always corporate in-fighting and gossip, and an underground info system that never quits. Boss says, "Let me worry 'bout that"

'Bout that time Harley Earl, the famous stylist chief from GM, dies. He had hand in "raising" Knudsen within GM and Harley was a "Smokey fan" and I really liked him. I was in Detroit for a meeting with Knudsen at Ford. When we finished, he said he was going to Harley's funeral in West Palm Beach, "Did I want to go?" I said, "Sure." As we were getting on Ford's plane, Knudsen asked the operations manager how Mr. Ford and Lee were getting along. (They both were in hospital, pretty serious stuff.) I made the mistake of saying something nasty about Lee and Knudsen really chewed my ass out. Mrs. Knudsen was on plane steps, and she said, "Atta boy Smokey," I think her intuition had the deal figured.

Three or four months later I was in Talladega for the first race. I waited for Knudsen to show up. I had a Mustang in a support race, and we had gotten the pole. I wouldn't race a Winston Cup car, the track surface and tires seemed like a movie set for a lot of bad shit. I got a call from Ford. Knudsen wasn't coming, Henry had canned his ass that morning and Lee got the steering wheel.

Well, now Knudsen got two giant kicks in the ass in 'bout eighteen months. I call him late that night. Man, he is a wounded duck. Really, in my opinion he never ever recovered the self confidence, vim and vigor he always had. I could tell it changed him cause he used to be cocky like a bantam rooster. You know, he wasn't a big man, but he acted like a 250 pound Marine before.

Also, with Knudsen gone from Ford, (I'm a Knudsen man) and especially with Iacocca in charge, I'm a dead player for four more years. I'm a minister without portfolio, no way to fly. I said, "Pay me till midnight and I'm gone." They said, "Bullshit, you're gonna sit on the bench four more years and we'll pay your salary but you can't race for us or anybody else." I had to get a good lawyer to explain to them that forcing me to stay and bench me, would make me a Lear Jet owner, and they wouldn't get anything for their expense. The money? Well hell – money ain't everything! It's only important when you're hungry. Don't they say it's the root of all evil?

It hurt Henry Ford also. I seen him later when he delivered a speech at an SAE meeting The speech was about how "the japs didn't scare him, they could not compete." Afterwards I said, "You're a brave man, you may have to eat that speech." I asked him, "What the hell was that all about?" Twenty months ago you told me Mr. K. was best car man in the world." He said, "Firing Mr. K. was toughest thing I had to do in my whole life," but his mother pulled a power play regarding a majority stock holder's threat that left absolutely no options 'cept can the Boss's ass. She loved "the mouth" and hated Mr. K. I can tell you Mr. Ford made it clear to me if he had the option, he would have swapped Lee for ten pounds of dog shit (maybe less).

Rite in here Henry Ford wasn't doing so hot either. President Johnson double-crossed him on the cabinet job, housing and urban renewal went sour. (Gave it to George Romney). His health was shaky and I believe he had one or two serious "split tail" problems. To tell you the truth, I quit being pissed at him and felt sorry for him. If I'd had an option to trade places with him then, I'd have turned it down. I got a feeling Ford was a better man than history will credit him. Maybe his medical problems never got under control, cause if you remember, he didn't last long after that, and he really wasn't that old. I liked his, "Don't ever complain. Don't ever explain," attitude and tried living by it. But I couldn't seem to stick to it.

Well, the Boss is down, but not out. White Motor Company here we come. Knudsen is the top cat. I get job developing alternative energy. In 1972 the world decides we are gonna run out of oil. So with a couple of bucks from White Motor Company, I build wind mills, solar collectors, develop ways to make hydrogen. Learn how to react it quite well in internal combustion engines.

Experiment with coal in fluidized bed technology, wave energy, temperature differential power, substitution of air conditioning fluids including air instead of fluorocarbons.

I investigate one road I thought then, and still do today, was the best. Liquid natural gas as a prime mover fuel is best and only immediate candidate to seriously contribute to reduction of environmental negatives. White actually then was more of a farmer-oriented company than a pure truck manufacturer. So environmental concerns were a hell of a lot more considered by practical farmer types than the normal captains of industry. Hell, they were the ignorant, greedy bastards that championed the mass pollution of earth. Matter of fact, they ain't doing too bad today still doing just that. They dump shit in the water bodies under the name of "sewage." That makes it better? How 'bout where you live?

Anyway, I worked for Knudsen personally at Pontiac, Chevy, Ford, White Motor Company. The sins of the past had pretty much boxed White company into a maze of financial dead-ends and the Boss couldn't steer her out of the rocks, so down she went. Well, he came damn close to taking the job of running BMW-USA, but it didn't happen. I never knew the whole story about this. We even owned a Jet Ranger helicopter charter service together. Hell, I taught him how to fly it and he flew it well.

1975, I'm surprised when I notice the Boss is kinda human and sometimes goofs up. In 1972 I wanted to take a stock block Chevy to Indy. I decided 205 cubic inches blown (turbocharged) to 90 to 100 inches could get it done power wise at Indy. I was working for Chevy and White Motor Company at the time. Piggins was the hi-performance boss at Chevy. He said, "If you take a Chevy to Indy we'll fire you, cause you'd make us look like we were violating the GM president's ban on racing." By then Ed Cole was a holy roller, screw racing advocate. For first time in my life I'm working for John Delorean who is the Chevy boss at this time, and getting paid 120 grand a year.

But I've made up my mind I'm gonna go to Indy with a "poor boys'" engine, and rescue Indy from the limeys. Mr. Knudsen is rich and he likes my idea. He says, "Fuck 'em. I'll pay the expenses, but no salaries." He paid the freight personally 1972, '73, '74, and '75. Remember when I told you he was a real racer? So I tell Piggins, " I'm going to Indy. I don't give a fuck what you or Chevy say." If I remember rite they never shit-canned me till John Delorean left as Chevy's boss. And really, their money paid for Ralph Johnson's and one other helper's time and we still did Chevy engine work, but not 120 grand's worth.

John Delorean

I got caught up in a John Delorean adventure where John was gonna buy hot vapor engine for the Delorean car and subsequently got sued by Delorean creditors, and bankruptcy lawyers. (What a bunch of crooked, money-grabbing pricks.) Mr. Knudsen was the "book" man for the hot vapor deal, I figured I needed someone with Detroit connections and business savvy on my team. Just before the shit hit the fan, the Boss drew up a new contract with me. I didn't even look at it, but it took him out of a legal liability position, and put whole load on me. When the creditor parasites come knocking, he gets "amnesia," and says he has no records. It cost me 45 grand in lawyers, and a year's time to avoid a 250 grand judgement against me. The suit and appeal were in a Federal court – if I lost I might have gotten life or the damn electric chair. Well, I was pissed, but I decided for all he did for me, I sure couldn't bitch. I'm sure the "new" Knudsen was caused by health problems. His wife Florence was a class act lady but she was gone, so I guess it's really tough plowing for the man.

He was a partner of mine in the hot vapor cycle engine deal until I sold it to Motor Tech. They bought him out for 380 grand. This is about 1983. He was pretty much retired then, but I notice his memory, is slipping, and slowly the Mr. Knudsen I knew was changing into a stranger to me.

Mr. Knudsen was one of the greats in automotive surface transportation. He had a giant part of the birthing of NASCAR. His support in the early days was invaluable.

By now you can see I sure had a great bunch of teachers to learn from. Too bad I wasted most of it. Sometimes now I think, if I had an accident when I was in my twenties, and accidentally got castrated, no telling where I might have gone. Mr. K, in his eighties, left us mid-summer 1998.

I hope one day soon racing will recognize his contribution with his installation in the International Motorsports Hall of Fame, or some other kind of a substantial honor from the automotive and racing clan.

I need to tell you about John Delorean. I consider this man to have been the most talented and most knowledgeable all around person Detroit had from 1957 to 1987. He wrote a book 'bout fifteen years ago called "On a Clear Day You Can See Detroit." (Or close to that, I got a copy but haven't read it yet). Actually his life, the parts of it I lived through with him exercised the extreme of every emotion known to humans except hunger. He hit homers with the bases loaded, came close to being hung by his balls, and was a world wide celebrity in both forms: a hero and an asshole.

John was a tall slim, good looking cat who maybe had Greek ancestors. He always had a big shit eating grin. He has way above average in intelligence. Must have had the IQ of a genius. He could add numbers in his head in the millions in seconds. He was educated as an engineer, and I believe his first job was with Packard. Somehow, when Mr. Knudsen was running Pontiac he hired John and that was to become very important. Mr. K became John's "grandfather." What that meant in motor company lingo was "don't fuck with John unless you're either the president or chairman of the board at General Motors." When I first met John in 1958, he was assistant chief engineer at Pontiac under Pete Estes at Pontiac.

Mr. Knudsen was the general manager, and a GM Vice president. In them days being general manager of a GM Car division was like being the king of Siam – you were a god.

John Delorean was an extra good engineer, but more important, he was especially talented in knowing what the public wanted in a car, and plus he had an exceptional taste in styling that the public liked. The 1962 to 1970 Pontiac was the work of John Delorean and Mr. K. – a production car reflected the General Manager's personality in his third year on the job.

I imagine you all have already formed opinions about John, and my guess is they are "not too good." My story won't parallel what you read. John Delorean was a goddam good, religious, honest, hard-working, extremely talented car man.

If nothing else, the fact that the Boss was John's grandfather tells you something. (Mr. K was a squeaky clean square.) Unfortunately, two things messed up John. If you're a male 30 to 50 years old pay attention, this could happen to you.

Number one: in board meetings (corporate) John differed with Cole, Smitty and several other old bean counting farts. No problem 'cept it was a major problem. John was almost always right. So be careful if you consistently out-think all your peers, you ain't gonna be too popular.

Right about that time John breaks the GM code of dress. He wears blue jeans and lacey shirt, with neck and hair hanging out, big gold chain with a half pound medallion, and loafers with no sox. Holy shit! No doubt all the previous presidents and board chairmen were spinning in their graves! Sure, some of the rest felt the same way, but didn't have the balls.

John's got a problem, but he don't know it. He decides to get in shape. Exercising, dieting, maybe a little help in an operating room. He tops it all off with a big surrealist portrait in his office. His original marriage has ended. What we got now? A good lookin,' rich, powerful, super intelligent, charming bachelor. Really, you guys pay attention here (the 30 to 50'ers).

John discovered pussy. He'd been so busy, so absorbed in his work he completely overlooked it.

This is a very standard disease for all. Maybe in my case it wasn't a problem (I discovered it when I was eleven and never forgot about it) Now John, don't get pissed, remember I lived through this with you when you thought you were having fun, and I guess some of it was.

GM had a company in the basement of the GM building called "Jam Handy." The world thought they made training and sales-oriented films, and they did. But they were also the CIA and FBI of GM. The big shooters at GM were looking for a way to blow John's ass out of the water cause he's on his was to being youngest president GM ever had. The guys who run the GM CIA were race fans, so when I got to a meeting early, or when my meetings started late, (and they usually were till I learned to have them between 7:00 and 8:00 am), I'd go to Jam Handy and read the reports and look at the film of John's adventures. Man, I envied him all night in a hotel suite on the island off of California (Capistrano), with Ann Margaret, Jill St. John and two other movie stars (I've forgotten their names). The time the various ladies left were noted, and a film of John coming out in the morning looking like you just finished a week at Green Briar. Well, I thought, "That son-of-a-bitch is tough. He would have made one hell of a racer."

Green Briar was a fancy expensive old farts very prestigious resort where GM had many of their rewards for "being good boys last year." It was really a rest camp and a status symbol for your peers to judge your climb up the GM management progression.

Well, John finally meets a nice young lady, one of Tom Harmon's daughters (Tom Harmon was a very famous Michigan football star.) Kelly was her name. I never did get to know her really, but Mr. K had three daughters, and Kelly and Mr. K's daughter were very good friends. (That's where John met Kelly). John was flat goofy over Kelly, so he married her and went straight. I know of one problem where an untruth ballooned into a major problem. Kelly was probably half John's age. I'm sure that didn't help, to shorten up the story. It didn't work out. Kelly took off.

Man that fuckin' near drove John insane (maybe it did a little). This got plumb serious. I was awake all night once trying to calm him down and talk him out of a very serious happening. During this period, the early 70s I was working for John at Chevy. Oh yes, he paid a lot better. (I think 120 grand a year.)

Meanwhile, John's problems at GM are getting bigger. He decides not to use a Cadillac, and has a Chevy limousine built. On the job, GM vice presidents had to use chauffeurs. Well, the GM president blew his stack. Said the Chevy limo was a waste of money, John had to have it scrapped. Actually it was two to four hours of getting his ass chewed out for building shitty cars. (This is the same guy who, when he is chairman of the board, tries to ride tourist on airlines to save money.

John started the rear engine Corvette and built the Blazer. A beautiful small pickup that looked like a Mack truck cab. He was gonna make Chevy a small GM inside of GM. Well, by now John's gotten his ol' buddy Pete Estes pissed. Chevy has a bad little car called the Vega. Can you imagine this piece of shit on top of the Corvair? Whew! (No apologies to Jim Musser either). This car don't help John and Pete's friendship at all. In short, 'bout the whole fuckin' board at GM is on John's ass.

Remember in 1970 John's grandfather, Mr. K, goes to Ford as president. According to the GM code of the hills, it's proper and expected that the defector (Mr. K.) is now an official asshole. Not to John, Mr. K. is still his friend. Take off ten more points. While working for John, my first job was to try and salvage a hemispherical head project Piggins had championed for the small block. Matter of fact, last time I worked at Chevy I worked with it. At that time it was a one half million dollar trip to Shitsville. Well, after three months we finally deep-six it for ever. About a dozen engines got out, but I think there were two hundred sets of parts.

John goes up another notch past Chevy. Now he and Cole and Estes play cat and dog five days a week. With John out of Chevy, Piggins and I ain't getting along too good and I'm out of grandfathers. So Vince offers me a chicken shit, 'bout back to the grand a month deal. I send contract back with a note that I was gonna apply for unemployment cause it netted me more. (You know, it probably would have). Well, Piggins is rid of me, only problem he's got now is Herb Fishel.

It ain't too far down the road and GM gets frisky enough either John quits or they fire him. I heard two versions of this. I never asked John for his version. John calls a year later, "I'm gonna build my own car, wanna job?" I pass. Actually I don't think it's gonna happen and I really wanted to start a push rod engine revolution at Indy, and was just dumb enough to think I could do it. Well, that deal was stillborn. Just took me three years to catch on. Between Indy experiments, I kept track of John through news media and mutual friends.

A financial institution Merrill Lynch asks questions 'bout John's car concept. Good or bad? Do you think John can do this single-handed? Texas, Puerto Rico, Ireland. Colin Chapman, a limey race wizard and a small volume car builder (Lotus) is in the deal. Johnny Carson, Sammy Davis, quite a few famous rich stock holders. Well, maybe.

I invented a different kind of engine in the late fifties. I kept improving it slowly, and in 1973 I put it in a car. It was a three-cylinder and it run good. I kept improving it along with other work. (This is the hot vapor cycle engine). I'm working for Buick in '79. Fishel is the Vince Piggins of Buick. (Piggins is rid of him – finally.) In 1981 I put a three cylinder hot vapor engine in a new Buick Skylark and entered it in a new engine show and tell. A competition between all GM Car divisions for budget approval.

I don't think I'm saying this egotistically, the Buick skylark with a three-cylinder vapor engine was the hit of the show. I also built a three-cylinder diesel for Buick, and demonstrated it in a new Volkswagen chassis. It was a finalist. Matter of fact for those of you who visited Disney World in Orlando in the eighties, that engine was used in the car of the future display for a long time. (The three cylinder diesel.)

John hears about the hot vapor engine and some knowledgeable people he knows drove it. John is now 'bout ready to sell his car. Circumstances put an aluminum V6 Peugeot engine in it. That engine was a bow-wow. Top of the scale John knows cars, and comes down to drive the hot vapor Skylark. He is so impressed he wants to buy the engine rights. I have given Mr. K. 25 percent of it thinking he could sell it.

John agrees to pay me twenty million for exclusive rights to engine. I've shown the engine to Ford and Chrysler as well. Matter of fact I built cars of theirs using their base engines to make hot vapor engines. Ford said, "I don't know, I doubt it." Chrysler said, "Let's make a deal."

Head Chrysler honcho, Harold Sperlich, a goddam good engineer, actually the cat that saved Chrysler's ass. Small world, John D. and Harold Sperlich were classmates in college. Sperlich finds out Knudsen owns 25 percent in final meeting in New York at the Four Seasons restaurant. Sperlich says, "Get rid of that bastard or no deal." I'm in a state of shock. I say, "Why?"

He says, "'Cause he fired me at Ford!" How's that for a kick in the ass? Here's the deal, John D. and Chrysler are gonna joint venture the engine, and Delorean will produce it in the US for both companies. OK, "Mr. K will you sell? And if so, how much?" "Five million!" Whoops, not bad, I gave him the 25percent. Well, John says, "I'll buy it myself" (Delorean Motor Company). He and Mr. K. work out contract and we all sign it. Right in here I got a friend in Houston name of Bunker Hunt, a billionaire. He has heard 'bout the engine and calls. Says, "I want to buy your engine." (Remember we were buddies from Indy 1960.) "Can't do it, John D. bought it." John D. hears 'bout it and says, "What 'bout a joint venture?" Bunker says, "OK, I got a son named Houston who I want to switch from geology (oil) to car manufacturing" (Bunker became a billionaire because of his dad's oil ventures and his own.)

Bunker says if John will train Houston and the factory is built in, or around Laredo, Texas, he will buy the deal and let John D. run it on some kind of joint venture deal between them. Bunker wants to build a small cheap Cadillac type car with no options, and hot vapor engine for power. The deal is worked out at my shop. Details are to be put into a contract. In meantime John's built 'bout 5,000 cars or more. He knows he needs to come out quick with something else. Turns out shortage of money caused John to make bunch of compromises that weren't good. This period consumed about a year.

John's remarried, a beautiful model, I believe her name was Christina Ferrari (like the car). I met her first time 1975 at Indy where we were getting ready to race. John's got two kids under six years old, I think a boy and a girl. John's new wife was a good kid. Funny, smart, and seemed to be a gung-ho John D. fan. Every week I'm hearing 'bout production and money problems on the Delorean car.

John's a real hero used in a big expensive scotch whiskey advertisement. The car's getting medium to not so good reviews, but still selling slowly. In the early eighties the car business went down into the shit house. The worst time in forty years to sell a car right when Delorean came out. I doubt too that John was best money manager. I can remember no matter how bad the economics, John told me it would always be resolved by next Wednesday. Never Monday, Tuesday, Thursday, Friday – always Wednesday.

I'd always thought I'd like to have a Lear Jet for a toy, but you know I never got excited 'bout the deal. My premonition was, "Something will blow the deal." I notice Christina ain't too damn happy. She's bitching John used her money, or won't give her what she needs. Ever hear that shit before? There are stories popping up that some good-sized hunks of money have disappeared. Car warranty problems, manufacturing accounts are running late. The British government got some people saying, "We got into a bum deal." They (the British) bankrolled the start up in Dublin, Ireland as a gesture of good will, (I think). Actually that stuff's over my head.

In short, suddenly John's world has gone from roses to dog shit. I can't imagine how one human could juggle that many balls. Where's Colin Chapman? I can't find out. So John has me doing some corrective work. Clutch took a gorilla to push down, etc.

Well, finally the hot vapor sale paper work gets done. Everybody's happy. It's Tuesday. Everybody will go to Houston Thursday to sign the Hunt-Delorean-Knudsen-Smokey deal. Tuesday night, 6:00 pm, TV news. John D. is in handcuffs. Selling coke! Goddam, it hit me like a sledge hammer. Knudsen calls and says, "Turn on TV, station so and so." Man oh man, more bad shit. Wednesday morning early, Houston Hunt calls. Won't even say the word Delorean. He says, "No deal Thursday Smokey, but dad will loan you five million at five percent so you can keep going."

I say, "Thank you, but I could never pay it back probably." He says, "Invest the money." Believe it or not 20 percent was not hard to get then. Even on a pretty safe deal. "Invest the money and operate on the 15 percent profit, and we will get together later." I turned it down. It's sixteen years later. I never heard from either Bunker or Houston Hunt again.

The Friday before that fateful Tuesday I talked to John and I smelled trouble – money coming from the Miami area. I'm convinced even today John Delorean had so much pressure on him those next five days he truly was temporarily goofy. His whole world was exploding in his face. I'd guess on the Tuesday he went down, he was one hundred million bucks short of successful survival. His actions those five days I regard as desperate, almost suicidal acts looking for a short term stall; for a miracle. He reminded me of a mouse in a corner. A mouse will even take on a gorilla when it's out of options.

Who the hell am I to judge what's right or wrong? In my life I can equate his predicament to an experience I had at Indy not being able to qualify a car and having to leave. A failure by your racing competitors standards and all race fans. My pain I was able to erase with the conviction that even though I failed, I did the best I could. To my critics I refused to let them know the depth of my pain. I spent years learning how to mask a large disappointment with absolutely no comment, and with no expression. But underneath, I'd think, "I'll be back next year you motherfuckers, and better prepared."

John Delorean went to church five to six times a week. He was a Catholic, he was the easiest touch there was for a destitute person. He was a sucker for every charity that ever approached him. I'm talking his money, not GM's. Delorean goes into St. Patrick's on his way to work in New York, he went in every day. John was not a liar, bullshitter or ego maniac regarding society. If John was a bad man you'll have to condemn him for having ambitions that exceeded his abilities.

But I look at life different. John D. had won the Indy of life, but in his attempt to win it again with an under-powered engine and a junky car, he crashed and there was a fire. John got badly and painfully burned. He recovered, but he is badly scarred. The kind that will never-ever go away.

We are still friends. Two years ago I got him to come along with me to Denver to speak to a large group of Pontiac lovers. The Pontiac-Oakland Club of the world, those people enjoyed him. But for those who think he wasn't punished, you're wrong. John's like a tiger that's been defanged, declawed, been beaten for fifteen years and lives in a ten foot square cage.

It's pretty easy for us to be over ambitious, that could be a curse rather than good. I've been around a very varied economic and social range from the richest to the poorest. In my opinion the happiest people I've ever seen were Ecuadorian Indians (Cofanes) who had no money, no more possessions than they could wear or carry, who ate off of the land, and I guess most important of all, were totally satisfied with everything as it was. Those people have no cancer, no lawyers, no taxes, no cops, not even a McDonalds. Be careful what you wish for, it may have hidden costs.

ROGER PENSKE

Another person you have certainly heard of is Roger Penske. I met Roger Penske in 1964. He was a fair sports car driver and a salesman. I think he worked for Alcoa. His dad was quite high in the company and Roger had married a wealthy young lady with the last name Stouffer – you know candy and hotels. I get to know him 'cause he is romancing Cole to get adopted by Chevrolet. He's adopted, and I get the job to show Roger's mechanics, Travers and Coon, ex-Indy hero mechanics for Bill Vuckovich, how to build the motors. I find out he's getting 120 grand a year for listening and watching me build Camaros and small block Chevrolets, while I get 12,000.

I think this is one sharp son-of-a-bitch. Well, they produce and win championship with Donohue driving ("Captain Nice"). Roger hangs up his helmet and is on his way to tearing up the Trans Am. Indy, Can Am and NAS-CARs Winston Cup, 'cept here he got whoaed. His record was expensive, lots of rule litigation and short in the W column. Never the less he became the best we had in America. 'Bout in here I decide he wants to own Indy. That don't even come close to flying. So he and Pat Patrick start their own association, "CART," and proceed to fuck Indy up and damn near succeed. I'm pushing to get stock block engines in at Indy and am doing good enough that Goodyear says

Roger Penske and Rick Mears.

Smokey we'd like for you and Roger to team up with Roger running the movie. Well, Roger is there and I tell Goodyear no way. I've been down that road once before. I'm not interested even if I drive. My guess is I'd do all the work and Roger would end up with the loot. He is so much smarter than me as a businessman I'd come out of the deal like Hogan's goat. Well, that ended that movie right quick. Roger's been in racing 40 years. I believe he has only two equals: France and Ecclestone. I'm looking for this shortly to be Penske and Ecclestone. I'm hoping Roger don't get another shot at owning Indy. He don't like losing. His motives I think are ego and money. I suppose that's not a crime but I'd like Indy to go back to a USA world class event open to American engines and chassis. Then if an international event is required, make that another race. In my view Roger should have two trophies: one in the Indy Hall of Fame and a new "Benedict Arnold Hall of Fame" trophy for fucking up Indy.

Dewey Ruff

Now I want to tell you 'bout another human who was a big part of my life. A colored man who came into my life in 1960, Dewey Ruff. He had just reached retirement age, qualifying him for the social security program so he came to work for me as a janitor. Dewey was such a good person he soon became a full-time personal assistant. He's had a key to my home and garage since 1961. Still living, still helping me. If they ever have need for another saint, Dewey's a damn good candidate. Dewey was kinda my wife Patt's personal helper, so he also helped raise Sam, Steve and Patricia. He was available 24 hours a day, seven days a week, 365 days a year and attended all holiday family functions. In the forty years I've known Dewey Ruff, he had devoted 90 percent of his life to helping people. How old is he? Remember what I told you 'bout Social Security? Dewey served in World War II in the China-Burma-India theater. Dewey today, if he talks to a woman, removes his hat. He comes from what I noticed society classified as an "Uncle Tom." I call it "good manners."

Well, this could at times be embarrassing. One day the Boss wanted a helicopter brought to West Palm. He had a beautiful vacation home there on Fisher Island, hi-buck shit everywhere. The deal is, I fly the chopper to West Palm. I've got my boys Steve and Sam with me. Dewey is gonna meet us at West Palm airport with a car. Neil Armstrong (the moon walker) is a friend of the Boss's and staying at his house, as is Kelly Harmon (John Delorean's ex-wife). The chairman of Eaton and TRW are there also. My boys wanted to spend time with Armstrong (maybe get a moon rock). Neil wants to get a helicopter license and is gonna use our helicopter to refresh and check-ride in and I'm gonna help him get acquainted with helicopters. The kids are in awe of Armstrong but Neil ain't no talker. You got to pry info out of him. Dewey's a fashion plate on Sundays and he is our chauffeur. Well, after a big introduction and hand shaking contest Neil asks Dewey what he does at the shop. Dewey removes his hat, stiffens up, and says "I'm Smokey's nigger." Holy shit! I wanted to disappear.

Dewey's getting awfully wobbly now. He's got heart problems and his memory has long gone some place. He refuses to accept pay for not working. One day soon Dewey's gonna leave us, but hell, he's liable to outlast me. Boy, if we had a world full of Deweys it would be a 1,000 times nicer place. Besides all the good stuff, his memory problems and his ability to break anything that is mechanical and to stand there and deny it, reminds me of when a little boy shits his pants and pretends it never happened. I'm not sure that part hasn't maybe removed a few hours of my life. Even if so, having him was more than worth it.

The System: Don't Get Mad, Get Even

I'm gonna give my observation of what made "Car City USA" tick, as I saw it, from 1950 to 1987. This is regard to both stock car racing and the general mode of operation. I'll use General Motors as the example: Ford and Chrysler were the same, but on a smaller, more fucked up scale. In the fifties, where this starts, I doubt even one percent of all vehicles used in the United States were not domestically made. There was no one else. The car business then was as secretive as the US Military. This is regarding Ford, GM and Chrysler. But that was the tip of the iceberg. The car divisions got their character, faces and clothes from styling, the doors had coded locks changed daily, and employees were officially assigned to specific areas daily, plus all doors had security guards to validate your clearances. The secrecy was as obsessive between all different GM divisions.

The operating staff of General Motors car and truck divisions were composed of about twenty or twenty-five super big shots. The Chairman of the board was one notch over God. The President was the Chairman's stooge. He told the world every day what the Chairman thought. They also set the fashion standards for the US business person, and all good second bananas wore the same color. If a boss wore black on Tuesday, with plain black GM shoes with one stitch line, one third of the way up the nose, and five lace holes, that was it. It took thick-sole wing tips till 'bout 1960 to make it. I believe Mr. Knudsen walked first pair of them into the GM building, and walked 'em on the fourteenth floor wood and carpets. John Delorean I think was first with enough balls to walk a pair of loafers into the elevator and push button number fourteen. Mr. K. was right behind John in loafers. But John was the first and only one to do it without sox. Not only that. He did it with tight fitting blue jeans and a lacey long sleeve shirt, unbuttoned half way down, with a big gold chain. No, he didn't last long after that – 'bout a year.

Most General Motors chairmen were bean counters. Didn't know their ass from a hole in the ground about cars, but they had the power to "OK" or "stop" and move any other person, regardless of his talent, and it would not be questioned. Nothing ever came up at a board meeting the chairman was not in favor of. The voting was a joke. Even this whole countries' favored analysis of a major political, emotional, sports or economic problem was, "If it's good for GM, it's good for the country." Little Smitty, the bean counter chairman in the eighties, I guess he was goddam good in his field – punching in numbers and pulling the handle. But when he talked about cars I could smell cow shit and envision him talking from the seat of a Farmall tractor. How did he get to be chairman? The system. It was his turn in the barrel. If you wanted a general plan on how to succeed in the car business, read this book, and do every single thing opposite the way I did it.

Let's get to it. Those who "made it" had to operate as brown-nosing "yes" men, master the "don't rock the boat" doctrine, play golf, (but never beat your boss) and laugh at the boss's jokes no matter how many times you heard them. It's human nature. I'm gonna like people telling me what a good kid I am. And later I'm going to like people who devote every second of every day making me look good.

So, for all white collar workers, the golden goal is to get appointed to staff. That's about twenty/twenty-five people. Once you get lifted to staff, you're made for life. Now you can get caught having anal sex with your secretary and get away with it. (You can just say you tripped).

As you climb above the staff level you see the next chairman and president. Maybe it's you! Now the last part of the game is to get those who have the power to nominate the successors to choose you.

At the corporate level this includes brown-nosing the board of directors. This is especially hard to do because by now you're pretty impressed with yourself and the odor does start to get very offensive. At the division level the General Manager has the power of a dictator to all in his division, and reports to the president and/or chairman, and maybe in the chain of command the lead horse for next chairman. At the division level you find a new player or element; sponsorship from a "grandfather". For example: Mr. Knudsen was John Delorean's grandfather. Herb Fishel's grandfather was Lloyd Ruess, etc.

If my grandfather is the General Manager of Chevy division, do you want to fuck with me? Not if you intend to be around very long, unless your grandfather had more stroke than mine, maybe he's corporation president or chairman.

Another part of the system is "don't get mad, get even." This puts you in a position of not knowing you're gonna get it up the ass until it's halfway up there. This condition is a lot more dangerous than the average person realizes. The General Manager, for example, never says or does anything bad to anyone, anytime. He has a designated hatchet man who gets the job done.

Then when you complain to the head man he says, "That terrible. If I had known about it in time I could have fixed it."

At the division level the staff is even more important, and more powerful. They operate with "all for one, one for all" principle. When they reach down and pull you up, they explain they can hang you just as easy. The price to be on board is, "We all hang together." No single staff member can be singled out cause all twenty-four of them signed the memo authorizing whatever happens. The damage here is, you'll never find out who the dumb fuck was that screwed up at the division level.

Here's another example of impossible execution of the system. I'm your boss and you're assigned to work on an engine I helped design three years ago. There is a warranty or durability problem.

You're a young five year man. I'm your boss and I've got twelve years in. You fix my mistake or improve my design, am I gonna tell my boss how you fixed my mistake or improved my design? That will never work. Instead of congratulating you, I'd like to make you disappear.

The system and it's interface with racing – to start with it was absolutely impossible. Race engines and good surface transportation engines are as different as day and night. Maximum power per cubic inch for racing and maximum economy, minimum pollution, maximum durability, safety and comfort for the public are two sets of goals at crossed purposes. They are also as different engineering-wise as a throat doctor and an asshole doctor in reference to technology. But it existed from 1950 till nearly 1990. So my criticism of Detroit's engineers is often unfair in the light of the fact that they had to operate with their hands tied behind their backs.

But few had the balls to stand up and tell the world what the problem was. I know if they did this it would have dead ended their careers. Yes, there were a few, like Ralph Johnson who had the balls, but it wrecked his career. Or like Dick Kenneth, who ended up at Opel in Germany. Maybe best engine man GM had. And what did he do to get banished? He fought to save a good engine design.

The manufacturers treated stock car racing like going to a whorehouse. "Yeah. I been in there." They were involved on the surface, but to the public they denied they ever "put it in." For first five years they gave us a couple bucks to race, but wouldn't even advertise a win. In 1955 you could buy a NASCAR legal 265 inch small block Chevy engine, race ready, for five hundred bucks. Today it's forty five thousand. Not one single stock part, even nuts, bolts, or gaskets is used in the NASCAR Winston Cup Chevy, Ford, Dodge or Pontiac engine. What Pontiac engine? There is no Pontiac V8 race engine, and hasn't been one since the late sixties.

Going back to my engineering criticism. The factory loved stock car racing (when their stuff won). When I'd go to Chevy engineering center in 1955 after a win, man, everybody was tickled.

"Great for the team," Ed Cole said. But the real story was, for Chevy to make the parts we needed, they would have been illegal regarding NASCAR's rules, because rules said parts had to be used, as in production, and that would have expensed racing immediately out of reach. So the racers groveled and begged for better stuff, and fought NASCAR's inspectors. This was in regard to safety and performance. Even today, only parts Chevy and Ford made are cylinder heads and blocks casting. These are not used in any production engine, and never were. They are a "race only" item. The facts today are: even better blocks and cylinder heads are available today from after market vendors.

Had the manufacturers built a special racing engine in 1948 and NASCAR approved it, no question in my mind it could have been done and done well. But the system of both the OEMs and NASCAR were hopelessly flawed, as borne out by today's national appeal for stock car racing. Which is as "stock" as a three-peckered billy goat. It is a completely special engine constructed out of a selection of after market parts vendors. They use a car manufacturers cylinder block as a signature of legitimacy.

So, when you examine Bill France Sr.'s "foresight and vision," in reality it was just shit-house luck. It made "it" in spite of the dumb fucking mistakes both OEMs and NASCAR made. I'm not trying to diminish France's creating a crowd pleasing event, but man by instinct likes to watch his fellow man get eaten by the lion. Auto racing is a form of lion eating. So it's kinda like who ever invented sex, would that be hard to sell?

Racing's growth as a spectator event is nothing short of astonishing. Nothing is forever. Nothing is perfect. The day is coming, and getting closer every Sunday. When a car gets into the grandstand, and a lot of race fans die, who will there be standing to defend auto racing? The manufacturers and sponsors will haul ass out of "dodge" so fast the vacuum will pull every advertisement method plumb out of the ground, and the silence will be eerie. It may very well turn out Bill France had a great idea, but greed let it get out of hand.

The race car speeds today, by in large, are as much as fifty miles an hour over any sensibility. Is it possible when they strayed from the simple three page rule book they have cloned a method of self destruction? Wouldn't a strictly stock race program cut cost, increase safety, and most importantly, help create a safer "drunk proof" car?

Let me tell you something about the system and Detroit's contribution, and NASCAR's brilliant development of stock car racing, and of the fifty greatest drivers of all time. I believe the drivers deserved all they got and more. But what about the Knudsen's, Bud Moore's, Banjo's, Humpy Wheeler's. The Harold

Brasington's, Don O'Reilly, Pat Purcell, Frank Swain, Red Vogt, Glen Wood, John Laux, Max Muhleman, Bennie Kahn, Joe and 'Lightning' Epton, John and Mary Brunner, Herb Fishel, Judy Jones, Annie France, Pete Depaolo, Carl Keikhaefer?. Those who died racing, and at least 25 more non-drivers. Most of you fans reading this don't have a clue who the above are. But without 'em, I doubt half as much would have happened in regard to NASCAR's success.

Now we have some grandstands named after drivers. Dead or alive is this to honor the driver? Or as I see it, just another fuckin' play to make money off of their ghosts? What do you think? If it hadn't been for several thousand mechanics and self-made vendors, there'd never have been the first race run. We will never know how many million man hours were dedicated to make a stock car go fast in the last fifty years. But we do know most of the time was gifted, not paid for. In this respect, I compliment NASCAR up to 1998. Unlike other sports and entertainment venues, the only effort to glorify and credit itself has been to honor Bill France Sr. I don't question the results of the feat, just the execution.

The 1998 50th NASCAR anniversary celebration is in fact a clever financial engine that coined millions under the guise of honoring the past heroes of NASCAR. They never appreciated our contributions then, why do it now? For thirty years I battled for improvements from manufacturers, then battled the genius France, whose ears were shut unless your conversation reflected dollar signs. I battled a battery of inspectors ranging from alcoholics to gasoline station egotists, to world class comic book digesters. Technical improvements in NASCAR offered these frustrations, but what tore my ass up the most were the engineers in charge of various areas where I was looking for advice, or offered advice or a plan, or developed a fix and presented it for test. It seems whatever I suggested was kicked to death by these engineers for two years before extinction or acceptance and implementation. I was left out of advance planning because of politics. In planning my input could be 'built in' rather than a suggested fix for somebody else's mistake. In short, it was 'bout like thirty years of trying to push a snowball up a wildcat's ass with a red hot poker, and ninety five percent of the time at about five bucks an hour.

The system at the manufacturer's level today is totally unknown to me. My last glimpse of the system was in 1987. So consider my story as history, not current fact. The system had a very serious negative then. In my experience, the truly gifted individuals in various fields as a rule are supremely dedicated, extremely talented, loners, or maybe a better word, just "different." They seemed to almost always nonconformist and most I've met were reserved, with absolute courage in their convictions. Man, these were about a perfect set of qualities for zero penetration into the system.

The point is, the best people got lost. 1960, the US automotive Big Three had the world by the ass regarding best-cheapest-safest surface transportation for the masses in the world. The rice burners, the sauerkraut gobblers, hell, throw in the eyetalians and the limeys and the frogs, nobody was in the same league as the us. The system was attacked in the early seventies by the greens. An example: a man without a driver's license writes a book, Unsafe at Any Speed (a cross-threaded brain named Ralph Nader) about a GM Car named "Corvair."

Somebody told him what a dangerous shit-box this car was, and factually he was correct. But. There was a German-made car called the Volkswagen, or lovingly called the "Beetle," cause it did look like a Japanese beetle. This car was probably 25 percent more dangerous than the Corvair, and to this day, 40 years later, is still revered as great vehicle. In reality it was a dangerous, gutless, no handling, piece of shit, but at a price many people could afford. It however had one very remarkable and important characteristic. It didn't break. I believe there will be a few still running that are 100 years old someday.

I worked as a consultant to GM in this time frame. I remember Nader's first visit to the tech center and GM's attempt to appease him. I also remember Murph of GM's CIA trying to film him as a "dickey licker" (Jam Handy). Must of been a fun place to work then, Detroit was so fucked up and into 500 cubic inch engines, fish fins, 5,000 pound gas guzzlers. The Systemites stuck their heads in the sand like ostriches in 1972, and when they looked up in 1982, The Japanese had cleaned their plows, and the Germans were hot on their tail. Think about this if you bend over and stick your head in the sand, isn't your ass kinda vulnerable?

The system has now been cut by a third. Fast forward: GM, second week of August 1998, all division General Managers will be de-balled in the next six months. All divisions get put in one pot, with one boss man? Maybe-maybe not? I mention the above as food for thought. I worked for four General Motors presidents, two Ford presidents, and several other highly place executives. I mention that to let you know I swam in the same river with those cats so my comments are not based on hearsay.

I'm not trying to impress you. For what I got paid up to 1969, I could have made as much riding on the back of a garbage truck. At that time I quit a ten grand a year job and then turned down an offer for same the job next day for $585,000 bucks a year. That day, I noticed loud and clear that I'd never get the Nobel prize for labor negotiation or for brains.

Racing With One Arm

'Bout 1949 or '50 a truck pulling a racing boat pulls up in my shop parking lot. A big cat named Bill Rittner hops out and asks, "Smokey, how would you like to be the head mechanic on a couple of race boats?" I answer, "It really never crossed my mind." Only boat experience I ever had was 'bout two weeks on a banana boat from Okinawa to Hawaii and then to Frisco and I didn't like it at all. Well, Rittner got me believing this was a great opportunity, so I say "OK."

He's got two boats, a three point hydro in the big 235 cubic inch class, and one the next size down…I believe 'bout 135 cubic inch. Both boats used flat head Ford engines, an 85 and 60. Rittner drove the big Ford and Frank "Rebel" Mundy drove the smaller boat. I knew Frank. We had raced modified together.

After a race or two I decide boat racers are a bunch of sissies, rich jack-offs, and wanna-be racers. This was a big mistake. My second mistake was estimating the amount of time the boats would consume weekly. We did OK, the races we entered were won by either Rittner or Sid Street from Oklahoma City. He had Clay Smith for the engine man. Here's where I find out how sharp Clay is. Clay's from Long Beach, and a self-taught engine genius if there ever was one.

Rittner and Sid both wanted the big-3 point hydro speed record. Well, every other week we'd switch who held the record. Meanwhile, the boat's eating up so much time my local business was going backwards, so I ran Rittner off. He owned the Brisco Box Company in Camden, New Jersey. I believe the big boat's name was "Wa Wa (something)." Well, Bill's idea of fair pay and mine differed pretty bad, so I told him in a nice way to get his fucking junk out of there and don't come back.

Eight months later he's back, but with one less arm. He got thrown out of the boat and the prop cut his arm off. I ask, "Well what do you want, 'One Arm?'" "I'll pay you whatever you want to get boats ready to run for Governor's Cup Race,"…a big race in Lakeland as I recall. Bill can't drive with one arm, so a hotshot from Canada is gonna drive big boat and Frank Mundy in the 135.

A month later we are to leave the shop at 5:00 am to go to the big race. Mundy don't show up,

And Rittner is pissed, "Fuck him! let's go!" The Canadian tries out the boat and quits. He says he can't steer "in." There's something 'bout the rudder, and it's un-fixable in the hour we got left. Now we have no driver.

Here comes Frank with a terrible hangover. Plan "B" was: Frank drives the "Wa-Wa" but in ten minutes Frank is fired…double, triple fired. Nobody then or since could have ever been fired better. Rittner talks to a boat builder named Couloe, and other drivers. "Nooooo way. Thank you very much but I don't want my

221

arm cut off too." Hmmmmm, seems like boat is exceptionally flawed. ('Bout like some of the female boat fans: fast, but can't be handled). A guy who was my service manager when I was off racing, John Sabotka says, "Bill, why don't Smokey drive it?" Rittner says, "Hell yes, John! That's a hell of an idea!" I say, "Horse shit! I ain't driving that thing against Sid Street cold turkey out of the chute."

Ten minutes later I'm circling around trying to follow Street to hit start/finish line full speed at zero starting on the timed course. The idea at the start of a boat race is to cross the start/finish line just after the gun goes off. I'm 'bout fifty feet behind Street at the start. The boat would haul ass, so by the time I get to first turn I'm still 'bout fifty yards behind street. Well, it's time to turn and, "Oh shit!" With all the strength in my body it won't turn. I have to back off and fuckin' near ran up on the shore anyway. At race end I've been converted, 125 miles an hour on water seems like 250 on land. There was no seat belt and a big wide seat, just to stay in the boat was a job. Also, the boat don't go straight for over half an inch. It jumps and leaps and you can't see a goddam thing. Seems like I never got out of the rooster tail whole race.

I don't remember how I finished. I know it wasn't good, fifth or maybe third. I get out of the boat and Rittner says, "Hell of a job, couple more races and you'll eat 'em up." I'm so goddamned pooped I don't even answer. I've changed my mind. The boat racers ain't sissies – those bastards are insane.

The next day here comes a boat expert with Rittner to the shop. "Smokey the problem with the boat is the rudder." This is Henry Lauderback, a very famous race boat builder and a world authority on rudders. In the race, I hurt my left arm so bad fighting to turn the boat, I can't move it.

Rittner says, "He's gonna give you a new designed rudder that will let you turn the boat with two fingers."

I ain't getting in that son-of-a-bitch. "If you can steer it with two fingers, you drive it one arm."

Next day we've got the rudder on. All I'm gonna do is test the new rudder. We put the boat in the river, got two chase boats in case something goes wrong, a doctor, and all the bullshit that goes with it. My shop's on the river, so as the boat gets up to top speed (125 mph) I'm right in back of the shop. I take deep breath, now or never.

Sure enough, boat turns easy. Wow! This is neat! I get a big grin. Yea! Maybe I will be a boat racer. "Oh shit!" It won't straighten up. I get out of the throttle (no brake pedal in boat). That thing missed hitting the Seabreeze Bridge pier fender by about a foot. We towed the boat in and pulled it out of the water. The rudder is bent 90 degrees into an "L" shape.

"One Arm," the boats, spare rudders, everything and anything that had to do with big time boat racing were gone before the sun set. Only thing I forgot. I should have fired John Sabotka, his idea started the damn deal. In cleaning up last year, I found one part I failed to load up, a new 60 crank. Know anybody who needs one?

Dear Bill

Dear Bill:

This is a request that you look into/investigate the Curtis Turner crash at the "Cotton Picker's 500." I did not see the accident, but Curtis Turner and about 200 other people have told me that, during and after the combination Hell Driver's Thrill Show and part-time race, it appeared as though Lee Petty, America's favorite driver, had a hell of a dislike for black and gold Fords with 31s on them, and kind of crashed it into the fence.

Now this may not seem serious, but let me explain just how Lee's attitude has affected my whole life. To start with, everyone said that if I took my cars to Darlington September 2, there would be a race there, and that I would win from $12,000 to $20,000. So after months of work, and quite a bit of money spent, we arrive at the racer's paradise. There we had to sweat out the gnats, inspectors, a dirty hole called "the inspection station" and the local female cotton pickers. After many anxious moments in the inspection station, I finally won the title of the biggest cheater, not to say anything of the mental hell we were going through as we staggered into our beds at the motel. As you know, it was very crowded there, and finding a place for everyone to rest was not easy. By this time, after reading the paper and listening to the radio and TV, I am so sure we will win that I start spending the money.

Finally, the great day arrives. Just before the race starts we change our clothes so we will look nice in the pictures, and we are off. About the 28th lap I hear a hell of a crash and notice that one of my little Fords is missing. Of course you know why, so I won't go into that. About this time I am getting a little suspicious, maybe the newspapers had the wrong dope. But anyway, we still have another Ford left, and I didn't spend the whole $20,000 yet, so I figured Curtis would just win the $12,000. So I stand on the wall and push the watches and give signals so Economacki (Chris Economacki, the announcer) can tell everyone what a good kid I am.

We had the lead at this point, so I figured I would just stay around till the last gas stop, and then go and lay down so I'll look fresh for the movies, have enough strength to carry the money and the trophies…and to kiss Miss Cotton Picker of 1957. All of a sudden my car is missing and finally I see it staggering around the bend, like a bowlegged Memphis beauty queen, just hit by a train on the way to the Town Park Motel. I rush to the window and Mr. Turner is purple, and hollers, "Lee put me in the fence!" I notice you don't stop the race and wait for me to fix the car. And now I realize that I am in one hell of a mess. Boy, I really got troubles now.

So we fix the car up and get it back out again. But in the meantime they are long gone. As I stand on the wall now I'm sorry to be living; the papers and the radio were just a bunch of liars. I won't get the money I spent, I don't have any more racecars and Paul is in the hospital. After the thing is finally ended, as I sit down, people slap me on the back and tell me what a good job we did. Some say Lee should get a trophy for the beautiful style he has of putting a car in the wall, others compliment me on having the best-looking wrecks at the track. Bobby Myer's car looked a little better, but Turner's looked worse than Petty's Olds, so I still won that event. But not only did I win this year, I won last year also, so I got that sewed up. I only wish Petty could have done it sooner so we wouldn't have had to use so many tires and do the pit stops. Last year we had much better luck. Paul and Herb Thomas were well wrecked long before the halfway mark.

So Bill, you can see why I seemed a little upset. Of course I realize I don't have any right to, but I guess I am not quite broadminded enough. A lot of people go to the races to see the wrecks, and after all, we have to keep them happy. You sure have a swell guy in Lee. He has done a beautiful job for almost two years now, but I'm afraid you will lose him one of these days. I guess someone will come along to replace him though. I hope when it happens it will really look good, so everybody can always remember him as the best. Maybe he can get up into the grandstand and really put on a show.

Besides all the things that happened up there, I can't work since I got home. Everybody keeps calling up and coming here to see and talk about the wrecks. Also, I am having to walk around. I was driving a black and gold Ford, and ever since Monday, any time I drive near an Oldsmobile the damn Ford runs into a ditch and stops. So you see, Lee really messed up my whole life. Also, like a damn fool, I got mad about it, and won't race any more for a long time. Look at all the fun I'm going to miss. If you would care to discuss this with me any evening you can find me around Second Avenue getting a reversing treatment as this is the fourth time this has happened. Do you think you could advertise in your newsletter for me? A two-inch square of Curtis's or Paul's car for $1.00 as a souvenir of the 1957 eighth annual you name it.

Sincerely,
Smokey

Note: Feb. 24, 1969 it happened...Lee tangles with the wrong man at Daytona and damn near died from injuries. That ended Lee's career as a driver. Would you believe 'bout 40 years later I had the honor or putting Lee into the Daytona Hall of Fame and during my presentation he objected to something I said. He jumped up and said, "I never did like you either!"

NASCAR's reply:
Dear Smokey:
Your very elucidating letter of September 7, 1957, to Bill France has finally reached it's resting place on my desk, and now it is en route to the files for a very honorable repose. I must congratulate you on the rhetorical value, as well as the pertinent information contained therein.

I have written to Lee Petty requesting his version of this episode, and it is my ardent wish that the final washing will not lead to the complete ruination of your life; you are much too lugubrious a character to pass from the racing scene.

Sincerely yours,
Pat Purcell
Executive Manager

Mexican Road Race

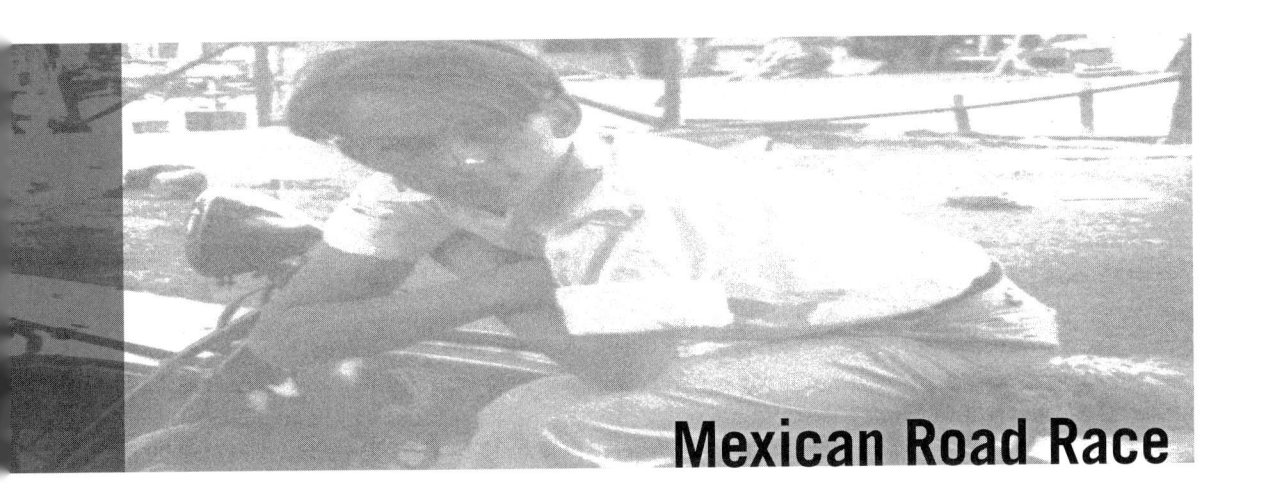

"Carrea Panamerica" means "Mexican Road Race" in Spanish. I don't know who dreamt this deal up, but if it had a main sponsor, it should have been the morticians of Mexico. Marshall Teague wanted to run a Hornet in the '52 race. Hudson says, "Yeah, we like that…here's 'bout 5,000 dollars…go tear 'em up!" We got three Hornets: a race car, a tow car, and another Hornet to pull a two wheel supply trailer. In the race it's Marshall and co-driver Les Snow. Les is a driver, and a pretty good one, from some rough suburb of Chicago…a nice guy. Also a damn good mechanic in general, though not an engine ace. One guy on the crew was from Marshall's gas station, Harry Van Driel. Harry was a damn good general mechanic and is still around. If I missed someone, I apologize.

We got 'bout 50 bucks a week and expenses. Some motor companies spent a fortune to try and win. Lincoln-Mercury were big spenders, with maybe the greatest mechanic that ever lived, Clay Smith as their main man. Watching Clay's behavior, and absorbing his preparation…it was a treat to watch one of our peers show you how it should be done: so perfectly and with seemingly effortless execution. Clay Smith was a genius. Probably the greatest so-called "racing mechanic" in the world at the time. But none of his ability impressed me as much as his helping his competitors with advice, and sometimes materials and tools. I'd watch him at 1:00 am, knowing he was as tired as I was, in the garage where we were preparing the cars for tomorrow's run. He would go help a competitor fix his carburetor so it wouldn't flood. True, the Lincoln budget was light years ahead of us, but he still had time for anyone who asked him for help. He did this in boats, Indy cars, midgets and stock cars. He even ground his own cam shafts. I think his 1st year to Indy, his car sat on the pole with a rookie driver, Walt Faulkner. In three point hydro in both classes…(racing boats) we run Ford 60s and Ford 85s…this was in the early 50s…I worked my ass off to beat him. Next week he'd come back and beat us again. The sad thing really is, to this day, racing has never come close to recognizing his contribution to helping build the foundation U.S. auto racing sits on. You know what really makes Clay Smith story so sad? He was killed at a way early age by his own race car. A sprinter that lost control coming off turn 2, and got in the pits and "nailed" him. The driver was one of Clay's best buddies.

Back to the race. There are a thousand stories 'bout the Mexican Road Race. Hell, in 1950 Bill France, Sr. and Curtis Turner co-drove an "up-side-down bathtub" (Nash) in the race. Well, we drive down through Matamoras (Brownsville, Texas). We have been told all kinds of horror stories 'bout the bad roads soon as you enter Mexico…('cept the Pan American' hi-way to El Paso). I'm driving one Hornet, towing the race car. We cross over into Mexico and hell, it's a good paved three lanes…for three miles.

Turn a corner…Bam!… running 60 and the asphalt stops no, one lane dirt… wrong road? turn around? down a little hill… hard turn… pow!! Wheeeeeee!!…river…no bridge… whooooeeeee… goddam near drove 'er in a small river. The river's got a flat deck barge, but river is way up from too much rain, (yet when we crossed the Rio Grande in Brownsville, it was damn near bone dry)… river's too wild… can't cross. Turns out five bucks gets river crossable (barely). Really, that was a very hazardous crossing. We could have lost everything we had. A single cable keeps barge from getting out of hand and you pull yourself across with rope-hand-power. Well, we manage the skinny, rough roads until we find the Pan American hi-way to Mexico City. (From there to Mexico City, roads good…very good) Mexico City…everything's same as today I think, 'cept then it was 90 percent smaller. Traffic rules are Russian roulette, kinda "don't let the other guy see your eyeballs." It's actually a game of "chicken." There were no traffic lights there. A very loud horn was best driving aid.

In Mexico City we work on car at the Hudson dealership. We can't speak Spanish, but the dealer's got a 15 or 16 year old son. A real nice guy and helper. He's going with us as our interpreter. (Good idea as it turned out.) Gotta have a place to stay for five days. Taxi driver says ,"Go to Angel's, best place in town." Angel's is a big house, 15 bucks a day for room and three meals…free booze part of rent…free hookers and dirty movies all day and night…all for 15 bucks a day. Yes, it was all good…for a dose of the crabs…quite an interesting place.

The owner took a liking to our driver. I observed her giving oral sex to him with a condom on. That puzzled and amused me. Actually…Les Snow, the co-driver, brought it to my attention… it was as interesting, I think, as the discovery I had made a few minutes earlier. After Les guided me to the room where our landlady was attempting to relax the driver, I then showed him my startling discovery. Remember, I said, "whiskey no charge." Well, if a tenant had sex with a waitress or bartender, an old lady would come in room after, and wash your sex parts with whiskey. Makes sense right? Well, on the second day I notice a door and I wonder, "Where does that go?" So, I open door and am startled to see an old lady pouring whiskey out of wash basins into a funnel stuck into a whiskey bottle. I realize, "Hey! That's what we were drinking"… (No wonder it had an unusual flavor) We soon solved that problem. We were able to buy a quart of good whiskey for 'bout three bucks.

I will always have a fond spot in my heart for Angel's place. Those young ladies actually taught me some things that the Californian's hadn't got to yet…(the deal with the beads in particular). Although that deal actually had a few draw backs – I got no rest at all. I told you about acquiring a group of annoying passengers in an area you see baseball players scratch all the time. Every time I see it on TV, I smile and say, "Wonder if they been to Angel's?" Piggins had made arrangements for us to stay in a private home in Mexico City, so when Les and I turned in our expenses, (5 days, $75 as medical expenses for the "Inca flu"). Piggins disallowed the expenses. I guess he was pissed we didn't invite him over there.

I'm really grateful to Marshall for including me in the race. It was an experience. When Marshall first invited me, I understood I was gonna be a co-driver. Now, co-drivers never drove. They just sat in right side of front seat and hollered…"Watch it!"…"Slow down!"…"Turn right you dumb shit or you'll never make it!"…"Whoo-ee!"…"Oh-shit!"…or when you passed someone in your class, give 'em the finger. But when the time came, Les got the co-driver job. The race was run on a new paved road (two lane) that run from El Paso in the United States to Tuxtla, at southern end of Mexico at beginning of Central America. One-half mile south of town, road went to jungle… not even dirt road. The Pan American hi-way race was 1,934 miles long in 1952, we ran it in five days: 1st leg: Tuxtla to Oaxaca; 2nd leg: Oaxaca to Puebla; 3rd

Effective Mexican Army crowd control.

leg: Puebla to Mexico City; 4th leg: Mexico City to Leon, 5th leg: Leon to Durango; 6th leg: Durango to Porral; 7th leg: Porral to Chihuahua; 8th leg: Chihuahua to Juarez. The race was a mountain road race, on a typical mountain…sharp turns… always either gaining or losing altitude…with no goddam guard rails and plenty of 5,000 foot straight down drops in case you slid off. Damn rite, somebody got wiped out 'bout every day… and sometimes spectators…actually, 26 people (mostly spectators) died in five years.

I left out something regarding Mexican culture and law. Radios and guns…it was not legal to have a radio capable of any distance to speak of…so getting car in country with radio was a son-of-a-bitch…and if that radio was gone when you tried to leave country…that was hell. So guess what would get stolen quicker than a cat could lick it's ass? Right…the radio. I took radio out, and antenna off, and hid them in with spare parts. Guns? gave 'em away in Brownsville coming in when I heard how that worked. More about guns later.

Now the little town where race started, is at the southern very end of Mexico. This is mountain… dry, poor, old-old town, but they had a Ford dealership there that was one half block square (inside). This dealership had a huge parts department. Very few cars, new or used…but at least one of every kind of tool to work on Fords, Lincolns and Mercurys made in the world, and take my word for it, them cats knew how to use 'em. They had some uncanny metal, or body men…threw away damn near nothing…straightened everything…like big Cadillac bumperette…How? Split 'em in four pieces… straightened each piece, then welded back together. They had a chrome plating facility that amazed me. The Mexican state troopers all run Mercurys. A wild bunch…you haven't lived until you get on latin country roads, including cities. No traffic lights, big-assed loud horns, and the code of the hills is "big is better"…so 100,000 pound tractor and trailer double, owned the road. (Yes, they had them…pulled by French tractors where 15 year old kids rode on both front fenders and hand oiled the valve gear… huge engines, diesel, 'bout 1,000 cubic inches.) For some reason these Latino truckers ride in the middle of a two lane hi-crown road and drive like a "bat out of hell." I swear, when they wind down out of the mountains and hit a town, they add 30 miles per hour and blow the horn like a freight train going through Fayetteville. Most Latinos can't drive worth a shit, but some of them cats with a little experience and good equipment, can race any son-of-a-bitch in the world.

Back to the Carerra Panamerica. OK… Here's how it works. Race starts around 6:00 or 7:00 am in morning (first daylight)…cars are flagged off a couple minutes apart… 'bout 10 classes, so "hot dogs" go first. Idea is to keep "hot dogs" from wading through "slow stuff." This is a real road course – no fences or guard rails either. The way they kept people and animals back, or kept regular cars off the road was to station soldiers within sight distance of each other on alternating sides of the road. (By the way, they drive on same side of the road we do.) It's a simple deal…in the race hours the road's closed. If an animal or human attempts to cross during the forbidden hours, the soldier shoots your ass "to kill." The race I was in, a young man right on outskirts of Tuxtla, crossed the road…soldier shot and killed him. A friend of mine, (well actually a friend of any racer), Don O'Reilly, had a magazine called "Speed Age" and witnessed this deal. He like to went "ape-shit" over it. I seen him a few months ago at his house, and we talked about the killing.

OK…pit crew: at the end of every "leg" you got lots of things to fix. (Reference: sliding off the road, tires, broken engine) so the pit crew gets cars ready to race, then you drive your ass off all night to get to next check-point, cause if you don't make it by "road closing," it's over for that team. Well, "we" (the Hudson team) are the Mexican Hudson dealer's son, Marshall's mechanic/employee, hi-buck 10-dollar-a-day-man Harry Van Driel and myself. The back of car is full of parts and tools, and we are pulling a two wheel trailer loaded with tires, parts and fuel. We had to carry everything we needed. At that time in Mexico, a gas station was a collection of 50 gallon drums along the road at a house. You stop…toot your horn and maybe. We all ride in front seat…either Harry or I drive. Let's call the son, ('bout 15) José OK? (I forgot his real name, sorry.). José is our interpreter, and a damn good one. Can speak English super…we have to really haul ass to get to next race checkpoint. First night, just 'bout midnight on Isthmus of Tojuanapec Road on the only straight level ground in whole race, ('bout sea level), all of a sudden… road block (with driftwood)! I'm asleep…car is lurching…tires screeching…horn blowing…guns going off. Harry, the dumb shit has decided to run through the road block, running 'bout 90, with the trailer flying all over hell behind. As I look in rear view mirror, I see what looks like career-ending flying experiment of a Mexican highway bandito. The trailer catches him, and he gets a trampoline type launch from the swinging trailer. I think "Harry can file at least one notch on side of the steering wheel"…(but probably two)…or we can paint something on side of car (kinda' like fighter planes did in war for a shot down enemy) …well nothing broke.

Next night Harry's driving again, I'm opposite side…José in middle. Hear brakes, then down-shift and wide-ass open engine. José's hollerin' "Stop!!!"…I look up… horses lined up across road, and up each bank…'bout 20 of 'em…all got rifles, and they are coming down. Twenty rifles are aimed at the windshield. I reach over, turn key off. Harry gets 'er whoa'ed 'bout five feet from the end of twenty rifle gun barrels. The boss-man is 'bout five foot four tall by five foot four around; got glasses and a mustache; got a "general" kinda hat with a strap to hold it on when his horse is going real fast. I can't understand him, but he is pissed! And Jose is talking his little diplomatic ass off to keep Harry from being turned into a very dead gringo son-of-a-bitch. (You know Harry, I doubt you have any idea how close you came to having a rock sitting in a cemetery, where the last thing on it said "1952.") Well 'bout nine-ten bucks was cost of "permission" to continue on our mission to next check-point at Oaxaca… You'd think by now I'd get thinking and put Harry's ass in the trailer and drive myself. Nope, I need some rest…ain't no way in hell it's gonna happen again rite?…so I doze off. Now we're in bad very-very twisty mountains, 'bout 4:00 am, Getting close to check point – one to one and a half hours out. Car's slowing… I hear José raising hell with Harry. I wake up…we are damn near stopped, going up real steep hill. I see 'bout 20 Mexicans…rocks across the road. One cat had a pistol…'bout 10 with machetes. Whoa Nellie! I wind window down…I'm opposite Harry, Jose in middle. Mr. Bandito is shit-faced drunk… Got a pistol with 'bout an 18 inch barrel, and he sticks it in my right ear. Harry don't see the pistol, and as men move around in front of car, and José tries to negotiate a peaceful arrangement which will let us continue to Oaxaca without any leaks in our blood carrying equipment, (engine's still running). I hear Harry say, "I'm gonna floor it and take off – road is clear now." I say, "Harry, before you do, check over here and see what's sticking in my right ear and note the drunken and unhappy attitude of the cat that's holding it." Well 'bout two quarts of wine (a departure present from the ladies at Angel's), about three or four bucks and one five gallon can of gas cured that deal. We get to Oaxaca an hour before road closure, so I decide to notify authorities about our terrible experiences. (Get the cops in the deal.) José says, "I don't think so"…I say, "Bullshit," so we go. It ain't far. Still dark as hell. As I walk into station I damn near have a heart attack. There sits Mr. Five Foot Four's twin brother (the horse bandit)…even the same clothes – boots and hat. I know it's impossible for it to be the same man…no vehicle passed us all night. Or was it the same man?…maybe there's another road? Anyway, José explains whole terrible deal. Mr. Mexican general rolls to the side, lets out a big fart, and eats José's ass out, and tells us, "Get our ass over to check-point garage and keep our damn mouths shut, or our ass is in jail." "OK, OK'… I've heard 'bout Mexican jails, and we ain't hurt. "Come to think about it, maybe it never happened…maybe I dreamt it." We got our stuff out to do our work, but still got to wait four or five hours. An American tourist…(big trout fisherman…fly rod champion of the world I think) is a Hudson Hornet lover, matter of fact, has a year old Hornet right outside. He can't go till race cars come and go (remember the system…"road closed to public and animals for a time.") He tells me about Mexican's trying to hold him up. He was fishing some place to our west, and came onto the Pan American highway 'bout 20 miles before "Mr. Long barrel pistol." They set up a road block with small rocks. He got scared and pulled a "Harry Van Driel," and run the road block. I said, "Did they shoot at you?…Did it hurt your car?" "Hell no!…I'm a good driver!"…I then notice a dark puddle under the engine, and a wet looking place at rear of the car, so I get a light and get close… You guessed it: oil and gas leaking. Turned out "Mr. Good Hudson driver" had 'bout no oil in oil pan (a rock from road block caused oil pan to flunk the "hit a rock with the oil pan at 60 miles per hour test") and "Mr. Very Lucky Champion Fly Fisherman Hudson-loving Good Driver-lucky Son-of-a-bitch, only had 22, yup…22 bullet holes in back of his "lucky black Hornet." Well "Lucky" decided he wanted to talk to the American ambassador to Mexico…said he knew him (maybe he gave him a free fish) about this outrage. So I directed him to the military headquarters and "General Fat-ass." I don't know what happened, but we left 'bout four hours later, and the "lucky black trout fishin' Hornet" with 22 bullet holes in it was still sittin' there, and the puddle of oil under engine was 'bout two foot in diameter. If you're still living "Mr. Champion Fisherman," I'd appreciate a note from you telling me how that deal ended. From there on, I never got to meet any more Mexican bandits, but I kinda' have a little idea how those people felt when they were on the stage coaches and they were attacked and robbed. I guess it's tougher the way we had it, cause only José knew what the bad guy was saying. (You know, Harry might have been a stage coach driver in a previous life.)

Another thing I haven't mentioned was the goofy spectators. Wherever anybody run off the road and got killed last year, that's where there would be 4,000 people – rite up to the edge of the road, and as a rule on the outside of turns. Then in Mexico City, you're coming in straight...running over a hundred...you've been off the road three or four times front and back. (What's the tires look like?). There's damn near a million people lined up for four or five miles with their toes on edge of asphalt, and you're going by 'em at over 100, rubbing your left and right door handles against their tits. What if a tire lets go? Those in back shoved those in front, and they couldn't back up. No, it never happened...maybe courtesy of the Inca gods...but in general, few races in the world extracted an unacceptable high cost in lives, sheet time, and inconvenience to the citizens as the Mexican road race. The same thing, reference crowds, happened coming into Juarez at end of the race.

Clay Smith and his Lincolns, and Bill Stroppe and his Mercurys dominated those races. Marshall and Les did pretty good. I think they ran from fifth, and I believe ended up seventh in stock car class and thirteenth overall. The whole deal took 'bout 22 hours racing time. Hershel McGriff, from Portland Oregon, won the first race which changed his life forever. I remember the car. An Olds 88, with a clever sign on it from Portland, Oregon "For You in Portland, a Rose Grows"... Who in the hell ever heard of a sponsor who sold roses in early '50s? Hershel I guess is still going... He turned out to be very good, and last I heard was 'bout 70, and still winning.

The Mexican Road Race was a wild chapter in American racing's early experiments while trying to find it's way, or to find a place where those who loved to go fast went to hear those loud, tortured engines. The hope was to establish at least an annual event that could fund the competitors sufficiently so that they could do it one more time next year. There are attempts to re-establish parts of that exciting time...but men, you missed the boat. It has come, and it has gone...like the Pony Express.

Mercedes won the race with a gull-wing coupe, with, I believe, a German driver (in 1952). John Fitch, a yankee American driver, was at his prime, and really doing the best job...but poor John got screwed by the Germans. They wanted a German driver to win, and as I remember, they had four or five cars in the race. At race end, Fitch gets disqualified cause he can't curse in German, and Karl Kling, a German race hero got the marbles. The Mexican Road Race ran many classes...from the fastest sports cars in the world to stock car to little shit-box sports cars with 'bout 100 horsepower at 8,000 rpm. So this race was between Mercedes and Ferrari. I guess the four things I remember most were: Number One – Angel's guest accommodations. Number Two – watching and working with Clay Smith. In my book Clay, you're "#1" by a ton. Number Three – The pit action of Ferrari and Mercedes...particularly the Germans: they performed as an army exhibition marching team, like robots with human minds. Watching John Fitch die a million deaths trying to get his car repaired (he developed brake trouble) But the real act was Ferrari.

No Keystone Cop movie can ever match the act those 20 "dago" mechanics, drivers and staff, put on at every pit stop. They were poorly equipped in all ways but bodies. At mid-point of a day's running, you have to fuel – change tires – and as a rule, change drivers...(Only the hottest sports cars had professional sports car drivers). Remember all these had co-drivers...(Some dumb shit who strapped his ass down in right hand seat, or left hand, as case might be) to yell at driver his observations, opinions, advice and/or criticism. Driving a race car is, as a rule, fun. But be a passenger in a fast car with a great driver, or even worse, with some terrible driver with tons of money and the balls of an elephant...and do this five to 10 hours a day for four or five days. As far as I'm concerned, is like sitting in an electric chair for that amount of time waiting on them to fix a problem in the system so they can fry your ass. Well, the drivers jump out, after sliding a quarter of a mile, and ending up running over their pit set-up. Why?…he is headed for the shit house… remember he's on 'bout on his fifth day of Mexican food. During a Carrera Panamerica stop, besides changing tires, (and fueling in case of sports cars), you had to, for sure, replace brake pads, and fix or "band-aid" whatever else is "not doing it." The Ferrari tire changers best act was to drop car without the wheel on yet…or put front tire on rear, or vise-versa. The fuelers, (with cans), dumping gas all over everybody and everything…and sometimes catch car on fire on re-start. The "soakers" getting smacked by the "soak-ee's" and the "soak-ee" attempting to dump gas on "soaker" to get even. But by far the best act was the water boys. They used garden water cans, (like your grandmother used to water her garden…with built in funnel…held 'bout a gallon and a half). The Ferraris run hot…so as tires, fuel and brake pad were being done, two to four guys open hood and start dumping water on radiator and into radiator. In the process, the brake pad, and/or tire guy, gets an unexpected bath, which pisses him off…so he jumps up, grabs the bucket and dumps it on radiator man, or the contest is even, and two guys are in a "bucket pulling contest," during which, driver accidentally gets a bucket of water down his helmet and back. Now mix in 'bout five officials, who don't know what the hell they're doing either, and Ferrari staff and race brass get into it…so now you got a mixture of Italian-Spanish, and maybe some English, French and German…cursing and lots of pushing and pulling…rule books, pit boards, and "motherfucker" in three to four languages. In addition to this, is a hoard of afficionados: ex-racers, wannabe racers, rich fans, about ten "Miss Italy's," and the news media (no TV yet). Every once in awhile throw in a Mexican policeman and farmer… (Wantin' to get paid, or "put your ass in jail" for a cow, donkey, pet or chickens you ran over last year.) And in Pueblo, a teen-age young lady with 'bout a three month old baby. Seems like a driver last year left some of his seeds with the little lady, and she wanted to talk to that driver about marriage, and a home in Italy…and it seemed like her father and brother had a different plan. They wanted to kill the son of a bitch. (This was in Ferrari pit.) Since big sports cars started first, and run fastest, we got to watch the deal from best seats before our cars came in. Number Four – the Mexican hi-way banditos, and their version on how to run a toll-road without any investment in it. Maybe Number Five could have been the "Inca trot," caused by not being cursed by it in Mexico City at Angel's, and my assumption, "I can drink the water and eat the vegetables…it don't bother me." I left a trail from Tuxtla to El Paso, and back into Florida…but it helped in later life, during the early sixties in my adventures in the jungle oil fields and gold mines in the Ecuadorian Oriente, I did not challenge the local medical wisdom of how to avoid the "toilet paper boogie."

Racing needed this five days of stupidity to guide us…but we didn't know it was a mistake until we did it…though it sure was a shame so many died. Actually, considering the scope of the race, the management did a hell of a job when you think of all the details of such an event. For those who would re-create this race today…some advice: just assemble all drivers in an auditorium and play Russian roulette instead. This spares the people who live on the race's proposed route the loss of several days of their lives, and the almost sure loss of several lives. Racing has "been there and done that." I learned one sentence "besame culo" in Spanish…(means "kiss my ass") and two Spanish words: "Adios" and "gracias."

"Adios" Carrera Panamerica… and "gracias."

It Didn't Say You Couldn't

Let's get right to it. In my day I was considered a cheater, ranked never worse than second. And you know, maybe I was. But, unless you were there, how in the hell would you ever know?

When NASCAR first started the rules were quite short – eight to ten pages covered everything both technical and business. Bill France Sr., Red Vogt and Marshall Teague wrote the technical part. France wouldn't have then made a big pimple on a good engine man's ass, but the other two, Teague and Vogt, were the peers of all of us. Can you imagine either one of them suggesting even one sentence that would block a horsepower increase?

OK, now how many of you have had a problem with the IRS, and talked to three or four IRS people, and gotten a different answer from every one? How about the law? You win, I appeal, you loose, another appeal. How many trials does it take? Maybe three, four or five; State Supreme Court, Federal Supreme Court. What I'm getting at is: rule interpretation is the same as law interpretation. You get caught drunk driving, you lose your license and get a big fine. The mayor gets caught, same deal, same cop and the verdict "not guilty." The 2000 presidential election is a great example of how effective good lying, loud-mouth lawyers are. So in NASCAR rules, like many other places, politics are very present.

Being in charge of a business puts you in a position where maybe you can make or lose money based on your interpretation of the "rules." Now, you're the most honest son-of-a-bitch in town, you're running a race association and you're working the razor edge of bankruptcy. Are you gonna side with a dirt poor racer and piss off Ford Motor Company? Come on, life ain't a delayed broadcast in slow motion. But, if you're real clever, you learn to talk in "gray," not "black and white." That way the rules are never really clear. Also, you never do the killing yourself. Always use a trusted "yes" man to do the hatchet work. Now, find tricky words and phrases to legislate with, and incorporate them into the company by-laws.

Nope, I didn't learn this from Bill France, I learned it from General Motors, Ford, and Chrysler (So did Bill). Bill just chose to implement these inconsistencies and call them rules. His Nobel prize winner was "not in the spirit of the rules," and/or, "not in the spirit of good competition." When he put that sentence on your ass you were a fucked duck. You now end up with a two word "Mexican standoff." I say "Why?" and he'd say, "Because." Probably the NASCAR attorney (also part owner at the time), Lewis Ossinsky, was the real author of those gems. But never mind the gray areas of the rules, we got a major problem to discuss next.

How in the hell do you legislate a fraudulent concept? Stock car racing, today the fraud is compounded

100 times from what was possible in 1950. Even if you're an eighth grader, you know stock car racing is at best, a good-natured lie. There hasn't been a "stock" car raced since 1970 in NASCAR. How in the hell can you legislate a V8 engine in a 2001 Chevy, with a rear drive, and call it "stock"? There ain't no such car. A two-door Ford Taurus with rear wheel drive, and a V8 engine with a carburetor? OK, you can legislate the current concept "if" you take every single separate piece of that vehicle and say categorically what it's correct specifications are. What you end up with, is a very fat rule book. One of the reasons the United States has two lawyers for every common laborer, is because lying to the public is not only legal in the United States, but a very honorable and lucrative profession (it and prostitution).

Gary Nelson, I hope you got more class than to get pissed about this, but somebody ought to ask him what he knows about Richard Petty's 4th of July (during President Reagan's visit) race-winning engine, under oath, with Bobby Allison as a sworn witness. Gary's biggest achievement as a cheater? I couldn't tell you. (Hopefully, there will be a book at a later date. I see no useful reason for him to reveal the details to you now.) Hopefully that "sinner" will choose to cleanse his soul with his own explanation some day. And then again maybe best idea is to "let sleeping dogs keep sleeping."

You know, it seems like when a human gets a lot, or maybe too much power over other humans, (I'm referring to athletes, business giants, political champs and entertainment personalities, and/or military heroes), invariably their power slowly becomes abusive to many. I guess it's just a normal human characteristic.

So if the inspector is qualified, and enforces rules fairly, he still has only one brain, where as the potential cheaters have about 60 individual brains at work. People like Yates, Elliot, Johnson, Roush, Pittman, Evernham, Childress, Foyt, and others plus the high performance wizards at Ford and General Motors and now Chrysler. How does one ex-bank robber outwit all the nations peer group of bank robbers? Can't be done by any one man. So in spite of everything, cheating is here to stay. Even if the prize is for who goes the slowest.

Now let's consider another variable. I've been down this road, so I know it exists. (I called it "shangri-la street") The inspector's boss has a business or personal reason to have a race end in a particular way. For example, motor company "X" wins, and motor company "Z" is pissed off because the rules limit their chances. So, the next race, instead of a 50-50 shot at it, company Z's chance is more like 90-10. Guess who gets the short end? (You know what I'm talking about don't you Junior J.?)

But that's life. Even if, as an inspector, you try and keep her in the middle of the road, you can't always call 'em like they are. Every once in a while you're gonna end up with a lit chain saw up your ass. Not just racing, but anything that concerns the opinion and interests of masses. The moral of this is, if you always call it like it is, you're gonna lead a lonely and probably, a low tax bracket life. And there's also good chance they will never name a grandstand after you.

Good thing Gary wasn't around with his big dollar fine system in 1968. Goddam…can you imagine what the fine would have been on the '67 Chevelle? The little car that could, but didn't? Point is, head inspector can't always have final word and remain there with desk with his name on the door. It's impossible to be the enforcer and win that outfit's popularity award. NASCAR's current chief inspector, should command respect. He is doing a pretty good job considering all the distractions that come with the territory, only way I'd want his job would be if the choice was between being inspector or getting infected with AIDS. Hell, dictators are human. You piss 'em off, they'll do same thing you'd do if somebody tried to jack you around. Big difference between being a boss and a dictator. 'Bout the worst a boss can give you is small flesh wound. The dictator, he can flat ruin your cotton pickin' ass rite quick. What do you think about that Cale? 50 "Big ones" for moving four little, bitty bolts a fraction of an inch, and never got to race it. Whoo-ee!

Back to my case, in regard to being nominated for first member of the "Cheater's Hall of Fame." I really just read the rule book carefully. If a nut, bolt, or part wasn't specifically mentioned, or a measurement wasn't given, I assumed those items were "fair game." Even where they said "stock," what the hell did that mean? They needed to say "stock as of a certain day." Hell, stock can change a lot depending on when and where a part was made. As a result of my reading of the rules, I think that by 1970, one half of the technical rule section of a NASCAR rule book, was dedicated to me – quite an honor actually.

I've been around race cars for 60 years or more now. There are really only a few things I consider cheating:

1. Big engine
2. Big gas tank
3. Hi-buck very expensive materials, in reference to weight saving
4. Blatant, very expensive aerodynamic rule violation.

Now three and four, I consider more "chicken shit" than cheating. These violations are unfair from an economic view point. Example, I've got money running out my ears so I put titanium every place I can on a car to save weight. Aerodynamics cheating: this, as a rule deals with taking advantage of the ignorance of inspectors, as compared to expertise of a world class aerodynamicist. Now, big engines and big gas tanks. I have no mental tolerance for either. Sure, if a poor-boy racer bores his engine .010, too big cause he can't afford a new block, I don't give a damn 'bout that. But that son-of-a-bitch who runs a "400-incher" against a 358, to me, he is a shit. Christ, it don't take brains to win that way. Same with "big tanker," if he goes a half-gallon over, I don't care. But that cat who was five or six gallons over, or with a hidden tank, in my book, he was dog shit. This was the cat who was gonna make four stops, to the legal cat's five.

What brains does that take?

Now I like racing like NASCAR was on "Day One," except for safety-related issues, and Indy rules in the 1950s and '60s. (You know, I can still write their rules 50 years later?)

– "Got to be at least -X- inches long."
– "No more than -X- inches wide"
– "got to run -X- gallons maximum of -X- fuel.
– "Engine can be X cubic inches max." For normal aspirated, and -X- max for blown."
– "Car must weigh at least -X- number of pounds"
– "the oil tank must be sealed."
– "open wheel car – no fenders, no roof"

As far as specifications for the car, that was it. (Oh yes, no bad words allowed on car or personal clothing. At my first Indy 500 race in 1958 we had to tape over the nasty word "damn" painted on the car, and Don O'Reilly had to cut "Smokey's, Best Damn Garage in Town" patch off of me and my crew's shirts before we were allowed on pit road race morning.) Now that's a set of rules a man can race by. We all had to run same tire – Firestones. They nicknamed 'em "Flintstones." Goddam, they were hard and stiff. I ain't kidding, a tire could be flat on race car and it would be hard to tell just by looking at it.

Cheat? How? Why? Engine rules were simple and easy to check. The fuel check was a simple sniff of the exhaust pipe. Any idiot could smell nitro. Weight, width, and length rules were safety oriented, and simple.

IT DIDN'T SAY YOU COULDN'T

My point here is, when you have simple rules it's easy to police and enforce. NASCAR was the same in the beginning, very simple. Don't change nothing, and nothing wrong with those rules, except cars were much too weak in suspension and brakes.

Now I'm sure you NASCAR "wheels," who are reading this are so pissed by now that you're gonna go to "Daytona USA" and rip any and everything out of there that has anything to do with Smokey, including anything painted black and gold. But you'll be a lot better off if you finish this, and then go tear all that stuff out. Just calm down. 90 percent of you reading this weren't even born when it happened, so how the hell you gonna dispute it? If Ray Fox, Ralph Moody, the Wood Brothers, or Frank Mundy, says it's bullshit, then listen. They walked the walk live, and in real time. Cotton Owens, Raymond Parks, Jack Smith, Bud Moore, Herb Thomas, and Lee Petty are also just as qualified to talk about it knowledgeably. Let's get back to cheaters and rules.

At first NASCAR said, "Nothing could be removed from cylinder head." OK, that's simple enough, but they didn't say, "You can't cut block, or jack up the pistons." Not at first anyway. The rules said, "Stock cam." I said, "What's stock cam?" To which they answered, "A cam with the same lobe shape and specifications as stock." OK, but they didn't say, "You can't move the lobe centers, and/or whole cam." Sure, I did all of that. But, was it cheating? After all, they checked the parts before the race and said, "You're legal." What self-respecting bank robber would write a letter to a bank and tell 'em when and how he was gonna rob the bank?

You gotta remember, this whole time there are a group of "Little Angels," like Teague, Fox, Vogt, Moore, Moody, Owens, Buck Baker, Shuman, Thomas, Petty, and about 30 more, all of whom could bend the rules into a pretzel, that I had to deal with on the track each race. Even though I only got through the 10th grade and some of the others really couldn't read or write, we all learned what tricks, legal or illegal, made a car go fast. (I'm not kidding. Don't believe me? If you could see some of the early sign-in sheets, and purse pay-out sheets, you'd find lots of "Xs," in the place where it says "sign here." If Johnny and Mary Brunner were still here, they could shock you with a recital of how "educated" the original crew were.) Maybe I just worked a little harder to find a little more speed.

I played with different length rods, offset pistons, off-set cranks, cam shaft lifter diameters, spark plug location, lightweight valves, rocker ratios… nothing in early rule book said you couldn't. Course the word "stock" was sprayed through all those pages, but hell, I've seen times when I don't think Ford built over 100 engines that were in all ways alike. It wasn't just that production changes made the word "stock" meaningless, they'd vary from plant to plant and country to country. The rule book didn't say you couldn't use a Canadian block or cylinder head. It just said "production block." It didn't say it couldn't be a truck part. My interpretation was, if a part was produced and stocked for some make or model, it was "stock." Go get an old rule book. It don't say "Chevy stock production," it says "stock production." Was I cheating? Can you refer this interpretation of the rules to a specific incident? Like "when I put the Chrysler pistons in the Ford block?"

Nothing in rule book said which way engine had to rotate, so if I reversed the deal, was I cheating? Actually, some of today's NASCAR engine men, will never know the thrill of an experiment that really worked. They'll never know the pleasure of walking out to the cars race morning, where you pull your pants up and look around at your competition and say, "All right you bastards, let's have a race" and watch your new invention "do it" to it.

We had so many engines…six cylinder Fords, overhead valve V8s, Olds, flat-head Fords, Cadillacs,

Hudsons, Pontiacs, Packards, GMC in line 6s, Nash, four cylinder Fords, Lincolns, Buicks, Studebakers, Chevy in line 6s and V8s. Also, in many of the makes we had more than one engine over time. Hell, in Ford alone, there were 'bout eight different engines. So we had a constant learning process and plenty of parts to experiment with. Now, in this steady stream of different engines and five buck an hour inspectors, who is kidding who? Lots of changes went unnoticed. In this time frame, you might say cheating was at it's glorious peak. Hell, we got so far ahead of the factories they were standing around as lost as the inspectors. Compare this variety of stuff we worked with to the last fifteen years of just two engines, Ford and Chevy 358 inch. These two engines started racing 45 years ago and every inspector now has a sample of every legal part. Of course, today they have higher paid inspectors too…six bucks an hour.

In the beginning, camshaft was considered 90 percent of speed or horsepower. Compression was the number two "supposed" horsepower magic. Actually, the real "hurt" in stock engines, was inability to get working fluid (gas and air mixture) in and out of the cylinders and the inadequacy of the exhaust system.

Since 1947, 90 percent of the power increase has come from improving the ability of the engine to fill it's cylinders at higher and higher rpm…it's just that simple. Almost all the "goody" has come from changes in the cylinder head, induction manifold, and exhaust systems. This evolution of the induction system also includes shape of combustion chamber (which includes piston dome shape).

Camshafts have been "beat to death," with one million different designs, which has now progressed to where 10 year old cams are the best (but with lots of lift). Compression cheating continued up to two years ago. When forced to reduce compression by the new rules, the racers found that when using gasoline, after they hit 12.5:1, it didn't get enough better to fool with. They also found that at low compression, alky was a big help, but at high compression, alky did very little to increase horsepower. Where I'm trying to take you here is this: much of cheating was counter-productive, and a waste of time, money and durability.

"Defensive cheating." You need to know about that so I'll give you an example. In 1962, I worked for Bunkie Knudsen, Pontiac head honcho at the time. He says, "Smokey, I want to win the Daytona 500, don't fuck me around with any bullshit, do it!." Well, everybody's running 28 gallon steel tanks. Legal tank size was 22 gallons; just a few drops difference, right? So I decide, OK I can't win with one or two extra fuel stops so I make 28 gallon tank like everybody else. I put a basketball in it. When I get fuel check, basketball is aired up with an aerosol can size of a paint can. Now cleared from inspection, with 22 gallons fuel capacity on race morning. I let air out of basketball through the aerosol can connection. Now I'm 28 gallons. We had equal fuel stops with all front runners. Was I cheating? We win the race, and go to inspection. I slide under car with an aerosol can and air up the basketball. I just need small hose and psssst, back to 22 gallons. I was shooting the shit with the inspector the whole time.

Fast time forward: 1966 and I'm cutting the lawn, on 'bout the 15th of June. It was a Sunday and France Sr. drives by, then comes back, pulls in driveway, gets out and says, "How come you ain't entered in the July 4th race?" I say, "I don't like to race and lose." He says, "What you getting at?" I say, "The goddam 28 gallon fuel tanks. I got a rubber fuel cell in my car that only holds 22 gallons, and I'll never race without it again." He says, "You mean to tell me you ain't smart enough to figure out how to match 'em?" I said, "Come on, we played that bullshit four years ago with the '62 Pontiac."

To make a long story short, to get me to enter the car, he agreed to put a sign four by eight foot saying, "After the race, all tanks on top 10 cars will come out and be inspected and an inspection hole will be cut in tank if outer dimensions are bigger than fluid capacity indicates." He agreed to put sign up in inspection area. I figured, if you knew for sure you were gonna get caught, no stupid bastard would play "game 28."

Well, I enter the car, and Curtis is gonna drive. I get to inspection for qualifying and there is no sign. So I turn around and start to leave. France catches up an says, "Where are you going?." I said, "Home, you lying asshole." Thirty minutes later the sign is up.

We "sand bag" in qualifying a little. On race day we got 'er made in the shade. We stop for our last fuel, but all my competitors decide to keep on going. We run fourth. Ray Nichels' Dodge, with Sam McQuagg driving, wins. Ray says after race, "Hey, I'll give you prize money difference after race, if you forget gas tank." And, so help me God, so does Bud Moore in second place, and Jim Paschals, who finished third. They all want to pay me some loot to forget tank. Jim Hurtibise, run fourth. He got screwed, and moved back to fifth and we got $3,000 bucks. (But Sam got $13,000).

Guess what? I swing into the inspection shed and the sign's gone. Friel's the chief inspector. I said, "You're supposed to pull tanks." He says, "I run this joint, and we ain't pullin nothing." I jump in the car and drive over to Bill's office. Can't go in, big victory party. Chrysler big shots and Bill and his cohorts. So I bust in. France is in his chair, and I say, "Come on to inspection, Friel won't pull tanks." France says, "Smokey I can't. Chrysler has released Dodge advertisements to the Associated Press and the United Press, etc. and they have all filed reports. I didn't know 'bout Friel, I'm sorry."

Well, I'm hot enough to fuck now, so I recited his pedigree, as I saw it, in front of Chrysler's big shots and local press. Next day, I get a letter hand delivered by a flunky from NASCAR and a note from Bill saying, "This ought to help the pain" and check for fifteen hundred bucks. The flunky was starting to leave. I stopped him. I told him I had a message for Bill that I wanted him to take back. I wiped my ass with the check, put it in envelope, and sent it back. No, I never heard no more 'bout it. (Oh yeah. If he couldn't see it, he sure could smell it.)

I guess to you, it sounds strange now, the "big hero" France Sr. getting his ass chewed out by a racer. But remember, back in 1950, I could pay my bills and had a couple bucks to boot. And he sometimes needed a little help from me business wise. And I ain't hurting him none around the race tracks, and last, but not least, there was a lot of shit that happened regarding "wine, women, and song" that I knew about. Knew about hell! I was in the middle of it. The big difference was, I didn't give a damn, but he did. I lived one day at a time, with the idea "don't put anything off till tomorrow – tomorrow is not guaranteed." We both drank too damn much.

The gas tank deal in '66 did it for me. I went my way, and I was totally disgusted with Bill, and had no real respect left for him, except to admire his skill and "balls" as an organizer, bullshit artist, and con-man. I was fascinated by his dual personality. To the big shots in industry he was "Bill-A" – to us racers he was "Bill-B." I can remember Mr. Knudsen saying, "Smokey, why do you dislike Bill? He's really a wonderful person." I'd say "Boss, the Bill you know is what you say, the Bill I deal with is not the same man you know."

I put 23 hard-hard years, with about a five dollar an hour average wage, but it was my choice. I got no regrets at all. Actually, I think I was lucky to have been part of the birth of stock car racing. I really loved the competition.

Nevertheless, it was never just about competition. A lot of the growth of NASCAR was from skillful maneuvering, planning, and management to keep the races interesting. Maybe 'bout 40 percent of the success was just shit-house luck. I think the same magnetism that seduced us as competitors did the same thing to the big shooters from motor companies and sponsors.

But let's stop beating around the bush. Since that time, when Bill Jr. replaced the old man, in spite of my firm conviction that "Young Bill" didn't have enough sense to pour piss out of a boot, Billy's probably out-did the old man three to one in profit and status. I recognize the possibility of fans reading this and considering hanging me by the balls, but the cold facts are: if you knew exactly how this thing came about – step by step – you'd puke. I know the part I lived, and I'm sure at best, I only knew half of it. Again, I say, "All I'm trying to do in this book, is tell you what I experienced in the 23 years I was directly involved in it."

By being involved as I was, in the races, I got to know many of the "captains" of this country's industry, politics, finance and communications media. Some I really admire, and am grateful for what they taught me, but seems like almost always, sooner or later all these activities come under the leadership of incompetent assholes, and sometimes outright crooks. I'm sure there is some logical explanation as to why the media has, in most cases chosen to report "half truths" to our citizens and those with money have continued to participate in a farce. But in my, perhaps negative and highly opinionated view, it's all about "greenies."

For 28 years I wrote a monthly column for Popular Science. I was their "Dear Abby" for cars. I also wrote for Circle Track magazine each month for 11 years. I think that if I had chosen to write in such a way as to avoid pissin' people off, today I would be a wealthy national celebrity. I'm gonna tell you something: you people who believe all the bullshit that news media feeds you daily are going to have trouble planning your life successfully. You're flying blind! How can the news media criticize their source of income? Can you name one neutral major media authority (of any kind)? Is there even one major media race reporter who is technically qualified to opinionate? (Except for ex-drivers or crew chiefs?) Are we being brain washed by a bunch of unqualified word wizards, bullshitters, and crack pots? How 'bout that goofy friggin' big mouth Geraldo Rivera? They talk the talk, but can't and never will walk the walk. Now if Gary Nelson or Ray Evernham come out of competition and decide to write, read that shit and you can take it to the bank.

Pontiac...How the Sweater Got Knit

The Pontiac, as you people know it, was born in 1956. Bunkie Knudsen had been moved over to be general manager of Pontiac, from General Manager of Allison division. (They made turbine engines and big automatic transmissions.) I never could call Knudsen "Bunkie," I called him "Boss." How the hell do you call the head cat "Bunkie?" I remembered a cartoon where there was a little baby with a lace trimmed hat called "Bunkie." I think it was "Barney Google." The Pontiac I first knew, had a flat head V8 and was called the "Oakland," 'bout a 1930 model. The engine wasn't worth a damn. When I first started working in a general car repair shop, I got to work on a bunch of them. They gave a lot of bearing trouble and they burned valves pretty bad. Couldn't take any pounding at all.

I mention this because in about five years, when I was a pilot in the Flying Tigers, my goof-off place was Calcutta. Guess what every damn taxi in Calcutta was, an Oakland touring car, with a convertible roof all. I mean all of them...and they all were driven by a turbaned Sikhs. The Sikhs were all big fellows as compared to Hindus and Moslems. These guys all had copper arm bands, never cut their hair or shaved and were really the most ferocious knife fighters in the world. (What did the copper arm bands do? Turn your arms green.) They drove those things 24 hours a day, seven days a week, at 20 miles an hour tops.

When Knudsen took over Pontiac, he really inherited a dog – 'bout like a Chevrolet, but with lots more chrome, and still no engine. A kinda of a "swoose" car. Half duck half goose. Well, it turns out Bunkie Knudsen's dad at one time was president of General Motors. He had Bunkie educated as an engineer. Also, when Bunkie was old enough to drive, his dad gave him a new Chevrolet in pieces. Bunkie had to assemble the car from blue prints and a service manual.

Also it turns out, Bunk's a "hot rod" at heart, and while at Allison, he personally owned a couple of midgets that Ronnie Householder drove and maintained, and they did pretty good. The Allison plants were right across the street from the Indianapolis Motor Speedway. They were so close that Mauri Rose worked at Allison and would walk over to the speedway on his lunch break to qualify his car.

Now it takes three years before a general manager got "his" car. Back then all cars at General Motors reflected the character of their general managers. Bunk "grandfathered" John Delorean, and had Pete Estes for a chief engineer. A hell of a combination. Bunk was a real car man. He could drive the shit out of a car and know if it did or didn't "have it."

John Delorean, who I'm gonna tell you rite now, was probably the best qualified automobile engineer in Detroit then. And for my opinion, still never matched. Remember now, John's a rookie. Bunkie hired

239

Marvin Panch's 1960 Pontiac that won Daytona in 1961.

him away from a dying player, (Packard). Bunkie saw something there and "grandfathered" " him through GM. You wonder what the hell this "grandfather" stuff means? Well, in General Motors then, and same with other manufacturers, talent alone would get you no place. John ain't gonna like this part, but politics, personality and brown-nosing were key to success, and also the key to the downfall of all American auto manufactures.

Well, John Delorean, as he got stronger, started showing the maverick in him, and when in meetings some dumb decisions were made, John would not go along. I'm gonna tell you right now, if John had of conformed to the General Motor's policy of "run with your head up your ass," and seen how much fun they (the staff) could have, he would've been the youngest, and could have been the most effective president General Motors ever had.

John Delorean in my view was the best all around executive GM ever had. He was a very sharp engineer, knew a little bit 'bout bean counting, but was, I think a little reckless with the greenies. John Delorean had more than enough talent to have been director of styling at General Motors, he just knew what the people wanted.

OK, one more player. Pete Estes, a goddamned good, engineer. He was rough, tough and could be a nasty SOB if you got his feathers up. So in '57 you got Bunkie, Estes and Delorean as a team who set out to make Pontiac a real outstanding car.

Knudsen spent many hours and days in the care of Harley Earl and his family. Now Harley was the greatest stylist Detroit ever had. He was a big, rough, tough cat and Bunkie learned from him.

I've got to give credit to the other great stylist that Knudsen, Estes, and Delorean had. It was Mrs. Knudsen. Yup, every upholstery combination you ever saw from 1958 to 1963, Knudsen had a necktie that had that pattern. Knudsen would take a prototype Pontiac home for the weekend for his kids and their friends to make comments. Knudsen made notes. Mrs. Knudsen discussed the upholstery and trim. Knudsen would take this back to styling, which was run by Bill Mitchell then. Bill loved Knudsen and gave him his way.

Back then the General Manager was "God." Nobody argued or even thought about crossing him, and

GM styling had total power over division styling, if you gave Bill Mitchell a bad time your ass was mud. Bill Mitchell was a "hot rod." He loved the big engines, 450 horsepower, and "no handling land-yachts." Bill must have been a fish lover. He added 150 pounds of steel to the ass-end of all GM cars. (When seen from the back they looked like big fishes and at night; their asses were all lit up.) But Bill knew how to control, and was a damn good car man. He couldn't drive worth a shit, and every time I had to ride with him could have been my last hour on earth.

More of the details of how the sweater got knit. Ed Cole had just hit a bases loaded homer with the '55, '56, '57 Chevrolet. But even though Ed was a good guy and a super car man, (he could half-assed drive a race car or race boat) somehow he and Knudsen decided they didn't like each other worth a shit.

In June of 1957 the American car manufacturers decide racing cost too much. So they said, "Let's all quit on the same day." And they all did (sort of). Man, this all happened over about 60 days, but wasn't made public till a week before they lowered the boom on the racing programs. Henry Ford II, he meant it, while Chrysler cheated like a son-of-a-bitch and kept her going under the table with the Petty's and Cole "back doored" Chevy high performance out of Atlanta. Olds, Buick, Cadillac, they didn't want it in the first place. Pontiac was left out in the cold. Chevy's back door deal, out of Nalley Chevrolet in Atlanta, was a secret. (Not over 10,000 people knew about it.) Piggins, Duntov and Mauri Rose directed this dumb frigging deal. It was called SEDCO: the Southern Engineering and Development Company.

OK, its November '57. Knudsen calls me and offers a job to build him a NASCAR racer. I turned it down, but he kept calling, and comes to Daytona one day. The truth is, back in them days he could have charmed the balls off of the Wall Street bull. He wanted a one race deal for the Daytona Beach Race in 1958. He offered 10 grand to do the job plus a couple of free cars.

In the '57 Beach Race, I ran a Chevrolet with Goldsmith driving (a fuel injected job). We led all the race, but last few laps an injector nozzle got partially plugged and we burnt a piston and a Pontiac wins (Cotton Owens, I believe). I think Banjo led it till his clutch went.

Well, Knudsen had hired Lou Moore, (a great Indy mechanic) as soon as he took over Pontiac to make a racer out of a" turtle." Lou did a good job, but way too much Indy stuff. This cost a fortune and the results were just "fair." My real plans were to find a way to go to Indy, but I was kinda pissed 'bout losing to Lou Moore the year before.

I knew they had to get off the beach. We now got so much power, cars were getting stuck in the soft sand from wheel spin. The track in Daytona was under construction and for some dumb reason I thought winning last beach race was important, so I took the job. Well, as luck would have it, we won the race. In them days we drove cars to the course on beach and back to the shop after the race. Remember these are "yellow bar" flat-tow days, nobody had trailer or tractor trailers yet ('cept for Kiekhaefer). As I was driving the six or seven miles to the shop, I get to thinking. Knudsen is gonna come to shop and offer me a deal to run again. He's got all the Pontiac staff with him to help talk me into it. So I decide to sell the car right away. Knudsen had already gotten rid of Lou Moore (or Johnny Moore) and has already hired Ray Nichels and Cotton Owens to race Pontiacs.

As I get to shop, I park the race car and close the door. Here's Cotton with a friend. He asks what I'm gonna do with the car. I said, "Sell it." It was common knowledge that it's a one race deal. He said, "What do you want for it?" I said, "Cotton, if you get this car out of here and pass under that traffic light in no more than five minutes, the price is 10 bucks." I figured Knudsen had been fair with me, and it was his personal money that had paid for the car. Cotton would maybe win more with it. Back then I had bad habit of giving stuff away. (I got over it finally, when I learned that only worked one way.)

He said he'd have to go back to motel, get a chain, etc. I thought, "I know most drivers were dumb bastards," but, I said, "Cotton you won't make it to motel and back in less than 10, 15 minutes." I had some rope handy so I threw it down, looked at my watch and said, "Cotton, you got four minutes to figure this out or you're a dead player." I had the title handy, and just signed it. I told him, "If you get it out of here on time, come back when there ain't no cars around and I'll give you the title."

Cotton was gone 'bout a minute before Knudsen and staff pulled up ('bout six carloads).

When I told Knudsen what happened he got pissed. I said, "Boss, the deal was one race and the car was mine. You just got it back for 10 bucks." I wanted to go to Indy, so I said, "I'm not gonna run any more NASCAR." While I was down at the beach I had a white work shirt on and Bill Tauss, who was then in charge of Grey Rock brake lining offered $300 to establish a "Smokey go to Indy fund." I had him write commitment on my shirt. The commitments, all written on my shirt, got up to $1,100. There were about nine total donors and they all paid. On way home from track I stopped at Mac's bar, the racers official watering hole at that time, and I picked up some more go to Indy money.

Strategy session.

Well, we go to Indy, qualify, crash, and come home. No money to play "Indy car" again. This was June 1958. In a month or so Knudsen pays my way up to see the '59 Pontiac, and offers me one. While I was there he also offers me a job. He wants me to organize and help manage a Pontiac race team and be the engine man to determine the specifications of upcoming models. This was a good deal. It paid 10 grand a year and all expenses. Plus, I get the race cars to keep along with any prize money. '59 is the beginning of the "wide track" deal and, man, them things were huge. But they've got a pretty damned nice looking engine (the 389). The whole car is heavy as hell, but with their engineering team and their willingness to change stuff it had a chance. See back then it had to be "strictly stock" and at Hudson, Packard, Chevrolet, Ford, and Buick, I had found out it took months to make a change, and then it would be half-assed. Having an engineering department that would work with racers would make all the difference.

Back then, there was the bread-and-butter work – production engineering, and then there was high-performance work. Bread and butter jobs brought greater glory and, most importantly, much more money. As of now, only man who ever made a decent payout of hi-performance, is Herb Fishel. I can give you an example of this; Joe Negre, at "General Motors Racing." He chose racing in 1980. Had he stayed in bread-and -butter, he had the talent to have been chief engineer at Buick 10 years ago at probably three or four times the pay.

Well anyhow, on the '59 offer, Knudsen says, "If you take the job, you're in total charge of racing." At a staff meeting there is some argument. Knudsen says, "Smokey runs it, period! If he don't get it done, I'll send his ass to Siberia. Do not second guess him."

I took the job, and then proceeded to over-book myself badly. I only had two paid helpers in racing. (The truck shop was same piece of ground, but the racing shop was fenced off). The truck shop was a combination GMC and International Harvester truck dealership, with Caterpiller, Cummins, Detroit Diesel and Bendix service franchises. It was 'bout a two million a year deal that had 20 employees.

I decide the '59 Pontiac NASCAR racer should have hydraulically controlled suspensions in the front, so driver could adjust front weight, and electrically controlled weight jackers for the rear.

I couldn't sell the rear deal to NASCAR and Pontiac sure didn't think much of it so it got shit-canned. (Cadillac used it.) I also decided to build variable ratio power steering and power brakes. Power for these brakes was supplied by residual pressure from the power steering pump.

Fireball Roberts drove the car. And I got it all working by March '59.

As a matter of fact , we won the first Atlanta race with it all working. Fireball didn't care too much for any of it after the first time he tried it out, but I was able to adjust brake and steering feel and effort, with pressure relief valve on brakes and by changing the viscosity of the fluid and diameter of the spool control valve. Fireball loved the hydraulic front suspension adjustment from the beginning. As soon as I finally got the steering and brake feel to his liking, NASCAR said, "Take that shit off, power steering and power brakes are needed like tits on a bull." I later started all this over at Chevrolet in 1963.

Frank Winchell, Chevrolet's head R & D man said, "American cars need that stuff like we all needed two assholes." Frank was smart, and a good engineer, I believe he is still living and working part-time for General Motors as a consultant, but Frank was also a stubborn, egotistical asshole.

"Balls" in action.

If I was of the "brown-nosing class," and waited six months or so, I could have pulled it off. His number two man was a brilliant young engineer named Jim Musser. But he really didn't have a good feel for what the public wanted, or needed. To prove my point, Jim was the chief engineer of the "Vega" some time later. When it came out, this was the second biggest piece of shit GM ever built. (The Corvair was number one.) They got the Vega fixed just before it got shit-canned. By the way, I installed one of my variable ratio power steering in Knudsen's personal car. Guess who got to call me for permission to use the idea in a Chevrolet? If you guessed Frank, you get 100. By the way, damn near every car in the world uses variable ratio power steering today.

Don't get bored about power steering yet. I told you we won first race in Atlanta, March 59. Well, Atlanta had a then and later, famous sports writer named Furman Bisher. Now in the stick and ball sports, I'm sure he was great, but he had as much use for stock car racing as I have for going to a symphony. For what ever reason, he interviewed me, and I gave him a good description of all the newly invented "goodies" on my car. At the time, they are gonna be legal 'cause Pontiac is gonna offer 'em as an option.

Well, General Motors manufactures these steering units by the thousands and sells them to all the other motor companies, even Ford. The part that gets interesting is, Frank Winchell, of General Motors, said, "Not interested at any price." Knudsen says, "Well Smoke, if Frank's negative, I can't push it." Well, I had enough money to get my patents started, but not by a long shot, for the whole nine yards. There were five inventions I believe: variable ratio power steering, power brakes from residual pressure of the power steering pump, adjustable height controlled hydraulically or electrically, an aluminum cross flow radiator, and a suspension that leaned all four wheels into corners. In 2000, I did a bullshitting session for the Ormond Kiwanis tribe. One of 'em asked a question 'bout a two-faced friend I have, Ray Fox. Ray told 'em I didn't invent nothing, that I had stole it all. I wish that asshole was correct now, when I consider how much money I spent on patents that didn't pay off.

Anyway, when Frank told me "no way," I quit fooling with patents for the stuff. But I wanted all this stuff for an Indy car which I was rebuilding for 1961. This car had all the inventions 'cept the ride height

Fireball on the pole. (photo: Don Hunter)

control. Roger Ward said, "It looked like a python that had swallowed a piano." This car was tested at Indy in 1961, you'll find the details in the 1961 Indy story. In 1963, I took Curtis Turner to Indy to learn how to drive Indy in "The Python." Not a real smart plan. The car was heavy, with some bugs in it. Finally, what took a year to build and assemble, Curtis disassembled on the third turn outside wall in about 1/2 second.

There's a story tied in with this car to Pontiac, General Motors and Chevrolet. After the turndown by General Motors on buying the rights to this stuff, I go to Phil Ziegler, general manager of Saginaw products. (Saginaw is then a subsidiary of GM) I show him my stuff and offer him rights to it for one set of chassis parts for the "flexible flyer," (all four wheels lean) also known as the "Python." I wanted 10-variable ratio power steering sets, 10 aluminum cross-flow radiators, 10 power brake units, and two sets of front spring hydraulic adjustment kits. (I made the rear electric adjustments myself)

I don't know if Phil is still with us, but he and I met in 56, when Ed Cole wanted to try air suspension and no steering wheel. Yup. A hell of a deal, Ed wanted my opinion on this experiment. The car had the dash removed, looked like an old buckboard wagon, and 1/2 of a baseball on left door arm rest, or on the center divider arm rest. This took the place of the steering wheel. By the way you could get comfortable with that steering in 30 minutes. The air suspension, as simple as it sounded, was loaded with technical problems. In other words, it handled poorly, sometimes dangerously poor. I'm sure they could have worked it all out, but it would be maybe too expensive. I've only ever seen one good handling air over hydraulic suspension. I believe it was on a 1958 Morris Mini Minor. Matter of fact, they had a car at Indy with that suspension. It didn't do any good, but I still believe it was best car that year. It was out of San Francisco. I believe the Cooper importer there had his race crew build it. It was a rear engine "funny car," as A.J.Watson named all 4-wheel independent suspension rear engine cars. The name Huffaker comes to my mind about this.

Anyhow, I get to use the no-steering wheel, air suspension 1958, Chevrolet while I'm in Detroit. I'm staying in a motel by the old city airport, Eastern Airlines used to land there. It's winter, and gets well below freezing that night. When I get up to go to a 7:30 am meeting with Cole, my car has been chopped and channeled to two inches off the ground. All four wheels are up to top of the inner fender wells and it can't move a wheel. Well, quick call to Phil Ziegler, and we got another problem I don't recognize. Public relations. "Goddam. Just can't let world know this happened." What happened? The air-water separator didn't get job done. It was plumbed with copper instead of steel. This is easier to work with in an experiment, but weaker than steel.

Well, the air suspension had hydraulic controls, so with frozen, broken control lines, the car body drops, the wheels can't roll over. Course, at that point it had no steering anyway. I can still see this gold, ugly, 1958 Chevrolet going slowly down the busy road hooked by two wreckers, one going backwards, headed to the tech center. I recommended that we pursue this suspension and steering in spite of this problem. I particularly liked the safety increases you could make with this concept but deal gets the deep six.

Well, going back to late '58. Phil agrees to do the deal (the flexible flyer racing suspension and the parts). Takes it on himself a kinda quiet under-the-table deal, but, "General Motors will finish patents." Phil's a damn good engineer. He looked like Casper Milktoast, but he had the balls of a lion. Well, almost, maybe a medium sized lion. He's got a number two man named George Edwards. I could never get his enthusiasm up to anywhere near Phil's, but being good at company politics, he pitched in. So after a while, Phil's gonna put my "flexible flyer" suspension on a '59 Buick prototype car. I can still remember the day. It was cold, snowing like a son-of-a-bitch. This experimental blue Buick with the "leaner suspension" is sitting there with no front end on, so we could see the suspension move. The car is driveable. I jumped up on the front frame horn to bounce the suspension. My heart stopped. It did it backwards – the suspension tilted in the wrong direction, opposite what would be useful. I looked at Phil and George. Phil turned white and I think George stopped breathing. The deal went through anyhow, but the Buick was never mentioned again. (By the way, the Indy leaner did it the right way.)

No matter how hard I try to stick to the story day-by-day, I can't. There are so many experiments, dreams and ideas that took one to five years to develop and even longer to surface as a visible adventure. In 1960, about the last of April (by the way, I've just agreed to co-chief mechanic Jim Rathman's Indy car with Chickie Hiroshima, for brand new car owners Ken Rich and Paul Lacey. (The "Ken-Paul Special" with which we won the race). I'm so broke in this period I'm living in an old laundry building. It's now our machine shop next to the main shop. I'm sleeping on an army cot and have only cold bath water.

Rathman is buying a Chevrolet dealership in Melbourne, Florida, from a friend of mine who now has had enough of the public, John Fordyce. This is a hell of a deal. Real cheap Chevrolet/Caddy dealership, lock, stock and barrel. Buildings, parts, land and used cars 'bout 120 grand. Jim's gonna have a partner named Denny Weinberg from California. Cole called me, and asked if I thought Rathman could handle it, cause he was gonna have to help sell the deal to the corporation. General Motors did not want any Jewish dealers or staff 'employees and Denny was Jewish.

Denny was also a wild son-of-a-bitch, but he had money and was a good businessman. Denny drove a stock car once in a while. You'd have to stretch it to call him a racer, but he did the drinking and screwing and partying of a world class racer. I always thought if Denny filled out a form asking his occupation he should have written in "fucker." As I saw it, that topic consumed 96 percent of his time. His favorite girlfriend was a famous singer. I'd tell you her name but I can't remember it. She liked to get between him and the steering wheel and have serious sexual experiences. Denny drove Cadillacs, and shortly before the dealership episode he and his singer gal were screwing away when Denny run a stop sign on a kinda country road. There were witnesses to the sexual experiment and the driving infraction, so Denny had to run a new Cadillac twenty miles with no water in the engine (yes, it was very expensive) to avoid explaining to his wife how he got on the evening news.

I liked Denny, but as I think about it now, and I bet Denny's still around the imperial valley someplace; Denny, is there any chance you knew Clinton and gave him a few pointers? Damn, if your method of operation and Clinton's don't seem to follow a parallel pattern. 'Cept for the lying, and the fact that Denny was a world class stud. Last I heard of Denny, his wife was adjusting his financial statement with division by two. Yup, divorce. Really, for 1960s Denny would of been a stereotype auto dealer.

Anyway, during the last week of April 1960, I got a letter from General Motors. "Dear Smokey, we feel we underpaid you for that stuff you gave Ziegler (variable ratio power steering, residual pressure power steering, adjustable suspension, aluminum cross flow radiators and leaning suspension) enclosed find a check for $15,000 bucks." Holy shit! At the time I'm dead assed broke, living like an animal, and I get this wonderful gift from those nice people at General Motors. I put check in First Federal bank here in Daytona. I been terminated as a husband within past few months in a very unfriendly arrangement where half of what I had (or everything actually, her 50 percent was 100 percent of what it brung) went to my former wife, so the money was like a godsend.

Next day 12:30 pm Rathman is on the phone crying. The deal for the dealership was to close at noon that day. Rathman had paid his half of $60,000 to Fordyce, but Dennis Weinberg didn't send his 60. Rathman couldn't find Denny on the phone, but Denny's brother said, "Ain't no money coming." Jim asks if I can, "Try and get John Fordyce to give him another day?" I get John on the phone. "He is not friendly." He is plumb pissed, ain't gonna give nothing. His whole life is fucked. Plus, he is supposed to start a world tour tomorrow and now he has to stay and run business – "Bullshit!" I get him calmed down, and I made him a deal. "I'll give you 15 grand in cash to apply against the balance, if you give Jim 24 hours." And guaranteed to get him the cash in two hours. John's a good person, so he says OK.

Well, the bank don't want to give me the cash. They say they've got to wait and see if the General Motors 15 grand check clears. Gil, the bank president and I had a conference. No, I didn't hit him. He decided he didn't want his wife to know he was screwing one of my lady friends. He particularly didn't like the two pictures my friend loaned me. He didn't look too good with no clothes on. (He's bald and got a belly and his head is in an area you don't see bankers very much.) In fifteen minutes, I had the fifteen grand, and sent my right hand man, William Harrison, to John with the money. It got there in time, but I was barred from doing any business with that bank again "forever." I knew Jim Rathman could probably borrow the last 60 if he could find Lindsey Hopkins. Lindsey had Indy cars and liked Jim as a driver. (Guess that's only way anybody could like him.) Jim Rathman turned out to be a first class asshole. Lindsey controlled the Pan American Bank in Miami. Lindsey's family were of the original Coca-Cola company, (his family owned the formula) Chapman Root's family from Terra Haute, Indiana owned the bottle and the bottling rights.

Sure enough, Rathman found Lindsey, John Fordyce got his money and got to take his trip and everybody was happy. A month later we win Indy, and Rathman's on his way to being a millionaire. I'm back to dead broke inside of 24 hours. Without even a receipt for my money.

Jim says I'm gonna be a partner, but I don't want to be a partner. By now I got him figured pretty good. Better than average driver, but a morally corrupt, selfish lying, egotistical, crooked, SOB. (And I never liked men who read comic books while they were getting a blow job.)

OK, day after the 15 grand episode, here comes a flannel mouth lawyer from General Motors. I think "hot damn. These are nice people. Even flies down to see if I got

Fireball's Pontiac from the 1960 Daytona race. (photo: Emap USA)

the money and thank me in person! Bullshit. Here's the deal. "We (General Motors) goofed-up. We never finished the patents." In the meantime Bendix has won both a variable-ratio-power steering, and a residual pressure power brake patent (two). And Bendix is suing General Motors for millions in royalties. The power steering is going like gangbusters, but power brake's stuck on zero. What can I tell him that would defend their position on "prior art"?

Know what this "prior art" is? In case you don't. It means if you get a patent on something, and I don't want to pay you a royalty, if I can prove some other person invented it a year before your patent was filed, then it is "prior art" and I do not have to pay. If the real inventor discloses the invention a year before you patented and the inventor doesn't file for a patent, he has given his invention to the good of his fellow man for free, and if any later patents have been issued, it would be voided. And no one could ever claim ownership to that particular invention.

Well, I'm really pissed now. The realization that General Motors didn't give a shit about me. The money was to buy me. I couldn't give him back the 15 grand and tell him to shove it up his ass. I ain't got it. I gave him Furman Bisher's address and phone number, and kicked his ass out in two minutes. I never heard another word about it, but prior art blowed up Bendix's patent. I can't remember much more 'bout '59

NASCAR Pontiac, but I did build, or more accurately totally change an existing car, for Indy. This did not end nice. I'll tell you 'bout that in the Indy '59 stuff.

In 1960 the Pontiac is really starting to be a neat car. Pontiac is also really starting to rule NASCAR. They got a nicer aerodynamic body. The performance image is growing elsewhere. Knudsen's got drag racer Mickey Thompson setting world records at the Salt Flats with a four engine Pontiac stream liner and NASCAR has gotten Pontiac into convertible racing. (That was an expensive, stupid deal to me – 'bout like trucks nowadays.) We've really got about 10 good NASCAR Pontiacs, and maybe five dogs. At the February Beach race, we blow up with Fireball leading. Bobby Johns runs second and Junior Johnson wins in a Chevy. Bobby Johns had the race won but his rear glass blew out and he spun. Well, by February 1960 Knudsen is wide-ass-open on racing and I'm getting paid with Pontiac checks.

Also, by the start of the 1960 season, we are changing part numbers every 10 minutes. This is possible because Knudsen and Bill France Sr. are on same page with complimentary loaner Pontiacs out-the-ass for NASCAR. Every race, Knudsen sent in 150 or more fancy Pontiacs for the elite and celebrities to drive. We called 'em "brass hat cars." After each race the local Pontiac dealer bought the cars real cheap, and made a fortune on them. In the sales pitches they used, usually Fireball drove 10 out of every 50 and I drove five out of every 50.

Well, as usual, I'm so busy working, I don't even know who's president. But I have picked up a leach, and it sucks blood out of me for three years before I wake up. Knudsen is pissing all over the AMA ban on racing so he needed dealer's name on the side of the car. The idea being, to the public, the dealer was paying for the race teams. As a result, Stevens Pontiac of Daytona Beach got a 3-year free ride from me. Jim Stevens made thousands of dollars in the "brass hat car" business, got to be personal friends with Knudsen and the Pontiac staff. Stephens also worked up a hell of a friendship with Bill France, Sr.

Need an example? Hell, I gave speeches to Rotary, Kiwanis, Racoons, Lion's Club, Elephants etc., to sell stock for the Daytona Speedway. Stephens don't do a damn thing 'cept furnish cars, (that he was making a fortune off of) booze and pussy for a week in February. I pay one dollar per share for speedway stock and Stephens gets 200,000 shares for 10 cents each. (This is an example of how well France took care of his racers.) We all paid a buck a share while a million shares went for 10 cents to local politicians, contractors, accountants, car dealers and magazine big shots. Remember France's grand slogan. "Load the wagon. The mule is blind." Hell, I didn't wake up to what happened for five years.

As I said, we did 'bout anything we wanted to, but had to have a part number in the book. In '60, Russ Gee, a young Pontiac engineer and personal right hand engineer to Knudsen is hand carrying cylinder heads and headers and parts on airlines to me in Daytona. (Russ eventually became very high in CPC (Chevrolet Pontiac Canada), as a matter of fact Larry Dickinson's number two man when Larry was the number one cat at CPC. Poor ol' Russ Gee is getting wore out as official " hi-speed pack mule." Through his efforts, we got aluminum brake parts, aluminum rear axle parts and we are playing two four barrels and three two barrels. I don't want the aluminum body parts or aluminum brake and suspension parts, or aluminum drive train pieces, but she's out of control now. (This aluminum stuff often wouldn't last 500 miles) Mickey Thompson's got 'em making aluminum cylinder heads. Even aluminum exhaust headers which usually melted in 10 laps.

For the 1960 Beach Race, I've made a set of stainless steel headers, sent them to Pontiac to get a part number and get copied. We had a young engineer named Bill Klinger to work with, and a sharpie named McKellar. I called him "cam head." Very good in valve dynamics, I think he actually knew what he was doing. The rest of the cam experts in Detroit were best described as "lost balls in the high weeds." Anyhow, I got my stainless headers bolted on, and aluminum hood, and aluminum front bumper. NASCAR's got a chief inspector named Norris Friel. Norris was a neighbor of Bill France Sr. when he lived in Washington, DC. He came from sprint cars, was 'bout 45-50 years old and was a real pain in the ass. He knew enough about cars to administer the program, but he dealt his authority in same way as France Sr. (a dictatorship). If you questioned some of the "wisdom" that came out of Friel's mouth and said "Why?" His answer was, "Because I said so." (France's favorite "duck the issue answer" was, "It's not in the spirit of competition"). How the fuck could you get a sensible solution with those two bull-shitters in collusion against you?

In all fairness to Friel, he treated us all about alike…like the stupid bastards we were to put up with his bullshit. I don't remember how he finally disappeared, and I've never cared enough to ask. In the real world, could anybody be a popular chief inspector in a racing organization? Really, no way.

Fireball racin' Darel Dieringer.

Well, if you go to the Talladega Hall of Fame museum, you will see a set of stainless headers that will fit a 1960 Pontiac V8, and an aluminum hood with faded black and gold paint and a red stripe, we never got to run a foot with the stuff. Even Knudsen couldn't overcome the "proclamation" that made those parts illegal. They were in the parts books, but too much was too much.

For inspectors, NASCAR started with Jimbo, then Buddy Schuman. They were OK. A fifth would 'bout solve any problem. Then came "Norris, the prick." Then "Gas away," a Bill France puppet and a world class comic book reader. Hopefully he saved all those comic books. You know, Spiderman, Superman, Batman, etc., it's my understanding that those old comic books are very valuable now. Maybe Bill's a millionaire now. (He's the dumb shit who gave me a list of 12 things to do to my '68 Chevelle in Daytona in one hour and 50 minutes remaining in qualifying. Number one on the list was "replace home-made frame with stock frame.") After him came Dick Beatty. He started off good, but in a couple of years he developed some hen-house ways. Had a pretty good temper, and it wasn't too hard to get him above his "pressure relief valve." He was born and raised a Ford man, and found it hard to treat all makes and racers alike. Oh hell, I left one chief out. Mr. Taylor. He took over when Friel left. But he never was his own man,

France Sr. called the shots.

After Dick Beatty retires, I noticed he must of had some friends cause I seen some good-bye stuff where some NASCAR people had tears big as horse turds. Dick knew the game, was a half assed good race driver, a half-good mechanic and he was all man. Well, after Dick left, here comes Gary Nelson with extremely fine credentials. He was one of the biggest cheaters in racing history if the truth was told. However, I don't give him full points for all he done. One, he cheated with management approval. That's a no-no. And two, I feel big engines and big gas tanks are chickenshit. No points for technical creativity there. I believe if a fair vote was taken, I could get my hunches seconded by a great driver whose name I don't think I should mention, but his initials are BA.

OK, Gary's still the head knocker at NASCAR tech. And probably will be for a long time. But it's possible, with the dramatic change in NASCAR's economics and stature as a premium entertainment and advertising vehicle, that there is a need for secret diplomacy and quiet penalty assignment. There's a lot of shit going on to equalize all cars. But this appears to have a legislative tilt towards all manufacturers getting something tangible for their investment. Well hell, they should.

How's a "has been" like myself gonna question the wisdom of this, considering the progress NASCAR had made in last 20 years?

Kind of reminds me of an old joke where the nice little rich girl tells her boy friend "the deal's off." Family don't like him cause he is uncouth. He says, "What's this uncouth shit?" The world I raced in has left, and to be able to criticize, you have to be actively in the game. So actually, my comments over last 20 years are unqualified really. I still get around the races and quietly watch and listen. No longer do I hear bitchin' and arguing with inspectors. It now operates like Detroit. Be nice to their faces. Hug 'em and kiss 'em, and when they can't see where it's coming from, stick it up their ass, smile, and say, "I'm sorry."

Back to 1960 Pontiac. No matter how hard I try, no way to tell the story without the numerous "side trips." What the hell's '60 Indy got to do with 60 Pontiac? Well, those air jacks worked so damn good at Indy, I built a set and put on our Pontiac for the 1960 Darlington 500. In practice, when my fellow racers saw that 3,900 pound Pontiac jump all four wheels off the ground in one second, they screamed together "Norris." Yup, here comes "The Prick" saying, "Take 'em off and give 'em to me." New Friel rule begun in February 1960 said, "all the stuff he said was "illegal," he kept or NASCAR kept." Two months later I found out about the new confiscation rules. That's why you see those headers in the museum at Talladega. When I thought about headers again, we removed the air jacks. Friel knew what his chances of getting them were, so I still have them. If anybody out there has that car, (I don't remember what happened to it) if you wonder what the funny looking square bracket with four corner holes in 'em are, that's where these air jacks used to sit, one to a wheel.

To this day I can't figure out why NASCAR mandates a very expensive hand jack, with a five foot long handle that puts the jack man's ass in front of all those left hand front fenders on pit road. What's chances of running over a jack man? Already been done and killed him. What are the chances, one day soon somebody is gonna catch one of those jacks in the head on that maneuver from right side to left side jackup? A set of air jacks would be "bullet proof" for a year and cost half of a high buck jack. Sure they weigh 15 pounds total, but what the hell's the difference? They all carry lead ballast anyway.

Same for fueling. It's just as primitive. At the first race in Darlington in 1950, we had fuel in open 50 gallon drum and dipped water buckets in it and dumped it into a funnel some guy was holding while smoking a cigar. Well, the fueling change in next year or two was to where they're at now. What's wrong with a two inch hose with a leak proof disconnect nozzle in case of accident, where maximum fuel in 14 seconds is 22 gallons? Such a system could shut off with vented fuel going back to the system. No more spilling at the end of that dangerous "dance" where two fuel men and two tire men play around the left rear tire and fuel filler pick-up holding two 11 gallon fuel cans, with two gallons of spilled vented fuel splashing all around. Also, the fuel should be in NASCAR's big tank and piped to every pit position. Do you have any idea of how much money is spent on boosted fuel and tricky extra fuel capacity? Hell, how fair a race is it if I got an extra gallon you ain't and I have to stop one less time than you? Did you ever see a race won by phenomenal mileage by the winner? I have.

Course, the last thing any race organization wants to do is disqualify the winner. Nowadays if you get caught you'll quietly pay a big fine. I mean a big fine. And then it's swept under the rug so you maintain your finishing position. There have been major rule infractions where the winning competitor was caught and you never knew it and never will. Hey, there's no brains involved in big gas tank or big engines, it's just chicken shit.

Well, let's get started with Pontiac '61. Not much change, but we got power up a little. We also have a better suspension with some stronger front spindles and a real nice homemade full floater, by then we were allowed to run a Ford third member. But we do have one major problem, tires. We've always had this problem. I mean from day one. But now the goddamned cars are in the 500 horsepower class so they are hauling ass. And remember, these things weighed right at 4,000 pounds.

Darrell Deringer, Richard Petty, Billy Wade and some others, hung their asses out, did a lot of testing and helped Goodyear come up with an inner tire. The idea with this being, when main tire blew, the car dropped an inch and rode on inner tire till you could get 'er whoaed.

A cartoonist did it best for me. At Charlotte he showed a cowboy pulling back on the reins of a horse who has just run off the end of a cliff, with about a mile of air under him, and the cowboy hollering "Whoa…you son-of-a-bitch, Whoa!" with reins pulled back damn near pulling the horse's head off. Well, Fireball and the Pontiac were the fastest horses, so as a rule, Fireball ran a live tire test every race. You just run behind him till he blew, and then went on at a slower pace. It happened so often, Fireball's official hillbilly song was "Hello Walls." To me it was the strangest feeling – it always sounded like a double barrel shotgun going off. The first "boom." (And you could hear it plain) was a tire blowing. A second or two later the "boom" was the car smashin' into the wall.

By now we can see the driver's superior skills and smart driving saving the car. But always, just as it seemed victory was in driver's grasp, he released his brake, opened his eye's and gassed her a dab. The son-of-a-bitch then went straight for the wall, and tore it all to shit. No matter how much trouble we had, Fireball always said, "Superior driving will see us thru." Sometimes we'd have to wait for him to regain consciousness for five minutes or so before he'd remind me, "No problem – superior driving."

I'm busy with 'factory' power goodies; two four barrels and three two barrels; more power, more power. I never wake up. We got more than enough power, but I don't know my ass from a hole in the ground about handling – chassis and vehicle dynamics. And if I did, wasn't much you could do to help it with rules as they were, but, yes, I could have done a lot better. Someone eventually won the race didn't they?

Knudsen is really gaining horsepower as a car man at General Motors and in the whole world really. Then trouble rears it's ugly head again. In '59, '60, '61 Ed Cole screwed up bad wanting a little car for Chevrolet. He hired Porsche's kid to build an air cooled, American Volkswagen engine, and they put it in a rear engine monstrosity called a "Corvair." This was an ill handling, dangerous car, but maybe not as bad as the

Volkswagen. For all you people who think the Volkswagen was a great car, you never drove one of the little sons-of-bitches 60 miles an hour on a windy day. Hell, half the women who drove 'em got out with their backs wet. Many of 'em were totaled simply from lack of control, while going straight and level.

Well, the Corvair is losing it's ass financially at Chevrolet, and Ed decides the way out is to build more volume. He decides that Pontiac should sell it also but under a different name. Well, Knudsen knew cars and knew the Corvair wasn't ever going to be worth a shit. He says, "No way, I'll build my own." And takes

Some of Fireball's handy-work. (photo: Al Swett)

off with another wet dream called a "Tempest." This car I believe was John Delorean's baby. I told you what a great car man he was, but I don't think he ever-considered cost. On his desk he had a big red button that said "money." If he pushed the button, the button asked "how much" and "when?" The Tempest damn near wore out that button.

Well the "Tempest" design was a front engine on conventional mounting with a solid shaft drive to an independently sprung rear suspension with power supplied through a solidly mounted transaxle, (manual or automatic). This stuff was sort of radical, but not unworkable. The real problem, as I saw it, was that John pioneered the belt driven overhead cam with hydraulic valve lifters in four, six, and eight cylinder versions. Remember the straight six overhead for a year or so?

Well, John run out of time on the four cylinder engine, and had to find a quick, cheap replacement for the Tempest first model run at least. Now maybe some of my views are not totally correct, cause I wasn't in on everything, but with the deadline approaching, everybody got uptight. Knudsen called me for a special meeting with Estes and the engine staff. I don't remember if John was there that day, I don't think so. I think at the time he was going crazy trying to get vibration out of that solid steel drive shaft. (Eventually they leaned against the shaft with a loaded bearing that, took a hell of a load but got rid of problem but with questionable durability) Anyway, at the engine meeting Knudsen says, "What are we going to use for a four cylinder engine?" When it is my turn I tell him I've made a four cylinder out of the right half of a 389 cubic inch Pontiac, and got 205 horsepower at 6,500 rpm and it's driveable. I add that it needed about a 45 pound flywheel and some motor mount work to make it acceptable in the shakin' and vibration department. I had seem the problem coming six months earlier and begun experimenting with carving up V8s. Pete Estes was pissed 'cause Knudsen likes my plan. I go home, get the engine, they dyno it and put it in production.

They then put me on a project to double turbo charge the 389. By June, I'm running twin turbo charged 389 on my dyno. At 20 to 25 pounds boost, we were making 600 to 650 horsepower. But the engine kept going lean, backfiring, blowing carbs and air cleaners into a concrete ceiling, hard enough to stick. At the time the best, biggest carburetor in existence, I believe, was a Carter that only flowed 450 cubic feet per minute with a tiny needle and seat, and small main metering system. With the small fuel delivery capacity we were in trouble even on normally aspirated stuff. The turbo job would get damn near two horsepower per cubic inch just before she sneezed and blew compressors, carburetors and air cleaners to shit.

'Bout then I got a guy working with me, an original Chevrolet small block engineer who is a carburetion wizard. He was in Daytona because he had wore out Detroit and the carburetor companies with his drinking and pussy-chasing. Ralph Johnson, the guy who helped me work out the Chevrolet fuel injector in 1957. I say, "Ralph, lets build a 800 cfm carb." He loved that. His last Detroit job was at Holley Carburetor, where he represented Holly to various car manufacturers and to Edelbrock. He knew a lot about Holleys, and we decided they had the most potential, so we machined, welded, and epoxy'ed (a lot of epoxy, Devcon, really good stuff.) We could drill air and liquid passages and half-ass thread it) a quick and dirty deal and took it to Pontiac. Ralph and I figured it was gonna cost 'bout 150 big ones to tool up.

Well, Bill Klinger runs a dyno test with that "quick and dirty" and only gets 10 horsepower more. In that prototype form it runs pretty ragged too, so he gives Pete, John and Knudsen a negative report. 150 Grand is a lot of money in '61, but maybe Bill's foresight was a little short.

We continue racing with the '61 (between crashes). Man we are 15 mph ahead of the available tires. Knudsen really wants to win Charlotte in the fall, so he says, "Build brand new car. But this car, I want to have personally at end of season." OK with me, he has done more for me than every body else put together in Detroit. I built a light, damn clean aero car. Cheating pretty bad, but it's kinda easy to get by with cause ain't anybody in NASCAR that can say the word "aerodynamics" let alone understand it. The car really runs, but comes to a terrible ending by the first third of it's first race. I hear the "shotgun deal." Boom, Boom – the tire, then the wall. And then a smash as Larry Franks T-bones him coming off the wall.

Well, Fireball ain't wounded too bad. In a day or so he knows where he is at, and his name. But the car is gone. I pull engine, give the car away and then realize, "I can't do that! Knudsen wants the car back. He'd told me he "don't care what shape it's in." Well, I "Indian-give" the car. I get it back. Hell, it ain't gone no where's, it's got no way to move. Somebody says, "I got an empty trailer if you want I'll bring it to Daytona." I've got to go to Miami, so I say, "Great." I have no real idea of this guy's name or really what he looks like, but I got to haul ass to catch plane to Daytona. The next day car shows up in Daytona. (I wasn't at the shop just then) and my guys unloaded it. (20 years later, I find out Peewee Griffin was the guy who brought it back. I never did pay, or thank you, but some forty years later, "Thanks Peewee.")

Well, "let's get this thing shipped to Detroit." Hell. Ain't no way, everything is ruined. I get a brain storm. I gotta send the car back as a matter of principal. So I go to local car squasher and he says bring it on. I'll squash it for you "no charge." I asked the operator after he got done if he could make the package smaller. He seemed reluctant to do any more, so I remembered the power of "greenies." I pulled out a 100 and said, "How much smaller can you get it if I transfer this "c" note to you?" He smiles and said "bout half." It came out under four foot square. (I think it didn't cost over couple thousand to fix damage on machine from the over-loading on the squashers.)

Well, the cars were in a four foot square. You can even see one of the "twos." I'm trying to get freight line to deliver it to Mr. Knudsen's house. He said originally, "Tow it to my house when your done with it." I can't get anybody to take it, because, "How we gonna get a tractor and trailer in a high-buck home, with wooded driveway?" and " how we gonna handle a bale of 2,500 pounds of iron?" Well, in a day or so Knudsen hears about it 'cause freight company sent someone to his house to see how they might deliver this. I guess mamma Knudsen said, "You ain't dumping that crap off here." So he calls me and says, "Goddam!, don't send that thing here."

OK, I lived up to my end of the deal, so I let just let the bale sit next to my race shop for 30 years. Like an idiot I sold it for scrap steel. What do you guess that thing would be worth in a museum or cut up in one inch squares?

When I look back now and recollect as best I can how we lived, we were nuts. We worked from 7:00 in morning to 1:00 or 2:00 am seven days a week. We would do damn near anything to get a couple bucks to be able to race next week. We lived on cold hot dogs and hamburgers, drank way too much, couldn't stay in a decent hotel, couldn't buy any insurance, couldn't borrow a dime from a bank, had zero credit cards and zero credit. You know, I think the conversation we got from race fans must have helped us think what were doing was good. But I never worried 'bout money. I always thought that somehow, some way I'd get what I needed.

But now, as I look a little closer, it was the invention money, and oil money from wildcatting that kept me going. Sure didn't get it from prize money. Most I ever got in NASCAR was 'bout 15 grand. Indy paid 160 grand (for one race). I gave all the cars away for a long time, same with used parts, or if they were new and didn't cost me anything. I figured if you raced it, that was its best use. I guess that's the way a racer thinks.

For the 12 grand a year I got, I assumed part of my job was to help you win, as long as you run what I run. I can remember sitting on pole, in February '60, with a Pontiac. A new Pontiac team had shown up from Arizona with Tiny Lund as driver and Lyle Stelzer the mechanic. Well, at the time Lyle knew enough about racing to be a go-fer, and Tiny he didn't know anything then 'cept how to half-assed drive. They run a Pontiac, and that's who I worked for so Tiny asked for any kind of help I could give him. After qualifying, cause we were on the pole, we had to pull cylinder heads for inspection to see if we were cheating. Well, we had a fast time and I thought, "What the hell, I'll give them my heads, carb, manifold and cam shaft." The parts are still warm. They take them to Friel, head inspector to be checked so they can put parts on their engine. Son-of-a-bitch if that damn Friel didn't rule them illegal. Why? Because he hated Lyle Stelter (the mechanic) 'cause Lyle thought he had the right to be treated like a normal human. (By the way, Friel didn't know where they got the stuff.)

Well, here comes Tiny and Lyle crying so I go jump on Friel (which really helped …HA!) in the verbal battle, I get the message. Lyle has run his mouth so much already, Friel hates the son-of-a-bitch. I finally got it settled, they bolt the parts on and in about two laps it blows all to shit, the bottom end was all fucked up. I asked Friel, "Why not be more fair?" Hell, if they were 500 cubic inchers, as rookies they still wouldn't know what hit 'em by the time we raced 500 miles and how the hell can you legislate and enforce rules based on who you do or don't like?

Point is, nobody in NASCAR seemed to give a shit 'bout helping new competitors getting going. Actually, they received much more stringent obstacles than we so called "regulars"…Very ass-backwards.

I knew Tiny a little. His first race with us was in West Memphis, a high bank, one 1/2 mile dirt, no good, killer track built of Mississippi River muck that would get three foot holes in it quick. Tiny and Fred Lorenzen started with us there on the same day. I think they were friends, and from Illinois. Both had '55 Chevrolets then. He and Lorenzen turned out to be as good as it gets. Tiny won Daytona with a Woods Brothers Ford not too many years later. Matter of fact, isn't there a big grandstand on the back stretch at Daytona named after Tiny?

You know, at the time, there was a zero training procedure to qualify for a Grand National Driver. You just built the car, took it to the track, went through a Mickey Mouse physical for five minutes, paid a fee, and you were a genuine NASCAR Grand National Driver. Hell, I drove in several races without a driver's license.

A word about "Fast Freddie" Lorenzen. He didn't stay with us long, but let me tell you, he won more than his share. When Holman and Moody took him into their Ford Camp this cat came alive. I think the reason I liked Freddie was, in my opinion, in the race car, he was actually scared shit less, but he wanted it so bad, he was able to mask his fear and drive the balls off of any decent race car and good enough to win very often.

One time at Darlington in practice, I seen him loose it coming off number four. He saved it, then proceeded to kill his self three times before he got it gathered up, down by number one. When he came in, he was trying to unhook his helmet, shaking like a dog shitting razor blades.

I think he ended up winning the race three days later. Let me tell you;,500 miles at Darlington in the 60s with lousy tires and really no shocks, 3,900 pound cars with 450 to 500 horsepower, with 30 hillbillies and 15 others, it took some balls to run in the top 10…let alone win it.

I rode around track at race speed with Goldsmith in a '57 Chevy, when he stuck it in number one the first time, I didn't close my eyes, I just quit breathing. I couldn't believe it could be done. The other aspect was the four to five hours of physically, brutally hot and intense work. Back before power steering, it took a ton of physical effort to run the corners. You gotta remember most of the drivers were not physical fitness fiends. Most drank too much, most ate junk food, most didn't go to bed before 2:00 am and really, most of 'em were lazy as hell – not all. A few worked their asses off, both on the race car and off the track.

The only way anybody ever run Darlington fast back then, and my guess it's the same today was coming out of the middle of either end of the racetrack, the car has got to have a touch of push in it. Well, when car is pushing, your right elbow is 'bout straight up aimed at roof, your left hand is down by your gut (with no leverage) so right hands doing 80 percent of the work. Them bumps really jar your arms. Most everybody run a ton of castor that's good for straight, but hard work when it's 130 degrees, inside the car. The guys had no driver's uniforms either, they just wore street shoes, blue jeans and a T-shirt. Also, then nine out of 10 drivers smoked. So in the left T-shirt arm, a pack of cigarettes is rolled in there for a yellow flag smoke. Hell, one year Fireball run whole race with windows up for speed. Can you imagine that for four hours?

The above is a handful, right? Well, now comes the good part. In first two years of Darlington, we tore track up "all to hell." Why? Well I guess the low budget and primitive equipment used to build and pave track didn't help either. Plus, who the hell anywheres in the world knew how to build and pave a high-bank asphalt track, where you hit the banks at 120 and every year got five miles and hour faster? It was decided by the local paving experts, "No way, but we know how to fix the problem." How? Well they decided the high lateral traction loads were the problem needing solution and they were dead right. So the night before the race here comes spray equipment (I think first time or two they did it with brushes.) and they apply this material to the race track groove in both ends of the track from going into one to coming out of two, same at three and four. We quickly name this modern miracle of paving technology "Bear Grease."

Boy, this now brings in a new dimension to the feeling. (like riding the edge of a razor blade at 120 plus.) As a matter of fact, I told Turner in '57 at Darlington I wasn't gonna put a seat belt in his car. "Just a trailer ball in the middle of the seat and cut a hole in his pants". Turner said, "You know that would work, but not AFTER the Bear Grease treatment."

In my opinion Darlington was the mechanism that got NASCAR moving. It was first race where results were discussed in days sport's report other than Indianapolis. The race fan with the dream and balls of an elephant was Harold Brasington. Talk about the baseball movie "build it and they will come." How 'bout 1949?...when a man did it in real life. I know Harold had some help. I can't remember all the players, but there was Bob Colvin, a smallish, bald firecracker and cigar smokin' ball of fire. This cat could talk a squirrel out of his nuts. Robert Colvin got it done. He became President of joint. Harold disappears – at least to me.

Harold Brasington took a cotton field (part in a swamp). I mean, if you opened your mouth 50 black gnats and three boll weevils would fly in. This is hot, humid, poor folks country, farm county, big-big "baccy" (tobacco) country. You know, the Lucky Strike auctioneer? He lived here. Also, this is cotton country – no-drinking, Southern Baptist "strong hold."

The first year the race track construction is running late. The race is on/off. A hundred of us racers show up, Yup a hundred. Half the cars were driven to track from "where-ever."

There was a small grandstand, the track, a race track control tower in middle of front straight away, on the inside of the track. The lower eight feet of the control tower is occupied by a single-holer-no-flush with a Sears and Roebuck Catalog (mostly shiny pages left.) On the outside wall a pay phone. Can you imagine the aroma and the line, both at the one-holer, and the phone?

After a rain shower the infield scene was enhanced by a sea of red mud. There was no paving, no pit wall, no pit paving. The pit area was all red mud and crushed stone.

(That's a movie that needs making...mules and all.) Harold, you have gone now. We finally got to recognize you in the Darlington International Hall of Fame just shortly before your retirement from the active living. Who was he? What was he? This was a man with a dream. I had always assumed he was a farmer or a road contractor. He told me, "Nope, I'm a truck driver." He told me he wanted Darlington to be a Southern edition of Indianapolis. I said "Don't look big enough, how big is it?" He said, "'bout one and a half miles," I said " Indy's two and a half miles," he said, "What difference is it gonna make?" His first conversation with me indicated he intended to run the open wheel cars, Indy cars and sprint cars as the main attraction, and fill in with some stock car races. You know, they did take the Championship open wheelers there and race. it was a disaster, mostly because of tires being totally incapable of the speeds they turned. The Indy car race didn't draw any people at all.

The first stock car race gave him his direction loud and clear. Harold, you never got near credit you should have received. But, hell Harold, in the long run, like you told me about the one mile difference in track length, what difference does it make? All that really counted was what you thought about yourself. Even if you weren't invited on race day, you could drive by and say you built the son-of-a-bitch off of your plans and dreams. You put Darlington on the map. I never heard of it in my life till you said, "I'm gonna build a racetrack." So Harold, I've told you this in person for myself, but now let me do same for all stock car racing fans: "Thanks for your vision and fortitude."

Bob Colvin, "thank you" too. I think you got a pretty fair deal financially, and recognition-wise, and a man would have to be stupid not to recognize Bill France Sr. was the "main course." Darlington would not have had a prayer to become the Indy of the South without NASCAR. Darlington would have gone back to the boll weevil and the black gnats, and maybe a good place for lovers to park and screw. (Remember, no motel in that area then.) Matter of fact, wasn't too bad for that, even with the race crowd.

Back to the '61 Pontiac. If I remember right, Fireball's got a three lap lead with a Pontiac and gets sick, so we replace him with our buddy Marvin Panch. Well, it don't work out. Nelson Stacey does us in with a "Yallar" Ford. We've already covered fall race Charlotte. Atlanta last race of year (the big "crash and squash" job).

So now it's '62 model time. Back in them days last three weeks of September, and maybe into first week of October was new model car time. Dealers put brown paper on their show room windows. This hype goes on for a month, then finally we can see in the show-room and all the new, glorious shineys are there for us to see, drive, touch, rub, feel, listen to.

We at Pontiac got a new 421 cubic inch engine, with a huge crank, 'bout like a Caterpillar tractor. Damn thing must have had about three inch mains. I liked the engine, but really got upset over the heavy crank.

Knudsen's 'bout to leave to go run Chevrolet. We don't know that, but I think he knows. I notice my control over engine program is long gone, cause over on the side of show room is the world's ugliest skinny car called a "Tempest." I open hood, yeah, there is the half of a 389, but it's half of a 421, big mains and all. Remember it's September '61, but the new models are '62s. When "Tempest" first got going it is a neat looking car on paper...say late '60. I know new engine's coming: overhead cam, hydraulic lifter, belt drive cams. Fours, 6s, V8s. Even saw a Bonneville with rear transaxle and independent suspension, a la Tempest. I've got double turbo going, but ain't getting anywheres, mostly cause we have so many weak spots. (crank, rods, pistons, carburetion) And I'm against the engine cause I figure it to be a high maintenance, 600 horsepower, young rich kid killer motor, with no practical application, not even for racing.

Well, time for '62 Daytona. Fireball's driving. It's same black and gold, with a red stripe. Even Knudsen got his personal car painted like a race car. During a Board Meeting at downtown General Motors Building parking garage, somebody sneaks a painter in and slaps #22 on each door (our race number) in water paint.

I get some cranks and blocks made with same bearing sizes as 389 (quietly). The grease was a case of Seagrams VO, and a pair of C-notes to some good guys in the foundry. The car runs good and Fireball wins everything there is to win, including a dandy Miss "something or other." Linda, do you remember who that was?

Knudsen has an artist make eight various poses of myself during practice and the race. He also has a famous artist make an oil painting of #22 Fireball Roberts in the Smokey Yunick Pontiac taking checkered flag. If you're 70 years old you know every Pontiac Dealer had a replica of that painting. It's a present for me for winning the race. Knudsen shows it to France at a party night of Atlanta race. The next time I see it, it's hanging in Big Bill's office. Somehow I feel, 35 years later, I'm never gonna get the painting. Knudsen is still going good, but I got a feeling he's forgot about "my painting," and Bill France Sr. can't say, "I forgot to give Smokey his painting." I do have a replica though. One day when I was at Monk King's Pontiac Dealership in Denton, Texas, I see the picture in a trash can still in good shape. (Pontiac made a cardboard copy of the painting for all the dealers. I took it home. I still got it. 'Bout six months ago somebody offered me 200 bucks for it but I couldn't bear to part with it. I'm pretty sure if we go back to my theory "we're all whores at heart," if someone offers a big enough stack of "greenies," I'll be able to part with it quite easily.

You notice I never say much about John Delorean, well he is the number three player throughout my whole nearly four years with Pontiac. We get along, but never really discuss anything. 80 percent was with Knudsen, 20 percent with "Iron Ass" (Pete Estes). Now shit hits fan quick. Knudsen goes to run Chevrolet, Pete Estes is running Pontiac, and John DeLorian is Chief Engineer Pontiac.

We got one more story before the lights go out at Pontiac. It involves a Tempest. John wants us to run a Tempest in a sports car race at Daytona. There are Corvettes and lots of other pretty good cars in the race. John wants to enter this skinny, ugly, tall 4-cylinder with the brakes of a bicycle (little bitty drums – nine inchers maybe) with a 40 pound transmission. I remember showing my boy Smokey his first look at a new, secret model car at Pontiac. Knudsen jerks the white cover off of the prototype. It's dark metallic green, and I gasped, I hadn't seen where they were, body-wise for damn near a year. I knew the car came in way over budget, and they re-did most of it.

Knudsen said, "What do you think?" I said, "That is the ugliest grill I've ever seen in my life." A pissed body engineer standing close by said, "I'd like to see what you can do for 45 cents." I got the message. Well, I did a lot of work on Tempest engine, and really surprised myself. Got 'bout 1.8 horsepower per cubic inch at 6500 rpm. I had a plan. About a year before I noticed people carefully cleaning up some "gooey stuff" around a refinery. You know, back then all refineries leaked some every place. I said, "Why so fussy 'bout how you handle that stinkin stuff? What is it?" The guy answers "propylene oxide." Not wanting to appear stupid, I said, "No shit!" He says, "boy that stuff burns hot!" I say, "Will it dissolve in gasoline?" "Yes" he says. So I make a deal and get 100 pounds of it.

I try various mixes of this stuff, and get nothing. One day I tried it on the Tempest engine in the dyno and for some reason choke plate was still in the carburetor I was using. It's supposed to be locked wide open. I had a piece of aluminum welding wire locking it, but the wire got bent so the carb had 'bout 25 percent choke. Course I don't know this. I fire up and son-of-a-bitch and get 220 horsepower at 6500. 210 cubic inches right around two horsepower per cubic inch. I happen to notice fuel flow is to the moon. I find the choke problem and fix it. Now I'm really gonna get some horsepower. Nope, nothing, back to 1.8 horsepower per cubic inch. I accidentally found out to run that stuff you had to go rich, rich as hell, and add some advance in ignition.

Well, somehow Goldsmith is the driver. Course he drives in Ray Nichels Pontiacs. At the time of the race it rains like a son-of-a-bitch. It pissed rain for the whole race and was so bad that Junior Johnson driving one of Mickey Thompson's Corvettes was sitting in water up to his ass. Well, Goldy must be a wet pavement driver. He blows my mind and wins the goddam race hands down. I'm in a state of shock.

John Delorean comes by and says, "Smokey, I want you to build me a couple more for a race soon in Silver Springs, Maryland. (24 hour race – I can't handle it.) I say, "John, you remind me of old joke. "I don't want to be a millionaire, just live like one." I said, "You want to get this pile of junk to act like a Ferrari, with no power, no brakes and no drive train, and with an old lady's suspension…I'm not even gonna try. There ain't no one can be that lucky twice." Lucky for me I guess, John is a good guy. He gave the job to Ray Nichels without firing my ass.

That 24 hour race comes on a Saturday. The phone rings 'bout 10 am (race in progress). I'm home working in the shop when Knudsen says, "There will be a jet at airport in five minutes, get in it." We get there in 'bout in first third of race to try and help but even God couldn't have fixed the mess they were in. It was a weird deal. All kinds of sports cars, were there along with rain, snow, sleet. A Go-Cart wins it with one driver going for 24 hours – a no-suspension, hot motored go-cart wins it. Yup, beat Corvettes, Porsches everything. Now John Delorean's got a double overhead cam belt driven V8, in-line six and a four banger all with hydraulic lifters. The plan was to bring out the four cylinder first, then a year later the six and the next year the V8.

Knudsen's at Chevrolet pulling same stuff he did at Pontiac. Pour it to it and argue 'bout AMA ban on racing later. "Fuck 'em," he said, "I want to build 10,000 cars and trucks a day" (and he did). The government is on GMs ass for "monopoly" and Knudsen says, "If they want to put someone in jail for taking 60 percent of the market, I'm their man!"

Remember the prototype carburetor that Ralph Johnson and I built and Pontiac turned down because of tooling cost? Well, soon as Knudsen gets to Chevrolet he says, "Come on over with me, I'll pay you two grand a year more." Well I hate changing. I want to but don't. He asks if he can borrow my 800 cfm carburetor. "Hell yes. why not?" Well, you guessed it. The Holley everybody runs today in stock car racing today is that carburetor. But there is more to the story. At this time Ralph Johnson is back at Holly Carburetor, and is Holly's Chevrolet Representative.

Well, Ralph does a job on that sucker finishing it up. God, there must have been 200 million of those things built so far. They are still building them ass over head. Ralph shortly later turned the fuel bowl in a more desirable plane that corrected for fuel behavior in reference to lateral-forward and stopping forces. Shortly after this, Ralph gets his ass fired again, and eventually comes to Daytona and helps me for about 15 or 17 years.

Neither he or I ever got a dime for that carburetor. "Thank you Holly Carburetor Company." Your Chief Executives should have been presented with a extra large diamond "screw-you" award for your treatment of Ralph and myself. I couldn't even get my fucking prototype carburetor back.

OK, one day couple months after Knudsen takes over Chevrolet he says, "Could you come by our Engineering Center, I'd like you to look at a new engine we have." Well, I'm busy as hell working for Pontiac but under strained conditions. I've started a new Indy car. I only got one helper, T.A. Toomes, and he has never seen an Indy car, but damn good stock car man. Ask Richard Petty. He'll tell you same thing. (Maybe not, in racing things change pretty fast sometimes) I don't tell anybody 'bout Indy car but T.A.

I forgot to tell you, back in the late 50's I kept Race Shop off limits to fans, bullshitters, race parasites but if you were a racer in a jam, I'd let you come in and work. I just covered up some of the stuff I was working on. Not for secrecy, but I hated to get into discussions about what I was doing with supposedly knowledgeable people. At times their opinions would confuse me, or cause me to lose my focus on what I was aiming at. You know, "Don't confuse me with the facts." Really, as I saw it the problem was that some of what was considered "engineering facts" in those days would be more properly filed under "ancient bullshit" or "incorrect data."

Anyway, I have to meet with Pete on turbo engine 8:30 am. Then in afternoon John D. and Klinger are gonna give the double overhead V8 birth, then we are gonna consider some valve gear problems on and about the hydraulic lifters and belt drives. On way to the 8:30 meeting I'm supposed to stop at 7:30 am at the Chevrolet Tech Center to take quick look at Chevrolet's new engine. Well, I figure 30 or 40 minutes at Chevrolet and 20 minutes travel to Pontiac I take quick look at the new Chev. It turns out to be the Mystery Engine and I tell them no way I'll say anything with less than six hours of looking. So OK, "Good-bye." I get to Pontiac 10 minutes late. Pete somehow knows I've stopped in to see Knudsen and calls me a "double-crossing bastard." I smacked Pete in the snoot. Well you can guess the rest – Bob Emerick, Pete's hatchet-man (he inherited him from Knudsen) – also once a Pro-Bowl Detroit Football Star gets deal stopped.

I quit. Pete fires me and hauls ass. But I feel like I got to finish day, so on to the engine room and dynos. I spend three hours there, long enough to say, "With that cam drive belt arrangement into those aluminum cam housings as tight as it is, won't that lock up the cams?" (Regarding V8; these were four valve engines with double overhead cams.) "Hell no," says Klinger. John say,s "I don't think so." In 10 minutes the engine is born and it runs. 10 minutes later at 3,500 rpm the engine gives a squeal like a stuck pig. A couple cams lock up, valves break, a valve head gets between cylinder heads and pistons, these parts run out of room and proceed out through water jackets, a rod breaks and the engine has about a four inch inspection hole in left bank. Boy, it got quiet. (I doubt that cost over 250 grand!)

Where we could make a one-of-a-kind crank for a grand, they might make it for 10 grand, etc. Making prototype castings with temporary tooling ain't cheap either and they'd usually make three or four of everything.

Just as I'm about to leave around 3:00 pm, Pete comes in, hugs me and apologizes for his mouth running in the morning. We kiss and make up, but really, it's over. I think Pete decided to back off of racing. I still talked with him once in awhile. Probably up to once every three or four months, before he checked out. But he never offered any explanation for his cooling off about racing. He and I meet again in 1969 when he's General Manager of Chevrolet and I worked for him again, and again in 1971 when he is President of General Motors.

I loaned (notice I'm getting smarter? – I used to give everything away) the '62 Pontiac to Fireball and Banjo Matthews, where they got the money I don't remember. I imagine Pontiac, through a dealer. They brought it back to Daytona's July 4th Race. I guess I helped them a little, and actually they ran two Pontiacs. Banjo drove one, I believe he had the Pole and led most of the race, but Fireball won. I think Banjo had a four speed transmission and a trans problem. My car had an Iron three speed, which was kinda bulletproof. Believe it or not. Banjo brought car back to me in good condition (less motor).

My friend, local Pontiac Dealer, Jim Stephens, offered me $2,500 for the car. (He said it was his anyway.). I think big reason he agreed was I owned it. (I also had a Bill of Sale saying I owned it.) I used to wonder how that could have happened, (the car was listed in NASCAR as Jim Stephens owned), but I think I know. Kinda makes you wanna hold your wallet when you're around some of them crooked bull-slingers don't it? Some one claimed the car owner money. I did us all up for twenty years.

That car still exists. Really is in very good mechanical condition, at the Talladega Hall of Fame, but it looks terrible, paint job is 37 years old. The engine, as it left me, was brand new 389 or 421. Everything else is real. It was driven away. The only thing I kept was Fireball's seat. I built it special for him and then made it into an office chair for myself. I still use it – My High-Speed office chair.

A cheap-assed Pontiac dealer recently asked to buy seat I just spent 150 bucks getting reupholstered (same stuff). Offered $200 cash, then called back and offered $500, but acting like it was robbery, so I offered him seat for $200 plus 10 percent compound interest from February 1962 till now. He said, "OK. How much is that?" I said, "Hell, figure it out and send check" – that was two years ago. Still no check. Figure the price I gave him you'll see why he chickened out.

I've also met some really fine people who were car dealers. Trouble is, they have a very low percentage. Remember when "Win on Sunday – Sell on Monday" first 20 years really worked? As I get older I get more pissed when I think how those son-of-a-bitches used us, milked us dry, and shit-canned us. Racing organizations promoters, manufacturers of vehicles and of parts, tires, fuel, etc. I asked Sales Manager at Chevrolet in 1955 how much is first place worth (they were second to Ford at the time). The Sales Manager

(I don't remember his name), Scotty, his Assistant Manager (Scotty was the originator and inventor of the Soap Box Derby) Scotty says "at least five million" (five bucks a car). Sales Manager says "at least." Well, Chevrolet got first place '56, with a lot of help from Herb Thomas and me (and other racers). Herb and I have exactly same privileges at Chevrolet that you have. Same at Pontiac. I'll bet you the head of Pontiac PR today doesn't have one clue about what I just told you in the Pontiac Story.

Is it fact? Is it baloney? This is June 20 something 1997. I'm sitting in a hotel in Minneapolis, totally deaf. I'm here trying to get some hearing back. been here a week waiting for a clearance to leave after an ear operation. July 10th, John Delorean and I (we are still good friends) are gonna give a two hour bull-slinging session with 2,000 or more proud Pontiac owners and lovers in Denver, Colorado. I'm 74 years old now, still work every day.

Consider this, I raced 35 years, I receive zero pension, zero medical, zero retirement.

I'm not complaining, just trying to write this in such a way that you can actually ride along with me during my life. The triple zero retired racers plan is offered to all who ever raced, and no longer able, because of age or loss of capacity to do so. You all read and hear about the money, glamour and grand life style of today's successful racing heroes. I don't begrudge them one dime of it.

The driver's risk so much as compared to a ball or ball and sticker, they still are sucking hind tit. But if they endorse something they get well paid. In my adventures, rules said "all rights to pictures and advertising belong to sponsors, and companies that put up contingency money and sanctioning body." But we did get free car polish and baseball caps with their logos on 'em. But you know, maybe that's how it's supposed to work. Racing's for the young. When you can't, or won't race anymore, get your ass out of the way for your replacement.

Well the '63 Pontiac Racing Program gets kinda mysterious to me. I get the feeling the train left without me. Seems like big deal at Pontiac is G.T.O. "Firebird." The cars got wider, man we had wide track. Hell, doors weighed 100 pounds. The Pontiac got too big and heavy to race, unless it was mostly aluminum, (and they were), and they did very well on drag strips for a little while.

Wore Out and Dead at 50

There was an annual event run for years called "The Mobil Gas Economy Run." From Pasadena, California to Detroit, New York, Boston, etc. In the winter of '58, Mr. Knudsen, boss of Pontiac then, says, "Smokey, do the Mobil Gas economy run for us." Which is quite easy, but required 'bout sixteen hours a day. Knudsen calls it a vacation for myself and Goldsmith and Fireball.

In the previous year's competition we have already figured out how to cheat like a son-of-a-bitch.

They run test runs over whole route. Learn how to draft off of a bus, coast down hill, time every stop lite, reference red-green-yellow, check all state and local and city laws. In Albuquerque, we find it not illegal to run on sidewalks, so pass on right, get up on sidewalks and beat the light. Yup, I went through Albuquerque once at high noon and never stopped once, but I did get up on sidewalk twice.

Ford Motor Company was biggest cheater of all, did the most planning and car preparation. They had Bill Stroppe ride heard over the deal for Ford, Lincoln and Mercury. Leo Villene did Nash, Piggins did Chevy and I did Pontiac, etc. In case I forget, Bill Stroppe was one of the finest men I ever raced against. Bill Stroppe deserves a statue in the middle of Long Beach, California for his contributions in racing and hi-performance automotive adventures. Simply stated: Bill Stroppe was a real talented, honest genius.

The cars we use have to be bone stock, 'cept for the tune up and other small details. So, before the performance run, you get a fleet of new cars to prepare. To get maximum mileage we loosened up the engines, upped the compression, changed camshafts, lowered the alternator output, shaved the water pump and opened up the oil pump to reduce pressure and parasitic power losses, unhooked the speedometers and ran them for 5,000 miles to reduce all component's friction. We also disassembled the engines and blueprinted the whole thing a la race engine preparation. From the factory we got special straight, light wheels and special hard tires made of an extra hard rubber compound with narrowed tread. We filled these tires with 60 pounds of air then changed an air pressure gage to read, 26 psi. These tires and the blueprinted engine then went into a chassis that had been built low and light with no sound deadener, and no undercoating. Finally, we'd jack the carburetor around very lean, lower the idle speed, and dial in very advanced timing. Yeah, a genuine "strictly stock" deal.

Even with all the stuff we did to the cars, the biggest mileage gain was in driving technique. You'd drive like you had an egg between your shoe and the accelerator. To give you an example of what a bone stock car could do after this treatment, we ran a Pontiac Catalina from Pasadena to Detroit averaging twenty-one miles per gallon. This car had a 389 cubic inch engine and the "real" mileage was 'bout 16 miles per gallon.

WORE OUT AND DEAD AT 50

The week before the run, getting ready to go was the fun part. We stayed at the Sands Motel in Hollywood. The restaurant there was full of would-be male and female actors. It was across the street from John Wayne's and Dean Martin's casting offices. Plus we met "Big Jim" a connoisseur and purveyor of sexual adventures with four hundred hookers under his leadership. By this point I've been totally around the world, and assumed I had experienced every kind of sexual perversion and unusual social behavior known to society. Not so. Big Jim called me a "Southern Square," and rated me a relative first grade student in the art of seduction and the arts of pleasing women.

In three years, I spent about a total of ten days being educated by Jim and his band of female entertainer/instructors. I met several "soon to be" movie stars, one established female movie star, one very famous singer and one very famous male movie star. Yes, Big Jim, as I reflect on my experiences at your place, I agree I was a hurting "square." The official attire of the ladies in training at Big Jim's was high heels and full stockings. Nothing else except ear rings allowed.

I later met a very famous major oil company chairman John Swearington who, when drunk, said his new wife, a younger redhead, served breakfast in exactly this costume. I asked him if he knew Big Jim from Hollywood. His strange look (without comment) made me think I may have hit a nerve.

I guess main difference in "love Hollywood style" from generally accepted practice is, instead of two participants, six to eight was about the normal procedure. If AIDS had been a problem then, all of Hollywood and the racing world would now be as extinct as the dinosaurs, so I have to assume it to be a more modern medical invention. The plan we were registered under at the Sands called for the attitude "there would be no tomorrow."

We soon had the motel manager and his secretary as participants, and Fireball figured out how to get the manager's wife pissed off enough about her husband, she jumped in bed with Fireball.

Paul Goldsmith did his share by corrupting several young starlets to be. My most memorable adventure was arriving at the motel at 8:00 pm after a long day getting cars ready and finding a beautiful female stranger unclothed in my bed. I know I should have called a policeman, but the devil got me, and I allowed her to give me a bath. I'm not catching on yet. Just before I left the garage in Pasadena, Bill Yeager, (nope, not related to Chuck 'cept maybe morally) says, "Your lookin low, take this greenie" (a green and white pill.) At this time in history California is inventing artificial motivation by drugs and they got a color for everything.

As this fine lady bathes me I'm puzzled by the lack of response my body is showing. There is a knock on the door. In comes a waiter and two steak dinners, courtesy of an anonymous donor. I start to eat, but I'm getting panicky. I've heard about this stuff, suddenly sexual powers disappear.

Well, let's get to it, to hell with the steak. But from the crucial part of me, zero enthusiasm. The lady is wired in, and she says, "Don't worry, I'll fix it." Well that little lady could have sucked the chrome off of a trailer ball, but zero. Nothing…goddam. I'm getting really worried.

There is a knock on the door. It's Fireball and he is pissed! (I put a live lobster in his bed.) He is wired in on the gag and wants to know, "If I need any help." "Oh hell no, everything's fine." But the lady says, "Yes, I could use a lot of help." There's a knock on the door. It's the manager's wife looking for Fireball, but she gets mad when she finds him. He is cheating on her after only one day.

Well, hell, soon it's like Grand Central station with eight or ten people in room. Another knock on the door. I open it up and here's the vice squad and they want to lock our asses up. Suddenly, I remember Mr. Detweiller describe the power of the greenie. His advice was, "In troubled times always test the ability of the greenies to solve your problem." Two won't do it, ain't enough. I get up to six one hundred dollar bills. That's the magic number. Now the vice squad is helping spread joy to the female attendees, including Mrs. Motel manager, with Mr. Motel manager cheering her on. I've always figured Fireball and I saved their marriage.

Mr. Knudsen and Pontiac Motor Company would have been proud of their team in the Mobil Gas economy run. No, we did not win in mileage, but we out-fucked every other motor company hands down.

I still don't know why I'm unable to perform. I'm planning on going to a hospital and get checked when party winds down, but I pass out. I wake up 6:00 am. Hot damn, it's hard! I run and take a piss and it's still hard! Yahoo, I'm cured! I eat breakfast, go to get my stuff (I need at work) up in the room. There is a knock on the door. A bouquet of roses are delivered with a card saying, "Thank you very much for a wonderful evening, Jeanie." Now the light comes on. That fuckin' Yeager had it all planned ('cept the vice squad)! Fireball stuck the lobster (now dead) in a hall light. Looks like all his bedding is out in the hall (yup, it don't smell too good). But it's a great day, my pecker's not ruined and I'm gonna go to bed early tonight. I'm pooped before we start to work.

Guess what? When the sun goes down racers start to rise, "and let's start a bran' new party." After all, wouldn't it be a sorry representation of Southern racers if we rejected the friendly and wild-assed California ladies? Yes, you're right. When we left we took few of them with us to show our appreciation of their help. As a rule though, when time came to part it wasn't always pleasant.

I believe 'bout 1962 the Mobil Gas Economy Run ended. A good thing too, I think in a few more years and the mileage would have got to 100 miles per gallon and the Pontiac team would have been wore out and dead at fifty.

The Little Car That Could...But Didn't

In 1964 I'm working for Mr. Knudsen, the top cat at Chevy. He has started secret project called "Chevelle." In late 1965 I go to see the number one prototype. It is a hand built car, metallic silver, with a 427 sitting high and centered over the front axle. "Try it Smoke, see what you think." I say, "I want to weigh it first, I don't like the high and forward 600-pound, boat anchor deal." Man, in my book it's awful, 62 percent – 38 percent weight distribution. Way heavy in the front. I drive it and turn the steering wheel hard. At even 50 miles an hour it just goes straight ahead. I hit the brakes and the rear tires light up. Knudsen says, "What you think?" I say, "Push the engine back four inches and down two."

Jim Primo is chief engineer and I'd say the best body man in Detroit, but he don't know jack-shit 'bout handling. Well, Jim's good, but can get real fuckin' nasty when a home made "expert" bad mouths his baby. Knudsen says, "Jim drop engine two inches and push it back four." Jim says, "goddamned Bunk, we've already got the firewalls' permanent tooling and blabbady-blah-blah and yackatty-yak finished." Knudsen says, "I'll be back Wednesday to ride it at Milford (proving ground)." That's five days including Saturday and Sunday. Real quick it looks like a 1,000 man hour job. Back in them days no questions asked. When the general manager said, "Do it."... you "did it." The big deal was to move firewall back three inches, that affects inside the car as well. Jim Primo I'm sure would have liked to tied me between two diesel tractors and pulled me apart, but he couldn't fuck with me 'cause Knudsen was my "grandfather."

It gets done. It took 'bout 50 men working 24 hours a day. I have a race over weekend and come back with Knudsen on Wednesday. The car's at the proving grounds and does much better; it's actually kinda racy. OK, it's a done deal. "Tool it up - let's go." I guess I don't have to tell you what kind of relationship I had with Jim after that do I? You know he was only living and fairly healthy engineer from the original "miracle 75" guys honored at the PRI "Small Block Chevy" 40th anniversary in 1995 that refused to come. So I guess he ain't healed up yet. If you're still peddling Jim, consider this: if you built the car the way you started, you'd of probably had the title of "sorriest handling car built in the US." (Which the '70 Mustang won when the Boss 429 was dumped in it).

Well, a week later Knudsen calls and says, "I want to race a new Chevelle at Daytona in 1966 (Feb)." I say, "How's that work? That's seven weeks away and I got no car?" He says, "Use the car you got." (I do have the silver prototype by now.) "The number one prototype?" "Yup." Normally these cars are never sold. They represent an immense liability problem. Normally they are tested to destruction. I bet that Chevelle was the first and only Chevy prototype ever to go into racing service.

I show up at track on time and the car ain't run an inch. I had no driver then, so I had gotten Mario Andretti to drive it. I'd seen the li'l guy run the shit out of a sprinter, (yup, back then I doubt he weighed more than 130 pounds) so I liked the idea. Knudsen and France liked the idea too.

The '66 Chevelle's chassis geometry front and rear was a dog. It had horsepower and was clean aerodynamically (relatively). But because the rear radius rods were too short, it had rear steer out the ass. That's when the rear end was changing wheel base with every bump.

It had a 22 gallon rubber fuel cell, the first one in NASCAR. The chief inspector said, "Get that inner tube outta here and put in a standard steel death trap." So I started to negotiate with him and said, "I ain't moving that tank nowheres – it stays." He says, "Then you're outta here." I say, "Fine, you can go take a flying fuck on a galloping duck, I ain't doing nothing." I tie rope on the car and proceed homeward. Just as I get to the tunnel, here comes the royal bullshitter France. "What's the problem?" I think this asshole's been on phone with Friel and Knudsen probably for 30 of the last 35 minutes. I say, "I just got a phone call from a guy that wants his garbage truck overhauled and I can make more money doing that than racing. See you next year, maybe."

France says, "Knudsen wants you to call him." I call Knudsen from the gas station on the corner.

Mario in the 1966 Chevelle. (photo: Don Hunter)

Boss says, "What's wrong?" I say, "Nothing. We are in the middle of the birth of a NASCAR Bill France engineering and safety breakthrough, the birth of a rubber fuel cell instead of a steel tank three inches off of the track and one inch inside the rear bumper." The Boss says, "I want to see that car run." I say, "You will. France wants Mario in the race more than he wants to screw Miss Pure Oil."

I hang up.

By then France had come over to the gas station, he asks, "What did he say?" I said "He said put it in the barn, then run it in USAC." France says, "Let me see the tank." "OK, Bill." He smokes it over a few minutes, then says "I'm gonna permit you to run it just this once, but you have to go back to our driver frying deal at Atlanta." I say, "They'll need snow tires in hell before I take that rubber tank out." He starts giving me a ration of shit but I interrupt, "You seen Fireball lately?" (He got bar-b-qued couple years prior with a steel tank.) France says "take it back to inspection station." Everybody say "thank you" to Firestone. (They built it for me using military helicopter specs.)

Car had power to spare, but the chassis was so fucked up God couldn't have drove it. After a crash or two, as I remember it, the engine mercifully blows early in the race and the infamous number one Chevelle is sitting in my shop resting and retired. I sold chassis to a modified hot dog out of Memphis, can't recall his name rite now, it was a very racy nickname and I believe that sorry suspension wore his ass and bankroll out.

Knudsen says, "Let's start early and run a '67 Chevelle." I say, "Boss, now I know a li'l something 'bout engines and aerodynamics, but if I took a dozen exams 'bout chassis I'd flunk every one." Knudsen says, "Well hell, we got Jim Musser and Frank Winchell running Chevy R&D, let's get them to build the chassis." I say, "Well, they should know the geometry, but I'm afraid we will get a heavy million dollar car." Knudsen calls 'em in. "Teach Smokey vehicle dynamics." Frank asks Mr. K, "You had any luck teaching him anything?"

So they built (well, start to build) the car in Chevy research and development. It gets heavy, it gets very expensive and they ain't gonna make it time wise. So we load all the shit up and take 'er to Daytona. They

Before Mario bent 'er up early. (photo: Don Hunter)

send down five or six technicians to help me finish it. I put it on a diet and we work around the clock. Some of those GM technicians were making two grand a week. We get done. This car broke every corporate rule there ever was.

Turner wants to drive it. Holman hired Mario when I gave up with the '66 Chevelle so Curtis gets the job. Everybody stand up and give a big cheer for Frank Winchell and Jim Musser, the car is very good handler. We sit on the pole by three miles an hour with an engine 23 cubic inches short of our allowable maximum. My idea was to shake it down with this engine then pull the gorilla 427 to qualify and race with. It came so easy (we practiced 20 laps, qualified, run 15 more laps) that we just parked it for the race. We run the 404 cubic inch qualifier in the race, but reliability was suspect. Turner got behind because of a terrible pit stop we gave him.

Mario gets the lead in a Holman-Moody Ford. Curtis has brain fade and mashed the gas hard. In a lap he catches him, but one of the connecting rods breaks. The million buck Chevelle looks like world's best mosquito sprayer. It blew all to shit. Oh yes... it had rubber fuel cell, the same one that was in the '66

267

Chevelle. This car was a li'l heavy, so it was the tire test car, but not on purpose. Luckily we passed the tire test.

You might say that with that Chevelle and at Daytona, I learned enough 'bout chassis to be dangerous, but I'm still horsepower happy. So for the next race at Atlanta, I've got a full house, 427 cubic incher with three, two barrels screwed in the Chevelle. This motherfucker paws the earth like a pissed off bull. It has 650 horsepower at 7,600 rpm, so when you mash the right pedal in this thing you need to have a good grip. We have also installed an expensive experimental GE radio in it (up till here no one could make radio work at speed). The car is hands down the "top cat."

For reasons never explained to me Turner and Cale Yarborough just flat don't like each other. Turner was so proud of this car that he wanted to show Cale a thing or two. Least that's the way he planned it. He started out of the pits in practice as Cale came off of turn four. He caught him and passed him going into turn three just half a lap later. Little did he realize the poor li'l Chevelle was five seconds from being a dead player. Going into number four the right side got into the grey and took off. First, it hit the outside guard rail kinda easy but this broke the watts linkage on the rear. The shit then hit the fan.

Listen to this: I had pictures of the car in the air tail first up over the last row of seats just off of turn four. It came down on any angle and centered the pit entrance guard rail not 15 feet from where I was standing. I had one helper, T.A. Toomes. In the middle of turn three I said to him, "Adios, one good race car." T.A. said, "Amen."

T.A. and I drug Turner out of the car. Curtis was out cold. He wasn't hurt too bad, just scared the hell out of us. He weighed 'bout 200 pounds, but when a guy is unconscious, trying to pick him up is hell. It's like 200 pounds of Jell-o. When he got out of hospital next day he said, "Something broke Smoke." I said, "You got that rite, after you hit the wall first time the race car was total junk." When I got to Daytona I

Notice the great gas fillin' technique...pit stops looked a little different back then. (photo: Don Hunter)

THE LITTLE CAR THAT COULD…BUT DIDN'T

(photo: Don Hunter)

pulled the engine and transmission – took it to Yorke's junkyard for a squash job. When they called to say it was squashed, I slipped the head squasher $100 to make it smaller…He got it four foot square like the Pontiac. It sat in the garage for 28 years. One day I sent it to Yorke's for scrap with the '61 Pontiac. You could still see the '3' on the Chevy and the '22' on the Pontiac.

Well now what?…Knudsen says, "Play it again Smoke." For the car in '68 I decided it was best to do everything in Daytona. I use a lot of good stuff Musser and Winchel taught me 'bout chassis and this time I used all I knew 'bout aerodynamics. I pulled the grill out, cut the air entrance in half and drained the air from the front and back wheel wells by creating negative air pressure pockets just behind all of 'em. I split front bumper lengthwise and add two inches. This kept air out from under the car and, together with the wheel well modifications, really helped eliminate front lift from packing air in the engine compartment. On the trunk lid we were allowed li'l chickenshit spoilers, but they were nowheres near enough. So, I still had a small rear roof spoiler, and slid the body back couple of inches and moved the wheel wells to fit the new contours front and rear. You might say this was just sloppy measurement on my part. With all these little changes I had pretty good control on the balance of down force front to rear. This car had to fit a set of templates and say it and NASCAR agreed. I think my plan on control in rear axle down force was biggest deal of the bunch.

I have a rotisserie in shop I built where I could fasten car at both ends and rotate the car a full 360 degrees either way. There were no rules against it then so I faired the bottom of the car in, including fuel cell, from front bumper to rear bumper I decided to quit fooling around and use the engine as a frame member to stiffen the chassis in twist. (Engine torque reacting against the rear axle tended to twist the chassis about the axis of the drive shaft, torsional twist.) I built a frame myself to eliminate twist. For weight and safety I installed a Lexan windshield and rear glass. Here's something that took a lot of work, I moved all the other glass damn near flush with out skin. To move more weight where it would do some good, I shoved the driver two inches to left and three inches back. This car was light, so I was able to add 100 pounds to left side. They didn't check the left to right weight bias back then.

The exhaust system in this car took me the better part of three months to figure and build. Each cylinder had the same flow and each bank was installed in an area where I had created some pretty good negative pressure. The pipe termination and the exhausts had sliding inner ventricles I adjusted to length to melt at 1,700 degrees – aluminum. I figured the scavenging of the relative vacuum after the aluminum melted was

Curtis and the '66 Chevelle at Charlotte. (photo: Norman Poole)

good for horsepower. To keep heat where it would do some good I also wrapped the whole exhaust system, insulated the fire wall and floor, built valve covers with heat deflectors.

If you heard the car run when we turned it to 6,900 rpm, you heard 13,800 firing the venturi in exhaust along with the oxygen inlet holes furnished enough oxygen for the secondary ignition.

These were 3/16 inch holes in each primary one and a half inches down from header face plate.

We passed inspection finally. Bill Gazaway was chief inspector, his brother was number two.

His brother conducted the inspection. Car finally passes inspection so I send it and Emory Lunsford, my helper, to the gas station for the last inspection deal the "first fill." Emory comes back and says, "They won't pass it, Bill Gazaway wants to see you." I think, "Yeah goddam, I haven't brought him any new Spiderman and Superman comic books to read and maybe he's pissed 'bout it." I get to "His Excellency's" dumpy comic book office. He's spins in his swiveley office chair, leans back and pitches me a sheet of paper.

"Ahem…"

#1 – Replace homemade frame with stock frame.

#2 – Remove all inner panels to let inspectors check for hidden fuel cells.

#3 – Replace all handmade beams joint suspension – replace with stock suspension….

And eight more dandies.

There is one and a half hours left to qualify, so I say, "My driver poor old Gordon Johncock ain't got a lap in the car, you got sixty seconds to tear up this paper and go give orders to OK my car or you'll see it leave in eight minutes." He just leaned way back in his chair and said, "Do it."

The car's still got a big tow rope tied to front bumper, so I started to tow car home but decided to put some gas in it and drive it home, and was gonna drive it to a track and take a couple laps. Well, Union won't give my helper Emory any gas to drive home. Who needs it, fuel line had one inch inner diameter and holds nearly five gallons. Well, that was all empty on account of the inspection. I go and get some gas, maybe three or four gallons and come back to the car. As I go to dump it in and one inspector tries to stop me from breaking the NASCAR seal to remove the filler cap. I've had enough. I knock him on his ass, jerk the seal off gas cap, dump some gas in it, hop in and fire her up.

I aim for track but run over the tow rope and realize I can't run a couple laps. So I head for the tunnel under the track. As I come out of the tunnel, Len Kulcher, number two in NASCAR is jumping up and down. "Stop! France wants to talk to you." I said, "I don't want to talk to the fucker, I want to kill the son-of-a-bitch." I believe I make it to shop in four minutes and it's five miles and twenty lights. France should have left me alone, but he followed. When he got there I damn near centered him with a four pound hammer. (Still got it if you wanna see it.) That did the trick, he hauled ass.

This car had power, aerodynamics and chassis. Too bad we never got to run it. I think it might have been interesting. Was this car a "cheater" Smokey? You're goddam rite it was…but not by NASCARs published rule book for 1968.

I'll tell you why I got so pissed. Two weeks before the race I got into a pneumonia deal. I was behind with the car and couldn't go 10 minutes without puking. I was hurting and exhausted so I was making mistakes left and right. So I jumped in a car and went to see him. I said, "France, I hear you've made a deal with Ford and Chrysler that no Chevy is gonna sit on pole and embarrass 'em like last year." (You see Ford won't contribute a dime and Ford and Chrysler were keeping NASCAR going). He said, "I'd never do that." I said, "Listen close…level with me, if it would be better for me to miss the race, I'll give up trying to make it. I ain't got a dime of insurance and I can't afford professional sheet time." He looked me in the eye and says "Nothing like that has happened." (without the "on my mother's grave" part of it).

Here's the rest of the story. A year later, 1969 and I'm working for Mr. Knudsen again but he's now president of Ford Motor Company. The big company joke was how they got the '68 Chevy kicked out. They and Chrysler said, "If that thing runs we cancel all our ads in your programs."

You've only heard my side of it. Billy France (Bill Jr.) didn't have a clue back then, but Kulchler and Gazaway may still be around. What do you guess on getting a straight answer out of any of 'em now? I ran my mouth so long on this because I believe this is the most famous race car in the world that never ran a lap in competition. As of today I've signed about 18,000, 24 x36 "Prolong" posters picturing the race car. It seems like this car will be argued about for the next 50 years.

Soon after the Daytona deal a strange thing happened. Firestone hired me and the car to do a tire test at Daytona in June of 1968. Three days before the test Firestone canceled because NASCAR found out it was the '68 Chevelle. The car was barred from ever competing on a NASCAR track by silent decree. I didn't get paid for the car. I'd sold it to Jerry Dorminey in Doe Run, Georgia. One day 'bout six years later I got pissed and decided to go get my car. I found it in the city dump. It had survived a garbage fire and the firemen had pushed it outside. It was in a hell of a mess from being used as a dirt track car. The front and back had heavy steel pipe guards and the fenders had been cut out with an acetylene torch. Luckily I had built a spare set of suspension parts when we built the car. When I sold the car it was less engine so I still had the original engine. Unfortunately the headers got lost in the deal so I put notice in paper up there offering a thousand dollar reward. I never got 'em back, but I'd have given three grand to get 'em back. Hell, it took me a month to build the new ones. So with $65,000 of paid parts and paint and about a year's time we got 'er back new in all ways.

I restored the car in 1985 and sold it at an auction to Floyd Garrett's muscle car museum in Sevierville, Tennessee. The car is race ready and is even more perfect today than the day I built it.

For you cats that think the car is a 7/8th scale version, I think Floyd might let you measure it up. I know Richard Childress has, he had it in his museum for a couple years, maybe ask him. I'm not gonna tell anymore. May be as time passes more will come to top of the water. Go see the car, but there's a hundred

I built the car…NASCAR made it a legend by not lettin' 'er run.

or more famous stock cars in the Floyd's museum. Let me tell you this, Floyd Garrett knows his shit on the complete muscle car era both stocks and drags. He collects the Detroit iron as built for circle track and any other stock car competition. He has 40 years experience collecting and restoring and, for my money, one of the very few people left where his handshake is as good as a 30 page contract. With the above I'll leave you to your thoughts.

Floyd Garrett bought the car for 100 grand (yes, Mr. IRS, I paid the goddam tax; I got $60,000 they took $40,000. Every time I think of the IRS, I get mental picture of three big vultures sitting on a limb of a dead tree, watching us work, while they oil their adding machines. I was 75 years old in 1998. I still got a social security bill for $17,000 bucks. What really pisses me off is we elected these assholes that did that to us (some of them five or six times). That sucker is race ready, nothing phoney 'bout it. I bet with a new set of the best tires and Earnhardt (El Mustachio) and a current chassis set up, the thing would run over 200. Car got sold recently and I don't know where it is 'cept California.

50 Good Drivers and an Asshole

I raced with fifty-one drivers I can remember. I'm often asked who was, in my opinion, the "best driver?" I can't answer that. There are too many variables. Like when, what kind of car, luck good or bad, amount of money we had to race with, etc. But if you ask me who was the worst driver I ever raced with that's easy: Jim Rathman.

JIM RATHMAN

Rathman was by far the biggest asshole I ever run across in racing. They will have to bury him in waterproof clothes and goggles if I outlive him 'cause I intend to piss on his grave. I was co-chief mechanic on his 1960 Indy win. He says I was not, that I was just a mechanic working for him. The man who Rathman said was chief mechanic wasn't even in the pits till 350 miles into the race, and he showed up in street clothes then. This is a man I lent $15,000 to without a note, to save his $60,000 deposit on the dealership he still owns. I had only gotten the $15,000 the day before, was $90,000 in debt, and living in my machine shop sleeping on an army cot. After that the ungrateful prick denies I was the crew chief and mechanic for his Indy winning car. OK, now that I have the biggest asshole out of the way, let me tell you about a good person.

The winning team at Indy with my good friend, Jim Rathman, at the wheel. (photo: Indianapolis Motor Speedway.

Marshall Teague

Marshall Teague was the first driver I ever worked with. He was a real good human, a damn good driver, and one of the top three mechanics in racing in the forties and fifties. When we met he was eeking out a living as a machinist at Motive Parts. He was married with a young daughter. Marshall needed help to get to track on time, so when he asked for help, I'd help at night, and go to some races to help. Soon I was the "chief" in pits for both he and Herb Thomas. I guess he and Red Vogt were sharpest mechanics in stock car racing in the late forties, early fifties. They both taught me a lot.

Marshall was a flight engineer on a B-29 in World War II. Man he was sure proud of that deal. For some reason I felt different about my Air Force experiences. I was able to totally divorce myself from the whole deal and didn't talk about it much. Only interest I had was to keep flying planes somehow, even just as a hobby.

Marshall was one of the founders of NASCAR, actually the first secretary and treasurer. Marshall was very easygoing, but fiercely independent. Well, he and France constantly clashed over agenda and execution of Nascar rules. Also, Marshall overloaded his ass with the dual Hornet deal, he and Herb Thomas. Hudson hired me to do Thomas engines. Marshall wanted, and got to try Indy. This pissed France off, so he kicked Marshall's ass out. "Barred forever." Marshall goes to USAC as the stock car ace for Hudson. Well, it didn't work out too good for him.

Herb Thomas and I ran Nascar 1951, '52, '53 and '54. Together we won two championships, and ran second the other two years. By 1954, Marshall's trying to get back into NASCAR without much luck. Our relationship got strained. If Marshall had any bad habits, one might have been professional jealousy. He got me started, he goes to the shit house, and I go to Broadway. In 1955 I'm running Chevy racing program, and number 76 on the Chevy small block engineering staff. He wants in at Chevy. For some reason Chevy turned him down. I hear about it and got the horsepower to make it happen. But he don't know it. He tries to "Lone Ranger" the Chevy deal, to run without factory support. Again, bad luck and maybe lack of planning so not much happens with his Chevy.

Then the bad shit comes. Turns out in 1959 France makes him a deal. If he sets a world closed course record (180 mph), he can collect ten grand prize, and get back in NASCAR. That's an unrealistic goal. The car he is supposed to do it with, the Zumar Special, is seven or eight miles an hour short with real bad aerodynamics. It wants to fly the nose. It was a beautiful car, but wrong. Hell, aerodynamics, automobiles, 1959? Who knew? He wanted help. I said, "The car's body is wrong. We would have to rebuild it." He says, "Can't do that…no money."

One Saturday morning he calls 'bout 7:00 am or so. Says, "Come to race track and help me." I say, "I can't help you. Get the hell out of the car and quit it." I call France at 8:30 am, chew his ass out, and ask him to go to track and tell Marshall the "deal's off" but okay his return to NASCAR. It don't happen. France tells me to "mind my own god-damned business." At 10:30 Florence Rati calls from race track crying. Marshall's dead. Yup, Son of a bitch got air borne. Marshall's seat and all came out. Adios one stock car pioneer.

They named a grandstand after him, and put him in a couple halls of fame. He was finally back in good standing with NASCAR. The day I helped carry Marshall his last foot horizontally, and then six foot down, I started to feel a smoldering resentment towards France that never went away until about two years before France checked out. This was during a visit France paid me at the shop, and it dawned on me; life was like a race. Skill and brains could set up a victory, but the ultimate challenge of the variables of life itself dictated the winner or the loser. I also learned it's very difficult to really know if you won or lost. Did the man who lived to be ninety and was sick the last twenty-five years of his life, or did the man who died at thirty-five, doing what he wanted to do win? What do you think? Really, as I see it, if a man lived to be 85, is that as much as 85 seconds in real-time in the history of mankind since we used to be apes? I also always wondered how cave men walked around the young ladies without showing a hard on?

HERB THOMAS

Herb Thomas, he was a piece of work. A poor boy who worked his ass off, very average in intelligence, but a natural born racer. His ass was tuned to the last ten thousandths of "push" or "loose" a car had. He had the two things you gotta have at the highest level: (A) sense of balance (B) desire to win. I liked Herb Thomas as a driver and as a human. But we were from two different worlds. Herb's wife Helen worked very hard helping him, and went with him every inch of his journey. Since their lives were such a hard struggle, money became all-important. Smokey the racer did an awful lot of work for a very little part of the money, and you know I never noticed it till ten years after our racing together ended.

Herb was never in the running for America's male sex symbol and his interviews after he won won't be copied. A favorite comment of his on the difficulty of winning that day was, "Shaw, warn't no problem. I didn't have any competition." Herb Thomas, I think, had then, and maybe still the highest percentage of winning of any NASCAR Grand National (or Winston Cup) driver for the first seven years he drove. But even so, the money was woefully short.

A PR guy's dream.

Herb was an unusual driver. Did not drink, did not chase women, and worked like a dog on the racecar. (And other than engines and body work half-assed knew what he was doing). When the Hudson deal wore out, end of '54, I really didn't give a damn whether I raced or not. I finally woke up that those first seven years of NASCAR were a Bill France benefit performance

JACK NANCE

Jack Nance. Well somehow, I don't remember how, I got involved with Jack Nance at Packard. He was president and chief operating officer. Jack didn't know his ass from a hole in the ground 'bout racing. He was an electrical appliance wizard, especially toasters from GE. He was gonna "save Packard from a fate worse than death." As part of this salvation, he hired me to win the '55 beach race with a Packard. Well,

Packards came with an automatic transmission only, and the rules said you gotta run it. Like a damn fool I took the job. Herb drove it and it was a disaster. I believe we broke some valve springs on the pace lap. I retired as a Packard racer after one outing.

Well, you'd think that was enough wouldn't you? Nope. I also built a modified Chrysler coupe with a big, heavy, Hemi engine. The engine had the steam. But the car would have to have had a steering wheel for each wheel, with Herb, Curtis Turner, Marshall and Fireball steering each wheel. I believe it was Cotton Owens who had the terrible honor to try and drive it. This car was built to built to prove that Fish carburetor made more power. Best, kindest way to put it. "It was a first class no handling shit box." It disappeared to it's owner, a rich-man backer of Fish carburetors named Kekorian, (or kinda like that). I believe Vegas and Hollywood were Kerk's next adventures.

OK, more about Fish carburetor. This was a very simple invention by a Yankee named Bob Fish. This gadget gave you your choice, power or mileage. But you couldn't have both at the same time. It only had three moving parts, and I used to say none of them worked. But on a race car it would make power. No two ways 'bout it. The modified I first raced had a Fish carb on it. Fish carburetor ended up being in a building 'bout a block from my shop. Both of us on west bank of the Halifax River with the bridge between us. The building is still there at the Southwest corner of the Seabreeze bridge.

The Packard, the Chrysler modified, had convinced me that my future is in anything but stock car racing. But Herb wanted to run a Buick. The chief engineer at Buick, a real nice guy named Kelly, calls me and says, "If you want to run a Buick, I'll give you car, parts and lots of money." I say, "I'll let you know," but really have no intentions of calling him back. Next page of this story, you guessed it, Kelly sent Buick and parts, but check I guess is "still in the mail." It hasn't got here yet. Well, we want to run the Buick first time at Langhorne in the spring of '55. I finish car and engine way late, Thursday night 'bout 4:00 am. Got one goofy helper, Junior Robbins. (Goofy cause he works so long and hard for no pay.) I got to try car out. I have a mental target. Cars got to turn 6,000 in "high." That's 150 mph by my calculations. That figure includes slippage.

So 'bout 4:00 am, with no headlights (but moon light is good) I decide to go to Highway 92. At the time, 92 was a very level and straight two lane to Deland. That is good, but it's also a brick road then, and very-very narrow. (I had my own Indy test track.) We get to place I'm gonna try car out. Jr. Robbins is with me. His job is to use a cigarette lighter and check rpm. He's on his knees (no seat) holding onto dash. But fate's fickle finger slides in, the roads foggy as hell in places. In the fog you can't see shit. Well, I decide to "Do it" anyway and poor Junior ain't got a vote. Junior just sat there, had to've been nervous runnin' through that fog. That son-of-a-bitch really ran, and in about a mile we hit the six grand.

So, I ease it back to shop, finish up, load up and head for Langhorne. We are leading with 10 laps to go, and get a big horse track fence spike in left rear tire. Herb pulls in and says, "Change it quick, we'll win 'er yet." Well, Langhorne's rough and fast. No we didn't win and Herb says he wants to run the Charlotte fairgrounds next Sunday. I say, "Bullshit, I'm gonna sell the car. Kelly's never gonna send the money, and I can't get him on the phone." (Always don't call him, he'll call me.) Herb's arguing more so I say, "We have to change rear axle's and front spindles, and steering arms, and I ain't got 'em and I ain't gonna buy 'em." I fly home. Thursday comes and the Buick still ain't got to Daytona. I know then, the Buick's going to Charlotte.

In the Charlotte race, Herb's leading, the track has wooden fence, and the rear axle breaks. Now the Buick's got broken right rear axle, the right rear wheel is gone with half the axle and the fence has big hole in it. In stopping of a three wheel Buick with no brakes, driver's leg gets broke. (I didn't go to the race, secret deal.) Right there is where Herb Thomas should have retired. But you know he didn't. I never saw my Buick again. It disappeared. If you know where it went, call or write me. Herb never could seem to remember what happened to the car (as of April 20th, 1998).

OK, Buick's disappeared, that's the end of that. Why didn't you ever pay me "nail head exhaust valve Kelly?" Would you have liked to worked your ass off for 'bout 400 hours for nothing?

In late '54, Ed Cole, boss of Chevy, had a plan to race his new car, and for what ever reason, wanted me to captain the effort. Bill France was wired in after Ed's first attempt to hire me. Ed wanted a "pretty boy" driver. Kinda a role model type. Well, Herb would have run last in that class. After the third go-round Cole and I agreed to run a one race deal at Darlington in 1955. France picked some one beside Herb to drive it. I don't remember who, but I said, "Bullshit, Herb's the driver." Remember he is healing up from a badly broken leg. (First time he'd done "sheet time.") Well, I decide to do a good job at Darlington, we should try car out. There is a race in late August in West Memphis, Arkansas. One and a half mile hi-bank dirt, a bad-bad track with 30 degrees plus. I wasn't too smart in that deal. Anyway, we go and in practice and qualifying I'm shocked. Fearless Herb, the one-handed driver who drives with one hand and picks his nose with the other "don't live there any more."

This is my first race experience at a race with Mauri Rose. And he says, "Smokey, I don't understand, this guy looks like a stroker not a charger." I say, "Mauri, I see what you see. Maybe he just decided to cool it and save the car," but I knew we were in big trouble. Lots of times when a driver experiences a serious "sheet time," he can't "do it" anymore. The other side of this is, it's like it never happened. Oh well, "Maybe." Sometimes sun shines on your ass so you can't do no wrong. At Darlington in 1955, we run a 500 mile race with a storybook ending, Herb wins. We finish out '55 season with the "Motoramic" blue and white Chevy number 92. The car was an optional model really built to sell cigarettes, yup cigarettes; "coffin nails" we called 'em. The car came with no backseat, had a plywood floor into the trunk. How 'bout that for a career switch for Mighty Mouse? From cigarette peddler to ferocious racer. We won some more in '55.

Now it's Beach Race time, new '56 car. My suspicions that Herb's not a happy driver are confirmed (at least as I see it). The windshield on the '56 Chevy was so sand blasted you could not see a thing. Herb's a "follower" now. We run 'bout fifth. As Herb's wife Helen snaps the big brown alleygator pocket book shut with the few dollars the car won I said, "Adios Herb. In my opinion you should quit. You go slow, and have seat gap. Take what you got and go back to fighting the boll weevils and raising coffin nail filler." You're right, he didn't agree. (I didn't expect he would) But right or wrong, by my code he was a candidate for serious sheet time or termination. I wasn't mad. Just convinced "it" was used up.

I was running the Chevy race program with Mauri Rose, so I offered Herb the race car and a new Chevy convertible race car, and three or four engines. Also, Ray Fox worked for me and he had about a belly full of me. I'm very hard to work for (a know-it-all son of a bitch), and I figured Ray wanted to go fly on his own. So I offered Ray to go with Herb, and have Chevy pay Ray and Herb a salary. So much a month to rent a shop in his hometown, Sanford, North Carolina. You know, pay his expenses. It was a good deal then, but a long way from today. Nobody could buy Lear jets on the deal.

How did they do? They actually they won the championship. But Kiekhaefer and France pulled a chicken-shit deal end of year, and added two races. Last race Herb's still leading for championship. A bad wreck and Herb ends up doing about five years sheet time. He ended up driving a tractor-trailer for a long time before going back to fighting his sworn enemies, the tobacco worm and the boll weevil. Oh, he tried to come back as a driver, but it didn't work.

He then tried being a car owner, even won a race with a free engine I built for him. Well, actually for 400 bucks he never paid me. Marvin Panch won West Memphis with that engine. Well, that did it. I got pissed and moved him into the "asshole" category. But in last ten years I've decided if I'd of had to go through what the poor guy did, I'd probably not got everything right either. What caused the big wreck? Ask Speedy Thompson, I wasn't there. (He can't answer you either, he don't live here any more.)

BOB FISH

Bob Fish was a book in himself, Inventor of the Fish carburetor. Had a good idea, but chose to operate in a mode that suggested the government, major oil companies and automotive manufacturers were out to destroy him and Fish carburetors because it gave too much mileage. A real nice person. In reality his carburetor was not for the US, but would have been great in the third world countries.

In the 1955 beach race, see if you can figure this one out: Fish has hired the granddaddy of all stock car mechanics, Red Vogt, to build the car and engine, and Fireball to drive it. If I remember, Ray Fox helped

That's Bob Fish in the middle.

Red Vogt on it. A real winning team. Well can you believe this? Ray Fox came to see me in June of '98. He tells me that he built the Buick engine in this historic episode of stock car racing. Stayed up all night to do it. (All that Red had to do with it was to shorten the damn push rods). That car sat on the pole, and led every lap. Nope, it had regular Rochester carb on it. (For a while I thought it was a Fish carb). Tim Flock runs second with a Chrysler 300, a Kiekaefer production. Well, there's a problem here. Apparently France has sold his soul to Chrysler, but the goddam Buick is so much faster Fireball just runs away with the race. OK, the after race, inspection takes three days to settle. They gotta disqualify the Buick so the Chrysler can win.

Finally, they (NASCAR) buy a Buick engine and compare piece by piece until they hit pay-dirt. Red shortened the Buick push rods 'bout a hundred thousandths. He figured this would preclude a valve float.

The engine had hydraulic valve lifters and rules said can't change to solids. When Red asked me 'bout shortening them, I believed it was unnecessary. "Don't do it, just zero lash lifters." What I'm getting at is shortening the push rods didn't really help one goddam bit, but Red did it anyhow. He does it here so nobody will know about it. Remember, I had a Packard. I had no teeth to bite anything. Guess who found short push rods? Fonty Flock, Tim's brother. Tim flock wins, Chrysler wins, yahoo!

OK, now the chief inspector on the Buick fiasco was a guy named Frank Thomas, from Allen equipment. He called a month ago, all shook up. He feels threatened now for saying the disqualification was ordered by France and wanted to know if I'd back him up. "Hell, yes Frank, but I can't prove why." You know, only three players left out of twenty are Ray, Frank and myself. And I'm illegal (hearsay).

Ray Fox got it up the ass again at Talladega at the first Winston Cup race. His car sat on pole and won the race. Somehow Joe Epton got scoring goofed up and Ray and driver Jim Vandiver, got aced out of the hero's ring. Ray said "tell it like it was." When I told him I did, and at one point I called him a prick he left. Think that pissed him off?

Life's funny. Three days ago Cliff Whaley, one of Marshall Teague's early employees, and also one of Bill France's employees in the late forties (Cliff has become an electrical contractor, and was Mayor of Holly Hill for a long time. Holly Hill is next door to Daytona.) I have a electrical problem and after he fixed it he asked 'bout this book. Guess who bought counterfeit tire rationing coupons from Bill France? Ray Fox, Cliff and I did. No, Cliff didn't go to Bill's funeral. Why? It's not fit to print. Don't worry Cliff, neither one of us has that far to slide, and you did say, "Say it like it was." I know I'll sell some books, hell Cliff ordered one, that makes 'bout 100. You know, I can't find one damn person that lived in the beginning that says one nice thing 'bout France. All the same, and all bad!

Well, might as well tell you I doubt I was loved very much by my competitors. They called me "Smokey the bear." Believe it or not, when I raced I was quiet. But when a problem developed, I got very nasty. As a matter of fact, once in awhile I got the shit kicked out of me for misjudging my adversaries. But during this same time, more importantly, the opposite sex was, as a rule, extremely hospitable. I think "Smokey the Bullshitter and writer" all came as a replacement for the lack of competition as a competitive racer. I always told it like it was, but avoided the media and the public. I was called a loner, a rebel, a…(all the rest was much worse), but you know, I liked it that way. I figured how a man felt about his adventures was the ultimate test of his reason for being. He is at top of his career as a stock car racer.

Paul Goldsmith

As I watched the motorcycle races on the beach in '54-'55, I noticed a Harley rider named Paul Goldsmith (actually the US Champion plate #1). I really liked his style. He worked on his motorcycle at Marshall Teague's race shop, and I met and talked with him there. When Herb and I got "divorced," Paul came by one day and I said, "You want to race stock cars?." He said actually, that's why he came by. I'd decided to get someone with no car racing experience for a driver. But to find someone with very quick reflexes who had an extra ordinary sense of balance. I wanted a lean, strong cat and somebody who didn't mind working. After Herb left I built a new car and entered it in a road race at the airport in Titusville (50 miles south of Daytona). First, I gave Paul the reflex test, the coiled snake in the candy can. Damned if he didn't grab it first shot! Herb, Fireball, Marshall or Curtis couldn't catch it even knowing what was coming, so next test is he rides me around Titusville sports car course. Man, that cat is hauling ass and doing it like he's just going down the street to get a pack of cigarettes.

I've got a brake test I've built. How fast can you get your foot off the throttle, onto the brake, and get cylinder pressure to 1,500 psi? Fireball's got the record but Paul's faster. So Paul and I went racing. He was every bit as good as I guessed plus he worked his ass off, and was very pleasant to race with. We won a few races with the Chevys. People are really noticing Paul, and his stock is going up fast. We sit on the pole Beach Race '57 on seven cylinders, a plug wire fell off with me driving, I can't find Paul in the race. He leads till close to end when a fuel injector nozzle plugs up with a few laps to go. Lots of smoke, burnt piston, no cigar.

In March '57, I quit Chevy and go to Ford. Paul comes with me, and we don't win too much, but we sure give it hell till we crash or blow. By now Curtis and I have completed Paul's training as a NASCAR racer. We taught him about drinking, partying and wild-wild women, and also how to fly. (He really did learn the "wild women" part fastest). I think rite now would be place to say Paul was most natural born racer and pilot I've ever seen.

Paul and I had a wild 1957. But the motor companies pulled the plug in June 1957, and party was over.

Goldy was a helluva good driver and a hard worker. (photo: Norman Poole)

We finished '57 out with the Fords, and I think I should mention that when I went with Ford in 1957, I actually worked for Ford through Pete Depaolo. Now Pete was a class act. One of my life's good experiences was knowing him. Ford paid me 'bout four times what GM did, plus free everything, including old airplane, clothes, even paid for "traveling female secretary." Pete's instructions to me were, "Do anything you want, as long as you're going fast and are using Ford parts and keep trying to go faster." Pete was really funny, he knew every saloon joke there was. He knew every big shot in surface transportation in North America and Europe. Pete was a race driver, and a damn good one. He won Indy once. I believe the first to average 100 mph for the 500 miles. Pete was as good as it gets as an after dinner speaker. He was a master of dialects.

I put super brakes on a '57 Ford and took it to Martinsville. We drove all night to get to the track by 8:00 am, then worked and tested till 5:00 pm By five we are pooped and the brakes aren't good enough. We go back to our rooms at the Perriwinkle Motel. I tell my helper Junior, "Clean up and we'll go to eat." The telephone service was so slow that I go across to the shopping center to call back to the hotel to get Junior out of the room for supper. Even calling from outside didn't work. The damn switchboard in town was so slow that I jerked the phone and cord out of the pay phone. I then see a guy trying to make a call with the phone and the cord hanging nearly to the ground.

Where's Junior? We were supposed to eat at seven. I decide to go to his room to get him. The room is not locked. As I open the door a wave of water covers my boots. I look in the bathroom and there in the tub is Junior. Apparently he pooped in his bloomers as there is a giant turd in there with him. I shake him. Oh shit! He is dead. I gotta call the police and what am I gonna tell his wife and two boys?

Just as I decide that he is for sure dead, I notice the turd is moving away from his nose. The turd then stops and slowly comes back. He's not dead! He's breathing! I pull the tub plug and fish the feces out and into the toilet. In about five minutes Junior comes to.

In the meantime, the hotel owner has witnessed my rescue of my nearly drowned helper and is raising hell about who is gonna pay for repair to the walls and who's gonna buy new carpet. Right in here I decide this is super funny; the relief that Junior ain't dead and the guy with the busted phone cord. While I laugh, the motel owner continues to give me a hard time about the damage, so I decide that his plumbing may not be up to code. I call Dewey, my vice president of sanitation back at the shop in Daytona and put on like I am talking to my lawyer. I give him instructions to sue the motel before I call another friend of mine and act like I am talking to a Detroit lawyer who needs to sue as well. This got a damage release, but the damage bill might have been worth the good laugh and new floating turd method of determining if someone is alive I got from the deal.

Well, Paul and Curtis Turner used up the Fords in the '57 Darlington race. It was a bad day at Black Rock. Bobby Meyers (Chocolate Meyers' daddy), got into a hell of a wreck with Fonty Flock which cost him his life and wrecked Goldsmith. Then Curtis crashed. I was out of cars, so Goldy goes to drive for Holman and Moody for a while. Goldy and I teamed up again for the last Beach Race (on the beach) with a '58 Pontiac. With Paul's driving skills, along with a good "horse" and a little luck, victory was "our'en."

I've really got Indy fever now, even though we won the race and we split the money, I doubt I made over two bucks an hour. I found a three or four year old Kurtis Offy roadster for five grand, all apart. The owner was a young heir to the Texaco fortune and got killed on his estate driveway. Car wreck, big driveway, oak tree won, '55 Chevy and driver lost. I bought car from his grandmother. All I had was $4,500, she said "pay other $500 May 1."

Well, I don't know which was the biggest happening, picking out the Indy car pieces, or the adventure with the two ladies from Bell telephone, or maybe the fact that we survived the snow and icy roads from Detroit to Chicago to Atlanta.

Entry fee, paint, and a few parts eat up 'bout $1,800 bucks. April 30, off to Indy. "Here we come."

We start the rookie test. Just before Paul passes it everything goes to shit. Indy press says "neither driver or mechanic qualify to take the test. Zero past experience in AAA open wheel racing." Now, Don O'Reilly, editor of Speed Age, leads a split in the press, hollering, "Let 'em go!" Well, officials say, "OK, you'll never make it anyhow."

110 Entries, 33 will race and the rest will watch. 13 days after Paul first sets his ass in any Indy car, we're qualified 'bout middle of the field. We got so much ink in those two weeks it must have convinced the female race fans that givin' us a "little lovin'" it would help us go fast. Don't misconstrue this as a complaint.

By the time the race was over and I was five miles south of Indy, my poor worn out li'l peter needed a string tied to it to find it. Goldy? I think he got a black belt rating out of the deal also. But probably best thing is to ask him about it, he's still going good. Well, we crashed in first lap, actually leading the race. But Paul's stock was to the moon.

Firestone used an Indy test driver year round. Not a bad paying job. Ray Nichels had the contract to test Firestone tires. He wanted Paul, and Paul wanted what everybody does – fame and fortune. I think that deal changed Paul's life. Once he started testing, Paul's luck and race winning went to hell. He became "Harvey Wall-banger." But it's possible one of the greatest drivers there ever was never got his due. I was pissed for a few years, but then decided that was part of this game. We are still friends, and he has molded himself a very comfortable life style. For you who would like to see him, he owns and operates the airport in Griffen, Indiana. Only racing he does now is with a horse pulling a wagon. It's really too bad the racing public don't know him better, but when he quit racing he disappeared, and the press has ignored him. He should be in every of the Stock Car Hall of Fame.

Indy 1959 I had the car to win the race, and damn near did with Duane Carter.

Curtis Turner

Curtis Turner was a simple down to earth true Southerner. A big, good-looking, hard drinking, pussy-hound, he didn't give a shit 'bout nothing really 'cept "let's start a bran new party." Curtis Turner could flat fucking drive a racecar. There is no other way to put it. He was a mechanic's dream. As long as the car had horsepower, he'd figure out a way to get it around a racetrack. You could ask him how it handled, and the answer was always the same to me. "Perfect, don't touch a thing," when really it was terrible, and he was backing it through the turns. Curtis should have been a dirt sprint car driver. His best buddy was Joe Weatherly, an ex motorcycle champion and a goddam good stock car driver. Those two were one constant party. The popularity of both was very instrumental in building the NASCAR stock car fan base.

First race I seen Turner drive was the beach modified race 'bout 1949. He drove in dress shoes (wing tips), and nothing else but a pair of farmer's overalls and a helmet. Weatherly always wore black and white 'zoot suiter' saddle shoes. Watching Turner broad sliding that Ford modified into the North turn at the beach was a treat in skill and balls. Curtis showed me how to jam on the brakes and slide the back end around to turn around on a two lane road when running 60 miles an hour. He made it look so simple and easy, but every time I tried it, I crashed.

Curtis got serious and he and Bruton Smith decided to build the Charlotte racetrack. From there on, Curtis's life was one big mess of lawsuits, lack of operation money, and NASCAR suspensions. In short, nothing but trouble. He'd sign anything for a 90-day option on timber. He was a damn good timber man. I found a lot of high dollar wood in Ecuador, like rosewood, teak, etc. Took Curtis there to look at it and to negotiate a deal to buy it.

Curtis was a damn good pilot, but very careless, and with some dangerous flying habits. He had a twin-engine plane we were going to use to go to Rockingham from Charlotte. I was at the plane first and found one fuel tank missing the tank cap. It's raining, so I'm going to drain tank. He shows up half-drunk and says, "The water goes to the bottom, you've drained enough, let's go." Well, the weather is very bad and I'm flying cause he don't feel good (hung over). I start down runway behind an Eastern jet and as I become airborne I notice all the vacuum instruments are out. The artificial horizon, turn and bank, rate of climb, etc. I pull throttles back, but he rams 'em back in and says, "They will start working in a couple minutes." I say, "You fly it. I don't know how without instruments." (I'm IFR.) He takes over and in a couple minutes

Time for a "bran' new party!" (photo: Don Hunter)

everything is working.

Another time he has a new plane (twin engine), we are in Florence, South Carolina, both drinking, looking for two certain women. We find 'em in bed with a couple other race drivers, so Curtis wants to go back to Charlotte and start a brand new party at his house on Freedom Drive. Well, the weather is real bad. It's raining like hell with thunder storms all around. We get the two women dressed and add Ray Fox (somehow he shows up needing a ride to Charlotte). We got one passenger too many. Get to Florence airport and it's dark now. The airport is closed to commercial flying. No runway lights. Turner now is so drunk he slides off the front of the wing twice trying to get into the plane, so he decides I fly.

Well, I've never seen one of these things before, and I'm not too sober. But I figure I got better chance than him to make it. So off we go on a 45 degree path across ditches, runways, taxi strips. I got 'er in the air, but I can't find landing gear raiser upper. By time I find it, I notice I'm 'bout 100 feet from going through the roof of the motel that "Li'l Joe" is staying at. Sure, I made it. But I collected quite a few pine needles, branches, etc. How I got to Charlotte I don't know. It was really a rough trip, thunderstorms all the way. I find the airport and get clearance in just about the time Turner comes to (he's been passed out). All of a sudden I see power lines. The tower is hollering, "Pull up, pull up"! I ask Turner "over or under?" He says "under." No way in hell I could have got over that quick enough. Well, I heard and felt some unusual thing while going under that power line. There were big trees all around.

We land and when I get to hanger, the FAA says, "Come to the tower to talk." Well, I don't have a valid instrument ticket, so Turner is the pilot now. I say, "Why they want to talk?" Inspector says, "Cause you plowed through the trees." I say, "No way, not even close." Then I see the plane. Branches and leaves in every crack and hanging out of the wheel wells. (Yeah, does look kinda bad.) Good thing they were Smokey/Curtis fans.

Between the flight and Curtis doing two 180 degree turns at 60 miles an hour on the way to the motel, the girls are so scared and shook up sex is the furthest thing from their minds. Later on Curtis gets another new plane (an Aero Commander) pretty big one this time. I'm not with him, (I'm telling you what he tole me). Sunday morning 10:00 am, Curtis and Chevy dealer from Greenville, South Carolina are en route to Charlotte and decide to land on the street in front of Chevy dealership to pick up a case of whiskey. They land and get the whiskey. Curtis on take off has to go under a traffic lite, then turns the plane 90 degrees on it's side to get up through power lines and trees. Well, Curtis knows he's got big trouble when they land, so he goes to an isolated dirt strip. No-good, the FAA meets him there and adios license. At the trial it turns out an elderly lady and a deputy sheriff were waiting for the light to turn. They are both now FAA witnesses. When deputy was asked what he saw he said, "I'm waiting for light to turn, and here comes this goddam airplane with it's belly on the road, then turns sideways, up through trees, power lines." Well Turner has a new wife, Bunny so he gets her to get a private pilot's license and uses her for pilot. He rides, as so-called "co-pilot" Hardly slowed him up.

Curtis wanted to try Indy. I had built a car year before that I took to Indy as a second car that in the turns all four wheels leaned into the turns, kinda like two motorcycles hooked together. Poor Curtis, it's bad enough to try and learn Indy in two weeks, plus a wild new romance (no sleep, he fell in love second day we got to Indy). And to tell the truth, that car would have never been a contender for the Nobel Prize in engineering (even though I was it's daddy.)

We pushed too hard, and two days before qualifying in turn three Curtis and the Python tried to knock down the wall. We called the car "The Python." Roger Ward named it. He said it looked like a python that had swallowed a piano. (You know, it kinda did). Well, poor ol' python is junk. I'm out of money, so ends Turner's Indy career. "Let's start a bran new party." He's got an airplane. 'Bout a week later I noticed we're in Vegas. I'd better go home. Well, we raced together every once in awhile till about 1968.

Sometime later he was in bad shape financially (I'm trying to help). His best way to make a living was wholesale timber tracts. I'm waiting for him at Miami airport to go to Quito, Ecuador to sign big timber deal. I see a newspaper, lower right front-page "stock car racing star dies in airplane crash." Yup, it was Curtis. Well, I had to go to Ecuador to explain to timber people, because for them to get to Quito was a real chore ('bout a week's journey). So I didn't get to say "see ya later ace," and walk him on down. What really pissed me off was France was a pallbearer. With the suspensions and all he put on Turner, suddenly he loves Curtis. What a phony deal. But we had a deal 'bout funerals, "Ill go to yours, but only if you come to mine."

What happened? Hell, I have no idea. Plane crashed, don't know why. For years a couple of young men who told me they were his sons bugged me. They think he's still alive and living in South America. Maybe he and Elvis are hanging out together down there someplace. If so Curtis, and you read this, give me a call....let's have one last party before I run out of time.

There was only one of him. He was a "real racer." He lived and drove like there would be no tomorrow. For you race fans that never seen him drive, I doubt you can envision the circus he put on. I called it Southern style, belly to the ground, ears and tail straight back. He'd tell me, "If I can get the front end through, the rear end will follow won't it?" Well, most of the time yes, but not always. NASCAR's 50th anniversary came and went. Near as I can see, he never existed either.

He wrote a book "Timber on the Moon." Hell, he tried to rent the rockets to put up satellites in the sixties and started "Comstat." (Dumb hillbilly?) We enjoyed each other. No matter how outrageous my life was, his was just a cunt hair wilder. I really missed Curtis – he stayed heavy on my mind for ten years. Strange, it seems like at Charlotte and NASCAR there never was a racer named Curtis Turner. I consider that chicken shit. There is a lot more 'bout Curtis in the Indy section.

Fireball Roberts

When Fireball Roberts hears Paul is gone to Nichols, he comes by and asks to drive a '59 Pontiac I'm building for Knudsen. Well, even though we are kinda neighbors, and I consider him one of the four NASCAR driving aces, I'm hesitant to hook up with him. I have a total one paid helper and a couple of goofy volunteers (and I say that reverently, without 'em I could not of done one third of what I did). I also know Fireball has two allergies, asthma and work, and he don't like to tow the racecar. I don't enjoy towing either. (We are still flat towing the racer with the "yellow peril" (tow bar and steering cables). Fireball had the skill and the balls, and he was the smartest of the drivers. I think he was the first full time race driver. Everyone else had a "day job." He rated all his competitors, noted their shortcomings, considered all other racecars as to speed and durability and spent a lot of time developing pit strategy. He didn't care too much for my method of running a maximum or minimum lap time, don't get lapped, and start racing last one hundred miles. His plan was simple: Sit on the pole, and lead every lap.

I did decide to race with Fireball. We raced together damn near four years with Pontiacs, '59, '60, '61 and part of '62. If Fireball would have had a tire that could have stood up under the punishment he put on them, his record would be something that would have never been equaled. We won the first race at Atlanta. Linda Vaughn was the virgin beauty queen. That was her first exposure to racing. Fireball figured it was his duty to introduce her properly to the sport. I think it fair to say he did a very good job. She is still very much involved in racing

Fireball and the 1962 Pontiac that won everything at Daytona.

forty years later...forty years?

Now "Balls" wasn't much help on the race car "hands on," but he knew quite a bit about the total race car mechanically, so he could give me clues on how to make the car handle. Unfortunately for both of us, I didn't learn enough, so we ended up in every race running either a Goodyear or Firestone tire test.

In those days you could hear the tires blow. The deal was, the guy leading was running the tire test. How in the hell he could have set there for nearly four hours waiting for that goddamned "boom," knowing it was gonna hurt, is hard to understand. There was a hillbilly song called "Hello Walls," that was Fireball's official song. If there was a live band in a bar or nite club, soon as he walked in, the music stopped, and they switched to "Hello Walls."

Fireball did not get his nickname from racing. He went to University of Florida for a couple years, and got his nickname as a baseball pitcher. Around the track he was known simply as "Balls." Back then we spent about twice as much time at 500 mile race as they do now. Well, then they made us leave race track at 5:00 pm. For those of us who didn't bring the engine back to the motel to work on it, we were duty bound to get drunk and entertain the ladies, (the pioneer women race fans). You lady race fans today owe a little gratitude to those lady race fans who stayed up to 5:00 am partying with us, and having to go home, or to work with a terrible hangover and face their fathers, husbands and boyfriends. Every night but Saturday night was party night.

Fireball served a very important function in this process. Soon as he got couple of drinks in him, he'd get very friendly and invite the whole motel to his room. Yup, back then 90 percent of us stayed in same place. What happened next was a voluntary process that was referred to as, "Let's get naked and get in a pile." (It's a damn good thing AIDS hadn't been invented yet). We never got credit for it, but Weatherly, Turner, Fireball, Goldsmith and myself, with about five other drivers invented lady race car fans. Well, I credit quite a bit of the development of these social customs to Fireball. As the process became refined it wasn't unusual to get the motel manager and his wife involved in the festivities. I can remember our first year at Atlanta. The manager's wife called the police. Next race she had a much more benevolent attitude.

In 1962 Fireball won everything there was at the February 500 Beach Race including the beauty queen. I didn't witness the beauty queen part of it, so that may or may not be fact. In my opinion the tire wars had finally took their toll. (Remember, this is just my opinion.) So, when the party is over I say, "Fireball, it's time for our divorce. I don't expect you to agree with me, but I think it's time you pursued another profession." As you guessed, he said, "Bullshit!" So, I gave him and Banjo the Pontiac cars and engines and parts as well as got Pontiac to pay them a few bucks, and off they went. They came back 4th of July with the car. I helped them a little and Fireball won that race also.

Well, we remained half-assed friends, but he did resent my opinion.

About a year-and-a-half later, May 1964, I'm at Indy trying to get the capsule car qualified with Bobby Johns. A guard says, "You got a visitor." It was Fireball and his girlfriend, my sister-in-law-to- be, Judy Judge. What a surprise! Well, reason for visit is, "You were right Smoke, I do have a problem going fast." He is driving for Ford Motor Company, and has, number one, gotten Ford to let him out of contract at finish of Charlotte race and, number two, he is coming back from Chicago with a contract to work for a beer company (Falstaff) as a public relations man and, number three, is gonna marry Judy, my wife's sister. Four days later, Sunday, last qualifying day at Indy, and Charlotte 600 race day. We hit the wall in turn one trying to qualify, Bobby Johns driving, 'bout the same time Fireball crashed and burns at Charlotte. He holds on for a while in the hospital burn unit, but 'bout a month later comes the sad deal at the local "boot hill."

Shit happens. One race too many. Steel gas tanks got him. No guard in filler cap area.

BOBBY JOHNS

Bobby Johns – he and I just run couple races together, one at Daytona and one at Indy.

Bobby lived in Miami. His dad was a rough and tough ex-midget racer, Shorty Johns. Bobby was a little guy who had plenty of talent. Probably 'bout a nine. No not inches, nine on a scale of one to ten as a racer. Came very close to making "Broadway," but was a little short in the luck department. Bobby was pretty damn good mechanic as well as a good driver. Nice personality, but that little "something" was missing. He damn near won Daytona February '61 in my car. Had race won towing Junior Johnson, when Goddam rear window popped out and spun him right at the end. No fault of his.

At Indy, the goddam Rathmans, Dick and Jim, spooked him with criticism of driver position. This is the car we called "the capsule car." Driver sat outside of car, center left side. The car's in Indy Hall of Fame. See for yourself. Driver's position does look spooky don't it? I thought after '64 Indy, Bobby was on his way to the big time. In '65 Colin Chapman gave Bobby team car with Jim Clark.

Clark wins, but Bobby runs seventh, seven laps down. That didn't help Bobby at all.

There is a very dangerous deal in racing. I call it the "Black Hole." It's there all the time, every race, at every place in the world. You have to be extremely careful not to get too close to it. It has a tremendous vacuum, and can suck you into it, and you disappear forever. All racers, drivers, mechanics and owners are rated by the public and by sponsors, and by your fellow racers. Sometimes a racer is unfairly pushed into the black hole. Also, if your luck is running bad, and your line of bullshit is not too good, or if your desire to win gets a little wobbly, in the black hole you go.

Bobby Johns and Fireball.

Chances of crawling back out some day are slim to none. I think the black hole got Bobby.

A.J. FOYT

A.J.Foyt has been in and out of my life since May 5, 1958. He and Paul Goldsmith and I were all Indy rookies. I met him at around midnight first week of May, 1958 in Gasoline Alley. I was working late in garage area at Indy. He drove for Dean Van Lines and Clint Brawner was his chief mechanic. They too had to work late. He came by my garage and introduced himself, and announced, "This place (Indy) was nothing! He would sit on the pole." Well, I looked him over, 'bout six foot tall, good looking, brush hair cut, built like a brick shit house, shiny teeth, gum chewing, cocky son-of-a-bitch. In my world, I don't like braggarts. I like quiet cats who don't run their mouth and just "do it." He's got on his shiny white driver's coveralls, and driving shoes (loafers) at midnite. So I put him down as a bull-shitter, and continue working. Well, what the hell? Weren't all Texans back then bragging bull-shitters?

Next day Mr. "Put 'er on the pole" runs into a little problem, and the wall changes the look of his car. I notice this as wrecker brings his car back. I think, "Mr. Brawner (A.J.'s mechanic) will work late tonight"

Back in them days, believe it or not, very few had a second car. Mr. "Put 'er on the pole" comes by at midnight with a big band aid on his head from the wall around "this ain't nothing place." He explains it wasn't his fault. Well shit, what can I say? I didn't see it happen. I think A.J. and the wrecker driver met each other one more time in practice, and once in the race. The pole? No, not by a long way.

If you ask me now what an Indy car mechanic looked like in 1958, I'd show you Clint Brawner or Jean Marcenac (Novi chief mechanic). Clint was a racer, period, and a damn good one. He's gone now, and I think the time he spent racing with A.J. shortened his life span. A.J. Foyt, I think, was greatest race driver there ever has been in U.S. racing history so far. Yeah, I know you think he's an asshole, and are shocked by my #1 rating of him, but 90 percent of you never seen him drive. You rate him by his last ten years of driving, and current shitty social behavior from banging Lyendyke on the head to his tantrums when someone crosses him and his unusual (and ineffective) method of adjusting $7,000 computers when they make a mistake. All this aside, A.J. Foyt could beat your ass in anything that had a motor and wheels. In midgets, sprinters, Indy cars, stock cars and road racers. I don't think when he was still the greatest from '58 till the mid seventies, he ever had a good handling car. He was on bias ply tires, and would find some way to manhandle the goddam thing. It wasn't nothin' for him to whitewall the sidewall of the right rear tire qualifying at Indy.

John Laux and A.J. Foyt (photo: courtesy of John Laux)

Before you decide I had a love affair with Foyt, I will tell you this: he was the biggest pain in the ass I ever raced with, period. But I have to give the devil his due. It was sad to me to see him destroy his image when he continued to cram his fat ass into the cockpit, then look like a shadow of what he had been. But you can't compare the action of person that lived and did the things of a super racer with a normal human being. To start off with, you have to be nuts to expose yourself to serious injury or a crippling accident, or death 'bout 40 times a year for 30 years or more.

I think the biggest problem about any mechanic had working with A.J. was the fact he was a pretty damn good mechanic himself, and that gave him enough knowledge to be a genuine pain in the ass trying to get the car dialed in. If you had 60 springs and 20 sway bars and 50 shocks, you'd try 'em all in various combinations and usually end up in the race how you came into the track. He liked a car he could manhandle. Actually, no one in the world could drive his car. In his heyday years at Indy, he'd kill himself 30-40 times every race. He wrote a book long time ago and he gave a few sentences to me. What did he say? He said, "I was a big cheater." If I was, damn if that wasn't the pot calling the kettle black. If a book was written about cheating, and a prize was given for whoever did the most, I believe the money would be in A.J.'s pocket. But I need to expand on that. All his principle competitors cheated, so defensive cheating sometimes is unavoidable. He has raced the longest, in a more diversified way than any racer I know.

There was a time when I'd fight for him, work around the clock for nothing, loan him engines. Then I noticed if I wasn't helping him, I didn't exist. In racing we have a phrase for that. "A one way son-of-a-bitch, with hen-house ways." I lost my hearing over a year ago. I've seen him three or four times. He hasn't said a word yet. (You're thinking, "How would I know if he did." Nope, I'd of known.) The fourth time he spoke to me. Course he's helped me a few times. In '69 I wanted a fuel injector casting he had. He loaned it to me. Herb Porter owned part of it, and objected a little too much. A.J. smacked him one time and Herb fell hard enough to break his hip.

A.J.'s temper is like a land mine. You step on it and in one second it explodes. He can't control it.

One time an old-old, skinny guard at the old garage gates (at Indy), a really nice man, stopped A.J. from riding a bicycle into garage area. (Clarence Cagel, boss of the track outlawed bikes in garage area.) He put his hand out and said, "Mr. Foyt, please don't do that." Mistake he made was to hold A.J.'s arm. The temper went off. I grabbed A.J.'s arm as he aimed for the old guard. He picked my ass up off the ground with that one arm. Man that was a strong cat.

Yet I've also heard of quite a few people he has gone way out of his way to help financially and otherwise. And doing it in a secretive way, almost like he was ashamed of it. Go figure!

One time we went to Atlanta to run a NASCAR race (stock car). The car I had probably had 50 horsepower that nobody else had, but it was like most of my early cars, a terrible handling car. As a matter of fact all of his bragging 'bout how fast he was gonna go got him nicknamed "Cassius Foyt." Well, we did five days of the spring-shock and sway-bar boogie, and qualified lousy. The track had a big bump in number one turn. He wouldn't lift where I asked him to. So with all the power and speed he'd hit the bump…all four wheels would fly off the ground, then he'd look like a monkey trying to fuck a football, trying to herd it up again. Saturday morning we have to scuff tires in. I ask him if anybody ever took race car home before race that he was supposed to drive. He said, "No, and if anybody ever did he'd whip his ass." I said, "We may find out about that soon." I said, "If you drive that thing into corner like you been doing all week, I'll load 'er up and head for Daytona." Well, scuffing tires he did it right and his lap time was one and a half a mile per hour faster than the pole. 250 miles into race he had lapped the field. No, we didn't win. The clutch wasn't up to job and gave up (my fault).

I was at Indy 1998 six days qualifying. This is exactly forty years since we both started there. Foyt is still there, now as a car owner. How's he doing? The pole! And third fastest, and favorite to win. Ain't too shabby is it? P.S. Almost did win too, but the racer ran out of gas. (Foyt killed his computer. Serves it rite.) But who is remotely qualified to coach a driver and manage a race team at Indy as well as A.J.? Nobody!

For you who never seen him drive in his prime, you missed the best part of it. It's kinda like those who never heard the Novi when one of the "hot dogs" of the time got after the throttle. You missed a hell of a thrill. It wouldn't surprise me if after A.J. reads this he smacks me in the snoot next time he sees me. But when that old lion roars, with his 300 pounds, and poor ol' tore up feet, not too many gonna take off for the hills any more. I'm glad I had the opportunity to know and race with A.J. I'm just sad he didn't mellow with age and realize he's still only got one head, two arms and two legs like the rest of us. There is an awful lot more to A.J., but I'm gonna quit. My problem is there was a lot more good stuff 'bout him, but all I can remember is the bad shit. Wonder why? (There is some stuff he done that if known would disappoint a lot of A.J.'s fans.)

The Allisons

I met the Allisons, Bobby and Donnie 'bout 1966. They were out of Miami then, skinny little snot-nose kids with no money and a yellow Chevelle, at Daytona. Probably got the paint for nothing from state road department. I called it road stripe yeller. There was 'bout six or more Allisons with 'em; Dad, brothers, uncles, cousins, wives, and two or three babies. Really nice, polite kids that asked good questions. I sure didn't take 'em seriously then. No power steering yet. Back then steering a Grand National car was just not for skinny little farts. Look at them now. Hard to believe they were once 'bout under 140 pounds ain't it?

Well, them cats turned out to be racers, 100 proof racers. They did not know what the words "can't do it" meant. For whatever reason, money I guess, they (including Red Farmer) moved to the unlikely location of Hueytown, Alabama. They went up there with Saturday night local yokel shit boxes. Shortly, they owned the short tracks in the area. Local hell, that's all there was. Talladega wasn't invented yet. They made enough money to keep trying the Grand National from time to time. Finally Bobby wins his first race in New Hampshire, or Maine, with a junk engine a Chevy dealer gave him (a warranty failure).

By 1960, the Allison cats were getting a good reputation, and were driving fairly good cars and doing damn good. Bobby's impatient. He wants it all now. So he keeps moving around, looking for the car and team he can do it with. Donnie gets with Banjo, and they are a pretty good team.

Bobby gets hooked up with DiGard. Some pretty damn good mechanics, like Robert Yates, Gary Nelson and Mario Rossi. Now all of them are pure hell and have to be reckoned with. (We can only guess at Mario's disappearance.)

By 1969 both are as good as it gets. Most of you know how good Bobby was, but really, Donnie was 'bout as good. But he seriously busted his ass at Charlotte, and I guess it upset his super sense of balance, and he then had to struggle as opposed to driving with one hand and pickin his nose with the other like when he started. (Seat gap strikes again). Someplace in here Bobby drove for me. I don't remember where. But I do remember it was one of my "no-handling" models. And on top of that, engine blew before race got a good start.

Back then I couldn't relate too well to Bobby, but Donnie and I got along great. Matter of fact he tested my '70 Ford at Daytona, and I think at Atlanta. This was a car I got from Holman and Moody. A stock body three inches higher than any of their Fords. This was a typical John Holman deal. Ol' John was a real carney: "Don't ever give a sucker an even break." Funny thing is, partner Ralph Moody was such an opposite. You could take his word to the bank. Well, 'bout now we got a whole new deal. "The Alabama gang" Bobby, Donnie, Red Farmer (a new-comer), Neil Bonnett, and suddenly "Hueytown, Alabama" are racing buzz-words nation wide. Donnie and Neil Bonnett are badly wounded. Bobby is NASCAR champ. Red Farmer I guess kinda likes being a big frog in a small pond. He don't push too hard for the "big time."

Donnie backed down to Busch cars. It's really over for him. I'm pissing him off trying to get him to quit. I notice Bobby is starting to struggle. I suggest he throw in the towel. Matter of fact ESPN flew me up to Talladega for a day to interview Bobby and a couple other drivers. I even asked Bobby to consider quitting on the show. (They cut that part out). Well, three days later he put parts of his car in the grandstand. Didn't hurt him too bad. He has his own car now, a Buick with Miller (a horse piss manufacturer) as a sponsor. Finally, he is making some real money.

Well, by now Donnie's quit, Bobbie's son Davey is driving Saturday night specials and doing pretty good. Davey's got Bobby's backing, and teamed up with a new up and coming engine builder from the "boonies" in Wisconsin, Carl Wegner, and they are plumb tough. Davey gets a shot at Yates #28 Ford. The rest is history. I never really got to know Davey real well. But I'd of had to be blind not to see this kid was going to the moon. Funny, it seemed like in a year or so Davey went from a kid standing on the front seat of Bobby's pickup, holding the steering wheel and hollering "Yeadon! Yeadon!' to a Winston Cup star running second to his dad at Daytona.

Well, I talk to Bobby 'bout quitting some more. He gives me the standard bullshit. "I'm having so much fun." That reminded me of Richard Petty at Atlanta. Hotter than a son-of-a-bitch and Richard's "over center" and struggling. I say, "Quit. Before you bust your ass, you're starting a whole new career being Tail End Charlie." He says, "I'm still really enjoying it." Three hours later they pull him out of the car, he is lying on the ground passed out. They are giving him oxygen. A TV reporter is going nuts describing this terrible deal, and asked me what I think. All I can think of is: You dumb son-of-a-bitch, why are you concerned – can't you tell when a man's really having a good time?

In 'bout here Bobbie's son Clifford, driving a Busch car, nailed the wall at Michigan. Bad-bad ending, Clifford dies. Pocono time, car ain't rite. Maybe a Bobby error in judgment. He's got a tire going down, car spins. Bad-bad deal. Bobby is more dead than alive for best part of a year. Finally he gets back with us half-assed (serious head injury).

That whole Allison clan would be classified under a simple Southern saying, 'They're good people." Simple, religious, hard working, close family, from grandparents to grandkids, all racers, Male and female. Well, that family of Bobby's paid a hell of a price for the thirty years as world class racers. Bobby's sons, Clifford and Davey are gone. Clifford directly, Davey indirectly. Bobby's still wounded from the Pocono deal. His marriage almost came unglued. He

Me and Bobby Allison.

lost his home, his race team and his health. Yet through it all, I never heard him complain or moan. He was as good as it gets as a driver and he could drive the shit out of an Indy car. So could Donnie. One time Donnie drove one of A.J.'s Coyotes at Indy. Man, that was the most no handling son-of-a-bitch known to man. Should have been called "Tasmanian devil." That thing scared Donnie so bad, if he'd of had a trailer ball bolted to the seat, and he sat on it, he wouldn't have needed a seat belt. Yup, he finished the race, and his Indy driver career. Finished 4th. Not too shabby was it, for a no handling shit-box? How do know? I was his crew chief.

Bobby's first Indy car trial was at Ontario, California. In thirty minutes he is running faster than Mark Donahue. He qualifies real good, and he's leading, or hangin' right there near the front. But the engine kept blowing. They were running turbo Offies and the "rich kids," Travers and Coons, were Roger Penske's engine men. Yup, Roger was smart enough to figure Bobby could handle an Indy car. But you know, Bobby never got to like an Indy car. Why? I don't know. Ask him next time you see him. He told me he thought Roger's mechanics didn't like him and were trying to kill him. I knew Penske's car chief, Jim McGee, and I know that isn't true. But when Bobby got an idea in his head you had as much chance to change it as pissing into a 100 mile an hour wind.

Last Indy car race for him was at Pocono, I believe. He sat on the pole and was leading the race when the engine blew. He drove in behind pit wall and started undressing as he got out of the car. He reached the garage in his underwear. The uniform went in trash can, he put on his clothes, went to the airport and never sat his ass in Indy car again. Bobby was one of about a dozen drivers who learned to fly and owned aircraft to get around to all the races.

Bobby was like Schrader, he'd race anything, anytime, five times a week, 50 weeks a year. Near as I can tell his only real leisure in life left is flying. (He's got an old Aero Star he's put a pair of Allison turbines on that, I call it "the diesel.") And fishing, put him in a fishing contest, and whatever the top prize is, he'll get it. He should have a fishing show on TV. When he healed up enough from the bad crash to get his pilot's license back, I believe that's the high spot of his life since the big crash. Can he still fly good? Damn sure can! I flew with him in his diesel April 1998 and he does just fine.

I'll tell you what Bobby has got. He's got several million race fans who think he was and still is, the greatest racer NASCAR ever had. I doubt you can live off that, but maybe. Donnie is still Donnie. Course he don't weigh no 140 no more. (Man he is getting to be a fat ass). If you see him walking from behind, you know by his limpy way of walking, either a race car or a 15 foot alleygator ate on him. Yup, Donnie's still a racer and always will be. It's all he's ever done. When I look at the pair of them together now, and think of all they done for so many years, and know they won't get a dime of pension or retirement money, it really pisses me off. You know with all the money that's flying around in racing rite now, there is still in 1998, no plan to take care of old or wounded racers or their families. As I think about the need for improvement on this big oversight, I hear a very low voice saying, "Load the wagon. The mule is blind," and I get caught up in the thought. Goddamned racers really must be stupid to continue without a sound.

Bobby was pretty good chassis man. He's the cat who got us to switch to front steer, spent lots of money to make forgings of the spindles. Well, now they are gonna name a grandstand at Phoenix after Bobby. Big fuckin' deal. If he goes up to it cold, they'll charge him ninety-five bucks just like any other cowboy there. Now in '98, Visa card's building a TV commercial about the Donnie-Bobby-Cale Yarborough fight in turn three at the beach. Maybe that will keep 'em off of food stamps. Well, Smokey, what did you do about it in last fifty years? OK, You're right, nothing. Why? I didn't give a shit. I was gonna live forever, never get sick and somehow I'd find money to live on and, if all else failed, I'd just marry a rich lady.

A while ago one of the best drivers, Tim Flock got very sick, very expensive. As we tried to raise money to help, I got to thinking. What a shitty ending to this proud tiger who was part of the foundation of stock car racing. Maybe the Gordon's, Earnhardt's, and Wallace's won't need help ever. How 'bout your buddies, the cats who try every week, run in the shit house, don't make it some races? They get old, sick, crippled. Hey, if racing don't need provisions for life's negatives from competition, why do politicians and union people, and the stick and ball players? What's the difference? Even you got something going for your golden years.

Junior, with all the good press you get about your management, I think you got your head up your ass on this very-very important subject. You are going to have to give the government thieves 80 percent of your deal when you croak, and that won't be all that long if you keep smokin' and stay 50 pounds over weight. Why not take care of your workers and furnish them benefits all the rest of the working people get?

MARIO ANDRETTI

I got Chevelle number one in 1966. NASCAR said it was OK to run it with a 427 cubic inch big block engine. I'm working for Mr. Knudsen, General Manager, Chevrolet. This is a new model, new name plate, gonna be Chevy's hot rod, 500 horsepower, 180 mph off show room floor. Really a poor kid's revenge; many rich kids got adiosed with this car. I got a prototype, a silver pre-production, donkey. I had the boys in Detroit move the engine back four inches and down two so the thing would turn at all. Boss says, "Run 'er at Daytona Smoke. Who you gonna get to drive it?" Well I've had 'bout enough of "Paul Bunyan" (A.J.) for a while, so I notice this little Eyetalian, Mario Andretti, goes like Jack the bear, and looks like he really knows how to avoid expensive sudden stops. So I offer him the Daytona ride. He likes the idea. France loves it. Knudsen says, "Damn good thinking."

Well, car's too stock suspension wise, got too much horse power for the tires and it's nose heavy (bad 'bout pushing). So, with Mario's stock car inexperience, my ignorance about chassis

Me and Mario in the pits. (photo: Don Hunter)

(and the car is an aerodynamic disaster), we really didn't set any records or scare our competitors. So, the race didn't include any glowing press for the car, Mario or myself. We run the qualifying race, and got 100 bucks for 20th. Down three laps in 40. In the 500 mile race we crashed on lap 31, but we got even more money for nine less laps ($1,065.00). Mario was easy to work with. Very pleasant, very knowledgeable, loved horsepower, and wanted to go very fast.

Well stock car fans decided Indy drivers couldn't handle stock cars. The open wheelers call NASCAR racers "taxi cabs." Well, while the fans were having fun sending Indy drivers to hell, Holman hires Mario to drive a Ford in '67, and Mario won the Daytona Beach Race. "Andretti wins"! Yes, he was all over the racetrack, and killed himself 'bout ten times in the race. It was a miracle he and the car survived, but the cold facts are he won the son-of-a-bitch. And the fans went ape shit, they thought Mario was doing all that shit on purpose. I don't remember us ever crossing paths again, but I consider it a privilege that Mario and I raced together. Ain't too many are ever gonna top his act. Can you believe there was a time that cat weighed 'bout 130 pounds soaking wet? Mario, as I knew him, didn't get involved with us personally. I do know he was a genuine racer. But I guess a kinda private cat. I know his brother Aldo chewed my ass out for telling Mario to quit, that he was too old ('bout two years before he did).

Buck Baker

Man, Buck Baker was a 1950 stereotype NASCAR driver. His day job was driving a bus in Charlotte. When Nascar first got going Buck drove the shit out of some modifieds and was a consistent winner. Buck was really as tough as it ever got. This was back in the days when racing was slipping, sliding, manhandling. Mostly on dirt. As stock cars got going, Buck favored the Olds '88 Rocket. Really a Chevy with a different grill and a pretty decent V-8 for those days and times. Buck did great things for the reputation of a NASCAR racer. Apparently, he did a remarkable job in the hay, considering the number of well-stacked women who asked to be introduced to him and to those who knew him and couldn't find him.

We run Darlington in '63. I had a Chevy with power out the ass, but was just completely lost in the chassis. The rear radius rods were too short and we had rear steer so bad no one could have driven it worth a damn. Sad part about it, I was too dumb to know how bad it was, and I incorrectly blamed our sorry performance on Buck, assuming he had "used it up" and slowed down. The next year he won the race hands down in a Ray Fox car. Buck said that car was only car that ever carried the right front coming off of four at Darlington.

I think Buck was part Indian. Didn't take much to get him drunk, and when drunk he got very belligerent and wanted to fight. It might be said, some of his drinking episodes might have been more dangerous than the racing. Marshall Teague, Fireball, Buck, Fonty and Tim Flock, Herb Thomas, Lee Petty, Joe Eubanks, Cotton Owens, Banjo Matthews, Jack Smith, Frank Mundy, Curtis Turner, Joe Weatherly: they were the deal. 98 percent of the early racing stars. Week in, week out these guys raced, not drove, cars like there was no tomorrow. When race was over their hands were bleeding from the broken blisters. Their asses bleeding from sliding around on the seats. Their throttle foot blistered and burned from the exhaust. They were deaf for three days after every race. Believe this or not, it was not at all unusual for a driver to lose 15 pounds in five hours at Darlington. These drivers created the excitement that gave NASCAR its magnetism and fan appeal.

Buck runs several driving schools now, and his health ain't too good, but take my word for it. In his day he was a racer.

Bunky Blackburn

Bunky Blackburn was a really nice guy who really loved to race, but luck never favored him much. He wasn't a bad driver, but just a whisker short compared to the stars, probably not aggressive enough in getting a ride. When Talladega had first race they had a support race first. Mustang, Camaro, Chrysler "something" race. Bunk was helping us in the shop when I worked for Ford the second time in '70. Knudsen was President of Ford now, and I worked for him. He wanted me to run both the Mustang type race and the Winston cup race. I refused to run the Winston cup deal. In my opinion tires not capable, and the track was a flawed surface. Knudson finally said "OK, if you think the Winston race is too dangerous, run the Mustang in the support race.." Well damn, I'd just finished a Mustang Trans am car and no time to build another circle track car, so I had to switch the Mustang from a road racer to a circle tracker.

Now I don't have a driver. So I decide hell. We'll let our Bunky do it. He sat her on the pole, 'bout 180 miles an hour and led it to damn near the end when the push rods started coming through the rocker arms, which is what we expected. Who knows? If engine hadn't failed him that might have got him started to Broadway.

Tony Bettenhausen

Was an Indy car open wheel racer from the fifties and sixties. This man was as rough and tough and strong as a ten-foot rattlesnake. A farmer from Tinley Park, Illinois. Man, on the dirt with a sprinter or champ car he did as much as any one ever could do to make the front five rows of seats unsaleable. He'd simply bury those front seats in dirt and mud. When Daytona was new and France decided to run an Indy car race on it in 1959, I had a fair championship roadster, a Kuzma, so I decided to run it. I knew Tony from Indy, so I asked him if he wanted to drive the car. "Yup," he said, "I'd like that." Well, after we tested the car at Daytona Tony decides, "I don't think so." Well, OK, Paul Russo wants to drive it. Nope, a few laps later he decides he needs to go to Ohio. A.J. Foyt, a few laps now "Don't think so." What the hell's going on? No real reason given, just "thanks anyhow," so I decide I'll drive the damn thing myself.

The big concern was the cars would get airborne (no down force, no wings- etc.). Well, I climb in, run few laps half assed and decide "nothing to it." Look everything over, looks good. Now I'm gonna go fast. Whoa! whole new ball game. No problem 'bout flying, car has so much load from cornering I can hardly steer it, plus it's bottoming out on track at certain bumps. Next, I get lost. Yes, lost on the track. I thought I was in number one turn when I was in dogleg, and goddam near hit wall head on. Well, that scared the shit out of me so I pulled in and retired as the driver.

Dick Rathman, who I raced with Hudsons, laughed his ass of at my near wall job, so I asked him if he wanted to drive it. "Sure" he says. Guess who damn near centered the dogleg wall on his first hot lap. He decides he don't want it. Here's the deal, that track at speed was like being in a black barrel. I couldn't even see all the wall. You were squashed down, straining to turn it and hold it. Finally, Dempsy Wilson comes along and finishes the race. I don't remember where we finished. It was way down though. Turned out not a good idea. Couple drivers got killed in the race, and it was never tried again (yet).

Paul Russo

Tony Bettenhausen and I were good friends, so 'bout 1964, Paul Russo is driving a car like we won with, in 1960, a Watson, damn good car. Paul's having problems getting it going good enough to qualify. I try and talk to crew chief, but nothing comes of it. Paul asks me to come check car. I don't want to, cause I don't like attitude of crew chief. A nice guy, but short on racing experience in my view, and I don't like beer in garage icebox all the time – too much can impair a crew chief's judgement. Well, I try but speed is still short. I decide it has to go on Bear frame rack to check axle alignment. It don't happen. Paul asks Tony to drive car for suggestions to get it handling. I'm out of the deal now 'cause nobody is listening. Tony asks me what I think. I tell him, "I think car needs another crew chief who has raced more, this is Indy – no place for fuck ups."

Well, I'm working away on the capsule car in the old garage area. When I still had ears I could tell when something went wrong by the engine sounds, and when I sensed trouble I'd look at crowd in top of grandstand and see which direction they were looking. I stopped working, walked out, and looked at crowd. Looked like they were looking straight ahead. I walked to track gate and I seen a red car all wrapped up in chain link fence. Good-bye Tony boy. The drag link came unhooked coming off turn number 4. No steering. Adios the farm. Good-bye Paul Russo too. He hung it up after this wreck. He and Tony were very good friends. You know, in racing things change so fast it's hard to adjust. One minute you got the world by the ass and two minutes later you're so low you can walk under a snake's belly standing up with a hat on. I think watching and listening to Paul Russo in his prime, manhandling a Jean Masenac wrenched Novi in an early sixties Indy race was the most vivid memory I have of power, speed, balls and the indescribable voice of that Novi engine. I still get goose bumps thinking 'bout it.

DUANE CARTER

Another real racer from the beginning. An open-wheeler deluxe, midgets, sprinters, champ cars. Won in everything, but Indy. Going into his later forties, he retires and becomes director of competition for USAC. He hadn't run in five years when his USAC job pooped out. I'm at Indy with two cars: an old Kurtis roadster we ran in '58, and a chopped up year old Kurtis that did poorly in '58 with a good driver (Johnny Thompson). I get half ownership (no pay) to race it in '59 at Indy.

Art Lathrop, a wealthy Indy car owner with much owner experience, decides I'm new, hot prospect crew chief and car builder and that I might be able to salvage his investment in this pink, yes, pussy pink car. The press asks me why I chopped the fancy independent suspension off of Frank Kurtis's last year's inven-

Duane Carter (photo: Indianapolis Motor Speedway)

tion. I beat around the bush with a one-sentence answer: "It wasn't worth a shit." Well, that did it. Frank had a million fans, and his cars were the best before Watson. People who worked for Frank loved him. They wanted to lynch me. His million fans put me on a shit list. So, I went from "rookie hero" in '58 to "World Class Asshole" with one sentence in thirty seconds.

Frank blasted me in the press, and for twenty-five years I remained in the Kurtis fan club shit house. One day at Indy Frank came by and introduced me to his son and daughter, and said, "The feud is over. You were right. The front end wasn't worth a shit. Let's be friends." Took a hell of a man to do that. Sure made me feel good. From that day Frank had a million and "one" fans. Shortly after that Frank's health failed and he left us.

Back to Duane Carter '59. I have rebuilt the '58 Kurtis Paul Goldsmith crashed at Indy (it really wasn't hurt bad at all), and I had the chopped up pink pussy cat of Art Lathrop's which caused me a lot of trouble getting through inspection. Here's the deal: rules said all welding had to be electric "stick" weld, with a certain type of rod. I decided in re-doing the car, a new welding process would be better, "Heliarc." I had a drunken friend who was an electrical genius – a professor on drunk leave from Northwestern University. I bought a World War II surplus, Lincoln upright welder for twenty-five bucks. Frank (sorry, I can't remember his last name) and I built my first Heliarc machine. Total cost 'bout seventy bucks. Well inspectors said, "Take it home, cut out your illegal welds, do it rite, come back later." Well, that damn near ends Indy '59. No way to do it time wise.

The year of 1959 for me was a series of disappointments, and experiments in living on 20-25 bucks a week, but the fickle finger of fate saved my ass. The head inspector, Dr. Silberman, head of Magna Flux Corporation liked my idea and said, "Let him run, and every evening we'll check frame for any sign of failure." That's how Heliarc chassis welding got OK'd at Indy.

I got no driver. Lathrop wanted Roger Ward to drive it. I for some reason didn't like Roger. I didn't like his dog. Yup, back then a racer could bring his dog in the pits. Jim Hurtibise has a giant police dog strong enough to tow his car. Roger had a tiny, sissy dog. By the way, Ward won Indy that year. Well a famous Indy racer shakes down both my cars and I didn't safety the oil pressure check valve on either car yet. They both come loose, and both engines blew. (Plan was "run, check pressure, and then safety wire 'em.')

Oh, I forgot one more detail: the Smokey car is an Offie laying down to the left, and engine runs backwards to any other engine. The "Reverse Torque Special" was it's name. Nobody wants to drive either car. The old Kurtis is too old, and the new one is a Buck Rogers deal. OK, "Hell, I'll drive it myself." Back then a mechanic could go see Franky Bain and beg an OK to test the car if you promised on a stack of bibles "you wouldn't go fast." My master plan is learn how to do it, twenty laps a day for three days, by running half laps. Then do some full laps at qualifying speed and get OK'd to drive. Goofy? Remember the year before we pulled off the Smokey/Goldsmith deal.

Well, one major problem I can't, to save my ass, stick it in the number three turn like it needs to be done. Turn one didn't bother me, but three looked like trying to put a bulldozer through the eye of a needle at 200 miles an hour. Finally I come off of the number two turn, put my left foot on top of right foot, vow to die before I lift before the pine tree. When I get to pine tree I notice I've already lifted. So I retired, back off, go into pits gotta find driver. Car runs like a bat out of hell and the reverse torque really works great. I know the reverse torque car can win if it don't fall apart (and I get a driver). I only have one helper, Frank Cannon, a parts man out of our shop in Daytona. Frank's no mechanic, just "go-fer." But he disappointed me, he is afraid of the starter. Can't even run stopwatch good.

In my driving experiment I have to start engine, work throttle with a string, get half in cockpit, close hood and put in dzus fastener. (Half the time it would stall.) Then time myself every second lap. Big problem was the Offy vibrated so much, when you took your hand off of steering wheel it got about three inches wide, and was a son-of-a-bitch to grab again. Here comes Duane Carter, "Let me drive your car Smoke." Back then, a driver over 50 years old was unheard of. He hadn't driven in five years to boot. Well, what the hell, I'll let him run a day or two while I find somebody. Big surprise! (He does damn good.) I decide to sell the old Kurtis. Aggie's car crashed. Maybe he'd buy the old car (close…but didn't). Maybe I should take a chance of a top five with Duane. In a few days I'd got to like ol' Duane. He was 'bout like that guy in Li'l Abner where he always had a cloud and rain over his head. Maybe I liked him 'cause he reminded me of my problems ('cept for his women problems – Duane stayed constantly in soap opera mode).

Well, here it is Friday before qualifying. I need Duane to qualify the car quick on Saturday 'cause I gotta go to Charlotte to race '59 Pontiac Sunday with Fireball. I draw a qualifying number 'bout fourth or fifth. Duane's saying, "No way, next weekend." I say, "Bullshit. Now or never." Well he gets 'er done…Really not real fast, but plenty OK, 12th.

Well life's looking up. Now I got time to party a little, cause one-way or another, I'll shortly be rich.

Dusty Rhoades, president of Sun Manufacturing has agreed to copy my homemade cylinder leakage tester, and sell them, and I'll get a big fat fee as inventor and a royalty. (Well, all I get out of that was tester serial number one, and a lesson in verbal business arrangements). Yup, I got nothing, but I did pick up some new and interesting sexual adventures.

John Laux introduced me to a lonesome divorcee who had an unusually educated dog. You'll never believe this: she raised and sold pedigreed police dogs. You guessed it, she reminds me of Bill Clinton's statement: "He never had sexual relations with "Harmonica." Maybe not, but a thirty minute videos of the police dog raiser really wouldn't be showable, except to a very limited audience. Even with my generous views, I decided not to pursue this friendship.

Instead, I then moved on to an attractive fence bunny, a socialite who had a very unusual lifestyle. This lady was the most talented and perverted person I ever met (up to this time, including California). But I didn't care for the ending (seventy-year old husband watching from a closet). I was a Florida Justice of the Peace. I'm getting car finished for the race. I'm just about asleep when a friend of mine, Bill Yeager, asked me to marry him to a girl he'd recently met. I'm in a trench coat and boots, and nothing else with a motel Bible and witnesses. After ceremony bride and groom decide to take a bath before starting honeymoon. The bride decides to warm up by laying me, while talking to the bridegroom in the bathtub. I wonder if that was a first? I wasn't too surprised to learn marriage only lasted a week or so.

I'm not gonna describe the next adventure. (An interracial experiment that was a big-big mistake.) Nobody would believe it anyway. (I doubt I ever came that close to getting killed then or since.)

When Duane qualified he was reborn. Man he was happy. I had one problem I need Duane's help with. Offy engine just ain't oil leak proof, so some oil and it didn't take much, would get on the aluminum floor in drivers foot area. Here's problem: Duane's got a pair of "lucky" leather boots with leather soles he is gonna use race day. Well, I now have to put a rug on cockpit floor to keep lucky boots from getting oil on the soles. The shitty model clutch and poor torque of the Offy at low rpm made it very-very hard to do stall free start. Oil makes leather slippery as hell. Now problem is, if I put rug in there it's got to be fire-proofed. Usual normal rug can't be fire-proofed, has to be cotton I think. I'm having trouble finding the rite stuff (Duane don't want the rug). He says, "I'll get the rug, no rug, day after day. " Don't worry, I'll have it tomorrow." Rug never happens.

We have fastest car. Roger Ward has a Watson Super car and he is running his ass off, so we start to fall behind. No radios then, pit boards only. I'm trying to get Duane to pickup pace. Nothing works. Finally I give him his lap speed in mph (which is six mph short of his better laps). Man, next lap he's hauling ass. Then I realize he is embarrassed by slow lap time. (The fans see the shitty lap times.) Now we're in business. Take the two stalls time lost out of it, and we would of won the race easy, but he run seventh.

For thirty-five years after that I'd piss Duane off by telling how he threw away the '59 race.

Art Lathrop, my partner and owner of the other half of the car, sober was a real nice person, but drunk (and that was 70 percent of the time) he was such a pain in the ass that even while I was dead broke then, I gave him my half of the car rather than put up with his act when drinking. And I'll be goddamned if it didn't take me six months to get back the Pontiac station wagon Knudsen loaned me to tow with.

I think the Kurtis kids have found the car and restored it back to Frank's original design. Too bad I didn't save its snoot. I just cut it off at the firewall (and it was just like new), and then threw it away. As you can guess, Art and I weren't friends anymore. He only lasted a few more years. I met his son a month ago for first time. Art's wife is still going strong. Talk about a small world.

Duane Carter contributed his life and talent to auto racing. Take my word for it. Duane Carter was a racer, and a damn good one. He represented us well as a driver and as a spokesperson, and was a racer till the day he checked out. Duane, I hope someday your peers will give you the credit you deserve. (I hope you took your lucky boots with you).

DAREL DIERINGER

Darel Dieringer was an average early day racer. He loved going fast. He'd race anything, anyplace, anytime. He'd race you for a half of your popsicle. When he first showed up in late fifties, he did good. Go like hell and crash a lot. But hell, didn't everybody? I had a no handling Chevy at Rockingham, I believe Banjo tried to tame 'er and couldn't, and I let Darrell try to figure out a way to drive it. It didn't work. I couldn't get enough out of his description of what the car was doing to help him. Well, actually, I couldn't have helped him even if I could understand his description. That was again, a Chevy with too much power and rear roll steer (the short track bars problem). For the record, a hillbilly, Junior Johnson had enough "farmer smarts" to finally figure it out.

Darel finally landed in Bud Moore's car, a Mercury I think. They made a good team. A very formidable competitor every week. Darel stuck his ass out a mile and did the test-driving necessary to develop the inner liner tire concept. (Still used today.) There is no way to guess how many serious injuries and/or deaths that work avoided. Darel and Bud Moore, his car owner, did much testing for Goodyear, so in Darel's prime, he knew the tire story, and believe me even today that's half of the battle. Darel was never down, always laughing, joking, anything but a loner. He really enjoyed life. I don't think he was ever financially well off, but if the big "C" hadn't taken him away so early, I guarantee you he'd of been involved in racing somehow till he was ninety.

Bill Hall, the manager of the Charlotte Track's Cabbarus Suite and he were very good friends. Through Bill I kept up with Darrell's problems throughout the last several years of his life. Bill Hall is an example of an early NASCAR fan. Somehow they wove NASCAR into their lives. If you go in the Cabbarus Suite you'll find him still involved and lovin' it. Race fans truly picked out and loved certain drivers. Darrell had a very large following but not quite enough for Broadway. Darel was finally inducted into the Darlington Hall of Fame (fifteen years too late). But he sure was happy and proud. Shortly the big "C" took him away. Notice how almost every one of the pioneers get the shitty end of the stick in their so-called "golden years?"

JERRY KARL

Jerry Karl was Yankee driver from Pennsylvania. In 1973 I built a double turbo charged taxi cab motor to run Indy. It was a 208 cubic inch Chevy, and I put it into a Gurney Eagle chassis. I also built my own trans-axle, which allowed me to drop the engine 4" lower than if I'd of used a Hewland trans-axle. Well, again I've got an untried, unproven race car that I couldn't ask a driver with a pedigree to drive. Why? Well, a bunch of radical innovation is a good way for a driver to lose a year. The only new engine I ever remember winning first year was Mercedes in the early nineties. A Penske production, with little Al as a driver.

I gathered up some information from a friend of mine, who gave Jerry Karl a recommendation, so I decided to try him. Why is it OK with Karl? He's a rookie. Not much chance anybody's gonna put him in a good, proven car. Why is Jerry Karl a good prospect? He is quick, but not goofy. He don't wreck too much. He truly has balance, runs a consistent pattern, and has got balls big enough to keep the gas pedal down. Simply stated, likes to go fast, and can flat drive a race car. Off the track, he has most of the credentials a racer needs. He is lazy as hell, chases pussy like a hound dog and after dark, you hardly ever seen without a beer can in one hand, he ain't got a dime, he don't worry 'bout anything and has got an above average desire to win. If he had any shortcomings, it was he knew enough about race cars to be dangerous when being debriefed after some hot laps.

Jerry probably had a rough life and he didn't have a sparkling personality or a real good line of bullshit,

That's me, Ralph Johnson, Dusty Thatcher and Jerry Karl. (photo: Indianapolis Motor Speedway)

so he would have been real easy to overlook. I've always said, "There are at least always one hundred guys with Earnhardt and Jeff Gordon potential out there all the time. Jerry was one of them that fell through the cracks. If my car had of been a winner, I'm sure he'd of gone on to star status.

But I never could get the car fueled properly, and it either would run like a bat out of hell, or drill a piston. Power was no problem. It had 1,000 horsepower at 6,800 with a 208 cubic inch of push rod, Stove Bolt, small block. 1,000 horses from a 208 Chevy? I don't blame you for doubting, but ask anyone who drove it, or ask anyone who saw it run, or anyone behind it coming off the corner. If there were ten cars on front straightaway, all you'd hear was the little Stove Bolt. It had a gorilla voice all of it's own. Jerry wasn't afraid to mash the button, so we got her qualified.

Man, that was a struggle. Twenty hours a day seven days a week for five months, with 'bout ten "allniters" thrown in. You know when you qualify at Indy, as you return to qualifying ceremony area, you have to pass all of your competitors. I got a standing ovation from every one of them as I passed. I'm not a sentimental person, but I still get teary-eyed as I recall those few minutes. (Kinda like Earnhardt got from his competitors when he won the Beach in '98.)

Well, in the race we had nothing but trouble. Finally, mercifully, it burned a piston and put us out of our misery. It took me four months to heal the burns on my hands and arms from working with those red-hot blowers during the race. Well, Jerry didn't exactly set my ass on fire because he was so damn lazy. Every evening he'd disappear to run his "trap line." Ralph and I would work till 2:00 am getting ready for a bran' new deal for tomorrow at 9:00 am. Within a minute or two of track opening for practice we were out there trying to conquer the fueling problem. Jerry came back and drove the Chevy in '75. We were logged 10th and ended up 12th. (See the story in Indy '75)

Sammy Sessions

So, in 1974, I got a scrappy little guy, Sammy Sessions to drive it. The neatest, nicest guy you could find and pretty good driver. No, he didn't work either, but before he'd disappear for the day, he'd tell Ralph and I how sorry he was we had to work so hard. And every morning he'd compliment us on how much we'd accomplished. Sammy had driven for Mickey Thompson before. Now this really qualified Sammy for me. Mickey was goofier than me. Front wheel drive, four wheel drive, four wheel steering, 12 inch wheels, Buick's, Chevy's, titanium pistons and rods; I mean some weird shit. Don't get me wrong, racing owes Mickey. He did a ton of good (along with some not so good), but he was only guy who could hold a candle to Ralph and I on work hours.

Who is Ralph? Ralph Johnson was a big engineer who could have been chief engineer at Chevy except for his love of pussy and booze. And mostly because of his non-conformist attitude at GM. In those days it was the code of the hills to be a brown-nosing, two-faced, son-of-a-bitch to stay in the rotation to the top. Ralph had the talent, but he would not play the game. Much more about Ralph in the chapter of "important and influential people who taught me, helped me, or were two-faced assholes who hugged me while they stuck it up my gazoo."

The '74 Indy for Sammy and I was a weirdo deal. One qualifying weekend instead of the usual two. I drew a bad qualifying number, 'bout like 68. It rained both qualifying days. We were sitting with the engine running when the 6:00 pm gun went off and we never got a shot at it.

To be honest, I'd say we at best had a 50 percent chance to bump our way in. Some competitors who felt they were screwed in the experiment wanted to sue, and Sam and I had the perfect case. We never got out of line and just before it was our turn to dance, the band went home.

I asked Sammy if he wanted to join the law suit, he asked me how I felt. I said, "I come to race, not to fuck around with a bunch of vultures" (lawyers). He said, "I feel same way," so we kissed goodbye with no firm plans for '75. Sammy got killed in a skimobile race in the winter of '74. Sam was what I called "good people." Never put anybody down, didn't complain or make excuses. Sam tried to get through life being friends with everybody, and did a good job of it.

Joe Leonard

1960s motorcycle ace, Harley Davidson hero. Towing a trailer with a Nash car. I believe car and trailer were worth 'bout 800 bucks. Carrying the number 1 U.S. National Champion plate on the cycle. This was not 1912, this is the early sixties. He was 'bout six feet tall, 165 pounds, good looking, with personality of a hound dawg. Always grinning. Never quit sniffing. We called him "José." He was from San José,

California.

If there is such a thing as a natural born racer, this is it. He liked to go fast, very fast and knew how to do it. He decides that all that motorcycles are gonna pay ain't enough to live on. He has friends in four wheel racin' doing much better financially, and with the same benefit, regarding wine, women and partying. Joe had the genes of an early racer. As the sun slowly disappeared to the West, their peckers would start to rise. He was allergic to work, another trait 95 percent of best racers had.

By the mid-sixties he's driving one of A.J.'s "Tasmanian devil" Indy cars, (Coyotes) doing pretty damn good, but still not getting rich. 'bout this time Joe develops a bad habit. He forgets the contracts he makes verbally and/or written. In Indy cars then the big money came from Firestone or Goodyear. Joe Leonard

Joe Leonard. (photo: Indianapolis Motor Speedway)

had Indy in his back pocket in 1968 with nine laps to go. He was driving a turbine for Andy Granitelli and the goddam fuel pump tore up. Well, during the rest of the '68 year, and most of '69, Joe was on the master shit list of both Firestone and Goodyear. They boycotted him.

1969 was the official "fuck Joe Leonard year." I'm working for Mr. Knudsen, President of Ford Motor Company. It's now April 10th, 1969. He calls and says, "I want you to run Indy with a double overhead cam turbo'd Ford race engine." In them days Indy starts May first…so I say, "Why start so early?…I got twenty days to build engines, buy, or build a car, no driver." Knudsen says, "I'm serious, do it!," and hangs up. Gurney has a new '69 Eagle he hasn't sold and it was built to use a Ford 4-cam turbo. I buy it over the phone and in five days it's in shop here at Daytona. By then I've gotten two new engines shipped in from Meyer's shop in Indy. Lou Meyers has Ford contract to head up engine program. OK, now for a driver.

I don't know Joe Leonard well at all, but I know his number one buddy, "the coon-ass, Everett Brashear." I ask him what the deal is with Joe regarding he has no ride (Everett fills me in). I call Joe cold and offer him ten grand up front for expenses and 50 percent of prize money. "Meet me here in week to get controls and seat fit and figured." Joe gives me a line of shit 'bout money and other deals. I say, "OK, forget it." He says, "There ain't nobody else to drive that car." I say, "I know that, I'll strap a monkey in and drive it with remote control from a helicopter," and hang up. Ten minutes later he calls back, says, "I'll take it." He gets here and wants a contract. I say, "What for, you need some extra toilet paper?" So, from a somewhat rocky start, we go to Indy and start May 1. Course I'm fuckin' near dead from all the work. I only got two helpers and I'm still running a twenty mechanic truck dealership.

Well, Joe and I got along great. His feedback was super. No ideas, just clear picture of what car was doing. Also, Joe really is a great driver. Now I see what Foyt saw in him. But the car is a piece of shit, 1969 Eagle. (Sorry if that offends you Dan, but that motherfucker flew the nose and pushed its ass off. On second thought, I don't give a shit if it pisses you off.) Joe kept telling me, "It's pushing." I kept chopping off the nose and gaining, but very slowly. I had another problem. The car had a Bendix fuel injector, which wasn't worth a shit and a sorry piston, and combustion chamber configuration, as well as a very unreliable turbo waste gate.

A.J. lent me an injector casting he and Herb Porter developed, I found a Spitzer waste gate I liked, so besides tearing up the body work on car, and changing the air, we quickly redid induction system of the engine. This year at Indy, Ford has group of engineers run by a two-faced prick named Jack Passino. The deal is, they assign Ford engineer to each Ford-powered car for the race. Well there are so many Fords in the field, they are short of engineers, so, "Fuck Smokey and Joe, they ain't got a prayer anyhow." Big deal I guess, all of the engineers put together wouldn't have made a pimple on a good race engineer's ass. (Well there was one, but I can't remember his name.) OK, so it's Wednesday and pole qualifying will be Saturday. Joe and I look like we'll qualify fair (actually 11th).

Now let me fill you in on the tire deal. In 1967 Goodyear paid me a lot of money to run and teach Dennis Hulme the Indy race routine. I didn't run in '68, 'cause there was no money (nobody offered anything even remotely interesting). Matter of fact nobody offered anything. Well, as much as Goodyear wanted me in 1967, and although we didn't set the weeds on fire in '67 we did run 4th with a rookie driver, so I was shocked when Goodyear said no to ten grand for running their tires in '69. Their answer is, "Sorry, our budget is used up." (Goldsmith had warned me if I didn't kick back some money to Larry Truesale in '67, I'd be on shit list in '68) Well OK, it is 'bout May 1st, so I ask Firestone. Same answer 'cept, "If you make driver change, check back." Well, I guess I couldn't blame them for boycotting Joe, but it still pissed me off. (Maybe it was me they were pissed off at…who knows?)

Well by Thursday, two days before the pole, Joe's testing a new four-wheel drive car for Parnelli Jones in his spare time with Firestone tires. Tuesday, four days before the Pole Day, Goodyear and Firestone change their mind about their depleted budget, and to make a long story short Goodyear gave each of us, Joe and I, $60,000.00 to run their tires. Funny thing, by then I'd decided I was gonna run Goodyear's, money or no money. I signed a contract with Goodyear and gave Joe his sixty grand. Now this is the same son-of-a-bitch who is maybe gonna drive the four-wheel drive Firestone for Parnelli. They offer him 50 to drive it. Around 4:00 pm Thursday, I catch up with Joe and say, "You got 30 minutes to make up your mind what you're gonna drive Saturday, and if you pick the four-wheeler, you got to give Goodyear back their sixty Gs." Then I told him, "If he don't give Goodyear back their sixty, he ain't gonna drive nothing." I know Joe understood me, so he swore on a stack of motel Bibles he'd stay where he was.

Again the fickle finger of fate screwed Joe. He had the race won when a damn hose clamp from the earlier wreck of the Ernie Kneppner car gets picked up by Mario's left rear tire and gets throwed clean through our 4 inch thick radiator. (Joe had wanted to pass Mario for five laps for the lead, and I said "Wait," so I guess I screwed Joe out of the deal.)

This was Joe's second year in a row that fate rejected my "hero" driver. We got paid for 7th. Take my word for it: Joe Leonard was as good a driver, and man, as ever set his ass in an Indy car. But he had a problem. He gutted around for 20 years with very poor peripheral vision. He always had to wear trick glasses, but in 1970 his depth perception and peripheral vision went bad and Joe didn't know where the outside wall was anymore. Joe and I tried stock car racing a little, but before we got dialed in, my boss Knudsen gets fired. I get pissed and quit shortly after Joe busted his ass good at the Ontario track in the spring of '73, in an Indy car with Firestone tires. Well, "hurry up and heal for Indy" goes sour, and Joe's still limping around. His racing career was over. Joe had a rough life, but he is always the same. Even now he sees the good stuff. Forgets the bad shit. I'm real glad I got to race with and know a "li'l something 'bout "José" I learned from Joe. Most of it was "what not to do." Joe and I are still friends.

Banjo Matthews

Banjo Matthews was born in Ohio, but he was really from Miami. He was 'bout five feet nine inches tall, heavy set, with one half-inch thick goggle glasses. That's how he got named Banjo. I met him in 1947. He was a modified driver. He, Joe Allen (Bobby Allen's father), Marshall Teague, and Fireball were friends and Banjo was always picking Marshall's brain regarding engine speed tips. So when it got close to a big modified race, like the beach, Motive Parts in Daytona was the common meeting place at the time for stock car racing's top cats.

You would have liked Banjo. He was as common as dirt, worked his ass off, and had good manners, (too bad some of it didn't rub off on his son Jody). I knew him from time he was 17 till he died in his mid-sixties a couple years ago. Racing was his whole life from age 15 till death, and it was all in NASCAR. Banjo, you apparently didn't contribute a damn thing to stock car racing. In their 50th Anniversary celebration, I did not heard your name mentioned once. Banjo was a stereotypical NASCAR stock car racer. A gas station kid that loved to go fast, he had no real education but had a good head, and was a super absorber of information. He had a day job, but only to support his racing habit.

Here's the deal. It's 1947, World War II is over and the USA is in the first years of their second love affair with automobiles. We could build a decent modified for 450 to 500 bucks. The people who ran automotive type businesses felt a race car running out of their garage or gas station helped business and attracted good quality mechanics to their shops…and it did. So the Banjo's could find a place to work on their cars and also work a weekly job. Banjo grew up with NASCAR. He knew France Sr. and every single NASCAR player till at least 1985. He helped form the rules (France would ask Banjo about rule changes). At one time his race cars were winning 95 percent of the annual Grand National, which is now the Winston cup series races. He was the Henry Ford of cheap mass produced race cars. He built and sold good race cars for a grand, cars capable of winning anywhere.

Banjo was good people, really not a real racer in every sense of the word. He couldn't drink worth a shit and I always said he couldn't get laid in whorehouse with a credit card. But Banjo was a very good driver and mechanic. Kinda Marshall Teague number two. He eventually became a very good engine builder. Actually, he could do anything there was to do at the highest level of stock car racing there was. He was a successful car owner till he hooked up with A.J. Foyt. I really believe A.J. took five years off Banjo's life in the two or three years they raced together. (Banjo said it was more like ten years.) Banjo was really easy going and hard to piss off. But from the day A.J. and Banjo separated as race partners, Banjo never forgave whatever it was that was the last straw.

We all considered Banjo a chassis wizard. He was, but only on the Ford chassis as developed by Holman and Moody. Matter of fact his stubborn refusal to go from rear steer to front steer 'bout destroyed his business and reputation.

Banjo and I hooked up to run a Chevy at Rockingham and Charlotte. We figured with his chassis input as driver, and my strong engine we'd be tough. It never happened. The excessive rear steer in my car made it impossible to drive, and Banjo was defeated. He was using Ford tech

Banjo and Jack Sullivan.

on a Chevy chassis that had a major flaw. Banjo raced out of Miami to start with. In the early fifties he went to Asheville North Carolina to work on his car at his sponsor's shop. That did it. He fell in love with that early mountain country and climate. He spent the rest of his life there.

He had no hobbies, just worked and raced seven days a week, three hundred sixty five days a year. No hobbies until he became enamored with antiques, and collected tons of them. Banjo's wife Penny spent a large part of her forties and fifties fighting the big "C." When finally cancer took her, Banjo never recovered. He appeared to kinda half die starting shortly after her passing. Banjo's last ten years were full of pain and misery. By 1997 our poor Banjo had lost all will to continue living.

Junkyard had ten puppies. One of them looked like Banjo, so we sent him to Banjo as a present. ("Oil Pan" mysteriously died very soon in his sleep.)

I guess it's rite to say, mercifully Banjo's life ended soon after that. He was ready. For those of you who are interested in the history of stock car racing, for you to correctly understand the actual truth, you'd have to place Banjo in the top ten of the building blocks of NASCAR. I'll always believe his early days as a modified driver, with no exhaust system, and breathing the exhaust fumes rite out of the Ford block ruined his lungs.

I hope they have air-conditioned suites where you are Banjo, and you can watch what you helped create. I feel good 'bout you knowing how much we admired you before you left. I'm done trying to get the world to know you now. What the hell good would it do now? You finally got put in the International Motor Sports Hall of Fame in April 1998, eighteen months too late. I helped install Banjo in the Darlington Hall of Fame, and got him awarded the Champion Buddy Schuman award at NASCARs victory banquet in '97. Also, we awarded him the Smokey Yunick Life Achievement award at Charlotte. Maybe you knew how we felt about you and that helped. I hope so.

RALPH MOODY

Man, that cat goes back to the wooden frame days. Wooden racecar frames? Yup, and some run Indy. Ralph came to us from New England (I mean this cat was 101 percent Yankee). He is still going and still talks like he still lives in New Hampshire. The most unlikely NASCAR racer candidate there could be. Didn't drink, wouldn't come play with us at night. Only vice I know he had was he smoked like a freight train locomotive. Ralph's now aimed at eighty and still going pretty good. Same for his wife Mitzi. They've lived in Charlotte 'bout forty years.

Here's how we got Ralph. Ford had first place in car sales 1954-55. Ed Cole's invention, the 1955 Chevy, with its new chassis and the small block V8 is as big a success as Viagra is today. What you people today don't know is, accidentally, or on purpose, both the front and back seats of a '55 Chevy were best in the industry for sex and they were very safe cars to have sex in. No chance to accidentally bump gear shift into neutral and roll off. This next part is hearsay: I was told the National Motel Association and Ford Motor Company threw in together to stop the damage the li'l Chevy's were doing to the motel's shack-up deals and Ford's looming loss of first place in car sales. So, Ford hires Pete Depaolo, with instructions to race and improve Ford's on the NASCAR circuit. Oh, and most importantly, kick the shit out of Chevy's racers. Pete hires John Holman, who was Bill Stroppe's stooge for more time than John's ego liked to recall, and John is 'bout number one as an organizer. But they lack a chassis expert.

Well, Ralph came down and raced with us with his Yankee cars, and quickly showed us we didn't know much 'bout chassis. Ralph was a self-educated, cut-and-try, farmer-type, who really knows his shit. Plus he could drive 'bout as good as it gets, and he worked his ass off. You know, you can't beat a driver/mechanic combo that avoids the possible problem of miscommunication. (Off the subject for a minute…this is what launched Bill Elliott to stardom. He made his own chassis adjustment in the beginning and his ass told him where the deal was.)

OK, now we got Pete Depaolo, John Holman and Ralph Moody renting old Air Force barracks building at the Charlotte airport. Well, they hire 'bout four of best drivers and start getting it done.

Ralph supervised the car building, and does much of the test-driving, and wins a few races himself.

Shootin' the shit in the pits with Ralph.

Well, June 1957, motor companies go home and Depaolo's deal goes up in smoke. American automobile manufacturers agree to abandon auto racing. Chrysler cheats and keeps feeding money to #42. Petty blue roars on. Meanwhile, John Holman and Ralph got tons of Ford parts, the personnel and a couple bucks in the bank but they are orphans. Their "rich Uncle Henry" died and didn't leave anything in his will for them 'cept 150 tons of Ford parts.

Right in here John Holman and Ralph Moody save NASCARs ass – period! They can, and do build and sell a Ford race car, race-ready, including paint color you want, for ten grand. Wait a second, I mean a car good enough to win the race! You see, all support money from manufacturers had been retracted back to the "uppa-u-ass, Detroit, Michigan," except to a little town in North Carolina that painted race cars light blue. Well, Ford was extra good to me. They paid off the contract of 'bout two years and released me six weeks before even John Holman knew about it. So I decided to finish '57 with the car parts and money I had. The Holman and Moody cars kept racers on the track after the manufacturers had gone home.

Ralph was really a super person. He'd help any way; test the car for me, giving helpful chassis information, but John-boy was another story. Whenever I talk to him face-to-face I'd keep my hand on my wallet. Now, I liked John but he was a challenge. He'd lie like a son-of-a-bitch. He was really a carnie. He knew his shit, but buddy, when he came down the street he'd pick up everything not nailed down. John was not crooked, but he sure had hen-house ways. I imagine I'll end up which ever way John went so I suppose I'll hear about this later.

Ralph Moody did what he did quietly, and done it at the highest level. I don't know if he was, or is religious, but that cat ain't gonna have but damn few check marks on the "hot" side of the passport you get when you check out. If somebody asks me, "You know Ralph Moody?" I say, "Damn sure do, and proud of it." You're living proof there are good Yankees. I went back to Ford in 1970 and Ralph helped me with chassis again. He was damn good test driver.

Life's funny, and really unpredictable. 'bout 1990 Winston decided "Let's have an old-timers race, and see how many old hands we can crash up." Well, Humpy makes a flat quarter mile track in front of grandstand at start finish line (at Charlotte). They pick 'bout twenty-five old drivers. Moody's one of them. The cars are 'bout 500 horsepower. Some of 'em like Junior's and Childress's may have had more like 650 horsepower. Well, 'bout three hours before race, Ralph flunks physical. So somebody says, "Will you drive Ralph's car?." I think they are kidding. So I say, "If you're crazy enough to give it to me to drive, sure I'd love to do it." Well, in two minutes I'm getting physical, driver's uniform and stuff. "How's Ralph?" "Oh, he's OK." Well, it starts to rain; the practice is 'bout six laps.

The race is in the rain. I'm so fucked up just trying to stay alive I don't worry about losing my brakes. Caution flags are a joke, they just make some of us go faster. Junior Johnson passed me on a yellow to crash the pace car in the passenger door. (France Jr. was sitting there. I notice he retired as pace car passenger next lap.) 'Bout half the field are total junk, wrecked, write-offs. By now I am wondering "Did Ralph pull a Holman on me?" I bet he knew what was gonna happen and decided he'd rather not spend some sheet time again 'cause purse was still zero, and Bruton tripled it just before race started. Elmo Langley won it with Yarborough and Goldsmith hot on his ass. My boy Sam was watching, so was my wife Margie, (I think she peed her pants in the excitement) along with 90,000 people. My boy says, "Why didn't you run harder?" I thought I was flying.

Cotton Owens

Cotton Owens was the Spartanburg, South Carolina town hero. He was a small man, but with elephant balls. He was called "Cotton" cause of his very blond hair. He started with modifieds 'bout 1950. He was as tough a man to beat as there was. This is mostly dirt, small tracks on bias ply tires, lots of slipping and sliding. He drove a sorry handling modified for me at the beach in 1956, and when he finally got a good Grand National car he became a top contender and did his share of winning.

He got a break with Pontiac. Mr. Knudson was the boss man. He knew Cotton was a winner and backed him. Cotton became one of the first successful driver-owners. During my adventures at Pontiac from 1958 to 1962 we were involved in races and tests where I worked on cars that he drove. Cotton's still going, still in good shape. I seen him when he was here for the NASCAR 50th anniversary important people celebration.

Hell, he just recently quit driving the short tracks. You know why? He can't beat his grand kids anymore. He taught 'em too well. Cotton retired and became a very successful parts vendor, and I believe kinda runs a Chrysler-only junkyard. After his Pontiac days he became a Chrysler man. One of his driver clients was ol' Marty Robbins (the singer). Man, if he coulda' drove like he sang those hillbilly tear jerkers, he'd of been in all the racing halls of fame. But he didn't. He wasn't short on brave, just never got it figured out. He started too late and raced as a hobby, not for food on the table. For those who judged Cotton by his size, they shortly learned when racing him you better get your best hold, or he'd have your ass in a hurry.

MARVIN PANCH

"Starvin Marvin." A Californian who came to live with us in 1954. A very quiet, easy going, medium size cat who had a very long struggle to get into a real competitive car. I'd say Pete Depaolo, picking up Marvin in '57, showed us all his real potential. He finished second in Grand National championship. But when Ford went home it left slim pickins for '58. Bang...back to 18th in Fords.

Marvin moved from Charlotte to Daytona, so we are neighbors. Marvin has no ride worth a damn so he spends a lot of time around my shop. He wants to drive a second car in the Daytona 500 in Feb.'61. Well, I was surprised Fireball didn't object too much. He liked Panch. Everybody liked Panch 'cept cigarette, alcohol companies and wild women race fans. He don't smoke, drink or chase pussy. You might say he was "a freak among racers." Well, I'm glad he talked me into running the year old car for him cause with 13 laps to go Fireball's Pontiac suddenly looks like a mosquito spray truck. Bye-bye one/two finish. But Starvin Marvin is right there, and ends up with all the money ($20,500 bucks) and fame.

Well, Marvin and I try again at Charlotte in '61, but this time at 140 laps we have serious engine failure and expensive damage in the stopping process. (El Crasho.) We get $230 bucks for our efforts, no fame, no fortune and a basket case racecar. We try again, Southern 500 Fireball has got three-lap lead and 87 laps to go. Fireball is a sick, sore, pooped out racer. Marvin was driving a Petty Plymouth that poops out early, so we get Marvin and put him in Fireball's car. Don't know exactly what's going on. Maybe Marvin can't reach the pedals, or car don't suit him, but when we got seven

Marvin, his kids Richie and Marvette, Junior Robbins and Marvin's wife Betty after the 1961 Daytona win.

laps to go Nelson Stacey finally unlaps himself three times and passes Panch. Good-by glory.

We tried again, Charlotte '61 in October, lap 113, Fireball lucks out by crawling out alive and not hurt bad in the goddamnedest crash you ever saw. Lap 136 Marvin uses walls and other cars for brakes and it didn't really help the appearance of that car either. Well I'm out of race cars, so Marvin and I go separate paths to what ever the next adventure is gonna be.

I need to back up a little before I go on to next driver. Marvin would help and get his hands dirty, but he was like 'bout any racer struggling to feed his family, so he was not able to full time it, but he would tow and that was a big help. But Marvin hated tobacco smoke. I smoked a pipe then and he'd really bitch and get feeling bad from the smoke. So, next time we towed to Atlanta, fifty miles out of Daytona I threw him a World War II surplus gas mask. What do you think people thought as we passed 'em towing a race car and the driver or passenger looking like a little elephant?

JOHNNY PATTERSON

You probably never heard of Johnny Patterson. He came out of nowheres. Someone in Tennessee, or Kentucky asked me to build him a Hornet racecar and engine to run Darlington. "Driver's gonna be named Johnny Patterson." "Johnny who?" Turns out he'd raced with us, but for some reason didn't register with me. His car owner was Grady Akers. Never heard of him either. Well in the '52 Darlington race all of a sudden this young cat who qualified 42nd is leading, and doing a hell of a job. Herb and I have a Hornet there and we can't handle him. When smoke clears away Johnny P is second, and Herb Thomas is third. How do you like them apples?

Johnny, I'd guess was 'bout 19, 20 years old, good looking, 'bout six foot, curly hair. Don't give a shit 'bout nothing. Man, He'd of needed a bucket full of Viagra to half keep up with the potential business he was offered. Johnny thought I was superman he was so impressed with the car and engine. Ol' Herb was pissed. For whatever reason, I decided not to do any more for the car owner (I think we had a money dispute 'bout the bill). Racing is not the best way to establish lasting friendships. I guess it's because the people involved are goofy. Well, fate has funny way of dealing the cards. A few years later Johnny shows up here married with kids, and becomes my truck sales manager. International and GMC, mostly diesel. We got along great. He did a good job. Healthy, I thought, then without any warning (I can remember) he is gone. That stayed heavy on my mind. I decided to work less, party and drink more, and worry less. Indirectly Johnny, you caused me quite a few problems. That life style caused more bad days than good days. Johnny, too bad you didn't get a good full time ride. You may very well have been the first Jeff Gordon.

As you consider these drivers, and the character of all of us who were helping construct a foundation for something, we didn't have the slightest idea what we were building. It's hard to comprehend it's formula that led to such an economic and entertainment success. NASCAR, or stock car racing was built with these ingredients: illegal alcohol, unpaid bills, liars, con-men, carneys, extreme sexual adventures, cheating, broken families, extreme medical pain, sudden death, crippling accidents, work loads of 80 hours a week, an arrangement whereby all competitors had to pay for the right to work for nothing and quite a bit of physical fighting, and with quite a bit of loss of freedom from time to time (simply stated…jail). The above gave us a social status one step lower than the man who rode on the back of a garbage truck. We called 'em "'mon-backers."

Now consider the above. Mix it all up, and add water (or maybe whiskey) and it isn't too hard to understand how this mixture hardened good enough to support what now exists. Or more importantly, and intriguing to me, is it going to be able to support the massive weight now being placed on it? The few of us left from the class of '47 have got to remember that when last guy leaves, close the door behind himself. The journey was like we sat down in a chute with a down hill attitude and our asses greased and smoking. Ever down, ever faster.

I'm going to give you a partial list of names that NASCAR drivers used as their first names. This list comes from first nine years we raced, starting 1949: (these names came off of entry blanks)

Buzz…Fireball…Slick…Ace…Runt…Peck…Buck…Skimp…Chuck…Buckey…Reds…
Shep…Pewee Pap…Pappy…Lucky…Soapy…Red…Bud…Speedy Buckshot…Dink…
Cannonball…Shorty…Whitey…Chick…Slab…Cotton…Squirt…Fonty…Bub…Possum…
Jug… Rebel…Hub…Brownie…Tiny…Smokey…Tex…Pepper…Izzy…Buddy…Fifi…
Rocky…Sandy…Slow Poke Chick…Rusty…Tubby…Junie…Crash…Hap… Nuffy…Herk
Sonny…Fuzzy… Tojo…Woody…Bugs…Dizzy…Bo…Speedy…Jose… Buster…Tip…
Boss…Nook…Blackie…Hooker…Scotty…Pug…Gib…Giff…Spook…Wimpy…
Pop… Dutch…Roz…Bunk…Curly…Huck.

From this list of names do you get some sort of an idea how we stacked up educationally, and financially and morally? (I'm not talking sex here). These were my relatives. These were the wrenches Bill France used to build his empire. My guess is 90 percent of the above are dead now. Every single one got same reward…no pension, no retirement, next to nothing regarding medical insurance. Maybe it's what we deserve for being race car happy; for our addiction to noise, speed and extreme competition. I think it's important you know this. I'm proud to have raced with them. A few of the above were assholes, but it's the way of the world and nature. I got a million stories about 'em. You'd get bored reading them all.

Examples:

Be-Bop, alias Joe Weatherly, is in a modified race on the last lap running second to Sam DiRusso. He bumps Sam coming off of three, He gets wobbly and Joe gets the lead. Joe goes on to win and Sam comes in third. Joe refuses trophy and money, says it belongs to Sam. And then it does go to Sam.

George Bush drove a '52 Olds 88 sixty-seven laps at North Wilkesboro.

Joie Ray, first colored driver, drove a '52 Henry "J" at Daytona on the beach 1952. He crashed. Don't believe ever saw Joie again.

There's an old racing sports writer…lives in Spartanburg, South Carolina – Gene Granger. Only man who really recorded the NASCAR adventures anywheres near accurately. He's still with us…boy that cat has the stories.

Dick Rathman

Yup, the older of the two racing brothers. Dick was from my world in a way, but actually quite a bit further into the unconventional. He and I were throwed together by the Hudson Hornet race program. He drove a Hornet for a very nice man (Hudson dealer from Pennsylvania) named Walt Chapman. So from '51 to '54 we did much towing, traveling and racing together. Dick, Herb Thomas and I worked on our cars together usually at some Hudson dealer's shop, or at my place. Dick had a real good young helper, or stooge, who traveled and lived with Dick. His name was Bob McKee. Yup, same guy now president McKee Engineering, Lake Zurich, Illinois. Best way to describe Dick is 'bout six foot 1inch, good-looking, baldish, blond, nice smile. But he was a weird, crazy cat. He'd cry if he saw a wounded bird but would light matches and burn a rat's feet or tail.

Drive? Damn rite! He was a racer. Open wheelers or taxis. Went like Jack the Bear. He could 'bout do anything on a racer car and do it well, except engines. But he wasn't too shabby on rebuilding an engine. I think Dick just missed being a big hero by a whisker. He was so fucking goofy nobody took him seriously. Morally, he didn't have any problems – he didn't have any and did what ever the hell he felt like. Once in awhile, he'd drive a car I built engine for or worked on. When Dick had to, he'd work his ass off. When the Hudson deal wore out, Dick got serious 'bout Indy and ran hot and cold there, but not because he didn't mash the throttle…he'd go like a winner, then either the car or he would goof up.

'Bout 1964 or so Dick just kinda drifted off and didn't come back. Last I heard he lives south of me 'bout 100 miles in Melbourne, Florida. He's been there 'bout thirty years in the auto business. Dick Rathman was a rough tough racer with elephant balls, but he acted a lot of the times like he was standing behind the door when the brains were handed out.

Dick was a Californian. His dad had a butcher shop in San Gabrielle. So actually Dick was from that super crop of Californian racers that controlled and won most all of the open wheel circle track stuff including Indy. His pedigree was 100 percent racer. Remember I told you he was weird. His sense of humor put me in a position where I was a few seconds away from death in 1957. For those who chose him in a game of "chicken," he'd die before he'd back down. The 1958 Indy race accident in turn three was product of the game of chicken between Ed Elisian and Dick. He told me they went eyeball to eyeball into turn three wide open, waiting for Ed Elisian to back off. When Ed did back off it was too late. All hell broke loose, including Pat O'Connor losing his life.

One time Dick got hurt and couldn't start the Indy race. I said, "What happened Dick?" Well, he put both hands on his hips, and with his elbows turned frontward, and in his serious, patented "let's talk" stance said, "You know the colored cat house at "such and such" street at Indy? Well I was parked in the alley and…." Dick never won any super big races, but it wasn't cause of shortage of desire or skill. I guess you could say the Dick R. I knew went through those fifteen years sideways. One time we were racing Hudsons on a half-mile dirt track at Savannah. Herb Thomas was in the #92 Hornet and was running good. Dick was not getting it done. I start telling him what he is doing wrong. He don't say a word. Puts his helmet on me and says "show me." OK, he slides over to passenger seat (it's a bench on front seat, no back on passenger side. He's got no helmet, no belts. Second lap I say as I come off of #2 "tell me where you lift for #3." He shook his head and never opened his mouth. We went into three wide-ass open. Spun around a big-big-big light pole. Matter of fact, lost the driver's door handle spinning around the pole. Spun again at entrance of #4. Just missed three or four other cars. When it stopped, he said, "Don't stall it"

MAURI ROSE

A small man physically, but with attitude of a nine hundred pound gorilla. He weighed 'bout 125 pounds, and with 10 or 15 pounds of balls. I met Mauri on the hill where the main grandstand of North Wilkesboro is now, in early 1955. He smoked a pipe and when he started running "hot" that pipe would wiggle up and down. Kinda reminded me of a pissed off rattlesnake. Then somebody got bit. Didn't matter if it was a floor sweeper or president of General Motors. Mauri worked personally for Ed Cole. Ed carried #1 plate at Chevy then. This was the original meeting where Chevy wants to play racer, and France wants me to get 'em hooked good. Ed introduces around, and asked if I'd met Mauri before. I say, "Nope, just heard about him." Mauri says, "Yeah, what did you hear?" I answered truthfully, "I was told you were the most miserable, nasty 'li'l son-of-a-bitch that ever crawled in a racecar." The pipe wiggled for five seconds then quit. He took pipe out and said with a laugh, "I used to be…but I'm not anymore."

Mauri and I never had one problem. He was a racer. He also knew his shit and worked like a horse.

He was an engineer. He didn't have to do physical work. He didn't have to put in eighty hours a week.

He did cause he was a racer first, Chevy engineer second. Mauri lived with my family in Daytona for a year for convenience. His old Indy buddies would ask me, "How can you stand that li'l SOB?" I'd answer, he's best man I ever worked with."

Well racers, Chevy's stock car racing program was born in my ol' junk garage (June 1955). And the whole deal was run out of there till March 1957. Mauri helped me get going at Indy. He and I remained friends till he passed on. Poor Mauri, life never was too generous to him. He won Indy three times. I don't know how he stood it. He drove standing up kinda. He was small and solid but to steer an Indy car four-plus hours, he patented a way to do it. Stiff armed and twisting his shoulders. No seat belts. I guess then only sissies used seat belts. A helmet 'bout equal to a turtle shell for strong. A t-shirt, regular pants and street shoes. He had to have glasses to drive. Kinda like a skinny Mr. Magoo with a mustache. Even though he'd won Indy three times, he never got all the good shit most other winners got.

He had two kids he raised by himself, named Mauri and Dori. I want to tell you there were two of life's functions I dreaded with Mauri. Number one was eating with Mauri and the kids in a restaurant. Number two: was riding as a passenger in a car with Mauri driving for over ten minutes. The restaurant deal was macaroni flying all over hell. Mauri cleaning his pipe with the butter knife. Actually, if a video would have been made to show the absolute worse manners you could demonstrate in a restaurant, they would have received an Oscar. Mauri would laugh his ass off, and was as bad as the kids. The second deal was, ride with him. He accelerated to within two inches of car in front of him, back off. Get 15 car lengths back, and then do it again and again for three or four hundred miles. Now he never put a scratch on any car, but that drove me nuts. I tried wearing a blindfold, but he never changed. Just ignored my ass. Only way out was always use a car that was not so-called "his."

Mauri had a pretty good approach to helping drivers, especially at Indy. But if you were a phony he wouldn't give you the sweat off of his balls. He never got half the credit he deserved regarding Chevy's success in racing from 1955 to 1970 because of his nonconformist attitude. Simply put he was allergic to brown nosing and pelicans. If racers were ranked somehow from privates to generals, Mauri would have been a five star. Mauri got a lousy hand dealt in his last illness. In his early seventies, according to his son Mauri wrong medication made a minor problem fatal. Mauri Rose, Thank you. I learned a lot from you. You'd be proud of me. I believe I'm in the top ten regarding "nasty." Not long ago a reporter said I was "infamous." My wife was tickled, she thought that was good. I said, "Look it up in the dictionary." Then she wanted to kill the little bitch that printed it.

Mauri was a good speaker, funny as hell. Ed Cole wants me to learn how to bullshit a young audience, high school and college kids and young engineers, also car dealers. He puts me in front of 2,000 people and I get scared shitless and paralyzed. "No sweat," Ed says. "Dale Carnegie will fix that in two months." Well, don't work out. Dale Carnegie refunds money after six weeks and says, "Hopeless case." Mauri says, "Smoke, listen to me. I'll show you how, and it's a piece of cake." He says, "Just pick out somebody in back row, anybody and look at and talk to him or her." Hell, that's easy. " OK," the audience is 2,000 college kids. I get introduced (thought they were talking 'bout somebody else, so much good stuff). Now or never. I look back row over. Damn, there's Mauri back there. Yeah, this is gonna be easy.

I open my mouth to talk (Chevy wrote the speech). Mauri sticks his fingers in his mouth and makes a goofy face, so I change the first sentence to "Mauri, you asshole." Well, now I'm lost. Terror sets in for sixty seconds. Finally I start reading the speech. You're right. I was terrible. But the biggest laugh I got in the whole forty-five minutes was the first sentence. After it was over I decided hell, they won't fine you or shoot you for a lousy speech, and if you're lousy they won't ask you anymore. That was forty-eight years ago. Today I'm as good a bullshitter as most anybody. Thirty minutes or three hours. I don't need to have a written deal. I just wing it, and size of audience don't bother me, 'cept I don't like a real small audience.

Mauri Rose is a five hundred page book in himself. I'm just trying to give you an idea of his contribution to racing. For those of us who knew Mauri, his son Mauri is an uncanny exact carbon copy in all ways, 'cept 'bout forty pounds over. Kinda looks like Mauri Sr. with an air hose blowing him up a little.

Fonty Flock

'Bout like Tim, he didn't drive a whole lot for me, but he helped when somebody got wounded or they were between jobs. Fonty was one hell of a driver – second to none. 'Bout five-eleven, a little too many steaks and booze. Let's call him "portly." But like Foyt, if it had wheels (four) and a motor, he could drive it 'bout as fast as it could be done and make it look easy. And if it didn't handle he'd experiment with different grooves and technique till he made it go fast. Also, he was easy on a car. He could keep in contention without killing the equipment. Personally, Fonty was a clown, a world-class beauty contest judge. It's been said, "Being nice to Fonty was not the best way to lose a beauty contest he judged." I think you'll find this hard to believe. The racers of the forties, fifties and sixties deep down really liked each other but wouldn't show it.

One time in 1957 Paul Goldsmith and I went to Concord with a Chevy. Bruton Smith's half-mile hi-bank mud hole. Holman is crying 'cause Fireball, one of his four aces, ain't gonna make the race with his purple people-eater Ford. (Fireball has his own airplane now, but bad weather has him parked – no instrument ticket). John's only gonna have three cars in the race. So I say, "John, I'll drive it for you," and he figures maybe I'll kill myself and make life easier for him. I don't know. So the word's out: "Smokey's gonna qualify Fireball's Ford."

Fonty's driving an Olds. He comes over. Says, "Smoke, don't do it. The track's real bad. Slippery, and even before race, it's got big holes." I say, "Nope Fonty, I'm gonna do it." So Fonty says, "Best you're gonna get for practice is ten laps. I'll lead you around and pick it up a little each lap." He was so fast that the only way I even got close was run it like it was dry, and hope the holes didn't tear the wheels off. With Fonty's lesson I get 'er qualified fair. Meanwhile, Fonty tells somebody, "Let's put him in the swamp off of turn three. Trees there only three-four inches in diameter, they'll slow him down before he busts his ass."

My driver Goldsmith says, "Isn't it gonna hinder my performance here today when I got no pit crew and have to gas the car myself?" I say, "No problem Paul. I'll be I the pits in no more than fifteen laps if the right front don't fall off first." (I can't seem to miss the big hole going into number one.) "I'm gonna put it in the swamp. There is no wall there, just a wood rail fence." Paul says, "Would you like a little help?" I say, "No, might get one of your tires. I'll do it myself"

Ralph Moody is there and thinking a lot better than John H. He gets the plan figured out. Ralph figures maybe Fireball will show up at the last minute, but he doesn't. We're lined up to start race and here comes Moody along with Dale Earnhardt's daddy Ralph. Moody says, "Smoke, would you mind letting Ralph drive it?," so they hold up the start till we get switched. Guess what happens? With 'bout fifty laps to go, Earnhardt gets bumped, he ends up in the swamp exactly where I was gonna put it. Fonty don't know 'bout drivers switch, he's on the pole and I'm fifteen cars back. He keeps expecting to lap me, but it don't happen. When car goes out of ballpark, he can't see the driver either. He tells me, "I should start driving steady, I did a hell of a job." I didn't tell him the truth.

Next race he got even. He fixed me up with a fancy lookin' woman, but the joke was on me. It was a cross-dresser. You ever been down that road? Man that's a shock. All I could do is laugh. No, you're wrong, all I did was laugh. I went back to the bar and got Turner's girl (he was out of it). While in the bar, I got even with Fonty. I asked him if he'd laid the young beauty queen he was fooling with? He said, "Hell no." I said, "Good, local guy told me she had a bad venereal disease." Fonty turned white. I found out later he left track for a penicillin shot.

To me, Fonty was a showman who did his own stunts. Can you imagine today somebody running in front all day at Darlington in Bermuda shorts and sandals and a Hawaiian flowered shirt? He was part of the early circus that built the fan count. When Tim got kicked out of NASCAR, Fonty was pissed, and he started being "not there." Saddest deal was the end. One morning, I hadn't seen him in a year. He shows up 8:00 am with a ton a blueprints, happy as hell. "Say Smoke, I'm building a race track. Two-and-a-half mile, high bank gonna be fastest track in the world. It's gonna be a monument to the Flock family. It's in a place called Eastabooga, Alabama." I'm in a state of shock. I say, "Where the fuck's Eastabooga?" He says, "Just this side of Birmingham. I got the land bought, and a contractor partner. All I need now is two race dates. I want this and this. What do you think?" By now we're in my office. He's got the prints unrolled explaining whole deal. Man, about 75 pounds of blue prints. This is one happy Flock. Well, Eastabooga is actually what you call Talladega now. Same piece of ground, but named for bigger town not too far away. 'Bout 4:00 pm the same day, here comes Fonty driving a new Dodge cream-colored station wagon. Says NASCAR insurance on the door. You know, NASCAR's insignia then (maybe still, I don't know). Fonty jumps out hollering. "France loved it Smoke! He loved it. I got two dates. Blabbly-blah-blah. Smoke, he wants a part of it, five percent or so. And listen to this, he offered me the job of head of NASCAR insurance." Back then NASCAR was trying to complete with AAA in insurance and road service (with free Dodge station wagons from Chrysler). I said to Fonty, "My gut feeling is, you'd better keep plenty of Vaseline on your ass, cause I got the damnedest feeling you're gonna need it."

About one year later 8:00 am, here's Fonty pulling up in an old wore out looking Oldsmobile. He says, "Smoke, I need to talk to you." We go in the office and close the door, and this big-rough-tough, wild-ass racer starts crying like a baby. He says, "Smoke, the insurance deal is over. I have no job." He says, "I'm sick-very sick." I think I knew his illness was terminal soon. He tells me, "I don't own Eastabooga anymore. I don't even own one percent. That son-of-a-bitch has got together with my partners and governor George Wallace, and General LeMay, and I'm not even the janitor there. Zero. Totally screwed out of the whole deal." Man, I'm tore up and pissed big time. I was afraid of trouble, but never dreamt it would be so bad. I never saw Fonty again. He went back to Atlanta and died not too long after. What's shocking is, now, thirty some years later, nobody knows the real story of Eastabooga. Nobody really knows what a major part Fonty played in the foundation of NASCAR. 98 percent of NASCAR fans got no idea what a super driver Fonty was.

Writing this has got me really pissed off again. Course I only heard Fonty's story. Maybe? But I saw the blueprints – looked at 'em for an hour! France didn't know about it till after I knew about it.

CHARLIE GLOTZBACK

He shows up middle sixties. A hillbilly from 'round Louisville. This is back in the 200 mph days on "May Pops." That was a descriptive name Joe Weatherly gave Goodyear tires then. Charlie and I tried to race a little. We run fourth in Atlanta. Nichols grabbed him then.

Charlie, 'bout six foot, 175 pounds of country boy, but he would damn sure mash the pedal. His bravery and shortage of experience with the woefully inadequate tires caused some very expensive problems when you unexpectedly use a concrete wall, or other cars to stop your racer. If you run into Charlie someplace and he tells you he used to be a racer, take my word for it. He was! I bet you he could still turn a damn good qualifying lap.

Charlie won some races and would have done really good, but he was wired in with Chrysler, with Nichols and Goldsmith, and when they pulled out of Dodge Charlie was an orphan. So we'll never know just how tough Charlie was. You'd like him if you knew him. He was a "aw shucks, twarn't nuthin" type. I doubt they name any grandstands after you Charlie. But I'll vote for you as a genuine racer.

LLOYD RUBY

'Bout a half-Texan, half-hillbilly. Very quiet. Genuine hot-dog. Mostly an open wheel cat. I think only place we raced together was Sebring Trans-Am race. I had a Camaro that would go like hell, but had a bad habit of breaking before the end of the race. Now he was no slouch in a road race. He could heel and toe it with the best of them. He's still peddling. Still looks like he's only got 80,000 miles on him. He won Indy two or three times. (Well almost, things like leaving pits with a four inch fuel line connected didn't work out.) Rube maybe wasted some Indy years driving car that either wouldn't turn or seemed to prefer going through turns rear end first. Rube had a patented style of driving around everybody in the grey shit on top of the groove, especially turn three and four at Indy. When he came by on the outside in the marbles 'bout ten mph faster than people tip-toeing in the groove it must have flat demoralized 'em.

Rube was way short on luck. Always some weird-ass deal would pop up and knock him out of the tub. He was from the old school of roadster runners on skinny cast iron tires, 'bout five inch wide at the track with a built in contour, so fucking hard you could run over a Hertz "don't back up" deal and not hurt 'em. Hell, if they had no air in 'em the 50-ply sidewall would hold car up. Also, these tires run 40 to 50 pounds of pressure. Them things, when they were best they get, were like 'bout like running in our own oil for four hours.

If you see him ambling 'round Indy in his white straw hat and boots, he is looking for a card game. (A tip: unless you know your card games, don't plan on making any money playing against him.) He is one of the very few of that special breed of open wheel runners who drove like there would be no tomorrow and got away with it, other than their special trade marks (severe facial burns.)

JOHNNY RUTHERFORD

In 1963, I'd built a Chevy with the so-called "Mystery Engine" or porcupine engine, right at 600 horsepower – these things would flat haul ass. Should have never run 'em. Never was but 42 sets of parts. Actually these were 427 cubic inch, and very close to the big block as finally produced and sold in mass. They were not produced because they cost too much by Detroit standards then. I've not raced for a while, got no driver, I'm working for Mr. Knudsen. (He is Chevy general manager and a General Motors Vice President.) Knudsen is a racer, 100 percent pure. Goofy as us 'bout going fast and winning.

A friend of mine who works for a Pontiac dealer in Dallas, name of Monk King, calls me and says, "You ever seen the rookie Johnny Rutherford drive?" I say, "Nope, never heard of him." Well, Monk says, "I believe that boy is special." Now my ears perk up. I want a young driver to see if I can teach him to drive like I think it should be done. Now really what qualifies me as a driving instructor? (Course this is when I think anybody with big balls can go fast in a race car). I'm thinking, "If you have a good plan and follow it would be better than qualifying on pole and lead every lap. So, I go quietly and watch Rutherford run a couple times. I decide Monk's rite. This kid is special. Only reservation I have is I wonder if he has a depth perception problem. Or is his peripheral vision impaired? I see him get away with stuff that makes me wonder. Is he a dirty driver? Are his eyes less than perfect? Well, I think we can "handle that," so I call him in Dallas, offer him the ride in the Mystery Engine Chevy for the '63 Daytona 500. You can guess his reaction.

Next, I call Knudsen and tell him what I've done. He goes ape-shit. Johnny who? I remind him my job is to run the race shit as I see it. (I don't tell him how to run Chevy.) I say, "You'll really like him Boss. He is a very nice young man and perfect for speeches and personal appearances." Back then Johnny looked like Tom Cruise with Adler elevated shoes. Really, anybody who has met Johnny will back me up. John was, and still is good people.

Well, my competition is laughing their ass off. I show up too late to run for the pole, of course. We are having a hell of a time keeping the engine running. Oiling is a little weak, and rods are shaky. Johnny gets one half-day practice and sets fast time for all qualifiers. Goddam! Knudsen is tickled to death. What a smart move on my part.

Step number two: Johnny wins 125-mile qualifier. Holy shit! What a brilliant move to find Johnny. "How'd you know this kid was so good?" We are talking 'bout a rookie setting fast time and winning his first Winston Cup race. (That's never been done before or since.) This was his first race in a stock car of any kind (and no restrictor plates at Daytona to boot).

In the five hundred-mile race, lack of experience catches up and it don't happen, but I never expected it would. He run ninth.

Johnny and my son Smokey.

During that week or two of practice. Qualifying, 125-miler and 500 race, my suspicion of eye problem gets worse. Matter of fact in the 500, as he entered the pits once, I decided he either had a mafia contract to kill me, or his depth perception didn't exist. Maybe the most important thing in racing for me was, "Don't get anybody hurt real bad or killed." Johnny, don't get pissed 'bout this. I still think you're a great and very special racer. Hell, you won Indy three times. That ain't too shabby is it? But the 500 is over. I felt he did it with a serious handicap, poor peripheral vision, and below normal depth perception. I always rooted for John at Indy, or wherever they run those things, but to me Johnny was Mr. Magoo.

The race world goes ape-shit over Johnny, so I decide to skip a few races and try to get oiling better. Really, I want Chevy to pull the Mystery Engine out of NASCAR. (I'll tell you 'bout that in Mr. Knudsen's stuff). I let Bud Moore steal Johnny from me to drive his Mercury. Don't ask me why, but with fenders over the tires, Johnny never much pissed a drop. Sure, most of his stock cars were dogs, but he did have a few good ones.

Johnny's got a son coming on now as a driver. Maybe he can top his dad. But I believe he will have his hands full for next fifteen years just to match him. The sprint cars later 'bout ate Johnny's ass up. He did some serious sheet time from sudden stops on the hi-banks. To me his racing record is bigger than it seems to you.

Johnny is now an executive in Indy car. Hopefully, he finds enough to do to wind up his working life. He's a hell of a public speaker and a real credit to racing. John's not from the breed like Lloyd Ruby or Jimmy Bryan. He's from someplace in the middle between 1947 and 1997. If you see him around and get a chance to meet him, do so. You'll be shocked to find out how normal he seems to be in spite of his thirty years as a racing champion and doing it the hard way, in open wheelers.

Jim Reed

A Yankee from New York shows up out of nowheres. Does all his own work, car and engine. Everything off the blueprint of say, Marshall Teague. He was very good in all departments, including race strategy. He never joined in with us socially, but I think it was cause he didn't have the time. He had to "yellow bar" it every place, operating out of Peeksill, New York, plus build it and drive it, and run a repair shop.

Jim was 'bout a six-footer, 175 pounds, mild mannered, but by no means a push-over. Passing him was no easy deal. He wasn't around us too long before he was through. He ran rite behind Herb Thomas at Darlington in '55, and won it in '59 in a Chevy. Ed Cole wanted the 24 hour closed course record, so I got two Chevys ready and had Paul Goldsmith, Jim Reed, Betty Skelton, Tim and Fonty Flock drive 'em.

Jim did a hell of a good job, and we got the record just a little over 100 mph for 24 hours.

This deal is strange, in that there is no record of this at NASCAR, Darlington or Chevrolet. Yet it was a nationwide deal with one or two full page advertisements for a week. Jim didn't spend a lot of time with us. I figured he realized stock car racing was not really the road to riches at that time. His racing provided him with motor city contacts, and he became a car-truck dealer, and I heard a very successful one. You came south too soon Jim. Now days with your talent, you'd have your own Lear. Jim's seventy-four years old and still going strong as a truck dealer.

Swede Savage

A young, big, well-built, blond, good lookin sports car type, could have just as easy been a movie star. Somehow I put him in a 1969 Trans Am Camaro I built, and we gave Watkins Glen a try.

Well, Swede did his job, but I flunked my part. The front engine torsional dampener exploded cutting power steer lines, brake lines and water hose. A big loud noise was next, as the front of the car got it's shape altered in the stopping process at end of rear straight away, just before a full 90 degree to the right.

Well, I went out of the Trans Am business for a while. In 1970 I'm working for Ford again and I got a Talladega with a Boss 429 in it, 'bout 640 horses, and 'bout 200 pounds too much on the front wheels. I got Swede to drive it. Swede did his part but my engine exploded 'bout 130 laps before race was over.

Swede and I were from two different worlds, so no way we could have been a successful team. But Mr. Knudsen really liked Swede's style, maybe 'cause they were both Swedish. What I saw was Swede wanted Broadway quick, big sports car races and Indy. He found a home with Dan Gurney perfect for his plan, best Indy car and great road race connections. But 'bout time his star was really visible he got involved in a very serious accident at Indy in 1973 that took his life. He was on his way. He had led some laps and was a serious contender to win.

Les Snow

A big Illinois racer, his nickname was Junior. 260 pounds, six foot one. Jr? I met him at Marshall

Teague's shop. He was a half-assed Saturday night special runner. Poor boy…Les Snow could drive a race car and do it well, but he was simply too goddamned big and heavy to be a world-class racer.

'Bout like Jeff Gordon having to drive with a 65 pound block of concrete along each side of his seat.

I don't remember where we raced, except the Mexican Road Race 1953. Well, check this out. Marshall Teague is by now being called portly by the kinder writers, and fat-assed by the nasty ones. The car finished sixth in its class, but without the extra 220 pounds, maybe it would have given the Lincolns a tough time.

Les loved to run the Beach (the real beach), brought his own car down each year and worked on it at Marshall's gas station. Les was a stereotype 1950 stock car racer, loved to race, did all his own work, spent every dime he could get his hands on to build and maintain a race car.

Back then 90 percent of difference in real good fast racer and a shit-box was pure work and know-how, the way the rules were. And remember, there wasn't one fucking thing built for sale to make a stock car go faster except cam shafts (and a hot rod cam was illegal). Sure, there was a few pieces for flathead Fords. But we didn't race them except as modified, or sportsman, so brain and sweat were the speed secrets. Period. Well yes, maybe I left out another big help. Some called it ingenuity, creative thinking, or most times it was called cheating.

Les was a funny and interesting guy at work or at play. It didn't take long at all to qualify him for a real Southern racer's badge. Les wasn't the most eloquent person, so funding for him was a real problem. Unfortunately, he chose a method to supplement what he earned working on cars that was frowned on by society. Apparently he was appropriating and reselling state property. This then caused him to drop racing for quite awhile and enter a controlled environment. When he was released from the penitentiary, age hadn't been too kind to him, he tried to resume his racing career, but his health seemed to fail very suddenly. Poor Les never got 'er going again, and left the deal at a very early age.

Maybe you don't think too much of Les's lifestyle. Listen: to be goofy enough to race in the thirties, forties, fifties and sixties, racers were not composed of a group of potential Nobel Prize winners, but Les and his brothers helped build racing's foundations. At least Les could read and write (in English, and knew a few Spanish dirty words – we learned them at Angel's in Mexico City during the 1953 PanAm Mexican Road Race).

Jerry Grant

Here's a guy who is just too damn big and heavy to be a race driver. He is USAC's Tiny Lund.

Jerry really liked sports car racing best. Jerry's a West-coaster, and was in his racing prime same time Dan Gurney was kicking ass. Jerry and Dan became friends and go off to Europe to seek their fame and fortune, and they make a great team and win some pretty tough stuff. Europe don't have circle tracks. It's either a sports car track or road courses. You know, where besides running over other drivers, you run over roosters, dogs, cats, sheep, goats, donkeys. Run in the rain and at night (with headlights). Well Dan ain't no midget either, but he does squeeze into a Formula One car and does good. But, if they'd've jacked a Formula One car apart enough to get Jerry's big ass in, the car would have collapsed in the middle from weight.

So he comes back here and does pretty good running sports cars in the US. I first met him in early sixties. He was racing a Corvette at Daytona and run out of engines, I loaned him an engine and he won the race and he got to thinking I knew how to make horsies. Well, Grant gets bored with the half-assed sports car program, specially the money part and decides to run the Winston Cup.

He gets going pretty good, but he really ain't got a car, team, and amount of money you need to be consistent winner. He's got a good car owner friend Ken, but it seemed to me it was mostly for the fun and hell of it. Well, it don't happen.

Grant did very well for what he had. If he had gotten with a qualified outfit he'd have been tough in stock cars also. In 1974 I've got a turbo charged 207 cubic inch Chevy in an Indy car. I'm at Ontario testing, and Gurney is there testing with a turbo Offy in his chassis. I also have a similar chassis, a Gurney. I ask Jerry to do me a favor and try my car out. Dan OK's it, but I believe it was 'cause he wanted to know how much steam the blowed Stove Bolt had. Grant really liked the power, but in a few laps it gets dark. Maybe if Jerry had a few more laps, and we helped the chassis a little, we'd have gone real fast.

In them days at Ontario we were just under 200 mph laps. Matter of fact, when race was run there (Ontario), Jerry Grant set a new world's closed course record, qualifying at just over 200 mph. So looks like Grant's found his calling. He jacks around with Indy cars, but it goes 'bout same as sports cars and stock cars, almost, but not quite.

He then really goofs up. He owns an Indy car with a Nash V-8 engine. What a fucking expensive dog! Whew. In 1972 he shows up at Indy with no ride. But maybe...in a cliffhanger, he gets 'bout 10 laps practice in one of Gurney's turbo Offied 1972 Eagle and qualifies it. No sponsor, a big screwed up deal. Anyhow, he starts the race fifteenth. "The Mystery Eagle" they called it. Now get this part: he wins the race! But by accident he gets ten gallons of alky out of his teammate's fuel tank (in same pit, Bobby Unser's tank). Bobby's engine blew, and he is a spectator. I'll be a son-of-a-bitch if Penske don't protest it, and in all fairness, rules said you can't do that. (Because of a possible problem we were allotted a specific amount of fuel, and we had a boost control in cockpit. So if you kept boost up all day, you couldn't make it on fuel.) But Grant had fuel in his pit tank. I'll get to it. They penalize him a lap. Now he is 12th, and they give the race to Mark Donohue (Captain Nice).

How's that for a giant range of emotions? From "made for life" to "back in the shit-house." Soon after, Grant has to "hang it up." He's got kids to raise. So he became a Champion spark plug PR man, and a touring speaker. Well "Champion" was the word for spark plug for forty years, but they sat on their ass and run the deal into the ground. By 1987 they were so bad I wouldn't even put one in a lawn mower.

Champion gets sold to Cooper Industries. Grant goes with the deal, so over the next year as Grant and I talk about how far Champion has slid into the shit house. We get to a place where Jerry Grant's boss, President of Champion, Jerry Godwin, says, "Let's hire Smokey to help turn this deal around." Never having done anything like this, I didn't have a clue about what I'd agreed to do. We got a chief engineer who won't rock the boat. "Let's keep doing same ol' shit that got us in this mess" (Tribble and the snails). My job is, "What's wrong and how do you fix it?" Day one, all management gets to meet the "genius from the swamp of Florida." Well, by the end of the day I've pissed off every executive in Champion. They had a party for me that night that further dropped my stock. Jerry Grant and I will help guide the Titanic away from the iceberg. One engineer, Robertson, is real. Knows his shit and wants to get deal going. So, Jerry and I spend next two-and-a-half years pissing into 100 mph wind.

Jerry is director of motorsports, so we start giving spark plug seminars. I write for race magazines, and try to get people to reconsider us. You know, the usual crap when a fucked up company tries to reinvent itself without admitting their product was previously junk. I found it quite puzzling in that the fucker-uppers in charge were still there. If it had been up to me I'd of fired every motherfucker there except Robertson.

The number one racing expert there was expert in customer entertainment. He would have been perfect as a host for the life-style of the rich and famous. But from a racer's point of view, you had to find him, and then kiss his ass for advice. Plugs he gave freely. He had mastered a language I call "grey." Which when consulted for technical guidance came out "either way is good." In plain talk, he didn't know his ass from a hole in the ground!

I was told by the president of Champion "all expenses considered, each racing spark plug we gave away cost us $42.00 to make." (By the way, all Formula One cars run Champion, and that was the major expense.) Grant starts sending me to NASCAR races. Champion had a representative (name Parker), his dad and I had worked together for Champion years ago. Well, Parker had as much use for me as he did for a 12 foot rattlesnake, and to his credit, let me know it. Not the hypocritical act the Limey John pulled. Grant is going goofy trying to swim in this undertow.

Finally we get the third sort of president, a midget named "Little Jack," who had a curly headed asshole named Mike Smith he hired to finish fucking up everything Grant and I had accomplished. My contract is up. So is Grant's. I got the deep six. I suspect so did Jerry. My last straw was receiving instructions on how to handle racers from a pansy. This is 'bout five years later, 2000, it will be interesting to see how long Cooper-Champion can keep it's head above water. They sold out mid '98, wanna buy a plug company cheap? Note: 2000 March Champion bites the dust. Honeywell bought them out.

The above sounds like I got a hard on for Champion don't it? If you knew the real story 75 percent of all big business operates the same damn way. They as a rule are run by a bunch of pelicans (all they do is eat, squawk and shit). While giving their selves more stock options and a higher salary. Jerry and I still work together. Grant's 'bout sixty-one now. Is in good shape for the shape he's in. I'm kinda glad for the adventures we've had together. It looks like he is gonna be able to win the last badge a real racer gets. That is to have made it through life without having to have ever worked.

There is a slight possibility Jerry may not make it out of this world a sane man. He is being tested at the present time at about a "level ten" as the Director of Motorsports at Prolong Super Lubricants.

Hopefully, he makes it a couple more years. His golden years are just in front of him. I'd like to see one more old racer make it without having to sell programs at a race track.

JIM HALL

I doubt the world ever knew the real Jim Hall, or ever will. Jim was born rich to an oil wise family, so he could have lived a good life at a hell of a lot better pace. The area of Texas that Jim lives in (Midland, Odessa) really required a hardy pioneering soul to figure out how to enjoy it. (I know, but I'm not ever planning on going back there). Jim Hall was as good a racecar engineer as ever pushed what he built on a racetrack and said, "Let's have a race." Plus he'd climb in the son-of-a-bitch and drive it himself. And he wouldn't have to get up on the porch when the big dogs came around. When Jim was screwing around with his first Chaparrals I didn't pay much attention to him. Chevy research built his engines. Not quite one horsepower per cubic inch, 330 horsepower nothin' engines, but with all kinds of hi-buck light weight parts. But when Jim went to building his own engines and negative pressure down force cars, I got to lookin' close. I went to his place to test a road race Camaro. He was totally self-sufficient. Had his own track, 'Rattlesnake Raceway,' behind his shops and the shops weren't fancy. Galvanized tin ranch stuff. His racetrack was hooked up to computers in Detroit. This is back in 19-0-shit!

I guess the shop was full of secrets. I don't remember him ever inviting me in. At this point technologically Hall's not following anyone. He is designing and building way-out stuff. Actually at one point I thought that dizzy bastard is as goofy as I am, but his stuff mostly worked. Back then sports car stuff at the Can Am level was world news. I'll tell you this. Jim does not have an ego, and for a Texan you got to give him double points. It's a close call who can go the longest without saying a word, him or Lloyd Ruby.

Jim Hall, well I'd be more accurate to say, Jim and Bruce McLaren and Dennis Hulme came close to driving a Camaro I'd built to run in the Daytona 24 hour race 'bout 1972. Jim came from Texas, Dennis Hulme from New Zealand, and Bruce from Australia, to get fitted to the cockpit and controls. But a terrible thing happened in the inspection procedure. It seems like my interpretation of the rules and those of those inspectors were at odds. I believe the rules were being administered by the gentlemen racers of the driving cap and mustache (where you put your cap on backwards, and then your goggles). As bad as France wanted them to run, (plus he had two tickets to New Zealand and Australia invested), he couldn't budge the fuzz. There was no possible way to make the changes they wanted.

I believe it was big aerodynamic problem. The bottom my car as clean and shiny as the roof. It also had a strange looking deal that kinda looked like Indy car tunnels on each side. I think maybe brake rotors were accidentally a little too big in diameter and they thought engine was four inches back and two inches down. You know, a lot of "nit picking." They didn't like the air jacks at all. Nor the three inch wider and lower front bumper, or the full frame using the engine as part of the frame (a stressed member). They were also very critical of the acid dipped body, and Lexan windows, but they never even noticed it was supercharged by clutch fly wheel and bell housing modifications. Probably just as well, seemed like if I got too creative car would go like hell for a little while then break.

Jim Hall and I crossed paths quite a bit. I worked for Chevy engineering as a race consultant and Jim had a deal with Chevy racing sports cars (Chapparal). Bruce McLaren the same. He had a deal with Chevy regarding Can-Am cars, those big go-fast mothers with tractor puller motors. So we were really from same barn. Jim was formally educated as an automotive engineer – even that didn't destroy his talent. When Jim decided to go to Indy I snickered and thought, "He'll get a work out here." Guess what he comes up with? The first down force tunnel car. Paints it yellar, slaps a Pennzoil sticker on it, then put Johnny Rutherford in it. Blew our doors slap off and went home with biggest check (and also with Al Unser Sr.) Jim's still going. Finally wised up and turned in his racer badge. I haven't seen him since the Indy Car-Cart divorce. Jim, you were one of the first to move racing to the level it's at now. You were a big credit for auto racers.

ZORA DUNTOV

Zora Duntov was, among other things, daddy of the "tuxedo tiger" In 1955 Ed Cole, Chevy's boss man and my boss said, "Smokey, I want you to race the Corvette in road races." I was puzzled; I said, "Ed, you've driven in some road races. I believe in Sebring race for one. How in the Hell can you win a road race using a heavy car with three-speed "Grampa Jones" transmission bolted to an in line six cylinder with a rubber crank and using twenty year old brake technology all attached to the road with a suspension system just better than a manure spreader or hay wagon?" His answer, "Takes a six cylinder Corvette, put in a V8 engine. I'm sending Zora to drive it. Mauri Rose you already have for liaison. Frank Burrell will come down and help with the engines. Paul Johnson will help upgrade the brakes and Gib Hoffstetter will solve all transmission and clutch problems."

So we stuck one of Frank Burrell's 283 cubic inch V8s, the next bigger small block in our Corvette racer. Actually we made the switch in a day. You see, motor mounts, transmission and, drive shaft were all the same for the six and eight. We got Sebring rented for a month to turn this thing into a race car. I have an old Chevy flat bed truck and a grease rack we can drive the car on it with. At Sebring we build a wooden unloading rack. We drove to Sebring every morning to work on the cars. (from Daytona to Sebring, three-and-a-half hours). We left at 5:00 am and quit testing at 5:00 pm. We usually got home around 8:30 pm to fix the day's disasters. We'd "eat" about two to three transmissions a day, 'bout two sets of brakes, the engines held up a little better. Even with the wet sump and poorly baffled oil pan, with the skinny-assed tires, narrow rims and sorry chassis the car really couldn't punish the engine too much. The drive train limited rpm to 'bout 5,300 so the engines lasted a day or two, maybe more.

Zora stayed in Sebring. I first met him at Sebring unloading Corvette first day. I'd heard much about him, and held him in high regard. I was surprised by his very heavily-accented speech (I could just barely understand it). I can't even imagine him saying "y'all." Well, in a couple days I'm clued in. Zora really isn't gonna be listed in world's best drivers book. Maybe on a one to ten, 'bout a six.

Zora is gone now but we were friends for damn near forty years. And if you were still here Zora, you'd have to admit by time we met your driving wasn't much. You were by far a better engineer.

My main helper on this deal is Mauri Rose. He is one of Ed Cole's personal engineers, and at one time "Hell on wheels" (won Indy three times). Mauri is critical of Zora's driving, and does not keep it a secret. So Zora and Mauri had a running verbal battle. Mauri would hold stopwatch when Zora pulled in and say, "What's holding up the car Zora?" He would snap back, "The wheels goddam it!" Now this went on for a month. What saved my ass is that frustrating month was Cole sent three mechanics from Chevy's proving ground crew. A man 'bout sixty, Abe Bidwell, Charley Bear ('bout forty-five), and a young pollock (I'm half pollock) named Whitey, and Paul Johnson, a young engineer who eventually became Chevy's chief engineer. Those four people worked like dogs eighteen hours a day, seven days a week. Also, Mauri Rose was a working demon. I mean, do it! Not bullshitting, but turning wrenches. The Chevy mechanics shocked me at their willingness and first class fast work.

Frank Burrell and Gib Hoffstetter were "pelicans." 'Bout all they did was eat, shit, and squawk. Well, I guess you can't say they didn't work, cause in that time frame young engineers were in training to become staff engineers and they had to be proficient pelicans. I got to like Zora, but I was puzzled by the exercise. I'm trying to put disc brakes on, and a five-speed transmission on, and get a four-wheel independent suspension going, plus another 100 horsepower under the hood and get rid of three or four hundred pounds of fiberglass. (That body was, I mean, heavy!) But nothing changed. Same ol' shit day after day after day. The car wears out parts faster than Frank can get parts shipped in. One day 'bout three weeks into it we used up all transmissions, including the one in my personal car. I have to come back to Daytona from Sebring in high gear only. Last engine blowed, broke a valve and busted up a piston.

I don't know what's going on, so when I get to Daytona I make a pair of valves for it from something else. I weld up the piston and am machining new piston ring grooves in it when I hear Frank talking to Ed Cole on phone from my big red two buck office chair around midnight, saying, "I'm coming back in morning. We are out of parts. I need to go back to get more engines built to finish test." Then I hear, "The swamp farmer's welding up the last broke engine." Makes a big joke out of it. A year later, with the swamp farmer welded up engine, I won the standing mile on the beach against Ferrari and Zora in his special super CERV2 dandy big engine special Corvette. I won in what was the original home-made V8 test car.

Zora and I didn't always agree, so I got eased away from Corvette. You see, Zora had about dictatorial powers regarding Corvette, but actually had to operate with one hand tied behind his back. Chevy never came close to allowing him to make the changes it needed to be a world-class sports car. If they had of, the car would probably tripled in price. Also, a big negative was when Ed Cole moved to become president of GM in '68 he was against racing – 180-degree turnaround.

Zora loved road racing and hi-tech engines. He had about a six-year period he was able to design and build some very exotic engines…single and double overhead cam engines. They were not practical though. Hell, to install 'em in car you have to increase car length a foot, or open the front wheel track up a foot. Too bad Chevy didn't save those engines for all of you to see, but as in everything else they did, long range planning was omitted.

The division managers had awesome power, but at the top corporate level the power was complete, uncompromising and dictatorial. Maybe one word to best describe it: "absolute." Zora had to constantly juggle corporate criticism. After Ed Cole turned in his racer's badge, corporate constantly threw up challenges to deep-six the Corvette. Why? I was told Corvette never made one dime profit. I can't say how it did for GM after 1987 cause that's when I run my mouth negatively for the last time at a General Motors staff meeting.

I can tell you not to call their entire next year's models "shit boxes one and all" if you want to get paid by them. I know first hand that will piss 'em off. After driving all of '87 stuff a year or so ahead of production, after saying "all were junk" to president of GM Lloyd Ruess and five other General Managers and VPs, and when Lloyd said, "What do you propose we do about it?" My answer, "Monday morning, shut down for two years and fix 'em" (meeting was on Saturday). The meeting was quickly adjourned. It's been twelve years since and not even a phone call.

Back to Zora. Zora and I started a year later (1956) to jointly develop the Rochester fuel injection, but suddenly Cole changed his mind. Instead, he had my shop fenced with a twelve foot high chain link fence with a twenty-four hour security company controlling the entrance and we did the job here. ("We" being Ralph Johnson and myself). I went to one retirement party in my life, and only because Zora invited me to his. We stayed in contact till he passed away. Matter of fact I believe his last public appearance was at Columbus, Ohio at the PRI ceremonies to honor the seventy-five engineers who developed the small block engine. I was the master of ceremonies. Zora had much difficulty speaking that night. But we were glad Zora could attend. Very shortly he was gone. Zora, you surely left your mark on this earth, and I'm sure your contributions will be held in high regard for a long time to come.

John Fitch

Our association wasn't for very long. John was in 1956 considered "American Road Racer Badge #1." John was brought in by Ed Cole to be Corvette's big gun. Maybe Zora wasn't too anxious to share control of Corvette's racing destiny. As I said before, after the beginning of V8 Corvette racing, I was slowly moved out of that program into full-time stock car racing, (rite after Herb Thomas won Darlington with the new Chevy and new engine in 1955 and soon after the Sebring Corvette test).

Well, I'd seen Fitch drive in the Mexican Road Race. Actually, as I saw it he should have won, but he drove a Mercedes, one of those gull wing jobs, a factory racer. You know, maybe his didn't have a roof at all. Well anyway, it looked to me like they jacked Fitch around in the pit stops so a German driver would win. No question this cat is good. But he's from a different world. You know, the English sports cap (kind you put on backward, and put on your goggles when you run your MG fast.) A real educated yankee gentlemen from maybe Connecticut? Lime Rock strikes me as his territory. In 1956 and 1957 France had a big deal at the beach called the "Standing and Flying Mile" on the sand – hell of a big deal. You get a hundred idiots and a dozen manufacturers to pay a pretty tough fee to see who was the fastest in about fifty classes. Ed Cole swallows this one big…I believe fisherman call it "gut-hooked."

I'm to build "world's fastest pickup. Zora gets "world's fastest Corvette" ready, including his baby, called the "CERV One." (The initials meant something good and important, but I forgot what.) Well, I find out

John Fitch is Cole's lead man to introduce the Corvette to the sports car set. John drives several Corvettes in the standing and flying mile. I get the job of getting cars ready for the runs, so John and I spend a lot of time together. He was quite an experience for me. Didn't cuss, didn't drink, don't believe he smoked. He ignored all the pussy trying to test his manhood (at least what part I saw and heard). Matter of fact, if I hadn't seen his act in the Mexican Road Race, I'd of labeled him a "jack-off."

John was a slim "seat full," with his helmet rubbing the roof. A really pleasant, nice guy. I don't remember the details, but he was supposed to be a big part of Corvette's birthing, but somehow I don't remember it happening that way. I got the feeling Zora and Fitch weren't exactly asshole buddies.

BETTY SKELTON

Betty Skelton was, I believe, a world class air craft aerobatics pilot…American champion…friend of Bill France Sr.'s. I think aviation didn't pay enough to be a road to a wealthy retirement, and not too many aerobatics pilots lasted long enough to get gray hair. Betty was a cute, li'l 100 pounder, 'bout five foot two. She had guts, and half knew how to go fast. But she was not able to race. A stock car, simply stated, would wear her ass out in ten minutes. (Matter of fact, she helped drive in the 24 hour record run.) I had to spend some time with the steering box to decrease steering effort. In the middle of this "record deal," I had to run Langhorne with a '56 Chevy. Tim Flock was the driver. I left Paul with Betty at Darlington to teach her how to lap Darlington at 100 to 105 mph. When I got back from Langhorne I had a feeling Paul taught her a lot more stuff besides driving. (He did teach her to be comfortable at required speeds.)

During the 24 hour run she did her tank of fuel run 'bout as good as the men. In '56, 100 mph round Darlington was not like going down the street to get a pack of cigarettes. And to do it couple hours at a time, day and night was a pretty tough deal. Track had no lights at all. All they had was headlights. So Betty had talent, but neither France nor Chevy figured out exactly how to harness it in stock car racing, or how to sell Chevys with it.

Goldy, me and Betty Skelton on the beach.

I seen her fly her plane. I think it was a Pitts, (called the li'l stinker). Something maybe connected to a skunk. Now, I at the time figured I knew a thing or two about flying, but I would have been a poor second to her in aerobatics. She was a cheerful pleasant li'l thing, really didn't at all fit in with the stereotype stock car racer. I don't know what happened to her after 1960. I did work on some Corvettes she drove on the beach during the "Flying and Standing Mile" contests. She and Fitch were kinda the Chevy Corvette team.

TIM FLOCK

This racer was what I'd have shown you in 1955 if you were from outer Mongolia and had never seen a car race, and said "Smokey, what is a NASCAR race driver?" He ran in first NASCAR race, and it was his first race. His brothers Bobby and Fonty had experience and didn't want their little brother to get hurt, so they did all they could to discourage him. Didn't work. First race he run fifth to his big brother Fonty's second. (That's out of a thirty-three car field in Charlotte.) No, not the Charlotte you know. This was Charlotte Fairgrounds, 3/4 mile dirt scrabble track with three foot deep holes. His other brother Bob, who was the pole sitter run thirty-second. How's that for a start?

Tim was 'bout six foot two inches tall, thin, good lookin' with loose "don't give a shit 'bout nothin'" attitude. Remember, these drivers didn't have any Buck Baker driving schools to go to and they didn't get two years in Busch cars. It was all on in first lap of your first race, kinda like a live correspondence course. Tim also come into this you might say "cold." His brothers hauled "shine," and were plenty savvy 'bout the high speed feel of "just right" and "oh shit." Tim said he only ever hauled one load. Maybe, maybe not.

Before a race Tim was up-tight, but brother when the green fell, he'd get a shit-eatin' grin, and it was "on." He was kinda like they say, "a natural born." Whatever it was, Tim in a good fast car that didn't break, was 'bout impossible to beat. He had confidence out the gazoo. And once he got car and track figured he was the Orange Blossom Special, long-long gone.

The Flocks were from Atlanta. A tight family, 'bout a station wagon full of kids. Even had a sister (Ethyl - named after the gas) who could "mash it" and knew what she was doing. Tim drove a bunch of modified and sportsman races. What 'bout everybody's forgot, or what later arrivals both competitors and fans don't remember, is NASCAR was not born of stock cars in the strictly stock sense, but with the modified classes. A class of $400 to $500 total cost, '37 Ford coupes, with a well-massaged flat-head Ford engine. That's what did the bulldozing to clear the brush, to start building the Winston Cup foundation. These cars were born of a racing pioneer, the granddaddy of all NASCAR mechanics – Red Vogt. (Jerome "Red" Vogt) His vision, skill and knowledge furnished a road map, and the light when it got dark, for us to follow.

Bob and Fonty Flock, and Red Byron, were Red Vogt's favorite drivers. Behind this was a race lovin', self-made man, who if he had to could haul ass in a modified car, owner Raymond Parks.

This very important circle included a bootlegger, would be-racer, Bobby Watson, really, a Red Vogt "go-fer," and Tim's traveling "boot man" (stooge). The deal was, "Don't fuck with any of this gang, or you may have to deal with the hatchet man Billy W." But Billy wasn't really an Einstein, and he didn't last no time as a bootlegger, before the Federales had him in controlled environment for a while.

The treatment worked. Billy gave up hauling whiskey without tax stamps on it. He by the way, is happy, healthy and well off. If he offers you a ride on his boat take it. It's a big son-of-a-bitch.

Tim was the best known, and maybe the most colorful of the Flocks. But topping Fonty Flock was no easy deal. Tim was a great driver. NASCAR elected him as one of the fifty greatest drivers in NASCAR history, which he damn sure deserved. I would say "top ten." He too, had a large family to support, so he very much participated in the PR circus of early NASCAR. He rode around with a monkey in his car. (Well hell, France and the top cats at Champion Spark plug rode three miles on an elephant, with three quarts of whiskey and two hookers.)

Tim, Fonty and I had some remarkable adventures that were alcohol-fueled, and quite often involved elderly (eighteen to thirty year old) women who apparently felt over-dressed for our parties, and would remove their clothing. Then it seemed the devil took over, at least for me, and made me do things I wouldn't care to have shown on video to my family. Once in awhile things got out of hand and we'd get acquainted with some local police with very poor sense of humor. I can remember an evening in hotel in Philadelphia. We were running Langhorne. A lady got very unhappy with a joke Fonty pulled on her and it took all the strength I and Tim had to stop her from giving Fonty a quick sex change operation without anesthesia. Fonty was indebted to me for rest of his life. In those days we'd of preferred death to anything that would seriously impair our ability to get good grades from the ladies regarding our sexual performance. Fonty, Tim and I always referred to this event as the "hot cucumber deal."(I now call it "the almost Bobbitt" movie.)

In 1956 Tim got pissed at Kiekhaefer and quit. He asked me 'bout driving my Chevy at Langhorne in April. I said "sure." We damn near beat the Kiekhaefer freight train, but not quite, ended up third.

Same-old, same-old – you can't beat cubic inches. We had 283 cubic inches, they had over 300. We maybe ran a few more races, and again went off on separate trails.

In the summer of '60 France kicks Tim's ass out for life, or death, which ever comes first, for joining the racing union. France fought the union like a tiger. Threatened to shoot our asses, plow up the Daytona track and plant corn. All a lot of bullshit. If in fact the union had continued, nothing France could have done but accept it. There are times in life when you have to look down and see who's got who by the balls. Turner, Tim Flock, Goldsmith and Fireball got kicked out of NASCAR. Fireball had a change of heart and reneges on his membership, same with Goldsmith. I had the union's #1 mechanic's license (still do). Nothing happened to me. Guess I ain't important enough. I didn't like the deal worth a damn and, though we needed to get more for what we did, I argued with Curtis 'bout who we were unionizing under. I considered the teamsters a mafia bunch of crooks. Regardless, France made it rough for Turner and forced Curtis back into a corner. Yes, he did. Turner told me the whole story. Course I only heard Curtis's side of it, but I still believe Curtis.

Tim is at top of his career as a stock car racer. He was starving in NASCAR. In USAC it was worse. So Tim quit. Had to. I'm not going to try and list his wins, etc. He was a NASCAR champ a couple times, and all he won wouldn't be as much as one Daytona 500 pays for first place today. I wish I had the talent to be able to explain, or tell you about men like Tim who strapped their asses in those early stock cars races and endured the heat and punishment for three to five hours. Driven by an almost surreal desire to test the absolute limit of every sense they had. Where they put up an entry fee and their lives for a license to compete in a game of Russian roulette, except they used cars instead of guns. Not thirty times a year, but forty or fifty times a year

Bruce McLaren

Man. This cat is from a one of a kind world. Born a Scotsman, a homemade racer, builder, driver type. Kinda like a NASCAR racer from the fifties. I didn't know him too well, but I knew him from day one at Chevy. He had a shop in Detroit and got wired in at Chevy with his Can am program. Bruce to me was super easy to get along with, a very-very hard worker. Bruce could do anything there was to do on a race car, from a clean piece of paper to line it up and race it. He was a damn good driver. I believe he told me he'd run some Formula One races as a driver and builder. Bruce was a damn good engine man. Matter of fact when I first moved the spark plug in the small block cylinder head (the later called "angle plug head"), 'bout 1960 I modified a couple of heads, tested them and sent a pair to Chevy to test. I got 'bout 15 horsepower increase.

Bill Powell and the other Chevy research engineers ran the heads for Piggins, who was at the time the Chevy Motorsports boss man. Report was "ain't worth a shit." They sit on shelf about a year at Chevy research. Bruce spotted them and asked how they worked. They said, "We are getting ready to throw 'em away, They are no good." Bruce tested them next day, went back to Chevy and said they got him 15 horsepower, "Make some more now." Piggins and Fishel got their asses in a crack, so they had to set up a half-assed production line. I had to machine parts and weld them in the heads. Then drill and tap for new plug location, a lot of work. In about a year I read how Piggins and Fishel invented the angle plug head.

I worked for Chevy engineering quite a few years; I finally learned how to get a change. Give the idea to the engineer in charge of that program and wait two years for him to invent it. I used to show it to my boss first (the General Manager). That was the kiss of death. Believe it or not, I was starting to learn how to communicate with pelicans. Bruce was smarter than I was, and he had a way of getting them to do it and like it. I never learned how Bruce did it. Bruce, you're long gone now (he busted his ass testing one of his cars). I'd guess you would have to be one of he five greatest racers ever. Probably in the Ferrari and Colin Chapman, Harry Miller class for starters.

DENNIS HULME

Denny's gone now (notice, not too many racers hang around long in their golden years). I believe a truck ate him up in a race of some kind. Denny and three other European Formula One drivers wanted Indy in '67, and Goodyear said, "We will pay the bill." So in February 1967 Goodyear said "if you had your choice of Dennis Hulme and three more, all very successful Formula One big time racers, and we paid you to run Indy. Which one you want?" I said, "None, I've noticed racing hasn't been the road to riches, and if I apply those eighteen hour days to something else, maybe I'll do better." At this point I'm up to my ass in alternate energy projects. I ain't getting paid, but I'm betting on the "come." (The truth is, that was a loser also, even with White Motor Company's help). I also was committed to run a Chevy in NASCAR a little.

In April '67 in Atlanta, I'm eating supper alone at an airport motel. Goodyear's Larry Truesdale and one of his men ask, "Can we join you?" I said, "Sure" ('cause it would be a free dinner now). Larry asks if I'd reconsider the Indy deal. I got pissed and said, "Hey, we've been down that road in February and I don't want it." He then threw a check for forty grand on table and said, "How 'bout this?" Now I sit up straight. I'm a broke wobbly garage owner, making big-assed alimony-type payments, and paying off a hundred grand note (divorce oriented obligation). As I've said before, "We are all whores at heart, it's just a question of price." At that moment I remembered what an old up-country Dutchman told me (I worked in his gas station). "When you got 'em by the balls, their hearts and minds will follow." So I say, "I get the purse and split it with driver." "Yes sir" says Larry. "You pay for all help and expenses." "Damn rite" says Larry. "I own car after race." "Well, no," says Larry. "We want car back."

I push check back to him and get up. Larry says, "Sit down, you get the car." I'm really rolling now, and I say, "The deal is, I put the forty in the bank, you pay every bill involved in the race, including tools as necessary, including tow trailer and car." Larry sighs and says, "Yup, who do you want for driver?" I say, "The Limey." "Well, Andy Granitelli's spoken for him. "OK, I'll take the goofy Austrian." "Well so and so wants him and I promised." "Well, OK, Denny Hulme." "That's perfect" says Larry. "Sign here." I say, "Bullshit! Change the contract, bring another twenty for expenses in advance. I leave Sunday night at 6:00 pm. If you do what we agreed by tomorrow in writing, then deal's on." Little did I know Curtis was gonna wad the Chevelle up in practice, and I'd be leaving a day early. By 10 am Saturday I got signed contract and both checks. "Thank you, Mr. Detweiller," (the up-country Dutchman). I damn near chickened out on the car deal, but I held on because of your instructions. (By 1980 I decided Roger Penske had met the Dutchman also.)

Indy, here we come. I get a '67 Eagle, it looks like a cigar with some junk sticking out here and there. I get the car April 10th. I got twenty days to get it to Indy. I got one full-timer, T.A. Toomes, and my oldest boy Smokey for helpers. The engine is a four cam Ford normally aspirated, so I put a five-day kamikaze hot rod job on the engine (picked up 30 horsepower). Then started cleaning up the car with fairings and wheel covers and blending in rivets and skin joints. Don't get me wrong, Gurney's 1967 Eagle was the best Indy car going, but I wanted to blow everybody's ass off, rookie or no rookie. We make it to Indy May 1, half-dead from the work. It's a black and gold customized Eagle.

First day in Indy garage, here comes Jack Brabham and his chief engineer. (Sorry ace, but in my advanced age I can't remember it all – only the real good and the real bad stuff.) Also, a bright faced, stocky, not too tall man, who I assume is Denny Hulme. Yup, he was. I look him over, and I think, "How's he gonna get all that ass in a fifteen and a half inch wide seat bottom?" So we pleasantly bullshit each other for 15 or 20 minutes. Denny gets in cockpit and gives me a list of, "shorten this, lengthen that, normal race driver stuff." Now he says "seat's too tight." Jack Brabham says, "Denny, nothing he can do in that area." (Thank you Jack.) So I say, "Two things we can do, one is grease your ass, or the seat before you get in, or don't eat this month.." Next, I ask Denny if he's read his contract with myself that the Goodyear lawyers drafted for he and I. He said, "He had and it was fine 'cept for 'bout ten things." I had a copy and handed it to him, and a pen. Asked him to sign it and have Jack witness it. Denny says, "I will after you make changes." (The "When you got 'em by the ..." drifts around in my head) and I say, "OK. I'll go back to Daytona tomorrow and get contract fixed. I'll be back in two or three days." He decides to sign the contract "as-is." Then Jack hems and haws. I can tell he wants to say something he thinks I won't like.

Remember Jack and I are fairly good friends. We had many midnight conversations in the old Indy garages. We were next door to each other in '64. Jack was trying to qualify an in-line six cylinder he invented or something like that. But the engine was too small in displacement and he couldn't get her in. If you don't know, Jack was a Formula One champion himself. He knew his shit and had elephant balls. Finally, Jack "ahems" and says, "Would you consider letting myself and my engineer handle the chassis? And you handle the engine and everything else?" "No problem, Jack we'll do the work you order." What Jack don't know 'bout four wheel independent suspension at the time ain't worth knowing, and his engineer designed a Formula One championship winning car. This takes a load off my shoulders. Now everybody's happy. Denny's got supreme confidence in Jack. After all, they supplied the car he won the Formula One championship in. Denny is the sitting Formula One world champion.

Well, I don't know if Denny and I are gonna make a team. He calls "pussy" "birds" and I get the feeling if we drilled a hole in his head fifty pussies would fall out. Now that don't make him no bad guy, but at Indy I'm all racer from 6:00 am till 2:00 am seven days a week. But I decide a driver gets more slack. We work our ass off for a couple days. My son has disappeared; apparently he was not happy at Indy. Now its just T.A. and I, and Jack keeping us humping. We've been through seventy-five spring and shock combinations, as well as ten different sway bars, three chassis alignments, about forty attempts in changing weight distribution, with about 200 tire changes regarding stagger and tread compound. Then throw in some engine power increases. I'm watching this with amusement. I know what the problem is, and so does Jack. He's run here and knows to play with the big dogs at Indy and get qualified you got to run five miles an hour over your head, and that plan can really be hard on your future if one of them "Oh shits!" causes you to stop too fast.

Jack says, "Would you mind very much if my engineer and I left? I have some pressing business in Australia." What can I say? His help was a favor to Denny and myself. So I say, "Hate to see you go. Would you reconsider if I rent a kangaroo and tie it to the door?" (I think maybe they are just homesick.) Fifteen seconds later Jack and the brain are on 16th Street spinning tires on the way to airport.

In the seven days we've been there, Denny hardly ever talked to me. When he did it was regarding his adventures with the "birds." So maybe really he did have the genes of an early American racer. We have about four days left before first qualifying day. I hear he plans on going to Europe and we will qualify second weekend. I've got a stock car race problem second weekend. Also, by now I've learned "qualify it the first day is 50 percent of your chance to win or finish good." Denny says, "Don't worry, we'll get it next week." Friday, 6:00 pm, before the first qualifying round, I draw a fair number for an attempt. Denny and I go to garage, he says, "He's got to go to Monte Carlo." I say, "Let's read the contract." He says, "Don't need to, I have." I ask him if he has read the sentence where it says, "If he fails to make a qualifying attempt if I present the car for qualification on the first day, I have the right to replace him."

I reach behind the toolbox and hand him a copy to read. He says, "He's not ready." I had driven the car, so I asked him if the car darted on the straight always? He said, "Exactly." I said, "When you get back on it in the corner does it feel like you're on the edge of a razor blade between loose and push?" He said, "Exactly. It's almost like you were riding with me." I said, "Denny, I'm going over everything on this car tonight, every nut and bolt, every specification, toe steer, every wheel, and I'm gonna add about ten more horsies. I want you to drive it to where you should lift, and get back on it where I've told you at both ends." He says, "OK, if I kill myself it will be on your conscience forever." I said, "Denny, if you don't want to get hurt stay behind ten foot of concrete with me in the pits. However shitty your car feels, so do the others. Make up your own mind. If you leave, Jochen Rindt's skinny ass will be in that seat tomorrow." (I haven't even talked to Rindt).

So at 8:00 am Saturday, here is Denny. He looks like death warmed over. Man is he pissed.

Denny says, "I'll do it as you say, and if I bust my ass…(so on and so on)." T.A. says, "Smoke, that cat's scared shitless." I say, "Nope. He is a fuckin' good driver, and the car's good as any other. All he's got to do is get serious, and he is pissed enough, he'll do fine." On his third practice lap, he's four miles an hour faster. Good enough for the front row. Three more laps and he comes in. Goodyear engineers are swarming around him. I ask, "Does the car have any problems?" "Nope, don't touch it." The 65 plus was easiest first lap all month. Man he is grinning like a shit-eating cat. T.A. says, "Holy shit! That sucker can drive." If Denny listened to me qualifying he'd been in the front row.

He took one lap too many warming up. Threw away a 65 plus and ended with a two mph short fourth lap– the tires were too hot.

Well, now we are buddies – I mean "mates." From then on it was "matey this" and "matey that." I believe if I asked I could have gotten a kangaroo and a boomerang for presents. Readers, take my word for this: tail end of May 1967, Dennis Hulme was about as good as it gets as a race driver.

The race was really a bad one. We got rained out right after start then ran the next day with more rain problems. There were ten caution flags for over an hour and on the first lap of race got about a ten car spin and crash deal. We end up fourth. Not too bad for a rookie and crew chief that never really jelled. In '68 he went with Gurney.

Denny came back 'bout four more years. Did good in '68, was fourth again. Then he didn't do much next two years. Got burned one of those years pretty bad. I'll tell you, if you try a Formula One driver any place you don't run it "balls out" all the way around, put 18 inch tires on it and 17.5 inch brake rotors. They like to go one foot beyond impossible, hit the brakes and then down shift, and wide ass open again. I don't believe we ever talked from 4:00 pm, May 30, 1967, till the day we all met here to try and get cockpit in the Camaro to fit Denny, Jim Hall and Bruce McClaren in 1973. Denny and I never met or talked again. I mention the above because regardless of what happened. Good, bad or sideways, the NASCAR bunch lived like a bunch of gypsies, but we still kept track of each other.

David Hobbs

I met him strangely. He was a European racer, a road racer. Guess that's all they had in Europe. David had a friend in Canada (Godwin) who had some money and wanted to get into big time auto racing in the US. He touted Hobbs, idea being, Hobbs' European experience I think included one or more starts in Formula One. This was fair, I'd make him a desirable candidate for Winston cup or Indy, and Trans Am and Can-Am. Well Godwin, the Canadian, buys some engines from me for a Camaro to be driven by Swede Savage, and tested at Riverside.

I don't want to do it, but I'm working for Chevy, and Piggins decides to get involved with Godwin. The test is junk. Chief mechanic plumbs first two engines wrong. Three laps apiece. They are junk. Third engine was OK with plumbing done correctly. Well, Godwin stays in the game a year or so. Later I have built a twin turbo-charged 207 cubic inch Chevy to run at Indy in a 1973 Gurney Eagle. I've talked to David several times. He and I are nowheres near the same wavelength, but fate screws around, and I end up letting David try this abortion.

The engine either makes 1,000 horsepower or is in process of burning a piston. We have to watch it through the gears, 'cause in the low gears it explodes in rpm when it hooks up. Well, in two days David screws it up twice; I mean "bad." Calls for engine change (incorrect shifting). That engine didn't like 12,000 rpm. So right or wrong, I write David off as a jack-off driver that's an excellent bullshitter. So David and I to this day never have exchanged birthday cards or Christmas gifts. I'm sure David's opinion of my racecar and myself is equal to the driver's rating I gave him.

David does get a shot at Indy driving for Penske. Turns out he don't like it too good. He got in a minor accident on front straight. Jumps out. "Fuck it." Crew chief rams his ass back in.

David forgets to turn ignition switch on. The chief hit him so hard in the head to wake him up; I swear David's head spun 300 degrees.

He turned out to be a big time race reporter, but I didn't like that either. I couldn't understand what the hell he was talking about. Same with Jackie Stewart. But Jackie sure as hell knew how to make a race car go and last

Billy Vukavitch Jr.

While I was testing at Pocono with David Hobbs, Billy was testing for Goodyear. Billy came over and said he'd like to try out with the Chevy. I just finished chewing out the limey's ass for doing it again, so I said, "Sure, no problem. We are driverless rite now." Guess what? In about half hour, Billy misses a gear and the farm is gone again. This is like June 2 or 3, so I got to change engines again, and change was a two-man eight-hour working contest. The garages are small and poorly lit, so Ralph and I decided to change engine in the alleyway at 11:00 pm. I'm a son-of-a-bitch if it don't start snowing. Bad. (First week of June).

Now we are exhausted, freezing and starving. We haven't eaten since breakfast. So I say, "Let's load this shit up and get the hell out of here before they have an earthquake." When I came back to race, the garage area went 30 inch deep in water. Got rained out twice. So Billy V and I never did get to run a race together. I believe if we did it would have worked. His dad was as good a race driver that ever run Indy, and he was from the early class. He was a rough, tough, haul-ass racer.

Billy Jr. reminded me of his dad. Funny, loved practical joking. Did not like the press. 100 percent self-confident. Had a "then" racer vocabulary. That is, every sentence had to have "fuck," "shit," "son-of-a-bitch," or "motherfucker" in it. Now wait a minute, Billy Jr. was kinda an improved, tamed, educated version of his dad. He only said "fuck" every second sentence. Billy Jr. was a hell of a good driver like his dad. But there were two problems. People expected too much from him too quick and Billy didn't get the equipment his dad had. Bill Sr.'s mechanics were Indy's best – Jim Travis and Frank Coons. We called 'em the "rich kids," 'cause the car owner, Howard Keck, was best car owner around, and gave the rich kids a license to get it done. The money was there.

Billy Jr. reminded me of his dad a lot with his mannerisms. I don't think you can find anybody who raced with Billy Jr. who didn't like him. Bill Sr. was so damn tough at Indy, some of his competition was very jealous of him. Remember when they started booing Earnhardt? Same deal. Bill Sr. hated the press. I don't know why. First time I went to Indy and ended up stooging for Jack Beckley, Dave Garroway decided to do a Good Morning America, or something like that Indy, and I guess they are gonna broadcast the qualifying and race. This is 'bout 1956 or '57, the first time TV went to Indy.

The TV cats ask me to go on with Vukey at 7:00 am. Idea is how much different are Indy and stock cars? To me, "Hell yes!" My life dreams are to lay Marilyn Monroe and win Indy. So a TV start I think is great (at this point I'm still believing the stuff they write about me. I haven't wised up yet) Bill says, "No fuckin way."

I guess Howard Keck, the car owner, saw it different, so at 7:00 am in a pouring rain, the deal's on.

I'm wearing my red satin NASCAR Grand National Champion Speed Age jacket, white work pants with blue stripe, big-assed leather wallet in left rear pocket with chain to my belt so those goddam city slickers can't steal it, well-shined boots and a big-assed cowboy type hat. Now to be honest 'bout this, I wore the big brim hat cause we did not use sunglasses and the hat with big brim was a "must."

Shit, if I'd of had a pair of them Earnhardt and Gordon sunglasses then, wouldn't that have been a deal? Damn. I'm getting excited rite now thinking of what that would have been. Well, the TV deal's in an old restaurant behind the pit grandstand for us racers. An "el cheapo," but very adequate place to eat 'cept not too good when it got cold.

Garraway, for whatever reason, is soaking wet, and it is chilly. He starts with Billy Sr., who is really mad. He hates the cables strung all over the place. Actually, the only thing a morning like that was good for was screwing. (That's what Bill told me as I arrived, and I felt the same.) So when Garroway asked Billy a stupid question, "What did he think of the weather?" Bill said, "Piss poor," in a nice bass voice that sure went over very clearly. Well back then "piss" was a terrible word. Suppose he'd used better English and said, "Urine poor." Don't you agree it's not there? Well, if you watched that program you'd have had to been deaf-dumb and blind not to know Bill didn't want to be there.

I guess I made it half decent, to tell the truth, I think that was first TV thing I'd ever done, and I was scared shitless. What a difference fifty-three years make. Now days I can bullshit to a TV camera same as talking to my dog.

Take my word for it. Back then it was a different breed. Bill was quiet, no braggart but in this period he knew he was the best. For example, he had very strong hands. He'd grab a fellow driver's forearm muscle in his hand, squeeze his fingers hard enough to leave bruises and laugh and say, "How's a weakling like you gonna race me?"

BOBBY ISAAC

I'd heard 'bout Bobby on the local short tracks in North Carolina, and at their 1963 October race in Charlotte. I think we started with Banjo driving, but the same problem – horsies out the ass, car-handling 'bout impossible. I'm asleep, run with short stock rear radius rods. The rear axle of the car aimed all over the track from roll steer (the short radius rods caused the ass end of the car to turn right or left depending on the body roll in the corner). Yeah, I know. Jr. Johnson and Fox had it figured out and fixed it. I spent 75 percent of my time getting more power. I think maybe Darrell Derringer tried it to drive it also.

Well, Bobby jumped at the chance to drive the car. Little did he know what he was getting into. He held his breath and closed his eyes, and managed a fifth place qualification. But in the race, doing it lap after lap in heavy traffic and on junk tires, the number three wall said, "Your ass is mine." There was a lot of noise and the Chevy stopped – not by the brakes, but by various parts of the body being squashed.

Well, car's a dead player. I decided that car was beyond my conquering. What cinched the deal was shortly after the race I was in a small town out of New Orleans thinking 'bout drilling an oil well there. I was introduced to a very attractive race fan. Yup, Creole night club entertainer…this lady should have been on an Olympic team that competed in a love-making contests where the winner was whoever's body was airborne, rather than touching a mattress, or anything else for the most time in say, 30 minutes. Also, she was a voodoo expert. She and her friends were gonna do a deal to remove a hex they said Jr. Johnson put on my car. (Jr., did you really do that?) But at last minute they decided "can't do it to cars. Well, how 'bout doing it on Junior? I decided to get the hell out of there, because I was starting to believe some of that shit. When I got back to Daytona I gave the car away to somebody I didn't like, but I can't remember who.

Bobby had the talent. Shortly after he got grabbed by the Ray Nichols outfit. Seven years later guess who the Grand National champ was? When Bobby got together with K & K Insurance company (the greenie machine) and a damned good mechanic, Harry Hyde, they won the brass ring. Bobby didn't make a lot of noise, he didn't bitch much, he just did it. Bobby was well liked by his fellow competitors.

It would be nice if I could say he retired and so on. But his health failed him way early. 'Bout like at the halfway point, and suddenly he was gone. Nope, a racing accident was not it. I think his "ticker" got him, but at a race. Kinda like Ralph Earnhardt.

GORDON JOHNCOCK

I first noticed him as an open wheeler. A small man regarding how far his ears were from the ground. But about 145, 150 pounds of tough farmer, with an attitude. Yes, with an attitude.

I first seen him at Indy with a damn good self-made wrench. This was way before engineers. This was before the crew chief carried a briefcase. This was way before the hi-buck wooden briefcases with the super loaded locks that you could hear clacking for forty yards. Well they had a low buck deal with plenty of problems, but they qualified fifteenth, finished fifth. You'd have to be blind not to see Johncock was special.

Well in 1968 I built a new Chevelle. Curtis demolished the original in a bad landing from 75 feet in the air coming off of turn four at Atlanta. I wanted a race driver with balls and skill, who liked to go fast. I had Gordon figured as a very confident cat, who was having a ball going like a son-of-a-bitch. Well, in the inspection process NASCAR and I came to a piss poor ending. We never got to race, so maybe I shouldn't have included Gordy, 'cause all we did was fit the car to him. But I did, 'cause he said he wanted to drive it.

I see him once in a while. He is back in Hastings, Michigan. He sells beef (half or quarter, least I can do is give you a no cost commercial Gordo). Oh, I forgot. He won Indy a couple times after that.

(I seen Gordy at Charlotte July '98. The beef deals off, said, "Animals are a pain in the ass," so if you need beef, call Wickert.)

MICKEY THOMPSON

There ain't no way I can tell you really what this cat was all about. This was a very-very special human. He had the balls of a dinosaur and the persistence of a hungry tiger. His mode of operation was 'bout like a 95,000 pound 600 horsepower diesel tractor and trailer coming at you running eighty. That man did not know what "it can't be done" meant.

'Bout six feet tall, a little on the porky side (not bad though), red hair, freckles, good-lookin.' He'd show his teeth quite a bit. Could be nicest guy you ever met or could be a pure asshole if you crossed him. He had a temper 'bout like A.J. Mick was a live hand grenade with the pin pulled.

I met Mickey in early sixties when we both worked for Mr. Knudsen, the Pontiac top cat. Well Mick built a land speed record car with four Pontiac engines in it. He tried to set world's speed record at Bonneville and did (one way) but couldn't get the sucker turned around fast enough (you gotta make two runs, one in each direction, in no more than one hour). He ran 400 and something. So next he decides get world record on water. The boat is Pontiac powered also. Mr. Knudsen is advancing money (in the beginning, his own) for Mick to do this. OK, the boat deal fucks up. The boat don't hold up going over rocks and dry ground. Mickey got a bad broke back for starters.

Knudsen says, "Smokey, go to the Vegas hospital and get me the real scoop on Mick's condition." I met with his doctors a week after the accident. All three say, "That son of a bitch is nuts! He is paralyzed for life from his belly button on down. He's going goofy up in the room wanting exercise equipment to rehabilitate." In short, doctors say they can't, or won't work with him. Mick tells me, "I'm gonna walk out of this shit-hole hospital in one month." (Good thing it wasn't Reno. I was in hospital there one time – 13 hours walked in and walked out, $18,000. There are still a few bandits left in the Wild West.)

Mickey Thompson.

I go back to Detroit and tell Knudsen the story. His plan was to bring in European doctors, or send Mick over there. I tell Knudsen he is pissin' into a 200 mile an hour wind.

In one month Mick goes to the hospital door in a wheel chair. Stands up with a cane, steps through the door and falls on his ass. He drags himself back up into wheelchair and says, "I walked out of it in a month like I said." Knudsen says, "Check again with doctors." I do. They are so pissed now 'cause Mick's put the "bad mouth" on 'em so bad. The doctor's say, "We wouldn't touch that asshole with a twenty foot pole." In a year, Mick is walking and driving. He is curing himself with a bunch of equipment he's built. He has a seat like a spring baby seat. He hangs on springs. One word: "unbelievable."

This started a friendship we had for twenty-five years. Mickey called me every twelve to fifteen days for those twenty-five years to shoot the bull about engines and shocks. Well, to talk about racecars and racing gossip and politics. And before he married his second wife, about pussy. I considered Mickey a friend, and I damn sure was his friend. You know I believe at best it's a lucky human who has three or four friends. I'm talking about someone who will drop what he is doing if you need help. I'm talking 'bout a person that will help you financially if your luck's gone to shit. I'm talking 'bout somebody who will if necessary take a chance on getting his ass kicked helping you. I believe in those years I knew every move Mickey made. He constantly stayed in trouble. That should have been his middle name. Mickey "Trouble" Thompson.

Who is Mickey Thompson? If you're under thirty years old, it's very possible you'd ask that. Mickey was a drag racer, a land speed record driver, a off-road racer. Hell, I think he half-invented both drag and off-road racing. He was an Indy racer and he was 'bout one of the first mass merchandiser and manufacturer of racing parts. He started SEMA (Specialty Equipment Manufacturers Association) with a partner. He was a race vehicle builder. He built racing tires. He pioneered valve gear, exotic metals in reciprocating parts; he knocked Charles Manson on his ass for screwing up his daughter. He was a good pilot. I can remember him dropping a cardboard box out of his airplane to me with injector parts at the Ontario racetrack infield (I caught the box.) He was a kid from Elmonte, California, who loved going fast, and a kid with a curiosity bigger than a 747. He was not satisfied to be second best at anything. I can remember at the Salt Flats when we were there setting 24 hour records for Chevy with some Camaros. At 2:00 am, he, Curtis Turner and myself, and two USAC officials seeing who could piss the furthest. Yes, he out pissed us all.

Mick worked for Pontiac, Chevy and Ford at same time I did. So sometimes we'd get together on a sports car race, a Bonneville record run, even Indy. Mickey was a gambler. I'm talking Vegas kind of stuff. I always heard how much he won, but never got involved in reports on how much he lost. I got involved in drilling for oil in late 1960, and did real good. Well, Mick decided to become an oil tycoon also, and joined me in some wildcat drilling. First hole made some gas, but "fair" at best. Second hole was twice as expensive, and a duster. No oil. Zero. Adios 100 grand apiece. Well, we were there for the TD (total depth, finish of the hole). Laredo, Texas, Boys Town: a world-class whorehouse and nightclub, this is 'bout '62, I'm astonished. (I'm sober.) He's doing it again. Looks like he is gonna out fuck and out drink every son-of-a-bitch in Boys Town. There was a big-big colored sexy lookin gal that was considered the world's greatest. Yup. We had to carry him out.

Couple years later I'm involved in gold mining, oil concessions, consulting in oil field engines (big-big mothers), cannibals, head shrinkers in Ecuador, in the world's best jungle: "The Oriente," on the East side of the Andes. My 1960 Indy winning car owner (a wild-wild assed Dallas, Texan, Kenny Rich) gets involved in secret gold mines. (He picked up valuable tips about this is a bar in Dallas). Kenny and I then met another Texan from San Antonio, name Leonard Schorsch. This cat had gold fever so bad it usually killed the victim. And you know, several times it nearly did.

So now when Mick asks 'bout what's going on in Ecuador, and he hears 'bout oil, gold, cannibals, head hunters, jungle, 30 foot snakes, crocodiles (yes) crocodiles 25 foot long, the Humboldt Hotel in Guyaquil (the hotel that leans 'bout five degrees, like it's gonna fall into the Bay of Guyaquil), the hotel where there is at least one woman of every skin color on earth, and seemed like all were either models or beauty queens (and all descendents of minks). To me the most fascinating collection of women con-artists, soldierettes of fortune on earth. Even better than the great Sheppard Hotel in Cairo in 1945. (Mick said hotel isn't leaning. I put a nickel on edge and let go. Yup. Clean across the room.) Earthquakes, mountain slides, 300-pound jaguars, and the pirahnas (you know, man-eating fish), and also a short report on the habits of the ladies down there when the moon comes up. Man, Mick's frothing at the mouth to get in the act.

I have to go down there pretty often, so I say, "Meet me in Miami with a good passport and a couple of shots for Typhus fever, etc." I'm waiting for Mick. I've got a ticket for us to go to Quito, Ecuador. I go to meet Mick's plane from Los Angeles. No Mick. Seems like everybody had deplaned. I'm puzzled and guess he missed the plane. Nope. Here comes "Jungle Jim." Pith helmet, bush jacket, shorts, snake boots, knife and flashlite holder belt, two cameras around his neck, great big dark "Dale Earnhardt" sunglasses, short wave radio. I say, "Where's pistol and rifle?" He says, "In my luggage." Well, it takes first class bribery job by Leonard Schorsch to get guns and radio into Ecuador. I figure he'll be safe in the jungle. The Indians will laugh their asses off, and the animals will run from "this thing."

We have rented a nice apartment in Quito to live in but they are very very fussy about noise. In Ecuador, like in all Latin countries, a bullfighter is a national hero. It's considered an honor if he screws your wife. Next is the soccer player, and a close third is a race car driver. Well, at this particular time I introduce Mickey as the fastest motherfucker on earth, 407 miles an hour. Wow-eeeee.

Well, Hotel Quito has a gambling casino in the bottom. Member I told you Mick was a good gambler. Well, I'm pooped, so after I take Mick over to the casino I hire cab driver for the evening (Big deal, all night for eight bucks includes tip). "After he's finished gambling, take him to the Mirador (Spanish for mirror I think). Best, nicest whore house in Ecuador, run by a refugee Nazi SS man. Ecuador was loaded with Germans on the run from the war crimes police. Well, 'bout an hour after we left Mick at the casino I get phone call. "Get Mick out of hotel casino." They are gonna arrest him for cheating. "What makes you think he cheated?" "He's only person who ever won in the two year history of the casino." Well, it's only two blocks from apartment to hotel, and we know hotel owner, so I get Mick loaded up in the cab. He still has all the chips he has won. Every pocket is full, and a bush jacket is loaded with pockets (I guess to carry all the bullets you need to shoot up the bad-assed lions and elephants.)

The Mirador is on a hill in Quito, so steep, the cabs had to stop and turn around two blocks short, and back up the last two blocks. Why? Because reverse was a lower gear than first, and they wouldn't make it in low gear. If you go to Quito I bet you it's still there. And tell 'em I sent you. Well, we call the owner and tell him a "famous driver is on his way. Be nice to him." Well, shit, Mick and the SS cat fall in love with each other and Mick gets drunker. He is the life of the party. In a forty-girl cathouse, he (I was told this) is stuffing the chips into the girl's bras and underpants. It turns out Mickey has no racial prejudices. As a matter of fact, I first noticed it in Boys Town, and then at the Mirador he seemed to prefer black skinned women, and big women. The biggest sexiest woman at the Mirador was very dark complected. I seen her drive a big shot priest to stupidity in fifteen minutes.

How I know all this stuff? 'Cause the big boys told me 'bout it. 5:00 am all hell breaks loose. I'm asleep, cab driver I hired is beating on the apartment door. "What's the matter?" My friend is "loco," he has the big gal I told you about and a little younger gal in the cab. He's brought the big gal for me or Leonard, and the little girl for himself. The big gal didn't want to come. She is scared shitless of Mick and the SS cat. Mickey is so drunk he is impossible to deal with, he's drunk on a quart of poro (sugar cane whiskey we got in the jungle). The colored gal was so scared her knees were knocking. Honest. I've heard 'bout that, but now actually see it.

Well, Leonard has to calm down the manager. He wants us evicted immediately. Mickey decides to shoot the trouble making li'l Spanish motherfucker. He's found his pistol. "Where the hell's the bullets?" Wisely, the manager went back to his apartment, but we had to rent another place very shortly. We rented a nice house with some room around it. It had a stuffed condor in the main entrance, and one in the living room. I mean whopper birds – spooky lookin.' A condor looks like a giant buzzard to me. Mick's been in Ecuador ten days, has been in the jungle a week, bought 200 acres of land next to our base camp close to Puerto Napo, seen some Jivaros (head shrinkers), been down to cannibal country. But take this with a grain of salt. They were of the Wranni, or Alkas tribe. Another make of Indian said, "Not so. White gringos taste terrible." They wouldn't eat us.

Mickey's visit was never forgotten. As we were headed to airport the next morning, remember I told you he'd been drinking poro? There were no traffic lites in Quito then, and at the airport there was a big traffic circle with a big statue of two oxen pulling a plow with an Indian driving. Well, Mick got sick, opened door with his toes in the taxi, and with his hands on the window molding and his belly rubbing the ground, puked all the way around the circle. Well, I came back couple months later and there was a ring of flowers around the circle. We figured Mick fertilized them. From that time on it was known as the "Mickey Thompson Circle."

Mickey gave his guns away before he went home. I never carried a gun except if we got close to the river pirate country on the Napo River from Coca, Ecuador to Iquitos, "no-name" country. No law (this was 1960s). In Iquitos, nicest guy there was simply wanted for murder. Yet I never had a problem or felt spooky there.

The river pirates knew all about whoever was coming down river. Money, guns, number of people you got rated. Don't fuck with 'em, or easy mark? Or maybe, but won't be easy. How they know? Drums. Yup. Every morning price of gold came down 'bout 150 miles an hour. Mick never went back. The jungle is a dead player. At the beginning of the sixties Mick started his invasion of Indy.

Every year it would be a wild deal. First one was aluminum throw-away Oldsmobile V8, and I believe Dan Gurney drove it. Mick brought some good stuff, and some not so hot. Cars with 12 inch tires, four wheel steer; man-o-man that was a handful. He tried front wheel drive, revisited his own Small Block Chevy based engines, titanium pistons, rods, valves, cranks and rockers. We shared who was the goofiest car builder up there intermittently for 'bout ten years.

In the late sixties Chevy wanted a lot of records at the Salt Flats. Well, I built two small block and two big block Camaro's, and who better to help at the Salt Flats than Mickey? So I got Mickey and Curtis Turner to be the main drivers. I had two helpers and a truck driver. Mickey and the sheriff at Wendover were old buddies. The sheriff owned the motel, restaurant and the big garage and air strip behind his business. At north end of town is another town called "State Line," and I believe a corner where four states touched. We headquartered at the sheriff's compound.

State Line had gambling and booze. The motel and restaurant had all Mormon maids, waitresses. Same with ladies who worked at State Line casino. Now Bonneville record run time is also hunting season. So all the ladies husband's go hunting elk and bears and other kinds of poor furry animals who get their asses killed trying to find something to eat. Near as I can remember Mormon ladies didn't drink or smoke. But the minute their husbands, boyfriends and fathers took off to the hills, the Mormon ladies declared open season on Bonneville racers. In one week them descendants of Brigham Young, put us in a condition 'bout like used to be the punch line of what a 40 acre wheat field looked like after a wild church charity event, where the survivor says in describing the condition of the field the next day said, "Fucked flat."

Curtis was complaining. Two separate maids got him from 6:00 am to 7:30 am. Mickey had a "three-way" going with door wide open. Ralph Johnson, my main helper was in Hog Heaven. I think the third day of that was the first day since I was ten years old, I didn't think of pussy. Please don't misunderstand me. That is not meant as a complaint. Mickey had been to Salt Flats so much over the years he kinda had the keys to that little strip of Americana.

Well, we got 'bout 220 records, what Chevy wanted. Mick won a lot of money at State Line, and I spent two weeks there. So when Salt Flats talk gets going, I've been there and done that. I'm glad I did get the opportunity. It was a "must" in any good racer's resume. Kinda like the Mexican Road Race. Mickey was on the first one. His behavior did little to strengthen the relations between the US and Mexico.

Well 1969, 1970, Mickey says, "Lets go over 400 again," and again it's Mr.Knudsen (he is now president of Ford). It don't work out. Mr. K gets his ass fired by Mr. Henry Ford the deuce. Don't bother Mick. Instead of getting more speed records he invents off-road racing, and off-road trucks. Well, I know a lot of people get a big bang looking at that stuff, but to be honest with you, I'd just as soon watch it rain while on a dry porch along the Napo River in the jungle.

So, I got briefed in the trials and tribulations of those inventions. By now Mickey is quite an accomplished businessman. He has remarried, and seems to be very happy for first time I can remember. He seems to have a comfortable life style. But it's one problem after another. He has big trouble with a partner, guy named Godwin (or something like that) and his house goddam near burns down in forest fire. Mick saves his house but all the neighbor's are lost. His son Danny is comin' on as a driver, but business apparently ain't doing too good. Now Mick is in all kinds of deals: manufacturing, promoting, real estate, boxing, and more. Mick's phone calls are largely negative stuff now.

I can't remember him being so down except the day he caught his mistress doing "it" with a police dog. "Well," he says "I defeated my partner in a long running law suit yesterday. I expect him to try and kill me now." This is serious shit, rite? Three days later I get the phone call edged in black – Mick and his wife have just been murdered. So, we played the sad sorry game of seven men going to the graveyard and only six of 'em coming back.

Mick, I've missed you and your goofy adventures. You were one of a kind. I guess it's like a saying I heard as a kid, "They broke the mold after they made you." I don't think you have received the attention and credit for the thirty some years of three hundred sixty five days a year, eighteen hour days you gave to racing. If you'd have put that much time and energy in any business, you'd still be alive as a rich, old, know-it-all pain in the ass to the pelicans who came after you. But I learned from you to weed the bullshit out from the facts. I never said "thanks." (As least I don't remember. Maybe as you slid down in the damn hole they dug I did). I wonder what else was in Mick's coffin that day we barely made it to the hole? (Man, it was heavy).

Anyone who reads this page: This is a fact. Mickey Thompson was as good a racer as it's possible to be. Consider this: the man who willingly risks his life knowingly is not the same breed of cat as a man who goes to work at 7:00 am with a lunch bucket, and comes home at 5:00. You have to cut a real racer a little slack to understand the movie. I heard from Mickey's sister in July 1998. She said murder might be solved pretty soon. We all hope so. But really what will that do for you? For the years you had Mickey, you never wasted a second. I believe at your funeral was first time I seriously realized my turn could be not that far off, and appreciated my health and life style that much more. Man that was a sad-sad day. Mick's boy Danny is still struggling, trying to find good grip on his niche.

Bobby Unser

Is a book also. So let's start from the beginning. I think Bobby's great grandfather bought Pike's Peak from the Indians for 40 quarts of corn likker. The biggest and best tasting food animals lived near the top. No refrigerators then, so to get it down to the house before it spoiled was tough.

That trail they made become the Pike's Peak road.

Bobby's great grandfather sold the mountain to a guy named Pike. He changed the name from Unser's Peak, to Pike's Peak, and one day he and a stranger got into an argument in the Antler hotel bar, 'bout who could go up it the fastest (they got cars now). A local mechanic, Bobby's dad, was in the bar, and wanted in on the deal. A three man see who can do it the fastest. By the way I got this story from one of the Unser family, who was 'bout as drunk as I was. But I'm pretty sure it's true.

If you see Bobby ask him about it. There was a slight problem; he didn't have a car. So he built one out of the junk stuff around his garage. Well, guess what? He beats them both so bad he was now famous for a hundred mile circle. (Remember, no TV, radio, no racing magazines, only thing was Speed Sport News, but they never had been further west than Indiana. That's how it started.

All Unser's became race car hill climbers. Every male Unser from the time of that first race have won one or more races at Pike's Peak. There must have been 'bout seventy-five races by now. I think an Unser has won all but three of 'em. I believe Bobby's dad and Bobby were the best of all Unsers. That is in reference to going fast up a shitty road to the top of a mountain with no guardrails.

Well, you know Bobby and "Big Al" and "Little Al." And now you're noticing Robby and Johnny have started to run Indy.

But there was more. Bobby had two more brothers, Louie and Jerry. If you're as old as I am you'd know they could drive the shit out of a race car, too. Plus Bobby's mom was as much a part of USAC at one time as the Offy engine. She was a chili cookin' champion. That stuff was the best paint remover you could find at the time and tasted damn good. If it hadn't been for her chili, Tums would have never been invented.

May 1963, Bobby Unser, the second Unser to run Indy, a cocky funny, curly haired cat. Always laughing and grinnin.' I liked him 'cause he didn't bitch, and he drove the racecar. As opposed to so many that let the car do what it wanted to. If you knew anything 'bout racing you'd have been blind if you couldn't see this cowboy was a good racecar driver.

I don't know what's in those Unser's genes. But seems like all male Unsers were good racers.

Jerry Unser I met in '58 at Indy. Louie was, I believe, driving sprinters then, and he got dealt a bad hand and became handicapped (at least to drive). So he became a good engine builder (We spent some time together.) In '59 Jerry spun off of four at Indy practicing and had a fire that burned him in his groin area. Seemed like he was gonna be just fine when all of a sudden things went to hell, and Jerry was gone. Jerry was Johnny's dad.

I may goof up here, but give me some slack. There were, and are, a bunch of racin' Unsers. Another trait the Unsers have, for my money they are all good people. I've never met a Pike's Peak Unser that was an asshole (yet). Bobby could really get it done in a sprinter.

Once he got in the door at Indy he kinda slid out of the little cars and run champ cars, the Peak and wanted stock cars (in USAC). That's kinda how Bobby and I got involved with each other.

Well, Bobby's first two years at Indy were awful. Total of three laps in two cars ('63, '64).

In '65 he jumped in the Novi for Granatelli. Nope. Still nothin.'

In '66 a top ten (he is eighth). But in '67 Bobby and Gurney hooked up. They only run ninth, but you could see something was clicking here. The car, the mechanics, the money and the driver were a team. You guessed it. '68 Bingo. He does it. First Unser to win Indy.

I have a '68 Camaro road race Trans-Am deal. July 4th, France has a "Midnite ride of Paul Revere" race.

The racin' was done and we were on the prowl.

Headlights only. Oh yes. There was a pole and light bulb here and there, but I bet the electric bill for three hours wouldn't have been over three bucks. Bobby wants to drive it. I like that deal, so we team up. Engines 302 cubic inches, double four barrel, 'bout 570 horsepower circa 8,000 rpm. We finish car late, don't even get to qualify. Start in the rear. Pretty good competition. Ford's got Bud Moore, a three car team of Mercurys there, with drivers like Parnelli, Lloyd Ruby, George Follmer, maybe Mark Donahue in a Camaro. 'Bout thirty cars, Pitch dark, no moon. Race starts through the infield, and by time they are coming off of two (this is the Daytona 24 hour road course). Unser's in the lead. He gets into three-way, running 'bout

180. So far ahead, car's lights behind him don't help at all. Middle turn three lights go out. Yup. Zero. Main battery cable was too short, and it grounded. No lights, no engine, 180. Well, I imagine 'bout then Unser dropped my racecar builder rating to a one or zero. But I'm a son-of-a-bitch if he don't manage to get it done. No crash. Comes in the pits hollerin "fix it!" Well battery is melted, so is some of the wires, so I say, "Go change your shorts. This deal is history." There really was a funny smell, but Bobby said it was from burnt wire covering. Maybe.

If it had been me I'd of been pissed. Bobby thought it was funny. All he talked about was how strong that sucker was. Well, next I got a Talladega Ford, but same problem, short of time. Can't build a car in time, so my buddy John Holman gives me a car. A piece of shit 'bout four inches higher than any other Talladega. Typical "John deal." That's what friends are for right? We got horsepower out the gazoo, but pushing much air as a Greyhound bus. Fifty laps a crash puts us out of our misery.

'Bout rite in here Pike's Peak gets to be important for Bobby. He knows Knudsen pretty good, soon Mr. K. calls and says, "Say, let's build an engine for Bobby to go up Pike's Peak." He calls Bill Stroppe, a super car and engine builder, and a world-class racer. Bill furnishes the car and the crew.

Lined up on pit road before the race.

Well, I built him an engine you couldn't run at sea level, but the deal starts 'bout 8,000 feet. Engine had too much compression for sea level where air is heavier. Bobby set record that lasted 'bout fifteen years.

Bobby threw in with Gurney and started winning in champ cars. I'd say he was the "hot dog" from '67 to '75 – won Indy three times. Bobby Unser's main asset that made him a champion was his fierce and dogged determination to win. Man if you passed him, you might pass him five times a lap. He never gave up. He truly believed he was the best race driver in the world. Not in a bragging sense. His style was "just do it":

Well, he tried Formula One a few races in a less than first class car, and I think those 'Grand Pricks' taught him maybe he could be beat. I asked him when he got back how it was. His answer was, "Them guys go like there ain't no such thing as tomorrow and that didn't fit his master plan."

If you'd of met him in the seventies, and you found out he was a race driver, it wouldn't have surprised you. He had a confident, (maybe arrogant) manner. Even standing talking, his arms and feet never quit moving. He seemed to always be laughing or smiling. Always stayed slim and in shape. I don't know if that was from the strenuous outdoor life he lived, or from all the women he was playing with. Oh, hell yes, Unser was a world-class pussy hound. Matter of fact, only man I ever heard give an interview while getting a blowjob. (No…the TV guy didn't know it. Bobby talked through a window in a van.)

We got along real good. Still do (till he reads this) for over thirty years. Matter of fact he spent his honeymoon with Robbie's mother at our house. Bobby drove for Penske for quite awhile. Polished up his act and right at the top of his career he walked away. Said, "Thank you, it ain't fun no more."

He stayed very close to the circus by becoming a very good TV commentator.

In '97 he decided that job was too restrictive, and "Adiosed" it also. In 1998 he coached his son Robbie into a fifth place finish at Indy. So world, make room for another Unser, cause fifth place finish, and the "Rookie of the Year" at Indy is a damn good paragraph in any racer's resumé. Remember his dad run thirty-third and thirty-second his first two years (out of thirty-three starters). Course he didn't have a three-time winner for a coach either.

Bobby damn near died winter of '96 from a snowmobile adventure that went to hell. Never been beat at the Peak till July 4th 1998. Finally Roger Mears did it in an exhibition race. Course, I should tell you Unser had to drive with one arm. Yes, he is starting to pay for those "oh shits" and sudden stops

There was a time that if a rattlesnake bit him, it would have broke its teeth. Readers, if you met Bobby today, he don't cut the swath he did in the sixties through the eighties. Take my word for it, that son-of-a-bitch was as tough as it ever gets. Bobby Unser is one of the top ten racers of all times.

I think if there had of never been a Bobby Unser, A.J. would have been a six times Indy winner.

Al Unser

I met him in 1965 at Indy. He run ninth as a rookie. Al was momma Unser's baby of her four racing sons. Al was easy to like, easy person to get acquainted with, and seemed like an easy person to get to know. (Here's where 95 percent of race drivers he drove against flunked out.) He appeared to be conservative, didn't hardly make a sound to the news media. He masked his elephant desire to win with most of us. (I suppose the inner family knew his true target and desires). He was 'bout five foot ten, was slim, and in super physical shape. He was an outdoor cat. Boats, motorcycle, jet boats, off road four wheeler. Had a ranch. Never seen him ride a horse, or seen him punch a cow, but maybe he did. Matter of fact I worked with him for Prolong in 1998. He is still in very good shape; especially after thirty years of open wheelers 'cept he is goddam near as deaf as I am. You ladies who meet him and want to take advantage of him (he is easy and a true racer) holler in his ear, or he may seem to ignore you and hurt your feelings.

From where I sat in a 500-mile race or any long race, he spent first 100 miles checking car out so when it came time to "do it" he 'bout knew exactly what he could get out of the car. The next hundred miles I believe he identified what he considered was his real competition. The third hundred miles he got himself in a position to win. The last two hundred miles he raced as much as it took. He gave nobody nothin'. But if you look at the lap speeds when he got truckin,' hell…it looked like engine picked up 100 horsepower after three hundred miles.

Al raced anything with wheels and a motor. Mostly open wheel, and he kinda liked road racing but didn't really get a real good ride in them things. I had a Camaro around 1970 or '71 maybe even '72. I decided to take it to Sebring and beat Roger Penske and Mark Donahue. Well, getting the idea was easy but getting the job done was something else. So I asked Al Unser and Lloyd Ruby to co-drive it. As usual car goes like "Jack the Bear," but this is a twelve hour race, and long before race is over the valves and pistons try to occupy the same space at the same time, and we get so far behind we quit, and Roger and Mark get all the marbles.

Next deal, Al knows I built an engine to go up Pike's Peak for Bobby, and it was a winner. I'm working for Ford now and Al is running some stock cars in USAC. Al asks me to build him a 429 Ford shotgun motor. In this case it didn't work out. Car didn't win, and I lost some points from Al.

I think he had one of those Greyhound bus Ford Talledegas from Holman. Well, how good you gotta be to win Indy four times and all the other races Al has won?

Al's had a nice retirement. He raced against his son Al Jr., who come on up to the big time. Matter of fact in 1992 "Little Al" won, and Al run third, ten seconds behind his son. I believe in 1994 Al decided to quit trying to get qualified with ten laps of practice, and walked away. I think Al can still give most anybody all they want on a racetrack. Al's now the professor of Indy Racing League driving. He helps new drivers coming in, and helps drivers from other forms of racing get acquainted with Indy cars. He is very much in demand as a celebrity racer, and does a few speeches (at which he isn't worth a shit). He ain't afraid to wrassle 1,100 horsepower car around Indy, but he gets petrified in room of fifty people where he has to talk. Al Unser is a remarkable person. He represented us well to the race fans. Still does. When I compare him and his career against most of the modern stick and ballers, he looks solid gold and they remind me of dog shit.

Dempsey Wilson

Just 'cause you never heard of him don't mean he wasn't a good driver. He was an open wheeler, sprinter, Indy car cat. Like so many racers, never really had best equipment, money and crew.

Right after France built Daytona he decided to run the Indy cars on it. He asked me about it. I said, "Are you trying to get even with USAC for Harry Quinn throwing your ass out the back gate on the cinders?" As usual, my input was ignored. (I was afraid some people were gonna get killed. Regrettably, I was rite.)

At the time I had a 'bout four-year-old Kuzma yallar cucumber, with a 255 Offie here. It belonged to Art Lathrop, an Indy car owner society figure. Art said, "Get it ready to honk, and let's run it." I said, "Which driver do you dislike the most?" I was sure this was going to be an ass-busting contest (I wish I'd been wrong for this). In a month or so Paul Russo called me and asked to drive it. This was in the 1960-'61 time frame. Paul has driven the Novi at Indy. I doubt many of you readers place any significance on this, but it was a heavily super charged 163" mother that would light up the tires in the middle of the straight away making the goddamnedest roar any engine ever did. That thing would hurt your ears – I mean hurt 'em.

Just before practice Paul gets smarter and calls me and cancels. So Tony Bettenhausen decides to give it a try. He runs a few laps and decides he needs to go back home and plow the back forty.

Well shit. "I'll drive 'er myself." Art's half shitfaced and says "best idea yet." We were concerned the cars would get airborne and lose traction. That's not what happened. It was other way around. For what ever reason, the downforce bottomed out the car on both ends, with heaviest torsion gears we had we drug bottoms of race cars four or five places around the track.

My thinking at the time was, "No brains needed here, just balls and physical strength." Well, after ten-twenty laps making changes and excuses for not getting with it, I decide "now or never." Corner speed was determined by how much arm strength you had. Even down to three-degree positive caster, you just couldn't turn the son-of-a-bitch. After a few laps I got to thinking. "Being a watcher rather than a driver might be the better plan." But I'm in it so deep now, there is really no honorable way out 'cept to say "it scares me" and I ain't ready to do that yet.

I hear some other lap times and know I need to "get with it," so in a couple laps I'm able to take a breath every other lap. Now, here's the deal, in the turns all you see is black asphalt. It's like you're in a barrel. You can't even see the outside wall. Do you believe you can get lost on the Daytona track? Well, I did. And I got damn near centered the wall in the dogleg. Yup, the dogleg on the front straight away. That got the job done. I came in, got out and retired as a Daytona Indy car driver. I decided in a thousandth of a second, if I got that car away from the wall in the dogleg, I didn't give a shit what anybody said. My life wasn't much good then, but not that bad.

Dick Rathman watched that act. When I came in he laughed his ass off. He didn't have a ride yet, and hadn't turned a lap. I said, "Dickey boy, jump in there and show me how to do this thing." Guess who, on first hot lap, goddamned near stuck it in the dogleg wall? A.J. jumps in, runs a few laps and disappears. I don't remember exactly what all happened. But after 'bout four drivers all decided to go do something else, Dempsey comes along and asks to drive it. He jumps in her cold and wrassled that damn thing till he was completely exhausted. No complaints. If I don't know anything else 'bout Dempsey Wilson, he was a strong mother and had plenty of balls.

JOE WEATHERLY

Our official clown. Half of the Turner-Weatherly "let's start a bran new party" act. You know about rock concerts. Well, in NASCAR racing about the last three nights before the race the big deal was "at what motel the Turner-Weatherly party was gonna be at?" The Romans had a word for it: orgy. It was an unhurried drinking party that started at 9:00 pm and usually ended at 5:00 am, each wilder than the last. Joe was originally a champion motorcycle racer from Virginia with a very badly scarred face. I never asked him, and he never told me how it happened. Joe was 'bout five foot eight, stocky, solid and heavyset. Very seldom got angry, to him everything was funny. If he demolished his car and ended up in a hospital, he'd find something funny 'bout it. If you had just met him (I mean even sober) you'd get taken by this curly headed, scar-faced, joker who talked so fast he'd get his words mixed up. Joe had the absolute biggest "don't give a shit" attitude 'bout life it's possible to have. The combination of Joe's machine gun talk and very strong Southern dialect made him not understandable to many. Especially when he included the Weatherly coined dictionary. Tires were "May Pops," "No handling" meant a difficult anything: car, woman, race official or bank. His nickname was "Be-bop." He was scared to death of snakes. A rubber snake could undo him. And if "goosed" he'd set a high jump record.

Joe and Curtis Turner had a very-very rare relationship. Each liked and enjoyed each other on and off the racetrack. In racing, for whatever reason, seldom do racers associate with each other socially. Why? I guess for the reasons that affected and depressed Turner when Joe got killed at Riverside.

Turner was never the same in his flippety floppety take it one day at a time, ain't no problem, let's start a bran' new party, wild-assed Indian manner. I noticed he would get drunk early. (And actually he became an alcoholic.)

If all the ladies who partied with Joe and Curtis could get together and write a book about your adventures with those two, I believe it would promote the start of one more medically oriented treatment of social disorder. I went to an airport at Darlington to tie a plane down because of a very serious thunderstorm. It's pitch black. Here's Fireball's airplane, with engine running, and it's tied down. In the plane, Joe and Fireball are giving two mid-life women ('bout 18) their first airplane ride, and putting them into the mile high club.

Next day I asked the ladies how they liked their first plane ride? I guess you won't believe it, but they really thought they had flown for forty-five minutes. This got me to recall a game the French Foreign Legion pilots I flew with in Marrakesh on the African Gold Coast in early forties taught me. "Love me tonight, I may die tomorrow," without ever knowing what it felt like. I wonder if there is any chance of a rich lady (bout seventy now I guess) reading this whose family owned a horse track in Alexandria, Egypt? Can you remember an American B-17 pilot she met at the Great Shepherd Hotel in Cairo in the early forties? And does she remember "doing it" in the horse track grandstands at 4:30 in the morning (to protect the young pilot from the possibility of such a sad ending)?

Joe drove modifieds and sportsmen to start with, then kinda moved into the Grand Nationals. He drove for many people, but when he and Bud Moore hooked up that was the perfect fit. Weatherly and Bud were hell to be reckoned with from there on. On the surface they seemed to get along great, but really it was somehow strained. Joe was a damn good driver. Hell to pass, and hell to keep behind you. In 1962 Joe won the Grand National championship with Bud Moore's cars. In 1963 he did it again but with 'bout fifteen different cars. (Bud ran out of money).

In 1957 the Darlington 500 Curtis and Goldsmith drove a pair of Fords I had. Goldy gets in a bad wreck in 'bout twenty-five laps. He is hurt and car is gone. Turner's leading now, and Lee Petty's chasing him. Turn three, Petty puts Turner in the wall. Bad mess. Had to change radiators. Turner's in the hospital.

Weatherly, driving his own '57 Ford catches Petty and puts him in the wall then comes back in. By now I got Turner's car ready. Weatherly jumps in thirteen laps down and finishes eleventh. He unlapped himself twice in that wrecked up, bow-legged Ford. No way of knowing if a spindle would break or what. He drove that son-of-a-bitch like it was brand new, and there would never be a tomorrow. (And he taught Lee not to fuck with his buddy).

So he retires, and now is being honored for his part in the building of stock car racing – I wish. No, instead on January 19,1964, 'bout three months after winning his second championship, we're at Riverside, California. Joe's in Bud Moore's Mercury. Not a good day. Car's running in the shit house. All of a sudden coming up through the esses, the car slid into a concrete barrier sideways. Adios our "Li'l Joe."

Joe's death got NASCAR to put window nets in the rules, and I'm sure many serious injuries and/or deaths have been avoided since. Joe, you and your black and white saddle shoes, and your goofy grin are gone. But I'm proud to be able to say, "I knew him well. Raced with him for seventeen years." Joe, you were special. Also, you had maybe a fan collection second only to Curtis or Fireball in your day. You were a very important part of this foundation NASCAR's been built on, but I wouldn't know that if I had to depend on what I read or saw in 2000. Hopefully, you, Tim, Curtis, Fireball, Tiny all watch from an air conditioned suite and piss and moan 'bout how different money was from then till now. And specially 'bout the piss-ant airplanes you guys had compared to today's hero's, where anything up to and including a twin turbo prop is slow junk. But be glad AIDS wasn't invented yet in your time. If it had been, you'd surely all be dead by now anyhow, but I guess in a uglier, painful way. You'll soon have every last ass with you. 'Bout the youngest is seventy-five now. Then Curtis, you can start a bran' new party. How 'bout at the Holiday Inn in South Atlanta?

Junior Johnson

Last and by a long way not the least is Junior Johnson, an american hero. A success story if there ever was one. I'll bet he wears widest shoes you can get. That's what happens when you go barefoot from the first thaw to the first snow. I been there and done that. If you had to walk on a hot asphalt road bare footed best relief was to go stand in fresh cow shit. You don't believe me do you? Well, next time you see Junior ask him. Long handle overalls and shorts. Period. (Well, throw in a red bandana snot rag.) That's it. A genuine whiskey makin' five star hillbilly if there ever was one. Part of a clan who never accepted this country's insistence to collect so much tax per quart of corn whiskey. (Or in early racin' lingo "leg spreader."). Bootlegger was the common description of the pioneering bunch of quiet, reclusive, inbred, fiercely proud, freedom lovin' patriots. Very few of these various tribal members were candidates for the Nobel Prize in anything. Matter of fact high school diplomas was a hell of a deal and just being able to read and write put you in the top percent regarding being educated.

So how can Junior Johnson, in twenty-five years of self-education, become one of the best stock car drivers ever? How does this self-financed, self educated man put all the racing experts in a state of shock and awe when he becomes a car owner and starts winning every goddam thing there is to win with Fords, Chevys, Pontiacs, Buicks, Oldsmobiles? How does this hillbilly (and he is a hillbilly – you 'bout need a translator to understand his lingo) develop theories regarding engines that have Detroit and universities listening and copying? Also consider a gap in his life whereby he was deprived of his freedom and was free-housed as punishment for failing to pay federally mandated taxes on his families manufactured products.

I believe Junior was vice president of distribution for his family's whiskey still. This job forced him to understand the physics of an automobile with too much rear weight well enough to out perform the better weight balance of the taxman's vehicle. Honing one's driving skills was a big help in this early form of tax protest, but Junior quickly found out engine power was of supreme importance also. To his advantage, he didn't get brainwashed in reverse by the current automotive engineering agenda, and learned by the greatest learning process of all, the farmer's "cut and try."

I first noticed Jr. in 1960, February 500, Daytona. He qualified twenty miles an hour slower than my car and kept improving power wise during practice. Ray Fox was his crew chief. Junior figured out and invented "drafting." We were leading all day. At the end he sucked our rear glass out from the drafting. He won the race. And the whole damn race car was built in 'bout three weeks by three or four men, including Junior. Well, now that just about took the rag off the bush. Watching him with his success with Ray Fox and the Holman Moody teams I knew a new he-coon was in our woods. I guess our first deal together came in '63. It was about 1963 Corvettes with new 427 Mystery motors. Mickey Thompson got the cars ready and I did the engines.

Mick brought cars here and we helped him install engines and baby sat them. They had a sports car race at Daytona and Junior drove one of Mickey's three Corvettes. It rained like hell. The Corvettes filled up with water (yup they raced in the rain) from a hard-hard rain. Junior pulled in the pits and opened the door and I damn near got drowned in the water that flew out. Next, I built an engine and loaned it to Ray Fox for Junior to use at Riverside, and he won that race.

He survived for a long time as a successful team owner. And compiled a record winning career second only to Richard Petty. In 1975 Chevy asked me to help Junior with some small block engines for Darlington. He owned the team and Cale Yarborough was the driver; I was working with a new kind of synthetic oil, polyoester stuff called "All Proof." The car led race and everything looked wonderful, then the cam lobes wore off. Adios, big check and hero badge.

When I left NASCAR in seventy, poor ol' Junior inherited my position on the shit list. While Nascar was policing Junior the rest of the troops were getting away with murder. Result was Junior's cars didn't do shit for 'bout last five years he run. I watched in amusement. It was the "moonshiner" versus "the revenuer" all over. NASCAR being the "fuzz" this go around. NASCAR got tougher and tougher on Junior's case till finally he was 'bout handcuffed.

I first noticed Billy France was getting to Junior in the Legends Race in Charlotte 'bout 1991. We were on a yellow flag. I was behind pace car. Junior passes me and rams pace car in passenger door during the yellow. Guess who was sitting in the seat? Yup. "Li'l Billy France." I knew the end was around the bend. A couple of days later, France fines and suspends Junior for being a couple cubic inches over in the big Charlotte 500, race two days later. The couple inches helped 'bout like a mosquito bite on an elephant's ass.

Somewheres in here, Junior happens to look down, and notice who's got who by the balls. As I said earlier, Junior wasn't standing behind the door when the brains were handed out. Suddenly there's a "For Sale" sign out on the race shop and team. In a few months Junior tells me he don't own one damn nut, bolt, or part to a race car. Good night Irene, the party is over. He has, I assume, accumulated enough money to build a big house on top of the hill and pave the road, and fence it in. He's in good health I think. Got a new family. Got time to be a good daddy. Got a bunch of big, fat black cows eating up the grass and fertilizing the ranch. Probably even got a crick on it with a few fishes swimmin' round. I believe Junior may turn out to be smartest again when his racin' buddies consider how they enjoyed their golden years. The winner will not be the richest, or the one with the most toys. Winner will be those with the best health.

Junior did get President Reagan to forgive him for his wearing out all the revenuer cars, and failure to pay for liquor tax stamps. (Yup, negotiated a pardon. Jail record? It never happened). NASCAR says Jr. was one of their greatest fifty drivers. And I'd say probably in the top fifteen. Junior Johnson is kinda like the Legend of Sleepy Hollow. That story ain't going away any time soon. (Junior, however, had a genuine racer's outlook on life, and there's a chance his golden years may be something less than perfect. It's about impossible to keep a hound dog chained up.)

That's the deal folks. You've met some of the greatest drivers racing will ever have. Add in the other forty to fifty aces. (Imagine sixty to eighty of 'em on Darlington). If you can find a good quality film of the early stuff, you're gonna get a surprise. There is wall-to-wall excitement every single minute. I'm not going to infer that racing today is not great. What you will notice is the early breed was a totally different breed of cat. They seemed fearless in all categories. Danger, money, fame. It seemed like every one of 'em bet everything they had on every roll of the dice. For example: points, championships, amount of prize money, tomorrow, family, for most came second to winning today.

Maybe like your city commissioner, spending a hundred grand to get a job that pays ten a year. There was an indescribable magic that lasted for 'bout an hour after you got the job done.

I'm not a good enough writer to really describe that magic that made men knowingly risk their lives for three to five hours, forty to fifty times a year for what today is less than the price of a new 'Plain John' Chevy this year.

I was talking to Harvey Walters (Humpy's number one man in race control) at Charlotte while a race was on and he told me how he watched an old race start to finish. And how much he enjoyed it. And told me it suddenly dawned on him…the difference in racing today and yesterday was a kind of an evolution from a larger group of potential winners with little or no breaks in the struggles to win, with tighter running and .001 less than rubbing, where they raced every lap as if each lap was the winning lap. But with a major difference: in this respect, you could go to left, right, over or under the man in front of you. But you had the code of the hills: don't touch him. The excitement and suspense was heightened by the ever-present blowed tires. First Darlington race over six hundred tires were blown. The new rules have changed forever the game. I suppose that's the same in all sports.

Looking at attendance, it would be foolish to conclude today is bad. In a practice of comparing yesterday's racers and athletes to each other, my opinion is, it is not possible. They are not apples to apples…If yesterday was apple, today is half apple/half orange. If you got a grandfather race fan, ask him if the above is real. Who is his favorite? Fireball or Jeff Gordon? Yesterdays racer was a struggling tiger trying to get loose. Today's racer is a skilled surgeon working with calculated precision.

Family

I got to get my family sorted out. They come in and out of the story as they came in and out of my life. It's very hard to figure it out. OK, I had six children, four boys and two girls. Smokey, Rex, and Betty Ann were children of my first wife, Elizabeth. When they were about 12-13 years old their mother decided she wanted a divorce and the standard deal – everything. I said over my dead body. Her side said, "Makes no difference to us." I had just finished a fancy stone house with maid's quarters. It had a big fat payment book, but hell, in 30 years it would be all mine. It became my wife's in three years, not 30 and with an even bigger payment book that I got to keep up. Well, I can no longer sign checks by myself so all my dirty rotten plans to bankrupt the company go to shit.

Long before this point (13 years into my first adventure in the blessings of holy matrimony), I knew loud and clear I was in the wrong barn. At first I tried to be a good boy but I couldn't help and notice there were quite a few ladies around who wanted to play doctor. When this happened I tried to appease my wife. She said are you ashamed of them? No, I wasn't. So, I brought them home 'bout 2:00 am and woke the maid up to cook breakfast. My wife called 'em whores. Well, a man can't keep friends that way so I went back to the old secret deal. That brought on the deadly 'D.'

When we were first married, my wife made me promise I would never drive a racecar. I guess she loved me so much she didn't want to lose me. Or on second thought, no that wasn't it. Well anyway, a couple of weeks after she filed, the judge says, "Give her everything or sell it and give her the house and 100,000 bucks." I say, "Judge that's what it's all worth" and he says, "That ain't all, you've got to pay your kids' expenses and 200 bucks a month." (1959). That judge caused my undoing. I was helping him keep his 35-year-old secretary screwed. I mentioned that to him in court and it all went down hill from there.

OK, That's it. I'm a flop as a father. I decide I will now live this life as it comes, one day at a time. I was very hostile to ladies till the sun went down, then I became a sweet, lying bastard till I got their bloomers off. I could get fucked to death by 30 different, lonesome, middle-age (25 years old) ladies even though I was living in machine shop we'd built in the old laundry next door to the truck shop. There I had no heat or hot water and slept on an army cot with an air mattress. (till my dog bit the mattress and it leaked) In those days if a lady mentioned marriage, I'd set a new 100-yard record to my car or motorcycle. Mentally, I'd convinced myself marriage was invented by women. I got lucky and made a lot of dinero from oil and inventions.

I was so gun shy of marriage I honestly was positive I'd never ever even consider it. Well, I made it five years and a lady who was such a change from the usual changed my mind. She wanted to marry me, but wanted no strings attached. Her dad was the county district attorney. She signed a paper saying I could be unchained, no rules 'cept come home when you can. Man, I was happy. We had three children. (Actually four, the first came as twins but the boy died shortly after birth.) Patricia, the surviving twin was named after her mother, Patricia. Next came two boys a year or so apart, Sam and Steve. So a total of three children in less than four years. But a problem was developing. I didn't notice it, but I really was happy with everything like it was. But Patt was so busy with the three kids she left me too much rope. I restarted an earlier romance and it became a major problem. I then realized that I was lost again. Actually what I thought I wanted was both movies at the same time. I now consider that possibility the equivalent of successfully pushing snowballs up a wildcat's ass with a red-hot poker.

Then real, real bad stuff happens. The 'big C' gets Patt. Then when I looked in mirror I wanted to puke. We get Patt to the M.D. Anderson Clinic in 10 hours. Paul Goldsmith flies to Daytona from Chicago in five hours. Five hours more we are at M.D. Anderson. A friend of mine from the oil business, Dan Montgomery, had the door wired open to our arrival and admittance. After months of out patient care in Houston and being looked after by her sister, Judy, Patt comes home supposedly cured. I guess the cure killed her; it damaged her and her heart. Now we got three children – 13, 14 and 15 – without a mother. The teenage years are no place to learn the father business. After Patt's death, I continued to raise the youngest three children. Nope, didn't do perfect but maybe I should have got a 'C' as a father on second batch.

My mistress gets mad and says now or never. I say, "Stop the world I want to get off." My lady friend tells me to get lost. For first time in my life I didn't know what to do. So I do the obvious – nothing. I find it's a full time job to herd up the kids. In about a year I start up with women again. I'm all goofed up and I pick a girl about half my age. Every once in a while looks like marriage is in the cards. All the ladies were good but that certain magic you need didn't happen. Why? Hell, I don't know.

Then Margie's husband died suddenly. Soon as I saw her at the funeral I knew there might be something for us. Now I'm back in the soup again. Margie is a beautiful blond, stacked like a brick shithouse, who seemed to be very attracted to me. I was very aware of her. So after a couple of starts and stops, I was totally ape-shit over her. And it didn't hurt she was a wildcat in the hay. It just happened. I enjoyed her all day and all night long. Finally a peace came over me and most importantly I didn't try to hide from my reflection in the mirror any more. I started to get my self-respect back.

Margie wanted to get married. That was a zero to me. Every pair I knew who lived together and got married was a disaster. I was sure if I married her it would blow up in a year. But, I couldn't help but notice that socially us just living together put Margie in a less than first-class lady category. One day out of the blue I said, "Get dressed, we are going to Bunnell and get married." $69.50 total wedding cost at the Bunnell courthouse. Now if I ever did anything right that was it. We had about 15 years of perfect life then the 'big C' snatched me in the ass. I was a 24-karat asshole much of the time, a mental attitude where I got mad instantly over nothing. But Margie lives for me. I don't have any idea how I'd live without her.

Meanwhile, the kids grew up and got married. Sam moved away and married Sharon. They've got two boys Patrick and Michael, 'bout four and five and live in Jacksonville. He's a successful restaurant owner and has a computer business.

My other boy, Steve, married Kathy and has a baby girl, Kaylin. Steve's a motorcycle policeman in Daytona helping the mayor and the city council keep law and order here. (By the way, they enforce the laws year 'round except for Black College Reunion 'bout tail end of March. If you come down it will show you

Me and my son Sam down by the river behind the shop.

a live real sample of zero lawlessness for four or five days in living color. Ain't a bad place if you have a death wish.)

My daughter Patricia, I named Kilroy when she was little. Kilroy was in an Army cartoon in World War II. As a little girl of 'bout five or six she was just barely able to get high enough to see over the fence, she looked like the cartoon Kilroy, done by Bill Mauldin (Sad Sack was the series.) Kilroy has two children, Laurel 'bout 13 and Brayden, four. She runs a pet store next to the shop and helps me out every day. Kilroy, her husband Chris, and my son Steve also help me keep this old dump together.

Actually, I had two families 'bout 15 years apart. In the first family I had three children, Smokey, Betty Ann and Rex. A couple of years after my divorce, the first family moved to New Jersey. The kids were 13, 11 and nine and I lost all input to them. My daughter Betty Ann became a nurse. The three older children never did join my new family. My oldest son, Smokey, (it's now 2001) has finally become interested in helping me, which was a pleasant surprise. The other son, Rex, didn't fare too well. He died in 2000 from a drinking-related medical problem. It was a sad ending to a wasted life. No, he had plenty of chances to fly right.

Margie and age has got me to realize I had a young family but that was a vague and strange to me so it had no real meaning. Margie wanted to get married. I had no such intentions; guess I just didn't want to think about anything permanent. So we lived together and I finally woke up and realized Margie had me thinking about tomorrow. Probably 1990 I woke up. There was a family and Margie was my mate and it would be that way till the first of us died. I put together a bunch of loose ends in my life and made preparations for when I couldn't work anymore.

I have a grandson named Casey Yunick who may end up a racer. His first year in All Pro (2000), he won rookie of the year. Nope, I didn't help him much since he started. Only way I could help was in securing parts. Also, being out of his life for the first 20 years didn't help.

Today, March 9, 2001 I got medical news. I may luck out and beat this cancer. It's quite a change from January 1, 2001; dead by March 1 to maybe March 8, 2001. Kinda like I got a reprieve from the electric chair.

One thing I note now is that I have to be careful about how I run my mouth to keep from overloading my ass. But maybe I'll get my horsepower back. I'm kinda excited now, I'm hopin' I can unload the extra wagon Margie's been pulling for 18 months.

In the last 18 months ain't no way in hell I could have handled it by myself. The reason I fought so hard to live was Margie. I didn't want to leave her. The kids help Margie and I with our everyday life, problems and chores with lots of help from Chris Brown, Kilroy's husband. My biggest daily pleasures are my dogs, Goofy and Carbon and Brayden – Kilroy's three-year-old boy. That kid is all boy. I can't understand him very well yet. If I get my health back I will have reason to be very thankful for my life.

Real Racer's Proving Ground

This was my quest for a "real racer's badge."

Well, at end of '54 NASCAR season, I've had the experience of two championships, (and twice second), in four years. I'm building the '55 Packard for the February '55 beach race, which half way through construction, I knew in my heart was a dead player. It's about two am. I'm tired, cold, got half a bottle of Seagrams V.O. (The "good stuff"– six bucks a quart), so I go to my office (a red desk and chair and four bucks worth of office furniture) and turn out the lite. I sit in the chair, and study what the hell I'm doing. I finally finish the V.O. 'bout 5:00 am, and have concluded that the stock car adventure is over (for me), and at best, it's been the equivalent of a 10 mile walk over broken whiskey bottles bare footed.

I was drunk enough to talk to myself. You ever done that? I brought "Big Bill" into my illusionary meeting. I've quit stock car racing and Bill came by to try and talk me out of it. Bill had a tricky way in his bullshitting. That was to always use the word "we." "We are gonna do this and that."

I said, "Bill, what's this Lindbergh shit. We?" ('member Lindbergh airplane "we"?) Said, "Way I see it, 'We' (the racers) do all the work, and 'you' get all the fucking money. So as of now, the Bill France Benefit Show is over." 'Cause as I sat there and thought it out I was reminded again how France had a deal going where we paid him for the rite to work for him for nothing. (How goofy you gotta be to pay somebody for the rite to work for nothing, and maybe kill yourself doing it?)

You pay for membership and entry fee. We have to agree he has rite to sell our pictures and advertising space on racecars for nothing. It's the same today in all of racing. Some as bad, some better, some worse. But even today really, a young man going into racing is making one of the dumbest business decisions he could have made. The odds for success are 'bout 10,000 to one, you will not only not make any money, but you will plow 10 to 15 years worth of what you made someplace else into it. Some will pay the ultimate price. Even worse, some will suffer 10 to 40 years from their racing wounds. No other way to put it. All the good reasons to be a racer can be written on the head of a pin in capital letters. But for myself, fifty some years later; do I regret I used a major part of my life to be a racer? Hell No! In fact, I'm pretty grateful to have had the opportunity.

No, this is not meant to be a "thank you" to Bill France, really, he didn't really know any more than we did about where we were going. I can relate to it this way: I spent 33 years, part time, in the Oriente jungle in Ecuador, in oil and gold. The NASCAR trip for me, 1946 to 1971, was like sitting down in a dugout canoe in a fast moving jungle river. You try to aim it but the river is really in control. Really, you don't know where you're going. What you see takes your breath away or maybe horrifies and disgusts you. But you're going so fast you really can't grasp it all. When you finally get out of the canoe, you realize you cannot get back the way you came. You will have to invent a new adventure to get back, and some never do make it back. Some died in the 'down river' trip, some became too weak in one of many ways to make the trip back. Also, many times on the trip, you decide "this is actually further than I want to go." You want to go back, you can't. So you keep going to some place where you can see a way back.

But really, is that much different than just plain ol' eight to five with a lunch bucket? Probably not 'cept for the scenery and the speed of the current.

OK, for some reason to be identified as real racer was important to me. In my mind, the greatest automobile race in the world was the "Indy 500." I can't begin to explain the intrigue and excitement that race represented to me. You, who have not experienced it before 1975, won't know even remotely, what we saw in that race. From '75 to '95 it slowly became a foreign car, foreign engine, and foreign driver race. Oh sure, we still had 10 or 12 out of the 33 drivers. But engines and cars are now 100 percent "green card".

Me and Goldy at Indy – the shirt says it all. (photo: David Nearpass Photography)

Now Tony Hulman's grandkid, Tony George, is trying to put it back. But three years later, it looks like he's pissin' into a 100 mile per hour wind. Damn if he ain't doing it the hard way, but I'm convinced he will eventually get the job done. Tony, I think you need to go off in a nice, quiet place, and re-think the deal. 'Cause if you keep pissing into 100 mile per hour wind, it blows back on you – bad. You can't ignore it when it finally socks you. You get all wet and you smell bad. (I give you credit Tony, you're in a fast, expensive adventure.)

So in the illusionary meeting I had (chaired by the quart of V.O.) I decided stock cars were "out" and Indy was next stop. Well the Packard did even worse than I expected. I've got no racecar now so I go to Indy to find a car owner.

1955, '56, '57 INDY

I got my first sniff of Indy in '55. I was invited to the garage area as a guest helper in Lindsey Hopkins garage. Lindsey was a very wealthy car owner from Atlanta. Lindsey's family were kinda owners of Coca-Cola's syrup formula. Jack Beckley was Lindsey's high paid crew chief. $150 a week year round. That was 'bout the going deal then for chiefs.

Back then the chief repaired the metal chassis and body, built the engines, built the drive train, handled every aspect of racing and travel and sanctioning body politics, babysat the driver, fixed the owner up with pussy, also was the sponsor's tour guide. Some chiefs could paint, letter, and build a car from ground up, and once in awhile they'd build their own engine and drive train, including casting and machining their own wheels. I've seen cars where only store bought stuff was the tires. They were allowed to make their own fuel (no straight gas allowed in my time, '55 through '75)

Now, goddam! This is where I wanna be. Li'l skinny rule book. It specified a minimum weight, a maximum width and length, 75 gallons maximum fuel tank, open wheel (no fenders). There were two engine rules; one for blown engines and one for normally aspirated – just listed displacement. Kinda snooty though. No curse words (like damn), no booze, no drugs, and no tobacco ads. No women allowed in garage area – period (including lady car owners).

The garage area was open 24 hours a day. Yup, you can sleep in garage. Every entry gets his own garage and you can lock it and keep your secrets hidden. The garage is yours for the whole year (if you qualify). 100 entries, 33 race, no bullshit.

In NASCAR today 59 cars enter 43-car race, 16 walk if they miss. Tears big as horse turds, but they have spots for ex-champions, hi point-runners, promoter option, or any other reason down to "'cause we said so" to choose the field. At Indy, then (and still) the 33 fastest go racing, and the other 67 walk. Absolutely no exceptions, absolutely no other way to qualify. Each year more walk than race, but I liked that (I later walked three times). Back then, it was my belief that to qualify at Indy was equivalent of a racing doctorate, of a present license only available to about 100 people on a worldwide basis. In short, I felt qualifying gave you the right to answer when asked, "What do you do for a living?" – to say, "I'm a real racer!" It was very important to me because Indy was the only racing in the US that was accepted as a major event (1958).

At that time the Offenhauser was "the king of the hill." A beautiful, simple, four cylinder masterpiece of ingenuity from a self-educated engineer, Harry Miller. The "Offy" had a voice that shook the earth. Kinda like I figured a elephant would sound like if you had a brick in each hand and banged 'em together with his balls in the middle. The Indy cars had a special smell about 'em too. Maybe from the fuel and oil, kinda just second to a sexy lady in full heat.

The competition lasted 30 days. May 1 to Memorial Day. I can't explain it, but in the first week I believe "I will win this race soon." I already had eight years racing and had won a lot of races. But everything before seemed to be very unimportant. The garage area was a small special world as were the pits – all fenced off. If you had a magic badge you could go and do whatever you wished. These fences were lined with "fence bunnies," ladies rich and poor, young and not so young, who wanted to be part of our world. And they wanted to play with the monkeys in the cage with the race cars. Actually, a never ending parade of applicants for a "lady racer job." No ladies allowed in garage and pit area under penalty of death almost. (Oh yes, some did get in at night.)

The keeper of the racer's lair was Clarence Cagel, a no nonsense, hard-nosed and fair groundskeeper. Clarence was a racer: still is (he's 'bout 80). But I never saw Clarence in the bars, police stations, or wild-assed motel parties. In short; Clarence didn't fuck around.

1955 Dave Garroway decided to do some TV at Indy with his "Today Show" my second day there, (this is the beginning of the all-month, deal). I'm asked if I would "go on television tomorrow morning" with Bill Vuckovich Sr? The deal is "stock car and Indy car aces: what are the differences?" So I say, "Hell yes." (I'm still having trouble controlling my ego.) Not Bill, he says "shit no." Well, Bill's car owner, a rich oil man (owned Superior Oil Company), Howard Keck, he saw it different, so I guess he said "do it," in such a way that "Vukey" agreed it was a good idea.

Well, 7:00 am and the deal's in old restaurant behind pit grandstand. It's raining like a son-of-a-bitch. Garroway starts off with, "What do you think of the weather?" Vukey says, "Piss poor." Yup, caught 'em flat footed, and it went nationwide. After thirty minutes of this Dave gives up on Vukey and I'm in the big time. "Hot damn you all!"

I stayed 'bout ten days. Met a lot of Indy racers and car owners, but bottom line was, "You ain't got one mile of open wheel experience. Come back and see me when you get three or four years experience." I see real quick, 100 car owners, 5,000 guys willing to work on 'em for nothing. That plan won't fly. Chief mechanic's good pay at Indy was 150 bucks a week. 100 cars trying for 33 starting positions. Tough sledding, rite?

I got to know Vukey's mechanics pretty good (Jim Travers and Frank Coons). Jim and Stew Hilborn dreamt up fuel injection (which 50 years later is still working good, with next to no change). Strange deal was, they (Travers and Coons), wanted out of Indy, and wanted to try building engines for stock cars. Their car owner was so rich, he lived in LA, had his own jet, and commuted every day to Houston (he could fly the jet). He parked his Cadillac limousine on the side walk next to main entrance of building in Houston. (Yes, he owned the building, and "caddy" driver sat in it all day, ready to go "wherever.")

Well, that team owned Indy at the time. Driver, and mechanics, good as it gets. Plenty of money, and they all like each other. I watched and kept my mouth shut. I was real impressed with Vuckovich's savvy. Them days drivers "car hopped." If I had a problem with car, I ask "so and so" to try it for his input about it's running and handling. It was in their code of the hills. I watched Vukey try a car that just wasn't doing anything. He was good enough he'd run it some faster. Pulled in. Tells mechanics on that car, "If his car run that good, and handled that good, the race was over." Then tells his crew "What a shit box, won't run, and handles like a dog." Well, that tore the competitor's camp up. Mechanics are convinced "driver is junk, car is perfect." (You can imagine rest of the month on that team.)

1956

Back to Daytona. No racecar deal. So, I do what I usually do when whatever I want don't work. I decide, "The hell with it. Didn't want it anyhow! Let's have a little drink or two." When I was about 15, the old man who owned the gas station I worked in sometimes, advised me two ways. (Mr. Detweiller, an upcountry Dutchman. I later came to appreciate his wisdom). Talk around station was 'bout young women, and "who was screwing who." He said, "Son, in reference to sex matters, be your own counsel." Which was damn good advice. (I kept my mouth shut, and got twice as much as average cat. Then, I wrote this book and now I can't say that any more). The other was, he noticed me riding a girl around on the motorcycle, (who I guess was pretty easy to part with her bloomers) but a friend of mine had a car and took over. I got feeling bad about it. He said, "Son, sometimes you need to be careful what you wish for; you might get it." (She gave my friend a "healthy" dose of the clap.)

I went back to Indy in '56 and "stooged" for Jack Beckley again for a couple weeks. Still no luck.

By now Marshall Teague not only has the "Indy bug," but has secured a ride in a pretty good car, "The Sumar Special." Chapman Root is the owner. It's Pure Oil sponsored. Remember Marshall brought Pure into stock car racing (1951), a la Hudson. So I spend some time with his crew. I got the "Indy bug" bad. But still "no cigar." I made 'bout a one week visit three years ('55, '56, '57) during practice. In this time frame, Marshall Teague had qualified once for the race and I stooged for him for a week. I came home with an official Indy white satin "Pure Oil" racing jacket. Hot damn, I slept in the damn thing for a month.

The jacket didn't last long. I met a girl in Charlotte that really looked great in that jacket with nothing else on but black panties, silk stockings and hi-heels. Nope. Never got it back. Only knew her nickname was "Bunny." Should have been "minkey." Whew! What the hell. Easy come, easy go.

By now, the rich kids, Traverse and Coons, are out of Indy (1955 when Vuckovich got killed, I believe, was last race the Keck team run). They switched to stock car engines and continued building Indy engines (Offies) for other teams. In this time frame Travers and Coons owned the Indy farm, and were sliding into doing the push rod Indy engines for Roger Penske for Mark Donohue.

1957 & '58

Well, 1957 is the same deal. I go up to smell the alky-nitro and castor oil and stooge for Beckley and Teague some more. Not even a nibble, I left out that I was back running NASCAR again 1955, 56 and 57, with Chevy and from March '57 to October '57 with Ford. Goldsmith and I won the '58 Beach Race in a Pontiac. Then it happened. I made up my mind five minutes after we won the race. I was gonna buy an Indy car, and enter it, no matter what.

NOTE: Early February 1958 I get tipped off 'bout a two year old Kurtis in a garage in a suburb of Chicago, I believe the town's name was "Sinclair" or "St. Charles." A rich grandmom, heir to Texaco fortune, I believe named "Sinclair," owned it after her grandson hit a big oak tree in their driveway with a '55 Chevy at Christmas time, and it put his lites out. Well, I deal with grandmom on phone. "Five grand, take it or leave it." "Thank you ma'am. Can I pay you $500 down and finance it three years?" "Click." Grandma didn't finance. Well, hell, you never know till you try.

Paul Goldsmith winning the Beach Race in 1958.

I built a '58 Pontiac to run the last NASCAR Beach Race (on the sand). Paul Goldsmith won the race with it. I think we got about $4,500. I get half. So all I need is $2,250 more. While still on the beach, right after the race, I ask for associate car owner share holder money. Well, Bill Tauss, head racer at Grey Rock Brakes said, "We'll donate $400." I ask for pledges to be written on my shirt (it's white). Next fundraiser stop on my way back to the shop. (In this period, I could have used some Clinton savvy on scammin' money, but I never gave China a thought.)

I drop in at Mac's bar on the way to the shop, a famous Daytona racer's bar (at that time). Make a long story short, I get $1,500 pledged. "I hate to keep bothering you ma'am, but I now have four grand cash American money. Will you take that and a one grand note due May 31st?"

"No, I won't. But, if you make the note due

May 1, before you have a chance to wreck it, I'll accept your offer." "OK, we got a deal ma'am. I'll air mail check up and be there in three days to get it. And I'll send a signed note with the check." Grandma says, "Cash only." Well, like I said, she was a rich, tough, fair lady. She wasn't gonna let somebody gyp her out of anything so what the hell. Whatever's fair right?

Goldy and I have decided he would drive it, and he'd help me get the car to Daytona. This is a nasty, cold winter. Paul has a '55 Chevy Nomad station wagon. I had to be in Detroit for a meeting with Mr. Knudsen (boss of Pontiac). Paul lived in Detroit. The deal is after the Pontiac meeting, we rent a trailer, use Paul's station wagon to pick car up. Then Paul helps me to get to Atlanta with it.

I got a free pass to ride Eastern Airlines (Eddie Rickenbacker is Eastern's top cat. Eddie is real racer, and for whatever reason, he felt I rated a free seat with Eastern. Am I gonna argue 'bout it?)

The deal is, I give Paul my pass, he flies home, and I bring station wagon back to Indy. The day before we leave Detroit to go to get the race car, a blizzard hits. Snow, ice, I mean it's bad. Paul says we can get there in six or seven hours. We are in a bar at the time, and a couple nice looking middle-age women came in ('bout 21 or 22) without escorts. (Bell telephone operators) I say, "Paul, ain't we liable to get lonesome in that long ride?" He says, "You're right." So, we took the telephone ladies with us to Chicago.

Well, with the cold, nasty weather and the station wagon rigged as a bed in the back, nature took it's course. Paul and I took turns violating one or two of the commandments, with the complete and enthusiastic cooperation of "Bell's" very friendly employees. We never made it to Chicago though. We got to South Bend and holed up for the night. Next morning, "Grandma, we've been delayed, we can't make it till 'bout five tonight because of the icy and snow drifted roads." "I understand, five o'clock will be fine." But the roads are so bad we get there closer to 11:00 pm. By then there was no more screwing around. By the time we left South Bend neither one us was gonna be sexy for at least four hours. Whoo-eeee. Actually, the ladies were a big help. We get to the place, a huge mansion with big iron gates, a guard and about a mile driveway. "Who? Let me call the house." Grandma's asleep, "Don't wake me up," but has left instructions. "Go to the garage, get the racer, leave the money and the note on the workbench by the phone."

We get in garage, the lite is on, but it's not lit up too good. Inside there is the Kurtis Indy car, a midget, a sprinter, a Piper Super Cub, two motorcycles and a badly wrecked '55 Chevy. The wrecked car is not scattered, but everything else is totally apart. There is a big note on the workbench by the phone. "I'm sure you know what to take."

Well, hell, that's easy. I never worked on a Kurtis and I only half-assed knew the Offy from the Indy visits. We left the garage at 3:30 am. I was short about two small car items we were able to make, and had two or three pieces of the plane and sprinter, which should have been mailed back.

The ladies? They decided to go back to Detroit and we parted at the closest Greyhound bus station. No, they weren't mad, just had enough of that adventure and got homesick. (Well, maybe one was a little pissed, she started calling Paul "Mr. Dry Balls" after we left South Bend.)

I scraped up the $1,000 entry fee, made a deal with the city to name the car the "City of Daytona Beach Special," rebuilt that sucker, painted it black and gold. I get five grand the day I leave for Indy from the City of Daytona Beach.

Well, hell, nothing ever goes according to plan in racing. France is building the new race track, and says, "Before you go to Indy, come by new track and let us take a picture." I get there at 2:00 pm, no France. The "City of Daytona Beach Special" is on trailer ready to go. I look around and decide, "Hell, I believe I can take tow car, trailer and racer around by doing a little twisting between the paving equipment." When I get back to where I started, Bill is there with smoke coming out both ears. He wanted to be first one around track with a race car. Can't un-do it can I?

Back to shop. I didn't even tell France I was sorry 'cause it would have been a lie. Really, I kinda got a kick out of it after I thought about it. 3:00 pm, at the shop, Mayor Eubanks and all the local politicians and news media are there to give me the five grand and a hearty send off to represent them in the greatest spectacle in auto racing for 1958.

There is a minor problem. The original deal was: name the car the "City of Daytona Beach Special." That's when I first noticed politicians in general were a bunch of ignorant jackoffs.

The politicians twisted it around and decided it should be named "The Halifax Recreational Area Special." I told them cats I would not change the name and if I did, the five grand would be pissed in the sewer. (If you were a fan at Indy, could you have even guessed that "Halifax" name meant "Daytona Beach?") So, when they told the audience I'd change the name up there and gave me the check, it's my turn, and I say, "They'll have a snow storm in hell first and tear up the check. (I'm dead sober.) Well, there went my close friendship with Volusia county's version of a Southern mafia. Now, if I murdered somebody, I'd have to do at least a week in jail.

The local newspaper has a real good savvy race reporter named Bennie Kahn. Bennie and Don O'Reilly invented Smokey and Fireball. Bennie liked my act and got his ass chewed out for siding with me quite often.

Well, 'bout midnight I leave to get there for April 30th arrival. I got a used trailer with practically new tires in reference to tread wear, but 'bout three or four years old and they are dry-rotted. Up around Chattanooga one blows. I find a used tire. I'm down to 'bout 90 bucks 'cause I was counting on the five grand to pay balance of car. (One grand, remember?) That's gotta last for rent, food. By now nothing makes sense. Only credit card I got is Eastern Airlines courtesy "Uncle Eddie."

Next tire blows. I trade a new quarter inch drill for it, and get a tank of gas to boot, station owner's never seen Indy car or Offy engine, lets me keep the gas for free.

I get the deal to the track. I got no helpers. Them days, only help we had was free local people or nothing. I find a room half mile from track in Speedway, Indiana. (Bet you didn't even know that area round the track is it's own city. All the politicians are ex-racers. Name of the town is "Speedway," makes sense don't it?)

A room with two beds for Paul and I, ten bucks a week, includes breakfast for both. The family name was Goldsmith. Nope, no relation to Paul, but I notice the mayor of Indy now is a "Goldsmith." Mayor, are you one of the Speedway Goldsmiths?

The is Larry Shinoda's original drawing of the City of Daytona Special.

Well, I get a couple hundred from Daytona via Western Union. Paul had a little money. I make a deal for two meals a day at "Maryanne's" (or something like that), at a two-story house restaurant just other side of the railroad overpass across 16th Street. Lunch and supper 35 bucks a week for both of us, a "rookie special." Between them, the restaurant lady and the Goldsmiths, they saved our asses.

Paul never even sat in a Indy car till May 1. I had never worked on an Indy car, 'cept stooging for Beckley. We got two weeks till first qualifying Saturday. 'Bout ten days into the deal, news cats are saying, "Hey, looks like they got a shot." For what ever reason we get a break with the news aces, and they are wearing out their pencils talking 'bout us. Well, this produced some very unexpected benefits. It seems like the local ladies decided we could do much better if we got plenty of lovin'. So collectively, and this is not a complaint believe me, they goddam near screwed us to death in three and a half weeks.

The garage you're assigned is dirty from last year and buildings are very old and rickety, ain't even paved, outside is cinders. So a gallon a white wash and a couple of lite bulbs and it's shiny. We got our own phone for $15 a month. Some local reporter put our phone number in a story. Paul and I wrote the phone numbers of the volunteer lady entertainment therapists on the wall by the phone and started rating them from one star to five stars. (I believe it only fair to credit the ladies for their contribution. We didn't get much sleep, but what little we got was quality rest.)

Well, not bragging, but we had quite a list. (Our landlord saved by us missing breakfast and not using sheets.)

About the third day we were at Indy something happened that blew my mind. A very well-dressed man came by the garage and said, "Do you have a couple minutes to spare? I knew it was the "boss man," Tony Hulman, so I said, "Yup." He introduces himself and shook my hand. He said, "I want to welcome you and thank you for entering the race. Without people like you we could not have this race." As he talked, I realized he had a short biography about me, and complimented me and Paul as good racers. Holy shit, I'm dumbfounded. In the past I'm used to "shut up and do it," "If you don't like it hit the road," "Do it or else," "If you look at us cross-eyed your ass is disqualified," "Why?... Because I said so" and " Load the wagon the mule is blind." Indy was different. Here is the boss man telling a couple of rookies "Thanks for coming."

Tony Hulman was a class act. Next he handed me his business card and said, "Both my office and home phone are on it. If you have a problem short of murder, and including a possible financial crisis; call me, I'll try to help you." Tony did this to every entrant, every year. Take my word for this – Tony Hulman loved the track and the race. He gave that place a very special mystique and class. His methods established the Indy 500 as the most important race in the world, and he kept the rules so that any talented racer could make the cut there if he had the desire and the skills.

It was an all American event: American drivers, engines and cars. The buildings were old, but the place looked like a country club. Everything was white and trimmed in green. The grass was cut and trimmed with flowers in many places. The whole place was very efficiently run, and everything a racer needed was there for us. Hell, it was kinda, at least to me, a racer's heaven. You could do just about anything you wanted

Me and Bill France, Sr.

in building your racer to make it go against the best there were in the world, and then line 'em up race day, hitch your pants and look to your left and to your right and say, or think, "All right you motherfuckers, let's race a race for all the marbles there are in the world."

Next day a big-big cat 'bout 65 comes by. Well dressed, I mean even a Homburg hat and gloves. Big bushy eyebrows, full bushy head of hair. "Hi. I'm Eddie Rickenbacker. I want to welcome you to the track. Here's my card. If you need help call, I may be able to help you some how." (Eddie was then president of Eastern Airlines). "Say, I heard you flew quite a bit of combat, they tell me you flew with French Foreign Legion and with the Tigers in Burma, and you were a 17 pilot." (He's apparently forgotten he gave me a pass two or three years ago to ride Eastern Airlines at a 100 percent discount.) Next, comes what I got every year word for word till he didn't come anymore. "I flew a 17 in the Pacific (I think he used a B-17 for a transport – not to fight) and had to ditch it and live in a raft for several days, damn near died of thirst and it rained. Damn near starved and a sea-gull landed on the raft and I caught it and we ate it." Finally he gets rescued. I'm not trying to minimize the rough movie he played in, but goddam. It's a 15 minute deal word for word for quite a few years. (If you meet anyone who says he raced at Indy '55 thru '65 and he don't know the seagull story; he is a bullshitter). For you younger readers, Eddie was greatest World War One aviation fighter pilot ace.

But Eddie, I enjoyed you, and especially enjoyed knowing you when it came time to buy a plane ticket on Eastern, especially when all seats were sold out. One time Mauri Rose and I got stuck in Atlanta, the flight was overbooked. By the way, Eddie Rickenbacker loved Mauri Rose, may have been only other guy in the US besides me that did. Station manager gave Mauri a rash of shit (actually we had seats, but got bumped). Mauri is running some heat. I see the pipe wiggling up and down, I 'bout know what's coming. Mauri lets the Eastern cat have it. After this, the manager gets hot, shoves our suitcases off the scales, and calls a cop. Mauri get in phone booth, this is 'bout 9:00 pm. Remember phone booths with folding doors? Inside one, if you keep your foot against the bottom of the middle door hinge, no way can you open it from outside. The cop is pissed.

Mauri finally gets Eddie on the phone, plane has to taxi back to gate, station manager is carrying both mine and Mauri's bags.

You know, for a few years there, it was like I had a free airliner to anywheres I needed to go. Not only on Eastern, but Eddie gave us some kind of pass that worked awful good on all airlines.

I'm in trouble in here and don't know it. I'm getting to believe a lot of the shit they write about me.

Free Stetson hats, free boots, free cars, lots of clothes, free tools, and telephone credit card free. A great big ego deal is building. In '54 Herb Thomas and I are running a Hudson Hornet at Monroe, Michigan (half mile dirt). Race finishes a li'l late and I mean, I'm filthy. Eddie has the plane wait for me (a DC-3). The passengers see this mess get on (so bad, stewardess put a white sheet on my seat before I sat down) and bitch, "Who the hell is he to hold a plane for?" The stewardess? She cleaned me up in her apartment in Jacksonville. Eastern Airlines really took good care of their passengers.

I guess my ego snuck up on me and I recognized all the "freebies," but never noticed I was working for 'bout a dollar an hour, 80 hours a week, 365 days a year. Had I pursued what I really wanted to do, be in the hunt for and drilling for oil, ain't no telling what kind of life that may have been. I'm sure the financial rewards would have been much greater for the same amount of effort.

May 10th, 1958, trouble rears it's ugly head. Number one local (very powerful) Indy writer says the "push rod kids" are illegal, not qualified to run at Indy. Pretty serious. Indy office says, "Sorry, we made a mistake accepting your entry. We'll give you your entry fee back."

Now let me tell you 'bout how Indy was really run. When I pulled up to Indy "day one" and ask guard procedure to get to garage, he directs me to a little frame one-story house on Speedway behind grandstand, and just off Georgetown road. The boss man is big-big "he Coon"...a big "mother," ex-racer name Harry Quinn. He looks me over, walks round me, looks at car, asks a few questions, then 'bout five or six others circle round me, sniff me, ask some questions. They find out I ain't Bill France's biggest booster. It don't take long...'bout five minutes to figure out for some reason they really dislike France. 'Bout 30 minutes of this and Harry gives me a good drink, slaps me on the ass, and says, "You're in kid, we want to see your act." I know now that thirty minutes either made you or broke you.

Well, when the press jumped our asses to kick us out, Don O'Reilly and Bennie Kahn liked to wore their typewriters out fighting for Paul and I. Then Harry and the clan came by and said, "Keep digging, you ain't going nowheres, you're gonna get a shot at the bull." Mysteriously, in about 36 hours the problem was gone and we are gonna qualify (that is, try to qualify).

Disaster raises it's head and strikes again. Friday 4:00 pm the clutch goes ape-shit. Baker engineering says 265 bucks cash. If you knew Baker, you know you didn't fuck around with him. He is good, fair, reasonable, and the only game in town. "Credit your ass," he's been down that road long before we met and that's it. I ain't got it; ain't got a clue on how to get it. Mentally, I gave up.

You know, tomorrow is the day. (Nope, I couldn't get nerve up to ask Tony for money.) Saturday, the first day of qualifying. Let me tell you something, and believe this, within an hour, when those cats we were competing against heard we were out, I had offers of a gift or loan of at least 20 clutches and offers from at least 75 mechanics to help change the clutch. The guy who gave me a clutch to use actually missed the race by a few hundredths of a second. You know what the chances of that are today?

We qualify middle of the field on the first day. Man, I'm really one happy son-of-a-bitch. I'm a "genuine Indy racer," hot damn. All through this Indy adventure, I had Mauri Rose by my side helping Paul and myself. After all, a three-time winner ain't no bad advisor. You agree?

The phone number and the rating program has become a society item, and I notice a little number copying going on by our fellow racers. Paul's family is coming to the race and he feels those phone numbers and the stars could cause some discontent and unpleasant days, unless we make the wall all white again. At first I say, "Well, lets just tape some paper over it." I notice Paul seems uncomfortable about my solution, so I decide a little sacrifice on my part is better than an uneasy driver, so I go to the paging garage and announce we will paint the wall at 7:00 pm. Goddam, within minutes, there was a steady stream of racers copying the numbers and rating system. (Done, I'm sure, for historical purposes only.) I found out, when I returned in '59 to race again, that many of the number copiers had quite a few sexual adventures with the ladies of the 'Let's screw Smokey and Paul silly club – Indy chapter.'

On the way out to pits race morning, I'm steering the car. A guard says "hold 'er Smoke." Here comes chief steward, Harlan Fengler. "Either remove the word "damn" from your clothing and the car, or you're disqualified, and the alternate starter will take your position." Yes, that makes sense don't it? One hour to race time, and we've been there thirty days. O'Reilly was there and went ballistic. But he got a razor blade and cut the "Best Damn Garage in Town" patches off our shirts.

I taped out the word "damn" on the car. Whew! I didn't need that. I look around. Holy shit. There are 350,000 people there. 700,000 eyeballs watching. Suppose I fuck up? Hate to admit it, but I was kinda scared.

Here comes next surprise. Those Offys were hard to start, and 'bout every race somebody wouldn't be able to get car started in time. Tony finally says, "Gentlemen, start them Mothers!" (Or something to that effect.) 33 Offies packed together make one hell of a racket. You can't tell if your own engine is running. I got injector side of the hood up and am working the throttle. The starter is in nose of the car. It weighs 'bout 65 pounds and stays in pits (once engine is started).

I decide to hold throttle with one hand, holding pistol grip gasoline squirter in my teeth and other hand on exhaust pipe to feel the heat. (Gas was a big starting aid). First and only time I got the shit burned out of my fingers (and loved it). Can you imagine waiting all year and can't get it started? (Yes, it happens 'bout every year.)

The race was a giant let down. On the first lap, there was a bad-bad accident in number three. 'Bout a 25 car pile up. Goldy's luck runs out. He'd cleared the wreck, was coming off of three and would have been leading but 'Cousin Weak Eyes,' Jerry Unser, didn't catch the yellow and is going into three in full racing mode. While Goldy's just accelerating out of the mess Jerry comes from last to second then runs up Goldie's back and helmet and leaves tire marks on 'em. Jerry lands in parking lot outside the track on his wheels. Well, Goldy's got a weak neck so this puts his face in the steering wheel and now he can't see and tags the outside wall. The hit wasn't too bad but the oil cooler I installed there (an oil cooler that I didn't really need) springs an oil leak. So we go from 11th to first to shitsville in 100 yards. End of 1958 Indy race for car number 31, as well as for Goldsmith and Smokey. One lousy lap.

What was the skinny on the big lap one wreck on turn three? 'Bout 20 cars crashed and Pat O'Connor died in the mess. Here is what Ed Elesian told me a week before the race. I have no proof it's a fact, but Elesian told me he owed some bad-asses in Chicago some gambling money. Ed had the pole, but Dick Rathman is just as fast as Elesian. The bad guys told Elesian "lead the first lap or else." If he did, his debt was cleared. Note: it was customary for betting to be on who led first lap.

Rathman knew this, 'cause Ed asked him for a little help to be sure. Well, going down the backstretch eyeball to eyeball and the third turn's coming. Now it's a game of "chicken." Ed should have known Dick would have taken her in there "balls out" if that's what it took. The inevitable happens and it starts the biggest goddam mess you've ever seen. The moral of story: if I had sent the oil cooler back, instead of adding it to the car, the accident would not have put us out of the race. Kids, you can see here, honesty would have been far better.

I gotta get back to Daytona. I've been gone 30 days and shop is not doing too good, so I'm two hours down the road with the buggered racer by the time the race is over. (Prize money gets paid Monday night at banquet.) Paul and I qualified for the 1958 race in good shape for a total of six grand in prize money. I realize I'm broke. Well, here's the gas station I got free gas going up. So maybe I can trade something for gas. "No problem." I swap a used Indy tire for gas and he fills up three GI cans (15 gallons) and we tie 'em on the trailer. I made it from Indy to Daytona in 20 hours on about five bucks. In them days we got a lot of sponsor oriented wearing apparel free; some pretty good stuff, plus lots of polish, snake oil, oil and filters, jackets and hats. All good stuff to trade for gas, plus I let 'em see a real live wounded Indy racer still warm from the battle.

1958 Indy Guards

Special world, old traditions – no way to explain Indy without the guards.

These are a cadre of older (most cases retired) males (no guns), yellow shirts with lite blue lettering. In most cases, really nice retired race fans 60 to 75 years old, many with history of "ain't missed a race since nineteen o-shit." These guys work on a very small pay scale, they did it partly for money, partly 'cause they were fans and partly to meet and know the players on a first name basis. We had our own post office, and the guards had a communication center and paging system for us to receive phone calls and messages and visitors. So if Keeley Smith called A. J. five times a day, we all kinda knew what was going on. If Miss Universe called Peter Revson every hour or so, the guards got it posted on the inner hot line. You know, "Peter R. is screwing Miss Universe, but don't tell anybody," or that "good lookin blonde with the big titties from the governor's office is sure chasing Smokey." (Yup, she caught me.)

Sex was just a li'l part of it. How 'bout parts supplier, bill collectors, wives, news media. What I'm trying to get you to see is the guards got wove into our lives. The guards controlled people motion very, very efficiently. They were under control of Harry Quinn and Clarence Cagel. When push came to shove there were certain guards that didn't take any shit from anybody. I can still see two of 'em picking Bill France up by his ass and arms and flinging him out the back pit gate onto a cinder covered mud hole. The guards were there at every part, bad and good. Serious injury, death, they hurt when we hurt, they were happy when we were happy. My birthday is May 25th and it wasn't nothing for four or five guards to say, "Happy Birthday Smokey."

We had our own hospital. We knew the doctors and nurses by first name. We had our own restaurant, maybe not recognized as a five-star connoisseur's delite, but adequate and very reasonable – especially if you liked mashed potatoes, sauerkraut and horse cock (that's what we called Indiana's big sausages). We called chipped beef and gravy on toast (a breakfast delite) "shit on a shingle" (that came from the military). We knew each other's problems good and bad. If we saw a pretty little waitress down in the dumps and a driver who quit eating there, we decided she missed her period. Oh, hell yes, it'd be all over garage area in half hour.

While at Indy, we could work 24 hours a day, seven days a week. Lots of times I would sleep there, just work to 2:00 am, and fall asleep on floor or cot. Yes, on a cold night, a guard would come in, throw a Goodyear blanket over you and turn out the lights and lock you in. The Goodyear blankets were to cover the bodywork while you worked - a promo item. All garages had wood, double swinging doors, green and white with small windows in each. When those old garages were torn down, some older drivers bought a pair of doors to install somewheres where they lived. On occasion, guard locked you in with the outside hasp lock by mistake, and you needed to get let out. So they'd go by every half hour or so to see if you wanted out. (Never knew who went to sleep working.)

Guards had spare keys to everything. This brings to mind Clint Brawner, an ace mechanic from Phoenix. That cat had a hobby of picking locks. He could be looking at a lock as he walked toward it and be feeling his set of lock pickin' tools, have the right one in his hand when he stopped to pick the lock and do it in five seconds. His skills kept his long distance phone bills very low. He knew how to open up a pay phone and fix it so the call was free (or at least not charged to the user). Clint was not a crook, he just happened to like picking locks as a hobby. Damn good thing he didn't turn his attention to safes. We'd of probably lost one of best mechanics Indy ever had.

No women allowed, I mean big time no-no. You guessed it, a very high ranking means of entertainment was to sneak a lady "would-be racer" in, get her to pose in the nude in your garage, and, naturally sometimes one of the ten commandments would get badly broken. We could cover the windows and lock the doors from the inside. A picture of a naked woman in a garage holding a newspaper showing the date was pretty good proof that Cagel's secret service had been penetrated. But the guards figured it out in a few minutes. We'd bribe 'em by letting them ogle part of it.

There was a very strange deal, very hard to figure. A lady we called "silver tongue" used to show up in the competitor's parking lot every year. The lot was a cinder covered kinda pot-holey place. Her husband had a big ol' Buick.

He'd bring her after 7:30 pm. "Silver Tongue" was a good looking, nice lady 'bout 35 years old that loved oral sex, and apparently augmented the family's weekly earnings by exercising this passion. For ten bucks, either there in the Buick or at your room. (Daddy just got out of the car and wandered off till ol' Buick stopped bouncing.) Nope, no fucking, he would not stand for that. Not even for 100 bucks. 200? I don't know. She or any lady in parking lot was OK. Course, I doubt screwing there was OK. Hell, I think guards loved the game.

Another tradition then was 'bout twice a week round 7:30 to 8:00 pm the guard would get on the PA and announce, "Banana Boat leaving for Anderson in ten minutes." Anderson, Indiana must of been a legal whorehouse city. The "Banana Boat" was a school bus, 'bout 25 passenger, that the whorehouses sent over to take racers to the party and bring 'em back. I never saw Silver Tongue in action and I never rode the Banana Boat, but not because I didn't want to; I just never had time. My workday up there was full-on racer, 7:30 am to 1:30 am, seven days a week. Judging from conversation, the Anderson deal was on the wild side. Hell, I remember a driver who had been a fighter pilot in World War II. He was divorced and lived in his car. He'd paint a banana on side of his door every time he came back. (He also lettered cars on the side.) I bet if you go in the Old Timers club room at next race and holler, "Banana Boat's leaving for Anderson in ten minutes," you'll see quite a few smiles. Why do I tell you this stuff? Goddam it, that's the way it was!

Remember Clarence?

1999, some of the guards I'll see this year I saw in 1958. They are very proud of their association and longevity. If you see a guard bald or white haired in his seventies or more, you're lookin' at a real race fan. If he looks old enough, say, "Did you know Silver Tongue?" If you get a big grin, you'll know.

Notice I haven't mentioned officials nor complimented them. Reason is, I never got to really know them. Of course, we could not have raced without their control and administration as I saw it most were ex-racers. They had the experience to serve competently in their positions. I did get to know the chief inspector Frankie Delroy very well. I considered him an outstanding human. He took the nastiest job in racing, chief inspector, and did it better than anyone. No one else was even close.

There was a lady who had a lot of horsepower; June Swango. In the rare occasion I needed some help, she never failed me. I saw her as a rare example of authority and compassion. I rated her as good people. That was my highest ranking of a human. However, there were and I guess always are strong, politically connected, high officials that were genuine assholes. I've said over and over racing is for young people. Racing has no place in it's management for old farts. Why? The technology of racing is moving so fast and the speeds are so high there is no tolerance for shaky, partially informed rule makers especially those who operate with the "if it ain't broke, don't fuck with it" reasoning.

Clarence Cagel, man he run the joint in a fair,strict no nonsense manner. Though I couldn't figure out why he tried so hard to deprive the Indy ladies of any sexual adventures with us and once in a while he got carried away with his authority, Cagel did as good a job as could be done. We were a difficult crowd, and although he wasn't on the same page with me sometimes, I'd like to say this: Cagel is a real Indy 'Hall of Famer.' His contributions in the earlier days were invaluable. He controlled a very unusual breed of man in an unabrasive, fair and firm manner

1959

The smoke clears away. All I have is the old Kurtis I run in '58. Well hell, that's better than nothing. I decide to put it on a diet. I take off a hundred pounds. Do a kamikaze deal on the engine. I got enough old Offy parts to build a race engine and a quicky qualifier. It's only got to last 'bout ten laps. Then I figured I'd "Watson" up the suspension close as I could and get 'er qualified. There was always (then) about 15 older drivers – "once a year, Indy only." These guys were often broke, desperate drivers on "brave pills, with a little more help from an altered fuel recipe. Qualified is worth 40 to 50 "big ones," with a 50-50 purse split, we both eat for six months. If she makes the whole 500 maybe we get out of there with 80 or 90 grand. And most of all, I get to play Indy racer one more time.

I'm a 37-year-old, speed lovin' bachelor. Dead broke and 160 "big ones" down. Plus, I've been rejected by matrimonial law, my social privileges have been suspended; my moral classification is somewheres between a tomcat and the devil. Of course, none of which was true. (Well, maybe just a little bit). My "home" is an army cot in a former public laundry, which is now becoming a machine shop for the truck repair shop I run.

I need one hundred thousand to buy garage back, and sixty to pay the house mortgage (says the judge). And monthly I require a fairly generous amount of so-called 'alley-money', in addition to the necessary child support. As I understand it, half you males reading this know the movie. Not least of my problems, I had a very bad addiction to the devil's substitution for water. About three quarters of a quart a day with a quart or two of beer for chaser. For some reason I didn't want to call it whiskey to me it was 'loud mouth' or 'leg spreader.'

I worked seven days a week year round, 7:00 am till 1:30 am. I worked hard. So I guess most of the whiskey got sweated out. I'm obligated to run a Pontiac in the February beach race, matter of fact I ran two cars, the '59 Pontiac with Bobby Johns and a new car for Fireball. I got too eager with Fireball's engine. It was a "runner," but broke a rod early on while leading. Bobby looked like he'd win with the '59, but a couple laps from the end his rear glass got sucked out. He spun. Fame and fortune went to shit. He runs second.

I'm frustrated. I want to built an Indy car but don't have the loot to do it. I want to build a half car-half airplane with a cast magnesium tub with a wing over driver. Turbine for power with big offset to left of driver and engine. With a pair of 16 inch wide dual slick tires side by side on 18 inch rims, with a four inch gap between them enough for a drive shaft to a buried differential (in between tires) with no rear suspension (a la go-kart). I've spent about four or five hours a night on the army cot building this thing in my mind for months. Once in awhile I get an offer to chief a hopeless case. Nobody good wants a once a year chief (Indy only), and I don't want any open wheel 'cept Indy. There was a time I could build a working engine or racecar in my mind that run. Yes, I could just stack the parts up, then make notes. The capsule car was dreamt up and built that way. You say, "No wonder it was such a goofy lookin' car."

I feel the old Kurtis ain't got a prayer to win. Goldsmith has quit and gone racing with Ray Nichels, so I ain't got much to offer a sponsor. I think the Indy establishment racers and track officials liked my act, so one of the top car owners, Art Lathrop, came to Daytona and made me an offer. Art had bought a new car in 1958, a Kurtis with independent front suspension, kinda like a knee action old Chevy, a slick sharkey looking car, painted pussy pink. Johnny Thomson had tried to qualify the car. It just didn't do it. Art said, "I'd like you to take the car and do anything you want to get it to run good. I'll give you half ownership, but pay you no labor. Just pay for materials as needed." Well it was best and only offer I got up to July '58, so I take it.

Art has car brought to me by "wet back," a Mexican go-fer he had. (We called all Mexican racers then "wet backs" inferring they just swam the Rio Grande, and were just drying out.) Next, Art announces he is moving to Daytona and gonna live here and "help me." (I'm still drinking.) "Hell, whatever's fair." This was not a good move. Art has the world ass-backwards, he sleeps all day, gets up at 5:00 pm, drinks and fucks till 5:00 am, then goes to sleep. The deal is: apartment and all living expenses get charged to racecar. I left out, Art's a rich, social, big shooter in Indy, his wife is an heir to, I believe, the Adams Grader Company, and momma controls the money.

Well, by 10:00 pm Art's got enough to drink he is a pain in the ass, all he does is talk. So in a week I know three things:

1. Art ain't never ever gonna sweat because he is working.

2. Art is a world class drunk.

3. Art is a connoisseur of good-looking big titted blondes who love to fuck. I happen to have such a lady as a friend, who has just lost her sugar daddy because of a busted heart medical problem and 'bout two weeks in the cold-cold ground. (I always figured she screwed him to death). If you come right down to it, wouldn't that be the most perfect way for "it" to happen? Kinda reminds me of a Darlington/dog deal that happened once. (Do you notice everything reminds me of something?) You know I like animals. One really rainy night I'm running late to get to Darlington, towing, running 'bout 85. I come up on a pair of dogs hard at "it," with their backs to me. Too late. I can't do shit. I always hoped they were both in the best part of "it" when the end came.

I knew if I kept her I'd have to quit working to satisfy her, but not having any money shut that movie off. So I decided to introduce her to Art. Three days later she comes by and says she "needs some money." I say, "Why ask me? I ain't got any." She says she "is our new secretary and office manager in regard to the '59 Indy project." I haven't seen Art since he met this lady, so I figure this ain't all bad, but how can I get Art's wife to pay for Art's mistress? Simple, put her on the payroll. I see this as a deal that gets Art out of my hair. (This has a long way to go till May 1)

You know, as outstanding as she was as a beautiful, sexy lady, I can't remember her real name. But she became "I. Loveitt" (Art's assistant) on the bills I sent to momma. ($200 a week). Wait a minute. Two hundred a week in Daytona, 1959 was not too shabby. Well, she damn sure earned her money. 'cause after a couple drinks Art got his steering locked up and you couldn't do a damn thing with him. He just became a nice social bullshitter that never shut up and never-ever quit drinking when on duty from 8:00 pm to 5:00 am seven days a week. The liquor bills became "pistons and gears." Counting food, apartment rent and Loveitt's clothing he was averaging $1,200 bucks a week. Really not too bad. But five grand a month for nine months sure run the bill up.

You'll never believe this. In November '98, I met Art's son at Indy. Seems like a nice guy. He designs race car suspensions and his momma is still going strong. I hope they don't get pissed about this, but I told you I was gonna tell it like it was. Only way I can tell it and make all the shit fit. "I. Loveitt" quit with about a month to go, and Art decided I should finish it myself. He would return to family in Indy. I think his guts were getting in some serious condition.

I built a steel table with wheels on it. Put the pussy pink racer up on it, got a cutting torch and cut the son-of-a-bitch in half and threw the beautiful independent Kurtis suspension in the iron pile. (I never should have threw it away. I'll tell you 'bout it later.) My mind was made up. If you had a front engine rear drive car the conventional engine rotation was absolutely backwards. Look, if you've got a front engine car with rear wheel drive, open driver's door and leave it wide open, and then start engine without putting it into and gear goose the motor good. Notice how driver's door raises up, and right side of car goes down (this conversation is for circle track left hand turns only). With conventional engine rotation, you're-transferring weight to the right side of the car – when you turn left the weight goes there anyway. The idea of reverse rotation is, when you accelerate hard the weight comes to the left front and left rear, and pulls weight off of the right front. This more evenly distributes weight across the chassis, increases your lateral traction on the front and back end. You go faster.

Also, I was gonna use George Saligh and George Gilbert's idea from 1957 and lay the engine down to the left, but with exhaust down and intake up. This both dropped the center of gravity and I felt it contributed to faster turn speed. I built a conventional front axle assembly pretty close to what you see in the 1959 Watson cars.

Now, reversing the engine required changing engine components. This was 4-cylinder Offy. I had to get or make new tappet cups, cams, oil and water pumps, and magneto. The lay down required change in oiling system plumbing and sump. I also had to build a transmission that worked backwards but the big job was to build a rear axle to accommodate the reverse engine rotation. I had decided to turn the engine 6,000 rpm, so I lightened up the crank, pistons, connecting rods and clutch. In changing cams I decided to do away with the radius cups and go to a flat tappet to increase dwell, and I also gave new cams more lift. To keep from wearing through the hard chrome cups I had three minutes of angle on cam lobes to induce cup turning. I couldn't get Art Sparks to design the pistons the way I wanted, so I did it here. (I wanted short skirts and long rods, high wrist pins.) I don't think many would have doubted more rpm would add more power, but all figured there would be no durability.

I figured as long as I had to change transmission around, to put a much lower first gear in it to prevent pit stop stalls. (Damn if that wasn't waste of effort). I had to weld a patch on side of transmission to cover up the big low gear.

I also fixed the broke Kurtis from '58 and brought it to Indy to try and sell. Hell, it didn't cost anything to fix. It was all labor and I had some paint left. How do I get two cars to Indy with one tow car? Well I decided, why not rig up the trailer like today's tandem trailers? I got a house trailer dolly I made to come to Florida in '46, so I incorporate it and take it for a test drive. Hell, works great, except the sheriff sees me and follows me to the shop and says "when you get 100 yards out of this county (Volusia), or to first officer that sees that fucking rig going down the highway, they will put you under the jail." What the hell. If I'd of pulled it off, I might have started a new industry. Art sent "wetback" down to pull other car.

I had also decided to heliarc the car instead of stick weld it. I couldn't afford a machine, so with help of my alcoholic, electrical wizard professor we built my first heliarc machine here. I could weld 'bout 20 minutes before it got too hot to hold (hadn't water cooled the torches yet in '59). Man, this was not a smart move. Damn near got car kicked out of Indy. They specified chrome alloy tube and a certain kind of stick welding rod. "I missed the rule." "Yeah I know." The inspector said, "Grind out all welds. (All welds!) And reweld with correct rod." Holy shit. That's two week's work.

But the head inspector, Dr Silberman, a big shooter from Magnaflux, saves my ass. He says "Men, I think heliarc may be as good or better than the called for procedure. Let's let him run, and every evening, we'll check the welds for cracking." The inspectors agreed, but not unanimously.

At this same time Sun equipment came out with a factory production model cylinder leakage instrument off of my prototype.

I had to reverse the auxiliary starter we used (an old air craft starter). Then guess who forgot to reverse the ignition, and couldn't get it started for six hours? Yup, first time I heard it run was 4:00 pm, May 1, 1959. First time it moved under it's own power was 9:00 am, May 2, 1959.

I'm in sort of a quandary, I got two cars at Indy. The old Kurtis and the reverse torque special, and no driver. One helper, Frank Cannon. He is from our truck parts department. Never been to Indy. Knows zero 'bout racers, but he loves to watch 'em run. What did you bring 'em for? A

go-fer and someone to shake me when I started to doze off towing to Indy (a non-stop 24 hour deal, skinny assed wet roads, half the time can't pass. You know the deal. Pretty soon you get to taking big chances.)

Well, Art ain't too happy. He wanted me to hire Roger Ward to drive, and Roger wanted it. I don't know why, but I didn't have that "warm fuzzy feeling" 'bout him. Ward brought a dog with him in '58, and it was a li'l sissy dog. I figured a good driver got to like big dogs. I'm thinking "Paul Russo, Tony Bettenhausen." (Guess who won the '59 race? Yup, Roger Ward.)

Well, I go see Frankie Bain 'bout a mechanic driver's permit. "No problem, swear on your mother's grave you won't go fast, or may God strike you dead if you do."

"Frank. Start 'er up." ("My" Frank says "huh?")

So, I jump out, put starter in, show him what to do, and I notice we ain't getting no wheres.

He reminds me of the football player named Calhoun joke, where they say in the huddle "give the ball to Calhoun" and Calhoun says, "I don't want the mother-fucker." OK, "Frank. I'll start her, you just work the throttle and keep her running till I put starter away and jump in." I start it three times. Every time engine catches Frank lets go of throttle and jumps back. I say, "Frank, you got a silver Indy badge. That means you are an Indy racer, now goddamned do it!"

"OK" Whooom. Phhttttt. Same deal.

New procedure. I got a string to the throttle with right side hook up and I can work it where I get in car and got engine control (one out of three times).

"O.K. Frank close the hood, put three Dzus buttons in."

"Don't know how."

I got out, weld big ears on all three, demonstrate. Still can't do it. Just plain scared of the son-of-a-bitch.

I can get two of the three in. The hell with the front one.

"Frank, you time me with the watch after third lap." "OK."

I run five laps. "How fast'd I go Frank?"

"Well, boss I don't know. I forgot how to read this deal."

"Oh shit." I take the watch and time myself every other lap, but I can't run full lap because Frankie Bain would shut me down.

So far so good. Russo and others ain't too anxious to drive my car either. Probably figure "out to lunch, no good crew." Duane Carter says, "Smoke, I'd like to drive your car."

"Huh? Shit, you've been a retired driver, director of competition for USAC for five years. Hell, you're too old and rusty." He was the stereotype racer, lived from day to day, eeked a living somehow, some way in the business of turning money into noise. "Nope Duane. You might bust your ass."

Duane says, "Smoke, I'm broke, on my ass, help me." That done it. Well, you didn't know Duane Carter, but he was one hell of a man and one hell of a racer. Simply put, good people. But he didn't know his ass from a hole in the ground 'bout women, and that cost him no end of trouble.

Well, both cars seem race ready, 'cept I need to adjust the oil pressure hot. The best maneuver is adjust in between hot laps. The adjusters are subject to get loose and back off, which goes to zero oil pressure, and bearings burn up and crank locks up. I don't have 'em safety wired, 'cause I will do that at final adjustment.

Jim Rathman comes by says, "I'd like to try your reverse rotation for couple laps." He is contracted to Lindsey Hopkins. "OK, if you also run ol' sway back enough to set oil pressure..."

Can you believe both of them sons of bitches backed off and locked up both motors? Rathman says, "I caught 'er Smoke, and turned it off before it burnt it." Caught her my ass! Both of 'em are locked up tighter than a bull's ass going up hill at fly time. The reverse job ain't too bad, I was able to save the crank and had to replace one rod and all bearings. On my car, the Kurtis, the crank and all rods are junk. I get a break. Some car owner fires his engine man, wants me to overhaul his engine. He's got lots of money and lots of good used parts. I get crank, rods, and bearings. Everything I need to fix the Kurtis. Course it was a 20 hour non-stop deal. But in two more days I got both cars running and in good shape.

Here's Duane again. "Smoke, you need some laps on the cars, I need some laps to get rust off."

"OK, run a few laps in the reverse torque car." He laps a few times and I ask, "How do you like the reverse torque?" "Well, really I don't notice much, maybe nothing." He won't drive it like I tell him, so I decide to try it myself. Rathman never got a chance; he froze it up at end of warm up straight.

I know I can only do a half lap and my favorite "try hard" turn is number one. I warm it up, try a couple turns, finally decide "now or never," take 'er to marker three, four, and shut it off by the time I get to big oak on the front straightaway. As I go into one, the left front wheel is five or six inches off the ground. I aim for the short chute and nail that bitch. The left front wheel came down so hard my goggles (I had those big ol' wide strappers) just dropped down on my neck.

I laughed. Man, I was happy. It worked, it worked.

Well, I'm way too far into two, can't hardly back off much, can't touch the brake. I can't get in the throttle to get left side working. I'm pretty sure I steered and shut my eyes waiting for the big noise and some sheet time. Don't ask me how I made it. Well, I put-putted into the pits and after ten minutes I quit shaking. I then decide on a whole new deal; I'll drive 'er myself in the 500; just run half laps until I get it figured.

I only have a problem in getting into three. I can't get close to comfortable and am shutting off early. Right now I gotta tell you this mother hauls ass. I mean I'm seeing six grand on backstretch and I'm shutting off fifty yards too quick. Whowee! This is a bad news special.

The car darts around bad when it's real windy, it sometimes jumps two car widths when you go from track surrounded by grandstand to open area.

I talk to Tony Bettenhausen, he says, "Smoke, they all do that. Don't do any thing, she won't hit the outer wall, the air pressure between the car and the wall will stop it from hitting." "No shit?" Hmmmm-mmm. Well I still pucker my ass up when it does it, but I don't correct. Hell, Tony said, "It's normal." Tony is driving a new lay down (Offy), I believe Harry Turner built it. Harry was a midget hot dog ten years ago. Tony's having big problems trying to go fast. Chassis problems. I ask Tony how to brainwash myself into driving into three. I've been over there and all the hot dogs are driving to a certain ('bout ten foot tall) pine tree before lifting. I can't get closer than fifty yards before I'm lifting. Tony says, "Just sneak up on it a car length a lap. You get her in three once or twice the lite will come on and it will be easy after that. Once

369

you're in there you can't lift or brake." He says, "You'll figure it out."

"How?"

"Well, you got to, Smoke. You just steer it a li'l, then nail it to number four entry."

I ain't gained nothing twenty laps later.

Tony and Harry ain't gaining either.

They come to my location on pit road and Tony says, "Smoke, I was running behind you from one to two. What's in that engine? You pulled me five or six car lengths down the back straight and you shut off early."

Harry's decided he needs to test his car also. Tony tells him he bets a thousand bucks Harry can't come within five miles per hour of Tony's speed. Harry starts for his wallet and I say, "Harry, you better re-think it, or you're gonna work this race for nothing." Well Harry gives her a try. Frankie OKs him. Shit, 34 maybe 35 laps later Harry's still 'bout five miles per hour short of Tony. I believe Tony flipped the car later and adiosed it, and drove something else in the race.

Well, it's Wednesday before qualifying. Time to shit or get off the pot. I decide, "I'm gonna do it now." Coming off of two, I nail it down. Put my left foot on top of the throttle foot, and vow to die but will not lift till the pine tree…same deal. I lift early. I can't believe it. I'm pushing hard as I can with both feet (or so I thought). I pull in pits, jump out and go looking for Duane Carter. He ain't hard to find. He gets 'bout 100 laps in three days.

On Saturday, "Line 'er up, qualify it." "Oh hell no. I ain't ready. Next week." I say, "Duane, I've already drawn your qualifying number." I kinda got him by the balls. He don't have any other options. I've decided he's close, and another week will probably get him spooky. Shit, he pissed and moaned. Damn near had to hog-tie him and strap him in six minutes later. Two warm up and four laps after that he qualifies 12th overall. Man what a happy son of a bitch. He's got at least 20 in the bank.

Well, Art Lathrop's happy, I'm happy. Gonna stroke it tonight. Gonna go down to Mate's White Front and do some drinking. But first I decide to pull the engine and look at the cams. All that stuff is new and untried.

I get over to the White Front 'bout 9:30 pm. I've already had a few pulls out of shop bottle. Jimmy Bryan and eight or ten other drivers were there, plus two or three cops (I've already been to jail once this year for a fight here). They had a live band, I believe Spike Jones. (This was before he hit the big time.) I remember he introduced a new song he'd written – I believe called "Along Came Jones." I was a little overcharged and I thought it was about a dog named Bones. I can still remember the odd beat and loud unusual band.

The furniture is bamboo with high stools and high rattan tables. Alice, the waitress, every racer's friend, was putting up with the usual ass grabbing and bullshit, but a stranger insulted her. Bryan must of been part Indian. Two or three beers and he would go in orbit. Take my word for this. He was rock solid, 'bout 185 pounds of Marine-burr-haircut trouble.

Well, Bryan cold cocked the stranger and off she went. 'Bout sixty guys and three cops into a huge brawl. The poor bandleader was no fighter but was shit-faced, fumbling around trying to protect the band instruments. Every time I saw him he was flying across the room. (Tall skinny guy. Was Spike Jones tall and skinny in his younger days?)

I'm trying to keep from getting badly wounded. So I avoid the big mothers. Somebody swung, and in ducking I fell backwards, both elbows went through the two drums on the floor behind me. 'Bout that time someone kicked me in the balls. That done it.

As I unload at the police station, desk sergeant says "Goddam, that car of yours hauls ass, congratulations." He is a Duane Carter fan. "How much money you got?" "Nothing." "Damn, same answer as last time...Smokey, remember what your daddy told you when you were little? If you want to play, you gotta pay." "Goddam Sarge, you call that playing?" He says, "What you did to that guy who kicked you in the balls was really bad Smoke, don't ever grab anybody by the balls and drag 'em around again." I say, "You think I should have put rubber gloves on first?"

He says, "You know what I mean goddammit. I bet he is gonna be in the Methodist crash shop two or three days." "What do you think my balls feel like rite now?" He says "I'm willing to bet you will be getting

(photo: Indianpolis Motor Speedway)

excellent therapy before the sun rises." He continued, "There is no way the lieutenant is gonna stay off my ass without you donating 'bout twenty bucks and a couple race tickets," I say, "How would you like a 35 year old nymphomaniac for the rest of the month." He says, "Does her family own a liquor store?"

Bryan? Shit no. He slid outta' there and into his motel. Remember, I always said "racing is for young people." Some of these old farts driving and working on racers today would have been on the bench then. Hell, a low-buck operation was a chief and one go-fer. With one car and some spare parts, a car trailer and a station wagon. We were judged by our performance and our moral qualifications were placed in about a "two" (reference a "one to ten" scale). So, personal appearances were not done (except for previous Indy winners, they were accorded hero status by the world). All other personal appearances for us were in court or hospital.

Qualifying first day is big-big advantage. All month up till qualifying, I have to go through a daily weld inspection (remember, I heliarced car). The quarantine will be up (Thursday) when we get our final inspection sticker. Then, the son of a bitch can break in half then – no problem.

If we qualify I'll disassemble total car, sand blasting paint off, magna flux and zyglo everything, then start over.

Well, during qualifying there was a speed trap on back straight. The reverse torque special recorded the fastest speed ever run in there, including the Novi. So this now has 'em rubbing their chins 'bout reverse torque, so in total disassembly, I get lots of visitors from competitors and the racing press.

Historically the sports reporter assigned to cover racing was the second lowest paid job at the paper. The janitor got slightly less. They didn't stay on that job too long – they couldn't. Hell, they'd have starved to death. So they either moved up to stick and ball, or went back to the gas station pumping gas (pencil still behind their ears, but to fill out cash and charge tickets).

God help the racer who got sideways with three or four big city sports reporters. Example: Bennie Kahn, Daytona's number one sports reporter happened to actually love car racing. He invented me and "Balls." We could sit on the pole, lead and blow up and the next morning if you read his deal we got more ink than the winner. I was "a 29 year old, handsome (he said) speed lovin' bachelor." Marshall Teague was "a portly gas station owner." Fireball was "college educated, lightning fast with unparalleled skill and courage."

The technically unqualified race reporters reminded me of how the Alka indians operated in the Oriente in Ecuador. Anything they don't understand either eat it, piss on it, fuck it or kill it. They mostly killed the reverse torque technology. No problem to me. All I want to do is win the mother-fucker. I don't give a damn 'bout nothing else.

"Aggie," a rich Indy regular car owner who became wealthy with his masterful management of a large, used food business (he transformed garbage into big fat pigs). He ain't gonna make Indy this year, car wreck. So, I got a shot at selling the old Kurtis, but I flunked the deal. Car ran good enough to squeak in, but that was the Kurtis's last gasp.

Note: I ended up selling the Kurtis for 'bout fifteen hundred bucks (less engine) and it went up north and suffered a super modified fate. I believe Steve Himmel, one of Roush's chiefs found it and it's back to life as the "City of Daytona" (black and gold again). But I'm just going on what Steve told me a few years ago.

Back to Indy. Man, I would like to have a picture of the shit eatin' grin I must have been sporting when the reverse torque qualified, 'cause this was damn near a complete "Smokey car." As a matter of fact, I entered it as a "Smokey," but the Indy Mafia frowned on that, so I didn't argue when Harry scratched it out and wrote in "Kurtis."

Carburetion day went real good. Duane is getting confident. He is in the hunt, with the power and cornering advantage. I'm sure the car can win, but I'm spooky 'bout Duane 'cause of his age and long retirement period. I'm scared he might crash 'cause drivers coming out of retirement got a bad record 'bout getting dead or serious hurt. Plus, Indy was not a good track for Duane – ever.

Every year at Indy a physical fitness program would begin. A Dr. R.N. Sabourin, a chiropractor (to us a "bone crusher") gave free skeleton adjustments to any and all of us.

Each garage built a chair with an old arm shock for resistance to a standard steering wheel (the steering wheels were made out of used saw blades and wood and covered in rubber).

Next, all drivers had two hand grip exercisers, a semi hard rubber ball. On May 1, all drivers had calluses on their elbows from the beer drinkin' position, but for three and a half weeks they'd crank the steering wheel, squeeze the hand grip and forearm muscle strengthener, and always have one rubber ball in their pocket. Actually the steering wheel vibrated so much in the race car it put your arms to sleep. If you let go of the wheel with one hand it would get four inches around, and was a son of a bitch to re-grab. If you look at old movies you'll see drivers taking turns exercising each arm to ward off numbness, and trying to grab the wheel. To me it was actually comical. A very good driver told me the challenge was like masturbation and switching hands without missing a stroke. Compared to today's drivers fitness programs, the '50s, '60s, and '70s were Stone Age in physical fitness.

The abuse of driving in a race was phenomenal. It was not unusual for both of a drivers hands to be bloody from broken blisters. I've seen Bryan get out of his car with his ass soaked in blood from blistering. I've seen driver's feet with second degree burns. I've seen drivers sit in alky so long that the skin came off where the belts were. The helmets were next to nothing and the goggles fogged and oiled up. Hell, they drove half blind most of the time. Some had a powder puff sewed to back of glove to rub goggles, but only one in five wore gloves. There were no uniforms, just street shoes and slacks, a white t-shirt with pack of cigarettes rolled up in arm cuff for a smoke on a yellow. Exhaust fumes from cracked and broken exhaust systems would have drivers semi-conscious. Quit? Shit no. You'd have to drag 'em out. I seen one dragged out and he died right there on pit road. There was a special breed of tough motherfuckers around those racecars in the beginning.

Another weird deal, half them drivers (especially the older ones) only ran one race a year. There weren't enough championship cars that ran the whole circuit to keep all the drivers employed. The big deal was "get 'er in the show." They live most of the year off of that.

Qualifying for Indy required running five miles per hour over your head. You haven't sat in a car in 11 months, and now in 10 days and 100 laps you got to be able to shove 'er into the qualifying line. Finally, you're number one in line. The chief steward explains the procedure to the driver and crew. Everybody is vibrating like a banjo string.

Let me take you through the '59 qualifying with Duane. The car's in the hole. Duane is walking down, dressed in a flimsy uniform that burns half as slow as gasoline, carrying his helmet. He just dropped one glove. "Smoke, let's wait, I need more laps." I say, "Bullshit, we're gonna do it now." We're 'bout seventh in line to go out. "Well, OK but I got to go take a piss first." "Get your ass in that damn seat, if you can't hold that piss, wait and do it on straights so you won't spin in it." We're up. I put starter in, he's still not in the car. "My goggles are dirty." I say, "Get in that motherfucker now, lucky leather boots and all, in six and a half minutes you'll be in the hero circle grinning like a cat eating shit." "OK." He gets in, we start it up and he goes, I have to run my ass off to get back to the beginning of pit entrance to call shots on qualifying. Art's using the golf cart, "Got to have another drink."

Duane is on his warm up lap. I got a blackboard. First time by is a warm up, slow lap. He can either take one or two laps and then he must be on his qualifying run. Second time I see him coming off of four I have to decide, are we gonna start the run or take one more warm up lap? In this deal the driver watches me and I give him a "go," or "no go" signal. If I give him "go" he holds up one hand for the starter, who is watching him with field glasses. All I got is about 200 yards to make up my mind. Kinda reminds me of leaving it in to the last 100th of a second before you pull it out. As you know, quite often that don't work good.

Sounds good. Looks good. I have a green and a yellow flag. If I wave green the fuse is lit, if I wave the yellow the attempt is aborted. You qualify the car, not the driver. Each car gets three attempts. I can see Duane got off of four like a rocket, that li'l lay down, backwards-turning Offy is howlin' like a wild-assed

Indian going ape-shit. I wave the green. Duane shoves his hand up (not too far, or the wind will break it). He's on his way. The announcer screams "Hezzzonit."

Next come four consecutive laps (10 miles). The average speed of the four laps is either a ticket to one of the 33 starting spots, or to "return to sender." No radios. If he didn't get a good start and I missed it, I could 'cause a poor qualifying speed. I've made up my mind 142 miles per hour average would get the job done.

First lap, Hot damn! Damn near 143. That six minutes is a lifetime. Every year, they spin or blow on last lap.

Second lap, still a high 42. I give him lap speed on a black board, I know he's feeling good, he's half way home. Oh shit! Number three slipped a little bit, but still OK. Now for the giant sweat job. Last lap. Here he comes off of four. Looks good. Yup, high 42. Average 142.8.

Duane pulls in, not grinning…some of his old cronies say, "Not enough speed, may get bumped"

12th fastest out of 33 is how it ends up. Finally ,it's 6:01 pm Sunday, last qualifying day. At age 50, a brand new Duane Carter is born. If any human experienced a high that was higher than Duane was at 6: 01 pm that Sunday, he would have blown all to shit.

As you watch the qualifying, look closely that last three hours. You can see more human drama there if you know what to look for than there is in four thriller movies. We used to have two weekends. Four days not counting bad weather. Now they have one weekend. We'd have up to a hundred competitors, now maybe forty. (Still for thirty-three spots.) For the competitor, if you're on the edge of missing the cut it reminds me of first day in the aviation cadets, where you get your first plane ride and instructor is trying to make you airsick (immediate disqualification), the snap rolls, the loops, the chandelles, the stalls. I've been down all these roads.

You're so bound up you forget your own name. When you first realize it's over, you failed. Man you could walk under a snake's belly with a top hat on and not touch. Used to be we had a live audience of 300,0000 people watching the movie. My biggest concern when I knew it was over was to show zero emotion. For some reason I didn't want anyone to know how bad I was hurt.

I can remember not saying one word for 24 hours driving home (I was alone). Yes, including buying gas and a hamburger.

I was lucky in another way 'cause in 24 hours it was like it happened ten years ago. I see Jeff Gordon jumping up and down on the roof. I remember it different. Kinda like 200 pounds had just been removed from my back. To me, showing your teeth was kinda like bragging. I, for what ever reason, could shut off the 695,000 eyeballs. I could actually talk to you and not recall anything .

I concentrated so hard I wouldn't let you change my train of thought. I always felt if I made a mistake it could be the equivalent of sticking a pistol in driver's ear and pulling the trigger. Every Indy race I ever did, I lost 13 to 15 pounds, and it took me a month to get back in the real world again.

After the first sleep I'd get after the race, I'd wake up kinda, I think, in shock. I didn't feel good, nothing was right. I was very irritable, actually a quite nasty son-of-a-bitch – better left alone for a month. Win or lose, on the way home my mental computer recognized the pluses and minuses of that last adventure. Then for days I rebuilt the racer mentally. I thought out my mistakes and errors both mechanical and human. I've never been slow to acknowledge I fucked up, and if you were helping me and screwed up, I'd run your ass off in a heartbeat with no emotion on my part.

We could be friends, but I'd never trust you with a driver's life again – ever. We had so many sad movies that very quickly a racer had to decide how to cope. To me zero emotion and very little socializing with other racers was best I could come up with. I lived that way thirty-five years, plus five years in the Air force.

Well, race day, my second shot at the bull and all the marbles. I'm pissed. I need a carpet that could be fire proofed for a floor mat. It was impossible to run an Offy three to three-and-a-half hours dry. Whatever you did, the oil seepage got on floor of cockpit (belly pan is slick aluminum). And pedals are steel; Duane has "lucky" leather soled boots for race. Duane promised on a stack of bibles he'd have rug by race morning. Truth is, he didn't want it, and by the time I figured it out it's too late.

Even with the extra low gear I had in the transmission and the Borg and Beck English clutch we stalled the engine on two out of three pit stops. We came in running second and go out 15th. The "lucky" boots: oily leather and oily aluminum don't go together. Things get very slippery.

Duane started off running real strong but after eight or 10 laps he got a whisker slower every lap.

I'm going goofy trying to figure out how to motivate him to concentrate harder and mash that son-of-a-bitch a little harder. No radio, pit boards only. 'Bout 100 miles into it and he is six miles per hour slower than he started. Ward goes by. On the next lap I put speed on the pit board. There it is...I hit the jackpot. Duane knew the fans could see this also. In two laps, he caught Ward and passed him. All day it was the same thing. If I didn't keep lap speed showing every lap he'd start to get a whisker slower every lap.

Last pit stop, for tires and fuel. He comes in second and goes out 'bout 15th (engine stall). Best he could do was to get back to seventh. Well, hell, shake it all up in a bag and let it out. Maybe for a rusty driver, a weird-assed racecar and a near rookie Indy chief it could have been worse. Duane and I argued about them fuckin' lucky leather soled boots for 'bout the next 35 years. (Duane is gone now.)

Duane, I still think if you'd of got that goddammed rug I asked you to get, you'd have won the race and went down in history as the greatest "comeback" story in all of sports. An hour after the race I'm loaded and on my way back to Daytona. Money is paid at victory dinner next night. Art's there and he pays Duane the agreed 50 percent. The check I get is way short of 50 percent. It seems like a lot of the month of May bills were disputed. Turns out he says my expenses were not chargeable, as well as some tools and paint. I've got car here in Daytona. After a month of this phone bullshit, I say, "Send me any fuckin' thing you think I'm entitled to, then you got one week to get this damn car out of here or it will be sitting on the trailer on some parking lot the morning of the eighth day. There will be the title and a bill of sale for one dollar in envelope under the seat cushion. (Nope, never got the dollar.)

"Wet-back" was here on third day and the "Reverse Torque Special" was out of my life – 'cept for the hate all the Frank Kurtis fans had for me. One little sentence: a reporter at Indy said, "Why did you cut car in half and throw away the innovative front suspension Frank Kurtis presented the car with?" Answer: "'Cause it wasn't worth a shit!" That did it. I got hate mail, insults at Indy, people who worked for Frank wanted to whip my ass. Frank didn't exactly wear out all the good words usually used by one of your peers when he responded to my one line comment. Well, hell, remember in '55, Dale Carnegie said I was a hopeless case. (Note: in another section Frank and I kiss and make up 30 years later.) Frank Kurtis never ever came close to getting the credit he should have. He was one of the ten most important pioneers open wheel racing has ever had.

But confidentially, that front end was an experiment he should have never got around to doing.

When I first saw it I was impressed. It looked good, beautiful workmanship, but it was like a southern saying 'bout some gals. "A pretty face with naught behind it." I think Frank's kids have found the remains and rebuilt it back to the original blue prints (an independent front wheel design), all other cars then had a solid front axle.

1960

Jim Rathman calls and says he wants me to help him at Indy for the 1960 race. Knowing him I say, "OK, send check for 25 grand with a contract that includes 10 percent of purse." I know he ain't gonna buy that, but it stops the bullshit. Middle of March, – Rathman again, "Hey I hear you don't have an Indy deal." I say, "You're wrong, I've entered the old sway backed Kurtis. Already paid the entry fee and it's ready to go." He says, "Smoke, I've run second three times at Indy. This year I got good car owners, best new car (Watson), all I need is a good chief." I say, "Call Apache reservation in Arizona and ask for Geronimo" and hang up.

I've had a good education on "one-ways." (Example: France) I sure ain't looking for any more experience along those lines. My poor li'l ass has been abused enough that I need Novocain in the vaseline. Third week April, "Smokey, you got a call, Jim Rathman, line one." "Tell him I'm on a service call in Brazil." That night he drives up here (he lives in Miami now). Well, he talks me into agreeing to a conference call. The Jim Rathman I know is a very good open wheel driver, a bullshit artist from California, raised up with the Chicago "rat pack." A lying dog who made my morals look like the Pope's.

Next day conference call. Rathman, Kenny Rich, Paul Lacey, and Chicky "the jap" Hiroshima. Kenny and Paul are the rich Dallas car owners, Chicky is, at this time, chief mechanic.

The Ken-Paul Special (photo: Indianapolis Motor Speedway)

Phone call is, "We want you to run the deal." I say, "What about Chicky?" Chicky tells me on phone he, "Can't be chief, nerves are shot." Chicky had much Indy experience, was a riding mechanic way back. He is also the chief Offy assembler for Meyer and Drake, the manufacturer. He doubts he'll be in pits on race day. "You don't care if I'm chief?" Chicky answers, "Nope." I say, "I ain't easy to get along with and if I take this job you agree when I say "jump," you say "how high?" "Yas-sa boss. No problem." "OK, What's the pay?"

"Don't know." "How 'bout ten grand up front, 10 percent of purse?" They agree.

Plus refund my entry fee (which I get back on my own).

I don't remember if there was a written contract, but there was no question. Everybody's happy.

I forgot my Air Force training and decide to offer Chicky a co-chief deal, which we all agree on.

I get to Indy May 1 (I've never seen car at this point). Step one, go to registrar, Frankie Bain and sign in. After all the hand shaking, hugging and kissin' with the "USACers," I fill out race forms for credentials. Frankie says, "Wait a minute Smoke. We got a problem. You signed in as "co-crew chief" and Chicky signed in yesterday as chief." Should have known. Fuckin' japs, sneaky little bastards. All my Air Force indoctrination reappears. I say, "Frankie, I'll be back." I roar off to garage like a wounded tiger.

Everybody's there. Jim Rathman, Kenny, Paul and the rice burner. "What the fucks going on? First ten minutes and a double cross." Jim says, "Chicky you were a bad boy. Smoke, I'll go fix it rite now with Frankie." Actually, as it turned out I never did get officially registered 'cause Frankie rejected the "co-chief" papers. I never signed any more, so I guess I wasn't even at Indy in 1960. Not another word is said all month. Car's a new Watson. Chicky built the engine, it's very good, but not quite steamy enough, so we pull it and rebuild it to qualify. I do all but the cam and valve work. Chicky does that. He's damn sure qualified. He's probably built 500 of 'em, but still a li'l power short. I got a problem. I got to run a Pontiac at Darlington weekend of first Indy qualifying.

Thursday night I put in cams I had Crower grind for me. Yeah, kinda sneaky. I didn't tell Chicky.

Runs good Friday but Rathman's got his head up his ass, forgets to flip the high gear lock in and it jumps out of gear while hot lapping. Tach shows 9,000. It tagged two exhaust valves in number two cylinder. Not real bad, but I got to leave to go to Darlington Friday night in a borrowed, old junk-slow, airplane to run Fireball and the Pontiac. No way Chicky can pull block, replace valves and qualify Saturday, so I pull exhaust header and straighten the valve through the exhaust port with a hammer and brass knocker I made. I get the cylinder back to four percent leak down. I'm betting it won't break a valve in ten laps, but if it does, bye-bye 'bout five grand (new engine, ten grand). I go to Darlington. Work my ass off to sit on the pole and have one of the best wrecks in NASCARs history.

Nope. We got outside pole in Indy. Guess I ain't ready for my "Indy experts badge" yet. You'll notice I'll never say anything nice about Rathman and the rice burner Chicky. But Chicky fought for the US in the Army in WW II with an all Jap outfit. History says they fought with above average courage and skill, so I gotta give him a gold star for that. (I doubt Rathman was in military service, probably too fuckin' goofy).

In truth, J. Rathman may have driven one of the best Indy races ever run before or since. I gotta give the son-of-a-bitch credit for balls, skill and determination. He was a racer that day and victory came hard, believe me. Ward, his chief competitor had about the same movie going for him. They must have swapped the lead fifty times. Sometimes three times a lap. In 1960 Firestone was "it" and they had an orange strip of rubber that appeared when tire was worn out. When that showed up, you had one, maybe two laps at full speed before there would be two loud noises. First one, the tire blowing and then the inner tube couldn't stand the weight and the second noise was the car banging the wall and all the shit that goes with it, (usually fire). Ward got the "breaker," three laps to go. Deal is over. Rathman and the "Ken-Paul Special number 4" is the victor.

Let's go back to this "chief" crap. The first 350 miles of the race the rice burner is not in our pits. He shows up in street clothes after two hours of racing. There is an asshole reporter named Joe Scalzo, who has written a book like he was told to write it. His version is a bunch of bullshit. I think Joe's goofy, probably played with his peter too much when he was little. I worked for same magazine with him 'bout eight years (Circle Track). Say hello Joe, and wave you dumb shit. This is 'bout fifth or sixth history deal I know about that he's screwed up.

We had air jacks for first time. I fueled the car. I trained the crew on speedy pit stops. In 1959, fifty seconds was a good pit stop; A.J. Watson's car with Ward as driver. The car being the "leader car special," did the same. We each had three pit stops and total difference in three stops was three seconds. We were quickest. The pit stops average twenty-two seconds. The pit crew, J.B. Wilson and Bill Slater came from Smokey's. Bruce Crower and Bob Bubinick came from Crower's, Vince Conzi the rear axle and steering box whiz and Ronnie Kaplan, (a Chicago racer), came from their own little companies.

The victory celebration (photo: Indianapolis Motor Speedway)

Note: six or seven years ago Jack Martin, an Indy official and PR expert, then running the Indy car museum, polled all living members of the pit crew. All but one said same as what I've told you.

All but one...the driver. Had Rathman agreed with the others, the speedway was gonna correct the official records. Now, do you kinda see why I think Rathman is a prick?

The Indy special racing paper is printed and delivered thirty minutes after race is over by helicopter. Headlines read: "Rathman and Smokey win Indy 500!" If anyone has a copy of this paper, I'd like to get a copy of it. Now, you haven't won Indy, your life is probably gonna be just fine. So why am I concerned?

Well, Indy ain't easy to win. But if you did it, do you think it's wrong, selfish or chickenshit to want it in the records?

That month of May, for that Ken-Paul Special's owners, driver, and some mechanics, was a book in it's own. I was in charge of the check book. I paid the bills. The car cost $14,000, the engine $10,000, engine spare parts $4,000. Get this. Our motel then was the brand new Holiday Inn across from turn one, run by a nice guy named Smithy. The 31-day motel bill was pennies short of $40,000. We won $160,000. The driver got $80,000. We went forty in the hole and won the first race the team ever run.

Airline tickets, car rentals, some nights 18 rooms, cab fare, food, booze, booze, booze, laundry and dry cleaning, flowers, clothes, race tickets, hookers. Ninety percent of this was by the two owners and the driver. Remember I have to work about 16 hours a day. No paid help. Not much time for partying. I had to move fast, maybe like a mongoose, when opportunity appeared.

Troy Ruttman is engaged to be married to a very wealthy lady from Birmingham, Alabama. I end up in bed with her, she jumps out to turn Troy's picture down so he can't watch, and takes off the engagement ring. (Troy won Indy in 1952).

Bill Yeager, Rathman's "stooge," falls in love with a nurse. They want to get married (they have known each other three days). I'm a Florida justice of the peace (for truck dealer reasons), and I can perform marriage ceremonies. The wedding, flowers and all, were charged to the motel.

The bride, I can't remember her name. (She was a nurse.) It was a quickie deal for me. Preacher didn't show, so I threw on a trench coat and boots, otherwise naked as a jaybird, and married them while the groom was taking a shower and as she is talking to him, I started the bride's honeymoon with a "quickie." There was a reason: the groom painted his peter with dayglow orange paint the day before and all the skin peeled off.

Goofy, yup. They had aprons made then for a joke, where you flipped up your apron and they had a big red pecker sewed on that looked like, well kinda like, your peter was out. Yeager flipped apron and the real deal was there in dayglow orange (till all the skin fell off) You guessed it, he could hardly walk, let alone screw. But at the time he held the number one ranking as world's champion oral sex artist, so I imagine it wasn't a total loss. Yeager, by the way, was Rathman's personal go-fer and a pretty big help to me. No, not the famous rocket pilot.

Bill Yeager broke in and was trained by A.J. Foyt. Yeag was a pretty good machinist, but lazy as hell and if you knocked a hole in his head 2,000 pussies would fall out. We called this condition "cunt goofy." The month was a blur of 14 to 20 hour working days and I'm sober and still fighting the urge to drink. Our garage is over on the crew parking lot side this year, so the fence bunnies are even more plentiful here than '58 and '59.

I mention this because this led to two especially interesting and unusual sexual adventures. I was exposed to sexual adventures that included animals (police dogs) by a lady John Laux introduced me to. And on my own, I met a wealthy young lady with a very wealthy old husband who enjoyed watching his wife screw other men. Take my word for it, when right in the best part of "it," here comes the husband out of the closet for a closer look. Yes, it was a record time-wise from "hard" to "zero." This is maybe exciting when drunk, but sober, very distracting.

1960 Indy, month of May 1960, I don't know how to act at Indy. I got money to race with, got good place to stay, getting paid, got super car, and I've got driver who wants it worse than life itself, and has experience. I'm 37 years old, dead broke, and way-way in debt. I can carry everything I own in one suitcase

(suitcase, hell a paper grocery bag). My garage has a $100,000 lien on it (divorce stuff). Can't even write a check without a co-signer, living one day at a time.

I don't give a damn. Some way, somehow I'll get going... How? I ain't got a clue. My total furniture is a three-buck army cot (ain't got the air mattress yet). I don't even have a suit of any kind. Work and casual clothes only.

I'm doing what I want to do. I've just sold an invention and paid off the house mortgage (divorce deal; 60 grand). I've decided I don't give a shit if I lose the garage (I figure the debt is about 100 percent of it's value), and I'm thinking real serious 'bout wanting to try and make a life in the oil exploration business somehow. I've had a bellyful of truckers not paying, and li'l things like a garbage truck driver telling me we didn't fix his truck correctly, especially day after the GM president flew me to Detroit to look at an engine for my comments. I think only thing I wanted out of life was to win Indy. (Well, maybe also to lay Marilyn Monroe.) 'Bout May 4, 1960, I decided while going to sleep that when the smoke cleared away May 30th, I'd have that job done. The only "maybe" was bad luck in the race.

I totally dropped out of the world mentally, May 4th to May 30th. My world was a three-mile circle

Pit stop in 1960. (photo: Indianapolis Motor Speedway)

from my Indy garage. That was the farthest alternate bed. When 33 starters were established, I picked about ten competitors I expected to have a shot at it, and watched every fuckin' move they made up to one hour before the race. I picked the right ten. I had the Watson-Ward team rated as number one competition. Actually, I picked eight competitors. My secret weapon was air jacks, but I didn't install them till day before Carburetion Day. We fumbled around during the practice time changing tires and splashing fuel all over hell. But we are in the 25 to 27 second range. The year before an average good pit stop was 50 seconds.

Nope. Next day Watson has a set of air jacks, too. He puts his on. No way to practice in secret. We get down to 21 to 22 seconds.Watson can practice where we don't know how good they are, but really it didn't help or hurt when you're running wide open as it is. I notice Chicky ain't around much after qualifying. Watson's garage is 'bout three doors over, and he's over there all the time and not around after 6:00 pm.

I found out fueling with a three inch hose (we hold 75 gallons then) takes 30 seconds.

I re-plumb and go to four-inch diameter hose (21 to 22 seconds).

Watson pops up with four-inch hose.

All month I've been working on tire wear and mileage. I find all the tires ain't alike. I get to go through

I'm near the back of the car and Chicky's sittin' behind the wall. (photo: Indianapolis Motor Speedway)(photo: Indianapo-

'em and pick what I want for the race reference tire O.D. and hardness and tread shift.

I know I want tires that haven't been sitting in the sun.

In watching Watson I think, "That fucker is either a mind reader, or we are both on exactly the same wave length, or I have a Pearl Harbor deal in my garage." I know Chicky and Watson are very good friends. I see him in Watson's garage a lot and I don't care. Watson is good people and I want to do everything myself; every single bolt, every single assembly, every single re-check, and all the engine parts selection. One of my pit crew tells me Chicky is working on Ward's engines and he is pissed I switched cams for qualifying. I don't pay any attention. I'm in a mindset, I don't give a shit what anybody else does, we are gonna be the hot dogs. The race is 200 laps, we led 100, Ward led 58. Didn't leave much for anybody else did it?

We each stopped three times. We pitted 'bout three stalls apart. We came in together and went out together. Our three stops were both 66 seconds in total…Watson's total was 69 seconds.

Firestone asks me if I told Watson's crew about my tire selection. I didn't. Still never woke up.

When Chicky was up for Indy Hall of Fame he says, "Besides being the winning chief on Rathman's car, he also built Ward's second place engine." You smell anything funny in this?

Note: Chicky is in the Indy Hall of Fame, I'm one of the judges, I voted for him. He absolutely deserves it for what he did before and after 1960, because in 1960 he didn't have a fucking thing to do with it! After the race I went back to bad mouthin' jap cars and people.

I spend a lot of time checking each cylinder for even fueling. I used a temperature stick on the inside of exhaust header bends (shielded from motion cooling) to even out cylinder temperatures with fuel nozzle election. I'll be damned, I notice they bring Ward's headers over for Chicky to look at.

During the month I did most of the work myself. Chicky was gone quite a bit over to Watson's garage…I guess building engines for Ward's car. The pit crew were last minute pick-ups. Four or five with good Indy car credentials, but unpaid, 'cept for Bill Yeager. They visited other garages and friends, and enjoyed themselves, and then we had 'bout four or five days serious pit practice.

The car owner's sexual acrobatics were amusing and exciting. I never got to know Paul Lacey as well as Kenny Rich. Near as I could tell, Paul screwed every TWA hostess there was (but three) during the month and they were lesbians. Kenny stayed drunk the whole month and capped it off race day by getting thrown out of the racetrack 'bout half way into the race for being nasty drunk.

He watched the last part of the race at the motel across from turn one and concluded his act by throwing Smitty (the motel owner) in the swimming pool at the end of the race. He did make it back to victory circle for the celebration, but I doubt he knew it. Yup, Smitty done what all good motel owners do if you throw 'em in the swimming pool. Threw Kenny out and handed me a bill just shy of 40 big ones. The Ken-Paul team won the Indy race. Their first race ever as owners.

But that day was not to be their best day. Mrs. Kenny and Mrs. Paul unexpectedly showed up in Indy day before the race and were extremely unhappy about what they found in their husband's rooms: unclothed ladies, much personal clothing, (not of a school teacher type), considerable evidence of violated matrimonial vows, plus no other rooms available. So you can guess they didn't think much of sharing the room with the strange women. Nope, they didn't stay for the race.

Shortly after delivering quite a bit of negative criticism about conditions at the motel, both ladies hauled ass to Dallas where two law firms had very good income for the next three months, helping the car owners become single and considerably less wealthy, very shortly after the race.

Kenny and I had many other adventures, including the 1961 and 1962 Indy races.

I had a helper for the month of May. Bunker Hunt. Bunker made a big impression on me. In 1960, he came to Indy with Kenny Rich. Bunker spent a month with us staying in the garage 'bout all the time. Bunker was not a fashion plate. He had a short neck, a burr hair cut, and his nickname was "Winnie the Pooh" 'cause of his hairy features and clothing. He kinda looked like a brown bear. Bunker's dad was one of the original owners of the first big Texas oil play, "Spindle Top." H. L. Hunt was a tool salesman who represented oil field equipment manufacturers. Mr. Hunt was a very good poker player and Mr. Hunt accepted oil field interests as payment for gambling debts. The oil business was in it's infancy and the original players who were lucky, got rich real quick. Now Mr. Hunt Sr. was a very sharp, shrewd, gambling, hard drinking, pussy hound. I believe you've eaten food his company produced and you've probably listened to his radio station. (Biggest radio deal going I think.) And like so many other wild-assed cats, he got religious when he was too old to fuck, fight and party.

In that month I spent at Indy 1960, we ended up winning the race, so for the car owners it was their first race experience, and it was of course impressive. Bunker took me to his dad's office in Houston one day, the idea being for me to meet him, and he will join us for lunch. Right in the middle of Houston is this dumpy, 'bout two-story office building; Mr. H. L. Hunt's headquarters. Well. Mr. H. L. is in his late sixties, a smallish man in a wrinkled up grey pin stripe suit, wrinkled up shirt and necktie with food spots, one shoelace untied and hair messed up 'bout like it's been combed with a garden rake. Bunker introduces Kenny Rich and me. He says to his dad, "Hello. Wanna go eat lunch?" "No", he gets out a brown paper bag, yup a brown bag and starts eating. But starts chewing Bunker's ass out big time 'bout being a stupid son-of-a-bitch for getting fucked up in Iraq and not getting all his oil drilling equipment out of Iraq before Saddam took over. Then worked Bunker's ass over even worse for drilling two dry holes in Lybia. I mean that old bastard was 'bout as mean as a junkyard dog. Five years later Bunker sells his oil interests for four billion bucks to British Petroleum.

I was taken with Bunker's dad's bookkeeping system. Every deal had all its details laid out on a desk of it's own.

Bunker impressed me with his quiet demeanor and balls in business deals. That cat put his money where his mouth was, and he loved 500 to 1 (odds against him). In the mid-eighties we crossed paths again. I haven't seen or talked to him in twenty-five years and it takes him a week to decide to take a one hundred million buck deal with John Delorean and myself. During the previous five years, Bunker had played Russian roulette in the silver game. It came out all wrong, and I imagine even today, fifteen years later, he still has a sore ass from the screwing he got from the precious metal bunch in Chicago. They removed him from the "B" class (billionaire) and put him in the low "M's" in regard to personal wealth. He never even mentioned it, not one peep.

He set up a workbench with us at the shop with both suit coat pockets full of vitamins in plastic bags with rubber bands around 'em, telling jokes. He was only billionaire I've ever known, and he only had two arms, two legs, and one head like you and I. Bunker Hunt helped me get the job done at Indy. No, he didn't know his ass from a hole in the ground 'bout engines or race cars, but he knew a ton 'bout life and people.

I guess in 1960, I might have been out of control reference social behavior. I always kept my dealings straight forward, and didn't compliment anyone for favor or social credibility. So, if you were an incompetent asshole president of Firestone, you knew I wasn't your fan. I liked Mauri Rose's gift to me on how to handle assholes of any size. 99.9 percent of the time when you were introduced, they said, "I'm pleased to meet you." Mauri's reply was, "Why?" Man, that does it. Try it sometime. My life style is I run wide open all the time, shooting from the hip.

Watching Bunker and talking to him (I spent 25 days with him, 8:00 am to 6:00 pm, much of the time just he and I) I knew a lot about him regarding his oil adventures in Iraq and Libya. Remember, I was intrigued by oil exploration business. I liked the challenge to work with wrenches that had handles two to three miles long. I was fascinated by the odds. A million to one either way. I noticed how careful he was with his thought and word choice. Kinda reminded me of the "old bull" joke where the young bull sees ten cows in heat 'bout a mile off, and says to ol' bull, "Let's run down there and fuck one of those cows." The old bull says, "Nope. Let's walk down and fuck 'em all."

'Cept for the engine problem (bent valves), Friday before the first qualifying day, the month was pretty calm. The night 'fore the race I start getting jumpy. Rathman's got about fifty goofy friends asking stupid questions. Kenny and Paul are up to their ass in alligators over matrimonial indiscretions, (fucking around) and they got plenty of hi-buck friends in the way at the garage. I decide to sleep in the garage and give my room key to Kenny, and tell him "do what he wants with the room." If they stole everything I had, seventy-five bucks would have covered it.

Now, the main road to the speedway is 16th Street. The night before first qualifying day and the night before the race is a book in itself. Traffic is totally stopped, cars four or five wide. People lined up to get in come morning. Big deal is who's first in line every year. Some ol' boy from Arizona dressed like a Union Pacific locomotive engineer was first in line for years – Larry Bisceglia. Hell, he was famous. "Mr. #1 at Indy," he had credentials same as we did. He kept his GMC van in line for a month (slept in it).

Badges

I need to tell you 'bout badges. Indy was the only race in the world where you are issued a really nice metal badge. There were two kinds, bronze and silver. Silver means you are a genuine racer and can go 'bout any place – any time. Every year badge is different. Each year badge depicts some historical item or event in Indy's history. My guess is a complete collection would be worth moocho loot today. Nope. You're wrong. No good as a sexual bribe. No women allowed in garage area then (legally). Wish I'd saved 'em all, would have 'bout 44 of 'em (55-99). Man, first few years I was proud of them.

Back to 16th Street. Hookers would use newspapers to cover car windows. Amateur drunk lady race fans wrecking business giving it away, 'bout 25 fights going on at once over booze, pussy, tickets, who's gonna win. Every con artist in every racket is out there on 16th Street. This lasts for 36 hours, twice a year. (qualifying and race day) It's all there, booze and food, souvenirs, gamblers, card and crap games. I forgot murder. Yup, 'bout every year, one or two. When it gets out of control, there must be 500 cops there. Clarence Cagle is in the middle of it with trained police dogs, with the cops on horses.

This goes on non-stop till 5:00 am, gates open. All hell breaks loose. (This is totally gone now.)

350,000 maybe more people. Man that's 700,000 arms, legs, eyeballs of every kind of humanity that exists on earth. My guess is 100,000 people who attended then never knew who won. When it was over, they were shit-faced drunk. Big deal. "Bring basket, we'll have a picnic." Yeah boy. In turn one there was an area inhabited by the best beer drinking race fans in the US, probably the world. This was called "the snake pit." Poor ol' Clarence would go goofy trying to control this act, but couldn't even come close. They were screwing, oral sexing, flashing. (You know 'bout that?) Yup, they'd strip naked, male or female, and run around infield, even run on the track. Once, one run up to the starters stand, fell out, and was dead. Hell, in 1960 a rickety, wooden, fan-made observation tower fell and killed two people race morning. Do you get the message? Back then Indy was the biggest fucking deal going world wide, period.

I've seen the bull-fighting act in South America 40 years ago. Indy was bigger. I believe then it was considered an honor if the head bullfighter screwed your wife and some fans felt that way about race drivers. I can remember a socialite friend of Kenny's from Dallas with her husband. Before the race she sounded like the queen of England. After the race (she is now allowed in the garage), sitting on a work bench, pulls her dress up (she's drunk), and says "She got so excited she peed in her panties. Feel. " Well, OK, didn't want to be rude. Nearly a problem. Husband ain't that drunk and Yeager's trying to kiss it. Don't worry, social matron in Dallas. Even though you'd of let Yeager do it if your husband didn't veto it. I don't have a clue what your name was. Sue me? I got a witness; yup a reporter took a picture of it.

Speaking 'bout the Queen of England. During the February 1960 Beach Race, there was a (kinda next door to the shop) bar called "The Paleface Harbor." The owner called me 'bout midnite and said, "A lady over here want to see your race cars and meet you. Can I bring her over?" "Hell yes!"

Well, Freddie Keeser is over here in a couple minutes. Man. This deal is one tiny notch under Marilyn Monroe. Blond, stacked like a brick shit house, and with a British accent that won't quit. One of them kind that makes you want to paw the earth like a bull. Or like I used to say, "I'd walk over two miles of broken whiskey bottles bare foot just to be able to sniff it."

"Well, what do you do lady, besides walk around giving everybody a hard on?" "I'm Lt. Governor of Indiana's secretary." The lady is 'bout 25, and very over-full on hi-test.

I don't know who was the Lt. Governor of Indiana, but I betcha this gal caused him and his wife some problems. (Unless he was left hand threaded). "Well nice meeting you. I got to weld up some stuff, are you gonna be here tomorrow, maybe I can take you to dinner and tell you some good race stories?"

"Nope. Leaving tomorrow afternoon."

"Could I get your phone number in Lafayette. Maybe I can call you there?"

"Sorry, nope."

"OK" No reason. (Maybe married.)

1:30 am, I'm quitting. I live at garage, but now I got a clean room I built with a dandy bed.

Bang-bang on door…here's Miss Lt. Governor's Secretary.

"I want you to have a drink with me."

Hell. . I'm dirty as hell. She's all shined up in lite colored clothes.

"Well it's too late to go to a bar, I got a bottle here."

"That's fine." I let her in my room and in 45 seconds my pants are down around my boots and a lot of sex gets going.

I'm in shock (and it takes a ton to surprise me in them days). Well, that baby goes from the Queen of England to a drunken bitch that uses every dirty word I ever heard (by the way, the accent is gone now).

I got a bottle of V.O. and she is giving it real hell. Next part of act is turn sex on and off every minute or two, then a pause, and "here we go again." I can't handle it. 30 minutes later I'm trying to get her dressed and out the damn door. Can't do it, so I throw her ass and clothes out the door.

It's cold. She finds a stick and pokes it in heater fan, and now there's no heat.

Sheriff's office is right across the street, so I call radio operator and say, "Can you see a lady banging on my door?"

He says, "Wait a minute." Comes back and says, "Hell yes and she's naked."

I say, "Get her ass dressed and to where ever her motel is."

Big laugh. "You mean you can't handle that little girl?" Laughs his ass off.

The next 20 minutes two deputies and two Holly Hill cops can't catch her. She's disappeared. They give up. I just get to sleep. Guess who's trying to tear the door off? OK, I let her in, get her dressed and take her to her room. (Hell no, I hauled ass).

Two days later some cat come over here mid-afternoon and asks if I know miss "so and so." I say, "Yup, never forget her." Turns out she didn't go home. She moved in with bartender who was a music freak, and destroyed 'bout 2,000 bucks worth of music shit while he was working. I say, "What you want me to do? Buy you new stuff or sing to you?"

"No." He wants to find her and get her arrested, and for me to testify.

I tell him, "Ace you wanna play, lots of times you gotta pay. It's now your turn, I got no intentions of fuckin' with that wild cat ever again." Little did I know.

I'm at Indy, middle of May. She called me from her office (I thought). "Come to Lafayette and take me to dinner." "OK, next couple of days I'll call." (Yeah…'bout like I want to catch a ten foot rattlesnake bare handed. Hell. I don't even have her phone number). Hour later guard says, "You got a visitor at the gate. The ol' boy lets me know it's a brick shit house type lady. I see her too late. She hollers "Smokey, come meet my boss, Mr. Lt. Governor." This bitch is unreal. Her boss and I look each other over, in fifteen minutes my peter takes over and says, "Boss, you misjudged her, she is really a nice person." She asks where I'm staying and I've moved to the Mayfair Motel 'cause half of the time Kenny or Paul have given my room to friends, hookers, etc. But I don't check out of the Holiday. I'm gonna ask her to stay for the evening.

Her boss says "load 'em up."

I'm a son-of-a-bitch. 1:00 am I'm laying in bed at the Mayfair. Bam-bam at the door. I got no idea who's at the door. Hell. Nobody knows I got a room here. Yup. Little Miss "ten miles of bad road." And she's been drinking. The accent is gone. She wants a drink. Comes in. Removes her clothes. Zzzingo. The sex deal where she turns it off and on like a light switch. I decide to change the movie this time. I half-ass dress her then pull her out of the room, but give her the bottle. Two pretty well heeled race fan (car dealers) invite her in for a drink. I don't know what happened, 'cept next day, desk asked me 'bout lady who was looking for me and got raped and called the police (remember this act). Week later, race day. We've won. I'm back at motel, take a bath to get ready for a party but I fall asleep. 'Bout 11:00 pm somebody's at the door. "Fuck 'em. I want to sleep."

1:00 am. Well it's "Miss trouble" in the room. She talks the desk into giving her a key. Bottle lying on the floor, I'm bare-assed naked, she can get naked in 11 seconds, and we start playing doctor. Same damn deal. I put up with this for an hour. I can't get her out of the room, I throw her clothes outside, try to throw her out. She grabs phone and calls police. "I've raped her"(remember). I grab the phone. I'm really pissed now, and I tell cop my name and room number and tell him to bring an ambulance with him, 'cause she's gonna get some severe discipline training and gonna need medical help. He says, "Hey. ain't you the Smokey on the winning car?" I said, "Yes." He said, "We'll drive slow, but don't break anything on her."

I hung phone up and that baby is gone (minus under clothes and shoes). Cops got her at the front desk waiting for a cab. Yep, let her spend night in the clink to sober up. 3:00 am back to sleep.

This is the only time I stayed for victory banquet.

I get to garage 'bout 10 am. It's Tuesday. I've decided to leave car at Indy. Rathman and Chicky are gonna run some races with it. I'd collected a bunch of free stuff during the month, had it in a pile on an overhead shelf. I'm gonna ship it home. Well, guess what? It's gone, every fuckin' piece of it. Next, Rathman buys fifteen wrist watches and has the speedway jeweler engrave them to "the winning crew 1960 Indy," you know, the usual bullshit, and charges them to race expenses.

Do you wanna guess who he forgot? And who "would get one tomorrow" and still hasn't got it?

There were eight in the crew – fifteen watches?

The day after the race is an all day photo interview, happy bullshit day. There is a banquet that night, kind of a big TV deal. And, to "the winner goes the spoils," a 'bout 40 foot trailer full of stuff for the chief mechanic. Boy, in them days free food, clothing for a year, lawn mowers, every kind of recreational gadget made. Tools, toolboxes, 50 polishes and lubricants by the case, free bone crusher service, 30 race jackets and 50 caps. Watches, jewelry, luggage and on and on.

They work the banquet deal backwards. Giving awards from last to first. After an hour we get to chief mechanic of winning car..."Chicky Hiroshima." I'd started to push myself up and to go podium. And silence. In a second, it dawned on me the motherfuckin' japs had done it again and that Rathman was rotten clean through. I started to leave. Three or four guys from our table got me to stay till it quieted down, then I left. Actually I had less to go home with than I came with. I put it in a big grocery bag, left all the dirty uniforms, even left my work boots. I did bring my work hat back.

I didn't have a watch, I'd given a Pole award Rolex I had to a female admirer. As I left the Mayfair the two cops who arrested "Miss Bad News" saw me waiting for a cab, they took me to the airport. It was 'bout 1:00 am. You know first thing they asked? "Did I have her phone number?" I spent rest of night in TWAs pilot's lounge. Got a flight headed south 'bout 7:30 am I'm now in the "blank" mood. I will not let you see me hurtin'. As I sat in the plane, I reflected on the past two days. I thought about how in two or three seconds what a violent range of emotions it's possible to experience. I had one 'bout the same when in '44 when flack knocked a hole in my left window (on a B-17) Suddenly, it's 65 degrees below zero. No heat. No pressurized cabin (oxygen bottle, period). The flack is red hot, hits the lower back edge of my steel flack helmet hard enough to knock it off my head. Two pieces of flack 'bout a half-inch square with jagged edges, drops down between some clothing layers to about an inch or so below my shoulders, and of course burns me.

Mentally, I've got a big hole in my back, I'm gonna die, man it hurts.

Did you know extreme cold and extreme hot are 'bout impossible to tell apart using just the sensation of pain?

I talk to co-pilot, I want to swap seats. Hell, we are way the fuck up in Germany, five hours from Foggia (home base), I ask engineer to look and see if he can stop bleeding. In about a minute I find I'm burned, not leaking a drop. That sixty seconds from "sure death" to "no problem" was a mental yo-yo 'bout equal to the Indy banquet.

One other kinda shock was what I herded up into my hotel room in Memphis in '43 (which turned out to be a male cross-dresser). Yeah, that was a shock . (Nope, I kicked his ass out). I still got the flak, had cuff links made out of 'em in Italy. Can't wear 'em much. Too jaggedy (they turned green also). I did have some fun out of it though. The "wanna see my flack burns" deal was an excellent "step one" to finger sex. I end up with the 10 grand I was promised. No 10 percent of purse. Zero chief mechanic stuff. You think that was bad? Hell, I was stupid enough to do it two more years.

1961

Kenny and I stayed friends till he died, February 1999. In tail end of January 1961, I decided to quit drinking till the Beach Race was behind me. My thinking was sober I'd stand a better chance of winning, and in that time frame winning Daytona seemed important to me. Plus, I have a $1,000 bet I would not drink till after Beach Race with Jim Stephens, local Pontiac dealer. I had to stay off of it. No way I could pay off the bet.

Well, to quit drinking cold is kinda like being around ten naked female movie stars, all of which have made it clear you can "have a little any time you want, but if you do you lose the bet" and the devil keeps saying, "Do it Smoke, nobody will know." But you grit your teeth, drink coffee, chew gum and fight it off.

This bet was for a month. We won the '61 Beach Race and I decided to have the drunk of all drunks. But after the race I went back to the machine shop to get washed up and get all "pretty" for the ladies and woke up at 5:00 am the next morning. Still in race clothes.

Well, shit. If staying sober helped win Daytona what about Indy?

Well, "you never know." And since I live on a day by day basis...

Jim Rathmann in 1961. (photo: Indianapolis Motor Speedway)

Tuesday after Beach Race I decide "no drinking till after Indy." By now it's getting a little easier.

Nope, I never had any especially tough days staying sober. Biggest trouble I had was when the devil had my friends work on me. I got stubborn and run on the theory, "I'll drink when I'm goddamned good and ready. Not when you push me." I remember one of my "no drink remedies" was to switch from pipe to cigars. I now notice people who drink have stinky breath, funny it never occurred to me before, nor did it occur to me then, how bad cigars smelled, or how bad tobacco breath was.

Man. I really dug Indy. Your imagination was you limit. Not 150 pages of rules dedicated to the preservation of mass production shit boxes. By June 15th the 1960 Indy was "just a bad day at Black Rock." Tomorrow would be a bran' new party – fuck yesterday, it was irreversible. In June, after the '60 Indy race, the plan for the Ken-Paul Special was to run the rest of the USAC races. With the screwing I got from Rathman and Chicky along with the owner's inaction to give me what they agreed to. (half the crew chief spoils and 10 percent of the purse), I decided "to hell with it, I'd do what I wanted to do, build a car where all four wheels cambered into the turns. Right side wheels cambering negative and castor lengthening the right side wheel base and left side cambering positively and castoring to a shorter wheel base, a la two motorcycles hooked together and playing Dixie cup in the turns.

I wanted to have a cast magnesium chassis like a canoe and a fiberglass top. Engine and driver offset to left side of chassis and wheel center line, Offy powered, with 18 inch diameter wheels all way round, with slick eight inch wide tread, independent suspension with a ZF (German) limited slip drive axle, with constant velocity joints both ends of the drive axles.

Well to build this car I needed money and help. 1961, I'd do it better. GM was easy, I got styling involved 'cause Bill Mitchell loved Indy and innovation. Saginaw Steering, I got hooked by the curiosity and forward vision of the boss man there. A very unlikely racer type, actually a "Casper Milktoast" looking cat with the balls of a gorilla (well maybe a small gorilla). Owens Corning was easy to get in the deal, but getting money out of 'em was a task over my head. So back to my normal reasoning, I don't have a clue, but something will turn up and the money will pop up.

Phil Zeigler, the general manager of Saginaw and I had already been deeply involved starting late in 1958, when I ran out of money on patents regarding variable ratio power steering, power brake from residual pressure of power steering pump and hydraulic front suspension height control.

I ended up trading my rights to these three inventions for 10 power steering kits, 10 power brake kits and two sets of suspension height adjusters, two aluminum cross flow radiators. I just gave the leaning suspension away. Phil liked the suspension, and thought he'd try it on a passenger car (more on this elsewhere). I ended up in Hollywood with Phil (at the time, he and I were buddies). I think he got excited with my evening adventures and asks to be a player. I get a gal who works for Hollywood's Big Jim, who either is Ann Margaret or her twin. Nope momma, you don't need to get mad. Phil chickened out. That was 100 bucks shot in the ass.

Phil brainwashes himself into building the suspension and constant velocity axles. Here was mistake number one. Saginaw's engineers must have all had previous experience at Caterpillar tractor. This stuff was so over designed and heavy you couldn't believe it. What made it worse was everything had joints that were adjustable tapered fastening points with an expensive plastic poured in place for zero tolerance (like tie rod ends). To lighten it, we had a terrible problem to avoid ruining the plastic joint. My master plan was to play go-cart with rear wheels so that all compliance would come from the rear tires. I wanted to put the wheels and hard rubber mounts, no springs or shocks in rear.

The magnesium tub never got off the ground. Know why? That stuff is dangerous. When melted it wants to burn and it burns super hot. It was also very hard to heat treat. I could not find any one who would even consider doing it for money. I thought I had Dow talked into it, but they were not even close when it came time to commit. So we quit working on the patterns and I slapped a moly tube frame together for it.

Here's where Luigi Lesosky came in. He was capable of just winging it like I was. We made a good team. Luigi was probably the most talented fabrication artist racing has ever seen. He taught me tons of good stuff.

When the decision to go tube frame was made, GM styling said, "Soon as you get frame 'bout done, we'll send couple engineers and a couple technicians down to design body and build bucks for the fiberglass."

Owens Corning had said, "We'll work on the fiberglass." (You know, it's still painful today to relive

Making some adjustments during practice. (photo: Indianapolis Motor Speedway)

those days and their trials and tribulations.) November, Rathman calls and says, "Hey, we were a wonderful team, let's do it again, Chicky's gone, and you can have the whole nine yards. I want to win it again." Right there I felt a terrible pain in my ass. The job he done on me in May was like third degree burns and needed skin graft to fix. I never said a word when he came out with the word "team." I hung that son-of-a-bitch up like it was red-hot. A week later Kenny Rich calls and says, "Please come back and run the deal or we are gonna quit." There was the real reason that prick Rathman called me. I said, "No Kenny, I'm getting ready to go to Germany about limited slip rear axle." I ask how single life is? Momma is long gone along with most of his loot. Big deal here was she was loaded, heir to the Square D electrical fortune. He says, "Everything is great, I'm going to Ecuador to run some gold mines I bought." I asked, "How's Paul? "..."Well, not too good, his wife cleaned his plow, and he and I are having a race to see who can stay drunk the most. He's out of the race car."

Kenny says, "I want to come see you." I say, "I'll call you and tell you when I'll be here, I got to go to Tibet tomorrow on a service call, be gone a month or so." Next day he is at the shop. Deal ends up like this: I do the '61 Indy chief deal. Kenny's got his dad's company, Simonize Corporation to pay the bills. He'll pay for Germany trip and axle parts if I agree to incorporate it in the '62 car. Well, since I didn't have the money to go myself, and Popular Science was chickening out about expenses, (the original deal was, trip was for a story on ZF's transmissions and axles) this was tempting.

"What about my new car?" "Well," Ken says, "we'll pay some bills for first rights to race the car after 1961 Indy race." I'm starting to weaken. I say, "I've entered car and will run it also or no deal." Ken says, "Hell, if it runs better than the '60 winner, we'll run it." Now he's found the magic button. I'm happy with the deal. Ain't much you can do to a year old Indy winner when nothing good has happened and rules are the same, so I repaint it black and gold, take a few pounds off of it and put in the long rod, offset, lite weight pistons and flat cam followers and cams to go with it. (This is my '58 engine.) I also put on aluminum cross flow radiator, power steering, power brakes, and an aluminum fuel tank. It's race ready in January (the '60 winner).

I'm gonna call the new car "the Python" from now on. Ward told reporters the car "looked like a python that had just swallowed a piano." The body pieces come late February. Man nothing fits, I mean nothing. So Bill Mitchell sends five guys to Daytona to fix it. Luigi and I are moving Dzus fasteners locations up, down, sideways, the skin is getting lengthened-shortened; what a fucking mess. I itched for three months; fiberglass dust residual gets in your skin. Only thing kept me sane was the odor from the resin. We were three-quarters in orbit for three months.

One of the last straws, we're running late. It's late April, Luigi finishes the 75-gallon aluminum fuel tank, a very complex shape. A thing of beauty. Luigi does the most perfect aluminum gas welding of anyone in the world. We send tank to Orlando to get anodized so methanol won't eat it up. I install tank and forget it, but I notice something that makes me suspicious. I fill the tank with methanol, the son-of-a-bitch looks like a shower. It had a million tiny leaks, the anodize ate away some impurities in the beautiful welding and left holes. Took three, twenty-hour days to grind bad welds out and re-weld. But then it was perfect.

April 30th the Python is born and makes it's first worldly bellow. I drive it up Riverside Drive 'bout 100 miles per hour, put it in back in the barn, go to the sheriff's office to get hand cuffed and ride to jail. Cost 22 bucks and I lose three or four hours before they bring me back. I let the deputies sit in it for pictures. The sheriff says, "You gotta give me four tickets to the race. " I say, "You won't go. You been saying same thing since '58, but I'll give you a good phone number that will help you grow your hair back and help you shoot straighter." Rodney Thursby was a terrible shot. He couldn't hit a bull in the ass if he held him by his tail. Don't forget the sheriff's office is right across the street from me in this 10 years or so. So I can get in and out of trouble quicker than a cat can lick it's ass.

The '60 Watson run good right off the bat. I think if it wasn't the fastest it was close, so it gave plenty of time for the Python. Rathman runs it 30 or 40 laps, and is 'bout three or four miles per hour short of other cars. He comes in end of the day. The press is all there. "What do you think Jim? Well, "baldy" puts a baseball cap on sideways, makes a weird face like someone bewildered, and says, "Whoo-eee." That done it, to the press the "car is fuckin' junk, whole idea is stupid. " Next day I let Duane Carter run it 20 laps or so. He wants to try and qualify it. He runs it good enough that you can say "it may qualify."

Going by Rathman's analysis if I change car to be more conforming…maybe. Like a dumb son of a bitch, I damn near kill myself working around the clock and change it over to a conventional four-wheel independent suspension. Rathman rides it a few laps and comes in to pronounce it a dead player. Should have got Roger Ward's dog to piss all over it, photograph it, and then took it to race car heaven. Duane gives it another ride, 'bout same speed as before, but says, "Wish you hadn't changed it. " It's now Friday before first qualifying Saturday, so I decide to load it back on trailer and concentrate on the Watson.

Rathman don't like power steer, power brakes, so I jerk that stuff off. We qualify and I've been so busy, I forgot about "we will get the 1960 co-crew chief deal straightened out." Rathman and Kenny said, "We'll take care of it." So, I herd them up and we go to see Frankie to fix it. Frank says, "Hell, men, I'm up to my ass in alligators. Let's do it day after race." I say, "I won't be here." They say, "Yes you will, your probably gonna win race again." Same old shit, "Never put off tomorrow what you can put off today." I'm busy rebuilding car for a race. I'd rebuild every single part, replace every bolt and clevis pin, sand blast the frame, magnaflux, and zyglo everything, then repaint and wait for carburetion day to test the car.

Again the car runs good speed wise, but it don't sound right to me. To me, when the engine is right it's got a crisp sharp bite in the exhaust and sounds like it's doing it easy. I'm sure it's the magneto, but it's a new Joe Hunt magneto. I take it to Joe and say, "Check it Ace, it's got a problem." He brings it back and says, "Smoke, it's perfect." "What did you find Joe?" Joe says, "Nothing Smoke, it's your imagination." I say, "OK, let me have the mag off your car and you run my perfect mag." "No, can't do that" (by the way he had his own car qualified for the race). No, he didn't drive, he was a flight engineer for TWA with a side business building race mags. Joe was a racer, he won't change mags 'cause the timing was set and there was no more practice. It's all bullshit. It's about like setting time on a farm tractor bone simple and took two minutes.

'61 race day, 125 miles into the race, we are "the hot dogs, leading. Suddenly the noisemaker gets quiet. Rathman coasts her in. Magneto's dead. Yeah. I could have put another mag on and run maybe 10th. But I was so pissed I started walking back to garage area. Joe Hunt is just in sight. He sees me with the mag (I'm holding it by the plug wires) and asks about the most stupid question he could have, "What happened Smoke?" I spin mag around my head couple times and let it go, aimed at Joe and said, "This fuckin' "perfect" mag!" I missed Joe, but it hit a 50 gallon trash barrel and stuck in the barrel. Joe got the message and hauled ass.

There sat a jap motorcycle some dumb shit left sitting there with the key in it. I jumped on it, turned key on, and it starts. I'm off to the airport. I get to the airport, I park cycle on sidewalk (it's still running) and I holler, "When's next plane to Daytona?" The ticket guys are race fans and say, "Not till 9:00 pm, shit, you just missed one to Jacksonville." Another agent said, "He's taxiing to runway, ain't left yet." I holler, "Hold him," ran out the door, jump on motorcycle, I roar out to runway. It's a TWA Connie (I think), I jump off motorcycle, as the steps come down. Stewardess says "Captain said he's got a jump seat in cockpit if you want it. "OK." The captain gets the race on the radio, we land in Jacksonville and the race ain't over yet. We go into operations to hear the end of it.

I was at the track at 125 miles leading it and heard the end of it in Jacksonville, Florida. If that was your motorcycle I borrowed, can I say, "I'm sorry I did it" and "Thank You" at same time? Or, is it possible you lost your motorcycle at Indy in 1961 and never found out what happened to it? If so, I hope you had insurance. No, Joe Hunt never ever came close to me again. I had two helpers up there. They brought cars and parts back, including mag that failed. My giving the mag flying lessons really didn't hurt it. The trouble was the rotor was a quarter-of-an-inch too short, and that caused condenser to overheat and it then failed. I never used Joe's mags for anything serious after that race. I switched over to Mallory and Bosch stuff in '62. Joe, you're gone now. I'm glad I missed you with the mag. I liked you before and forgot about the '61 deal in a year or two.

Would you believe, in '62, I didn't like sound of engine and felt it was the mag, and swapped mags with Jack Beckley and finished. Jack's mag quit and his car was a contender for all the marbles. Nope, it wasn't a Joe Hunt. I believe that it was a Bosch. Back in them days, when I still had ears, I could understand engine talk.

This 1961 adventure ain't over yet. Coming home I go into passenger waiting area at Jacksonville. "Hey, Smoke." (it's Bob Anderson, general manager of some part of Chrysler, Plymouth maybe). He's 'bout half shit-faced. Says, "I heard you was at Indy racing, what you doing here?" "Long story Bob, don't feel like explaining it. Why you wobbling 'round in public? You're supposed to be a big shot." "Let's have a drink!"..."Damn good idea, but there ain't any here." I haven't told him yet that I'd quit.

Maybe I better tell you first part of this deal: several years before this ('bout '56) Bob was a project engineer for Chrysler and the engineer and chief mechanic on a yaller Plymouth that Wally Parks drove to a flying mile record on the beach (yup, the NHRA top cat). Bob needed a place to work so I let him work on his yaller racer at our place, and helped him a little. Bob's got big trouble at home and on the job. Maybe fired and divorced (don't remember), all I remember was he had plenty reason to be fucked up. "Come go with me to the Bahamas," he said. "Can't Bobby. I've been gone for a month, everything in Daytona is all screwed up." He begged me to go. I guess I should have, but I felt my problems were a little more important than his (at least to me). Plus, I know that advice in reference to matrimonial affairs, love affairs and drinking are a waste of time. You've probably been down that road and know what I mean. I'd already been run through that legal maze and I suppose Bob figured I could help him because I'd already played the game. I told him, "I can't help you, only advice I can give you is take the first deal you're offered no matter how bad you think it is, it will be your best deal. Especially if you've been a bad boy, and I think you probably have been." He said, "Just a little bit." While he went to find a drink I rented a car and went to Daytona. 'Bout five years later, no word from Bob, but I've kept up with him through the news and daily gossip. He's now CEO of Rockwell International, a big-big shooter.

Now, in February of '67 in the Daytona garage area, four or five extremely well dressed cats (it's colder than hell by the way) all in black overcoats. You know, Eskimo style, with gloves and hats. One of them has a Homburg hat on and a scarf (no spats). I'm in a trying period with NASCAR. Turner has put my car on the pole. Ford and Chrysler are pissed and GM ain't spent a dime (no leverage with NASCAR). Chrysler and Ford been supporting NASCAR for 15 months, so NASCAR's trying to find a way to disqualify the qualifying run. The Homburg asks quite a few questions, attempts to introduce me to his guests and I get annoyed. I look up and tell him to, "Get the fuck out of the way and go ask his goofy questions someplace else." I didn't want to offend him, but I believe I flunked the exercise.

I noticed the man looked like he's been hit in the face with a bucket of shit and disappeared a few minutes later, Sam Petok, who was Bob's hatchet man at both Chrysler and Rockwell, comes by and I said, "Sam, could I get one of those astronaut things you put out to celebrate going to the moon?" He's a little reluctant. Says, "I'll try, they are hard to come by." I say, "How's Bob?" He says "What you mean how's Bob?" Now it dawns on me who Mr. Homburg hat was. Nope, never saw him or talked to him again. If you're still peddling Bob, I'm sorry. You used to be such a sloppy kind of dresser, how the hell I know you'd gone Brooks Brothers? You know Bob, it was part your fault. You found out only thing helped you in Nassau was the booze and pussy, and if you'd of said, "That's not a very nice way to treat one of your old racin' and drinkin' buddies," I'd have wised up and we'd have hugged and kissed, and it would be all fixed. But nope, you've got a big head 'cause half the US was kissing your ass 'cause your over-priced shit got to the moon. You know Bob really was a damn good automotive engineer. Space engineer? I guess he had to be, they all came home.

Financially, Indy '61 was 'bout $2.50 an hour adventure. I'm involved with Pontiac up to my ass, so Daytona's Indy "ace" disappears into the hi-speed taxi world again, playing the push-rod boogie. About straightening out the '60 co-crew chief deal, that never happened. My big-big enchantment with Indy dims a little now. I wouldn't pull an Indy car from Daytona over half way with a rope now. I've found a new adventure. Cannibals, thirty foot snakes, gold, emeralds, oil, hi-speed rivers, earth quakes and mud slides, head shrinkers, volcanoes: the Oriente jungle in Ecuador. How? Kenny Rich, my Indy car owner landed down there running from divorce. He bought several wonderful maps to gold mines in a bar in Dallas, Texas. I don't need to tell you. You probably can guess what they really were worth. Cost him 'bout 150 big ones.

1962

Well, January, 1962 I break out in a rash. "The gotta go to Indy" disease. Kenny says, "Let's run the race car one last time." This will be ol' paint's swan song. (Really what the hell does swan song mean?) This meeting was in the biggest and best whorehouse in Quito, Ecuador. The "Mirador." Way up a steep hill. Run by a German ex-SS man on the run. You ever been there? Hill is so steep taxi's have to turn round and back up last two blocks.

I say, "Who you want to drive it? " He says "Baldy" (Jim Rathman). I say, "Kenny, I believe that ball game's over, he ain't gonna mash it anymore, it's over." "Well OK." It's a low budget deal. Nothing's going right. Dean Jefferies comes from California to paint the car (the race world's best painter). He fucks up the gold. It's a rosy gold, and he finishes day before I got to tow it to Indy.

The paint's not dry and hard, it's raining like a cow pissin' on a flat rock, so I put a tarp over it. Mistake number one. The wind causes the tarp to wind burn the paint (ruins some of it). Car's starting it's third year, gets named "Ol' Paint" after some famous horse (I think).

Finally, I'm on my way to Indy. I'm so tired. I'm towing by myself, been 40 hours without sleep, I get to right along side the Holiday Inn South (Atlanta), and the car gets in deep ditch in front of the motel. I mean a big-big ditch.

Don't know if the car thought we were gonna stay there that night 'cause that's where most of us push rodders stayed when running Atlanta. But I think truth is, I fell asleep.

With a miracle I got it back on the road, no damage, right then engine goes "phhttttt" and gets quiet. Oh shit! Out of gas. I kick it out of gear. I got enough steam left to coast it up to the gas pump (that gas station, next driveway past Holiday Inn).It's so close I have to kinda stretch the hose.

OK, full of fuel…nobody hurt yet. I think for a minute or two. I decide, "Smokey, you have used your luck up for next year or two, don't push it any more." Don Bailey, good NASCAR chief (I got his phone number) is living with his girlfriend in Atlanta, a super racer gal, Rosie. 4:45 am "Rosie. Sorry to wake you up, I need to talk to Bailey."

"Smokey, he is asleep/unconscious/drunk."

"Great! He'll be a big help. Rosie I need help to get racecar to Indy. Pack a three-day bag for you and Bailey, I'll be there in thirty minutes."

I find her house. Bailey cannot be awakened. "OK, Rosie, you keep me awake till he comes to." We throw Bailey in back seat and off we go for 'bout eight hours. I'm in big trouble now, truck stop, no-doz, coffee. 100 miles more, now I'm sleepy and goofy too. "Rosie you drive it." Still can't get Bailey to wake up. Now it's cold and raining like a son-of-a-bitch.

Well, Rosie just can't do it. I get the deal within a hundred miles and I'm history. Rosie stops me, turns off the key. I'm starting up a super hi-way going wrong way. Fate wakes Bailey up and tells him he's 'bout to piss his pants. I wake up in front of the Speedway Motel. Bailey brought 'er in. Rosie stays three days. I have to thank her for her help, only decent thing to do, but Don don't see it that way. (He got pissed because Rosie moved in with me.) I send Rosie home on the big silver bird and Don stays and helps me through the '62 race.

When you're at Indy today, if you see a tall lanky cowboy with a deputy sheriff's badge on in the pace car garage (he is in charge of pace cars and drives the real pace car in the race, and has probably for the last ten years or more), that's the Don Bailey I kidnapped in 1962. He stayed at Indy. He was a mechanic on Tony George's daddy's car, Elmer George. Then became Tony Holman's guest ranch supervisor in Jackson Hole, and still is, 'cept now it's owned by the Chapman Root family. Don damn near became a drunken mental case 'cause for some weird reason he lost his sexual powers for a few years. I'm happy to tell you, well at least one of his girlfriends five years later told me, "he was back to a "ten" in one department and a "ten plus" in

The wing car in '62 during practice. (photo: Indianapolis Motor Speedway)

the other." No, he hasn't grown a mustache.

The '62 race was a wasted year. The driver was spooked. His wife told him she dreamt he was gonna die. When I wanted him to practice it was "too windy," "too hot," "too oily," "can't learn anything." This is a bad sign, another is "got a cold" all the time. The third is religion becomes important. "Motherfucker" is replaced with references to God.

The car has power steering, power brakes, aluminum cross-flo radiator. This year I ain't taking 'em off. We don't run good. We can qualify but are no longer a contender. We also try a wing over driver. Yup. I had the first winged car at Indy. Bruce Crower's from San Diego and he's got some buddies from consolidated in airplane manufacturing who built the wing for us (no cost). Wing ain't Baldy's favorite thing. Remember I told you he ain't much for innovation. If all racers thought like him we'd still be racing steam engines.

The wing has way too much camber in it, straight away and turn speed is identical, but engine is laboring all the way around and driver don't want to play with it. Course when we put wing on, all the media runs over and attacks it in their contributions daily to racing fans. When Baldy turns his baseball cap sideways and goes into that bewildered cross-eyed pose in the press interviews, not much help is gained by the media's comments. The wing had potential. Well, hell, the world of Outlaws lives by 'em today. (We had wing right over the driver). So wing got put on a shelf up over the workbench. Don't have any idea what happened to it. I doubt engine would have survived the wing for three-and-a-half hours.

Why didn't I try in subsequent years? It was banned very shortly after, and showed up much later over rear axle and low on the nose in tandem with down force tunnels. I had a rough month trying to baby sit the driver. Race morning, I find him just before start of race, puking down 'round turn two. In the race a new clutch clevis pin broke in first fifty miles of the race. (Car now has no clutch release). On first pit stop he indicates "no brakes." We catch him and fuel him. Yes, without a clutch. He manages to get out of pit.

He was too fucked up mentally. He drove that whole race, finished I think ninth, thinking he had no brakes and it was in reality no clutch. We, the pit crew had to catch the car three times in pit stops. What kind of "cold medicine" you reckon he was taking?

More to story, it's got power brakes and power steer. He didn't like the brakes. How 'bout this? The race for us was so boring, I fell asleep in the pits between pit stops. He finally decided he liked the steering, so after the race here comes the sideways baseball cap and crossed eye pose.

"If I had brakes I think I could have won again."

Let's back up 20 minutes. I'm so puzzled 'bout brakes. Car is still at far end of pits. Crowds in garage area. I've told my pit crew, "I'm leaving in an hour and a half, get trailer in a loading mode up at a 30 degree angle." I jump in the car to

(photo: Indianapolis Motor Speedway)

The whole team…when the brakes were still workin'. (photo: Indianapolis Motor Speedway)

steer it to our garage, I notice clutch pedal is against firewall; brake pedal is in normal position. What the hell? I hit the brake pedal. Hell, it's got full pedal. One helper I have with me is from my Daytona shop, a young man, Vernon Blank. I say, "Vernon put starter on it and wind me up." The engine fires and the guard runs over says "Shut 'er off Smokey, ain't allowed." I say, "OK, " put it in low, run it up to 'bout 60, hit the brakes and fuckin' near come flying out of the car. If you wanted to see a genuine hot motherfucker that was me. Vernon hooked the tractor to me and took me back to our garage. Rathman is in the middle of explaining why he didn't win. I have crew push me up on trailer, put brakes on and holler to Rathman, "What do you think is holding this car up here?" Then I release, coast back off then have crew push me back up with no assist to hold me there till they drop nose of trailer. I jump out and tell Rathman what a no good. lying, two-faced son-of-a-bitch he is, and tell him "If he sees me coming down the street get the fuck on the other side" and I say, "If I see you first, I'll cross over."

He still owes me 15 grand (dealership buy money I loaned him year before), I tell him I want the money in 48 hours or I'll be in Melbourne to collect it. The money arrives in 36 hours. That was race day 1962. To my knowledge I've never spoken to him since. Three or four years ago I heard he died. I damn near came out of retirement as a drunk to celebrate. But someone told me "not so." But I've finally woken up. That was a million years ago, I don't even think about it unless I see him at Indy. I know I'm 'bout over it. Last two times I didn't even get the urge to puke when I see him.

I believe "Ol' Paint" got sold, 'bout a month later, to A. J. Foyt, the car and every other part of it for 15 grand. I still have the original upholstery and a few odds and ends off of the original car.

1963

By now I own 20 percent of some of Kenny's gold mines in Ecuador (for being a good racer), and I've found a perfect world for me. No phone, electricity, television, radio, newspaper, no mail. You get up at sunrise, get ready to sleep at 7:00 pm, money is next to worthless, no restaurants, no rooms to rent, no roads, no airports. Women of every kind. Catch 'em and try to train 'em. Big surprise, they're not very wild, but bad bad jealous. A dugout canoe or a burro is the equivalent of Hertz. Kenny's done with Indy forever.

I'm working for Chevy on racing and production problems. Curtis Turner comes to visit in Daytona. This is very unusual. Even though we were friends, we only socialized at races. So I say, "What you need Curtis?" Standard question when a fellow racer called or visited. He says, "Smoke, do you think I can run Indy?" I say, "Why fuck around and waste all that time and money. Just take a pistol and blow your brains out. Be easier on everybody and cheaper." He says, "Why do you say that?" I say, "You'll try dirt tracking them mothers on those rock hard skinny tires, you'll either spend six months at the Methodist on 16th Street or be six feet under in your ol' home town." He says, "Smoke, I gotta do it." I say, "OK, I got a half-assed car, the Python, they'll let us put 16 inch slicks on 'em now. If you take out an insurance policy for a million and pay up the policy for three months, we'll give it a try." (The 16 inch slick tire story is in the inventions section.)

I decided since Curtis don't beg for nothing, for some reason I gotta help him. Sponsor? Hell ain't no way after I painted it black and gold instead of Owens Corning red and white from '61.

Car's considered a wet dream. Curtis never sat in an Indy car. We are both temporarily financially embarrassed. Curtis is drinking pretty bad. I got a wealthy lady in Indy to pay for a room at the Speedway Motel for the month, but one room for the both of us. You already guessed her reason haven't you? Guess what? The second day we were there dear ol' daddy had divorce papers served on her. I think he wants pictures to show the jury. Room's paid for, she can't come near us. Daddy no longer wants to watch her getting laid. Curtis has a buddy in Indy, rich Lincoln-Mercury dealer with racer genes. He kinda supports Curtis for the month. We are gonna put something (an advertisement) on car when we qualify.

Driver's test goes OK, but nothing sensational. About the fourth day at Indy, a beautiful young thing, wants to be a "Miss Something." I met her in a nightclub parking lot late one night. She couldn't get her car started, so of course I rode up on my big white horse and fixed the car.

She said, "Wow can I ever repay you?" You wanna write in the next couple hours? Curtis said, "You have all the luck." He said, "How can you get so lucky?" I

Design model of the python.

said, "Easy. Go out in the parking lot and pull the coil wire out on her car 'bout 11:00 pm."

He really dug that baby, so I tell her, "Curtis not only is a racer, but he has a movie company and is looking for talent." Turner was a good looking, big, curly headed, "aw shucks" man. The little blond went ape-shit over Turner. Next day he disappeared 'bout 4:00 pm to get hair cut, buy shoes, a suit and shirts. First date. I slept in tow car that night, 'cause when I got back to motel at 1:30 am, Curtis was interviewing (I think), the blond in bed in a most unusual position for conversation. They go out for breakfast, lunch, and dinner for the next two days. I tell Turner, "Two nights in tow car is my limit." Third night slept in my bed. Hell, they never noticed me. They say love is blind.

Next day Turner passed his driver's test. He says, "Smoke I'm gonna marry that gal 'fore I leave here." "Oh shit," I say, "Turner the little thing's an alley cat, a hooker." Damn, he swung at me. The goddam love bug had him by the balls. I thought, "Shit, I gotta think fast." Next day he's got a thousand buck engagement ring.

A very famous Indy mechanic also had his eye on this li'l gal big time. I told him "George, her mother needs a cancer operation, I believe if you offer her 200 bucks as a contribution to her mother's medical problems she'll go out with you." I took night off 'bout 10:00 pm took Turner to bar-restaurant I knew George would take her (she told Turner she had to go home to stay with her sick mother). When they left

In the pits when she still looked good. (photo: Indianapolis Motor Speedway)

the nightclub, we follow 'em to George's room at same motel we were staying at. (I guess to talk about her mother's illness). But Turner saw it different. I said, "Calm down. How much do you owe on the ring?" He said, "'bout $900."

I figured she'd meet George at the speedway for a nooner, I'm at the restaurant for lunch and nabbed her coming in. I told her, "Turner stole the ring," cops were in motel looking for her 'bout the ring. That scared the shit out of her. I continued, "Let's get ring, let me take it back, and I believe it will end." She don't have ring, "will bring it tomorrow. " I say, "Good luck with cops," and start to leave. Suddenly, as I get to my car, a sweet li'l hand hands me the ring. Turner took ring back. All he was out was the $100. Would you believe George actually married her soon after? Nope, didn't last six months.

Next day I say, "Curtis we got two days left for you to pick up three miles per hour or we get kicked out of here with our tails between our li'l asses." He says, "What you suggest?" I say, "Trying to go faster, and if it scares you, tell me what it's doing and where." Couple hours later and 'bout one mile per hour faster, the yellow lite comes on. A guard says "Say Smoke; the Python was trying to take the wall down in number three." I go back over to the hospital. They say Turner's OK. Curtis says, "Sorry Smoke, I don't think it's hurt too bad." I say, "You OK?" "Yup."

The car shows up at garage. Best way I can kinda describe it's condition is it reminded me of how my

And Curtis told me she wadn't hurt too bad. (photo: Indianapolis Motor Speedway)

dog Pluto looked like when he got in a bad fight with a couple of coon huntin' dogs and got a few pieces of bird shot in his ass and tail. He was laying on his belly with front paws over his ears and his rear legs spread out flat on the ground. Muddy all over and a little blood on his ass end.

Only difference was Pluto made kinda whimper noises when I checked him over and the Python was dead silent and getting colder every minute. There was no question, it was a dead player. I said, "Curtis, go out to meet the media and announce your retirement from Indy competition for 1963, and tell 'em you'll be back in '64 and get it done. Then go crank up your airplane and go home right now, tomorrow you ain't gonna be able to move." But here comes the Lincoln dealer buddy, so Turner says, "Time to start a brand-new party." I never put car inside, didn't even lock the door just left with them. "Thank you," whoever loaded the poor ol' Python on the trailer and pushed her in the garage.

Two days later we were in Las Vegas finishing the party and I got back to Daytona with the remains in 'bout a week. I think the Python was cremated. It's remains went to Japan and came back in the form of a Honda motorcycle (probably two of 'em). The python may have well been my most unmemorable Indy adventure (at least at the track). We did extinguish any burning desire Curtis had to conquer Indy.

NEW YEAR'S DAY 1964

I'm at the shop and I decide, "If you expert asshole writers think the Python was wild, you ain't seen nothin." I start drawing the capsule car. I got one helper, T.A. Toomes. He's a good push rodder. Came from Petty country. T.A. is slow, very thorough, but a very hard, faithful worker. He is a racer. Hours don't mean shit to him either. He's never seen an Indy car or an open wheel racer. T. A. can't weld or run a lathe, a grinder or a milling machine. He can't do much metal work or fabrication 'cept stuff that's straight and flat. And he's never done fiberglass or rubber fuel cell stuff.

I sketch what we're gonna build. It's gonna be a turbine powered car that never changes offset weight or front to rear weight balance. It's gonna have a fiberglass body that weighs five ounces to a square foot, including color and lettering. It will have one spring leaf as the total front suspension and upper front spindle supports (transverse leaf replacing the a-frames). The brakes will be Tempest aluminum drums with centrifuge iron liners (in here lies the major flaw) The rear brakes will be the same, but inboard mounted on an experimental Corvette aluminum independent suspension drive assembly. The rear suspension was a 4-bar De Dion (another mistake). This car would have rubber fuel cells (this was very complex). Remember, we still carried 75 gallons. The biggest deal is the driver will sit in a small capsule, a completely separate component bolted to mainframe with five bolts. Also, this will be a one pedal car. Brake and throttle are combined in one dual function control. The clutch and gearshift will be in gearshift control, in one lever. This control has three gates, three cams and three cables, and weighed five pounds (five inches x six inches x one inch thick). It worked like a dream. Three speeds forward, and reverse with just cams and cables. Well hell, what do you expect from a drawing on a sheet of three foot wide, brown paint masking paper? We got 119 days to build it.

On March 1, I call the turbine company, say, "Ship me the turbine, I need it now." They say, "It's ready, send check for $34,000." "Huh? You said you'd loan it for free." "We will, but the overhaul charge will be $34,000 and that's bare cost." Well, I couldn't come up with $3,400 bucks, let alone add another zero, so "Adios turbine." I got enough stuff to put an Offy together.

Now I've got a partner and a sponsor. The partner is a weasley central European sharpie named George Chalik. Always wore couple giant diamonds. An old, rich bastard, owned a rubber company of some kind. The cat was sharp. I signed a worthless contract with him. He owned half the car, never put any money in it, I billed him but couldn't collect, legal deal. I said, "This ain't fair." He said, "Next time you'll learn how to read a contract." "OK, you got me," but I mentally ignore him. I won't even let him in the garage. When he did get in I'd take his glasses and give 'em a hardness test with a ball peen hammer on both lens. They failed. That then changed his number one problem from getting in the garage to getting another pair of "cheaters." Without 'em he couldn't see shit. Second time I tested his goggles, he got the message. Without glasses, if you grabbed one of those rings, and acted like you were gonna pull it off his finger he'd go goofy.

George Hurst put forty grand up for sponsorship. That's what I had to use, plus I guess 'bout twenty grand I scraped up.

So you're thinking, where in the hell did you get the plan to build such a goofy car? Over Regansburg Germany, in 1944, I was driving a B-17 carrying ten tons of remodeling equipment up there to an aircraft bearing factory, when I see a very skinny fuselage airplane hauling ass with a small capsule on one side, with a pilot in it. Turns out two small shapes with same total frontal area as one single shape has less parasitic drag. I was always told those weenie gobblers were sharp, so I paid attention. But it wasn't till 1962, I got the answer from that trip to Freidseckhoven, Germany.

I replace turbine with Offy, not too tough, but one aspect is how you gonna cool the radiator?

The Bluhm und Voss 141

I give my first idea a try in my wind tunnel and first shot out of the barrel I got it. Man, simple and effective as well. Aluminum cross flow radiator (remember, very lite). Only people can make 'em then was Harrison Radiator in Rochester, New York. A famous tech writer in a wheel chair wrote it would run hot, and in general wrote eight pages of negative stuff. Turned out he was as full of shit as a Christmas turkey. Somehow I got the Harrison engineers pissed off (really not all that hard for me to piss off engineers and lawyers). They say, "Don't ever come back." "OK, if that's the way you feel 'bout it, fuck you too." This was not a wise move.

I write a good bit of this book flying around the country, and I've noticed one of the perverted ways we amused ourselves yesterday, was to read the toilet walls message centers for information regarding homosexual adventures, some subtle, some advertising ladies by first name and phone number and a brief description of her sexual specialty. I always believed these were a form of revenge or a weird sense of humor. Lots of racist material, some seemed to be the work of new or infrequent travelers marking their trail of exciting new experiences. These as a rule are dated. You know like "Kilroy was here December 3, 1961." Quite an assortment of artistry, mostly very graphic and sexual. In short I became aware many of my fellow travelers were pretty fucking goofy. Today that art has disappeared along with the Pony Express rider, blacksmiths and pinstripers. The walls are now sterile and bare, made out of material you can't write or draw on. I think, but I can't prove it, that the production speed in toilets has picked up at least 25 percent. Hell, sometimes it would take five minutes to check out these publications. I've also heard those who read the wall were possibly with faulty credentials. What do you think 'bout this? I know, nuthin' to do with Indy. But I found it interesting.

Back to '64 capsule car.

Got to have a driver. I need a smaller size hero. Bobby Johns. Right size, brave, pretty damn good driver, never really got a shot in first class equipment, wasn't a wall banger. Well, maybe not goofy enough to want it. Never know if you don't ask right? Answer is: "Hell, yes. I've been wanting to go to Indy my whole racing life." No question. I hit the deal dead center. "Come on over to shop so we can fit you in the capsule." He ain't got a clue, never sat in an open wheel car, and when he sees how tiny this car is, and where he sits, I'm sure it dampened his enthusiasm some. But it's a deal. No nothing, just 50-50-prize money split. Hurst gearshift was the sponsor. I think maybe George Hurst gave Bobby couple bucks for expenses.

The gearshift puzzled him. It took some getting used to. The combination brake-throttle pedal got the deep six, it's now a two pedal car. With three days to go, I'm checking bump steer on the rear axle. Right in here I got an old friend, Bradley Dennis, to help for a few days to finish up. We discover the rear axle is

George Hurst really wanted to make this car heppen. (photo: Indianapolis Motor Speedway)

locked up in roll as a four bar, fixing it as a four-radius rod setup is next to impossible in time frame. No way in hell. The car's all painted. Man what a mess.

Well, in 48 hours non-stop, I changed it to a two bar set up and if I say so myself, "pretty fair job."

Look at it when you go to Indy Museum Car Hall of Fame and see what you think. Well, hell, it run fast enough to qualify.

Next a new rule pops up. I've got to have bumper front and rear. This pisses me off. Kinda getting like NASCAR now. So, for front bumper I trace li'l Smokey's hands on some moly plate, and chrome 'em up. A pair of steel hands, fingers stretched out, are front bumper. Yup, passed inspection. Much of the car's specifics are in "what did you invent section." I know it's a pain in the ass to switch back and forth, but how would you do it any different?

When we get to Indy the unveiling put half of the experts in a state of shock, including the officials. I heard it whispered, "That fucker is nuts...this proves it." But there was a very important one person who loved it. His name was Tony Hulman. Not a bad ally. He owned the farm. And a pretty fair racer from Europe named Colin Chapman, just stared at it for hours. We had garages pretty close to each other. I knew him for several years, but he ignored me like a commoner. He might have been "sir" something by then (to

Me and Bobby Johns. (photo: Indianapolis Motor Speedway)

me he was "Sir Don't Make 'em Strong") Oh, hell yes, I respected and admired his talent, but not his game of cut 'er close on "safe." I got to know him quite well in next three weeks. He was probably one of five best in the world, but he had an ego size of an elephant. Collectively, we (the Americans) set a goal to teach him to use "motherfucker" in his speech patterns. Nope, I never heard him do it, even with all the instruction he received. To say it is easy, but to use it correctly to emphasize a level of negative or positive state of reality, that's the trick. His word for emphasis was "bloody." Didn't make sense to me at all. He'd go on 'bout the "bloody car." I got to thinking his cars were all females and they had periods from time to time. Chapman had some further adventures you can find in the people section.

The "Capsule Car" is like the pied piper. 200 people follow its every move around the garage and pit area. An every day visitor for a progress check was Tony Hulman. The inspectors were very critical, but also very fair. First three or four days it was touch and go on whether the li'l car could try. The two main problems were the quick removable steering wheel and the capsule fastening. The car had a rectangular wheel to give knee and knuckle clearance. It had a collet locking device that secured it. They wanted it safety wired. Well, then the driver couldn't leave quick unless he carried a pair of side cutters. This being Indy's first quick removable steering wheel was the real problem. They were afraid locking device could

The capsule car in the pits at Indy. (photo: Indianapolis Motor Speedway)

come loose. Finally, I unscrewed total locking deal and put it in Don Cummins pocket (the head inspector). And said, "If you and your buddies can get the wheel off in 10 minutes I'll take the car home. Nope, they couldn't. Same with capsule. I removed five attachment bolts, put 'em in Don's pocket and again gave the ten-minute challenge. I won again. I think I made some friends with some of the inspectors that day and finally got the sticker.

The Rathman brothers of course knew Bobby Johns and proceeded to brainwash Johns into believing it was a death trap (the capsule location). I saw their act. They were effective because Bobby used them as a sounding board for advice and explanation. Bobby could ride it comfortable 'bout two miles per hour short of qualifying speed. With five days to go, I had to tell him "It's time to do it or get back behind the concrete wall with me." My buddy Mauri Rose was trying to heal the damage the Rathman's were causing. You gotta remember Bobby never sat in an Indy car with engine running before May 1, 1964. Well, he starts running 'bout one good lap out of five. I decide he needs more laps. We will go the second weekend.

Remember, I told you if you don't do it first weekend you're a candidate for 100 ways to miss the race. Bobby can't tell me what car's doing, 'cept feels spooky. What does "spooky" mean? Loose? Pushing? Both? Where? I never studied Halloween or ghosts; so spooky to me is like a 24 letter word. I didn't know what it meant. I try guessing. I finally find out it needs rear sway bar. I've got one. Just never tried it. But weather goes bad. We don't get much lap time. Suddenly it's Sunday of the second weekend and it's now or never. He's been plenty fast, but very inconsistent. I'm sure the car's twitchy (that means unstable), but the asshole Rathman has got him so confused we gotta guess what's wrong. That never worked worth a shit. We do have a problem that I understand: the rear brakes are very very hard to work on, they are too small for the application. Problem is, this is pretty much a rear engine car. Another problem is that with sintered iron linings, they need warming up.

Qualifying comes and it's 2:00 pm Sunday, the last day to do it. I've got four hours left. The first warm up lap is good enough. For the second lap I'm where the chiefs stand, signal and time. (Remember this is before radio.) I guess he got too deep into turn one. Hit the whoa-shit and the brakes were erratic. That backed 'er into the wall. The damage was not too bad, but the ass end of the car was the oil tank and oil cooler, all custom-made crap. Bobby's not hurt, but Indy 1964 just went to shitsville. That deal is an example of how fast life can change. And you know really nothing terrible happened. No red stuff spilled. It was just a twenty "G" mental crash.

THE MIGHTY INDY BULL

To me the Indy challenge had a main character that I conjured as a Paul Bunyon-sized bull. A huge-huge bull with big horns that hung out in turn one. This bull says, "Only four or five of you hundred or so racers will survive. My obstructions come in many forms: death, serious injury, weather, spins, oily race track, wet race track, engine failure, shortage of money, personal life interference, lack of speed, driver problems, alcohol interaction, tire problems, mistakes, ignorance, live animals, streakers, and on and on. The bull allowed zero tolerance for any man oriented mistake or inferior performance. That bull was our supreme controller. I go look at the mess in turn one. Our engine's life blood (oil) has been spilled. "How long it take to fix it Smoke?..."Damn, It ain't bad, but at least five or six hours." We've only got three and a half hours left before qualifying is over, closed, beat it, come back next year, get your shit out of the garage, go home. Well the motormouth Rathman's crap 'bout the 'deadly' capsule car is incorrect. The driver is walkin-n-talkin', no leaks, no broke parts. It sinks in. Load 'er up, I can hear alligators faintly, "Smokey come home, Smokey come back."

Max Muhleman, a reporter suddenly interrupts my loading concentration. Sez, "Hate to put this on you Smoke, Fireball just crashed at Charlotte, burned bad, 10 percent chance of climbing out." Goddam can't be. He was just here Thursday and told me after the Charlotte race he retires. They must have bum dope. I have a helper and an old truck for parts and tools. I say, "Get some sleep, load rest of the junk in morning and start back to Daytona. I'm going to Charlotte with the wounded capsule car and then on to Daytona." I get to Charlotte 5:00 am. "No, you can't see Fireball."

"OK, Let me talk to the doctor"..."At 5:00 am? You out of your fuckin' mind?"

"Bullshit! " I go to his room. He's out of it, they got him hooked up to all kinds of gadgets. A savvy nurse race fan gets me in hall and gives me the real dope. Says his worst burns are in the groin area.

REAL RACER'S PROVING GROUND

I say, "Leave out the boring details. When can he screw again?"

She says, "Smokey, if he lives, that part of his life is over with." Well, knowing Fireball, he's already dead.

I go back to my tow car, skin up a trailer fender getting turned around (I was in a hurry and came into hospital the wrong way). I decide to take a nap before I do something really stupid. Cop wakes me up, says, "Move, or your ass goes to jail." I say, "Does your jail have a good bed?" He gets wired in, he's a big Fireball fan, so I get escort to an Indian reservation the North Carolinians stole from Indians and named "Rock Hill." By 1:30 pm, I got the mess back to Daytona and I finally sleep. After a month or so, the phone call edged in black comes: Fireball's gone. Time to play the seven and six game. You know, this shit is happening much too often. Marshall and Fireball on each side of the Boot Hill road, 100 yards apart. Too many? Is about 25 too many for 15 years?

I don't think the capsule car episode can be closed without a brief description of the performance George Hurst our sponsor put on. How often do you think one man and one woman fucked for 14 days non-stop, 24 hours a day? Thought so. Now I'll explain this event, George is a neighbor of mine in Daytona (next door). He's married to, I believe, a nice German lady, and parks her in Daytona. The Hurst Gearshift Company, in 1964, is 'bout number one racecar aftermarketer in the United States. George is a nice guy. Sharp, hard worker, but born with 40 percent tomcat genes. He could go from a serious business conversation to the twist of the head, "I'll meet you in the parking lot" deal in five seconds. Just before we leave for Indy, George gets me to one side and says, "I won't be able to get to Indy much because of all my business commitments, but when I do come to visit, see if you can find a nice lady with a strong sex drive who will help with my phobia 'bout being in a locked room by myself."

Just what I need. Besides presiding over the birth of the capsule car, Bobby Johns rookie tribulations, I gotta be a pimp for George. 'Bout the fourth day at Indy I meet a lady who is an ex-beauty queen and is doing odds and ends for Goodyear. She comes by to compliment me on the goofy capsule car (and she's got her eye on Colin Chapman). I say, "Thank you, and you sure have a sexy li'l ass, plus a pretty neat set of titties, if they are real." She says, "I was Miss Italian Airlines." I say, "I have a job in mind for you, but I need to interview you in a less public place (we were at the pit fence). I say, "How 'bout a sandwich?" She says, "Good, I'm starved." I have a room at Mayfair Motel for the month for George, it's ten minutes away. We get in car. By the time I hit 16th Street my zipper is down and she disappears. An hour later, I stagger out of the room leaving her there. 2:00 pm the phone rings. "Hi, I'm at airport. Can someone pick me up?" "Sure George, 15 minutes."

I go back to his room. She says, "Oh good, can we do it again?" I say, "You are now George Hurst's personal secretary, 100 bucks a day till June first, with a $200 clothing allowance. Take me back to garage. You pick Hurst up at airport." I never saw Hurst, and never saw the lady again till May 20th. They stayed in that room 24 hours a day for 14 fuckin' days (literally). She came by the garage on the 15th day and told me she could hardly walk, and that George was the only man in the world who ever satisfied her. (Hell, I thought I did a pretty good job.) By the way, one of her boyfriends was George Wallace (yup, the governor of Alabama). So, I think in all fairness it can be said George was a world-class fucker besides his other "attributes." George Hurst was a good man who got all fucked up. I really don't know the story, but one sad day several episodes later in his life, he terminated himself.

The car got it's wounds repaired and some of the negatives were fixed. Gonna go back to Indy in October for a Goodyear tire test. Disaster rears it's ugly head, a USAC rule change has historied the car. A rule aimed at Granitelli's turbine car and Mickey Thompson's "roller skate" cars, caught the capsule car. "No part of body can exceed a line pulled from inner rim tire edge from front to rear." The capsule intruded into this space with no way to change it to conform. Oh shit, fucked again by the fickle finger of fate.

First week of February, 1965, Tony Hulman calls and asks, "Smokey, I don't see an entry for your car." I say, "Tony, a new rule killed it." Tony says, "I want to see car run again, can I bring Henry Banks, vice president of competition who is an automotive engineer, to look at car and help devise a way to conform to new rule?" "Sure, come on." After a day Henry says to Tony, "He is right, no way." I say, "Change the rule, it would take three minutes to fix it with a pencil." In real life, it never happens, so after pigeons roosting on car and shitting all over it, we clean it up and donate it to Indy museum (three years later).

It resides up there in the museum in the Indy Hall of Fame mostly in the cellar. It's 36 years old now, and could use some cosmetic repair, but it's runable and still a mental challenge to the purist open wheeler experts. The capsule car had some very good chassis features, with a little luck, if car had qualified; I believe several of it's concepts could have established a simple front suspension trend. The racing world is famous for its "what if's," the capsule car was a very viable example.

So, in February '65, there was no way to run and nobody offered me anything that had any promise. Rear engine cars are in now. I like that. V-8 engines seem to be on verge of taking over and somehow this affected me like 50 gallons of ice water. Foreign engines, foreign chassis. Actually a Ford push rod masterminded by Colin Chapman (a limey) won the '65 race. I tried to get Chevy to tackle Indy with a single stick overhead cam in a special stock block classification. What really happened was the one car racer with his innovations was now up against major automotive marketers who suddenly dedicated large-large budgets (by our standards) to position chosen Indy contenders. Strangely, the experts were foreigners, although Dan Gurney gave 'em hell till 1970. I was raised in an era where it was 100 percent American, the flag, apple pie, hamburgers/ French fries, and Ford cars. In 1965 Indy without realizing it started selling out to a "world concept" rather than the "American format" as used for the previous 25 years. Indy started as an international event, staggered around from 1911 to 'bout 1925, and then the race became quite Americanized by the Miller engine. By the way, as far as I'm concerned the Miller and the Offy are one and the same. Nope, Chevy never come close till 1955, Chevrolet brothers and all. Chevy was a 4,000 pound lead sled that couldn't even spin a wheel if your rear wheels were sitting on oiled asphalt.

I guess the '64 capsule car finished branding me as a kook. I'm hot on gold mining and finding oil in Ecuador, I'm deep into alternate energy – solar, wind, geothermal, hydrogen, electric cars, wave technology, ocean temperature differential. Everything but atomic energy. (I was then, and still today, of an opinion that unless someone finds a way to neutralize nuclear waste, "Don't fuck with it." It's half life is beyond my comprehension – let alone it's full life) I listen to '65 race in jungle on a short wave radio (very poor reception) while helping on a "fishing job" at 11,000 feet.

Jim Clark/Colin Chapman with a Lotus car, all English, wins. Only American deal is Firestone tires and NASCAR's Wood Brothers lightning fast pit crew. The door to Indy is wide open to any and all comers, reference nationality. This was step one in the give-away of Indy to the green carders.

Here's the problem. The Indy drivers, tech people, in short, the whole Indy family needs to be American, because the fans have to know 'em and care who wins, have to follow their adventures from "day one" to "lights out." The American race fan wants to know and understand the fundamentals we race by. "He" or I should say "she and he" are first, driver fans; cars are second, engines third. If NASCARs drivers could competitively interchange into Indy cars, Tony would need a million seats around that joint (if they drove

REAL RACER'S PROVING GROUND

American cars with American engines).

Read this two or three times Tony.

1965 and 1966, I had no offers to race Indy. Oh sure, couple chicken-shit loser deals. So, I proceed to wean my way away from racing. The Ecuadorean adventures with cannibals, head shrinkers, 30-foot snakes, 25-foot crocodiles, gold and diamond hunting, oil drilling and production adventures, learning to live off the jungle. My dreams are of volcano heat and waterpower. Had as much excitement as I could handle. In 1966 I'm settling down a little. Oil, gold and alternate energy have me so preoccupied, plus my work with the "hot vapor engine," that I don't seem to miss Indy, and I still got a plate full of stock car racing activities. The '66 Indy race is won by Graham Hill and Lotus, both English, using a special overhead cam Ford Indy V8. Now it's four foreigners out of top ten. The car owner, John Mecom Jr., and Firestone tires, are only American stuff in the deal. The change is underway. The Limey's got a grip on our balls now. Again, I listen to race in South American jungle oil field. I miss it, I want to play, but have no idea how to compete against the new competition, which has very expensive financial requirements and now is a year round job, no longer a four or five-month effort. This era birthed the sponsor, a serious sponsor. And in eight years the game's gone from three zeros to six zeros. Man, that's inflation. That is inflation.

1967 I get offers. None worth a shit, 'cept one, the deal I took – Goodyear. Around December 1966, Goodyear's Larry Truesdale, the boss then, asked if I'd consider a chief job for Indy '67.

Chevy was working the hell out of me. I was way behind in the February '67 Chevelle project. The Indy deal included a rookie Formula One driver. I'd learned best way to say "no" was to say, "Sure, send 100 grand with a contract." March '67, I'm at Atlanta with the Chevelle and Turner driving. We'd sat on pole in Daytona and "blew" around the end of the race, and we were the fastest car at Atlanta. I'm having dinner at the airport motel by myself. Here comes Truesdale and three lieutenants. Ask if he can, "sit and talk." I say, "Sure." He throws a 40 grand check on table and says, "Here's a contract, you sign, you own the check." I push it back saying, "I don't want to work for anyone," and thank him for the offer. He says, "What do you want?" I say, "I own the car and the driver gets 50 percent, I have right to fire driver if he don't stand ready to qualify first day, Goodyear pays for any help and special tools I need for the job, and all travel expenses, deal ends midnight of race day." He says, "No way." I say, "Gentlemen, this meeting is over, thank you and good-bye." (I learned this from Cole.) I also learned a good chief needs a fancy wood hi-buck brief case with very loud locks. Nope, never did get one.

9:00 am the next morning, here's Truesdale with contract like I wanted. I took the 40 Gs, three hours later Turner gives the Chevelle it's first flying lesson coming off of four. That didn't hurt it, but a bad landing totally ruined it. Total junk, a squash job. Local car squasher made it a 4x4 cube I set by the shop door. The only car I can get is a Gurney Eagle; matter of fact Gurney was building it for Goodyear. 'Bout April 4, we get it off a plane in Chicago and truck it to Daytona. It is a cigar looking car without an engine. On April 6th this car is entered with a Ford four-cam engine, normally aspirated, 255 cubic inches. I get couple engines from Ford by April 8. Hell, I never saw one till I opened the crate. I've got 22 days to show up at Indy with a race ready car. I've got one full time helper, T. A. Toomes and my boy, Smokey ('bout 18 years old at the time)

I put the engine on the dyno. I'm disappointed. I decide to clean up the race car body, fare in the engine, run inner and outer wheel discs and backing plate fairing to reduce wheel drag, and use elliptical metal for suspension components. For the engine, I get more aggressive cams made, and open up the cylinder head ports; in short, I run it 500 rpm more and picked up 40 horsepower.

409

Got no sponsor...what about a driver?

This whole deal was bad. Goodyear getting four Formula One drivers Indy rides. All rookies at Indy: Mike Spence, Jochen Rindt, Dennis Hulme, the current Formula One champion, and I can't remember the fourth driver. I say, "I'll take Spence." "Sorry he's gonna drive for Granatelli, a turbine car." "OK, I'll take Rindt." "Well, so and so wants him, we've half-way promised him." I say, "I'll take Dennis Hulme." They say, "Great." That's what they wanted. We arrive at Indy last day of April half dead. T. A. Toomes, Smokey Jr. and myself, with a bad motel deal. In a real-life a whorehouse catering mostly to black patrons, but that's not the problem. It is too damn far away from the track.

May 1, 9:00 am, "Hello driver." A New Zealander 'bout five foot nine, a little on the porky side, ruddy face. This don't turn out to be love at first sight. He has a friend of mine, Jack Brabham, with him and a famous racecar engineer I know a little, Brabham's chief designer. (Can't remember his name.) Jack was Denny's car owner and Jack's company designed and built the Formula One championship car Denny won the championship with. Jack says, "Would it hurt your feelings if the engineer and I did the chassis brainwork and you do the engine?" "Hell no." How can I get pissed, I got two world's best chassis men free. (Jack had already won the Formula One championship himself.) Jack calls the shots and we do the work.

Denny's got a little problem; he has read too many of his press stories and has a standard racer problem. He's pussy goofy. He's like the dog Pluto I used to have, he's either doing it, looking for it, or just finished it.

The starting grid just before the race. (photo: Indianapolis Motor Speedway)

The first week is driver's test and then we work up to speed. The whole week we are in a spring, shock, and sway bar changing contest. 7:30 am to 1:30 am ('bout five days). We run a week. He's four miles per hour short and bitching.

Meanwhile, Smokey Jr. is missing. He is fed up with my slave driving and yelling and goes to Asheville, North Carolina to Banjo Matthews' shop and goes to work. To this day he's never discussed this unusual method of job termination. Smokey is his real name. A mistake on my part. Next sentence is always "What's your real name?" Love could have been a part of this movie. Shortly afterwards, I was told Smokey got married in Asheville. Nope, I didn't get invited. I think three or four years later I saw him again. By now he is a super welder and fabricator with race car driver's aspirations.

Back at Indy '67, it's now it's T.A. and me. More chassis changes regarding static settings, ride height, caster camber, toe in. On the tenth day, Jack says "Do you mind if we leave? I've got to get back to feed my kangaroos and wallabies." By the way, Jack's driven Indy couple times by now, he knows the problems. What can I say, 'cept, "Thanks for the help you've given me." I think 30 seconds later I could hear their tires screeching as they came out of the tunnel and turned right on 16th street headed for the airport.

The car I had was 'bout as good as any of the top five or six, but, as I've explained, to qualify at Indy you have to drive five miles per hour over your head. If you don't you ain't gonna be one of the 33 fastest, and that's the name of the game. The Thursday before the first Saturday qualifying, I hear "I'm going back to England first qualifying weekend, and qualify last weekend, I need many more laps and car has to improve."

"Pussy" to Denny was called "bird," women were "birds." (I guess in New Zealand you have to catch 'em like a rooster does to screw 'em.) At track closing, 6:00 pm, Denny was long gone after a bird. Friday, one day left. Denny says "I'm going to England tonight." We are stuck two or three miles an hour short and getting no place. 6:00 pm Denny changes clothes. I ask for a few minutes. I ask if he's read his contract, he says "Certainly, and so has his barrister" (whatever that was – apparently a lawyer) I said, "Did you notice I have a right to kick your ass out and put Jochen Rindt in tomorrow? " "No-no, not so." I say, "Here's a copy, read the shit colored yellow." He hates the idea of being replaced, he complains car ain't right. I say, "Does car dart on straights sometimes jump two lanes either way? " He says, "Exactly, it's as if you rode with me." I continue, "In the corners does it feel like it's on ice and you are on the edge of push or loose all the way through the corner in the 'on throttle' parts?" He says, "It's as if you are in the car with me, man it's bad." I say, "If you get a good shot off of four and two do you get a little wheel spin? And does the car get twitchy?" He said, "Exactly! " I said, "Denny, you need to make you're mind up whether you want to risk your fat ass or get behind the concrete wall with me. Every fuckin' car out there that's in the running does all that bad shit and more. If you ain't willin' to extend yourself, go back to Europe." I told him, "I'm gonna give you 'bout 25 more horsepower for tomorrow. I'm gonna bump steer all four wheels to damn zero, by 9:00 am tomorrow morning this car will be as ready as it ever will be to qualify." I said, "Either go to driver's meeting and draw a qualifying number or I will. I'm gonna get qualified tomorrow with you or without you." "If I leave who you gonna get?" "Jochen Rindt" (course I've still never even spoken to Rindt).

He is pissed, he says, "If I stay and kill myself tomorrow it will be on your conscience forever."

I say, "If you believe that shit go home. I've never had anybody hurt bad, let alone get dead."

(By the way, I have already driven the car here enough to know its character.) I told him, "You are a good fuckin' race driver or you'd of never won that champion ring. But you've been fuckin' off here all month chasing pussy and waiting for this deal to come to you." (T.A. and I stayed all night working)

9:00 am Saturday morning practice, as he gets in I tell him, "The car and tires are good as it gets, drive it like I tell you, stay off the brakes and when you get back in it, stay in it." Man, he is pissed. I get the bullshit 'bout "if I get killed" again. Three warm up laps and then the fifth, sixth and seventh lap are fast enough to sit outside front row. I bring him in. Goodyear is going ape-shit. Denny is grinning like a hog in a mud hole. First time he calls me "mate." He says, "It's easier going fast than going slower." I say, "No shit."

In qualifying I tell him to give signal to start qualifying run second time he passes big oak tree coming off of four. You won't believe it. The dumb shit wastes his best lap, forgets to put his hand up. By the fifth hard lap tires are gone, so instead of front row we wind up 'bout in fourth row. He is one happy son-of-a-bitch. Suddenly he remembers he hasn't been laid in 24 hours. Said, "He couldn't sleep a wink Friday night." He disappears till noon Sunday. We run all week with full fuel load, traffic, hot days, windy days, damp days. I hate to report, Saturday night after we qualified him, I ate and got bench racing at the Holiday Inn North and ended up in a depraved adventure with three hookers from Dallas, who worked the Kentucky Derby and figured to come back for Indy qualifying. I guess they figured best way to get in the racing world was to advertise. They were the most aggressive three-some I ever saw, and when they wore me out they found ways to continue without me.

Next day, I put 'em in Denny's room and when he came in with a "bird" he caught, he had three naked "Dallas birds" in his bed. He never thanked me or even mentioned it, but those ladies did learn racing, and I think very profitably. I guess what I did was kinda "pimpy," but remember I never took any money. Samples? "Yes," but hell you would have done the same thing.

OK, It's show time, but weather goes to shit.

We start but rain stops us. It takes two days to get it done 'cause of the weather. This is bad-bad deal. The mental drain of one start is bad. The second try compounds the spooky mental gymnastics you experience. By then I've learned to use the word "spooky" for all unknown or unpredictable happenings. Kinda like flying in icing conditions for two hours with no de-icing boots on your wings. We sit under the tarps lined up on track waiting for rain to quit, asking and answering same dumb questions a thousand times. We are all 'bout as spooky as 100 cats in a room with 100 rocking chairs.

When the race finally happens, Denny shows he is a racer and despite all the distractions he ends up fourth. I don't go to dinner to get the money, Denny gets check, we split it by mail. He is gone from my life as if we'd never met.

Goodyear calls couple days after I get home, says, "Lindsey Hopkins lost two cars, one before Indy and one at Indy." Would I "mind lending him my car if he agreed to return it in good condition? " "It is just for the Milwaukee race? Roger McCluskey is the driver." "Sure, come and get it." Next day "Say, could "so and so" borrow your spare engine? We'll return it overhauled in three weeks." "Sure." This is 39 years later, I've never seen the car since and the engine ain't back yet. I hope who ever has the car is taking good car of it. I have the original title and bill of sale to the car and one day I may decide to take it back. Matter of fact I know where it is now. Isn't it illegal to sell somebody's car and give phony title info?

Well, 1968 rolls around. Nothing exciting pops up. I hear Denny is gonna drive for Gurney. After running fourth in '67 and Goodyear stealing my car and spare engines, I thought they would be glad if I asked for a job for '68. Nope, the reception I got was colder than a well digger's ass: "In a meeting," "out of town," "He'll call you, don't call him." Goldsmith, who was really wired in at Goodyear by then said, "You fucked up Smoke, you should have give Larry Truesdale some money back, so you're on the shit list." Well, OK, I'm up to my ass in alleygators working for Chevy and the alternate energy projects, Ecuador gold mine and oil field plays. I'm also deep into the hot vapor engine, so I've got no time to give money to anybody. My code of the hills had zero tolerance for this kick back shit anyway. Actually it really pissed me off. South America operates every thing that way and I hated it. (That is in '60s, '70s '80s, today I don't know)

For the '68 race I can remember being on a well in Alka (cannibal) country with a little Sony short wave radio walkin' in circles, climbing up the derrick trying to keep tuned in to the Armed Forces radio broadcast. Bobby Unser wins. Buck (a partner in an oil field service company) and Leonard (other partner) were there on a fishing job. Buck gets lucky and gets it on the second entry. I found a big snail and some yucca. I remember eating yucca soup and the snail for supper and thinking "what a difference a year ago." Nope, I didn't miss it that day. I loved the jungle, I was happy for Bobby Unser and was sound asleep by 8:00 pm. Ecuador is an eastern time zone schedule.

1969 Indy

During '68 and early '69 I left Pete Estes and Chevy to go to work for Mr. Knudsen, then president of Ford. Knudsen says, "I want to quit running the special double overhead cam and now turbo charged Ford engine. I want you to run Indy this year, and then start to build a 350 pushrod engine for 1970." I want to quit using special non-stock engines after Indy '69. "You build a new building and store those double overheads and maybe give 'em away, but go to Indy now ('69)."

I say, "Well, shit, ain't it a little early? It's only April 2, that leaves 29 days to show up at Indy race ready. I'll need a car won't I? Only one I can buy is a Gurney. Remember money is not a problem when the Boss says, "Do it!" "You do what ever it takes." Well, Gurney was the Indy car champ with his '67 and '68 eagles, but his '69 eagles should have been called a "goofy bird." Man, it was a high drag, nose flying, no good motherfucker car. ("You're welcome Dan." This is how I make friends. By the way your treatment of me never got to be like a long lost friend.)

Cash deal, I get car April 7. No engine, "engines are here." Car is built to take a four-cam turbo Ford. I'm running the turbo Ford in dyno. Man, I have trouble with fuel injection. It's a Bendix product and I just can't get to like it, same with turbo chargers and waste gate.

Car? I don't have a clue, so all we do is "black and gold" it. I walk around it, sniff it, it's damn sure not love at first sight I can tell you that. Who's gonna drive this 42,000 bucks worth of Eagle tech? Joe Leonard, who I figure can drive the shit out of an Indy car, has jacked around too many people to get a ride anywhere else. He's pissed off Foyt, Firestone, Goodyear for starters, and I smell "boycott." Joe is targeted for the bench for Indy '69. So I call some of his friends (most racers both motorcycle and car, liked Joe). Everett Brashear, a coon-ass who raced Joe on cycles (Everett's 'bout as real as it gets, and savvy). Everett says, "Smoke, I believe you two would make a tough team." I call Joe. "Wanna drive my car?" "Maybe, I'm sorting out 'bout ten other offers." April 14? I say, "I need answer in 48 hours, I'll pay ten grand and 50 percent." He says, "Whoa man. You need to kick the "ten" way the hell up." I say, "Joe, you are gonna be pounding the alleys at the garage area and gonna end up in a shit box on second weekend. The equivalent of going from the Yankees to a "d" league team. You're blackballed and you are flat fucked. You got sixty hours to be standing here for a cockpit fitting and paper signing, or don't bother to even call back." He says, "Nobody but me left worth a shit, without me, you get a second weekend ol' stroker." I say, "You're right Joe, if you don't want to drive it I'll put a chimpanzee in it and run it with a remote control from a helicopter." He says, "No deal."

I hang up. An hour later, "I'll be on the red-eye tonite…be there 'bout noon tomorrow."

Joe gets here as advertised and I like him right off the bat. He says, "Can I get copy of contract to wire my attorney right away? " I say, "There won't be a paper contract unless you're short of toilet paper, I've checked you out and apparently you can't read, 'cause you don't pay any attention to contracts." I offer my hand and say, "Here's your contract, a handshake and a check for ten grand." He says he "needs a contract." I tell office manager to call a zoo and see how much we can rent a chimpanzee for. I tell Joe, "Good-bye." He says, "OK, we got a deal" and shakes on it.

Let me tell you, this Joe Leonard was a race car driver, that son-of-a-bitch didn't fuck around with the

I like 'er better with the new turbo. (photo: Indianapolis Motor Speedway)

wind, hot oily track, he run the shit out of it and came in and told you what it was doing.

If you listened and fixed it, he went faster the first hot lap after. Well, car would push, had big area wide nose. Simply stated, faster you went, more nose lifted. I kept cutting it off. To be honest, I was guessing, it could have been chassis. But, Dan drove one himself and he couldn't get it going. Of, course Dan was doing it the hard way with 319 cubic inch Weslake headed stock engine. So we can't help each other, and if he could have helped me, he wouldn't have.

I think Dan Gurney was just about a perfect man. Super driver, good car builder, smart, gentleman, didn't drink or smoke, chase girls, didn't even curse. So, you see, he was an oddball racer, a social misfit with us. I didn't mind that he was a polite citizen, but Dan Gurney had a trait I didn't like. He was a self-centered egotist. But, he didn't complain if he got screwed around by competition. Well, hell, who's perfect?

I remember in 1967 I was trying to get Dennis Hulme some help in driving pattern, along with brake and throttle management (in them days no way to flat foot it), I ask Dan if he'd help. "Sure," he says. I get Denny, take him to Dan who says, "Just come down this straight away and when you get close you'll see turn one, turn left. You can't miss it. Then do the same thing three more times and you're back where you started from." Do you remember Danny boy? Don't get me wrong. Dan's one of ten best US racers of all time, but he did have a few hen-house traits. I guess he was allowed.

Well, we know we'll qualify, but the engine is a can of worms. I can't get it to drive like it should.

Before I came to Indy, I called both Goodyear and Firestone 'bout same deal: money. Ten grand to run either tire (they were about 'even steven' really).

Both said, "Ain't got any money, spent our budget." OK, guess we ain't scaring anybody yet. Foyt's got a pair of castings for a Hilborn injection kind of a deal. Something he and Herb Porter did together. I asked A.J. for a pair of unmachined castings. He said, "OK," but Herb Porter got pissed (guess I wasn't on his list of good guys). He complains to Foyt a little too strongly so Foyt smacks him in the snoot. Herb falls back and breaks a hip (I think). Whatever it was it lasted several months and several pair of crutches. Well, you know you have li'l disagreements like this in racing and I think Herb Porter has earned his Indy stripes maybe three times to whatever I achieved. But Herb, when he smacked you one time and you spun around and hit the ground I did laugh. I just couldn't help it. Like so many others in those days, "Don't fuck with Super Tex."

We build up our own fuel injector copy of A. J. and Herb's. I change blowers and waste gates, and doctor up some cams. I met a guy named Charley Sarle who worked for Schwitzer, an Indy company that made crankshaft torsional balancers, turbo chargers and wastegates. I like his stuff better than Bendix, so I modified our exhaust system to mount Schwitzer stuff. It's now 'bout six days from first qualifying. We are running.

You can see we got an engine, and if we can tame chassis a li'l more, number 44 is gonna be trouble. Now the sun is shifting and is starting to shine on Joe and me. Ford engineers, along with Firestone and Goodyear had ignored us up to here. Larry Truesdale, Goodyear's big shooter comes by, says "Say, I found ten grand for you." I say, "Larry, Ford's paying for this deal, and I'm going to go with whatever tire I figure is best. Thank you very much." Right behind Truesdale is McCreary from Firestone. "Say, I'm going out on a limb, but I can give you ten grand to run our tires." I give him the same story. Two days later I got sixty for me and sixty for Joe. One hundred twenty grand for one race.

Ford's engineers are now asking, "What can we do for you?" I tell 'em, "Stay the fuck out of our garage is probably biggest contribution you can make." Ashland's Valvoline oil is the next problem. In my view it can't handle the extreme pressure, and won't get job done. I find old Ray McMahon, the Mobil Oil wizard. He gets me a drum of Mobil FR 50 SAE. Now I'm in business. I cut oil pressure to 100 pounds from 180. I believe all 33 starters had Mobile FR in 'em that came out of Valvoline cans. Jack Stamper was Valvoline's head honcho on Indy cars. Ask him when you see him if that's a fact.

Meanwhile 'Jose' (Joe's nickname, he's from San Jose) has decided to fuck with the world again. He's got sixty in the tomato can, I'm busy and Parnelli Jones has a new four wheel drive fuckin' monstrosity that Firestone's sponsored, and with mucho Firestone loot in it. Next thing I know Joe's test driving it. This is Wednesday, three days before qualifying starts. The deal is, if he can qualify it, he gets 50 Gs plus 50 percent of the purse. Wednesday evening I corner him 'bout 6:00 pm, and say, "Joe, you decide by 9:00 am what you're gonna drive. If you drive the Firestone car and don't give Goodyear back their sixty, you ain't gonna drive anything 'cause you're gonna spend some time at the Methodist hospital." I say, "If you return Goodyear money to me you can keep the ten I gave you and still be healthy."

Well, he says, "He's sorry, he'll drive "the platypus" (that's what I called the nose flying eagle). I called it the platypus 'cause it had a wide flat nose. (Remember, by now I'm damn near "Jungle Jim"). Nobody got the Firestone four-wheeler in the show. I don't think it ever raced, ask Parnelli.

Ralph Johnson worked his ass off helping me full time and Dusty Miller helped us quite a bit as a go-fer. He was local, had a body shop, helped part time, but really his help was very important. We had other free help and I feel kinda shitty not remembering their names. I got a suggestion. If you're a new racer and

Looks sorta like a platypus, don't it? (photo: Indianapolis Motor Speedway)

intend to make your life racing, keep a diary (in a safety deposit box), so if you decide to write a book you'll have all the dope in order.

Caution: I kept a diary of my World War II adventures. When I'd been married a year or two my wife found it and read it. I can't tell you how much fuckin' trouble the goddam book caused me. Plus, now I could use it to clear up some of what I've forgotten or got dim. Or maybe keep this part a lot more accurate. (Hell no, I never saw it again.) I was never a racist, and with my earliest adventures being in Africa playing with the French Foreign Legion pilots. I was single. I got married in 1940. War's over. My "then" wife seemed quite put out that I apparently didn't let race or color limit my sexual adventures. Hell, I'm not sure it wasn't as good or better, but kinda shakey in real hot weather.

Racing would have never happened without those thousands of go-fers and helpers we found in our travels. A go-fer was a 101 percent race fan, and in many cases as qualified as a peer in his field. They solved many of our problems, turned a lot of nuts, washed a lot of parts and used hundreds of cans of racecar polish. The go-fer is extinct now. He has been exterminated by the hard card carrying, green carder, and by the funding changes whereby permanent employees (multi-functional) staff race crews, see to unanticipated needs, and provide even a percentage of excess help at show time.

We got 'bout a fifth place car, I never cured the "push," and even if I had of, at best we'd have been a second place car due to some extenuating circumstances regarding how to properly calculate the engine's displacement, where instead of two and two equaling 163 cubic inches for a turbo entry, two and two equaled 255 cubic inches for a few of the cars. I'm gonna skip the whole story here because if I told the real truth it would turn some of Indy's greatest moments to cheating shit. Even now, as I think about it, I want to puke. Sad part is, it wasn't necessary, competition was good enough to do it straight up.

As I tell you this story I need to tell you I probably cost Joe Leonard the race. At 300 miles Joe is the toughest kid in the game. Three or four hot shots were in trouble, or "out." Fifty laps to go. Mario's leading, Joe is right behind him stroking, begging me to let him pass Mario. Pit strategy, race management, call it whatever, I got a plan, which ends up to be a trip to shitsville. Joe has to limp around with a cane now, and has had to for thirty years. Maybe if I hadn't been so "race smart" Joe's life would have been 180 degrees opposite what it is today.

We need to pit at 50 laps to go. So does Mario. The night before the race, 'bout 2:00 am, I'm working on my car. Here comes Clint Brawner, Mario's chief mechanic. Clint is the stereotype Indy "chief." Been there many years and he is 'bout good as it gets. I'm talking '40s, '50s, '60s and '70s. Clint is chief on the STP car, Andy Granatelli's car, Mario's car, called "the Hawk III." The poor ol' hawk has rear end problems. Clint got some bastard kind of transaxle. Or at least a bastard ring and pinion. He's got four pair of gears (ring and pinion) that apparently got mixed up. He's also got a sharp rookie mechanic named Jim McGee. Together they can't get a decent tooth pattern.

He says "Smoke, can you help me? You're sharp on gear mesh." I'm nearly caught up, just gonna work few more minutes and take a nap in the garage so I say, "Hell, yes." Clint's always been good to me. Well 'bout 5:00 am, it turns out there ain't no good match possible in any combination. I tell Clint, "Here's all I can do, I can get this deal right when engine is pulling, but when Mario decelerates, then there will be a high wear problem, but he can help this enough to make it. Get braking started before decell to keep teeth together on the good side. Gonna take more brakes, but that's not a problem."

At 300 miles, I notice when Mario decelerates his rear axle is really whining, he's apparently forgot, or never heeded my driving tip. Well Joe wants to pass Mario. I decide we'll fuel shortly; we hold 75 gallons (475 pounds). At 375 miles we are "one" and "two," nobody close, so I figure, "Hell. Let's wait till we fuel. The extra weight will force Mario to abuse those gears more and they will fail before 500 miles." (Hey, when the green flag drops, so does the buddy-buddy shit).

We are using blackboards, no radio. Joe don't know what I know about Mario's rear axle.

As he goes by he jabs his finger at Mario, I shake my head "no." Here comes Lady Luck and the fickle finger. Just before half way Arnie Knepper crashed coming off of turn four. In the clean up they miss one hose clamp, a genuine Stant hose clamp. Lap 147, Mario's left rear tire picked up that fuckin' hose clamp and threw it through the four-inch thick brass radiator on Joe's car. Only thing we know is water temperature went to the moon. Lap 150, the ball game's over. If I'd let Joe pass, no hose clamp.

Yup…I keep it on the wall over my desk.

Next movie: Joe takes uniform off; Joe goes over to the scoring tower to be interviewed. Mickey Thompson says, "Smoke, if you had a radiator would you go back and run?" I say, "Sure." In a total of 13 minutes and 54 seconds Mickey Thompson ran a half mile to Dan Gurney's garage, took the radiator out of Dan's spare car (broke garage lock), I install the radiator, and we get Joe to abort the interview and re-dress and are back in the race. Joe ran 193 laps to Mario's 200. Joe run laps at 55 seconds, seven laps behind equals six minutes and 41 seconds. When Joe got going again ('bout 163 or 164 laps into it) he lapped Mario seven times in thirty-six laps. But we ended up sixth. No tears, we gave it hell. I fucked up.

When race is over I congratulate Clint and Jim. (Clint's long gone now). I ask Jim, "How's axle look?" He says "It's great!" I say, "Bullshit, pull rear cover off. It's easy to get to for quick gear changes. When he pulls cover back instead of black grease it was silver with pieces of bearing cages and gears. The ring gear was so worn you could have shaved with it. Mario was like Joe, snake bit at Indy, but I want to tell you, the fact Mario's car lasted is a very special miracle. I'm sure Mario could hear all the trouble and died a million deaths in the last fifty laps waiting for the rear axle to quit, but this was a race of no finishers. A handful of cripples split up the loot.

For a mechanic first or sixth don't amount to much of anything. But to a driver, to win Indy then was a brand new world that lasted forever. That year only four cars run 200 laps, fifth place was three laps down and seventh place was ten laps down. Wait. There's more. In 1968, Joe's driving a STP Turbine, got the race won. A wreck, ten laps to go, on restart Joe's turbine goes "phttttttt," fuel pump pooped out, two years in a row Joe's all but got the golden ring. Five years later Joe gets in a big wreck at Ontario, California – he's on Firestone tires, suddenly a tire loses 'bout 50 pounds of air pressure. Ka-bongo! A broke leg. In a giant "hurry up to heal for Indy," something goes bad wrong, Joe's leg won't heal. Too many antibiotics I heard (nobody knows better then). 'Jose' the motorcycle champ and damn near Indy champ ('bout three times), is history. Damn shame, but really in racing a very old movie. Joe's still limping around, still laughs. But as a friend I gotta tell you he was dealt quite a few bad hands then, and not much better today. Joe and I are still friends. We had several other adventures you'll read about in the stock car and jungle parts of these books.

Something of interest: Dan Gurney with his Weslake stock Ford engine finished second in the same lap and on six cylinders for about 100 miles (it was a V8 engine) with same kinda car Joe and I had (a '69 Eagle). This has to do with luck, both good and bad. It shows what a driver Gurney was and it might have been the sorriest Indy race ever run? Was you there? What did you see?

1970

When I got back from Indy I took that car apart to the last rivet. I vowed it would never run again ('cause of it's doggy handling). From some of it's parts, and part of the rear engine Corvette, I started to build a down force car in '70 that I lost because of a hot baked potato that Tony Mucho shoved in his lovin' wife's mouth to quiet her down. Yes, Mamma Mucho run Tony's ass off. Tony run into some medical problems and shortly departed this life. By time I got around to finding out how Tony and his burned mouth wife were doing, a deal was consummated between a junkman and the widow Mucho and the 1970 Indy down force car most likely was turned into a little puddle of steel and aluminum. I couldn't blame Mrs. Mucho, to her it was junk. It got caught in a kinda social cleansing – "Get racing out of Tony's garage." Back then not too many racers wives were race fans as well.

The '69 Eagle looked like a doorstop. The '67 Eagle looked like a cigar. I wish Dan had liked fish, I think a car like a flounder would have been a good shot. Well, with my 1970 invention down force car disaster, I decide "the hell with it." You know, quite a bit of work and 'bout ten grand was invested in the down force car. I tell about the rear engine Corvette in the tech part of my book, but the 1970 down force car act saved the rear engine Corvette's ass. For those of you who see it in the museum at Bowling Green, that car was headed for a junkyard, Herb Fishel saved it's ass by loaning it to me.

Mr. Knudsen gets fired from Ford (August '69), I'm hot to get the hot vapor cycle engine invention in an Indy car. I quit Ford Motor Company. Gold and oil in Ecuador with Kenny Rich and Leonard Schorsch is wide open. I'm talking alternate energy speeches at colleges, judging alternate energy proposals, trying to get government money to get hot vapor engine going. I'm hob-nobbing with atom smashers, space, wind and solar experts. In total, 'bout ten alternate energy possibles. I'm running engines on hydrogen. I'm build them here in Daytona and helping the Perry company run a submarine on one of my hydrogen engines. I'm so busy saving the world I lost my "hard on" for Indy.

I'm not sure what motivated me in '70. I was like horseshit in 1915, I was everywhere. All over the US, South and Central America, Europe. We are gonna run out of oil by 1982 (I thought), and I'm hunting a new form of energy. Atmospherically clean energy. Indy happened and I'm not sure I even went there during the month of May. I spent a lot of time going to sleep thinking and dreamin' 'bout my fighter pilot buddies from Foggia, Italy – the two pollocks. I don't know why. The dreams were weird and upset me. There was a message there but I never understood it. I'd wake up hollering, fighting. I'd break out in a cold sweat, breathing hard. The witch doctors (shaman) that we lived among would shrug their shoulders and say in Quecha 'malaria.' No, it wasn't, that hadn't happened in 15 or 20 years by then.

1971

Only Indy offers are long shots, very poorly financed, no driver, one hundred to one shots. I'm still running 20 hours a day seven days a week on alternate energy and South American gold and oil. Foyt calls and asks me to crew chief Donnie Allison in a year old Coyote. I know the car and I know what workin' with A.J. was like and that right there, was worth two grand a week in cash. But I really liked Donnie, and I foolishly thought maybe I can help him enough to do it to it. Ha! Little did I know what was in store for me at Indy.

Within 48 hours after I arrived at Indy I realized I was in the condition referred to quite frequently as the "Hogan's goat" situation. I was fucked. A.J. called all shots. The year old car should be used as an example on what not to do to a chassis. Poor ol' Donnie was driving his balls off and he was still at least one mile per hour short for a safe qualifying and it was scaring the shit out of him, two out of three laps. Now, Donnie run fourth at Indy in '70 in an Eagle, and won "rookie of the year," so it ain't like Donnie was lost.

Here's the movie; we qualify, Steve Krisloff is next in line to go in a Granitelli STP car. Steve is gonna bump us. This had major significance for both the 'spaghetti bender' and the 'Mad Texan.'

Foyt withdraws Donnie's sick, year old Coyote and gives us a new Coyote. Now we are in business, almost. The rear wing is too high; we get by with it for qualifying. Donnie got shoved in qualifying line with ten practice laps, but race morning disaster struck. Wing's too high. Well, dropping the wing was like a human with a triple dose of ex-lax, very, very loose in the ass end. He can't drive it. Soon as someone got close behind him, Donnie was like on ice, a very delicate feeling. They watch pit stops like a hawk, so we can't help Donnie by raising the wing. But here's what makes it so rough, in this time frame, A.J. was hands down the best and his specialty was going fast in no handling shit boxes. Specially if they were Coyote yallar and had Foyt engines.

Well guess what? Foyt had to drop his wing race morning (or did he?), to pass inspection. And man he had a handful. He did finish third, but in the 200 laps he killed himself 78 times at least.

Coyotes? I called them things "Tasmanian Devils" – untamable, wild cars that could certainly be called mother fuckers. These cars were built by one of Indy's greatest car builders, Eddie Kuzma. Independent suspension and aerodynamics were two areas the old hands had trouble seeing from behind the dinosaurs. Donnie never went back to Indy. I said, "Because that '71 ride scared him so bad," but he says, "Nope, it thrilled him much-much more than he wanted, but had no bearing on his never coming back." Why? I can't answer your question; ask him, he's still going strong in NASCAR. We finished sixth. One good thing 'bout the deal. It didn't raise my income tax ten cents. But really, you could have done it. I was just a robot that A.J. programmed.

Working in the garage. (photo: Indianapolis Motor Speedway)

1972-'75

The 1972 Indy story is about four years long from concept to trash can. Only way I know how to write this so you can follow, since there are so many players, plus this period had an accelerated evolution (most of it not good). Economics and politics were going through rapid and significant changes. The whole concept of Indy racing, as Tony Hulman and his family and employees had established, was being very subtly attacked. Kinda like how a little hole in a dam slowly gets bigger, unnoticed. So only way I can tell this is as you and I are talking, with you asking questions, and with me anticipating lots of your questions. I do have a problem. It's not possible to make this all clear to all race fans. There is such a tremendous difference in racing knowledge from the dyed in the wool, open wheel Indy fan and the fan who has seen one race from a poor seat, or the new electronic breed fan, (TV and Internet) the 110 volters who also read race rags and magazines for explanation, definition and gossip. Unfortunately, most of the editorial they get is highly opinionated, with two major flaws:

(A) Not enough experience from both the writers and the readers.

(B) Influence from potential customers and advertisers.

Some is very accurate and well done, but only a small percentage. OK, Let's plow into it.

'Bout in here it's very clear:
— The day of the "hot shot racing mechanics" with a "good, brave driver" backed by some rich cat with a race season budget of 100 grand was over.
— The day of the once a year Indy racer is over.
— The days of the one car racer are over.
— The days of the race team with a tow car and trailer are over.
— Sponsors are around that will put up a million a year to run the USAC schedule.
— The days of the two-man race team are over.
— The chief, his go-fer and local free help are history.
— The pick-up pit crew is over with. The pit crew is now a paid, drilled, skillful six to eight man bunch of athletes
— The portly 50-year-old beer guzzling race fan, ex-racer, "All I want is a silver badge and a team uniform and jacket," is not competitive. You're talking two laps down.
— The big-big change is: the fun is gone.

Actually, one man turned Indy on it's ass. Roger Penske. He too, had a dream; "Own Indy." Well, he couldn't buy it, so he started "CART, " where he got control of chassis, engines and huge chunks of sponsor money. His act made it very clear if Indy was run as a year round business with the cream of the crop mechanics and drivers, they would control Indy. It became obvious that a team with a $600,000 budget would be ground under the heels of a two million buck budgeted team. I see Indy, the Indy I loved so much, disappearing. Foreign cars, engines and drivers will soon kill the American flavor of Indy and it's 45 American racer heroes in American cars with American engines and American tires. Apple pie, hot dogs, french fries. And all are headed down the tube when the CART cats pushed the flush lever. "Back home in Indiana" survived, the only reminder of an era gone by.

In mid-1971 I decide to build a car and use a push rod Chevy. Indy allowed 208 cubic inch turbo charged. To me a turbo charged engine is like a .45 caliber pistol. It makes the li'l guy and the big shooter equal. So my plan was a pair of turbo's, a $30,000 buck engine in a 40 grand chassis. I never believed the exotic hi-buck engine meant anything to Indy. The magic was the fans knew the drivers and crews, also the gossip, the sound of the racers (un-super charged), the danger, the unpredictability of the race outcome. It was the most important sporting event of the year in the world, and it was accessible to talented American racers.

Well, shit, I thought, if I can build enough power to compete and am short on durability, twenty-five other race teams will join in and in two or three years push rods will be the affordable power source for our new "would be" Indy racers. What we called among ourselves "the real racers." If I'd had my way you'd have to be an American citizen to be accepted at Indy, and cars couldn't cost over 80 grand. You run one car, one driver, and no teams. If you totaled your car and didn't have time to fix it. "Come back next year." There'd be one make tire per year, with one left and one right side tire. Period. The rookie test would decide acceptance or rejection. Age is 18 to 52. No exceptions. (Some guys can still go at 60, but a very low percentage. Good drivers don't want to quit. So as age creeps up on 'em when they have a bear by the tail. They don't know how to let go. As a rule, two bad things happen. The old timer cheats a newcomer out of his shot, and the old timer is a high-risk accident candidate. Why? Eyes, ears, reflexes, brain function, physical condition, are all by natural processes something less than they were. Plus the instinct for self-preservation becomes stronger.

Sure, you say, "Look at Dick Trickle, 60 and still going good." He is one in 100,000, and if he don't quit, he is gonna bust his ass bad. Sure, I know this pisses you off Dick. But if this in any way gets you to your retirement in good shape, I don't give a shit. Dave Marcis: same deal. Petty and Foyt should have been kicked out at age 52. I like 'em all. Still do. They were damn good racers, but that movie is over. A lot of people all the time tell me if I decided to race again, they wouldn't know what hit 'em. The truth is, I would not be competitive. The effort required is way beyond even a 60 year old. Racing is for young people, it's very hard to do a world-class level. (It would be me that didn't know what hit him.)

The test donkey I used for the Indy engine happened to be a 302 cubic inch Trans Am engine. I hung a pair of big turbo's on it and used carbs. For starters, at 4,000 rpm, 780 pounds of torque. It bent all eight rods into a shallow "c." I'm working for Chevy at the time. Vince Piggins is the boss, but my contract is with John Delorean, who is the general manager at Chevy. Vince says, "What the hell are you doing?" I say, "I'm gonna play the push rod boogie at Indy." He says, "If you don't stop I'll fire you." We (GM) are in a lying sneaky "we ain't racing period." "You going to Indy will make it look like we are involved." I laugh and say, "Do what ever's fair." John then calls and says, "Do you want to get fired?" I say, "Not exactly." He says, "Piggins wants to fire you." I'm getting 120 Gs a year working for John, not the usual 12 grand, but I tell John, "I'm going to Indy in '73. If that will 'cause you to need and use "Preparation H" due to criticism from your peers let him fire me. I'm going to Indy: rip, shit, or bust." John says, "Do you what you want to. I need you to come up. I'm building a rear engine Corvette, a Chevy limousine and a half-ton pickup that is like you think will sell. Gonna look like a Mack square cab truck, even have wooden floor boards screwed in." "Am I fired?" "No, but when I get promoted or fired I guess you will be, but not right now." "OK. Say, could I get a raise? I hear you're getting two and a half million and I work harder than you." I believe I heard a faint "fuck you" and he hung up. Seems impossible to please everybody.

Vince shuts up, zero Indy talk, I still do my Chevy job but I only give them 40 hours, and the other 40 go on the Indy job.

When I was at Indy in '71 with Donnie Allison, I went down to the big oak tree in turn one real early one morning. I said, "Old bull, if I come here with a 'jiggler' in '73, would you give me a li'l extra slack?" The old bull let out a big fart, swished his tail and said, "Hell no, this place has one set of rules, 'cept I can't help but favor American racers." He also said, "You better hurry Smoke – the almighty "greenie" is coming like a freight train." In the middle of '72 I get lucky. Mr. Knudsen had quit GM, got fired at Ford and was now head honcho at White Motor Company. Somewhere in here John D. and GM get a divorce. Why? Quit? Fired? I don't know – what the hell difference does it make? He ain't there no-mo.

My new boss, McDonald has as much use for racing and outside consultants as he has for a dose of the clap. Now Vince has the upper hand. Finally, sixteen years later, he's the driver. "Yup Smoke, the budget etc., we gotta cut your pay." I can see a guy on a big black horse galloping towards me holding a big sign saying, "12 grand." I tell Vince, "I'll call you later." (I'm learning to use their shit).

Five things GM taught me very loud and very clearly:

(a) "The price of progress is trouble." (Kettering)

(b) "Don't get mad, get even." (Ed Cole)

(c) "Don't get in a pissing contest with a skunk." (Knudsen)

(d) "Hug 'em as you shove it up their ass." (Estes)

(e) "You don't have to know what you're doing if you got the right friends." (McDonald)

Herb Fishel worked for Piggins. Herb liked the Indy idea, so he busted his ass, took career chances and helped me get the block fixed before the lights went out. Iron block? Yup, iron blocks couldn't handle 1,000 horsepower as it was in '71. We had to make 'em a little thicker here and there. Also, had to beef up the heads in the deck area. Believe it or not, at one time Herb was a racer. He'd work his ass off 20 hours a day seven days a week and probably did to get me those stronger blocks. I was able to put block and heads on a diet. The block race ready was 147 pounds and I got 10 pounds off of each cylinder head with a Bridgeport, doctored patterns and chemical milling. Why all the iron? Rules said so, but the head inspector (a real racer) Frankie Delroy let me know inspectors were stock block fans. They told me, "We won't carry any magnets and there is good black paint that sticks good to aluminum and is polarized."

But they were forced to inspect the shit out of us. Man what a pain in the ass. With the Offy, the limey engine, and the Ford, they measured displacement through the spark plug hole. What a joke. On a Ford for example, you could have a phony balancer with bottom dead center marked in the right place, and you could sneak a 255-inch Ford in where rules called for a 163 incher. Anybody do it? Hell, poles and races were won that way. But the stove bolt, we had to pull both heads every time for qualifying and for the race. Sure, inspectors would hand me the mikes, and once I gave 'em bore and stroke they'd come out to 350 cubic inches. They just wrote it down and OK'd the engine. Did I run big? Nope. To me things like "big engine," "big fuel tanks," were really chickenshit. It don't take any brains for a 255 inches to beat a 163 incher does it?

Why didn't I go aluminum? Power was no problem. 1,000 horsepower at 6,800 and 90 inches boost was easy. 1,300 horsepower at 6,800 with 120 inches boost was there as well. So my problem was durability, not power. Of course I was 70 pounds heavy as compared to aluminum, but I was also sure if we got going good we'd run into rule trouble. The genuine rules said "iron block and heads." I had to use iron even with Frankie Delroy as inspector.

It's a damn shame the racing world never gave Frankie the credit he deserved. He was a life long racer, a Yankee from New Jersey, I believe. He was a riding mechanic, a chief, he did it all. In the seventies he's the chief inspector for USAC. I first met Frank with a problem regarding rule interpretation. I got hot and Frankie came by to settle the deal. My mind's made up; Frankie is a dumb motor mouth Yankee. After fifteen minutes I thought, "This cat is sharp, fair, and got some horse sense." Life is weird. We settle the problem then we both need to take a piss. Well, back in them days in the old garages the pisser and hand washer were in a common area. When Frankie, standing next to me whipped his "tool" out I thought "Holy shit, Donkey Dick the second" (look at the stuff I wrote about Cuba). I'll bet Frankie was a fence bunny favorite in his day. Frank could also see what I saw. Indy was going foreign. He thought the push rod might save the deal.

Well, I'm kinda unemployed as a factory race "anything," but we are giving the Indy turbo project hell. I know we can be competitive on power and now we need a car and go test. I told you I got lucky in '72 when I left Chevy. Knudsen was president of White Motor Company and he hired me to do alternative energy work for White. Big part of White's customers were farmers, so wind generators, solar energy, animal waste fuels, water power, crops produced for energy like ethanol, gasahol, wood conversion to liquid fuel, etc. had possible farmer product potential. Also, Knudsen had seen my hot vapor engine and wanted White Motor Company to be in a position to buy into it. The White job was half my time.

One day Knudsen was here at the shop when I made a 1,300 horsepower dyno run with the li'l Chevy. I told you he was a real racer. Man that thing lit his fuse. "Take it to Indy." "Hell of an idea boss, but I ain't able to buy a car, I'll have to build one, and that's a year's work." He says, "I'll put 100,000 grand in the deal, do it!" Mr. K was also concerned about the foreign intrusion at Indy. His 100,000 grand was his gift to Indy racing. To hopefully keep it American. You know Mr. Knudsen is another major contributor in the evolution of auto racing from nothing to Broadway, who has never been accorded a "thank you" for his involvement, contributions from his own bank account, as well as the coffers of several major motor companies, and his 30 years as a spokesman for auto racing.

Again, the only car available quick is a Gurney Eagle, 1972 model. Looked like a chicken that was losing it's feathers. The front half of the car looked like a racer, but from middle back, everything is uncovered and topped off with a wing. It also cost 42,000 bucks and has three months lead time till delivery for one built to take a small block Chevy with a Hewland transaxle, "a roller." Even then Dan didn't appear too anxious to take my money. You kinda had to kiss his ass to get any response. This came hard for me. I still believed all people should have good manners, and that all humans were 'bout equal. It don't cost anything to practice good manners, and really no excuse for any of us to be dirty. Dan was only game in town, so I had to accept it or build my own car. What stopped that idea cold was I don't think any racer should try Indy with new car and new engine same year (and with a new driver). I knew the '72 Eagle was a good racer, so that gave me a solid foundation to build my dream on.

I made a big mistake. In the beginning I chose to use special carburetors Ralph Johnson and I built (very modified Holleys), but let me tell you, this injection never equaled the power or very good fuel mileage carburetors gave us. I guess I wasted eight months building carbureted engines and doing track test with carbs. The fuel would slosh vertical in the bowls on the banks and the inside jets would get uncovered, and we'd drill a piston (too lean).

Well, I make an injection system from Kinsler parts. Didn't work at all. I couldn't get it to go from a 1,000 horsepower tiger at full throttle back to a 250 horsepower pussycat at cracked throttle.

I then made an injector out of Hilborn pumps and nozzles and check valves. I play the "burn a piston boogie" for three years. Hate to admit it, but I never got it right. I got it real close four-five times, but then I'd get lost trying to make it better. I ended up putting 'bout 25 percent of the fuel into the compressors and 75 percent of the fuel in the separate fuel plenums. I had the plenum pretty close in early '73 when I built one common plenum, but gave up too quickly on it. Remember, I'm doing it manually. Computers ain't here yet. But don't take that sentence as an excuse. Other engines, the Offy for example, did it manually with a little valve Hillborn called the "brain" and did it pretty damn good. Somehow my brain couldn't cope with the problem of changing fuel flow 75 percent in a hundredth of a second strictly with a mechanical pressure differential hardware. Sure I tried the Hillborn Offy deal, but the stove bolt was so responsive the Offy deal wasn't quick enough. Nothing in my whole racing life gave me the challenge, the hours and hours of work, and a steady stream of defeats for three solid years.

Maybe my only vindication is, neither did anyone else then or since. In 1972 I was computer illiterate. In 1999 I'm in same posture. I'd still rather fuck with an eight-foot rattlesnake than a computer. You've heard about the 'Peter Principle?' Well I think when computers invaded racing I hit my limit. Mentally I tried to solve every problem with physics and chemistry. But electronics was gonna be a very important advancement. I failed to recognize it.

I would however like to say the perfect engine or prime mover in the future will not depend on a computer. Once complete combustion is mastered and fuel is improved, a computer will not be necessary. There's an old saying, "The more things change, the more they stay the same." A full circle will happen, and engines will again be quite simple.

Gettin' ready for practice at Ontario. (photo: Jim McFarland)

We test at Indy, Michigan, Ontario, Pocono with various pick-up drivers. We raced at Indy, Michigan, Ontario and Pocono, qualifying anywhere from almost on the pole to the shithouse.

But all this goes on while I'm doing 50 other deals and running a heavy-duty truck dealership.

But every day the lack of money presented roadblocks. You see, by now a million a year for a car was not a wild dream. I really need some fueling help, I didn't realize how badly. Part of this problem was I couldn't afford the cost of help. So in my world, "tomorrow I would fix it." But tomorrow never came. I also was working with a handicap I never had before. That was doing it sober, and the peyote had run out.

There was one more important negative. I counted on others joining me on the jiggler deal and expected some help from collective input of stock blockers. Nope, not even a whisper. Apparently I was a one-man band trying to change the world and my voice simply got drowned out with the accepted state of the art. That, as a rule, is common if the singular voice cannot pick up support. This lone ranger was pissing into a strong wind. It ain't gonna happen. I suppose a major motivator in humans is "does it make life easier with less work?" At this time the racer was sniffing a race ready engine. Only effort required was to 'sign the check.' So, in general nobody else decided to do the "push rod boogie." None of this should be taken as a complaint from me.

The Indy car gave me a fair shake. The average guy after a couple of years would give up. Not me. I'm gonna make a push rod engine winner or die trying. I'm gonna save Indy, but shit, Indy don't want to be saved.

1973 rolls around, I'd entered Indy. Dan's late as hell with the car, and man, we (Ralph and I) work from

8:00 am till 1:30 am seven days a week to get it ready. I need a driver. To me I must pick a "has been" or a rookie. It wouldn't be fair to a current "hot shot" to maybe waste a year on somebody's wet dream. I think, look and ask questions. Finally I'm impressed with Jerry Karl. A Yankee driver who never got a shot at good equipment, but looked to me like he knew how to go fast, had the desire, and I thought, would pitch in and help. In about a week I figured out part of his problem of why he didn't get a shot at the big time sooner. He's a poor boy fighting tooth and nail to get a shot at it, but with the personality of a brick. Well, shit, back then that was common to quite a few good drivers.

For any up and coming drivers reading this, it would be a good idea if you read this part twice. The more a driver knows about the total racecar, the better he will perform. Why? Very seldom does a racecar do everything so to speak, "perfect" for the total race. A good driver can and will adjust his driving pattern to compensate for the developed problem because he understands the physics, including aerodynamics, tire technology and the effect of weather and track condition changes during the race. A good driver will study and work on race cars from day he starts to day he quits. 40 to 60 hours a week, year round. The crew chief depends on driver feed back before and during the race. The accuracy of driver's interpretation of what the car is doing and his ability to give input and understanding to crew chiefs race and pit strategy, is as important as speed itself.

I'd say 75 percent of races won were because of clever and precise pit stops (done with a fast car), that is in references to races long enough to require pit stops. No one in racing today or yesterday knows it all. (Nor will the man that comes tomorrow.) Every week a good racer's skill is honed sharper. Know why? The real race is not between drivers or cars. It's a contest between the driver, car combination and nature.

Setup discussion with Jerry. (photo: Mike Teeguarden)

We have to include planning and luck. They are very important variables which driver and/or crew chief can influence one way or the other.

Whey Foyt was in his prime he could set up the chassis and build the engine and call all the pit stops and changes. So could other so called "special aces." Today that ain't gonna happen. The tech is too complex. But a good driver is still listening and learning. The racecar develops a vibration. What is it? Tire? Engine? Drive line? If driver has a clue he can maybe save the day by pitting, or providing input to crew chief. No race team will ever be successful unless the driver, chief and money like each other and operate off the same page every day. A good driver knows every crewmember by name, as well as each crewmembers trials and tribulations. No driver will ever win a big hi-buck race without a race crew that really busted their asses for him. I don't know of any driver today who does that, but I of course don't know 'em all.

Herb Thomas and Paul Goldsmith were the two good drivers I raced with that were 100 percent involved, and worked their asses off. So did Foyt, but really he went off the deep end too much and could be a real pain in the ass. Fireball and Turner were too busy partying.

Well, back to Indy '73, Jerry Karl is what I expected. Got balls, pushes the button and knows how to steer a race car. Input from him is junk, but we had so goddam much engine trouble we never got a chance to dial chassis in. What surprised me was Jerry showed a strong distaste for work.

He had standard racer traits. As the sun descended towards St. Louis (west) his one hand encircled a beer can and the other hand had fingers dialing for pussy. Not best way to be loved by a two-man crew, working

Trying to keep Jerry's head screwed on. (photo: Indianapolis Motor Speedway)

19 or 20 hours a day, with some 48 hours in a row deals.

I also noticed, he'd never win the Nobel Prize for brains. Herb Fishel was then number two at Chevy, and working his ass off as a go-fer for us. Herb could be an entry into a good Winston Cup ride. Well, Herbie's found a little fence bunny and seems to be quite happy with his discovery. My guess is Herb wasn't too lonesome in bed. I'll be damned if Jerry don't hit on her, and I believe he blowed Herb out of the tub. Next day the cheerful "good morning" disappears, and Herb decides to go back to Detroit. Losing a helper wasn't what I needed.

Jerry did good in driver's test and quickly passed. He's doing a good job hot lapping, but we are in deep

427

shit in the fueling department. It's just burning pistons left and right, no other trouble. Well, the heat generated in the piston burning gave the exhaust valve seats hell as well. Plus, exhaust valve seats are in trouble, rapid wear. I get some alky mixed up with four cc's of tetra ethyl lead per gallon. That takes us out of valve seat wear. The little Chevy had a voice of it's own, it drowned out all other cars and when it was right, it could flat "walk the dog" down the straights. But it didn't hook up clean and sharp off the corners. I'm, almost defeated. Ralph is so pooped out that 3:00 am last qualifying day he is on his knees by the pit fence puking. He won't go to the motel.

Ralph and me during a long ass day. (photo: Indianapolis Motor Speedway)

We finish up 9:00 am, no sleep. The night before three hours of sleep. Here we go, our turn to qualify. It's now or never. Warm up lap is good. First lap is real good. Second and third lap's good. Fourth lap down some, but it's qualified and in good shape.

I'm at the entrance of the pits giving Jerry instructions with sign board and flags (no radios yet) which is all the way opposite from where car goes for qualifying pictures and interviews. I have no golf cart so I have to walk. I'd guess that walk was about three or four minutes, past about fifty race crews and cars. As I got to the race crews those guys gave Ralph and I a standing ovation the whole way down. It never dawned on me that our competitors were watching our struggle, or even gave a damn. Nobody really gave the car a shot in hell to qualify. That deal stirred my soul. I had tears all the way down to the qualifying area. That three or four minute exhibition suddenly made the two-year struggle worth it. The bond that racers had for each other is maybe the biggest loss auto racing experienced in last fifty years.

I watched Penske's teams miss the race in 1995 after winning 10 Indy races, and the exact opposite happened. The racers and fans cheered 'cause they failed to quality. Of those fifty teams congratulating us in '72, at least 20 of 'em didn't make the race.

The '73 race for us was a disaster. In twenty laps we had blower trouble. I patched it up. Soon after another blower problem. By now, after second patch job, I've got 'bout ten first and second degree burns on my hands and arms. The motherfucker then burned a piston and mercifully put us out of our misery. Unsuccessful race results don't do much to strengthen team relationships. As I returned to Daytona I decided Jerry Karl was history in my world. I can only guess Karls' mindset. I think a lot of teams were impressed with Jerry's exhibition of being capable of running Indy and offered him some choices for '74.

The Bull

'Bout 1950 I started having dreams about Indy. Always in the dreams there was a huge bull that sat under the big oak tree close to #1 turn. He, I found, could talk. Man, this sucker had horns two racecars wide. Kinda like a Paul Bunyan bull. I said, "What do you do here, Mr. Bull?" He said, "I am the race, and one way or another I will eliminate all but four or five of all who try and conquer this race. I represent the 1,001 ways for all of you to goof up." Sure, there were other animals in the dream, but you soon had it figured, the bull worked for Mr. Hulman (track owner). Once in a while there was no winner, like 1969, the year Mario won.

If you're gonna get the straight scoop out of this you may have to bone up a li'l on other Indy publications, like Floyd Clymer's year books. Wait a minute, before you start bitching, go see the tons of text and pictures in the archives.

From the dreams I decided to try and stay wired in with the bull. This was second in importance to Harry Quinn's friendship. ('Member in '55 Quinn threw France's ass out in the mud and cinders.)

I learned some of the bull's tricks by listening to him. No way in hell a phony could get by him. When I said, "No winner in '69, that was no reflection Mario wasn't qualified to be a winner, it just meant the bull won and the race went to a bunch of cripple." Hell, Mario's rear axle was cooked. Second place was a stock block (a V-8) on six cylinders.

In '60, day 'fore the race, I said, "Mr. Bull, would you give me a li'l slack for the extra difficulty in dealing with a sneaky, lying driver and co-chief mechanic?" He said, "Nope, you made the deal so you gotta live with it".

Well, 1973 rolls around. I ask the bull, "How bout li'l help on American stuff?" The old bull answered with tears in his eyes; a sad and profound statement. He said, "Smoke, I can't do anything for you. I'm fired after this race, the Limey's, through Penske and Pat Patrick and Carl Hauss, will take this joint over next year."

Well, I never went back to Indy as a racer again so I don't know what happened to the old bull, but I heard Penske sold him to a dog food company.

I notice that the guys who fucked Indy up are gonna run there this year. I wonder what wonderful improvements them assholes will invoke on the joint this time.

OK, I got a year to solve the fueling problem, but I unwisely chose to race Michigan, Ontario and Pocono. Plus, I decided to build my own transaxle, which would let me drop the engine four inches and turn transaxle around where transmission was in front of drive axle. Getting rid of big negative counter weight a Hewland had in their design. Pete Wiseman and his wife, the transaxle gear wizards from California, helped me. $5,500 for first one, and $2,500 for a spare. Can you believe it? For less than a Hewland, I had a better transaxle. We did a lot of the work ourselves, but it was an example of poor boy racing at it's best.

In '74, I decided to cover up the engine and fair all the parts in (the car's in the Indy Hall of Fame Museum if you ever want to take a look at it). The fuel injection, the turbos and fueling scheme is all new and better (we hope). In the dyno, everything is great. For the 1974 Indy race I get together with a neat li'l racer, Sam Sessions. I got to know him from his Mickey Thompson's Indy 1973 thrill show, front wheel drive, four wheel steering and more. So Sammy qualified as the "I ain't scared of weird cars" driver. Now Sammy had the personality of a politician. He was a simple, honest man, who loved to race, and raced anything. Sam, as best as I can put it, was what I called "good people." His word was good. He showed up at 8:30 am and left at 6:00 pm. Nope, Sammy didn't get his li'l fingers dirty.

Working with him was a pleasure 'cept in the chassis feedback department. He was a lost ball in the high weeds. But all the wonderful fueling work was junk, we actually had more trouble than in 1973. We burn pistons every day, work all night to change engines. Every morning we are first out at 9:00 am, By 5:00 pm we are changing engines. Now to change engines in that son-of-a-bitch it was a good eight to

10 hours of hard work. We got another major problem, too. This is an experimental year. Instead of two qualifying weekends, gonna do it all in one weekend. I drew number 64 to qualify. The two qualifying days both had rain. At 6:00 pm on Sunday we are in the starting gate when the closing gun goes off. Shut 'er off, it's over.

We never got a qualifying attempt. To be honest we didn't have any better than a 60 percent chance the car could have qualified. Disappointed? Sure. Bum deal? Yes, it was. But hell, it was all on the entry blank. I signed it and paid entry fee. Did I read it? Hell no, I never did. Well, that evening, 'bout ten teams decided to sue Indy. I had the best-case 'cause we never got out of line and never got a shot at it. "Will I join 'em?" I'm packing up and got my tail tucked in under. This is third time I flunked the test. I say, "Nope, I came here to race, not to make the world safe from various pitfalls that can fuck up a racer's life style." I figured they had a legitimate bitch, but picked wrong cat to play with. Who's got the most friends in the Indiana court system? I already know the answer to that one. Mr. Tony Hulman, in Indiana, reminded me of the story, "What do you give an 800-pound gorilla." Answer is "any damn thing he wants."

So in 1975 I'm gonna take the same deal back to Indy. Sammy has left us. He was in a snowmobile race and the snowmobile got tangled up in a fence and ended his life. So the lights are dim, but Jerry Karl and I decided to try it again in '75. The Indy rules now required a large reduction in boost so much power is lost. Again, a whole new injection fueling system with some turbo changes, but same ol' trouble. Won't drive out of the pits, is erratic taking the throttle coming off the corner. There are times it's doing it almost right, but never like we want it. We have another rough month. By the way, for years the standard Indy deal was "open speedway up for practice on the first day of May, and race on Memorial Day." We were there the whole month.

We get it qualified, but again a terrible struggle. First qualifying day is Saturday. Saturday morning go to breakfast 7:00 am. By 9:00 am I go to the infield hospital. "Doc what you got for a bad belly ache?" In 'bout 20 minutes doc says, "I'm sending you to Methodist hospital. I think you have a kidney stone."

"Kidney stone – what's that mean doc? " "Well, you're gonna have an operation where two doctors who are world renowned experts in going down through the hole in your peter to grab the stone and take it out. They are known as "the fishermen." Second, if they can't get it, you will have to be cut in half and it will be 'bout six months fore you're worth a shit." I say, "Doc, I got to qualify today. I can't go to hospital." He's a smart ol' cat, and says "Oh, I see. OK, see you later."

I walk out of hospital and the pain puts me on the ground by the fence. 'Bout five minutes later doc comes out (he's been watching me all the time). Says, "I thought you went back to qualify your car." I say, "I can't move doc," and I puked. He says, "You want to go to hospital?" I say, "No." I come to in emergency room at Methodist hospital. Man. I got the misery. I hurt so bad I'm trying to bribe nurse with two hundred dollar bills for a shot to knock me out. She won't do it.

'Bout fifteen minutes, here comes the merry fishermen. Oh hell yes. I've seen 'em at the track.

They give me a shot. In five minutes I'm wanting to live again. They say, "x-ray shows this. It's a tiny deal, 'bout like a broke off pencil point. We're gonna try and fish it out in about an hour." I feel a lot better. I say, "No, I gotta go qualify." "Oh I see," says one of the docs. Hey, we are scheduled to work at track hospital in thirty minutes. We were gonna cancel, but if you're going back to the track, hell, ride with us." "O.K. Just a minute, I got to use the bathroom." Five minutes later I'm on the floor puking in the toilet. The door opens and the doc says "Come on Smoke, we are gonna be late at the track." I woke up in the recovery room. The famous fishermen say, "Bad news Smoke. We couldn't hook the li'l son of a bitch. Gonna have to do the whole deal. You're gonna be in here two weeks so I guess you'll have to withdraw your car."

I call Ralph, tell him the story round 9:00 pm, I felt pretty good than so I say, "Come to the parking lot at the emergency ward." My clothes are in the closet, so I then do the goddamnedest TV movie 'sneaking out of hospital room' stunt. I work till 2:00 am, go back to hospital, and sneak back in. Nobody says a word. Pretty slick, no operation Sunday, so I sneak out Sunday night feeling pretty good now. I work till 5:00 am then sneak back into the hospital. Nobody says nuthin'. Monday doctors say, "Maybe we should wait and see if you pass the stone as long as you're not in any bad pain, but you gotta stay here so we can watch you." "Oh sure." As soon as they leave I get ready to sneak out but I've got a visitor. A lady who has driven a long way to see me. In a few minutes it's decided it's possible some sexual therapeutics might make the stone come out. This ends kinda bad. Zora Duntov and Vince Piggins arrive at just about the end of the treatment. (You know you can't lock those hospital doors). I guess it was a li'l embarrassing, but it seemed to work. At least I felt pretty good.

Tuesday night doctors came by and say, "We are releasing you tonight. Here is a tea strainer we want you to pee through so you can check to see if you pass the stone." I say, "Doc, I smoke a pipe and when I piss I need one hand on the pipe and one on my peter. How am I gonna hold the strainer?" I also ask 'em, "If a person swallowed one of those li'l stones was it medically a problem?" They asked me to explain the question. I doubted it would raise my social status, or help, so I declined. As I was checking out the doctors told the nurse to give me a discount since I didn't use the room most nights. Hell, they had it all in writing. The time I had walked out till time I came back, every time I'd snuck out. Nope, they did not give me the discount.

Listening to the engines at Indy in 2000.

Well, we qualified second weekend. I backed power down and we run halfway decent. Through all the '73, '74, '75 race and testing, I'm using a new synthetic oil called "All Proof." A polyolesther (acid and fat) as used by jets. An invention of an old cat from Duluth, Minnesota, I believe named Fagan, a real self-educated brain. ('bout 85 at the time). He told me he invented STP. The trick was to get the polyolesther modified to do all things lube has to do in a reciprocating engine; no one else was able to do. The oil really worked better than any other oil but it did have some unsolved problems.

The reason for this oil story is this: Mr. Knudsen was president of White Motor Company and Mr. Knudsen was my backer on the car. I had the only car qualified for the '75 race not on Valvoline. This pissed off the asshole (their president) who ran Valvoline. He put pressure on Knudsen to get me to use Valvoline so they could claim the whole field. Valvoline had order in for 'bout 90 White over the road tractors.

I'd guess 'bout 25 grand apiece back then. The deal is, "if he don't switch oils we'll cancel our truck order." I say, "Well hell, we'll use their oil." Knudsen asks me if I think it will hurt our chances. I say, "Yes, All Proof is better." Knudsen says, "Then use it! Fuck that son-of-a-bitch." I like that kind of attitude.

In the race, we run 10th with one stall and a fuel run out. A giant rainstorm ended the race short. Frankie Delroy says, Sorry Smoke gotta pull it down, you're 10th. We get it 'bout apart and Clarence Cagel comes by and says what you doing? I say special training to tear it down fast. He says bullshit, you're not in the top 10. I get pissed and ask why they don't all get on the same page? Clarence hates stock blockers and is just about ready to tear my ass up and he caught in the corner of his eyes the crazy pollock was on about a three on a countdown to blast off. He hauled ass. I did the same. Hey 10th or 12th, what's the difference?

August '75

I got a feeling and I try it on dyno. Hmmm, looks pretty good in dyno so I call Goodyear. Can I test in the fall with you? Hell yes. Late August 75 at an international press conference. "Dick what's future for stock block? Dick, president of USAC says, " The stock block has got no place at Indy, now or ever." I dropped my wrenches like they'd turned red hot. In one second another racer died, but I didn't know that. How come I didn't know? I have no idea. You 'spect me to be a friggin' brain doctor also? I went home from racing for the last time after May 1975. I never brought my racer back. 25 years ago I was 52 years old. A 30-year journey that ended in a heart beat. You wanna see my Chevy racer? It's in the cellar of Indy Car Hall of Fame. Nope, don't come out much.

Indy Qualifying

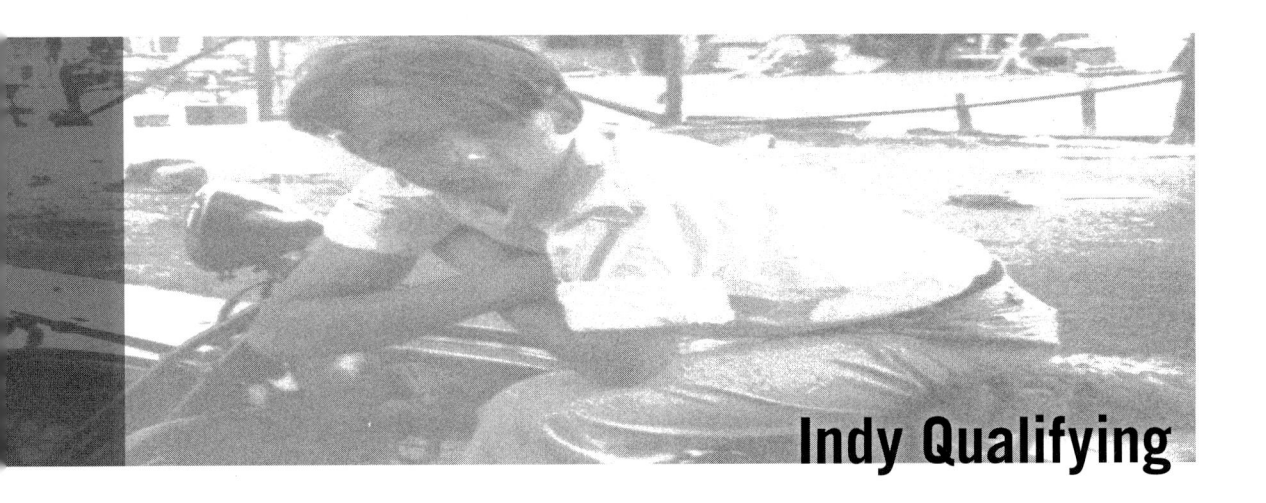

Let's go through the qualifying procedures at Indy. It's very complex. Friday night before first qualifying Saturday a representative from each entered team draws a number out of a container. These numbers are your qualifying order on first day. Nobody wants to go early, everyone prefers 5:00 to 6:00 pm. Why? Track's fastest then because air and track temp are cooler which is better for speed. There are three classes of drivers:

1. Rookies never been goofy enough to try it before
2. Qualified drivers got good current Indy experience
3. And the refresher driver who missed one or more Indy races but has driven in the race before.

Today, any self-anointed driver can request a driver's test. There is a panel of Indy drivers and racing peers who can either grant or refuse the candidate, based on his record and this test. The driver had to pass a physical first by the sanctioning bodies physicians. Glasses can't be over half-an-inch thick, no pace makers allowed. (I've kinda pulled their leg cause physical ain't too strict.) The test is in four phases of increasing speed (10 miles per hour increments) and it is aimed at close to guessed qualifying speeds (say within five to seven miles per hour).

Today's drivers, as a rule, they are pretty nice people. Why you say today's? 'Cause sponsors are a must and sponsors insist on a clean boy image. The sponsor wants a 23-year-old virgin, with movie star looks. Ideally he is a college-educated cat who's never been arrested, has no drug record and no paternity suits. Well, on drugs if he or she never inhaled it's okay. On the sex part no scandal 'cept maybe a li'l masturbation would be OK. I've noticed some of the new breed might not pass the old fashioned test of who do you like best boys or girls. Each year there are maybe three in the world who are capable of winning the race. How do we find them? Usually after we trip over 'em three or four times.

Indy's qualifying rules and the drama that goes with it are a 500-page book in itself. Every year one or more competitors loses a real chance to make the race because of mistakes made in the qualifying planning. Many times decisions made in qualifying are about the equivalent of a $500,000 roll of the dice at Vegas. And this happens every damn year. Here's the deal: the driver has to be qualified medically and professionally. Once that's accomplished he or she can drive any car that meets the technical standards.

An Indy racecar has to pass a tech inspection and receive a primary sticker (a paste on). Before it can make a qualifying attempt it must have demonstrated sufficient performance during its use in practice. Once it does, the car gets it's final sticker, which proclaims "this car is a genuine Indy race car that conforms to current rules and goes like a son-of-a-bitch."

The qualifying procedure is: one warm up lap, then as many as two laps to get up to speed, then four laps must be run consecutively. The average speed of the four laps is your official and only qualifying attempt for that car for that year. At Indy the car gets qualified, not the driver. Each car gets a maximum of three attempts to qualify. But if the entrant lets the car complete any run "that's it." No more attempts to better the speed is allowed.

Before in-car radios, on the warm up laps the crew chief went to the upper end of the pits in a designated area with a blackboard and a two flags – a green and a yellow. The officials for qualifying were 15 feet above the track at the start/finish line equipped with binoculars. They watched the driver and the crew chief to start the run on either the first or second warm up lap. The driver and the crew chief have to get together with signals to qualifying officials. Typically, the driver would raise one hand partially up, and crew chief would wave his green flag. Then the announcer on the PA system would scream, "Hezzzzonit!"

OK. The decision to take one or two warm up laps. Why the option? Mainly tire temperatures and driver preference. The trick is to be wound up to full speed and come off of number four turn in good shape so as you cross start/finish line for start of lap one. You've got to have a good start. The decision to take one or two is as a rule the crew chief's call. The driver watches crew chief's flag. And if he sees green, he puts his hand up. Not too damn far though, or wind would cause serious arm trouble.

Now during the next four laps it's up to the crew chief to judge whether those speeds are good enough to be at least 33rd fastest of all the competitors. There could be a total of 50 or there could be 100 qualifying attempts. Well, what's fast enough? How 'bout when crew chief waved green flag? How's he sure car is fully wound up? How's he know if driver has car under complete control? He could have over driven the corner and be off the throttle. There are a lot of variables that only experience can help you determine.

Now, anytime during the next four laps the crew chief can wave the yellow flag. This officially cancels the attempt and no harm done. Still got two more attempts. Here's an important part.

If crew chief lets car cross start/finish line on fourth qualifying lap an then waves the yellow, it's too late.

If your car is one of the fastest, you know your speed will be good enough, 'cept for possible driver error, or a car mechanical problem. It's pretty easy to handle the qualifying of a top ten runner. You run maybe little slower, or even a li'l faster than you hoped, but you have a spot.

You expect to see your car at so many seconds coming off of number four on the first qualifying lap, and if you think driver's on schedule at that point you take a breath and wave the green flag you have that tells the officials, and the driver, the next four laps are for a qualifying spot.

Four consecutive laps and the average speed of those laps is your official speed. The fastest 33 cars start. No exceptions. If you won it last year and was 34th fastest your ass is mud, go home come back next year. Go turn in your hero badge. OK, if your car compiles an average speed as fast or faster than you guesstimate you jump up and down and grin like a shit eating cat and run down to the starting line for qualifying pictures. Or if you have a buck or two you ride down in a golf cart. But it ain't over till 6:00 pm last qualifying day. Your guesstimate may be wrong. You got to remember in the qualifying area, you'll be interviewed: don't forget to grin, wave to the crowd and thank everyone who made a tire or any part of your car. Hug your mechanics and thank them for their wonderful help. Your world is perfect right now.

Maybe you were going for the pole and you decide at start of 4th lap you're short. You yellow the deal to try later. Or, maybe you got a car that is border line speed wise. And in those days I'm talking about you only got one car, and 90 cars entered is not unusual. For these cases there was a procedure that complicates this some more. Friday evening before the first qualifying day, all competitors have to draw a number. This number is your qualifying order.

Now, suppose your speed so far in practice is not too good and you draw number two. You're gonna be second to qualify. You have to somehow, from the practice speeds up to qualifying, decide what minimum speed to accept. That is a tough choice. Compare this to a guy with a medium speed practice that draws number 64 out of 68 total. As the other guys try to get fast enough, the guys with high qualifying numbers will get lots of information to go by. The question of what to accept. Here's the deal: you're not sure what to do, so you abort your drawn qualifying position. There is no penalty, but when you do, you go to the end of the qualifying order. No problem? Wrong.

In here comes the biggest factor of all, weather. No matter how smart you are, weather can screw you right out of the race in many ways. Rain can eat qualifying time badly or heat can change lap speeds three or four miles per hour up or down. Wind can have a huge effect. Man, this can take the best man out there and cause a three miles per hour speed drop on a lap. Hell, the time of day can change lap speed three miles per hour up or down, 5:00 pm to 6:00 pm is ideal cause the track cooler, 1:00 pm to 4:00 is the worst time (track hot and slow, tires get too hot). Basically clouds are good, sun is slow. Other variables like qualifying after an engine failure is slow (Oil and oil absorbent on the track). How much grip do you loose? Or worse case: you spin; no damage, or you loose it and crash. Spins, crashes and car failure pepper every qualifying day. These unpredictables and the weather can screw even the best car out of the race.

Note: Today there are two major changes to all the above. First, qualifying is now limited to two days, (one weekend) essentially half the time we had ('cept for '74 experimental one weekend deal). Second, the other is a competitor may have as many as four race cars at his disposal. So, his qualification games are endless. The game is, if you're unhappy with a qualified car's speed, withdraw it and push next car in line. I don't like these options. Why? It lets money grease your chance to qualify. Based on his financial resources a competitor now has many options. (News flash: 2001 back to old qualifying procedure – two weekends)

33 cars will start and they usually keep the 34th fastest qualifier as an alternate starter in case a qualified car cannot start for whatever reason. There are more pieces to the puzzle. When 33 cars have qualified, the field is full and if weather goes ape-shit, that can be the end of the game. Yes, you can do everything correctly, have a fast enough car and never get a chance to qualify. This happened to me in '74. The weather went bad, I had drawn a high qualifying number so we were sitting at starting line with the engine running when time expired ('bout five seconds short). In truth, had we got to run our speed would have been shaky.

Here's a fact: anybody who don't qualify first day is in deep shit. Back in the double weekend days the drama got ever more intense. And you had an extra week to wear out your stuff. 'Bout Thursday of the second week drivers got desperate to get going and start crashing. Drivers also began to "car hop" looking for a faster mount. Back in my time drivers had no contracts.

I've seen the two Novi's fastest by far, entered in the race and miss the race because of weather and a car owner playing "deal money" games. I've seen Penske miss race completely with two drivers and six cars after having won it 10 times. I've seen slowest car in the field sit on the pole (a weather deal).

How tough is it to judge what's good enough and what ain't? Every year qualifiers and losers were separated by a few hundredths of a second. Nowadays it's like a couple of thousandths of a second. How the hell can you be sure? At best you only have 80 percent of the information. You don't know last lap guesstimate.

Hell, you've only got two or three seconds to make the call. The whole damn year and…maybe?

Qualifying, yesterday, many times was 90 percent of a well-known drivers food for a year. Today a million or more can be bucks shot to hell over that decision. I've seen cars wave off a speed that would have made the race and get backed into a corner. Had to accept a slower speed and didn't make it. The starting positions are determined this way.

On the first day the fastest gets the pole and 100 to 200 grand in goodies. Qualifying starts 11:00 am and ends 6:00 pm to the second. (On the 6:00 pm part, an official opens a window in the control tower and shoots a pistol) First day qualifiers line up according to speed. As a rule 25 to 30 cars would qualify on the first day. On the second day, no matter how fast the fastest is, he is put in the starting grid right next to slowest from the first day. Now when you got 33 qualified, whatever day the field is full and to get in the race you must exceed speed of slowest qualified car. You get the position that car had. This is called 'bumping.' The drama here is so thick you can see it, damn near hold it and feel it and smell it.

An unusual deal at Indy in qualifying is the four lap average. Not one, two or three laps or a total time, but your average speed is the boogey. When the track announcer says the four-lap average is "blah-blah. He has bumped car number 'X.' That bumped car, in a few seconds, experiences a mental let down probably just next to being sentenced to jail, being told you've got AIDS or when your wife shows you a stack of pictures of you and some gal in the hay. I never experienced that (getting bumped), but I sure seen the pain. As a rule you knew the wounded. The bumping can continue till all qualifying time has been consumed. In the bumping procedure, there is a game going on: what position to place your car in qualifying line. Once all entrants are afforded a qualifying opportunity, then you line up by position in line.

Here's more to put into the equation: before you qualify you have to be checked for technical correctness, and then double-checked after you qualify. Here's a giant problem: in the past there were opportunities to cheat and it still goes on. You know how "so and so" ran this morning speed-wise, but some drivers never show all their cards until it's "show time," and "who got by the inspectors with a two miles-per-hour lap-speed cheater."

With turbocharged engines there were many little ways to trick the jury with turbo. A locked waste gate on a turbo engine is good for around 100 horsepower. Did it ever happen? Hell yes, every year. There was also wing magic, changing the wing location outside the rules for just a little less drag. Then there was the possibility of petro-chemistry, of talented competitior using a liquid fuel of his own recipe. Of course there is always the "big engine" possibility.

Did you ever cheat Smokey? At Indy? Nope. As a rule, I never had a horsepower problem. I was so busy battling all new chassis, new body shape and engine durability, I just didn't have time to cheat. My problem was to get the son-of-a-bitch to last four laps, and I'd always have problem of trying to team up with a new driver (to me). So I really never had the need to consider cheating.

I, however, from time to time, was unable to resist the temptation to demonstrate my personal fuel "recipes." This item really has nothing to do with qualifying. Yet I guess it was a factor.

During 'Happy Hour,' you wanted to show your stuff, so that's when fuel experimentation was in effect for me. You got to know this to play "Indy car expert." The 'Happy Hour' phrase is over 50 years old. I describe the coolest part of the day, historically between 5:00 and 6:00 pm. A cool track means more tire grip and this is more speed. There is PR, sponsor and mind game value to being the fastest of the day in practice, so drivers and crews put extra effort in preparation and driving. And they cheat a little on car's configuration regarding aerodynamics. The top prize for fastest of the day was free dinner for two at a top restaurant. So sometimes qualifying speeds of the "hot dogs" is short of expectations because the last ritual before qualifying is technical inspection.

Yesterday, technical inspection was pretty iffy and hectic. A sharp cat could cheat pretty easy, especially with turbo charged engines. But now, it's a whole new ball game. A company named Race Specs, from Forrest, Ohio has developed equipment that is jigged, computerized and staffed by about a dozen very qualified technicians that keep every one even rule-wise, on chassis and body. This system is the invention of a former sprint car driver and machine shop operator, Ray Marshall. A super feature of the system is it takes about five minutes for a bulletproof check (course, that's not including the engine). Ray is a self-made man; a great example of the American system. NASCAR could use a Race Spec system big-time. Formula one also uses the Race Spec system. (Who is Formula One? The most expensive racing in the world.)

If I was an Indy car fan, I'd want a high seat in the area behind the pit fence in line with qualifying cars position for final instructions to driver with a pair of field glasses and an accurate watch. This is an action packed movie with cliffhangers, joy, disappointment, villains, heroes, frustration, fuck-ups, tempers, and confusion. This all in real time with an advertised penalty that could be in the millions of dollars, or even the supreme sacrifice from being permanently crippled or dead. A stone cold movie.

But this shit ain't no movie. It's as real as it will ever get. No other form of auto racing ever approaches the difficulty and excitement of Indy qualifications. A grown man cries because he will miss a good chance to die on race day. He will sell his soul to the devil to start in the Indy 500.

You know all of the racing movies there have been – none has even scratched the surface of the real Indy story. Next time you go to Indy, consider what I've told you about qualifying. I think you'll get a hell of a lot more for your time and money.

Now I got to remind you 'bout the "Big Bull" in turn one? All of the above is part of his plan to defeat you at Indy. Why a bull and not an elephant or a lion? Hell I don't know. In the dreams I had in the fifties I saw a big bull. Sure. Snakes, rabbits and squirrels too. But they just ran across the track once in awhile, playing "chicken" with the racecars. Yup. Some lost also. (I'm glad this part's over, I'm tired of the word "qualifying").

When qualifying is concluded that's it. No more running until Thursday before the race. This is called 'Carburetion Day' from the very early days (but they haven't used carburetors since the early fifties.) By '55, we all used mechanical fuel injection. Although in 1973, I did try to run a pair of carburetors on the turbo charged, Chevy. Power-wise they were better, but the tremendous lateral acceleration grip we had with wings closed those doors. The fuel went into a vertical position and uncovered main metering jets. This was accompanied by a big puff of blue smoke.

What was known on the track as a "motherfucker burnt piston."

Anyway, on Carburetion Day we each got 45 minutes of practice and they allowed half the field on the track in two groups (to avoid a bad crash). This way always made it quite interesting since at least one engine was blown every year and at least one spin or crash would occur. Can you imagine being one of the favorites to win, blowing an engine in the last practice and spinning and crashing in your own oil? Can you imagine the range of emotions from being fastest in last practice to a near fatally wounded car with a very sore driver? Telling all how he "damn near saved it." When really his arms were braced, brakes full on and eyes shut when the son-of-a-bitch hit the first and second time.

Up to the sixties, the race cars had straight front and rear axles and a very strong frame. The wheels didn't fly off. In real life the driver was at least twice as vulnerable to serious injury or death than in 2000 and 'bout about 100 times more likely to get burned. Back then all veteran Indy drivers had facial and hand burns and all limped a little (some a lot).

Those drivers seemed immune to the reality of a crippling injury or death. But all drivers feared fire. The reality of being trapped in a burning car was impossible to ignore by even the bravest of the brave. Methanol, when burning, is not visible especially in a bright light. There is another bad aspect of methanol when burning, if you inhale it by mouth or by nostril, it continues to burn as it enters your lungs. By the way, methanol or 'alky' is the mandatory fuel for Indy cars from the thirties till today. Today's cars are 100 times less likely to burn because of many mandatory rules aimed at reducing the risk of fire. For example, we used to carry 75 gallons, today it's 35 gallons. Although today the drivers seat is the front of his fuel tank, today's fuel tank has leak proof quick disconnect and about crash proof filler hardware, plus it is a non-metal fuel container with fire extinguishers. Compare that to the 1940s no helmets, no seat belts, no fire-proof clothing and 75 gallons of alky and nitro, all on skinny-assed rock-hard tires, inflated to 50 pounds of air. Who were these mothers? What drove them? Were they human? Did they get here in flying saucers?

How do you like that deal? The older race-cars (pre-sixties) were hell for strong and heavy, 'bout 1,800 pounds Compared to today (1,500 pounds). But "strong" had some serious negatives. The human body can stand 40 Gs for .005 of a second before serious injury or death occurs. There are three principle reasons. The brain, the heart and the kidneys all of which are not actually fastened inside the body. They are suspended, and kept in a general area by tubes and various parts of the thinking, digestive and blood flow systems. These three body parts can collide with skull, ribs, etc., and are severely damaged if they suffer a deceleration over more than I stated above. (If you want to dispute the above, talk to my mentor, who I consider the number one world authority, Colonel John Paul Stapp. Remember him? A military physician that conducted all the tests for super sonic aircraft, space and surface safety retention systems, the granddaddy of your car's safety belt technology) Col. Stapp personally survived acceleration from zero to 632 miles per hour and back to a dead stop in six seconds strapped to a very strong wooden chair with an open faced helmet and nothing else. Talk about balls. Whew!!!

So, by transformation from very strong to a system where the vehicle collapses and sheds parts in it's deceleration, there is a much less chance the driver will exceed the limits his body has. But this plan has some very serious and deadly negatives. In a three-month period in 1999 at least six people have been killed with flying car parts, along with about a dozen injured (spectators). They will ultimately have to let the walls absorb some of the energy of a wreck. Some times the rules are determined by some brain-dead old farts.

Consider this: those human limits were probably the same when man first evolved, and the likelihood is those parameters will stay the same till man joins the dinosaurs. Indeed, I believe man has become more fragile in the last 100 years because of life style changes. I started to say "improvements." I'm no longer convinced all this new electronic shit is good. I get to thinking, in another 50 years we'll have gone to a change where at night when you sleep, our feet will be plugged into an electronic receptacle (or in a male, maybe plugged in by his penis) What do you think 'bout this?

The Fan

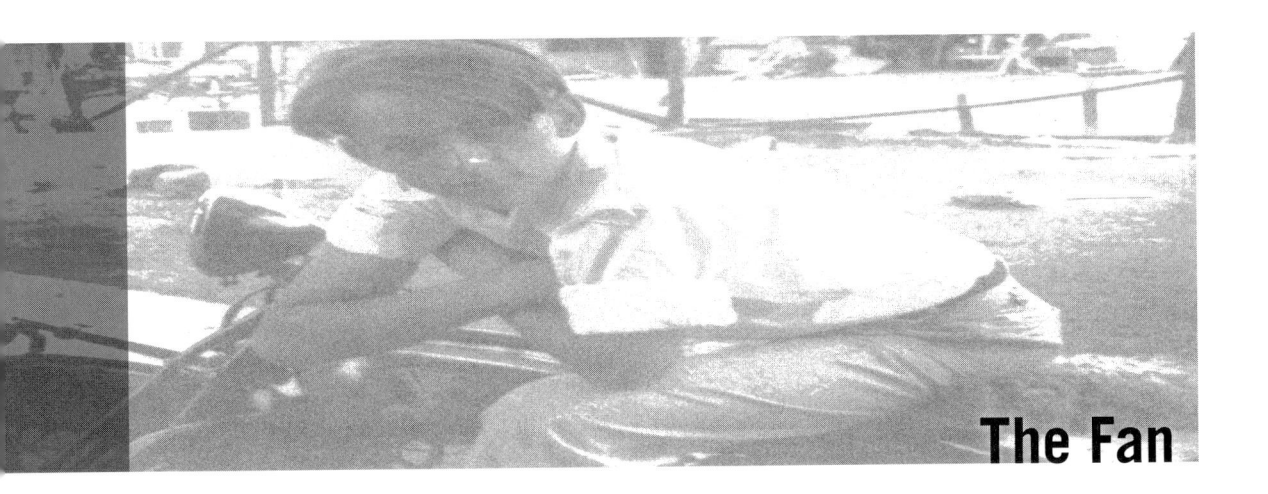

Did you ever see a book written 'bout the race fan? Shit no!

And yet the fan is racing's biggest and only economic support. Couldn't do it without 'em. You say what about TV? If race fans didn't watch it there would be no TV coverage.

You say automobile factories would pay for racing? A dollar amount equal to cost of racing is charged against every car, tube of toothpaste, box of corn flakes, every tire, every battery, every single thing needed to make it possible. Who buys this shit? You do, the race fans.

The fan supports the sport both at the track and at the market, yet we sit 'em in the rain, under 100 degree sun, or in 30 degree snowstorms. We tie 'em up for four hours in traffic coming and going. We keep raising prices for same stuff, same seats. We work on ruining their ears with cars that are too damn loud. And at race time hotels, restaurants and bars double and triple prices. Clever race ticket packages are being invented, mass marketing geniuses are getting so creative and so greedy that not only does the fan need Vaseline for the screwing he is getting, they need to add novocaine to deaden the pain.

The race fan is the greatest, most loyal and most enthusiastic fan there is in the whole world.

We got every kind: young, old, male, female, rich, poor.

They clothe themselves and their children in their hero's likeness. They eat, drink, sleep where their hero gets his sponsorship. They buy all kinds of dated memorabilia at very high prices. They invest in race-oriented games, stock, information schemes.

They join fan clubs. They buy and read race personnel books, (maybe even this one), news media rags and magazines.

It's time racing started treating the fan like the important customers they are. Give them a softer seat, a couple extra inches of room, a roof overhead to keep the water and sun off and, most importantly, keep the pricing of food, drinks, parking, tickets, hotel, motels, restaurants, so a fair 10 percent net is realized. That's right, stop price gouging with legal changes regarding pricing.

In Daytona they put a ticket scalper in jail, but they let the motel-restaurant-bar-parking and all other race related goods and services screw-rape-rob-scalp, in short, fuck fans silly. The mayor, the commissioners, and all elected city, county and state officials including the Governor and sometimes the President sit in air conditioned suites at the track, drinking free booze and getting fatter eating free food. From their air conditioned roost hey remain silent. Kinda like the three monkeys "see no evil, hear no evil, speak no evil." (Deaf, dumb and blind) The race fan is the golden goose. I'm positive that goose can be killed.

Indy car '99 shows the goose is pretty sick. Open wheel racing is showing signs of cancer, but look at how easy that would be to cure. Take all of the fan's problems into consideration when the events are planned. Greed is one of man's natural instincts. So is murder. So is being lazy.

I believe racing today has let itself become the most expensive spectator event of all major so called "sports." I doubt you can legislate greed out of existence. Therefore, I believe racing needs one major group of racing peers without vested interests to form a sort of constitution for the general good of the fans, competitors and the owners of the racing facilities. Hell, to own a NASCAR Winston Cup track you at best have one year of guaranteed racing dates. How the hell can you pay off a one hundred million buck mortgage with that for starters?

There are two things that can put racing out of business overnight:

(a) the fans

(b) a race car in a full grandstand.

If you piss the fan off, he will quit coming. Hey, a bunch already have. Ask the small track owner.

Actually NASCARs Winston Cup, Busch races and the World of Outlaws are the only venues doing great. Their success has colored the whole deal rosy, but it really ain't. The best and cheapest way to operate is "preventive maintenance" not "fix it when it breaks." 'Cause if the love affair race fans have with racing ever gets over, it may be un-fixable.

There is another segment of Indy fans who are treated like dog feces. Notice I don't use Southern Racing English. The ex-driver, mechanics and go-fer. I'll give you concrete example: Paul Goldsmith (driver) only way he can get credentials (maybe) is to kiss about 10 asses and go through a written request sequence unknown to him. An ex-mechanic, John Fisher, worked in A.J. Foyt's crew for 'bout 20 years and three Indy victories. There is no road, paved or dirt, for a ticket. He has a job at the track requiring his presence. The normal procedure is buy your ticket. He is no different than you who are a first time spectator. Now 'bout me, Indy still treats me like an alumni. Couldn't be any better 'cept race day, I have to have a ticket. (I buy it). I'm not complaining, but I did promise you in the beginning I'd tell it like it was or is. Now, when you go to buy a ticket race week some places there ain't any. As a result I'm very aware of the garage area crowding. I'm also aware for a price you can tour the garage.

The third neglected Indy fan – the go-fer. He has worked with a race crew for nothing from five to 25 years. My example is Cecil Taylor from Kansas City, Missouri. He worked for free for 20 years for A.J. Foyt. He is now a retired telephone engineer. He's got some miles on him and like an old faithful dog ain't allowed in the house any more cause he ain't as useful as he once was. Like a dog that smells bad and has got a skin problem, just take him to the dog pound and gas that sucker away. Don't tell me what you did for me yesterday – whatcha gonna do for me today?

What you getting at Smoke? Goddamit, racing should collectively offer free credentials to any and all who gave to the creation and advancement of auto racing. It's not a lot, most of the old timers are dead or are tired of ass-kissing and don't want to go. Can you imagine A.J. having to buy an Indy ticket? Don't cry after you read this part. It is July 13, 2000 and has been this way since mid 1970. Unless a race track invites me and finds a way to furnish me credentials, I can't get in. Companies I work for tried to buy a hard card for me and were refused.

I have attended every Beach Race since 1971 (for half of it). I have paid for a tunnel walk in ticket all but two of these years. Mr. Knudsen president of Ford asked me as his guest one year, Circle Track magazine invited me to the 2000 race. The last ticket I bought in '99 was 75 bucks. I forgot, one year a ticket taker refused my money and insisted I go in free. After that confession, maybe I'll have to send NASCAR 60 or 65 bucks. I don't remember the year. Remember there are always two or more sides to a life story. Maybe NASCAR has very good reason for their views. One thing is sure, I damn sure am not gonna kiss any rectums. I'll accept whatever I might have earned good or bad. I'd also like to repeat an old southern saying: "The sun don't shine on the same dog's ass all the time."

Indy Pace Car

Around 1995, I received a call saying, "How'd you like to drive the Indy pace car this year?"

I said, "Thank you very much, but I can't think of any good reason (at my age) to drive the pace car – give up a month of my life and possibly do something stupid for one billion people to watch." The voice says, "Hey, wait a minute. The minimum to you would be 50 grand and the car. Maybe as much as 100 grand." I say, "Whole different ball game." (He's way exceeded my prostitute minimum.) He says, "Can't be sure yet. One camp wants you, but there is another that wants Tom Cruise." I say, "What's he know 'bout racing?" Then it dawns on me, he's won the Winston Cup Championship in a shitty movie. He says, "Odds are you'll get it. Tom and his studio don't like the idea." (Probably too sissy for him after being Winston Cup Champion.)

It's February, Beach Race time. My ol' buddy, Bobby Unser comes to see me. He's the ABC TV sportscaster champ now. I tell him 'bout the offer. I notice he is really absorbing everything – names, etc. A month later I hear no more from the deal. I guess they gave it to Cruise. I pick up paper one day and guess what, "Bobby Unser To Drive Pontiac Pace Car" is the headline. Bobby never did tell me the story, but the guy called me and said, "They were led to believe I had no interest in the deal." If you see Bobby's Pontiac pace car think, "Smokey damn near had that car."

Nope, I didn't get pissed. I wouldn't have used the car (I don't like big cars). It would cost 'bout 3 grand a year for insurance, batteries, wash, shine, paint, lubrication changes and dry storage. By the time Bobby sells it for 35 grand, he'll have 45 grand in it including interest. The 100 grand? Nope, I don't need a house in Mexico. Who knows if I'd have got it anyhow.

While I'm at it I may as well tell you 'bout another close call with fame and fortune. Remember the movie "The Right Stuff," 'bout Chuck Yeager and the original bunch of astronaut candidates?

Well 'bout 3 months before that movie came out the Delco division of GM wanted a spokesman for their products. Again a two camp deal between Chuck Yeager and Smokey. One million a year is number, I heard (hope you didn't go for less Chuck). Well, that movie done it. Shit, I didn't have a prayer. If they'd chose me they'd of been goofy.

Chuck knocked 'em dead for 'bout 3 years. According to what I learned 'bout Chuck and the other test pilots and their social behavior, that boy had all the right stuff to have been a very good racer. Remember, I had quite a bit of Air Force experience. (We heard all 'bout the shit you cats were pullin' off Chuck.)

Chuck might have become the most successful and celebrated pace car driver of all time 'cept a friend of mine, Jim Perkins, a GM vice president with racing aspirations, and more importantly, the General Manager of Chevy, which is nearly the perennial pace car at Indy. Jim wanted to do the hero shit himself. Course, in that race, Chuck was running with four plug wires off. Adios Chuck Yeager the pace car driver.

From what I heard from the ladies around Indy Chuck would have been a good presidential candidate. I believe he could have out-screwed Clinton hands down. Shit, he could be delivering bombs personally. All Clinton can do is say "do it." I can see it now, Chuck flies a secret, high-speed helicopter in, grabs Milosevic by the ass, puts him in helicopter, brings him back to Washington and shows him on Saturday Night Live. Plus, look at the money we'd save. Chuck could fly the big mother Clinton uses and save us a pilot's salary. I also think Chuck could have saved us a shitpot full of money by stopping all the phony expensive wars Clinton gets us in. I think Chuck had a bellyful of the dumb shit 15 years ago. But, we'll never know. I doubt Chuck's dumb enough to try it now. You racers behind this, Chuck Yeager was a he-coon from outer space. Also, a very special human. Tell you about him? I can't. Yeah, I can. Try the Jeff Gordon word: awesome.

The Beaver Patrol

During the month of May '58, I noticed a lot of the old racers walking around with binoculars hung around their necks and I was kinda puzzled. I assumed it was to see the cars, but I half-assed noticed they were mostly pointed up and straight ahead. In '59 I hear a waitress in our restaurant talking 'bout the "dirty old men in the beaver patrol." (Note: for racers, women (when discussed in regard to sex) were sometimes called "beavers." Why? Hell, I don't know. I honestly have never had a good close up look at a real beaver, I just know "pussy" and "beaver" were synonymous.)

Now the light's starting to come on. If you look at the spectator stands in front of the pits, you'll notice the seats are on an angle from five to 50 feet in the air, and just across the track from the pits it's the same story. You starting to catch on?

Slacks and shorts were not common in the 50s. Dresses and skirts were the ladies' normal form of dress. Well, it seems like some ladies preferred fresh air and various other undergarments to panties. The beaver patrol was, simply put, yesterday's racers. I'd say from age fifty on and I later noticed some young racers were performing internship for future beaver patroller's badges. I never got to see their rule book, but I remember "no panties" got highest points (one hundred). Black lace was worth eighty points, and so on.

Well, apparently word of this innocent form of entertainment leaked out and the ladies had, I think, the anti-beaver patrol defense. As the field was scanned, a lady would position herself to attract attention of all avid beaver watchers. Then she'd spread her legs even more and place a "fuck you" sign where it could best be read via binocular. Some of the ladies had their own binoculars, and it was whispered around that certain racers exposed their sexual organs. "Cagles raiders," the safety patrol, tried to clean this game up a little. But this posed a major problem. The safety patrol were all past sixty, and probably the biggest fans of this contest. Well, it soon became commercial.

When the legs exposed the black lace or natural scenery, they also exposed a phone number. I don't know if this still exists. I doubt it, since television and the Internet goes way past the binocular "flash." But, I do remember one day in the early seventies when a well-endowed, cross-dressing male gave the patrol an interesting and shocking three or four minute masturbation exhibition.

Of course, the chant "show us your tits" was often rewarded by many bra-less ladies lifting up (or down) their tops, to show off their charms much to the appreciation of all beaver patrollers lucky enough to be watching. Along with the evolution of technology regarding surface transportation I witnessed at Indy from 1955 to 1999, I've also noticed the evolution of accepted sexual behavior.

THE BEAVER PATROL

Next at Indy came the "flashers." They simply got bare-assed naked (male and female) and ran all over the damned race track down in front of the "snake pit." The snake pit may not be fondly remembered by all racing historians, or by the Speedway cadre, but it was an area in the infield at the turn one entrance. There is still (1999) a big oak tree there. They had cheap bleacher seats behind a second fence 'bout 150 feet from inside of turn one. In dry weather it was a grassy, well-mowed, nice smelling area. But on a wet number one qualifying day, or race day, it became a filthy, fuckin' mud hole. 'Bout two to three thousand snake pitters would be a close guesstimate. Clarence Cagle could give you an hour-and-a-half of wild-assed tales 'bout every sexual, drug-related and alcohol-induced perversion known to humans and sometimes practiced by animals.

At times over one hundred lawmen were in there battling the "gooneys" with horses and dogs.

They sure were race fans, but they represented an ugly form of lawlessness that I kinda attach to the age of the hippie. Those motherfuckers that bitched about everything, wouldn't work, and imposed their will and expenses on the taxpayers. What was interesting, their actions were defended by a bunch of politicians called "Presidents," "Senators" and "Congressmen." Including a bunch of old farts called "The Supreme Court." Kinda reminded me of Bill France's, "'cause I said so." The main license to this mess was a war with a bunch of poor farmers in a jungle and swamp called Vietnam. A so-called "war" where our politicians and military leaders showed the world they didn't have a clue, and we couldn't fight our way out of a paper bag without the big atomic bomb. These hippies, as they became older, invented a new election system whereby industry could buy laws and rape the taxpayers, and for monetary reasons force the media to color horse shit as a bouquet of roses. From this sorry mess came today's politicians and lawyers; word magicians who tax your ass slap off and get you to believe they are doing you a favor.

Taxation as I see it today is like fucking in a car. Starts off with the sweet talk and feeling around. The politician is the male and we taxpayers are the female. Politician gets us believing this is gonna lead to something good and gets you believing his bullshit. Then comes the inevitable lost art – you're getting fucked. Review the Clinton impeachment proceedings. A terrible example of an American adult male with a support cast of social trash. Members of the Congress and Senate bullshitted this country, and world, with their doctrine of are you gonna believe me or your goddam lying eyes? Our only consolation is inevitably these types finally go one step too far and end up finishing their own destruction. Don't believe it? Review the ending of every dictator or imperialist for the last 500 years.

I write this in May of 1999. Yugoslavia gave us the "Yugo," but I think what we are doing to them now is way too much to get even for the little shit box car. Why do I think I smell the same odor I did when we decided to teach the Vietnamese to do what we told 'em to?

If we're so smart, how come we got this damn Cart/Indy Car crap? We had it by the ass from '25 to '75. When the Penskes, Patricks, etc. decided to "fix" it, it took me fifteen minutes at 9:00 am on first day of qualifying (pole day), to get in and get parked fifty feet from entrance to Gasoline Alley in 1999. In 1960 that would have been a three-hour exercise. The cause being that there were ten times more fans then. I know we'll get back on track, but it sure makes you rub your chin watching this four-year-old movie. The snake pit '99? Nope, it's now just a couple sticky pages in a history book – it's gone.

What Did You Invent Smokey?

COMBUSTION CHAMBER SHAPE

If you're not into engine technology, or are not able to comprehend engine development and evolution, skip this section as there are very few juicy personal stories. If, however, you are technically qualified, and would enjoy someone's version of "how it unfolded," don't miss this part. I was in it up to my ears.

Well, I'm gonna run through it year by year best as I can recall. In 1950 I went to a surplus military sale at Melborne, ('bout 100 miles south of Daytona). I wanted to buy a Jeep and arc welder and maybe a drill press or a lathe too. At the auction I seen a funny looking black narrow box like deal with a glass front that said "smoke tunnel." It was a device that blowed smoke in a laminar fashion across air foils where you could see lift, laminar air flow, turbulence, chaos. The effect of flaps. You could see it with your eyes. The Navy used 'em as training aids for air crew and maintenance crew training.

Five bucks will get two of 'em (one for spare parts). You lit a kerosene burner, and an electric fan distributed the smoke through a vertical wall of tubes blowing smoke – laminar smoke flow.

What if you narrowed up a valve space was 'bout 1.5 inches wide and watched smoke for best treatment of valve face and edges? And what's best angle? You agree no way air and fuel can go through valve. It must go around it. Here's where I learned the best seat valve angles. The better the smoke looked the better it flowed in the cylinder head.

Well, it turned out the middle 75 percent of the valve either way. Air coming or going didn't have a damn thing to do with it. You know tulip valves, flat valves machined valve heads and under head, polished valves that don't do a damn thing to help or hurt air flow. Here's the deal. The air column in the manifold and cylinder head port ain't moving. It's dead stopped till when you crack the valve open .010. The pressure drop is to absolute minimum. The velocity of that column jumps from zero to sonic speed almost instantly.

The Otto cycle engine operates on the pressure differential between 28 inches of negative pressure and 15 pound per square inch of positive pressure (atmospheric pressure at sea level). That's what we had to depend on to fill the cylinder in a normally aspirated engine.

To me the engine is a series of machines hooked together to produce energy that can be harnessed to do work. Therefore, the ports and physics of working fluid are a machine that can be built to do a specific job to a maximum level. Be it speed, power, mileage, cost or ecological considerations, etc. These specific jobs at a specific level means that they can be efficient only in narrow rpm ranges.

Next, it turns out in a wedge type cylinder head. A la Winston Cup. Ford and Chevy 1999, about 60 degrees of both the intake and exhaust valve are too closely shrouded to flow in a linear manner for 360 degrees. Instead the shrouded area behaves in a chaotic, tumbling and fluctuating manner. Shrouding – the effect of a cylinder wall or combustion chamber encroaching upon the open valve. They may not touch, but the wall will inhibit air flow. Note that this is subject to change as the valve moves into the cylinder. Well hell, that 60 degrees is 'bout useless. But in a flat head no shrouding or shielding. You almost get the full 360 degrees of flow, even when you consider the gasses moving all the way across the cylinder, but the cam timing can have longer valve dwell at full open because of lack of interference.

What the hooker here is, soon as valve starts to open cylinder wall shrouds about 30 degrees of flow. Well now I graduate and build a one cylinder flow machine with everything working but not running, being motored at variable speed with live flame burning a rich mixture of kerosene. Now I have flame and smoke in a glass cylinder. Man-oh-man. What an eye opening thrill this was. First time I saw it live was second only to sexual climax. Surprise again. Flame starts in narrow area between intake and exhaust valve. Why? Guess it's the most uncontaminated (reference exhaust gas) area in cylinder.

Laminar flow testing device.

Also, first 90 degrees of reaction stroke burns good, last 270 degrees burns weaker and weaker and kinda goes out. Why? I say it runs out of oxygen, 'cause remember you had a cylinder full of 12 to one air fuel at top of the firing stroke. Half of the unreacted fuel is still in there, but at this point, for example, so is one half of it's displaced volume with exhaust gases. Remember, both valves are closed here.

What is the actual air fuel ratio of the last half of fuel reaction?

Damn sure ain't 12.5 to one is it? Wouldn't it be closer to six to one?

I go back to Indian brain magic (peyote) for this conclusion. But the deal ends up with no better answers and a pissed off lady. (I forgot a planned sexual adventure and made mistake of leaving door unlocked in my machine shop "budwaur." Yup, my performance was jus barely ahead of homo. Well what the hell, nobody's perfect.)

I call my buddies in Houston at the fancy petro lab. I ask "What's heavier, 10 cc of unreacted fuel, or 10 cc of exhaust gas? Answer: bang. Exhaust gas is lighter. (Shit house luck). This was a part of a complex test they did for someone in the space program. But answer "is a secret; don't tell a soul." "Oh, hell no. On my mother's grave." Hell, this is forty years later. I'm sure it ain't secret no more. I get a brain storm. I've got a centrifuge. I feed vaporized air-fuel mixture in to it running, trying to see how I can keep a gas vapor a vapor. Because flowing wet with a glass spider manifold on a small block, I always have eight rivers of fuel and the same of a running engine.

It all came out of carburetor as a vapor, but before cylinder uses it, a little river of fuel appears along with the vapor. Centrifugally mixed and storing in a five gallon glass jug no better than 20 seconds or less it starts to liquefy. In here, I got interested in sonic cleaners.

General Electric had a big well equipped laboratory in Daytona, and one day I found a pretty big sonic cleaner in their surplus equipment. I'm kinda wired in. Some of their big shooters were race fans (big time). In particular was an engineer named Don Wolfe. Donny helps me get the sonic cleaner cheap. I notice, when operational, the cleaner turns liquid into vapor. Here we go again. What if? What if we passed the fuel over a sonic device for vaporization? How long would it stay as a vapor? How about twenty minutes? OK, that would get rid of the little rivers of fuel that's wasted. Liquid fuel won't react, period.

Well, there's negatives. I can't figure out how to overcome the electrical power requirements and size of contraption is impossible to hide in a NASCAR Grand National engine.

By now I've learned using pure oxygen instead of ambient air 'bout doubles the power of a one cylinder motorcycle engine. I built a 25 horsepower, water-cooled disc brake dyno for this experiment (by the way, still got the li'l dyno and the sonic cleaner and the two smoke tunnels).

I now find pure vapor produces 'bout 10 percent more power than conventional partial vapor (at least). Don't try the 100 percent oxygen deal. It don't get along worth a shit with oil, but it about doubles the horsepower till the "big boom." I don't have the one cylinder motorcycle engine any more for that reason.

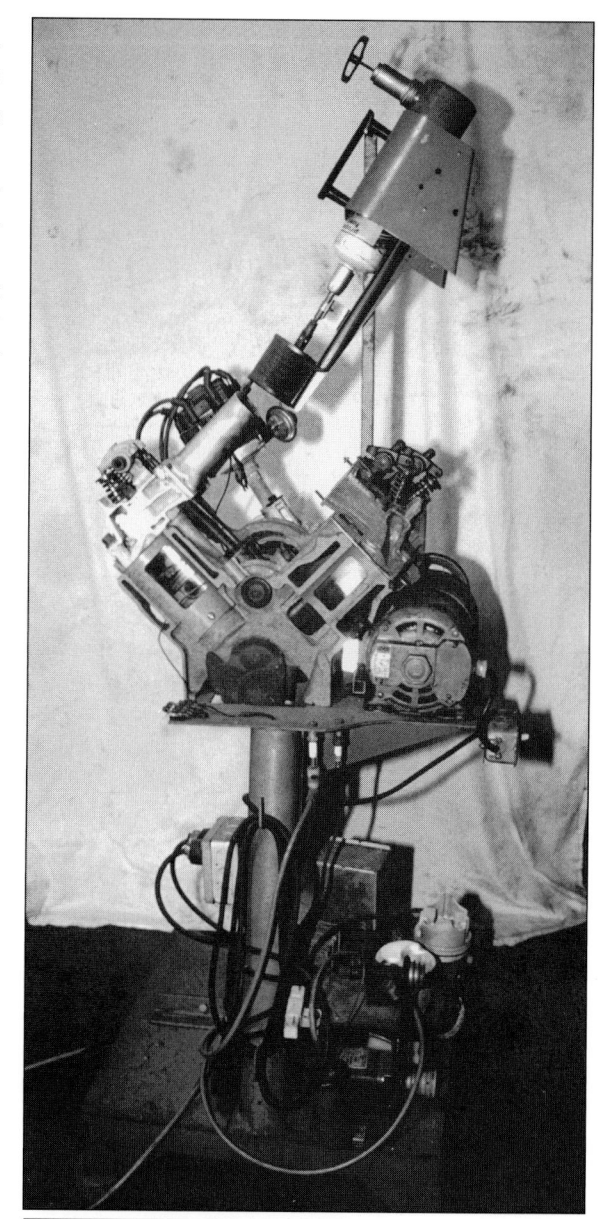

What did you invent Smokey out of all this?

My combustion viewing contraption.

Spiral combustion, and I got it patented. How much you make off of that one smoke? Zero. But came close once. What the hell is spiral combustion? A. Exhaust gas is lighter than unreacted working fluid. B. The Chinese yin-yang philosophy (no two things are ever absolutely alike, two of anything and one is male while one is female). Male represents the stronger, and visa versa. Now make a combustion cavity in cylinder head that's shaped like one side of a two bladed boat propeller. Yup, valve fit in super and at

WHAT DID YOU INVENT SMOKEY?

Close-up of the cylinder.

The spiral combustion patent.

most desirable angles. Next, make a piston that matches that helix so if piston is at TDC. Made it so that if you fill combustion cavity with cold setting rubber, remove head, pull rubber out, you got a rubber two bladed propeller. Yin-yang kicks in. The male side of propeller dictates direction of rotation.

In the glass cylinder engine, you can see the fuel spinning and burning, and the faster the machine is rotated the faster the flame spins. You can see it clear as day. Don't forget, fuel starts to react in the center of the combustion cavity, that's why that's the place spark plug belongs. The heavier unreacted fuel goes to outer diameter of cylinder, and exhaust gasses remain tucked in center. You react all the way to the cylinder wall. The big deal is, you keep reacted and unreacted fuel seperated and maintain air fuel ratio in the power stroke. This proves the "so called cold wall theory" is bull shit.

How do you know it works Smokey? I run it at Indy in 1975. Finished 12th with an iron 207 cubic inch Chevy (blowed). Agreed, nothing to brag about, but not too shabby if you knew all the details.

Other proof? Grass don't grow on a busy street. Only carbon on any piston crown was 1/8th inch wide figure "s." Which defined the mating inner face of the inner edge of the propeller half way across and vise versa for the rest of the way (the outer edge of propeller). No carbon anyplace else.

I showed it to some GM big shot engineers in 1975. Seven out of 10 said, "You're right." Three said, "We don't see a damn thing." One who saw nothing was heaviest hitter at GM Research, Chuck Amann. I knew bucking him would be past my potential and everybody else was afraid of him politically. He went off on something called "trilogy." I never figured out what the fuck that was, and I believe after many millions of dollars of GM money pissed in the sewer on that

449

one. My guess is those ten years of bullshit were dutifully buried with no birth certificate or death certificate for any historian to find. You know anything about it?

I later run into this asshole again ('bout 1985) regards to my hot vapor cycle engine. Nope, he didn't help that either. He tried to spin me out again. He had a favorite expression that was pretty close to the noise a rattlesnake makes just before he bits your ass. The sentence was, "You have a very cavalier attitude Mr. so and so." Man, that ended any support I might have had. (What the hell does "cavalier" mean? I thought it was a hi-buck fish product). But hell, he was probably making 500 to 700 grand a year to my ten. So there's a good chance my side of the story is flawed. Did you ever meet an inventor who said his invention wasn't worth a shit?

IGNITION AND SPARK PLUGS

'Bout 1980 multiple spark plugs reared it's ugly head again for about the tenth time. So this time I got an air cooled, one cylinder, motor cycle engine and made a head for it with five spark plug locations and run it with two magnetos, each firing one or two plugs at once. I found that one plug in right location did just as good as four at once. But, I found in artificially aspirated engines with high boost and high rpm (firing), multiple spark plugs reduce misfires percentage and simply stated, makes a little more power with increased durability, but for a Winston Cup engine, once you get in right place, one plug will get it done just fine.

I spent a lot of time experimenting with various types of electrodes on spark plugs, spark plug gaps, diameter of center wire, center wire radiuses, center wire flat multi-ground electrodes, surface gap, flame ignition or plasma ignition. Various ceramics qualities in regard to dielectric strength, heat range, center wire sealing and the battle to remove all moisture in the center wire seal area. Remember I worked as a consultant twice for Champion Spark Plug. Matter of fact, the first complete Champion plug lab with dyno was at my place 'bout in 1957 time frame and came back as a consultant again in the early '90s. So you could say I am half way qualified to talk spark plugs.

I found small diameter center wire and a glass seal the best. The ceramic material formula and heat treat are very crucial to dielectric strength. Sharp edge, flat center, electrodes are the best, rounded electrode is very negative. More gap, say like .075 is best, but takes a very good ceramic with a no moisture center wire

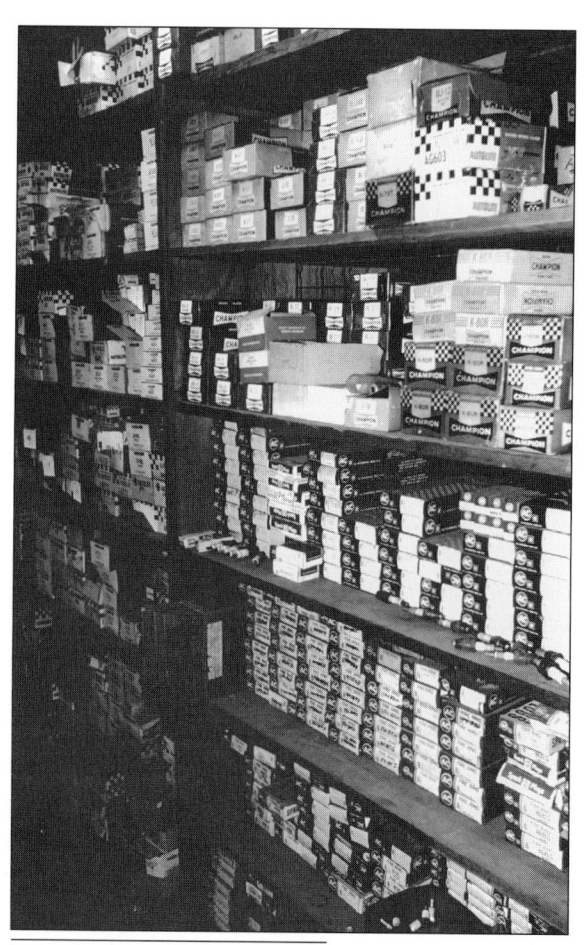

A history of spark plug development.

seal and a strong ignition in amperage and duration. This then puts plug wires in trouble reference leaking. As a rule no plug wire can handle it as good as a wire with added protection from a premium wire shield like Moroso blue. Seems like multiple ground electrodes are a little better, less misfire, especially late in race when oil control weakens. (This is not a power tool for round track racers.) This was durability medicine. I found we, as a rule, used too cold a plug.

I think ceramic should be 'bout 1100 degrees F for best ignition, the heat reduces the chance for misfire because of oiling or incorrect air fuel ratio. Plug gap should be all the system can stand reliably. I believe in individual coils for each cylinder with no plug wires. Here's a five cent tip on coil or condenser reliability: if either one gets so hot it burns when you touch them, that engine will soon quit making noise. Remember, it's harder to transmit electrical energy in elevated temperature without a significant loss of voltage also.

Comparing a three foot plug wire to a one foot plug wire, about half the voltage is lost. Now this information is nowhere's near as critical to normal surface transportation engines as in state of the art racing engines. With a coil per cylinder we run without plug wires so I did the best I could. I plugged coil into spark plug surrounded with a heavy silicon boot for mechanical and dielectric strength and a sleeve which increased the dielectric strength of the wire. When we had to run plug wires.

How 'bout platinum or other precious or exotic metals for spark plug electrodes? My experience is these expensive metals add life and durability, but for say a 500 mile Indy race they wouldn't be any advantage at all because all the race plugs are replaced every race. Where multiple electrodes are part of design only one pair of electrodes will react, that being the pair (current and ground) that offer the least resistance, so multiple electrodes offer one advantage, optional electrical path in case of fouling of the normal or primary pair.

The spark plug is now damn near 100 years old, and essentially the same since day one.

Flame or plasma will react a much greater range of non-stochiometric cylinder charges.

Only predecessor a spark plug has would be striking a pair of flint stones, or rubbing two sticks together.

INTAKE MANIFOLDS

In 1970, while working for Ford, I decided to build a variable length intake runner to use with the 302 engine as used in Trans Am racing. Ford kinda liked this idea. Next thing I knew they decided to build it for me. My plan was for a cross ram arrangement whereby the three sides of runner remained full length, but top of runner had a vacuum controlled gear activated retractable runner roof. Man, what a "Rube Goldburg" deal this was, but believe it or not it showed remarkable potential. As rpm increased, runners effectively became shorter because negative pressure dropped at high rpm. Shortly after prototype was tested my Ford deal blew up, so I quit work on it. At an auction I had here in 1987 some Ford lover in South Carolina bought it for five grand and had it on exhibition in his little race museum at his fueling plaza.

I built two other very different intake manifolds. One with a what I call a "heart valve." A one way rubber check valve so at valve overlap, if exhaust back pressure was stronger than induction current, valve blew shut. It worked, but couldn't take the heat, and, if we had a lean back fire, blew the checks all to shit. Kinda like having two intake valves.

The third manifold was the tunnel cross ram I built for the engine that was used in Trans-Am. This manifold had a rubber liner in each port and intake negative pressure reduced inner dimensions, but not length. Boy, this worked like "jack the bear" in acceleration. This was damaged in a cold start fire about the time Ford and I got divorced in 1970. Someone stole the thing and I never tried to finish the job unfunded.

Just a few of the experimental manifolds.

I offered it as a possible adventure to Chevy later. They seemed as interested in it as a good dose of the clap, so I dropped the idea.

CAM THRUST

In 1956 I became concerned with small block Chevy cam having no control of forward movement of cam shaft, which in design depended on a few minutes or cam lobe negative angle to rotate lifters to retain cam against at the timing gear rear interface with block. The cam bore had a couple of minutes of angle, so cam always had a slight inwards pressure, 'cept roller cams they had no provisions for rotating the lifters. I machined the block to accept a hard trust surface, then machined the timing gear to leave room for a Torrington thrust roller bearing – idea number one.

Next, I drilled and tapped cam shaft nose to accept a threaded stud, mounted small Torrington thrust bearing. This was adjustable to as to just touch inner time gear cover, then a boss was welded to water pump housing in correct position to interface with the center of the Torrington front cam thrust stop. This water pump boss was threaded for adjustment to give cam approximately .005 to .010 of lateral movement. Later this bearing was changed to simply pilot in timing gear center hole and held in place with the cam bolt mechanical lock shoulders. What did you invent Smokey? Well I did the deal, but an after market supplier (Isky maybe) supplied the first hardware. I got nothing out of it. At the time I was so busy racing and living it never dawned on me to try and capitalize off of it.

CLUTCH

In about here we were running stock cast flywheels, very heavy, with a twelve inch clutch. Well, "what if" I used a steel flywheel with standard size ring gear and used a eight inch multi-disc clutch made in England, loaded to 2,500 pounds? Well hell, it worked great on short tracks. Helped in acceleration enough to see on a stop watch, but later on long tracks didn't help. I even went the other way in Daytona. A 54 pound fly wheel and heavy 12 inch pressure plate. I brainwashed myself into believing that was better. But after a couple years went back to lightest, smallest diameter. No matter how you cut it, "heavy" took longer to accelerate, and closed throttle braking was reduced. Fords in particular were hell on heavy-big diameter flywheel clutch assemblies. Hell. That stuff would have worked on a D-8 Caterpillar tractor.

In the late sixties and early seventies a new problem popped up. We are turning up to 7,600 now and flywheels are flying apart. I mean bad shit considering where your feet are when this happens.

Instead of fixing the problem with a much stronger flywheel and much smaller diameter, we went to a stamped steel bell housing.

Well, this set the stage for a new after market millionaire (Joe Huradka?). It was a good move in as much as it was much lighter and stronger than production cast iron, and much-much stronger than production aluminum.

In the late sixties and early seventies remember stock cars weighed 4,000 pounds, And have 430 cubic inch engines with 550 feet pounds of torque. Clutch failure was suddenly a problem. I ended up with 2,700 pound loading on clutch disc to hold them babies. The technical inspection wizards would slide right under. Jerk flywheel cover off and the shit would be in the fan. Rule book said production clutches. If it flew and apart and cut your feet off, tough shit. The small diameter multi-disc had to be benched for the steel bell housing.

In 1965 I started using the engine as a stressed frame member, rules called for stock engine mounts which I had, but for looks only. I had a front motor plate and mounted steel bell housing solid to the frame as well. Man, this stiffened things up tremendous in torsion. Only negative, took long time for engine change.

We were always short of room for exhaust headers on the left side because of steering gear on the left side and the starter on the right side. The right hand drive Australian cars had a reverse mounting. I'd get Australian steering gear, mounting it on left side outside the frame. Now I had tons of header room. Then with steel bell housing I reversed the starter rotation and mounted it high and inside the car facing the rear. Now I had wide open sailing for left and right hand headers.

Things are changing fast now. We got 650 horsepower, 4,000 pound locomotives running 190 mile-an-hour laps at Daytona on 180 mile-an-hour tires. Actually, in here we had to add another strap in the safety harness one from floor to seat belt so driver couldn't slide down and get the "whoa" load in his guts. Big problem here was there was about a foot of balls in this area, as carried by the "hot dogs" of this time frame. (A sudden stop could curtail the driver's sexual adventures for a few days).

PAPER AIR CLEANER

In 1951 we still run mostly on dirt tracks, only air cleaner we had was an oil bath type. If you put enough oil into it to do some good, it would slosh over in the turns and hydraulic the engine, causing a large expensive engine failure, so for all practical purposes we run a dry system that prevented rocks and lug nuts from going down the carburetor. Of course, one race was about all you could get out of a set of rings. Well, in talking with the Purolator engineers, I was experimenting with a "steel wool soaked in oil" idea, which was fair at best, one of the young Purolator people said, "how 'bout paper air filter?" I said, "Couldn't get enough air, and doubted it would be strong enough." Well, I was part right. It could get a hole in it too easy, and we found out one hole size of a pencil was enough to cause serious damage. On 'bout third try, paper could stand it. Also changed from a wire mesh to a stamped screen to back paper up and went to a pleated design for big area increase.

I was running a Hudson Hornet, which, with Hudson air cleaners, restricted air flow even with carburetors half big enough. Well, inside of two years the paper filter idea went from ridicule to "invention of the year." I still have a few new ones from "day one." Also, what was to become a pattern of my adventures in engine and race cars. Three things usually happened. It took two to four years for idea to be accepted. " And by then I "didn't have anything to do with it." And then, of course, I never got paid for it.

DYNO

In 1952 "horsepower" was the buzz word. But we based our numbers on educated guessing. Well, I decided to buy a dyno. That was taken care of in a 10 minute phone call to Clayton Dynamometer Company in California. ($5,500 bucks, American money, three months delivery.)

Right, $5,500 bucks then was 'bout equal to $75,000 today.

So necessity became the mother of invention. No money, so we will build our own out of junkyard bargains. A small diameter multi-stage water pump hooked up to a leverage system where five pounds of engine torque was one pound on a 100 pound fish scale. I borrowed from Durham's fish market next door. I still have the scale. Never gave it back. Well, it sure wasn't that accurate. But we had first NASCAR dyno, and we had a number to talk about. So if we gained (pulled fish scale down further, car went faster). You know I looked at the scale the other day and I swear it still smells like a dead fish. Maybe it's my imagination.

Well, in 1954 I sold an invention, and Clayton dynamometer built me a kinda special dyno for stock engines. Six grand less freight. Mickey Thompson, a buddy of mine, lived in El Monte, California where Clayton was, and got me 'bout a $1,000 discount. The dyno is still operational, and in running condition, and is at Don Gartlits' museum in Ocala, Florida. Now, if that dyno could talk it could fill a 600 page book on the growing pains of NASCAR. Being the only one, it ran damn near all the time…with about every make passenger car engine…some trucks…with about every kind of chemical that would react to an electrical spark and compression.

OCTANE ENGINE

Rite about here I got my first octane rating engine, and started a gourmet gasoline program like Wynns and Bardol for NASCAR approval. I decided to make my own additives. I diverted from the NASCAR plan (which called for their approval for a substantial fee and contingency awards). I elected to use my product quietly, with no real intent to sell to the public. I'm sure you can understand, I was interested in going faster, not in a manufacturing business. Well, I discovered many interesting chemicals, like ether, benzene, hydrazine, indoline, acetatone, (nitro, both as a gas or liquid) propolene oxide, alky, tetraethyl lead, and many others that produced interesting results and quite a few fires, explosions and several severe engine failures (as well as quite a few visits to doctors due to breathing some of the fumes.)

I never used drugs except when I was in the Flying Tigers in India. And that was for experimental purposes only in Calcutta, Agratella, Chittigong or Luliang, China. But some of my fuel experiments caused me to – I guess the word is – "get high."

A common octane rating machine was used world wide then and still is. To rate all gasoline as to its "octane rating" in both it's research value and motoring method value. Add 'em up. Divide by two, and you got it. Simply stated, it could load an engine that had a selection of three carburetors that had three sample kinds of fuel and you could switch on the fly, and also vary the compression (while running) from seven to one to fifteen to one. Air fuel ratio and ignition timing was adjustable while running also when the fuel reached it's detonation limit, it would record knock, and it's severity. So name of the game was: sit engine on twelve and one half to one compression, and keep mixing various concoctions that could stand more compression, more ignition timing, and more load. This is all related to more useable power.

NITROUS OXIDE

One day I had a bad toothache, and my favorite toothache medicine was Seagrams 7 Crown. Well, toothache stayed. All I had was a headache, empty 7 Crown bottle and tooth worse. So, I went to see local dentist. I gotta tell you, I've always been scared shitless of tooth repairs. Still aint crazy 'bout going to dentist. Though once I had my teeth cleaned in California by a topless dental assistant. I didn't mind that at all, nope (she was a muff diver). Well, back to toothache.

Dentist said, "Tooth is shot. Gotta pull it." I said "OK. Do you have any whiskey here to get me in the mood?" He said, "Nope, I got a better deal." It was a pale blue bottle of gas called nitrous oxide. Trade name "laughing gas." Well, no question, it helped. But the "painless" claim was 'bout like all the guarantees we hear on television. 99 percent bullshit!

As I was paying the fifteen bucks charge (plus five bucks for the "painless gas"), I asked him, "What is that stuff?" He said, "concentrated oxygen." I said, "Nothing else?" He said "Nope, just oxygen." Man, that perked my ears up.

"Where do you get it?" "William's Welding Supply." "How much it cost?" "Eighteen bucks a full cylinder." (Cylinder just loaned to you on a two month deal.)

Well, serial number 10002015 bottle started riding around race tracks in 1951. In qualifying the bottle was filled with "Smokey's fuel additive nitrous" (laughing gas). So, if you are old enough to have been there and saw the two rooster tails coming off the rear tires of my car, you were witnessing the birth of a new industry. I never even told the drivers 'bout it, or anyone. I just slit the seat 'bout five-six inches, shoved bottle in down between springs crossways, pull metering rod out of carb, pulled valve up while I helped with the seat belt. Time bottle run out, the party was over. I think Jack McGrath, a very good driver-mechanic from California stumbled on to it shortly after I did.

Back in them days tail pipe sniffing around Indy gave my curiosity fuel for questions, and further chemistry education. The biggest problem in the missionary work was that to find a better fuel turned out to be dangerous. For example a drop of tetra ethyl lead on a cut, and you're on your way to the final checkered flag. Some, so unstable, if you dropped it, it would react. Some would trigger at elevated temperature as low as 90 degrees Fahrenheit.

Yup. The blue bottle is still here. (Just sniffed it. Still got some stuff in it). But Williams Welding Supply is long gone. No, never did buy the bottle. Just inherited it I guess. Naw, I didn't steal it, did I?

Actually many things that were learned here, as in the whole world, were accidents, or mysteries that sometimes took ten to twenty years to really understand. Well, apparently fuel additives were not that lucrative, and pure oil became the official fuel. And then it became Unocal. Actually Unocal 'bout owned half of NASCAR in a stock deal. Next thing I know fuel additives are banned. But nitrous was an oxygen additive, not fuel. But I decided I'd lose that rule interpretation with France invoking the catch all bullshit rule "not in spirit of competition." So blue bottle #1000112015 has been resting behind a filing cabinet for around forty years.

BORE/STROKE

In 1953 I got looking at bore-stroke relationship. Big bore, short stroke, square engine or long stroke small bore. The math is over my head. I asked Detroit as best as I could, and noticed nobody agreed on anything along the bore-stroke story. 'Cept long stroke for low rpm, high torque (truck), and visa versa for autos and power was an important part of vehicle's image.

Well back to the fish scale.

By welding on one journal of a scrap crank to increase, or decrease stroke (long tedious job of welding, machine and grinding and boring and/or sleeving of the cylinder wall.) (I later machined crank journal down to 1.5 inches then made a series of eight split crank throw spacers where I could vary stroke a quarter inch at a time from three inches to five inches. I then made a series of sleeves to change the bore from three inches to five inches.) I used 150 pounds of shop air to blow piston down from top to dead center and observe the fish scale for more of less pounds on the home made torque measuring deal, I made an arrow like a telltale tach to read accurately. OK, that worked. But I noticed at top dead center were I started from with a piston with an "on-center" wrist pin no amount of air would turn crank. I called this "crank lock up," and decided it was wrong for power to waste six degrees to 12 degrees of crank movement at highest cylinder pressure to lockup.

OK, what choices? Number one: simple, offset wrist pin. Number two: offset crank in an in line six cycle (for example) off set cylinder bores in case of a bolt together crankcase to block. (Example: Offenhauser). Well, turns out all the above has been used). My favorite, because is was easiest, was about .060 offset wrist pin.

Note: from 1953 till I run my last race in 1975, I never run engine in race that if you put a piston on TDC and put air pressure in cylinder with valves closed, that piston wouldn't go to bottom dead center in direction of engine rotation.

Yes. This showed a small gain on the fish scale. I'm not inventing anything new, but I'm finding a lot of specs. In passenger car engines are based on cost. Not on quality. Also I'm seeing you change any one part of an engines geometry it effects as many as five components in reference to maximizing power.

By 1954 I've decided I need a little more bore rather than more stroke. I do easiest thing to prevent cylinder lock up. By now I'm finding how big should bearings be, or? How many piston rings do I need. And where should they be?, How long should connecting rod be? Too big a connecting rod or main bearing is worse than not enough. Why?

Too many feet per minute of bearing speed can overcome oil's ability to lube.

What is ideal shape for a piston? I've got a problem that makes me very dubious of so called "engine engineering" being correct, or best for stock car racing. In early 1955 I was in a quiet way totally divorcing myself from anything stock specification wise being ideal or correct for racing. So I guess you could say, in 1955 I decided to use the rules for the existing engines as no more than a bunch of parts that needed modification or changes, and everything was fair game except block and cylinder head castings and maximum allowable displacement. (And any rules specifically set in plain English with simple understandable math (example: compression ratio). I asked a quite famous engineer how much I could turn an Olds 88 engine. (A quite popular race engine in the early fifties). In a day or two I received an answer "5,450 rpm If I exceeded that, pistons would seize. Lack of lubrication at that number of feet per minute of piston movement." Absolute answer.

Well shit! I'm really confused cause we've been turning it 6,000 and no piston problem. I guess I'll have to figure this out myself.

Connecting Rods and Detroit's Finest

Next: how long should connecting rod be?

I built a model with two connecting rods six inches and 12 inches long. The difference in amount of pull on the fish scale was day and night. Well, no way to use 12 inch rod, but if I had engine with 5.7 inch rod, I damn sure stretched it to the absolute limit. I'd like to add this to the observation: the short rod wasn't just plain stupid engineering. But required, to be able to close the hood on the styling that was mandated. Engineer had no choice but to chop off the height of the block, which left no room for long rod.

There really weren't any specific rules about this. Hell, by 1952, 1953 several of us, Red Vogt being the leader of the pack, (Clay Smith, Marshall Teague too) could double the power of a mass produced engine in a week. From 1946 to 1986 Detroit engineers, in regard to horsepower per cubic inch, were at best, a bunch of lost balls in the high weeds.

In their defense, maximum horsepower per cubic inch was not their game. But their egos held us up to where what we could have done in 10 years took 45 years. By 1953, I never met a Detroit engine expert who knew his ass from a hole in the ground in regard to racing or about gasoline except it smelled bad, don't drink it, and it burns (and it don't burn). Hell no. You can't burn anything. "Burn" is a slang word for "reaction."

Today is February 25, 1998, still pretty near 100 years later. The gasoline is "reacted" with an electrical spark, when a flame is much-much more efficient for the job. Modern engines have a stroke rod length ratio of less than two to one. When four to one still isn't too much. It took twenty years to get long rods and offset pistons to be re-accepted from day one we had piston, wrist pin and piston ring trouble.

PISTON RINGS

Piston rings were totally, and woefully short. Only attempt any one made to make a piston ring suitable for racing in the US was Perfect Circle. They were represented by a sharp man at the time, given the state of the art. Gene Stonechiper. If you were working on Indy cars, and you wanted piston ring help, you went to paging garage at Indy and asked for "Stoney" to go to garage "so and so." A tall, slim, 'bout 40 year old male with riding britches and hundred dollar riding boots would be at your garage in 10 minutes or less. He would fix you up with state of the art rings if you were working on an Offy. But stock cars, cast chrome top ring, cast iron scraper and a three piece 3/16ths oil ring.

Well, the top ring wasn't near strong enough. Least bit of detonation and the top ring broke. The scraper ring did not get it done, and oil ring had way too much cylinder pressure. The chrome top ring was very hard and next to impossible to get seated, but they were free, and the service was good.

I wanted nodular iron top ring, or steel with a soft interface, with the cylinder wall.

I wanted a reverse torsional twist cast iron scraper ring, and cut way back on oil ring static pressure.

I also wanted a top ring that was directly loaded with working cylinder pressure (a la dykes ring) and a 1/8th inch oil ring instead of 3/16ths inch.

Neither of the ideas were too good, matter of fact 1/8th inch oil ring, when I finally got it was an oil pumper. In short, "stupid idea."

The pressure back ring could be considered a "fair idea," but really not worth the effort considering reliability.

Well, Stoney was kinda like Model T Fords. (Any color you want, as long as it was black).

Perfect Circle wasn't about to take engineering suggestions from a hillbilly, wild man, stock car racer.

'Bout 1951 we're having pretty good luck with Grant piston rings, but they weren't strong enough in top ring, and if you run hot top ring, annealed, and ball game was over.

One day in the early fifties a real nice engineer that worked for Pedrick Piston Ring Company, from Philadelphia, PA., showed up at shop. Said "Pedrick would supply rings to my specs if I was interested." (Got to find engineer's name – Bob?). Man, he was as welcome as the end of winter. So it was as if some one gave me my own piston ring factory. Anything I wanted to do they tried.

Pedrick was an old-old company. But weren't in too good a financial condition. I'm afraid I helped them finish going broke.

They pioneered the moly coated ring (top ring) for me. We had so many failed applications ideas and that was very expensive. They also spent a lot of money working on my pressure back ring ideas. First the dykes type ring, and secondly the top ring tension controlled by orifices machined or drilled into top ring groove from the piston crown to meter a given gas pressure to top ring regarding cylinder wall contact.

Well, when we finish a successful manufacturing method, and they put it in production it was slow catching on, and imitators jumped on board 'bout time the moly coated ring got rolling, but this was too late for Pedrick. Also, the cost to build the 1/8th inch oil ring, and find it wasn't gonna work didn't help. It caused warranty problems. (Didn't drain enough oil).

Well, now we have a strong (nodular iron) top ring with a quick break in, and better cylinder wall sealing. Finally, a moly coating that stayed.

An interesting side to the ring adventure with Pedrick was Mr. Ferrari, the spaghetti bender genius who owned Ferrari. Every winter some Ferrari's ran in the 24 hour race at Daytona in this time frame ('bout 1960). Mr. Ferrari couldn't speak English, and only Italian I knew was in reference to sexual discussions with young Italian ladies. (I lived in Italy for a while driving B-17s, and hauling bombs up to, at the time, our enemies the Germans. I lived in Foggia italy for a year or more. Matter of fact owned my own home there. Built it myself out of sawed lime stone block and a tent roof, and heated with aviation gasoline.)

Ferrari had an interpreter, and needed space to work on his cars. I could spare the room, so I let them work here. Ferrari asked to see our dyno, flow bench and engine room. Well, hell, I was flattered, so I said, "Sure." Well, he made a mistake and decided to copy my pressure back ring experiment. Next year he came back and asked me "how it worked out." I said, "not worth a shit. I screwed up two or three engines." He laughed and said "he screwed up a couple also." You know, even with our language barrier I learned quite a bit from him. I got a kick out of his paint jobs. The red with a brush and the silver with a spray bomb. He said, "Who can tell on the track?" I don't think they make racers like him any more.

Rings are good now, but rod and main bearings are really getting unable to handle the program.

It's 1955, and I'm working for Ed Cole on the V8 Chevy, and got some input horsepower.

Connecting rod is too short, and much too weak, but rules say "run stock," so all we can do is forge the rods instead of casting them. The rods were notoriously weak in the bolt head area because of stress risers and shitty rod bolts. I pissed and moaned about rod bolts from 1948 to 1987, and it never sunk in. Finally ARP came along, and we could finally get a good rod bolt. Yes, I know Carrillo had good rods, and good bolts, but they were not allowed, "period." It wasn't until the late seventies, early eighties, before it was allowed. Typical NASCAR head-up-their-asses approach. But if a vendor was willing to pay fifty grand, plus a contingency ('bout another fifty) it would be OK.

This is now 1998, and those dumb shits are still running flat tappet cams. Goddam Gary. If I didn't know better, I'd think you owned a flat tappet lifter company. Goddam, even production cars run roller lifters now. In 1998, Winston Cup is running hard over lay cams and high buck lifters (solid). Very-very expensive, and they, at best last one race. Come on Gary, you know better. You run the rollers any time you figured you could get away with it.

I've been seeing piston ring leakage even with the best rings. So, one day I honed an engine on a CK 10 Sunnen cylinder hone. I still have it serial number one. I seen it at McCormack's place in Chicago at a engine rebuilders convention. I was working as a mouthpiece for a company that sold engine Ex-Lax – Rislone. A damn good chemical for constipated engines for last 70 years or so. Well, I was so impressed with hone demo up there. They had a sharp sales manager named Del Pico. He knocked off a couple bucks, and when show closed shipped 'er to Daytona. After hone job all eight cylinder bores "dead nuts." Round every which – way.

I bolt in a pair of cylinder heads, torque 'em in, no crank in it. Slide a dial bore gauge in the holes from the bottom, and couldn't believe how bad cylinders were twisted out of round up at the last two inches from the top where all the work is done.

Next move: bore through cylinder heads and leave heads torqued in place. Much better, but not good enough.

Step two: have heads cast solid and bore through again. Pretty good, but not practical. So I use a four inch steel plate. This don't do it good enough, so I decide to drill mike centers in each end of stud. I decided to use studs instead of bolts, and wanted to torque to .006 or .007 of stretch.

Why .006 or .007 stretch? Experimentally I stretched .010 To.015. When I released the torque, fastener was longer, so I assumed I'd taken the fastener to yield, and in effect, ruined it. Why stretch at all? I reasoned if I clamped two pieces of metal together with a fastener that had the ability to exceed the real world load with some stretch (the stretch was to be my lock washer-safety wire, or any other chemical or mechanical locking idea). My thinking, with the help of my alcoholic metallurgist, was in situation where the clamping ability exceeds the work load, the fastener will never fatigue. It don't know that it's doing anything. I found different lengths required different torque. Short one didn't stretch as far at a given torque. Also found out, had to use hardened washers, had to have very straight threaded studs, and found out 'bout all lubricants effected stretch differently.

Another mistake I made was not recognizing for uniform results had to use same head gasket by type, number and manufacturer and torque in sequence, and lastly, top of cylinder block varied in ability to twist the bore. In short, I found out deck needed to be thicker, and have blind stud or bolt holes. But thicker deck also increased cylinder wall temperature at top of stroke. Why? (No water where you add metal). Well by removing metal here and there on the four inch deck plate we could end up with eight bores within .002 torqued up…then I quit.

Oil

Well, not quite. I spent a year screwing around with hot honing, pumping 250 degrees F oil through water cavities in the block. I decided it wasn't worth the trouble. (This was in late fifties).

Another area we had a major problem was keeping oil clean. Oil filters in 1950 were either not available, or an extra cost accessory.

If you examined a "then" filter. They had 3/16ths oil lines. The filter caused a 20 pound pressure drop and a roll of toilet paper in a steel container even worked as good, but still woefully short.

But most importantly, I'd guess 25 percent of the oil got filtered 75 percent of the time. Actually, a "then" oil filter was about useless.

Again, Purolator rode up on a big white horse to the rescue. But the goddam horse walked slower than my old horse "Big Bill." (see 'Where Do Racers Come From?') What we needed was more area with less pressure drop. A major problem was in Detroit. I tried four years with Hudson, then one year at Chevy, to get a true fully filtered system. In 1956 best I could get was a cast in the block nearly full filtered lube system. But they insisted on a 35 pound relief valve (in case owner run with plugged filter). A warranty consideration. Well we'd block that deal off easily, but if something started to fail and trash was in oil in the pan, we never devised a way to stop this contaminated oil from going through the oil pump or being splashed up the cylinder bores. Even to this day the band-aid is: filter the sump oil (this is dry sump only) before reservoir, and re-filter after pressurization at the pump. 'bout 80 percent effective. But "no hurry" it's only been eighty years. Is some of this planned obsolescence? And Henry Ford number one story: "Sell car at cost? OK, just give me all the new parts business."

What did you invent regarding the above Smokey? Nothing really. I just kept making farmer cut and try band-aids, and kept my finger in the filter people and engine manufacturers asses. What did I do? I moved the oil filter from 3/16ths inch steel tubing to number 10 Aeroquip, and got filters area-wise big enough and filter mesh size to 30 microns instead of too tight 10 microns to cut pressure drop to 7 or 8 pounds at 10 gallons a minute oil flow. Hell, I found one 90 degree fitting could cost you a five pound pressure drop. So 90 degree fittings were out of my vocabulary from then on.

Lubrication was maybe our number one enemy from day one. Man the state of the art in 1940's was still in the Barney Flintstone age. In fairness to lube people, what they had was good enough for your grandmother, who'd never been over 30 miles per hour in her life. Engine would last 40 or 45 thousand miles. But boy, if the grand kids got ahold of that sucker, one good 30 minute run would mortally wound that heavy antique. So the lube was as good as the equipment and the roads.

I'm not knocking either the lube or car people. Back aviation up 80 years and you're sitting along side of the Wright brothers.

From the beginning, we fought water temperature. Consider all our tracks were dirt then. On top of a poor cooling system for double the rpm and horsepower the engines were developed for. Plus mud plugging the radiators, etc. High water temperatures pointed out head gaskets and head bolt technology short-comings, and radiators were hurtin' big time.

I believe it could be said that over the last fifty years the whole damned car and all it's parts as raced in Winston Cup, including engine, drive train, chassis, suspension and aerodynamics, have become especially created for "stock" car racing. The bull shit "win on Sunday, sell on Monday," is a crock. Any fan who buys a Ford, Chevy or Pontiac, or eliminates the consideration of a Chrysler product because of what's happening at the race track, is a little on the dingy side. But in 1950, 1955, 1960, 1965 it was real. By 1970 the water's starting to get pretty muddy, by 1975 you can't see anything in the water any more. By 1980 all you can see is crap and toilet paper floating on the top (regards to stock cars). As I see it, "stock car" racing started in 'bout 1936 and ended in 1965. From 1965 to present, best name or description would be "nascars." Does the above piss you off? Then you probably still think Clinton didn't do it either.

Back to oil 1947. Back then they put up a tower 'bout 100 feet tall and bout 8 feet in diameter, with seven spigots on towers side, 'bout 15 feet apart. Put bunch of crude oil in bottom of tower, light a fire at bottom of tower. Everything that came out of the third spigot up was put in oil cans, fourth spigot up diesel, fifth spigot is gasoline, etc. Well, I started trying to self educate myself on oil same time I'm playing the "mad chemist" with fuel. Two things help me. One: getting jobs in domestic oil fields working on big diesels and natural gas engine conversions. I cultivate friends, or anybody who will teach me about fuel and oil.

I notice someone scraping up goop around refinery joint and couplings that leak out and semi hardened. I ask, "What is that stuff?" Man says "Propylene oxide." I say, "What's that good for? Man says, "Burns hot as hell. They make antifreeze, whole bunch of other commercial applications." And, it turns out, mixed with gasoline in correct air/fuel ratio, makes much power.

I notice small lube company in Dallas, home brewing oils and greases for the major oil companies to use in the oil fields. Don't that seem odd? Turns out better oil and better grease cost more money, but to experts more than worth difference in maintenance cost. The major lube and fuel producers are just like the motor companies, they want to be best on a scale of one to ten against each other, not on a one to ten scale in quality.

I say, "What's in oil that's better?" The answer is 'bout five specific areas, but one perks my ears up. Extreme pressure. That's where we are hurting. We need protection at 2,500 psi or better, but store bought gas station stuff is barely over 2,000 psi How you get it higher? Man says, "Various forms of zinc and or chlorinated paraffin." I say, "no shit." You see I've been brain washed.

There were two basic types of oil in the US. Asphaltic base from Texas and paraffin base out of Pennsylvania. The story is: (1950) paraffin is no good. Sludges up and plugs up stuff and causes rings and valves to stick. So I get some of each and experiment with which is best, or both. I ended up putting both in. Parraffin better? Seemed so to me. (For a short period). We'd change oil every week.

Same stuff with grease. Our grease and oil test was: smooth anvil, smooth four pound hammer, put oil on anvil and smack it. Observe if anvil is dry or still wet. "Still wet" wins. I can't say I invented anything in oils or greases, but I got oil companies trying to get me to use their stuff and give 'em "feedback." "Did you get any money for it?" "Hell no!" But we got free product, that helped, and once in awhile we'd get a jacket with their name on it, or a baseball cap with their logo on it.

I now have about 5007 baseball caps, sometimes at Indy 15, a race. If they advertised race results, it was after they increased France's bank account. (News flash 1999 I find hat collection invaded by bugs. I'm down to 'bout seven hats now). I may be wrong, but by 1970, I assumed France owned NASCAR lock stock and barrel, so a check to NASCAR was a check to France.

In the beginning of a long race we'd start with SAE-50, at end of 500 miles it was SAE 150 gear grease. Light ends vaporized from the prolonged high temperature and shearing. Actually, when I first started (1938), best oil was a bean oil called castor oil. In actual lubricity, it's even today, maybe the best. But considering the pressure and heat, the oil was exposed to under racing conditions, castor bean oil flunked the pressure and heat requirements of racing engines of the fifties. This abuse of oil manufactured some serious negatives, such as shellacs, gums, varnishes, and metal to metal contact which quickly started the engine into a failed mode. It's obsolete now. Useful mostly to look at in museums. Smells good when burned. I get a whiff of castor oil now and I can hear the Novi and the Offy running again.

By 1963 I'm hiding dry sump systems, tricking radiator and water pumps to lower water temperatures, reduce radiator plugging (from dirt) and adding oil coolers. Standard radiator would have, say, 10 fins per inch. We'd build 14 fins per inch, but they plugged much more. (On dirt). By 1970 gas station oils can do the job in engines making 'bout one and one half horsepower per cubic inch, but it seemed like anytime oil temperature got over 280 degrees Fahrenheit in the sump, it was thirty degrees higher at the bearings, and driver and crew would-be loading up 'bout fifteen minutes later.

I used various forms of petroleum based oils up till 1972. Mobil was the best as I saw it. I used their "FR" oil in everything. I spent 1973 till 1980 trying to run a synthesized polyoester oil (acid and fat). Keeping additive package in suspension was 'bout impossible, especially the extreme pressure additives. 1980 I gave up and went with Mobil 1, which I found to be best, or equal of, or in a peer group of, Elf and Shell.

Testing oil is toughest job of all phases of a reciprocating engine's components. It has so many important and influencing variables, like heat, pressure, humidity, geological conditions, ingested contaminates, time (oil can be rendered to junk just by inactivity over a prolonged period). Takes about four years to really test a lubrication innovation. This is 1998, I'm still involved in lubrication up to my ass believe it or not fifty-five years later. I've lived through and into what to me is phase four in lubrication. As usual it's quite controversial, but not as bad as the flack I took over going from mineral oil to synthetic oil in 1973. Man, Ashland Oil wanted to hang me by my balls. Only car in Indy race 1973 and 1975 not on Valvoline, and using a polyolester oil, "All-Proof." Worked great in race car. Could stand 1,000 degrees Fahrenheit, but had a bad problem regarding passenger cars. In four years of normal driving, it would freeze all piston rings in the ring lands tighter than a bull's ass going uphill in fly time. Also establish a growth in intake ports that reduced useable area by 75 percent in four years of real world use.

In 1962 I met a cat named Deschamps plugging a synthetic lube named "All-Proof," a true polyoester oil. All jets and turbine engines use it cause temperature in those engines approach 1,000 degrees in some lube areas. Dechamps had rights to All-Proof, the invention of an old man from some cold fuckin' icebox part of Minnesota or Wisconsin, Duluth I think. His name was Fagan. Now Fagan did his petro-chemistry on the kitchen stove. Matter of fact he told me he invented STP (his story to me) and got screwed out of the deal. My need was for a lube that could take more temperature and more extreme pressure. The polyoester was better in extreme pressure, but not good enough.

So the problem was, nobody could keep a zinc-based, extreme pressure additive in suspension in a polyoester oil. It simply had a higher specific weight and in a week went to the bottom of the oil can, or engine oil pan. Fagan made it happen. You see jets and turbines turn very smooth and balanced, they don't need extreme pressure protection in the lube. (No recapture of reciprocal parts.) The Germans tried to copy All-Proof. I sold them oil for four years. At my last conversation with them I asked them "How come, as smart as Germans are supposed to be, how come a li'l old man could outdo you with a kitchen stove?" They said, "Smokey, we know exactly what's in it, and have known since first week. The problem is there are 13 million possible combinations of pressure, temperature and sequence."

How much All-Proof pay me? About 100 cases of oil. Company went broke. (Mr Fagan's mind unwound. At 85 that's not unusual is it?) But I believe I kicked the door open for synthetic oil to take over race car lubrication, including my stubborn hard headed friend, world's champion sprint car and midget engine builder, Earl Gaerte. I think Earl got the job to close the door on the history of mineral racing oil. As he switched "finally," a very knowledgeable manufacturer of oil field equipment, who incidentally owned and managed two Indy winners in the fifties. Jack Zink, who I feel fortunate to call a friend, said something the other day, "What's synthetic oil?" I thought I knew. Today I'm not sure.

Who the hell's Jack Zink? Well if you know anything 'bout Boy Scouts or Girl Scouts you know about the Zink Ranch in Oklahoma. Jack Zink was a day one racer, but not at all related to early NASCAR racers. Jack is surely a credit to auto racing and our country, with his technical talent and his consideration of his fellow man. Again, did I invent anything here? I doubt it. But I sure kept quite a few oil companies asses in gear to get involved in motorsports. Bearings, rods, mains and cams. Man, with shitty contaminated oil, much too hot oil, wet sump systems, little pans without good baffling, and with putty soft bearings we had a hell of a time with all hi velocity and heavy loaded parts. Minimum surface area and in some areas too much bearing speed.

Bearings

Cam bearings, at the time were able to borderline handle their job. Why soft bearings? The engineers reason "embedability." Soft bearings lets foreign abrasive trash jam into soft bearing so as not to damage the crank shaft, cam shaft or pistons. Well after 'bout three-four years trying everything known to man, the Clevite 77 bearings are the best for wear, but still trouble. Big time.

Up to 1955, all rod and main bearing shells, when clamped in their respective positions were as close to round as you could get, and here in laid the enemy. The connecting rods when going to top dead center and then captured by the crank and had their directions reversed, were not strong enough to maintain their dimensions, so where the rod and rod cap indexed, that area stretched, and in doing so described an elliptical shape smaller at the parting line, this condition pinched the bearing shell into the crank journal. The result was not only no clearance, but a severe dragging effect of bearing on the crankshaft journal, which instantly broke down the oil film as we went metal to metal. Sure, stronger rods and main caps etc. would help. But rules said "can't do it." No inspectors, never, were so drunk or ignorant that if they had a stock rod or main in their hand, they couldn't notice a hand made item.

Remember, this is before there was any vendors for this stuff. (Well, one, Fred Carrillo.) Enter a genius, or shit-house luck. In one shot, he outdid the world in connecting rod design and had the balls to manufacture it. His design was simple. Effective, cheap, light and hydrodyromaticaly quite corrrect.

I had a friend who lived in New Mexico. A college professor, who was big on natural remedies. You know, like mary wanna, cocaine, etc. He is living in Daytona on a leave of absence from a college so he can find out how quick your guts give up if you keep 'em soaked in alcohol. He gave me a miracle cure. (he said), for making you think clearly and deeply. I said, "What is it?" Answer was, "Peyote."

I'm drinking, so is he. What's peyote? Answer was: a derivative of cactus, perfectly harmless (he says), matter of fact he said he has discovered that's how come Sitting Bull kicked the shit out of General Custer and the American Army. Well that's good enough for me. If this stuff is good enough to help one friggin' Indian whip the US Army, it's good enough for me. I tried sitting on my haunches like he told me, but my knees got too sore, but goddam, it did work (kinda) and it was fun. Hell, you'd see dinosaurs, all kinds of shit, just out of the realm of "for real." If you ever tried it you'd know why. My vision of "fix" came in a mind-boggling burst of brain power. That is, "Where it pinches the crank, remove some metal." So, simply stated: when it's distorted it never gets smaller than required for lubrication. So I scraped my ass off on all bearings for 'bout eight to ten hours an engine. Oh, hell yes, it helped. But it was a corn cobby way of doing it.

This is 1955. I'm working for Ed Cole, Chevy's top cat, and at the time he likes me. I ask for bearing made .002 bigger at the parting line and I see my chances of him recommending me for the Nobel prize in engine design wavering. Finally, "OK, but don't tell anybody else. Get a price from TRW" "OK." I know the head cat there (Harold McCormack). A real nice capable engineer. Mac says, "Let me do you a favor. Forget it. It won't work." Now I realize it's gonna be hard to do on his production machinery, so I ask him, "How much to do something you don't want to do?" He hems and haws and finally, "150 Grand'. I think, "That's hi-way robbery," and tell him, "Forget it. I'll get Federal Mogul to do it." He says, "OK, see you later."

Federal Mogul throws me out. They think I'm a kook, so I have to go back to TRW. Mac says, "I got an idea." And I say, "I don't wanna hear your fuckin' idea. I got an OK to pay for tooling from Chevy by Mr. Cole." But he argues. Still don't want to do it. I get pissed and leave. (We meet in St. Louis in his office) next day he called and said, "Deal's on." I think Dick Keineth, a very sharp Chevy engineer took it from there. It flat got the job done, but when combined with the Clevite 77 rod bearings with a lead idiom overlay we had that problem by the ass. I guess it's safe to say I got the elliptical bearings game going. It's still getting it done today (in racing).

I kept experimenting with solutions, and when I gave up the chase I was running hardened crank surface and hardened rod interface with a special lubrication process (and rod bearings stayed on the shelf). The negative, still not totally solved, was need for extremely clean lubricant and absolute collection of worn metal particles. (Magnetic fields did pretty good job reference ferrous metal).

Caution regarding inventions and who did it first: even in patent law, Elisha Gray and Bell had a hell of a mess back then. Inventor was first to patent. Now we're back to first to invent. Seems like Bell was by five minutes first to file. If he'd filed six minutes later we have the Gray phone companies instead of Bell.

Written history, being by nature seems to be a biased well polished bunch of lies, where the biggest ego and richest camp wins. Note: NASCAR is writing their own history. This is a story of my adventures as best as I can reconstruct it. I have no interest in trying to convince you I was a wizard, or Rhodes Scholar material.

Matter of fact in last six years, adventures of a Rhodes Scholar name of Clinton, have put a serious doubt in my mind of it's significance. On the other hand, it is something special when a cat with a three inch pecker can become president of the United States and screw half of Arkansas and all of Washington, D.C. I remember him coming to the Darlington 500 race in September '91. A very impressive introduction. Even had two airplanes pulling signs 'bout him around the track for six hours that he didn't pay for. Banners said, "We don't want a draft dodger for president." Richard Petty lost all his points with him. He refused to shake his hand at driver introduction. (Think that had anything to do with his poor showing when he ran for chief dog catcher in state of North Carolina?) Maybe it wasn't dog catcher. But it was a kinda low pay job with a big title. You know, up till then I figured he could of been governor anytime he felt like it. Maybe what did Richard in was banging that guy on the hi-way with the big butting Ram Charger pickup with giant tars. Now I wonder if 'Black Bart' could be governor if he tried? Margie met Clinton, but wasn't impressed with him. Nope, I never met him. I avoided him because of what all J.V. Brotherton from Mena, Arkansas told me about him several months prior to September '91. (You know J.V., he is Brodix).

Connecting Rods

Connecting rods gave us fits first twenty years. Two problems with rods. Remember still stock, even with factory "so-called heavy duty," from '56 to '70. The other problem: rod bolts. NASCAR had their head up their ass and wouldn't allow a Carrillo rod to be used. Carrillo was a custom connecting rod manufacturer in California, who had mastered the weak connecting rod and weak connecting rod bolt problems for all engines. Way back in the early fifties and today same damn rod handles the program. That gives you an idea of how sharp that Fred Carrillo was. 'Bout thirty-five years ahead of "Detroit's Finest."

Fred was a racer also, and run at Indy some. Got caught switching cars and engines and they drummed him out of the race. Kinda like when you get kicked out of the French Foreign Legion for not feeding your camel, and they cut all the buttons off of your coat then fling you out into the desert to die. They did Fred a favor that probably saved him five million bucks.

The factories, GM, Ford and Chrysler, wasted fifteen fuckin' years with band-aids. Subtle changes, metallurgical changes in composition, forging dies and temperatures. Different vendors of rod bolts.

As a matter of fact, never did solve the prob-

A few of the rods laying around my shop.

lem. Can you believe one home made engineer solves a problem all of Detroit can't? Well, in defense of Detroit, their rods cost ten bucks apiece, and Fred's cost eighty bucks each, but if a ten buck rod failed, what's the real price in lost races and blowed engines? Order extra truck load of Sta-Dri.

I think maybe NASCAR owns the Sta-Dri company. Maybe that's why it took so long to allow using Carrillo rods. This is 2000 and Fred's got ten competitors now, but NASCAR owes him a golden connecting rod trophy. Fred's top man Jack Sparks is a sharpie, and now that Fred's off buying all of Nevada ('cept Las Vegas), he keeps improving the formula enough to keep ahead of the curve. He ain't too sharp on rod bolts. He don't use ARP (well, so far).

Right here let me try and get you to understand the difference between "hard" and "strong." The harder metal is, the less elasticity it has. I think a paper clip is good way to demonstrate it.

Remember when your girlfriend called you and said her period was ten days over due, and you knew her husband was sterile? You picked up a paper clip and started bending it. A nervous band aid. Remember it got hot? Then when she called ten days later and said it was gonna cost three grand. And as you kept twisting the paper clip it got hot then broke? The strength of metal is based on it's proportions of various chemical and various percentages of more expensive metals, like carbon, tungsten, nickel, chrome, manganese, etc. The hardness of metal is mostly due to it's grain structure and heat treatment. And also it's ingredients. Some parts we want to be hard and ridged, like a wrist pin. Some parts we want to be strong and flexible, like a fastener. Or specifically, a rod bolt.

OK, energy in resisting bending is stored as heat in the part in tension or compression, unless the part is more than capable of resisting deformation, or does not exceed it's yield strength – they can last indefinitely. Fasteners, bolts and studs were totally omitted technology-wise till the late sixties and early seventies. A Californian named Gary Holzapfel, who loved drag racing, went into the fastener business (ARP by name). Gary took us from the dark ages in fasteners to a capable state of the art where fasteners are no longer a weak link in the engine or chassis. ARP makes the best rod bolts now. But Jack still uses SPS Bolts…well hell, nobody's perfect (and SPS is world class).

PISTONS

Again, what did you invent here Smokey? Nothing really, except helped motivate solutions. How'd you do that? Tell 'em their stuff is 'bout equal to dog shit till they fixed it. Jack Spark's daddy was racing's first racing piston manufacturer, he was located in the Los Angeles area.

Art Sparks. He was to early racing pistons what Champion was to spark plugs, what Perfect Circle was to piston rings. We are backed up into the late twenties now. Art takes his profession seriously and pokes around in every corner of the world for every grain of improvement. Art's customers were sports car racers, aviation engines, Indy racers, OEM, experimental engines from all over the world, and I guess he manufactured pistons for limited production non-automotive engines. What was important to me, was he talked to Porsche and Ferrari. And all the engine geniuses around the world. Plus he'd already tried everything you could think of. We had piston trouble big time. We broke 'em and we burned 'em. In the early flat head days we raced cast steel pistons, but in forties everything went to aluminum.

A company called Zollenor made an aluminum piston with a steel strut reinforcement cast in for added strength. Detroit loved it cause it was quieter than steel or cast iron and lighter.

Aluminum melts at say, 1,700 degrees Fahrenheit. Combustion temperatures can and do exceed 2,000 degrees Fahrenheit. Nope, don't melt unless you detonate, have premature ignition, run maximum lean, or have too much ignition timing, or a sharp metal projection in the chamber. The top ring drains heat from piston crown and oil absorbs lots of heat from inside and bottom of piston crown. Anyhow, as long as everything is as it should be, it won't melt.

I got to include weight in this discussion. The weight of everything that spins. The weight of everything that goes up and down is critical to racing because of acceleration, deceleration, durability and vehicle cornering capability. This includes pistons, wrist pins, rings, connecting rods, crank shafts, clutch assembly, front vibration dampener (if used). I call it the reciprocating mass.

Aluminum pistons are either cast or forged, steel reinforcing has gone by the boards. Forging is stronger than casting. Not a hell of a lot of metallurgy in aluminum. 'Bout biggest difference is amount of silicone in the aluminum, but that's not for strength, that's for durability. Hi-performance pistons are made of virgin metal. No, that don't mean all the men or women who make the metal are virgins. But it means they can't be made out of used budweiser beer cans. Why? Guess the beer weakens the aluminum.

Heat treatment of aluminum is dirt simple. Heat to "x" and dump in one hundred fifty degree Fahrenheit water. Heat to "x," hold for "x" hours and re-cool. We as stock car racers, got piston problems out the ass. They break, they melt, they get vertical scratches and score. Bores like wise. We have a built in vertical leak at ring gap interface. Pistons deform from too much heat. This causes pressure leakage, loss of oil control, the oil burns hotter than gas and has a much lower detonation tolerance. So shortly a major failure. "The big white smokeroo." We gall wrist pins and wear and deform wrist pins and wrist pin bores. We have a terrible time keeping wrist pin retainers in their respective place of residence.

Here is an example of piston weight reduction to reduce reciprocating mass.

They deform from heat and cause loss of clearance, loss of lubrication and try to weld their selves to the cylinder walls. We melt pistons and jerk wrist pin bosses out of piston. When suddenly your favorite, (or least favorite) race car lets out of wall of whitish smoke, that, as a rule, means that motherfucker just burnt a piston, melted it, and the oil is burning.

(Note: when referring to any racing engine major failure, the engine always is referred to as a "motherfucker." That denotes the seriousness of the tragedy, and I guess in a way, the extreme cost. A less serious, less expensive failure is a sumbitch.)

When you see that sudden and dramatic wall of smoke, you can estimate the cost in a Winston Cup unrestricted engine at about twenty-five thousand bucks. An IRL car, 'bout seventy thousand bucks, and a CART car 'bout one hundred fifty grand. Top fuel drag cars? I don't know, but I bet it's at least fifty grand. A restricted Winston Cup engine 'bout thirty five grand.

OK, you agree with me now. Pistons are serious shit.

One other negative: it's a very interesting few seconds as a rule that follows the burnt piston. Oil gets all over your rear tires. This problem is unsolveable. You do nothing. Quit breathing. Pucker up your asshole. Hit the brakes. Shut your eyes and brace yourself. Then say, "Oh shit!" real loud. A driver can tell how bad the accident is gonna be. If it hits between the "oh" and the "shit," it's gonna be a bad one with some sheet time.

Well, in 1956, I'm working on Stove Bolts, (thats southern for Chevrolet) – the small block piston as made for cars and trucks is nowheres near adequate. Back in those days racing was really a kind of big mystery. Which of three things would happen first, a blown tire, a blown engine or the race would be over. In 1956, after a bad day at Black Rock with a failed piston problem, I asked Ed Cole for permission to make a piston we could race, and he could sell as a heavy duty part (to be legal). He said, "Sure. I'll get them started." I said, "Bull shit! We've already been down that road three times. Lipstick and face powder ain't gonna get it. We need to start gound zero." "Well, then." he said, "OK, make me a drawing." "OK" I grab a napkin and start to draw piston. He says, "Dammit! You know that won't get it." I say, "Hell, I heard they drew plans to first atom bomb on a restaurant napkin." He said, "Do what you think is the fix. I'll see 'bout getting the money." Hal McCormack is top cat engineer TRW, "How much to make a piston like this?" He says, "Make me a drawing." I said, "You make the drawing. We'll pay for it. I want a forging that has short skirt with an offset wrist pin (.060) with much stronger pin bosses and oil ring land, oiled wrist pins. I wanted it to be round at four hundred degrees Fahrenheit the top ring, .150 from top, scraper ring .100 below it, oil ring .100 below it. I want 1/16th ring lands for a 'D' wall ring for compression and scraper and a 3/16ths oil ring. The was the main part of the gain I was looking for. The '55 Chevy as manufactured had offset piston to reduce cold idle noise (piston slap), I put 'em in backwards to get more power.

I told him alloy I wanted (I got it from Sparks). You know, aluminum is a wonderful metal (magnesium is more so). Add 'bout six other metals in total less than one percent, and six to nine percent silicone, and you got an alloy that does 80 percent of racing. The heat treat, 8th grade stuff. Heat to 1,000 degrees F, hold for 10 or 12 hours, dump it in hot water then age at around 300 degrees F for one to six hours to establish hardness. I learned the hard way when you heat aluminum past 300 degrees F you're starting to soften it. So if you get in a jam and can't get a new piston, weld the old one, heat it up till you melt the 800 degree temperature stick. Throw in hot water (150 degrees F) it will shrink a couple thousandths, but you can stretch the skirt with a sand bag and ball peen hammer. Yup, good enough to win with. Same thing with cylinder head, block, anything aluminum don't forget to re-harden.

Back to piston specs. They get a thicker deck, bigger radius in all stress risers. I asked for a double Tru-Arc wrist pin retainer. I asked for valve reliefs to parallel valve head so it contact was made in a valve float mode head of valve wouldn't be bent and break. In 'bout six or seven months we got samples. I try 'em. We make minor changes. Couple more months and the Comformatic piston is born.

The piston solved our problems, and soon all racing stock car pistons seem to be copies (to me). Near as I can see, today's piston is a slow evolution of stronger and lighter of the original Conformatic. I got no patent, no extra money to my already exorbanent salary of ten grand a year.

Although piston was successful, I lost out on the offset and shorter wrist pin. Nor do they put in double Tru-Arc spec wrist pin retainer grooves. This is a major fuck-up. Now we have to remachine the retaining ring area and it's a bitch to do engine by engine with a Bridgeport, plus many racers don't have a milling machine. But you know the engineers holding back the engine development worked kinda like nature's balance. The engineers kept us from over-running development of the tires any worse than it was. You've

467

noticed how much I put down the Detroit engineers. The problem was real. But it was not because all Detroit engineers were idiots. It was all a product of the system. I describe the system in another more appropriate section, actually our guys were world class for cheap, safe, reliable surface transportation. But in '18 o-shit for thermal efficiency, a few engines were pretty good or close. This is not horsepower related. It's mileage and pollution talk.

Oiling System, Pans, Windage

The oiling systems from 1948 till to 1965 were stock stone age. Wet sump 'bout five to eight quarts of oil flying around in home made oil pan, with two hundred ideas how to properly baffle the oil so oil pan pickup wouldn't get uncovered in cornering, accelerating, and braking. Uncover the pickup for .100 of a second…"Good-bye rod and main bearings." In late fifties I'd experimented with all kinds of baffling and all kinds of oil pick-ups. Here's where I ended up.

An early oil pan with a diamond cut screen.

Directional diamond cut screen just missing rotating parts with a small round rotating pick up, with oil pressure across the joint to prevent air entry for road courses, and for circle track, right hand pocket added to oil pan aimed at eight quart capacity and baffling to keep pickup submerged in lateral- acceleration and deceleration modes. Thirty years later the industry went to directional diamond plate screen. You want to know why this works? OK, I'll tell you. With reciprocating parts just missing directional diamond screen a pressure drop is created below the screen and pulls oil down into the sump. Did I invent anything here? Hell no. I got the idea off of a 75 year old farmer appliance. 20 years later racing accepted it.

I think Moroso led the charge. You know the big "C" just got him, just before his golden years.

Dick Moroso contributed a great deal to all kinds of racing 'cept open wheel. Too bad you didn't get to know him. He was a fucking racer, with impeccable credentials. He'd done every bit of it. World class. Nope. It wasn't all wonderful. Our life style cost him a son, Robbie. Dick was a real example of a local yokel, nickel and dimer who, with his balls and 100 hour weeks made it to Broadway. Dick had one hell of a helper in Bob Hone. They were the Mutt and Jeff of racing.

Nope, no happy ending there either. Racing don't promote long time friendships.

I guess reason was, racers from 1940 to 1980 were essentially a goofy bunch of individualist, loners that operated at wide open throttle 18-20 hours a day, 365 days a year.

Dick Moroso would listen.

Plug Wires

We had big time trouble with leaking plug wires and burned plug wires. I found a very good plug wire, seven strand stainless with a extra good dielectric strength (silicone made it's debut here). Then I found a commercial sleeve that had both diametric strength and the thermal barrier that just slid over the wire. Add silicone boots and we finally had a good dependable wire. Then I made special supports to preclude cross fire and grounding. Moroso got the stuff painted light blue, hung a "blue maximum" name on it and to this day I still get a royalty check (that helps me donate involuntarily to help pay for blowing up all the countries that don't do what "Pinocchio" tells 'em)

I also invented the Moroso water front head outlet that prevented left to right pulsing in water return to radiator, carb spacers, cylinder leakage testers, and several special engine tools. This may be biggest exception in my total adventure reference money. I got paid a royalty, and an extra exception, on the level. Every other royalty deal I've ever had, and I had a bunch, I got a royal fucking. And, every other one, down to and including collector cars and models (including "Upper Deck"). What I've received regarding the 50th anniversary of NASCAR wouldn't pay for 1,000 mile round trip air plane ticket...I ain't complaining, just bragging on Dick Moroso.

Dry Sump

The swinging pick up? Worked most of the time, but was really like a rattlesnake. When you relaxed and dropped your guard the son of a bitch would bite you...in short...a loser.

Well, rules say "stock oiling." I begged France to allow dry sump from 1955. We run 'bout forty races a year for about seventeen years. The lousy oiling caused at least five blowed engines a race, so a rough guesstimate was: refusing dry sump cost 3,400 blowed engines from 1948 to 1965.

Well, let's not rush into things. Right? 1963 I had a bellyful of this shit, so I used regular oil pump for scavenge pump, hid a ten quart tank in the left front lower cowl compartment, and took a chance using a power steering pump for the pressure pump. I told inspector I was trying power steering. Every once in awhile, inspector would look quizzically at the plumbing, but after 'bout a year of this, my nerves were saying, "Let's quit." Well, I then took a flat round pump out of a hydramatic transmission, made a timing cover looking, aluminum casting, and buried this pump into lower part of casting. It was driven by crankshaft key way, and a dog type interface.

The front pully (modified slightly) covered it totally up. Cheating? Sure! Like a son-of-a-bitch. I lost 'bout seven or eight extra horsepower, but no more blowed engines because of uncovered wet sump pickups. Actually, it cost me a few horsies but saved lots of engines. I never got caught with it.

Finally, dry sump was legal. Avaid in California had pump ready at a reasonable price. Wanna see what it looked like? Come on by. I'll show you one I saved. What did I invent? Nothing.

What was dry sump? It's an oiling system where you use one oil pump to remove oil from the engine in a vacuum mode and transfer it to a remote lubrication reservoir. The reservoir services the second oil pump, which serves as the pressure system to all lubrication points. The above, as opposed to oil supply reserve and oil pressure pump, all reside in a common vessel. We call it the crank case, or oil pan. Oil is returned to oil pan simply by gravity, and leaking around lubricated parts. Why's dry sump better? It is positive lubrication regardless of lateral or forward or stopping forces. It eliminates some of the loss of power from crankshaft rotating in a viscous fluid.

It reduces oil temperature that is created if engine parts are rotating in a liquid and it reduces oil temperature because the reserve oil resides in a separate vessel away from operating engine heat and away from contact with recripical parts, less heat, less horsepower loss.

Dry sump was invented in late 1910s. Strange that dry sump deal of mine is still not exploited commercially, and it's still better than any pump today. Why?

(A) don't need a drive belt.

(B) requires less horsepower to operate because no friction loss

(C) not likely to fail from belt loss or minor accident.

Why less power? More efficient liquid compression design.

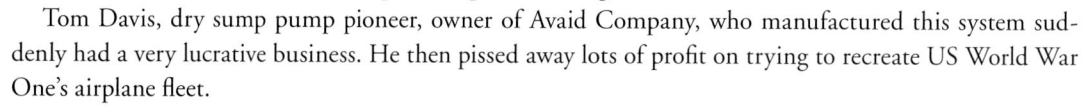

My experimental "power steering pump."

Tom Davis, dry sump pump pioneer, owner of Avaid Company, who manufactured this system suddenly had a very lucrative business. He then pissed away lots of profit on trying to recreate US World War One's airplane fleet.

Tom was an example of early birth of racing after market vendor.

Tom and several hundred other (mostly Californians) who had exceptional talent and an entrepreneurial spirit, were an important and necessary part of the evolution in auto racing 1948-1999. This group started with five hundred bucks. Worked fourteen hours a day, seven days a week. Some didn't make the cut, mostly because the nature of the pioneer is classically a piss poor business person. (Tom's gone now.) But some did very well, and became extremely successful and wealthy. An example would be Vic Edlebrock. I'll elaborate more on this in another chapter. Without these people there would be no auto racing at world class level in the United States.

Needle Roller Cam Bearings

In 1958 I got serious about cam bearings, which historically were very soft. The cam bearings were pressurized leaks that in conjunction with crankshaft splashing oil on cam shaft supplied oil in a haphazard, half-assed way. It seemed to be satisfactory for standard mass surface transportation, but very unreliable for high performance or racing engines.

Cam shafts mostly were machined, chilled cast iron billets (very hard and brittle). We had to increase valve spring pressure on the seat, approximately 100 percent (over passenger car design.), (80 psi standard, race 160 psi.) Even way back in 1958-1960 we were trying to turn the smaller engines (say 300 cubic inches or less) 8,000 rpm. Well, cam lobes couldn't handle it. Mickey Thompson and Isky got a roller rocker program going that was better than the stock slip and slide, but NASCAR said, "Nope. Couldn't use it." (Maybe Harlan Sharp was number one.) Another head-up-the-ass management decision: NASCAR Winston Cup…which to this day (1998) is still the same.

Both the slip and slide lifters, and the rollers rockers have made dramatic gains in durability.

Interestingly, common surface transportation has moved to roller lifter. NASCAR still mandating ancient history in Winston Cup, but Busch is rollers. Go figure.

In 1958, working with the Offenhauser engine, the cam bearings were aluminum with 'bout 140 psi on the seat. To do certain assembly and valve clearance adjustments required much hand rotating of cam shaft against full spring load. Wow, the effort to turn cam shaft was tremendous. Also history of these aluminum cam bearings was very shaky reliability.

I decide to replace aluminum with needle bearing in a pair of half shells like a connecting rod bearing. Well, this took a year. The Bearing Company of America made several sets for me to test. I should add, if it hadn't been for Mauri Rose's friendship with BCA management, it never would have happened. Finally the great day comes. A dyno run. I'm expecting 'bout 8-10 horsepower gain, but the facts were…zero, no power gain.

Well, I'm going to Indy – 1959. I try the deal at Indy, but elect to go back to original configuration.

I feel we have good chance to win, and I'm afraid I don't have enough running time regarding durability. The lap time at Indy bore out the dyno information. No gain. Well, in 1960 I took cams with me to Indy again. And again I decided against them. I had in the '60 Indy pit crew Bruce Crower, a cam shaft manufacturer for race engines. One night when I wasn't in the garage, he found these cams housings with needle bearings while nosing around my spare parts, and shortly after the Crower Imperial Needle Bearing cam system arrived and fell flat on it's ass. There was no more power, but there was more durability when engine rpm increased to over 9000 rpm, with ungodly pressure on valve springs. 200 on the seat, 600 across the nose, but there was oil pressure loss at the needles and need for seals. Today the needle bearing cam bearings are a fact of life in the Winston Cup for durability reasons. They plugged the cam bearing lube sysem and oil by splash. Yup. Works good.

Again, a patent search showed it had been done long before 1959. I think I'm ahead of myself here in time frame.

Flow Bench

I go to Detroit on some Hudson business and get to examine equipment used to check various parts for air flow. I want to buy a book with pictures and dimensions. I want a book that tells me about shapes and sizes. I'm shocked to find out some manufactors don't own or use air flow equipment. Some, like Buick, Olds use equipment that ain't worth a shit. Chevrolet air flow bench 1958 was a 6-71 Detroit Diesel super charger, driven by a 10 horsepower electric motor. So help me God. I sat down and called every place that had anything to do with air flow equipment. Even the aviation engine people. No one made anything that was acknowledged accurate in a 7,000 rpm range. I bought about five SAE papers on air flow, but I became confused. All were different from each other. By 1960 I decided nothing published could be proven correct. Then decided to figure it out for myself unless I met a tiny human who could stand in combustion chamber, in a fire and heat proof suit and watch it first hand. Also, I decided to be my own counsel in the experiment. Discussions with peers distracted and confused me. Back to the peyote.

I decided to get a pump big enough to flow 1,500 cubic feet of air at 28 inches of water (this is a negative pressure, or vacuum mode). I got this number of feet guesstimating biggest engine and highest rpm I would ever test. In next two years more shock treatment. A company called Stuterbuilt makes such a pump, but it takes 100…yup…100 horsepower electric motor to turn it. Twenty five grand to own one. Well, I've sold an invention and I've got fifty grand. One year fast forward: flow bench is complete. Dry flow, wet flow, I can handle stuff up to 75 cubic inch per cylinder, 8,000 rpm. Eighty five grand is now gone. But I got the biggest, most powerful, most accurate flow bench in the United States. This flow bench run damn near year round from 8:00 am to 2:00 am, for twenty years, seven days a week. This son-of-a-bitch makes so much noise it takes a pair of mufflers that weigh a ton apiece to half way quiet it down to 'bout 100 decibels at twenty feet.

I quickly learned the best control valve was like a camera iris. The best port was straightest, that air flow around a poppet valve was controlled by subtle things, like radiuses, and sharp edge, angles were better than radius alone if over nine degrees of direction change as required.

I learned there is no way to change one parameter without adjusting every other variable.

Most importantly I learned Otto cycle engine, no mater how perfectly done, would never give maximum performance for longer than a 300 rpm range unless valve timing, port shape, size and length, could be altered on the fly. I learned the Otto cycle engine could never be perfected. It is a basket of flawed systems. But it's also, as of today, August, 1998, the best and most viable system known to man considering every aspect, and all parameters to be met to be the state of the art of viable surface transportation. I learned the Otto cycle engine would be replaced with a machine at least two to two and a half times better in thermal efficiency. I learned the entropy of the Otto cycle is flawed because of the tremendous increase in the size of the combustion cavity. But man, for a quicky deal 'bout 100 years ago, we owe Otto a hell of a lot more than we gave him. I've learned it's possible to have roughly no emissions, and consume nearly all the hydro-carbons (a la external combustion). But in a confined environment.

I learned if we don't consume all hydro-carbons completely, this world won't be fit to live in in a hundred years. You know what one hundred years is in real time? 'bout one hundred seconds.

Same goes for the carbon in wood and coal, or any other combustible solid.

I want you to consider this one sentence carefully.

Water is wonderful as it is, and as we understand it. Maybe one day in the near future water may contribute a solution to our current trajectory of world genocide by atmospheric pollution. Just as water may one day save our asses it can also destroy civilization by the lack of potable water. I live on a river (the Halifax River, Daytona Beach, Florida), fifty-three years ago it was as clear as drinking water ('cept brackish and some salt), with a brown sand bottom (this is a big river). Today it is filthy. People and cities shit in it, pour oil, gas and diesel in it, dump toxic waste, detergents, fertilizer and garbage in it, pump tons of engine exhaust in it. Our government and industry and water toys are the greatest polluters. My solution would be to make the polluters drink it and bath in it till it kills 'em. You know, we've been one hundred years fucking up the natural ecology system. I'd like to remind you it will take approximately the same length of time to unfuck it...how the hell did I get into this sermon?

Well, my flow bench gets to meet many various engine manufacturers engine components regarding air and fuel conduits, cylinder heads, manifolds intake and exhaust and carburetors and air cleaners.

Eventually Chevy showed how to do 'bout the same thing for 'bout a million bucks. Small, affordable flow benches are now offered to the racers. Nowadays all racers of any stature have a flow bench. So air flow is as big a topic in race oriented publications as is chassis technology. It's too bad most of it is bullshit. The technology of air flow is no different than of a liquid. Air is of course not possible to totally observe visually, but the physics is the same, the difference being the specific gravity of each.

I put the "what if" to it. What if you colored the air? Colored the smoke? Yup, it worked. You can see what's happening.

The ability to maintain a correct air-fuel ratio with a computer controlled positive pressure fueling equipment reduces errors in air fuel ratio that carburation for example is unable to adjust for because natural physics is almost capable, but not totally capable to monitor a correct air fuel ratio under all conditions.

Why? Hell, I can't answer that. Ask God when you see him. He figured this shit out several million years ago. As of now, he still keeps some of His stuff secret.

If computer controlled fuel systems were allowed in the Cigarette Cup, laps on round track speeds would hardly budge. But, if these systems were used at Watkins Glen and Somona road courses, lap speeds would jump up markedly. Why? With computer you could hold a desirable air / fuel ratio 100 percent of the time. Not possible with a carburetor that would conform to rules.

In all the work I done with carburetors I could never establish and hold a wanted air-fuel ratio at any and all times. Let me qualify that sentence.

At all and every driving mode, and in reliability and in emissions.

A great lesson I learned from the flow bench was: everything is available in three states. As a gas, liquid or solid.

There are two factors that can cause a limited or total phase change. Those being temperature and pressure. Changing gasoline to a gasoline vapor is an example of "phase change."

Actually, there is a third factor present that deals with one or more elements interfacing with the working fluid. In this case, air and gasoline.

That last deal we'll call "sequence."

So my experimenting self-educated me by accident that temperature, pressure and sequence are as big a part of petro chemistry as are the ingredients.

Simply put: if you had the complete and accurate formula for a chemical product except for the sequence, temperature and pressure, your chances to make same product would be less than one in a million.

I could teach you in two days how to build correct size intake and exhaust manifolds, and correct size carburetor in two days if the parts were not cluttered up with pistons, cylinder walls, head bolts, water passages and push rods and rpm range.

It turns out best push rod cylinder head will be the best known series of compromises. And assuming all parts are not adjustable, the maximum rpm operating range will at best be 300 rpm for maximum efficiency.

Holley 4150

Maybe for some of you this shit's getting too deep. But fifty years of engine research is hard to get on fifteen pages. So if you're lost, move on to some of the more entertaining stuff. Maybe when we assemble this into a book we can add some pages of pornographic pictures with substituted heads of some of the early racers to make this section more interesting. (I almost got a centerfold in a women's magazine once. Also almost got one in "Hot Rod" magazine). Grumpy Jenkins did.

We've touched on carburetors, so let's go to the carb most stock car racers use.

The Standard Holley Four-barrel Double Pumper

The biggest carb we had in passenger cars up to and including 1962 was about 450 cubic foot at an inch and a half, or 28 inches of water. That was restrictor carb racing, 'cept very few knew it.

A 400 cubic inch engine at 7,000 rpm needed 'bout 850 cubic feet of air fuel mix. So generally speaking we need a carburetor 'bout twice as big as anything around.

This was 427 cubic inch time, or seven liters.

I worked as a consultant at Pontiac for Mr. Knudsen.

I had an ornery fucker, 'bout half-genius, named Ralph Johnson, working with me (because he got throwed out of half of Detroit and couldn't get a job). Why? He wouldn't brown nose and play "yes man." He was a heavy drinkin,' pussy-hound and he loved to be around race cars. He and I knew carburetor was too small. By the way, he was an engineer and a damn good one. And really a carburetor or fueling engineer to boot. I tell Mr. K. we need a bigger carburetor (I'm at Pontiac now). Carter, Holley, Rochester have told me, "We ain't gonna spend our money to make one that big. We don't need it." Damn. We are at 421 cubic inches, headed for 500.

Mr. K. says, "Do it." So Ralph and I, and honestly, Ralph did 75 percent of it, modify a goofy Holley truck carburetor to 1-11/16 throttle plates, primary and secondary both, put in staged secondary and 'bout double size of everything. We can flow carb wet or dry. Course this is right down Ralph's alley. Well, when we get done in a month or so (we still have to race also) the carb looks 'bout like it does today. But it's half bondo (a plastic we mix up), one fourth aluminum, and one fourth pot metal. We try it on 389 cubic inch Pontiac. Runs shitty, won't idle. But we gain 10 horsepower Well, hell, first shot out of the barrel, not too shabby. Well, I work with a nice project engineer up at Pontiac named Bill Klinger, so I take carburetor up there to be checked. I figure when they see a gain with that cobbled up mess I'll get OK to finish it and get OK for money to get carburetor tooled up.

Well, Bill gets 10 horsepower, but I got standard problem. "We don't want no fuckin' swamp farmer telling us how to build engines." So Pontiac engineering tells the boss, Mr. K., "Ain't no good." Knudsen says, "I'm not gonna overrule engineering and piss Pete off (Pete Estes was chief engineer). I'm good and pissed, so I get my carb and go home. See, all I got was one side of the story. At this time Knudsen knew he would be at Chevy driving that deal soon, and Delorean told Mr. K. carb was good idea. At the time, John is number three at Pontiac, Estes is Knudsen's co-pilot, but the carb don't set his ass on fire. (And he knows he will be running Pontiac in a month).

Soon as Mr. K. gets to Chevy he calls and offers me a job. I decline. He then say,s "We'll talk 'bout this later, but could he have the home-made carb to look at. Maybe get Chevy to pay the tooling. Maybe get Rochester to build it." "Sure. It ain't doing no good here sitting on top of a workbench."

Well, I'll be damned, three months later Knudsen says he, "made a deal with Holley carburetor to tool it up and build it as an 850 cfm." I say, "Great, but send the bondo prototype back. I'd like to keep it." "Oh, hell yes, you'll have it in couple days." Thirty-six years later…it ain't back yet. Usual deal was: "Don't know where it is, but we'll find it." This goes on for one year, then to the standard second year deal: "Nobody knows where it is." Third year: "Quit bothering us. Your getting to be a pain in the ass." "Oh, the hell with it. Probably Holley will give us a sizable fee if it's successful."

I'll bet you two hundred million of those things were sold up to now, and they are still the standard racing carb of the world. You couldn't buy a hamburger for what Ralph and I got. 'Course now, maybe they forgot.

I'm sure the prototype is in some trophy area in some Holley engineer's collection as evidence of him being it's inventor. Or possibly a Chevy engineer. The original had a couple of flaws. We didn't mount the fuel bowl in the best plane to preclude cornering fuel ratio instability, and we only had one accelerator pump. Should have been two. Ralph, shortly after carburetor was accepted went to work for Holley and made those two changes.

I've since met engineers who improved the carb. I've met vendors who have modified it to be much better, but what puzzled me is, only changes I see in a new 1998 carb is better quality workmanship and improvements that make it easier to calibrate to given engine and given track. Also, there is now a very long range of sizes which help custom fit best qualities needed for specific types of racing. You friggin' genius Holley carb "experts" need to say, "Thank you Ralph," every time you pay your income tax and at least give me a t-shirt. I'd like you to be honest also and say you had nothing to do with it…Ralph and I did.

HONING FINISH

In 1956 I'm working for and racing Chevy's. I decided to try and solve the mystery (to me) of the vertical scratches in the cylinder bore and on the piston skirts and on the compression rings. In general it was covered with a blanket reason for all cylinder bore imperfections that came with use: "It's dirt and metal particles in the oil."

Well, it happens to grandma's engine as well as a racing engine. I know engine was clean when I put it together. So standard answer is an accepted guess. I kept looking at the bores. I noticed when I finished honing bore was like a mirror, but on overhaul I could see some cross-hatch. Well, hell. I didn't leave a cross-hatch.

I preferred to control oil with scraper and oil ring.

Reverse torsional twist scraper and oil land drainage drilled or machined.

I saved a cylinder bore out of a ruined block, and then cut it in half and studied it with a magnifying glass.

There was the answer. The honing process dug grooves (the valleys) then folded the peaks over into the valleys.

Let's stop here a minute. You start honing with a rough grit. Why? It cuts fastest.

So, first stone is 100 grit (100 cutting pieces per square inch), Then to a 200 or 300, the to a 500 grit.

You change stones three to four times. Last cutting stone mostly polishes.

Now right here I finally realized a hone does not cut anything. Nor does any grinding procedure. (Hones and grinders tear metal out).

What the hell can we do about it?

Well, somebody makes a brush wall bore cleaner (poor man's cylinder hone), 'bout 25 bucks. I notice it pulls folded metal out (some) of the valleys but not all. So I use it after each stage of honing as I go finer in grit (my method of knowing how much of the folded metal I got out with a ball hone on a scrap sample cylinder). I'd paint it with muriatic acid, then after eight hours I'd brush hone again and examine with a 20 power magnifying glass).

Back 'bout 1985 I heard about a company called "Osborne" from Kansas instruments, sales manager John Goodman, who made a tough plastic brush you could fit into a CK 10 stone holder. The plastic, I believe had an impregnated cutting material (industrial diamonds) embedded in the plastic. Well, 30 years later this system solved the vertical scratching problem and bore seal got six or seven percent better and improved engine life very noticeably.

Peterson Machine Tool recognized the merit and marketed it to us. Joe Glaser from Osborne taught me the tricks on how to use it. This technology was a real exception. It was one of the few ideas racers didn't argue about for three to five years before they accepted it.

I think Osborne hit a homer, bases loaded within a year.

What did I invent? Nothing.. Did I get paid? Nope, I got the unusual, I was thanked by some of the company executives.

Why mention Goodman and Glaser? I'd like for you to know at least by name, some of the thousands of peers in their fields who helped me learn. No one man could possibly do it all.

I also got my ass chewed out by the grandson of the inventor of the ball brush hone I used at first. Why chewed out? I wrote a feature story in Circle Track and gave all the credit to Osborne. Grandson said, "Bullshit! Grampa did it!." I told the grandson to, "Get me the facts, I'll write a story if you're right and tell the world I screwed your grandpop out of credit he was due."

I never wrote the story. Why? Grandson never came up with dope, plus I used his grandpop's deal for 25 years and it didn't really do a super good job of overlaid peaks.

Grandson. I tried to find your company name to credit grandpop with recognizing problem first, but I can't remember, and I couldn't find it in any recent ads. Don't bitch. If you'd done what you said you were gonna do, grandpop would be grinning at which ever way he went. (But maybe if it was wrong way, they can't get magazines there because of heat).

You know…I think you'll notice by the time you get to the end of "What Did You Invent Smokey?" chapter you'll notice maybe I am a mechanical nymphomaniac…I liked doing it so much, I gave it all away.

If I'd of had a male madam, or pimp (what's the normal handle – business manager?) collecting for me I'd be rich. Maybe.

Valve Technology

'Bout 1960, valve spring technology was 'bout like tires – way short. In a two-valve engine the intake valve is much bigger and weighs more than an exhaust valve, so I decided to try titanium intake valves to stop valve floating. I had TRW make samples for Chevy, a two-piece valve stem and head. Between TRW and Chevy bureaucracy this was a real pain in the ass. Titanium stems hammered out at the rocker interface and valve stems galled badly.

Fusing a hardened valve stem tip was easy, and solved one problem, but coating the valve stem we must have went thru 15 failures in a material and material bonding search. At one point I had to buy $7,000 worth of valves with my money to keep TRW working on it (I resold valves eventually). TRW was losing their ass on this deal. Over half the valves were scrapped, didn't meet specs.

We finally found a hi-temperature moly and a good bonding technique…suddenly victory was "ourn."

Valve float in stock car racing is caused by the weight of the valve, valve spring, valve spring retention parts. Well hell. Everything on the valve side of the rocker shaft or pivot.

As rpm increases, the acceleration of the mass increases amount of effort necessary to control the valve motion as dictated by the cam lobe. If there is not enough energy to make valve follow cam lobe exactly, valve float occurs. Float in most cases is where a valve accelerates into a mode where it's lift limit is valve spring coil bind. The damage caused, and it can be very severe, occurs on the closing side of the lobe where the valve closes in a bouncing mode, and shock loads are destructive to all valve train components. Push rods, rockers, lifter and cam lobes are in a "will fail" mode, and as a rule causes contact between piston and valve. Then valve usually breaks.

The problem in a nanosecond, is usually a piston failure next followed with a cylinder block rupture which produces the giant white smoke screen and the "oh shit" part is initiated in that same thousandth of a second when you saw the smoke. If driver's able to talk after this, he says "The motor broke."

Valve spring research includes much more investigation than spring alone. Therefore all the beating around the bush in what follows. There is room here for a "hero badge." Poppet valves are 200 years old and a piss poor way of letting working fluid in and out of the engine. Don't study how to make a poppet valve deal. Better study how to junk the deal and go to a better mouse trap.

Doing the exhaust valve was easier because lube coating technique was known. So all we had to sweat was bore finish of hollow stem that needed to be slick. Why? Sharp machining lines are stress risers and failure is soon. What made most all of this rough was, anything you changed had resistance from both staffs (the vehicle manufacturer and the parts vendor). The "don't rock the boat" and the "if it ain't broke don't fuck with it" mentality was part of their holy grail. Well, sure you can't make a mistake if you don't change.

Cam shafts and rocker arms were badly neglected by the OEM. In 1955 they abandoned the flat head engine concept because of inability to have a higher compression ratio and maintain valve to cylinder head clearance. And because overhead valves clearly had much better flow potential.

The simplicity and lower cost of the flat head no longer could be used as justification for the poor power and thermal inefficiency this design had.

The Hudson Hornet was the last flat head that ever sat, grinning and panting, in a victory circle.

Take it from me, that son-of-a-bitch was a running mother. Believe it or not it took up to 1955 before the flat-head/overhead valve debate was finally conceded to the over headers, and I'll be damned if I didn't see Chrysler working on it again in 1985. Part of my original agreement with Ed Cole was I could put in a shaft mounted rocker if the mickey mouse production deal (standard '55 Chevy) was no good. Well, to my amazement with an rpm limit of 6,000, it was good enough from a power point of view, but I screwed up bad in accepting that system too quickly. It had terrible durability. Matter of fact it was 75 percent of our trouble. The one-and-a-half rocker ratio was not good. We had to put too much in the cam lobes, and we had a lifter 'bout .200 to .300 too small in diameter to get all the action in. Well, those days NASCAR doesn't have any Nobel Prize winning genius as inspector. So I bored lifter bores to the Ford lifters size (bigger). Use big block rocker arms one-and-three-quarters ratio by simply moving rocker stud .185 away from valve. But cylinder heads were so small port wise, engine never saw the "goody." I battled Chevy's engine brains off and on for 13-14 years to get ports to flow 300 cubic feet intake and 240 cubic feet exhaust. They gave in about two percent a year.

The one-and-three-quarters rocker deal was a durability flop then as well as an insignificant power improvement. We then got ahold of some aluminum after-market heads. Opened and welded ports up. Made a shaft rocker deal with positive oiling. Running a 1.8 intake rocker ratio and 1.60 exhaust…now that mother got to honking! 'Bout same time I moved the spark plug (you know it now as the angle plug) heads. All this was rejected by Chevy engineering, except 'bout 18 months later angle plug head was accepted.

All through here valve spring research goes on. Two coils, dampers, three coils, 50 kinds of steel. We slowly inch up in rpm, but in a nut shell, "we ain't fixed it." One day Bruce McClaren seen the original pair of welded up angle head prototypes I'd sent to Chevy to test. We got 'bout 15 horsepower with the new plug location. Bill Howell, a Chevy product engineer, and not really a Smokey fan. (And that was OK, I didn't rate him very high as an engine genius. Matter of fact he was a pain in the ass.) Bill had tested the heads at Chevy and said "didn't do a thing." The heads were on a shelf in Chevy research laboratory. Been there a year. Bruce wanted to try them. Bill says, "Take 'em if you want too. I'm getting ready to throw 'em in the scrap." Well, Bruce gets 15 horsies next day. Tells Piggins, Chevy's racing boss. So Piggins gets a small off-line modification project going. The head got a part number and off they went. I liked that. I'd been running the heads for 'bout a year-and-a-half and it was a pain in the ass to modify standard heads here.

I soon read about how Vince Piggins and Herb Fishel invented this great advance. Don't know why they didn't get the Nobel Prize for engineering for the breakthrough. Ed Cole and I argued 'bout that from day one. Remember?

Stock Quality – Caps, Blocks, Rods

About in here, we are making 'bout 1.8 horsepower per cubic inch and turning 8,000 with the three inch stroke 302 engine. A new rattlesnake moves in. Head gaskets can't handle the program. I spend hours and hours making a pair of copper head gaskets by hand.

I try gas filled rings around cylinders. Nothing is good. I find trouble in both the block deck and the head deck are too weak. So I get some blocks made with half inch thick deck with big upper radius inside the casting and blind stud holes. And get a thicker cylinder head deck.

Lastly, we have to make head studs in three different diameters to get same stretch at 85 pounds of torque with oil for lubricant. Well, this gets head nailed down but twists the upper bore badly in the last inch up. There ain't no end to it. Making the head plate solved that bore distortion, now main and rod bearings can't handle it.

We four bolt the mains, make steel main caps ('cept for rear). Rods remain border line as do rod bolts, but we get forging dies shaved. Get better and cleaner steel and forge hotter and get rods that if you x-rayed 'em, we get 40 percent scrap rate. (From dirt and inclusions due to forging too cold and unclean steel).

Believe it or not Chevy was never able to solve the rod bolt problem.

I still today must have twenty different kinds. But Gary Holzapfel of ARP gets it done first shot out of the barrel. I also found we had to remachine all machined surfaces plus spend about two hours a rod removing stress risers and then re-shotpeen. Then refinish bores of the big and little end of the rod. Chevy never ever made a good useable rod up to 1985 that I ever saw.

We could buy eight good Carrillo rods with good rod bolts for 750 bucks. We spent more in man hours for lesser quality, but NASCAR said "use stock shit." Jr. Johnson and Chevy tried making small block rods out of big block forging. They were stronger, but too heavy. A band-aid on a cancer. I still get pissed thinking about the hundreds and hundreds of man hours I spent trying to make that shit into roses.

Well, guess what now, the cranks start breaking and they do step up to that. We get bigger mains and rod journals, but what we really needed was a good forged no-twist crank. I'll bet I spent four years of my life cleaning up crank shaft forgings for stress relief and oil drag. Finally, after-market crank was OK'd… and the Carrillo rods.

Moldex got so rich (he told me through Whitey, his number two man), he wouldn't talk to anyone but his girlfriend anymore. Them cats at Moldex made beautiful billet cranks on old wore out machinery that George Washington used making guns to shoot the British in 17-0-shit. I can't even remember boss man at Moldex's name any more, so I can't credit him with his pioneering. After Whitey told me 'bout no phone calls, I threw away the business card. (I just remembered it. Bob Gillelan). This shows again the disruptive power of the li'l wooley booger.

Lifter bores, believe it or not we had to rebore them to get 'em aligned with the cam correctly. Boy that was about a two day pain in the ass, cause after you bored 'em you have to sleeve 'em back to standard. With a Bridgeport, I did it the easy, best way (put bigger Ford lifters in, NASCAR hadn't woke up yet). The deck on each cylinder bank were cut usually twisted opposite to each other. It was done with a broach zap, and over with. Cylinder bores were same way. Off the print and varied with length of time since tooling was adjusted. When tooling was nearly new and had just been retooled and re-set, blocks and heads were fair, but as production progressed, the quality recessed. You know some of the original tooling for small block Chevy was cannibalized from in line six cylinder tooling and in general the tooling was too weak. Today's tooling is massive compared to 1947. It was not unusual for the specs. Of a 1957 engine to vary 3/16ths from pan rail to carburetor mounting flange. That happens when the plus's or minuses all lined up same way (the tolerances on the blueprints). Called "stack up." This was true of all American manufacturers.

Mystery Engine

In 1963 I came back to Chevy from Pontiac to help develop the Mystery Engine for racing. (Still screwing with valve springs now getting German spring tech and got some from Sweden on the way.) I think that particular engine was closest to the small block Chevy in a mass production cheap world-class horsepower per dollar. I'd say it was second. But in my mind too big, too powerful and much too heavy for a sensible passenger car. I loved it's power and potential, but shit, why not a 16 cylinder, 1,000 horsepower that weighed 1,600 pounds and was 7 feet long? Along with the Mystery Engine work, I built a pair of 427 cubic inch small blocks. The Mystery Engine 427 cubic inch finally produced 650 horsepower on three two barrels at 7,600 rpm, but the 427 small block produced 550 horsepower first shot out, at 5,500 rpm with one four barrel. (These two engines, small block 427s terrorized South Georgia for about three years on the dirt and small paved tracks.) Well, Piggins is running Hi-Performance and he likes the 427 big block. So does Mr. K., so I lose the argument. But so do Mr. K. and Piggins after 'bout 18 months. France wakes up and says, "No big engines – back to 355 inches." By now I've built a 427 small block, where I added half inch to the bore length, raised the cam shaft. All this by machining methods, and got a couple pair of big-assed port heads made, used Carrillo 6.25 inch rods. First time we dyno'd this sucker 605 horsepower at 6,500.

I'm bucking to make the small block bigger and forget big block, 'cept for trucks.

Well Piggins bad mouthed that combination so bad I decided not to even show it to them. I decided to do some Indy stuff instead, and murdered it, along with the big pile of shit the re-engineered big block was and still is.

If you saw the Mystery Engine and a 427 side by side without exhaust headers, 98 out of 100 of you readers couldn't have seen the difference. But the clever things that engines now have to make them both thermally and power efficient the Mystery Engine had in 1963. It's main flaw was in about 100 pounds of unnecessary weight in all the cast iron components. It's principal designer was a young cat named Dick Keineth. Dick actually worked for Zora Duntov. I was working for Pontiac. Knudsen asked me to come look at Mystery Engine for my opinion. 7:30 am, Chevy Tech center…I'm in one of the secret rooms. They have totally disassembled Mystery Engine that had 'bout 10 hours of hard dyno time. Room full of big shots: Ed Cole, Mr. K., Zora Duntov, Harry Barr (chevy chief engineer) and Rosy (asst. chief engineer), and a medium-size cat with a burr haircut, black suit, pants two inches too short. You can see the white sox good, and black grandpa's GM five holers shoes, Suit coat too short and sleeves too short, clean white shirt and necktie.

Shirt looks like a cow chewed it. All wrinkled necktie (whopper big green job with a big bull frog on it), skinny end of tie an inch below fat side…by no means a dandy dresser. Burr hair cut and half inch thick black rimmed goggles.

We've been in room 'bout an hour with two technicians, also Walt Sprinkle and another technician.

Through the whole deal Dick never opened his mouth. Duntov, Cole, Barr and Walt answer questions. Knudson says, "What do you think?" I say, "Looks like a 200 pound Marilyn Monroe."

Barr asks Cole "what that means." Knudsen answers, "Good looking, but too heavy." I ask, "Who designed his engine?" Burr head finally speaks (and very loud), "I did." Holy shit. I'm surprised. I expect Duntov to take credit. But Dick left no room for doubt. He did it and was damn proud of it. I walked over, shook his hand and said, "I got a feeling 'fore you're done here lots of people gonna know 'bout you." I think Dick Keineth was the most talented engineer all of Detroit had in 1963 in reference to gasoline engines.

I gotta clear this part up. The "so called Mystery, or Porcupine Engine," never made production.

Only 42 sets of parts were ever made. The bean counters killed the Mystery Engine (too expensive to manufacture). Dick Keineth's masterpiece was handed over to a bunch of butchers to cut production cost. Dick run his mouth pretty bad 'bout them ruining his engine and he got second worst punishment GM can hang on a bad boy engineer's ass…assistant chief engineer at Opel, in Germany. Number one worst punishment was to be sent to Argentina. Remember, this was back in early sixties. As a rule, two or three years in either Germany or Argentina and the victim either committed suicide, went goofy or quit. (Dick survived and took early retirement). But they ruined the best engine man Detroit ever had. Some just quit and leave and some quit and stay.

Intake Designs, Heat Shield Pontiac, Edelbrock "Smokeram"

Rite in here I've built a new manifold for the Pontiac where I incorporate a lower floor in the intake casting to keep from inner engine heat, and hot oil from heating bottom of intake runners.

My boss is Pete Estes, a good engine man. I ask him, "Should I patent it?" He says "I doubt that does any good really." Well, I should not have listened to that bit of advice.

Next, I built a single four-barrel cross ram manifold for small block Chevy with same principal and made a deal with Vic Edelbrock to manufacture and sell it. I called it the air gap manifold. Edelbrock called it the "Smokeram." All performance manifolds now use that principle.

I invented it and I believe Vic's bank account appreciated it. The Smokeram really worked on engines up to 327 cubic inches. I paid for half the tooling and was to receive five bucks a manifold. My half of tooling was taken from royalty, but my manifold sales were taking sales from other Edelbrock manifolds (with no royalty).

I asked a friend at Edelbrock why sales were slowing. He said, "Pick up the phone and call our technical help dept. I got the answer. The answer, "technician said cross ram was junk. Use a spider type." Shortly, Edelbrock canceled the manifold. I tried to buy Vic's half of the tooling. He wouldn't sell it…just dared me to try and get it legally. If he'd of come to Daytona the next year I still had the legal juice to convince him to have better manners. But he didn't show. 'Bout then I said, "Fuck it. It ain't worth it." I was puzzled, Vic's dad was such a goddam nice guy. Where did Vic inherit his hen house ways from? (Recently he tried to pull a deal on me 'bout a model car. I just don't get it. Maybe he has a plan where he can take it with him.)

'Bout that time Vic got cross ways with a manifold designer named "Brownfield." Now Brownie taught Vic's lawyers a lesson about who was the daddy of the spider series manifolds. Vic, you need to look back at your tracks and go back and fix some of it before you run out of time.

As you get older the time seems to pass at an ever increasing speed. I ain't mad at Vic, but I notice when I finish some pages, maybe this will end a beautiful friendship. But again. I'm telling it like it was. If someone takes offense to me telling what they did…good or bad…"tough shit."

Cold Air Plenum

Carburetor air, to you I guess that's not an exciting topic, but really if you're a racer that topic can change your style of living. For every ten degrees Fahrenheit you cool the air you gain one percent in power. OK, we got 500 horsepower and the under hood temperature is 200 degrees Fahrenheit, outside air is 80 degrees.

That's a 12 percent difference in power. Five times twelve is 60, right? 60 horsies if you can give the engine unheated air. OK, now if you can pressurize the air going into the engine by ten pounds you can easy increase horsepower 25 percent. 500 horsepower + 25 percent = 625 horsepower.

Well, in the early 60s just below bottom of wind shield there was a big opening to receive ambient air (outside air) for heater and air conditioner. And as air hits the windshield, it's possible to put a positive pressure in that box. I put an opening in the front of the fire wall in the upper right hand corner. Then made an elbow to fasten to the air cleaner to interface with hole in the fire wall, and used a rubber cut from a truck tube to make a flexible joint and positive seal to force the plenum air into the carburetor air cleaner. By blocking all exits except carburetor air cleaner, I got much cooler air and some positive pressure close to one pound. Lastly, I covered everything with a thermal barrier to preclude engine heat increasing temperature of all metal components of the system. What I get? 'Bout a 20 horsepower gain nominally speaking. Like the ol' lady said when she pissed in ocean, "Every little bit helps."

Flywheel Supercharger

I find out when the engine is at high rpm, there is a pressure in the bell housing area…hmmmmm. What if? All my life I've been a "what iffer?" What if I put a hole in the right place in the bell housing for air to come in, and another hole in the bell housing for air to come out. Then made sure all other leaks were sealed. The fly wheel and it's teeth, and the pressure plate are impellers inside a housing. Now if I have everything clean inside and stick a bottle of urethane at a hole and press the buttons, everything inside gets full of foam. Let it harden. Now crank engine up and cut a path for rotating parts. Then what if you opened the entrance and exit area up with a knife, then cut room for throw out bearing and fork. Then run engine up to 7,000 rpm and find you get ten pounds of pressure, and are pumping 800 cubic feet of air a minute with no parasitic losses? What if the air cleaner crossed the area where the "out hole" was in the bell housing, and you have a three inch collar, inch long both places, and you had a short piece of hose to connect them in a leak proof mode up to ten pounds or so? What if air cleaner had an inner valve that blew closed at two or three pounds of pressure so pressurized air couldn't go back out the plenum and had to go into engine? What if that increased horsepower 25 percent? I run that deal two years, no one ever said a word. Biggest problem is keeping it a "one man deal." Not even the driver knew.

Get an old rule book, early sixties, see if any part of this is classified as illegal. Was it cheating?

You say, "How do you do this and nobody catches on?" Damn, if they can put the lady in the box and saw her in half, how hard is it to slip an air cleaner down one inch inside of a three inch rubber collar? What did you invent Smokey? Nothing. I went to patent it and found about twenty patents going back to 1919 reference flywheel superchargers.

Iron Blocks

'Bout 1957 main bearing caps and block strength got to be a major problem. I set up a Pontiac block by it's bell housing bolts to a plate and beam that can't move. I have a free spinning crank. No rear seal, with easy end play. Next, I fasten a beam on front of block and put a 300 pound twist on it. Crank's locked solid. Man, that was a shock. Hell. Engine got over 400 foot pounds of torque. Well, put cylinder heads on and intake manifold that should take some twist out of it. It does, but you can tell crank can feel it. It's not locked, just hard to turn. That explained some of the goofy main bearing stress we saw. OK, go to .003, .0035 main clearance and the binding ain't bad now.

This is an example of why I've never favored an aluminum block, and I still don't believe in aluminum for hi-torque engines. Sure if you get horsepower at 14,000 rpm with 20 pounds of torque, aluminum is great. How 'bout magnesium? It's stronger than aluminum. I was involved in a comparison of an aluminum and iron Chevy bow tie block as cast by Yamaha in Japan using a proprietary casting technique. It machined out as light and a little stronger. Hell, this was fifteen years ago. The good shit is bearing clearances on iron block stay much better. Iron is twice as strong as aluminum, but weighs twice as much. So the trick is how to cast thin iron sections.

The reason I avoid aluminum if I can where part needs to be strong and maintain its tolerances and the aluminum coefficient of expansion is double that of iron.

Historically all stock car engines (American manufactured) had a cast iron main bearing cap held in place with two big bolts. We could see metal chaffing and metal transfer between main cap and block. Main bearing would exhibit excessive wear and/or distress, all over the 360 degrees of area in a very irregular pattern. So, I made steel main bearing caps and added a second bolt, and tapped the block to accept this modification. Now we got four bolt mains.

Ford came with cross bolting finally, by good old farmer cut and try, we found the extra main bolts should be at an angle to supplement the clamping force with stabilization in the lateral plane

The V6 Buick was an exception so we made a three-quarter inch steel plate that with a little machining on main caps, tied all mains together with the pan bolt, perimeter bolts as well. It worked but was a pure pain in the ass to get assembled without block distortion. Block distortion in twist was a shock to me. I had to overcome it when I first used engine as a stress member in a '66 Chevelle.

Moroso Manufacturing sold the block girdle for Buick, I guess I wasn't first guy to do it, and one day a lady chewed my ass out big time. Said I stole the idea from her husband. Remember what I said about "who did it first." Now this snake is dead.

Along with the steel main caps I decided to get serious with fasteners: bolts, studs, washers, locking systems, lubrication and retention of fasteners, plus the metallurgy, heat treat and various high manpower input. Stuff such as hardness test and control of polishing and shot peening, threading one at a time as well as protective and/or cosmetic coatings. Racers, take my word for this; fastener technology and manufacturing expertise are a life time adventure for an educated and talented engineer or technician. I've self educated myself for sixty years, and my last twelve years as a student of ARPs manufacturing adventures. I can say this in a very qualified way. No one will ever be a successful engine builder in high buck racing who cannot get a passing grade in current fastener technology.

At this time (2000), ARP is the target for quality and state of the art. Mechanical fasteners locking ideas for safety engineering is a past art for 98 percent of all application the correct method is stretch and with a limited amount of chemical locking. The chemical locking and sealing wizards for my money, is the Loc-Tite Company. They offer a manual to technicians to educate rookies and world class winners on the mysteries of chemical locking and gasketry. Gasketry and fasteners are a common combination that requires a lot of "know how." Done correctly it's very simple effective and reliable. Done in a guessing or half-assed way is about a guaranteed failure. I found if a fastener was designed correctly it's life would be infinite. That statement includes rod bolts. (This assumes the connecting rod design and execution was correct.)

If you think this part's boring, how would you like to have lived through 50 years of probably 20 failures a year in one or more of the various categories we've covered, and will cover before we visit all the problem areas a racer experienced from day one of stock car racing? Remember, there were no vendors. And if there were, they were "not allowed." And as the chief or car owner you did it all, plus trying to cope with NASCAR politics and world class gas station mechanics as inspectors. It was kinda like walking through a room (bare footed while blind folded) that had twenty rattlers on the floor. But to be honest 'bout it, we could have said "fuck it" and quit. Nobody forced us, 'cept maybe our egos and our needs to compete and win. Here we are, back to our number one nemesis again. I told you we'd get to it.

Valve Springs

Valve springs were a problem on day one and still are today fifty-five years later. I tried, I bet, 200 different ideas to have a valve spring that simply put, "got the job done" with radical (very radical) cam lobe profile and designs. Most of the experimenting was with various steel formulas, also much time was spent in heat treat. An area that turned out to be very important was time consuming detail regarding removing all stress risers. That kinda means wire has to be very-very diametrically uniform and very smooth. The real problem is the valve spring is a manufactured resistance to alternate directional motion. The fact that it is a coiled spring it has a series of resonant frequencies where, I guess simply stated, it does goofy stuff. The most common description is "valve float."

We want the valves to follow the cam profile, but they go ape-shit and fly up off the cam lobe and bounce three to five times on the closing side, and as a rule, cause a very serious engine failure.

Considering the competitive view and the economic implications like championship points, race purses and sponsors, this failure also can trigger a race car total destruction. Valve failure (most times) causes a rupture in the water or oil containment system and oil or water gets under rear tires. Then comes the big "Oh-shit!"

A valve spring is principally an energy storage machine. The glaring problem is, the machine is too small. The obvious fix is a valve spring that is longer, bigger in diameter and with more coils of heavier wire. But this creates problems (like not enough room). There are no inexpensive fixes for two valve push rod engines. Here's the deal: with two valve engines you need bigger valves to flow more air at higher rpm. No sweat, but the bigger valves weigh more. Herein lives the rattlesnake 'valve float.' OK, there are engines that turn 13,000 with springs. Yes, but they are four valve, five valve design and the valves are like a feather, very small diameter. Get it? Four valves pass as much or more air with half the weight each.

But it's gotta be stock right? Well, that will change soon, when they let the Asian and European cars compete in NASCAR (and they will). They have multi-valve overhead cammers…yup, soon.

Yeah, I know over Chevy's dead push rods. Watch and see the power of the greenie rear it's ugly head before too many more moons.

You see, if the energy necessary to open the valve stayed stored in the valve spring, that energy would be repaid when valve closed. But since spring mass is too small, a lot of energy is lost in the form of heat. The oil in a Winston Cup engine is the hottest in the exhaust valve spring seat on a small block Chevy. Wanna know why? Well, exhaust gas is 'bout 1,500 degrees Fahrenheit. It's one quarter of an inch below spring seat, and there is no water in that area to help cool the spring. I devised a way to flood the lower one and one half coils and cool them in oil, and that helped quite a bit. They do it now by spraying oil on the spring. I tried that in '60 and '61, but didn't help me enough. Guess I didn't flow enough oil. The valve spring still today is an imperfect machine. But successful by custom building it for a narrow rpm range (that's talking push rod). We liked light push rods, but found they flexed, so heavier push rod walls and bigger outer diameter push rods had to happen. The Formula One cars have an air actuated valve which of course doesn't have the negatives of a spring's dynamics, so 17,000 rpm for them is now quite reliable. But it is expensive.

Maybe not though. A very good valve spring can cost over one hundred bucks and be good for one race only. So sixteen hundred to thirty two hundred a race and a number of DNFs a year can run into serious money and sponsorship problems.

What did I invent? Not one damn thing, 'cept I found 'bout 150 things that didn't help. So many little things were bad. Example: on a humid morning, just starting the engine could break a valve spring, humid weather on a cold morning makes water droplets on bottom side of wire in a vertical installed valve spring. When you compress springs, all but a couple of coils come together. Water won't compress. This can crack and break the spring wire.

I tried two, three, even four springs in a combination arrangement, tapered wire, tapered springs, every shape you can imagine. Nope, never tried a square spring.

In a nut shell no spring is the best. Maybe a electrical solenoid, which I worked with, and still dislike, desmodramic (no spring mechanical guidance in all motion). I learned weight of everything on the valve side of the rocker stud or shaft was critical the spring, valve, valve spring retainer and that side of the rocker, but on opposite side. Weight of push rod and valve lifter. I couldn't prove a gain or loss in rpm from an inaccurate valve motion based on weight. The importance of stress risers turns out to be a major durability factor. Polished valve springs are better. I don't know wider is for sure better but I know polished is.

Titanium is a good material for a valve spring. It's not as heat sensitive and is light, but again very expensive and still harmonic plagued. In short, valves and springs are a pain in the ass and always will be. Answer? Get rid of 'em. Yup, it can be done. (I might tell you how if you're nice to me. But not now.) In 1955, 75 pound spring pressure on the seat was 'bout standard for a mass produced surface transportation engine with 'bout .375 lift. At Gainesville drags, March '99, 975 pounds on the seat and one inch lift at 8,500. Whew!

Ignition Sleeves, Coils and flames

In 1953 I noticed the common state of the art for ignition origination was a point type distributor. Did a good job up to 4,500 rpm, if coil was not over 15,000 volts. But at 6,000 rpm at high cylinder pressures in general, very unreliable. In running the ignition system in a test made in a dark room at high rpm and in a maximum power mode, the electric leaks look like St. Elmo's fire or the Fourth of July fancy fireworks demonstration. The wires, distributor cap, the spark plug ceramics, the nose of the coil – everything is leaking visible electric energy. I decided to build a distributor with eight sets of points exactly 90 degrees apart. After two months work, a test, real power in dyno. Not one horsepower better or worse. Each set of points talked to a common coil.

So, next I reversed the deal and put a coil with a two inch coil wire right to the plug (no so-called plug wires, no distributor cap, no rotor). Used one set of points to trigger 12 volts to the coil primary with each coil having it's own capacitor. Now this deal said, "You're on the right track, keep coming." But I never made it past first inspection. I was told "had to put a distributor cap on and a plug wire to each spark plug." Apparently never noticed the eight coils.

Watching a juke box in a half-crocked stupor one night, I was intrigued by the magic eye (actually an electric sensor). I had a drinking buddy who serviced and sold juke boxes. With his electrical expertise we built an ignition that utilized the electronic juke box eye to replace the points on an accurate 90 degree interval, but again with no power advantage. But accurate and 100 percent firing at high rpm (We used to have a hell of a time with point bounce.)

I found the biggest problem was the length of the plug wires and their insulation. Every foot of plug wire 'bout halved the output of the coil. I also found the longer the duration of the electrical energy to the plug was much more critical than the maximum voltage the coil put out in regard to improving power. What did I invent? Nothing in the distribution system except plug wire leakage sleeves. I found a sleeve that had a very strong dielectric strength and was a strong thermal barrier (exhaust headers used to burn our wire and short 'em out). I slid the sleeve over all high voltage wires. Eventually Moroso marketed it. You've probably used it. (It's blue, Blue Maximum, buy lots of it.) I do receive some money every year from it.

In here, I was curious if the individual spark plug distributor cap rotor pickup terminals were far enough apart. Nope, they were not. And with an unvented cap the jumping electric charges turned the atmosphere inside the distributor and cap to ozone. Ozone is extremely easy to conduct current through as compared to air. So accurate plug firing was just a mess. (A vented cap helped.)

So I invented the big diameter distributor cap. That, of course, helped, but with the help of MSD in their early days, Jack Priegle, their resident genius then, and now owner, made me a big diameter distributor cap that 'bout doubled the terminal spacing, and man that helped. All racers should say, "Thanks MSD." They single handedly did more for ignition than everybody else put together, and they never quit making it better.

I was still very confused about ignition in that time frame I had about ten 50 gallon empty gasoline fuel drums, probably about two months spacing on their being empty, and from 18 months open to 10 months open (vented to atmosphere) and sat them outside with the big two inch bung hole open. Drums upside down. I wanted to make a trash can out of one, so I wheeled the torch out. Rolled the oldest empty barrel over (had been empty at least 18 months). Lit up the cutting torch, put it where I want to start cutting, pull the trigger.

I hear a loud noise and am knocked on my ass. My face feels funny – I look in mirror and notice I don't have any eyebrows and I have a severe sunburn.

I now figure out how they make oil drums. They have two round ends and one flat middle. They roll the pieces together in a leak proof mode. The explosion flattened the vertical metal in the drum and blew both ends off. Well, in 18 months what could the air-fuel ratio of that have been? 100 to 1 or 1,000 to 1?

I still got nine empties, so next day (I ain't burnt too bad, just hurts when you laugh or frown.) I make the proverbial 10 foot pole, 'cept I make it 15 foot long. I stand barrel up, put a shop rag on end of 15 foot pole, dip it in gas and light it. As I aim it at empty bung hole, 'bout a foot from the hole…you guessed it…Kabooooom. That mother did it again. Well, I ain't hurt, but I see clearly the deal.

Takes 'bout 15 minutes to explain to cops and firemen nothing's wrong. Funny, the day before that, which was a Sunday, nobody come and I could have been dying. OK, barrel number three same deal. I hook up a Model T Ford coil so it's doing it all the time. Hook it to a spark plus with .035 gap. Got a transformer supply of DC current to fire the Ford coil. Plug has steady blue spark. With the 15 foot pole, I lower spark plug into the open bung hole ('bout two inches in diameter). Slowly, slowly to bottom of barrel and then slowly back up. It comes out of barrel still sparking it's ass off. Nothing happens.

Back to 15 foot pole and gas soaked rag. I got an expert helper now, a Hudson engineer. I say "light the rag for me." He says, "OK, but she won't blow." I say, "You sure?" He says, "Hell yes."

I say, "Sit on the barrel." I lay it down sideways. He won't do it. As he walks away from it, I put lit rag close to bung hole. Well, he was incorrect. I can still remember the look of terror in his eyes when the air pressure hit him in the ass and the noise filled his ears. When he picked hisself up, I said, "What was that?" And why do we now have another three piece barrel? And "What's that funny smell you got when I get behind you?"

So that triggered my search for flame ignition. I found in 'bout six or seven years, if I made a spark plug looking thing with a 3/8 inch hole half inch deep and put on insulated electrode in the center and with the shell being the ground when I fired the gadget with 23 amps and 500 volts, it would shoot out a flame strong enough to blow a hole in a piece of newspaper. I had the help of a local general electric engineer, Don Wolfe, who was the electrical brains. Now I'm making a full set of plugs, or igniters, for a Buick V6 racing engine. Don's got power supply ready. Minor problem. Don't touch the output. It will kill you. Gonna test it tomorrow. Hell, by now it's 1980 or '81. I've always wanted a Lear jet like the good racers now have, but I decide not to order it till I finish the test. Well shit. Don't make one goddamned more horsepower, but I can get down to 24 to 1 air fuel and still fire, but power is down 'bout 50 percent as well (lean burn bullshit). This would work in the toughest class of draggers, but that ain't no place for somebody with 'bout five percent of hearing left. I still got all the stuff.

Along the adventures I've experienced I found the failed experiments are almost as valuable as the successes. You know why? Inventions are all a large quantity of "what ifs?" The flops are one of the "what ifs?" The failure is really a black hole in our search for improvement, and I don't waste any more time going there again. The other thing I've noticed is all problems have a main governor that is holding up the works. Many times you resolve the immediate governor, a gain is made and it takes one to ten years to figure out why, the result being a breakthrough…can be kind like giving up on a gold mine, while your heel is on a five pound dirt covered nugget.

I believe flame or plasma ignition will be the ignition for tomorrow. From day one all racers were concerned with getting air into engine, so we made racy lookin' things to funnel air into the carburetor and intake area. The idea being the faster you went, you rammed air into the engine, a sort of supercharging. Well, it made us feel good (car went a li'l bit faster), but really, it was an exercise in mental masturbation.

Results 'bout the same as when thinking about sex. Can't get anybody pregnant, or catch a venereal disease. The power improvement was really nothing to do with air compression. It had to do with cooler induction air. The dyno taught me the importance of induction air temperature.

One percent gain for every 10 degrees Fahrenheit air temperature decrease.

Heat Wrap

'Bout in here I'm dreaming of an adiabatic engine. (Adiabatic is for even exchange, i.e., put 100 BTUs in, get 100 BTUs of work out.) This required extensive thermal damming, dealing with a maximum of 2,000 degrees Fahrenheit, and hoping for 100 percent or as close to it as we can get for thermal containment. This steered me towards Union Carbide, Carborundum, and United Technologies, for answer about materials that were both thermal dams and/or thermal absorbers.

Carborundum had a division called "Fiberfrax." A line of thermal dams. With the help of Bill Long, a Carborundum engineer and Charlie Boos, a Carborundum technician, thermal damming was born (in racing). It's now all over the exhaust systems and turbo gas passages also fuel and lubrication conduits and air conduits and thermal damning of driver's compartments and driver's clothing.

What did you invent Smokey? Again, nothing, but we did open the door and whet the appetites of racers and others to the point where it's now a common place state of the art system being developed further and with maybe 100 participating manufacturers. The space and aviation programs paid the huge development costs. We racers got a lot of help from it.

Also say "Thank you" to Wright Patterson development for their contributions to us racers. They pioneered strong, light-weight, non-metal fabrication materials and the technology, also thermo management materials. "Thank you," Dick Kavalauskas and all the geniuses who worked out the extreme performance stuff you cats dreamt up and perfected, but this was high priced tech. "Whew!" Did you know the hi-tech in Formula One and Cart, and Indy Car carbon fiber body work was all born in Columbus, Ohio, Wright Patterson? (Tell me 'bout European and Asian engineering superiority).

You know, if you're a foreigner reading this, I'd say welcome to the United States of Goofy. We are the richest, most spoiled, laziest, mixed bag of humanity on earth. I'm not sure which we are gonna do first; either fuck ourselves out of space or pollute the earth down to one square foot of livable space. We are trying to direct our democratic society into a condition where no one works and everyone gets at least $100,000 a year. We have so many lawyers now who have fucked up our laws and our language so badly that combined with the shithead politicians who have discovered how to buy an election and by industry that will pay for it. We pay the President of the United States 200 grand a year, and a basketball player 45 million. A filthy trash-mouth rap singer 10 million, murderers can buy their way out of prison…say hello O.J. A president who is slap pussy-happy and perhaps the biggest bullshitter known to the human race. If there was a Nobel Prize for lying motherfucker of the year, he would win it every year. But what's most interesting is 75 percent of all of us think he is doing a wonderful job. We have the most valuable right any human can have, the right to vote on a one to one basis with any citizen of this country. 65 percent of the stupid assholes, male and female don't vote. Nope, but boy do they run their mouths about stuff that don't suit 'em. (How 'bout you? Do you vote?)

The politicians are slowly sliding into a group of radical minorities (and how's best way to say cocksuckers, sexual deviants, crooks, and quite a few racists but with a twist. He's now black, and a man. Turn a TV camera on 'em and those cats, they can rattle off bullshit like it was coming off a high speed newspaper printer. They are like robots. Loaded and wound by the top cats and just turned on and turned loose. We got a president who rides around in a half billion dollar airplane ('bout half a billion a year to pay for the expense) using it like it was a Chevy pickup truck.

That ain't the worst part. Every time that son-of-a-bitch lands, he jumps off and gives somebody another billion or more. We are so smart, we are fixing every goddamn problem every country in the world has…yet how come tonight and every night grown and young people are sleeping on the riverbank behind my garage? Drugs all over are getting worse, sick people with no money, kids without food or a place to live. Hi-jacking cars, home invasion, worse every day. Sexual twist-offs in every form of government. Corporate robbery, stock and bond rapes. Lawyers stealing money, overcharging by the billions. Corporate top people paying their selves up to 150 million a year. Education has slid into a stinking sewer of unqualified, under-paid, poorly-administered personnel. Doctors, who used to be most respected people on earth, now by and large are greedy opportunists with sub-standard skills. Don't it make any sense, before we fix Somalia, Israel, Iraq, Palestine, Mexico, Central America, Japan, China, Russia, Korea, we ought to fix ourselves?

How many billions of dollars have American people paid for our goofy-assed politicians adventures in global economy and military security? How can an American president, most powerful man on earth, say, while wiggling his finger to the whole fuckin' world on TV that he had a gal give him 25 or so blow jobs and never felt anything sexual? (I wonder what he thought she was doing? Maybe he just didn't want to hurt her feelings, so he let her (while he was on the phone). Do you reckon it was a reaction from tobacco that's dipped in pussy juice that gives you a type of memory loss? Ain't this whole movie goofy?

We had the world by the ass in safe, economical, viable surface transportation in 1975. In twenty years we gave 30 percent of it away to the Europeans and Asians. Plus one of the "Big Three" is now owned by the sauerkraut guzzlers. Our world class "Cadillac" standard of the world in automotive excellence is 'bout number five or number six and ever moving closer to the shit house and "out." Ain't that goofy?

Does the whole impeachment deal sound goofy to you? I pay 'bout at least half my income a year in taxes, yet I see a lady in front of me in a food store driving a new Cadillac paying for her stuff with food stamps. (I drive a '78 Fiesta) I still think the United States of Goofy is best place in the world to live, but can't anything in the world be ruined if it's over abused?

Look at the Indy race – hands down the greatest race in the world. From 1975 to 1995 the race was destroyed by Cart. Gave it to foreign cars, drivers and engines. Only thing left American, Goodyear tires, but really the rice-burners are in process of taking that away under the cover name of Firestone. Yup, the japs gobbled up Firestone 15-20 years ago. Gotta give 'em credit. They're building good racing shit. Usually it takes 'bout as long to un-fuck something as it takes to fuck it up, so maybe we still have to put in a lot more goofy time at some point and soon, we better get our heads out of our asses and get back to basics.

Maybe something as simple as the ten commandments. 'Cept maybe take the one out you can't stop. The one 'bout don't screw your neighbor's wife…and replace it with "we each take care of ourselves and our tribe." I'm long passed pissed 'bout "paying half what I earn" while the government subsidizes the "sit on your ass" game for the trash people and commercial leaders who suck on taxpayer's tits. I'm sure I could have never had the life I've had any other place in the world, but if it isn't my age screwing up, my ability to comprehend this whole deal is headed for shitsville at about 100 miles per hour. Would you believe this; today I read a famous kook artist canned his own shit and it brought $28,800 at an auction for a one pound can. Is this goofy? How does the buyer know if it's authentic, or counterfeit shit from China?

Cams and Intakes

Cam shafts were the racers number one weapon from day one. There have been one million two hundred thousand different cam grinds since 1915. We are now going through these for the second-third, maybe fourth time. (I'm talking Otto cycle engine).

There is no perfect cam shaft, never will be unless you can move lobes of both intake and exhaust cams on the fly and also be able to adjust lift, and to retard or advance lobes. At the same time be able to adjust the size and length of intake and exhaust orifices. It turns out in a multi-cylinder engine with a common induction plenum there are many pressure changes from negative to positive. The motion and behavior of the working fluid (air and fuel) is affected by pressure and temperature. Next, the velocity of the working fluid has a bearing on it's state of vaporization. It's specific density (Bernoulli's law). As speed increases pressure decreases, and the reverse of this, as speed decreases pressure increases. Next multi-cylinder induction common conduits are effected by valve overlap, and length of working fluid column. These air fuel columns are affected by any change of direction over eight to nine degrees. And very important, affected by and variation in column configuration considering length of radiuses (short side, long side). This results in a general condition called "chaos." It can never be predicted, measured or explained.

Artificial aspiration turbo or super charging becomes only way to effectively address this condition. Artificial aspiration, say about 10 pounds or more of induced pressure overcomes the smaller effects of temperature, velocity, small amount of conduit variation and cam shaft overlap.

It's not perfect but it stabilizes cylinder charging with working fluid and scavenging to a point that results are very positive for power.

A cam shaft's job is to fill the combustion chamber to 100 percent or more depending on induction system design. Well, with fixed design for all rpm, you can at best attain 99 percent volumetric efficiency for a 300 rpm range (with a normally aspirated engine).

Stock car racing has legislated into it, a very poor method of valve operation. Simply explained for "cost considerations," and I think that is a wise position. We can easily exceed any sensible power need with this very simple and crude design. It's a credit to their ingenuity of the engine builders of today who rule wise are bound to so called stock engines. To be able to produce over two horsepower per cubic inch and race in the 9,000 to 9,300 rpm range reliably for three to five hours every Sunday, and as many as 24 hours once or twice a year. However, my guess is today 8,500 to 8,900 is the maximum in 2000. And I should add, race gasoline is not too much different than pump premium fuel.

I bet I spent 10 years of my life collectively studying the cam shaft and it's associated components that introduce and scavenge the working fluid to it's cylinders. I bet I have still have remnants of about 500 experimental cam shafts, 200 different kinds of valve springs. Probably 100 different methods of operating the valves. From push rod to pneumatic operation. The true cam shaft is a life's work in itself. I don't recommend any young person plan on making it his life's work because the ideal cam shaft would be no cam shaft, no valve spring, no valves.

OK, Smokey, you spent so much time on cams and are supposed to know quite a bit about it…what did you invent here? As honestly and as best I can remember, not one damn thing.

I think cam shaft knowledge is most important. Like a guy with a three inch peter. It ain't what you got, it's how you use it.

Every time I did something that helped and started to puff up about it I found hell, somebody did that in the 1920s. If there was anything in the world this sentence "the more things change, the more they stay the same," it would be the four-cylinder Otto cycle engine. Today Winston Cup engines retails at 40 to 55 thousand dollars range. The 390 horsepower 'restricter plate' engine's the most expensive. A non-restrictor engine makes 780 horsepower. 1960 engine cost $8.00 per horsepower. Year 2000 it's 70 bucks per horsepower Here's the goofy part; the restrictor plate engine costs $10,000 extra to lose 400 horsepower

Edison and Bell got praised up one side and down the other, but really, if Otto was the inventor of our present engine, how come it's a secret? You know a cam shaft is kinda like a music roll in an old player piano. As you turn it, music comes out according to where the bumps are, and how fast you turn it.

COLD AIR INTAKE

In 1958 I was adding a new section to my collection of buildings. (If you look at my collection of old buildings, each leaning on each other, kinda like a stack of dominos. Looks like if any one falls they'll all collapse. Anyhow, each building represents an invention sale, an oil well that did it big, a big race won or a specific development contract.

Why I mention this is, one day in the early 60s I accidentally made a discovery. I'd installed the air system plumbing in a new addition, but I missed soldering two joints adjacent to each other. I had someone turn on the air supply and right where I was, air pressure blew two lines away from a tee that was the air supply. One side was 'bout three inches long, opposite side 'bout seven inches long. I, by instinct, foolishly grabbed the blown off lines and tried to force them back into the tee (150 pounds-per-square-inch pressure air supply). I quickly let go. I thought the short side was hot. Puzzled, I quickly seen it was very cold because the short side was cold enough that frost was coating it. I then made several prototypes to investigate this further and found if I optimized the lengths of each side, and the orifice size, I could have 35 degrees F on one side and 90 degrees F on the other, with the supply pressure approximately 75 degrees Fahrenheit (with 150 psi).

Well, I puzzled with this for several years, trying to understand it. Accidentally I found answer in an encyclopedia under the explanation of a German inventor named Haley (this was 'bout 1920).

Haley built a very large apparatus kinda like this to cool a deep coal mine. It was very noisy. The system was named "Haley's Demon." But no explanations. Well, "Professor Peyote" came through. My professor from Northwestern University supplied the dream potions, and in an all night "what if?" we got answer.

Energy in air pressure being released changed from pressure to heat. (Yes, 35 degrees is still heat. considering 360 degrees minus is absolute zero.) Vortec makes a device like this to cool machine tools and it is used in many places today. OK, what's all this above bullshit wasting space for? I found the hot side pressure to always be above ambient temperature and cold side was the same, always cold. The temperature of both divided by two equaled the incoming line's pressure.

COLD AIR CAMARO HOOD

So, the cold air Camaro hood was born from this. I slotted from bumper two inch by 14 inches for ram air. Slot pressure was linear with vehicle velocity, but pressure controlled by length and size of conduits release of air at both hot and cold side. So, I put cold air in carburetor and directed the hot air vertically to the ground to get an air curtain that prevents air from going under the car. The negatives were already and mandatorally paid for. This system had no parasitic losses. This system was installed on a '72 Camaro road racer I built for A.J. to drive. Car even painted coyote yallar (or is it orange?).

We tested the deal at Sebring. Carburetor air was down 40 degrees, power up four percent – 'bout 25 horsepower (guesstimated from lap speed). Air dam worked. How much I don't know. But if you blocked air curtain off, car pushed. If you let it work, no push and lap speed was better by two tenths. I can't remember why we never raced it. Couple years later I sold this car. (Unusual for me – maybe I was starting to catch on.) I sold it to a road racer in Belgium. We took it to a dock in Jacksonville and I never saw or heard from it again.

I never tried it in the Winston Cup. If you're running a front bumper two inches too wide, I don't believe it to be a good idea to also cut a horizontal slot in it do you? (Might attract too much attention.)

My wind tunnel…it's seen better days.

I'm deep into alternate energy in this time frame, so I get deep into thermal conservation, thermo damning and into ceramic engine components. This puts me working with Carborundum, the nations peer in thermal management. If you go look at the number 13 Chevelle in Floyd Garrett's muscle car museum in Sevierville, Tennessee, you see all headers, all induction conduits and drivers compartment, all thermally damned with various products from Carborundum's Fiberfrax division (1966).

A new dimension has now been added to racing. It was first used in turbo charged engine hot sections. Yeah, I started it. Did I invent it? Hell no. Thermal management has been around since day one. Who ever invented clothing invented thermal management. Maybe Barney Flintstone?

How 'bout in early part of World War II? I was in Marrakesh, Africa waiting and flying with the French Foreign Legion. The Arabs wore heavy wool clothing (now here's an example of thermal management). Covered up even their heads. In short, wrapped in a wool garment from head to the ground. Of course they sweated like a son-of-a-bitch. But as the sweat vaporized it gave you a feeling of cold. I tried it. Works great. There is however an odor in there that I imagine our ladies would not go goofy over. I can attest personally. The ladies who used this method of air conditioning weren't in much demand for sex.

An Otto cycle engine is a clever heat management machine. The fuel creates the heat, which makes the pressure that makes everything go roun' and roun.'

Re-ignition

Let's back up to '62. I'm playing with cam shafts. We know size and length and shape of both induction and exhaust. We got to a point where we had too much valve overlap in the end of the exhaust and beginning of the induction cycle. "What if" I added ambient air into the exhaust gas stream at proper location and of the proper size to support secondary combustion before it exited the exhaust system? Thereby keeping exhaust gas temperature at it's maximum, which reduces pressure in exhaust system because it increases gas velocity, at same time reducing it's specific weight. All the above simply stated was aimed at getting rid of the same amount of exhaust gases with less cam over lap. Therefore cylinder operating pressure would be higher. Presto, more power per unit of fuel so wheels go faster.

Headers

Did it work? Hang on. Got another bunch of stuff that factors into this. By 1959 I've experimented enough with headers, I can take a '60 Pontiac and gain 25 horsepower by removing stock manifolds and bolting on a set of light stainless steel headers I've made. Well hell, I think most of us knew stock manifolds were dog shit from 1950. But "Big Daddy" says don't you fuck with the exhaust system, or I'll make you go stand in the corner. This is in writing by specific part number. Well no way to interpret this to say it's OK to put headers on.

Remember, I told you France and the Boss (Mr. K.) were exceptionally good friends? So in late '60 I made a set of headers that fit a '61 Pontiac (our new race car then), sent them to Pontiac to be copied and get a part number. "Heavy duty exhaust headers" get in part book. I put 'em on for the '61 Beach Race.

You ever been to Talladega? Well if you've been in their Hall of Fame Museum, and you saw a pair of stainless steel headers in the confiscated parts department, that's them.

Nope, they never run an inch in a race. Friel grabbed them. By time I woke up they were long gone. Racers, that four intake pipe collector you all use with a venturi, say "Thanks, Smoke." It was born here. Nope, I couldn't buy a postage stamp with what I got out of it. By the way, if you are a race fan, (and if you're not, why are you reading this?) if you haven't visited the International Motorsports Hall of Fame Museum, you should. Tell them I told you to come. There's a lot of racing history there. Also they need money to make it bigger and better. So buy a t-shirt and eat some stuff. (The museum is in Eastabooga, Alabama in front of the Talladega race track. Say "hello" Mr. Eastabooga mayor.) He calls it "Talladega," 100 years ago "Eastaboga" was five miles east of "Boga." Boga got canceled.

Re-ignition, Next Page

Well, next page. 1963, got a Chevy Cup racer. Headers now legal. The boss (Mr. K.) is running Chevy now. In the meantime I've discovered if I drill a hole to let air in the headers of the right size in the right place (3/16ths inch hole one-and-a-half inches from the valve), I can get re-ignition in exhaust pipe at 53 inches down stream (a product of the oxygen addition), therefore helping scavenge exhaust gases more efficiently and have also discovered if I put a venturi of the right shape and size in the right location exhaust gas flows better (faster), less inner pipe pressure.

I've made these venturis out of aluminum. Easier to machine and lighter. I slide 'em up and down exhaust secondary pipes till I maximize power in dyno. At the track we start with dyno location, but slide 'em on a race car. Turns out 'bout a three inch difference in distance in the car. 3.5 inch ex-pipes 56 inches from end of primaries. Did it work? Yup, the aluminum melted at 1,750 degrees Fahrenheit. The exhaust gas temperature 1.5 inches out of the cylinder head was 1,475 degrees. The surprise was how little it took of more oxygen to effect re- or secondary ignition of exhaust column. Also a surprise was in one hot lap quarter panel was coated with aluminum. The exhaust gases pulled a "Houdini" on the venturis. They are gone. Consider this: that aluminum melted at 1,720 degrees F. (We go to steel ventures when we get dialed in). Now make another cam, closed exhaust valve five degrees sooner, (reduce overlap). 'Bout in there, the car could flat walk the dog.

This is a weird sounding mother. If you heard it run, the reason it sounded funny, was if it was turning

7,500, you heard 15,000 explosions not 7,500, 'cause in re-ignition it barked again. Now I got me a tail pipe splitting son-of-a-bitch. I finally learned how to make it last a long race.

Do you see how everything leans on each other?

Air Under Hood

The '63 deal is insulated headers with air injection, with venturi secondaries much reduced exhaust valve closing point and plenum air (outside air) which is cooler and we keep cool with thermal air cleaner blankets and insulated headers plus an aluminum heat shield on the headers to further reduce temperature of under hood air.

Nope…ain't done yet. I noticed in '57 under hood pressure was a serious negative. By now the '57 tunnels I made to drain under hood pressure are outlawed. The long arm of NASCAR bullshitters has struck again. And once more the fickle finger of fate has been inserted in my rectum by the champions of technical retardation. Well, good-bye tunnels. So I find a plenum properly arranged can produce a positive pressure to the carburetor. Granted not much, but remember the old lady who pissed in the ocean. "Every little bit helps."

In here we butchered the fender wells to leak under-hood air out, and added some sheet metal to form a venturi to suck under hood air out at the lower fire wall which was reshaped to recirculate air much easier. Also, location of exhaust pipe exits were such that with some subtle sheet metal changes and additions we built an artificial low to dump exhaust into. Then I used the hot air and shape of the remaining under body of the car control path and velocity of exit of under car air to add or decrease down force at rear of the car.

I started using a manometer in the car (had to sit on the floor to read it). By now we are in bucket seats. Take my word for it, it is hot on your ass and the hot steel floor banging on your ass at 190 miles per hour. May be good therapy to reduce a fat ass, but to a bony ass like me; extremely uncomfortable to say the least, no seat belt didn't help either.

Well, we finally get 'bout 14 inches of water of positive pressure. Now we got a 600 horsepower, 3,900 pound, no handling death trap. I'm so busy trying to out-Otto Otto that I built a totally unmanageable racer with rear steer out the ass.

Buck Baker, A.J., Banjo, Bobby Issac, Johnny Rutherford, Bobby Allison and some others couldn't do a thing with this no-handling son-of-a-bitch. If I'd of snuck a look at what Junior Johnson and Ray Fox were doing with rear axle long truck radius rods. I believe we'd have made some money with that car.

Exhaust flow

Is that it? Nope still left out one part, headers. Remember by '57 I got good flow equipment, so I want to maximize exhaust scavenging. By now I know both sides of engine regarding working fluids work like a musical instrument, the distance the pressure travels, the size of it's exit orifice, affect sound we hear, and these factors have harmonics, oh say first, second, third order, very tricky shit that I could not master mathematically.

But back to farmer cut and try. Project number one, make orifices and conduits so all cylinders get exactly the same opportunities. Make sense? I decide number one deal is, total length must be equal all cylinders. Well turns, out equal length isn't always equal flow. If you don't include air flow measurements you still ain't equal. Real answer was equal air flow. Bends over nine degrees are very negative. In this time frame I find torque and horsepower are not the same. Many times maximum torque at correct place beats maximum horsepower at top end. On a short track maximum torque off the corner beats horsepower. It's king at end of the straight (short track). Long track (Daytona, Talladega) maximum horsepower is the name of the game, either with or without restrictor plate, so length of primary and inside diameter of conduit is critical to each track. Same for secondary exhaust systems – could easily be a man's life's work.

Example: in a two stroke engine exhaust system technology doubled, yup doubled, horsepower - in two years.

'Bout 1960: a big enemy of tube headers is durability. Believe it or not cheap carbon steel is good for headers reference cracking. Not used in hi-buck racing because of weight. They use stainless, titanium and inconel. Damn right, titanium is for the hi-bucker. Would you believe 8 to 10 grand for a set of pipes? This part done yet? Nope, it turns out if a balance pipe is run between left and right bank right behind primary pipes, car gets back little quicker, so we put four into one, two into two (this is eight cylinder stuff).

In short, we tried eight different combinations. Guess what was best for most applications?

Give up?

Eight to one, reason: most V8s fire every 90 degrees, in a standard firing order there can be as much as a 270 degree pause between firing in a four-cylinder header. (Right or left bank)

The pause lets ambient pressure get into the pipes, don't forget ambient pressure nominally speaking is 15 psi. So, exhaust of a normally aspirated engine has to overcome 15 pounds of pressure to start gases flow out. In an eight into one, there is an exhaust pulse every 90 degrees you have a positive pressure pulse…bottom line, easier for exhaust gas to get out. What you invent Smoke? Nothing really. Yet I did the equal length technology, the length and size, the distinction between primary and secondary and the four pipe collector I first made is still the favorite today, 45 years later.

We found slowly increasing pipe inner diameter helped a little (in the primary). I got headers started in NASCAR, but actually it was Mr. Knudsen's persuasion of France that did it. Indy cars, champ cars, sprinter and midgets used a crude four into one header back to day one. Most all were four cylinders. From my first attempt at headers in 1955 to today, I continue to learn new neat little tricks about that mousetrap. Any changes made in the engine's breathing and exhaust systems, as well as any change in cylinder firing pressure and also fuel character differences and ignition total effectiveness all effect not only horsepower, but torque and power at the most desirable rpm

None of this is Einstein stuff separately, but when considering all parameters of ideal engine design it then requires some thought.

If you think the last few pages confusing, it shows you were a goof off in high school and you either slept through your physics classes or your high school lacked physics, 'cause the school board and principle has their heads up their asses and didn't think physics was essential.

However, if you got a kid or a grandkid that's a good student in a good hi-school, get him to help you understand. Is this the end? Nope. I first checked all induction and exhaust ports individually. Experience taught me to air flow total system in as much of their entirety as possible. So I changed our flow bench so that on intake side we had oil pan, cylinder block, cylinder head with valves, timing cover and engine sealed in total intake manifold carburetor and air cleaner in place. (See flow bench chapter for more on the flow capacity.) I had a deal to open intake valve as much as I liked (usually .600). The oil pan had a four inch fitting for a four inch air flow pull.

Ambient air came through air cleaner entrance. We pulled 28 inches of vacuum on total system. Name of the game: "get all cylinders flow equally." I think I should tell you the block was in a wheeled stand at bench height. We did same thing on exhaust flow measurements. I added the exhaust header we intended to race with exhaust valve open .600. I pulled 28 inches of water on the exhaust pipe collector at end of primary and measured air supplied through four inch fitting in oil pan.

I checked all cylinders in this manner in both intake and exhaust sides. Are you done yet? Nope. What'd you invent? Don't know. You decide.

I'm getting tired writing 'bout this particular tech. I have trouble remembering what I already told you. But nope. It's not over by a long ways.

Oil Filter Invention

I've always been concerned about starting an engine without oil pressure, so in the '80s I invented and patented a system where auxiliary pressurized oil supply charged engine to 40 pounds per square inch before engine turned over. Oil change and oil addition is at best a poor way to keep abrasives out of the lubrication supply, so I invented a new method of changing oil where oil is filtered as it's being added and priming the oil system with pressurization before crank rotation by adding a quick change disconnect fitting to bottom of the oil filter, oil is filtered from the outside to center. Even if oil you're putting in had sand in it, the filter stopped it. How much money you make with all this investment in time and money? I couldn't buy one of Jeff Gordon's or Dale Earnhardt's cheapest die cast cars with it.

Wind Tunnel/Water Tunnel

'Bout the same as I got for trying to get water tunnels to be built and used rather than air tunnels.

You wanna guess where the real answers are coming from today? Ask Ford if water is better than air. Ask the Navy. How'd you get that brainstorm Smoke? By sitting on a fast creek river bank and watching water flow over various rocks and observing what happens when I turned the rocks 90 degrees.

In 1955 I built my first wind tunnel. Still got it, I need to find a new home for it. Later I switched to water. I remember some of the mail I got when I wrote about this in Circle Track (1980 or so). Lucky I wasn't impeached. Aerodynamics consumed about two months out of every year of my life from 1942 to 1980. That is in reference to reading and experimenting and actual race car hardware. From '41 to '47 I was fascinated by aviation and it was in my best interest to learn as much as I could since it had quite a bit to do with how long, and in what way my adventure here on earth would proceed.

I took all I read and was taught at face value. This is (Air Force and GM) except for one sentence "all aerodynamic reactions are linear with speed." In the real world, speed affects temperature and pressure. Therefore, what is negative at 100 miles per hour might be zero at 200 miles per hour and can cause a neutral to total change in character. Wind tunnel information confused me to where I no longer accepted (in my mind) the results. Fast running small rivers or big creeks in Ecuador, starting in 1961, were my mental stabilizers. All rocks were smooth shaped by how ever they were arranged by nature. I experimented by turning the rocks, representing yaw, and now I start really learning. At least I'm totally convinced of this then and still today.

1959, I had a quarter-scale wind tunnel (still have it). I took various car models with me to Ecuador when I went there on the gold exploration and later in the oil field adventures. This is pure jungle. I get Indians to dam the creek in such a way to increase water velocity and found model behavior varied with velocity. But the real eye opener was what happened with model half inch off the bottom as compared to one foot off of bottom. At this point (1961), I've bought a helicopter, and have found what is now referred to as "ground effect."

In all this, a constant problem occurred if the submerged shape caused the water to change direction too much (as in un-laminar flow), all hell would break loose regarding the turbulence around the rock or object. For lack of a proper description of its condition and with the unpredictability of what would happen,

I decided to call this chaos.

Kinda reminded me of my younger days when I had too much to drink. It's 1:30 am and I haven't found a way to ask a lady who I met fifteen minutes ago. Bar closes in 30 minutes. I go back to basics and ask the lady if she wants to fuck. Sometimes you got, "I thought you'd never ask" or all hell would break loose and I'd get slapped and get told that was, "No fucking way to talk to a lady." If her boyfriend happened to be on the next bar stool this is where the chaos stuff could happen. Unpredictable and unmeasurable.

Air flow or water (any fluid) as long as the presentation of the object doesn't cause a change of flow over nine degrees is quite predictable and understandable. To me chaos is unpredictable and ever changing. Therefore impossible to calculate or measure. Only measurement is farmer cut and try. The proverbial can of worms deal. What did you invent Smokey? Hell. Nothing. I suddenly realized I knew less about it than did a fish or a bird. But this is a fact: straighter the port, the closer you get to where you need to go. Also the best shaped valve is no valve. A valve like a camera iris is best compromise, but not viable. Any change in flow over nine degrees, chaos and compromise are the game.

Edge Versus Radius

Here comes more trouble for me from my peers. I decided when fluid flow needed or had to make a change in direction of over 15 degrees it was better to do it with two 7.5 degree changes and with a sharp edge rather than a radius. Why? I noticed in water, the sharp edges created much less chaos than did the radiuses. You ever take a good look at the stealth fighter? Notice how race cars are getting 'slabby' lookin? Talking that shit in 1960; the aero peers would holler for somebody with a big net. In 1957 I decided with some sports cars, and looking at Indy cars, that independent runners were better than a common conduit serving two or more cylinders. But you know this is 40 years later and I've never been able to solidly prove it.

Multi-cylinder induction conduits are able to reverse some of the negative of valve overlap, reversion, fuel stand off. I now believe a common plenum is best when you're dealing with individual injector supplying fuel to each cylinder. I've found by being able to pressure the fuel delivery to over 100 psi, you can increase the volumetric efficiency (a little) and in a longer rpm range (more than 300 rpm). I've been as high as 400 psi with special fuel (not gasoline) and over 4,000 psi with diesel. Simply put, you're blowing fuel in a very positive mode which increases mixing-vaporization and combats the working fluid being blowed back out of the induction conduits.

My experiments with direct cylinder injection were never as good as port injection. You gotta consider the fuel is really a big part of the mass: in gas it's a 12th, with alky it's a 7th and with top drag fuel an equal 1 to 1. So dry flow is very deceptive. You can actually be half big enough as in the case of the nitro burner drag car. I assume the petro-chemistry that says air (which is both oxygen and nitrogen) must be mixed with fuel vapor was correct, therefore direct injection really don't have time to mix and homogenize fuel with the air. Volumetric efficiency on a normally aspirated engine depends on the cylinder presenting a high negative pressure for longest period of degrees in the intake stroke including consideration of the positive pressure of the exhaust gasses, which weakens the total negative signal in both singular or plural induction conduit. I also found size-length-shape and temperature dictated every individual cylinder's ability to achieve maximum and equal volumetric efficiency. Well, the shit's getting deep here, so if you say, "What did you invent here?" Maybe three things for sure. The 1970 Ford Trans Am cross ram, the early '60 Smokeram manifold Edelbrock sold and the air gap method of isolating the induction conduits from the engine radiant and oil heat and water heat. (I also moved the front water passage away from front runners).

I say perfect distribution requires all working fluid be same temperature, as well as all combustible cavities and temperatures in all combustion cavities have equal temperature in their total surface area. Nope, no patent, no greenies: the Smokeram gave it away as prior art.

If you're dealing with artificial aspiration turbo or super chargers the case for a common conduit on engines with multiple cylinders is clear for a very large common plenum. Early stock manifolds forced us to have a lot of exhaust heat in the intake manifold. Especially the center cylinders. That was for cold start of mass surface transportation. But the problem was this was negative as hell for power. So, we had to figure out how to block this off in such a way NASCAR's technical eagles couldn't find it, (plugged cylinder head passage).

Cam Oiling

In 1961 I started running into trouble with standard or stock cam shafts. They were made from a chilled cast iron casting. To get to 8,000 rpm with a small Chevy with the wild assed cams, we'd migrated to 160 pounds or 180 pounds on the seat and 500 pounds at top of lift. .650 lift, with 280 degree, 300 degree duration cams were not unusual, and lobe centers of 98 to 100 not unheard of. I noticed after several failures, the lobes would get hot and burn. The lifters lubrication would break down and metal to metal contact in 60 seconds was enough to start the deal. Once any galling occurs the end is right around the bend.

I accidentally found a new cam and lifter assembly was more susceptible to failure than matching parts reused in original as installed locations (lifters in same holes). I found start of failure usually occurred in first twenty minutes. I found worst place in reference to rpm was slow. I found running race car slow around bottom of race track very bad for new cam assembly. Why? Solid lifters need to be slowly turned as they work to control heat, and therefore wear. So each lifter has a slight radius, and the cam lobe has a slight angle (in minutes not degrees). Therefore, at interface there is built in physics to slowly turn lifter. New cam, new lifter has a problem, the contact area new might be as small as a .030 circle. This puts a tremendous pressure on the small interface which puts the lubricant into an inadequate mode reference extreme pressure. But in as little as 20 minutes of running at medium rpm, the interface increases in area ten-fold. Now the lube has a chance also. Stop and think. The only oiling the cam lobes and lifters get in a "so-called" stock engine are splash from crank, connecting rod leakage at top of stroke, so the slower the engine ran, the drier the assembly ran.

What do you do? Heat oil and water and metal parts with an in the block electrical water heater and then warm up starting with at-speed laps. My main fix was, drill a .025 hole from oil gallery as to be aimed at each cam lobe flank (pressure oil the cam lobes). This caused a big drop in oil pressure, but a correct sized pressure section and proper tension on oil pump relief valve spring (wet or dry sump) got pressure back up, but pumping more oil volume, more horsepower was wasted in parasitic loss and oil temperature went up. It worked, but not absolute, and with some negatives. Even today at 9,000 plus rpm, cams are lubed in a "Flintstone" fashion. But I notice they are no longer laughing at needle bearing cam bearings and pressure lubing cam lobes.

Man, what I would have give for "Prolong" then. Finally, I ended up either with short rocker ratio like one to one, or pull out inner spring for 15 or 20 minutes and run at 2400 to 2800 rpm, then reinstall inners. A big time consuming pain in the ass. (Called "breaking in the cam shaft assembly".)

Finally, using the "Smoketron" with the pressure lobe lubrication for 30 minutes was easiest and fastest, and best way to break in a cam assembly and a set of heads with full spring pressure.

I also found out when doing any maintenance that required removing cam shaft, you must keep lifters and lobes in sequence similar to how they ran on reassembly. Why? The mated contact areas.

Wrist Pin Locks

In about '59-'60 we suddenly run into a problem where wrist pin would get up against wrist pin lock and kinda hammer on the lock every revolution. Finally drive the wrist pin lock out and cause a very major failure. Well, we tried spiral locks, round locks, even plastic buttons. Nothing really worked. What the hell was causing this?

Well, with the "Smoketron" and a glass pan and a camera I found, unless connecting rod was dead center of wrist pin, and unless both the upper and lower bore of the connecting rod were exactly in parallel for 360 degrees of rotation, or if rod bearing had any taper in it's width, in short: to keep every thing in perfect plane was next to impossible. So the connecting rods actually describe a "figure 8" motion in every 360 degrees of rotation. It wasn't much of a motion, but enough to hammer on the wrist pin locks. The round wire lock and the spiral lock wear pretty good, but a real pain in the ass to get out. So I took a page out of the Torrington bearing cam end travel story. I cut retainer groove to take a pair of Tru-arc in the way they were manufactured, putting the two coined, rounded faces of the locks against each other. They worked like a bearing, and being hard, and in a very oily area. Problem solved.

What did you invent Smokey? I just told you.

Slicks

1961, for Indy, I had Firestone make me some 16 inch tires, slick, no tread and no contour as Indy tires had. Also these tires had a eight-inch foot print. 'bout twice the Indy tire. I believe these were first slicks at Indy. Although, the real approved Indy tire had next to no tread and it was contoured, my slick wide tires had much more flexible side walls, but I'll tell more about them in my Indy adventures. Did you get any fame or fortune? Nope. Actually got my ass eat out and was refused permission to use them. Maybe you won't believe this, but I think if anything I ever did along the lines of an invention was ever accepted and recognized as a useful contribution when I first offered it, I would have been surprised. I was totally conditioned to be ignored, ridiculed, or quietly copied.

In the 55 years I've been around the race track I haven't seen over 15 real innovators with balls enough to "just do it" and defy tradition and go off into the jungle. The most successful mechanics never have a paved road. Kinda reminds me of going fast at Bonneville. If you spin out, you don't do anything and you won't hurt a thing (this is up to 200 miles per hour)

I think the big money is bad in racing for the "what iffers?" Now days it's, "win or your ass is mud" – no room for experiments.

Championships are always won with fastest known chassis and fastest known engine with a known ace driver. My heroes were Frank Lockhart, Harry Miller, Clay Smith, Jean Marcenac, Mickey Thompson, Bruce Crower, Ed (Isky) Iskenderian, Kenny Weld, Red Vogt, Marshall Teague, Winfield, Frank Kurtis, A.J. Watson, George Bignotti. Almost all self educated workaholics with uncanny confidence of their convictions. I'm sure I've omitted some who deserve to be recognized, but I only know about what was in my world and what remains in my "suspect" memory.

Tires Pumping Air

Talking 'bout front fender wells. In 1965 and 1966 I was working for Chevy and they had a clever engineer named Don Gates who was a sharp cat. Very good on instrumentation, who really liked racing. I wanted to instrument a car to measure steering wheel degree of motion, throttle position, wheel travel and frequency, engine temperature by cylinders, exhaust gas analysis and weight on each tire. But all these measurements were to be recorded at any and all positions the race car had on the race track.

So I had a 12 foot van one-and-a-half ton Chevy truck 'bout 15 years old and Don worked out a deal where the running tape recorded everything and we could very easily see what was happening any place on the track. At the speed we are running and the lateral traction we are showing the right front tire is in trouble (overloaded), but the wheel travel says, "can't be."

Turns out treaded tire in a tight wheel well (in them days, tires had tread patterns) is the impeller of an air pump and holding up the right front corner. So tire sees weight indicated by spring compressed length change, plus the weight being held up by the positive pressure in the wheel well.

"Bullshit" you say? OK, spend four hours drilling 1/16th inch holes in fender well to make the wheel well a screen. Guess what? Next, run wheel travel shows 2,800 pounds plus on the right front tire now everything checks out. We added a double check, I painted rings around the tire sidewalls, and photographed the fender edge in reference to wheel travel to which we did a calculation for a tire rate. With the drilled fender well the spring collapsed to the ring where it mathematically should have dropped to. What did you invent? Nothing at all. This shit is just plain ol' physics.

The more aggressive a tire's tread is, the less lateral traction it will have (less actual tire-track interface). And there is one more negative. The aggressive tread pattern, due to it's pumping action, has a lot of parasitic drag. In short; a tire is an impeller of an air pump. You want to go fast (on paved surfaces)? The tire needs to be smooth, no tread and smooth side walls. Even so, it still pumps some air.

Notice today's Winston Cup cars…ain't got much for fender or tire walls up front.

Note: the same applies to rear tires and the games there are very complex. Why? That pumping action can be used to control down force, and/or parasitic drag from too much down force or entrapment of undercar air flow. You can play one hell of a game in this area.

I learned from instrumentation even the driver doesn't realize some of the things he is doing or experiencing, so verbal feedback is very possibly tainted.

In about here I decide the fastest thing on earth would be a flounder in a vacuum.

Magnetism and gravity are the same.

Electricity is nothing but polarized heat.

Oil didn't come from dead dinosaurs.

I also decided a ton of anything would always remain a ton of something no matter what you did to it.

If not, the amount of carbon we've reacted wood, coat and oil, would have lightened the earth up so much it would go out of it's orbit and we might bang into the moon.

I'm 75 and still don't understand how a lousy match works. Everybody who explains it to me says it different, and some I've had educate me were very heavy hitters. The problem is all explanations have some difference.

How can a stick of dynamite have so much energy when exploded as compared to how much energy it has if consumed in a slow time frame. Say like fire?

Yes, dynamite will burn and not explode. Don't try it till you get the rest of the story.

I'm talking BTUs either way.

A pound of gasoline has same BTUs if exploded or reacted over a half hour time period.

If perpetual motion is not possible, what keeps the earth suspended in same place for a gillion years?

What do you reckon earth weighs? What holds it in air? Can you prove it?

I'm far out in here ain't I? Nope. I'm not if you are a real racer the "what ifs?" the "whys?" just form a circle that just gets ever bigger in proportion to how hard you study and how many pages you jerk off the calendar. I'll tell you this. I've never been bored. The adventures of a racer got to be someplace in the top three. My other choices would be space or aviation. And make energy number four. If you think about it as it is. Dale Earnhardt's real competition is not Jeff Gordon, it's nature's physics. If he pushes less air, makes more power and has better lateral traction both ends of his car, uses less fuel and moves the steering wheel less than any other car, he wins. (I left out – if he keeps the pedal mashed down.) If it don't break and he don't crash, no fucked up pit stops. Sure, drivers make a difference, but you get my point don't you? You want to be a racer? Stay awake in physics. Find a way to study thermodynamics (aerodynamics is a spin-off of physics.)

Drum Brakes

We had hell with brakes from day one. We were four wheel drum brakes with organic lining. One good decell from 150 miles-per-hour every two minutes was about it. Our weapons were lining only, and to tell the truth some of it wasn't much better than hi-grade cardboard but even the best we could find in a couple of quick stops the resin holding the stuff together would rise to friction surface and then glaze it and drop the friction coefficient to about nothing. Along with the lining trouble brake fluid would boil and we would go for the brakes and "Oh shit." It would hit the floor. Pump your ass off and pucker up your tail and steer. Maybe be able to get a breath in on next straight.

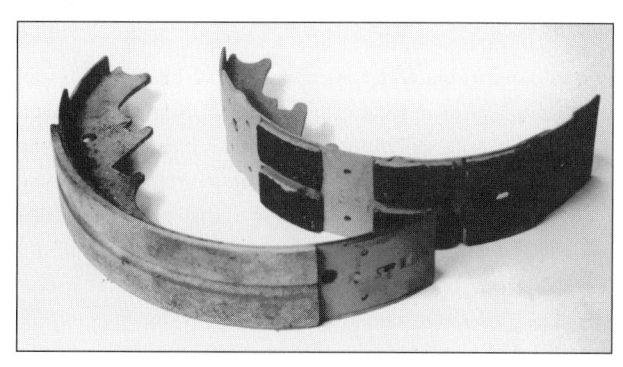

This deal would get everything so hot in the hub area the heat would kill the grease. Now you got no brakes and burned up wheel bearings. Yup, you get to meet the wrecker driver in that area. (Well, not always…sometimes you didn't wake up for a little while, and you met the ambulance driver or fire crewman.) This helped in the PR department 'cause if you crashed good you made the paper.

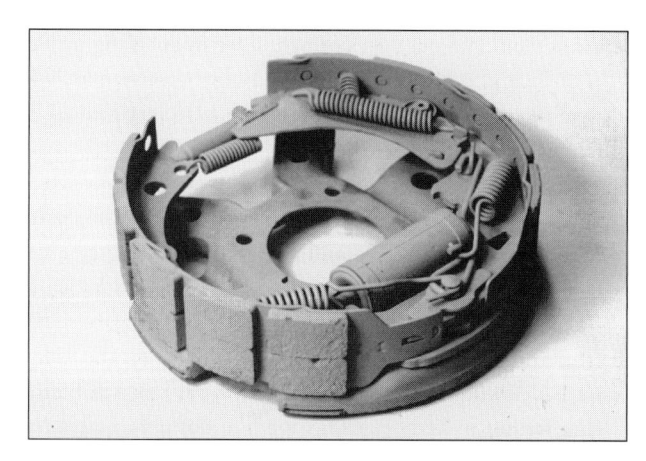

Bigger diameter drums, wider lining cooling ducts, drilled drums, fancy brake fluid from Formula One would just last few more laps and then "same ol' deal." I got some help from aviation. They had a sintered metal type lining used in a disc type brake. I got a brake company to form it in a shoe shape. We'd jerk it off the rivets. OK, now double rivet and go to big drums and three inch wide shoes. The pressure and heat would fold the shoes down. Now brace shoes with small tubes welded from web of shoe to lining surface. Now take this mess with a 4,000 pound car to Martinsville for 500 laps. What brakes? I try splitting brake shoes in half and make a double primary and double secondary arrangement with sintered iron lining. Failure took place sometime longer, so you essentially rationed your brakes or you lost 'em.

For me, I never got to where disk brakes were allowed, 1971 still drums all the way 'cept on road racing. I don't know how many millions of dollars were wadded up in race cars using each other or the walls for brakes. France would not consider allowing disc brakes, he very reluctantly allowed air ducts and the band-aids I told you about. Another interesting deal was rear axle failure. The axles flat couldn't handle the program, and when one broke, number one it was always in a corner with a full lateral load so, number two you lost the wheel and your brakes at same time plus, number three you can't steer the ass end, so usually you had enough time to say, "oh shit" twice before the big boom. Except if it was a Hudson Hornet. They kept wheel trapped and you got the "end over end" deal. Not too many survived that maneuver.

Full Floater

In 1959, I had enough of it and modified the rear end to use a full floater hub like a three-quarter ton pickup had. If axle broke, no big deal. Still got wheel and brakes. I had 'em on a '59 Pontiac, showed it to France. He said, "Can't do it." I said, "Fine, then the son-of-a-bitch can run USAC." I took it to Atlanta and we won the race. Nobody said shit. (NASCAR Grand National).

That car also had hydraulic weight jackers for front wheels, electric weight jackers for rear wheels, power steering (variable ratio), power brakes off of the residual pressure of the power steering with a 1- inch master cylinder, a cross flow aluminum radiator. Fireball drove, it and really wasn't a happy camper till race was over. France and associates outlawed every damn bit of it next day. Then "Balls" was pissed. ("Balls" was Fireball's shortcut nick name).

There were four inventions on that Pontiac I believe:
– variable ratio power steering
– power brakes from residual pressure of power steering pump
– adjustable height control hydraulically or electrically
– aluminum cross flow radiators.

180 Degree

In 1970 I decided 180 degree V8 would make more power than a 90 degree engine. What's a 90 degree engine? It's got a crankshaft that has rod journals every 90 degrees. What's a 180 degree engine? An engine with a crankshaft that has rod journals every 180 degrees. The 180 degree engine sounds totally different. We had to make our own crankshafts and different cam shaft.

Also, the 180 degree induction and exhaust conduits needed to be re-thought. Well, I battle the 180 degree for two years before I could equal the power of a 90 degree. But on a race track, seemed like 90 degree engine was a whisker quicker in lap time. I can't prove why.

I loved the sound of a 180 degree (we are talking V8s here). I even went so far as to run 180 degree engines (Chevys) at Indy, but gave up, lap time a li'l short, but vibrated like a son-of-a-bitch. So, I figured durability would suffer. 'Bout time I gave up on 180 degree in 1975, seemed like Junior Johnson picked it up and the different sound, coupled with his cars being the fastest, it was decided the 180 degree was the hot tip. So millions were spent in about four years while the racers chased their asses. The more I told them they were wasting time and money and sacrificing some durability, the more determined they were to 180 it. Back in them days race magazines printed my adventures, and I always gave them the straight skinny. Sometimes I kept quiet about some stuff, but I never blew smoke at 'em. In 1974 I'm a retired 180 degree fan. "Good-bye forever."

Combo Brake and Throttle

In 1963, I decide a race car could be best driven with one pedal, a combination brake and throttle. And use an automatic transmission? Nope, manual. The start of this idea was in Italy in 'bout mid '40s. I got into a swap deal with the limey's where I let them fly a B-17 (mine), and they let me fly clipped wing Spitfire, with it's narrow landing gear and a tail dragger to boot. It required concentration to keep from changing it's shape (ground loop). I let them fly a B-25, they let me fly a Mosquito. My favorite plane. You strap it on and do any fucking thing you can think of. In an American plane if you wanted left or right, or both

We tried a single pedal in the capsule car, but changed it before qualifying. Also had a removable steering wheel.

brakes, you pushed left-right-or both pedals regardless of rudder pedal position. The limey stuff you had to establish rudder position left-right or neutral for left-right or both brakes (neutral for both). You want left brake you gotta push in left rudder and tip the pedal, etc. I liked that deal in strong cross wind.

I figured there were times you needed brake and throttle at same time. I never got this to work very well mechanically, but worked pretty good with a hydraulic throttle. I tried it using a dyno with a running engine and brake load control and a pressure gauge on master cylinder and assuming 1500 pounds-per-square-inch full brakes on a 16 to one mechanical advantage on the master cylinder. I never got real happy with my invention, so I put it on hold. (I thought then, and still do, entering a turn left rear brake only would help a ton, and more power on the right rear wheel coming off would help.)

Clutchless Gear Shift

Now, the clutch gear shift, I had this down pat. I used a pair of cams and a pair of cables that had 100 pounds of control in both push and pull. You simply pull gear shift lever towards you. A third cable disengaged clutch. You keep pulling clutch. Clutch cam goes neutral, but first gear is engaged. You keep pulling shift lever. And gear shift cam went neutral and clutch is engaged. I had three gates: 1st and 2nd, 3rd and 4th, and reverse. The total travel in all gears was same as a manual Hurst gear shifter. Big, heavy, complex?

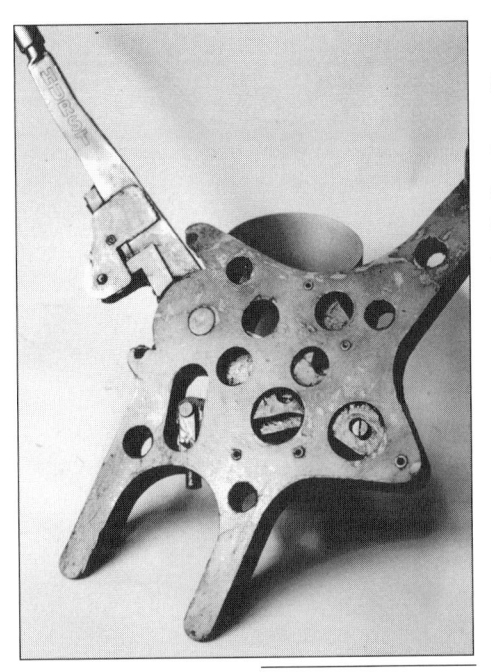

1 1/8th inch wide, five inches by six inches. Total weight five pounds.

How did it work? Ask Bobby Johns. I built three of them. One is on the Indy '64 capsule car. One I put on the general manager of Chevy's Caprice (Mr. Knudsen), and I still have the third one. Hurst shifter was the capsule car's sponsor ($40,000) and they got the rights to the inventions patents. But to be honest about it, I got an awful lot of help on this invention from an engineer who worked for George Hurst. I'm sorry I can't remember his name. His long suit was designing machines to knit cloth which use cams and cables extensively.

The capsule car was a one pedal car, throttle and brake. I chickened out in the final design and separated the brake and throttle and made up a bleedless hook and unhook connection.

TILT WHEEL, ADJUSTABLE COLUMN

To get in and out of the capsule the steering wheel had to be removed no other way to get in or out. Here comes first removable steering wheel. I used a collet and spline that could unlock in a second, since no exit possible for driver with steering wheel on. It still works, December 4, 1998 I removed the wheel to get in it at the PRI show in Indy.

At this time I also decided a round steering wheel in a race car is unnecessary, so I removed the lower 150 degrees of the radius and went straight to gain room for drivers upper legs. I also removed 100 degrees of the top of the steering wheel radius, ending up with a rectangular looking wheel, with rounded left and right hand grips. I never finished patents of removable steering wheel. First prototype had a cable steering shaft and tilt wheel feature.(cable like a big speedo cable) The tilt wheel was worthless in this capsule. If you tilted the wheel your knuckles either go into the windshield or the dash board. So I decided I was gonna have trouble with being too radical and maybe inspectors at Indy would cause me trouble or disqualification's. I think Saginaw division of GM ended up with patents on cable steering column and tilt steering wheel feature.

I also had adjustable steering wheel height again this was useless in the Capsule Car for same reasons as the tilt wheel. No room. Reason

I still have the third one.

The first removable steeering wheel.

for all this moveable stuff was seat was in a forever position. Only way to adjust for drivers was extremely flexible steering wheel position and adjustable brake and throttle location.

I might as well tell you about my experience in fiberglass right here. I decided to make a fiberglass body or covering. I ended up using a very light approach whereby the body weighed five ounces per square foot with body color in the gel coat. But this required a design to allow inner body pressure equal to outside pressure. It worked in spite of some experts' ridicule. What'd you invent Smokey? I'll let you decide.

V-belts

Let's back up in time a little to 'bout "day one." In the 40s stock car racers had trouble keeping generator-alternator and/or water pump drive belts (a v-belt drive of some kind) on and from flipping over. "Nope. Got to use stock." You see, looking at the front of an engine, let's talk V8s (95 percent were V8s) belt turns clockwise from the front. So right side of the belt had pulley pulling and keeping it tight but the left side of the belt in is effect pushing and not tight. You guessed it. Left side of belt would get to dancing at high rpm, then twist and roll over in the pulley. "Adios the deal." Belt's off or breaks. There went water pump, cooling and electrical charging system. Three laps later you're sitting in the pits watching. You say to your buddy, "The number 92 is smokin!" Your buddy knows 'bout engines. Says, "Yup, white smoke. That sumbitch is hot."

If he ain't a Herb Thomas fan he gets happy. He knows it's over for ol' number 92 today.

The stock '55 Chevy V8 had generator mounted on front left exhaust header. Big long push configuration just hopeless card trick number one. I get busy. '55 Chevy V8 gets a right exhaust header cast with mounting bosses for generator that lengthened the pull side but really shortened the push side. Believe it or not NASCAR never noticed.

In '56 production all were moved to right side. Even had trouble with it on production cars and trucks. We spent 'bout 12 years fighting v-belts at high rpm. I find a flat cogged belt and got Gates to make some quality samples. Damn right it was way better, but the long arm of NASCAR's law reached in and wiggled it's long stinky finger and sez, "no deal. Write on blackboard 1,000 times, 'Don't fuck with flat cog belts.'"

Wind Generator

I'm flying a Super Cub one day, somebody loaned me,. I notice generator has quit. Generator is driven by small propeller, it's mounted in the air stream. As I find it with my eyes, the light comes on (without even a drop of peyote). I get back to shop, get a small generator, whittle out a one foot propeller, fasten it on, put it behind the grill on my car and 50 miles per hour, 10 amps. Hot damn. We got it!

I buy an aluminum propeller. Find out Prest-O-

Lite makes a small aircraft wind generator. I hide it back of the grill. By now we got dual belts stock, so when I gut the alternator no load to pull, water pumps got it's own belt, when belt flies off, who gives a shit right? Lasted 'bout 10 races, a banged up grill exposes the wind generator to the prying eyes of my competitors, this brings league of inspectors to: "A-ha! Look at that crooked deal." Need a good wind generator? I still got it.

There is no telling how far stock car racing could have progressed if in the beginning NASCAR had a Clinton type chief mechanic who was technically inclined and combined with the line of lying bullshit he's got there would have been a champion with 35 wins a year. France and his 'Keystone Kops' wouldn't have had a chance. Somebody asked me if something like this might be going on now on the 24 car? Don't know. Why not ask Ray Evernham? Maybe he would know. Or how 'bout Jack Roush. Reckon he'd know? Wonder if NASCAR's got an impeachment clause in their charter? If they don't they should put it in, don't you think? If a blow job ain't sex, can you do it in front of a cop and not get arrested? I envy the younger sexually active people. goddam. We had to go through all kinds of deception to hide what's totally legal and morally acceptable now.

ZF Limited Slip

In late 1960, we had won the '60 Indy and was getting ready for '61 Indy and I decided I wanted to run a limited slip rear axle instead of a full locker, (a one-piece axle). I thought the solid rear axle was a heavy power draining deal because of the quick change gears and built in stagger in tires and the long straight at Indy. That was a way of life for a sprinter or a midget. Throw a paper cup on the floor (empty) and kick it. Watch it make a circle, that's stagger. Little wheel, big wheel. Also, if you have various length paper cups you'll notice the shorter they are the tighter they turn.

In looking at limited slip differentials I found the clutch type useless in steady service (got to slipping). The best looker, the Detroit Locker not rugged enough (for Indy Offy). I saw a drawing on a ZF (German) limited slip that looked super to me. Very simple and I assumed with good durability. How do you get one? Don't sell 'em in the US. My mind is made up. I'm gonna go with some kind of limited slip. I'm the Popular Science "Dear Abby for cars." I call up and say I want to write a story for Popular Science about ZF drive train parts. Germany? Well, hell yes! When you wanna do it? Tomorrow? Well, in two weeks here I am at the tar paper covered factory in Germany (Friedrickshaven).

I been there before but at 32,000 ft. Well hell, don't look too bad. Maybe we missed it. Not too unusual with the famous Norden bomb sight.

Got a meeting with chief engineer. I see the ZF limited slip, looks real good and strong also.

"Can I get two assemblies? How much?" (including changes I needed to get it to fit in an Indy car). "How long it take?" Price is cheap, delivery ain't bad. Now one thing left. "I want spare parts." I notice chief engineer's feathers look ruffled. He says, "You won't need any spare parts."

Well, shit. It's great to have faith in your product, but it's a long way from Indy to Germany. So I insist. I'm a son-of-a-bitch if he don't jump up and leave the room. I insulted him (I was told by the interpreter) by insisting on spare parts. Yup, we got the parts. I used one differential in the '62 Python (the four wheel leaner car) and I still have one.

Yup, it worked really good, but I'm not sure solid axle wouldn't have been as good, cause then we at best could get was half inch of stagger in legal tires for the joint. You know, this is damn near 40 years later, and if I needed a limited slip drive axle, I'd still like that simple effective design (the ZF). I'll tell you this. German engineers then, and probably still, think they are the most brilliant bunch in the world, and are no trip to Paris to get along with. You know, I'll bet on this regarding the Chrysler/Mercedes merger, a lot of Chrysler big shooters are gonna have a hell of a time adjusting to this German mind set. Boy, I can imagine Iacocca being top dog at Chrysler trying to adjust to the kraut guys. Zero. Be like Dewey says, "Lord have mercy."

The Bald Eagle Tire

In the mid-sixties I decided to build a silent tire that had an additional 20 percent of tread patch contact. I found at 40 miles per hour, tires made more noise than everything else combined. Do you know your tires make more noise than your engine? The main objective was better traction in the lateral, acceleration and braking planes. A non-treaded tire (a slick) offers more road to rubber interface for the same contact patch. Make sense? But on wet roads slicks are big trouble, hydroplaning. Simply put, the tire gets up on top of the water and coefficient of friction goes to zero. You may as well be ten feet in the air. Mud is also a negative for non treaded tire. Snow and ice some worse. In loose, sandy, soil works like a champ.

I got this urge from racing a spin off of our transition from treaded to slicks. I arrived at Indy, 1961 with slick tires, and was refused permission to use them. Why? Ground rule, all tires used must be tested first. My tires were Firestone race tires, but they were untested (1962, they were legalized for Indy).

Tires, generally speaking, displace water. My invention was a tread that blew the water away from the contact patch. (This is 1965) My idea was to turn tire slowly, then have a razor sharp tool that looked like a threading device cut the slick tire surface in a thread like pattern of four slices per inch, a half inch wide, then move over a half inch and do it again until we crossed the total tread area. I set the depth to the approximate bottom of the tread thickness. A six inch wide tread had 12 rows of spiral slices.

By accident I find a machine made in Mississippi by a man named Ken Currey. His machine was named "Ken-Tru." It's main purpose was to true up tires that had distorted wear patterns. Ken, at the same time had found this spiral slicing made tire run cooler. Truing tires by shaving off a spiral slice was called "sipping."

Well, I got a machine and modified it to create a tread configuration I called the Bald Eagle." I had a set of Goodyear Eagle tires retreaded with slick cap. Therefore my name – 'Bald Eagle.' Well how does this work? A tire is round, but where it touches the road, particularly with a biased ply tire (remember, this is mid 1960) the tread flattens out. This caused the cuts to open up, when tire started back to round, the cuts closed. This opening and closing created a fairly strong air wall which blew the water away from contact patch of tire. No hydroplaning. Ken and I are new partners. We register a trade mark "Bald Eagle."

I get Goodyear to conduct a three day test at their San Angelo tire proving ground. The tire is silent and as good as anything they have in all ways 'cept mud. But I found we hit a nerve when Goodyear's lawyers woke up, they had the copyright "Bald Eagle" rescinded.

(If you make a tire you can't use 'Eagle.' Vulture, hawk, robbin, parrot, any kind of other bird is OK, but don't fuck with 'Eagle.')

Now, Goodyear makes up 100 special tires. We are gonna do a big test (I still got the tires). My good friend Bob Mercer, who is CEO of Goodyear, kinda lets me know chances of Ken and I making any money on the deal are slim. NASCAR bans my idea. It really worked good on race car, even helped on dry track.

Ultraviolet is bad news on tires, it causes rapid oxidation of certain chemistry normally used in tread stock. My tire design reduced this negative. (By the way my Bald Eagle was nearly silent).

The Bald Eagle runs much cooler. Consider this: you cannot wear a tire unless you have heat and abrasion at same time. Heat alone and tire would just melt. Friction alone will not wear rubber. Try a piece of tread stock, a grinding wheel, and a garden hose. You can hold it on grind stone all day but if it's cool it won't touch it.

The ultraviolet from the sun affects the chemical composition of the tread. For example: if you weigh a new tire very-very precisely then put in the sun for six months, tire will weigh less. Why? Vaporization of some of the tread chemistry by ultra violet. Also a phase change slowly occurs. Tire gets harder and harder in a linear way considering the length of time the ultra violet got to the tire. Moral of story: tires and roads should be white. Damn sure not black anyway.

Why? Black acts as a blotter, sucks in ultraviolet. White repels it to a degree by reverse radiation.

Ultraviolet did same to asphalt, so in normal tire, these two negatives added up to two. If they don't care if the sun wrecks their tires, fuck 'em. (This was in 1968.) Do you notice now (1999) tires in the pits are covered with an advertisement adorned total light barrier? I wonder why?

Only connection I got to tires is, I own some Goodyear stock and own part of a rubber plantation (I never got a dime out of it either. But that's only been 'bout 30 years).

Yup, I know how to make the rubber from step one, ending up as a 100 pound ball on a stick. Kinda like a popsicle, 'cept it's done with heat. Do you know natural rubber is pure white?

Yes, natural rubber is still important in tire manufacturing. How much you make with the "Bald Eagle" Smoke? I'm afraid that was a four year exercise as is normal when a major corporation has a possible innovation development from the world of "not invented here." Best described as pissing into a 100 mile-per-hour wind. You and I pay same price for tires, but you didn't have to smell the rubber smoke for weeks to learn.

Flow Bench

Flow Bench: A short biography of the development of auto racing's first and most flexible air-fuel tool.

In 1951 after I'd worked for Hudson for a year building engines for Herb Thomas, I came to an opinion: no one in the automotive industry really understood anything about air and fuel flow in both the induction and exhaust systems. Therefore the best possible way to gain net power and at same time get the most power for BTU input was to understand the working fluids (air and fuel), and then capitalize and also use that information to enhance future engine designs.

I next visited any and all engine test facilities I was permitted to examine. I really got a shock. Most all systems were different from each other, or didn't exist. For example: the Chevy motor company air flow equipment up to 1960 was a 10 horsepower motor driving a 6-71 Detroit Diesel supercharger.

I talked to many engineers looking for guidance to build a machine to knowledgeably examine and test real movement and quantity of both the air and the fuel. Well, I wasted a year. All guidance offered, differed. I decided to continue, but completely on my own, as the varying advice confused me. This took me on a 30 year $350,000 journey.

My biggest mistakes were to build machines that were too small. Another mistake was neglecting to recognize the importance of temperature, humidity and pressure of the working fluid, and how it was modified in transit from it's entrance to the induction system, to the combustion chamber. Yet another mistake I made was in assuming the working fluid composition remained constant from its entrance in the fueler to combustion. I was searching for a simple bullet proof machine that could measure air and fuel independently, singularly or plurally. Also, how to measure air and fuel in each independent fueling conduit. By 1957, I think after 1,000 man hours building various concepts (labor then was cheap, 'bout $10 an hour). I'm down 'bout 150 grand in motors, chambers, custom hardware to fit various engines.

Now, I decide I will work on engines with this equipment from 50 cubic inches to 1,800 cubic inches. I've decided the best info was obtained at high negative pressure 28 inches of water. I set out to build Flow Bench number three.

Now, another surprise. An air pump big enough to do this, and it's associated hardware cost $80,000 and weighed 3 1/2 tons. This equipment is big and heavy and now consumes over 600 square feet of space, and is as much as 15 feet tall indoors. The power necessary to drive the air pump was 100 horsepower, 440 volts at 200 amps for a Roots design blower. This was very noisy and required a huge muffler system that weighed about 3,000 pounds and was 20 feet tall. Finding a good valve to control the air pump was about a three month search. A four inch iris valve as was used in early cameras proved to be the perfect solution for a linear and very sensitive air flow control (it actually came from a huge camera). I chose four inch as the size of all conduits from the air pump to any of it's functions. I choose a four inch laminar flow element manufactured by Meriam instruments. Matter of fact I used all air flow measurement equipment from Meriam instruments (good stuff – very expensive)

   A. Barometer
   B. Inclined manometer
   C. A very accurate pressure instrument for negative pressure read out.

Now I built the flow bench to use a stock or modified cylinder head as the conclusion of the combustion chamber. I then built a system where I could open one or more of the valves and measure the airflow very accurately. And again I stress, we read the real air flow quantity. But I had to correct for temperature, humidity and barometer. (can't change the weather) We made up graphs for computing. Once this equipment is up and running, I have enough muscle so I deal in real numbers, nothing is extrapolated. Now we

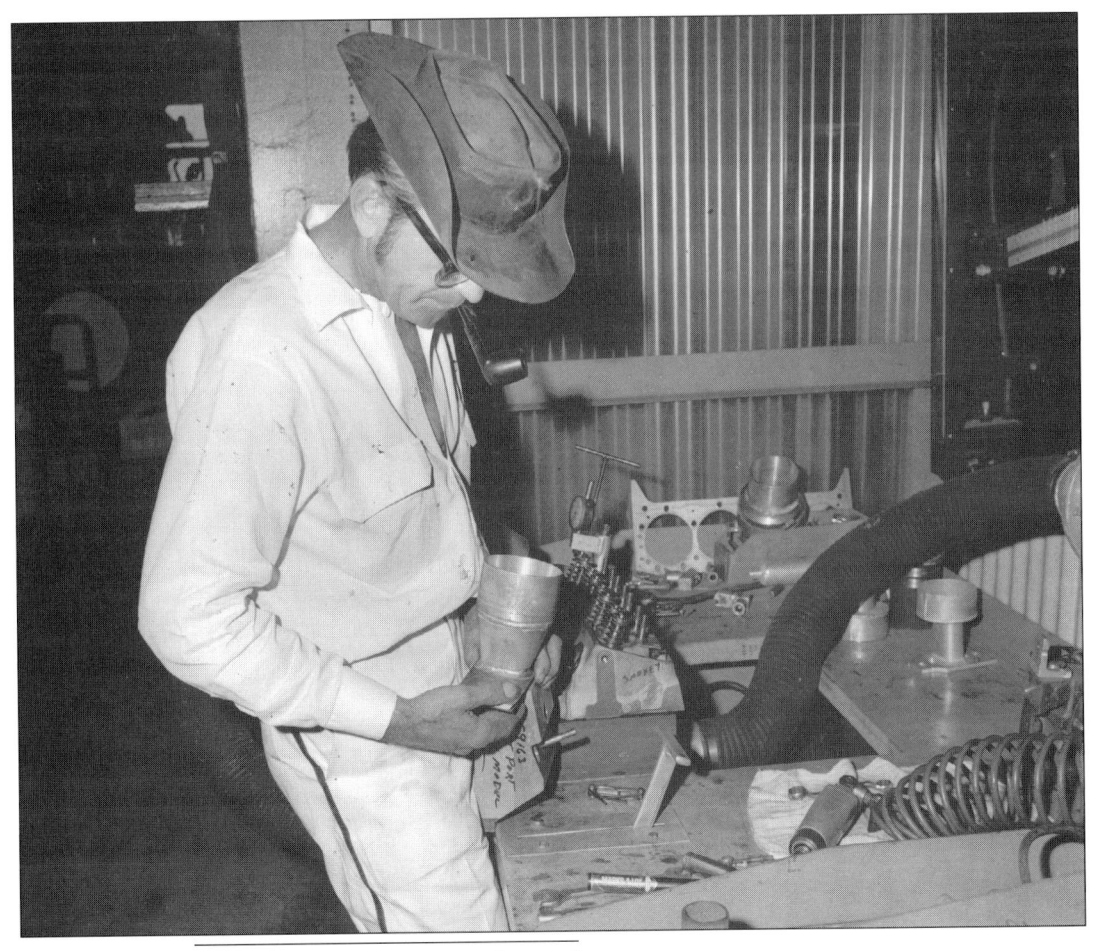

The Flow Bench. (photo: EMAP-Pertersen)

are off.....

This equipment works slick as a whistle. And we run it 18 hours a day uncovering hundreds of unknown idiosyncrasies that occur to the working fluid due to pressure and temperature changes incurred as the velocity and pressure changed due to orifice shape and size.

Now, I could flow any cylinder head very accurately and I got enough business from Detroit to keep this machine working 7 days a week. At this point, I added transparent ports and colored smoke. This exposed a major flaw in air flow measurement of a conduit in an intake manifold that served or a multiconduits from a common plenum. What we discovered was vaporized fuel under certain conditions would fall out of phase and go back to a liquid. Liquid gas will not react to a flame, it has to be vaporized. This affected air/fuel ratio immensely in a negative way. This discovery created the need to super vaporize the working fluid so that conduits that slowed or heated the working fluid had enough speed or low enough temperature to stay in a vapor phase. Now we have substantiated investment in the glass 'see in' manifolds, adapters, and sample intake runners.

In this time frame, I had to devise a way to get a sample of each conduit. This led to the quick setting rubber technology we used to make sample conduits from. The manifolds, with windows to observe colored smoke travel in multi conduit models that showed fuel fall out due to design errors. (In the early 1960's Chevy showed how to duplicate our flow equipment for a million bucks.)

'Bout in 1970, I decided to prepare a complete engine so it could be air and fuel flowed in both dry and with fuel, through all of it's components such as air cleaner, carb, induction system, cam shaft, cylinder heads, and same for the exhaust system. This showed air flow of a cylinder could be very misleading and incorrect. Again, many prototype parts had to be fabricated. We now have engine in a stand, complete with air cleaner, carb intake manifold cylinder heads complete with valves, sealed with oil pan and timing cover, crank shaft with rods and pistons (pistons have many holes for air passage equal to or greater than maximum air flow would be). We put crank shaft in position of maximum lift on the camshaft and flowed each cylinder. This is how we flowed each valve intake or exhaust. On intake flow, oil pan had four inch hole with an air tight joint. Carb was in wide open position. Carb had four inch adapter to laminar flow element, so by pulling on the pan we measured air flow through total combustion chamber and complete induction system, and each conduit individually.

I motored the engine when measuring flow. After six months of back to back checking, I decided the "holey" pistons were a negative step so we removed the pistons. And I stopped motoring the engine and simply opened the valves mechanically with a precision adjustment.

We adopted .650 as the optimum opening at 28 inches of water. We use to flow at every .050 increments from .050 to .650. In this time frame we abandoned all flowing except the above specs. (.650 at 28 inches of water barometric pressure). The same system was used to flow exhaust system. This include all components, including exhaust header and with or without exhaust pipes.

These changes produced a very stable result. Any increase in air flow always produced an increase in horsepower with the exception that the intake and exhaust systems had to be sized in correct proportion to each other. (Example: 1.580 exhaust valve and 2.050 intake valve in 1975 was ideal for a 350 cubic inch small block Chevy).

By 1975, this flow bench had shown no cylinder head available had big enough intake ports and the small exhaust port and valve were nearly ideal, but we were unable to confirm this without dyno and track testing. The flow bench taught us size and shape of ports and sizes relative to intake and exhaust changed with intended use.

In 1970, I wanted to investigate the character of wet flow vs. dry flow. New equipment was prohibitively expensive, so about $50,000 worth of used equipment did the job. (Note: measuring air fuel ratio was easy, so available equipment did the job nicely). This created a need for new hardware in regard to a series of adaptations for interface between dry and wet flow benches and the intake and exhaust ports. Also carburetor and exhaust systems as well as air cleaners. This took several years of cut and try, and much dyno running to correlate our flow numbers to horse power. In this time frame we learned driveability was directly related to sizing of all engine systems.

In 1978, I discovered cylinder wall interference and subsequent reduction in actual air-fuel flow as th valve was moved to increase lift. This changed our ideal valve motion, to valve motion moving away from cylinder wall shrouding.

Development of the total air and fuel flow consumed about 50 man hours a week for thirty some years plus electricity to run flow bench and material to make adapters. This flow bench pioneered technology of air and fuel flow. Particularly on common plenum multi-cylinder fuel distribution conduits. This flow bench taught the science of air flow wet must be customized to the race track and to the race car. And it had some negatives we could not overcome (using carbs) Also, the driver's technique was a critical part of good performance. This flow bench teaches there is no perfect way to fuel a high performance engine with a common plenum manifold. My experience in carbureted air fuel flow pointed out some of the advantages of fuel injection. This machine teaches further that the Otto cycle engine is a series of compromises, and to extend it's rpm range and maintain maximum torque is not possible, but what is doable is to have maximum torque at a chosen 300 rpm range between say, 3,000 rpm to 6,000 rpm

I'd like to pass this machine and my 50 years of experience into the hands of a teaching institution...particularly to one with a curriculum of advanced study of prime movers for exceptionally talented engineers with a faculty headed by a technology leader such as Dr. Hoekstra.

Air/fuel flow technology singularly is a life's work for an engineer. Air flow technology is still in it's infancy. Huge rewards still remain to be discovered.

A Greased Chute to Shitsville

You may find this chapter boring as hell, however this is supposed to be a story of my life, and I did spend about fifteen years in this adventure. Consider this: I actually did all this work for no pay to try and save your ass from a cold dark world so least you can do is read about it. It's part of the price of the book. Hell, no use wastin' it.

Being deeply involved in business of wildcat drilling partnerships from 1961 to 1972, I correctly, or incorrectly, felt oil as a fuel was a finite commodity, and that shortly, maybe by 1985, there would be a world shortage of crude oil. I also felt then, as I do now (2000), no matter if we never run out of oil, the petro-chemical negative of reacting those fifty million barrels a day (or to my guesstimate of 100 million barrels a day.) by 2010, will be a world loaded on to a greased chute to Shitsville. (By the way, I still believe this.) You don't have to be an Einstein to be very concerned when it's too hot or too cold. Or if the whole state of Florida is being consumed by forest fires (June '98), or when your eyes, nose and throat are offended by atmospheric conditions.

I've lived in Daytona Beach close to fifty-five years. We've had a huge change in our weather.

Considering the damage we have inflicted on the normal natural ecology system by paving half the state and polluting every water body. Then consider the cause: crooked, greedy, politicians, lawyers and industrialists. Consider the silence of the state professional legislative bureaus, receiving enormous salaries to cater to the various industries that are raping the state, with absolutely no relief in sight. And in most cases without a pain killer. It's hard to live with it, knowing we, the average citizen are absolutely powerless to contain the exploding decay of morality as it pertains to simplest laws of man.

By 1965, I'm convinced some concerned knowledgeable group of neutrals must investigate all alternate known forms of energy and explore ideas conceived by the brains and experiments of the world at large. We need a form of energy to replace hydrocarbons. We need an energy producing commodity: cheap, clean and available to the world – that is infinite.

Sure, tall order. But is it really? Considering what's at stake? Do you care what kind of world your great grandkids will have in sixty or seventy years? Someplace in here soon, you better do a much better job of voting. Based on the performance of our present Congress and Senates in state Capitols and in Washington, you and I have elected the biggest bunch of crooked do-nothing assholes in US history. (Or should I say your not voting elected?) We have sat on our asses and given them a license to do any damn thing they and their friends want to. Consider this: If it took fifty years to fuck it up, it will take at least that long to unfuck it.

Between 1965 and 1972 I'm self educating myself on wind and solar power. I find in five years the efficiency of a solar collector falls 80 percent due to oxidation of it's components internally and externally. Here's the plan I devised to consider all optional and alternate forms of energy.

(A) How many BTUs does it take to create it?
(B) How long before it pays those BTUs back?
(C) How many BTUs does it cost to maintain it?
(D) How many BTUs will it yield in a salvage mode?

I spent fifteen years, 'bout half the time or more, investigating anything that seemed to have a chance to be a viable and commercial that could reduce the need for hydrocarbons. Here's how it looked to me in short term: only one viable candidate and it was a hydrocarbon – natural gas. In both the gaseous and liquefied state. And I preferred the liquid natural gas for most all forms of surface, water, and much of the air transportation. My research also said natural and liquid gas were by far the best fuel for industry and farm operations. I preferred liquid natural gas because of its ability to furnish a consistent energy value as opposed to the gaseous form, which varies in BTUs content as much as 50 percent. That's same as trying to run gasoline that varies in octane from 100 to 75.

I had four main interests:
1. electric powered vehicles for short term
2. hydrogen fuel – hydrogen then replaces gasoline for long term.
3. solar collectors – short and long term
4. wind generators – short and long term

None of the above qualified when subjected to the BTU Test.

1. Electric vehicles fail because whenever you exchange one form of energy for another there is a loss in the form of heat. For an electric vehicle to become commercial you must produce electricity and then consume it as electricity – that is, without cost for power transmission.

2. Fuel cell technology is well known and has been used in space technology for years. Today it's touted as a done deal, with fuel cell cars just around the corner. In the real world it's a very expensive, impractical dream being exploited for PR purposes, and quite a few greenies. Fuel cell advocates make a hell of a living teasing the world with half truths reference it's progress. Sure, it works, but it's practicality today is zero. Tomorrow? Could be, but it's main usefulness today is in furnishing politicians, the military and part of industry, especially the surface transportation industry, with PR which indicates progress in fuel cell technology is dramatic and almost here. Get a ride in a fuel celled vehicle (don't forget your ear plugs). While your getting your ride try and imagine you and your family members being able to correctly operate one of these deals.

The above has been repeated for fifty years in the seeming simple search for a viable electrical storage device called a battery. Example: I had an electric car forty years ago that would revolutionize the world soon as a "better battery was developed." (I used lead acid batteries).

Hydrogen Fuel

I found hundreds of ways to make it, but all at the equivalent price of five dollars a gallon or more. But it took me ten years to wake up. Even if I could make it for an equivalent fifteen cents a gallon as compared to gasoline storage problems destroy hydrogen potential. I mastered using hydrogen in an Otto cycle engine to a commercial success technically, but a disaster economically. Reason: hydrogen in a gaseous form – the container for the equivalent of nine tenths of a gallon of gas weighed ninety pounds (a cylinder) so a container to hold equivalent of twenty gallons of gasoline weighed two thousand pounds. Probably too heavy, but that's not the problem. OK, now hydrogen in a liquid form, in the most expensive cryogenic container, like a high pressure thermos bottle, 'cept at higher pressure, and nearly three hundred fifty degrees Fahrenheit below zero still 'loses' one percent a day. Today, the normal shelf life of gasoline out of refinery to your engine is ninety days. Get the message? Shelf life of hydrogen would be 'bout same. You lose ninety percent in the so called "pipe line."

There was a third form. I tried a hydride system, but simply reported it also weighed approximately two thousand pounds for equivalent energy of twenty gallons of gas. Dangerous? Nope, I do not agree. Sure the Hindenburg syndrome exists, but I'm sure it would be no more of a problem than gas or alcohol as consumed in an Otto cycle engine today that would include natural or liquefied natural gas. Hydrogen is like electricity. It would have to be made and consumed in the vehicle to have commercial value.

I expect to see electricity, hydrogen, and fuel cell technology, pursued by vehicle manufacturers. If the above technology had recognizable potential wouldn't you expect the major development to come from a consumer of energy rather than a seller of energy? So don't hold your breath. Four items never discussed are cost, weight, size, and complexity of operation and maintenance. For example: if a turbine engine became viable for surface transportation, it's operational expertise would be over the ability of 75 percent of the motoring public to cope with. A simple mistake in a hot start sequence could cost the equivalent of a whole Otto cycle engined car. Durability of a turbine is outstanding, but fuel consumption at sea level prohibitively expensive. Hell, at sea level 12 percent thermal efficiency would be razor edge of the technology as compared to 35 percent in an Otto cycle engine. Emission wins with turbine and hydrogen - they hit a homer with bases loaded. Electric cars, if battery powered, are an environmental disaster, but never elaborated upon Battery emissions and lead, a toxic favorite battery component are not safe environmentally.

Solar energy

It's potential varies with weather, and atmospheric conditions. On a sunny, clear day one and a half BTUs per square centimeter, but as low as one tenth of BTU per square centimeter on a very cloudy day. But the killer on solar was that in approximately five years the deterioration of efficiency reduces the collector's efficiency by 'bout 80 percent. Why? Environmental outside and inside negative deposits. A solar collector by in large is a looser on BTUs out. I had at one time every kind of solar collector known to man. We made electricity, hydrogen, and heated the building. Also heated water. Across the board a looser. Sure, in a location where no electricity is available it beats nothing, but in no way an energy bargain.

Wind was a similar deal. Every place in the world I found lots of wind had no people. Too hostile an environment. Wind generators require costly supervision 365 days a year. Wind generators: I've had two bladed and wind turbines. I built one, put it up in a hundred foot tower, and could make 10 KW in a 30 mile-an-hour wind, but at 10 mph, 600 watts. A ten year recording of wind in Daytona beach averaged 9.9 miles per hour. Again, the BTUs in and BTUs out, a very decided looser. I fooled with wind generators for fifteen years. It's not possible to transmit AC current over long distances without substantial losses (heat is the enemy). Actually, we have two choices; DC or AC. DC requires storage, AC requires transformer, changing of DC to AC. Again, a big penalty regarding electrical losses, and with a heavy cost regarding batteries. You see, to make useful AC, you have to hold a steady generation RPM say within 20 rpm of 1,800, (or any multiple of 900 rpm) because of the 60 cycle requirement in the United States. This is do-able, but tough. Why? AC has negative and positive cycling at 60 cycles per second in the US. To make AC to interface and enter it into an AC grid, you must stay in exact sequence regarding negative and positive cycling.

I was able to make hydrogen, electricity, air condition, heat, water, heat building, with solar and wind. But at a very high cost, and the systems were very sensitive to normal and particularly abnormal atmospheric conditions. It's feast or famine. A wind turbine capable of 10 kilowatts had 780 pounds of torque in a 30 mph wind. In a 60 mile-an-hour wind, we'd have to lock it down. We couldn't control it, and physically we could not make it strong enough. Think of this: at 30 miles an hour, with the 16 foot wind turbine we had, it had the equivalent power of a 6-71 Detroit Diesel: over 700 foot pounds of torque.

Hell, at one time around 1972, all the alternate energy deals I had running were a cover story with Popular Science. But the bottom line was I wasted fifteen years, and a lot of money. I couldn't have done it without help financially from people like White Motor Company, (spelled "Mr. Knudsen"). I actually built a hydrogen-fueled engine for a submarine building company in Palm Beach Gardens called Perry. This was a converted Chevy small block that easily pulled a 100 KV generator. Did it work? Hell no. The storage problem again defeated the plan. I told Perry it was an unsolvable problem. He said he'd handle that part. It was a Captain Nemo scenario, with one page of the story missing.

Next adventure: the air conditioner we had to have was a prime mover that used power supplied by solar energy. A local inventor named Emmett Oliver invented a clever machine that I modified into a Rankine cycle engine that could use air as a working fluid instead of a fluorocarbon. Matter of fact US Army got interested in it, but not too serious. They wanted to test several systems at my expense. I was again short on money, and no longer trying to save the world from itself, so I said, "I'll let you know." But really, in that time frame I noticed 99 percent of the people could care less.

Again, I'm involved in the thirsty horse deal. I get him to the river and he won't drink. By 1970 I'm getting a reputation as Popular Science's alternate energy Einstein and get invited to judge alternate energy concepts in a top fifty college annual contest. I'm one of ten or fifteen judges who are supposed to understand the difference between viable possible alternate energy concepts and impossible wet dreams. Now, I'm a tenth grade drop out, but this contest was held at Sandia Laboratories in Albuquerque, New Mexico. Then next year at Sanford Washington at the Atomic Energy Control Center. As I'm involved in the judging, I'm in a state of shock as I looked at work done by MIT, University of North Carolina, The University of Florida, etc. These colleges have the leading people in every one of the possible energy concepts, and several impossible concepts. I could not believe the primitive construction and partially completed technology, and the stuff that was absolutely junk. I'd ask, "How come?" from a students, the answer was always same, "The expert was not paid extra to help, so the hell with it." Plus, funding for the projects was really poor. I had an idea of how much money these colleges get annually to fund research. It's a ton. So the sad realization on my part was, really, this too, was a political exercise.

About 1970 I was asked by the Society of Automotive Engineers (SAE) to deliver a key note speech in Chicago. I spent one hour outlining about fifteen alternate energy concepts or possibilities. Following my speech the head cat thanked me and more or less chewed my ass out for not talking about Indy cars. He then dumped 500 gallons of ice water on my deal by saying it wasn't viable or practical. Turns out he was correct, but maybe one or more of the 2,000 engineers would have found the holy grail if the top cat hadn't sent it to hell.

Collectively the colleges were only giving lip service to the available governmental funding feeding troughs. I think this part of my life did an awful lot to sour me regarding my, or anyone else's efforts to contribute to solutions of national, world, or local problems that affected us all in economical, environmentally and in a moral sense. Control was in the hands of indifferent, greedy and incompetent people. Some talented people with interesting solutions to alternate and renewable energy were denied funding and were ridiculed at the same time. One way trips in futility were revisited for the second and the tenth time. Fuel cells, gasahol, ethanol, various coal schemes, electric cars, hydrogen fuel, solar collectors, wind generators, perpetual motion contraptions, atomic variations…alchemy.

It's thirty years later now. Not one, not a single one of the above has become commercial. I even remember Ed Cole at General Motors giving money to play with a steam engine Greyhound bus. And then millions in experimental Rankine cycle engines (turbines) for surface transportation! It wasn't all a trip through a mirror maze. I learned quite a bit.

Rule Number 1 – don't fuck with nature. Its power dwarfs all that man can even imagine.

Rule Number 2 – forget nuclear power. Its kinda like the genie in the bottle. Once you let it out you can't get it to go back. Do we really know everything there is to know 'bout that stuff? In my adventures as a judge in alternate energy contest I got to know the atom squashers who invented and attempted to harness this energy. To a man they said, "Don't fuck with it anymore until you find a way to handle the residuals (as in spent fuel and contaminated materials) that accumulates in maintenance." None had any doubt a safe machine could be built. The unsolved problem is contaminated waste disposal.

A funny thing came out of this. I have now maybe an unreasonable respect for water. I never realized how magic water is. When I see how cities abuse water bodies I'd like to string the legislators who allow this up by their balls. We need a simple law, and we need to enforce it: "Do anything you want to any fresh water body as long as you're willing to drink it." (All government personnel must drink untreated river or lake water. I did all the time in the jungle.) The most important thing I learned in those fifteen years was how short sighted man is (this is on a world wide basis). Ten years is at best, the maximum time frame considered by our industrial and political leaders. I find myself saying. "Man, I'm sure glad I won't have to face the consequences of what's going on now." You older readers, you ever think that way? Wanna guess what the history book is going to say about the blind assholes who controlled the game in the 1900s?

Lastly, the world is like a space ship. It was loaded with everything that it was ever gonna have. If we use some of it to extinction, there ain't gonna be any more is there? If you don't believe that, show me one live dinosaur. My point is, we'd better consider waste much more importantly. How 'bout you with your Lincoln Navigator Ford pick-up, with forty thousand dollar seats and thirteen miles per gallon? Or you with that big-ass Chevy Suburban, with those giant tars, and big engine, 500 cubic inches, ten miles per gallon? (After you threw the cat converter away and put on them "California straight-thrus.") How's that new fancy hi-buck radar catcher workin? Ain't your problem, right? Fuck 'em. You inherited your money or your business, and you're important enough you do as you goddamned please. "My old man's Senator Foghorn, what's your badge number? He'll have your ass in forty-eight hours." "Goddam. Look at that motorhome comin.' Betcha it's running ninety miles-an-hour." "Big-ass diesel. Did you see the big number 2 - Miller? Shoot man, that's Rusty's deal. Holy shit, I heard it cost 3/4 of a million." "Shoot," driver says "try one point two." "That you driving Rusty?" "Shit no, he's got a jet. He just sleeps in the motorhome race night." Waste?

I can hear it very faintly (1950), but it gets little bit louder each passing year. "Load the wagon boys, the mule is blind." I think I hear faint music with it now, it sounds like the Cannonball Express. Margie says I lost my sense of humor. I think she's right, but if you hadn't had a drink in damn near forty years, didn't smoke, was half way between seventy and eighty, and when the sun goes down, instead of getting horny you get sleepy, plus you get to thinking you have more fun with your wife, and take her with you where ever you go, what the hell you gonna do to be funny?

Last week I made two official looking signs and named the new Seabreeze bridges after our dogs, Junkyard and Goofy. Well, the climb up those big poles on the bridge at night, no help, watching out for cops, and installing those heavy signs. Hell, it's kinda hard then to be funny when your daughter finds out what you done and she is embarrassed and thinks I've flipped my cork. (Her comment, "How hard will it be to take 'em down?") My wife laughed herself silly when she seen the signs, but, "I've lost my sense of humor." Why did I do it? It's bad luck to leave a new bridge unnamed. You see we got two new bridges and five commissioners. All five of 'em want bridges to have same name they have. You get it? So, game is, "play waiting game" 'cause five other local bullshitters and politicians got same idea.

OK, Daytona is so dry (atmospheric pollution?) that it starts burning. Well actually, all of central Florida is burning. Now I'm puzzled. The very reverend Jerry Fartwell says it's 'cause Orlando blessed and OK'd corn-holing. Remember, he said "because of Orlando doing it the community is going to burn in hell." Wel,l consider the size of this earth, and consider the control center for God may be be millions of miles away. It wouldn't be hard to miss a few miles, and Daytona gets it because of Orlando. But after careful consideration, I decide God can get stuff to happen to the inch and to the second. The fire's got to be bad luck over the bridge deal. Would you believe the idiots took the signs down in less than forty-eight hours? (Yup. I got 'em back). But what's happened? Three hours after I put signs up it rained. First time in seven weeks. Day after they took signs down 100,000 acres, and lots of houses burned down. Wait. There's more!

I believe the damn fire is gonna last another month. Now it took me a week, and 'bout seventy-five bucks to make the signs. I was ignored regarding the bad luck and fire cause. The Pepsi Cola 400, where Coca Cola is the official drink (Sound goofy to you? Does to me.) and the only official dope allowed, has been canceled. 180,000 fans were headed this way. You can't see shit. We are smoked out. Right now as I write this my eyes are watering. Our official cat is laying on the floor (I'm at the shop) with both front paws over his eyes. The official dogs won't hardly go out to take a piss because of the heat, smoke and falling ashes. It's been three days since they took the signs down, and would you believe they still haven't come and begged me to put 'em back up?

Listen to this. Right now we got enough rolls, hamburgers and hot dogs for 180,000 people for three days. The colas and horse piss can keep, but watch your ass on hot dogs and hamburgers (e-coli) for the next month or so. The food, drink and hotel people are crying with tears big as horse turds. They went from tripling the price (What's the proper words for pricks that do that…"price gougers" or just plain "greedy pricks?") to owners of a lot of tube steaks with nobody to eat 'em. If you can come to Daytona to see a race stop fifty miles 'fore you get here and lubricate you ass well, cause your gonna be hurting even worse if you don't. Well now in all fairness to Daytona gougers, let me say all cities and towns do it where ever the race is.

They are evacuating all around here. (The whole county next to us). I don't know what they did to piss God off. Flagler County is a hurting place. Lot of good people who like to live in the woods are losing all their worldly possessions. Mark Martin, who don't live in Daytona, is supposed to get a key to city of Daytona Beach today. But you know, they should have given him a fire extinguisher. Our TV is 24 hours wall to wall fire and people tragedy, but what about the snakes, foxes, deer, turtles, birds, skunks, raccoons, alligators, etc,…what the hell did they do to deserve this? They had nothing to do with the unnamed bridges, or queers in Orlando. Preacher Fartwell, I hope you talk to God and reverse your punishment regarding the queers cause a lot of race fans and local people are suffering. Reverend, you got any idea what we're gonna do with a half million hot dogs, hamburgers and rolls if the goddam power goes off tonight? How many cows and hogs will have died in vain if this comes to pass? (I'm not sure if pork is in either, so maybe it's just cows.) I have heard some hot dogs have mice and rat parts in 'em, but I think that's not on purpose. Reverend, would you be interested in a deal where you could get me some divine help to get 'bout 800 horsepower out of a 358? If so, and the price is right, I'd start back racing again.

But preacher, it's got to be done on the level. No cheating.

I know this fire reminds me again of how insignificant a human is singularly or plurality as compared to nature's wake up calls like fire, tornado, hurricane, flood and earthquake. You know if you rake up a pile of leaves and set them on fire here, they fine your ass 'bout three times what we got to win a NASCAR race in 1949. Do you suppose just maybe the "tree huggers" got their facts fucked up? Burning natural residual and living stuff ain't the problem. It's man made industrial products and their manufacturing processes. If the tree huggers are right, don't come to Florida for fifty years, and if you got any kin folk in Florida, write 'em off. We've eaten enough smoke in last three weeks in Volusia county and Flagler county to make it through three generations of pensioned fire fighters. Now I have an idea what a smoked turkey feels like.

As I worked those fifteen years trying to come up with short term and long term alternate energy, I noticed groups with vested interests who owned the senate and congress, climb in on our experiments and begin to manufacture alcohol supplemented fuels. Facts are alcohol blended gasoline has been, and still is nothing but a fucking rape of American taxpayers. Same with electric cars, hydrogen fuel, diesel cars, solar collectors, wind generators, atomic power, fuel cells. OK, I've stepped on many toes here and I doubt you reading this agree. You the reader, I bet you in your lifetime you will never see the viable commercial adaptation of anything I mentioned using any technology available today (well, maybe fuel cells). I don't care if you're fifteen years old and live to a hundred. The problem is so huge and so critical, and the time frame for solution so short, it scares me to think of what it's gonna be like for my grandchildren and great grand kids. I gave up in 1972 and have joined the rest of the ostriches. My head's in the sand and my master plan is, "I'll be out of here before the shit hits the fan." I remind you again, in the ostrich position your are in a wide open target for exploitation. I don't recommend the ostrich solution considering the unprotected attitude your ass is in.

Today there is hope for major change, but you gotta look close. Maybe an engine invented in Australia may cut fuel consumption in half (and maybe not). I've been involved in this a li'l bit.

In Tulsa, Oklahoma a process to turn natural gas into white petroleum. This would double world hydrocarbons. Make fuel cheaper and cleaner. (no sulfur, no nitrogen). I've been sniffing this since 1972 and it may be "real" now. Plus, new lubrication hybrid systems may greatly increase life of all mechanical systems. I work on it every day, still.

The Smokey BTU Juggling Contest

In around 1955, I started thinking we wasted too much heat in the Otto cycle engine. Racing wasn't as much fun as it had been. This is in reference to NASCAR's rules and politics. We didn't know what the hell was going on regarding France's wheeling and dealing.

I had this idea. Build an engine that could run in a sealed container that was a thermal barrier to ambient and just have two holes in the box. One to let air into the engine fuel induction system and the other hole to emit reacted exhaust gases. What the hell's going on in my mind? Why do I give a damn about running out of oil. Why do I even consider not messing up the air and water?

Hell, I'll be dead and gone before the shit hits the fan. I can't answer why, suddenly stuff like this seemed important concerning tomorrow. I never before thought about tomorrow, it was not guaranteed.

This was a strange part of my life. I had an all concrete shop back of the truck shop where I built race engines and race cars. Nobody allowed in there 'cept driver and one or two part time helpers, and Dewey, the vice president of sanitation. I paint the windows black and keep doors locked. From seven pm till 1:30 am I'm Thomas Edison. Man, I got ideas coming out the ass. I lay in bed and build this stuff in my mind part by part. I can't wait till tomorrow night to make parts. Why secret? Not because I wanted full compensation, but because I'd found out in discussing my ideas with a peer, their thoughts confused me. In this time frame I notice I got kids and relatives who may end up living in a cold, dark world. I decide to help devise a plan to double the usefulness of a barrel of crude oil or it's equivalent in gas. Enter twenty-five years of the Smokey BTU juggling contest.

The engine in a sealed box? What is it? Now I've collected a whole bunch of physics and chemistry books and dictionaries especially concerned with physics and chemistry. I think I'm going goofy. I very seldom read anything since the Air Force, and if I did it was a book that taught me either physics or petro chemistry. Note: in the Air Force I collected and digested all the technical literature I could find if it was related to air planes or weather. Why? Well in those days my life depended on luck, airplanes without holes in 'em, good weather, and engines that kept making noise till I got it back on the ground. There is no education to this effect. Flying a good airplane in good weather was easy, but the more I knew about the plane and the weather, the less likely my day would be fucked up.

Back to my nighttime experimental efforts. In this period I change friends. I change from hard living pussy-hounds to an alcoholic metallurgist, another social misfit who was a thermodynamicist, a hard-drinking petro-chemist, an early retirement physicist who spent a lot of his time in Goofyville. An electrical genius who said Edison was a phony and Nikola Tesla was the genius.

Even had some discussions with Von Braun the rocket scientist. We both wrote for Popular Science then, and he lived in Melbourne (100 miles south of Daytona). And local wizard Emmit Oliver (a real brain) who had the ability to invent practical and useful stuff totally different. Example: the spinning reel instead of the winch type fishing reel. Emmit was a master of mechanical motion and harnessing electricity and magnetism.

I learned a new word: "adiabatic." A Greek word that means "even exchange." My engine in a box would hopefully give back, in mechanical energy, as much energy as was put into it thermally.

Therefore the adiabatic engine was born. Did I invent the adiabatic engine? No, and I doubt anyone else will either.

Strangely this was more fun than racing. I worked every night from 7:00 pm to 1:30 am, five days a week and all day Saturday and Sunday. Emitt Oliver, Dave Bennett and I built an engine that ran and ran well, that Von Braun said would never run as an external combustion machine. Not only run, but maybe the most efficient expander cycle engine up till then. Matter of fact General Electric considered it as a 40,000 horsepower generator prime mover for an electrical power plant. And General Motors was inspired by it to build a running model in a Pontiac experimental car that I last saw in 1996 at the Pontiac Oakland International annual meeting in Denver. Small world. John Delorean and I were both the speakers for this assembly.

Workin' on one of the hot vapor engines on the dyno.

My whole life is a circle that started off as a very small deal and just got bigger and bigger as the years passed. The first adiabatic engine was a search for metals that could stand the very high operating temperatures and for a lubricant that could stand 800 to 900 degrees operating temperature. When in 1958 I first run the engine, in fifteen minutes I found a major problem. Gasoline as a fuel was out. The limits of gasoline vapor control was approximately 235 degrees F. And I didn't know it. Well the engine detonated it's ass off. Experiment was junk.

I don't give up. I have an option. Use diesel as a fuel, but by now I've already decided diesel was not a candidate fuel. Environmentally and medically it was a bigger loser than gasoline so the search now was how to modify gasoline or it's reaction process to be controllable to 400 degrees Fahrenheit. I found the speed or velocity of the gasoline vapor was a big factor. I found if the gasoline was homogenized into a vapor with air, and then super heated quickly enough, then the molecules of fuel would be of more equal octane value and detonation would occur at a much higher temperature. I know this is boring and confusing to most of you. But goddam it, how can I skip over it and write a story of my life and leave out 35 years of an adventure that maybe consumed the biggest part of my awake life?

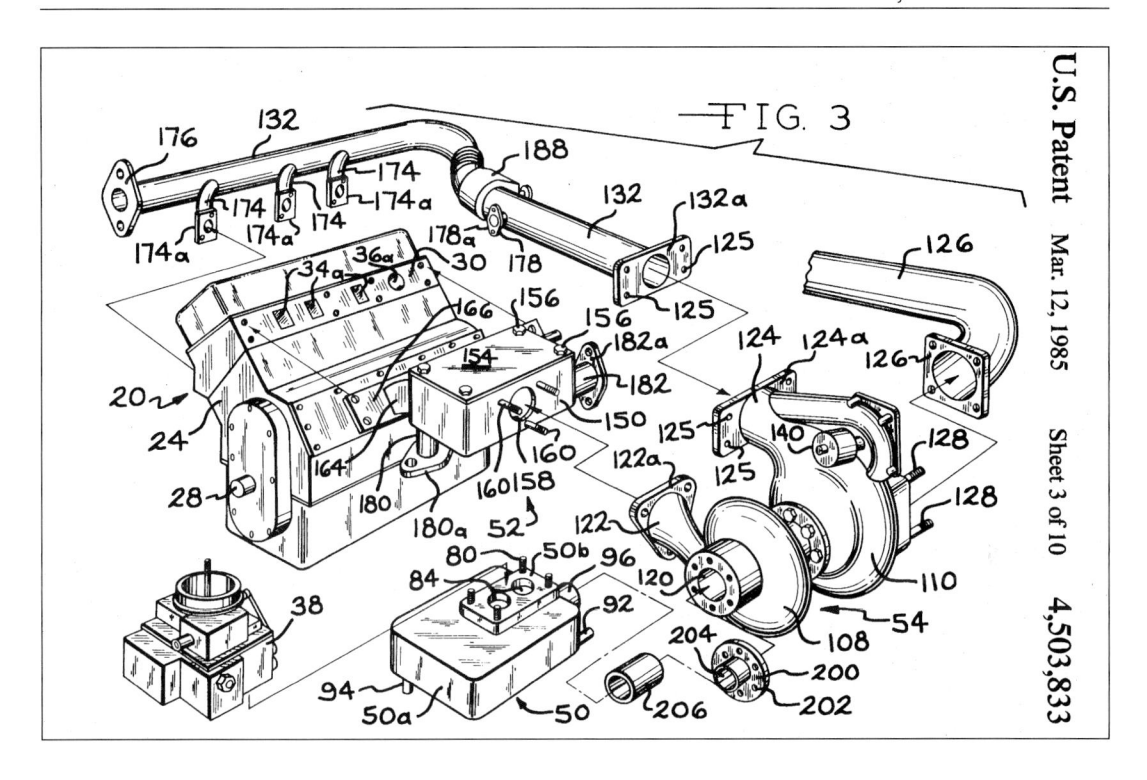

'Bout 1968 or so I was so sure oil was gonna run out 'bout 1982, I started thinking alternative energy. What's that stuff? Anything that don't change the quality of the air we breath and live in when reacted to furnish energy for all the inventions man has discovered in the name of bettering the quality of human life. Here's where I launched the second attempt to build an adiabatic engine. I started the project in around '54. It was a metal engine then. In '68 my master plan was ceramics and composites.

Yes, there are several inventions in this adventure. Since this trip took damn near forty years, I'm gonna tell you 'bout it in one go-round. My dream was to build an engine that could operate in a sealed box. That is one hole to let air in and a second hole to let exhaust out. Idea being no radiant heat be lost. No cooling. Another way to put it would be, if the engine consumed a fuel that had 10,000 BTUs at full utilization, the engine produces 10,000 BTUs of work.

Of course I didn't expect 100 percent, but at the time the boogey for a four-cycle reciprocator was 'bout 33 percent (state of the art 1950s). 100 percent conversion brings the Greek word "adiabatic" into the game. Adiabatic in Southern Race English means "even swap." In 1954 my first experiment with this dream crashed when engine detonated so bad in five minutes I have to shut it off. What a shock.

I never considered the problem of loss of fuel reaction control due to heating the fuel and it's condiments to over 235 degrees F, where I lost control of a smooth reaction and experienced reaction in form of explosion (detonation). I knew by now diesel fuel could handle higher temperatures, but by 1954 my experience with diesel engines lead me to believe that if the diesel exhaust fumes offended my nose and eyes so strongly it had to be a non-candidate fuel for medical reasons. So, I tried alternate fuels: propane, natural gas, liquid natural gas, alcohol, methanol, hydrogen, methane gases from coconut husks, cow shit, horse shit, pig shit, chicken shit (by the way, cow shit was best of the methanes, chicken shit second and horse shit last). Yes. I got all of the above to operate a six-cylinder Chevy engine. OK, I decide we got to with gasoline as the fuel or nothing.

Lucky I had friends in the petro-chemical labs, in Houston. I found gasoline drop by drop varied as much as seven or eight octane numbers in a pound of gasoline. 100 octane gas drop by drop varied from 95 to 103 octane. Now I found how fast you heat or cool fuel affected it's character kinda like tempering steel. The faster you cool it the harder it gets. I found the faster you heated gasoline the more stable it got. You see, gasoline is as a rule, 'bout 100 different species of hydrocarbons, and they all had their own octane numbers. Fast heating gave the fuel less time to departmentize, reference light ends and heavy ends.

I decide to do this heating in three separate stages. First I re-use coolant heat. I devise a dual wall first stage heater section (with engine coolant) where by fuel is partially vaporized to about 190 degrees F. then is sucked in and thrown against a hot wall with an impeller turning 'bout 150,000 rpm. This intake pressure pump is essentially a hi-speed centrifugal exhaust gas heated, dual wall blender. This now allowed me to operate at over 300 degrees with gasoline. I made this device out of a turbocharger compressor, and used exhaust gas to drive it. I call this "the homogenizer." It super mixes and heats air and gas vapor very-very fast. No time for phase change or separation of ingredients.

Here's the deal, to run an Otto cycle engine you need 'bout 1,600 degrees F. average working temperature of the working fluid in cylinders. To make good power with a carbureted engine the air fuel goes into the manifold 'bout 36 degrees F, damn near and sometimes icing. (Yes, even on a 90 degree day. So you have to use fuel to get the 1,600 degree average. Well, I could get 25 percent of the way for nothing. How? Well, first heating stage 200 degrees with engine coolant. Second stage heat the vapor in the homogenizer to 300 degrees. And the last step, use exhaust heated induction conduits to peak the temperature at 350 to 375 degrees F.

If you're bored with this, flip a few pages. But if you're a gear head, read slower and I think I can tow you through here without losing you in the weeds.

The hot vapor engine in a rabbit…it'll still smoke the tires.

If you vaporize gasoline and heat it, the pressure of the vapor will rise, and then most of it will try to flow back out of the induction conduits back to atmosphere. I need a check valve. I got the homogenizer to automatically always have a half pound of pressure pushing against the induction manifold pressure regardless of what it was, by sizing of the turbine and homogenizer wheels. Also I got the homogenizer to always have a least six inches of vacuum pulling in ambient air regardless of what was going on, again this is done by sizing.

So now we got an engine artificially aspirated with it's own waste heat and I could get induction pressures of 20 to 25 pounds over atmospheric by controlling heating from exhaust system.

Now consider this: the specific density of the heated working fluid was same as at ambient temperature because the fluid was not allowed to expand but the pressure rose dramatically.

Essentially this doubled the horsepower and improved the thermal efficiency by quite a bit – much better mileage. We also get an important gift. A cleaner burning engine in regard to emission. Matter of fact, regarding hydrocarbons and carbon monoxide, we could run steady state damn near zero, but NOx (nitrogen oxide) was a problem. We could pass emissions in (1987) with a carburetor and point ignition, zero computer controls, but NOx was at the limit.

After many years of cut and try, I finally found a way to build a commercial, part adiabatic engine. I quit drinking in 1960, so I slowly lost my academic camaraderie at the watering holes, and then death seemed to claim most rather quickly. This adventure started in 1955, has now consumed 15 years – it's 1980. I build

This is the hot vapor engine that is headed to the Smithsonian.

a three cylinder engine 120 cubic inches. I call it a "hot vapor cycle" engine (adiabatic seems too distant to be factual). I installed it in a front wheel drive Buick called a "Skylark." This car could have been more appropriately called the "shit bird." Terrible brakes, very poor powertrain and body. It had a fair engine but a nightmare to work on and it's electronic fuel controls were from Mickey-Mouseville.

I got the deal working good in 1981. GM was looking for new engines in 1980 and 1981, so there was a big show and tell for the president of GM, Pete Estes and his soon-to-be successor, McDonald. I'm working for Buick under Herb Fishel and Lloyd Ruess both in hi-performance and in conventional surface transportation. Lloyd Ruess, General Manager of Buick was forced to get diesel literate by the corporate idiots, so he hired Ricardo in England to make a V6 diesel. They made it out of a modified beefed up V6 gasoline engine. Nope, that never works. It was junk. Two years and much loot shot in the ass.

For the show and tell (in the "all divisions show and tell"), I get the job to build a three-cylinder diesel and install it in a Volkswagen diesel car. Idea is, Buick is to supplement their car line with a competitive car to the Volkswagen diesel. I get thirteen weeks to do it. I have two helpers and my pay is $1,000 a month for me and the shop. (My helper's pay is greater than mine) I bill Buick for helpers and material, I pay insurance, taxes and maintenance. That should give you an insight to my IQ. Buick sent an engineer down to help me. A snot-nosed, wet behind the ears genius who couldn't pour piss out of a boot. He's probably chief engineer of something at GM now. We make it and Buick says, "bring up your three cylinder hot vapor car also." We have to pass emissions with the three-cylinder diesel and do at GM staff engineering. I already had the three cylinder gas job certified for emissions at Southwest Research. Well, I ride with Estes and McDonald in both. They try to make a deal with Buick for the gas job. "The diesel is ours," they say (and it is really), so we'll keep it at staff engineering." The chassis was a new Rabbit diesel. If you saw a three-cylinder diesel-engined car at GM's car exhibition at Disney World in Orlando around 1981 as the car of the future, guess where that diesel engine came from?

Hell, I've still got the three-cylinder gas car I took up there. This was a running son-of-a-bitch, and on the strength of one thirty minute ride in it, GM, Ford, and Chrysler, John Delorean, Volvo, Volkswagen and BMW all said, "What kind of a deal can we make where you do all the work and we get to understand it and figure out how to do it without paying for it." Everybody except John Delorean, he immediately offered twenty million for total ownership. By 1984, I've built one, two, three and four cylinder hot vapor engines and have all of them running in cars. I have that one cylinder in a Fiesta, the two cylinder in a Volkswagen and the three cylinder in a Delorean and in a Buick Skylark. I've got a four cylinder in a Ford and a Chrysler and also in a Pontiac Fiero. GM, Ford, Chrysler, Volkswagen, Volvo, BMW have been here riding and smoking the stuff over. They have given me cars to test, furnished engines and drive trains, and once in awhile a couple of bucks. We have been to Southwest Research in San Antonio and passed emissions with the Buick and the Delorean. We passed emissions on the Pontiac at Pontiac and the Ford at Ford, and I have been at Ford's and GM's test tracks in Michigan for mileage, performance and driveability runs. These things start as a little conversation and like a hurricane get spinning faster and faster and I guess, where the inventor generally gets blowed out the side someplace, then the wind and rain goes away and in thirty days it's like it never happened.

As it stands today the Smithsonian has inquired about a hot vapor engine for their museum. Maybe you can go check it out there, if they never get into vehicles. They've also got one of my work hats.

Slippin' Outta Sync

A lawyer told me 'bout all men do exactly the same thing subject to their financial position. He said, "Their behavior is so predictable it was almost comical." I said, "What am I gonna do?" He answered, "Same as you've been doing – buy a fifth of cheap-ass Three Feathers whiskey, work and drink till midnight then go across the road to Danny's Bar and bullshit a lonesome divorcee off the bar stool over to your army cot. This seduction routine will go on four days a week, and you'll disappear three days a week with your race car."

Well, Kenny Rich did it in extra special style (he still had money). He bought a couple of secret gold mines in Ecuador off a bar stool in Dallas from a slick dago named Eduardo Bottenilli. You know Ecuador had tons of gold it is said, gold that had been hidden from the Spanish when that prick Pizzaro went down there and killed all the reigning Indians (Incas). (How come Pizzaro was so invincible? Easy, the Indians thought the horse and it's rider were some kind of a two piece indestructible invention of the gods.) All this shit happened to the head Inca (Atahulfa) in Archidonna and Bottenilli knew where the gold was buried. It had been hidden for 450 years, but Kenny had the secret map, and he gave me 10 percent of it 'cause he liked me.

Kenny calls and says, "You'll soon be rich, come down to Ecuador with me next week." Well hell, I got to race the '60 Pontiac with Fireball, do the 1960 Mobile Gas Economy Run, write for Popular Science plus I'm building my own Indy car and getting Kenny's Indy car ready, I've got some production problems for Pontiac to play with, and I'm a GMC Truck dealer with 20 mechanics to ride herd over and a million bucks worth of trucks to sell (this list is just for starters). So I take the easy way out and say "Thank you very much, but I don't want any goddam gold mines – I'm up to my ass in alleygators as it is."

Three months later it's Kenny again, back for a short visit. He wants to know, "Can I come down?" It looks like they've 'bout located the gold, but need some help with a diesel water pump on a dredge. I'm tempted, but remember I'm dead broke and I owe 165 grand so I answer "Nope, can't do it." 'Bout a month later every fuckin' thing that could go wrong goes wrong. I've got money, pussy, dealership, and racing problems out the ass. I call the airlines. They need 400 bucks and two days to get me to Ecuador. I send telegram to Kenny at his headquarters in Guyaquil, Ecuador, at Imperial Hotel. I leave a three page note for office and service and sales managers. I leave with an Eastern Airlines ticket charged on my credit card and 40 bucks. With me I've got two changes of work clothes in a paper bag with a razor and tooth brush.

I got a passport but I need a vaccination. Something that takes five days to tell if it took (small pox).

Luckily the ticket honcho is a race fan. I rode to Miami on a motorcycle, leave it in a hanger and the ticket man says "Shit, what they gonna do if I let you get off the plane? Hell, they ain't gonna shoot you (I don't think)" I agree, "We'll worry 'bout that when I get there."

The plane from Miami to Panama is a four engine DC-4 war surplus, a slo-slo boat to China. I sleep on a bench in the Panama airport. The next plane, to Guyaquil, is a C-46 war surplus job packed solid (including the toilet) with government papers, chickens and ducks. Five damn, long hours to Guyaquil – filthy, half-assed, short runway, and a hot, stinkin' terminal.

"No shot?" (small pox) "OK, Gotta have one, cost 16 sucres." ('bout 85 cents)

(That day 18 sucres of their money equaled one dollar, today it's 'bout 11,000 to a dollar).

Ecuador's money is called "sucre." I cashed 15 grand into sucres one day in Quito. My pal Leonard and I both had two giant brown grocery bags full and walked it ten blocks to deposit in another bank (it was 200 to one then).

I'll be damned, Kenny's there when I get out of customs. Off we go to Hotel Imperial.

It's right on the Bay of Guyaquil…it is a pretty nice place. They've got electricity and running water most of the time. Hot water? Nope! "Cold water is better" (they say). Here's the deal, you can't drill for water. Don't ask me why, I don't remember. All the fresh water comes from rain caught in cisterns, so water is short. This is actually odd as it's really jungle and swamp country with big rivers close by, but the rivers are filthy from both pollution and mud. The city is big, but really dirty and poor-poor-poor. They are at the time the banana kings of the world. Seafood and fruit are abundant and cheap. So are coffee and tea. Yucca (a tuber kinda like a potato) and rice are the main staples. Next day it's "off to gold mine," the "Sterra Honda," 'bout 100 year old Indian dry placer deal. A "dry placer" is where a dry river bed has been pushed up by an earthquake.

At the mine I meet Bottenilli. You guessed it, a first class bullshitter. Wears 100 dollar slacks, 200 buck shoes and forty buck shirts in the jungle. Eduardo has an Ecuadorian girlfriend named Nellie. Her family invented Ecuador and the money, (sucre). That's her last name. Nellie would work her ass off in the jungle during the day with panning for gold, making camp, cooking, carrying 80 pounds all day. Bottenilli? Hell no, he never did any work, just bullshits 'bout "millions tomorrow." Eduardo's secret is about a 10 inch peter that never goes down, and Nellie apparently likes that action. Every night in sleeping bags Nellie would giggle and squeak and squeal seemed 'bout like all night.

The mine is junk (played out), but they just got a new better mine on the Esmaraldes River. This is way the fuck into the jungle, right in the middle of the head-shrinker country (a tribe called the Jivaros). It don't take me long to figure out the gold deal is zero, but I find I like the jungle. The jungle is like going 250 years back in time. I like a jungle cattle town called "Quininde," in cattle country, where cowboys ride into town Saturday night on beautiful horses and shoot the town full of holes as they get drunker and drunker. The hotel there has no doors or windows, one toilet and dining room with a dirt floor and chickens, dogs and pigs running through your feet. All this with one dirt street on one side and a beautiful, clean, cold river on the other side. A room there and three meals were 'bout 75 cents a day. (Laundry 18 cents extra a day).

I find I like the life where you live a few hours at a time. Communication, survival, food, shelter, travel and health are problems that have no solutions available for money alone. The law of the jungle is don't get hurt and don't get sick 'cause the consequences are very bad. I like living a life that has two parts only: living or sleeping. In the jungle, you go to sleep when it gets dark and wake up with the sun. Clocks? Hell no, there is no place in the jungle that you can't hear a rooster at daybreak. After ten days I decide I gotta

The Andes.

go home. I tell Kenny I think the gold mine stuff is bullshit. It takes me 'bout five days to get home, but truth is I'm addicted to the jungle. While I'm there I keep hearing about the "Oriente." What the hell is the "Oriente?" They say the word means "jungle." It's on the east side of the Andes mountains. You see, all of my travels were on the west side of the Andes up till now. A narrow strip of jungle with the Pacific Ocean on the western side and the Andes mountains on the eastern side.

At home I miss the adventures such as where you come up on a tribal type war and you pay five bucks so they stop the war long enough for you to pass. I miss watching the Peruvian Air Force bomb the farmers market in Guyaquil, with coconuts. Back at home I can't quit wondering about the Colorados Indians with their "limey sports car-looking" mud hats (with termites in 'em). I wonder 'bout them painting their bodies in loud color with no clothing; just a kinda leafy jock strap (and it can get cool at night). I found it hard to understand the Indian was not the least bit curious 'bout the big silver bird and his lack of interest in money. I found the jungle Indian to be fearless of everything but a cold. I was told snake bite and bronchial pneumonia were about equally the two biggest killers of Indians. They had no visible fear of the snake, but if they got a cold they'd be scared shitless. When they talked to each other they held a cloth over their mouths, and wouldn't face each other, kinda like pitcher-catcher talk on TV. A cold could cause death in 48 hours. Near as I could tell mid-life Indians were only concerned with three things: eating, fucking and sleeping. And maybe a little bit of hunting and a li'l bit of fishing. I am fascinated by jealousy with which they guard their big-titted women and the ferocity of their ways. I saw one slit another open from his peter to his upper rib cage, I watched his inner guts drop to the floor as he died, all this without a sound from either. Snakes, I hate 'em. But in less then two weeks I saw two men die because of a couple of pissed off snakes. Ecuador is the snake capitol of the world. It was as if I suddenly found myself in 1700 instead of 1961. I don't expect you to believe it, but I preferred it to the world I lived my life in.

'Bout three months after my first trip to Ecuador, Kenny called and said, "I've purchased part of gold mine in the Oriente, near a town called "Puerto Napo," 'bout 50 miles south of the northern origin of the Amazon river." Holy shit! This I had to see. Remember, in this time frame I'm a 39 year old speed lovin,' unattached male. It's Christmas here: in the States, in my world of Detroit and racing, everything shuts down December 15th and re-cranks up January 15th. This time I fly to Quito, Ecuador. Man, I lucked out. It was clear around Quito and the land below looked like a beautiful patch work quilt. Quito is 10,000 feet up, kinda in the middle of the Andes. I clear customs quickly as this time I got no medical problems.

Kenny is there to meet me and to the hotel we go. It was the former Japanese embassy operated by a German that came to Ecuador in 1940 and began South American life as damn near a slave. You see, during

World War II, Ecuador gave access and sanction to the Germans for submarine service and supply. After the war Germans could start over and, if necessary, "maybe" get residential safe haven from war criminal prosecution extradition. Fredrick slowly escaped his servitude and saved up enough money to buy the old embassy. The only reason I tell you this, is if you see the huge, beautiful "Hotel Colon" in Quito, that was the result of Frederick and his wife's hard work. His is a rag to riches story if there ever was one. The first floor of the hotel had concrete columns as poured. I tried to get him to tile them. He really resented my kidding him about it.

OK, some food then some sleep. The next day at 5:00 am we're off to the jungle. At this time an Ecuadorian named Galo Burbano was minister of customs and getting paid 'bout five grand a year. Kenny and he had become friends. Galo was race car crazy and Kenny was an Indy car owner and winner. "Next year we'll pay your way up there." (Get the message?) Galo agreed to take us as far as a vehicle can go. He was a frustrated race driver and how we survived those three days was a real miracle. 90 percent of the journey was over very-very poor, dirt, one lane roads cut into the side of mountains as high as 15,000 feet. There were no guard rails and one lane. Every mile or mile-and-a-half, they find a place to widen to two cars wide. You play chicken by watching oncoming dust in daytime and lights at night to see who backs up to or stops at the wide spot. Horns are a must. Galo and other Ecuadorians could not possibly drive one mile without a horn. They blow the horn, close their eyes and floorboard it. Every time the road enters a li'l town our horn's steady wide open with Galo going 20 miles an hour faster. I never found out why.

Amazingly we never hit anybody. But animals, people, vehicles, goats, burros, chickens, and ducks were smothered in the flying dust and bellowing horn. After second day he let me drive, and I relaxed some till I came up on a stalled truck in a steep, very hilly area. The truck slipped backwards. I couldn't find the goddam horn. Crunch – one squashed hood and I'm a passenger again after that.

When we'd gotten ten miles out of Quito the road changed from a nine to a four (that is on a scale of one to ten). A very-very real danger there is rock or mudslides. In the thirty-three years I worked in Ecuador, I'll bet I was affected by about 50 of 'em. Some for hours, most for a day or two, some for months. Ecuador taught me the true power of nature. Man at best is a

Colorados Indian and Margie.

Cleanin' up after a mudslide.

microscopic dot when compared to the forces of nature.

This is world class earthquake, mudslide and avalanche country. We came to a city ("Ambato") where Galo was raised. Something I never understood, the cabbages there, in and around Ambato, they looked and tasted just like ours, but could weigh as much as 75 pounds. (The price 'bout 10 cents.) Yet tomatoes, lettuce, onions, cucumber, carrots were all the same size as here.

Ambato has well paved roads that are shot at each end. Galo showed me his old home, which was at the river's edge at the bottom of the valley. But when he lived there, it was a mile up a hill 'bout 1,500 foot higher.

We head out of town, away from decent pavement to the next town, Pelileo. To me it was "earthquake city." I believe an earthquake buried thousands there. A kind of a short squatty Indians lived there we nicknamed the "brown hats." Man, they hated gringos, especially Americans. The story I got was that when an earthquake hit, our Red Cross did a very sad job, for which up to 1993 we ain't come close to being forgiven, and the town was never rebuilt. Last I saw of it, center of old town was a huge open-air farmer's market. I can tell you this, "Don't hang around that town, gringo."

The road slowly became more unstable for next 50 miles, to a nice li'l town called "Banos." That means "hot springs." With certain minerals supposed to heal 'bout anything. About "Banos." Five or 10 miles out of Banos we pass a beautiful waterfall, go through a road tunnel and then, whamo, the road goes to 'bout a "three." The last hint of civilization is another 50 miles into the jungle, a town called "Puyo." Well, we find a hotel in Puyo called the "Hotel Turlingulia," owned and operated by an ex-pate German. This place is very clean, with good food and running cold water, wood floors, windows and doors and even had an in-room toilet. (Instructions were: don't put the paper in the toilet, it must go in bucket on the side) He says the water will help you keep it up all night. I told hotel owner it didn't do anything for me he said you ain't doing it rite. He called for an attendant told her to wash me. Yup, the water seemed to work then. But sex at high altitude has unexpected effect, kinda like running up hill.

The owner loved and tamed wild animals, and walked them on leashes like dogs. He had ocelots, margays, honey bears, water raccoons, a lot of stuff, but no jaguars. In fact I never saw a tame jaguar. All the jaguars I ever saw wanted to bite my ass up. He tamed birds, too. There were parrots, macaws, myna birds around in cages. He taught 'em to talk, but in Spanish or German. His place had about a ten-acre orchid farm – he had at least one of every kind of orchid in the world. Nope, not one black one.

Puyo is a big jungle town with 'bout 2,000 full-timers. On a Friday or Saturday night the population can go to 75,000. The town also had a big farmer's market and one street of supply stores to supply all variety of man made items from safety pins to ten ton trucks. Available in the farmer's market were two cheap, legal trouble-brewers: a sugar cane whisky called "poro," and a nasty dark green drink made out of a tree like plant. This was called "ayahuasca" (eye-au-wah-ska) I think. Each were about a buck a gallon and would get you shit-faced pronto. The cane whiskey was just about like US moonshine – powerful, cheap, and big time discomfort during the sobering up process.

The ayahuasca was the Quichua Indian's "peyote." It too was evil brew. Friday night mamma and poppa get the jug out and start sipping on it. The juice is a hallucinogenic drug. Sure I tried it, you see all kinds of goofy, weirdo, happy shit. 'Bout like peyote, but with more horsepower and it caused a loss of the normal train of thought. Anyway, momma and poppa would sit and talk about their visions all night long. That's their TV, their movies – in short, their favorite part of life. Trouble is, the juice's effects don't go away. Suddenly, for no reason, a year or as much as two years later, it can come back, and it affects you as if you just took it.

I knew a gringo oil field hand that got to playing with it. Soon as it kicked in he'd want to get naked, not for a sexual reason – just got happy and would not wear clothes. Well, the cops in Puyo didn't like naked gringos walking around in a crowd on Saturday night, so they flung him in the caboose. I can remember him being in jail for a month. When they are set to let him out, Leonard buys him clothes and shoes as a favor to the mayor. They turn him loose dressed and I see him an hour later, naked as a jay bird, a mile out of town running out of a sugar cane field.

One of the markets.

Yup, a buck a gallon. I always wanted to bring a gallon back and climb up the water tank tower and put it in the water to see what the hell all would happen. Can you imagine 100 naked people driving, walking into bars, restaurants, stores, churches? You know, that stuff still intrigues me. If you want some you can get it on a good road in Umbato. Couldn't be that's Clinton's problem? Has he fucked with it? Could happen without you knowing it. Could be called a herbal tea maybe. If you got someone in the family who gets naked a lot, consider what I've just told you. I get to wondering, could it be somebody's got the stuff in the Hollywood water? I decided to leave it alone when I thought 'bout it. I decided if it came back on me when I was going to a meeting at GM they'd probably be pissed if I showed up naked or seeing purple dinosaurs with yellow polka dots.

The Quichua was the servant Indian of the Aztecs. Their south American headquarters is five miles into the jungle west of Puyo. It could be reached by what would have been an insult to the word "road." Believe it or not, they understood unions, five-day work week, and time-and-a-half for over 40 hours. Historically they would work three or four months and then quit because they had accumulated what ever they needed money for. They never save money but rather live off the land completely and use barter instead of money in general. Same for their homes, the materials came from the jungle and the labor was communal. The Quichua word for this was "minga." Generally speaking, the national code is: if you employ a person for 90 days, you must keep them for at least eleven months, and then give them one month's pay and a month off for so called "vacation." So common practice is for employers to lay off and swap employees on the 89th day.

Of course the Indian's game is to work the 90th day. It's not unusual for an Indian to quit with a month's pay coming, and come back a year later to get his money. Nope, they don't forget. As I saw it there were only two things civilization had that the average Indian coveted: an outboard motor and a chain saw.

Can you see why I liked the jungle so much? Every day something surprising and interesting popped up. From Puyo to Puerto Napo the road is a one or two on the one to ten scale, barely one lane. I can remember an Indian running on old Inca trail to Napo, and that's 'bout 25 miles, and he got there when we did. Them cats could run all day. They didn't eat. Instead they carried 'bout four banana leaf pouches of chi-chi, an alcoholic white juice made out of yucca. They got their energy sucking on the chi-chi. Have you ever eaten yucca? If you did, you'd like it…it's kinda like a potato.

In 1961 it's my third trip to Ecuador. Gonna look at a gold mine Kenny is planning to buy. The place is a "dry placer" up in "The Oriente." Goddam, the name alone sounded mysterious and dangerous. Now this was real deep-deep jungle. I'm guessing it's 'bout 10,000 square miles. Only about 4,000 Indians estimated to live there. Five miles from "Tina" (the capital of the Oriente) is Kenny's new gold mine. Well hell, it's 10 percent mine. The so called road ends five miles from the mine.

If you go southeast down the river from Tina it's 2,000 miles to next road. The amazon starts 40 miles north of our mine. We are gonna meet the gold mine seller and employee partner, Leonard Schorsch, a six foot tall, 180 pound, good lookin', 100 percent German ancestry guy from Jordonton, Texas. Leonard Schorsch had prospected the Oriente with a helicopter (Bell 47). The copter crashed – killed the pilot. He lives at the Hotel Jaguar in Napo. We pull up to a two story building with 'bout 10 rooms and a restaurant, and a kinda country store. "Where's Leonard?" The guy in the store answers, "Don't know, try his room" His room is first one. It's got no windows but it had a door. This door ain't locked. I look in to see a cot, a table, a closet, and a US Army surplus short wave radio, but no Leonard.

Leonard.

The cook is behind the restaurant squatting on his haunches. He says, "I think he's down by the river in the Hotel Napo bar." I ask Galo, our customs boss guide, "What's he doing, Galo"? Galo asks him and then tells me "He's pickin the rat shit out of the rice." Big joke, ha ha ha. Later he said the reason our meal didn't taste so good was "taking the rat shit out ruined the flavor"

It's raining like hell. (Why is rain always cold?) We walk down to the edge of the Napo river to the Hotel Napo. Leonard's in there, chewing an American soldier of fortune's ass out because he wants to borrow his water pump to pan some gold. Turns out a $250 water pump in a hardware store in the States is one thing. The same pump way in the jungle is whole new ballgame. Leonard has enough poro in him, I'd guess he'd be 'bout 300 percent drunk if he blowed in a drunker meter – it's around 11:00 am.

The gold mine I came to see is 'bout six or seven miles up the Yancama River, with 'bout a four kilometer walk. Half of this hike is in a swamp where you're in two to four feet of water, mud, and snakes.

Some of those snakes are bad mothers too – if they bite, you bleed through the pores of your skin.

We eat on a screened in porch at the hotel Napo about 40 feet above the river and overhanging it.

When you're hungry like we were, the food tastes better, rat shit or not. After an hour-and-a-half of bullshit I say "Leonard, I want to go to the gold mine" (it's Saturday). He says, "Can't, river's too wild – maybe tomorrow." Here's the deal: Napo is in the bottom of a 2,500 foot valley. All around are mountains up to 18,500 feet. So it can rain 75 miles away and suddenly the river will rise three to five feet and pick up to say 35 miles an hour of current. By the way, the water is 'bout one degree warmer than freezing. The snow line is 'bout 12,000 feet.

I'm pissed. I come all this way and this cat knew I was coming and he is shit-faced drunk and gonna waste a day of my time. "OK, OK, you smart-assed gringo. I'll take you up the fuckin' river!" He bellows some Spanish to Wilfreddo, his boat captain. Leonard has a 50 foot long dug-out canoe and with 100 horsepower Mercury. (All boats, I mean every fuckin' boat in the Oriente is a dug-out from 10 to 50 feet. You know how much in American money in '61? – a buck a foot) Wilfreddo says "Can't go – river's bad." When river's bad you should not go boating. Trees come down the river, some of them 100 foot tall with root ball and all. This weighs maybe 20 tons and is moving at 40 miles an hour.

I say, "Bull shit! We're going." I don't have a clue how stupid my talk is. I think the river story is bullshit cause Leonard is drunk. Well, I get Leonard pissed and he tells Wilfreddo, "We are going with or without you." Reluctantly he decides to go. It didn't take but 'bout ten minutes for me to get the message. There were places where even with that 100 horse Merc wide open we'd lose ground. Goddam trees and trash coming ass over head and the river's full of rocks up to 15 foot in diameter. I say "OK, Let's go back." Leonard says, "You smart ass gringo, you wanted to go, you're fuckin' going!"

We gotta go 'bout five miles up river. First to a place called "Momma Rosa's." It's on north side of the river, high and dry, but immediately surrounded by swamp. She's an Ecuadorian/Spanish kinda lady who pioneered this area 25 years ago looking for gold. Her husband died, she raised five or six kids by herself. She was the area's gold buyer. Years ago, to keep goats, burros,

Fishing camp.

cattle and critters in the compound, they planted a fence around 'bout four acres. This hedge was made of a kind of cactus. Well when I first see it, it's 12 or 15 foot tall, and I swear a D-8 Cat could not go straight through it. Biggest problem was, this cactus fence is now 30 to 40 feet wide and full of sharp needles and snakes. In fact, the son-of-a-bitchin' fence is snake headquarters for the Oriente.

It was the home of four or five poisonous kinds like the bushmaster, fer-de-lance, a diamond pattern swamp snake, the chi-chi, and a luminous chartreuse colored snake that averaged six to eight feet and had

Somewhere around the mine.

no known anti-venom. With that kind it was 'bout 15 minutes to "adios" 100 percent of the time

'Bout 20 years later, momma set fire to the fence to get rid of the snakes. Hell, there were four to eight grandkids around there by then. I bet 1,000 snakes over three feet long came out of the cactus. After it burned for a week they were able to clear the roots out with a dozer. By then there was a dirt road 'bout a mile behind her place we cut in there. But you know, when this fire started bare-footed Indians were running around in there killing and catching snakes with clubs, rocks and bare handing some into bags. The skins, meat, and venom had a market and value. Machetes? Not "no," but "hell no." The Indians called snakes "machankas" and though all Indians carried machetes always, when you heard the snake word, you heard every machete hit the ground and they went for sticks and stones. Why? I guess trying to cut a snake's head off with a machete had about a 98 percent bad ending. A snake can't climb a dirt bank over four foot high. Why? Soon as they get beyond what the tail can push from the flat, they tumble down. (I didn't say trees.) This don't include boa's and anaconda's. They could get huge and could go 'bout anywheres a man could.

OK, so we get to Momma Rosa's. She loves Leonard (no husband and I ain't too sure she and Leonard didn't play doctor once in awhile). Back then Momma didn't look too bad. She gives us a snack and says "Stay the night and go in the morning." I say "Nope, I want to get to the mine," so we get ready to go. We've got sacks of flour, rice, sugar, salt, beans, and coffee we're bringing in with us. These sacks weigh 80 to 95 pounds and the Indians weigh 115 to130 pounds. She says "Put the gringo's on horses," and she loans up three for myself, Galo and Kenny. "Not me, I don't need a horse – I can walk it with Leonard and the Indians."

The swamp was bad, but in a couple hours we're past it and are high and dry, but we gotta gain about 1,500 feet in about a mile. Holy shit! In 1961, I'm still in pretty good shape ('cept I smoke too much) and I'm dying from the climb. It's hot ('bout 90 degrees) and we're getting to 'bout 4,000 feet. The li'l indians are out walking me with an 80 pound load and I ain't got nothing to carry. Leonard is so wobbly drunk he walks bent over at 45 degrees using his hands to balance.

'Bout 5:00 pm I see the camp. It is made out of bamboo, palm and chuaka, a tall, skinny, branchless, palm- looking tree. The shelters are made without nails. Everything is tied together with vines and or palm strips.

Well this deal is eight foot off the ground to protect against snakes and varmints. It is big enough to sleep a dozen comfortably. No kitchen and the toilet was the garden. Nope, don't piss in it, just shit in it. The

Indian said the best fertilizer in the world is human poop. Well, I kinda knew that from my farmer experience. (Wanna guess how a lot of produce health food nuts buy is fertilized?) Well, as we arrive Leonard is confronted by a young lady 'bout 17 or 18. She is plumb ape-shit. She and her husband are caretakers and watchmen at the base camp and gold mine. They get free rent and food from the garden, chickens, goats, and pigs that live there plus four bucks a week.

Her husband is not there when we arrive. She had been working in the garden and a seven foot anaconda had just gone after her baby ('bout a year old) on a blanket under a yucca plant. She got the baby in the house, and when we get there an Indian boy 'bout 12-13 years old has just found the anaconda and killed it. Welcome to the jungle. Soon as we got there they started to fix the evening meal. One dead snake does it.

It starts getting dark there at 6:00 pm and it happens in 30 minutes. In sitting there relaxing after the tough walk, I watch chickens fly up to cistern edge to roost for the night. The fresh water supply is a 200 gallon cistern up on poles 'bout six foot high. Cistern is 'bout six foot in diameter and four foot deep. Well, we got running water for shower (bamboo split in half overlapping, going slightly down hill from bottom of cistern to end of bamboo pipe. Interestingly, I notice as they ring the cistern that the chickens turn around to where their tails are toward the middle. I think, I wonder, I go look. There's 'bout three inches of chicken shit all the way around the inside of the tank. Well, the drinking water, coffee and cooking water, is laced with chicken shit. What do you care when you're hungry and thirsty? Maybe chicken shit is why cancer is unheard of in the jungle in 1961. I'm not recommending it, but just throwing it in for your consideration. Next morning cistern got un-chicken-shitted.

Gold mine looks real. I like Leonard. 'Bout six foot, hard worker, college graduate geologist. He knew his mining shit. We make some gold there. He's down to earth, makes sense and is a fairly good geologist. We need to build a base camp close to the dirt road in from Puyo. We

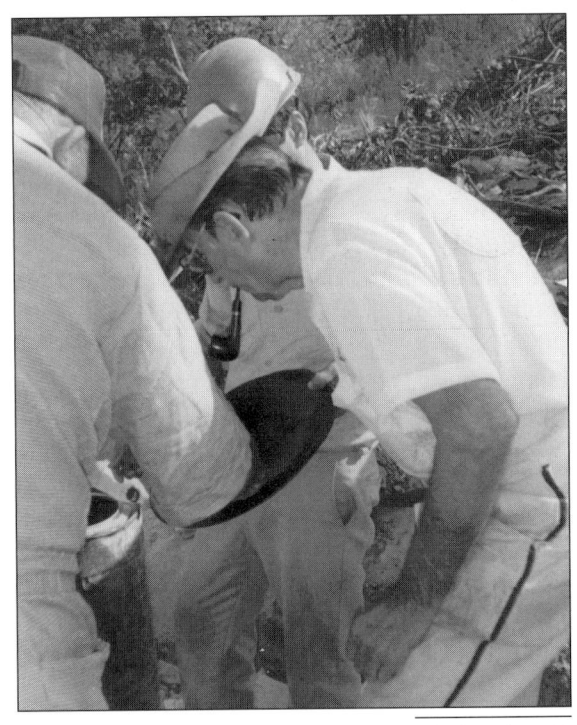

Checking for gold.

buy 200 acres. I buy a bulldozer and low boy. I gather up a bunch of tools, stuff like a one bag cement mixer. I got Ford Motor Company to give me a three-quarter ton five-man cab, four-wheel drive, air-conditioned pickup, an F-8 with the same cab, and a 16 foot flat bed dump with all wheel drive, and ship 'er down. With Bill Stroppe's help, get we get a low boy and a dozer into the Oriente (first one with low boy) and set about building a base camp to house 40 men. I'm there through it all. Step one: build a road from main road to camp living quarters. Its raining like hell. I got the bulldozer, the low boy, the F-8 and the pickup stuck trying to dig ditches and haul rock in for the road base. We got supplies and food in and a tent to sleep under (pretty big – 25 foot x 20 foot). I am sleeping on blanket, on the ground in the tent. By 2:00 am and there is water in tent and 'bout 2:30 am the tent half blows down. I end up sleeping in a wheel barrow…cold…wet. I get to thinking I could be a li'l goofy to work my ass off for nothing…to be shivering in a wet wheelbarrow trying to sleep, instead of a room at the Holiday Inn, and getting paid to boot.

Now I gotta tell you 'bout "dark" in the jungle: when you're on the ground under the trees at night it's plumb dark. Wanna know what it's like? Shut your eyes. You can't see nothing, so if you try to walk without a reference for balance, if you step on a one inch rock you're gonna fall on your ass.

We build the camp, and in the process build a cheap sawmill, start a farm to grow corn, pineapple, cocoa, coffee, yucca, tomatoes. At the camp we've also got wild oranges. Gold mining requires the dozer for efficiency, so we next build about a five mile corduroy road with the dozer and cut down trees. The minute we got the road going, Indians moved in, built houses on both sides of the road we made, and started clearing and farming. In the jungle if you clear it and farm it, it's yours. Well, we gold mined for a year or so, and it ain't that good.

I sold an invention in '61 for 100 grand and got hooked up with three "wildcatters" (independent oil drillers) and in two years my deal was worth five million. With this I really found something I enjoyed. I liked the million to one odds. I liked working with three-mile long wrenches. I liked the company, most everything done on a handshake.

I tell you this to get you to understand how I started getting "oil happy." I traded the five million for an "elephant" play that ended in a six million buck blow out and fire. I got out with zero. You heard the "easy come-easy go" shit. People wired in said, "Didn't that really shake you up losing five million?" I said, "Sure, but I knew the risk and I lost." You wanna play, be ready to pay – ain't it always been that way? What I really lost was 100 grand.

I once met a guy named "King," "J.L." I believe. He made millions as a wildcatter with lawyers and doctors for limited partners. Last time I saw him he was in a $200 Chevy pickup. The time before was a Lear jet. We were at the Lemon Tree in Dallas eating. A cat ribbed him 'bout losing his ass and he told this smart ass, "I, however, did get some satisfaction out of the trip. And I did the same thing to limited partnerships in oil, that panty hose did to finger fucking."

Leonard's got an Ecuadorian buddy who is the minister of minerals, a five grand a year job. Leonard had helped when his family was hungry in the past. Some wildcat types said "there's oil here big time." Course it's just the opinion of an educated geologist. I'm sure there's oil in the Oriente too. However, Shell Oil was there '40-'45 and pulled out. All they found was "heavy oil." This stuff was too thick to be useful and was unproduceable at four bucks a barrel, 200 miles from a shipping terminal. But that was in the Puyo-Postanza area, 75 miles southeast.

To make a long story short: through this minister of minerals guy, Leonard, Kenny and I got the whole fuckin' Oriente oil concession, 'bout 13 million acres, for ten grand, with fifteen hundred down, for two years. We then hauled ass up to Chicago trying to get a partner. Looked like best place to start would be in Lago Agrio. 9,500 foot to total depth, an estimated one million dollar helicopter hole. I can remember the land man for Unocal in Chicago sitting on edge of his desk laughing, and saying to Kenny, (he knew Kenny from Texas – by the way, Kenny was a big wildcatter when he lived in Dallas) "Kenny, don't try to con a con man. You know there ain't no oil in there. Shell tried and gave up 20 years ago." We offered Unocal half of the thirteen million for cost of first hole. We lost the concession two years later.

The government sold half of our concession for over twenty million bucks. The "Lago One" hole came in at 9,000 barrels a day, of 29 gravity, no sulphur oil and produced for thirty fuckin' years.

The Oriente still today produces 300,000 barrels a day 29 years later. Gold? I did end up with 'bout 100 pounds of it. But that's a long story I'm not gonna tell.

After the oil adventure in Ecuador, Kenny decided to build an "Acapulco on the coast." The Ayangage coast had white cliffs, warm water, pretty beaches, fishing of every kind, 10 pound Lobsters and 2,000 pound Marlin. 'Bout 40 miles from where Hemingway wrote "The Old Man and the Sea" (Salanias). Though it was a beautiful place, this was a dumb idea that cost Kenny 'bout 300 grand.

I got a buddy at Chevy, Herb Fishel, who is in Chevy racing and has led a sheltered life. I decide he should enjoy a little more excitement. "Wanna go to Ecuador Herb?" "Hell yes, when?" We leave 'bout a month later. By now I work as a consultant to Gulf Oil, Texaco and sometimes the Ecuadorian government. My consulting is mostly about engine maintenance on oil field and pipe line engines ('bout 150,000 total horsepower by then in this oil field). Typically I get called, "We need help, we're burning valves and turbo-turbine wheels." I hop a jet and (usually) solve the problem. Herb and I leave from Miami to Quito. We now have a big house in Quito with two great stuffed condors in front room and hall. When I get there I find our housekeeper has quit. Well hell, I decide to put the word out in Quito's finest whore house, (the "Mirador," ever been there? way-way up a steep hill). "We need a housekeeper, interviews tomorrow."

Herb was single, and I believe he got involved in some sinful games. I notice when I got up at 7:00 am he was bare-assed naked dancing the bugaloo with our first housekeeper applicant, a middle-aged woman 'bout 18. As a matter of fact I still got a couple of pictures of that. I doubt he'd want them blowed up and hung on his house or office wall, but really, by today's standards, he'd be well within the limits of today's Emily Post's rules. As a matter of fact, in one of the pictures, by president Clinton's interpretation, Herb is not involved in a sexual act. (Maybe an experiment in reverse resuscitation.) Yeah, that bugger sowed some wild oats. We are going to the jungle in morning and Herb's new friend wants to go. I decide "damn good idea" as many times as we have flat tires, she'd come in handy to blow up a tire.

I introduced Herb Fishel to ways of Latin women, and then to the jungle, it's people and it's day-to-day trials and tribulations. I was kinda caught up with work, and I'd been wanting to go to where Ernest Hemingway went to drink, fuck and write a book 'bout a hand line fisherman called "The Old Man and the Sea." I thought Herbie might end up a big shot at GM. (And I got that part right, 2,000 years after the coming of the Lord, Herb is the number one man in any and all high performance activities at GM, that reads "racing.") So I think it's only right that I groom Herb for a career in high places. I decide he needs to have experience in the broadest possible spectrum, 'cause who knows? Herb might someday rule an international activity. I figure this trip to Hemingway's former haunt is actually an adventure in the realm of the arts. For example, Mr. Knudsen knew and fished with Hemingway in Cuba and West Palm Beach. He became a talented and respected automotive executive. Do you get where I'm going?

It's 'bout a day's journey from Guyaquil, to Salanias. That evening we find relatives of the old fisherman in the book. Actually not hard. I think every person I met 'cept one was related to the fisherman (this cat was coal black). We rent the place he stayed in. This story, I found out, was true. And probably duplicated twenty times a year there (even today). By the way, marlin record for sport tackle is like 1,900 pounds. All world record holders are doctors. After they stick it up our asses and rob us, seems like one favorite deal they use the money for is, buy a bunch of high-high buck fishing stuff, then fly down there and drive up and down the ocean in a big-assed fishing palace to catch huge fish. But down at bottom of page in record book, in fine-fine print, it reads something like, "Hector Gonzoles, hand line, 2,890 pounds."

This is also supposedly the greatest sailfish, marlin, swordfish and huge tuna area in the world. They say this is the closest to shore, and smoothest big game fishing spot. I think, "15 miles out is close?" Most world record fish come from here. I saw a fishing club north of Salanias that had a two mile driveway, and the fence on both sides was the spine and tails of marlin buried in the ground. This is the place to catch a fish.

Well, a crisis arises. Leonard's buddy from Punta Carnero who has a nice fishing boat (he's the guy who found a sunken Spanish ship, recovered it's gold quietly and built the most beautiful hotel on the barren stinkin' remains of Ecuador's first oil field – a place called "Libertad"), unexpectedly has a wealthy client who charters the boat for a week. But, he has a buddy in Punto el Mucho who was a great drinking buddy of Hemingway's, was in charge of rounding up pussy for the "big H," and is a great fishing guide with a nice boat.

We get to the "nice fishing boat" 'bout 5:00 am. It is a 20 foot long piss-ant cruiser with a gasoline Volvo motor, and the bilge that smelled like sticking your nose in a five gallon can of gas. So Leonard, Kenny Rich, Herb Fishel and I are gonna be the fishermen. We go out on this shitty boat. The "smoothest sport fishing water" turns out to be more like straight up one side of a wave, then straight down. After half-an-hour of this I make another observation. In the likely event this fuckin' boat quits, we can walk to shore on the backs of the sharks around us in the water. Blue, gray, white, brown…this is shark city. (This is also a big commercial fishing ground with floating fish factories, and the scraps, I guess, attract the sharks).

I notice Herb is not feeling well, and Leonard is real quiet. Kenny has a good supply of scotch, soda and ice cubes. He just keeps drinking. He feels great. An hour later we are 15 miles out into "the world's smoothest big game fish waters." By then Herb looks like his neck and face are painted a light green. He is laying on a bunk puking out the boat window. "You wanna turn around and go back?" "No-no, I'll be better in a while." Herb was skinny, but that day I know he lost 15 pounds. He must have puked for five hours. Leonard's fishing was 'bout the same, 'cept maybe half as much puking. As for Kenny hell, he ate sandwiches and kept drinking whole trip – never fished.

Now the captain, he gets sick too, but he's got a helper who knows the deal. I start fishing, I'm rite on the edge of stomach problems, but I start catching fish round 50 to 100 pounds. As I reel them in, we got a problem. The boat driver knows no English. The only Spanish I know is "Where am I?" "Where's a place to get food?" "Where's a place to sleep?" "Would you like to play doctor?" and "You sure got a pretty ass." None of that applies here, so his instructions are of no use to me 'cept gestures. Leonard, who would have been the translator, is of no use. He is at some point of misery where even death would be ignored.

I decide to land one last fish, a big dolphin. A shark cuts 'em in half right at the boat. Well hell, nobody fishing but me. "Lets go back." I can't get the boat driver to understand this when all of a sudden…zzzzzzzz zzzzzzzzzzzzzzzzzzzzzzzzzz. Something on my line! Turns out it's a 165 pound sailfish, 'bout 11 feet long. (Nope. I'm not stretching it – I can see it from where I sit writing – come by and measure it) Well now, a sailfish, this is more like it. 'Bout hour later it's beside the boat. I then realize that no one will eat it. Hell I don't know why, but I find out that down there they don't eat sailfish. They make fishmeal out of 'em for chickens to eat. I tell the Ecuadorian, "cut 'em loose." He won't do it, and pulls fish in the boat. It pisses me off to see that big beautiful fish croak for no good reason. (I find out later the fish was so pooped out a shark would have gotten it in a minute if we had cut it loose. Hell, apparently even fish have unfriendly neighborhoods.)

Now we start back. While I'm being sorry for myself in this piss-ant boat death trap, I notice sail boats, towing out past us a six foot by six foot balsa wood raft with a three by two hole in the middle. A fisherman gets on at 5:00 pm and drifts and fishes all night on those rafts five days a week for a dollar a day. There are 'bout 24 or 30 or 'em. Remember what I tole you 'bout the sharks.

We get to shore and the fish gets hung up for a picture. "Naaah, I don't want a picture." I want to go back to hotel and shower and eat. "Well OK, one picture" Everybody says, "Why don't you get it stuffed to hang on your office wall?" I look over a few feet, they are hanging up a big fish with a wrecker 'bout 800 pounds and half of it lays on the beach. (The deal ain't high enough.) Mine now looks like a baby fish. A voice says, "Gimme five bucks, I'll skin the fish and send it to Miami to have it mounted." I'm tired of the fish, so I give him five bucks and head for hotel. (Ain't no way he can skin fish and ship it to Miami for five bucks. To me this was the easiest way out – big mistake.)

At the hotel, Leonard and Herb start recovering, but slowly. That evening I found three girls who knew Hemingway very-very well. Near as I could tell, seems like he screwed all but two or three of all the women between 15 an 30 years old at the time. Well, neither Herb or Leonard were interested in a one night course in the sexual customs of the women of Punta el Mucho. However, I think they missed something. After that experience I doubt TV would attract a large audience there after dark.

Three months later a phone call from Miami. "We have a beautiful sailfish skin you wanted mounted, send 450 bucks and we will proceed." Hey, hold it. I never dreamt that cat down there was on the level. I just said OK to end the bullshit. "Well, what the hell," I send the money. Three months later. "Your fish looks wonderful, send 350 bucks and we'll finish it up." 800 Bucks for a friggin' dead fish? Well hell, they already got 450. Maybe I will hang it up in the house. "OK," I say and send 350 down. Regarding the fish, it is becoming unclear who caught who. Three months later; "your fish is done and came out beautiful. Where do want us to send it?" "Send it to the house." Two weeks later my wife calls and says, "a truck is here with a big crate COD…510 bucks – final payment and freight."

It's still hanging in the shop.

I go home, open the huge crate, gonna put him on the wall. Nope, his beak is in the ceiling and tail is on the floor. There ain't no place in the house I can hang or put that fish. (Well, I guess could add a room to the house to hang it up). Moral of this story, if you catch a big fish, watch your ass, I got clipped for 1,310 bucks. If you'd like this fish, he is hanging on the wall in the shop here. Come on by, maybe we can make a deal. Be a hell of a lot cheaper than going down there to catch your own.

OK, let me tell you 'bout the Humboldt Hotel in Guyaquil, Ecuador. The hotel is a book by itself. It sits above the bay of the world's largest banana shipping source (I'm talking 1961). The hotel has a problem. It's leaning five degrees west towards the bay. What's the big deal? Well, that little fact just helps set the atmosphere. It's about a 75 year-old hotel. It reminded me of the Great Sheppard Hotel in Cairo, or the Great Eastern hotel in Calcutta. The clientele were a cross section of every race, every color, everywhere. They were business and con men (and women), drug peddlers, criminals on the run, soldiers of fortune, weapons dealers and other mysterious women and men running from something. There always seemed to be secret service types from many countries tailing people and law officers en route to and from arrests with and without prisoners in restraints. In a one hour period sitting on a bar stool, you'd be offered hot diamonds, gold bullion, shares in secret gold mines, "sure thing" oil well leases, sex of any kind with any of about 40 nationalities, money laundering services, guide service, treasure maps, false credentials, gambling opportunities, protection or annihilation services, even couriers (I took to be both legal and illegal). The place was also a hangout for ex-military pilots and helicopter pilots, also crop duster pilots. As pilots they found instant, often illegal, job opportunities all over the world in the third world countries.

One of the shops in town.

I remember the biggest fuckin' marlin head sticking through the bar wall – that thing must have weighed 2,400 pounds when it was hauled in. I gave the head bartender a racing jacket and he kept us wired in on much of the activities. Sitting there trying to guess the patron's purpose for being there amused me. Kenny put word out I was a big rubber trader from an American company called "Trojan." Kenny met a girl there who ended up clipping him for a couple grand and a dentist in Quito for a couple grand of dental work. A meal in their restaurant on the roof was a buck and a half for a five course dinner with a five pound lobster. If you had a couple bucks in your pocket you could find all the excitement, trouble, adventure, your li'l heart could handle.

But no women allowed in your hotel room unless she's family. Yes, a maid sits on every floor and looks at all people entering and leaving. If you sneak a lovely in, after 'bout ten minutes the hotel security is there. Yet the women in the bar have a way of magically appearing in your room. (Again, witness the power of the "greenie.")

I took Mickey Thompson and Joe Leonard to this hotel separately. When word got around that there were famous speed kings they experienced treatment second only to bull fighters and champion soccer players. Mickey described to hotel management and a German engineering company how to straighten the hotel up. Joe Leonard fell in love with a French movie actress and damn near went to France. He was so drunk I bet he never knew how close he came to ending up in France (Air France stopped in Guyaquil). I really enjoyed sitting in a big rattan chair in the courtyard.

One night I meet a rich gal from London who is looking for something, and wants someone to take her to Inquitos. Inquitos is 600 miles south-east of Quito, a jungle town at the intersection of the Amazon and the Maramon. It is an interesting place 3,000 miles up the Amazon where everything is mud, no rocks, no easy access to wood, no road, no airport, no radio. Only way in and out is boat or seaplane. Inquito has no law, no cops, no soldiers. (I'm talking early sixties)

Why live there? I can't even guess, 'cept in my experience, seemed to me, nicest cat in town was only wanted for murder. A cross-section of the world's meanest people. Inquitos would be perfect place to hide from the law. Seemed like Inquitos is known world-wide but when I was there I had no apprehension of danger from the inhabitants.

Why did I go there? I heard about it and wanted to see how a bunch of people got along without law. Them days it wasn't Peru or Ecuador, as I saw it, it was part of Ecuador, but they didn't claim it. (It now belongs to Peru and it's an oil country prospect and operations center with a jet port.) I had about ten tourist women, all I'd have to guess with some loot, that I met in the Hotel Colon Bar in Quito between 1961 and early 80s that wanted to go to Inquitos. Well, I tell this limey gal I can take her to Cocoa on the Napo river, and there she can catch a river freighter to Rocafuerte at the border of Peru and Ecuador, but that leaves 'bout 400 kilometers to go, and river has many river pirates. She says, "How much you charge me to go with you?" I say "Lets go to my place so I can talk to Leonard to see if we got room." This gal is 'bout 30, from England, in high heels and white evening gown (and that's 'bout how the rest of 'em were also). She says "OK."

We go to house (with the condors). Leonard says "Yes, we have room." It's 1:00 am and we are gonna leave at 5:00 am in the five-man cab Ford. I tell her to go back to hotel, get her stuff and come back at five. You already guessed it haven't you? 'bout two hours of mattress boogie and a short nap and it's time. I say, "Hey, take a cab and go get your stuff." She says she "Ain't got anything there that would be useful." I say "Call and check out." She says, "The hell with it."

I pick up her purse and dump it out, I want to see how much loot she got. Goddam, 'bout five grand. I make her take off her jewelry and leave it at the house and we're off.

'Bout noon I ask her if she wants to stop and go in the bushes to pee. "Nope, she's fine."

'Bout 4:00 pm as we get ready to go through Ambato, I stop where they sell clothes, buy her a pair of khaki pants and shirt and a pair of sneakers and a belt. I tell clerk, "put dress in a bag" and she says, "leave it." So I trade the dress for the clothes and get her a couple pair of bloomers and a head cloth thrown in. Goddam dress probably cost 500 bucks or more. Still no rest room. "Wanna go in bushes?" No-no, She's "OK." 45 minutes later we come up to a rock slide, it's raining, and looks like couple hours or more to continue, and maybe all night.

Finally, she's gotta pee. We're standing there in the rain and mud in the middle of 150 people. There is nothing to do but piss off the steep side of the road. Down come the pants, she's got her feet on my boots while I hold her arms. Pride, "Miss Manners" and embarrassment go out the window. She's pissing like a cow on a flat rock.

We got to Puerto Napo and the Oriente Hotel next night. This gal is gone jungle goofy. She loves it the rougher it gets. At the hotel is an Ecuadorian surveyor. A small, pretty good-looking pussy-hound 'bout 40 years old that is hung like my old dog Pluto. Well shit, the minute we introduced them to each other, it was on. The surveyor is famous and in great demand. Apparently the only cat who surveys at night using the stars. This technique is apparently much better in jungle conditions. Inquitos? Forget it. She stayed there for two months, even when the surveyor's wife came down from Quito and emptied her revolver at

It was hot down here, but all I had was boots.

him while he was hauling ass (lucky for him she couldn't hit anything). I never did find out how that ended, or ever see "Miss England" again, nor did I ever see the surveyor again.

By 1965 the "gold fever" is cooling down. Ecuador is filling up with oil field promoters and con artists. Ecuador is changing. The mining laws are changing and things are getting bad for prospecting. We get into timber. We buy a plantation that raises tea, coffee, cocoa, fruit, and has a factory to process the tree fruit they make lipstick out of, and another bush they use to make perfume. But the most profitable deal for a while was "papauquine" (pa-pa-een), the main ingredient they use to make meat tenderizer. It's a papaya juice you take before fruit ripens. Just slash a young papaya and catch the white juice with folded banana leaf cups. Just 'bout like collecting rubber tree juice, turpentine, or maple syrup. Except, if you have a cut and that juice got in it, you'll probably lose at least the finger. It was even worse on bones. If you had seen how powerful this stuff was you'd never use meat tenderizer.

After we collected the juice it was put in shallow trays. It dried out, curled up, and was pure white. It looked like shredded coconut but had the most horrible odor you ever smelled. It stank like rotten fish. Man it was bad. (Racer's have a word for this odor.) If I sprinkled a half teaspoon on a two inch thick piece of meat, in 20-25 minutes it would dissolve the tissue into a liquid and make a hole in the meat you could drop a quarter through. It was at this stage a powerful enzyme. Side problem with this was our papan fields were a snake bedroom community. The whole place was full of bushmasters, one bad-bad nasty son-of-a-bitch. They'd chase you like a dog and the poison? Damn rite! 'Bout an eight or nine on a one to 10 scale, but there was an anti- venom for it.

How 'bout this? Our plantation also had a silkworm factory. They eat mulberry leaves, so we had to grow three or four varieties of mulberry. Our property also had free gold several places and in two rivers that were our north-south and south boundary. Course we raised rice and yucca and sugar cane. The place was 'bout 150,000 acres with 'bout 80,000 acres of timber (teak, rosewood and 'bout three others, hi-buck wood trees). I made down payment of seven grand and Kenny was gonna take it from there. We lost it 'bout 18 months later. Kenny never made first payment.

So you think all I do is fuck around with racecars, but I'm learning 'bout perfume, lipstick, silk, meat tenderizer and the hi-buck timber business. I also absorb practical things about how to live in the jungle. Things like how to outrun a damn bushmaster, how not to piss them or the natives off, how to make sugar cane whiskey. If you cultivate cocoa and poppies (they seem to grow wild there), the Quichias (Indians) explain the process of how to turn it into bad-bad hi-buck shit. Hell no, not me. Ecuadorian law said "You screw with that stuff, it's either life or death." Now getting away with it for a while was not too hard 'cause the military were the cops. The "ruralies," ran the back country and everything was for sale. In the military, even up to highest level were poorly paid. Yet if a guy stayed in 'bout 20 years he seemed to be quite well to do. Down there, maybe the same as here, the power of the greenie is real, expected and it works. But this power can shift quickly, based on who's offering how much.

Ecuadorian women picked certain leaves off of cocoa trees and chewed 'em like chewing tobacco. They chew, spit, the whole nine yards. They got a slight buzz off of it. You could make an alcoholic drink out of yucca, kinda like vodka maybe. I know this, it would knock you on your ass if you didn't watch it. I wonder why we don't grow yucca and breadfruit here in the states. Neither can stand a freeze, but both are sure super foods.

Breadfruit: wanna know what it is? You start with a seed, and in three or four years it's a tree 15 feet tall and 40 feet wide with huge leaves and produces a deal 'bout eight inches in diameter. This fruit looks like the a green coconut. When ripe, the big deal falls off the tree. They are pretty heavy, 'bout one to four pounds. Inside it's full of whitish goop (like snot – yuk). I didn't like putting my hands in it, Margie didn't mind so she fished out the nuts. In a minute or two they had maybe 60-100 nuts. Brown. Maybe looked like pecans. You wash 'em off, boil 'em in salty water. When cooked you cracked the thin shell, peeled it off and it was very tasty, and I guess very nutritious cause 'bout a third of the world depends on breadfruit for much of their food. Down in the jungle some Indians near 'bout live on yucca and breadfruit and rice.

Breadfruit and yucca at the local market.

I'd always walk around with a pocket full of boiled nuts (unpeeled). Well, a drilling superintendent (a gringo) asked me why I carried and ate them. I told him it kept my peter rock hard 24 hours a day. They were reworking the "Lago One," the oil well that started the Oriente oil field. Leonard's company (Poole) had a rework rig over the hole. The job had problems and was running over usual time. We're there 'bout 11:00 pm. It was raining like hell and as I left I gave the superintendent 'bout 50 nuts. 'Bout two weeks later we revisit the hole. (I believe it had some collapsed casings from the volcano eruption 'bout 60 days prior.) Here comes the "super" ass over head, "Smokey you're rite! I've eaten breadfruit every day since you left, and I'm the terror of that big whore house in Lago." (Prostitution is legal there.)

I've learned the average human can be brain washed and manipulated by the power of suggestion. Especially easy when the game produces a hoped for result or illusion. For the next six months every farmer's market run out of breadfruit. The oil hands (ex-pate gringos) were each eating five pounds a week. Hell, even Margie was bragging on the power of breadfruit. Well shit, they ain't got no rhinoceros to cut the horns off of in South America. But they've got plenty of breadfruit.

Try it at your own risk.

I brought some seeds back and tried to raise it in the Daytona Beach Community College greenhouse, but lost my communications with the person in charge. I went by there a year ago and the greenhouse is shut down. No huge breadfruit trees growing through the roof, so I guess it didn't work. Ones I planted at shop got 'bout four feet tall and froze.

The tea we grew in town just north of us, Postaza, commanded the highest price of any tea in the world. I heard the soil and climate were most perfect for tea flavor. I always figured the firecracker inventors (Chinese) grew the best. The tea farm was a series of mounds with tea bushes all over each mound. Growing and harvesting tea is very-very labor intensive. Each leaf is picked by hand by women. About 25 percent of them carrying a baby in a pouch. Right here I'd like to inject something that has always puzzled me: Why don't poor country babies cry? If you don't believe it, take a trip and see for yourself. Sure, if they are hurt or sick they cry, but for the most part they are just watching the world go by.

We also grew quinine trees at the plantation to make malaria medicine. Also grew Indian palm. Its fruit was processed for oil which was very useful in medicine. This may sound goofy, but I saw a shaman (witch doctor) cure an awful lot of serious shit with their home-brew medicine.

Matter of fact they were the inventors of hallucinogenic drugs and pain killers. Their remedy for the "Inca flu" (diarrhea) is better than anything else. Same with their cure for motion sickness or an ear-oriented loss of balance.

In the education of hunting for gold, I meet a friend of Leonard's, a geologist named Chester Sellers. When we met he lived in Cuinca, was in the copper and silver mining business and was just barely eeking out a living with a small production facility using ground up ore. So I half-assed get a condensed education on copper and silver. Ain't never a dull minute. Believe it or not, all this helps me with engines and vehicles. I learned a lot about copper in physics, chemistry and the polarization of electrical energy. As today's man understands it, such technology is used to create the products: food and medical contributions that make our lives easier and more difficult, safer and more deadly. Stuff like electricity, the car, airplanes, all make our lives easier, maybe better. But they can also kill us instantly. Another example is cigarettes. Doctors, lawyers, mortician, hospitals and drug manufacturers owe two-thirds of their income and a large number of jobs to that simple invention. That is just a direct result. Look at how many of our current racers and race related business this simple device has furnished them life styles of the rich and famous.

In 1993 I visited a museum in Cuinca. A Catholic deal run by a priest 'bout 90 years old, Father Creaszy. Been there 60 some years now in kinda in an Alzheimer mode. Pretty goofy, but he has some interesting stories. First off he's branded a communist, and they (the locals) burned his museum and damage it pretty bad. He can speak English, and I get a one day interview with him. Most of the stuff is real – like Spanish suits of armor from Pizzarro's time, but some looked like it was made last week of spam cans. Remember the book and movie "The Chariot of the Gods"? Well that book was Father Creaszy's creation. He believed all that stuff. Hell, I ended up looking at his porcelain lined caves full of fancy birds. Cuinca is an area a glacier moved over a jillion years ago. Pretty heavily mineralized. In that area there were many natural freaky deals. Compasses go ape-shit, hot springs, place is full of Inca buildings. If you drop down a ways into Peru there are rocks weighing 50 tons, 50 miles from their origin moved 10,000 feet up a mountain. (Machu Pichu). We ain't got equipment that can put it back today. How in the hell did it get up there? (Maybe teams of big condors?)

Too bad Father Creaszy didn't get checked out while his mind was in good shape. He came to Ecuador as a young priest and has been there 60 years. I once met the cat who pumped the ol' boy for his version of the Inca world and put it into a best seller and movie. According to the priest he wasn't sending Christmas cards to the guy who pumped him (named Von-something) - spent 'bout a year there according to the ol' priest. In religiously proper language (Catholic) the priest said the "Von" boy gave him a royal fucking. Matter of fact, I was told by Chester Sellers to make a donation of 'bout 20 bucks. Well hell, it was a bargain. I spent four or five hours looking at stuff from 15-0-shit with my mouth open, and eyes big as silver dollars. If his tip on the white porcelain-lined cave was real and I found it, that would have been worth millions. He said cave had all kinds of gold in it. He warned, "But be very careful, very slippery because of bird and bat shit."

As long as we are on Father Creaszy, let me tell you a couple more Catholic priest stories. I now know how the mafia got idea 'bout monthly pay. In say, Ecuador, my guess is 95 percent of everyone is Catholic. In the jungle, all churches, schools, and hospitals (damn near) are provided and run by the Catholic church. No little, inexperienced task. Well to fund this, once a month the priest jumps in his 50 foot dugout canoe and has his Indian boat runners take him to every village in that priest's territory. The going rate for Catholics world wide is 10 percent of your income. Now you know lots of Catholics cheat in the States (probably 'bout 99.5 percent), but the Indian gets his ass chewed out if he don't pay up. Now pay is usually not in money. Nope, usually it's gold. Remember there is free gold in most all the rivers, and (I should have told you this before) every hut, village or town is on a navigable water way. It is like this 'cause they've got no roads. To get around you use a boat. Hell, chop a tree down, and with an ax, lots of labor, and even burning, you gut the log. Then whittle out a paddle and you got "wheels."

So anyway, the Indian gives the priests gold, food, minerals, animals. Anything of value to represent 10 percent of his monthly efforts. Maybe a one dollar value for the month, but it's considered a "must," or priest wires ahead and if you croak you're going to hell with highest priority. One time I needed to get from the jungle to Guyaquil, in a hurry to catch a plane to the States, and a recently retired priest was the pilot. I knew him, but did not know his collar was canceled. I called him "Father." He said "I'm no longer father of spirit, I am now father of children." Well, hell, I don't know why, but I always figured the priest got all the pussy they wanted. When we got to Guyaquil, I think I said, "I think you should go back to paddling your canoe. Or at least forget flying." That son-of-a-bitch could not fly for shit. 'Bout six months later, he found out when you run into a mountain with an airplane, the sudden stop will kill you.

Another priest was at a Catholic mission on the Napo river with an Alka (Guarani) museum. The mission was on the east side of the Napo, I believe on an island. This is Alka country (they will kill any outsiders), but they don't use boats and therefore can't cross water over five foot deep.

The little village across the river is called Phoenix (I believe). The priest is 'bout 40 years old. Has been there 'bout five years (replaced a curly red-haired priest who'd been moved to cocoa, fifty miles closer to civilization – a big town by jungle standards). By the way, this priest was a good looking pussy hound (this was 'bout 1991). I'm sure by now he's either screwed himself to death or out of the church. A real nice "do-gooder."

The jungle mission priest specialty is the Alkas (cannibals). They still hate gringos and hell, anybody. He shows Margie all the Alka stuff in his museum and explains it while he tells her how misunderstood the Alkas are. Down the river 'bout 100 miles there is an oil drilling deal going in on the west side of the Napo (way-way down, 'bout to the Tiputini river, damn near to Peru). Well, this was Alka territory. Nobody with any sense would go in there 'cept heavily armed in a group of ten men or more. There is a band of Alkas who paint their legs red. They're called 'Rojas Alkas' and they are bad-ass, mean motherfuckers and they are fighting the shit out of the oil company. The government is trying to get along with them but getting no place. For example, the head "red legs" wants a freezer. The government gives him one and he's pissed cause meat and fish still spoil. He didn't know he needed an electric generator to run it. The red legs starts raising hell because their new fridge doesn't work.

This priest and a couple of nuns were flown by helicopter, 60 days after we saw him, into the oil patch base camp to calm down the red legs. When he didn't return in four hours a squad of soldiers went in there looking for them. Between the nuns and the priest they had 'bout 175 spears stuck in 'em. All deader than Hogan's goat. The priest and the nuns carried in a bunch of gifts.

After listening to what this priest had told Margie, I said, "If he believes that shit 'bout the red legs being misunderstood, he was gonna need a lot of help from some unnamed source, or he would never go bald or grey." The 175 spears is not an exaggeration. The first Alka killing I remember was Leonard's cook in '61. The Alkas stuck about 70 spears in him in five minutes within sight of Cocoa around five one afternoon. Leonard shot and killed the chief, but the rest got away. If they get you, don't worry 'bout getting cooked and eaten. The word was "gringos taste terrible" – they don't eat 'em.

You wanna know what made those Indians so mean and nasty? It was Henry Ford and Harvey Firestone. Way back when, this tribe of Indians who lived in the west side of the Napo river, from about Napo to Cocoa. They were captured and forced to work on rubber plantations, where they were treated like animals. After 'bout ten years of this they escape. The rubber plantations were abandoned. The soil was played out. These Indians apparently hated and taught their young to hate the gringo and so-called "white man." You know, "only good gringo is a dead gringo."

We're lucky they don't have lots of dogs, or I suppose they would have made dog food out of us.

They were still pissed as of 1999.

Here's a story that's part of the Alka's deal. 'Bout 1940 a preacher from the Detroit area got intrigued with the Alka story and decides to go down there and make them Christians to save their souls. At the time they mostly lived between Puerto Napo and Cocoa, on a triangle of jungle between the Napo, Curaray and Arajuno rivers. You can walk across these rivers most of the time. This preacher has perfect last name, "Saint." I believe his name was Bob Saint. He is an amateur pilot and he and his

brother-in-law clear a landing strip on the west bank of the Napo dead in the middle of Alka country. Man, this took balls. Course they had about five or six helpers, and were well armed. The local Indians would go in during the day and work, but not stay there after dark. They, probably 100 Alkas or more, watching in the jungle for a chance to kill 'em. Saint built a kinda church-school-hospital deal, a la the Catholic game.

The rest of this story reminds me of the deal where a man is training a horse to live without eating. Just as the horse finally got trained he croaked. After 'bout a year of coaxing them out for presents, and a few hung around for medical help, Saint flew up to Quito for supplies, and when he got back the Alkas got pissed and had the two or three Americans surrounded in the school. Saint was trying to calm 'em down (tough sledding, he couldn't speak or understand their language yet). The brother-in-law gets scared and shoots one of the head Alkas. End of story. The Alkas killed 'em all (and ate 'em so the story goes). Well, this somehow gets out of Ecuador and is world news.

Now the story I saw gets going. Saint's got a sister named "Rachel." A good-looking, smart, gutsy, gal who contends to be qualified to go to Ecuador and finish the dead missionaries mission. This was in 'bout 1950. She easily raises a fortune from the world's holy rollers to construct a compound in Alka territory.

Fast forward to 1961 and I'm down in the Napo area looking for gold. I get lost. Really lost. We see a DC-3 land a mile in front of us. We're in a dugout canoe with a 50 horsepower motor. In a few minutes we see a clearing 'bout 30 feet above the river. I walk up the bank to find a grass and gravel strip that looks to be 4,000 to 4,500 feet long. The DC-3 is parked at the far end from the river. This place is 80 miles from last vestige of civilization, and here is a walled, guarded town: "Limon Cocha."

"We are hungry, can we get a meal? Can we spend the night?"

"Yes" to both, 'bout four bucks a piece for super and a place to sleep.

We are not welcome and they make it clear, "In the morning get out and stay out."

Rachel Saint at this time has largest, most powerful radio station in the world dedicated to religious programming, just out of Quito. Limon Cocha is a fortified compound with schools, an infirmary, a church, and offices. The whole place is serviced by three airplanes (a DC-3, a push-pull Cessna Skymaster and another Cessna, maybe a 205?). There are about 50 Alkas there going to school. They have a power plant, two walk-in coolers. Looks like Rachel is shacked up with big-big Negro stud. I'm talking height and pounds (not inches). Remember the amazon queen stuff? Here it was, but with only one queen.

Would I? Damn rite. She was a sexy lookin' and movin' thing. But I believe I was 'bout as interesting to her as a pound of jaguar shit. "How 'bout a ride to Quito."

"Sure. In three days – 150 bucks."

A couple of Caiman.

There's a big lake right outside the compound with a big building, kinda like a motel. When we got close guards raised their rifles and chased our asses way. That lake I bet had 2,000 caiman in it. Know what a caiman is? It's a south American alleygator 'bout two to eight foot long. They eat 'em down there, especially the tail.

I went back there around 1990. Matter of fact took Margie there. I'd heard they knew how to tan snake skin that would stay in good shape for 25-30 years. I wanted to get some boots made outta' this stuff in Quito. They cost 25 bucks a pair. They did a pretty good job, but size was a problem. Every time for 30 years, when I get some made, the boots would be an inch too short. Damn if I know why. You'd stand on a piece of paper and they'd trace your footprint. Maybe that was just for show and they only knew how to make one size boot.

Leather pants cost 40 bucks a pair. Margie said my balls smelled like a new Cadillac after a day in leather pants. Speaking of leather pants, I got brand new pair of pants chaps made of genuine goat fur just like those Indian cowboys wore around Tiputini (the end of the railroad south of Quito). Margie took some pictures one Saturday night of some mean drunk cowboys with these kind of pants and we had to haul ass to keep from having a big problem. I don't know what model those Indians were, but they were mean mothers who made it clear they didn't like gringos. Actually worse than the brown hats from Pelileo. (They didn't wear shoes and ground was dry cool-cold and full of things like sand spurs. Didn't bother them.)

They wore lamb skin with fur out. Pants-vest-coat. Why? Seemed ass backwards to me.

I was gonna wear my stuff to a GM meeting, but after I got the pants they haven't hired me (since 1987). Maybe that "shit box" meeting wore out my usefulness. If you plan on moving down in the Tiputini area maybe we can make a deal on my fur pants.

Back to oil.

White Motor Company owned an engine company called Alco. They made big-big locomotive and stationary engines – up to 5,000 horsepower diesels. Gulf and Texaco started drilling in the late sixties. As a matter of fact they drilled first on our number one location, the "Lago One." White has another make, a smaller engine in the oil field called the "White Superior." This becomes quite important 'bout six years later when we start using them to pump production oil to the main pipeline.

1971 and on. When we lost the oil concession in the mid sixties a wildcatter from Conroe, Texas came in and drilled some stuff 25 to sixty miles further into the jungle east of Lago Agrio. I mean this is tough-ass jungle. (It still is 35 years later.) Well, I invested in the company, Cayman, and got involved in the deal. Our first well called the "Fannie One" was a fucked up mess of inexperience. You had to take everything in there by helicopter. This meant no piece over 20 feet long and no piece over 4,000 pounds. We had to fly in the drill and living quarters, mess hall, little hospital and all supplies, including fuel. Flew it all in with Vietnam War surplus Huey helicopters furnished by a Colombian company called "Helicol." God-dam, what a mess. You'd have to take off at daybreak to beat the heat. For lifting power, you'd have to get 40 Indians pulling ropes to run into the wind to help the copter into transitional lift. This was because of the heat and load. You can imagine this ain't no way to live to be 85. Cayman battled the jungle and really, there was no book on helicopter holes in the late sixties.

The Columbian helicopter mechanics surprised me. They were good. And worked hard under terrible conditions. The Fanny One ate up a fortune through rework, re-entry, twist offs and collapsed casings. It made oil, but was no barn burner.

The next adventure, fifty miles further east was a pure helicopter hole. Even today there is no road close. It too had oil, but it was heavy oil – very heavy – 'bout 15 or 16 gravity. It would flow to surface, cool off and you could shovel it. It wouldn't flow. No pipe line, etc., so it was a loser.

'Bout that time I met an oil man in the Detroit area named "Pat" Patrick. His real first name was a goofy thing I believe started with a "u." He had a resume 'bout like H.L. Hunt 'cept Pat got fucked up in Vietnam (I think), and would never run the mile in four minutes. He was an oil field tool salesman who had run into an extra sharp geologist (last name "Scott"). Scotty and Pat made a good team. Pat had the balls a wildcatter needs to survive, and Scotty had a good oil field nose, so they were quite successful.

Pat wants to play "Indy racer" 'bout '70 or '71. He knows some people at GM and Penske. He offers me a job cause he wants to "build his own car." But Pat was, in my book, a stubborn, nosey cat that I believed would be a fuckin' pain in the ass to work for. Shortly, he and Don Gates find each other and the "Antaries" race car gets built. It was a goofy lookin' disaster. I like Pat, and Don Gates and I are friends, so I kinda know all of Pat's adventures both in oil and racing. By the way, he does win Indy with his own car, later called "The Wild Cat," with Gordon Johncock as driver in 1982. But, his team had already won their first Indy in 1973 in a Gurney Eagle, so you see, Pat didn't fuck around. If he set his mind to it, it happened.

Why all the Patrick and Indy stuff? In the early seventies Pat was taken with my Ecuador oil field adventures and thought he wanted an oil concession there. I was in a position to take him to the head cat in Ecuadorian oil politics. So Pat flew down and I got him wired in, but not much came of it. Probably Pat and Scotty didn't like the odds and the players. But, it seems Pat did take a fancy to Ecuadorian women, based on a story a lady told me five years later as I lent her enough money to get back to Ecuador. (I know there are two sides to every story, but based on her version, my guess is Pat won't be going to Quito for vacations. Remember Ecuadorian ladies when pissed are bad about cutting off the offending male's peter, a la John Bobbitt.)

Well by '71, I'm 'bout out of gas in Ecuadorian oil. No pun intended. I work as a consultant. Sometimes for Texaco-Gulf-Ecuadorian Government consortium. I'm kinda desirable 'cause I can fly choppers and am pretty handy around engines. Kenny Rich is in Quito and got the new deals going. He's gonna create Acapulco number two and he is introducing American hamburgers to Ecuador. He started an American-style Lemon Tree restaurant like there is in Dallas. A house turned into restaurant and drinking joint with customized food and drink. Really a private gringo social club for oil people, con artists, players, dreamers, fuck-offs, and CIA jerk-offs. But I do mean there was some hi-buck pussy in that joint at times.

By '75 I've been walkin,' driving, and bouncing around Ecuador on horses, burros, canoes, you name it, and the truth is, I kinda knew 'bout most all the mineral and various "get rich" schemes that follow an oil and gold play in a poor country. I really liked Ecuador and it's diversified people, and what's most important, I enjoyed my time there very much. Goddam…for me it was a new movie every day. I wouldn't stay in civilization a day, I'd invent reasons to go to someplace I'd never been. I never made any money to speak of there, but every day I'd come close.

Leonard got disgusted with Kenny's ever changing plans and had to do something or starve. By now he had an 18 year old mistress, an ex-hooker from Guyaquil and 'bout three kids official or unofficial. The old Dutchman told me one day "it's a wise man who knows who his father is." I thought about it for a week and decided he had an important point there. So I said, "You should write a book Mr. Detweiller, and put all these things in it." He said "I got that out of a book a Chinese cat wrote named Confucius." Anyhow, Leonard went to work for an oil field work-over company named "Poole International" out of San Angelo, Texas, as a personnel director. Leonard could speak Spanish, English, German, Portuguese, and enough Quechia as well as three or four other Indian dialects. He could really handle men, but regarding women he was flat fucking lost.

He soon became the camp top dog. He ran the whole damn operation and that was no easy task.

He's taught me enough 'bout the jungle to fill many lifetimes. Hell, by then it had been 17 or 18 years. You know, if Leonard had of run for president of Ecuador in 1980 I believe he'd have won.

I never ever was in a town or village that hadn't heard of him and I never met anyone who didn't like him. Leonard was a 100 percent German and 100 percent Texan. He had about the right kinda genes to be any fucking thing he wanted to be.

When I first met Leonard he had gold fever, I'd say just shy of fatal. He'd come to Ecuador in 1959, sent in by the Securities and Exchange Commission. They sent him in, a gringo gold prospector with a Bell 47 helicopter and Mexican mining experience, to check out a guy from Indianapolis named Clifford who supposedly pulled a stock scam in the states called "The Golden Sands." This guy actually got a dredge in to the Napo river just below Puerto Napo. I mean a big mother. My guess 150 to 200 tons - assembled it and got it operational. The logistics to get it that far through the mountains and that far into the jungle as I saw it looked like a job for Merlin or God. But I guess you could say there was a problem. Turns out not enough gold there to be commercial. You guessed it. "The Golden Sands" went belly up and lots of stock holders lost their money.

I once met Clifford at Indy at race time. He seemed like a nice guy with dreams and a good line of bullshit. His was the typical game where greed (and we all have some of those genes) overcomes your brains and you're ripe for plucking (no matter how you spell it) by the con artist. But you know, I think Clifford really believed he was gonna get rich, because gold was there. But exactly "where" was the problem. Right in here I'm suspicious the CIA, not the SEC, sent Leonard in.

At this time Ecuador's got several hundred good and bad-ass Germans on the run from war crimes and other various possible illegal activities, related to World War II.

When Leonard goes in, he is just another gringo gold prospector with a Bell-47 helicopter and Mexican mining experience. He's looking for the "mother lode." This is always in hi-country (talking 'bout river gold). Leonard and his crew are working the river "Juten Yacu," 'bout 10,000 high. The helicopter is wrecked from a flying mistake. Though the pilot and mechanic survive crash, the pilot drowns trying to get out of a canyon where they crashed. I met Leonard 'bout six months later at Puerto Napo, where the Juten Yacu river flows into the Napo river. The original meeting of the first gold trip in the Oriente (1961).

In 1962 I met in Quito a very sharp geologist who worked for Union Carbide. This guy, J. Armstrong, was goofy about snakes. I mean nuts! He wouldn't think nothing 'bout grabbing a 15 foot anaconda from a canoe in 10 feet of water and 'rassling with it in the river till he could put it in a big burlap bag. I've sat in his Quito office on a couch and felt something like a bug on my neck and turn around to see a boa head flicking it's tongue. I'd open a drawer to see a mineral sample, gold or diamond, and there would be a snake in the drawer he forgot about.

Last adventure I almost had with him was North Ecuador in South Columbia. He'd heard about a snake with a head on both ends and a gold play (river wet placer) at 12,500 feet. The snake deal was at lower altitude but in same area. (Snakes freeze at 35 degrees and you can use them for walking sticks; ain't dead, just can't move.) I think he misrepresented his mission. I believe he worked for Union Carbide, but was looking for uranium or some other rare mineral for the Atomic Energy Commission. I seen equipment they use in checking radioactivity and bags of samples locked up and separated from stuff he showed me. I wish I'd of gone with him, but I think it was 'cause I didn't want a week above the snow line. Too damn cold and wet.

This cat made a good profit out of supplying snakes to a snake zoo in Chicago. He'd get orders for snakes once a month. Well, a red-tailed boa was on the list so he told me, "A five foot red-tail boa brought five grand." We had one I saw quite often at our base camp close to Napo. "I'll bring one back with me," I said. "OK, I'll give you $2,500 when you bring it."

Well, we got a Canadian working for us named Ralph. Not really an Einstein, but he has 'bout 10 years jungle time, can run a dozer, a saw mill, and knew 'bout dry placer gold. He's on the dozer, sees our red tailed boa, and drops the blade on him and skins him. When I ask him to get the Indians to put him in a bamboo tube (that's our snake suit case). He says, "Hell, I've got him" and brings me the skin.

By the way, I don't know how big snakes get, but our guys killed and skinned a big boa. He was on the wall of our base gold camp for ten years. 25 feet-five inches long and 72 inches at widest part. I found out there was a reward for a 30 foot "any kind" of snake in good physical condition. The New York Zoological Society still had Teddy Roosevelt's original $10,000 reward. He'd said, "ain't no such snake."

The reward in 1990 was $75,000. Shit, I knew where there were some anacondas 30 to 35 feet long. At the same place there were 25 foot crocodiles, 250 miles from the ocean. The snakes were in a swamp just 'bout five miles south of the Colombian border. The swamp formed the head waters of the Cuyabeno River.

We got the permits from the government, made a deal with New York to come get the snake, built a box to put him in, and made a deal with kinda the best Indian "snake doctor" to keep it healthy.

Leonard and Buck (Leonard's partner in the late eighties) had built a fishing camp on the Cuyabeno just about three miles west of the swamp. Well, in this time frame this part of the jungle is going bad. The Colombian cocaine manufacturers and the Peruvian suppliers of cocaine mush sent the stuff up from Peru to the Ecuadorian border via the Napo to the Aguarico river then up the Cuyabeno river. The mush then went through the swamp to the San Miguel river. This is the Colombian border. No road here. The stuff is moved farther up river to the cocaine factories 'bout 10 to 20 miles east.

Now people, this is so isolated and so protected the army won't go in there. I never crossed the San Miguel there, let alone head east. Only place I crossed the San Miguel was north of Lago Agrio, then decided to get back quick 'cause I suddenly realized gringos were good ransom stuff.

Me, Margie and C. J.

I did kinda slide over the coke factory in a helicopter one day. (Now, in 2001, Columbia and the world still got a big-big problem in there).

Matter of fact I took C.J. Baker, publisher of Circle Track magazine to this big snake area in about 1990. Leonard wanted to check on the fish camp and do some repairs on it. The cocaine cowboys must have used it at times cause it was in bad shape. Actually the building (bamboo, palm and chucka wood put together with no nails, tied together with palm and bamboo) had collapsed to where floor was on ground on one end and three feet up on other.

Why a fish camp here? Ever hear of a fish called peacock bass? This big, beautifully colored, very tasty, fish lived here. (So did piranha.) We got there at 5:00 pm. It was an all day trip from last town on the river (125 miles). We are hot, so after the Indians swam around quietly a bit (that's when I know Indians feel those piranha are not to be a problem). I told Margie "OK, Let's wash up." Well you bathe in river bare-assed naked and soap and scrub each other off. This water is cold, 'bout 60 degrees. I tell C.J. "Take a bath," it's very important to stay clean in jungle. Bacteria grows like lightning cause it's so hot and humid, and you can

These buggers make swimming interesting.

go from OK to damn near dead in 36 hours.

When he finishes I ask him if he felt any piranha nibbling on him? He figured I was bullshitting, so I had Indians catch four or five in 'bout five minutes for him to look at. He took some pictures and he never-ever would go in the river again. There or anyplace else down there. (Think he paid for it with a bit of fungus, but in his mind it was a fair trade).

I don't know why piranha will eat your ass up one place and others "no problem." I've been places we'd have to throw a dead pig in the water then hurry across while the fish had their meal. When you seen the bad-assed piranha eating flesh…it's a frenzy. If a man got in the water in wrong place it would be all over in two or three minutes. (Did you ever see the teeth on those things? They look like sharp human teeth.) In other places you could swim all day and never be touched. I've probably heard 10 or 15 stories, but have no way to separate the bullshit from the facts. I always treated it as a local issue. If the local Indians swim, I swim. That worked for me and I've never been bitten.

Margie found a spot with no piranha.

You know, you never think about food 'cept at meal times. In the jungle you never quit looking for good fruit (bananas, oranges, pineapples) a big snail, yucca, corn, tomatoes, eggs. I don't mean you just take stuff. You buy it if it's domestically raised. You carry rice, flour, salt and some sugar (and a live chicken if you want to make sure of supper). Let me tell you 'bout jungle chickens. They run all over hell and those chickens, after you cook 'em eight hours, are so tough you can barely drive a nail in 'em. And parrot? Hell, they'd make a good tire tread. They are all muscle. Snakes, howler monkeys, piranha – I could never get that stuff down. I could, and sometimes did, live on just yucca and fruit. Bananas are everywhere. A strange deal, wild oranges grow a lot of places too. They are a very unappetizing shade of pale yellow and they are hard to get. The trees have no low branches so you got to climb to get 'em, or pick up those that fell off. But I've never eaten a sweeter, more tasty orange anywhere.

In the wild there are also orange-looking fruit trees. They have big, beautiful looking orange things that are limes and taste worse than battery acid. Man, I can remember being thirsty and hungry, coming up on an Indian village and seeing this beautiful fruit. I take one, peel it, and take a big bite. It was a shock.

You know how hungry you are determines taste. I met up with Leonard one time when I hadn't eaten in 'bout 36 hours. When I got there he had a stew cooked and I think that was the tastiest meal I've ever eaten in my life. I asked him what he did to make it so tasty – said he threw his old socks in it. Meat? Remember no refrigeration. If you kill it today, in 24 hours it's going bad. So I ate 'bout no meat down there.

Boy, I sure wish I'd of kept a diary. Leonard wrote in his every day. You know his diary would make 'bout ten movies and the facts would be straight.

In the early eighties a goofed up geologist named Ray Haskins shows up in Quito. He came for the oil play but he missed the boat. He visits our big gold play in the Napo area and falls in love with our deal. We ain't doing anything there, so we lease him the mine. I really am against it but Kenny and Leonard figure maybe he'll find something. Well, in my first meeting with him he describes his previous night in Quito. He says he can fly like a bat, and flew over and around the city for four or five hours stark naked. Quito is at 10,000 feet elevation and 'bout 50 degrees at night.

How in the hell can he flap his arms fast enough to fly in that thin air? How come he don't freeze? Why naked? Ayahusca?

He said he could read people's minds. Maybe that's why he and I didn't become buddies, 'cause I figured him to be a fruit cake. As you may have guessed by now, he spent about a year mining, going into debt, and not paying us. He gets pissed off and burns the camp down. Sure, we put him in jail, but he ain't worried, he's gonna fly out first chance he gets when there is a full moon. This cat went gold goofy. He'd be up at dawn and pan till dark. Every next pan "he'd find the mother lode." Like a drunk or drug addict. "Just one more drink" – "one more fix" – "one more pan."

On the subject of Ecuadorian jails; if you go down there, behave yourself. The jails are filthy and rough beyond description. At the time they had no provisions to feed prisoners. You could buy food cheap, but from time you were arrested to time you're put in jail all prisoners are penniless.

No attempt is made to locate help for you. Oh yes, if you can get enough money you could buy your way out. Only thing you couldn't buy your way out of was drugs or anything considered subversive politically.

They took drug money freely as long as you weren't caught. But once you got a legal drug violation charge it was a "new game." There was an exception to the drug crime payoff but it was like fifty grand and up. My partner, Kenny Rich, had a boy 'bout 18 years old living down there and he went off of the drug deep end 'bout 1980. I believe Kenny pulled a high roller deal to get him out. (He was looking at life in prison.) I think Kenny didn't do what he promised and he had to get the hell out of Ecuador.

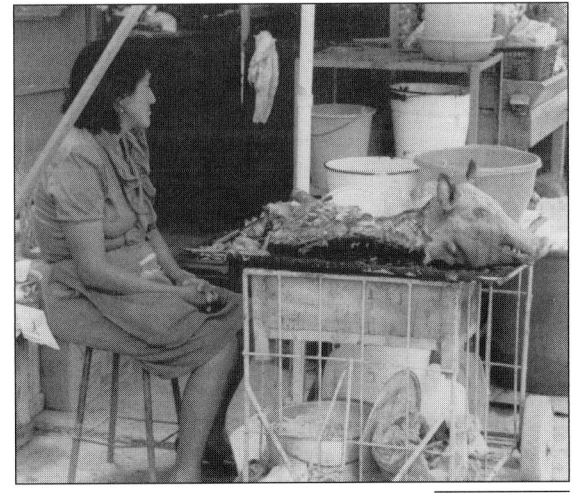

Fast food stand.

Ever hear of the Peace Corps? I've never been ashamed of being an American 'cept when I'd watch American Peace Corps assholes, stoned out of their minds, dirty and filthy, wearing weird-ass clothes, holed up in some village, raising dope and processing it for their use under the guise of helping the Indians and Ecuadorians learn how to make a better living. They had an unending flow of money from the States to support their lifestyle. Hell, they weren't trying to live like the locals, when they were in Quito you'd see 'em stoned all the places gringos were found: airports, stores, restaurants, hotels. Every third one carrying a guitar.

Hell, Misahualli was way in the Oriente. There was a small island within a mile that had so many small parrots living there that when they flew between you and the sun it got darker. You wanna know why? There were warm springs rite there and the birds bathed and played in that warm mineral water. I went to see what the attraction for the birds was besides the warm springs and I saw five acres of marijuana and poppies and an ayahusca bottling operation with a sign over the compound "US Peace Corps," complete with new Ford tractor and a couple of Jeeps. I also saw a young man fuckin' near die in some quicksand he was told to stay away from. It took 'bout five of us to get him out. There was a steel cable bridge 'bout 100 yards long to cross to get to the island. Driving a pickup across that bridge reminded me of driving over a big bunch of Jell-o. (Maybe stoned it seemed OK.)

Leonard has been at Poole a couple years. He worked up to be the operations manager, and got a li'l nervous 'bout a steady job with limited future, so he bought some cheap acreage (400 acres) close to Poole's camp. Poole was the only work-over equipped company in Ecuador. Work over companies do maintenance and remedial work on oil or gas wells. Their equipment, some of it at least, was very similar to an oil well drill. It's a dangerous, rough, hard life.

Their camp was close to a fair-sized jungle town called Shushufindi. In his spare time Leonard put up a shed and a secure tool house 'bout 20 feet by 15 feet and hung a sign on the side that said "Minga." Minga is a Quichua Indian word for community work tradition (very similar to US barn raising by early settlers). Minga was a seed company hopefully to become an oil field service company. What's oil field service company? Can be 100 things and 100 technologies and 100 professions. He took the machinery I'd shipped into our gold and sawmill operation at Puerto Napo (yup, we had a sawmill) took it all down the river to Cocoa, then to Shushufindi.

Oil fields need machine shops, pipe threading and handling, fishing equipment (for stuck stuff down hole), wire lines, welding. Hell, an oil field can have, say 150,000 horsepower of engines and turbines in it. They need a lot of attention and parts. Plus, oil fields need roads and bridges. I've seen oil field service companies spread out over 200 acres.

Leonard and I continued to be friends. We jointly had a friend then from Houston, a geologist name of Britt Wherry. Britt was a damn good geologist, but bad luck was his specialty. He became badly-badly crippled with arthritis. He was a dreamer and poor business man, and when oil was discovered there (Ecuador), he kept missing the boat. After three or four years he decided to start an oil field service company. Leonard, Britt Wherry and I each owned a third of the company Leonard called Minga. We needed money and I had a friend that had a business our government frowned on. He wanted a business in a secure area from our government's claws in case he was threatened with loss of his freedom. He invested forty grand, and was to add another one hundred sixty grand. I got voted out of the company which suited me, but I was surprised I never got any part of my equity back.

One of the engines I had to keep runnin'.

Well, Leonard needed all things for a machine and welding shop, and equipment for vehicle and oil field related machine and tool repair. This is stuff I had, and/or knew where a bunch of it was cheap. So over a five or six year period, I shipped quite a bit of equipment to Leonard with the understanding (at least as I understood it this way), that someday I'd have an interest in the business and get a few bucks to pay part of my costs to get it to Ecuador. This business grew very rapidly and Leonard left Poole to run Minga full time. Leonard took all the tools and equipment out of the gold camp 'cept the low boy and bulldozer.

Kenny was smart enough to take them back to Quito before Leonard gobbled it up. I'll be goddamned if on the trip back to Quito with the dozer, an International 'bout like a turboed D-7 Cat, they dropped it off the low boy and it fell 5,500 feet. Nope, hardly hurt it, so we got it back up by disassembling it to 500 pound sections and in two days got it all up on the road with about 200 Indians and ropes. Yes, nothing but rope and Indian home made rope at that. The operation kinda reminded me of a bunch of ants carrying food to the nest. The boss Indian ran it like clockwork. With a single long cadence, where everyone repeated the cadence loudly and in total rhythm. Hell, I guess the frame weighed several tons, and it couldn't be disassembled. With ropes and hand power they drug it back about one mile straight up in about four hours.

The company cafeteria.

Well, Minga grew and grew. By 1985 I'd say they were netting about a million American a year.

Still no talk of me getting back my third of the company. When it first started I gave up my third to appease the money man who paid a little and hauled ass. 'Bout 1990 Minga added a partner, Buck, a professional "fisherman" (nothing with fins or gills, a guy that does the down hole removal or recapture of foreign material blocking the hole). Story had a bad ending. The other one hundred sixty grand never happened, Britt Wherry's arthritis killed him, then the third partner (Buck) dies. Leonard ends up with an eight million dollar company.

An adventure I experienced in Ecuador was the possible creation of resort in the style of Mexico's Acapulco. Kenny Rich found an area on the pacific coast, a town called "Ayangue." This area had a pretty white beaches and white cliffs. There was enough high area to accommodate the buildings and fixed facilities of a private resort town. The area was 'bout four square miles. The ocean gave Ayangue a beautiful circular harbor. Those beaches probably had best spear fishing grounds in the world. Marine life (like lobsters) was very plentiful and huge. Hell, the place even had some six foot lizards. (Probably got lost looking for the Galapagos islands). Also, natural gas was bubbling through cracks in the rocks so, "free energy."

The place had no vegetation 'cept desert stuff. It hadn't rained there in 13 years when I first saw it. That, by the way cost me four or five hundred bucks. I'd see it pouring within a mile, bet a hundred that rain would come and lose it. Hell, I have seen it within 100 yards and lost again. By the way, here was a lesson in ecology. This, in 1935 was jungle where it rained 100 to 120 inches a year. Oil was discovered 20 miles away. The oil wells had part salt water, and as always, some crude was wasted into a dug pit. Over the years this stuff spread, penetrated the ground and got into the rivers and in thirty years killed all vegetation. The lack of vegetation created a negative for rain clouds. In 35 years a jungle turned into pure desert complete with cactus and tumble weed. (Nope, no sidewinder snakes.) The oil field has played out and it's headed back to jungle now. Yup, it rained in the 14th year.

Well Kenny fenced in three sides. The cliff of course didn't need it. Kenny called it "Playas si Branncaas" (the beaches and cliffs). Well 'bout like all Kenny deals, much money was wasted.

A law which said a gringo can't own ocean side property was not able to be changed after ten years of trying. Nothing changed 'cept the wild burros in the fenced area with a little bit of water. That was a lesson on the need for population control. That four square miles was wall to wall burros when then son-of-a-bitches finally knocked the fence down. There must have been 1,000 of them things and let me tell you a plumb wild burro ain't no friendly critter.

Ecuador, from day I first went there, was not a country loved by the US. It seems that during World War II the Ecuadorians let the Germans park their submarines for fueling, provisions, maintenance and to let the sailors get some poontang to take the pressure off the "drop the soap in the shower game." Plus, after the war, a lot of ex-military and civilian Germans hid there who had reason to believe their activities in Europe during the war might bring prison or execution. Then there was the deal where President Roosevelt gave Peru a big part of Ecuador's swampy jungle. Wasn't worth a shit, 'cept now they've found oil. How come he had the power to and why he did this I don't know. But Americans were not any better off in Ecuador during the sixties than negroes were in the South in the forties. We were one notch above dog shit. I suppose it's standard procedure for people to hunt an ethnic bond in a foreign country. They all did, so Americans hung out together, same with limeys, Germans, Japanese, etc.

This kinda US ethnic hangout group included the American embassy and it's personnel. In addition I noticed quite a few American males, 'bout say in their forties, with no real reason to be there - no visible form of financial support that played a role kinda like a soldier of fortune. They dealt in diamonds, gold, oil, and minerals (like copper, etc.). I think this group were kinda like advanced peace core, or senior hippies. I'm pretty sure some of them were CIA trying to find out what was going on with the Germans and the Japs. This group did very little to get the world to love us.

Hey, this is another revelation; if you get in a jam in a foreign country and depend on help from the American embassy, from what I saw, forget even trying to talk to 'em. They are too busy having parties and getting refrigerators, Mercedes, TV sets, jet skis, outboard motors, etc., shipped in for their supposed use. (Sure, they buy all that shit with government money or subsidy and then sell it to make their personal fortunes). They ain't got time for nuthin' else – I'm serious. What ever they are supposed to be doing ain't got anything to do with helping Americans in trouble. The head cat is a political ass-kisser and donator, usually a wealthy retired business man with a dickey licker thrown in here and there. They are professional pals of government (hi-buckers) that can't be fired, and ride the gravy train for 20 years and then triple dip on retirement. Guess how the tax deal regarding pay works? Man, what a racket. The system is bad enough to make you puke.

Kenny had a Volkswagen van with an American embassy designation displayed on it. I'm sure that for this we were picked on in traffic.

I'll tell you something that surprised me. It was a real eye-opener when Rockefeller was running for vice president and came to visit Ecuador. This damn near caused a paint shortage in Ecuador. Besides being a gringo, he owned big part of "Nestle," a Swiss company that owned a huge plantation in Ecuador ('bout six million acres) that grew coffee, cocoa, tea, pineapples, Indian palm, rice, bananas and hell, I don't know what all they grew. The Ecuadorians hated the Nestle operation. In Ecuador the law says "all must vote, or lose their citizenship." Most can't read or write, so political opponents are identified by color, and the word "lista." So a good ad is to paint a big rock red and paint the word "lista" on it. All rocks, walls, and buildings are used for political messaging. When Rockefeller got there the Ecuadorians must have used used a half a million gallons of paint calling him a "murderer," "crook," "cheater," "scumbag gringo." I remember seeing him going down main street in Quito in an open limousine and all the way to the palace was solid signs on the walls on both sides saying bad-bad shit 'bout him. Then consider all the paint needed to paint over it. Them walls and rocks got 'bout an inch of paint on 'em.

I noticed an unusual custom practiced in South America. It was common for the boss at siesta time to have his secretary go to company garage and get in the back of his Mercedes and lay on the floor (covered with a blanket). The boss then drove to a motel, entered room from a rear garage (each room has a garage and a window where food and drink is delivered, which you order by phone.) So you sneak your secretary or girlfriend in the room and get some food, drink and pussy. Pay through the window (one way glass).

Pretty slick and sneaky right?

Guess what, momma ain't sitting home knitting. It's OK for her to have a young stud to screw. For this it is the same deal. Nobody can see who the mystery guest is. Momma's liable to be in same motel with daddy if they ain't careful.

You hear so much about "we should have diesel cars." I've been in Latin cities where they had a 25 percent diesel vehicle population. The food tasted like diesel, if you walked down the street you're eyes were watering and your nose was offended, the hotel smelled like diesel, and if you bought a shirt or pair of pants they smell like diesel. If the goofys in this country re-fire up on diesel and make it happen, remember what I just told you. Can you imagine sex with both partners wearing "Wild Diesel" as a romantic odor?

By 1985 gold was on back burner. Oil was on. But in the service arena only. No chance to own any oil production any more, so my game was tagging along on Leonard's equipment franchise deals for Minga. I was always trying to buy some equipment or vehicle for Minga. We also shipped them odd-ball parts. I was on the board of directors till the laws made directors potentially liable.

Magnificent views were everywhere.

By 1985 I've been 24 years in the jungle (part time) along with the racing, truck dealerships, inventions, alternative energy, prospecting and oil wells – talk about a jungle college.

I invented a portable oil field hone (helicopter moveable)…jungle oil field helicopter flying…half-invented a looper refinery for cleaning vanadium out of crude oil…half invented an extra tough overlay for valves that were used in crude oil burning engines…alluvial gold mining…copper and silver mining.

I got a look at the diet and habits of people who had a 20 percent life expectancy of 100.

A good look at earthquake power…same for volcano power.

A real variety of religious beliefs and customs, including cannibalism and head-shrinking.

An astonishing observation of the power of the shaman and his jungle-oriented medicines and pain killers.

Maybe the biggest single thing I learned was that the average human, if put naked in the jungle, could probably adapt and survive and live a pretty decent life without the inventions of the last 200 years and really not miss it, even having had it once.

I found to feel good all you need is not to be hungry, not to be cold, to be able to sleep without fear, to have shelter and most of all have friends who truly give a damn, that will help if you're in need. I found it takes 12 hours of a day (all the daylite) to fill the needs of an average human. So this precludes time for so called "advancements" in lifestyle. Would you believe the Indian and the so-called poor Latino do not envy us. In fact they consider themselves superior to us "the gringo."

I found insects can tell the difference between healthy and unhealthy people, they will leave a healthy person alone but will eat all over the sick man.

I found out that animals know when we have fear, and are much more aggressive when they sense it. If you find yourself in an environment of wild animals, wear clothes that say "No Fear" all over 'em.

I've seen in nature the survival of the fittest. It looks cruel, but it also looks like the only plan that works.

Sea lion.

I saw some things in the jungle that there is no logical explanation for. In particular, how were huge, heavy rocks placed where they were? We don't have a way to do it today, the year 2001, four or five hundred (or more) years later.

I watched 'em for 33 years slowly but surely destroying huge-huge areas of forest full of plants, animals, and bodies of water.

I've watched the environmental rape (in the name of resource exploration). The effects of man's exploitation of natural resources, with seemingly no regard for future generations, nor for the negative consequences, such as water-ground and/or air pollution, erosion, and interference with the flow of natural water bodies.

Destruction and extinction of so many species of animals, fish, plants, insects, birds and their normal, natural habitats

You would be astounded looking at the stars at night in southern Central America. There are so many and they are so bright. You know why? In the US there is so much air pollution that maybe as many as half are obscured to man's eyes.

But you know what's even worse? The Indian who have lived there from, I suppose, "day one" are being squeezed even further back, away from their normal habitats and food chain. We introduce our modern diseases to them and apparently their immune systems are not capable of defending against them. How bad is this? In some cases rite to total extinction of specific tribes.

Big lizard.

An example: If you tried the water they drink, the food they eat, you would probably start the most effective diet known to man besides sewing the mouth shut. You will also experience the greatest shitting contest of your life. Yet you can, in a month or so, adjust to that particular bacteria and go back to normal. (An interesting item, no medicine available here is any where's near as effective as the homemade cure – course you may go blind taking it).

Religion is a topic I may be the least knowledgeable about. It seems they have as many religions as they have dialects of language. Seems like modern religion is actually a form of control or government. A majority of Indian religions or worship involves animals, stars, planets, snakes and, in particular, the sun. Yup, to many Indian tribes the sun is their main comfort. I'm glad I didn't live with some of their religious beliefs where human sacrifice was an early day form of taxes.

Bored? Never. Every evening, every rainy day, I was trying to absorb and understand this culture that was so profoundly simple as compared to us in Y2K. Their computer is a string, and how many knots it's got where. If a guy wants to know how many cows he's got, he pulls out a string and count the knots. Battery never goes dead. The Energizer Bunny can forget running around in the middle of South America, ain't no place to put batteries. I suppose you could make a blow gun with a light on it to shoot more accurately when light is poor in the jungle. Come to think 'bout it, the lighting is poor in the jungle all the time.

Without really noticing it, these adventures got myself and Margie to just about every place

Rush hour.

that Ecuador had industry or remarkable geography. How would you like to be awakened at 5:30 am in a rented room by a cow licking your ass? (They really have rough tongues.) Interesting, don't you agree? Especially since last thing they told you night before "Check the floor and your boots for snakes in the morning." And a boat driver telling you 'bout a 65 foot anaconda that climbed up on a raft he was sleeping on 100 yards from the bed you're in. Nope, I didn't believe stories 'bout anything over 35 feet.

One day we were headed for a new oil discovery 300 miles down the river Napo from a road. It was 100 percent jungle all the way. Around 5:00 pm the river's getting up and nasty so we need to quit for the day. We spot an Indian house on the bank. Maybe, hell yes, it's the "Holiday Inn of something" $2.00 apiece for supper, breakfast and a bed. This seems a little high, but we can't shop around. The house is bamboo, palm and chucka. It is up in air five feet to keep out the snakes. It hasn't got a shower so they use the river. They have a balsa raft with two foot hole rite in the middle. Jump in the hole and even though the river's solid mud from the big rain behind us it felt good. We dry off and eat supper. Hi-buck meal, snails-yucca-rice and fruit. "Where's the toilet deal?" "The hole in the raft." Well, OK the current is 'bout 25 miles an hour, but Margie felt like the plan wasn't too good. Well, our belly's are full, it's cooled off. "Want some tea?" "Hell yes." Margie notices, "what a beautiful china teapot so far in the jungle." They go fill it up with water, wanna guess where?

A little shade was hard to find in town.

The bed is plywood five feet, 10 inches long and I'm six feet tall. Yes, you can sleep with your feet hanging out over plywood. It rains like hell all night. As for relief that night, sure, just stand at edge of room and piss out the window (no doors – no windows). Not so easy for ladies, they get muddy feet. I helped Margie…I shine the flashlight out the window for her. I say, "Watch out for snakes." Complaining? Hell no, I wouldn't trade that deal for 1,000 bucks.

A day or so before we slept on a split bamboo floor in an empty schoolhouse on the river bank. A rainy, cool night. That goddam night was 48 hours long. I would trade that for 1000 bucks.

We always brought cheese and bread and watched for food to buy or find all day long. Eating the local fare could have negative consequences. One night we ended up at a new oil site damn near in Peru in a town called "Tiputini." This town was 'bout 15 buildings and three or four stores. We need to spend the night there so the General store owner says he has some rooms to rent on second floor. This building is built out of rough sawed lumber probably 25-30 years old.

It is a first class shit hole complete with a tin roof and 1,000 big rats and 500 bats flying around and running all over hell up in the rafters.

Margie won't listen to me and eats some spoiled "ah-hi." (homemade salsa). By 4:00 am that li'l gal's got such a bellyache she'd have to get better to die. At day light we head for civilization, but that's two days away by canoe. We are just below the Equator on the Napo river, so the sun's rite over your head all the time. It's 'bout 90 degrees. Margie is wrapped up in a couple of blankets, still shivering like a dog shittin' razor blades. All she can do is drink, puke and shiver. Second night we found a real nice place to clean Margie up – with a good place to sleep, and got a li'l food in her. Two days she was good as new and 15 pounds lighter.

Listen to this. We had a guest couple with us from Birmingham, the female was a nurse named Marty. That dirty bitch had all kinds of medicine with her (in case they got sick) and never offered Margie anything, nor did she give a shit 'bout Margie's sickness. I didn't find that out till she got better. Marty, you are a dirty, rotten, no-good cunt in my book. Hopefully you'll get paid back for your selfish, inconsiderate and pig-type manners. I should have gave you to the Alkas (cannibals) on way back from Tiputini.

I need to tell you 'bout my favorite hotel in the world. It is in Puerto Napo, Ecuador. When I first saw it in 1961, it's name was the "Hotel Oriente" It had 14 rooms, a barber shop, a restaurant and a small general store. It was about 40 feet above the Napo river, right at the barge crossing. The owner's home was across a dirt road from hotel. This hotel, the "Jose Johnson" as it came to be known, was very special to me.

Then it cost fifty cents a night and 25 to 30 cents a meal. Haircuts were 25 cents. You could buy cigarettes there, or anything else, for gold you panned and wrapped in a banana leaf. The gold price in 1961 was 200 bucks an ounce. The hotel had one cold water shower for all and one toilet for all (it went straight into the Napo river – guess they learned that from us.) But the part I loved was a 40 feet long screened in porch 40 feet above the river. Kinda like a box seat in an opera house. We had 'bout 15 rockin' chairs to watch the action on the river crossing barge and the smaller cable trolley for people crossing just a few feet above the hotel. Out there we had candle light at night. Sometimes we had electricity, but very seldom. We called the porch "the worrying porch."

OK, in the jungle it rained a lot. Hotel is on east side of the Andes and they top out in there 'bout 15,000 feet. Puerto Napo is 2,500 feet. So when it rains up in mountains, time we'd see it, water would raise river fifteen feet in thirty minutes and river was really hauling ass – 'bout 40 miles an hour. The porch to me was greatest therapy for rest and relaxation I ever had. When it rained we couldn't work, and the rain would

Hoping one will jump in the boat.

cool the air. So we all sit on the porch talking about what all we'd do when it quit raining, at same time hoping it would never quit. We solved all problems, told and listened to all kinds of stories, adventures, lies, dreams. Consider the people on that porch Leonard, Kenny and myself, experienced with ten years or more in gold, oil, cannibals, snakes, jaguars, Indian and pussy stories filled the cool air. Some starving gold prospectors, some first day jungle players, some natives who worked for us, plus canoe drivers, guides, laborers, holy rollers, sometimes rich, lost souls (mostly females looking for something, but they didn't know what it looked like) joined us on the porch.

The worrying porch was delicious during the day when it rained hard back up in the mountains and the river couldn't be crossed or used. We sat there all day hoping it wouldn't quit raining, talking about what all we'd do when the river went down. We'd also talk about the biggest snake, jaguar, gold nugget – the dying and the close calls of the rivers and jungles and earthquakes and volcano eruptions. There were tales about the biggest fish, the worst place for piranha, the secret gold mine, cannibal and head shrinker stories, the two-headed snake stories, hidden treasure stories, you name it. I guess that porch was kinda like a mild form of ayahusca – exciting, border-line believable, interesting and amusing. I always hated it when first cat said, "It's nine o'clock. I'm gonna go to bed." In 15 minutes, party was over, and that ice cold shower was next. Only thing made me do that was how good it felt when you dried off and warmed up. In the jungle you've gotta stay clean – bacteria gallops down there. As a rule Indians bathe twice a day. Serious scrubbing with soap. Women washed with a dress on, a "three-holer" that used to be a sugar or flour sack.

This porch and the Hotel Oriente was at the end of access by vehicle in the Oriente. The other road north and east ended way short in Biazaea. We had salesmen with wrist watches up both arms, a small farmer's market, a military camp, and last store for fuel, beer, coke, cigarettes, clothes, hardware and kitchen utensils. Monday morning 30 people lived on our side of the river.

Saturday evening there were 400 people coming and going. Two people could live there very well for 12 to 15 bucks a week with a full time servant. I spent two or three New Year Eve's there dancing in a muddy street with local musicians. One gallon sugar cane whiskey (poro) – one buck.

(Now beer was expensive, and not too cold) Would you believe I've seen Coca Cola for sale 500 miles from closest road at little river bank town. Price is cheap except if you don't return the bottle, man! Bottles were a problem the whole thirty-three years I worked there. Both beer and soft drinks, no cans, period.

Our hotel had a dirt road to the river, and there a big flat barge was only way to get anything heavy across. The barge was tied to a cable to stop current from sweeping barge down the river. And barge had two 75 horsepower outboards to push it. The river was 'bout forty feet below the hotel on our side. 75 yards north of the hotel was the pair of 'people' cables also.

They had two cables that were stretched across the river 'bout 30 feet above it, where they had a flat six foot by four foot deck below a pully frame, with a rope that was tied to either bank connected to a big drum hand-powered wench. (The river was about 100 yards wide here) When the platform was released and pushed off, the cable sag would make the platform and it's passenger and freight go like hell to the middle, then the winches had to pull it up hill to the other bank. We had two cables side by side. One called Lufthansa, the other Braniff. Charge (one sucre) five cents per passenger, and freight was negotiated at 'bout a nickel per hundred pounds. Burros ten cents, little pigs a nickel, big pigs a dime in their money (sucres) Dogs, cats and pets were free.

OK, the best entertainment was watching the loading and unloading of cars, trucks, animals on the barge. This was a never ending comedy of bad thinking, arguments, minor fights, buses, cars or trucks falling in the river. Oh hell yes, all the time. There was about ten miles of road across the river. One road, 'bout five miles, went to Tina, capital of the Oriente province, one road down the Napo five miles to Misahualli, a big canoe loading-unloading spot. The barge could carry a Mercedes fuel truck, 4,000 gallons fuel that weighed 'bout fifty thousand pounds total. In the loading process, nose of truck ends up in river (four foot of water), and rear wheels on river edge. Same with buses. A bus there, generally speaking, was a truck with a locally made wooden body and a roof, no doors or windows, wood bench slats, ten people wide. Ten people side by side in a ten foot wide bench and each bus held about ten rows of seats. The roof of the bus was like a stage coach for freight, animals, chickens, produce, building materials, assorted baggage and mail. Every driver had two passengers on his left (he drove left handed, American style), and seven passengers on his right. Well, sometimes a bus would fall in the river in the loading and unloading mode.

Now this is all rite under your rocking chair like a movie. Nine times out of ten, problem is caused by overloading. Seems like biggest real problem is the inability of those people to listen and stubbornness. They never seem to pick and follow a leader. When a bus slides off you got one hundred people in the river. Babies, old people, animals, luggage, fruit, produce, bicycles, auto or truck parts, tires, you name it. Water ain't deep, but it's cold (always 'bout 36 degrees fahrenheit). Now to make it more interesting, at the road's sides it's grass and weeds, and full of little poisonous snakes we call "che-che" and little no-see-em bugs, that when they bite, make you itch for weeks. Next hazard is you wanna guess how many people use this area for a toilet immediately after they get off or just before barge leaves? I guess you could say after a barge incident you're up to your knees in shitty snakes and bugs.

Now Indians have pet animals, so owning a dog is a big deal. In the jungle they are the shittyest, scariest dogs in the world. Dirty-skinny and lots with skin problems. The dogs go everywhere it's master goes, bus included. At the hotel we got our own official dog. A pretty big, part Airedale, part police dog. Kinda a mustard colored snaggled tooth, skinny, and as a rule, good-natured. (Came with the hotel purchase). But most of all, the horniest dog in the Oriente. Here's the deal: ol' Firp would pace back and forth till barge landed and nail first female dog off the barge. Wham! Firpo was bad 'bout getting hung up, and he'd jump on any size. This looked kinda goofy, him dragging around a twenty pound dog, barking and yelping. In 1961 no two dogs looked alike. In 1992 every dog in the Oriente looked like our dog "Firpo." Firpo was the name of a famous, giant, prize fighter from Argentina in the thirties and forties. Firpo, not only was the finest fucker in the jungle, he was also the Mike Tyson of jungle dogs. You know, both Firpo's ears had pieces out of 'em, and old Firpo was a very good ear eater himself.

Back to Lufthansa and Braniff the cable crossing. Every couple hours, cable platform gets overloaded, or maybe two or three drunks on, and in the river the whole shitteroo goes.

Burros, people, pigs, chickens (feet tied together), bananas, food, cigarettes, watch salesmen with twenty-five watches on each arm and inside the coat. Actually 35 feet into 36 degree water - not deep, just three to six feet unless it's raining. Oh yeah, the river is full of piranha. (They eat 'em every day.) Piranha are not vicious all the time, but I don't know how to tell you what to look for. (I watch Indians…if they get in, I get in.) Nope, I never seen anyone or animal die, drown, or even get a serious injury from a cable dumping.

At first I'd get in that fuckin' water and try and help salvage, but I soon quit that. There was even an unofficial rescue crew on duty to help at all times. Their pay was salvage of the freight, and quite a bit of poontang from the grateful ladies. You see, if the weight distribution on the platform became unequal it would twist, and everything would slide off. The code of the hills here was if you're married lady - no screwing around. But widows seemed to be afforded a much more lenient code. So if the salvage crew had an interesting looking male, one sucre (one nickel) got you to the middle of the river and you on purpose jumped off the platform and got rescued at river's edge thirty foot below with plenty of room to disappear for half hour. Official female costume was dress, nothing else. Not at all unusual for rescued ladies to reappear in anything but distressful mood. Ladies, where else can you get your pick of the town stud for a nickel? By the way, that cold water problem only lasts for a few seconds, then feels good.

This cable car was the movies – the television. You know how long it takes to get used to doing without anything that has a wire going someplace? 'bout one week. The worrying porch was my entertainment and my school. Yup, my school. It taught me if my belly was full, if the roof don't leak, I felt good and my shoes didn't have holes in 'em, I had more than enough to be thankful for.

That porch taught me fame was bullshit maybe, and probably a curse. Money was just another form of living off the land. I learned everything we do after dark ('cept sex) is unnecessary. We should be sleeping. I think them people who had nothing but each other were the happiest people I've ever been around in my life.

(How you get a milk cow or bull 300 miles down river? Ain't easy.) By river boat or canoe. A canoe has a round bottom, very-very easy to flip in the river. River boat round trip cocoa to Neuvo Rockaforte is 300 miles, cost 20 bucks and takes a week or eight days. The river boat captain weighed 300 pounds and had the best looking hooker from Cocoa living on the boat with him. He is chief trader for the boat company, he barters all the way up and down. Besides being a freighter and people mover, he has stuff to sell or trade, like fuel, rice, sugar; kinda like a general store on the river. Damn right, when he's busy loading and unloading at the stops, his live in love might be off in the bushes doing some business also. Boy, that would piss him off.

I saw that deal change from the primitive river boat to a hotel on water, a jungle tour for tourist. In 1990 they paid 1,500 bucks for three days…in 1962 it was 20 bucks for eight days (but didn't include food) and you sleep on deck in the open. The tourist deal hardly went half way up river and turned around.

I guess I'm goofy, but to me the jungle was like a movie that never ended, and never repeated itself. When I got off the plane from the states I couldn't get in the jungle quick enough, and I dreaded the day I had to start back. 'Bout 1970 "we" bought the Hotel Oriente, or I should say "I" bought it, for $5,000 bucks. Leonard shut it down as a commercial hotel about two years later and used it as his family's residence. We never kept it up and it slowly went to hell.

In 1974, I renamed it the "Jose Johnson" and painted it's corrugated tin roof orange. Got the name copyrighted in the Pacto Andino. I didn't have a sponsor for the 1975 Indy race. Best offer I had was for twenty-five grand. So I decided I'd rather starve than go for twenty-five grand. So I named the car "the Jose Johnson Oriente Express, Puerto Napo, Ecuador." After we got the roof painted orange, we had a sign made "the Jose Johnson Hotel" with the race car's picture painted on it. Pat McDougle made it, a real unusual sight that modern Indy car hanging on a deep jungle hotel. (Someone stole the sign.)

The last time I used my "royal suite" across from the hotel, one end of it dropped 'bout two feet. (house was on two foot chucka posts). Termites and dry rot had ruined my house. Eventually the Hotel too got rotten and fell in the river. Last time I saw it, vegetation was 12 to 15 feet high, as if it had never been there. Nature foreclosed it's mortgage on the Jose Johnson Hotel and repossessed it. It would be interesting to know how that property got into Leonard's name without my signature. I guess the hundred or so nights on the worrying porch were worth the five grand.

Fifteen years later in 1975 the jungle adventure was changed from gold and diamonds.

I forgot 'bout the great diamond episode. The original gold mine in the Oriente was called the "Sardinias." J. Armstrong, who worked for Union Carbide…a world class geologist. I always thought he was looking for exotic minerals associated with nuclear energy. Kind of a secret cat and a li'l goofy.

Well, at one point in the six or seven hour journey to the gold mine we pass an area (pretty big) where clay is the prevailing surface. The clay is baby blue and baby pink. I mean this clay looked like heavy paint. Here's the deal: diamonds and pink and blue clay go together like matches and fire. And to make things interesting this clay was loaded with quartz. The deal gets tough now, quartz and diamonds (in the rough) look alike, and weigh about the same. How you tell which is what?

Armstrong says, "Put stone in your ass and then suck on it. If it's dull it's quartz. If it's shiny it's a diamond."

I personally took that as a non-answer. A subtle way of saying, "It's beyond amateurs." We took 50 to 75 pounds of samples to Quito and shipped 'em to Brazil for testing. No diamonds. I don't think we got a phony report. If those had been diamonds in the samples, in a month we'd of had 100 diamond hunters there.

I'll tell you what this place did have was a snake called the bush master. This is a truly bad-assed snake that can get 'bout six or seven foot long. Nasty son-of-a-bitches would chase you like a dog. They're flat black when full grown and have bright yellow diamonds in mid-life. Like a caiman (the south American alleygator) it could travel 'bout one inch a minute less than I could.

In 'bout 1990 my master plan was to give the kids the keys and title to whatever I had in Florida, take a few bucks, then go to Ecuador with Margie. I wanted to build a house in the high jungle and spend the rest of our lives living off the land and visiting new (to us) places. I never got bored there and never wished for any more than we had. We found we didn't need wires, cars or airplanes. We found out how important food, shelter and health was.

I had some stock in a gold mining company in Bolivia (Battle Mountain). This stock wasn't worth a shit. The company was run by some people out of Houston, probably ex-gas station attendants.

They were using a fairly new process of leach mining (acid) that I thought would work in a new gold mine Leonard had acquired on the Ecuadorian-Peruvian border, close to Macarra, an army town. Main Street was 4,500 foot landing strip. This town had airplane hangers next to hotel, and in between stores. It was built in a desert area, but with some water and amazingly fertile due to volcanic residual of some sort.

As a stock holder I asked for permission to visit the mine in Bolivia. The answer was "You gotta ask in La Paz, Bolivia?" Well, OK, I wanted to show Margie Lake Titicaca, the highest lake in the world. I also wanted to show her the park where the Sundance kids tied their horses up in La Paz before they robbed a bank. So off we went.

La Paz is way high. The airport is over two miles high and the city is way down in a bowl type valley. I don't know if a horse could carry you up from city to airport. It would have to be a tough horse. I suspect they don't need any fire engines; not enough oxygen to burn much. When we arrived we got a run-around 'bout being allowed to visit the mine. "Got to wait till Monday." I decide to visit the island where they make reed boats and reed islands to meet the cats who built the Kon-Tiki. (Remember the ocean going reed boat that guy (Von Daniken?) drove from South America to where it finally sunk?) Yup, the boat builder was home. We ate a trout and the kids hit us up for matches (don't know why matches were so important to them). 'Bout seven or eight hundred people live there. They were supposedly all interbred over and over but they seemed pretty normal to me.

I never get over how small the world is getting. Here we are, way the hell and gone from the civilization at a lake in the top of the world in a foreign country, and somebody says "Hey, are you Smokey Yunick?" Turns out that 25 people from the Charlotte area are there working for Motorola, putting in a new phone service for the Bolivian government. All race fans.

Turns out we can't get permission to go to gold mine. It's way the hell and gone inland 300 miles and high up. "Fuck em," I say and we rent a Jeep and driver ('bout 350 bucks a day). We leave at 4:00 am. It's cold and we don't have enough clothes. Eight hours later we are lost and we are up 'bout 15,000 feet in a big-big tin mining town. You guessed it, they say "where Paul Newman and Robert Redford got killed in the Sundance saga." (Margie saw the tree).

Everything regarding minerals and hydrocarbons is a secret in Bolivia. By luck we find the mine. It is fenced and guarded. The guards asks, "What do you want?" I answer, "I'm stock holder and the president in Texas said it would be OK to visit." "Bullshit, we don't have anything that says that."Call Houston – this is an outrage!" A man comes in the guard office and asks, "Are you Smokey Yunick?" "Yup," I answer. "Well goddam, you hungry?" We lucked out from "can't come" to "honored guest, wanna place to stay tonight?" (Thank you but no, not with a Jeep rented at 350 bucks a day.) We got fed royally and then get a three-hour tour of the mine. It is up at 13,500 feet and they are basically cutting the top off of a mountain. Dynamite blasts every few minutes. The bulldozers, drag lines and loaders are really huffing up there. "Got any ideas how to get more power?"

Gotcha!

The leach process they were using looked good and better than anything else I'd ever seen, but I was shocked at the low value ores they were working. I sold the stock I had. It was twelve bucks and had moved down to a buck and a half.

Ecuadorian oil fields in late eighties and early nineties had field horsepower around 150,000 horsepower and growing. We are running most everything on crude oil 'cept some turbines, and they are on casing head gas. Problem is there is still no refinery to feed these engines in the area. I'm helping smooth out wrinkles like exhaust valves and turbochargers failing very prematurely.

I find vanadium in the crude is the culprit doing the damage. I get TRW to come up with a valve face overlay that triples valve life, but don't help the turbo exhaust impeller. So with the help of a friend of mine in Houston, Malcom McCants, we develop a crude oil looper to centrifically, and with a few small clean up steps, pass the vanadium on. With this in the oil supply line the turbo impeller gets relief.

Well 'bout in here, early nineties, Ecuador takes over the whole operation. Gulf is long gone, Texaco has been booted out and Cepe (name of Ecuador's oil company) express interest equivalent to us wishing to get AIDS or cancer, in my fuel. But they got a new problem I'm interested in. They found a bunch of heavy oil – 15 to 18 gravity – too heavy to pump, so Malcom invents a new process called a "vis breaker," which can get the heavy crude transportable by pipe.

They look it over, get all excited, cancel a 90 passenger flight out of the jungle, fly Margie and I to Quito. We're set for a big meeting 'bout our new technology. I'm looking at used Lears, Malcom and I are gonna be rich. It's nine years later and I haven't heard anything more 'bout it. I've now decided I'd rather have a Cessna Citation if they decide to do it.

Just before the vis breaker action, some of the wells had been in production 15 years or so and needed some help to produce. The average hole was 10,000 feet and produced 'bout 7,000 or 9,000 barrels a day. Damn right, really great. Well Reda pumps and oil drive was installed (artificial lift). The oil drive worked good, but the crude had lot of acidity and abrasive material in it and wore the pump cylinders out every two or three months. To replace the pump was about a 35 to 50 grand job (just for the rework rig). The hones necessary to salvage the cylinders weighed 'bout three tons and were in Midland, Texas. So freight to and from, duty and hone cost, causes a "buy new" decision – the hell with rework ($2,400 bucks apiece).

By now they got a mountain of worn cylinders. I tell Texaco, "Why don't you build a portable hone that you can carry in a Huey helicopter?" Kobe, the oil drive systems producer says, "Ain't no way." I say, "Bullshit." Texaco says, "Build it." I give the job to my son Smokey, he has a nice welding and machine shop.

I tell him what I think would work. Six months later I'm getting chewed out for running my mouth and not producing the stuff. By the way, the factory hone cost 240 grand. This was hard-hard shit, and they wore funny – big in the middle. I go to see where Smokey is with it. I'm shocked to find out $800 to a grand would pay for material and labor he has expended on the hone. So I get pissed and pay him off and take what he has to my shop. I got Leonard and Britt's company to get an agreement to hone all the Kobe cylinders for 500 bucks each and advised them to own the machine. It took me two weeks with one helper to make the thing. We built it in a walkway between machines. It weighed 1,300 pounds and cost 13 grand to build. Included in hone's cost was a new special 45 inch long dial bore gauge. I had Starrett build it to go with the machine.

I got Del Pico, Sunnen's sales manager to keep trying various cutting stone formulas. In 'bout six weeks we got it. Average cylinder, start to finish – 20 minutes and every bit as accurate as a new cylinder. Where we are at this point, I own the invention, Minga (Leonard and Britt's company) have the honing contract and two men to operate it. They can do three cylinders an hour ($1,500 bucks). The cost for this, two men, honing oil and electricity per hour is maybe two bucks. Yup, two bucks. Three shifts equals 70 cylinders a day.

I got Minga to build a windowless, well ventilated, tall roofed room. I taught his Indians how to use it. Reason for no windows and one locked door was, if Texaco saw how much money they were making, it would cause trouble. Within a month they have shown everyone the machine and bragged on the income. In two years Texaco forced Minga to sell them the machine and the honeymoon was over.

That hone deal was a one in a million shot, where you get a brain storm that flat gets it done and had durability. I tried to get Del Pico, Sunnen's sales manager, interested in building and selling the hone – "no sale." That total hone episode (five years) was kinda like trying to milk a cow on a hot day in a dirty stable. The cow's tail has wet cow shit on the end and every time a fly bites the cow, she swishes her tail and you get foot of long cow tail hairs, shit-covered, wrapped around your face. At this point you have several choices.

   A. Quit milking the cow.
   B. Cut the cow's tail off.
   C. Clean the stables and spray it for flies.

I chose to quit milking the cow. The last time I saw the hone was '93 in Cocoa. Like the Eveready rabbit, still going. There's a moral to this story. In our modern world "Fuck your friend first, then say you're sorry." I applied for a patent on the hone when I built it, but dropped it when I couldn't find a manufacturing partner.

Well, I still own half of the gold camp and two hundred acres, but in my last visit to Ecuador Leonard says "I don't remember you owning half of that property." I know that means I don't anymore, so I decide I'll wait till Leonard clears up some of these mysteries. I don't even know if he is alive. He is damn near three years older than me. Hard man to figure. When he got to be seventy he discovered pussy. With the help of a "peter mechanic" in Houston, and his knowledge of the human body and the behavior of a simple mechanical mechanism called a spring, he made Leonard a relative of the Eveready rabbit. Unfortunately Leonard's genes were attracted to very young females, late teens, early twenties. I guess this led to some expensive and maybe unverified conception miracles. You'd have thought Leonard would have known the best sex was more likely to be understood by older females.

Well, life's full of goddam unusual twists. Sometime later in a shop accident, an engine falls to the floor off of a three foot high bench. Unfortunately for Leonard, his new toy is between the cement floor and the engine. It hurts me to even think about it. Nope, I haven't seen him since this accident. I have visions of the ladies now calling him "flat dick," or maybe the mechanical peter wizard in Houston has recertified Leonard's toy and he's back terrorizing the young ladies looking for a rich, old, gringo husband. Thirty-three

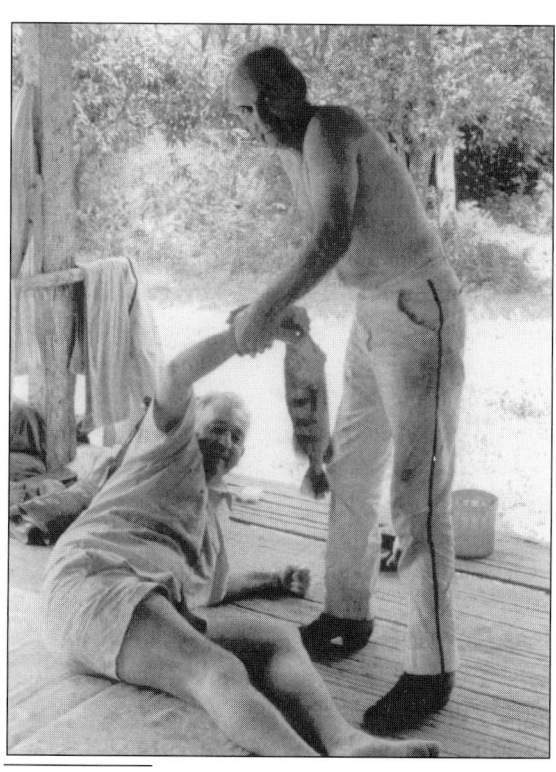

Catch of the day.

years we worked, dreamt and enjoyed each others friendship. In my whole life I've never experienced any disappointment as deep as my realization that there never was a real friendship. It was an almighty exercise in money.

What did I learn from him? Probably nothing worth knowing, but there is no way for me to describe to you what all I learned about what really constitutes real wealth, health and happiness. Family and friendship are offspring of happiness. Sense of accomplishment is personal examination of our lives frequently for a mental self-rating of good or bad.

Maybe the most important and shocking part was to see that wild animal and man were deadly enemies, and so were humans to each other. You doubt me? Try taking food away from a hungry child with it's mother or father is there. I don't expect you to believe this, but consider what the world would be like if murder was not a capital crime. Think about it carefully…I spent a lot of time in those 33 years where there was no law, and I observed seeing the law of the jungle in real time. I learned from the Indians, who I could only communicate with by gestures or with a very crude limited vocabulary.

The jungle gave me a very important present in showing me all of us are microscopic little nothings as compared to the natural forces of this universe. Your family – how you feel about yourself and your health – those are the real measure of your success or failure in a human's short adventure called life.

What can you do walking around in a jungle for thirty-three years? Find and produce oil, same for gold, look for diamonds…grow coffee, tea, pineapple, yucca…catch birds, animals and snakes…learn to make a dugout canoe…raise silkworms, learn the timber and sawmill business…raise rice…work on pipe lines, drilling, workover and oil field testing and production equipment…build rock crushing and gold mining processing equipment…learn how to raise Indian palm and collect it's oil…learn how to collect rubber and process it for the market… learn about many medicinal benefits of things that grow in the jungle…learn how to use dynamite and nitro…study earthquakes, volcanoes, geology and melted rocks…learn how to make diesel, motor oil, gasoline, methane, methanol, butane, propane…how to process casing gas and burn it in turbines, diesels and gasoline engines…how to make a truck, bus or car run on cow shit, chicken shit, cocoa husks, charcoal…how to build steam engines…I never could eat howler monkey that was cooked on a rotating stick …looked like a two-year-old human.

Lookin' over "Leonard's" gold camp.

I learned what it was like to use ayahusca, a hallucinatory drink – buck a gallon…'bout like peyote. I learned how to raise fish (tahatchuja), watched witch doctors (shaman) make medicine from local vegetation and perform sometimes unbelievable cures or relieve intense pain.

Learned not to drink gasoline for snake bite poison. (Diesel OK.)

Learned papaya juice, when fruit is still green is a meat-eating enzyme. Learned to grow plants that are used in perfume and cosmetics.

Learned how to run water for miles without pipe. (Bamboo…only works downhill).

Learned to grow and process sugar cane and how to make sugar cane whiskey. Learned in a jungle town on the Esmerealdas river (almost all people Chinese – ship wreck 150 years ago) Chinese girls don't go cross wise.

Never did learn to ride a horse or burro with a wooden saddle without getting two huge sores on either side of my ass.

Never learned to like snakes. Man, Ecuador is snake capitol of the world.

I'm not sure the jungle isn't a natural free university. I learned about people…actually, deep down we are all enemies of each other.

My 33 years in the jungle was 'bout like a 30-year college course about the mysteries, power, and wonders of planet earth. From all this I'm convinced at least two major discoveries in force remain to be discovered, and someday to be understood. This jungle course taught me that the world's population better start doing a much better job of using this earth's resources. I do not believe any of it is infinite. I'm convinced we can abuse nature to the point it's check and balance system could be forced to eliminate civilization and life for a "Let's start over from ground zero movie." Simply put – man may be the next dinosaur.

I brought back part of meteorite I found and gave it to someone at the University of Florida to examine. I guess it vaporized. Could never get it back. Did you know rock can be melted?

I don't know how it's done, but I've seen it many times. An exposed wall of rock, say a quarter mile square that looked like a shiny wall of a strawberry milkshake (like porcelain).

I used to travel, walk, ride horses and finally drive past an active volcano. "Reventador" was 'bout 15,000 feet. We passed on a trail road at 'bout the 5,000 foot level. Every night it made the sky red-orange (never quit). One day though, it must have burped. It didn't do the deal with the lava, but it changed 50 miles of valley. From the shaking that whole damn volcano done it moved rivers, mountains, villages, like they were a piece of paper. This volcano, from the air, don't look any different but the valley is a whole new deal.

I couldn't believe it – after the eruption I saw a 300 pound catfish hanging in tree. "300 pounds?" you say. Yup, biggest I seen on a every day basis was 50 pounds. An Indian said there were 300 to 400 pound cats in there. I believe now that there had been, but after the volcano deal they had to start over from one pounders. What's gonna happen some day if Reventador really lets go? (I'd day dream 'bout drilling holes in and running pipes out for steam to supply half of Ecuador with electricity.)

Ever hear the deal "curiosity killed the cat?" It applies to humans and I have never been able to figure this out. In the Latin countries of South and Central America, a never ending series of revolutions, guerrilla shoot 'em ups, violent strikes, inter-tribal conflict, mass protests, natural disasters, floods, earthquakes, mudslides, volcano eruptions and hurricanes seem to always be in process. Why do people out of harms way go goofy trying to get where the bad stuff is happening? For example, in the middle of a city a rebellion is in gear. There is shooting, tear gas, fire, bombs, and buildings falling. I'm busting my ass to get as far from it as I can get, but I'm crushed by hundreds of dumb bastards who want to see what's happening. As you can guess, their's is not the best plan to get to live to 100. I've been in six or seven or them deals and every one was alike. My biggest problem was not the disaster or combat, but those blocking my retreat, while running into the jaws of death or serious injury.

Being a part of this dangerous shit does not fit into my low-key travel method. My free advice: If you plan to check out Ecuador for yourself, don't overdress, over-equip yourself or meddle in local affairs. If you do you're instantly a loud mouth, rich, fucking gringo. Trouble then appears in big bunches. In seconds, for you there is no help. You are in what racers call "deep shit" – a real easy way to get dead. Believe me, when "push" comes to "shove" the nationals will join hands and you became a dog-shit gringo.

I witnessed for 33 years the slow but steady destruction of the jungle. It's plants, animals, birds and it's primitive people.

I've watched the abuse of natural resources. Water mainly. I'm pretty sure many species of living animals, birds, fish, bugs and plants were driven into extinction by abuse and greed. These species were probably important to nature's balance and useful to man's health. I'll never forget in the late sixties, Indians asking if we knew what was turning the snow black. Yup, it was the prevailing winds that send some of our pollution across the Andes, all the way down to Chile. Next time you fly over it, if it's not cloudy, look and see it for yourself.

In the 33 years I attended jungle university I learned something every day. My appreciation for water and natural resources constantly increased. At the same time I slowly became more and more hostile towards those who unnecessarily or selfishly violated 'bout every natural function that nature had provided for the continuation of animal, plant, and human existence.

It was a school that kept you on your toes. A list of sudden, unexpected heart stoppers:

– As you support yourself down a hill you notice your hand was 6 inches from the mouth of a sleeping poisonous snake for which there is no anti-venom.

– A blowout in the oil field. Suddenly over a half million pounds of drill stem, two miles long, in 40 foot sections are raining down out of the sky like Coca-Cola straws. Run? Which way?

– A week search looking for the supposedly tanned skin of world record jaguar. (We found it, but it's lost – tanning job was no good.

– Get permit to capture a 30 foot anaconda and the arrangements ($75,000 reward).

– Locate/place 25 foot crocodiles live. Gonna show ol' Crocodile Dundee what a big crocodile looks like.

– One of our Indian workers disappears taking an evening bath in the small river by the Sardinas gold mine. We find him in belly of a 25 foot five inch boa constrictor (72 inch in circumference at biggest place).

– See a rock slide start on mountain road. Suddenly a village is buried.

– Flood in canyon. How 'bout 30 foot rise in 25 minutes?

– The ever present latest story on where the Inca gold is.

– The con jobs. Even to a Colombian Indian with a quart of gold (it was silver, gold plated). He conned a 30 year river gold trader.

– Watch a volcano erupt and move rivers. Move billions of yards of rock and earth. Fill valleys and make valleys.

When you see the power of nature against man's efforts to contain it, you get the feeling of being a piss-ant trying to dictate to an elephant. I think what surprised me most was how quickly the need for water, food and shelter overshadowed the desire for cars, airplanes, electricity, hot water, bathrooms, air conditioning, restaurants, motels, TV, radio, newspapers, telephones, etc. I think one of the big surprises was nature's system of support for the able or disabled. That was handled by the family, not by the society. The weak or malformed were abandoned. Cruel? It sure seemed like it, but examined closely it might be the only answer.

I believe someone who was a peer in human behavior studies would find the Indian or say primitive people, interesting. All seemed to believe there was a form of control that should be obeyed or celebrated. The spread in beliefs ranged all over the place. The sun, the moon, a body of water, an animal, a volcano, a mountain. So, apparently it's not possible for humans to co-exist with same form of government. Very interesting to me. The same system was used by any and all of small groups or tribes as we use in the so called civilized world. A group of bullshitters, we call politicians, establish and enforce laws that force or cause the majority to support the minority in elevated life styles and system for their control.

How 'bout this? Can you imagine our world without lawyers? Nope. I never saw one Indian lawyer in 33 years. So you'll notice where ever you travel in any jungle, there are no BMW, Mercedes, Porsche, Jaguar or Lexus dealerships. But down there jails were not evident. Their system worked like an off-on electric switch. Punishment, as I seen it, was terminal and swift. I noticed one favorite deal was sacrifice of human or animal life. Modern society has renamed this as war, jail and tax.

Down there I learned our worldly possessions and toys commit us to life styles un-normal. I watch gold flakes wrapped in banana leaves being traded for one or two cigarettes.

The worrying porch school taught me I could very easily have walked away from today and lived the jungle life with no regrets. One expatriate worker said, "Smokey, you say that but you know you can leave any time you want – if you had to stay here it might be different." Yeah, maybe, but if I could move around in the jungle there is more here to see and wonder about than there are days in a lifetime.

I know where there may be lots of gold. I think I know where there are diamonds. I believe I know a real good place to drill for oil. I know a real good place to put a hydro-electric plant. I believe I know where some stuff grows that might cure cancer. I think I could get enough heat from the side of a volcano in Ecuador called "Reventador" to generate enough electricity to power the northern half of Ecuador. I believe I know where huge food crops could be grown without fertilizer or bug killers.

Well, "Why didn't you stay there Smokey?" I don't know. Could have been a lot of things. Like my shock and disappointment of Leonard going money goofy. Hell, how come you didn't become a firemen or a jet pilot or a race driver like you wanted to? Maybe it was because I'd already seen that movie and I subconsciously didn't want to be a part of wrecking that wonderful real-real world. Margie could have handled it easy. She walked the jungle till her feet bled, slept on bamboo floors, washed in icy and piranha rivers, learned to live off the land. Leonard built a real good oil field service shop and built up a big beautiful and profitable farm. I helped him from day one (1961), but maybe his pure German lineage made him autocratic and greedy. I don't know, maybe as I aged, I was the one who slipped out of sync with the real world.

I learned from the Indians, anything you don't understand, eat it, piss on it, fuck it or kill it. But never leave any major life decision unsettled. After my last trip there (I believe 1993), I said "Fuck it" and I forgot it.

Adios.

Ocelot

I'd been working in the jungle oil and gold fields of Ecuador 'bout three years and had brought home some live animals I shouldn't have (although it was not illegal then). Critters like kinkajoos (honey bears), ocelots, and margays (miniature tigers). We had two live honey bears living in a big bay tree back of the house. They were nocturnal and when I came home at 12 or one or two in the morning, one of 'em could drop down out of the bay tree around my neck and scare the hell out of me. Actually they were very affectionate as long as they understood the game…but scared they were bad news. They had five razor blades in all four corners, so you had to be cool and not startle them unless you didn't mind 100 or so stitches. By now, after seeing our ocelot de-fanged, claws removed, sex organs altered, plus living with the honey bears, I was opposed to trying to tame wild animals.

Right or wrong, and even though my daughter Kilroy has had a pet store for twenty years…I'm against trying to capture and tame wild animals or birds. In short, I'm very opposed to any living thing being held captive. By 1963 I was retired as "Jungle Jim, the animal catcher"…well almost. I've got a friend named Roy Jones. I knew him in 1947, and in 1949 he followed me down to Daytona and helped me for a year or so. Now, Roy was a good mechanic and a world class welder. Fireball keeps his modified at the shop. Jonesy falls in love with racing. He and Fireball get along super. After about a year Fireball, Jonesy and the modified are a real pain in the ass. So I kick 'em out into the cold cruel world. They moved to the Charlotte area to seek their fame and fortune as racers. In two or three years they are back 'bout twenty pounds lighter each. They survive off of racing, but not too well. Roy's got a wife and baby now and gets a job as a welder at Cape Canaveral to help get people to the moon. 'Bout 1965 Roy says, "Could you bring me an ocelot for my daughter?" I say, "Yup, I could, but I ain't gonna." His daughter begged me to do it and like a damn fool, I agreed.

Next trip we get couple ocelot cubs. I give 'em to an Indian to raise and tame for 'bout eight months. The day before I get a job near (within fifty kilometers) where the cubs are supposed to be, the Ecuadorian friend of mine who placed the cubs with Indian to housebreak them, drowns in a whirlpool a mile from his home while coming back at night in a dugout canoe. He is only person who knows where cubs are, and the "Oriente" is a big-ass jungle. To make a long story short, I can't figure out where they may be, but I've got to come back with an ocelot. A couple of days later I'm in a good size jungle town, Tena, capitol of the province Oriente. I see about a twelve-year-old girl with an ocelot on her shoulder. Next thing I know I get snookered. I'm suspicious the cat's drugged and wild, but the girl's dad says "No, no, we've raised it from a week old." My partner Leonard who lives in the area (a Texan from Jordan, Texas) questions girl and her dad and says "I think deal's on the level." You see the Indians would bring snakes, monkeys, big birds like parrots and macaws, and cats like ocelots and margays to town to sell to tourist gringos (suckers). Back in the early sixties a trip to the Oriente was considered (and usually was) one hell of an adventure. I first went in 1961 and when we got back to Quito, people born and raised in Ecuador sixty years old and more, including government officials, would ask you what it was like. The Oriente was truly a jungle. Next problem, daddy says "fifty bucks." Well, shit! Usually five to fifteen bucks would do it, but daddy knows he's got the only cat in town this weekend. Finally forty bucks including a Indian wooden cage gets ownership transferred.

We are staying in a dump of a hotel owned by the mayor, a guy named "El Loco." Yup, everybody called him "Loco" or "Fatso." It was called the Hotel Danube. At five o'clock in the morning, the roosters in the lobby, and in the community bathroom would start crowing. Nobody in a jungle town needed an alarm clock. The fucking roosters were so noisy you had to be deaf to sleep. (I could now I think.) So we get up to have breakfast in hotel dining room. I look at the cat in the cage and the "light" comes on. I've been "had," this goddam cat is plumb wild. I doubt over two days caught – the very worst kind. (The dope's wore off and the cat is pissed). The Indians made a drug out of a certain plant that would calm down a full grown tiger for a day I believe. OK, I go buy a few doped bananas from a local bird seller. No deal, the cat won't eat. Next, I get a piece of raw chicken from kitchen. The chef tries to dope it and get the cat to eat it...no deal. All that happens is the cook somehow digested some and he is floating around in some dream world.

Well, no problem, El Loco, the mayor, is now the cook.

As we eat, three or four pigs are around our feet. Kenny Rich (remember him?...my 1960 Indy car owner) is there. We also own a gold mine 'bout fifteen kilometers away. Kenny is always drinkin.' Hell yes, Scotch and water 5:30 am. Well, he gets pissed 'bout hogs in the dining room and kicks one. Ecuadorian pigs don't like getting kicked by a gringo. Only place for medical attention of any kind is Catholic church and infirmary. 'Bout an hour later Kenny's foot is stitched up. (It took 15 years to heal). A traveler's tip: I recommend, if you're eating in a restaurant and there are pigs under the table, don't kick at 'em.

We've chartered "Captain Von Zepplin" and his push-pull Cessna to pick us up here at the Tena International Airport (2,000 ft. grass strip with cows and burrows walkin' around). Kenny's leg, and finding a dead man in vacant lot across the street holds us up 'bout a hour (I'm a witness). El Loco, the mayor fills out death report, "heart attack" but I notice his belly is cut open from just above his pecker to top of his gut. Looked like a Colorados Indian gut job to me, done with a machete. But maybe he had a heart attack and fell on his own machete, make sense to you?

We go to airport. Von Zepplin has plane running. "Hurry up, the weather is going to shit over the top of a mountain range, we've got to cross now." "Oh shit! I forgot goddam cat." We send Indian "Jesus" who worked for us to get it. Yes, Jesus (hay-suz) is a very common first name there.

OK, we're off. In two or three minutes we are in the clouds. Von Zep makes two and a half-climbing 360s and is aimed for Quito climbing hard to clear top of mountain. Lowest place is 14,500 feet. I also know it's all the plane can do loaded to clear the top with over two to three hundred feet. (All this shit is dead reckoning: no radio or radar). Jesus is sitting in the back with the cat cage on his lap. A very strange thing happened – in the one-and-a-half hours back, the cat pissed for one hour and fifteen minutes into Jesus's lap. The temperature is 'bout 25 degrees F – how much piss can a cat store up? I told Jesus "frozen ocelot piss was in the US...a famous sexual aphrodisiac...'bout 500 bucks a treatment." He then quit shivering.

OK, I'm going back tomorrow. That cat's got to have certain shots to clear US Customs in Miami. Quito has a very-very famous veterinarian. Jesus takes cat over. It's Saturday, and it takes a lot of bullshitting from Leonard and the minister of customs, a friend of ours who works for us part time. (Minister of customs, Ecuador 1961, annual pay 'bout five grand.) His name is Galo Burbano, a hell of a fine friend.

So we talk our way into an appointment, but the cat tears world famous doc up. Never got the shots in her. (Turns out it's a female.) Well, now what? I get Galo to get me a phony shot report. It happens. Now we are set. I'm going home tomorrow on a Braniff 707.

Saturday night I get cat out of its Indian wooden cage in the kitchen. (I forgot, we have an apartment in Quito at the Colon Apartments. The apartment kitchen has one way in and out – a sliding door.) I lose control of the cat as I'm tying it to the stove (it had an Indian rope around it's neck 'bout eight foot long) "The hell with it!...I'll worry with it in the morning." And shut the sliding door.

Saturday evening I had bought a blue, el-cheapo suitcase and cut three holes on one side, and put travel stickers over the holes. It's 5:00 am and I'm gonna put cat in suitcase. Jesus, Kenny and I go to the kitchen. "Oh shit! The cat's dead - it hung itself" I grab a kitchen knife and cut it loose and get it on the floor. This was the first big mistake of the day. That cat ain't dead and has started to eat my arm. After 'bout five minutes, Jesus, Kenny and I are standing on top of kitchen table.

After all the commotion, here comes "Jungle Jim Leonard" (bare-footed) into the kitchen. He laughs his ass off..."three grown men held helpless and captive by a little twenty pound pussy cat." The Indian wooden cage and blue suitcase are on floor in middle of the kitchen. Soon the cat decides it don't like Leonard either. Leonard jumps up on the Indian cage. The cat then stamps both Leonard's bare feet with both front paws. Now "Jungle Jim" is on kitchen table with us. Finally, I manage to grab the rope and pick cat off of it's feet. Now I'm in charge. With gloves and towels we get the goddam cat in the blue suitcase, with 'bout eight inches of rope hanging out. The extra rope is gonna be my handle to get it out in Daytona.

In the custom report the agent says, "What's its name?" Man, I'm ready after all this. I say, "Culo" (in spanish that means "asshole"). Galo Burbano, the custom's boss, meets us at airport and says Braniff ain't happy with the forged medical paper, so Galo says, "Carry her on and keep the suitcase back of your legs." Yeah, hell of an idea, I've only got to sit that way 'bout four-and-a-half or five hours. I get on the plane. This flight has a huge Ecuadorian male flight attendant. He grabs my blue suitcase just before I sit down and says, "No anne-mols allowed dis plane." "What animals?" I look at his snoot, then I decide this steward is not gonna budge. Well, I'd waited till the last minute to get on because of the cat. It is now time for the plane to leave. Here comes Galo the custom minister. He meets my suitcase and the steward at the bottom of the steps. He jerks the suitcase away from "Jumbo," the steward, and there's 'bout a five minute argument at foot of the stairs. All engines been running seven-eight minutes now. Soon, here comes an Ecuadorian cop. He jerks my ass out of the seat and off the plane. So I can join (or at least observe) the big-big bull shitting and screaming contest going on. By now I'm trying to think of a new worse name for the cat. Suddenly Galo wins. I get put back in my seat. The baggage door opens and my blue suitcase is thrown in. I'm not too popular with anyone on the plane as I've caused it to be delayed fifteen minutes or so.

Back in them days (I was in first class because of Galo's sister who was a stewardess), they fed you something every fifteen minutes. I was afraid to eat, figured ol' Jumbo would poison me. He took defeat very badly. You'd think that was enough wouldn't you? Shit no...it was just getting ready to get good, me and the cat haven't even hit the US yet.

We arrive Miami. My big suitcase full of dirty clothes I open for inspection. The blue cat bag I don't.

The cat is silent. I'm pretty sure it's dead from cold and lack of oxygen. Custom guy says "What's in that one…the blue one?" I say, "An ocelot." Well now here we go again. "Open it up" he says, "I want to see inside." I say, "Not good idea" The customs area got 'bout five hundred people, and a mile of glass everywhere, not a good place to liberate a pissed-off ocelot. The custom guys start to get nasty. I say OK, "I'll open the goddam bag soon as we agree on who's gonna put him back in, or you agree I ain't liable for what happens after I open the bag." He says, "I think it's dead anyhow." I say "I agree, but just in case that motherfucker ain't, you agree I don't have to put it back in?" Well he pushes a button and here comes Mr. Chief Customs Inspector. After he got the story he tells me to "Open it up." I say "Bullshit! You open it." He says "How I know you ain't got box full of drugs?" That does it. "OK, I'm gonna open it rite now." The chief, for some reason changes his mind, holds suitcase down and says, "Get that fucking thing out of here." I'm pissed he's called me a drug transporter. "Let go of it!" (I'm gonna open it up.) Mr. Chief Customs Inspector has apparently had a bad day before me. He's also got both hands pushing down on the suitcase while he says, "Get that out of here while you're still ahead!" I notice his face indicated possible murder…so I took bags and left.

Done now? Hell no! I got to catch an Eastern flight, a twin engine Eastern Falcon to Daytona. In preparation I go to souvenir place, buy some more stickers to put on air holes of dead cat suitcase. I notice rope hanging out of suitcase so borrow a porter's knife to cut off rope. The rope made it look real suspicious. I call Roy Jones in Daytona, "Meet me at airport in two hours, your cat is on it's last journey to your daughter. Get several pair of welding gloves and bring the new cage for the transfer at the airport." All set. Roy's happy, his daughter is delirious with joy. "What's it's name?" She asks. "Culo"…"Oh, what a lovely name." It's about dark and I'm headed for the Eastern plane. An Eastern agent stops me. I'm carrying the blue suitcase. He says "Sir, Eastern doesn't allow animals in the cabin." Holy shit! How could he possibly know the bag had a cat in it? Well, I'm too far gone to quit now. I go on down to the flight and I'm first on. Got the suitcase behind my legs with a trench coat dropped over my legs. Here comes pretty stewardess. "How are you?" etc. The "dead" cat goes "grrrrr" loud as hell. I turn around and look at stewardess. She's stopped with one foot in mid air. I start coughing and barking. She buys it. It's still fifteen minutes till flight time, but not another sound.

Finally, Daytona. No fancy shit. Come down steps and walk to terminal. "Pappy" the boss of Eastern in Daytona, says "Let me carry that." I say "No" but he insists. I figure I'm tired of the bull shit. He says "What's in the bag? Feels heavy." I say, "An ocelot." He laughs like hell…he knows that's bullshit.

Well Jonesy and daughter are there with station wagon and cage. By now I decide transfer will be at his house. I get him off to the side and tell him cat may be dead. Still not another sound. Ten minutes later at Roy's house, we put on welding gloves and open the blue suitcase to look. Dead my ass. That sucker came out of there like it had a 500 pound spring in it's ass. OK, it's in the cage, but rope still on it's neck. Got to get it off. Well, in process of taking the rope off the cat, it makes leather shoe laces out of Jonesy's welding gloves.

Finally the job is done. "Well, Jonesy you got to get the cat it's shots." There's a lion farm fifteen miles south, bound to be a vet there that can handle it. Nope, that didn't work. This cat still has all it's female sex parts. (They can and do emit a spray and odor that's pretty skunky…worse than the Budweiser commercial.) They leave cat out of cage. It tears furniture to shreds and gets on top of refrigerator. It won't let 'em in to get anything to eat for days. In four months it destroyed all the furniture in the house, and the house stinks like a pig barn. It chews up some wood furniture and digs holes in the walls. Really a cute, wonderful family pet. One day Jonesy's asleep on the couch. Cat decides to eat his hand that was hanging over the couch. Well, Roy's able to go back to work three months later…the bite got bad infected.

"Well Smokey, would you like this wonderful pet back?"

"Fuck no!"

So lion farm says, "We'll take it and breed it, and give you pick of the litter."

However, in between visits lion farmer disappears and "adios Culo." I don't think it cost Jonesy over fifteen grand to get home back to normal. And only lost 'bout ten grand in missed wages. If you have a daughter that wants a cute ocelot as a pet, see if you can interest her in a eight-foot rattlesnake instead.

Smokey Yunick, Ph.D.

In 1963 a friend of mine then, Gary Cunningham, said, "How 'bout lending us some tractors and trailers?" I was a heavy duty truck and trailer dealer. "Who's us?" "Us" is local civic leaders, with some foresight, who have been mesmerized by a bullslinger named Jack Hunt, to bring a broke down aviation school from the Miami area to the Daytona airport, utilizing the old left over military barracks here.

Jack Hunt was real. When I called him a bull slinger, (he was that) I say it reverently. Besides his talent to sell using only one medium (speech), Embry-Riddle's birth, if examined by experts, would be acknowledged as very effectively and skillfully presented. With my background in aviation, naturally I'm a candidate to vote yes to a flying school in Daytona.

"Us" gets Embry-Riddle moved up here in a month or so. Everything put together maybe was worth fifty grand. I mean some of this shit dates back to 1929. The airplanes were old, with band-aids and patches. Maybe kindest thing I could say is, they were refugees from the South American process. (That's the last stop for wore out airplanes.) Jack comes by to say "thanks." I'm prepared to write it off as a Gary Cunningham and Jack Mullins exercise in dreamland.

Jack Mullin really was 'bout most visible and noisy booster of this deal, but I hate to report his over-zealous pursuit of the insurance policy (Yup, Jack was a big-assed insurance man.) Somehow he pissed off Jack Hunt. Mullins gets shit-canned out of the deal and now Gary's the top cat with Jack Hunt.

This deal is based on dreams. No money, no credit, really a hopeless future, but Jack was a very famous cundrum pilot (you know, big silver deal, US Navy, kinda looked like a big silver hot dog. Maybe to you – I know what they looked like to me.) Jack received the Harmon trophy from President Eisenhower for flying one of these for 'bout two weeks non-stop from US to Europe, Africa, Puerto Rico then Cuba, 364 hours non-stop and no fuel added. In aviation the Harmon trophy is 'bout like winning the Winston Cup or the Super Bowl: it's big.

I notice Bill France ignores the whole deal. To me that's strange. Bill's now an avid pilot himself, and not too bad. Facts are, in a year Jack says, "France is a big egotistical prick." France tells me Hunt's "a dumb fly-by-night hustler who couldn't pour piss out of a boot." (I said, "You mean like your kid Billy?") Well, I think, "Damn, that Hunt's not to dumb, he figures France out rite quick"…so that gets him a lot of points with me. You see, I was pissed when France refused to help.

When France went public to sell Speedway stock I made seven various speeches to the local Rotarians, Moose, Lions, Raccoons, Kiwanis, you know the deal. (Nope, not the Ku Klux Klan.) This was before I found out us racers were charged ten times as much for the same stock he sold to his friends. If you get the idea I'm down on France, you're wrong. All I'm doing is telling you what happened, and how it happened. You're only getting my side of it in this book. You decide for yourself if you think Bill Sr. had a pointy head, or if he should have been screwed into the ground when he left. Keep in mind I raced in NASCAR twenty-four years, and some of that well after the birth of Embry-Riddle.

I also paid $1.00 a share for 1,000 shares. (I saw a receipt for 200,000 shares for ten cents a share to the local Pontiac dealer who did nothing but kiss France's ass and make a fortune off of Pontiac brass hat cars.) Every Pontiac picture you ever saw of a Pontiac NASCAR racer saying "Stephens Pontiac" was free to Stephens. I see now he owned the 1962 Pontiac I owned. I never checked. Believe it or not, I never knew there was car owner money at year end. You guessed it, he didn't help in the Embry-Riddle deal either.

One day after six months of moving up here, Jack says "Smokey, I need you on the board of directors." I looked at him and I ask "Jack, do you use drugs?" He says, "Hell no I don't. Why do you ask?" I answer "How in the hell can a high school drop-out be on a board of directors for a university?" Course I'm flattered, so I say, "OK." I'm still racing and going to board meetings is really a pain in the ass. By now I really like Jack, and I think I believe this son-of-a-bitch is gonna pull this off. In the board meetings we discuss and argue for three hours or so 'bout once a month, then I have to come back to work on the race car till

The Board of Directors of Embry-Riddle.

2:00 am. But as years slide by, school's really going now, headed for 5,000 students. (I know that's not that much, but we started with 'bout fifty students.) I notice that in real life Jack usually does the opposite of what we directors voted on. It's a waste of my time to go to the board meetings, and that's something I ain't got enough of as it is.

Also, in examining my usefulness as a director (by now I'm thinking of quitting), the facts look like if Jack had of followed our (the board's) recommended procedures, Embry-Riddle would have been bank-

Me and Bunkie after graduation.

rupted within two years. By now being a director on Embry-Riddle board is very desirable to the local upper crust. Local upper crust is, as a rule, a collection of a community's successful business types and politicians who are socially connected in various exclusive membership arrangements, who operate on clever arrangements, like "who's scratching whose back, one hand washes the other, don't go across the street to get gypped, let me do it."

Jack says, "Don't quit," but he don't cry too much, 'cause he learned how to use these social egotists to his advantage.

A rare thing happens. A really good, sincere person replaces me. The Chevy dealer, Spence was his name. In that time frame he was more useful than I could have been. Believe it or not, ten years after Embry-Riddle came to Daytona the community still ignored 'em. Spence started a successful "Let's appreciate the economic contribution the University has brought to the area" campaign.

This high school dropout has a doctorate in aeronautical engineering (honorary). Jack decided to honor me and Mr. Semon Knudsen with the honorary degrees. Mr. K. was president of Ford Motor Company at the time, and my boss at Ford. Jack had me do a graduation-key speaker deal. Since then my adventures in high education abruptly stopped. I'd like to think I helped Embry-Riddle happen, but I can't prove it no way. You decide for yourself.

Jack was running wide-open like a 600 horsepower diesel tractor and the big "C" bit him in the rear. Nope, he didn't whip that one. In a year he was gone. I really liked him. I know I learned from him, but I'm not sure what. His funeral was a big deal at the University. It was absolutely packed, and at the end the Jack I knew came back. In his last wishes he requested a song to be played at the end of this very-very somber and sorrowful ceremony. Wide-ass open, loud, they played "There's a Diesel on My Tail." It threw

Me and Bunkie after graduation.

everyone into shock. In a few seconds I recovered and started laughing, and thought, "You son-of-a-bitch, you did it one more time."

One day they named the Daytona airport after Jack, but it was not blessed by the local politicians and bullshitters. Shortly after they built a new 58 million dollar airport that we needed like another asshole, Jack's big plaque never made it to the new air port, and Jack, you never happened anymore. It's now Daytona International Airport. It's down to one airline now (Delta). If they pull out we'll have two terminals we don't need. And some flights from a piss-ant midget jet? As of 1998 Delta's talking 'bout leaving. I believe there is a major lesson here. I think all county commissioners and city officials should have to take eighth grade test in all subjects to be qualified to run for office. Right now we're getting a new international terminal, but no airlines. I wonder if that will hurt attendance at the local races?

I'm glad I kept a picture of me in the stuff you wear to get a doctorate – cause you might not believe this part. Now? All I get from Embry-Riddle after Jack died was requests for money. When I got tired of that, I don't even get a free key ring any more. Last time I was over there I got a parking ticket and fine.

Don't misunderstand this as a complaint. I mention it only as an example of maybe our not quite perfect society, where the etiquette is, "Don't tell me what you did for me yesterday, whatcha gonna go for me today?"

Daytona does have a multi-million buck golf course and headquarters for pro golf. But no tournaments. How are they gonna fund a tennis capitol? A hi-buck marina (empty). We have financed 'bout 6 million for a motel. Now we financed a big parking garage that's losing it's ass. Our town is paralyzed for four days for a colored person orgy completely out of control. This town is owned by NASCAR and the motel association. Governed by a bunch of nitwits in their pockets. The fix is so easy. Vote those mothers out and enforce the laws as they were 30 years ago.

Funny-lookin' Grasshoppers

Italy-Naples…I've been transferred out of the 97th Bomb Group, a B-17 outfit, to the 1st Emergency Rescue. What did that mean? I'm not sure exactly, but we sure had lots of secret stuff.

I assumed it was an easy goof-off job. Well, maybe, and maybe not. Some of the assignments could be real hazardous to a man's future. This assignment was punishment for the Russian bombing I did in Budapest, and also for taking and losing General LeMay's flak suit in the process. No question 'bout it, you should of been able to get a better insurance rate in the 1st Emergency than in the 97th. My first deal is this: strap a Higgins boat to the belly of a 17 and drop it to a crew of a ditched airplane in the ocean. A Higgins boat is equipped with engine and sails and supplies to take care of sixteen men for a month or more. (A really nice boat – all wood).

Here's the deal. You get to 1,000 feet and slow down to just over stall ('bout 100 miles an hour), pull the salvo ball and drop the boat. It has three big chutes, and when it hits the water, it automatically shoots 'bout four lines out for survivors to grab before the sharks snap their asses up.

I know, I know, "What the hell does this have to do with helicopters?" I'll get to it in a minute, just hang on.

So I've dropped a couple boats in practice and everything went OK. There's this big deal today in Naples, the US Air Force is gonna demonstrate a jet airplane. So at this show is this new jet built by Bell aviation, the B-17 belly-boat rescue invention, and something that looked like a big grasshopper with a propeller coming out of the back of it's head parallel to the ground, a sideways propeller coming out of it's ass. This whole damn thing hangs on about a two inch diameter steel shaft. Sikorsky, a Russian kinda name, is the manufacturer. I looked at it and thought, "How bad do you have to fuck up to be put in one of these things?" Little did I imagine 1960.

Well, here we go to demonstrate these three new war winners. The jet melts its tail half-off during take-off. Oh shit! Next, I drop the boat. Yup, the chutes screw up. The hi-buck Higgins boat is now two million tooth picks in the Bay of Naples. So far our new stuff is not too impressive. The helicopter does like it's supposed to. I don't know the reason, but that thing really intrigued me. So I go ask pilot to give me a ride and show me how to fly it, and I'll give him a ride in a Higgins boat. No cigar.

Fast forward to 1960. I'm a GMC dealer in Daytona. Cape Canaveral space station is being built ass over head and a contractor wants to buy twenty dump trucks at 'bout thirty grand apiece. Here's the deal: it's a bid deal. Each dealer gets twenty minutes to present bid and give trucks a sales pitch. I'm last. My time is 3:40 pm to 4:00 pm and the bid will be awarded 4:05. Well, it's one-and-a-half hour drive, but I cut it too close. I can see the motel I'm meeting customer at 3:20 pm. But I have to cross the Banana River, and it has an open draw bridge. When the clock says 3:55, I see a helicopter going across the river. I get to motel 4:05 pm and the customer is gone. GMC Orlando got the deal. Man, I was pissed, but on the spot I vowed "never again."

The next day I called every son-of-a-bitch I knew in aviation and asked, "Where you buy a helicopter?" Well, what I assume is the answer is "on an island off coast of South Georgia," place called St. Simons Island. So I call the Hughes helicopter dealer. Yup, he has a couple, "Wanna see one." "Yup"…I'll be down tomorrow." "Bullshit!" This is Tuesday and I have to qualify race car Friday. "How about I come down today? OK? See you in two hours"…and he does.

Man, this is really a goofy looking thing, a Hughes 269-A. With no wind, runnin' wide-ass open she'll do 100 mph. "How much?" I ask. "Twenty five grand and it's new." Well, that's not too bad. I'll start with it then after a year or so get a better one. So in forty-five minutes I own it. Had the cash from an invention. The money?…well this is the late '60s and I've moved from dead broke to not too bad money-wise. Little did I know disaster lurked 30 days ahead, and my net worth would be back in two figures.

Dealer says flight training goes with the deal. It's a two week school with flying and ground school. I'm thinking, if I could fly all the shit the Air Force had, including 29s, I don't need any help to fly this goofy lookin' piss-ant thing. The dealer is smart, and says "When you gonna fly it?" By the way, all this is in back of my shop where he'd delivered it, back there I've got several open acres. I say, "In 'bout an hour." I notice when I come out to learn to fly this thing he's around. I try to start it and I'm having trouble. He asks, "Could I help you start it?" I agree, "Yeah, good idea." He starts it. "OK, sure, that's easy…thanks."

OK, take off…Whoa boy!…This thing is a little sensitive. I ain't too sure if I got it up, I'll be able to get it down. The dealer walks over, "Could I help you take it off?" I agree, "Yes, thank you." Well now we're in the air. At fifty feet I've got more than I can handle, but I'm gonna land it. As you can guess the dealer landed it. He told me if I went back to his place and studied and flew two full days he thinks I'd "have it." Well we get up there at night. I go to a video ground school (cold as hell). Dealer doesn't show up till 10:30 pm. To shorten the story up, by Friday afternoon at 5:00 he tells me I need another week.

Man, I'm really hot. This cat, once he had the money didn't do anything he said he would. The airfield is big and we are 'bout one half mile from his hanger. I land and tell him to get out. When he

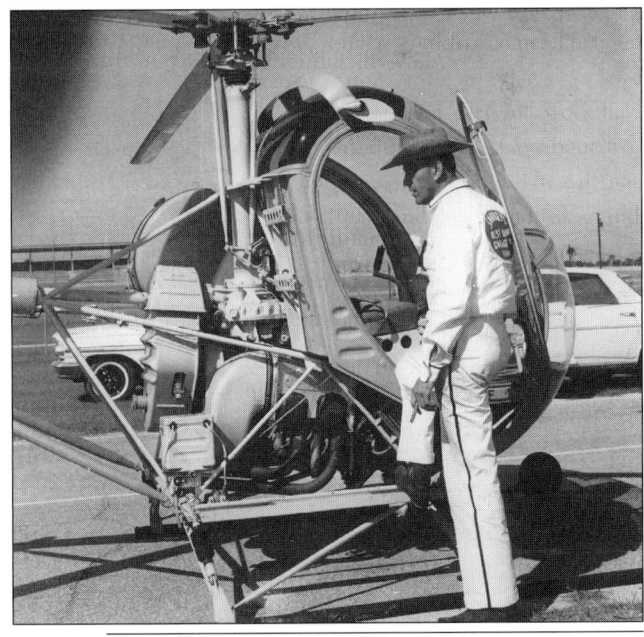

It used to really piss France off when I flew it over to the track.

does, I take off for Daytona. I know fuel's gonna be close, but I figure it will just make it. Well, when I get there, it's blacker than a well digger's asshole. I guess it took me five more minutes to get it on the ground.

I flew it for a couple weeks every day I was here for an hour or so, and was able to pass an FAA check-ride in a month. Part of the test is emergency landing with engine off. (This is called auto-rotation.) That ain't easy for a rookie helicopter pilot. Well, I lucked out. My inspector didn't like going to the ground in a 269-A. That last five feet is the tough part in an auto-rotation and apparently it was especially rough in a 269-A.

I had a lot of fun with that thing, but France really would get mad when I'd land it in the garage area. Course that made it even more fun. And he'd get pissed if I followed race cars around the track.

It was good for other things, too. The helicopter taught me ground effect. If I was at five hundred feet and set up a rate of descent of two hundred fifty feet per minute, you couldn't get to the ground. At 25 to 30 feet above the ground it would quit coming down. The shop's backyard is normally four feet above the river. So if it took off and just stayed a foot above ground and headed to the river soon as I left ground it would drop to a few inches above the water. (Idea was, don't move the collective controls and see how the thing reacts.) OK, now I'm gonna build an Indy car with a tail rotor and steerable rudder over each rear wheel. I've really looked rule book over, and no problem. I've even experimented with ropes tied to tail boom and tried to measure how much side force tail rotor had. I was dragging men around back yard of the shop the force was so strong.

My private heliport in the back of the shop next to the river.

I never should have called and double-checked the rules 'bout tail rotors and steerable rudders. Shortly after, there were rules in reference to controllable airfoils. But we did try a wing over the cockpit in 1961. Yes, they let us try it, but I gave up when lap speed was same. We could run wide open all way around, the corner speed was same as straightaways. But the total was not enough to get around the track faster

One day two things happened that killed my affection for the li'l Hughes. A salesman landed with a French "Gazelle." This is a turbine helicopter with enclosed tail rotor. He gave me a ride in it. We got to 165 miles an hour faster than a cat could lick it's ass. Next, I have to take mine to go to Melbourne, Florida ('bout 100 miles south). So I'm along side of I-95 headed south and I look down and see a Volkswagen. It's pulling away from me. I'm in 'bout a 35-40 mile an hour head wind getting dusted by a VW. Man, that done it. I had just sold another invention for 'bout 100 grand and was flush. I called a friend I had at Bell in Hurst, Texas 'bout gettin' a Jet Ranger.

He said "Come on out, I'll get you a supreme deal" ('bout 10% over list – 140 grand). I rode one for two or three hours. After this I want one bad. Unfortunately I'm 'bout forty short, so another good idea shot in the ass.

I'm working as a consultant for Mr. Knudsen at Chevy, and tell him 'bout my "almost Jet Ranger." I'm surprised when he says "I've always wanted one myself." Hmmmm…I say, "How'd you like to own half a Jet Ranger?" (He has a home in West Palm Beach) He answers, "Hell of an idea."

So I order it from Bell and four months pass. I've put up a $10,000 deposit. The phone rings. My buddy at Bell says, "The price went up to $155,000, either agree or we'll return deposit." Knudsen says "Let me handle it." The next word I get is, "Bring $155 grand in certified funds when you come." Knudsen says, "Bullshit, I'll call president." I go out with my half of certified funds and sit there for two days till Knudsen's half gets there. I thought, "He called the president of Bell my ass." (Shit, I found out that even the US Army had to pay in full for each and every helicopter before they flew it out.) Bell had no delinquent balances. I watched Westinghouse pilot wait for 4-5 days for money to clear.

The Jet Ranger satisfied me. We kept fooling with it and souping it up to get it faster and smoother. If you pushed it, it would run 145 and very smooth. Movie and TV people liked to charter it because it was so smooth. We taught Mr. Knudsen how to fly it (no, I'm not kidding) and fly it pretty damn good. But he had a medical problem and couldn't pass the physical. I never found out what it was.

During the 1980s the insurance was going up every year (from four grand to thirty-one grand per Ranger. In 1987 I finally ask insurance man "What the hell's going on?" He explains, "Here's the deal: nobody wants a helicopter pilot over sixty, so we just raise the premium till the pilot drops out." I said, "You got the job done." The insurance plus expenses, meant we had to charge 400 to 450 bucks an hour to make a profit in the charter company. (About in here most all of our customers quit us.) Also, there were about ten helicopters in South Florida that drug dealers had and chartered for any price to write off a Jet Ranger. They didn't have a charter license and nobody did anything about it. So I have to sell my best and only toy. It broke my heart to end the helicopter deal cause I really enjoyed what all you can do with a helicopter. Even if you had enough to afford a Lear jet and have a business, a helicopter really gives you much more time to maneuver. For up to 250 miles it's faster than a jet. The back of the shop is still a licensed private heliport, and only one in Daytona.

Sometimes newlyweds would charter the Ranger. Man, let me tell you this from all the reports and observations I have, the first helicopter ride will make a virgin out of a hooker for two hours. It's bad news regarding sexy. Helicopters are hard to fly, much harder than airplanes. I can't think of anything that can eat your ass up quicker if you goof up. I believe 'bout anybody could learn to fly one, but to fly one for a lengthy period of time, say 5,000 hours, and stay alive, you have to be an expert at thinking five minutes ahead of where you are now, every time you open the door and climb in one.

Me in the Jet Ranger.

Mr. Sikorsky, I admire your engineering talents in pioneering the helicopter, but I can't help but believe you were a little dingy to have had that dream. And to have gone to the trouble to make the helicopter commercial that took vision and faith, 'cause the helicopter is just one notch past the bumble bee and the guys who were building airplanes with wings that flapped in 1915. Still, I wish it was still like it was. There was a time where I could be on my way in the air in five to eight minutes from this desk at the shop.

If I've excited you with the helicopter story, and you got a couple of bucks– forget it. Today a good helicopter is close to a million, and cost 'bout two hundred grand a year including interest, insurance and maintenance. Here's the ironic part of the helicopter adventure: I never again had a truck deal where having a helicopter was useful.

Helicopters can get you in a lot of trouble in a hurry. For example, I was landing into the sun once, and got between the upper and lower wires of some 13,000 volt stuff. The wires got to galloping up and down and you have to follow their rhythm or you get toasted. Just as I backed out and turned, the tail boom antenna touched a wire. That filled the cockpit with smoke. I remember seeing some kids playing underneath so I'm blind, trying to land in an arc away from the kids. I land on a hill at a bad angle and here comes cops and fire engines. To keep from being arrested for landing on a hill in town I decide to take off. (The cops ain't got no jurisdiction over helicopters do they?) In the process, I have to jiggle the cop off of the landing skid by bouncing the copter while 'bout eight feet off the ground. I did get to meet some state highway police because I landed at a Gulf station for gasoline once.

Birds and wires are the biggest ruination of helicopter pilots. I've found out no birds live in the swamps or in desolate uninhabited areas. They have all moved to town. I'm serious. For you bird lovers, it looks like in another fifty years you'll all be walking around town on a foot of bird shit. Man....there are millions of 'em around every town.

The biggest benefit I had from the helicopter adventures were the awareness of ground effects relating to aerodynamics. I built a ground effect prototype car for Indy in 1972 with ground effect tunnels. I had decided to let Tony Mucho in Detroit make the actual body out of aluminum, so the prototype was in his shop up in Detroit. You'll never believe how I lost the car. Tony got into an argument with his wife (this is what he told me) while eating dinner. He shoved a hot baked potato (too far) in her mouth to shut her up. By the time they got it out, the divorce was planned by his burned wife. Next Tony gets sick and croaks. Mamma sells all the shit in the shop. By the time I wake up to all this, it's "adios" Indy racer. He never had the decency to call me and tell me he was gonna die, and come get your racer pieces.

Who knows, one lousy baked potato may have changed the course of aero race car history. In spite of this, I'll still vote for Tony the racer...would you vote for him? All I got to show for it are three badly time worn pictures.

But for you Corvette lovers, when you see the rear engine Corvette in the Corvette Hall of Fame, this ground effect Indy project saved that car's ass. It was dead by decree and waiting to be destroyed and converted to scrap. I got Herb Fishel to get it out of the morgue and got Chevy to loan it to me for experimental reasons involved in a ground effect design. Chevy did not participate in this project 'cept loan me the car.

The story about using the car for aero test was a ruse to save the car. It would have been the only Corvette prototype missing. This car was 100 percent John Delorean.

Incidentally, the car was flawed. I can remember driving it out of Chevy research and development, and getting front wheels three foot off the ground before I got to the guard shack. Hard acceleration would wind up the front end like a Fordson tractor.

Well, finally Chevy said "cut car in four pieces – furnish pictures and an affidavit confirming destruction." No way to stop it now, so one day I lit a torch and cut the son of a bitch down the middle and then across the seat area. I still have the original death certificate, 'bout 24″ x 30″, framed and signed by Herb Fishel. They made it big for photos. Herb wrote on it to "Rest in Peace," etc.

Well, I bring pieces back from junkyard (Herb don't know this) and I cover 'em up. I showed it once to a potential restorer and he got tears in his eyes big as dinosaur turds (a real Corvette lover).

Four or five years later I meet a goofy Chevy dealer from a hick town around St. Louis…Steve Tate was his name. He was at the shop and accidentally saw the pieces and when he heard the story he wanted to buy the pieces. Well, my master plan was to give pieces to a rich, dumb Corvette lover for a bonded agreement to restore it. To get Steve out of the loop, I tell him I want eight grand, and agreement that he restore it. I'm sure that will shut him up and end the story. Goddam! He says "sold" and whips out the loot. Well, I'm fucked now. I can't back out, I've done said it. I'll be damned if 'bout three years later he's got it running. Well, at best it's kinda "corn cobby," it lives again.

Steve had one of the afflictions that most of the then car dealers had…he drank too much. Well, finally the world crashed down on him and the car is sold. I don't know whole story, but after a rough series of ownerships, the car ends up in Chevy's possession, or I guess I don't know who owns it, but as you look at that thing, visualize that laying on the ground, cut in four pieces with a torch.

Champion Hound Dog Tamer

Margie. To tell you about Margie, I got to kinda beat around the bush a little.

Most of this book is written in a period when I'm deaf, and trying to get back some ability to hear again…nine months and six ear operations, as of now…nope, still can't hear.

Update: seventh, eighth, ninth and tenth operations got the job done. Thanks to Dr. Lundy and Mayo clinic I now am able to hear some, and I am hopeful for more improvement as things heal up. Thanks also to Dr. Earl Harford at "Starkey" for hearing aids.

Last night, five days after operation number seven, I woke up and had totally lost my ability to orient myself. The room started spinning and I was puking and having lots of weird, bad feelings.

I've had this experience before, but not for over five minutes.

In high altitude formation, hauling bombs in a B-17, when we had weather that caused us to make vapor trails. We flew very close – overlapping wing half-way, in a diamond, 20 or 30 feet over or under other cat's wings, 'cept for "Tail End Charlie." He flew close but low. Well, that's where I usually flew. Nobody wanted it because of turbulence and shell casings through the props and windshield. I liked it cause I had maximum room to move. Up in the vapor trails, lines of clouds streaming and spiralling past you at three hundred miles an hour, I'd get thinking I was sliding backwards, and get to jerking with the throttles from "closed" to "wide open." After much of this disorientation, I'd get nauseated, and finally hand it to the co-pilot for five minutes so I could recover. No, everybody who flew behind vapor trails had the same problem. The real truth was, I and nine other guys were in a position to die real damn quick. The co-pilot I had hated bombers. Like all of us he wanted to fly a fighter, so he would sit there with his arms crossed, scared shitless. We can't and don't talk (radio silence) and really, he can't fly a B-17. (Who would know that better than me?) But when I got hurting real bad, I honestly did not give a shit about living. I think it must be that way for everyone. Have you ever been really hurt and felt this way?

OK, now in my life I have been very badly injured and run into some very serious medical problems because of a life-style based on "do it today, tomorrow may not happen." Which turns out to be a bad approach, because it's like taxation on taxation, you pay twice.

When it calmed down a little (the room spinning slower), I thought, "Goddam, I got to tell you about the most important part of my life" or maybe at my hi-mileage condition I won't get a chance to. (Hell, let's face it, if I was a used car, I'd be parked in the last row, out in the weeds.) Nope, that ain't sad, it's the way it's gotta be! Now you and I never think about this much, but none of us want to die, yet we all know

CHAMPION HOUND DOG TAMER

we will.

One day in July, 1997, I was attending the annual dinner of the Pontiac Oakland International Club with Margie and John Delorean. We were the speakers ('bout 1,500 people at the dinner that preceded the annual awards presentation). Well, there are many awards, and many judges, and simply put …the awards presentation was all fucked up. It ends too soon so now the host, president, and master of ceremonies, Mr. Lloyd Burger, is in deep shit. He's gotta kill some time.

So he decides to give a nice resume of my racing career, but it's still not enough time used. So he puts me "on" to kill time. Well, even though I'm deaf, we have figured out a way to communicate. With Margie writing questions from the audience and me answering, we can go on for hours. Well 'bout 10 minutes into the deal, someone asks "What was the greatest experience, or event in my life?" Without any hesitation, I said, "Getting together with Margie."

I'd never thought about it. I'd have guessed it might have been when four or five times I was sure the story would end in seconds or less. Maybe winning a big race, Indy, Daytona, Darlington. Or maybe induction into a hall of fame. Nope, in a flash the answer was "Margie." We have been together 'bout 17 years, and not all of it was smooth and perfect. My whole life I lived kinda like a hound dog…"Don't chain me up – I can't handle that." "Just let me be me, and I will always come home sooner or later." Well now, from the hound dog's point of view that's pretty good, but from a female point of view I'm sure it rates about a 98 percent bullshit vote. Margie I guess, was a natural born hound dog trainer. And with a little help from nature (regarding older hound dogs), I guess you might say she tamed me.

Now you all know about love, and all the stuff that goes with marriage, but not very many people ever really know, or experience "mating."

These pictures speak for themselves.

Where you enjoy each other's company, you don't notice each other's negatives, you really try to make each other's day better, you feel each other's pain or joy,…you really are a team. I can't imagine what it would be like without Margie. She's like a part of me, and what I am, and what I do. I respect her even though she's got the instincts of a 18-year-old go-go dancer. No, she was not that way when I got her, I trained her. Nobody ever sees her in a negative mood, always funny and laughing.

For you ladies reading this, I doubt I'm an easy person to live with. I came from a world that doesn't exist anymore, where you worked your ass off, regardless of hours, till you got it done. Where just doing it was nothing, doing it as good or better than anyone else, was the target.

From a world where it was OK to say, "I'm sorry, I fucked up." From a world where it was allowed only once to make the same mistake. I came from a world where a handshake was as good as a fifty page contract. I came from a world where if you smack somebody in the mouth and say "I'm sorry" it was unacceptable 'cause it still hurt. I came from a world where the politicians were as crooked and rotten as they are today, but nobody knew about it. So maybe, I hope, after you females read this, you find something in it to make you appreciate your life with that fat, bald, lazy, asshole you married.

What I'm getting at is you could have a lot to do with "baldy's" life-style.

Maybe Margie should write a book on "how to remodel, groom, feed and train defective hound dogs." Margie has made me a better person. I bet without her right now I'd be a 100 percent miserable, old, asshole sitting in this dump of a garage waiting to die. ("What do you think Bryson?…What do you think Grant? Bill France Jr., I don't give a shit what you think.")

But Margie had good material to work with. If you get a subject that's 85 percent defective, it's lots easier to show a big improvement than if you start with someone only 15 percent defective. I first met Margie in 'bout 1957. She was going with a friend of mine who was a world class, champion pussy-hound. She was a receptionist at the Lincoln-Mercury-Edsel-Ford headquarters and to sit up there you had to look like a movie star and be stacked like a brick shit house. Man, she was beautiful. I would have went after her like a 10-year-old tiger that hadn't had any in two years, 'cept in my 10 commandments, I would never mess with a friend's woman (unless she asked me…and she never asked me). So I told her "if her deal didn't work out…whistle." 'Bout 22 years later, her husband died…and the rest of the story was gonna happen just like you know the sun will come up every morning.

You know racers, when we are young, and even when we head into the "autumn years," and get ready for the "golden years," (that's a lot of bullshit) we can make it halfway decent by ourselves. But Margie gave me a wall plaque 'bout 18 years ago, that says, "A man who has no problems to solve is out of the game." Here's where you really need a mate. Because when you "bark" and nobody "jumps," or you have to finally admit your creativity is slowed way down, you forget. Or maybe you just got too much wedge in left rear (money). It's like you're turning 8,500 and it's coming hard, and some young cat comes by you at 9,300. And now you realize it's gone…you can't do it and it doesn't upset you. Men, that's where we all need a Margie.

She says "Maybe you can't race anymore, but your better in the hay than ever." I smile and think, "If I'd got hold of you 20 years sooner, I wonder if you'd say the same." You know what I mean? Your partner sees a lot of other good things we can do. Sometimes I get to thinking 'bout Tim and Frances Flock, Herb and Helen Thomas, Ralph and Mitzi Moody, Lee and Elizabeth Petty, and I wonder (they all been married 'bout 50 or more years), if it was as good for them the whole time as it has been for me with Margie. If so, they are very lucky people. The message is: if you got a Margie, don't take any chances on losing her, there ain't that many around. Also, for those where it's not fun and good, it's, in my opinion, no indication you're doomed. I think for the male's, probably the first time you got married your pecker outvoted everything else put together.

For the females, you were in too big of a hurry to have a home, kids, fancy clothes and vacations. You didn't notice he farts in bed, don't smell too good as a rule, rolls over and goes to sleep soon as he "comes," leaving you hanging from the chandelier…or you didn't notice you weren't getting all his "business," but you got a good idea now your losing your only customer. I'm afraid the only fix is "give up and back off and watch,"…or go look for someone who matches your specification for a good mate.

To me marriage is bullshit. I never got to vote on the deal. That was all decided 1,000 or 2,000 years ago. How did they work it then? Did they have marriage license, preacher, churches, etc.?

I really believe pussy has caused more wars, killing, misery, than any one thing on the face of the earth. I'm married to Margie only because I could see she felt inferior, like a second class lady. She was living with me and some "friends" treated her poorly cause she didn't have a ring. I was sure the marriage would blow up the good deal we had. Well, lucky for me it didn't change anything. I didn't need the ring or the piece of paper. You couldn't have pulled me away from her with a bulldozer. But to her it was important and that's what counts.

So what it gets to is "whatever's fair" and "whatever turns you on." "Love" is a four letter word that has as many meanings as the four letter word "fuck." We need a word that means "respect," "admiration," "companionship," "helpmate" and "sex." How about "rachs?" I know it's got five letters, all I'm trying to do is get something started for a new word…the right word. If I was smart enough to be able to solve all the world's problems, I wouldn't be sitting in this junky garage Christmas Day writing about my life. I'd be on some fancy island with my own jet and 100 foot yacht outside, living a miserable life with a young, sexy, cheating bitch that I couldn't handle in the hay. Trying to keep her from spending money and screwing the boat captain, pilot, chauffeur or maybe the gardener. Why not write at home?…a lot nicer…don't know…I seem to need quiet…no interruption, to keep a line of thought. Haven't you noticed how I start in one direction and ramble off into a totally different world some places?

You want to know why? So much has happened in my adventures, 1936 seems to be as far back as I can remember, and as I write, I start remembering things, and writing them down for you to read. When I re-read to correct, I think, "What the hell did you stray so far for?" I don't know. All I can tell you is that's how it comes out. I'm sure this is not the way a "pro" writes a book. Well, hell, I ain't no "pro." This is first and only book I'm ever gonna write about my life. I don't want no "pro" telling you about me in the correct form…just pouring on the good stuff and leaving out the warts and blemishes. This is the fourth time I've rewritten this whole book. I'm trying to give you the high spots of 60 years or so of my life.

I think my adventures will never be repeated. Not because of any reason except the world changes every day. If you wanted to discover America, too late. Some Spanish cat named Columbus did it in 1492 (or something). If you want to be a Pony Express rider, too late. They use jets now. Want to be in on the beginning of big time stock car racing – too late. The train left 50 years ago. So I'm writing free hand (which is pretty shitty). Margie has learned how to translate this with a computer. She gets it down where it can be read. Between the two of us, you're still dealing with two amateurs, so you, the reader, will have to bear with us, and try to figure out and understand the history. I'm sure no one else will ever tell it like it was, for business reasons. And let's face it, there are at best only 50 people left that could tell it and five or six times a year we lose another. But remember, I've lived it all. Within a mile from where it came from, and there's a good chance, even though I sure never knew all that was going on, I didn't miss much. Not for business, or being nosy, let's just say "probably pillow talk" on a near daily basis from people who lived every day off it (and some of it in a horizontal position).

I wonder what Margie thinks when she comes to some of the parts where society would criticize my behavior? I did very few things I thought were wrong. I figured what I thought was right was OK, but sometimes I exceeded my personal limits. You won't believe this, but when that happened, I'd feel real bad, and try never to do it again. But there was a period when after the sun went down, my breed of racer started to get thirsty and started getting hard. (I think about 7:00 pm.) The devil would take over the mind of the model racer, so when I couldn't come up with a reasonable reason for by behavior, I'd file it under "I don't know…I think the devil made me do it."

Worked then, but I know now it was just a crutch.

Margie's "two cents":

I was twenty-seven years old when I met Smokey and have considered him a friend from "day one." I loved his sense of humor, and was entertained by his romantic adventures, professional efforts, victories and defeats.

We were all single at the time, and as attracted as I was to Smokey was afraid he was too "wild" for me. So I married his friend, and because of that, Smokey has remained a constant thread in the fabric of my life for forty years. We always kept track of each other, and when times got bad for me, there was always the thought…"What if?"…"I wonder." But there were five children yet to be born, and all of them treasured. I had two children (a boy and a girl). He married and had three (a girl and two boys).

Smokey's wife Patt, became very ill and passed away. A couple years later my husband, Wally Hink, died of a heart attack. Smokey and I got our second chance, and the timing was right.

Nothing you read here shocks me, cause I've already heard it all. I knew what I was getting when we got together, and I've always known he was a "keeper." Smokey is my best friend and, lucky for the world, "our time" didn't happen sooner. Of course, there were those five children waiting to be born, and it might possibly have really messed up a good book. (Not that a lot of this stuff wouldn't have happened if I were in the picture sooner, I just might have never known about it!) I am enjoying this re-visit to Smokey's past. And can tell you the reader to "hang on, you're in for one hell of a ride." Enjoy…It's all true.

As to the ladies who got to him "first" I say, "Thank you one and all…you taught him well."

Margie

Eleven Rose Bushes

I told you about my dog Pluto, my companion from 1936 through 1941. Well, the war, my fast and furious racing schedule, and other adventures didn't leave any time for a lot of good stuff like dogs, fishing, holidays, vacations, kids, etc. So after Pluto, and after the war, the dogs at our house were small, belonged to the family and lived at the house. Hell, sometimes they didn't know whether to wag their tails or bite me, I saw them so seldom during daylight.

'Bout 1985 my daughter had a Great Dane boy dog, that was 'bout a year old and had all his genes working. Well, that dog became a big burden to her, running away, barking, you know – all the bad shit that comes with a 180-pound, horny, boy dog. So she tries to find him a new home, but no luck. Dog pound and the gas pipe are only deal left.

Dewey, my vice president of sanitation says, "We need a big-big dog to protect the shop." I say "Hell, ain't had a guard dog for 35 years, why now?" Dewey says, "World's changed."

OK, we got 'bout four to five acres fenced in so the Great Dane moves in on trial.

For what ever reason, the dog will never get over six inches away from me. I go to get a license for him. "What's his name?" they ask. I decide real quick, "Deputy Dog." Why? Hell I don't know, guess I liked the "Deputy Dog" cartoon, 'member that?

Deputy Dog turned out to like race cars. When the engines roar in the dyno room, hell, he just lays down beside where I'm standing and covers his ears with his paws. This sucker is big too. Every time I leave for over an hour and come back, he puts his front paws on my shoulders and washes my face with his tongue. (Ever notice how boy dogs spend so much time licking their balls and asses? I considered this method of washing my face unsanitary and would get decidedly pissed, but ol' Dep never got the message.) I tell Dewey to take him to the dog pound every day for first two weeks. Dep liked me to walk him with a leash, so every night just 'fore dark he'd 'bout bring the leash to me. Deputy Dog got adopted and his citizenship papers in the third week.

I had a "cracker" customer, a 'coon huntin,' loud mouth, know it all son-of-a-bitch (you know anybody like that?) Man, I didn't like him. (Still don't). Well Leonard (the cracker) goes to pick his truck up one evening from the back parking lot. (Which Deputy Dog has annexed as his domain). Next thing I know the bullshitter's on the roof of his Autocar (big-big tractor). I notice the dog…and the 'coon hunting expert is very upset and his ass is kinda hanging out (apparently Dep removed part of his pants to get a better grip on his ass). I'm not sure if that was the hardest I ever laughed…if not, it's in the top three. You know a lot of hunters are real rough on their dogs, I liked seeing the dog having control of the "mighty bull-shitter." Nope, he didn't come back for a long time, but I didn't give a shit. I'd just as soon starve to death as work for people like him.

Deputy Dog's College Adventure

When it's decided Dep was gonna be part of our shop family I noticed he had no manners. He never listened to anybody, was pretty dirty and smelled bad, so I had Dewey tie him to a small truck and wash him with soap and water (with a hose). If you're gonna give a big dog (180 pounds) his first bath, don't do what we did. Dep like to have strangled his self. Dewey was exhausted, and wetter than Dep. From that day on Dep hated garden hoses of any color or kind. Oh yeah, we finally figured out how to get him to kinda like it. (A tip: it's a good idea not to get a lot of soap on your dog's asshole, balls or pecker.)

Well, OK, Dep smells better, but what about manners? We check every dog college in town and find the supposedly "best" (for sure the most expensive) dog college around. The fee must be paid in total and is "not refundable" if you fail to bring the dog to class. Pay fee and wait for position in next available class. It was a surprise to me, but the dog's owner, or owner's proxy, must bring dog and attend all classes. Shit, I thought for that money they'd send a bus for him. Nope, it's six or seven miles away. Even got to send his pedigree for them to see. (Yup, Kilroy, my daughter, had one). Kinda like getting into Yale or Harvard.

I can't go, so Dewey, who is Dep's godfather is appointed. Goddam classes are 7:00 to 9:00 pm. Dewey showed up in dress clothes – a double-breasted suit coat, hat, and a necktie. Things don't go well. 'Bout the third week college president calls and says I should come, "Dewey is not handling Dep correctly." I say, "Can't come, I gotta work." A week later, "Your dog disrupts the total class." "Huh?" Seems like Dep tried to screw a lady police dog in the class. Well, goddam, don't all boy dogs want to screw a lady dog who thinks it's a good idea? Next week Dewey says, "He had to bring Dep home early, he started a big fight and 'bout ten dogs got tangled up in it."

President of "Bowser U." calls, "Your dog is out, expelled, don't bring him back." "OK, Give me my money back, your college failed." "Nope, we ain't giving nothing back it ain't our fault, it's your dog's fault." "I'll be at next class with Dep and a lawyer."

Bowser U. says, "Let's try it one more week with Dewey." Dewey gets back to shop early. Dep bit another dog owner cause when Dep was sniffing his dog's hind quarters, he socked Dep and Dep got even. (Hell, that's like a hello hug in dog land). Oh hell yes, immediate expulsion, kinda like getting drummed out of the French Foreign Legion. Only thing they didn't do was cut the buttons of Dewey's double breasted suit coat.

Next morning office gets a call, "We are mailing a full refund of Deputy Dog's tuition." I then trained Dep myself. I got him to mind me (if he agreed.) If not he'd just sit down, cock his head and look at me with kinda a "fuck you" look. Dep showed me all I knew about training dogs could be written on the back of a match cover. Well hell, a man can't be good at everything.

In a few months he became so over protective that if you shook hands with me he might decide to bite your ass. Now when ol' Dep clamped down, 'bout every time the "bitee" would have four leaks in his blood pressure system. As rule it was a transient bum or a snow bird messing around in the back parking lot, but sometimes it would be a customer coming to pick up his truck and Dep would have him up on the cab roof bellowing for help. I don't recommend this kind of protection as good business practice. Dep got where he could about piss "Goodyear" on the sand in one pissing. You know this is a racer's type dog for sure. He didn't like Firestones, and would piss on every one he got a shot at.

He never bit any racers, but for some reason he didn't like A.J. You ever notice there are some people dogs don't like? I got two boys, Steve and Sam. Dogs love Steve but they avoid Sam and seem to mumble bad stuff about him. I wouldn't have got too pissed if Dep put his brand on A.J.'s ass. Maybe I got a perverted sense of humor, but A.J. seemed to always push people around. Truth is, I think A.J. knew ol' Dep wanted some of his ass and was afraid of him.

Deputy Dog loved to ride in a car or truck (I guess most dogs like to ride). Goddam, you'd open the truck door and in a hundredth of a second Dep was sitting in the passenger seat with his head bumping the roof. In 1987 I decided I had a belly full of motor companies, racing and the truck business, so I committed motor company consultant suicide with a lot of negative criticism in Popular Science from 1975 to 1987 in reference to shitty American cars. I then started telling the complete line of GM Vice presidents and general managers, and Lloyd Ruess, GM President, all their 1987 prototypes were shit boxes. Next, I closed the truck business down. All that was left was Dewey and Deputy Dog.

Motor Tech (the company that was in a joint development contract with GM regarding the hot vapor cycle engine) didn't want to fund the hot vapor cycle engine after GM said, "You pay from here for further development." Motor Tech "bailed," so the hot vapor idea got shut down. I decided that since the truck sales and service business had been a money-losing, pain in the ass for 16 years, it should close for "reorganization." That was thirteen years ago, I'm still not reorganized, but all parts and tools are still sitting there and if I want to reopen tomorrow, every thing I need to do it with is still there.

Seems like every so often (seven years?) A man's priorities change, and when I change it's all over in thirty seconds. I joined the Aviation Cadets that way, I left the Air Force that way, my first marriage ended that way, I left NASCAR that way, I quit Indy cars in the same way, I walked away from the motor companies that way, I quit Popular Science (after 28 years) that way, I left Circle Track (after 11 years) that way, I left the jungle oil and gold stuff (after 33 years) that way, I quit drinking (after 30 years) that way, and I quit smoking (50 years of that) that way. I don't recommend this system to any one, but seems like there is a point where I decide, "Fuck it… it ain't worth the hassle." There is no question this is a bad way to become a wealthy, know it all, pain in the ass old fart, but a man's gotta do what he's gotta do.

With the truck shop closed, I fence in the shop property, hang "No Trespassing" signs, shit-can all the phones. The message is zero business done here – stay out. I got new phone number (it's listed) and just me and Deputy Dog and Dewey, vice president of sanitation, and Bill Davidson, the office manager. I've got enough new shit started that it will take forty years to finish it, and I'm 65, so I ain't got time for anything else.

Now I find myself talking to Deputy Dog. I do what I want to do – when I want to do it, and don't have to listen to the goofy fuckin' motor company politicians. Don't have to bust my ass and listen to the fucking idiots at Motor Tech (hot vapor engine). Don't have to deal with ass-kissing, lying half-truths published to gather advertisers compliments and dollars.

This sounds like I'm right and the world is wrong. Nope, not at all. In my makeup I can mesh or turn the same rpm or run in the same gear, but with very few people. I ran wide open not just to do it – I insisted I had to try to do it the best. I never considered money after I made a deal.

If I lost my ass I never cut back a dime. I expected my bosses to be peers in whatever their profession was. I expected all people and organizations I dealt with to be honest, to govern knowledgeably and be fair. Trouble is, that is a dream world that if ever it did – don't exist anymore. So maybe I'm the lost ball in the high weeds who zigs when he should zag, etc.

The wheelbarrow wasn't big enough for long.   *They wore my ass out.*

Maybe society had it right in 1948, racers are social misfits.

Whatever turns you on or whatever's fair, suits me. I'm gonna finish it up like I started, still trying to do it best. I like the army deal…"Be the best you can be," but not just at game time.

Dep was so faithful…that dog would die for me, and I hadn't been that good to him. In 'bout here, when I'd tell Dep about something I was gonna do and he'd cock his head and act like he understood, I guess I seen what Dewey saw in him. He is getting up in age for a Great Dane… 'bout seven years is it. Don't ever get a Great Dane for that reason, they are almost human.. You get very attached and "zoom," it's all over.

I get to thinking, he has lived his whole adult life at this garage and has never experienced sex, never fathered puppies. Who knows what a dog gets out of that part of life? One day I mentioned to Margie I was gonna try and find a lonesome female Great Dane. My daughter, Kilroy, heard me.

In about a month it was Christmas and my daughter gave me a big cardboard box and in it was a 40 pound, light brown Great Dane, girl puppy. Yup, eight weeks old and already weighed forty pounds. She had paws big as your hands, fur like velvet, dark ears, eyes and nose (giant eyes).

"What are you gonna name her?" I instantly said, "Junkyard." Now this puppy became an 185 pound lady Great Dane and she lived at the house, but came to work with me everyday and Margie picked her up at 4:00 pm to take her home. Dep scared hell out of her for 'bout a month, so I told ol' Dep "better be nice to her, one day soon you may change your thinking."

Junkyard was funny, bouncy and playful; actually damn near human. Dep taught her 'bout biting and guarding. Yeah, boy! I doubt any four humans without weapons could have survived Dep and Junkyard if they were trying to harm me. When Junkyard is eight months old ol' Dep has discovered pussy. He and Junkyard play all day, but "no sale" on Dep's ideas 'bout playing "doctor." In about a month's more time, Junkyard has decided she likes the sex stuff, and man they really go to it. Once Junkyard got cranked up she wore poor ol' Dep's ass out. It don't take long before the puppies were coming. (I got screwed too, the birth ended up costing $5,000.)

I build a nice dog house. 'Bout 8:30 pm the first puppy arrives. I go to bed 'bout 11 pm after five puppies. At 2:30 am the tenth and last puppy is born…Margie is pooped. The next eight weeks of Margie's life she was as surrogate mother for Junkyard's puppies. In two weeks, original dog house ain't half big enough. OK. I build a "big mother," 10 foot by 10 foot, and put it in the car garage. Junkyard can't make enough milk, so Margie bottle feeds half of 'em. In a couple days, Junkyard's decided to let Margie do it all. I think maybe Deputy Dog should go live at the house for awhile, if nothing else, to give Junkyard moral support. He goes over but seems to ignore the whole deal and don't want to play with the puppies.

Hell, I figured he'd get a kick out of seeing what he'd helped create. Nope. OK, back to the garage. In about eight weeks each puppy weighs forty pounds. But in order to weigh forty pounds, each puppy has shit eighty pounds. In order to clean their 10 foot by 10 foot pen daily, I put puppies in a wheelbarrow and take 'em to a fenced in dirt pen for the day, if it isn't raining. Then every evening I wheelbarrow them back up to garage for their inside house. Margie is plumb wore out. She has been feedin' some puppies with a bottle, taking 'em to the doctor to get their shots, washing 'em, cleaning up dog shit two hours a day. She even had to take Junkyard to the doctor cause she gets sore and infected feeding the puppies.

One day I notice I can barely push the wheelbarrow and Margie says she had to take couple puppies to vet. I ask, "What they weigh?" She says, "40 pounds." Holy shit, no wonder I couldn't hardly pick up and push that wheelbarrow – 400 pounds of wiggley dogs. Deputy Dog and Junkyard were racing dogs, so I decided to give the puppies to racers.

"Crankshaft North" went to Humpy Wheeler at Charlotte Motor Speedway.

"Lug Nut" went to Richard Childress and Chocolate (one of his crew).

"Oil Pan" went to Banjo Mathews.

"Cam Shaft" went to A.J. Foyt.

"Thunder" to Jack Bowser.

One went to a ranch in Florida and two went to minor league racers. My son Rex got a big black one just like the one we kept. (He called his dog "Woobie," don't know why).

We kept a big beautiful male, black and shiny like a marine's dress shoes. His name was "Crankshaft" (south). Man he became a whopper. 'Bout 190 pounds and nine feet from the ground to top of his front paws standing up on his hind legs. This dog was the most gentle-natured…even more human-like than his mother.

Boy, by the time this ends, ten weeks after birth, with air freight, dog shipping cages, shots, papers; five grand is shot in the ass.

Twelve weeks later guess what? Junkyard and Dep are starting a new batch.

Well, this may make you mad, but Junkyard had an abortion and her momma stuff shut off.

Junkyard.

Hell…the first deal half-killed her, and wore out Margie, and I really wasn't in the mood to do it all over again. So we made a kid's play house out of the big dog box for our granddaughter, Laurel.

Crankshaft was born with a bad heart (we didn't have a clue). We have possums and 'coons in the back yard and Crankshaft loved to chase and catch 'em. Well one night a "he" 'coon wore Crank's ass out and the heart trouble was discovered. Margie took him to experts at University of Florida, kinda the Mayo Clinic for dogs. But they said his condition was terminal and time was short. It 'bout broke Margie's and my heart, 'fore he was two, he died a tough way. He couldn't breathe. But Crankshaft and his dad Deputy Dog are still here. They are down by the river, side by side, in a nice grassy place with some flowers.

Dep made it to 'bout seven years old and his hips gave out…then seemed like everything went wrong. You know it's 'bout like someone in the family. That's why I say don't get a Great Dane, they don't live long.

Junkyard's laying here watching me write. She's ten years old now and having rear hip problems.

I'm dreading what I'm afraid will come soon. She sure has been my buddy since I got her.

I know Margie will be hurtin' also, when the time comes for Junkyard to go down by the river, Margie loves Junkyard.

GOOFY

When Crankshaft died my daughter said, "If you got another dog, what would you get?" I said "I'm gonna get an elephant, they live a long time. Or, maybe an Orphan Annie dog – an Airedale. You guessed it, next Christmas I find an Airedale puppy under the Christmas tree. (The reason I considered an Airedale was cause of "Firpo," the South American dog I tole you about in my jungle adventures: he was such a smart, tough, loyal feller. He never got broke – so no vet fees…) Well, I found out all Airedales ain't alike.

Whooee, that puppy liked to put Margie in an insane asylum. But either we got used to her, or she got better. She was originally named "Raggedy Ann." But I once commented that "she was the goofiest looking and acting dog I ever saw," and Margie said, "That's perfect…that's her new name."

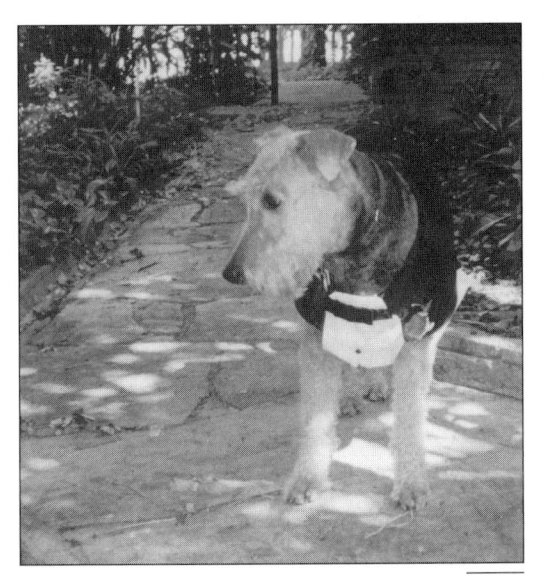

Goofy.

Goofy needed some medical attention and the vet said, "How come you call that fine dog such a name?" When Margie went to pick her up the vet said, "I see why you named her Goofy."

Nope, we won't ever have any Goofy puppies to give away. I believe one Goofy is as much as the world needs. If you got a good place for a dog to live and you're up in miles and out of warranty, it ain't no bad idea to get a big dog. Could help you cope with the crazy shit that's going on in our world today. Dogs are good stuff.

January 1999, our boy Steve gets married at the house. Big fancy deal, even got the reverend Hal Marchman, racing's number one preacher to do the job. Margie is organizing the deal. You know, tuxedos and all the hi-class bullshit you can pile on. Steve's sister, Kilroy, made tuxedo's for Junkyard and Goofy, and I'll be damned if they didn't wear 'em for three hours perfectly. Ever see a dog in a tux any place? (They looked as fine as anyone there, and better than some.)

Requiem for a wonderful creature that blessed Margie's and my life for eleven years and looked like a brown lady Great Dane dog we called Junkyard.

August 30, 1999 was for me a bad-bad day. My second best friend in the world, Junkyard, is going to leave her, mine, Margie and Goofy's world.

Just shy of eleven years old, Junkyard was a brown female Great Dane, 185 pounds of gentle loving companion, or 185 pounds of a lightning mouthful of teeth. She would die for either Margie or I, without hesitation. Junkyard was as close to human as it can possibly get. She picked me to be her master. In those eleven years that dog never let me out of her sight, if she could help it.

If I was a lollipop I'd have had 200 pounds licked off of me. Junkyard licked everything and everybody, including cats.

In my advanced age maybe I'm getting goofy, I talked to Junkyard. When I got home I took Junkyard off like I took off my clothes. She slept at the foot of our bed and in the morning when I got dressed I put Junkyard on. As I worked Junkyard's barks told me "it's kinda serious," or "minor." Dogs pick one person to attach too and even though Margie fed, tended to her medical needs and actually did more for her than I did, I was Junkyard's number one. I guess Junkyard's eleven years were 'bout like a human's ninety years. Last year or so she started losing her mobility…'bout like people. Six months ago we could see it was getting serious. A month ago her right rear leg started swelling ('bout like in our knee area).

The vet said, bone cancer, a tumor, no way out, six months at best, very painful. She lay there, licked the sore place and looked at me like "goddam it boss, can't you make this go away? You and Margie always have before." Junkyard's got a five-year-old buddy – an 85 pound. Airedale we named "Goofy." Goofy's world is Junkyard. I can tell she knows Junkyard is hurtin.'

She licks Junkyard's snoot, comes over to me with a look like, "Please do something to make Junkyard's 'bad' go away." It gets worse fast. Junkyard's foot swells up till it looks like a giant lion's paw. She can't hardly get up – even pees herself cause it hurts to get up. We get the super pain pills and all there is, but it ain't enough. Junkyard hasn't eaten in four days. She still wags her tail and still follows me no matter how much it hurts. She loves to ride and no matter how much it hurts, somehow, someway, she gets in the car to come to work and go home to Margie.

Sunday, August 29th: I bring Junkyard and Goofy to work, I sit in my chair all day thinking and watching her. The doctor said ten days ago to send her on. She's still smiling, still wants to be rubbed. She tries to follow me and falls down. After 'bout six hours I know it's time. As I sit there, having decided, I can't help it…I start crying. The crying upsets Junkyard. She struggles to get up and push her head into my lap like she wants to console me, but a big sadness kinda envelopes me. I've decided Junkyard will only see one more sunset. I tell her about it, and tell her she will be with her husband, "Deputy Dog" and her favorite son "Crankshaft." She starts nudging me with her nose, this is was her "take me home to Margie" act.

When I walk in the house with Junkyard I tell Margie what I've decided. It tears her up, but she agrees letting her suffer would be selfishly wrong. Junkyard will not eat and has a bad night pain-wise. Margie calls the veterinarian and he agrees to come to the shop at 11:00 am and put her to sleep. We, my son Steve, myself, and daughter Patricia (Kilroy), wait for the vet while Margie waits at home with Steve's wife Kathy. Dewey and Brian dug her grave in the middle of the orange trees where she loved to roll in the grass.

Dewey was part of Junkyard's life every day of her life. When I told him Junkyard was gonna go back to her maker he broke down and cried like a baby. We wait from 10:40 till 2:00 pm. The vet don't show. We take Junkyard to another vet's office. The shot ended her life quickly, and I'm sure without pain. She looked at me as always and listened as I thanked her for the happiness she brought to Margie and I, and told her I hoped she'd get to play with Deputy Dog and Crankshaft.

I told her I hoped I done the right thing, but if I didn't – forgive me. You know, she had that same pleasant look till she closed her eyes. I heard the doctor say, "She is gone." I stopped crying and left the room. I have one last bad job to do – bury her. It was very hard to pour the dirt over her.

When we finished, a kind of peace came over me. Margie came to me and we held each other, both 'bout pooped out. That was a part of our lives that showed us happiness is not really free…but neither of us would have missed Junkyard's contributions to our lives, regardless of the pain of August 30, 1999.

Man, writing this has been tough. Wonder what it's like if you have to play this game with a human you love? Whew….

Goofy's world has exploded. Her beloved Junkyard just disappeared. She looks and paces back and forth. Every morning and every evening she runs all over house and garage property sniffing and looking. Every day, four or five times I tell her, "Junkyard's gone and will never come back, maybe someday you'll join her" (if in fact there really is a "page two"). I doubt she understands. But hell, what else can a man do? This is our fourth day, we've got a long way to go. I think dogs are kinda lucky. In a couple of months they forget, but Margie and I will never forget our Junkyard. Though I think later as we remember we will smile, today it is still tough.

It took Margie hours to type this. She'd get to crying and her glasses would get messed up from tears. This morning Goofy's looking for Junkyard in our back yard…she's standing at Junkyard's grave alongside the 11 rose bushes – one for each year – but ain't no way I can tell Goofy, "she's asleep rite under you're paws."

Carbon

I had to go to Darlington the Friday after Junkyard died for the 500 race. Margie and I got home early, 'bout 8:00 pm. I'm sitting in a chair thinking, and I hear a noise. Suddenly a black "thing" with a big red ribbon falls into my lap. Hell, it's a dog, a puppy, a black girl Labrador of 'bout 20 pounds and 'bout the blackest live thing ever made.

The puppy is scared, but gives me a big "hello" lick across my snoot. Did you ever really look at a labrador puppy's snoot? Ain't no way you can't like 'em. My kids, Steve and Kilroy got the puppy and I'm pretty sure Margie half-assed knew what was going on. Their idea is, "this will help us miss Junkyard less." Goofy comes over and she's pissed – she still can't find Junkyard, and now a strange dog moves in.

Well, it's five weeks later as I write. "Carbon" (the li'l dog's name), is soaking wet, asleep under my feet. Goofy's 'bout five feet from me sound asleep with a kinda grin on her snoot. Carbon is Goofy's new world. Although she was nasty to her for two or three weeks. They play all the time and Goofy watches out for Carbon. We live on, and the shop's on, a river bank. Carbon loves to swim.

The puppy come kinda like an unwanted pregnancy, but this li'l (now 30 pound…yup, don't take long) ball of energy has got Goofy, Margie and I grinning again, and has sure helped ease the pain of Junkyard leaving our lives. In spite of Margie running around with new age chemistry to remove the negatives of puppy piss, eat up slippers, chewed up chairs, and eat up flowers. Nope, no problem 'bout crying and barking.

I guess you can call this part, "Let me tell you 'bout our grand-dog."

Since I Quit Racing

"The sun don't shine on same dog's ass all the time"...my mental explanation of the bad day.

MY LIFE IN RACING SINCE 1975

The checkered flag at Indy '75 was last race I was a competitor. They said "you're 10th, take your engine down" for inspection. Then an hour later…"Nope, you're 12th, we took away last lap run under green." (Race was rained out short) I was very tired, very disappointed …10th…12th…Who gives a shit? In my book if you didn't finish in the lead lap you flunked the course.

I had absolutely no intentions of quitting. Hell, I was only 52 years old. We had four or five, of those two days and two nights with no sleep between February and the last of May. I noticed what a struggle they were as compared to ten years ago. I knew I was exceeding my physical limits. Thirty years of cold tube steaks and drinking two day old black coffee, I think, was catching up. I was so tired I fell asleep laying on the floor on a Goodyear race blanket. When I woke I thought, "How smart is this? Three years, zero pay. You see, everyone else had switched to foreign engines and many to foreign chassis. I would not switch to a foreign engine. I had to make the push rod work. Well, after Indy '75 race I rebuild car.

I'm gonna do a Goodyear tire test in November. In August of '75 Dick King, president of USAC was giving an international news conference briefing on Indy. A reporter asked a question. "What's the future of push rod engines at Indy?" Dick replied, "Push rod engine has no future at Indy – now or ever." I dropped my wrenches like they were red hot. That did it. To me Indy was American, period: chassis, engines and drivers.

If I had my way today, 2000, the first rule would be "open only to Americans, with American cars, American engines and American drivers on American tires. No chassis costing more than $100,000 allowed, no engines allowed costing more than $40,000, all wheels be protected from a competitors wheels (in reference to incidental contact."

I know you open wheelers want to hang me by my balls. I don't give a shit. That's what I believe.

I'll also predict if open wheelers don't do the above they will be legislated out of existence by legislation or cost (reads "dead fans"). This is 2000, not 1940-'50-'60-'70-'80-'90-etc.

I know Foyt and Tony, for starters, think I'm fuckin' goofy. Watch it play out. Every week on TV you see the injury and destruction wheel contact causes.

The Indy 500 was at one time hands down the greatest automobile race on earth. It's losing out for last 10 years. Rite now if seating was available and pricing was equal, the Brickyard 400 would outdraw the "real" Indy.

After I quit the Indy movie I'm finally out of options. In my last conversation with France regarding NASCAR in 1971, I told him "I'm long gone." He said "You'll be back." I said, "If you don't think I'm gone, count the days till I come back. If you see me coming down the street, get the hell on the other side. If I see you first I'll cross over. If you ask me what time it is, the charge will be 100 bucks." In my world, the Bill France benefit is over – in my world, I'd have died before I'd have come back.

Everybody says "Don't you miss it?" "Yeah. 'Bout as much as I'd like to get AIDS." Ask Jr. Johnson how much he misses NASCAR. By 1970 the NASCAR-Smokey rules and inspection follies had become an annual ritual. It actually sold tickets. I liked racing you on an even playing field with 'bout 15 black or white rules. I liked racing where bravery and skill counted. But not under conditions where driver was semi-kamikaze pilot. By 1970 racing was just about money for France.

1976: By now the shop had wind mills, solar collectors, engines running on hydrogen, coal dust, cow shit, fluorocarbons (freon), ammonia, hot vapor, natural gas and liquid natural gas. Ever since 1962 when I decided we had to get off of prime movers as we knew then in the sixties – hydrocarbon dependent. Why? They polluted way too much, and we'd run out of enough oil in the mid eighties. (Big mistake in my research.)

By the way, in regard to the alternate energy adventures from 1962 to 1990, I made many big mistakes. Biggest one was "hydrogen will replace hydrocarbons." I wasted ten years on this.

All the time I was racing since 1955 I kept playing with various world saving ideas for example: electric cars, wind and solar machines, ocean energy, wave machines, temperature differential schemes.

I spent eight years on a Rankine cycle engine that used fluorocarbons for the working fluid.

Being the "Dear Abby" for car and truck problems at Popular Science from 1959 to 1987 drew me into many interesting and educational areas. The world's full of "what-if'ers." 45 years of listening to their plans wasn't a good allotment of time. 96 percent of it was pure bullshit. But hey, you never know.

My real goal was to build the "hot vapor cycle engine" in three separate stages, where by the third state would be say 95 percent adiabatic.

I'm able to keep current in racing by development contracts from manufacturers of mass surface transportation and racing parts manufacturers. Also, by being spokesperson for several manufacturers. Being the racing "Dear Abby" and monthly feature story writer for Circle Track magazine for eleven years helped keep me in the game also.

By 1975 it seemed all racing rumors, gossip, scandal, rules, politics, had to be reported to me for comment and analysis. This includes all forms of racing 'cept formula one and draggers ('cept for twice a month one hour phone meeting with Mickey Thompson, which was in reference to draggers and off road adventures. Plus phone calls from all over the world 24 hours a day).

Nope, I never, ever had an unlisted number. All you needed to talk to me was one head, two arms, two legs and some times I'd waive those restrictions.

After I'd been gone from racing 'bout a year I decided no one should be allowed to legislate racing rules, who had a current vested financial interest or had no peer experience in the topic. All forms of racing should have a special built racer that has two seats in it and the rule-makers take turns driving and riding this vehicle in competition before rules are poured in concrete. In other words, "Don't talk the talk, if you don't walk the walk." I also feel the official's shorts be presented for examination by the media (as removed) after the test ride. Consider this: you read criticism, praise, explanation of events and accidents from a reporter or official who's never ran a hot lap in his/her life. Does this mean the hotel advertisement that says if you spend a night there you become an expert in race competition is for real? As they represent in their commercial reference wild bear management?

I've kept going to open wheel and taxi cab races, a few drag races. Damn near no sports car races (What the hell's a sports car? Seems like that includes one of every kind of racing there is.) Truck racing hasn't done shit for my soul. That's a sales tool where fan pays for the truck manufacturer's advertisement. I expect a new class of racers, soon. Truck chassis with Pepsi-Cola, Dr. Pepper or Seven-Up, Marlboro, Phillip Morris and Frito-Lay vending machines for bodies.

Margie gave me a plaque 'bout 1982. Said "He who has no problems to solve is out of the game." I can see it happening to me. Ten years ago I got 20 calls a day, five visitors, 15 letters. Now I get the same, 'cept in a month. From 1975 to 1985, I decided to listen good, keep my mouth shut most of the time and be even more cautious 'bout painting anything "black or white." I've learned there are 1,000 shades of gray in between, and as you get older your eyesight deteriorates badly therefore you don't see all the details as clearly. So you need to be more careful 'bout running your mouth.

In 1976, I finish the first phase of the hot vapor engine and install it in a car. 'Bout same time I got in a joint development deal with Carborundum, a company that leads the world in ceramic technology. We worked on the manufacturer of ceramic and composite parts for prime movers. Next, 'bout '77, I entered into another one of my famous $1,000 bucks a month consulting deals with Buick to make a rose out of a pig's ear (Buick V6 into a racing engine) and to help solve production problem with the V6. I worked with Lloyd Ruess (chief engineer) and Herb Fishel (director of high performance vehicles) during this period.

I do more and more work in the jungle oil fields. I'm still writing monthly for Popular Science and have made a mistake in accepting a deal where I visited various colleges and gave speeches and seminars on alternate energy. The audience was the new "hippie." My best simple description of my audiences as a rule was like talking to between 1,000 and 2,000 hogs.

If you're wondering why the country's fucked up now, these students are now running the country politically and industrially. Last one I did was University of Ohio, halfway through the deal I just shut up, walked out and went to the airport. I doubt they knew I was gone. I've watched these jackoffs become presidents, generals, labor and religious leaders and captains of industry, educators. I see our country control half the world with the biggest collection of crooked, greedy, egotistical assholes in the history of mankind. I bet you this plan will not fly much longer. Hey, it just can't. Today I see a pro football player knock an official on his ass on national TV for throwing a penalty flag in his eye. What's tomorrow? The player jerks his head off?

The alternative energy adventures kept me hopping. Speeches, seminars, judging new ideas, and an engine invention of my own and Emmet Oliver (mostly Oliver). A Rankine cycle engine that used fluorocarbons as the working fluid. This was aimed at recovery of waste heat in various industries. It was a six or seven year waste of time and money.

25 years later industry is more wasteful than ever, but is polluting less. I judged two years of an alternate energy contest between the 50 top colleges. That was a shocker. My fellow judges were the world's top brains in energy. Hell, today we got up to 50 foot long 30,000 pound, luxury motorhomes and 6,000 pound SUVs gettin' eight miles to a gallon.

Motorhomes costing up to a million dollars that need 600 horsepower diesels to push 'em 100 mph. 'Bout any time you look up at the sky you see a big jet consuming tons of fuel a trip.

I now make big mistake number one regarding the hot vapor cycle. I offer Mr. Knudsen 25 percent of the invention free. Thinking his endorsement and know-how will get the job done easy sales-wise.

GM gets pissed, don't want nothing to do with Mr. K. (Remember he quit 'em, if you quit GM, you never lived). We just go around in circles. Now I'm making a hot vapor cycle engine out of the four cylinder 150 cubic inch (Iron Duke) Pontiac engine. Next I go to Chrysler and deal indirectly with Harold Sperlich. Man this cat is one of the real car men in Detroit. Actually his engineering and Iacocca's bullshitting saved Chrysler's ass. I knew him from Ford. He engineered the car, built the tooling and damn near single-handed gave the world the 1978 Ford Fiesta. At the time, the finest small car in the world. He got in trouble at Ford over this car. It sold well but Henry Ford didn't like it and wanted to kill it. Sperlich fought for the car like a tiger.

Mr. K is Ford's president at the time.

Henry told Knudsen to fire Harold and so he did. (This rears it's ugly head later.) The Fiesta dies.

Iacocca hires Sperlich and history is on it's way. Mini-vans. Neat, little, tough, four-cylinder cars. Hal had as much to do with saving Chrysler's ass as Iacocca. Iacocca may be is the world's greatest bullshitter-salesman, but he wouldn't have made a pimple on a good engineer's ass. They, as a team, were a class act of (just do it). Hal Sperlich was like Delorean. He knew what the people wanted. Would you believe they were classmates in college? Hal gives me some porky asshole to work with (Sinclair, I believe) and a cat named Robertson. Sperlich had me do some exhaust manifold work on his four-banger. I got along great with him, but Sinclair and Robinson did their damnedest to shit-can the hot vapor engine.

Sperlich came to Daytona with Robinson and Sinclair and drove the hot vapor, three-cylinder Buick with a three speed manual and ended up shifting from 1st to 3rd, skipped 2nd. And he chewed Robinson's ass out for asking for a five speed for the future Chryslers.

That done it. Now Chrysler give me a chicken-shit offer for the engine. I get pissed and quit fooling with Chrysler. I still have a four cylinder li'l car Chrysler gave me to install a hot vapor cycle engine into. For this car I modify their engine into a hot vapor cycle. This really turned out well.

Zero to 60 in 6.1 seconds, 54 miles per gallon highway and 32 mpg city cycle. Hal never rode in this car.

I next get John Delorean to take a ride in the three cylinder Buick Skylark. Man he went ape-shit over it. In a month I've got a Delorean and am building a three cycle hot vapor engine for it. John and Mr. K are putting together a 20 million dollar deal whereby the Delorean Motor Company owns the hot vapor cycle. We get a signed deal. Delorean then talks to Sperlich about the engine and it's agreed verbally that Chrysler and Delorean will joint venture a deal. Sperlich and Delorean say, "Come to New York and we will sign the deal. Delorean will manufacture the engine for use both in Chrysler and Delorean's…papers will be ready 5:00 pm. Let's go to Four Seasons restaurant have dinner and sign the contract."

Bunkie Knudson, me, John Delorean and Bunker Hunt.

Remember, at this point John D. has contract buying the invention for 20 million bucks. At the dinner, Hal finds out Mr. K owns 25 percent of engine and he says, "Bullshit. Get Knudsen out of the deal or there is no deal." I'm in shock. So is John. I say, "What in the hell did Knudsen do to you?" Hal says, "The son-of-a-bitch fired me at Ford." (I didn't yet know that.) It's 7:30 pm I decide to go to airport and try and patch a way home. I spent the night there. First plane out 7:00 am. Two giant kicks in the ass by two out of the big three cause of Knudsen. Delorean loved Mr. K. Still he was hurt by some of Knudsen's criticism of him and his car. But even today John is a Knudsen fan. Well, Mr. K. was John's "grandfather" at GM. I ask Mr. K 'bout it. He denies he fired Sperlich. (Turns out he did.)

I ask Mr. K. how much he will take to get out. He says "ten million." My bank balance is in the four figures, so I can't play that game. OK, I get a phone call from Bunker Hunt. It's a small world. In the "Indy" part you'll find out we became friends in 1960. Bunker says "I've heard about your engine, is it for sale?" I say "Nope. John Delorean has bought it but hasn't paid for it yet." He asks to come see me, I say, "Hell yes." I go to meet him, I figure he'll come in private jet. Nope, he's riding a Delta "tourist." (At this time Bunker is rated at four billion plus. Bunker is good people. The world come down pretty hard on him 'bout the silver deal, but way I see it, the US Government and those crooks who run the Chicago commodities markets screwed Bunker beyond comprehension.)

Here's the deal: (by the way, John Delorean is at shop when Bunker comes). This ain't a perfect deal. Bunker is pissed 'bout a helicopter deal John peddled to Bunker couple years ago, but Bunker says, "John's best in car business." He has a son just out of college named Houston, who is a college trained geologist. (Oil) Bunker says, "I believe it's time for another motor company, a cheap "baby cadillac," no options but color, built on the tex-mex border." He'll put up the money, Houston gets trained to switch careers, John Delorean will head it up, Chrysler gets the "deep six."

We rock along for a month. This Thursday we will sign final papers in Daytona, and Bunker gives me five millions of operating capital. I'm gonna re-do shop (got three acres), Knudsen gets five million to leave (Bunker wants no part of him. Go figure. I ain't got a clue. I thought the world loved the Boss). Tuesday 6:30 pm, Knudsen calls. I'm still at work. "Turn on your TV, channel "x." " There's John, handcuffed. Cocaine deal. I stare in disbelief. John? Cocaine? This cat went to church five days a week – a Catholic. His office was in New York City. He had an apartment close by and walked to work past St. Patrick's church, and would go in every day.

8:00 am Wednesday morning Houston Hunt calls me, says "Dad says deal's off as to final papers being signed Thursday." (He won't even say the word "Delorean." Says, "Dad will put up the five million at 6 percent. A five year loan." I say, "Well thank you, but I couldn't pay it back." Houston says "Smokey, we'll show you where to invest it at 21 percent interest. You can operate off the interest till we work up another arrangement." (Yes, 21 percent, no special deal then). I say "Thank you, but I'll continue as I am."

By now I have three cars with hot vapor engines running: the three-cylinder Buick, a li'l Chrysler car and the Delorean with a three-cylinder engine. All three have passed emissions with carburetors and points at Southwest Labs. I also have a four-cylinder Ford Taurus I'm turning into a hot vapor cycle car. (Ford gave me the car.)

John's in deep shit. In jail, his contract is junk – didn't pay. We're up to 'bout 1982. I get a call from Pittsburgh, Kopper's Coke venture capital company. "Is your engine for sale?" "Yup." Well in 'bout three months I get one-and-a-half million and a third of the company "if"…get this now…if Knudsen is out. Knudsen agrees to take 385 grand to go "bye-bye." (This comes out of my one-and-a-half million) I give Ralph Johnson my helper 100 grand or so, I don't exactly remember. Now Koppers has two or three partners in the deal, Continental Insurance and how the hell Crane Cams wiggled in there for five or 10 percent, I can't remember.

Big mistake #2, Crane Cam had an older man running the company and a mouthy sales manager named Gene Ezell. The old man kept me fucked up with his second guessing and his ability to use his small interest (Crane Cams), to control the two-thirds majority. So in reality my one third was about as useful as tits on a bull. Ezell was a great sales manager, but with aspirations for the Crane presidency, which he soon got. Ezell knew as much about engines as your grandmother. But he was a sneaky motherfucker, who played games with a real pain in the ass lawyer named Kaney.

The name of this adventure was "Motor Tech." This deal lasted 'bout four years.

GM decided in August '87 not to pay any more development money. The deal blows up – Motor Tech violates the sales agreement. I get the invention back. I'm so pissed off with the way Motor Tech and GM handled this deal I get disgusted and park the deal. This is September, 1987. I've battled the world over the hot vapor cycle for over 30 years. We came so close to Broadway. I decided it was time to move on to new adventures.

Maybe I was getting goofy. If the world don't agree for thirty years, there's a good chance I'm the lost Indian. From time to time since '87, Honda won the Formula One championship copying it, it's been called one of "the top ten engine developments in the world." Once in awhile I get a nibble 'bout it, but in my "Smokey world," I've taken you to the river when you are thirsty. If you don't wanna drink I'm not gonna sit on your head and force you to drink.

I doubt this movie is over with. I've told you I suspect man will discover one or more other beneficial laws of motion. Could be that point that resists a force could be as productive as the force itself if harnessed properly, as in counter-rotation forces. The hot vapor cycle engine is a simple example of energy salvage by utilizing the physics of phase change and the latent heat of vaporization. For you young people reading this, hopefully you'll notice the application of physics and chemistry.

To do useful work for man is exciting, interesting, and with some potential for economical rewards. One thing for damn sure, we've just scratched the surface of knowledge. But I'm a long way from sure that that's good. Example: my lifetime so far: electricity, telephone, television (black and white, color), computers, microwave, jets, turbines, rockets, space exploration, autos, medical advances, disease control, atomic energy. The list goes on and on. (Including my personal favorite, king-sized beds). All this is in 90 years. Can you imagine someone predicting these developments in 1900?

Here we are starting the 21st century. To me it's kinda scary. We have the option of making the world a better place to live. But we go for the almighty greenie and continue to pollute and rape nature while screwing over whoever we can now and future generations…in short, operate in a "hooray for me, fuck you" attitude. Some place here soon, you under 25 all are gonna have to learn to work, vote and honor at least half of the ten commandments, 'cause my generation is handing you a royal fucking mess. It's beyond my comprehension. We elected and support a male human as our president who don't know what the word "fuck" means. If we get this kind of thinking from a Rhodes Scholar, what do we get from a plain, rich-kid hippie? I advise you to buy stock in Vaseline, 'cause with the screwing we get from today's politicians and business leaders, considering a linear state of evolution as in past ten years, every citizen will need to purchase 100 pounds of Vaseline a year to keep from bleeding to death because of an overly abused asshole.

October 1987, I decide to abdicate from the world of Detroit, quit Popular Science and close garage. Fence in the property and operate with office manager, a janitor and one technician. I got zero income. I now do what I want to do, when I want to do it, and how I want to do it. And if anybody don't like it they can kiss my ass. The parts, tools and supplies still sit in same place they were 13 years ago (reference the truck shop). Course some stuff is a li'l rusty. A big sign in front says, "Closed for Reorganization." (I learned that phrase out of the Wall Street Journal.) Anything that is morally, socially, or economically bankrupt can – like going to confession (as in Catholic church, state your sins, ask for forgiveness, and it is pardoned).

'Bout 1980, when I looked in the mirror when I shaved I noticed I didn't like what I saw.

I'd ask myself, "Where you going? What do you want?" I'd answer, "I don't know, I think I'm lost." I had a good wife and three good kids, but I hardly knew them. I had a serious relationship with another lady. I didn't like what I saw in the mirror. A loud mouth, know-it-all, two-faced, cheating asshole. And what's worse I couldn't see a clear path to fixing it all. Fate had it's own special movie for me. My wife got cancer. In worst way, and she was gone in nothing flat. And I mean, she got instant best care at M.D. Anderson Hospital in Houston.

Fate said, "Nope."

Now I'm 'bout 57 years old, three teenage kids I hardly knew and a mistress who is very unhappy. I'm really a lost soul – very disappointed in myself. I don't like what I see in the mirror. Somewheres in next four or five years, I could start to see a way back to a half-decent human.

Round 1994-95 I got involved in a very interesting racing adventure. A man comes in here, C.J. Baker sent him. Says, "I want to hire you as a race consultant. I want to build a Winston cup track in Vicksburg, Mississippi." He's got armload of plans and horseshit. I say, "Mister, get the fuck out of here – I got work to do." He says, "I'm willing to pay…are you nuts?" (I ignore the question, but he may have a point.) He comes back second time and says, "I'll pay you three grand a month for a year to help me." I say, "Go away, if I took your money it would be like stealing it. If you searched the world over for the person least able to help in NASCAR politics, you've just found him. There ain't no dates available for any more Winston cup races, and a few that will be squeezed in will be to France and company, or "biggies" like Bruton. You're pissing into a 100 mile and hour wind. Go home." He says, "OK, do you have any ideas how we can do this? We want race tracks in places gambling casinos can be built. We don't care if track makes a profit, just break even, we want that race crowd." Oh shit, the mafia wants in racing now. I say, "Meeting's over, you're game is a con game. I'd rather go sit on the sea wall and play with my peter and starve to death first."

He then gives me some song and dance 'bout "gaming people," not "gambling bad-asses."

My brain lights up…maybe. "Mister, can your group write a check for one billion dollars that won't bounce?" He says, "I believe we can, but we have no plans for that large an investment." I get up, put my hand out, say, "Goodbye. This meeting is over. Don't forget your artists rendition of your track. I just remembered I forgot to take Junkyard to the river. For our daily meeting." Junkyard loves the river.

He's back in a week. "What's your plan?" My idea is, his outfit owns all the casino-hotel action. I start a NASCAR two and call it "the American Racing League." The members of the

The beginnings of the ARL.

American League own the sanctioning body, and share it's profits. The gaming people that own the track are guaranteed zero liability, and full compensation for track operating expense. This includes recapture of track cost over thirty years.

Idea is: you said "if track breaks even," the ARL gets TV money, all profits and expenses for 32 races a year. ARL pays prize money. In short, gaming finances ARL for rights to all gaming activities; that is till the ARL pays out. Then we remain partners but with separate identities. We're gonna build 16 tracks, all exactly alike, one-and-a-half miles, low bank, 10 degree, 12 degree and 14 degree bank, three lanes. Concrete, no asphalt anyplace a race car goes. We get so far as hiring engineer who maintains Indy to make preliminary drawings. Hire A.J. Foyt as a PR (not my idea) deal, hire Clarence Cagel as a consultant (I wanted Clarence). Clarence and A.J. are against concrete track. Year is up in August same day as first Brickyard race. No contract. The people I'm dealing with say we must have control over ARL as well. I say this meeting has just ended. Stick to original deal. Have contract for me to sign tomorrow or take your bullshit someplace else. End of adventure.

My deal had racer retirement, medical care pensions and bonus program. All tracks alike exactly. Covered grandstand and lights use rain tires, no rain outs. Air jacks mandatory, fuel furnished by track pipeline and quick disconnect. 22 gallons each in six seconds. Pits covered. No spectators allowed in garage area but will be allowed 12 feet overhead. All interviews and autographs will be at upper level accessed by undertrack tunnel at start finish line with tire and car understructure visible. Why? To police tire condition. Big big deal was outside 360 degree road behind pit wall for emergency vehicles. Outer wall all a movable barrier that you can hit at 150 mph and walk away with maybe a headache. This project used a year so, I can't describe it all. My idea was at season end, have a championship contest (a la baseball or football) for us, maybe a championship with NASCAR.

A strange thing happened to me today. A TV reporter looked me in the eyes and said, "What's it feel like to win?" Can you believe I've never thought 'bout it before and no one ever asked before. The question caught me by such surprise I couldn't answer. Then suddenly (and this was live), I blurted out, "Maybe equal to, or same as the ultimate feelings of sex." Yup. That's it. Your emotions explode, you have only one feeling…happy. You can't feel heat or cold or pain. It's probably the only ten seconds in a person's life when, if asked if, "You could be granted a wish, what would it be?" You'd answer "nothing more." For me the feeling lasted no more than three or four minutes, and then I'd return to earth and the training I imposed on myself took charge again, and the game was "show no emotion." I think this was a defense for disappointment, maybe a defense against race fans and competitors who didn't want you to win.

I know it was a defense against disappointment. It could have been for something else. A race car, besides being the basic part of a game, could be a dangerous, unforgiving weapon in the hands of incompetent or distracted technicians. My plan was, when it was "show time" to hypnotize myself in such a way that fans and all other humans except my teammates were blocked out. If you were an official, I could hold a brief conversation with you without interrupting my train of thought and never remember the conversation. For example: 350 thousand fans at Indy, I don't see or hear them till my car is at rest and it's over. A distraction that would cause me to make a mistake could be equal to me putting a pistol in driver's ear and pulling the trigger. In racing your emotions fluctuate between thrills, agony, joy, misery, pain, disgust, exhaustion, fear and anxiety. My advice, if I was asked by a newcomer to racing, would be, "Mask your emotions as do poker players in a hi-stakes game." I think you agree, a human life is as high as the stakes can go.

When we asked if crashed driver would be OK, and at that juncture the person who was at fence breaks eye contact, we know. Another Indian just bit the dust. How else would you proceed in a long race if a friend of yours just got killed in it? As cruel as it may seem to you, I never grieved the dead much. I had learned how to accept it when I was still a teenager. What I had trouble with was the living dead (the cripples and vegetables). For you who have access to garage and pit area, consider what I've said when you engage the technicians in conversation. You're damn sure not doing that team's chances any good. (Well, maybe if you're a good lookin' thing, and you tell the driver "If he wins, you'll give him a li'l." That's OK.)

How 'bout "l-u-c-k" in racing? We hear so much about it. Is there such a thing as "good" or "bad" luck? Can you expect divine intervention if you are a good Christian? If so, does that apply to Jews, Arabs, Moslems, etc? How about an atheist? Is he out of the game? When pieces of a race car go into the grandstand and kill people, does God aim that stuff at bad people? Is luck the random "luck of the draw"? Or do we, to some degree, make our own luck? If you know you're gonna crash, is it better to say, "Lord, help me!" or "Oh shit!"? To me, I lived by what Confucius said…"The sun don't shine on the same dog's ass all the time."

Damn rite he had dogs. Where you think those wrinkly, goofy, fat-looking dogs came from?

So, to a degree you make your own luck, but life is really more like a lottery. You can't win if you don't gamble. The odds are against the gambler always. I bet you the real word for "luck" is a four letter word. For a change not "fuck," but "fate." I believe the answer to "what is fate?" is as elusive as what happened to the dinosaur?...How did the world get formed?...Who did it?...Where did oil come from?...Does Clinton know yet what intercourse is?

I don't think the driver who crashes 15 out of 30 races can get lucky next week with a rabbit's foot. Answer is: as a driver he ain't worth a shit.

I kinda seen it as, "The harder you work, the luckier you get." Still, life's full of choices, even the best of the best sometimes "zig" when the correct answer was "zag." So the real accounting of success: "What's your average?" I spent 'bout 35 years of my life writing for magazines.

28 Years as the "Dear Abby of Cars" in Popular Science, 11 years as a race tech writer for Circle Track magazine and various other similar time and tree-wasters (all the above was part time).

No question we need a news media to function as a tool for educating people as to current events and news on a universal basis, but I came away from this experience very disillusioned. For those of you who believe everything you read, you are lost in the middle of a thousand mile jungle. Or in Southern Racing English (pre-Winston Cup): "a fucked duck," or "Hogan's-type goat."

I found advertisers get pissed off if you say or print their products ain't worth a shit, regardless of if they are or are not.

I found without advertisers there are no magazines, newspapers, radio or TV shows.

I found what Mr. Detweiller told me to be 100 percent true: greenies, greed and pussy rule this world. Hello Donald. I don't know you but I've spent some time watching your act. Are you sure you're not lost? Unfortunately the guys with the big piles of greenies get bigger piles of greenies. This then seemingly never ends until another event eventually happens. I don't know who said it first, might have been A.J. Foyt. "Nothing is forever." (Maybe it was Davy Crockett at the Alamo). When the deal wears out, I guess a stack of lies makes a very shaky foundation, and eventually the apparatus fails from simply it's own weight.

Oh yes, Clinton will end up with his correct nomenclature on his dog tags, as will Bill Gates, Billy France, Roger Penske, Tony George, Herb Fishel, yup, every one of us. Here's the part that gets all of us...you can bullshit every one in the world, except yourself.

The immediate news is 75 percent bullshit, flavored by money and, sadly, history is recorded as seen by the best financed and influential liars of our now political and industrial leaders. Before my writing experience I believed George Washington told his ol' man he cut the tree down. After watching the Simpson murder trial and the Clinton impeachment circus, I don't believe a fuckin' thing in the history books any more. The only thing I believe 'bout Washington was the part where he was gonna cross the Delaware river and first thing he said was, "Get in the boat." Now I'd be surprised if the Washington's ever had a cherry tree.

Popular Science, as it got bigger and bigger (two to two-and-a-half million circulation), slowly lost control of "tell it like it is" for two reasons. Mainly from the slow erosion of the manufacturer code of ethics, and by the slowly increasing leverage of the greenie. Let me give an example: Firestone came out with a new expensive tire around 1980. They spent a fortune promoting it, but it had a serious flaw. The tread would get pretty warm at legal speed limit and get dangerously close to failing the tread-to-carcass bond. But at heavy loads and/or speeds above the speed limit, for 30 minutes or so, the tread would simply fly off, and quickly deflate. Causing serious accidents, injury, deaths, inconvenience and economic negatives. Matter of fact, the tire bankrupted Firestone Tire Company (among other things).

Just after the tire came out I received a flood of negative letters. Then I got a set of tires and tested them. The test was very bad. I asked for and got more tires. I blew five tires in a 475 mile course running a steady 85 mph. The fifth blow out caused $575 quarter panel damage. I wrote answers to unhappy customers (after talking to high Firestone brass, and finding out they did not intend to recall tire.) "Get rid of tires immediately." Popular Science would not print my answer for three months. I called, said, "Print on fourth month or I quit." Editor and publisher said, "I'll get fired if I do." I said, "I got contract saying you will publish what I write without correction." He says "OK, I'm getting tired of New York anyhow."

The week the story broke in Popular Science a senate sub-committee was investigating these tire failures. Tire was shit-canned and Firestone shortly fell into the hands of the rice burners (now Bridgestone). Nope, Lucky, the editor, didn't get fired, he got gold star.

Same kind of story 'bout Mobil One oil. In early eighties Mobil gave misinformation about product to public (but the product was good). This created a major problem. (We'll quit our advertisements unless you shut that damn Smokey up.) Course you know me, so you didn't see a Mobil ad for awhile in Popular Science. All big magazines take a monthly poll from readers to find out what readers like, don't like, etc. When I first wrote for Popular Science, Von Braun, the space genius, wrote for Popular Science and he was always number one in reader's poll. In 'bout six months my column, called "Say Smokey" became number one, and stayed there for years.

The public likes straight talk, but can be trained to eat bullshit as well. It slowly got worse.

Popular Science would change my answers, so I said "I quit." They said, "Oh, hell no. Don't do that. It will bankrupt the magazine. We are gonna give you a special honor and dinner in Los Angeles to celebrate your being oldest employee (28 years)." Two weeks later, editor and publisher are fired, dinner canceled, letter comes saying "We think you're quitting is a hell of a good idea. We will publish two more issues, we have enough answers."

To this day, 13 years later, I've never heard from Popular Science, and they never mentioned my disappearance in the magazine. Popular Science was part of the Times News chain. About the cheapest bastards on earth. I started at $300 a month and 28 years later was getting $650 a month. I got from 50 to 2,000 letters a month, spent 15 to 20 hours a month on column, and 'bout 20 hours a month on visitors and personal letters. If I wrote a feature story, I got a big one-fifty.

The first editor I worked for there was Bob Crosley, he was real, a fine man, only bad thing was he was first guy to talk me into working in a whore house. My second adventure into the world of wasting trees and printed bullshit was Circle Track magazine, a Petersen publishing company, monthly auto race criteria publication. A friend of mine, C.J. Baker, talked me into that in the early eighties. This time I knew better, but I liked C.J., and the deal was to be the "Dear Abby of Racers" for a couple years to help get the magazine going (a new publication). Same deal (ditch digger wages, watch your language, kiss Billy France's ass every third paragraph, don't step on any of big three's toes (Chrysler, Ford, GM). This deal lasted 11 years. The magazine was a success (at least I thought so).

More and more, every day, news stories are really infomercials, or technomercials. So much of it is outright lies. I expect in a year or so I'll see ads where a phone company pays you a nickel a minute to use their service. I think the most printed word in the English language is "free."

Really, anybody ever give you anything for free in your life? Take my advice soon as you see word free in print – haul ass after throwing the stuff in the trash. The definition for free in the dictionary should be "bullshit." (They even charge you to send in your tax check).

C.J. helped me as much as he could, but slowly C.J.'s boss, John Diana, a Sears and Roebuck washing machine salesman, who had bullslung his way into a Peterson vice presidency, became C.J.'s and my enemy. Why? I don't have a clue. I always considered him an incompetent asshole – but assumed that was common knowledge. I suppose John could sense my rating of him, but I never got involved in Petersen's politics. By the way, it's no longer Petersen's magazine, it belongs to a limey corporation now. Maybe good people. Don't know. Hope so, let's give 'em benefit of the doubt. Diana got on C.J.s case and got him scared shitless, matter of fact, flat out fired him 'bout five years ago.

C.J. now is helpless to help me.

Diana's picking the editors, dictating editorial. I'm trying to get the hell out of there. Finally, the last straw. Diana hires an editor named Grissom. This cat wouldn't have made a pimple on a race tech magazine editor's ass.

I want you to realize my criticism of people is my personal opinion, and possibly flawed because of the large number of assholes and pelicans I have had in my adventures. It's very possible I'm hard to get along with. I try the, "Quit, I need more money" routine, and goddam after working me like a dog for nothing for years, they agree to 36 grand a year for 12 columns and 10 features a year. The first eight years was about eight to 12 grand a year. I spent 'bout 80 or 90 hours a month on that ride.

Poor ol' C.J.s 'bout reduced to eating dog shit to hang on. Grissom is goofier than a three-peckered billy goat. I'm in a constant "hot enough to fuck" mode because Grissom is jacking with my answers. Circle Track got Grissom from Jack Priegle at MSD Ignition. He was their tech writer.

Jack told me how happy he was to be rid of him and asked how it was going. Everything I told him, he laughed and said, "Amen, same thing here." Now Grissom, as a human, is a nice slap happy idiot who is a tremendous bullshitter, but really a stereotype pelican (you know, eat, squawk and shit routine). The publisher of Circle Track 'bout in 1995, ain't a Smokey fan, so he tells editor of Circle Track (then Peter Sauracker), "Fire the old son-of-a-bitch." Pete won't do it. He gets shit-canned (not all because of me).

Hell, just 'fore the end at Circle Track Grissom would call me and identify himself as "the pelican." I'm disgusted with Circle Track, CJ and Grissom. A good magazine is going straight to hell. So I go back to the old reliable and say, "Pelican, I want a raise to 42 grand a year." He says, "Can't handle it." I say "Hell, you're getting 90 and you don't do shit." That does it. Formal answer is "Adios." Grissom is from the bean bandit school, but without the "know how" (they were racers). Johnny D. you win, Smokey's gone. Is Circle Track better for it? What do you guys think?

This is 'bout 1994 to 1996.

The Pelican lasts 'bout two years and then he bites the dust. John's got C.J. beat to a pulp with a rolled-up, fucked-up Circle Track magazine. Guess what? Justice triumphs. Li'l John's been a pussy-hound from day one, and in summer of '99, John gets 'bout half shit-faced at a company party, grabs wrong female by the ass and puts the move on her. It was a company employee's wife. There are witnesses. In less than 24 hours John-boy is a dead player.

Consider this, Clinton and John D.: one gets fired for just asking and the other gets a bunch of blow jobs and it's OK. This goes back to prove nothing's forever and 99 percent of us end up shooting ourselves into deep-deep reverse once we forget we are not special humans with exceptional privileges. I hope the new breed at Circle Track will let C.J. regain his manhood and he gets recognized for his contributions and knowledge of racing. But goddam it C.J., speak your mind and quit letting them shit on you. No

Dep said piss on it…so I did.

one knows the story as well as you 'cept maybe Economacki. Li'l John, you got your just reward. Actually, I could care less, it's good to see the bad guy lose too. Here the facts: Chris Economacki, C.J. Baker and Dick Berggren are #1 #2 and #3 regarding auto racing reporting. Collectively, 'bout 110 years experience.

In the fall of '87 GM decided not to further fund development of the hot vapor engine any longer. That meant Motor Tech, who owned the license, had to spend a minimum of 20 grand a month on development. They elected not to. Which triggered a provision whereby I got the patents back.

The truck business, which had been losing money for 16 years (my fault) was scaring me. Workmanship and pride had slipped so bad among the technicians, I had nightmares about a technical mistake or poor workmanship causing fatal accidents. I also received complaints from customers and employees. I personally felt our performance was slipping. Up till '85 I figured we were the peers in our business. In '87 I was ashamed of our performance. One Monday morning with a bad start of the day, I went back to the river bank with Deputy Dog and sat there chewing on grass stems like Dep, and pondered what to do. I said, "Deputy, what should I do?" After 15 minutes or so, Deputy got up, walked over to a palm tree, lifted his leg and pissed on it.

That instantly gave me the answer. "Piss on it." I walked up front to service manager's office, then parts, and then office manager, and said "We'll have a meeting at 5:00 pm…all employees must attend." I asked them if they were underpaid, overworked. All said "yes." I then said, "I'm sorry I have made your life so tough, I'm gonna do the best thing for you all. In two weeks this place is closed. So you can all get a better job. For those who wish to leave earlier, you can draw your pay and pro-rate vacation pay at any time from today on." I, and whoever stayed, finished all started work and redid any warranty work necessary. 13 years later, (2000) all parts, tools and equipment still sitting same place. I hung big sign "Closed for Reorganization," and it's still there. Shortly before Deputy died I asked again what to do. He turned to the tree by the river and did it again, pissed on it.

I held my breath for a year regarding a serious accident because of poor workmanship. Lucked out. Nothing happened.

Yup, Junkyard died September 5, 1999. Her hips gave out. Mine and Margie's and Goofy's companion for 11 years left all of us very sad, but better people from her examples.

Next I quit all jobs I had with motor companies. Lastly, I put a fence up surrounding the place.

I hired an office manager, kept my clean-up man (made him and Deputy Dog and Junkyard vice presidents) and withdrew from the world.

I worked seven days a week doing what I wanted to do when I wanted to and how I wanted to. I had about 30-40 years of unfinished experiments to finish and I was 69 years old. In this time frame I decided I fucked with the hot vapor cycle engine for 35 years and failed to get the world to agree it was worthy of commercialization, so I shoved it off in a corner and got started on two projects I had a strong interest in.

#1. Make crude oil out of natural gas, or put another way, make gasoline and diesel fuel out of natural gas competitive with natural crude, but would be cleanest fuel in the world.

#2. I restarted experiments to lubricate prime movers without a liquid lubricant, and experimented with engines without rod or main bearings (no soft interface).

At the same time I noticed the garage was filled with tons and tons of left over parts. Cars, engines, etc. but in various states of disassembly, and some stuff deteriorating from oxidation (rust). I hired a "wannabe racer," Bill Ellis, who helped me several years and then the racing bug infected him so bad I got Dick Moroso to hire him on his son's Busch team. Bill was a real racer, and did very well.

When I closed down in '87 I was overwhelmed at the accumulation of racing stuff I had. Man, if you looked at, say the spark plug collection, it was the evolution of spark plugs 1946 to 2000. Same for rings, pistons, carburetors. Hell, just everything. Well in '88 I decided to auction off all the stuff and scheduled it for February '88 (figured the race crowd would eat it up). The auction was maybe the biggest cluster fuck of my life. We had stuff all over the covered floors. Say two acres, and then two acres of it outside uncovered. We had auction experts help us, and maybe they were overwhelmed also. We run into some major trouble.

#1. The weather turned to hard-cold rain with mucho wind – the whole time.

#2. I didn't have a clue what the stuff was selling for, so we "gave" a lot of it away (so to speak). But some stuff sold for prices that shocked me. Like 35 to 40 grand for a Chevy mystery engine…five grand for an intake manifold…three grand for air cleaner. 80 bucks for dirty old Exide thermometer.

I was lucky in picking the auctioneers. I got Joe Bonomo and his partner Joe from Indiana, they had the knowledge and the temperament to keep things half-way orderly in spite of the mess. It was supposed to be a hell of a deal. Mickey Thompson had t-shirts made for us to sell commemorating the event. But we had a problem, most of the people were fans just wanting to look, and the "real" buyers couldn't come. The race had all the airlines, hotels and rental cars sold out.

Hell, you just never knew. They wanted my work clothes off my back. $1,500 for dirty ol' work hat. I ended up in shorts and a t-shirt with a Goodyear engine blanket wrapped around me. (Got 'bout five grand total for clothes I wore. Nope. Nobody bid on shorts or sox). We sold my '67 Chevelle. The car that NASCAR barred from not only competition, but tire test as well. We got 100 grand for it, and five grand for my original neon sign. But we only sold 'bout 5 percent of the stuff.

We tried again a year later, much better prepared and with fair weather, sold 'bout 5 percent more. So there is still 'bout 50 tons of it left.

For starters: 45 complete engines, 100 cranks, 50 blocks, 50 sets cylinder heads, 250 cams, 2,500 pistons, some sheet metal, some trim. It's Hudson, Chevy, Ford, Pontiac, Buick, Offy, Indy car, Delorean, GMC, Fiesta, Volkswagen. A li'l of everything from 1946 to 1987. Little by little I get rid of some of it to museums, colleges. If you're kinda goofy and like old race car stuff, and have two tractor and trailers and mucho loot, come down and I'll help you load it. It's been a full-time job keeping the stuff clean, oiled and dry (expensive too). My goal is "get rid of the stuff, get up on the roof with 20 gallons of gas, spread it around and light it. The goddam garage is 55 years old and it's getting in really poor shape. We had two hurricanes in '99 and the roof looks like a chicken with most of it's feathers off.

I had hurricane insurance. Take my word for this: those pricks with the full help of the state insurance commissioner charged me three grand for policy, the damage was over $23,000 – they paid me three grand.

The insurance commissioner, Nelson, today is running for state senator. Man, I wouldn't vote for him to be cesspool inspector. I've been paying insurance for 20 years. That asshole wouldn't make a good used car salesman.

I have never stopped working and still in 1999, worked every day including Saturday and Sunday.

I get there late, 'bout 11:00 am and leave at 7:00 pm. Even tho' I haven't been a competitor since Indy '75, I still go to enough Winston Cup and Indy car races to be half-assed current with the tech.

What made this work was I got jobs, like representing Champion Plugs and ARP Fasteners, so in helping the current competitors use the products I represented, our dialogue keeps me pretty much up to date. This puts me in the position to compare yesterday and today.

I couldn't have in my goofiest dreams imagined how ape-shit this country has gone over taxi cab racing. The tremendous increase in compensation to the race teams blows my mind. The social status of the racer has changed dramatically also. Today's front runners enjoy a near mythical worship from the fans and general public, whereas in my time, at best we were 'bout like paroled felons with small following of what was to be the embryo of a modern Winston Cup race fan.

A puzzling paradox is the reversal in popularity of open wheel racing as compared to "so-called" stock cars. I can't imagine what would happen to someone who caused a TV with ten people watching to quit working during a Winston Cup race with ten laps to go.

I'd get many requests to speak or do seminars, but until '87 avoided all but alternate energy topics. In refusing a speaking offer a man said, "Where else can you make five grand an hour? Now this hit home. "You mean?" "Why, hell yes." "You got a point there." So I did a couple, and was astonished that I could get five grand or more for maybe one to three hours of my time. For damn near as often as I cared to do it. And much to my surprise I found I was able to amuse and to educate (to a point) large groups.

In the beginning, say from '55 to '75 I wrote the speeches (what little I did), and am quite sure I was boring as hell. One day I lost my speech. Hell, I was pissed. I had no choice, I had to get up and wing it. Hell, it was ten times easier, and I think ten times better. Ever since I just stand up there and let it fly, getting clues on which way to go by listening to questions from the audience.

I did lots of speaking engagements…that's Bob Florine of ARP…a good company that paid me to talk about their fasteners.

In 1995, I lost my hearing. Do you think a deaf man could do a question and answer deal with a 600 person audience for four hours and they didn't know he was deaf? We did it with question cards. Margie kept 'em coming. In between questions I picked what I thought was best.

How did you lose you're hearing Smokey? Well, I only had one ear, left ear was 100 percent deaf since 1970. In 1995, I had to do a li'l speaking in Birmingham, Alabama and there were to be some big shooters (like George Bush) there, and I thought if I got my working ear cleaned I could hear better. So, I go to an ear doctor I've been to before, but don't trust. Turns out he was only one that could clean my ear on short notice. The dumb son-of-a-bitch ends up sticking an air hose in my nostril…gonna blow out a plugged "something."

Well, in three minutes my middle ear feels like it blew up. I end up going to this Alabama ear doctor who bills himself as "Ear One" I get operated on by "Ear One," two days after ear blow job. In a month he says "Ball game's over…I can give you an implant for 'bout 17 grand, but let's wait couple more weeks." I go back in two weeks (I'm totally deaf now, hearing aids can't do anything). I manage by carrying a Mickey Mouse writing board and easy erase felt tip. Ear One checks me over saying "hmmmmmm" and rubbing his chin, then writes, "Only hope is ear implant."

I say, "How much." He writes "'bout 35 grand." Whooooeeeee…less than 30 days and price doubles. "I'll let you know doc. Any chance you'll have a clearance sale and cut the price a little?" "Nope. If we can't do it tomorrow it may be too late even for an implant."

My little inner brain says "Haul ass outta here Smoke. Once you go the implant route it's Russian roulette. If it don't work there are no other options. You're gonna use a lot of Mickey Mouse boards and felt tips till lights go out."

When I first got in ear trouble bad enough that hearing aids were necessary, I got lucky. With the help of Bobby and Al Unser, I got directed to Doctor Earl Harford at a big hearing aid company in Minneapolis ("Starkey"). Doc Harford, his boss man Bill Austin and Gary Anderson, their chief tech guy, busted their asses to help me. Starkey rides and has rode in some pretty important ears. How's this for starters: Richard Petty, Bobby and Al Unser, Bobby and Donnie Allison, Red Farmer, Chris Economacki, Stan Musial, Frank Sinatra, Ronald Reagan, Johnny Rutherford. A tip to anybody who is gonna need hearing aids: there is no easy-perfect fix. If you don't really give those hearing aid people your complete confidence and make some adjustments mentally to accept a lesser ability to understand, you're gonna waste a lot of money and suffer many disappointments. The above is aimed at people who have a serious hearing loss. The biggest problem with hearing aids is background noise. Another kinda tip: hearing impaired people seem to be ignorant of the imposition their problem is putting on their families. I damn near drove Margie goofy by winding up the TV volume and refusing to recognize the extent of my hearing loss.

I decide to use Dr. Harford as a "guide dog" regarding any further ear maneuvering. He says, "Hell no!" Implants at best ain't good, and at worst is like rollin' snake eyes.

Doc Harford through the grapevine finds a doctor Lundy at the Mayo Clinic in Jacksonville, Florida, who has a "Merlin rating" as an ear magician. I'm totally deaf now. Two famous ear surgeons say after four operations, only hope is ear implant in right ear, left ear is zero. No way to get it going. Six operations and one year later, Doc Lundy's got both ears working (granted, half-assed, but good enough to get by with hearing aids) If you got serious ear problems find a way to get Doc Lundy at the Mayo clinic in Jacksonville to check you out. His first name should be "Magic."

Racers, take this seriously. You must be much more protective of your ears. Racers are at serious risk, but believe me. So are the fans, and sadly those most damaged by excessive noise are infants and the very young. I love loud race cars, but racers you better muffle your racers before someone makes a public crusade out of this. Make up your mind 90 to 95 decibels are your limit. Today in a grandstand, close to front and lower rows, I've measured 135 decibels. Specially when cars are bunched up at the start or restart. A fact you should know about most deafness: it is very hereditary, so strict precaution does much to help minimize the damage but will not avoid it…it can't. This damage is kinda like smoking. It's cumulative, and it will absolutely appear in time to affect your life in a negative way. You wanna get an idea what I'm talking 'bout? Put a good set of ear plugs in your ears. Now leave 'em in for half a day on your job. I don't care what your job is…nope, can't take em out to answer phone.

I now know why most companies retired their staff and employees at 60 to 65. I see two reasons. One is, after you pass 40 everything starts to slo' down a little. Don't believe it? Ask your wife.

Sure, you may still be pretty good in the hay, but if momma is honest she'll tell you "you're still great, but you can't do the mile in less than four minutes anymore." Momma's noticing she's slowly getting to be the star in your sex movies. Well, hell, that's the way it's supposed to be.

Any other scenario and we would have annihilated the human race for lack of adequate food a million years ago. Ol' cats are real good sounding boards, they "been there and done that" a long time ago. But their advice could be flawed. Technology changes faster than the ol' dogs can totally absorb, comprehend and accept. People are really creatures of habit. Think about it. The unknown of anything is an uncomfortable position to feel relaxed with. Kinda like, "Did he say that snake was or was not poisonous?" Specially if the damn thing just bit you.

Every day now I realize I really had a wonderful life. Ain't a day goes by somebody in an airport, at home or at work, at a race track or conventions, trade shows, seminars – somebody tells me I helped them some way. I don't get all the feedback. People don't go out of their way as much to tell you you were an asshole. I finally realize I got a family who support me and care about my welfare. I doubt there's any way I can tell you how much Margie has affected my life for the better. For the first 60 years, I run wide open, turning 'tween 8,500 and 9,000 rpm, and just as I could barely see the place I had been aimed at, I'd see a place over the next hill I needed to go to.

Now I realize loud and clear, racing is for young people because it requires so much of what a person over 60 ain't got any more. A good racer is hungry, full of energy, willing to sacrifice, very talented in people management without even knowing it. He's special. Yup…every one of 'em is a "he." And at one time there are only 20 in the whole world. Could a woman do it? Yes, but with a handicap. Every one of them unwittingly dedicate their lives to racing and sorry to say, for some it's not gonna have a good ending.

That kind of stuff I'm good at now. I watch the Ray Evernham and Jeff Gordon story unfold. It's an unhappy, and I imagine, bitter time between them, but I've seen it so often I know it's part of nature. It takes a team – money, driver, crew chief. If it clicks they are next to unbeatable. Lose the special comradeship and they can't piss a drop. The Ray and Jeff story is not news to me it is an old movie. It's in its retake 'bout number 15. Who is right? Who is wrong? Nobody, that's what the movie is about.

Back in Gordon's early days.

Dale Earnhardt

Dale (The Mustache) and I never raced together. I knew his dad well and damn near raced with him. When Dale came to the big-time, I remembered his adventures driving the Wrangler car for Bud Moore. I couldn't help but feel this li'l shit might be a real racer so from time to time, I'd be able to help him a little. His questions 'bout car and driving and his ability to control the car in some of the goddamndest situations lead me to believe he had a very extra special middle ear which gives that driver a razor's edge know-how of push and spin. I think Gordon's got it, the Wood brothers and the new kid on block Harvick. I'm sure several others. I don't get to see 'em enough anymore. Earnhardt had the balls of a 900 pound gorilla, but I wasn't fond of his methods. In the beginning, we all felt leader owns the track. You can go around him either side, under him or over him but you can't touch him. 60 years later I still feel same way. I've said earlier in this book to criticize 2001 racing you must have 2001 experience. So 60 years had too many changes...most for the best. I rather doubt Terry Labonte feels that way, but nevertheless, I was proud of the tough ass for his skill and courage.

Race fans I wish you'd digest this part: driver privacy doesn't exist any more. They have to ride in a million buck motorhome then jump out and run in the racer. You want to say hello, wish him good luck. He ignores you. Some place in here just 'fore a big race starts all drivers get in a nervous irritable mode. Now they're helpless to do anything. They're strapped in there so tight it hurts to fart. Also, he realizes he may be beginning the last hours of his life. I watched Dale at Darlington, climb in car, talked normal then start the race unconscious. I felt it was a medication backfire, but all I know 'bout medicine can be written on a postage stamp.

For you up-and-coming drivers and fans you ain't got a clue what sacrifices a winning driver goes through to get there. The heat, the three-and-a-half hours feeling like you're running on ice and knowing any second you're a wall job. There's places in race you'd need a four pound hammer to drive a 20 penny nail up the driver's ass. Try that 35 or 40 times a year.

Four drivers, including the Best, died in a year. By the way, the real total is over 10.

'Bout two years ago I realized Earnhardt put me in a new classification and I understood his position, so I kept away from him. No one can read that much shit 'bout himself without some major personality changes. Consider his case...got the world by the ass. I heard within 300 and six more zeros at 50 and in .500 of a second the movie ends in baddest way. You are willing? Would you trade what he had for early death? So, I guess drivers need to also consider when and how to jump off that bronco before the shit hits the fan.

All this to tell you I was in first International Hall of Fame induction. Dale Earnhardt did the induction speech. Goodbye Dale and all you stood for. Your leaving further confuses me on life. I guess only way not to get snake bit is don't fuck with 'em. In my book you are without a peer. You represented us without comparison. The Earnhardt crew, Richard Childress; owner (the elephant hater), mechanics like Danny Lawrence and Mike Hawkins, the Earnhardt family…I figured if ever a person had a perfect dream-world life, it was Ironhead E.

What pisses me off…I seen all this shit on the wall at night 10 years ago in my dreams. That voice seemed like it blew back at me at 100 mph. Moveable walls, concrete tracks, fueling by computer, air jacks 'stead of the 30 pound flying sledge hammers they use, mandatory retirement age, etc. When the hell they gonna get to doing something? Maybe after next Ace gets it? When they gonna get rid of the fucking restrictor plate and go to smaller engines? Don't give me that horseshit answer you can get killed in a bathtub. It's this simple: who ever's running NASCAR has got his head up his ass. Course that's just an old racer's opinion. Some of these things, Billy, remind me of a kid who played with his peter too much when he was little.

The Smoketron

In 1958, I decide I want to air flow the engine both in the motoring mode and in the running mode. Ever hear of something called a Smoketron? Well, I built five Smoketrons, each bigger and better.

Well, first I bought a Navy surplus 50 horsepower spin tester. All it could do was take 4 cylinders (half the engine) to 7000 rpm the cam and springs only. Wow, I under estimated the power requirements a ton. I had to build a dummy crankshaft for oiling reasons and found out quite a bit. I found weight on valve side of the rocker pivot critical i.e. valve, valve spring, valve spring retainer, valve keepers. A giant surprise was that the weight of rocker, pushrod and lifter next to no effect on the rpm of valve float. Faults of Smoketron number 1: it runs hot and not enough power. I want to pull whole engines so the second model has 100 horsepower. It is still way short of power. Still runs hot (oil) pulling all 8 cylinders with heads and valves only (no crank). I started receiving cams and valve springs to test. More faults become apparent as I test.

By 1968, I got contract with Graftex, a division of Exxon. They had a division in North Carolina that made composite parts. In the first test, soon as I hit resonant frequencies of the push rod I had dust instead of a push rod. In mean time I bought an Optron (strobe) to watch valve gear.

By 1979, I found we'd spent 120 grand, took in $15,000. I now know it's gonna take a 300 horsepower motor to get to 8500 rpm. This is after wasting 20 grand getting a 200 horsepower specially wound motor that wasn't up to it. (Note: reciprocators are engine, electric power is motors.) In the beginning, I built the Smoketron to do valve gear analysis only. Turning the whole engine might allow more testing. Well, to get a 300 horsepower system that had accurate control you're talking 50 big ones just for the motor.

In 1983, I decide to build the real deal. Clint Folsom, a Birmingham entrepreneur, inventor and race car nut wanted to be a partner. (his idea). We had a contract but he fell on bad times. A real race pussy-hound and the whole nine yards. He built the gear case; a heavy monstrosity out of steel case and all. I expect prototype to cost 300,000 grand. It would run a Winston Cup engine complete at 9,000 rpm This machine would include a dyno and flow bench equipment. Clint's company, Seal Tech, contracted to build and market the deal for 250,000 each. However his company went to shit because of lack of attention (my guess) and interest in the great wooly bugger. He quit and forfeited his interest. Now I'm stuck with finishing 'em.

By now machine is getting computerized, has automatic air flow measurement including subtraction of blow by and all corrections. Damn patents of Smoketron were close to 100 grand. Had to be portable, run on 440 volt three phase, have dyno with a gear shift, had to have electronic capabilities to photograph any and all parts in motion and display it on tape.

That most recent one was completed in 'bout 1993 and patented. At this point I got 'bout 600 or 700 thousand in the Smoketron. But it can motor a Winston Cup engine in it's entirety to 9,000 rpm. Guess how much horsepower it takes to turn a Winston Cup motor 9,000 rpm? 'Bout 300 horsepower. (How 'bout this: just pull spark plugs and it takes 300 horsepower to get to 6,000 rpm. Why? You figure that out.)

Any of that surprise you? I decided real air flow is what goes into fueler in total, but also measure how much gets blowed back out at overlap, subtract overlap and you got the real answer. We had it worked out so one piece of equipment does this, plus calculate correction for temperature, barometric pressure and humidity. I read one number, constantly corrected air flow. Well in this method we've found the absolute cylinder volumetric efficiency is limited to the 99 percent range. I've never seen 100 percent, let alone 114 percent (the fancy words mean "how full is the cylinder of air and fuel").

Another surprise: the worst cylinder filling is at "idle." Why? (Cam overlap intake opens while exhaust is still open and it retards flow.) Hell, at idle cylinders are only 35 to 40 percent full.

This bothered me the most. Maximum cylinder filling is no longer than a 300 rpm range!

So where do you want maximum torque? Maximum torque is maximum cylinder fill (makes sense: most potential energy = most working fluid in cylinder). With the Smoketron we can see valve float and print it's motion at all times. We can tell which spring or springs are floating and if it's inner or outer spring or both. We can draw a picture of the actual motion of any parts motion with a printer. We can aim a synchronized light and a camera at a part (synchronized also) and watch or freeze the part in a stressed or failure mode. We have glass oil pan, valve covers, timing covers, glass manifolds and glass valley covers. We can produce a video in color to see the behavior of these components.

A cam shaft timing chain is broken because of hysterisis (a stack up of tolerances and reactions).

We found under certain high rpm conditions with a timing chain the slack side of timing chain can be in tension. For this to happen physically, cam shaft must stop for a millionth of a second (this is where timing chains and cams are busted).

With the Smoketron in a motoring mode we could choose every component and examine it's contribution or obstruction in the complete breathing system (both sides) intake and exhaust, then place maximum torque at damn near any rpm we wanted. However there is a compromise that must be considered. That is the race track. Specifically, fastest lap time is a consideration of maximum torque at right place along with maximum horsepower at right place on a given track. (This is assuming chassis, driver and aerodynamics are good with open differential). We found too much horsepower at wrong place on track is worse than not enough. Why? You grind the right rear tire off.

We found all engine components no matter how expertly manufactured or prepared, no two pieces were really alike. Example: Chinese yin-yang philosophy. Yin-yang says no two or more of anything are 100 percent alike. Therefore if you had three carburetors you assumed alike. In real life all will be something different. Not much. But if you're running for 50 grand for the pole, it's important. The Smoketron is so expensive, mostly because of the need for a 300 horsepower electric motor that can be set at any rpm between 100 and 9,000 rpm and stay in a two to three rpm range. This turns out to be 50 grand or more right here. Also lots of electric measuring, photographing and printing equipment. An important feature is, I can use the electric motor and in a few minutes shift gears and go to a live engine mode and measure horsepower. The friction measuring capabilities are accurate to one half of one foot pound of torque. So water and oil pumps can be measured for gains or losses. Valve spring tension is a big horsepower eater.

The Smoketron points out the most desirable manufacturer or what is best modification for that particular component. Example: oil pressure horsepower costs sometimes are eye openers. The Smoketron can measure water or oil flow or both. We have a system on the machine that can measure the amount of air in the oil. That is a very interesting revelation that most oil systems both wet and dry sump impregnate the oil with air. Normally speaking, in 30 minutes we have a 50-50 air oil mix. We found a metal mesh and metal stacked plates filter (like a Cuno) put less air in the oil than paper filters do and eventually learned why. I found they do not let atmosphere into engine. A one way check valve pressure out only, for minimum air-oil contamination. Look at an Indy or Formula One engine. You'll see an air separator somewhere in the oil loop. Without air separator those engines will fail in ten miles.

What's best cam?

What's best valve lash?

Should you advance or retard it?

What's best header diameter and length for primary?

What's best intake manifold?

What's best air cleaner?

Which carb? What size? (Smallest for max flow, so it will drive.) Because we know a long track maximum volumetric efficiency needs to be at highest point in rpm range we will run in. For a short track we aim for highest volumetric efficiency at rpm coming off the corner.

The Smoketron taught me the oil holes in a crank, rods and mains need thought in regard to position timing in a 360 degree arch of the rod journal. The hydrostatic wedge needs to originate just prior to maximum bearing pressures.

What's the effect of compression in regard to what fuel you use and in reference to maximum mechanical and/or maximum thermal efficiency, they are not alike. Maximum power is rich, say 12.5 to one. Maximum thermal efficiency is round 14 to one.

What does water temperature cylinder to cylinder have to do with the deal?

What oil temperature and viscosity have to do with power?

What's best cam drive? Is chain best, or three-gear or two-gear, or belt?

What's best combustion chamber cavity shape? And what's piston crown shape got to do with efficient combustion for power and/or emissions? I learned best combustion chamber is no combustion chamber with a flat head concave piston dome.

If somebody got a miracle oil or treatment (regarding friction), what's it do?

Did you gain? How much? Or was it as usual a bunch of bullshit and nothing happened?

How much power do you gain or lose with oil pan fluid level?

When you look at crank running hard with glass pan you see big gobs of oil flying off of the rotating mass intermittently. What about balance? In real life we balance to a gnat's ass. Here is two or three ounces flying off. Tell me 'bout perfect balance.

You make a piston ring change, various wall pressure various ring material, try pressure back top ring. Go to a two ring deal. Compare different ring tech reference width of ring. Did friction go up-down? What happened when you double check and fire up and read power? Did it correlate?

What's best bore finish? Real slick? Rough cross hatch?

A major power surprise was: where does the spark plug belong for power in a combustion cavity? Answer: the cleanest spot reference scavenging exhaust or reacted gasses. You wanna know here it is? Rite where intake valve and exhaust are the closest to each other. Did I invent that? Nope. A cat named Ricardo from England taught me that deal. Would a third valve work in road racing in braking? Works in trucks don't it? The Smoketron was what showed me by accident in 1960 how to use the flywheel and pressure plate and bell housings as a free supercharger. I learned best combustion chamber was no chamber. Do it with the piston.

I learned not to vent the engine to atmospheric instead use one pound check valve for venting blow-by. This is in reference to air-oil contamination.

I learned if I built a carburetor where when throttle was water tight on close, that at 7,000 rpm a quick full closure would shear throttle shaft out of the carb.

I used it to measure spark plug ceramic temperature to run close on heat range. Looks like ceramic temperature of 1,100 degrees F. is the ideal.

The Smoketron confirms long rod length and offset wrist pins by cylinder pressure and torque readings.

This is world's best "what if?" machine. You can get 90 percent of the answer before you ever heat the exhaust pipes. Answers to questions like:

How many gallons of oil you need to flow?

What's right sized oil pump?

How many scavenge sections? (Dry sump). And where from?

What's oil temperature at the rod bearing? (The main bearing, etc.)

What's oil temperature at bottom of exhaust valve spring?

How much oil spray on valve springs should you have?

What's air fuel flow look like in intake runners? How much chaos?

Any rivers of fuel? (With glass intake)

What's the cylinder temperature and pressure in each cylinder running?

The ability to read, instantly, detonation and it's degree of danger.

How 'bout reading crank case pressure and percentage of blo-by, running hard?

How 'bout read torque and power from a simulated lap and develop an ignition advance or retard curve, and maybe discover at maximum torque what the best timing is. Say eight degrees less than at best power? (This is short track and yellow flag restart stuff).

How 'bout testing coated bearing surfaces, piston rings, cylinder walls, cams, valve springs and other motion parts for how much benefit is it?

How much friction did it take out? Or did it?

Various thermal dams, piston, valves, combustion chamber. Power increase? Or nothing? Maybe a loss? How? If it don't flow more air running you ain't done anything. You can try various bore stroke combo looking for maximum cylinder pressure and find the winner without heat.

The Smoketron points out that a good engine man needs a mind like a professional card shark. That is, a need to be able mentally to assemble and envision about 50 factors that either compliment or oppose maximum performance for a specific engine task. I believe a good engine man can layout all the engine components in his mind and then describe it good enough in writing and sketches that it can be built. The Smoketron is a single portable machine that is the summation of all I learned about the physics and chemistry of a four cycle engine. The current valve motion study machines commercially available are knock-offs

The Smoketron is at UCF.

of maybe Smoketron number two from 1960. Every successful hi-buck engine builder will have to have a Smoketron type machine within five years.

Off the top of my head that's most of what the Smoketron will do. I think this is best tool in regard to the physics of air-fuel management in the world today. Did I invent anything? Yup, the Smoketron is patented. After Clint Folsom and Seal Tech bailed, I offered it for sale for $450,000 to $500,000 patents and all. Never did get a deal I figured would hold up so I donated it to the University of Central Florida where it now resides under the command of Dr. Bob Hoekstra. They have a Smokey Yunick engineering course for graduate engineers to earn a Ph.D. in race car engineering.

Power Secrets

In 1980, Larry Schreib started bugging me to write a tech book on race engines. I had written for Popular Science 'bout 20 years by then (and hated it) and a few stories for other magazines, and had no interest in it at all. For example: I was the "Dear Abby" for cars at Popular Science for 28 years. Every month a column (called "Smokey Sez")… 336 Columns and a few features. The most I ever got was 500 bucks a month.

Can you imagine the mailman dumping 300 to 2,000 letters a month on the floor…(every month)? Popular Science says, "he reads every one and picks the best." Some of them letters were ten pages long. I learned this loud and clear in a couple years…if the president of every motor company had someone read'em all…the guidance those letters gave I consider invaluable.

A pattern would show up by category and frequency that showed me what people wanted and expected, and what new features they liked or disliked. Some was pathetic, some was hilariously funny, some sad. Most of it valid and well written. Of course the main premise was "how do I correct" a perceived fault in my car or truck. There was always some fucking kooky stuff way out in left field, but no more than five percent. In that 28 years I watched Detroit (Ford, GM and Chrysler) operate with their heads up their collective asses and they never woke up and listened to their customers. I've been both ways, working for GM at a big car show they passed out questionnaires…

"What kind of car would you like?," answers always the same.

– "zero to sixty, five seconds"
– "40 miles per gallon"
– "six passenger seats that can be made into beds"
– "no repairs or maintenance for 100,000 miles"
– "cost no more than $2,000 bucks"
– "cruise speed 'bout 100 miles per hour"
– "lots of chrome"
– "automatic pilot"
– "automatic wash and shine button"
– "entertainment center"
– "a kitchen for long trips"

…but if they read the letters I got they would have known people wanted small cars, mini-vans, nicer pick-ups, safer, longer-lasting, better mileage, better brakes on slick roads, better handling vehicles. They would have learned a station wagon, a two-door, a four-door and a convertible only fit maybe 50 percent of their customer's garages. They would have discovered the Americans loved their wheels.

GM, instead of having five divisions, all having the same cars 'cept for price, should have had each division build four or five models to fit various niches with no same ability between divisions. Same with Ford and Chrysler. Hey, I can remember when foreign car sales were one percent. The head cat at GM said, "A perfect car had to have five good seats and also have room for a dog." Do you agree?

I notice now the car buying public is goofier than ever…you've gone pickup nuts. A pickup in inclement weather is inherently dangerous (ain't got enough weight on rear wheels). Why would you choose a more dangerous vehicle? You tired of living? Hey, you got a pickup and have used it three years, what you ever haul in it? The inner body looks brand new to me. How many times did you ever use the 4-wheel drive? Yet 4-wheel drive is a safer driving mode when inclement weather is encountered…you with those giant tars…ever notice 'bout every time you make last lunge to get up in the seat you fart? Can you hear your wife quietly cursing you as she gets in with one foot even with her tits? Especially those who got to eating way too much when bored. I never got any letters from ladies who wanted a woman's pickup. Sure, if you're a rancher, farmer, trucker or are in construction, etc., you gotta have it, but what 'bout all those pick-ups at the country club? What's that shit?

How 'bout the million buck motorhome towing a 4-wheel drive sports utility with a cross-country motorcycle on rear bumper, parked in motel parking lot? Sign on back of motorhome "the kid's inheritance." How 'bout this, (regarding Popular Science letters) "My wife and I wanted a new Cadillac, I retired, we bought one… got electric everything. It's 13 months old, our fortunes went to shit, wife is invalid now. Electric door locks have quit working. Dealer says to fix will cost $1,800…got to cut doors and re-weld and repaint all four doors, warranty has ended at 12 months. I ain't got the money, do you know of a cheaper way to fix? My solution was to remove the rear seat and drag my wife through the trunk up to the front seat area." I showed it to president of GM, he like to pissed his pants laughing.

How 'bout this: "Bought a limited edition Chevy, has special upholstery, I'm in a car pool, five of us, we all wear three piece suits, before we get out of car we have to take our shoes off because as we slide across the seat to exit, soon as the first shoe hits the ground we get shocked in the balls."

How 'bout this: "I'm a retired railroad conductor. I've never had enough money to buy a new car before. So as a gift to ourselves we bought a new four-cylinder Chevy, but it has a problem. I've had it back to the dealer six or eight times. Every time I turn left it stalls. I have a letter from the dealer saying, "It's not fixable this time, stay in touch." My wife will not ride in the car any more unless I can plan a route where we never turn left."

Or: "I bought a new Buick, some times it runs away. I've had one fairly serious accident, have avoided one by driving up on a sidewalk. My wife won't ride in it and I'm now renting a car. The Buick is five months old, dealer says, "Nothing is wrong with it."

I could give you a thousand of these. I showed 'em to top man of all divisions mentioned. All laughed like hell. And what did they do? Nothing. Were these kooky complaints? Hell no! Every one of them showed up as most frequent complaints of those makes and models.

Mr. Knudsen (Remember him? He built ten million GM cars). His sister bought a new Caddy, electric everything including hood lock. Got automatic head light turner-on-ers, it's dusk, Cleveland shopping center. Electric headlight turner-off-er don't do it, an hour or so shopping, she pushes the button and the driver's door opens. All windows are up (cold weather) The car don't start (normal result of battery being low cause head lights stayed on). She still don't know it. OK, gotta get out and call service (no cell phones yet) Oh shit! battery is so low door lock won't work. OK, wind window down and holler…nope, not enough juice. OK, holler at people through window, gesture, etc. Turns out this lady has a phobia 'bout being locked in. Her frantic verbal and physical contortions lead passers-by to decide she's drunk. Finally, a neighbor spots the deal. OK, gonna be fine, I'll have a service truck here in five minutes. In twenty minutes he gets there. "Sorry, couldn't get away, you know how it is." "Pull the hood lock ma'am." She says, "I have pulled it, dead battery." Well, they break a window, drag her out, cut an eight-inch hole in the hood over the lock (a Caddy technician told them where.) The tow truck guy put a battery in it and took it to GM executive garage for repairs. What did they do besides fix that as official job for a week? Nothing!

Check this one out: I'm sitting in vice president of CCS Engineering's office, a friend of mine, Larry Dickinson, Saturday morning. I've given him five runaway letters…two Pontiacs, three Buicks. He glances at 'em, says "Smokey, we bought a BMW and an Audi to check that rumor out. It don't exist." I say, "How 'bout these letters?" He says "operator goof up." Believe me, this happened: five minutes later we get in a new especially prepared, most expensive yallar Pontiac (there's 50 miles on it). Only the guys who work in executive garages can tell you how these supposedly rite off the line cars go through their special checks. Larry tries a different car every week. We only got to go from the Fisher building to the Chevy engineering center, hardly a mile. The floor is grey paint (slick). We jump in… Larry fires it, pulls it in gear (runaway) all wheels sliding, spinning. Turns key off. Whew! no damage. I look at Larry's eyes – they are bigger than two piss holes in the snow. I say, "Goddam, you're getting wild in your old age." He's sitting there talking to himself, going through it in sequence. OK, restarts the engine, got a death grip on the steering wheel, got the brakes on hard, waits a couple seconds, puts her in drive, touches the throttle…runaway number two. I get out and look. Black marks are on the floor from front wheels pulling and rear wheels sliding. I pull letters out of my pocket and say, "This car seems to be acting like these in the letters. "Get in goddam it, we are going."

I see big black Caddy 30-40 feet away, I push the wheel little to the left and say "if it does it again you're aimed at the exit door, you'll have plenty of time to get things under control." Nope, didn't do it again. He backed it into a parking spot at executive Chevy garage, but with a glaring mistake, when he had it aimed to back in, he turned key off at 'bout five miles an hour, but he lucked out. He got it stopped before the big noise. (When you turn key off you lock the steering.)

What did they do? Surprise, next day they started a department called "unusual and mysterious car behavioral problems," six months later person in charge wanted any letters I had on items like this. I asked him "what they'd found on that Pontiac?" "Nothing, maybe this, maybe that." You know Larry, I kidded you at the meeting we went to when I told them 'bout "you dreamed runaways." I said then, and still believe that you smelled a little funny after the second runaway that never happened. You want me to tell you what I think happened? I have no absolute proof, no one ever said "we'll pay you to find out." All they wanted me to do was be a professional witness and explain to the jury what happened. The Corvair professional witness adventure cured me of any desire to play that game again.

I had a friend here in Daytona, Bill Gordon. I referred all those deals to him. Some of those I heard about were fatal, some very funny. Specially the expert tow truck driver who needed to move a runaway to get it hooked to his wrecker and he backed through a second level concrete block wall.

After 27 years I got thinking how in the hell did I get in this rat race? And seriously decided to quit. I called publisher, he says "Smoke, you must be a mind reader, I was just gonna call you. You're the oldest employee Popular Science has, in March it will be 28 years. We are gonna honor you in Los Angles with a big dinner. By the way, they're honoring me too, I'll have 25 years in February 1st." Get plane tickets, 800 bucks, week before the dinner phone call, publisher fired, dinner canceled. Took three months to get my plane ticket money back.

I ask my friend Mr. Knudsen how to quit without pissing everybody off. He says ask for them to double your salary. I call new publisher, he's from the computer world, with a long dago name.

He don't talk to contributing editors, "stay in line of command." Before I can tell him to stick his job up his ass he hangs up. I call right guy, he says, "We can't pay you twelve hundred dollars a month." I say, "Good, I quit." He says, "Goddam you, don't do that, you got two million readers who will go ape-shit and bankrupt this magazine. Don't do anything, I'll get a director's meeting and see what we can work out."

Two weeks later he calls and says, "March will be last of your monthly column." I say, "Ain't you worried 'bout the magazine going bankrupt?" They never published one word 'bout terminating the column, and I see they are still in business twelve years later. It was an experience, and an interesting adventure. Popular Science had a real neat editor in 1959, Bob Crosby. He loved racing. He knew Tom McCahill got lots of help from me and Bob wanted to use me to compete with Tom McCahill at Popular Mechanics. I try it for three issues, also I was gonna replace a monthly feature called "something Gus" (I can't remember) with "Say Smokey." Well, they run a survey every month. Crosby pours it on me 'bout how popular it is. Hell in three months I'm running second to Von Braun (the rocket wizard). Well, I still want to quit. Von Braun invites me to the Cape to talk about a prime mover a friend of mine, Emmit Oliver, invented. I got something to do with that. Shit, I'm hobnobbing with some real brains here. Hell of a deal. (My ego is a problem here.)

Six months, "Bob, I want this to be last column." "Oh damn! Smoke, we buried Gus last month, stay six more months." "OK. Bob, six months up now, I quit again." Meantime Popular Mechanic hires Dan Gurney to parallel my stuff in Popular Science. I've eat McCahill's ass up. Dan don't do the writing, his PR guy, Max Muhleman is writing the column with tech answers by (probably) Phil Remington. It don't work, too much racing. "Bob, I hate this deal, plus I could make more money cleaning shit houses." "Smoke, you can't quit, you're number one now, you've passed Von Braun." I'll bet you for the lousy 300 to 400 bucks a month I'd spend a hard 20 to 25 hours writing and 20 hours a month on phone with readers and offended or happy advertisers. If you ever saw me at an airport of on a plane I'd be reading and writing answers.

I find out McCahill supposedly gets 50 grand a year. I get $4,800. McCahill don't know anything really 'bout cars or driving, but his bullshit apparently sells, and most astonishingly to me, the car manufacturers are scared shitless of him. They give him cars, wine and dine him: hell, Bill France treats him like the king of Siam. I'd like to have a 30-minute movie of a scene in a New York Hotel room (at an early year NASCAR championship banquet), of France, Paul Whiteman, Tom McCahill, Xaviar Cugat and his wife Abby Lane, Miles Warmer from Time Magazine. Add in a couple of gays and 'bout two straights (NASCAR secretaries) and three hookers. My first good look at what is explained when you look up the word "orgy" in the dictionary.

I'm really getting a deep shock as I start to realize how phony the news media is, how powerful the industrial community is, and most of all, the top people in our major corporations, politics, finance, military and law enforcement are really there because of brown-nosing and family connections, plus manipulation of the system by those with the aspirations to become the leaders. Clinton would be maybe the prime example of how a slick, smart bullshitter can take 'er all the way to the moon.

Bob Crosby's deal with one was, "If you're sure of your ground, I'll publish it with no special consideration to anyone." I can call it real! Firestone comes up with a bad-bad tire (721 I think was designation). Major problem was tread separation. I got bunch of letters. People getting hurt, people getting killed. I got friends at Firestone. I call and say, "Your new tire is junk, come look at my mail." "No Smokey, tire's good… it's this-that-etc." I say, "Bullshit, I've read these letters long enough I know if you don't stop building that tire you're gonna lose your ass." The boss man at Firestone says, "I hear you're concerned 'bout the tire, what kind of car you got?" "A new Caprice Chevy loaned me," "I'll send you a set of tires, put 'em on your car and try 'em." I already knew these will be special, x-rayed, with all kinds of special not normally done care and checking.

I tell him "problem is sustained high speed on super hi-ways overheats tire and in an hour or so tread separates." He says, "Not a problem, you can run 'em 100 mph all day long." "Yeah…how 'bout 90 mph?" "No sweat." I put 'em on (he sends five); I mount and balance 'em all. I'm going to go I-95 Daytona to Miami via the Alleygator's turnpike. Only stop to pay toll once each way. Run tank to tank at 90 mph. I leave here 9:00 pm. I got five more wheels mounted up (had to take back seat out). I take a good jack.

At 5:00 am I blew the fifth tire leaving Melbourne. I was half asleep and it got away from me. When the tread came off it did 'bout 500 bucks damage to right rear quarter panel. I damn near flipped it when it blew, first thing it did was go down in about an eight-foot ditch, but it was pretty smooth and grassy. I got it back up without rolling it. I called him at 9:00 pm and recited my adventure; he said," I'll send you five more." I said, "Will you pay for the quarter panel, fuel and toll and loan me a test car?" He hung up.

So I blasted the tires. But Popular Science didn't print it. Next month trouble getting worse, got a neighbor, Dr. Snodgrass, blew four from Daytona to Maine (after I told him they weren't worth a shit). Nobody dead or hurt but he wants me to call Firestone. I say, "Doc, I ain't sure I want you to advise me." (Apparently a man can get to be a doctor with a lousy IQ.) Second month, still won't print it. New publisher. (Bob's got fired for something, probably telling the truth). Lucky new headman says, "Smokey if I print it I'll get fired, I just bought a new sail boat and I need the job."

I say, "Don't get fired over me, I quit. You've ruptured my contract with magazine." He says, "No, I'll print it, I know now you're correct. Why did the tread come loose?" "Hell I don't know for sure. But I guess it either wasn't fastened good enough or it got bigger than the carcass. Hell, if I knew all this shit I wouldn't be writing goddam column for 300 bucks a month." Yup, he printed it.

He was told his ass was gone, but rite at that time so much trouble came from those tires (I guess they were failing on all the politicians freebie tires and Firestone wouldn't pay to fix their quarter panels), a senate subcommittee was investigating the tire, and subsequently came down on the tire bad. Lucky's ass got saved; he was able to pay off the sailboat. Firestone went to the shithouse and ended up a rice burner possession. Can you imagine Firestone, Henry Ford and Thomas Edison's drinking buddy, having to suffer the humiliation (even after death)?

Mobil Oil did some bull slinging when they first played synthetic oil. All I did was keep 'em straight, but "Lucky" damn near got the deep six again. Last column I wrote they junked correct answer 'bout a GMC Jimmy's air conditioner with a phony GM answer. My answer was "A/C is too small, don't waste any money trying to fix it, either buy a bigger system or drink lots of Kool-aid and carry a cooler." GM's answer "use would over temp the working fluid and turn it into phosphorus gas."

The truth was, 'bout 1980 the cars had gotten so much more complex that readers couldn't afford tools and equipment needed to trouble shoot and repair, plus, I no longer had every answer in my head. The column is used up like the pony express…it's over.

But they didn't want to change the format or kill the damn deal. In between '60 to '87 I'd written some stuff for other magazines and a tech book. Petersen Publishing took their best tech writer and had him start up a new magazine called Circle Track. C.J. Baker was "father" of this new child in the Peterson world of racetrack tech, personalities, old news and race stories. You know, the concept of a monthly magazine to report race news is about as sensible as tits on a bull.

Actually, stuff I wrote today was as least three months old when it got read. So in August I could tell you 'bout Indy last May.

C.J. decided to feature tech, but he had a boss, John Diana, who had no balls, no imagination and insisted Circle Track become a close copy of Hot Rod. Well, Hot Rod has peaked, and headed to the shit house 'cause it tried to be all things to all performance fans to where they became so fucked up kissing advertisers asses and trying to be 12 magazines in one that the published result by '85 was a "What the fuck is it?" It wasn't a swan or a duck or a goose… maybe it was a swoose. If John had kept his nose out of Circle Track it would have went to the moon as the tech bible of auto racing world wide.

C.J. had the correct vision, too bad John shit on his parade.

C.J. wanted me to write a "Dear Abby" column for Circle Track, a la Popular Science. I wanted to do that 'bout as much as I wanted to be an astronaut (then…I'm ready to go now).

I really enjoyed C.J., I think I was his first interview assignment as a Hot Rod reporter. He came as a burr haircut ex-soldier who'd been living like a mole in underground silo that had nuclear weapons in 'em out in the cornfields of Iowa. He seemed to know enough 'bout racecars to wash parts and sweep the floor, but he had the desire and personality to get cooperation from the racers. C.J. was a smart country boy who caught on fast and I felt in 5-6 years he was best tech writer Petersen had.

I don't know how Petersen was so successful, cause I remember him way back as what I called a "zoot-suiter," good lookin,' goofy clothes with carney traits. Kinda like a young barker with his horn telling 'bout diver gonna dive 250 foot into 431 gallons of water two foot deep. His early guys, photographers and editorial, were good hard workers …Hell…Wally Parks was one of 'em. But by 1980 the brass were a bunch of hi-paid stuck in the mud fuck-offs. Grey Baskerville as a picture shooter was as good as it gets and fifty years later, still around. "OK C.J. I'll do it for a year if you think it will help you." I really want him to succeed. But I'm puzzled, 'cause I'm not noted for being a mild, easy going conformist. Matter of fact my nickname was "Smokey the Bear," and the postman didn't get overloaded bringing me Christmas cards. Maybe 'cause I crossed my name out and re-addressed sender's name on same envelope and sent it back next year. True, some were offended…No, my justification "to save the tree so squirrels would have a place to live didn't seem to get much credit." My idea to date the used Christmas card for a three-year time span didn't go over either.

How many people die a year licking those shitty tasting stamps? (You know how I'd make 'em taste?)

Well a year passes, but as far as I'm concerned, deal's a flop compared to the flood of questions I got at Popular Science.

C.J. says, "Go one more year." Tell you the truth; three month old news is like selling recycled food in my way of thinking. In second year, enough good tech starts to get in. Letters pick up and it's off to the races. Trouble starts to rear it's ugly head, near as I can see there's a plan to keep Circle Track small ('bout 100 to 120,000). I've been in six or seven company deals where the brass is incompetent …they micro manage enough to keep all your brainstorms and ideas out of the pipeline.

631

No talented, qualified, lower level executive can survive this for over three years till they quit, just stay drawing pay, or try and live with it, but slowly give up working. "What's the use?" or if you're like me…quit and worry 'bout paying bills later. Well, C.J. has a family, mortgage payments…hell…what was a $35,000 house in Daytona is 300 grand in the L.A. area. You can't quit, you have to stay and eat the crap. It's kinda like castrating your best bull – all he can do now is eat, beller and shit. That's it. Many-many companies lose their best men that way. They are looking for a manager for a weak area when they have the best man in the country for the job rite now.

'Bout the time Circle Track got going good they put C. J. in sales, and as far as I'm concerned greased the skid for their magazine to slide backwards. Would you be surprised to know C. J. and five other people started and run Circle Track for several years. Don O'Reilly and his wife Edith and one helper named Vince started and ran Speed Age, the original pioneer monthly racing skinny paper. To people my age, Sears catalogues and magazines were our toilet paper. The shiny pages were no good (no, ain't gonna explain it). So we distinguished between skinny and plain (shiny paper though was better than corn cobs.)

I read every letter and answered every one. Those not printed got short answer from me or a phone call. There is no tech writer or editor school, and with C.J. on the road selling ads, we go from inexperienced to incompetent to just plain dumb and lazy bullshit artist for management. I get paid late, underpaid, and got editors fucking with my answers. That does it. They get a guy named Grissom, that cat took the rag off the bush. Hoooo-ee…he knew enough to be dangerous, lazy as a Mexican burro, 'bout a six-inch mouth and questioned 'bout everything I did. This one-year deal is now ten years old. It's kind of a shame. I'm doing a lot of good with readers, C.J. is helpless, he hired Grissom and Diana fell in love with him. In a little while looks like Grissom out ranks C.J. I couldn't figure it out, then I decided Grissom had a picture of Diana doing something he shouldn't.

After ten years I'm finally getting paid good and almost on time. 36 grand a year…I'm damn near in McCahill's class (30 years later). Grissom is really a nice human being but I think his real calling would have been pumping gas in El Paso…or a landscape gardener.

In my advanced age my tolerance is on a scale of one to ten regarding pelicans is 'bout one and a half. I remember Knudsen's advice, "Ask for more money" well 'bout last five years going back to manual, the cry at Petersen was "get rid of that old bastard…his ideas are outdated." I believe the real reason was "he won't kiss our ass and do what we tell him and he pisses off some of our advertisers who sell junk." Let me say this: the physics and chemistry, the thermodynamics, the aerodynamics, the petro-chemistry, the vehicle dynamics, that determine cars at speed, have been the same last 90 years, and stand a good chance of staying that way until eternity (however long that is).

You guessed it…asking for raise got job done. The "old bastard" gets shit-canned. Why? Ask the readers. The answer is a well thought out conclusion…it was a business decision." Remember that line the next time you need to fire somebody. Did I deserve it? Probably. Predictions of the magazines demise without me, now five years later were apparently bum dope. Magazine is still going and I understand profitably. Only Circle Track emotions I have is, I'm very sorry to see the treatment C.J. got, and for what it did to him as an energetic, talented human.

For you who believe all you read, I caution you – you are daily being brainwashed for profit by extremely effective psychology with very little regard to factual accuracy. In short, you're at the mercy of the world's greatest bullshit artists with the morals of a stray tomcat. Shorter yet…watch it, you're on the edge of getting fucked again.

Across the Pond

Just 'bout the time I decided no more new adventures, I get an invitation to go to Goodwood Festival of Speed. Goodwood – what the hell's that? Well, "Goodwood" is the name of a 200-year-old private estate, about 1,200 acres of beautiful woods and meadows where this three-day festival of speed is to be held. Yeah, I had heard a little 'bout it, but thought it had to do with European road racing and Formula One, probably attended by 10 or 15,000 old farts still living the 20 to 75 year old "used to be." I accepted, and after one rough day of travel, Margie and I are in "bloody old England."

The Earl of March and his wife, the Countess, preside over this event, which damn near blew my mind with its size. There were nearly 100,000 people there. I have no idea of the number of really old (1900 or 1910 kinda old), and interesting current racecars there are. Actually, the surprise is how many were preserved through a series of strange events and discovery even today.

If the cars were presented chronologically you can just about see the evolution of the modern car from steam to gasoline to diesel to turbine to fuel cells.

Who in the hell could orchestrate such a huge event 150 miles out in the boonies? A pretty young Englishman named Richard Sutton, that's who! His ability to juggle 10 balls at once and keep everyone happy is an amazing feat. An attempt is made to have all cars run in a short demonstration of their authenticity and for all of us to hear the various sounds their birthing produced. The range is enormous. From the deep-throated sounds of low rpm huge bore and strokes to the high rpm screamers with a feminine, shrill sound.

If you spent your life exploring surface transportation from normal to the very highest performance machine, this is the encyclopedia and history book of a fantastic 100 years in man's attempts to manipulate himself into becoming part machine and part human. Kinda like Pizzaro had the Inca indians believing that rider and horse were able to perform as both human and or animal or as half-human and half-horse.

At Goodwood you see the adventures of not only going fast, but of stopping fast.

The adventures of aerodynamics and its effects on safety, speed, fuel economy, and the current American trend to ignore it. I noticed price of fuel now in England is 'bout six bucks a gallon. Now, if price of fuel here gets to those prices, will that affect your thinking on future purchases?

If you look close you see the adventures to find the optimum method to cool and lubricate today's car. You gotta notice that fifty years ago a car that run 100,000 miles was one in 100,000.

Today some don't change plugs till 100,000 miles, and it's not really rare to find vehicles with 300,000 on one engine. (That's been made possible with a lot of work and a lot trial and error.)

A good book on what I saw at Goodwood and the curiosities it awoke in me could easily be 1,000 pages. Hell, it's 100 years of all of man-kind's brains put together in one place, English, American, German, French, Italian. And much of the 100 years was spent on one-way streets to no place, but that's as necessary as the productive steps. You only walk the mistakes one time.

While I was there tragedy finally took two lives and there were some serious injuries as well.

Don't know why, but my guess is something broke. Also it's possible age and inexperience are ever present negatives when operated by "wanna- bees."

I, nor no one else can totally explain the Goodwood Festival of Speed. You must visit it for yourself. It's like going through three days at the Smithsonian with everything operating and doing what it's supposed to do. I'll bet you if I estimated the value of what was on exhibit there at a billion dollars it would be short.

For you motorcycle fans, they had a very large collection showing the evolution of motorcycles, but I believe the Barber collection in Birmingham, Alabama to be much greater.

Who do you see there? I sure don't know all the European champs, but I recognized John Surtees, Dan Gurney, Tony George, Jack Brabham, Phil Hill, Jr. Johnson, Herb Fishel, and Sterling Moss for starters.

"How in the hell did you get to Goodwood Smokey?" you ask. Here's the deal, Dick Mittman writes a nice story 'bout the capsule car in the May issue of "Old Timer's News" (Indy stuff) 37 years after it raced. Goodwood had asked the Indy Hall of Fame for loan of most unusual entry ever at Indy. It's decided that the capsule car was that entry. I didn't know anything about this till Dick called me for some details 'bout car and asks, "You going to Goodwood with the car?" I say, "Nope, no one said a word 'cept during the week of Indy they asked for a bill of sale." (Turns out I still owned it.) I sign it over to them. I have no interest in the trip, but I think, "Hell, Margie's never been to Europe, she'd love it. Old castles, princes, dukes, countesses and sirs." So I call Shelby and ask him if he can find out whether they intend to invite me. I've got lots of stuff to do in June and July. Turns out Shelby is a big buddy of Richard Sutton, the boss of the festival.

I think Shelby caused Richard to invite me by phone. He calls, but it is a "no expenses" deal. Well my code of the hills is, "I don't pay any expenses to be honored or used in promotion." Look, I raced for 30 years for peanuts. I've got no complaint, but I'll be goddamned if I'll be used in any more ego trips. I worked my ass off for 30 years for a "good racer license." I finally earned it, so I'm at peace with my soul. People pretend they didn't know why Lee Petty refused to attend various ceremonies to celebrate his fame and achievements. Hell, I knew before he told me. He raced for chicken-shit prize money. Why should he let racing continue to exploit him living, and then his ghost? I didn't blame Goodwood – hell, I figured nobody in Europe knew me anyhow, so I turned it down.

Elton Alderman, President of Prolong, said he'd go if they invited him and he'd pay Margie's and my expenses. I've made a mistake in here, 'cause Margie ain't feeling good and don't want to go. But I've already accepted the deal. Margie's in terrible ear pain during the trip and for next three days, but pain eases last two days. We have a terrible trip over. Elton cancels out, now he can't make it.

Mistake number two shows up. We've sent 1,200 posters and some product to Goodwood. The posters are 36 x 24 pictures of the capsule car. I figured they wouldn't know me. Wrong! Damn, I signed over 2,200 autographs in three days!

The capsule car was a major attraction. The people (100,000) were friendly as hell. They really enjoyed examining the car. Too bad it wasn't runable. As an attraction it was a flat "homer with the bases loaded."

I don't get it. For 37 years it sat over at the museum with little notice. This always struck me as odd. When the car run at Indy, the biggest fan the car had was Tony Hulman, Indy Speedway owner, and Colin Chapman, England's most productive race car designer.

I really enjoyed my visit to Goodwood. I'm glad I was invited, and that Prolong made it possible to go. Thank you Goodwood for a very pleasant chapter in the sundown of my adventures. I believe even Margie is now glad she went.

If you're a race fan of any kind I recommend you try and visit Goodwood during the Festival of Speed at least once in you lifetime. It's much more than a profitable, race-oriented event – it's a history of the evolution of the automobile, and a tribute to the thousands who gave a major part of their lives over the last 100 years to make the automobile a better mouse trap.

I wanted to end my racing with a position in Indy's Hall of Fame, although I was kinda sure I didn't do enough up there to deserve it. So when at Goodwood I thought, "Wonder if I could get a deal like Jack Brabham or Sterling Moss, and get called "Sir Smokey," but I found out that door will never open. You know I think that's good, really. If you get everything you want, what incentive would you have to keep on living? Think 'bout it.

My wife Margie gave me a plaque 20 years ago that said, "He who had no problems to solve is out of the game." I'm thankful I still play a small role.

Back in the Game

The longer I live life, the more I am surprised by the twists and turns of life. A high school dropout getting an engineering course and a chair named after him. The University of Central Florida did this the first part of October 2000. This was one of the last pieces of the puzzle of my life…how to transfer what I've learned and what I've accumulated to the future. Dr. Robert Hoekstra, an engineering professor at UCF, was the answer.

He has the only course in automotive engineering in the US where you need a degree before you can start getting your master's degree in High Performance Engine Design. OK, what's the big deal? Racing, you agree, has progressed significantly in the last fifty years. The motor companies not only recognize racing, but support it financially and functionally. The manufacturers have now intertwined their whole product line with high performance. They have again discovered that performance sells, but not in the original way. They now use racing as a hip "in" thing. The amount of wins is certainly a factor, but nowhere near what it was. The new turn of events created driver heroes. Race teams, a collection of super, near mythical humans. So racing technology had to take a giant step forward and create a system to educate engineers and pick the outstanding candidates to guide the technology into the future.

The NASCAR teams must have engineering supervision just as they do in Formula One racing. By the way, these top engineering jobs will be very high paying, easily up to a million per year. So, having input in this kinda jabbed my ego a little. As you quit hitting homers with the bases loaded, you're ego kinda follows your sexual physical abilities. You're in a period where you're returning slowly to an adolescent, so being back in the game makes me feel useful again.

I've helped pick a board of advisors for the course:
– Robert Yates
– Jack Roush
– Richard Childress
– Ray Evernham
– Dave Bowman - "Shade Tree Mechanic"
– John Kilroy - PRI.

How's that for a start to blend yesterday and tomorrow? We'll have about six or seven more. Herb Fishel, Don Davis and Jim France have been invited.

Auto racing will soon be America's number one or two sport. (Man, I had a hell of a time calling racing a sport.) Safety and fan appreciation with a large increase in their amenities are on the front burners now. This push to further the education of various specialists is an immediate "must." Safety will be helped tremendously when the medical profession is consulted. Names like Angus Ruppert, MD, PhD and Bill Muzzy will be familiar to us all.

The other problem is fan treatment. Much more engineering is coming in race facilities regarding weather, comfort, convenience and safety. Rainouts will become very rare. I have no idea if training is necessary to materially help it. This problem is greed. What's the medicine for moderation in this area?

Racing stock cars will finally have to legislate in new technology. The carburetor is great but ancient history. Racer's lives will soon be invaded with atoms and electronics beyond Buck Rogers. If Einstein were still alive he'd have to go to school to educate himself to the lightning speed of today's electronic technology.

The medical profession will soon play a major part in the selection of future drivers. Yup, they will "bullet-proof" the selection of driver candidates. Right now there is a giant need for driver training. The old system we had (that is still in use) is as antique as high button shoes. A real race driver can drive any damn thing there is if he (or she) wants to. Driving schools will pop up that have a European flavor. Daddy will get hit with a 200 or 300 grand bill for this, but junior will come out running and able.

The biggest hit on daddy's wallet is the cost of junior's race miles and mistakes. Sadly, the local boy with talent but no funds will fall through the cracks. Same with technicians. But I expect racing to become much more lucrative financially to those who choose and struggle to educate themselves to the top ten percent of their fields.

Even Humpy Wheeler, boss man at Charlotte, who pioneered lights, nice track garages, track cosmetics, higher purses, and suites will have to start all over and redo most of his past innovations. That man should be the high commissioner of US racing (a non-political appointment) at a higher salary than that of those who control stick and ball sports. Every woman fan owes Humpy a big thank you. He probably cut the number of wet panties in half. He is the champion of women's rest rooms.

Maybe this deal at UCF will be able to develop a plan to help a few deserving "would-be" racers climb on board this fast moving train. I've seen it work at Embry-Riddle, an aeronautical university. I was on the original board of directors there. I believe in ten years a degree in Racing Engineering from UCF will be a badge of competence on an international basis.

The Final Final Chapter

December 20, 1999, Mayo Clinic: looks like, you got a-credit-card Anemia (Myelodysplasia). Damn! Yesterday, you said I didn't eat enough meat and was low on iron. There were 'bout five doctors and all but one looked real, real sad. It was kinda like jury foreman giving me a one-year delayed death sentence. The one doctor acted like "serves you right for living bad."

They say I've got to start chemotherapy, but it probably ain't' gonna do any good…too old. Well, I don't like working with people who give up when you hit an unscheduled pit stop. I want a second opinion so it's off to Texas.

At M.D. Anderson in Houston they say, "Yep, you're fucked up." We've got a new treatment made out of ground up horse's feet (ATG). It may save your ass…wanna try it? Since I like experimenting I say, yup. The first three days went great 'cept I kept wanting to whinny like a horse all the time. I get the fourth and last treatment while exercising. I feel weak so I lay down and doze off. When I wake up in 30 minutes, I can't move left side. It's paralyzed on January 5, 2000.

I'm discharged next morning. I keep the bad shit quiet. I just wanna go home. Of the 300 people on plane 290 are Chinese tourists going to Disney World. I go to bathroom, and coming out, I fall down. Immediately all 290 chinamen try to pick me up. Pilot comes back and asks if he should turn around. I say "Hell no, just help me get in my seat." We get home to phone message from M. D. Anderson telling us to go to the Mayo Clinic immediately. Turns out I have E. coli in my blood.

In eight hours and 10 minutes I'm taken out of a deep freeze room and put in a room that's just behind a jet engine. (A sterile room?) I get out of bed middle of next night and crawl into a hallway. I won't stay in that room. The noise and cold just about drove me nuts. They send a Catholic priest to give me Last Rites. He gets pissed cause I don't want any. (Read early war, Italy). Mayo wants me to go back to M. D. Anderson to croak.

In the next two weeks I passed two kidney stones and paid for half of all of my sins. I get a second offer of Last Rites. I told priest of my rejection of Catholicism. I also said now that I hurt so bad and am maybe ready to check out, I ain't gonna turn holy roller and beg. I tell the guy that, "I am what I am, but if you'll get me some pain relief I got two 100 dollar bills I will donate to your church." No deal. Why do hospitals let people hurt so much? Is there a medical reason? In that month there were times I was sure the race was gonna be flagged short. I got scared. Course, I wanted Margie to say adios to.

In a couple of months I got back in the world again only…problem is my left leg is zero. After a couple months of therapy, wheel chairs, walkers, cane…I go home, but keep the therapy going. I find a whole new world…good and bad. I find out my family is supporting me every day, all day. I'd lived my life as a one-man band till Margie and I teamed up. It took her about 10 years to get the kids to love and respect her. Margie had made a family out of five lone rangers.

The prognosis looks like, with intermittent blood transfusions, I will keep living. In my attempt to learn to walk again, I see in many rooms. What I see are poor and rich, all skin colors, male and female who smoked a lot and did other bad things to their health. We all had one thing in common: we all thought, "This will never happen to me." From a healthy person who administers care to these people, they consider us (and perhaps rightfully so) the walking dead. We never get better again, they just change disease names. Many of these people, if they were bad, don't need to be sent to hell, they lived in hell for a few years before they died. What's the message? Just this: good health is more important than any single item in life. I'll leave the religion for people qualified to discuss it. My definition of a good life is to be healthy for 80 years and then die having sex! What is cancer? Is it everything that kills people that we don't understand? Spend a day in the hospital section that deals with venereal diseases and see walking dead people 15 to 25 years old. Mostly it was drugs that brought those people there. I couldn't get an OK to observe it, I don't know why. But in talking to the people who work in those areas, it too, is a horrible way to exist. Folks there have little chance for a total cure.

In my case, I change from doing great to flat on my ass in six hours. I believe best plan is to work every day and work out at a gym to get help from a stranger, a physical therapist named Raymond Long. I get to where I can handle 60 pounds upper and lower body.

Whammo! On January 13, 2001, I get a routine blood test followed by bad news. The doctor says I have switched to Acute Myeloid Leukemia. I don't understand, but my wife's face turned white and I could see tears in her eyes. I thought, "Oh shit, this looks bad." Doctor says I've got 90 days unless a miracle. The Mayo Clinic doctors say, "Too old for chemotherapy." Well I'm gonna take chemotherapy. Hell, I got no choice but it kinda looks like March, 2001 is the end of the book. My real fear is that I don't want to leave Margie.

I think I have kids' financial needs taken care of. Taxes and all the many places the government gets into. In Florida, the state takes first 55 percent, then 40 percent or the rest for IRS.

I hope you who were too lazy to vote get your plows cleaned also.

I never worry 'bout the weather or anything else I have no control over.

Would I change anything? Nope. For those who read my story you'll see very, very few people lived a fuller or more exciting life. Only deal I'd make is: "Devil, if you give me some more time with Margie, I'm ready to listen to the price." Again I feel life gave me a special deal. I get a couple months to get ready. Am I gonna forgive all my enemies? Hell, that happened long ago, but that don't change the movie. I forgave the dead…but the living…I still won't let the living bad guys get behind me. I get mail 'bout five times a week that makes me feel good. I get thank you's from people I helped along the way, I've got drawers full of them. I've even got thank you's from people like Steve Lewis, the boss man at PRI. From Prolong? Nope, they seem to intend on driving me goofy with Elton's visions of how to run a railroad. I set 'em up in a million plus deal and their thank you was a 40 percent pay cut. But that's life…it's part of living. Blame someone else for what ever is wrong. I watch this wondering if they will ever figure it out, but man, if you're not honest with yourself you're a lost soul swimming with the 15 foot crocodiles.

I'm coming back from L.A. and Prolong. I think I should use my remaining hours doing good and useful stuff. I don't believe I'm running on an hourly schedule, but I know it will take a miracle to change the movie.

Yup, I still think maybe.

I wondered what emotions condemned criminal experiences when the countdown gets real close, once there is no more hope? Seems like the best plan is do it. Very little progress has been made with the big "C." Twenty years ago it killed Kilroy, Sam and Steve's momma. We were all the time hoping for a last minute cure. Now it's my turn and still the same story…maybe tomorrow. If you don't got anything else out of this book, make your number one priority your health. For you "it ain't gonna happen to me" dreamers, you'll feel very helpless when you find the big "C" has just poked it's fangs into your ass.

I've been involved with racing about 55 years. There will never be any way to justify even one life. It is February 20, 2001 and the whole world has gone ape-shit. The last lap of the Daytona race, with 11 seconds till the end, and Dale is dead…deader than Hogan's fucking goat. Yes, Dale is dead! No Dale can't be dead, he has hit many times much harder.

Why did they lie and withhold news of his death? I'm old, but not stupid. Why did they lie to me? Why tell me five days later that we know a lot of shit that you ain't allowed to hear? What gives you the right to strangle the media? A lot of good men have died since the 1700s defending our democracy and our rights. Among these rights is freedom of the press. Are you gonna let them roll us in the shit now or are you gonna stand up on your hind legs and say racing needs help? Consider how quickly gravel and sand traps fixed Formula One. Is there a point where it turns from accident to murder?

I've had a bad one-and-a-half years making simple decisions. I've been told twice in the last year I'd be dead March 1 and doomed. If you pick a 68 year old man to run a two billion dollar company…NASCAR will never be completely well again. Consider this: Billy, you can bullshit everyone but yourself.

The Dictionary According to Smokey

Across the nose - measurement taken on a cam at maximum lift

Air Fuel Ratio - amount of fuel and air by percentage

Alky - alcohol

Ass - as in "get some pussy"

Asshole - a person who is not liked

Bagel Burner - Jewish person

Balls - as in "bravery"

Band Aid - temporary-fast patch job

Bean Bandits - Mexican racers

Bear Grease - slippery shit put on the track to limit lateral traction and keep heavy cars from tearing up the asphalt.

Beaver - female sex organ

Bench Racing - talking about racing or race cars, often involves booze.

Bird - in Australian - women

Bird - in United States - kinda a one fingered "salute"

Bitch - as in "complain"

Blowed Off - out run by a competitor badly

Blowed (or Blown) - as in engine ... artificially aspirated

Blowed - as in sex...... oral sex... as in "Clinton"

Bone Crusher - chiropractor

Bore - diameter of a cylinder

Bow Wow - as in dog.... regarding a female who was a poor companion

Brass - regarding controlling executives , or simply "control"

Brave - reference lack of, or abundance of, courage

Bullshitting - just talking

Bump Steer - measuring and adjusting the amount the caster, camber and toe-in a suspension changes throughout its range of motion.

C note - hundred bucks

CFM - cubic feet per minute usually the amount of air / fuel mixture that could flow through a carburetor

CERV 1 - experimental Corvette - looks like a spaceship

Camber - amount the top of the front wheels tilted in toward the car. A lot of negative camber means the wheels tilted in past vertical.

Caster - the inclination of front wheel pivot axis that tended to return wheels to straight ahead.

Chickenshit - unfair, hung up on details, 'one way'

Chunk - see Pumpkin

Cobby - crude construction

Cocksucker - reference mostly a male you didn't like but sometimes just an adjective to describe a competitor.

Coffin Nail - as in cigarette

Compression Ratio - reference the ratio you compressed an air fuel mixture above standard atmosphere

Coon Ass - a native of Louisiana

Cool it - as in shut up

Coon - colored person

Corn Holer - anal sex among males

Cotton Picker - poor, under standard, dumb

Crash House - hospital

Cubic Inches (cu. in.) - size of one or more cylinders in total

Cunt - a female asshole

Cunt Hair - a tiny amount

Deep Six - death

Dick Head - a male you didn't like

Dick Tracey - was used in reference to bravery or recklessness

Dickey Licker - oral sex - either male or female - same as "Cock Sucker"

Dope - a Coke or information

Dog - as in unattractive woman

Dog Shit - as in "no good", worse than junk

Donkey - does hard work

Donuts - tires

Down Force - a term to describe artificial force to hold car down on the track by aerodynamic design.

Drag Coefficient - regarding how easy or how hard it would be to furnish energy to attain a maximum speed.

Dry - referring to race car without water, fuel or oil in it

Dyno - short for Dynomometer - a device that measures horsepower by determining torque at a given RPM

Dzus - a shortish fastener with two spiral ears used to attach panels onto racecars. It's ears twisted one quarter turn over a spring wire set in a hole on the chassis.

Eating at the 'Y' - oral sex; as in male to female

Elephant - any real big deal

Extremely Pissed - someone is hanging over the edge of control or safety

Fearless Fosdick - as in brave (from Dick Tracey comic strip)

Fence Bunnies - girls who stayed at pit or garage fences to be noticed and approached for meeting racers.

Finn - five bucks

Fishing Job or Fisherman - pertains to recovery of unwanted obstruction in an oil well

Fucked Duck - indicates failure

Fuzz - cops

Firing - as in engine reacting fuel and air

Flat Out - means doing what ever it is as hard and as well done as you can possibly do it

Flat Rate - a term used by auto manufacturers to describe amount of hours it takes normally to do a specific maintenance or repair task.

Front Steer - car with the steering linkage in front of the front axle center line. Tended to allow oil sump in back of motor.

Get Some Head - as in oral sex

Glued Together - as in "fix it"

Gobbler - female oral sex expert

God Father or Grandfather - a person in high position who steers you in an advancing social, sport, political or working path.

Go-fer - a helper to do menial tasks and run errands at no pay.

Greenies - Money

Grey - the grey is the slippery parts of a oval where there is no rubber laid onto the track, not the groove

Groove - the groove is the fast line around a track

Hauled Ass - as in "fast"

Hauling the Mail - regarding speed meaning fast, or good

Heat - as in police

Heavy Oil - oil too thick to pump in an oil field

Heebie Jeebies - caffeine induced jumpy state

Heliarc - electric welding where the molten puddle is protected by a gas shield coming from a nozzle around the electrode

Hen house ways - making big trouble out of a little deal, one way.

Holy Roller - a very religious person

Honkers - women who are very good at and desire oral sex rather than sexual relations sex. If you're confused, call and ask Clinton.

Horny - sexy

Horsepower or Horsies - describing an engine's power, or a person's power - politically, financially or legally.

Import - a girl who you pay her expenses to attend weekend races with you.

I F R - instument flight rating - can fly a plane using instruments only (and actually get where you're headed)

Jackoff - lazy, ineffectual, a negative person regarding task at hand.

Jack you around - give you undeserved trouble

Jerkoff - lazy, same as Jack-off.

Jiggler - southern for pushrod engine

Juice - power; social, political or economic

Jungle bunny - colored person in the forties and fifties

Junk - material from which things can be built or something that is worthless

Knockers - breasts, female

Left hand threaded - homosexual

Leg Spreader - booze

Lift - when you back off from full throttle, or an aerodynamic term that describes relative negative pressure on top of an airfoil, flying

Lit Chainsaw - big-big trouble

Loot - money

Loudmouth - booze

Mag - magneto

Magnaflux - crack checking method for ferrous metals- uses magnetic field to pull luminous fluid into a crack so it shows up under blacklight.

Marbles - loose sand, dirt and bits of rubber outside the groove, no traction situation

Methodist - the crash house in Indy

Mexican Chrome - aluminum silver paint

Mexican Socket Set - an adjustable wrench

Mexican Stand off - nobody wins... a tie

Moly - very strong steel alloy made with chromium and molybdenum.

Mon-Backer - socially and economically poor person.... the person behind a garbage truck backing up.. ("mon-back, mon-back")

Monkey Fence - the fence separating fans from racers. They hang on it entertained by the monkeys in a cage.

Monkey Fuckin' A Football - monkeys will try to fuck just about anything, this term describes an unsuccessful technique

Mother Lode - as in finding a big pile of gold or a major victory in business - economic or social advancement

Motherfucker - very good or very bad event, person, place or machine

Motha-fucker - A southern mother fucker

Motor - actually means engine

Mule - un-expert; does hard work

Naked - start of sex

No Handling - person or machine that is difficult to predict or control

Nose Flying - car with front end prone to lift off at speed

O E M - Original Equipment Manufacturer, as in auto maker

One-way - will freely take help or advice, and not return it.

Out the ass - a lot of

Pelican - a person who is ineffective at "what ever" as in a pelican: all they do is eat, shit and squawk

Peter Principle - Where we are likely to exceed our ability and find ourselves in over our heads.

Peyote - an hallucinogenic product invented by Western Indians and used as cocaine, but an aid in deep thinking.... (maybe yes.... maybe no)

Plugs - spark plugs

Pole - a term that denotes the fastest qualifier

Poon-Tang - sex adventure

Prick - a racer's term for a person who is unfair and one way.

Pumpkin - same as third member

Pussy - means "woman" and/or "sex"

Put Lipstick On It - as in "cosmetic patch job"

Rack - as in sex - a bed

Rag, On the - term describing a lady having her period

Rankine Cycle - using expansion of heated working fluid in a closed loop with a condenser to effect mechanical motion

Red Devil - early tow bar without steering cables or remote brakes. It was essentially a pair of steel "hands" with one common wrist that clamped on the back and front bumper. The whole device was about a foot long and six inches wide.

Rear steer - condition where changing geometry of rear axle causes car to push or get loose regardless of what front wheels are doing or steering linkage behind the center line of the front axle; often had clearance problems with the oil sump.

Riceburner - Japanese person

RPM - revolutions per minute - loosely describes how hard an engine (or person) is working

Rubber - as in tires

Sack - bed, or denotes maybe a sexual experience.

Sack Time - sleep

Sawbones - doctor

Seat Gap - the gap between a driver's back and the seat that indicates they are nervous and no longer enjoying what they are doing.

Screwed - where you were unfairly treated - Or had sex

Sheet Time - regards hospital or convalescence time

Shittin' and gettin'- hauling ass

Shot in the Ass - experimant that was not productive

Sitting on the Pole - the fastest qualifier

Stroking - not doing what ever it is well

Sixty-Nine oral sex between male and female simultaneously

Smoke Over - look over something carefully before giving an opinion or reaction

Snake Oil - oil additives as in S.T.P. - Rislone - Slick 50 - Prolong

Sneeze in the Heater - as in oral sex

Son of a Bitch - anything difficult or negative to you. It can be a task or a human. As a rule does not apply to a person's lineage.

Southern Style - regards going fast, as in a dog running belly to the ground - tail straight out and ears back

Spagetti Bender - Italian person

Split tail - a woman

Stacked - well built female (as in brick shit house)

Stove Bolt - a Chevy

THE DICTIONARY ACCORDING TO SMOKEY

Stroke - refers to engines; how far piston goes up and down or amount of influence a person has

Stroking - going slower than you need to in order to be competitive

T Bone - car wreck grille to door

Take the rag off the bush - revealing the truth

TDC - top dead center - when a piston reaches the top of its bore. Ignition timing is generally referenced as degrees before TDC.

Third Member - the removable center of a straight rear axle setup with differential, ring and pinion as in a Ford "9 inch"

Ticker - heart

Tits - the protrusion most females have in upper front and that part racers like to nibble at

Toe-in - amount the front of the front wheels are set inward. This helps keep a car moving straight.

Torque - describes the ability of an engine to accelerate and one of the ingredients that dictate horse power

Training films - porno movies

Transaxle - combined transmission and differential, independent axles bolt to this.

Trots, The - as in diarrhea

Tube Steaks - hot dogs

Vibrating - getting excited

Walk The Dog - going very well and very fast

Wiener Guzzler - German person

Wet - when a race car has all it's fluids installed

Wheelbase - distance between center of front and real axle

Wheelies - as in "fast start"... pick front wheels off the ground

Wild Catter - drilling for oil with a minimum bankroll and as a rule in a class "B" location.

Wired in - current on the insider information

Whoaed - as in "stop"

Wobbly - anything of questionable durability, including humans

Wooley Booger - 1940 to 1960 slang for colored person

Yellow Peril - early tow bar with steering cables, usually painted yellow

Yhtbktbwa - you have to be killed to be written about

Zizzer- throttle on a vehicle

Zoomies - exhaust made with one pipe per cylinder

Zyglo - crack checking method for non-ferrous metals